EFFECTIVE

- **A powerful way for students to learn how to apply and use core concepts covered in the text chapters.**
  More and more professors who teach strategy courses are finding that simulations are every bit as effective as case analysis in providing students with a means of applying what they have read about in the text chapters.

- **Students are assigned a senior executive role.**
  Students' strategy-making and decision-making skills are put to the test. In this learn-by-doing exercise, students gain hands-on experience in crafting a competitive strategy and in making decisions relating to product quality, production, work force compensation and training, pricing and marketing, and financing of company operations.

- **Assurance of Learning.**
  Wonder how well your students perform globally, or perform against accreditation standards? A Learning Assurance Report is automatically produced and displays how well each student performed relative to all other students worldwide.

See what the buzz is all about.

Visit the Web site **www.mhhe.com/thompsonsims**, to register for a demonstration and to read what your colleagues are saying about BSG and GLO-BUS.

Strategic Management

Formulation, Implementation, and Control

Strategic Management

Formulation, Implementation, and Control

Eleventh Edition

John A. Pearce II
Villanova School of Business
Villanova University

Richard B. Robinson, Jr.
Moore School of Business
University of South Carolina

McGraw-Hill
Irwin

Boston   Burr Ridge, IL   Dubuque, IA   Madison, WI   New York   San Francisco   St. Louis
Bangkok   Bogotá   Caracas   Kuala Lumpur   Lisbon   London   Madrid   Mexico City
Milan   Montreal   New Delhi   Santiago   Seoul   Singapore   Sydney   Taipei   Toronto

McGraw-Hill
Irwin

STRATEGIC MANAGEMENT: FORMULATION, IMPLEMENTATION, AND CONTROL
Published by McGraw-Hill/Irwin, a business unit of The McGraw-Hill Companies, Inc., 1221 Avenue of the Americas, New York, NY, 10020.

1 2 3 4 5 6 7 8 9 0 DOW/DOW 0 9 8

ISBN   978-0-07-338136-7
MHID   0-07-338136-5

Editorial director: *Brent Gordon*
Publisher: *Paul Ducham*
Senior sponsoring editor: *Michael Ablassmeir*
Editorial coordinator: *Kelly Pekelder*
Senior marketing manager: *Anke Braun Weekes*
Project manager: *Bruce Gin*
Senior production supervisor: *Debra R. Sylvester*
Lead designer: *Matthew Baldwin*
Senior photo research coordinator: *Jeremy Cheshareck*
Photo researcher: *Keri Johnson*
Senior media project manager: *Susan Lombardi*
Cover design: *Kami Carter*
Typeface: *10/12 Times New Roman*
Compositor: *Hurix*
Printer: *R. R. Donnelley*

Library of Congress Cataloging-in-Publication Data

Pearce, John A.
   Strategic management : formulation, implementation, and control / John A. Pearce II,
Richard B. Robinson, Jr.—11th ed.
      p. cm.
   Includes index.
   ISBN-13: 978-0-07-338136-7 (alk. paper)
   ISBN-10: 0-07-338136-5 (alk. paper)
   1. Strategic planning. I. Robinson, Richard B. (Richard Braden), 1947–II. Title.
HD30.28.P3395 2009
   658.4'012—dc22

                                  2007052594

www.mhhe.com

To Susan McCartney Pearce, David Donham Pearce, Mark McCartney Pearce, Katherine Elizabeth Robinson, Corporal John Braden Robinson, and Chance Robinson—for the love, joy, and vitality that they give to our lives.

About the Authors

John A. Pearce II   *Villanova University*

John A. Pearce II, Ph.D., holds the Villanova School of Business Endowed Chair in Strategic Management and Entrepreneurship at Villanova University. In 2004, he was the Distinguished Visiting Professor at ITAM in Mexico City. Previously, Professor Pearce was the Eakin Endowed Chair in Strategic Management at George Mason University and a State of Virginia Eminent Scholar. He received the 2004 Fulbright U.S. Professional Award, which he served at INTAN in Malaysia. Dr. Pearce has taught at Penn State University, West Virginia University, the University of Malta as the Fulbright Senior Professor in International Management, and at the University of South Carolina where he was Director of Ph.D. Programs in Strategic Management. He received a Ph.D. degree in Business Administration and Strategic Management from the Pennsylvania State University.

Professor Pearce is coauthor of 36 books and has authored more than 250 articles and refereed professional papers. The articles have appeared in journals that include *Academy of Management Executive, Academy of Management Journal, Academy of Management Review, Business Horizons, California Management Review, Journal of Applied Psychology, Journal of Business Venturing, Long-Range Planning, Organizational Dynamics, Sloan Management Review,* and *Strategic Management Journal.* Several of these publications have resulted from Professor Pearce's work as a principal on research projects funded for more than $2 million. He is a widely recognized expert in the field of strategic management, with special accomplishments in the areas of strategic planning and management, including strategy formulation, implementation, and control, mission statement development, environmental assessment, industry analysis, and tools for strategy evaluation and selection.

Professor Pearce is the recipient of several awards in recognition of his accomplishments in teaching, research, scholarship, and professional service, including three Outstanding Paper Awards from the Academy of Management and the 2003 Villanova University Outstanding Faculty Research Award. A frequent leader of executive development programs and an active consultant to business and industry, Dr. Pearce's client list includes domestic and multinational firms engaged in manufacturing and service industries.

Richard B. Robinson, Jr.   *University of South Carolina*

Richard B. Robinson, Jr., Ph.D., is a Moore Fellow at the Moore School of Business, University of South Carolina. He also serves as Director of the Faber Entrepreneurship Center at USC and Assistant Director of the Center for Manufacturing and Technology in USC's College of Engineering and Computing. Dr. Robinson received his Ph.D. in Business Administration from the University of Georgia. He graduated from Georgia Tech in Industrial Management.

Professor Robinson has authored or coauthored numerous books, articles, professional papers, and case studies addressing strategic management and entrepreneurship issues that students and managers use worldwide. His research has been published in major journals including the *Academy of Management Journal, Academy of Management Review, Strategic Management Journal, Academy of Entrepreneurship Journal,* and the *Journal of Business Venturing.*

Dr. Robinson has previously held executive positions with companies in the pulp and paper, hazardous waste, building products, lodging, and restaurant industries. He currently serves as a director or adviser to entrepreneurial companies that are global leaders in niche markets in the log home, building products, animation, and visualization software industries. Dr. Robinson also advises more than 250 students each year who undertake field consulting projects and internships with entrepreneurial companies worldwide.

Preface

This eleventh edition of *Strategic Management: Formulation, Implementation, and Control* is a comprehensive revision designed to accommodate the needs of strategy students worldwide in our fast changing twenty-first century. These are exciting times, and they are reflected on the many new developments in this book and the accompanying McGraw-Hill supplements. This preface describes what we have done to make the eleventh edition uniquely effective in preparing students for strategic decisions in tomorrow's fast-paced global business arena. They include:

- A chapter dedicated to corporate social responsibility and business ethics
- A chapter dedicated to structuring effective 21st century organizations
- Extensive coverage of globalization as a central theme integrated and illustrated throughout this book and in a separate, updated chapter of the global business environment
- A major section on leadership including numerous examples and illustrations that help provide practical guidelines young, emerging leaders can use
- A NEW chapter focused on innovation and entrepreneurship
- "Top Strategist" boxes highlighting the world's best new leaders as strategists
- 100 NEW *BusinessWeek* Strategy in Action boxes
- NEW coverage of the pros and cons of outsourcing and the reality of what is now a truly global economy

Top Strategist
Jean-Pierre Garnier, CEO of GlaxoSmithKline

Exhibit 3.12

When Jean-Pierre Garnier took over as CEO of GlaxoSmith-Kline in 2000, the company's reputation on corporate social responsibility was at its nadir. As part of a coalition of 39 pharmaceutical companies, the drugmaker was suing Nelson Mandela's South African government for voiding patents on prescription drugs. Mandela's top priority was giving desperately sick patients access to HIV treatments, and GSK—the world's largest supplier—was standing in the way. "It was a public relations disaster," Garnier concedes.

The experience convinced Garnier that GSK should lead the crusade to improve access to medicine. In 2001, GSK became the first major drugmaker to sell its AIDS medicines at cost in 100 countries worldwide. In fact, GSK sells 90 percent of its vaccines, in volume terms, at not-for-profit prices to customers in the developing world. In 2005, it set a new paradigm in the vaccine industry. It chose Mexico over other, wealthier nations as the launch pad for Rotarix, a new vaccine against gastrointestinal rotavirus. "We wanted to get the vaccine to the children who needed it most," Garnier explains.

Creating medicines for the Third World while still posting a profit required fancy financial footwork. GSK has formed 14 different partnerships with the World Health Organization and other nongovernmental bodies, and with philanthropies such as the Bill & Melinda Gates Foundation. Garnier says he is drawn to GSK to make a diff admired for it, company, he says engaged workfor competitors."

Source: Excerpted from Getting AIDS Drugs January 29, 2007, p.

Strategy in Action
Helping Big Brother in China Go High Tech

Exhibit 3.7

Cisco, Oracle, and other U.S. companies are supplying China's police with software and gear that can be used to keep tabs on criminals and dissidents.

Google, Yahoo!, and Microsoft endured a wave of Public disapproval in 2006 over their compliance with Chinese censorship of their Web sites. But another striking form of tech commerce with China is taking place below the radar of the U.S. public: major American manufacturers are rushing to supply China's police with the latest information technology.

Oracle Crop. has sold software to the Chinese Ministry of Public Security, which oversees both criminal and ideological investigations. The ministry uses the software to manage digital identity cards that are replacing the paper ID that Chinese citizens must carry. Meanwhile, regional Chinese police departments are modernizing their computer networks with routers and switches purchased from Cisco Systems Inc. And Motorola Inc. has sold the Chinese authorities handheld devices that will allow street cops to tap into the sorts of sophisticated data repositories that EMC Corp. markets to the Ministry of Public Security. "It's a booming market," says Simon Zhou, the top executive in Beijing for EMC, which is based in Hopkinton, Mass. "We can expect big revenue from public security" agencies in china.

The scramble to sell technology to Chinese law enforcers seems, for starters, to be at odds with the intent of an American export law enacted after the massacre of hundreds of pro-democracy demonstrators in Tiananmen Square in 1989. The Tiananmen sanctions prohibited the export "of any crime control or detection instruments or equipment" to China. "We wanted to undermine the effectiveness of the police in rounding up, imprisoning, and torturing political dissidents, not only those involved in the Tiananmen Square movement, but for year to come," explains Representative Tom Lantos (D–CA), who helped draft the law. Despite the improvement of its image on the world stage, China still has a dismal human rights record. The U.S. State Department says that the Communist government is holding at least 260,000 people in ideological "reeducation" camps.

The upshot is that "manufacturers of handcuffs aren't allowed to sell their products to China's police, but Cisco and other companies are selling Chinese authorities much more useful technology," Harry Wu, a former Chinese political prisoner living in the United States, told a House subcommittee on human rights in February 2006. His testimony was eclipsed by the panel's heavily covered excoriation of Google, Yahoo!, and Microsoft for their agreement to block parts of their Chinese Web sites as a condition of operating in the country.

Source: Excerpted from Bruce Einhorn and Ben Elgin, "Helping Big Brother Go High Tech," *BusinessWeek*, September 18, 2006, p. 46.

- 14 NEW *BusinessWeek* end of chapter cases providing practical, interesting, contemporary applications of chapter topics
- 30 NEW *BusinessWeek* cases that represent the best of *BusinessWeek* from around the world and developed by *BusinessWeek*'s top correspondents
- 20 NEW traditional strategy cases covering contemporary business situations from around the world

- NEW cases and illustration modules about companies founded and run by women and minorities
- NEW Chapter material, cases, and illustrations examining the accelerating pace of global and technological change and its impact on companies, markets, and industries
- Comprehensive supplemental material and industry leading e-book support
- Comprehensive Web site for both the student and the instructor
- A proven model-based treatment of strategic management that allows for self-directed study, easy-to-understand presentation—in a package that represents the most cost effective book on the market today
- A proven author team recognized with more than 20 research awards from various professional organizations including five "Best Paper" awards from the prestigious Academy of Management

The eleventh edition of *Strategic Management* is divided into 14 chapters. They provide a thorough, state-of-the-art treatment of the critical business skills needed to plan and manage strategic activities. While the text continues a solid academic connection, students will find the text material to be practical, skills oriented, and relevant to their jobs and entrepreneurial aspirations.

We were thrilled to have access to the world's best business publication, *BusinessWeek*, to create examples, illustration modules, and various cases. The result is an extensively enhanced text and cases benefiting from hundreds of contemporary examples and illustrations provided by *BusinessWeek* writers worldwide. You will see *BusinessWeek*'s impact on our discussion case feature, our Strategy in Action modules, our cases, and our Web site. Of course, we are also pleased with several hundred examples blended into the text material, which came from recent issues of *BusinessWeek* or *www.businessweek.com*

AN OVERVIEW OF OUR TEXT MATERIAL

The eleventh edition uses a model of the strategic management process as the basis for the organization of the text material. Adopters have identified this model as a key distinctive competence for our text because it offers a logical flow, distinct elements, and an easy-to-understand guide to strategic management. The model reflects strategic analysis at different organizational levels as well as the importance of innovation in the strategic management process. The model and parallel chapter organization provides a student-friendly approach to the study of strategic management.

The first chapter provides an overview of the strategic management process and explains what students will find as they use this book. The remaining 13 chapters cover each part of the strategic management process and techniques that aid strategic analysis, decision making, implementation, control and renewal. The literature and research in the strategic management area have developed at a rapid pace in recent years in both the academic and business press. The eleventh edition includes several upgrades designed to incorporate major developments from both these sources. While we include cutting-edge concepts, we emphasize straightforward, logical, and simple presentation so that students can grasp these new ideas without additional reading. The following are a few of the elements of this text that deserve particular note:

Corporate Social Responsibility and Business Ethics

Because of the public's heightened sensitivity to the behavior of strategic managers, we developed a new chapter for the eleventh edition that focuses on Corporate Social Responsibility and Business Ethics. Always important in our text, we are pleased to bring these important issues into the foreground of informed classroom instruction. A key feature of the new Chapter 3 is its emphasis on "naming names." We identify dozens of corporations that are taking steps to assure that their stakeholders are properly represented in their communities and the world. Our goal is to help students to understand how Corporate Social Responsibility and Business Ethics can be managed properly.

Sarbanes-Oxley in 2010 and Beyond

Responding to highly publicized corporate and executive misconduct in recent years, the Sarbanes-Oxley Act was passed by the U.S. Congress requiring certifications for financial statements, new corporate regulations, disclosure requirements, and penalties for failure to comply. Chapter 3 provides in-depth coverage of the act, including discussions of the provisions restricting the corporate control of executives, accounting firms, auditing committees, and attorneys. Particular attention is given to its impact on the governance structure of American corporations, including the heightened role of corporate internal auditors who now routinely deal directly with top corporate officials, after its initial years in existence.

Agency Theory

Of the recent approaches to corporate governance and strategic management, probably none has had a greater impact on managerial thinking than agency theory. While the breadth and measurement of its usefulness continue to be hotly debated, students of strategic management need to understand the role of agency in our free enterprise, capitalistic system. This edition presents agency theory in a coherent and practical manner. We believe that it arms students with a cutting-edge approach to increasing their understanding of the priorities of executive decision making and strategic control.

Resource-Based View of the Firm

One of the most significant conceptual frameworks to systematize and "measure" a firm's strategic capabilities is the resource-based view (RBV) of the firm. The RBV has received major academic and business press attention during the last decade, helping to shape its value as a conceptual tool by adding rigor during the internal analysis and strategic analysis phases of the strategic management process. This edition provides a revised treatment of this concept in Chapter 6, Internal Analysis. We present the RBV in a logical and practical manner as a central underpinning of sound strategic analysis. Students will find several useful examples and a straightforward treatment of different types of "assets" and organizational capabilities culminating in the ability to determine when these resources create competitive advantage. They will see different ways to answer the question "what makes a resource valuable?" and be able to determine when that resource creates a competitive advantage in a systematic, disciplined, creative manner.

The Value Disciplines

A new approach to generic strategy centers on delivering superior customer value through one of three value disciplines: operational excellence, customer intimacy, or product leadership. Companies that specialize in one of these disciplines, while simultaneously meeting industry standards in the other two, gain a sustainable lead in their markets. Chapter 7, Long-Term Objectives and Strategies, provides details on these approaches with several examples of successful company experiences.

Bankruptcy

Many revisions in this book are driven by changes in business trends. Nowhere is that more evident than in our discussion of company bankruptcy. In the 1980s bankruptcy was treated as a last option that precluded any future for the firm. In the first decade of the 2000s the view has dramatically changed. Bankruptcy has been elevated to the status of a strategic option, and executives need to be well versed in its potentials and limitations, as you will see in Chapter 7, Long-Term Objectives and Strategies.

Executive Compensation

While our text has led the field in providing a practice-oriented approach to strategic management, we have redoubled our efforts to treat topics with an emphasis on application. Our revised section on executive compensation in Chapter 10, Implementation, is a clear example. You will find an extended discussion of executive bonus options that provides a comparison of the relative merits of the five most popular approaches, to include the current debate on the use, or overuse, of stock options and the need to accurately account for their true cost.

Outsourcing

"Outsourcing" of jobs and functions has become a global business necessity in the majority of companies in the U.S., Europe and indeed throughout the world today. It has moved from simply seeking low cost manufacturing options to having product development, product design, and indeed core innovation sought by some of the world's best known companies actually done outside that company by an "outsourced" provider. Chapter 11, Organizational Structure, along with an excellent special *BusinessWeek* case, reviews the pros and cons of outsourcing along with a practical look at the post-outsourcing reality of an interconnected global economy.

Structuring Effective Organizations

The accelerating rate of change often driven by the sudden emergence of opportunities in global market niches demanding quick decisions and immediate action places unprecedented demands on an organization's use of people and resources. Forward thinking entrepreneurs and business leaders have responded to this new reality by crafting organizational structures that are fluid, open, virtual networks of people, expertise, and knowledge. Doing so is absolutely essential in implementing twenty-first century strategies. Chapter 11, Organizational Structure, helps students understand how to structure effective organizations in these types of market settings. We identify numerous organizations that illustrate effective structures, and explore ways to incorporate key advantages associated with traditional organizing principles into organizational structures that are at the same time ambidextrous, fluid, boundaryless, and comprehensively responsive. And we examine Web-enabled virtual organizations that are rapidly emerging as new "structureless" business organizations.

Leadership

Developments of the last few years that highlight corporate and executive misconduct along with the unprecedented challenge faced by companies seeking to survive and prosper in a dynamic, constantly changing global business environment highlight the critical need for solid leadership more than ever before. Chapter 12, Leadership and Culture, provides a completely new examination of leadership, the critical things that good leaders do, and a look at ways young operating managers can develop specific skills that will help them become outstanding future leaders in what will be an incredibly dynamic global economy.

Innovation and Entrepreneurship

In a global economy that allows everyone everywhere instant information and instant connectivity, change often occurs at lightning speed. So leaders are increasingly looking for their firms to embrace innovation and entrepreneurship as essential foundations from which to respond and find opportunity in overwhelming uncertainty. Indeed this rapid change and steady uncertainty is the ideal setting within which start-up entrepreneurs and disruptive technologies typically thrive. Chapter 14, Innovation and Entrepreneurship, examines innovation, different types of innovation, and the best ways to bring more innovative activity into a firm. It examines the entrepreneurship process as another way to build innovative responsiveness and opportunity recognition into a firm, both in new venture settings and in large business organizations. Finally, it looks at the Web-enabled ways businesses are linking worldwide with people who are not part of their organizations, yet are key players helping to innovate and create their businesses' future.

Strategic Control

Rapid change necessitates control that is at once loose and flexible yet also tight and focused. Chapter 13 examines four ways strategists create "steering" controls over a firm's overall direction to keep its long-term objectives in focus. Conversely, operating activities and periodic review seek to dissect performance so as to ensure efficient and effective use of company resources. Chapter 13 provides new treatment of approaches to do this including the latest on the Balanced Scorecard approach, Six Sigma, CCC21, continuous improvement and the evaluation of deviations in short-term performance.

OUR STRATEGIC ALLIANCE WITH *BUSINESSWEEK*

We have long felt *BusinessWeek* to be the unquestionable leader among business periodicals for its coverage of strategic issues in businesses, industries, and economies worldwide, and we are proud to include articles and cases which illustrate relevant and compelling examples which resonate with students and instructors alike.

Personal surveys of collegiate faculty teaching strategic management confirmed our intuition: While there are many outstanding business magazines and new publications, none match the consistent quality found in *BusinessWeek* for the coverage of corporate strategies, case stories, and topics of interest to students and professors of strategic management. From our point of view, this is a unique four-way win-win; teachers, students, authors, and *BusinessWeek* all stand to gain in many ways. The most direct way you can see the impact of the *BusinessWeek* alliance is in three book features: discussion cases, Strategy in Action modules, and 30 short cases.

Strategy in Action Modules

Another pedagogical feature, Strategy in Action modules, has become standard in most strategy books. We have drawn on the work of *BusinessWeek* field correspondents worldwide to fill 100 new *BusinessWeek* Strategy in Action modules with short, hard-hitting current illustrations of key chapter topics. We are energized by the excitement, interest, and practical illustration value our students tell us they provide.

Short Cases

As professors of strategic management, we continually look for content or pedagogical developments and enhancements that make the strategy course more valuable. Some shorter cases play a role by facilitating a focus on one incident, or allow for a discussion of only 20 to 30 minutes so that the case topic can be used in concert with other materials, or provide a springboard for discussion of "real time" situations, perhaps supplemented by Web site and Internet-derived information. These short cases generate useful class discussions while allowing coverage of other material during the case portion of the course or as a supplement and source of variety during the text portion of the course. We think you will find it useful. We have included 30 such cases in the eleventh edition while continuing to include 20 longer cases.

CASES IN THE ELEVENTH EDITION

We are pleased to offer 50 excellent cases in this edition. As noted earlier, these include 20 comprehensive cases and industry notes that adopters expect in a strategic management textbook. The remaining 30 cases are short cases built on solidly developed *BusinessWeek* articles from the most recent editions of that magazine. Both sets of cases present companies, industries, and situations that are easily recognized, current, and interesting. We have a good mixture of small and large firms, start-ups and industry leaders, global and domestically focused companies, and service, retail, manufacturing, technology, and diversified activities. We explore U.S.-based companies, European-based companies, Asian-based companies and emerging Middle Eastern economies.

OUR WEB SITE

A substantial Web site has been designed to aid your use of this book. It includes areas accessible only to instructors and areas specifically designed to assist students. The instructor section includes supplement files, which include detailed teaching notes, PowerPoint slides, and case teaching notes for all 50 case studies, which keep your work area less cluttered and let you quickly obtain information. Students are provided company and related business periodical (and other) Web site linkages to aid and expedite their case research and preparation efforts. Practice quizzes are provided to help students prepare for tests on the text material and attempt to lower their anxiety in that regard. We expect students will find the Web site useful and interesting. Please visit us at www.mhhe.com/pearce11e.

SUPPLEMENTS

Components of our teaching package include a revised, comprehensive instructor's manual, test bank, PowerPoint presentation, a large collection of videos designed to complement many of the cases in the book, and a computerized test bank. These are all available to qualified adopters of the text. Professors can also use a simulation game as a possible package with this text: the Business Strategy Game (Thompson/Stappenbeck). The Business Strategy Game provides an exercise to help students understand how the functional pieces of a business fit together. Students will work with the numbers, explore options, and try to unite production, marketing, finance, and human resource decisions into a coherent strategy.

Acknowledgments

We have benefited from the help of many people in the evolution of this project over eleven editions. Students, adopters, colleagues, reviewers, and business contacts have provided hundreds of insightful comments, suggestions, and contributions that have progressively enhanced this book and its supplements. We are indebted to the researchers and practicing managers who have accelerated the development of the literature on strategic management.

We are particularly indebted to the talented case researchers who have produced the cases used in this book, as well as to case researchers dedicated to the revitalization of case research as an important academic endeavor. First-class case research is a major avenue through which top strategic management scholars should be recognized.

Several reviewers provided feedback to us for the eleventh edition. We are grateful for their honest and compelling suggestions, which facilitated the revisions to this edition:

Mitch Ellison
Quincy University

Sally Fowler
Kogod School of Business, American University

Richard L. Jines
Oakland City University

Timothy S. Kiessling
Eastern Kentucky University

Michael D. Meeks
San Francisco State University

Michael D. Pfarrer
University of Maryland, College Park

Michael W. Pitts
Virginia Commonwealth University

Douglas E. Thomas
University of New Mexico

Marta Szabo White
Georgia State University

Scott Williams
Wright State University

Beth Woodard
Belmont University

The development of this book through eleven editions has benefited from the generous commitments of time, energy, and ideas from our colleagues. The valuable ideas, recommendations, and support from these outstanding scholars, teachers, and practitioners have added quality to this book:

Mary Ackenhusen, *INSEAD*; A. J. Almaney, *DePaul University*; James Almeida, *Fairleigh Dickinson University*; B. Alpert, *San Francisco State University*; Alan Amason, *University of Georgia*; Sonny Aries, *University of Toledo*; Katherine A. Auer, *The Pennsylvania State University*; Henry Beam, *Western Michigan University*; Amy Vernberg Beekman, *University of Tampa*; Patricia Bilafer, *Bentley College*; Robert Earl Bolick, *Metropolitan State University*; Bill Boulton, *Auburn University*; Charles Boyd, *Southwest Missouri State University*; Thomas Boyle, *Seton Hill University*; Jeff Bracker, *University of Louisville*; Dorothy Brawley, *Kennesaw State College*; James W. Bronson, *Washington State University*; Eric Brown, *George Mason University*; Robert F. Bruner, *INSEAD*; William Burr, *University of Oregon*; Gene E. Burton, *California State University–Fresno*; Edgar T. Busch, *Western Kentucky University*; Charles M. Byles, *Virginia Commonwealth University*; Jim Callahan, *University of LaVerne*; James W. Camerius, *Northern Michigan University*; Sam D. Cappel, *Southeastern Louisiana University*; Richard Castaldi, *San Francisco State University*; Gary J. Castogiovanni, *Louisiana State University*; Jafor Chowdbury, *University of Scranton*; James J. Chrisman, *University of Calgary*; Neil Churchill, *INSEAD*; J. Carl Clamp, *University of South Carolina*; David R. Conley, *Louisiana State University at Alexandria*; Earl D. Cooper, *Florida Institute of Technology*; Louis Coraggio, *Troy State*

University; Jeff Covin, *Indiana University*; John P. Cragin, *Oklahoma Baptist University*; Larry Cummings, *Northwestern University*; Peter Davis, *University of North Carolina-Charlotte*; William Davis, *Auburn University*; Julio DeCastro, *University of Colorado*; Kim DeDee, *University of Wisconsin*; Philippe Demigne, *INSEAD*; D. Keith Denton, *Southwest Missouri State University*; F. Derakhshan, *California State University–San Bernardino*; Brook Dobni, *University of Saskatchewan*; Mark Dollinger, *Indiana University*; Jean–Christopher Donck, *INSEAD*; Lon Doty, *University of Phoenix/San Jose State University*; Max E. Douglas, *Indiana State University*; Yves Doz, *INSEAD*; Julie Driscoll, *Bentley College*; Derrick Dsouza, *University of North Texas*; Thomas J. Dudley, *Pepperdine University*; John Dunkelberg, *Wake Forest University*; Soumitra Dutta, *INSEAD*; Harold Dyck, *California State University*; Raed Elaydi, *University of North Carolina-Chapel Hill*; Norbert Esser, *Central Wesleyan College*; Forest D. Etheredge, *Aurora University*; Liam Fahey, *Babson College*; Mary Fandel, *Bentley College*; Mark Fiegener, *University of Washington–Tacoma*; Calvin D. Fowler, *Embry-Riddle Aeronautical University*; Mark Fox, *IUSB*; Debbie Francis, *Jacksonville State University*; Elizabeth Freeman, *Southern Methodist University*; Mahmound A. Gaballa, *Mansfield University*; Donna M. Gallo, *Boston College*; Diane Garsombke, *Brenau University*; Betsy Gatewood, *Wake Forest University*; Bertrand George, *INSEAD*; Michael Geringer, *Southern Methodist University*; Manton C. Gibbs, *Indiana University of Pennsylvania*; David Gilliss, *San Jose State University*; Nicholas A. Glaskowsky, Jr., *University of Miami*; Tom Goho, *Wake Forest University*; Jon Goodman, *University of Southern California*; Pradeep Gopalakrishna, *Hofstra University*; R. H. Gordon, *Hofstra University*; Barbara Gottfried, *Bentley College*; Peter Goulet, *University of Northern Iowa*; Walter E. Greene, *University of Texas–Pan American*; Sue Greenfeld, *California State University–San Bernardino*; David W. Grigsby, *Clemson University*; Daniel E. Hallock, *St. Edward's University*; Don Hambrick, *Pennsylvania State University*; Barry Hand, *Indiana State University*; Jean M. Hanebury, *Texas A&M University*; Karen Hare, *Bentley College*; Earl Harper, *Grand Valley State University*; William B. Hartley, *SUNY Fredonia*; Samuel Hazen, *Tarleton State University*; W. Harvey Hegarty, *Indiana University*; Edward A. Hegner, *California State University–Sacramento*; Marilyn M. Helms, *Dalton State College*; Lanny Herron, *University of Baltimore*; D. Higginbothan, *University of Missouri*; Roger Higgs, *Western Carolina University*; William H. Hinkle, *Johns Hopkins University*; Charles T. Hofer, *University of Georgia*; Alan N. Hoffman, *Bentley College*; Richard Hoffman, *Salisbury University*; Eileen Hogan, *Kutztown University*; Phyllis G. Holland, *Valdosta State University*; Gary L. Holman, *St. Martin's College*; Don Hopkins, *Temple University*; Cecil Horst, *Keller Graduate School of Management*; Mel Horwitch, *Theseus*; Henry F. House, *Auburn University–Montgomery*; William C. House, *University of Arkansas–Fayetteville*; Frank Hoy, *University of Texas–El Paso*; Warren Huckabay, *Sammamish, WA*; Eugene H. Hunt, *Virginia Commonwealth University*; Tammy G. Hunt, *University of North Carolina–Wilmington*; John W. Huonker, *University of Arizona*; Janice Jackson, *Western New England College*; Stephen R. Jenner, *California State University*; Shailendra Jha, *Wilfrid Laurier University–Ontario*; C. Boyd Johnson, *California State University–Fresno*; Troy Jones, *University of Central Florida*; Jon Kalinowski, *Mankato State University*; Al Kayloe, *Lake Erie College*; Michael J. Keefe, *Southwest Texas State University*; Kay Keels, *Brenau University*; James A. Kidney, *Southern Connecticut State University*; John D. King, *Embry-Riddle Aeronautical University*; Raymond M. Kinnunen, *Northeastern University*; John B. Knauff, *University of St. Thomas*; Rose Knotts, *University of North Texas*; Dan Kopp, *Southwest Missouri State University*; Michael Koshuta, *Valparaiso University*; Jeffrey A. Krug, *The University of Illinois*; Myroslaw Kyj, *Widener University*; Dick LaBarre, *Ferris State University*; Joseph Lampel, *City University–London*; Ryan Lancaster, *The University of Phoenix*; Sharon Ungar Lane, *Bentley College*; Patrick Langan, *Wartburg College*; Roland Larose, *Bentley College*; Anne T. Lawrence, *San Jose*

State University; Joseph Leonard, *Miami University–Ohio*; Robert Letovsky, *Saint Michael's College*; Michael Levy, *INSEAD*; Benjamin Litt, *Lehigh University*; Frank S. Lockwood, *Western Carolina University*; John Logan, *University of South Carolina*; Sandra Logan, *Newberry College*; Jean M. Lundin, *Lake Superior State University*; Rodney H. Mabry, *Clemson University*; Jennifer Mailey, *SUNY Empire State College*; Donald C. Malm, *University of Missouri–St. Louis*; Charles C. Manz, *University of Massachusetts*; John Maurer, *Wayne State University*; Denise Mazur, *Aquinas College*; Edward McClelland, *Roanoke College*; Bob McDonald, *Central Wesleyan College*; Patricia P. McDougall, *Indiana University*; S. Mehta, *San Jose State University*; Ralph Melaragno, *Pepperdine University*; Richard Merner, *University of Delaware*; Linda Merrill, *Bentley College*; Timothy Mescon, *Kennesaw State College*; Philip C. Micka, *Park College*; Bill J. Middlebrook, *Southwest Texas State University*; Robert Mockler, *St. John's University*; James F. Molly, Jr., *Northeastern University*; Cynthia Montgomery, *Harvard University*; W. Kent Moore, *Valdosta State University*; Jaideep Motwani, *Grand Valley State University*; Karen Mullen, *Bentley College*; Gary W. Muller, *Hofstra University*; Terry Muson, *Northern Montana College*; Daniel Muzyka, *INSEAD*; Stephanie Newell, *Eastern Michigan University*; Michael E. Nix, *Trinity College of Vermont*; Kenneth Olm, *University of Texas–Austin*; K. C. Oshaughnessy, *Western Michigan University*; Benjamin M. Oviatt, *Georgia State University*; Joseph Paolillo, *University of Mississippi*; Gerald Parker, *St. Louis University*; Paul J. Patinka, *University of Colorado*; James W. Pearce, *Western Carolina University*; Michael W. Pitts, *Virginia Commonwealth University*; Douglas Polley, *St. Cloud State University*; Carlos de Pommes, *Theseus*; Valerie J. Porciello, *Bentley College*; Mark S. Poulous, *St. Edward's University*; John B. Pratt, *Saint Joseph's College*; Oliver Ray Price, *West Coast University*; John Primus, *Golden Gate University*; Norris Rath, *Shepard College*; Paula Rechner, *California State University–Fresno*; Richard Reed, *Washington State University*; J. Bruce Regan, *University of St. Thomas*; H. Lee Remmers, *INSEAD*; F. A. Ricci, *Georgetown University*; Keith Robbins, *Winthrop University*; Gary Roberts, *Kennesaw State College*; Lloyd E. Roberts, *Mississippi College*; John K. Ross III, *Southwest Texas State University*; George C. Rubenson, *Salisbury State University*; Alison Rude, *Bentley College*; Les Rue, *Georgia State University*; Carol Rugg, *Bentley College*; J. A. Ruslyk, *Memphis State University*; Ronald J. Salazar, *Human Skills Management, LLC*; Bill Sandberg, *University of South Carolina*; Uri Savoray, *INSEAD*; Jack Scarborough, *Barry University*; Paul J. Schlachter, *Florida International University*; Greg Schultz, *Carroll College*; David Schweiger, *University of South Carolina*; John Seeger, *Bentley College*; Martin Shapiro, *Iona College*; Arthur Sharplin, *McNeese State University*; Frank M. Shipper, *Salisbury State University*; Rodney C. Shrader, *University of Illinois*; Lois Shufeldt, *Southwest Missouri State University*; Bonnie Silvieria, *Bentley College*; F. Bruce Simmons III, *The University of Akron*; Mark Simon, *Oakland University*; Michael Skipton, *Memorial University*; Fred Smith, *Western Illinois University*; Scott Snell, *Michigan State University*; Coral R. Snodgrass, *Canisius College*; Rudolph P. Snowadzky, *University of Maine*; Neil Snyder, *University of Virginia*; Melvin J. Stanford, *Mankato State University*; Romuald A. Stone, *DeVry University*; Warren S. Stone, *Virginia Commonwealth University*; Ram Subramanian, *Grand Valley State University*; Paul M. Swiercz, *George Washington University*; Robert L. Swinth, *Montana State University*; Chris Taubman, *INSEAD*; Russell Teasley, *Western Carolina University*; James Teboul, *INSEAD*; George H. Tompson, *University of Tampa*; Melanie Trevino, *University of Texas–ElPaso*; Howard Tu, *University of Memphis*; Craig Tunwall, *Empire State College*; Elaine M. Tweedy, *University of Scranton*; Arieh A. Ullmann, *Binghamton University*; P. Veglahn, *James Madison University*; George Vozikis, *University of Tulsa*; William Waddell, *California State University–Los Angeles*; Bill Warren, *College of William and Mary*; Kirby Warren, *Columbia University*; Steven J. Warren, *Rutgers University*; Michael White, *University of Tulsa*; Randy White, *Auburn*

University; Sam E. White, *Portland State University*; Cleon Wiggins, *Park University*; Frank Winfrey, *Lyon College*; Joseph Wolfe, *Experiential Adventures*; Robley Wood, *Virginia Commonwealth University*; Diana Wong, *Eastern Michigan University*; Edware D. Writh, Jr., *Florida Institute of Technology*; John Young, *University of New Mexico*; S. David Young, *INSEAD*; Jan Zahrly, *Old Dominion University*; and Alan Zeiber, *Portland State University*.

We are affiliated with two separate universities, both of which provide environments that deserve thanks. As the Villanova School of Business Endowed Chair at Villanova University, Jack is able to combine his scholarly and teaching activities with his coauthorship of this text. He is grateful to Villanova University, Dean James Danko, and his colleagues for the support and encouragement they provide.

Richard appreciates the support provided within the Moore School of Business by Mr. Dean Kress, Dean Hildy Teegen, Dr. Brian Klass, Cheryl Fowler, Susie Gorsage, and Carol Lucas.

We want to thank Dr. Ram Subramanian, Montclair State University, for his outstanding contributions in this instructor's manual and ancillaries for the eleventh edition. His dedication and attention to detail make this a better book. Likewise, we are most grateful to Dr. Amit Shah, Frostburg State University, for his excellent earlier contributions to this project.

Leaders at McGraw-Hill/Irwin deserve our utmost thanks and appreciation. Gerald Saykes, John Black, John Biernat, and Craig Beytein contributed to our early success. The editorial leadership of Doug Hughes and Michael Ablassmeir helps to assure that it will continue in this eleventh edition. Editorial coordinator Kelly Pekelder and project manager Bruce Gin helped us to produce a much improved book. The McGraw-Hill/Irwin field organization deserves particular recognition and thanks for the amazing sales record of this text.

We also want to thank *Business Week,* which is proving to be an excellent strategic partner.

We hope that you will find our book and ancillaries all that you expect. We welcome your ideas and recommendations about our material, and we wish you the utmost success in teaching and studying strategic management.

Dr. John A. Pearce II
Villanova School of Business
Villanova University
Villanova, PA 19085–1678

Dr. Richard Robinson
Moore School of Business
University of South Carolina
Columbia, SC 29208

Brief Contents

Table of Contents

Part **One**

Overview of Strategic Management

The first chapter of this book introduces strategic management, the set of decisions and actions that result in the design and activation of strategies to achieve the objectives of an organization. The chapter provides an overview of the nature, benefits, and terminology of and the need for strategic management. Subsequent chapters provide greater detail.

The first major section of Chapter 1, "The Nature and Value of Strategic Management," emphasizes the practical value and benefits of strategic management for a firm. It also distinguishes between a firm's strategic decisions and its other planning tasks.

The section stresses the key point that strategic management activities are undertaken at three levels: corporate, business, and functional. The distinctive characteristics of strategic decision making at each of these levels affect the impact of activities at these levels on company operations. Other topics dealt with in this section are the value of formality in strategic management and the alignment of strategy makers in strategy formulation and implementation. The section concludes with a review of the planning research on business, which demonstrates that the use of strategic management processes yields financial and behavioral benefits that justify their costs.

The second major section of Chapter 1 presents a model of the strategic management process. The model, which will serve as an outline for the remainder of the text, describes approaches currently used by strategic planners. Its individual components are carefully defined and explained, as is the process for integrating them into the strategic management process. The section ends with a discussion of the model's practical limitations and the advisability of tailoring the recommendations made to actual business situations.

Chapter **One**

Strategic Management

After reading and studying this chapter, you should be able to

1. Explain the concept of strategic management.

2. Describe how strategic decisions differ from other decisions that managers make.

3. Name the benefits and risks of a participative approach to strategic decision making.

4. Understand the types of strategic decisions for which managers at different levels of the company are responsible.

5. Describe a comprehensive model of strategic decision making.

6. Appreciate the importance of strategic management as a process.

7. Give examples of strategic decisions that companies have recently made.

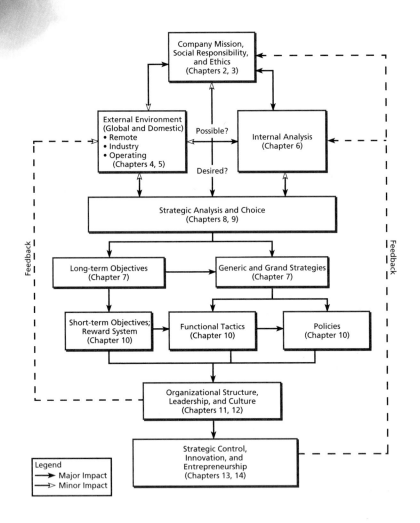

Company Mission, Social Responsibility, and Ethics (Chapters 2, 3)

External Environment (Global and Domestic)
• Remote
• Industry
• Operating
(Chapters 4, 5)

Possible?

Internal Analysis (Chapter 6)

Desired?

Strategic Analysis and Choice (Chapters 8, 9)

Long-term Objectives (Chapter 7)

Generic and Grand Strategies (Chapter 7)

Short-term Objectives; Reward System (Chapter 10)

Functional Tactics (Chapter 10)

Policies (Chapter 10)

Organizational Structure, Leadership, and Culture (Chapters 11, 12)

Strategic Control, Innovation, and Entrepreneurship (Chapters 13, 14)

Feedback

Feedback

Legend
→ Major Impact
⇢ Minor Impact

THE NATURE AND VALUE OF STRATEGIC MANAGEMENT

Managing activities internal to the firm is only part of the modern executive's responsibilities. The modern executive also must respond to the challenges posed by the firm's immediate and remote external environments. The immediate external environment includes competitors, suppliers, increasingly scarce resources, government agencies and their ever more numerous regulations, and customers whose preferences often shift inexplicably. The remote external environment comprises economic and social conditions, political priorities, and technological developments, all of which must be anticipated, monitored, assessed, and incorporated into the executive's decision making. However, the executive often is compelled to subordinate the demands of the firm's internal activities and external environment to the multiple and often inconsistent requirements of its stakeholders: owners, top managers, employees, communities, customers, and country. To deal effectively with everything that affects the growth and profitability of a firm, executives employ management processes that they feel will position it optimally in its competitive environment by maximizing the anticipation of environmental changes and of unexpected internal and competitive demands.

To earn profits, firms need to perfect processes that respond to increases in the size and number of competing firms; to the expanded role of government as a buyer, seller, regulator, and competitor in the free enterprise system; and to greater business involvement in international trade. Perhaps the most significant improvement in these management processes came when "long-range planning," "planning, programming, budgeting," and "business policy" were blended with increased emphasis on environmental forecasting and external considerations in formulating and implementing plans. This all-encompassing approach is known as strategic management.

strategic management
The set of decisions and actions that result in the formulation and implementation of plans designed to achieve a company's objectives.

Strategic management is defined as the set of decisions and actions that result in the formulation and implementation of plans designed to achieve a company's objectives. It comprises nine critical tasks:

1. Formulate the company's mission, including broad statements about its purpose, philosophy, and goals.
2. Conduct an analysis that reflects the company's internal conditions and capabilities.
3. Assess the company's external environment, including both the competitive and the general contextual factors.
4. Analyze the company's options by matching its resources with the external environment.
5. Identify the most desirable options by evaluating each option in light of the company's mission.
6. Select a set of long-term objectives and grand strategies that will achieve the most desirable options.
7. Develop annual objectives and short-term strategies that are compatible with the selected set of long-term objectives and grand strategies.
8. Implement the strategic choices by means of budgeted resource allocations in which the matching of tasks, people, structures, technologies, and reward systems is emphasized.
9. Evaluate the success of the strategic process as an input for future decision making.

strategy
Large-scale, future-oriented plans for interacting with the competitive environment to achieve company objectives.

As these nine tasks indicate, strategic management involves the planning, directing, organizing, and controlling of a company's strategy-related decisions and actions. By **strategy,** managers mean their large-scale, future-oriented plans for interacting with the competitive environment to achieve company objectives. A strategy is a company's game plan.

Although that plan does not precisely detail all future deployments (of people, finances, and material), it does provide a framework for managerial decisions. A strategy reflects a company's awareness of how, when, and where it should compete; against whom it should compete; and for what purposes it should compete.

Dimensions of Strategic Decisions

What decisions facing a business are strategic and therefore deserve strategic management attention? Typically, strategic issues have the following dimensions.

Strategic Issues Require Top-Management Decisions   Because strategic decisions over-arch several areas of a firm's operations, they require top-management involvement. Usually only top management has the perspective needed to understand the broad implications of such decisions and the power to authorize the necessary resource allocations. As top manager of Volvo GM Heavy Truck Corporation, Karl-Erling Trogen, president, wanted to push the company closer to the customer by overarching operations with service and customer relations empowering the workforce closest to the customer with greater knowledge and authority. This strategy called for a major commitment to the parts and service end of the business where customer relations was first priority. Trogen's philosophy was to so empower the workforce that more operating questions were handled on the line where workers worked directly with customers. He believed that the corporate headquarters should be more focused on strategic issues, such as engineering, production, quality, and marketing.

Strategic Issues Require Large Amounts of the Firm's Resources   Strategic decisions involve substantial allocations of people, physical assets, or moneys that either must be redirected from internal sources or secured from outside the firm. They also commit the firm to actions over an extended period. For these reasons, they require substantial resources. Whirlpool Corporation's "Quality Express" product delivery program exemplified a strategy that required a strong financial and personnel commitment from the company. The plan was to deliver products to customers when, where, and how they wanted them. This proprietary service uses contract logistics strategy to deliver Whirlpool, Kitchen Aid, Roper, and Estate brand appliances to 90 percent of the company's dealer and builder customers within 24 hours and to the other 10 percent within 48 hours. In highly competitive service-oriented businesses, achieving and maintaining customer satisfaction frequently involve a commitment from every facet of the organization.

Strategic Issues Often Affect the Firm's Long-Term Prosperity   Strategic decisions ostensibly commit the firm for a long time, typically five years; however, the impact of such decisions often lasts much longer. Once a firm has committed itself to a particular strategy, its image and competitive advantages usually are tied to that strategy. Firms become known in certain markets, for certain products, with certain technologies. They would jeopardize their previous gains if they shifted from these markets, products, or technologies by adopting a radically different strategy. Thus, strategic decisions have enduring effects on firms—for better or worse. For example, Commerce One created an alliance with SAP in 1999 to improve its position in the e-marketplace for business to business (B2B) sales. After taking three years to ready its e-portals, Commerce One and SAP were ready to take on the market in 2002. Unfortunately, the market changed. The "foolproof strategy" got to the market too late and the alliance failed.

For years, Toyota had a successful strategy of marketing its sedans in Japan. With this strategy came an image, a car for an older customer, and a competitive advantage, a traditional base for Toyota. The strategy was effective, but as its customer base grew older its strategy remained unchanged. A younger customer market saw the image as unattractive and began to seek out other manufacturers. Toyota's strategic task in foreign markets is to formulate and implement a strategy that will reignite interest in its image.

Strategic Issues Are Future Oriented Strategic decisions are based on what managers forecast, rather than on what they know. In such decisions, emphasis is placed on the development of projections that will enable the firm to select the most promising strategic options. In the turbulent and competitive free enterprise environment, a firm will succeed only if it takes a proactive (anticipatory) stance toward change.

Strategic Issues Usually Have Multifunctional or Multibusiness Consequences Strategic decisions have complex implications for most areas of the firm. Decisions about such matters as customer mix, competitive emphasis, or organizational structure necessarily involve a number of the firm's strategic business units (SBUs), divisions, or program units. All of these areas will be affected by allocations or reallocations of responsibilities and resources that result from these decisions.

Strategic Issues Require Considering the Firm's External Environment All business firms exist in an open system. They affect and are affected by external conditions that are largely beyond their control. Therefore, to successfully position a firm in competitive situations, its strategic managers must look beyond its operations. They must consider what relevant others (e.g., competitors, customers, suppliers, creditors, government, and labor) are likely to do.

Three Levels of Strategy

The decision-making hierarchy of a firm typically contains three levels. At the top of this hierarchy is the corporate level, composed principally of a board of directors and the chief executive and administrative officers. They are responsible for the firm's financial performance and for the achievement of nonfinancial goals, such as enhancing the firm's image and fulfilling its social responsibilities. To a large extent, attitudes at the corporate level reflect the concerns of stockholders and society at large. In a multibusiness firm, corporate-level executives determine the businesses in which the firm should be involved. They also set objectives and formulate strategies that span the activities and functional areas of these businesses. Corporate-level strategic managers attempt to exploit their firm's distinctive competencies by adopting a portfolio approach to the management of its businesses and by developing long-term plans, typically for a three- to five-year period. A key corporate strategy of Airborne Express's operations involved direct sale to high-volume corporate accounts and developing an expansive network in the international arena. Instead of setting up operations overseas, Airborne's long-term strategy was to form direct associations with national companies within foreign countries to expand and diversify their operations.

Another example of the portfolio approach involved a plan by state-owned Saudi Arabian Oil to spend $1.4 billion to build and operate an oil refinery in Korea with its partner, Ssangyong. To implement their program, the Saudis embarked on a new "cut-out-the-middleman" strategy to reduce the role of international oil companies in the processing and selling of Saudi crude oil.

In the middle of the decision-making hierarchy is the business level, composed principally of business and corporate managers. These managers must translate the statements of direction and intent generated at the corporate level into concrete objectives and strategies for individual business divisions, or SBUs. In essence, business-level strategic managers determine how the firm will compete in the selected product-market arena. They strive to identify and secure the most promising market segment within that arena. This segment is the piece of the total market that the firm can claim and defend because of its competitive advantages.

At the bottom of the decision-making hierarchy is the functional level, composed principally of managers of product, geographic, and functional areas. They develop annual objectives and short-term strategies in such areas as production, operations, research and development, finance and accounting, marketing, and human relations. However, their

EXHIBIT 1.1
Alternative Strategic Management Structures

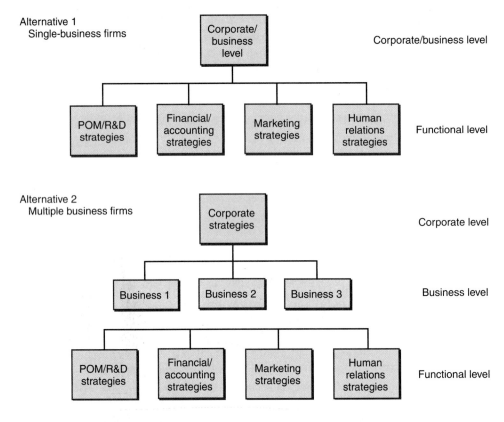

principal responsibility is to implement or execute the firm's strategic plans. Whereas corporate- and business-level managers center their attention on "doing the right things," managers at the functional level center their attention on "doing things right." Thus, they address such issues as the efficiency and effectiveness of production and marketing systems, the quality of customer service, and the success of particular products and services in increasing the firm's market shares.

Exhibit 1.1 depicts the three levels of strategic management as structured in practice. In alternative 1, the firm is engaged in only one business and the corporate- and business-level responsibilities are concentrated in a single group of directors, officers, and managers. This is the organizational format of most small businesses.

Alternative 2, the classical corporate structure, comprises three fully operative levels: the corporate level, the business level, and the functional level. The approach taken throughout this text assumes the use of alternative 2. Moreover, whenever appropriate, topics are covered from the perspective of each level of strategic management. In this way, the text presents a comprehensive discussion of the strategic management process.

Characteristics of Strategic Management Decisions

The characteristics of strategic management decisions vary with the level of strategic activity considered. As shown in Exhibit 1.2, decisions at the corporate level tend to be more value oriented, more conceptual, and less concrete than decisions at the business or functional level. For example, at Alcoa, the world's largest aluminum maker, chairman Paul O'Neill made Alcoa one of the nation's most centralized organizations by imposing a dramatic management reorganization that wiped out two layers of management. He found that this effort not only reduced costs but also enabled him to be closer to the front-line operations managers. Corporate-level decisions are often characterized by greater risk,

EXHIBIT 1.2 **Hierarchy of Objectives and Strategies**

Ends (What is to be achieved?)	Means (How is it to be achieved?)	Strategic Decision Makers			
		Board of Directors	Corporate Managers	Business Managers	Functional Managers
Mission, including goals and philosophy		✓✓	✓✓	✓	
Long-term objectives	Grand strategy	✓	✓✓	✓✓	
Annual objectives	Short-term strategies and policies		✓	✓✓	✓✓

Note: ✓✓ indicate a principal responsibility; ✓ indicates a secondary responsibility.

cost, and profit potential; greater need for flexibility; and longer time horizons. Such decisions include the choice of businesses, dividend policies, sources of long-term financing, and priorities for growth.

Functional-level decisions implement the overall strategy formulated at the corporate and business levels. They involve action-oriented operational issues and are relatively short range and low risk. Functional-level decisions incur only modest costs, because they depend on available resources. They usually are adaptable to ongoing activities and, therefore, can be implemented with minimal cooperation. For example, the corporate headquarters of Sears, Roebuck & Company spent $60 million to automate 6,900 clerical jobs by installing 28,000 computerized cash registers at its 868 stores in the United States. Although this move eliminated many functional-level jobs, top management believed that reducing annual operating expenses by at least $50 million was crucial to competitive survival.

Because functional-level decisions are relatively concrete and quantifiable, they receive critical attention and analysis even though their comparative profit potential is low. Common functional-level decisions include decisions on generic versus brandname labeling, basic versus applied research and development (R&D), high versus low inventory levels, general-purpose versus specific-purpose production equipment, and close versus loose supervision.

Business-level decisions help bridge decisions at the corporate and functional levels. Such decisions are less costly, risky, and potentially profitable than corporate-level decisions, but they are more costly, risky, and potentially profitable than functional-level decisions. Common business-level decisions include decisions on plant location, marketing segmentation and geographic coverage, and distribution channels.

Formality in Strategic Management

formality
The degree to which participation, responsibility, authority, and discretion in decision making are specified in strategic management.

The formality of strategic management systems varies widely among companies. **Formality** refers to the degree to which participants, responsibilities, authority, and discretion in decision making are specified. It is an important consideration in the study of strategic management, because greater formality is usually positively correlated with the cost, comprehensiveness, accuracy, and success of planning.

A number of forces determine how much formality is needed in strategic management. The size of the organization, its predominant management styles, the complexity of its environment, its production process, its problems, and the purpose of its planning system all play a part in determining the appropriate degree of formality.

In particular, formality is associated with the size of the firm and with its stage of development. Some firms, especially smaller ones, follow an **entrepreneurial mode.** They are basically under the control of a single individual, and they produce a limited number of

entrepreneurial mode

The informal, intuitive, and limited approach to strategic management associated with owner-managers of smaller firms.

planning mode

The strategic formality associated with large firms that operate under a comprehensive, formal planning system.

adaptive mode

The strategic formality associated with medium-sized firms that emphasize the incremental modification of existing competitive approaches.

products or services. In such firms, strategic evaluation is informal, intuitive, and limited. Very large firms, on the other hand, make strategic evaluation part of a comprehensive, formal planning system, an approach that Henry Mintzberg called the **planning mode.** Mintzberg also identified a third mode (the **adaptive mode**), which he associated with medium-sized firms in relatively stable environments.[1] For firms that follow the adaptive mode, the identification and evaluation of alternative strategies are closely related to existing strategy. It is not unusual to find different modes within the same organization. For example, ExxonMobil might follow an entrepreneurial mode in developing and evaluating the strategy of its solar subsidiary but follow a planning mode in the rest of the company.

The Strategy Makers

The ideal strategic management team includes decision makers from all three company levels (the corporate, business, and functional)—for example, the chief executive officer (CEO), the product managers, and the heads of functional areas. In addition, the team obtains input from company planning staffs, when they exist, and from lower-level managers and supervisors. The latter provide data for strategic decision making and then implement strategies.

Because strategic decisions have a tremendous impact on a company and require large commitments of company resources, top managers must give final approval for strategic action. Exhibit 1.2 aligns levels of strategic decision makers with the kinds of objectives and strategies for which they are typically responsible.

Planning departments, often headed by a corporate vice president for planning, are common in large corporations. Medium-sized firms often employ at least one full-time staff member to spearhead strategic data-collection efforts. Even in small firms or less progressive larger firms, strategic planning often is spearheaded by an officer or by a group of officers designated as a planning committee.

Precisely what are managers' responsibilities in the strategic planning process at the corporate and business levels? Top management shoulders broad responsibility for all the major elements of strategic planning and management. They develop the major portions of the strategic plan and reviews, and they evaluate and counsel on all other portions. General managers at the business level typically have principal responsibilities for developing environmental analysis and forecasting, establishing business objectives, and developing business plans prepared by staff groups.

An executive who understands and excels at the strategic management process is Richard Lenny, CEO of Hershey. You can read about the challenges he faced, the strategies he led, and the successes he achieved in Exhibit 1.3, Top Strategist.

A firm's president or CEO characteristically plays a dominant role in the strategic planning process. In many ways, this situation is desirable. The CEO's principal duty often is defined as giving long-term direction to the firm, and the CEO is ultimately responsible for the firm's success and, therefore, for the success of its strategy. In addition, CEOs are typically strong-willed, company-oriented individuals.

However, when the dominance of the CEO approaches autocracy, the effectiveness of the firm's strategic planning and management processes is likely to be diminished. For this reason, establishing a strategic management system implies that the CEO will allow managers at all levels to participate in the strategic posture of the company.

In implementing a company's strategy, the CEO must have an appreciation for the power and responsibility of the board, while retaining the power to lead the company with the guidance of informed directors. The interaction between the CEO and board is key to

---

[1] H. Mintzberg, "Strategy Making in Three Modes," *California Management Review* 16, no. 2 (1973), pp. 44–53.

Top Strategist
Richard Lenny, CEO of Hershey

Exhibit
1.3

An ambitious restructuring plan and a move into new-product lines such as premium chocolate and snacks for nutrition-conscious consumers have Hershey predicting a sweet future. CEO Richard Lenny has also bolstered sales of higher-margin, single-serve snacks aimed at on-the-go consumers and is making changes in distribution by expanding the brand's presence beyond grocery stores and mass merchant chains to home improvement and other specialty stores. Overseas, Hershey faces strong competition from Mars and Cadbury Schweppes, but a venture with Korea's Lotte Confectionery will help it make inroads in China and other Asian markets. To increase its competitiveness, Hershey plans to cut its workforce by 10.7 percent or 1,500, and shift more of its production overseas. These moves should bring savings of $170 million to $190 million by 2010.

Source: Reprinted with special permission from "The *BusinessWeek* 50—The Best Performers," *BusinessWeek*, March 26, 2007. Copyright © 2007 The McGraw-Hill Companies.

any corporation's strategy. Empowerment of nonmanagerial employees has been a recent trend across major management teams. For example, in 2003, IBM replaced its 92-year-old executive board structure with three newly created management teams: strategy, operations, and technology. Each team combined top executives, managers, and engineers going down six levels in some cases. This new team structure was responsible for guiding the creation of IBM's strategy and for helping to implement the strategies once they were authorized.

Benefits of Strategic Management

Using the strategic management approach, managers at all levels of the firm interact in planning and implementing. As a result, the behavioral consequences of strategic management are similar to those of participative decision making. Therefore, an accurate assessment of the impact of strategy formulation on organizational performance requires not only financial evaluation criteria but also nonfinancial evaluation criteria—measures of behavior-based effects. In fact, promoting positive behavioral consequences also enables the firm to achieve its financial goals. However, regardless of the profitability of strategic plans, several behavioral effects of strategic management improve the firm's welfare:

1. Strategy formulation activities enhance the firm's ability to prevent problems. Managers who encourage subordinates' attention to planning are aided in their monitoring and forecasting responsibilities by subordinates who are aware of the needs of strategic planning.

2. Group-based strategic decisions are likely to be drawn from the best available alternatives. The strategic management process results in better decisions because group interaction generates a greater variety of strategies and because forecasts based on the specialized perspectives of group members improve the screening of options.

3. The involvement of employees in strategy formulation improves their understanding of the productivity-reward relationship in every strategic plan and, thus, heightens their motivation.

4. Gaps and overlaps in activities among individuals and groups are reduced as participation in strategy formulation clarifies differences in roles.

5. Resistance to change is reduced. Though the participants in strategy formulation may be no more pleased with their own decisions than they would be with authoritarian decisions, their greater awareness of the parameters that limit the available options makes them more likely to accept those decisions.

Risks of Strategic Management

Managers must be trained to guard against three types of unintended negative consequences of involvement in strategy formulation.

First, the time that managers spend on the strategic management process may have a negative impact on operational responsibilities. Managers must be trained to minimize that impact by scheduling their duties to allow the necessary time for strategic activities.

Second, if the formulators of strategy are not intimately involved in its implementation, they may shirk their individual responsibility for the decisions reached. Thus, strategic managers must be trained to limit their promises to performance that the decision makers and their subordinates can deliver.

Third, strategic managers must be trained to anticipate and respond to the disappointment of participating subordinates over unattained expectations. Subordinates may expect their involvement in even minor phases of total strategy formulation to result in both acceptance of their proposals and an increase in their rewards, or they may expect a solicitation of their input on selected issues to extend to other areas of decision making.

Sensitizing managers to these possible negative consequences and preparing them with effective means of minimizing such consequences will greatly enhance the potential of strategic planning.

THE STRATEGIC MANAGEMENT PROCESS

Businesses vary in the processes they use to formulate and direct their strategic management activities. Sophisticated planners, such as General Electric, Procter & Gamble, and IBM, have developed more detailed processes than less formal planners of similar size. Small businesses that rely on the strategy formulation skills and limited time of an entrepreneur typically exhibit more basic planning concerns than those of larger firms in their industries. Understandably, firms with multiple products, markets, or technologies tend to use more complex strategic management systems. However, despite differences in detail and the degree of formalization, the basic components of the models used to analyze strategic management operations are very similar.

Because of the similarity among the general models of the strategic management process, it is possible to develop an eclectic model representative of the foremost thought in the strategic management area. This model is shown in Exhibit 1.4. It serves three major functions: (1) It depicts the sequence and the relationships of the major components of the strategic management process. (2) It is the outline for this book. This chapter provides a general overview of the strategic management process, and the major components of the model will be the principal theme of subsequent chapters. Notice that the chapters of the text that discuss each of the strategic management process components are shown in each block. (3) The model offers one approach for analyzing the case studies in this text and thus helps the analyst develop strategy formulation skills.

Components of the Strategic Management Model

This section will define and briefly describe the key components of the strategic management model. Each of these components will receive much greater attention in a later chapter. The intention here is simply to introduce them.

EXHIBIT 1.4
Strategic
Management Model

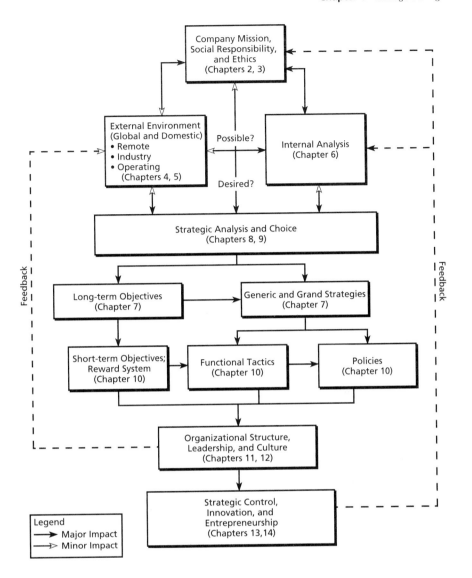

Company Mission

The mission of a company is the unique purpose that sets it apart from other companies of its type and identifies the scope of its operations. In short, the **company mission** describes the company's product, market, and technological areas of emphasis in a way that reflects the values and priorities of the strategic decision makers. For example, Lee Hun-Hee, the new chairman of the Samsung Group, revamped the company mission by stamping his own brand of management on Samsung. Immediately, Samsung separated Chonju Paper Manufacturing and Shinsegae Department Store from other operations. This corporate act of downscaling reflected a revised management philosophy that favored specialization, thereby changing the direction and scope of the organization.

Social responsibility is a critical consideration for a company's strategic decision makers since the mission statement must express how the company intends to contribute to the societies that sustain it. A firm needs to set social responsibility aspirations for itself, just as it does in other areas of corporate performance.

company mission
The unique purpose that sets a company apart from others of its type and identifies the scope of its operations.

Internal Analysis

The company analyzes the quantity and quality of the company's financial, human, and physical resources. It also assesses the strengths and weaknesses of the company's management and organizational structure. Finally, it contrasts the company's past successes and traditional concerns with the company's current capabilities in an attempt to identify the company's future capabilities.

External Environment

A firm's external environment consists of all the conditions and forces that affect its strategic options and define its competitive situation. The strategic management model shows the external environment as three interactive segments: the remote, industry, and operating environments.

Strategic Analysis and Choice

Simultaneous assessment of the external environment and the company profile enables a firm to identify a range of possibly attractive interactive opportunities. These opportunities are *possible* avenues for investment. However, they must be screened through the criterion of the company mission to generate a set of possible and *desired* opportunities. This screening process results in the selection of options from which a *strategic choice* is made. The process is meant to provide the combination of long-term objectives and generic and grand strategies that optimally position the firm in its external environment to achieve the company mission.

Strategic analysis and choice in single or dominant product/service businesses center around identifying strategies that are most effective at building sustainable competitive advantage based on key value chain activities and capabilities—core competencies of the firm. Multibusiness companies find their managers focused on the question of which combination of businesses maximizes shareholder value as the guiding theme during their strategic analysis and choice.

Long-Term Objectives

long-term objectives
The results that an organization seeks to achieve over a multiyear period.

The results that an organization seeks over a multiyear period are its **long-term objectives.** Such objectives typically involve some or all of the following areas: profitability, return on investment, competitive position, technological leadership, productivity, employee relations, public responsibility, and employee development.

Generic and Grand Strategies

generic strategies
Fundamental philosophical options for the design of strategies.

grand strategies
The means by which objectives are achieved.

Many businesses explicitly and all implicitly adopt one or more **generic strategies** characterizing their competitive orientation in the marketplace. Low cost, differentiation, or focus strategies define the three fundamental options. Enlightened managers seek to create ways their firm possesses both low cost and differentiation competitive advantages as part of their overall generic strategy. They usually combine these capabilities with a comprehensive, general plan of major actions through which their firm intends to achieve its long-term objectives in a dynamic environment. Called the **grand strategy,** this statement of means indicates how the objectives are to be achieved. Although every grand strategy is, in fact, a unique package of long-term strategies, 15 basic approaches can be identified: concentration, market development, product development, innovation, horizontal integration, vertical integration, joint venture, strategic alliances, consortia, concentric diversification, conglomerate diversification, turnaround, divestiture, bankruptcy, and liquidation.

Each of these grand strategies will be covered in detail in Chapter 7.

Short-Term Objectives

Short-term objectives are the desired results that a company seeks over a period of one year or less. They are logically consistent with the firm's long-term objectives. Companies typically have many **short-term objectives** to provide guidance for their functional and operational activities. Thus, there are short-term marketing activity, raw material usage, employee turnover, and sales objectives, to name just four.

short-term objectives
Desired results that provide specific guidance for action during a period of one year or less.

Action Plans

Action plans translate generic and grand strategies into "action" by incorporating four elements. First, they identify specific actions to be undertaken in the next year or less as part of the business's effort to build competitive advantage. Second, they establish a clear time frame for completion of each action. Third, action plans create accountability by identifying who is responsible for each "action" in the plan. Fourth, each "action" in a plan has one or more specific, immediate objectives that identify outcomes that the action should generate.

Functional Tactics

Within the general framework created by the business's generic and grand strategies, each business function needs to undertake activities that help build a sustainable competitive advantage. These short-term, limited-scope plans are called **tactics**. A radio ad campaign, an inventory reduction, and an introductory loan rate are examples of tactics. Managers in each business function develop tactics that delineate the functional activities undertaken in their part of the business and usually include them as a core part of their action plan. **Functional tactics** are detailed statements of the "means" or activities that will be used to achieve short-term objectives and establish competitive advantage.

tactics
Specific actions that need to be undertaken to achieve short-term objectives, usually by functional areas.

functional tactics
Short-term, narrow scoped plans that detail the "means" or activities that a company will use to achieve short-term objectives.

Policies That Empower Action

Speed is a critical necessity for success in today's competitive, global marketplace. One way to enhance speed and responsiveness is to force/allow decisions to be made whenever possible at the lowest level in organizations. **Policies** are broad, precedent-setting decisions that guide or substitute for repetitive or time-sensitive managerial decision making. Creating policies that guide and "preauthorize" the thinking, decisions, and actions of operating managers and their subordinates in implementing the business's strategy is essential for establishing and controlling the ongoing operating process of the firm in a manner consistent with the firm's strategic objectives. Policies often increase managerial effectiveness by standardizing routine decisions and empowering or expanding the discretion of managers and subordinates in implementing business strategies.

policies
Predetermined decisions that substitute for managerial discretion in repetitive decision making.

The following are examples of the nature and diversity of company policies:

A requirement that managers have purchase requests for items costing more than $5,000 cosigned by the controller.

The minimum equity position required for all new McDonald's franchises.

The standard formula used to calculate return on investment for the 6 strategic business units of General Electric.

A decision that Sears service and repair employees have the right to waive repair charges to appliance customers they feel have been poorly served by their Sears appliance.

Restructuring, Reengineering, and Refocusing the Organization

Until this point in the strategic management process, managers have maintained a decidedly market-oriented focus as they formulate strategies and begin implementation through action plans and functional tactics. Now the process takes an internal focus—getting the work of the business done efficiently and effectively so as to make the strategy successful. What is the best way to organize ourselves to accomplish the mission? Where should leadership come from? What values should guide our daily activities—what should the organization and its people be like? How can we shape rewards to encourage appropriate action? The intense competition in the global marketplace has made this traditionally "internally focused" set of questions—how the activities within their business are conducted—recast themselves with unprecedented attentiveness to the marketplace. *Downsizing, restructuring,* and *reengineering* are terms that reflect the critical stage in strategy implementation wherein managers attempt to recast their organization. The company's structure, leadership, culture, and reward systems may all be changed to ensure cost competitiveness and quality demanded by unique requirements of its strategies.

The elements of the strategic management process are evident in the recent activities at Ford Motor Company. In 2006, Ford undertook to create a strategy to lower costs, increase efficiency, improve designs, and increase brand appeal. These improvements were needed to keep cash flows up to cover rising pension costs. For Ford to accomplish this new strategy it had to improve operations. New executives were brought in to lead product development and financial controls. To break down the bureaucratic boundaries, a committee was created that included employees from the major functional areas, and it was given the assignment to reduce the time needed to develop a new-concept vehicle.

Strategic Control and Continuous Improvement

strategic control

Tracking a strategy as it is being implemented, detecting problems or changes in its underlying premises, and making necessary adjustments.

Strategic control is concerned with tracking a strategy as it is being implemented, detecting problems or changes in its underlying premises, and making necessary adjustments. In contrast to postaction control, strategic control seeks to guide action on behalf of the generic and grand strategies as they are taking place and when the end results are still several years away. The rapid, accelerating change of the global marketplace of the last 10 years has made continuous improvement another aspect of strategic control in many organizations. **Continuous improvement** provides a way for managers to provide a form of strategic control that allows their organization to respond more proactively and timely to rapid developments in hundreds of areas that influence a business's success.

continuous improvement

A form of strategic control in which managers are encouraged to be proactive in improving all operations of the firm.

In 2003, Yahoo!'s strategy was to move into the broadband and Internet search markets. However, even in its early implementation stages the strategy required revisions. Yahoo! had formed an alliance with SBC to provide the broadband service, but SBC had such limited capabilities that Yahoo! had to find new ways to reach users. Yahoo! also needed to continuously improve its new Internet search market, given competitors' upgrades and rapidly rising customer expectations. Additionally, for Yahoo! to increase its market share, it needed to continually improve its branding, rather than rely largely on its technological capabilities.

Strategic Management as a Process

process

The flow of information through interrelated stages of analysis toward the achievement of an aim.

A **process** is the flow of information through interrelated stages of analysis toward the achievement of an aim. Thus, the strategic management model in Exhibit 1.4 depicts a process. In the strategic management process, the flow of information involves historical, current, and forecast data on the operations and environment of the business. Managers evaluate these data in light of the values and priorities of influential individuals and groups—often called **stakeholders**—that are vitally interested in the actions of the business. The interrelated stages of the process are the 11 components discussed in the previous section. Finally, the aim of the process is the formulation and implementation of strategies that work, achieving the company's long-term mission and near-term objectives.

stakeholders

Influential people who are vitally interested in the actions of the business.

Viewing strategic management as a process has several important implications. First, a change in any component will affect several or all of the other components. Most of the arrows in the model point two ways, suggesting that the flow of information usually is reciprocal. For example, forces in the external environment may influence the nature of a company's mission, and the company may in turn affect the external environment and heighten competition in its realm of operation. A specific example is a power company that is persuaded, in part by governmental incentives, to include a commitment to the development of energy alternatives in its mission statement. The company then might promise to extend its research and development (R&D) efforts in the area of coal liquefaction. The external environment has affected the company's mission, and the revised mission signals a competitive condition in the environment.

A second implication of viewing strategic management as a process is that strategy formulation and implementation are sequential. The process begins with development or reevaluation of the company mission. This step is associated with, but essentially followed by, development of a company profile and assessment of the external environment. Then follow, in order, strategic choice, definition of long-term objectives, design of the grand strategy, definition of short-term objectives, design of operating strategies, institutionalization of the strategy, and review and evaluation.

The apparent rigidity of the process, however, must be qualified.

First, a firm's strategic posture may have to be reevaluated in response to changes in any of the principal factors that determine or affect its performance. Entry by a major new competitor, the death of a prominent board member, replacement of the chief executive officer, and a downturn in market responsiveness are among the thousands of changes that can prompt reassessment of a firm's strategic plan. However, no matter where the need for a reassessment originates, the strategic management process begins with the mission statement.

Second, not every component of the strategic management process deserves equal attention each time planning activity takes place. Firms in an extremely stable environment may find that an in-depth assessment is not required every five years. Companies often are satisfied with their original mission statements even after a decade of operation and spend only a minimal amount of time addressing this subject. In addition, while formal strategic planning may be undertaken only every five years, objectives and strategies usually are updated each year, and rigorous reassessment of the initial stages of strategic planning rarely is undertaken at these times.

A third implication of viewing strategic management as a process is the necessity of feedback from institutionalization, review, and evaluation to the early stages of the process. **Feedback** can be defined as the analysis of postimplementation results that can be used to enhance future decision making. Therefore, as indicated in Exhibit 1.4, strategic managers should assess the impact of implemented strategies on external environments. Thus, future planning can reflect any changes precipitated by strategic actions. Strategic managers also should analyze the impact of strategies on the possible need for modifications in the company mission.

A fourth implication of viewing strategic management as a process is the need to regard it as a dynamic system. The term **dynamic** characterizes the constantly changing conditions that affect interrelated and interdependent strategic activities. Managers should recognize that the components of the strategic process are constantly evolving but that formal planning artificially freezes those components, much as an action photograph freezes the movement of a swimmer. Since change is continuous, the dynamic strategic planning process must be monitored constantly for significant shifts in any of its components as a precaution against implementing an obsolete strategy.

feedback
The analysis of post-implementation results that can be used to enhance future decision making.

dynamic
The term that characterizes the constantly changing conditions that affect interrelated and interdependent strategic activities.

Changes in the Process

The strategic management process undergoes continual assessment and subtle updating. Although the elements of the basic strategic management model rarely change, the relative emphasis that each element receives will vary with the decision makers who use the model and with the environments of their companies.

A recent study describes general trends in strategic management, summarizing the responses of more than 200 corporate executives. This update shows there has been an increasing companywide emphasis on and appreciation for the value of strategic management activities. It also provides evidence that practicing managers have given increasing attention to the need for frequent and widespread involvement in the formulation and implementation phases of the strategic management process. Finally, it indicates that, as managers and their firms gain knowledge, experience, skill, and understanding in how to design and manage their planning activities, they become better able to avoid the potential negative consequences of instituting a vigorous strategic management process.

Summary

Strategic management is the set of decisions and actions that result in the formulation and implementation of plans designed to achieve a company's objectives. Because it involves long-term, future-oriented, complex decision making and requires considerable resources, top-management participation is essential.

Strategic management is a three-tier process involving corporate-, business-, and functional-level planners, and support personnel. At each progressively lower level, strategic activities were shown to be more specific, narrow, short-term, and action oriented, with lower risks but fewer opportunities for dramatic impact.

The strategic management model presented in this chapter will serve as the structure for understanding and integrating all the major phases of strategy formulation and implementation. The chapter provided a summary account of these phases, each of which is given extensive individual attention in subsequent chapters.

The chapter stressed that the strategic management process centers on the belief that a firm's mission can be best achieved through a systematic and comprehensive assessment of both its internal capabilities and its external environment. Subsequent evaluation of the firm's opportunities leads, in turn, to the choice of long-term objectives and grand strategies and, ultimately, to annual objectives and operating strategies, which must be implemented, monitored, and controlled.

Key Terms

adaptive mode, *p. 8*	functional tactics, *p. 13*	short-term objectives, *p. 13*
company mission, *p. 11*	generic strategies, *p. 12*	stakeholders, *p. 14*
continuous improvement, *p. 14*	grand strategies, *p. 12*	strategic control, *p. 14*
dynamic, *p. 15*	long-term objectives, *p. 12*	strategic management, *p. 3*
entrepreneurial mode, *p. 8*	planning mode, *p. 8*	strategy, *p. 3*
feedback, *p. 15*	policies, *p. 13*	tactics, *p. 13*
formality, *p. 7*	process, *p. 14*	

Questions for Discussion

1. Find a recent copy of *BusinessWeek* and read the "Corporate Strategies" section. Was the main decision discussed strategic? At what level in the organization was the key decision made?
2. In what ways do you think the subject matter in this strategic management–business policy course will differ from that of previous courses you have taken?
3. After graduation, you are not likely to move directly to a top-level management position. In fact, few members of your class will ever reach the top-management level. Why, then, is it important for all business majors to study the field of strategic management?

4. Do you expect outstanding performance in this course to require a great deal of memorization? Why or why not?

5. You undoubtedly have read about individuals who seemingly have given singled-handed direction to their corporations. Is a participative strategic management approach likely to stifle or suppress the contributions of such individuals?

6. Think about the courses you have taken in functional areas, such as marketing, finance, production, personnel, and accounting. What is the importance of each of these areas to the strategic planning process?

7. Discuss with practicing business managers the strategic management models used in their firms. What are the similarities and differences between these models and the one in the text?

8. In what ways do you believe the strategic planning approach of not-for-profit organizations would differ from that of profit-oriented organizations?

9. How do you explain the success of firms that do not use a formal strategic planning process?

10. Think about your postgraduation job search as a strategic decision. How would the strategic management model be helpful to you in identifying and securing the most promising position?

Chapter 1 Discussion Case

Carlyle Changes Its Stripes

1 In the two decades since private equity firms first stormed the business world, they've been called a lot of things, from raiders to barbarians. But only one firm has been tagged in the popular imagination with warmongering, treason, and acting as cold-eyed architects of government conspiracies. The broadsides got to be more than David M. Rubenstein, William E. Conway Jr., and Daniel A. D'Aniello, founders of Washington's Carlyle Group, could take. "It was nauseating," Rubenstein says.

2 Carlyle, founded 20 years ago in the shadow of Washington's power centers, long went about its business far from the public eye. Its ranks were larded with the politically connected, including former Presidents, Cabinet members, even former British Prime Minister John Major. It used its partners' collective relationships to build a lucrative business buying, transforming, and selling companies—particularly defense companies that did business with governments.

3 Carlyle might have continued happily in that niche except for the confluence of three events. First there were the terrorist attacks of September 11, 2001. In the aftermath, conspiracy theorists seized on Carlyle's huge profits, intense secrecy, and close dealings with wealthy Saudi investors. The scrutiny reached a crescendo in Michael Moore's documentary *Fahrenheit 9/11,* which made Carlyle seem like the sort of company image-conscious investors like public pension funds might choose to avoid. The second factor was the tsunami of

capital that has been sloshing around the globe for five years, providing almost limitless funding for the kind of dealmaking that is Carlyle's specialty. All that liquidity has brought with it immense opportunity as well as stiff new competition. Finally, there's the succession issue. Carlyle's baby boomer founders can see retirement around the corner. And they badly want the firm, their legacy, to outlast them.

4 At this make-or-break juncture, Carlyle's founders, billionaires all, decided to refashion their firm radically—to transform it into something more ambitious, more diverse, and more lasting.

5 Stage I of what some have dubbed the Great Experiment was largely cosmetic. The founders asked members of the bin Laden family to take back their money. They sat down with George H. W. Bush and John Major and discussed, improbable though it might seem, how the two were no longer wanted as senior advisers because they hurt the firm's image. Out went former Reagan Defense Secretary Frank C. Carlucci as chairman. In came highly regarded former chairman and CEO of IBM, Louis V. Gerstner Jr., along with former Securities and Exchange Commission Chairman Arthur Levitt, former General Electric Vice Chairman David Calhoun, and former Time Inc. Editor-in-Chief Norman Pearlstine, among others, to underscore Carlyle's commitment to portfolio diversification and upright corporate citizenship. Carlyle also pared back its defense holdings dramatically.

6 Stage II went much further and, indeed, might come to redefine the very nature of private equity. While other major buyout firms raise a few massive funds that hunt big prey—companies they can take private, rejigger financially, and, eventually, sell off or take public again—Carlyle has spread its money among no fewer than 48 funds around the world. Whereas the other giant firms—Blackstone Group, Kohlberg Kravis Roberts, and Texas Pacific Group—manage just 14, 7, and 6 funds, respectively, according to Thomson Financial, Carlyle launched a mind-boggling 11 in 2005 and 11 more in 2006.

7 More important, Carlyle now deals in a broad swath of alternative assets that include venture capital, real estate, collateralized debt obligations, and other investing exotica, which now make up a third of its assets. Rubenstein expects that percentage to grow to half by 2012. By getting into so many different areas, Carlyle seeks to exploit lucrative opportunities now and gain flexibility later when the booming buyout market slumps. The risk lies in getting it right. Having never managed such disparate assets before, Carlyle is on a steep learning curve. And it will be competing with traders and managers who have seen every kind of market—up, down, sideways.

8 Carlyle's radical makeover has turned the firm into the biggest fund-raising juggernaut the private equity world has ever seen. By the end of this year it expects to have an unprecedented $85 billion in investor commitments under management, up sixfold from 2001 and more than any other firm expects. Rubenstein sees the total swelling to as much as $300 billion by 2012. This year alone, Carlyle plans to raise a record $34 billion. Thanks to the surging debt markets, which are pumping up leveraged buyouts, that easily translates into more than $200 billion in purchasing power, enough for Carlyle to take out, say, Yahoo!, Caterpillar, and FedEx and still have $100 billion left over. "People probably look at them with a bit of envy," says Joncarlo Mark, a senior portfolio manager at California Public Employees' Retirement System (CalPERS), which owns 5.5 percent of the firm. Texas Pacific co-founder David Bonderman considers Conway, Carlyle's chief investment officer, "one of the best in our business."

9 So what, exactly, is Carlyle? Part buyout shop, part investment bank, part asset-management firm, it has set out on a course all its own. "There are going to be some major financial institutions that emerge from the phenomenal growth [in private equity] of the last years," says Colin Blaydon, director of the Center for Private Equity & Entrepreneurship at Dartmouth's Tuck School of Business. "Carlyle is very deliberately moving in that direction. It looks a bit like the mid-'80s, when a handful of big, multiline investment-banking firms emerged as the bulge bracket."

10 Make no mistake—Carlyle is already massive. It owns nearly 200 companies that generate a combined $68 billion in revenue and employ 200,000 people. Last year it bought a new company approximately once every three days and sold one almost once a week—all while dabbling in increasingly esoteric investments.

Such feats might qualify Rubenstein for Master of the **11** Universe status, but his New York office certainly doesn't announce it. Bespectacled and tightly wound, Rubenstein, 57, sits behind a dark mahogany desk so spare it's hard to believe he ever uses it. And the place has none of the typical trappings of the private equity elite. No photographs of Rubenstein with famous people (although he knows plenty). No artwork. No "love me" collages of degrees and awards. "[Carlyle] is a serious money-management business," says Rubenstein, "and we have to operate it that way if it's to have duration beyond the founders." Besides, he says, his austere offices in Washington and New York serve as reminders that he could lose everything at any moment. "I don't have things on the walls because I might have to take them down," he says. Rubenstein is ascetic by nature. He shuns red meat, avoids alcohol and desserts, and limits his business attire to navy pin-striped suits.

Rubenstein doesn't have much time to gaze at the walls **12** anyway. With money flowing in so fast and opportunities increasing exponentially, the firm's expansion is creating problems buyout shops have never had to deal with before.

Coping with the hypergrowth is Stage III of the Great **13** Experiment. Carlyle has overhauled its management structure, decentralizing decision making in a way that would shock the typical larger-than-life buyout baron. Now, instead of relying on the founders to bless every deal, it sprinkles investment committees around the firm, each made up of managers from different funds and backgrounds. Before memos reach THE TOP, they have to make it through each fund's committee. If a big deal in, say, Japan, looks tempting, the Japan fund might solicit money from bigger Carlyle funds, which perform their own due diligence. This is management more along the lines of a professionally run, shareholder-owned corporation than a private partnership where the founders' dictates, wise or not, carry the force of law. In the annals of business, it's the juncture at which many a hot boutique has failed. Rubenstein says big private equity firms, including his own, will one day be publicly held.

The new setup allows Carlyle's founders, known inside **14** the firm as "DBD" for David-Bill-Daniel, to concentrate on what they do best. Rubenstein travels the globe 260 days a year to raise funds. The fiery Conway, 57, scrambles to put the money to work. D'Aniello, 60, is chief operating officer and, in many ways, the glue of the operation. Underneath DBD and Chairman Gerstner, a web of investment managers runs money while seasoned executives not only manage companies but beat the bushes looking for deals. Carlyle estimates that at any one time it has headhunters conducting 10 to 15 searches for high-level talent. When Carlyle and its partners landed Calhoun, they were willing to pay him $100 million. Carlyle has promoted 50 of its people to the level of partner—a path that typically takes 12 years. Below them sit associates, who earn about $150,000 to start.

15   Central to Carlyle's Great Experiment is old-fashioned risk management. The more diverse the assets, say finance textbooks, the better the risk-adjusted returns. Carlyle has long been known as one of the most risk-averse of the major firms. Its main U.S. buyout fund has lost money on only 4 percent of its investments, making it one of the most consistent performers in an industry that typically sees losses on 10 to 15 percent of its positions, according to Hamilton Lane, an institutional money-management and advisory firm. Thus far, Carlyle's aversion to risk hasn't come at the expense of returns. Quite the opposite: Since its founding in 1987 it has generated annualized after-fee returns of 26 percent, compared with the industry average in the mid-teens. But already, DBD is telling investors they shouldn't expect private equity returns of 30 percent a year to continue.

16   Carlyle's longtime focus on small and midmarket deals—less than $1 billion—has also set it apart from the other megafirms. In buyouts, KKR and Blackstone concentrate on the biggest acquisitions, while Texas Pacific Group is known for doing difficult deals that other firms won't touch. Carlyle's specialty is turning small deals into big successes. Even its most ardent former skeptic praises the approach. Stephen L. Norris, one of the firm's original five founders, split in 1995 in a bitter fight over Carlyle's direction. "I was wrong," Norris says flatly. "David is a billionaire, and I'm not." (The other original partner, Greg A. Rosenbaum, left during the first year.)

17   But overheated debt markets have changed Carlyle's formula, at least for now. When interest rates plunged earlier in the decade, deal financing got much cheaper, and Carlyle took full advantage, making successively bigger purchases. Founder Conway acknowledges the worry. "Our business right now is being propelled by the rocket fuel of cheap debt," he says. "Rocket fuel is explosive, and you have to be careful how you handle it." Daniel F. Akerson, co-head of the firm's U.S. buyout fund, says one bank last year offered to give Carlyle twice the financing it needed for an acquisition. "That's when you say to yourself: 'Wow.' That's the craziness of it."

RED FLAGS

18   Such easy access to capital now can set up big trouble later on. To paraphrase Alan Greenspan, the worst of deals are made at the best of times. Right now almost all dealmakers look like geniuses. But history tells us that when the cycle turns, many who are riding the current wave of hope and euphoria will be washed out to sea. If interest rates rise, opportunities to refinance debt will disappear. Cash flows will shrivel. There will be bankruptcies.

19   Carlyle has a longer and more lustrous record than most firms, but there's no doubt it's getting increasingly audacious in its financial footwork. In June, along with partners Clayton, Dubilier & Rice and Merrill Lynch, it collected an unprecedented $1 billion dividend from rental-car company Hertz just six months after taking it private for $15 billion—and

then promptly took it public again, a lightning-quick flip in buyout land. Carlyle estimates it has already earned back 54 percent of its $765 million investment and points out that it and its partners still own 71 percent of the company and are managing it for the long term.

20   Conway makes no apologies for returning money to investors—institutions, pension funds, and wealthy individuals—as quickly as possible. He's paid to spot opportunities and seize them. For example, in 2002, Carlyle beat a pack of other firms to buy the Dex Media Yellow Pages Division from struggling Qwest Communications International for $7 billion with partner Welsh, Carson, Anderson & Stowe. Then the largest buyout since RJR Nabisco, the deal was beset by regulatory hurdles and was ultimately carried out in two stages. (Carlyle made 2.6 times its investment when it took Dex public in 2004 and exited last year.)

21   When Stephen A. Schwarzman, CEO of Blackstone Group, called Rubenstein last August to gauge his interest in Austin (Texas)–based Freescale Semiconductor, Carlyle's Great Experiment was put to the test. Schwarzman gave Carlyle only a few weeks to decide. So 40 investment professionals from the firm's U.S., Asian, Japanese, and European buyout funds got to work. They probed Freescale's ability to service its clients worldwide, researched its management team, and wrestled with the risks involved in the company's valuation, which had more than doubled in two years. Buyouts of tech companies, with their high capital expenditures and boom-and-bust product cycles, have been rare. Ultimately, the group decided the deal was worth the risk, and Carlyle bid alongside Blackstone.

22   Such moves have raised red flags among regulators. Carlyle is one of several firms that received letters from the U.S. Department of Justice last fall asking for information on club deals. And the firm's sprawling portfolio is beginning to raise eyebrows, too. On January 25, 2007, the Federal Trade Commission told Carlyle it could complete a $27.5 billion buyout of energy-distribution holding company Kinder Morgan Inc. only if it agrees to give up operational control of another company it owns. Carlyle has gotten so big and so diverse that it's actually raising antitrust concerns—a first for a buyout firm.

23   Back in 1987 no one would have imagined that Carlyle's founders would one day count themselves among the private equity aristocracy. Rubenstein was an unhappy lawyer whose main calling card was a stint as a domestic policy adviser in the Carter Administration. Conway had dealt with junk-bond czar Michael R. Milken as treasurer and chief financial officer of MCI Communications but had little experience buying companies. D'Aniello's expertise was handling hotel financings at Marriott Corp. "People laughed at us," Rubenstein recalls.

24   With a bankroll of just $5 million, Carlyle struggled. It began by marketing Alaskan tax write-offs to corporations—hardly the stuff of Wall Street or Washington folklore. Its first attempt at a buyout turned into a painful learning experience. Carlyle hit up one of its founding investors, the

Mellon family of Pittsburgh, for money to buy the restaurant chain Chi-Chi's. Then the group made a pilgrimage to Milken to get the rest of the money. They lost the auction to a company called Foodmaker and learned afterward that Milken had financed each of the four bidders. "It was stunning to us," recalls D'Aniello of his introduction to the buyout business. Milken was not available for comment.

25   Their fortunes turned when they wooed former Defense Secretary Carlucci to the firm in 1989. He delivered a sweet deal in his first year—a defense think tank called BDM International that was involved in large projects like manned space stations and, eventually, the deployment of Operation Desert Shield. "All these little jewels were coming available from larger companies that were looking to [pare their holdings to] find their core competencies," recalls D'Aniello. Carlyle was able to sell BDM in 1997 and make its investors 10.5 times their initial stake. The firm went on to become a force in the defense industry: Carlyle was one of the nation's 15 biggest defense contractors from 1998 to 2003, according to the Pentagon.

26   By 2005, thanks to the diversification strategy, it wasn't even among the top 100 defense contractors. Today, investment professionals in New York, Washington, Los Angeles, and London buy and sell loans, stocks, bonds, and other securities. Their largest holdings are in secured bank loans. But on the 42nd floor of Carlyle's New York office, some now trade in the securities of deeply distressed companies—the kind that Carlyle's buyout business once refused to touch.

ACROSS THE GLOBE

27   The seeds of that business were sown in 2002, when debt was getting cheaper and Managing Director Michael J. Zupon convinced DBD that there were profitable opportunities in distressed companies. He had taken a position in the bonds of an aerospace company at less than 50 cents on the dollar, and the company's executives pitched him on buying preferred stock. Keenly aware of Carlyle's expertise in aerospace, Zupon consulted with one of the firm's senior dealmakers in the sector. The two decided that Carlyle's high-yield fund and its U.S. buyout fund should buy the $15 million stake. Its value soared to $45 million in 18 months. "That was the catalyst," Zupon says. The business has since expanded into buying companies outright. One of the group's first purchases was titanium-component maker Stellex Aerostructures Inc., which Carlyle had once considered acquiring. The distressed team bought it after it emerged from bankruptcy in 2004. Two years later it sold for 6.3 times what Carlyle paid.

28   At the other end of the investing spectrum, a group of 50 people spread out in Washington, San Francisco, Mumbai, Beijing, Shanghai, Hong Kong, and London are looking to put $3.6 billion to work in venture and other deals. "We're seeing a set of opportunities with strong growth attributes but

which just don't lend themselves to the traditional leveraged-buyout approach," explains Brooke B. Coburn, who co-heads Carlyle's American venture fund. Most of the group's investments are in small businesses and fledgling divisions carved from companies. For example, the U.S. venture group paid $44 million for the English-as-a-second-language instruction division of publicly traded Laureate Education Inc. in 2005. Carlyle's venture team saw a chance to expand dramatically. The company's revenues have surged 70 percent, to more than $120 million.

Increasingly, Carlyle is also backing entrepreneurs who **29** have little more than a patent. One investment is with a group that patented the idea for an advanced liposuction machine. In theory it damages fat cells with ultrasound waves so they can be secreted naturally, eliminating the need for surgery. "We've been in [that investment] for five to six years, and [the company] has no revenue at this point," says Coburn. Carlyle has invested $6.7 million.

In China, Carlyle's venture fund focuses on consumer- **30** oriented investments like Ctrip.com, the Chinese version of Travelocity. Carlyle invested $8 million, took it public, and reaped $117 million. In India, Carlyle is backing technology, including a company called Claris Lifesciences Ltd., which makes low-cost medicines and hospital-care products.

Carlyle may soon become even more far-flung. Its recent **31** hiring of a team of traders from hedge fund Amaranth Advisors, which lost $6 billion last year on bad natural gas bets, has prompted speculation that Carlyle is preparing to launch a hedge fund. There's also talk that the firm may start new buyout funds focusing on emerging markets. On January 28, 2007, Carlyle announced the hiring of a dealmaker in Cairo to oversee investments in Egypt and North Africa. Citing SEC restrictions, the firm declined to comment on potential new funds.

Investors like the new, diversified approach. "The remark- **32** able thing about the firm [is that] a lot of their funds have done exceptionally well," says CalPERS' Mark. "But you [also] have the safety net of the broader organization."

The biggest question facing Carlyle is whether it can **33** maintain the discipline and top-notch performance it has been known for through this period of hypergrowth. The tension between Rubenstein rushing out new funds and Conway racing to find the financial expertise to keep up is palpable. Good investment professionals "don't grow on trees," Conway complains. "You talk to a headhunter who says: 'I know 50 of those people.' Then you hire the headhunter and . . . the 50 becomes 3.''

With so much money flowing in, finding and keeping **34** talent has become an obsession. D'Aniello, who oversees Carlyle's real estate and energy investments, has been moonlighting as the firm's management guru. He has hired human resources staff to attract top people, implemented 360-degree performance reviews, started succession planning, instituted Carlyle's annual management retreat, and spearheaded an initiative called "One Carlyle," designed to encourage teamwork across borders and silos. What could be more corporate-sounding?

35   "We don't want isolationists," D'Aniello says of the employees he's trying to attract to sustain his firm long into the future. "We also don't want crybabies. And we don't want mercenaries—people who are here to put a notch on their own gun. We want people to help us build a cannon."

Source: Reprinted with special permission from Emily Thornton, "Carlyle Changes Its Stripes," *BusinessWeek*, February 12, 2007. Copyright © 2007 The McGraw-Hill Companies.

DISCUSSION QUESTIONS

1. What do you believe are the keys to success in the venture capital industry?
2. What do you believe are the keys to success in the private equity industry?
3. How would Carlyle define its business strategy?
4. What current conditions in Carlyle's external environment favor its success?
5. What are the keys to Carlyle's future strategic success given its impressive and stiffer competition?

Part **Two**

Strategy Formulation

Strategy formulation guides executives in defining the business their firm is in, the ends it seeks, and the means it will use to accomplish those ends. The approach of strategy formulation is an improvement over that of traditional long-range planning. As discussed in the next eight chapters—about developing a firm's competitive plan of action—strategy formulation combines a future-oriented perspective with concern for the firm's internal and external environments.

The strategy formulation process begins with definition of the company mission, as discussed in Chapter 2. In this chapter, the purpose of business is defined to reflect the values of a wide variety of interested parties. In Chapter 3 social responsibility is discussed as a critical consideration for a company's strategic decision makers because the mission statement must express how the company intends to contribute to the societies that sustain it. Central to the idea that companies should be operated in socially responsible ways is the belief that managers will behave in an ethical manner. Management ethics are discussed in this chapter with special attention to the utilitarian, moral rights, and social justice approaches.

Chapter 4 deals with the principal factors in a firm's external environment that strategic managers must assess so they can anticipate and take advantage of future business conditions. It emphasizes the importance to a firm's planning activities of factors in the firm's remote, industry, and operating environments.

Chapter 5 describes the key differences in strategic planning among domestic, multinational, and global firms. It gives special attention to the new vision that a firm must communicate when it multinationalizes.

Chapter 6 shows how firms evaluate their company's strengths and weaknesses to produce an internal analysis. Strategic managers use such profiles to target competitive advantages they can emphasize and competitive disadvantages they should correct or minimize.

Chapter 7 examines the types of long-range objectives strategic managers set and specifies the qualities these objectives must have to provide a basis for direction and evaluation. The chapter also examines the generic and grand strategies that firms use to achieve long-range objectives.

Comprehensive approaches to the evaluation of strategic opportunities and to the final strategic decision are the focus of Chapter 8. The chapter shows how a firm's strategic options can be compared in a way that allows selection of the best available option. It also discusses how a company can create competitive advantages for each of its businesses.

Chapter 9 extends the attention on strategic analysis and choice by showing how managers can build value in multibusiness companies.

Company Mission

1. Describe a company mission and explain its value.

2. Explain why it is important for the mission statement to include the company's basic product or service, its primary markets, and its principal technology.

3. Explain which goal of a company is most important: survival, profitability, or growth.

4. Discuss the importance of company philosophy, public image, and company self-concept to stockholders.

5. Give examples of the newest trends in mission statement components: customer emphasis, quality, and company vision.

6. Describe the role of a company's board of directors.

7. Explain agency theory and its value in helping a board of directors improve corporate governance.

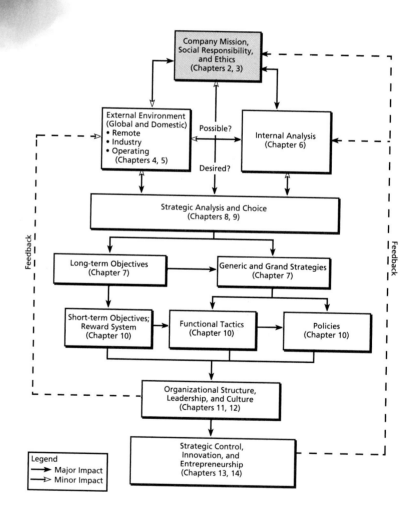

Company Mission, Social Responsibility, and Ethics (Chapters 2, 3)

External Environment (Global and Domestic)
• Remote
• Industry
• Operating
(Chapters 4, 5)

Possible?

Desired?

Internal Analysis (Chapter 6)

Strategic Analysis and Choice (Chapters 8, 9)

Long-term Objectives (Chapter 7)

Generic and Grand Strategies (Chapter 7)

Short-term Objectives; Reward System (Chapter 10)

Functional Tactics (Chapter 10)

Policies (Chapter 10)

Organizational Structure, Leadership, and Culture (Chapters 11, 12)

Strategic Control, Innovation, and Entrepreneurship (Chapters 13, 14)

Feedback

Legend
→ Major Impact
⇢ Minor Impact

Mission Statement of Nicor Inc.

PREAMBLE

We, the management of Nicor Inc., here set forth our belief as to the purpose for which the company is established and the principles under which it should operate. We pledge our effort to the accomplishment of these purposes within these principles.

BASIC PURPOSE

The basic purpose of Nicor Inc. is to perpetuate an investor-owned company engaging in various phases of the energy business, striving for balance among those phases so as to render needed satisfactory products and services and earn optimum, long-range profits.

WHAT WE DO

The principal business of the company, through its utility subsidiary, is the provision of energy through a pipe system to meet the needs of ultimate consumers. To accomplish its basic purpose, and to ensure its strength, the company will engage in other energy-related activities, directly or through subsidiaries or in participation with other persons, corporations, firms, or entities.

All activities of the company shall be consistent with its responsibilities to investors, customers, employees, and the public and its concern for the optimum development and utilization of natural resources and for environmental needs.

WHERE WE DO IT

The company's operations shall be primarily in the United States, but no self-imposed or regulatory geographical limitations are placed upon the acquisition, development, processing, transportation, or storage of energy resources, or upon other energy-related ventures in which the company may engage. The company will engage in such activities in any location where, after careful review, it has determined that such activity is in the best interest of its stockholders.

Utility service will be offered in the territory of the company's utility subsidiary to the best of its ability, in accordance with the requirements of regulatory agencies and pursuant to the subsidiary's purposes and principles.

Source: Nicor Inc., http://www.nicor.com/

WHAT IS A COMPANY MISSION?

company mission
The unique purpose that sets a company apart from others of its type and identifies the scope of its operations in product, market, and technology terms.

Whether a firm is developing a new business or reformulating direction for an ongoing business, it must determine the basic goals and philosophies that will shape its strategic posture. This fundamental purpose that sets a firm apart from other firms of its type and identifies the scope of its operations in product and market terms is defined as the company mission. As discussed in Chapter 1, the **company mission** is a broadly framed but enduring statement of a firm's intent. It embodies the business philosophy of the firm's strategic decision makers, implies the image the firm seeks to project, reflects the firm's self-concept, and indicates the firm's principal product or service areas and the primary customer needs the firm will attempt to satisfy. In short, it describes the firm's product, market, and technological areas of emphasis, and it does so in a way that reflects the values and priorities of the firm's strategic decision makers. An excellent example is the company mission statement of Nicor Inc., shown in Exhibit 2.1, Strategy in Action.

The Need for an Explicit Mission

No external body requires that the company mission be defined, and the process of defining it is time-consuming and tedious. Moreover, it contains broadly outlined or implied objectives and strategies rather than specific directives. Characteristically, it is a statement, not of measurable targets but of attitude, outlook, and orientation.

The mission statement is a message designed to be inclusive of the expectations of all stakeholders for the company's performance over the long run. The executives and board who prepare the mission statement attempt to provide a unifying purpose for the company that will provide a basis for strategic objective setting and decision making. In general terms, the mission statement addresses the following questions:

Why is this firm in business?

What are our economic goals?

What is our operating philosophy in terms of quality, company image, and self-concept?

What are our core competencies and competitive advantages?

What customers do and can we serve?

How do we view our responsibilities to stockholders, employees, communities, environment, social issues, and competitors?

FORMULATING A MISSION

The process of defining the company mission for a specific business can perhaps be best understood by thinking about the business at its inception. The typical business begins with the beliefs, desires, and aspirations of a single entrepreneur. Such an owner-manager's sense of mission usually is based on the following fundamental beliefs:

1. The product or service of the business can provide benefits at least equal to its price.

2. The product or service can satisfy a customer need of specific market segments that is currently not being met adequately.

3. The technology that is to be used in production will provide a cost- and quality-competitive product or service.

4. With hard work and the support of others, the business can not only survive but also grow and be profitable.

5. The management philosophy of the business will result in a favorable public image and will provide financial and psychological rewards for those who are willing to invest their labor and money in helping the business to succeed.

6. The entrepreneur's self-concept of the business can be communicated to and adopted by employees and stockholders.

As the business grows or is forced by competitive pressures to alter its product, market, or technology, redefining the company mission may be necessary. If so, the revised mission statement will contain the same components as the original. It will state the basic type of product or service to be offered, the primary markets or customer groups to be served; the technology to be used in production or delivery; the firm's fundamental concern for survival through growth and profitability; the firm's managerial philosophy; the public image the firm seeks; and the self-concept those affiliated with the firm should have of it. This chapter will discuss in detail these components. The examples shown in Exhibit 2.2, Strategy in Action, provide insights into how some major corporations handle them.

Basic Product or Service; Primary Market; Principal Technology

Three indispensable components of the mission statement are specification of the basic product or service, specification of the primary market, and specification of the principal technology for production or delivery. These components are discussed under one heading because only in combination do they describe the company's business activity. A good example of the three components is to be found in the business plan of ITT Barton,

Identifying Mission Statement Components: A Compilation of Excerpts from Actual Corporate Mission Statements

1. Customer-market	We believe our first responsibility is to the doctors, nurses, and patients, to mothers and all others who use our products and services. (Johnson & Johnson) To anticipate and meet market needs of farmers, ranchers, and rural communities within North America. (CENEX)
2. Product-service	AMAX's principal products are molybdenum, coal, iron ore, copper, lead, zinc, petroleum and natural gas, potash, phosphates, nickel, tungsten, silver, gold, and magnesium. (AMAX)
3. Geographic domain	We are dedicated to total success of Corning Glass Works as a worldwide competitor. (Corning Glass)
4. Technology	Control Data is in the business of applying microelectronics and computer technology in two general areas: computer-related hardware and computing-enhancing services, which include computation, information, education, and finance. (Control Data) The common technology in these areas relates to discrete particle coatings. (NASHUA)
5. Concern for survival	In this respect, the company will conduct its operation prudently, and will provide the profits and growth which will assure Hoover's ultimate success. (Hoover Universal)
6. Philosophy	We are committed to improve health care throughout the world. (Baxter Travenol) We believe human development to be the worthiest of the goals of civilization and independence to be the superior condition for nurturing growth in the capabilities of people. (Sun Company)
7. Self-concept	Hoover Universal is a diversified, multi-industry corporation with strong manufacturing capabilities, entrepreneurial policies, and individual business unit autonomy. (Hoover Universal)
8. Concern for public image	We are responsible to the communities in which we live and work and to the world community as well. (Johnson & Johnson) Also, we must be responsive to the broader concerns of the public, including especially the general desire for improvement in the quality of life, equal opportunity for all, and the constructive use of natural resources. (Sun Company)

a division of ITT. Under the heading of business mission and area served, the following information is presented:

> The unit's mission is to serve industry and government with quality instruments used for the primary measurement, analysis, and local control of fluid flow, level, pressure, temperature, and fluid properties. This instrumentation includes flow meters, electronic readouts, indicators, recorders, switches, liquid level systems, analytical instruments such as titrators, integrators, controllers, transmitters, and various instruments for the measurement of fluid properties (density, viscosity, gravity) used for processing variable sensing, data collecting, control, and transmission. The unit's mission includes fundamental loop-closing control and display devices, when economically justified, but excludes broadline central control room instrumentation, systems design, and turnkey responsibility.
>
> Markets served include instrumentation for oil and gas production, gas transportation, chemical and petrochemical processing, cryogenics, power generation, aerospace, government, and marine, as well as other instrument and equipment manufacturers.

In only 129 words, this segment of the mission statement clearly indicates to all readers—from company employees to casual observers—the basic products, primary markets, and principal technologies of ITT Barton.

Often the most referenced public statement of a company's selected products and markets appears in "silver bullet" form in the mission statement; for example, "Dayton-Hudson Corporation is a diversified retailing company whose business is to serve the American consumer through the retailing of fashion-oriented quality merchandise." Such an abstract of company direction is particularly helpful to outsiders who value condensed overviews.

Company Goals: Survival; Growth; Profitability

Three economic goals guide the strategic direction of almost every business organization. Whether or not the mission statement explicitly states these goals, it reflects the firm's intention to secure *survival* through *growth* and *profitability.*

A firm that is unable to survive will be incapable of satisfying the aims of any of its stakeholders. Unfortunately, the goal of survival, like the goals of growth and profitability, often is taken for granted to such an extent that it is neglected as a principal criterion in strategic decision making. When this happens, the firm may focus on short-term aims at the expense of the long run. Concerns for expediency, a quick fix, or a bargain may displace the assessment of long-term impact. Too often, the result is near-term economic failure owing to a lack of resource synergy and sound business practice. For example, Consolidated Foods, maker of Shasta soft drinks and L'eggs hosiery, sought growth through the acquisition of bargain businesses. However, the erratic sales patterns of its diverse holdings forced it to divest itself of more than four dozen companies. This process cost Consolidated Foods millions of dollars and hampered its growth.

Profitability is the mainstay goal of a business organization. No matter how profit is measured or defined, profit over the long term is the clearest indication of a firm's ability to satisfy the principal claims and desires of employees and stockholders. The key phrase here is "over the long term." Obviously, basing decisions on a short-term concern for profitability would lead to a strategic myopia. Overlooking the enduring concerns of customers, suppliers, creditors, ecologists, and regulatory agents may produce profit in the short term, but, over time, the financial consequences are likely to be detrimental.

The following excerpt from the Hewlett-Packard statement of mission ably expresses the importance of an orientation toward long-term profit:

> To achieve sufficient profit to finance our company growth and to provide the resources we need to achieve our other corporate objectives.
>
> In our economic system, the profit we generate from our operation is the ultimate source of the funds we need to prosper and grow. It is the one absolutely essential measure of our corporate performance over the long term. Only if we continue to meet our profit objective can we achieve our other corporate objectives.

A firm's growth is tied inextricably to its survival and profitability. In this context, the meaning of growth must be broadly defined. Although product impact market studies (PIMS) have shown that growth in market share is correlated with profitability, other important forms of growth do exist. Growth in the number of markets served, in the variety of products offered, and in the technologies that are used to provide goods or services frequently lead to improvements in a firm's competitive ability. Growth means change, and proactive change is essential in a dynamic business environment.

AOL's strategy provides an example. In 2003, some analysts believed that AOL Time Warner should change to a survival strategy because of the amount of debt that it was carrying. They believed that AOL should try to reduce debt and regain some market share that it had lost over the previous year. AOL did decide to reduce its $7 billion debt by the end of 2004, but not simply to survive. AOL was trying to position itself for the acquisition of either Adelphia or Cablevision. AOL felt that if it could acquire one of these two companies or possibly both, it could increase its footprint in the market. AOL believed that growth for its company would have to come from the cable TV market and that the only way to grow was to serve more markets. Luckily, AOL's top competitor, Comcast, was in the same debt position as AOL and could not immediately preempt the acquisitions.

Hewlett-Packard's mission statement provides another excellent example of corporate regard for growth:

Objective: To let our growth be limited only by our profits and our ability to develop and produce technical products that satisfy real customer needs.

We do not believe that large size is important for its own sake; however, for at least two basic reasons, continuous growth is essential for us to achieve our other objectives.

In the first place, we serve a rapidly growing and expanding segment of our technological society. To remain static would be to lose ground. We cannot maintain a position of strength and leadership in our field without growth.

In the second place, growth is important in order to attract and hold high-caliber people. These individuals will align their future only with a company that offers them considerable opportunity for personal progress. Opportunities are greater and more challenging in a growing company.

The issue of growth raises a concern about the definition of the company mission. How can a firm's product, market, and technology be specified sufficiently to provide direction without precluding the exercise of unanticipated strategic options? How can a firm so define its mission that it can consider opportunistic diversification while maintaining the parameters that guide its growth decision? Perhaps such questions are best addressed when a firm's mission statement outlines the conditions under which the firm might depart from ongoing operations. General Electric Company's extensive global mission provided the foundation for its GE Appliances (GEA) in Louisville, Kentucky. GEA did not see consumer preferences in the world market becoming Americanized. Instead, its expansion goals allowed for flexibility in examining the unique characteristics of individual foreign markets and tailoring strategies to fit them.

The growth philosophy of Dayton-Hudson also embodies this approach:

The stability and quality of the corporation's financial performance will be developed through the profitable execution of our existing businesses, as well as through the acquisition or development of new businesses. Our growth priorities, in order, are as follows:

1. Development of the profitable market preeminence of existing companies in existing markets through new store development or new strategies within existing stores.
2. Expansion of our companies to feasible new markets.
3. Acquisition of other retailing companies that are strategically and financially compatible with Dayton-Hudson.
4. Internal development of new retailing strategies.

Capital allocations to fund the expansion of existing Dayton-Hudson operating companies will be based on each company's return on investment (ROI), in relationship to its ROI objective and its consistency in earnings growth and on the ability of its management to perform up to the forecasts contained in its capital requests. Expansion via acquisition or new venture will occur when the opportunity promises an acceptable rate of long-term growth and profitability, an acceptable degree of risk, and compatibility with Dayton-Hudson's long-term strategy.

Keith Rattie, the CEO of Questar, is a top strategist who has been consistent in using his company's mission to guide its growth. Read Exhibit 2.3, Top Strategist, to learn how he helps create success by designing and executing strategies that are consistent with long-term business goals.

Questar traces its roots to a natural gas discovery in Wyoming back in 1922. Today, the Salt Lake City outfit is one of the nation's top-performing energy companies. The reason for its success? Focus. Under CEO Keith Rattie, the company has rapidly added new natural gas reserves at low cost by staying close to its Rocky Mountain beginnings. Questar combs over old fields at greater depths than ever by using the latest drilling technologies. Its biggest natural gas field, Pinedale, is still just 150 miles from that 1922 strike in southeastern Wyoming. The company reaps most of its revenue from exploration, but it also owns gas pipelines and a natural gas utility serving more than 800,000 customers in Utah. Revenue from those other businesses provide a nice cushion to help offset the ebb and flow of natural gas prices—and keep Questar's earnings and dividends flowing.

Source: Reprinted with special permission from "The *BusinessWeek* 50—The Best Performers," *BusinessWeek*, March 26, 2007. Copyright © 2007 The McGraw-Hill Companies.

Company Philosophy

company creed
A company's statement of its philosophy.

The statement of a company's philosophy, often called the **company creed,** usually accompanies or appears within the mission statement. It reflects or specifies the basic beliefs, values, aspirations, and philosophical priorities to which strategic decision makers are committed in managing the company. Fortunately, the philosophies vary little from one firm to another. Owners and managers implicitly accept a general, unwritten, yet pervasive code of behavior that governs business actions and permits them to be largely self-regulated. Unfortunately, statements of company philosophy are often so similar and so platitudinous that they read more like public relations handouts than the commitment to values they are meant to be.

Saturn's statement of philosophy, presented in Exhibit 2.4, Strategy in Action, indicates the company's clearly defined initiatives for satisfying the needs of its customers, employees, suppliers, and dealers.

Despite the similarity of these statements, the intentions of the strategic managers in developing them do not warrant cynicism. Company executives attempt to provide a distinctive and accurate picture of the firm's managerial outlook. One such statement of company philosophy is that of AIM Private Asset Management, Inc. As Exhibit 2.5, Strategy in Action, shows, AIM's board of directors and executives have established especially clear directions for company decision making and action based on growth.

As seen in Exhibit 2.6, Global Strategy in Action, the philosophy of Nissan Motor Manufacturing is expressed by the company's People Principles and Key Corporate Principles. These principles form the basis of the way the company operates on a daily basis. They address the principal concepts used in meeting the company's established goals. Nissan

Saturn's Statement of Philosophy

We, the Saturn Team, in concert with the UAW and General Motors, believe that meeting the needs of customers, Saturn members, suppliers, dealers, and neighbors is fundamental to fulfilling our mission.

To meet our customer's needs . . .

- our products and services must be world leaders in value and satisfaction.

To meet our members' needs, we . . .

- will create a sense of belonging in an environment of mutual trust, respect, and dignity;
- believe that all people want to be involved in decisions that affect them, care about their jobs and each other, take pride in themselves and in their contributions, and want to share in the success of their efforts;
- will develop the tools, training, and education for each member, recognizing individual skills and knowledge;
- believe that creative, motivated, responsible team members who understand that change is critical to success are Saturn's most important asset.

To meet our suppliers' and dealers' needs, we . . .

- will strive to create real partnerships with them;
- will be open and fair in our dealings, reflecting trust, respect, and their importance to Saturn;
- want dealers and suppliers to feel ownerships in Saturn's mission and philosophy as their own.

To meet the needs of our neighbors, the communities in which we live and operate, we . . .

- will be good citizens, protect the environment, and conserve natural resources;
- will seek to cooperate with government at all levels and strive to be sensitive, open, and candid in all our public statements.

Source: Saturn Corp., http://www.saturn.com

focuses on the distinction between the role of the individual and the corporation. In this way, employees can link their productivity and success to the productivity and success of the company. Given these principles, the company is able to concentrate on the issues most important to its survival, growth, and profitability.

Exhibit 2.7, Strategy in Action, provides an example of how General Motors uses a statement of company philosophy to clarify its environmental principles.

Public Image

Both present and potential customers attribute certain qualities to particular businesses. Gerber and Johnson & Johnson make safe products; Cross Pen makes high-quality writing instruments; Étienne Aigner makes stylish but affordable leather products; Corvettes are power machines; and Izod Lacoste stands for the preppy look. Thus, mission statements should reflect the public's expectations, because this makes achievement of the firm's goals more likely. Gerber's mission statement should not open the possibility for diversification into pesticides, and Cross Pen's should not open the possibility for diversification into $0.59 brand-name disposables.

On the other hand, a negative public image often prompts firms to reemphasize the beneficial aspects of their mission. For example, in response to what it saw as a disturbing trend in public opinion, Dow Chemical undertook an aggressive promotional campaign to

Growth Philosophy at AIM Private Asset Management Inc.

AIM's growth philosophy focuses on earnings—a tangible measure of a company's growth. Because stock prices can gyrate widely on rumors, we use earnings to weed out "high-flying" speculative stocks.

In selecting investments, we look for:
- Quality earnings growth—because we believe earnings drive stock prices.
- Positive earnings momentum—stocks with greater positive momentum will rise above the crowd.

Our growth philosophy adheres to four basic rules:
- Remain fully invested.
- Focus on individual companies rather than industries, sectors or countries.

- Strive to find the best earnings growth.
- Maintain a strong sell discipline.

Why growth philosophy?
- Investment decisions are based on facts, not guesses or big-picture economic forecasts.
- Earnings—not emotions—dictate when we should buy and sell.
- AIM's investment managers have followed the same earnings-driven philosophy for decades.
- This approach has proven itself in domestic and foreign markets.

Source: AIM Private Asset Management Inc., http://sma.aiminvestments.com/

---

fortify its credibility, particularly among "employees and those who live and work in [their] plant communities." Dow described its approach in its annual report:

> All around the world today, Dow people are speaking up. People who care deeply about their company, what it stands for, and how it is viewed by others. People who are immensely proud of their company's performance, yet realistic enough to realize it is the public's perception of that performance that counts in the long run.

Firms seldom address the question of their public image in an intermittent fashion. Although public agitation often stimulates greater attention to this question, firms are concerned about their public image even in the absence of such agitation. The following excerpt from the mission statement of Intel Corporation is an example of this attitude:

> We are sensitive to our *image with our customers and the business community.* Commitments to customers are considered sacred, and we are upset with ourselves when we do not meet our commitments. We strive to demonstrate to the business world on a continuing basis that we are credible in describing the state of the corporation, and that we are well organized and in complete control of all things that determine the numbers.

Exhibit 2.8, Strategy in Action, presents a marketing translation of the essence of the mission statements of six high-end shoe companies. The impressive feature of the exhibit is that it shows dramatically how closely competing firms can incorporate subtle, yet meaningful, differences into their mission statements.

Company Self-Concept

A major determinant of a firm's success is the extent to which the firm can relate functionally to its external environment. To achieve its proper place in a competitive situation, the firm realistically must evaluate its competitive strengths and weaknesses. This idea—that the firm must know itself—is the essence of the company self-concept. The idea is not commonly integrated into theories of strategic management; its importance for individuals has been recognized since ancient times.

Principles of Nissan Motor Manufacturing (UK) Ltd.

	People Principles **(All other objectives can only be achieved by people)**
Selection	Hire the highest caliber people; look for technical capabilities and emphasize attitude.
Responsibility	Maximize the responsibility; staff by devolving decision making.
Teamwork	Recognize and encourage individual contributions, with everyone working toward the same objectives.
Flexibility	Expand the role of the individual: multiskilled, no job description, generic job titles.
Kaizen	Continuously seek 100.1 percent improvements; give "ownership of change."
Communications	"Every day, face to face."
Training	Establish individual "continuous development programs."
Supervisors	Regard as "the professionals at managing the production process"; give them much responsibility normally assumed by individual departments; make them the genuine leaders of their teams.
Single status	Treat everyone as a "first class" citizen; eliminate all illogical differences.
Trade unionism	Establish single union agreement with AEU emphasizing the common objective for a successful enterprise.
	Key Corporate Principles
Quality	Building profitably the highest quality car sold in Europe.
Customers	Achieve target of no. 1 customer satisfaction in Europe.
Volume	Always achieve required volume.
New products	Deliver on time, at required quality, within cost.
Suppliers	Establish long-term relationship with single-source suppliers; aim for zero defects and just-in-time delivery; apply Nissan principles to suppliers.
Production	Use "most appropriate" technology; develop predictable "best method" of doing job; build in quality.
Engineering	Design "quality" and "ease of working" into the product and facilities; establish "simultaneous engineering" to reduce development time.

Source: Nissan Motor Co. Ltd., http://www.nissanmotors.com/

Both individuals and firms have a crucial need to know themselves. The ability of either to survive in a dynamic and highly competitive environment would be severely limited if they did not understand their impact on others or of others on them.

In some senses, then, firms take on personalities of their own. Much behavior in firms is organizationally based; that is, a firm acts on its members in other ways than their individual interactions. Thus, firms are entities whose personality transcends the personalities of their members. As such, they can set decision-making parameters based on aims different and distinct from the aims of their members. These organizational considerations have pervasive effects.

Ordinarily, descriptions of the company self-concept per se do not appear in mission statements. Yet such statements often provide strong impressions of the company self-concept. For example, ARCO's environment, health, and safety (EHS) managers were adamant about

General Motors Environmental Principles

As a responsible corporate citizen, General Motors is dedicated to protecting human health, natural resources, and the global environment. This dedication reaches further than compliance with the law to encompass the integration of sound environmental practices into our business decisions.

The following environmental principles provide guidance to General Motors personnel worldwide in the conduct of their daily business practices:

1. We are committed to actions to restore and preserve the environment.

2. We are committed to reducing waste and pollutants, conserving resources, and recycling materials at every stage of the product life cycle.

3. We will continue to participate actively in educating the public regarding environmental conservation.

4. We will continue to pursue vigorously the development and implementation of technologies for minimizing pollutant emissions.

5. We will continue to work with all governmental entities for the development of technically sound and financially responsible environmental laws and regulations.

6. We will continually assess the impact of our plants and products on the environment and the communities in which we live and operate with a goal of continuous improvement.

Source: General Motors Corporation, http://www.gm.com/

emphasizing the company's position on safety and environmental performance as a part of the mission statement. The challenges facing the ARCO EHS managers included dealing with concerned environmental groups and a public that has become environmentally aware. They hoped to motivate employees toward safer behavior while reducing emissions and waste. They saw this as a reflection of the company's positive self-image.

The following excerpts from the Intel Corporation mission statement describe the corporate persona that its top management seeks to foster:

> Management is self-critical. The leaders must be capable of recognizing and accepting their mistakes and learning from them.
>
> Open (constructive) confrontation is encouraged at all levels of the corporation and is viewed as a method of problem solving and conflict resolution.
>
> Decision by consensus is the rule. Decisions once made are supported. Position in the organization is not the basis for quality of ideas.
>
> A highly communicative, open management is part of the style.
>
> Management must be ethical. Managing by telling the truth and treating all employees equitably has established credibility that is ethical.
>
> We strive to provide an opportunity for rapid development.
>
> Intel is a results-oriented company. The focus is on substance versus form, quality versus quantity.
>
> We believe in the principle that hard work, high productivity is something to be proud of.
>
> The concept of assumed responsibility is accepted. (If a task needs to be done, assume you have the responsibility to get it done.)
>
> Commitments are long term. If career problems occur at some point, reassignment is a better alternative than termination.
>
> We desire to have all employees involved and participative in their relationship with Intel.

Newest Trends in Mission Components

Recently, three issues have become so prominent in the strategic planning for organizations that they are increasingly becoming integral parts in the development and revisions

Mission Statements for the High-End Shoe Industry

ALLEN-EDMONDS

Allen-Edmonds provides high-quality shoes for the affluent consumer who appreciates a well-made, finely crafted, stylish dress shoe.

BALLY

Bally shoes set you apart. They are the perfect shoe to complement your lifestyle. Bally shoes project an image of European style and elegance that ensures one is not just dressed, but well dressed.

BOSTONIAN

Bostonian shoes are for those successful individuals who are well-traveled, on the "go" and want a stylish dress shoe that can keep up with their variety of needs and activities. With Bostonian, you know you will always be well dressed whatever the situation.

COLE-HAHN

Cole-Hahn offers a line of contemporary shoes for the man who wants to go his own way. They are shoes for the urban, upscale, stylish man who wants to project an image of being one step ahead.

FLORSHEIM

Florsheim shoes are the affordable classic men's dress shoes for those who want to experience the comfort and style of a solid dress shoe.

JOHNSTON & MURPHY

Johnston & Murphy is the quintessential business shoe for those affluent individuals who know and demand the best.

Source: "Thinking on Your Feet, the Johnston & Murphy Guerrilla Marketing Competition" (Johnston & Murphy, a GENESCO Company).

of mission statements: sensitivity to consumer wants, concern for quality, and statements of company vision.

Customers

"The customer is our top priority" is a slogan that would be claimed by the majority of businesses in the United States and abroad. For companies including Caterpillar Tractor, General Electric, and Johnson & Johnson this means analyzing consumer needs before as well as after a sale. The bonus plan at Xerox allows for a 40 percent annual bonus, based on high customer reviews of the service that they receive, and a 20 percent penalty if the feedback is especially bad. For these firms and many others, the overriding concern for the company has become consumer satisfaction.

In addition many U.S. firms maintain extensive product safety programs to help ensure consumer satisfaction. RCA, Sears, and 3M boast of such programs. Other firms including Calgon Corporation, Amoco, Mobil Oil, Whirlpool, and Zenith provide toll-free telephone lines to answer customer concerns and complaints.

The focus on customer satisfaction is demonstrated by retailer JCPenney in this excerpt from its statement of philosophy: "The Penney Idea is (1) To serve the public as nearly as we can to its complete satisfaction; (2) To expect for the service we render a fair remuneration, and not all the profit the traffic will bear; (3) To do all in our power to pack the customer's dollar full of value, quality, and satisfaction."

A focus on customer satisfaction causes managers to realize the importance of providing quality customer service. Strong customer service initiatives have led some firms to gain competitive advantages in the marketplace. Hence, many corporations have made the customer service initiative a key component of their corporate mission.

Quality

"Quality is job one!" is a rallying point not only for Ford Motor Corporation but for many resurging U.S. businesses as well. Two U.S. management experts fostered a worldwide

35

Visions of Quality

CADILLAC

The Mission of the Cadillac Motor Company is to engineer, produce, and market the world's finest automobiles known for uncompromised levels of distinctiveness, comfort, convenience, and refined performance. Through its people, who are its strength, Cadillac will continuously improve the quality of its products and services to meet or exceed customer expectations and succeed as a profitable business.

MOTOROLA

Dedication to quality is a way of life at our company, so much so that it goes far beyond rhetorical slogans. Our ongoing program is one of continued improvement reaches out for change, refinement, and even revolution in our pursuit of quality excellence.

It is the objective of Motorola Inc. to produce and provide products and services of the highest quality. In its activities, Motorola will pursue goals aimed at the achievement of quality excellence. These results will be derived from the dedicated efforts of each employee in conjunction with supportive participation from management at all levels of the corporation.

ZYTEC

Zytec is a company that competes on value; is market driven; provides superior quality and service; builds strong relationship with its customers; and provides technical excellence in its products.

emphasis on quality in manufacturing. W. Edwards Deming and J. M. Juran's messages were first embraced by Japanese managers, whose quality consciousness led to global dominance in several industries including automobile, TV, audio equipment, and electronic components manufacturing. Deming summarizes his approach in 14 now well-known points:

1. Create constancy of purpose.
2. Adopt the new philosophy.
3. Cease dependence on mass inspection to achieve quality.
4. End the practice of awarding business on price tag alone. Instead, minimize total cost, often accomplished by working with a single supplier.
5. Improve constantly the system of production and service.
6. Institute training on the job.
7. Institute leadership.
8. Drive out fear.
9. Break down barriers between departments.
10. Eliminate slogans, exhortations, and numerical targets.
11. Eliminate work standards (quotas) and management by objective.
12. Remove barriers that rob workers, engineers, and managers of their right to pride of workmanship.
13. Institute a vigorous program of education and self-improvement.
14. Put everyone in the company to work to accomplish the transformation.

Firms in the United States responded aggressively. The new philosophy is that quality should be the norm. For example, Motorola's production goal is 60 or fewer defects per every billion components that it manufactures.

Exhibit 2.9, Strategy in Action, presents the integration of the quality initiative into the mission statements of three corporations. The emphasis on quality has received added emphasis in many corporate philosophies since the Congress created the Malcolm Baldrige

Examples of Vision Statements

ALLIANCE CORPORATE VISION

Alliance is the most innovative and feature rich ACH processing platform available to client originators today and will remain on the cutting edge for electronic funds transfer services.

AMD CORPORATE VISION

A connected global population.

CUTCO CORPORATE VISION

To become the largest, most respected and widely recognized cutlery company in the world.

FEDERAL EXPRESS CORPORATE VISION

Our vision is to change the way we all connect with each other in the New Network Economy.

FIRSTENERGY CORPORATE VISION

FirstEnergy will be a leading regional energy provider, recognized for operational excellence and service; the choice for long-term growth, investment, value and financial strength; and a company committed to safety and driven by the leadership, skills, diversity, and character of its employees.

FORD MOTOR COMPANY CORPORATE VISION

Ford Motor Company's vision is to become the world's leading consumer company for automotive products and services.

GENERAL ELECTRIC CORPORATE VISION

We bring good things to life.

MAGNA CORPORATE VISION

Magna's corporate vision is to provide world class services that help maximize the customers ROI (Return on Investment) and promote teamwork and creativity. The company strongly believes in the corporate philosophy of fulfilling its commitments to its customers.

MICROSOFT CORPORATE VISION

Microsoft's vision is to enable people and businesses throughout the world to realize their full potential.

Quality Award. Each year up to two Baldrige Awards can be given in three categories of a company's operations: manufacturing, services, and small businesses.

Vision Statement

vision statement

A statement that presents a firm's strategic intent designed to focus the energies and resources of the company on achieving a desirable future.

Whereas the mission statement expresses an answer to the question "What business are we in?" a company **vision statement** is sometimes developed to express the aspirations of the executive leadership. A vision statement presents the firm's strategic intent that focuses the energies and resources of the company on achieving a desirable future. However, in actual practice, the mission and vision statement are frequently combined into a single statement. When they are separated, the vision statement is often a single sentence, designed to be memorable. For examples, see Exhibit 2.10, Strategy in Action.

An Exemplary Mission Statement

When BB&T merged with Southern Bank, the board of directors and officers undertook the creation of a comprehensive mission statement that was designed to include most of the topics that we discussed in this chapter. In 2003, the company updated its statement and mailed the resulting booklet to its shareholders and other interested parties. The foreword to the document expresses the greatest values of such a public pronouncement and was signed by BB&T's chairman and CEO, John A. Allison:

> In a rapidly changing and unpredictable world, individuals and organizations need a clear set of fundamental principles to guide their actions. At BB&T we know the content of our business will, and should, experience constant change. Change is necessary for progress. However, the context, our fundamental principles, is unchanging because these principles are based on basic truths.

BB&T is a mission-driven organization with a clearly defined set of values. We encourage our employees to have a strong sense of purpose, a high level of self-esteem and the capacity to think clearly and logically.

We believe that competitive advantage is largely in the minds of our employees as represented by their capacity to turn rational ideas into action towards the accomplishment of our mission.

The Chapter 2 Appendix presents BB&T's vision, mission, and purpose statement in its entirety. It also includes detailed expressions of the company's values and views on the role of emotions, management style, the management concept, attributes of an outstanding employee, the importance of positive attitude, obligations to its employees, virtues of an outstanding credit culture, achieving the company goal, the nature of a "world standard" revenue-driven sales organization, the nature of a "world standard" client service community bank, the company's commitment to education and learning, and its passions.

BOARDS OF DIRECTORS

Who is responsible for determining the firm's mission? Who is responsible for acquiring and allocating resources so the firm can thoughtfully develop and implement a strategic plan? Who is responsible for monitoring the firm's success in the competitive marketplace to determine whether that plan was well designed and activated? The answer to all of these questions is strategic decision makers. Most organizations have multiple levels of strategic decision makers; typically, the larger the firm, the more levels it will have. The strategic managers at the highest level are responsible for decisions that affect the entire firm, commit the firm and its resources for the longest periods, and declare the firm's sense of values. In other words, this group of strategic managers is responsible for overseeing the creation and accomplishment of the company mission. The term that describes the group is **board of directors**.

board of directors
The group of stockholder representatives and strategic managers responsible for overseeing the creation and accomplishment of the company mission.

In overseeing the management of a firm, the board of directors operates as the representatives of the firm's stockholders. Elected by the stockholders, the board has these major responsibilities:

1. To establish and update the company mission.
2. To elect the company's top officers, the foremost of whom is the CEO.
3. To establish the compensation levels of the top officers, including their salaries and bonuses.
4. To determine the amount and timing of the dividends paid to stockholders.
5. To set broad company policy on such matters as labor–management relations, product or service lines of business, and employee benefit packages.
6. To set company objectives and to authorize managers to implement the long-term strategies that the top officers and the board have found agreeable.
7. To mandate company compliance with legal and ethical dictates.

In the current business environment, boards of directors are accepting the challenge of shareholders and other stakeholders to become active in establishing the strategic initiatives of the companies that they serve.

This chapter considers the board of directors because the board's greatest impact on the behavior of a firm results from its determination of the company mission. The philosophy espoused in the mission statement sets the tone by which the firm and all of its employees will be judged. As logical extensions of the mission statement, the firm's objectives and strategies embody the board's view of proper business demeanor. Through its appointment

Hello, You Must Be Going

When Catherine West arrived at JCPenney Co.'s Plano (Texas) offices in June 2006 as the new chief operating officer, she brought a gold-plated record. Penney CEO Myron E. Ullman called her a "world-class" executive. He was so confident she had what it would take to succeed that he gave her a contract guaranteeing a $10 million payment when she left the retailer, even in the remote event that she took off in less than a year.

That's just what happened. By December 28, 2006, Ullman felt no holiday goodwill toward West. She was terminated "due to her failure to satisfy performance objectives," primarily "gaining an understanding of the company's operations," Penney reported.

At Wal-Mart Stores Inc., two marketing managers and the head of global procurement left, all in under 12 months. Home Depot Inc. lost its head of marketing and merchandising, Tom Taylor, in similarly short order. Gap Inc. said good-bye to veteran Liz Claiborne Inc. manager Denise Johnston after only 9 months in her role heading up Gap Adult. Software maker Adobe Systems Inc. and retailer Sears Holdings Corp. both lost chief financial officers within 6 months. And Ford Motor Co. continued to crank through executives, among them Chief Operations Officer Anne Stevens, who lasted 11 months in that role.

The brutal reality is that executives have less time than ever to prove their worth. Tough global competition, more diligent regulators, increasingly engaged boards of directors, and demanding investors have combined to create an environment in which a new hire has to show results almost from Day One. In 2006, there were 28,058 executive turnovers, including board members and executives from CEO down to vice-president, a 68 percent increase over 2005, according to Liberum Research's analysis of North American public companies.

When a company ejects a high-profile hire in under a year, the problem is usually not one of ability but of style. The person clashes with the CEO, inspires resentment in co-workers, or pushes for too much change too quickly.

The new high-pressure climate reaches to every member of a company's top management. At large companies, chief financial officers are turning over at a rate of 22 percent a year, according to Russell Reynolds Associates, because CFOs are under pressure in the regime of Sarbanes-Oxley, but also because they are the face of the company to Wall Street.

But if there's one job that is most firmly in the danger zone at present, it's the chief of marketing, a spot with a dangerous combination of lofty goals and quickly measured returns. So while the typical CEO today has a five-year tenure, search firm Spencer Stuart has found the chief marketing officer has only 23 months in the job.

Source: Reprinted with special permission from Nanette Byrnes and David Kiley, "Hello, You Must Be Going," *BusinessWeek,* February 12, 2007. Copyright © 2007 The McGraw-Hill Companies.

of top executives and its decisions about their compensation, the board reveals its priorities for organizational achievement.

Evidence of the high level of involvement of the board of directors in providing active direction for their businesses is the increasing rate of CEO replacement. Exhibit 2.11, Strategy in Action, provides an interesting discussion on the short tenure that CEOs frequently experience.

AGENCY THEORY

Whenever there is a separation of the owners (principals) and the managers (agents) of a firm, the potential exists for the wishes of the owners to be ignored. This fact, and the recognition that agents are expensive, established the basis for a set of complex but helpful ideas known as **agency theory.** Whenever owners (or managers) delegate decision-making authority to others, an agency relationship exists between the two parties. Agency relationships, such as those between stockholders and managers, can be very effective as

agency theory
A set of ideas on organizational control based on the belief that the separation of the ownership from management creates the potential for the wishes of owners to be ignored.

long as managers make investment decisions in ways that are consistent with stockholders' interests. However, when the interests of managers diverge from those of owners, then managers' decisions are more likely to reflect the managers' preferences than the owners' preferences.

In general, owners seek stock value maximization. When managers hold important blocks of company stock, they too prefer strategies that result in stock appreciation. However, when managers better resemble "hired hands" than owner-partners, they often prefer strategies that increase their personal payoffs rather than those of shareholders. Such behavior can result in decreased stock performance (as when high executive bonuses reduce corporate earnings) and in strategic decisions that point the firm in the direction of outcomes that are suboptimal from a stockholder's perspective.

If, as agency theory argues, self-interested managers act in ways that increase their own welfare at the expense of the gain of corporate stockholders, then owners who delegate decision-making authority to their agents will incur both the loss of potential gain that would have resulted from owner-optimal strategies and/or the costs of monitoring and control systems that are designed to minimize the consequences of such self-centered management decisions. In combination, the cost of agency problems and the cost of actions taken to minimize agency problems are called **agency costs.** These costs can often be identified by their direct benefit for the agents and their negative present value. Agency costs are found when there are differing self-interests between shareholders and managers, superiors and subordinates, or managers of competing departments or branch offices.

agency costs
The cost of agency problems and the cost of actions taken to minimize them.

How Agency Problems Occur

Because owners have access to only a relatively small portion of the information that is available to executives about the performance of the firm and cannot afford to monitor every executive decision or action, executives are often free to pursue their own interests. This condition is known as the **moral hazard problem.** It is also called shirking to suggest "self-interest combined with smile."

moral hazard problem
An agency problem that occurs because owners have limited access to company information, making executives free to pursue their own interests.

As a result of moral hazards, executives may design strategies that provide the greatest possible benefits for themselves, with the welfare of the organization being given only secondary consideration. For example, executives may presell products at year-end to trigger their annual bonuses even though the deep discounts that they must offer will threaten the price stability of their products for the upcoming year. Similarly, unchecked executives may advance their own self-interests by slacking on the job, altering forecasts to maximize their performance bonuses; unrealistically assessing acquisition targets' outlooks in order to increase the probability of increasing organizational size through their acquisition; or manipulating personnel records to keep or acquire key company personnel.

adverse selection
An agency problem caused by the limited ability of stockholders to precisely determine the competencies and priorities of executives at the time they are hired.

The second major reason that agency costs are incurred is known as **adverse selection.** This refers to the limited ability that stockholders have to precisely determine the competencies and priorities of executives at the time that they are hired. Because principals cannot initially verify an executive's appropriateness as an agent of the owners, unanticipated problems of nonoverlapping priorities between owners and agents are likely to occur.

The most popular solution to moral dilemma and adverse selection problems is for owners to attempt to more closely align their own best interests with those of their agents through the use of executive bonus plans.[1] Foremost among these approaches are stock option plans, which enable executives to benefit directly from the appreciation of the company's stock just as other stockholders do. In most instances, executive bonus plans are unabashed attempts to align the interests of owners and executives and to thereby induce

---

[1] An in-depth discussion of executive bonus compensation is provided in Chapter 10.

executives to support strategies that increase stockholder wealth. While such schemes are unlikely to eliminate self-interest as a major criterion in executive decision making, they help to reduce the costs associated with moral dilemmas and adverse selections.

Problems That Can Result from Agency

From a strategic management perspective there are five different kinds of problems that can arise because of the agency relationship between corporate stockholders and their company's executives:

1. Executives pursue growth in company size rather than in earnings. Shareholders generally want to maximize earnings, because earnings growth yields stock appreciation. However, because managers are typically more heavily compensated for increases in firm size than for earnings growth, they may recommend strategies that yield company growth such as mergers and acquisitions.

In addition, managers' stature in the business community is commonly associated with company size. Managers gain prominence by directing the growth of an organization, and they benefit in the forms of career advancement and job mobility that are associated with increases in company size.

Finally, executives need an enlarging set of advancement opportunities for subordinates whom they wish to motivate with nonfinancial inducements. Acquisitions can provide the needed positions.

2. Executives attempt to diversify their corporate risk. Whereas stockholders can vary their investment risks through management of their individual stock portfolios, managers' careers and stock incentives are tied to the performance of a single corporation, albeit the one that employs them. Consequently, executives are tempted to diversify their corporation's operation, businesses, and product lines to moderate the risk incurred in any single venture. While this approach serves the executives' personal agendas, it compromises the "pure play" quality of their firm as an investment. In other words, diversifying a corporation reduces the beta associated with the firm's return, which is an undesirable outcome for many stockholders.

3. Executives avoid risk. Even when, or perhaps especially when, executives are willing to restrict the diversification of their companies, they are tempted to minimize the risk that they face. Executives are often fired for failure, but rarely for mediocre corporate performance. Therefore, executives may avoid desirable levels of risk if they anticipate little reward and opt for conservative strategies that minimize the risk of company failure. If they do, executives will rarely support plans for innovation, diversification, and rapid growth.

However, from an investor's perspective, risk taking is desirable when it is systematic. In other words, when investors can reasonably expect that their company will generate higher long-term returns from assuming greater risk, they may wish to pursue the greater payoff, especially when the company is positioned to perform better than its competitors that face the same nominal risks. Obviously, the agency relationship creates a problem—should executives prioritize their job security or the company's financial returns to stockholders?

4. Managers act to optimize their personal payoffs. If executives can gain more from an annual performance bonus by achieving objective 1 than from stock appreciation resulting from the achievement of objective 2, then owners must anticipate that the executives will target objective 1 as their priority, even though objective 2 is clearly in the best interest of the shareholders. Similarly, executives may pursue a range of expensive perquisites that have a net negative effect on shareholder returns. Elegant corner offices, corporate jets, large staffs, golf club memberships, extravagant retirement programs, and limousines for executive benefit are rarely good investments for stockholders.

5. Executives act to protect their status. When their companies expand, executives want to ensure that their knowledge, experience, and skills remain relevant and central to the strategic direction of the corporation. They favor doing more of what they already do well. In contrast, investors may prefer revolutionary advancement to incremental improvement. For example, when confronted with Amazon.com, competitor Barnes & Noble initiated a joint venture Web site with Bertelsmann. In addition, Barnes & Noble used vertical integration with the nation's largest book distributor, which supplies 60 percent of Amazon's books. This type of revolutionary strategy is most likely to occur when executives are given assurances that they will not make themselves obsolete within the changing company that they create.

Solutions to the Agency Problem

In addition to defining an agent's responsibilities in a contract and including elements like bonus incentives that help align executives' and owners' interests, principals can take several other actions to minimize agency problems. The first is for the owners to pay executives a premium for their service. This premium helps executives to see their loyalty to the stockholders as the key to achieving their personal financial targets.

A second solution to agency problems is for executives to receive backloaded compensation. This means that executives are paid a handsome premium for superior future performance. Strategic actions taken in year one, which are to have an impact in year three, become the basis for executive bonuses in year three. This lag time between action and bonus more realistically rewards executives for the consequences of their decision making, ties the executive to the company for the long term, and properly focuses strategic management activities on the future.

Finally, creating teams of executives across different units of a corporation can help to focus performance measures on organizational rather than personal goals. Through the use of executive teams, owner interests often receive the priority that they deserve.

Summary

Defining the company mission is one of the most often slighted tasks in strategic management. Emphasizing the operational aspects of long-range management activities comes much more easily for most executives. But the critical role of the mission statement repeatedly is demonstrated by failing firms whose short-run actions have been at odds with their long-run purposes.

The principal value of the mission statement is its specification of the firm's ultimate aims. A firm gains a heightened sense of purpose when its board of directors and its top executives address these issues: "What business are we in?" "What customers do we serve?" "Why does this organization exist?" However, the potential contribution of the company mission can be undermined if platitudes or ambiguous generalizations are accepted in response to these questions. It is not enough to say that Lever Brothers is in the business of "making anything that cleans anything" or that Polaroid is committed to businesses that deal with "the interaction of light and matter." Only if a firm clearly articulates its long-term intentions can its goals serve as a basis for shared expectations, planning, and performance evaluation.

A mission statement that is developed from this perspective provides managers with a unity of direction transcending individual, parochial, and temporary needs. It promotes a sense of shared expectations among all levels and generations of employees. It consolidates values over time and across individuals and interest groups. It projects a sense of worth and intent that can be identified and assimilated by outside stakeholders, that is, customers, suppliers, competitors, local committees, and the general public. Finally, it asserts the firm's commitment to responsible action in symbiosis with the preservation and protection of the essential claims of insider stakeholders' survival, growth, and profitability.

Key Terms

adverse selection, *p. 40*
agency costs, *p. 40*
agency theory, *p. 40*

board of directors, *p. 38*
company creed, *p. 30*
company mission, *p. 25*

moral hazard problem, *p. 40*
vision statement, *p. 37*

Questions for Discussion

1. Reread Nicor Inc.'s mission statement in Exhibit 2.1, Strategy in Action. List five insights into Nicor that you feel you gained from knowing its mission.
2. Locate the mission statement of a company not mentioned in the chapter. Where did you find it? Was it presented as a consolidated statement, or were you forced to assemble it yourself from various publications of the firm? How many of the mission statement elements outlined in this chapter were discussed or revealed in the statement you found?
3. Prepare a two-page typewritten mission statement for your school of business or for a firm selected by your instructor.
4. List five potentially vulnerable areas of a firm without a stated company mission.
5. Mission statements are often criticized for being lists of platitudes. What can strategic managers do to prevent their statements from appearing to be simple statements of obvious truths?
6. What evidence do you see that mission statements are valuable?
7. How can a mission statement be an enduring statement of values and simultaneously provide a basis of competitive advantage?
8. If the goal of survival refers to ability to maintain a specific legal form, what are the comparative advantages of sole proprietorships, partnerships, and corporations?
9. In the 1990s many Nasdaq firms favored growth over profitability; in the 2000s the goal of profitability is displacing growth. How might each preference be explained?
10. Do you agree that a mission statement provides substantive guidance while a vision statement provides inspirational guidance? Explain.

Chapter 2 Discussion Case

BusinessWeek

Anger over CEO Pay Has Put Directors on the Hot Seat

1 A new era for directors dawned with the passage of the Sarbanes-Oxley Act of 2002. Then board members were hit with the frightening prospect of real financial liability in a smattering of lawsuits that followed the corporate crime wave. Now the heat on directors is growing more intense. Their reputations are increasingly at risk when the companies they watch over are tainted by scandal. Their judgment is being questioned by activist shareholders outraged by sky-high pay packages. And investors and regulators are subjecting their actions to higher scrutiny. Long gone are the days when a director could get away with a quick rubber-stamp of a CEO's plans.

2 The old rules of civility that discouraged directors from asking managers tough or embarrassing questions are eroding. At the same time, board members are being forced to devote more time and energy to many of their most important duties: setting CEO compensation, overseeing the auditing

of financial statements, and, when needed, investigating crises. That's the good news. The bad news is they are so busy delving into the minutiae of compliance that they don't have nearly as much time to advise corporate chieftains on strategy. Many board candidates no longer find the job attractive.

The hottest issue for boards is executive compensation. For the **3** first time ever, companies are required to disclose a complete tally of everything they have promised to pay their executives, including such until now hidden or difficult-to-find items as severance, deferred pay, accumulated pension benefits, and perks worth more than $10,000. They will also have to provide an explanation of how and why they've chosen to pay executives as they do. The numbers are likely to be eye-popping. Michael S. Melbinger, a top compensation lawyer in Chicago, thinks that when all the proxies are filed, there could be 50 companies or more with CEO pay packages worth $150 million-plus.

4 And this is, believe it or not, coming as just as big a surprise to many directors as it will be to investors. Up to now, most directors have never seen a tally for the total pay they've promised to executives. "Pay was all compartmentalized: Boards would approve a salary, a certain amount for a bonus, or a certain amount if he got fired, but no one ever added it all up," says Fred Whittlesey, the head of pay consultants Compensation Venture Group.

5 It's not just compensation committee members who find the world changing. Audit committees used to meet only twice a year: once when it was time to take the audit in and once more to ratify it. Dick Swanson, chair of the audit committees of two NASDAQ-traded companies, says he now holds 8 to 12 meetings a year for each committee. In addition, he spends many more hours keeping up on what all the other board committees are doing, especially focusing on any risk—financial, operational, or otherwise—that the company may run. "It's not like the old days when you could join a board for the twice-a-year dinners," says Swanson.

PLAYBOOK: BEST-PRACTICE IDEAS

6 The New Rules for Directors

Pay

7 Companies will disclose full details of CEO payouts for the first time in their 2007 SEC filings. Activist investors are already drawing up hit lists of companies where CEO paychecks are out of step with performance.

Know the Math

8 Before OK'ing any financial package, directors must make sure they can explain the numbers. They need to adopt the mindset of an activist investor and ask, What's the harshest criticism someone could make about this package?

Strategy

9 Boards have been so focused on compliance that duties like strategy and leadership oversight too often get short shrift. Only 59 percent of directors in a recent study rated their board favorably on setting strategy.

Make It a Priority

10 To avoid spending too much time on compliance issues, strategy has to move up to the beginning of the meeting. Annual one-, two- or three-day offsite meetings on strategy alone are becoming standard for good boards.

Financials

11 Although 95 percent of directors in the recent study said they were doing a good job of monitoring financials, the number of earnings restatements hit a new high in 2006, after breaking records in 2004 and 2005.

Put in the Time

12 Even nonfinancial board members need to monitor the numbers and keep a close eye on cash flows. Audit committee members: prepare to spend 300 hours a year on committee responsibilities.

Crisis Management

13 Some 120 companies are under scrutiny for options backdating, and the 100 largest companies have replaced 56 CEOs in the past five years, nearly double the terminations in the prior five years.

Dig In

14 The increased scrutiny on boards means that a perfunctory review will not suffice if a scandal strikes. Directors can no longer afford to defer to management in a crisis. They must roll up their sleeves and move into watchdog mode.

DISCUSSION QUESTIONS

1. What influence do you believe shareholders have over a company's board of directors?

2. What is an appropriate compensation package for a CEO?

3. What relationship do you see between a company's board of directors and the development of the business strategy?

4. Do you believe that a company's board of directors can change the ethical standards in a business? How can they do it?

5. Would you like to serve on a company's board of directors? What do you think that you could accomplish? What do you believe would be fair compensation to you for your contribution and personal liability?

Chapter 2 Appendix

BB&T Vision, Mission, and Purpose

BB&T Vision

To create the best financial institution possible: *"The Best of The Best."*

BB&T Mission

To make the world a better place to live by: helping our clients achieve economic success and financial security; creating a place where our employees can learn, grow and be fulfilled in their work; making the communities in which we work better places to be; and thereby: optimizing the long-term return to our shareholders, while providing a safe and sound investment.

BB&T Purpose

Our ultimate purpose is to create superior long-term economic rewards for our shareholders.

This purpose is defined by the free market and is as it should be. Our shareholders provide the capital that is necessary to make our business possible. They take the risk if the business is unsuccessful. They have the right to receive economic rewards for the risk which they have undertaken.

However, our purpose, to create superior long-term economic rewards for our shareholders, can only be accomplished by providing excellent service to our clients, as our clients are our source of revenues.

To have excellent client relations, we must have outstanding employees to serve our clients. To attract and retain outstanding employees, we must reward them financially and create an environment where they can learn and grow.

Our economic results are significantly impacted by the success of our communities. The community's "quality of life" impacts its ability to attract industry for growth.

Therefore, we manage our business in a long-term context, as an integrated whole, with the ultimate objective of rewarding the shareholders for their investment, while realizing that the cause of this result is quality client service. Excellent service will be delivered by motivated employees working as an integrated team. These results will be impacted by our capacity to contribute to the growth and well-being of the communities we serve.

Values

"Excellence is an art won by training and habituation. We are what we repeatedly do. Excellence then is not an act, but a habit."—Aristotle

The great Greek philosophers saw values as guides to excellence in thinking and action. In this context, values are standards which we strive to achieve. Values are practical habits that enable us as individuals to live, be successful and achieve happiness. For BB&T, our values enable us to achieve our mission and corporate purpose.

To be useful, values must be consciously held and be consistent (noncontradictory). Many people have conflicting values which prevent them from acting with clarity and self-confidence.

There are 10 primary values at BB&T. These values are consistent with one another and are integrated. To fully act on one of these values, you must also act consistently with the other values. Our focus on values grows from our belief that ideas matter and that an individual's character is of critical significance.

Values are important at BB&T!

1. Reality (Fact-Based)

What is, is. If we want to be better, we must act within the context of reality (the facts). Businesses and individuals often make serious mistakes by making decisions based on what they "wish was so," or based on theories which are disconnected from reality. The foundation for quality decision making is a careful understanding of the facts.

There is a fundamental difference between the laws of nature (reality), which are immutable, and the man-made. The law of gravity is the law of gravity. The existence of the law of gravity does not mean man can not create an airplane. However, an airplane must be created within the context of the law of gravity. At BB&T, we believe in being "reality grounded."

2. Reason (Objectivity)

Mankind has a specific means of survival, which is his ability to think, i.e., his capacity to reason logically from the facts of reality as presented to his five senses. A lion has claws to hunt. A deer has swiftness to avoid the hunter. Man has his ability to think. There is only one "natural resource"—the human mind.

Clear thinking is not automatic. It requires intellectual discipline and begins with sound premises based on observed facts. You must be able to draw general conclusions in a rational manner from specific examples (induction) and be able to apply general principles to the solution of specific problems (deduction). You must be able to think in an integrated way, thereby avoiding logical contradictions.

We cannot all be geniuses, but each of us can develop the mental habits which ensure that when making decisions we carefully examine the facts and think logically without contradiction in deriving a conclusion. We must learn to think in terms of what is essential, i.e., about what is important. Our goal is to objectively make the best decision to accomplish our purpose.

Rational thinking is a learned skill which requires mental focus and a fundamental commitment to consistently improving the clarity of our mental processes. At BB&T, we are looking for people who are committed to constantly improving their ability to reason.

3. Independent Thinking

All employees are challenged to use their individual minds to their optimum to make rational decisions. In this context, each of us is *responsible* for what we do and who we are. In addition, creativity is strongly encouraged and only possible with independent thought.

We learn a great deal from each other. Teamwork is important at BB&T (as will be discussed later). However, each of us thinks alone. Our minds are not physically connected. In this regard, each of us must be willing to make an independent judgment of the facts based on our capacity to think logically. Just because the "crowd" says it is so, does not make it so.

In this context, each of us is responsible for our own actions. Each of us is responsible for our personal success or failure; that is, it is not the bank's fault if someone does not achieve his objectives.

All human progress by definition is based on creativity, because creativity is the source of positive change. Creativity is only possible to an independent thinker. Creativity is not about just doing something different. It is about doing something better. To be better, the new method/process must be judged by its impact on the whole organization, and as to whether it contributes to the accomplishment of our mission.

There is an infinite opportunity for each of us to do whatever we do better. A significant aspect of the self-fulfillment which work can provide comes from creative thought and action.

4. Productivity

We are committed to being producers of wealth and well-being by taking the actions necessary to accomplish our mission. The tangible evidence of our productivity is that we have rationally allocated capital through our lending and investment process, and that we have provided needed services to our clients in an efficient manner resulting in superior profitability.

Profitability is a measure of the differences in the economic value of the products/services we produce and the cost of producing these products/services. In a long-term context and in a free market, the bigger the profit, the better. This is true not only from our shareholders' perspective (which would be enough justification), but also in terms of the impact of our work on society as a whole. Healthy profits represent productive work. At BB&T we are looking for people who want to create, to produce, and who are thereby committed to turning their thoughts into actions that improve economic well-being.

5. Honesty

Being honest is simply being consistent with reality. To be dishonest is to be in conflict with reality, which is therefore self-defeating. A primary reason that individuals fail is because they become disconnected from reality, pretending that facts are other than they are.

To be honest does not require that we know everything. Knowledge is always contextual and man is not omniscient. However, we must be responsible for saying what we mean and meaning what we say.

6. Integrity

Because we have developed our principles logically, based on reality, we will always act consistently with our principles. Regardless of the short-term benefits, acting inconsistently with our principles is to our long-term detriment. We do not, therefore, believe in compromising our principles in any situation.

Principles provide carefully thought-out concepts which will lead to our long-term success and happiness. Violating our principles will always lead to failure. BB&T is an organization of the highest integrity.

7. Justice (Fairness)

Individuals should be evaluated and rewarded objectively (for better or worse) based on their contributions toward accomplishing our mission and adherence to our values. Those who contribute the most should receive the most.

The single most significant way in which employees evaluate their managers is in determining whether the manager is just. Employees become extremely unhappy (and rightly so) when they perceive that a person who is not contributing is overrewarded or a strong contributor is underrewarded.

If we do not reward those who contribute the most, they will leave and our organization will be less successful. Even more important, if there is no reward for superior performance, the average person will not be motivated to maximize his productivity.

We must evaluate whether the food we eat is healthy, the clothes we wear attractive, the car we drive functional, etc., and we must also evaluate whether relationships with other people are good for us or not.

In evaluating other people, it is critical that we judge based on essentials. At BB&T we do not discriminate based on nonessentials such as race, sex, nationality, etc. We do discriminate based on competency, performance and character. We consciously reject egalitarianism and collectivism. Individuals must be judged individually based on their personal merits, not their membership in any group.

8. Pride

Pride is the psychological reward we earn from living by our values, that is, from being just, honest, having integrity, being an independent thinker, being productive and rational.

Aristotle believed that "earned" pride (not arrogance) was the highest of virtues, because it presupposed all the others. Striving for earned pride simply reinforces the importance of having high moral values.

Each of us must perform our work in a manner as to be able to be justly proud of what we have accomplished. BB&T must be the kind of organization with which each employee and client can be proud to be associated.

9. Self-Esteem (Self-Motivation)

We expect our employees to earn positive self-esteem from doing their work well. We expect and want our employees to act in their rational, long-term self-interest. We want employees who have strong personal goals and who expect to be able to accomplish their goals within the context of our mission.

A necessary attribute for self-esteem is self-motivation. We have a strong work ethic. We believe that you receive from your work in proportion to how much you contribute. If you do not want to work hard, work somewhere else.

While there are many trade-offs in the content of life, you need to be clear that BB&T is the best place, all things considered, for you to work to accomplish your long-term goals. When you know this, you can be more productive and happy.

10. Teamwork/Mutual Supportiveness

While independent thought and strong personal goals are critically important, our work is accomplished within teams. Each of us must consistently act to achieve the agreed-upon objectives of the team, with respect for our fellow employees, while acting in a mutually supportive manner.

Our work at BB&T is so complex that it requires an integrated effort among many people to accomplish important tasks. While we are looking for self-motivated and independent thinking individuals, these individuals must recognize that almost nothing at BB&T can be accomplished without the help of their team members. One of the responsibilities of leadership in our organization is to ensure that each individual is rewarded based on their contribution to the success of the total team. We need outstanding individuals working together to create an outstanding team.

Our values are held consciously and are logically consistent. To fully execute on any one value, you must act consistently with all 10 values. At BB&T values are practical and important.

The Role of Emotions

Often people believe that making logical decisions means that we should be unemotional and that emotions are thereby unimportant. In fact, emotions are important. However, the real issue is how rational are our emotions. Emotions are mental habits which are often developed as children. Emotions give us automatic responses to people and events; these responses can either be very useful or destructive indicators. Emotions as such are not means of decision or of knowledge; the issue is: How were your emotions formed? The real question is, Are we happy when we should be happy, and unhappy when we should be unhappy, or are we unhappy when we should be happy?

Emotions are learned behaviors. The goal is to "train up" our emotions so that our emotions objectively reinforce the best decisions and behaviors toward our long-term success and happiness. Just because someone is unemotional does not mean that they are logical.

Concepts That Describe BB&T

1. Client-Driven

"World class" client service organization.
Our clients are our partners.
Our goal is to create win/win relationships.
"You can tell we want your business."
"It is easy to do business with BB&T."
"Respect the individual, value the relationship."

We will absolutely never, ever, take advantage of anyone, nor do we want to do business with those who would take advantage of us. Our clients are long-term partners and should be treated accordingly. One of the attributes of partnerships is that both partners must keep their agreements. We keep our agreements. When our partners fail to keep their agreements, they are terminating the partnership.

There are an infinite number of opportunities where we can get better together, where we can help our clients achieve their financial goals and where our client will enable us to make a profit in doing so.

2. Quality Oriented

Quality must be built into the process.

In every aspect of our business we want to execute and deliver quality. It is easier and less expensive to do things correctly than to fix what has been done incorrectly.

3. Efficient

"Waste not, want not."
Design efficiency into the system.

4. Growing Both Our Business and Our People

Grow or die.
Life requires constant, focused thought and actions towards one's goals.

5. Continuous Improvement

Everything can be done better.
Fundamental commitment to innovation.
Every employee should constantly use their reasoning ability to do whatever they do better every day. All managers of systems/processes should constantly search for better methods to solve problems and serve the client.

6. Objective Decision Making

Fact-based and rational.

BB&T Management Style

Participative
Team Oriented
Fact-Based
Rational
Objective

Our management process, by intention, is designed to be participative and team oriented. We work hard to create consensus. When people are involved in the decision process, better information is available to make decisions. The participant's understanding of the decision is greater and, therefore, execution is better.

However, there is a risk in participative decision making: the decision process can become a popularity contest. Therefore, our decision process is disciplined. Our decisions will be made based on the facts using reason. The best objective decision will be the one which is enacted.

Therefore, it does not matter whom you know, who your friends are, etc.; it matters whether you can offer the best objective solution to accomplishing the goal or solving the problem at hand.

BB&T Management Concept

Hire excellent people
Train them well
Give them an appropriate level of authority and responsibility
Expect a high level of achievement
Reward their performance

Our concept is to operate a highly autonomous, entrepreneurial organization. In order to execute this concept, we must have extremely competent individuals who are "masters" of BB&T's philosophy and who are "masters" in their field of technical expertise.

By having individuals who are "masters" in their field, we can afford to have less costly control systems and be more responsive in meeting the needs of our clients.

Attributes of an Outstanding BB&T Employee

Purpose
Rationality
Self-esteem

Consistent with our values, successful individuals at BB&T have a sense of purpose for their lives; that is, they believe that their lives matter and that they can accomplish something meaningful through their work. We are looking for people who are rational and have a high level of personal self-esteem. People with a strong personal self-esteem get along better with others, because they are at peace with themselves.

BB&T Positive Attitude

Since we build on the facts of reality and our ability to reason, we are capable of achieving both success and happiness.

We do not believe that "realism" means pessimism. On the contrary, precisely because our goals are based on and consistent with reality, we fully expect to accomplish them.

BB&T'S Obligations to Its Employees

We will do our best to:

Compensate employees fairly in relation to internal equity and market-comparable pay practices—performance-based compensation.

Provide a comprehensive and market-competitive benefit program.

Create a place where employees can learn and grow—to become more productive workers and better people.

Train employees so they are competent to do the work asked of them. (Never ask anyone to do anything they are not trained to do.)

Evaluate and recognize performance objectively, fairly and consistently based on the individual's contribution to the accomplishment of our mission and adherence to our values.

Treat each employee as an individual with dignity and respect.

Virtues of an Outstanding Credit Culture

Just as individuals need a set of values (virtues) to guide their actions, systems should be designed to have a set of attributes which optimize their performance towards our goals. In this regard, our credit culture has seven fundamental virtues:

1. Provides fundamental insight to help clients achieve their economic goals and solve their financial problems: We are in the high-quality financial advice business.
2. Responsive: The client deserves an answer as quickly as possible, even when the answer is no.
3. Flexible (Creative): We are committed to finding better ways to meet the client's financial needs.
4. Reliable: Our clients are selected as long-term partners and treated accordingly. BB&T must continue to earn the right to be known as the most reliable bank.
5. Manages risk within agreed-upon limits: Clients do not want to fail financially, and the bank does not want a bad loan.
6. Ensures an appropriate economic return to the bank for risk taken: The higher the risk, the higher the return. The lower the risk, the lower the return. This is an expression of justice.
7. Creates a "premium" for service delivery: The concept is to provide superior value to the client through outstanding service quality. A rational client will fairly compensate us when we provide sound financial advice, are responsive, creative and reliable, because these attributes are of economic value to the client.

Strategic Objectives

Create a high performance financial institution that can survive and prosper in a rapidly changing, highly competitive, globally integrated environment.

Achieving Our Goal

The key to maximizing our probability of being both independent and prosperous over the long term is to create a superior earnings per share (EPS) growth rate without sacrificing the fundamental quality and long-term competitiveness of our business and without taking unreasonable risk.

While being fundamentally efficient is critical, the "easy" way to rapid EPS growth is to artificially cut cost. However, not investing for the future is long-term suicide, as it destroys our capability to compete.

The intelligent process to achieve superior EPS growth is to grow revenues by providing (and selling) superior quality service while systematically enhancing our margins, improving our efficiency, expanding our profitable product offerings and creating more effective distribution channels.

The "World Standard" Revenue-Driven Sales Organization

At BB&T, selling is about identifying our clients' legitimate financial needs and finding a way to help the client achieve economic goals by providing the right products and services.

Effective selling requires a disciplined approach in which the BB&T employee asks the client about financial goals and problems and has a complete understanding of how our products can help the client achieve objectives and solve financial problems.

It also requires exceptional execution by support staffs and product managers, since service and sales are fundamentally connected and creativity is required in product design and development.

"World Standard" Client Service Community Banks

BB&T operates as a series of "Community Banks." The "Community Bank" concept is the foundation for local decision making and the basis for responsive, reliable and empathetic client service.

By putting decision making closer to the client, all local factors can be considered, and we can ensure that the client is being treated as an individual.

To operate in this decentralized decision-making fashion, we must have highly trained employees who understand BB&T's philosophy and are "masters" of their areas of responsibility.

Commitment to Education/Learning

Competitive advantage is in the minds of our employees. We are committed to making substantial investments in employee education to create a "knowledge-based learning organization" founded on the premise that knowledge (understanding), properly applied, is the source of superior performance.

We believe in systematized learning founded on Aristotle's concept that "excellence is an art won by training and habituation." We attempt to train our employees with the best knowledge/methods in their fields and to habituate those behaviors through consistent management reinforcement. The goal is for each employee to be a "master" of his or her role, whether it be a computer operator, teller, lender, financial consultant or any other job responsibility.

Our Passions

To create the best financial institution possible.

To consistently provide the client with better value through rational innovation and productivity improvement.

At BB&T we have two powerful passions. Our fundamental passion is our Vision: To Create The Best Financial Institution Possible—The "World Standard"—The "Best of the Best." We believe that the best can be objectively evaluated by rational performance standards in relation to the accomplishment of our mission.

To be the best of the best, we must constantly find ways to deliver better value to our clients in a highly profitable manner. This requires us to keep our minds focused at all times on innovative ways to enhance our productivity.

Corporate Social Responsibility and Business Ethics

After reading and studying this chapter, you should be able to

1. Understand the importance of the stakeholder approach to social responsibility.

2. Explain the continuum of social responsibility and the effect of various options on company profitability.

3. Describe a social audit and explain its importance.

4. Discuss the effect of the Sarbanes-Oxley Act of 2002 on the ethical conduct of business.

5. Compare the advantages of collaborative social initiatives with alternative approaches to CSR.

6. Explain the five principles of collaborative social initiatives.

7. Compare the merits of different approaches to business ethics.

8. Explain the relevance of business ethics to strategic management practice.

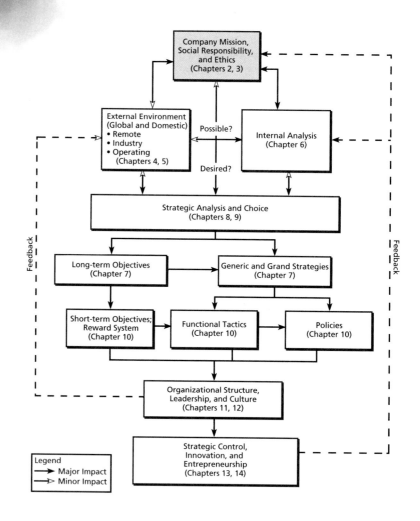

THE STAKEHOLDER APPROACH TO SOCIAL RESPONSIBILITY

In defining or redefining the company mission, strategic managers must recognize the legitimate rights of the firm's claimants. These include not only stockholders and employees but also outsiders affected by the firm's actions. Such outsiders commonly include customers, suppliers, governments, unions, competitors, local communities, and the general public. Each of these interest groups has justifiable reasons for expecting (and often for demanding) that the firm satisfy their claims in a responsible manner. In general, stockholders claim appropriate returns on their investment; employees seek broadly defined job satisfactions; customers want what they pay for; suppliers seek dependable buyers; governments want adherence to legislation; unions seek benefits for their members; competitors want fair competition; local communities want the firm to be a responsible citizen; and the general public expects the firm's existence to improve the quality of life.

According to a survey of 2,361 directors in 291 of the largest southeastern U.S. companies,

1. Directors perceived the existence of distinct stakeholder groups.
2. Directors have high stakeholder orientations.
3. Directors view some stakeholders differently, depending on their occupation (CEO directors versus non-CEO directors) and type (inside versus outside directors).

The study also found that the perceived stakeholders were, in the order of their importance, customers and government, stockholders, employees, and society. The results clearly indicated that boards of directors no longer believe that the stockholder is the only constituency to whom they are responsible.

However, when a firm attempts to incorporate the interests of these groups into its mission statement, broad generalizations are insufficient. These steps need to be taken:

1. Identification of the stakeholders.
2. Understanding the stakeholders' specific claims vis-à-vis the firm.
3. Reconciliation of these claims and assignment of priorities to them.
4. Coordination of the claims with other elements of the company mission.

Identification The left-hand column of Exhibit 3.1 lists the commonly encountered stakeholder groups, to which the executive officer group often is added. Obviously, though, every business faces a slightly different set of stakeholder groups, which vary in number, size, influence, and importance. In defining the company, strategic managers must identify all of the stakeholder groups and weigh their relative rights and their relative ability to affect the firm's success.

Understanding The concerns of the principal stakeholder groups tend to center on the general claims listed in the right-hand column of Exhibit 3.1. However, strategic decision makers should understand the specific demands of each group. They then will be better able to initiate actions that satisfy these demands.

Reconciliation and Priorities Unfortunately, the claims of various stakeholder groups often conflict. For example, the claims of governments and the general public tend to limit profitability, which is the central claim of most creditors and stockholders. Thus, claims must be reconciled in a mission statement that resolves the competing, conflicting, and contradicting claims of stakeholders. For objectives and strategies to be internally consistent and precisely focused, the statement must display a single-minded, though multidimensional, approach to the firm's aims.

EXHIBIT 3.1
A Stakeholder View of Company Responsibility

Stakeholder	Nature of the Claim
Stockholders	Participation in distribution of profits, additional stock offerings, assets on liquidation; vote of stock; inspection of company books; transfer of stock; election of board of directors; and such additional rights as have been established in the contract with the corporation.
Creditors	Legal proportion of interest payments due and return of principal from the investment. Security of pledged assets; relative priority in event of liquidation. Management and owner prerogatives if certain conditions exist with the company (such as default of interest payments).
Employees	Economic, social, and psychological satisfaction in the place of employment. Freedom from arbitrary and capricious behavior on the part of company officials. Share in fringe benefits, freedom to join union and participate in collective bargaining, individual freedom in offering up their services through an employment contract. Adequate working conditions.
Customers	Service provided with the product; technical data to use the product; suitable warranties; spare parts to support the product during use; R&D leading to product improvement; facilitation of credit.
Suppliers	Continuing source of business; timely consummation of trade credit obligations; professional relationship in contracting for, purchasing, and receiving goods and services.
Governments	Taxes (income, property, and so on); adherence to the letter and intent of public policy dealing with the requirements of fair and free competition; discharge of legal obligations of business-people (and business organizations); adherence to antitrust laws.
Unions	Recognition as the negotiating agent for employees. Opportunity to perpetuate the union as a participant in the business organization.
Competitors	Observation of the norms for competitive conduct established by society and the industry. Business statesmanship on the part of peers.
Local communities	Place of productive and healthful employment in the community. Participation of company officials in community affairs, provision of regular employment, fair play, reasonable portion of purchases made in the local community, interest in and support of local government, support of cultural and charitable projects.
The general public	Participation in and contribution to society as a whole; creative communications between governmental and business units designed for reciprocal understanding; assumption of fair proportion of the burden of government and society. Fair price for products and advancement of the state-of-the-art technology that the product line involves.

Source: William R. King and David I. Cleland, *Strategic Planning and Policy*, © 1978, by Litton Educational Publishing, Inc., p. 153.

There are hundreds, if not thousands, of claims on any firm—high wages, pure air, job security, product quality, community service, taxes, occupational health and safety regulations, equal employment opportunity regulations, product variety, wide markets, career opportunities, company growth, investment security, high ROI, and many, many more. Although most, perhaps all, of these claims may be desirable ends, they cannot be pursued with equal emphasis. They must be assigned priorities in accordance with the relative emphasis that the firm will give them. That emphasis is reflected in the criteria that the firm uses in its strategic decision making; in the firm's allocation of its human, financial, and physical resources; and in the firm's long-term objectives and strategies.

Coordination with Other Elements   The demands of stakeholder groups constitute only one principal set of inputs to the company mission. The other principal sets are the managerial operating philosophy and the determinants of the product-market offering. Those determinants constitute a reality test that the accepted claims must pass. The key question is, How can the firm satisfy its claimants and at the same time optimize its economic success in the marketplace?

The Dynamics of Social Responsibility

As indicated in Exhibit 3.2, the various stakeholders of a firm can be divided into inside stakeholders and outside stakeholders. The insiders are the individuals or groups that are stockholders or employees of the firm. The outsiders are all the other individuals or groups that the firm's actions affect. The extremely large and often amorphous set of outsiders makes the general claim that the firm be socially responsible.

Perhaps the thorniest issues faced in defining a company mission are those that pertain to social responsibility. Corporate social responsibility is the idea that a business has a duty to serve society in general as well as the financial interests of its stockholders. The stakeholder approach offers the clearest perspective on such issues. Broadly stated, outsiders often demand that insiders' claims be subordinated to the greater good of the society; that is, to the greater good of outsiders. They believe that such issues as pollution, the disposal of solid and liquid wastes, and the conservation of natural resources should be principal considerations in strategic decision making. Also broadly stated, insiders tend to believe that the competing claims of outsiders should be balanced against one another in a way that protects the company mission. For example, they tend to believe that the need of consumers for a product should be balanced against the water pollution resulting from its production if the firm cannot eliminate that pollution entirely and still remain profitable. Some insiders also argue that the claims of society, as expressed in government regulation, provide tax money that can be used to eliminate water pollution and the like if the general public wants this to be done.

EXHIBIT 3.2
Inputs to the Development of the Company Mission

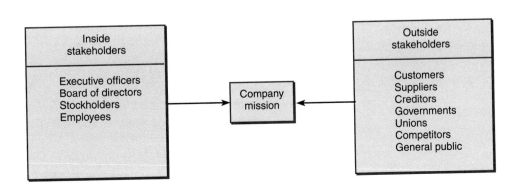

Beyond the Green Corporation

BusinessWeek

Under conventional notions of how to run a conglomerate like Unilever, CEO Patrick Cescau should wake up each morning with a laserlike focus: how to sell more soap and shampoo than Procter & Gamble Co. But ask Cescau about the $52 billion Dutch-British giant's biggest strategic challenges for the twenty-first century, and the conversation roams from water-deprived villages in Africa to the planet's warming climate.

The world is Unilever's laboratory. In Brazil, the company operates a free community laundry in a Sao Paulo slum, provides financing to help tomato growers convert to eco-friendly "drip" irrigation, and recycles 17 tons of waste annually at a toothpaste factory. Unilever funds a floating hospital that offers free medical care in Bangladesh, a nation with just 20 doctors for every 10,000 people. In Ghana, it teaches palm oil producers to reuse plant waste while providing potable water to deprived communities. In India, Unilever staff help thousands of women in remote villages start micro-enterprises. And responding to green activists, the company discloses how much carbon dioxide and hazardous waste its factories spew out around the world.

As Cescau sees it, helping such nations wrestle with poverty, water scarcity, and the effects of climate change is vital to staying competitive in coming decades. Some 40 percent of the company's sales and most of its growth now take place in developing nations. Unilever food products account for roughly 10 percent of the world's crops of tea and 30 percent of all spinach. It is also one of the world's biggest buyers of fish. As environmental regulations grow tighter around the world, Unilever must invest in green technologies or its leadership in packaged foods, soaps, and other goods could be imperiled. "You can't ignore the impact your company has on the community and environment," Cescau says. CEOs used to frame thoughts like these in the context of moral responsibility, he adds. But now, "it's also about growth and innovation. In the future, it will be the only way to do business."

The accompanying table on page 55 lists corporations and the actions that they have taken to be judged as having made important contributions to social initiatives.

Source: Reprinted with special permission from Pete Engardino, with Kerry Capell in London, John Carey in Washington, Kenji Hall in Tokyo, "Beyond the Green Corporation," *BusinessWeek*, January 29, 2007. Copyright © 2007 The McGraw-Hill Companies.

The issues are numerous, complex, and contingent on specific situations. Thus, rigid rules of business conduct cannot deal with them. Each firm *regardless of size* must decide how to meet its perceived social responsibility. While large, well-capitalized companies may have easy access to environmental consultants, this is not an affordable strategy for smaller companies. However, the experience of many small businesses demonstrates that it is feasible to accomplish significant pollution prevention and waste reduction without big expenditures and without hiring consultants. Once a problem area has been identified, a company's line employees frequently can develop a solution. Other important pollution prevention strategies include changing the materials used or redesigning how operations are bid out. Making pollution prevention a social responsibility can be beneficial to smaller companies. Publicly traded firms also can benefit directly from socially responsible strategies.

Different approaches adopted by different firms reflect differences in competitive position, industry, country, environmental and ecological pressures, and a host of other factors. In other words, they will reflect both situational factors and differing priorities in the acknowledgment of claims. Obviously, winning the loyalty of the growing legions of consumers will require new strategies and new alliances in the twenty-first century. Exhibit 3.3, Strategy in Action, discusses a wide range of socially responsible actions in which corporations are currently engaged.

Who's Doing Well by Doing Good

Automobiles

Toyota	The maker of the top-selling Prius hybrid leads in developing efficient gas-electric vehicles.
Renault	Integrates sustainability throughout organization; has fuel-efficient cars and factories.
Volkswagen	A market leader in small cars and clean diesel technologies.

Computers and Peripherals

Hewlett-Packard	Rates high on ecological standards and digital tech for the poor.
Toshiba	At forefront of developing eco-efficient products, such as fuel cells for notebook PC batteries.
Dell	Among the first U.S. PC makers to take hardware back from consumers and recycle it for free.

Health Care

Fresenius Medical Care	Discloses costs of its patient treatment in terms of energy and water use and waste generated.
IMS Health	Places unusual emphasis on environmental issues in its global health consulting work.
Quest Diagnostics	Has diversity program promoting businesses owned by minorities, women, and veterans.

Oil and Gas

Royal Dutch Shell	Since Nigerian human rights woes in 1990s, leads in community relations; invests in wind and solar.
Norsk Hydro	Cut greenhouse gas emissions 32 percent since 1990; strong in assessing social, environmental impact.
Suncor Energy	Ties with aboriginals help it deal with social and ecological issues in Canada's far north.

Retail

Marks & Spencer	Buys local product to cut transit costs and fuel use; good wages and benefits help retain staff.
Home retail group	High overall corporate responsibility standards have led to strong consumer and staff loyalty.
Aeon	Environmental accounting has saved $5.6 million; good employee policies in China and Southeast Asia.

Communications Equipment

Nokia	Makes phones for handicapped and low-income consumers; a leader in phasing out toxic materials.
Ericsson	Eco-friendly initiatives include wind- and fuel-cell-powered telecom systems in Nigerian villages.
Motorola	Good disclosure of environmental data; takes back used equipment in Mexico, United States, and Europe.

Financial Services

ABN Amro	Involved in carbon-emissions trading; finances everything from micro-enterprises to biomass fuels.
HSBC	Lending guidelines for forestry, freshwater, and chemical sectors factor in social, ecological risks.
Ing	Weighs sustainability in project finance; helps developing nations improve financial institutions.

Household Durables

Philips Electronics	Top innovator of energy-saving appliances, lighting, and medical gear and goods for developing world.
Sony	Is ahead on green issues and ensuring quality, safety, and labor standards of global suppliers.
Matsushita Electric	State-of-the-art green products; eliminated 96 percent of the most toxic substances in its global operations.

Pharmaceuticals

Roche	Committed to improving access to medicine in poor nations; invests in drug research for Third World.
Novo Nordisk	Spearheads efforts in diseases like leprosy and bird flu and is a leading player in lower-cost generics.
Glaxo-Smithkline	One of few pharmas to devote R&D to malaria and TB; first to offer AIDS drugs at cost.

Utilities

FPL	Largest U.S. solar generator; has 40 percent of wind-power capacity; strong shareholder relations.
Iberdrola	Since Scottish Power takeover, renewable energy accounts for 17 percent of capacity; wants that to grow.
Scottish & Southern	Aggressively discloses environmental risk, including air pollution and climate change.

Occidental Petroleum faces issues of corporate social responsibility in addressing the needs of the many stakeholders involved in the firm's oil exploration in developing countries. Many parties that have potential to be affected by the company's endeavors, including local inhabitants and government, environmental groups, and institutional investors.

Despite differences in their approaches, most American firms now try to assure outsiders that they attempt to conduct business in a socially responsible manner. Many firms, including Abt Associates, Dow Chemical, Eastern Gas and Fuel Associates, ExxonMobil, and the Bank of America, conduct and publish annual social audits. Such audits attempt to evaluate a firm from the perspective of social responsibility. Private consultants often conduct them for the firm and offer minimally biased evaluations on what are inherently highly subjective issues.

TYPES OF SOCIAL RESPONSIBILITY

To better understand the nature and range of social responsibilities for which they must plan, strategic managers can consider four types of social commitment: economic, legal, ethical, and discretionary social responsibilities.

economic responsibilities
The duty of managers, as agents of the company owners, to maximize stockholder wealth.

Economic responsibilities are the most basic social responsibilities of business. As we have noted, some economists see these as the only legitimate social responsibility of business. Living up to their economic responsibilities requires managers to maximize profits whenever possible. The essential responsibility of business is assumed to be providing goods and services to society at a reasonable cost. In discharging that economic responsibility, the company also emerges as socially responsible by providing productive jobs for its workforce, and tax payments for its local, state, and federal governments.

legal responsibilities
The firm's obligations to comply with the laws that regulate business activities.

Legal responsibilities reflect the firm's obligations to comply with the laws that regulate business activities. The consumer and environmental movements focused increased public attention on the need for social responsibility in business by lobbying for laws that govern business in the areas of pollution control and consumer safety. The intent of consumer legislation has been to correct the "balance of power" between buyers and sellers in the marketplace. Among the most important laws are the Federal Fair Packaging and Labeling Act that regulates labeling procedures for business, the Truth in Lending Act that regulates the extension of credit to individuals, and the Consumer Product Safety Act that protects consumers against unreasonable risks of injury in the use of consumer products.

The environmental movement has had a similar effect on the regulation of business. This movement achieved stricter enforcement of existing environmental protections and it spurred the passage of new, more comprehensive laws such as the National Environmental Policy Act, which is devoted to preserving the United States' ecological balance and making environmental protection a federal policy goal. It requires environmental impact studies whenever new construction may threaten an existing ecosystem, and it established the Council on Environmental Quality to guide business development. Another product of the environmental movement was the creation of the federal Environmental Protection Agency, which interprets and administers the environmental protection policies of the U.S. government.

Clearly, these legal responsibilities are supplemental to the requirement that businesses and their employees comply fully with the general civil and criminal laws that apply to all individuals and institutions in the country. Yet, strangely, individual failures to adhere to the law have recently produced some of the greatest scandals in the history of American free enterprise. Exhibit 3.4, Strategy in Action, presents an overview of seven of these cases that involved executives from Adelphia Communications, Arthur Andersen, Global Crossing, ImClone Systems, Merrill Lynch, WorldCom, and Xerox.

An Overview of Corporate Scandals*

ADELPHIA COMMUNICATIONS

On July 24, 2002, John Rigas, the 77-year-old founder of the country's sixth largest cable television operator was arrested, along with two of his sons, and accused of looting the now-bankrupt company. Several other former Adelphia executives were also arrested. The Securities and Exchange Commission (SEC) brought a civil suit against the company for allegedly fraudulently excluding billions of dollars in liabilities from its financial statements, falsifying statistics, inflating its earnings to meet Wall Street's expectations, and concealing "rampant self-dealing by the Rigas family." The family, which founded Adelphia in 1952, gave up control of the firm in May, and on June 25 the company filed for bankruptcy protection. The company was delisted by NASDAQ in June 2002.

ARTHUR ANDERSEN

On June 15, 2002, a Texas jury found the accounting firm guilty of obstructing justice for its role in shredding financial documents related to its former client Enron. Andersen, founded in 1913, had already been largely destroyed after admitting that it sped up the shredding of Enron documents following the launch of an SEC investigation. Andersen fired David Duncan, who led its Houston office, saying he was responsible for shredding the Enron documents. Duncan admitted to obstruction of justice, turned state's evidence, and testified on behalf of the government.

GLOBAL CROSSING

The SEC and the Federal Bureau of Investigation (FBI) are probing the five-year-old telecom company Global Crossing regarding alleged swaps of network capacity with other telecommunications firms to inflate revenue. The company ran into trouble by betting that it could borrow billions of dollars to build a fiber-optic infrastructure that would be in strong demand by corporations. Because others made the same bet, there was a glut of fiber optics and prices plunged, leaving Global Crossing with massive debts. It filed for bankruptcy on January 28, 2002. Chairman Gary Winnick, who founded Global Crossing in 1997, cashed out $734 million in stock before the company collapsed. Global Crossing was delisted from the New York Stock Exchange (NYSE) in January 2002.

IMCLONE SYSTEMS

The biotech firm is being investigated by a congressional committee that is seeking to find out if ImClone correctly informed investors that the Food and Drug Administration (FDA) had declined to accept for review its key experimental cancer drug, Erbitux. Former CEO Samuel Waksal pled guilty in June 2003 to insider trading charges related to Erbitux and was sentenced to seven years in prison. Also, federal investigators filed charges against home decorating diva Martha Stewart for using insider information on the cancer drug when she sold 4,000 ImClone shares one day before the FDA initially said it would reject the drug.

MERRILL LYNCH

On May 21, 2002, Merrill Lynch agreed to pay $100 million to settle New York Attorney General Eliot Spitzer's charges that the nation's largest securities firm knowingly peddled Internet stocks to investors to generate lucrative investment banking fees. Internal memos written by Merrill's feted Internet analyst Henry Blodgett revealed that company analysts thought little of the Web stocks that they urged investors to buy. Merrill agreed to strengthen firewalls between its research and investment-banking divisions, ensuring advice given to investors is not influenced by efforts to win underwriting fees.

WORLDCOM

The nation's second largest telecom company filed for the nation's biggest ever bankruptcy on July 21, 2002. WorldCom's demise accelerated on June 25, 2002, when it admitted it hid $3.85 billion in expenses, allowing it to post net income of $1.38 billion in 2001, instead of a loss. The company fired its CFO Scott Sullivan and on June 28 began cutting 17,000 jobs, more than 20 percent of its workforce. CEO Bernie Ebbers resigned in April amid questions about $408 million of personal loans he received from the company to cover losses he incurred in buying its shares. WorldCom was delisted from NASDAQ in July 2002.

XEROX

Xerox said on June 28, 2002, that it would restate five years of financial results to reclassify more than $6 billion in revenues. In April, the company settled SEC charges that it used "accounting tricks" to defraud investors, agreeing to pay a $10 million fine. The firm admitted no wrongdoing. Xerox manufactures imaging products, such as copiers, printers, fax machines, and scanners.

* This section was derived in its entirety from "A Guide to Corporate Scandals," MSNBC, www.msnbc.com/news/corpscandal front.

ethical responsibilities
The strategic managers' notion of right and proper business behavior.

discretionary responsibilities
Responsibilities voluntarily assumed by a business, such as public relations, good citizenship, and full corporate responsibility.

Ethical responsibilities reflect the company's notion of right and proper business behavior. Ethical responsibilities are obligations that transcend legal requirements. Firms are expected, but not required, to behave ethically. Some actions that are legal might be considered unethical. For example, the manufacture and distribution of cigarettes is legal. But in light of the often-lethal consequences of smoking, many consider the continued sale of cigarettes to be unethical. The topic of management ethics receives additional attention later in this chapter.

Discretionary responsibilities are those that are voluntarily assumed by a business organization. They include public relations activities, good citizenship, and full corporate social responsibility. Through public relations activities, managers attempt to enhance the image of their companies, products, and services by supporting worthy causes. This form of discretionary responsibility has a self-serving dimension. Companies that adopt the good citizenship approach actively support ongoing charities, public service advertising campaigns, or issues in the public interest. A commitment to full corporate responsibility requires strategic managers to attack social problems with the same zeal in which they attack business problems. For example, teams in the National Football League provide time off for players and other employees afflicted with drug or alcohol addictions who agree to enter rehabilitation programs.

It is important to remember that the categories on the continuum of social responsibility overlap, creating gray areas where societal expectations on organizational behavior are difficult to categorize. In considering the overlaps among various demands for social responsibility, however, managers should keep in mind that in the view of the general public, economic and legal responsibilities are required, ethical responsibility is expected, and discretionary responsibility is desired.

Corporate Social Responsibility and Profitability
CSR and the Bottom Line

corporate social responsibility
The idea that business has a duty to serve society in general as well as the financial interest of stockholders.

The goal of every firm is to maintain viability through long-run profitability. Until all costs and benefits are accounted for, however, profits may not be claimed. In the case of **corporate social responsibility** (CSR), costs and benefits are both economic and social. While economic costs and benefits are easily quantifiable, social costs and benefits are not. Managers therefore risk subordinating social consequences to other performance results that can be more straightforwardly measured.

The dynamic between CSR and success (profit) is complex. While one concept is clearly not mutually exclusive of the other, it is also clear that neither is a prerequisite of the other. Rather than viewing these two concepts as competing, it may be better to view CSR as a component in the decision-making process of business that must determine, among other objectives, how to maximize profits.

Attempts to undertake a cost-benefit analysis of CSR have not been very successful. The process is complicated by several factors. First, some CSR activities incur no dollar costs at all. For example, Second Harvest, the largest nongovernment, charitable food distributor in the nation, accepts donations from food manufacturers and food retailers of surplus food that would otherwise be thrown out due to overruns, warehouse damage, or labeling errors. In 10 years, Second Harvest has distributed more than 2 billion pounds of food. Gifts in Kind America is an organization that enables companies to reduce unsold or obsolete inventory by matching a corporation's donated products with a charity's or other nonprofit organization's needs. In addition, a tax break is realized by the company. In the past, corporate donations have included 130,000 pairs of shoes from Nike, 10,000 pairs of gloves from Aris Isotoner, and 480 computer systems from Apple Computer.

In addition, philanthropic activities of a corporation, which have been a traditional mainstay of CSR, are undertaken at a discounted cost to the firm since they are often tax deductible. The benefits of corporate philanthropy can be enormous as is shown by the many national social welfare causes that have been spurred by corporate giving. While such acts of benevolence often help establish a general perception of the involved companies within society, some philanthropic acts bring specific credit to the firm.

Second, socially responsible behavior does not come at a prohibitive cost. One needs only to look at the problems of A. H. Robbins Company (Dalkon Shield), Beech-Nut Corporation (apple juice), Drexel Burnham (insider trading), and Exxon *(Valdez)* for stark answers on the "cost" of social responsibility (or its absence) in the business environment.

Third, socially responsible practices may create savings and, as a result, increase profits. SET Laboratories uses popcorn to ship software rather than polystyrene peanuts. It is environmentally safer and costs 60 percent less to use. Corporations that offer part-time and adjustable work schedules have realized that this can lead to reduced absenteeism, greater productivity and increased morale. DuPont opted for more flexible schedules for its employees after a survey revealed 50 percent of women and 25 percent of men considered working for another employer with more flexibility for family concerns.

Proponents argue that CSR costs are more than offset in the long run by an improved company image and increased community goodwill. These intangible assets can prove valuable in a crisis, as Johnson & Johnson discovered with the Tylenol cyanide scare in 1982. Because it had established a solid reputation as a socially responsible company before the incident, the public readily accepted the company's assurances of public safety. Consequently, financial damage to Johnson & Johnson was minimized, despite the company's $100 million voluntary recall of potentially tainted capsules. CSR may also head off new regulation, preventing increased compliance costs. It may even attract investors who are themselves socially responsible. Proponents believe that for these reasons, socially responsible behavior increases the financial value of the firm in the long run. The mission statement of Johnson & Johnson is provided as Exhibit 3.5, Strategy in Action.

Performance   To explore the relationship between socially responsible behavior and financial performance, an important question must first be answered: How do managers measure the financial effect of corporate social performance?

Critics of CSR believe that companies that behave in a socially responsible manner, and portfolios comprising these companies' securities, should perform more poorly financially than those that do not. The costs of CSR outweigh the benefits for individual firms, they suggest. In addition, traditional portfolio theory holds that investors minimize risk and maximize return by being able to choose from an infinite universe of investment opportunities. Portfolios based on social criteria should suffer, critics argue, because they are by definition restrictive in nature. This restriction should increase portfolio risk and reduce portfolio return.

CSR Today

CSR has become a priority with American business. In addition to a commonsense belief that companies should be able to "do well by doing good," at least three broad trends are driving businesses to adopt CSR frameworks: the resurgence of environmentalism, increasing buyer power, and the globalization of business.

The Resurgence of Environmentalism   In March 1989, the Exxon *Valdez* ran aground in Prince William Sound, spilling 11 million gallons of oil, polluting miles of ocean and shore, and helping to revive worldwide concern for the ecological environment. Six months after the *Valdez* incident, the Coalition for Environmentally Responsible Economies (CERES) was formed to establish new goals for environmentally responsible corporate behavior.

Mission Statement: Johnson & Johnson

"We believe our first responsibility is to the doctors, nurses and patients, to mothers and fathers and all others who use our products and services. In meeting their needs everything we do must be of high quality. We must constantly strive to reduce our costs in order to maintain reasonable prices. Customers' orders must be serviced promptly and accurately. Our suppliers and distributors must have an opportunity to make a fair profit.

"We are responsible to our employees, the men and women who work with us throughout the world. Everyone must be considered as an individual. We must respect their dignity and recognize their merit. They must have a sense of security in their jobs. Compensation must be fair and adequate, and working conditions clean, orderly and safe. Employees must feel free to make suggestions and complaints. There must be equal opportunity for employment, development and advancement for those qualified. We must provide competent management, and their actions must be just and ethical.

"We are responsible to the communities in which we live and work and to the world community as well. We must be good citizens—support good works and charities and bear our fair share of taxes. We must encourage civic improvements and better health and education. We must maintain in good order the property we are privileged to use, protecting the environment and natural resources.

"Our final responsibility is to our stockholders. Business must make a sound profit. We must experiment with new ideas. Research must be carried on, innovative programs developed and mistakes paid for. New equipment must be purchased, new facilities provided and new products launched. Reserves must be created to provide for adverse times. When we operate according to these principles, the stockholders should realize a fair return."

Source: Johnson & Johnson, http://www.jnsj.com

The group drafted the CERES Principles to "establish an environmental ethic with criteria by which investors and others can assess the environmental performance of companies. Companies that sign these Principles pledge to go voluntarily beyond the requirements of the law."

The most prevalent forms of environmentalism are efforts to preserve natural resources and eliminating environmental pollution, often referred to as the concern for "greening." Exhibit 3.6, Strategy in Action, provides cutting-edge methods by which Bank of America is helping promote environmentalism in the construction of its new office building in New York City.

Increasing Buyer Power   The rise of the consumer movement has meant that buyers— consumers and investors—are increasingly flexing their economic muscle. Consumers are becoming more interested in buying products from socially responsible companies. Organizations such as the Council on Economic Priorities (CEP) help consumers make more informed buying decisions through such publications as *Shopping for a Better World,* which provides social performance information on 191 companies making more than 2,000 consumer products. CEP also sponsors the annual Corporate Conscience Awards, which recognize socially responsible companies. One example of consumer power at work is the effective outcry over the deaths of dolphins in tuna fishermen's nets.

Investors represent a second type of influential consumer. There has been a dramatic increase in the number of people interested in supporting socially responsible companies through their investments. Membership in the Social Investment Forum, a trade association serving social investing professionals, has been growing at a rate of about 50 percent annually. As baby boomers achieve their own financial success, the social investing movement has continued its rapid growth.

Strategy in Action

Exhibit 3.6

Bank of America Tower: The World's Greenest Skyscraper

BusinessWeek

The world's greenest skyscraper is set to open in 2008 near Times Square. The $1.3 billion building will be New York's second tallest. The energy-efficient design of the Bank of America (BoA) building has several unique features.

- **Water from sky and earth.** Not a drop of rain that falls on BoA Tower is sent down the drain. Rather, it's collected, routed to flush toilets, used to irrigate the green roof, and to run the air conditioning (AC) system. The tower also harvests water from condensation that drips from AC systems, which in turn are cooled by groundwater that seeps in from the bedrock before being added to the rainwater tank. All this promises to save enough fresh water to supply 125 homes per year.

- **Daylight savings.** Sunlight helps students learn and workers focus. It will also help cut BoA Tower's lighting energy needs by 25 percent. Floor-to-ceiling windows, 9.5 feet tall, are made of low iron glass manufactured by PPG Industries and assembled by Permasteelisa. This lets in more visible light than normal glass, yet still insulates well. Inside, sensors control ceiling lights, turning them down when daylight is plentiful or rooms are empty.

- **Chill factor.** Heat rises. That simple force lets BoA Tower virtually do away with costly, overhead chilled-air ducts and fans. Instead, cool air is pumped into a void under raised floors. As it warms, the air rises to ceiling vents, pulling more chilled air up from below. Since this works passively, under low pressure, the AC can be set to 65°F, rather than 55°F. And eliminating miles of moist ductwork—where pathogens can play—helps improve overall building health.

- **Aired out.** Clean, oxygen-rich air delivers big productivity gains, too. BoA Tower draws in air 10 floors up or higher—far above the stew of tailpipe emissions. Filters catch 95 percent of particulate matter, allergens, ozone, and other compounds that can cause illness. Oxygen sensors trigger injections of fresh air into crowed spaces to help prevent "meeting room coma." When the used air is vented from the building, it's still cleaner than the outside atmosphere.

- **Homemade juice.** A super-efficient power plant, running on clean-burning natural gas, nearly trebles the tower's overall energy efficiency. By reusing waste heat and eliminating losses caused when electricity is shipped via power lines over long distances, the turbine meets four-fifths of the tower's peak needs. The setup wastes just 23 percent of the energy from the fuel source, far better than the 70 percent lost at a conventional grid-connected building.

- **No parking.** In gridlocked New York, a project this big would normally have hundreds of basement parking spots. BoA Tower has practically none. Instead, the tower enhances midtown's network of public transport. New pedestrian tunnels connect the tower to 17 subway lines and commuter rails. With secure bike storage and shower access, bicycling is an option, too. And if a car is a must, BoA uses OZOcar, New York's first hybrid-only fleet of liveries

- **Ice storage.** The twenty-first century's most advanced skyscraper takes a lesson from Victorian-era ice houses that collected lake ice in winter to use in summer. In the tower's basement, 44 squat cylindrical ice tanks will make ice at night, when power is cheaper, to help cool the AC system during the day. The trick cuts by 50 percent the energy needed to run the tower's AC on the hottest days, enough savings to pay for itself in three to five years. Made by CALMAC Manufacturing, the ice promises to cut pollution, too. When demand for power spikes on hot summer days, utilities fire up their least efficient, most polluting plants. BoA Tower won't need to tap much of his dirty power.

- **Waterless urinals.** For male tenants, at least, the tower's most noticeable water-savings trick may be Falcon Waterfree's flushless urinals. Made of an antibacterial, superslick material, these fixtures will save 3 million gallons of water a year. They funnel urine into a tank filled with a liquid that floats on top, like oil on water. Urine settles to the bottom and drains out to sewers.

Source: Reprinted with special permission from Adam Aston, "Bank of America Tower: The World's Greenest Skyscraper, Set to Open Early Next Year, is Rising Near Times Square," *BusinessWeek*, March 12, 2007. Copyright © 2007 The McGraw-Hill Companies.

While social investing wields relatively low power as an individual private act (selling one's shares of ExxonMobil does not affect the company), it can be very powerful as a collective public act. When investors vote their shares in behalf of pro-CSR issues, companies may be pressured to change their social behavior. The South African divestiture movement is one example of how effective this pressure can be.

The Vermont National Bank has added a Socially Responsible Banking Fund to its product line. Investors can designate any of their interest-bearing accounts with a $500 minimum balance to be used by the fund. This fund then lends these monies for purposes such as low-income housing, the environment, education, farming, or small business development. Although it has had a "humble" beginning of approximately 800 people investing about $11 million, the bank has attracted out-of-state depositors and is growing faster than expected.

Social investors comprise both individuals and institutions. Much of the impetus for social investing originated with religious organizations that wanted their investments to mirror their beliefs. At present, the ranks of social investors have expanded to include educational institutions and large pension funds.

Large-scale social investing can be broken down into the two broad areas of guideline portfolio investing and shareholder activism. Guideline portfolio investing is the largest and fastest-growing segment of social investing. Individual and institutional guideline portfolio investors use ethical guidelines as screens to identify possible investments in stocks, bonds, and mutual funds. The investment instruments that survive the social screens are then layered over the investor's financial screens to create the investor's universe of possible investments.

Screens may be negative (e.g., excluding all tobacco companies) or they may combine negative and positive elements (e.g., eliminating companies with bad labor records while seeking out companies with good ones). Most investors rely on screens created by investment firms such as Kinder, Lydenberg Domini & Co. or by industry groups such as the Council on Economic Priorities. In addition to ecology, employee relations, and community development, corporations may be screened on their association with "sin" products (alcohol, tobacco, gambling), defense/weapons production, and nuclear power.

In contrast to guideline portfolio investors, who passively indicate their approval or disapproval of a company's social behavior by simply including or excluding it from their portfolios, shareholder activists seek to directly influence corporate social behavior. Shareholder activists invest in a corporation hoping to improve specific aspects of the company's social performance, typically by seeking a dialogue with upper management. If this and successive actions fail to achieve the desired results, shareholder activists may introduce proxy resolutions to be voted upon at the corporation's annual meeting. The goal of these resolutions is to achieve change by gaining public exposure for the issue at hand. While the number of shareholder activists is relatively small, they are by no means small in achievement: shareholder activists, led by such groups as the Interfaith Center on Corporate Responsibility, were the driving force behind the South African divestiture movement. Currently, there are more than 35 socially screened mutual funds available in the United States alone.

The Globalization of Business Management issues, including CSR, have become more complex as companies increasingly transcend national borders: It is difficult enough to come to a consensus on what constitutes socially responsible behavior within one culture, let alone determine common ethical values across cultures. In addition to different cultural views, the high barriers facing international CSR include differing corporate disclosure practices, inconsistent financial data and reporting methods, and the lack of CSR research organizations within countries. Despite these problems, CSR is growing abroad. The United Kingdom has 30 ethical mutual funds and Canada offers 6 socially responsible funds.

One of the most contentious social responsibility issues confronting multinational firms pertains to human rights. For example, many U.S. firms reduce their costs either by relying on foreign manufactured goods or by outsourcing their manufacturing to foreign manufacturers. These foreign manufacturers, often Chinese, offer low pricing because they pay very low wages by U.S. standards, even though they are extremely competitive by Chinese pay rates.

Cisco, Oracle, and other U.S. companies are supplying China's police with software and gear that can be used to keep tabs on criminals and dissidents.

Google, Yahoo!, and Microsoft endured a wave of public disapproval in 2006 over their compliance with Chinese censorship of their Web sites. But another striking form of tech commerce with China is taking place below the radar of the U.S. public: major American manufacturers are rushing to supply China's police with the latest information technology.

Oracle Corp. has sold software to the Chinese Ministry of Public Security, which oversees both criminal and ideological investigations. The ministry uses the software to manage digital identity cards that are replacing the paper ID that Chinese citizens must carry. Meanwhile, regional Chinese police departments are modernizing their computer networks with routers and switches purchased from Cisco Systems Inc. And Motorola Inc. has sold the Chinese authorities handheld devices that will allow street cops to tap into the sorts of sophisticated data repositories that EMC Corp. markets to the Ministry of Public Security. "It's a booming market," says Simon Zhou, the top executive in Beijing for EMC, which is based in Hopkinton, Mass. "We can expect big revenue from public security" agencies in China.

The scramble to sell technology to Chinese law enforcers seems, for starters, to be at odds with the intent of an American export law enacted after the massacre of hundreds of pro-democracy demonstrators in Tiananmen Square in 1989. The Tiananmen sanctions prohibited the export "of any crime control or detection instruments or equipment" to China. "We wanted to undermine the effectiveness of the police in rounding up, imprisoning, and torturing political dissidents, not only those involved in the Tiananmen Square movement, but for years to come," explains Representative Tom Lantos (D–CA), who helped draft the law. Despite the improvement of its image on the world stage, China still has a dismal human rights record. The U.S. State Department says that the Communist government is holding at least 260,000 people in ideological "reeducation" camps.

The upshot is that "manufacturers of handcuffs aren't allowed to sell their products to China's police, but Cisco and other companies are selling Chinese authorities much more useful technology," Harry Wu, a former Chinese political prisoner living in the United States, told a House subcommittee on human rights in February 2006. His testimony was eclipsed by the panel's heavily covered excoriation of Google, Yahoo!, and Microsoft for their agreement to block parts of their Chinese Web sites as a condition of operating in the country.

Source: Reprinted with special permission from Bruce Einhorn and Ben Elgin, "Helping Big Brother Go High Tech," *BusinessWeek*, September 18, 2006. Copyright © 2006 The McGraw-Hill Companies.

While Chinese workers are happy to earn manufacturer wages and U.S. customers are pleased by the lower prices charged for foreign manufactured goods, others are unhappy. They believe that such U.S. firms are failing to satisfy their social responsibilities. Some U.S. workers and their unions argue that jobs in the United States are being eliminated or devalued by foreign competition. Some human rights advocates argue that the working conditions and living standards of foreign workers are so substandard when compared with U.S. standards that they verge on inhumane. A troubling twist on American corporations' role in the human rights debate about conditions in China arises from the sale of software to the Chinese government. Developed by Cisco, Oracle, and other U.S. companies, the software is used by China's police to monitor the activities of individuals that the Chinese government labels as criminals and dissidents. A fuller discussion of this issue appears in Exhibit 3.7, Strategy in Action.

SARBANES-OXLEY ACT OF 2002

Following a string of wrongdoings by corporate executives in 2000 to 2002, and the subsequent failures of their firms, Washington lawmakers proposed more than 50 policies to reassure investors. None of the resulting bills were able to pass both houses of Congress until the Banking Committee Chairman Paul Sarbanes (D–MD) proposed legislation to

The following outline presents the major elements of the Sarbanes-Oxley Act of 2002.

CORPORATE RESPONSIBILITY

- The CEO and CFO of each company are required to submit a report, based on their knowledge, to the SEC certifying the company's financial statements are fair representations of the financial condition without false statements or omissions.

- The CEO and CFO must reimburse the company for any bonuses or equity-based incentives received for the last 12-month period if the company is required to restate its financial statements due to material noncompliance with any financial reporting requirement that resulted from misconduct.

- Directors and executive officers are prohibited from trading a company's 401(k) plan, profit sharing plan, or retirement plan during any blackout period. The plan administrators are required to notify the plan participants and beneficiaries with notice of all blackout periods, reasons for the blackout period, and a statement that the participant or beneficiary should evaluate their investment even though they are unable to direct or diversify their accounts during the blackout.

- No company may make, extend, modify, or renew any personal loans to its executives or directors. Limited exceptions are for loans made in the course of the company's business, on market terms, for home improvement and home loans, consumer credit, or extension of credit.

INCREASED DISCLOSURE

- Each annual and quarterly financial report filed with the SEC must disclose all material off-balance-sheet transactions, arrangements, and obligations that may affect the current or future financial condition of the company or its operations.

- Companies must present pro forma financial information with the SEC in a manner that is not misleading and must be reconciled with the company's financial condition and with generally accepted accounting principles (GAAP).

- Each company is required to disclose whether they have adopted a code of ethics for its senior financial officers. If not, the company must explain the reasons. Any change or waiver of the code of ethics must be disclosed.

- Each annual report must contain a statement of management's responsibility for establishing and maintaining an internal control structure and procedures for financial reporting. The report must also include an assessment of the effectiveness of the internal control procedures.

- The Form 4 will be provided within two business days after the execution date of the trading of a company's securities by directors and executive officers. The SEC may extend this deadline if it determines the two-day period is not feasible.

- The company must disclose information concerning changes in financial conditions or operations "on a rapid and current basis," in plain English.

The SEC must review the financial statements of each reporting company no less than once every three years.

AUDIT COMMITTEES

- The audit committee must be composed entirely of independent directors. Committee members are not permitted to accept any fees from the company, cannot control 5 percent or more of the voting of

---

Sarbanes-Oxley Act of 2002

Law that revised and strengthened auditing and accounting standards.

establish new auditing and accounting standards. The bill was called the Public Company Accounting Reform and Investor Protection Act of 2002. Later the name was changed to the **Sarbanes-Oxley Act of 2002.**

On July 30, 2002, President George Bush signed the Sarbanes-Oxley Act into law. This revolutionary act applies to public companies with securities registered under Section 12 of the Securities Act of 1934 and those required to file reports under Section 15(d) of the Exchange Act. Sarbanes-Oxley includes required certifications for financial statements, new corporate regulations, disclosure requirements, and penalties for failure to comply. More details on the Act are provided in Exhibit 3.8, Strategy in Action.

the company, nor be an officer, director, partner, or employee of the company.

- The audit committee must have the authority to engage the outside auditing firm.
- The audit committee must establish procedures for the treatment of complaints regarding accounting controls or auditing matters. They are responsible for employee complaints concerning questionable accounting and auditing.
- The audit committee must disclose whether at least one of the committee members is a "financial expert." If not, the committee must explain why not.

NEW CRIMES AND INCREASED CRIMINAL PENALTIES

- Tampering with records with intent to impede or influence any federal investigation or bankruptcy will be punishable by a fine and/or prison sentence up to 20 years.
- Failure by an accountant to maintain all auditing papers for five years after the end of the fiscal period will be punishable by a fine and/or up to 10-year prison sentence.
- Knowingly executing, or attempting to execute, a scheme to defraud investors will be punishable by a fine and/or prison sentence of up to 25 years.
- Willfully certifying a report that does not comply with the law can be punishable with a fine up to $5,000,000 and/or a prison sentence up to 20 years.

NEW CIVIL CAUSE OF ACTION AND INCREASED ENFORCEMENT POWERS

- Protection will be provided to whistle-blowers who provide information or assist in an investigation by law enforcement, congressional committee, or employee supervisor.
- Bankruptcy cannot be used to avoid liability from securities laws violations.
- Investors are able to file a civil action for fraud up to two years after discovery of the facts and five years after the occurrence of fraud.
- The SEC can receive a restraining order prohibiting payments to insiders during an investigation.
- The SEC can prevent individuals from holding an officer's or director's position in a public company as a result of violation of the securities law.

AUDITOR INDEPENDENCE

- All audit services must be preapproved by the audit committee and must be disclosed to investors.
- The lead audit or reviewing audit partner from the auditing accounting firm must change at least once every five fiscal years.
- The registered accounting firms must report to the audit committee all accounting policies and practices used, alternative uses of the financial information within GAAP that has been discussed with management, and written communications between the accounting firm and management.
- An auditing firm is prohibited from auditing a company if the company's CEO or CFO was employed by the auditing firm within the past year.

A Public Company Accounting Oversight Board is established by the SEC to oversee the audits of public companies. The Board will register public accounting firms, establish audit standards, inspect registered accounting firms, and discipline violators of the rules. No person can take part in an audit if not employed by a registered public accounting firm.

The Sarbanes-Oxley Act states that the CEO and CFO must certify every report containing the company's financial statements. The certification acknowledges that the CEO or CFO (chief financial officer) has reviewed the report. As part of the review, the officer must attest that the information does not include untrue statements or necessary omitted information. Furthermore, based on the officer's knowledge, the report is a reliable source of the company's financial condition and result of operations for the period represented. The certification also makes the officers responsible for establishing and maintaining internal controls such that they are aware of any material information relating to the company. The officers must also evaluate the effectiveness of the internal controls within 90 days of the release of the report and present their conclusions of the effectiveness of the controls.

Also, the officers must disclose any fraudulent material, deficiencies in the reporting of the financial reports, or problems with the internal control to the company's auditors and auditing committee. Finally, the officers must indicate any changes to the internal controls or factors that could affect them.

The Sarbanes-Oxley Act includes provisions restricting the corporate control of executives, accounting firms, auditing committees, and attorneys. With regard to executives, the Act bans personal loans. A company can no longer directly or indirectly issue, extend, or maintain a personal loan to any director or executive officer. Executive officers and directors are not permitted to purchase, sell, acquire, or transfer any equity security during any pension fund blackout period. Executives are required to notify fund participants of any blackout period and the reasons for the blackout period. The SEC will provide the company's executives with a code of ethics for the company to adopt. Failure to meet the code must be disclosed to the SEC.

The Act limits some and issues new duties of the registered public accounting firms that conduct the audits of the financial statements. Accounting firms are prohibited from performing bookkeeping or other accounting services related to the financial statements, designing or implementing financial systems, appraising, internal auditing, brokering banking services, or providing legal services unrelated to the audit. All critical accounting policies and alternative treatments of financial information within generally accepted accounting principles (GAAP), and written communication between the accounting firm and the company's management must be reported to the audit committee.

The Act defines the composition of the audit committee and specifies its responsibilities. The members of the audit committee must be members of the company's board of directors. At least one member of the committee should be classified as a "financial expert." The audit committee is directly responsible for the work of any accounting firm employed by the company, and the accounting firm must report directly to the audit committee. The audit committee must create procedures for employee complaints or concerns over accounting or auditing matters. Upon discovery of unlawful acts by the company, the audit committee must report and be supervised in its investigation by a Public Company Accounting Oversight Board.

The Act includes rules for attorney conduct. If a company's attorneys find evidence of securities violations, they are required to report the matter to the chief legal counsel or CEO. If there is not an appropriate response, the attorneys must report the information to the audit committee or the board of directors.

Other sections of the Sarbanes-Oxley Act stipulate disclosure periods for financial operations and reporting. Relevant information relating to changes in the financial condition or operations of a company must be immediately reported in plain English. Off-balance-sheet transactions, correcting adjustments, and pro-forma information must be presented in the annual and quarterly financial reports. The information must not contain any untrue statements, must not omit material facts, and must meet GAAP standards.

Stricter penalties have been issued for violations of the Sarbanes-Oxley Act. If a company must restate its financial statements due to noncompliance, the CEO and CFO must relinquish any bonus or incentive-based compensation or realized profits from the sale of securities during the 12-month period following the filing with the SEC. Other securities fraud, such as destruction or falsification of records, results in fines and prison sentences up to 25 years.

The New Corporate Governance Structure

A major consequence of the 2000–2002 accounting scandals was the Sarbanes-Oxley Act of 2002, and a major consequence of Sarbanes-Oxley has been the restructuring of the governance structure of American corporations. The most significant change in the restructuring

The New Corporate Governance Structure

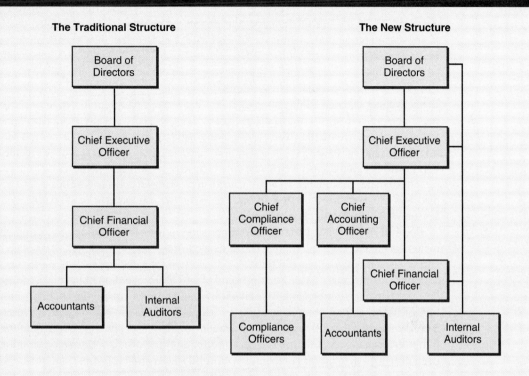

The Traditional Structure

- Board of Directors
- Chief Executive Officer
- Chief Financial Officer
- Accountants
- Internal Auditors

The New Structure

- Board of Directors
- Chief Executive Officer
- Chief Compliance Officer
- Chief Accounting Officer
- Chief Financial Officer
- Compliance Officers
- Accountants
- Internal Auditors

is the heightened role of corporate internal auditors, as depicted in Exhibit 3.9, Strategy in Action. Auditors have traditionally been viewed as performing a necessary but perfunctory function, namely to probe corporate financial records for unintentional or illicit misrepresentations. Although a majority of U.S. corporations have longstanding traditions of reporting that their auditors operated independently of CFO approval and that they had direct access to the board, in practice, the auditors' work usually traveled through the organization's hierarchical chain of command.

In the past, internal auditors reviewed financial reports generated by other corporate accountants. The auditors considered professional accounting and financial practices, as well as relevant aspects of corporate law, and then presented their findings to the chief financial officer (CFO). Historically, the CFO reviewed the audits and determined the financial data and information that was to be presented to top management, directors, and investors of the company.

However, because Sarbanes-Oxley requires that CEOs and audit committees sign off on financial results, auditors now routinely deal directly with top corporate officials, as shown in the new structure in Exhibit 3.9, Strategy in Action. Approximately 75 percent of senior corporate auditors now report directly to the Board of Directors' audit committee. Additionally, to eliminate the potential for accounting problems, companies are establishing direct lines of communication between top managers and the board and auditors that inform the CFO but that are not dependent on CFO approval or authorization.

The new structure also provides the CEO information provided directly by the company's chief compliance and chief accounting officers. Consequently, the CFO, who is responsible for ultimately approving all company payments, is not empowered to be the sole provider of data for financial evaluations by the CEO and board.

Privatization as a Response to Sarbanes-Oxley

privatization

A restructuring in which the ownership structure of a publicly traded corporation is converted into a privately held company.

A trend in financial restructuring that supports internal growth is **privatization**, in which the ownership structure of a publicly traded corporation is converted into a privately held company. There has been a dramatic upswing in the number of privatizations, due largely to negative manager and investor responses to the increased government regulation required by Sarbanes-Oxley Act of 2002. In 2006, a record number of 322 publicly traded companies with a combined value of $215.4 billion were taken private in the United States.

Some privatization deals are prompted by the huge funds attracted by private equity firms, which exceeded $280 billion in 2006, that allow a premium to be paid over the current stock price. However, the motivation in most cases of privatization is that privately held firms are not subject to the costs of complying with regulations for public companies stemming from the Sarbanes-Oxley legislation. Sarbanes-Oxley legislates that outside firms must audit a company's internal controls. The cost of hiring outside firms, maintaining systems to meet compliance standards, and establishing an audit committee on the board of directors to ensure that these activities are monitored is estimated to be $500,000 on average for the 16,000 publicly reporting companies.

Because of Sarbanes-Oxley, much more time is needed to manage reporting requirements for publicly traded companies. Managers must attest to the accuracy of quarterly financials and provide frequent releases of specified information, such as same-day notification of insider trades. In addition, general counsels are spending much more of their time on compliance activities, with 36 percent of companies incurring the cost and complication of hiring a chief compliance officer. Litigation costs have also risen because of the increased personal liability of board members and key executives, especially in the form of higher insurance premiums. The cost of directors' and officers' insurance premiums has risen nearly 40 percent for companies with solid sheets and clean financial histories.

Certain industry sectors are especially attractive for privatization strategies. In the technology sector, firms that were posting double-digit growth throughout most of the 1980s and 1990s are now having trouble growing their maturing businesses. Although Applied Materials, Dell, EMC, Intel, and Hewlett-Packard have considerable cash flow, equity investors have little interest in these slower-growing companies, cutting off a favorite source of equity funding and making them attractive privatization candidates.

Another active sector for privatization is real estate. In the first half of 2007, the stock prices for real estate investment trusts (REITs) were below the net asset value of their underlying real estate portfolios. This meant that investors believed that REITs were worth less as a company than the total value of their properties, creating an opportunity for investors to acquire the portfolio at a discount.

In the maturing technology sector, where slowing growth is lowering the price to earning multiples, executives look to other sources of funding outside of equity financing. Privatization offers a good alternative because it allows managers to avoid the distractions of short-term technical investors and traders, who react especially strongly to any unanticipated performance variation.

Exhibit 3.10, Strategy in Action provides an example of the role of private equity in the strategic activities of a company. Samsonite Corporation was taken private with the expressed intention of repositioning it as a public firm once its competitiveness had been reestablished.

CSR's Effect on the Mission Statement

The mission statement not only identifies what product or service a company produces, how it produces it, and what market it serves, it also embodies what the company believes. As such, it is essential that the mission statement recognize the legitimate claims of its external

Sleek. Stylish. Samsonite?

BusinessWeek

Marcello Bottoli had a gilded career as the chief executive of Louis Vuitton when, three years ago, he left to run Samsonite Corp. It was a move from one of the world's great luxury brands to a company that had been mistreated by its private investors, was still recovering from a sharp drop in business after September 11, 2001, and had, in fact, come dangerously close to declaring bankruptcy for the second time in a decade.

And Bottoli's plan is obvious; even he says so. He wants Samsonite to find its place in the expanding world of accessible luxury.

Since it was founded by Jesse Shwayder almost 100 years ago in Denver, Samsonite has been a near-complete reflection of the best and worst inclinations of the business world. Now Samsonite is in the hands of new private-equity investors (Ares Management, Bain Capital, and the Ontario Teachers' Pension Plan), who brought in Bottoli and gave him a piece of the business (management owns 10 percent of the company).

The owners, ready to cash out, want to take the company public again, perhaps this spring. This time, though, they would like Samsonite to be traded on the London Stock Exchange. That would make it among the first U.S. companies to have its primary listing outside the country. "But," says Bottoli, "we stick to and are proud of our American heritage."

Bottoli, who is 45, also hopes to give Samsonite a modern sensibility and fashion edge. To that end, he has brought in designers such as Alexander McQueen, the haute couture celebrity, to create signature lines of Black Label luggage. Bottoli hired the company's first creative director, who has gone back to the archives to create a vintage collection. The company is starting to sell leather shoes (they've been available in Italy for years), wallets, and stationery. Bottoli has doubled the amount Samsonite spends on marketing and persuaded inveterate traveler and showman Richard Branson to appear on the company's behalf.

Bottoli, like many chief executives brought into companies best by problems, had to determine how thoroughly to upend the status quo, staff included. Frank Steed, a former president of Samsonite USA and now a licensee for the company, says: "People there are trying to move along as fast as Marcello wants." Sales for the first nine months of 2006 were $784.4 million, 9.3 percent higher than the previous year's.

Source: Reprinted with special permission from Susan Berfield, "Sleek. Stylish. Samsonite?: The Brand Has Been Kicked Around for Years: Now Marcello Bottoli Wants to Take It Upscale," *BusinessWeek*, February 26, 2007. Copyright © 2007 The McGraw-Hill Companies.

stakeholders, which may include creditors, customers, suppliers, government, unions, competitors, local communities, and elements of the general public. This stakeholder approach has become widely accepted by U.S. business. For example, a survey of directors in 291 of the largest southeastern U.S. companies found that directors had high stakeholder orientations. Customers, government, stockholders, employees, and society, in that order, were the stakeholders these directors perceived as most important.

In developing mission statements, managers must identify all stakeholder groups and weigh their relative rights and abilities to affect the firm's success. Some companies are proactive in their approach to CSR, making it an integral part of their raison d'être (e.g., Ben & Jerry's ice cream); others are reactive, adopting socially responsible behavior only when they must (e.g., Exxon after the *Valdez* incident).

Social Audit

social audit
An attempt to measure a company's actual social performance against its social objectives.

A **social audit** attempts to measure a company's actual social performance against the social objectives it has set for itself. A social audit may be conducted by the company itself. However, one conducted by an outside consultant who will impose minimal biases may prove more beneficial to the firm. As with a financial audit, an outside auditor brings credibility to the evaluation. This credibility is essential if management is to take the results seriously and if the general public is to believe the company's public relations pronouncements.

Careful, accurate monitoring and evaluation of a company's CSR actions are important not only because the company wants to be sure it is implementing CSR policy as planned but also because CSR actions by their nature are open to intense public scrutiny. To make sure it is making good on its CSR promises, a company may conduct a social audit of its performance.

Once the social audit is complete, it may be distributed internally or both internally and externally, depending on the firm's goals and situation. Some firms include a section in their annual report devoted to social responsibility activities; others publish a separate periodic report on their social responsiveness. Companies publishing separate social audits include General Motors, Bank of America, Atlantic Richfield, Control Data, and Aetna Life and Casualty Company. Nearly all *Fortune* 500 corporations disclose social performance information in their annual reports.

Large firms are not the only companies employing the social audit. Boutique ice cream maker Ben & Jerry's, a CSR pioneer, publishes a social audit in its annual report. The audit, conducted by an outside consultant, scores company performance in such areas as employee benefits, plant safety, ecology, community involvement, and customer service. The report is published unedited.

The social audit may be used for more than simply monitoring and evaluating firm social performance. Managers also use social audits to scan the external environment, determine firm vulnerabilities, and institutionalize CSR within the firm. In addition, companies themselves are not the only ones who conduct social audits; public interest groups and the media watch companies who claim to be socially responsible very closely to see if they practice what they preach. These organizations include consumer groups and socially responsible investing firms that construct their own guidelines for evaluating companies. An excellent example of a company that worked with an environmental interest group to turn opposition into collaboration is shown in the case of the private equity takeover of a major Texas utility company, as described in Exhibit 3.11, Strategy in Action.

The Body Shop learned what can happen when a company's behavior falls short of its espoused mission and objectives. The 20-year-old manufacturer and retailer of naturally based hair and skin products had cultivated a socially responsible corporate image based on a reputation for socially responsible behavior. In late 1994, however, *Business Ethics* magazine published an exposé claiming that the company did not "walk the talk." It accused The Body Shop of using nonrenewable petrochemicals in its products, recycling far less than it claimed, using ingredients tested on animals, and making threats against investigative journalists. The Body Shop's contradictions were noteworthy because Anita Roddick, the company's founder, made CSR a centerpiece of the company's strategy.[1]

MANAGEMENT ETHICS

The Nature of Ethics in Business

Central to the belief that companies should be operated in a socially responsive way for the benefit of all stakeholders is the belief that managers will behave in an ethical manner. The term **ethics** refers to the moral principles that reflect society's beliefs about the actions of an individual or a group that are right and wrong. Of course, the values of one individual, group, or society may be at odds with the values of another individual, group, or society. Ethical standards, therefore, reflect not a universally accepted code, but rather the end product of a process of defining and clarifying the nature and content of human interaction.

ethics
The moral principles that reflect society's beliefs about the actions of an individual or group that are right and wrong.

[1] Jon Entine, "Shattered Image," *Business Ethics* 8, no. 5 (September/October 1994), pp. 23–28.

Hugging the Tree-Huggers

When William K. Reilly was plotting the private equity takeover of Texas Utility TXU Corp., he foresaw one potential dealbreaker. Says Reilly, "We decided the walk-away issue for us was not getting environmentalists' support." So Reilly called Fred Krupp, president of Environmental Defense, whose Texas attorney, James D. Marston, had been waging an all-out war on TXU's plans to build 11 coal-fired power plants. Krupp told Marston to hop on a plane to San Francisco for a top-secret meeting with Reilly's team.

The ensuing negotiations were often tense. After a marathon 17 hours, Reilly ended up giving Marston a big chunk of what he wanted: commitments by the new TXU owners to ax 8 of the 11 proposed plants and to join the call for mandatory national carbon emissions curbs. Meanwhile, the corporate raiders got exactly what they craved: public praise from Environmental Defense and the Natural Resources Defense Council (NRDC) for the deal.

The TXU takeover is a sign of a remarkable evolution in the dynamic between corporate executives and activists. Once fractious and antagonistic, it has moved toward accommodation and even mutual dependence. Companies increasingly seek a "green" imprimatur, while enviros view changes in how business operates as key to protecting the planet.

Examples of this new relationship are everywhere. Wal-Mart Stores Inc. turned to Conservation International to help shape ambitious goals to cut energy use, switch to renewable power, and sell millions of efficient fluorescent bulbs. When the CEOs of 10 major U.S. corporations converged on Washington on January 22, 2007, and issued a call for mandatory carbon emissions limits, sitting with them at the table were Fred Krupp and the president of the NRDC.

Source: Reprinted with special permission from John Carey, "Hugging the Tree-Huggers: Why So Many Companies are Suddenly Linking Up With Eco Groups. Hint: Smart Business," *BusinessWeek*, March 12, 2007. Copyright © 2007 The McGraw-Hill Companies.

SATISFYING CORPORATE SOCIAL RESPONSIBILITY

Corporate social responsibility has become a vital part of the business conversation. The issue is not whether companies will engage in socially responsible activities, but how. For most companies, the challenge is how best to achieve the maximum social benefit from a given amount of resources available for social projects. Research points to five principles that underscore better outcomes for society and for corporate participants.[2]

In 1999, William Ford Jr. angered Ford Motor Co. executives and investors when he wrote that "there are very real conflicts between Ford's current business practices, consumer choices, and emerging views of (environmental) sustainability." In his company citizenship report, the grandson of Henry Ford, then the automaker's nonexecutive chairman, even appeared to endorse a Sierra Club statement declaring that "the gas-guzzling SUV is a rolling monument to environmental destruction."

Bill Ford has had to moderate his strongest environmental beliefs since assuming the company's CEO position in October 2001, just after the Firestone tire scandal. Nevertheless, while he has strived to improve Ford's financial performance and restore trust among its diverse stakeholders, he remains strongly committed to corporate responsibility and environmental protection. In his words, "A good company delivers excellent products and services, and a great company does all that and strives to make the world a better place."[3] Today, Ford is a leader in producing vehicles that run on alternative sources of fuel, and

[2] This section was excerpted from J. A. Pearce II and J. Doh, "Enhancing Corporate Responsibility through Skillful Collaboration," *Sloan Management Review* 46, no. 3 (2005), pp. 30–39.

[3] "Ford Motor Company Encourages Elementary School Students to Support America's National Parks," www.ford.com/en/company/nationalParks.htm.

it is performing as well as or better than its major North American rivals, all of whom are involved in intense global competition. The new CEO is successfully pursuing a strategy that is showing improved financial performance, increased confidence in the brand, and clear evidence that the car company is committed to contributing more broadly to society. Among Ford's more notable outreach efforts are an innovative HIV/AIDS initiative in South Africa that is now expanding to India, China, and Thailand; a partnership with the U.S. National Parks Foundation to provide environmentally friendly transportation for park visitors; and significant support for the Clean Air Initiative for Asian Cities.

Ford's actions are emblematic of the corporate social responsibility initiatives of many leading companies today. Corporate-supported social initiatives are now a given. For some time now, many *Fortune* 500 corporations have had senior manager titles dedicated to helping their organizations "give back" more effectively. CSR is now almost universally embraced by top managers as an integral component of their executive roles, whether motivated by self-interest, altruism, strategic advantage, or political gain. Their outreach is usually plain to see on the companies' corporate Web sites. CSR is high on the agenda at major executive gatherings such as the World Economic Forum. It is very much in evidence during times of tragedy—as seen in the corporate responses to the Asian tsunami of December 2004—and it is the subject of many conferences, workshops, newsletters, and more. "Consultancies have sprung up to advise companies on how to do corporate social responsibility and how to let it be known that they are doing it," noted *The Economist* in a survey on CSR in 2005.

Executives face conflicting pressures to contribute to social responsibility while honoring their duties to maximize shareholder value. These days they face many belligerent critics who challenge the idea of a single-minded focus on profits—witness the often violent antiglobalization protests in recent years. They also face skeptics who contend that CSR initiatives are chiefly a convenient marketing gloss. However, the reality is that most executives are eager to improve their CSR effectiveness. The issue is not whether companies will engage in socially responsible activities, but how. For most companies, the challenge is how best to achieve the maximum social benefit from a given amount of resources available for social projects.

Studies of dozens of social responsibility initiatives at major corporations show that senior managers struggle to find the right balance between "low-engagement" solutions such as charitable gift-giving and "high-commitment" solutions that run the risk of diverting attention from the company's core mission. In this section, we will see that collaborative social initiatives (CSIs)—a form of engagement in which companies provide ongoing and sustained commitments to a social project or issue—provide the best combination of social and strategic impact.

Jean-Pierre Garnier, CEO of GlaxoSmithKline, believes that the economic and CSR goals of a company are best met by pursuing them simultaneously. Exhibit 3.12, Top Strategist describes some of his corporation's recent strategic successes.

The Core of the CSR Debate

The proper role of CSR—the actions of a company to benefit society beyond the requirement of the law and the direct interests of shareholders—has generated a century's worth of philosophically and economically intriguing debates. Since steel baron Andrew Carnegie published *The Gospel of Wealth* in 1899, the argument that businesses are the trustees of societal property that should be managed for the public good has been seen as one end of a continuum with, at the other end, the belief that profit maximization is management's only legitimate goal. The CSR debates had been largely confined to the background for most of the twentieth century, making the news after an oil spill or when a consumer product caused harm, or when ethics scandals reopened the question of business's fundamental purpose.

Top Strategist
Jean-Pierre Garnier, CEO of GlaxoSmithKline

Exhibit
3.12

When Jean-Pierre Garnier took over as CEO of GlaxoSmith-Kline in 2000, the company'sreputation on corporate social responsibility was at its nadir. As part of a coalition of 39 pharmaceutical companies, the drugmaker was suing Nelson Mandela's South African government for voiding patents on prescription drugs. Mandela's top priority was giving desperately sick patients access to HIV treatments, and GSK—the world's largest supplier—was standing in the way. "It was a public relations disaster," Garnier concedes.

The experience convinced Garnier that GSK should lead the crusade to improve access to medicine. In 2001, GSK became the first major drugmaker to sell its AIDS medicines at cost in 100 countries worldwide. In fact, GSK sells 90 percent of its vaccines, in volume terms, at not-for-profit prices

to customers in the developing world. In 2005, it set a new paradigm in the vaccine industry. It chose Mexico over other, wealthier nations as the launch pad for Rotarix, a new vaccine against gastrointestinal rotavirus. "We wanted to get the vaccine to the children who needed it most," Garnier explains.

Creating medicines for the Third World while still posting a profit required fancy financial footwork. GSK has formed 14 different partnerships with the World Health Organization and other nongovernmental bodies, and with philanthropies such as the Bill & Melinda Gates Foundation. A collaboration with the Gates Foundation led to a vaccine that provides a minimum of 18 months of protection against malaria.

Garnier says efforts such as these give the company several advantages over its rivals. Top scientists are drawn to GSK because they want their research to make a difference. Doing good, and being admired for it, also boosts general morale at the company, he says. "This creates a more aligned and engaged workforce, which helps us outperform our competitors."

Source: Reprinted with special permission from Kerry Capell, 2007. "GlaxoSmithKline: Getting AIDS Drugs to More Sick People," *BusinessWeek*, January 29, 2007. Copyright © 2007 The McGraw-Hill Companies.

The debates surfaced in more positive ways in the last 30 years as new businesses set up shop with altruism very much in mind and on display. Firms such as ice cream maker Ben & Jerry's argued that CSR and profits do not clash; their stance was that doing good led to making good money, too. That line of thinking has gained popularity as more executives have come to understand the value of their companies' reputations with customers—and with investors and employees. But only recently have business leaders begun to get a clearer understanding of the appropriate role of CSR and its effect on financial performance.

In the past, research on the financial effect of CSR produced inconsistent findings, with some studies reporting a positive relationship, others a negative one, and others no relationship at all. Since the mid-1990s, improvements in theory, research designs, data, and analysis have produced empirical research with more consistent results.[4] Importantly, a recent meta-analysis (a methodological technique that aggregates findings of multiple

[4] J. J. Griffin and J. F. Mahon, "The Corporate Social Performance and Corporate Financial Performance Debate: Twenty-Five Years of Incomparable Research," *Business and Society* 36 (1997), pp. 5–31; R. M. Roman, S. Hayibor, and B. R. Agle, "The Relationship between Social and Financial Performance: Repainting a Portrait," *Business and Society* 38 (1999), pp. 109–125; and J. D. Margolis and J. P. Walsh, "Misery Loves Companies: Rethinking Social Initiatives by Business," *Administrative Science Quarterly* 48 (2003), pp. 268–305.

Exhibit 3.13
Continuum of
Corporate Social
Responsibility
Commitments

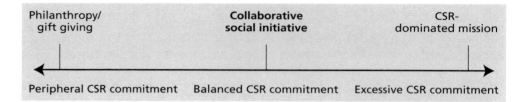

studies) of more than 10 studies found that on balance, positive relationships can be expected from CSR initiatives but that the primary vehicle for achieving superior financial performance from social responsibility is via reputation effects.[5]

There is no shortage of options with which businesses can advance their CSR goals. The greater challenge is finding the right balance. Philanthropy without active engagement—cash donations, for instance—has been criticized as narrow, self-serving, and often motivated to improve the corporation's reputation and keep nongovernmental organization (NGO) critics and other naysayers at bay.[6] However, redirecting the company toward a socially responsible mission, while seemingly attractive, may have the unintended consequences of diverting both managers and employees from their core mission. Exhibit 3.13 presents a simple illustration of the range of options available to corporations as they consider their CSR commitments.

What managers need is a model that they can use to guide them in selecting social initiatives and through which they can exploit their companies' core competencies for the maximum positive impact. As a starting point, research confirms that a business must determine the social causes that it will support and why and then decide how its support should be organized.[7] According to one perspective, businesses have three basic support options: donations of cash or material, usually to a nongovernmental or nonprofit agency; creation of a functional operation within the company to assist external charitable efforts; and development of a collaboration approach, whereby a company joins with an organization that has particular expertise in managing the way benefits are derived from corporate support.[8]

Mutual Advantages of Collaborative Social Initiatives

The term *social initiative* describes initiatives that take a collaborative approach. Research on alliances and networks among companies in competitive commercial environments tells us that each partner benefits when the other brings resources, capabilities, or other assets that it cannot easily attain on its own. These *combinative capabilities* allow the company to acquire and synthesize resources and build new applications from those resources, generating innovative responses to rapidly evolving environments.

It is no different with collaborative social initiatives. While neither companies nor nonprofits are well-equipped to handle escalating social or environmental problems, each participant has the potential to contribute valuable material resources, services, or individuals' voluntary time, talents, energies, and organizational knowledge. Those cumulative offerings are vastly superior to cash-only donations, which are a minimalist solution to

[5] M. Orlitzky, F. L. Schmidt, and S. L. Rynes, "Corporate Social and Financial Performance: A Meta-Analysis," *Organization Studies* 24, no. 3 (2003), pp. 403–441.

[6] B. Husted, "Governance Choices for Corporate Social Responsibility: To Contribute, Collaborate or Internalize?" *Long Range Planning* 36, no. 5 (2003), pp. 481–498.

[7] N. C. Smith. "Corporate Social Responsibility: Whether or How?" *California Management Review* 45, no. 4 (2003), pp. 52–76.

[8] Husted, "Governance Choices for Corporate Social Responsibility."

the challenges of social responsibility. Social initiatives involve ongoing information and operational exchanges among participants and are especially attractive because of their potential benefits for both the corporate and not-for-profit partners.

There is strong evidence to show that CSR activities increasingly confer benefits beyond enhanced reputation. For some participants, they can be a tool to attract, retain, and develop managerial talent. The PricewaterhouseCoopers (PwC) Project Ulysses is a leadership development program that sends small teams of PwC partners to developing countries to apply their expertise to complex social and economic challenges. The cross-cultural PwC teams collaborate with NGOs, community-based organizations, and intergovernmental agencies, working pro bono in eight-week assignments in communities struggling with the effects of poverty, conflict, and environmental degradation. The Ulysses program was designed in part to respond to a growing challenge confronting professional services companies: identifying and training up-and-coming leaders who can find nontraditional answers to intractable problems.

All 24 Ulysses graduates still work at PwC; most say they have a stronger commitment to the firm because of the commitment it made to them and because they now have a different view of PwC's values. For PwC, the Ulysses program provides a tangible message to its primary stakeholders that the company is committed to making a difference in the world. According to Brian McCann, the first U.S.-based partner to participate in Ulysses, "This is a real differentiator—not just in relation to our competitors, but to all global organizations."

Five Principles of Successful Collaborative Social Initiatives

There are five principles that are central to successful CSIs, as shown in Exhibit 3.14, Strategy in Action. When CSR initiatives include most or all of these elements, companies can indeed maximize the effects of their social contributions while advancing broader strategic goals. While most CSIs will not achieve complete success with all five elements, some progress with each is requisite for success. Here are the five principles, along with examples of companies that have adhered to them well:

1. Identify a Long-Term Durable Mission

Companies make the greatest social contribution when they identify an important, long-standing policy challenge and they participate in its solution over the long term. Veteran *Wall Street Journal* reporter and author Ron Alsop argues that companies that are interested in contributing to corporate responsibility and thus burnishing their reputations should "own the issue."[9] Companies that step up to tackle problems that are clearly important to society's welfare and that require substantial resources are signaling to internal and external constituencies that the initiative is deserving of the company's investment.

Among the more obvious examples of social challenges that will demand attention for years to come are hunger, inadequate housing, ill health, substandard education, and degradation of the environment. While a company's long-term commitment to any one of those problems embeds that issue in the fabric of the company, it is more important that the company can develop competencies that allow it to become better at its social activities yet be able to keep investing in those outputs. It is also important to identify limited-scope projects and shorter-term milestones that can be accomplished through direct contributions by the company. Solving global hunger is a worthy goal, but it is too large for any individual company to make much of a dent.

Avon Products Inc., the seller of beauty and related products, offers a fine example of a long-term commitment to a pervasive and longstanding problem. In 1992, the company's Avon Foundation—a public charity established in 1955 to improve the lives of women and

[9] R. Alsop, *The 18 Immutable Laws of Corporate Reputation* (New York: Free Press, 2004).

Five Principles of Successful Corporate Social Responsibility Collaboration

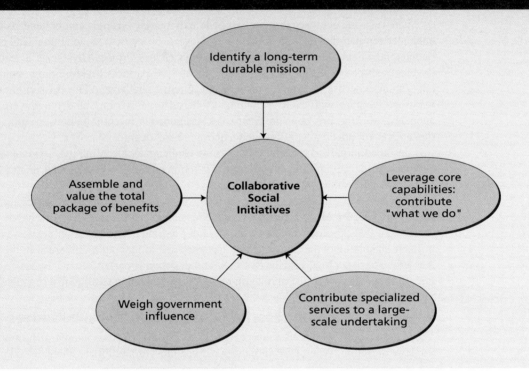

their families—launched its Breast Cancer Crusade in the United Kingdom. The program has expanded to 50 countries. Funds are raised through a variety of programs, product sales, and special events, including the Avon Walk for Breast Cancer series. The company distinguishes itself from other corporations that fund a single institution or scientific investigator because it operates as part of a collaborative, supporting a national network of research, medical, social service, and community-based organizations, each of which makes its own unique contribution to helping patients or advancing breast cancer research. The Crusade has awarded more than $300 million to breast cancer research and care organizations worldwide. In its first 10 years, The Avon Walks program raised more than $250 million for research, awareness, detection, and treatment.

Another example of a powerful CSI is found in IBM Corp.'s Reinventing Education initiative. Since 1994, IBM works with nonprofit school partners throughout the world to develop and implement innovative technology solutions designed to solve some of education's toughest problems: from coping with shrinking budgets and increasing parental involvement to moving to team teaching and developing new lesson plans. This initiative responds to a nearly universal agreement that education—especially education of young girls and women—provides the essential foundation for addressing a range of social and economic challenges in developing countries. Overcoming the existing educational deficit requires a long-term commitment to achieve school reform, such as methods for measuring learning.

One element of the Reinventing Education initiative is a Web-based "Change Toolkit" developed by IBM and Harvard Business School professor Rosabeth Moss Kanter, with sponsorship from the Council of Chief State School Officers, the National Association of Secondary School Principals, and the National Association of Elementary School Principals. The program has been lauded as a compelling model to systemic school reform.

The Home Depot has identified housing as its principal CSI. In 2002, the company set up its Home Depot Foundation with the primary mission of building "affordable, efficient, and healthy homes." Thirty million Americans face some sort of challenge in securing dependable housing, including living in substandard or overcrowded housing; lacking hot water, electricity, toilet, or bathtub/shower; or simply paying too high a percentage of their income on housing. Hence, Home Depot's long-term commitment in this area is unassailable. Its Foundation works closely with Home Depot suppliers and with a variety of nonprofits, placing a strong emphasis on local volunteer efforts.

2. Contribute "What We Do"

Companies maximize the benefits of their corporate contributions when they leverage core capabilities and contribute products and services that are based on expertise used in or generated by their normal operations. Such contributions create a mutually beneficial relationship between the partners; the social-purpose initiatives receive the maximum gains while the company minimizes costs and diversions. It is not essential that these services be synonymous with those of the company's business, but they should build upon some aspect of its strategic competencies.

The issue was aired at the recent World Economic Forum gathering in Davos, Switzerland. "We see corporate social responsibility as part and parcel of doing business, part of our core skills," said Antony Burgmans, chairman of consumer-products giant Unilever NV. "The major value for Unilever is the corporate reputation it helps create."

The thinking is similar at IBM, where, as part of its Reinventing Education initiative, the company contributes financial resources, researchers, educational consultants, and technology to each site to find new ways for technology to spur and support fundamental school restructuring and broad-based systemic change to raise student achievement. In effect, IBM leverages its technological and systems expertise, and its experience providing systems solutions to educational clients, to meet a broader educational challenge. Says Stanley Litow, vice president of Corporate Community Relations at IBM: "IBM believes that a strong community is a key to a company's success . . . To this end, a key focus of our work has been on raising the quality of public education and bridging the digital divide."[10] IBM gains significant goodwill and brand identity with important target markets, in some ways repeating Apple Computer Inc.'s successful strategy in the 1980s under which it donated computers to schools as a way to gain recognition.

There are many comparable initiatives on the procurement side. Retailers such as Starbucks Coffee Company now source much of their bean supply directly from producers, thereby ensuring that those farmers receive fair compensation without being exploited by powerful middlemen. Many retail supermarkets have followed with their own versions of the "fair trade" model.

3. Contribute Specialized Services to a Large-Scale Undertaking

Companies have the greatest social impact when they make specialized contributions to large-scale cooperative efforts. Those that contribute to initiatives in which other private, public, or nonprofit organizations are also active have an effect that goes beyond their limited contributions. Although it is tempting for a company to identify a specific cause that will be associated only with its own contributions, such a strategy is likely to be viewed as a "pet project" and not as a contribution to a larger problem where a range of players have important interests.

A good example is The AES Corp.'s carbon offset program. AES, headquartered in Arlington, Virginia, is one of the world's largest independent power producers, with 30,000 employees and generation and distribution businesses in 27 countries. Some years ago, the company

[10] "Reinventing Education," www.ibm.com/ibm/ibmgives/grant/education/programs/reinventing/re_school_reform.shtml.

recognized that it could make a contribution to the battle against global warming—a significant environmental threat with serious consequences such as habitat and species depletion, drought, and water scarcity. AES developed a program that offsets carbon emissions, creating carbon "sinks," a practical and effective means of combating this global problem.

Research has concluded that planting and preserving trees (technically "forest enhancement") provides the most practical and effective way to address the CO_2 emissions problem. Trees absorb CO_2 as they grow and convert it to carbon that is locked up (sequestered) in biomass as long as they live. AES leaders believed that if their company could contribute to increasing the standing stock of trees, the additional trees might be able to absorb enough CO_2 to offset the emissions from an AES cogeneration plant. This approach became one of the many mitigation measures now accepted in the global climate change treaty—the Kyoto Protocol—as a means of achieving legally binding emissions reduction targets.

For its part, packaged-foods giant ConAgra Foods Inc. helps to fight hunger in partnership with America's Second Harvest, an organization that leads the food recovery effort in the United States. Set up as the nationwide clearinghouse for handling the donations of prepared and perishable foods, ConAgra's coordination efforts enable smaller, local programs to share resources, making the food donation and distribution process more effective. In October 1999, ConAgra joined with food bank network America's Second Harvest in a specific initiative, the Feeding Children Better program, distributing food to 50,000 local charitable agencies, which, in turn, operate more than 94,000 food programs.

4. Weigh Government's Influence

Government support for corporate participation in CSIs—or at least its willingness to remove barriers—can have an important positive influence. Tax incentives, liability protection, and other forms of direct and indirect support for businesses all help to foster business participation and contribute to the success of CSIs.

For instance, in the United States, ConAgra's food recovery initiatives can deduct the cost (but not market value) of the donated products plus one half of the product's profit margin; the value of this deduction is capped at twice the cost of the product. To encourage further participation of businesses in such food recovery programs, America's Second Harvest generated a series of recommendations for the U.S. government. The recommendations seek to improve the tax benefits associated with food donation, including a proposal that tax deductions be set at the fair market value of donations. Tax deductions provide economic enticement for companies to consider participation, as Boston Market, KFC, and Kraft Foods have publicly acknowledged. Donating food also allows companies to identify the amount of food wasted because it is tracked for tax purposes.

Similar efforts are being applied to reforms that will ease businesses' concerns about their liability from contributing to social enterprises. The Bill Emerson Good Samaritan Food Donation Act, enacted in 1996, protects businesses from liability for food donations except in the case of gross negligence. Building on this federal U.S. act, all 50 states and the District of Columbia have enacted "good Samaritan" laws to protect donors except in cases evidencing negligence. Many companies and nonprofits would like to see more comprehensive tort reform to support their efforts.

Government endorsements are invaluable too. The Home Depot's partnership with Habitat for Humanity is actively supported by the U.S. Department of Housing and Urban Development (HUD). This support takes the form of formal endorsement, logistical facilitation, and implicit acknowledgement that the partnership's initiatives complement HUD's own efforts. Home Depot is assured that the agency will not burden the program with red tape. In the case of AES's efforts in the area of global warming, organizations such as the World Bank, the Global Environmental Facility, and the UN Environment and Development Program endorse and encourage offsets via grants, loans, and scientific research.

5. Assemble and Value the Total Package of Benefits

Companies gain the greatest benefits from their social contributions when they put a price on the total benefit package. The valuation should include both the social contributions delivered and the reputation effects that solidify or enhance the company's position among its constituencies. Positive reputation—by consumers, suppliers, employees, regulators, interest groups, and other stakeholders—is driven by genuine commitment rather than episodic or sporadic interest; consumers and other stakeholders see through nominal commitments designed simply to garner short-term positive goodwill. "The public can smell if [a CSR effort] is not legitimate," said Shelly Lazarus, chairman and CEO of advertising agency Ogilvy & Mather USA. Hence, social initiatives that reflect the five principles discussed here can generate significant reputation benefits for participating companies.

AES's commitment to carbon offsets has won it several awards and generates favorable consideration from international financial institutions such as the World Bank, International Finance Corporation, and Inter-American Development Bank, as well as from governments, insurers, and NGOs. In the consumer products sector, Avon receives extensive media recognition from the advertising and marketing of cancer walks, nationwide special events including a gala fund-raising concert, and an awards ceremony. Avon has become so closely associated with the breast cancer cause that many consumers now identify the company's commitment—and the trademark pink ribbon—as easily as its traditional door-to-door marketing and distribution systems.

While difficult to quantify precisely, the potential value of the pink ribbon campaign, and the brand awareness associated with it, generates economic benefits for Avon in the form of goodwill and overall reputation. Avon's strategy of focusing on a cause that women care about, leveraging its contributions, and partnering with respected NGOs has enabled it to gain trust and credibility in the marketplace. "There needs to be a correlation between the cause and the company," said Susan Heany, director for corporate social responsibility at Avon. "The linkage between corporate giving and the corporate product creates brand recognition. Both buyers and sellers want to achieve the same goal: improving women's health care worldwide."[11]

Assembling the Components

A range of corporate initiatives lend themselves to the CSI model because they share most of the five key attributes we have described here: they have long-term objectives, they are sufficiently large to allow a company to specialize in its contributions, they provide many opportunities for the company to contribute from its current activities or products, they enjoy government support, and they provide a package of benefits that adds value to the company. Exhibit 3.15, Strategy in Action, summarizes five very successful CSI programs and their performance against each of the five principles.

Of the five principles, the most important by far is the second one. Companies must apply what they do best in their normal commercial operations to their social responsibility undertakings. This tenet is consistent with research that argues that social activities most closely related to the company's core mission are most efficiently administered through internalization or collaboration. It is applicable far beyond the examples in this chapter; to waste management companies and recycling programs, for instance, or to publishing companies and after-school educational initiatives, or pharmaceutical companies and local immunization and health education programs.

[11] "Corporate Social Responsibility in Practice Casebook," *The Catalyst Consortium*, July 2002, p. 8. Available at www.rhcatalyst.org.

Strategy in Action

Exhibit 3.15

Five Successful Collaborative Social Initiatives

Program	Pursue a Long-Term, Durable Mission	Contribute "What We Do"	Contribute Specialized Resources to a Large Scale Undertaking	Weigh Government Influence	Assemble and Value Total Package of Benefits
ConAgra Foods' Feeding Children Better	Individuals needing food from charity in the United States grew to more than 23 million in 2001. In the United Kingdom, the total was 4 million people in 2003.	ConAgra uses its electronic inventory control systems and refrigerated trucks to assist America's Second Harvest's food rescue programs.	ConAgra fights child hunger in America by assembling a powerful partnership with America's Second Harvest, Brandeis University's Center on Hunger and Poverty, and the Ad Council.	The Bill Emerson Good Samaritan Food Donation Act protects businesses from liability for food donations.	ConAgra's brand-sponsored support of food rescue programs sustains its image as provider of "the largest corporate initiative dedicated solely to fighting child hunger in America."
Avon's Breast Cancer Crusade	Breast cancer is the second-leading cause of death in women in the United States and the most common cancer among women.	Avon's commitment to being "the company for women" is shown by their 550,000 sales representatives who sell Crusade "pink ribbon" items.	Avon distinguishes itself by supporting a national network of research, medical, social service, and local organizations to advance cancer research.	Government agencies often match individual contributions; local governments provide logistical support for fundraising walks.	Avon receives media recognition from the advertising and marketing of cancer walks and nationwide special events, including a gala fundraising concert and awards ceremony.
IBM's Reinventing Education	Education in developing countries requires a long-term commitment to school reform, such as methods for measuring learning.	IBM uses its leading researchers, educational consultants, and technology to spur and support fundamental school restructuring.	IBM monitors the program with rigorous, independent evaluations from the Center for Children & Technology in conjunction with the Harvard Business School.	IBM teams with the U.S. Department of Education and the U.K. Department of Education and Employment on many reinvention projects.	IBM views a commitment to education as a strategic business investment. By investing in its future workforce and its customers, IBM feels that it promotes its own success.
Home Depot's In Your Community	30 million Americans face housing problems, such as overcrowding, no hot water, no electricity, and no toilet, bathtub, or shower.	Home Depot offers help with the construction of homes, plus donations and volunteers to help provide affordable housing for low-income families.	More than 1,500 Home Depot stores have Team Depot volunteer programs to support Habitat for Humanity, Rebuilding Together, and KaBOOM with the help of its 315,000 company associates.	Home Depot's partnership with Habitat for Humanity is actively supported by the U.S. Department of Housing and Urban Development.	Home Depot's volunteer programs and "how-to" clinics "invite the community into their stores." Hundreds of thousands of potential customers participate each year.
AES's Carbon Offsets Program	Global warming is an environmental threat. Carbon offsets or "sinks" are one proven, effective means of combating this problem.	AES is a leading international power producer with extensive knowledge of developing countries and their resources, including the dangers from cogeneration plants.	AES has teamed with the World Resources Institute, Nature Conservancy, and CARE to find and evaluate appropriate forestry-based offset projects.	The Environmental Protection Agency, European environmental organizations, U.N. Development Program, and other agencies support carbon offsets.	AES has committed $12 million to carbon offset projects to offset 67 million tons of carbon emitted over the next 40 years—the equivalent of the emissions from a 1,000-MW coal facility over its lifetime.

The Limits of CSR Strategies

Some companies such as Ben & Jerry's have embedded social responsibility and sustainability commitments deeply in their core strategies. Research suggests that such single-minded devotion to CSR may be unrealistic for larger, more established corporations. For example, some analysts have suggested that the intense focus on social responsibility goals by the management team at Levi Strauss & Co. may have diverted the company from its core operational challenges, accelerating the company's closure of all of its North American manufacturing operations.

Larger companies must move beyond the easy options of charitable donations but also steer clear of overreaching commitments. This is not to suggest that companies should not think big—research shows that projects can be broad in scale and scope and still succeed. Rather, it suggests that companies need to view their commitments to corporate responsibility as one important part of their overall strategy but not let the commitment obscure their broad strategic business goals. By starting with a well-defined CSR strategy and developing the collaborative initiatives that support that strategy by meeting the five criteria we have identified, companies and their leaders can make important contributions to the common good while advancing their broader financial and market objectives.

CSR strategies can also run afoul of the skeptics, and the speed with which information can be disseminated via the Web—and accumulated in Web logs—makes this an issue with serious ramifications for reputation management. Nike has been a lightning rod for CSR activists for its alleged tolerance of hostile and dangerous working conditions in its many factories and subcontractors around the world. Despite the considerable efforts the company has made to respond to its critics, it has consistently been on the defensive in trying to redeem its reputation.

Touching on this issue at the World Economic Forum, Unilever chief Antony Burgmans noted the importance of "making people who matter in society aware of what you do." His point was amplified by Starbucks CEO Orin Smith, who invited the authors of an NGO report critical of Starbucks' sourcing strategies to the company's offices and showed them the books. "In many instances we ended up partnering with them," he said.

The Future of CSR

CSR is firmly and irreversibly part of the corporate fabric. Managed properly, CSR programs can confer significant benefits to participants in terms of corporate reputation; in terms of hiring, motivation, and retention; and as a means of building and cementing valuable partnerships. And of course, the benefits extend well beyond the boundaries of the participating organizations, enriching the lives of many disadvantaged communities and individuals and pushing back on problems that threaten future generations, other species, and precious natural resources.

That is the positive perspective. The more prickly aspect of CSR is that for all of their resources and capabilities, corporations will face growing demands for social responsibility contributions far beyond simple cash or in-kind donations. Aggressive protesters will keep the issues hot, employees will continue to have their say, and shareholders will pass judgment with their investments—and their votes.

The challenge for management, then, is to know how to meet the company's obligations to all stakeholders without compromising the basic need to earn a fair return for its owners. As research shows, a collaborative approach is the foundation for the most effective CSR initiatives. By then adhering to the five key principles outlined in this section, business leaders can maintain ongoing commitments to carefully chosen initiatives that can have positive and tangible effects on social problems while meeting their obligations to shareholders, employees, and the broader communities in which they operate.

Enron: Running on Empty

BusinessWeek

The fall of mighty Enron Corp. (ENE)—once one of the most valuable companies in America—was a collapse of mind-boggling proportions. In 2001, Enron had $101 billion in revenues, a stock-market capitalization of $63 billion, and a chairman who was a high-profile confidant of President Bush. Yet in a sickeningly swift spiral, the powerful energy trading company tumbled to the brink of bankruptcy in late November 2001—the victim of a botched expansion attempt, an accounting scandal, and the overweening ambition of its once widely admired top executives.

The end came quickly because Enron had over-extended itself—and because investors and customers lost faith in its secretive and complex financial maneuvers. With legions of traders working out of a Houston skyscraper, the company put together trades so exotic that they mystified many Wall Street veterans. Under Chairman Kenneth L. Lay—who pressed the administration to embrace a controversial policy of electricity deregulation—and former CEO Jeffrey K. Skilling, Enron had become largely a trading operation, dubbed by some the Goldman, Sachs & Co. of the energy business.

Enron's success depended on maintaining the trust of customers that it would make good on its dealings in the market. But that trust evaporated as it shocked the market with changes to its nearly incomprehensible financial statements. "If you are running a trading operation, you have to be like Caesar's wife, beyond reproach."

The fall of Enron—to 61 cents a share on November 28, 2001—wiped out more than 99 percent of its stock-market value. Banks that lent billions to Enron will have to fight for a share in bankruptcy court. Enron's biggest lenders are J. P. Morgan Chase & Co. and Citigroup, which together have an estimated $1.6 billion in exposure. Of that, $900 million is unsecured. Other losers: Enron's customers, who traded everything from electricity, gas, and metals to telecom bandwidth, credit insurance, and weather derivatives.

Already the once-arrogant Enron has become vulture meat. In addition to clamoring creditors, it faces class actions by shareholders and employees, whose pensions were heavily invested in Enron stock. That raises questions about how much value is left in the company, which will probably be dismembered and sold off in parts.

Who's to blame? Perhaps the biggest culprit was arrogance, which has caused Enron to be compared to past self-proclaimed masters of the universe such as Drexel Burnham Lambert Inc. in the 1980s and Long-Term Capital Management in the 1990s. Many fingers are pointing at Skilling, the longtime Enron financial engineer who took over as CEO in February and Lay and Andrew S. Fastow, who was ousted as chief financial officer on October 24, 2001. Fastow put together several partnerships that were intended to streamline Enron's balance sheet by taking on certain assets and liabilities. That created a conflict of interest for Fastow, who made over $30 million from his partnerships.

The most poignant aspect of Enron's failure is the damage to its own employees. "People have had their total savings disappear," says William Miller, business manager of the International Brotherhood of Electrical Workers union local in Portland, Oregon, which represents employees of Enron's Portland General Electric Co. subsidiary. "Some lives have been pretty well destroyed." Enron flew high, but when it fell, it fell hard.

Source: Reprinted with special permission from Peter Coy, Emily Thornton, Stephanie Anderson Forest, and Christopher Palmeri, "Enron: Running on Empty," *BusinessWeek*, December 10, 2001. Copyright © 2001 The McGraw-Hill Companies.

Unfortunately, the public's perception of the ethics of corporate executives in America is near its all-time low. A major cause is a spate of corporate scandals prompted by self-serving, and often criminal, executive action that resulted in the loss of stakeholder investments and employee jobs. The most notorious of these cases was the failure of the Enron Corporation, as described in Exhibit 3.16, Strategy in Action. The obvious goal of every company is to avoid scandal through a combination of high moral and ethical standards and careful monitoring to assure that those standards are maintained. However, when problems arise, the management task of restoring the credibility of the company becomes paramount.

External stakeholders are not the only critics of the current state of business ethics. Exhibit 3.17, Strategy in Action, presents the findings of a major survey of human resource managers in which they indicate that strategic managers have much work to do to establish high ethical standards in their organizations.

HR Professionals Believe Ethical Conduct Not Rewarded in Business

A major survey indicates that nearly half of human resources (HR) professionals believe ethical conduct is not rewarded in business today. Over the past five years, HR professionals have felt increasingly more pressure to compromise their organizations' ethical standards; however, they also indicate personally observing fewer cases of misconduct.

The Society for Human Resource Management (SHRM) and the Ethics Resource Center (ERC) jointly conducted the 2003 Business Ethics Survey, with 462 respondents. The survey results show the following:

- 79 percent of respondent organizations have written ethics standards.

- 49 percent say that ethical conduct is not rewarded in business today.

- 35 percent of HR professionals often or occasionally personally observed ethics misconduct in the last year.

- 24 percent of HR professionals feel pressured to compromise ethics standards. In comparison, 13 percent indicated they felt pressured in 1997.

- The top five reasons HR professionals compromise an organization's ethical standards are the need to follow the boss's directives (49 percent); meeting overly aggressive business/financial objectives (48 percent); helping the organization survive (40 percent); meeting schedule pressures (35 percent); and wanting to be a team player (27 percent).

Source: Society for Human Resource Management, www.shrm.org/press.

Even when groups agree on what constitutes human welfare in a given case, the means they choose to achieve this welfare may differ. Therefore, ethics also involve acting to attain human goals. For example, many people would agree that health is a value worth seeking—that is, health enhances human welfare. But what if the means deemed necessary to attain this value for some include the denial or risk of health for others, as is commonly an issue faced by pharmaceutical manufacturers? During production of some drugs, employees are sometimes subjected to great risk of personal injury and infection. For example, if contacted or inhaled, the mercury used in making thermometers and blood pressure equipment can cause heavy metal poisoning. If inhaled, ethylene oxide used to sterilize medical equipment before it is shipped to doctors can cause fetal abnormalities and miscarriages. Even penicillin, if inhaled during its manufacturing process, can cause acute anaphylaxis or shock. Thus, although the goal of customer health might be widely accepted, the means (involving jeopardy to production employees) may not be.

The spotlight on business ethics is a widespread phenomenon. For example, a 2004 survey by the Institute of Business Ethics helps to clarify how companies use their codes of ethics.[12] It found that more than 90 percent of Financial Times Stock Exchange (FTSE) companies in the United Kingdom have an explicit commitment to doing business ethically in the form of a code of ethical conduct. The respondents also reported that 26 percent of boards of directors are taking direct responsibility for the ethical programs of companies, up from 16 percent in 2001. The main reasons for having a code of ethics were to provide guidance to staff (38 percent) and to reduce legal liability (33 percent). Many of the managers (41 percent) also reported that they had used their code in disciplinary procedures in the last three years, usually on safety, security, and environmental ethical issues.

Approaches to Questions of Ethics

Managers report that the most critical quality of ethical decision making is consistency. Thus, they often try to adopt a philosophical approach that can provide the basis for the

---

[12] Accessed in 2005 from http://www.ibe.org.uk/ExecSumm.pdf.

consistency they seek. There are three fundamental ethical approaches for executives to consider: the utilitarian approach, the moral rights approach, and the social justice approach.

utilitarian approach
Judging the appropriateness of a particular action based on a goal to provide the greatest good for the greatest number of people.

Managers who adopt the **utilitarian approach** judge the effects of a particular action on the people directly involved, in terms of what provides the greatest good for the greatest number of people. The utilitarian approach focuses on actions, rather than on the motives behind the actions. Potentially positive results are weighed against potentially negative results. If the former outweigh the latter, the manager taking the utilitarian approach is likely to proceed with the action. That some people might be adversely affected by the action is accepted as inevitable. For example, the Council on Environmental Quality conducts cost-benefit analyses when selecting air pollution standards under the Clean Air Act, thereby acknowledging that some pollution must be accepted.

moral rights approach
Judging the appropriateness of a particular action based on a goal to maintain the fundamental rights and privileges of individuals and groups.

Managers who subscribe to the **moral rights approach** judge whether decisions and actions are in keeping with the maintenance of fundamental individual and group rights and privileges. The moral rights approach (also referred to as deontology) includes the rights of human beings to life and safety, a standard of truthfulness, privacy, freedom to express one's conscience, freedom of speech, and private property.

social justice approach
Judging the appropriateness of a particular action based on equity, fairness, and impartiality in the distribution of rewards and costs among individuals and groups.

Managers who take the **social justice approach** judge how consistent actions are with equity, fairness, and impartiality in the distribution of rewards and costs among individuals and groups. These ideas stem from two principles known as the liberty principle and the difference principle. The *liberty principle* states that individuals have certain basic liberties compatible with similar liberties of other people. The *difference principle* holds that social and economic inequities must be addressed to achieve a more equitable distribution of goods and services.

In addition to these defining principles, three implementing principles are essential to the social justice approach. According to the *distributive-justice principle,* individuals should not be treated differently on the basis of arbitrary characteristics, such as race, sex, religion or national origin. This familiar principle is embodied in the Civil Rights Act. The *fairness principle* means that employees must be expected to engage in cooperative activities according to the rules of the company, assuming that the company rules are deemed fair. The most obvious example is that, in order to further the mutual interests of the company, themselves, and other workers, employees must accept limits on their freedom to be absent from work. The *natural-duty principle* points up a number of general obligations, including the duty to help others who are in need or danger, the duty not to cause unnecessary suffering, and the duty to comply with the just rules of an institution.

CODES OF BUSINESS ETHICS

To help ensure consistency in the application of ethical standards, an increasing number of professional associations and businesses are establishing codes of ethical conduct. Associations of chemists, funeral directors, law enforcement agents, migration agents, hockey players, Internet providers, librarians, military arms sellers, philatelists, physicians, and psychologists all have such codes. So do companies such as Amazon.com, Colgate, Honeywell, New York Times, Nokia, PricewaterhouseCoopers, Sony Group, and Riggs Bank.

Nike faces the problems of a large global corporation in enforcing a code of conduct. Nike's products are manufactured in factories owned and operated by other companies. Nike's supply chain includes more than 660,000 contract manufacturing workers in more than 900 factories in more than 50 countries, including the United States. The workers are predominantly women, ages 19 to 25. The geographic dispersion of its manufacturing facilities is driven by many factors including pricing, quality, factory capacity, and quota allocations.

With such cultural, societal, and economic diversity, the ethics challenge for Nike is to "do business with contract factories that consistently demonstrate compliance with

Nike, Inc. was founded on a handshake. Implicit in that act was the determination that we would build our business with all of our partners based on trust, teamwork, honesty, and mutual respect. We expect all of our business partners to operate on the same principles.

At the core of the Nike corporate ethic is the belief that we are a company comprised of many different kinds of people, appreciating individual diversity, and dedicated to equal opportunity for each individual.

Nike designs, manufactures, and markets products for sports and fitness consumers. At every step in that process, we are driven to do not only what is required by law, but what is expected of a leader. We expect our business partners to do the same. Nike partners with contractors who share our commitment to best practices and continuous improvement in:

1. Management practices that respect the rights of all employees, including the right to free association and collective bargaining.
2. Minimizing our impact on the environment.
3. Providing a safe and healthy workplace.
4. Promoting the health and well-being of all employees.

Contractors must recognize the dignity of each employee, and the right to a workplace free of harassment, abuse or corporal punishment. Decisions on hiring, salary, benefits, advancement, termination, or retirement must be based solely on the employee's ability to do the job. There shall be no discrimination based on race, creed, gender, marital or maternity status, religious or political beliefs, age, or sexual orientation.

Wherever Nike operates around the globe, we are guided by this Code of Conduct, and we bind our contractors to these principles. Contractors must post this Code in all major workspaces, translated into the language of the employee, and must train employees on their rights and obligations as defined by this Code and applicable local laws.

While these principles establish the spirit of our partnerships, we also bind our partners to specific standards of conduct. The core standards are set forth below.

FORCED LABOR
The contractor does not use forced labor in any form—prison, indentured, bonded, or otherwise.

CHILD LABOR
The contractor does not employ any person below the age of 18 to produce footwear. The contractor does not employ any person below the age of 16 to produce apparel, accessories, or equipment. If at the time Nike production begins, the contractor employs people of the legal working age who are at least 15, that employment may continue, but the contractor will not hire any person going forward who is younger than the Nike or legal age limit, whichever is higher.

To further ensure these age standards are complied with, the contractor does not use any form of homework for Nike production.

COMPENSATION
The contractor provides each employee at least the minimum wage, or the prevailing industry wage, whichever is higher; provides each employee a clear, written accounting for every pay period; and does not deduct from employee pay for disciplinary infractions.

BENEFITS
The contractor provides each employee all legally mandated benefits.

HOURS OF WORK/OVERTIME
The contractor complies with legally mandated work hours; uses overtime only when each employee is fully compensated according to local law; informs each employee at the time of hiring if mandatory overtime is a condition of employment; and, on a regularly scheduled basis, provides one day off in seven, and requires no more than 60 hours of work per week on a regularly scheduled basis, or complies with local limits if they are lower.

ENVIRONMENT, SAFETY AND HEALTH (ES&H)
The contractor has written environmental, safety, and health policies and standards and implements a system to minimize negative impacts on the environment, reduce work-related injury and illness, and promote the general health of employees.

DOCUMENTATION AND INSPECTION
The contractor maintains on file all documentation needed to demonstrate compliance with this Code of Conduct and required laws, agrees to make these documents available for Nike or its designated monitor, and agrees to submit to inspections with or without prior notice.

Source: www.nike.com/nikebiz, 2007.

standards we set and that operate in an ethical and lawful manner." To help in this process, Nike has developed its own code of ethics, which it calls a Code of Conduct. It is a set of ethical principles intended to guide management decision making. Nike's code is presented in Exhibit 3.18, Strategy in Action.

Major Trends in Codes of Ethics

The increased interest in codifying business ethics has led to both the proliferation of formal statements by companies and to their prominence among business documents. Not long ago, codes of ethics that existed were usually found solely in employee handbooks. The new trend is for them to also be prominently displayed on corporate Web sites, in annual reports, and next to Title VII posters on bulletin boards.

A second trend is that companies are adding enforcement measures to their codes, including policies that are designed to guide employees on what to do if they see violations occur and sanctions that will be applied, including consequences on their employment and civil and criminal charges. As a consequence, businesses are increasingly requiring all employees to sign the ethics statement as a way to acknowledge that they have read and understood their obligations. In part this requirement reflects the impact of the Sarbanes-Oxley rule that CEOs and CFOs certify the accuracy of company financials. Executives want employees at all levels to recognize their own obligations to pass accurate information up the chain of command.

The third trend is increased attention by companies in improving employees' training in understanding their obligations under the company's code of ethics. The objective is to emphasize the consideration of ethics during the decision-making process. Training, and subsequent monitoring of actual work behavior, is also aided by computer software that identifies possible code violations, which managers can then investigate in detail.

Summary

Given the amount of time that people spend working, it is reasonable that they should try to shape the organizations in which they work. Inanimate organizations are often blamed for setting the legal, ethical, and moral tones in the workplace when, in reality, people determine how people behave. Just as individuals try to shape their neighborhoods, schools, political and social organizations, and religious institutions, employees need to help determine the major issues of corporate social responsibility and business ethics.

Strategic decisions, indeed all decisions, involve trade-offs. We choose one thing over another. We pursue one goal while subordinating another. On the topic of corporate social responsibility, individual employees must work to achieve the outcomes that they want. By volunteering for certain community welfare options they choose to improve that option's chances of being beneficial. Business ethics present a parallel opportunity. By choosing proper behaviors, employees help to build an organization that can be respected and economically viable in the long run.

Often, the concern is expressed that business activities tend to be illegal or unethical and that the failure of individuals to follow the pattern will leave them at a competitive disadvantage. Such claims, often prompted by high-profile examples, are absurd. Rare but much publicized criminal activities mask the meaningful reality that business conduct is as honest and honorable as any other activity in our lives. The people who are involved are the same, with the same values, ideals, and aspirations.

In this chapter, we have studied corporate social responsibility to understand it and to learn how our businesses can occasionally use some of their resources to make differential, positive impacts on our society. We also looked at business ethics to gain an appreciation for the importance of maintaining and promoting social values in the workplace.

Key Terms

corporate social
responsibility, *p. 58*
discretionary
responsibilities, *p. 58*
economic
responsibilities, *p. 56*

ethical responsibilities, *p. 58*
ethics, *p. 70*
legal responsibilities, *p. 56*
moral rights approach, *p. 84*
privatization, *p. 68*

Sarbanes-Oxley Act of
2002, *p. 64*
social audit, *p. 69*
social justice approach, *p. 84*
utilitarian approach, *p. 84*

Questions for Discussion

1. Define the term *social responsibility.* Find an example of a company action that was legal but not socially responsible. Defend your example on the basis of your definition.
2. Name five potentially valuable indicators of a firm's social responsibility and describe how company performance in each could be measured.
3. Do you think a business organization in today's society benefits by defining a socially responsible role for itself? Why or why not?
4. Which of the three basic philosophies of social responsibility would you find most appealing as the chief executive of a large corporation? Explain.
5. Do you think society's expectations for corporate social responsibility will change in the next decade? Explain.
6. How much should social responsibility be considered in evaluating an organization's overall performance?
7. Is it necessary that an action be voluntary to be termed socially responsible? Explain.
8. Do you think an organization should adhere to different philosophies of corporate responsibility when confronted with different issues, or should its philosophy always remain the same? Explain.
9. Describe yourself as a stakeholder in a company. What kind of stakeholder role do you play now? What kind of stakeholder roles do you expect to play in the future?
10. What sets the affirmative philosophy apart from the stakeholder philosophy of social responsibility? In what areas do the two philosophies overlap?
11. Cite examples of both ethical and unethical behavior drawn from your knowledge of current business events.
12. How would you describe the contemporary state of business ethics?
13. How can business self-interest also serve social interests?

Chapter 3 Discussion Case

BusinessWeek

The Poverty Business

1 Roxanne Tsosie decided in late 2005 to pull her life together. She was 28 years old and still lived in her mother's two-room apartment in a poor neighborhood in southeast Albuquerque known as the War Zone. She survived mostly on food stamps and welfare. The Tsosies are Navajo, and Roxanne's mother wanted to move back to a reservation in western New Mexico where the family has a dilapidated house lacking electricity and running water. Roxanne, unmarried and with four children of her own, could make out her future, and she didn't like what she saw.

2 With only a high school diploma, her employment options were limited. She landed a job as a home health care aide for the elderly and infirm. It paid $15,000 a year and required

that she have a car to make her rounds of Albuquerque and its rambling desert suburbs. A friend told her about a used-car place called J. D. Byrider Systems Inc.

3 The bright orange car lot stands out amid a jumble of payday lenders, pawn shops, and rent-to-own electronics stores on Central Avenue in the War Zone. Signs in Spanish along the street promise *Financiamos a Todos*—Financing for All. On the same day she walked into Byrider, Tsosie drove off, jubilant, in a 1999 Saturn subcompact she bought entirely on credit. "I was starting to think I could actually get things I wanted," she says.

4 In recent years, a range of businesses have made financing more readily available to even the riskiest of borrowers. Greater access to credit has put cars, computers, credit cards,

and even homes within reach for many more of the working poor. But this remaking of the marketplace for low-income consumers has a dark side: innovative and zealous firms have lured unsophisticated shoppers by the hundreds of thousands into a thicket of debt from which many never emerge.

5   Federal Reserve data show that in relative terms, that debt is getting expensive. In 1989 households earning $30,000 or less a year paid an average annual interest rate on auto loans that was 16.8 percent higher than what households earning more than $90,000 a year paid. By 2004 the discrepancy had soared to 56.1 percent. Roughly the same thing happened with mortgage loans: a leap from a 6.4 percent gap to one of 25.5 percent. "It's not only that the poor are paying more; the poor are paying a lot more," says Sheila C. Bair, chairman of the Federal Deposit Insurance Corp.

6   Once, substantial businesses had little interest in chasing customers of the sort who frequent the storefronts surrounding the Byrider dealership in Albuquerque. Why bother grabbing for the few dollars in a broke man's pocket? Now there's reason.

7   Armed with the latest technology for assessing credit risks—some of it so fine-tuned it picks up spending on cigarettes—ambitious corporations like Byrider see profits in those thin wallets. The liquidity lapping over all parts of the financial world also has enabled the dramatic expansion of lending to the working poor. Byrider, with financing from Bank of America Corp. (BAC) and others, boasts 130 dealerships in 30 states. At company headquarters in Carmel, Indiana, a profusion of colored pins decorates wall maps, marking the 372 additional franchises it aims to open from California to Florida. CompuCredit Corp., based in Atlanta, aggressively promotes credit cards to low-wage earners with a history of not paying their bills on time. And BlueHippo Funding, a self-described "direct response merchandise lender," has retooled the rent-to-own model to sell PCs and plasma TVs.

8   The recent furor over subprime mortgage loans fits into this broader story about the proliferation of subprime credit. In some instances, marketers essentially use products as the bait to hook less-well-off shoppers on expensive loans. "It's the finance business," explains Russ Darrow Jr., a Byrider franchisee in Milwaukee. "Cars happen to be the commodity that we sell." In another variation, tax-preparation services offer instant refunds, skimming off hefty fees. Attorneys general in several states say these techniques at times have violated consumer-protection laws.

9   Some economists applaud how the spread of credit to the tougher parts of town has raised home and auto-ownership rates. But others warn that in the long run the development could slow upward mobility. Wages for the working poor have been stagnant for three decades. Meanwhile, their spending has consistently and significantly exceeded their income since the mid-1980s. They are making up the difference by borrowing more. From 1989 through 2004, the total amount owed by households earning $30,000 or less a year has grown 247 percent to $691 billion, according to the most recent Federal Reserve data available.

"Having access to credit should be helping low-income 10 individuals," says Nouriel Roubini, an economics professor at New York University's Stern School of Business. "But instead of becoming an opportunity for upward social and economic mobility, it becomes a debt trap for many trying to move up."

Happy as she was with the Saturn (GM) she bought 11 in December 2005, Roxanne Tsosie soon ran into trouble paying off the loan on it. The car had 103,000 miles on the odometer. She agreed to a purchase price of $7,992, borrowing the full amount at a sky-high 24.9 percent. Based on her conversation with the Byrider salesman, she thought she had signed up for $150 monthly installments. The paperwork indicated she owed that amount every other week. She soon realized she couldn't manage the payments. Dejected, she agreed to give the car back, having already paid $900. "It kind of knocked me down," Tsosie says. "I felt I'd never get anywhere."

The abortive purchase meant Byrider could dust off and 12 resell the Saturn. Nearly half of Byrider sales in Albuquerque do not result in final payoff, and many vehicles are repossessed, says David Brotherton, managing partner of the dealership. A former factory worker, he says he sympathizes with customers who barely get by. "Many of these people are locked in perpetual cycle of debt," he says. "It's all motivated by self-interest, of course, but we do want to help credit-challenged people get to the finish line."

Byrider dealers say they can generally figure out which 13 customers will pay back their loans. Salesmen, many of whom come from positions at banks and other lending companies, use proprietary software called Automated Risk Evaluator (ARE) to assess customers' financial vital signs, ranging from credit scores from major credit agencies to amounts spent on alimony and cigarettes.

Unlike traditional dealers, Byrider doesn't post prices— 14 which average $10,200 at company-owned showrooms— directly on its cars. Salesmen, after consulting ARE, calculate the maximum that a person can afford to pay, and only then set the total price, down payment, and interest rate. Byrider calls this process fair and accurate; critics call it "opportunity pricing."

So how did Byrider figure that Tsosie had $300 a month 15 left over from her small salary for car payments? Barely a step up from destitution, she now lives in her own cramped apartment in a dingy two-story adobe-style building. Decorated with an old bow and arrow and sepia-tinted photographs of Navajo chiefs, the apartment is also home to her new husband, Joey A. Garcia, a grocery-store stocker earning $25,000 a year, his two children from a previous marriage, and two of Tsosie's kids. She and Garcia are paying off several other high-interest loans, including one for his used car and another for the $880 wedding ring he bought her this year.

Asked by *BusinessWeek* to review Tsosie's file, Byrider's 16 Brotherton raises his eyebrows, taps his keyboard, and studies the screen for a few minutes, "We probably should have spent more time explaining the terms to her," he says. Pausing, he adds that given Tsosie's finances, she should never have received a 24.9 percent loan for nearly $8,000.

17   That still leaves her $900 in Byrider's till. "No excuses; I apologize," Brotherton says. He promises to return the money (and later does). In most transactions, of course, there's no reporter on the scene asking questions.

18   A quarter century ago, Byrider's founder, the late James F. Devoe, saw before most people the untapped profits in selling expensive, highly financed products to marginal customers. "The light went on that there was a huge market of people with subprime and unconventional credit being turned down," says Devoe's 38-year-old son, James Jr., who is now chief executive.

19   The formula produces profits. Last year, net income on used cars sold by outlets Byrider owns averaged $828 apiece. That compared with only $223 for used cars sold as a sideline by new-car dealers, and a $31 loss for the typical new car, according to the National Automobile Dealers Assn. Nationwide, Byrider dealerships reported sales last year of $700 million, up 7 percent from 2005.

20   "Good Cars for People Who Need Credit," the company declares in its sunny advertising, but some law enforcers say Byrider's inventive sales techniques are unfair. Joel Cruz-Esparza, director of consumer protection in the New Mexico Attorney General's Office from 2002 to 2006, says he received numerous complaints from buyers about Byrider. His office contacted the dealer, but he never went to court. "They're taking advantage of people, but it's not illegal," he says.

21   Officials elsewhere disagree. Attorneys general in Kentucky and Ohio have alleged in recent civil suits that opportunity pricing misleads customers. Without admitting liability, Byrider and several franchises settled the suits in 2005 and 2006, agreeing to inform buyers of "maximum retail prices." Dealers now post prices somewhere on their premises, though still not on cars. Doing so would put them "at a competitive disadvantage," says CEO Devoe. Sales reps flip through charts telling customers they have the right to know prices. Even so, Devoe says, buyers "talk to us about the price of the car less than 10 percent of the time."

22   Tsosie recently purchased a 2001 Pontiac from another dealer. She's straining to make the $277 monthly payment on a 14.9 percent loan.

23   Nobody, poor or rich, is compelled to pay a high price for a used car, a credit card, or anything else. Some see the debate ending there. "The only feasible way to run a capitalist society is to allow companies to maximize their profits," says Tyler Cowen, an economist at George Mason University in Fairfax, Virginia. "That will sometimes include allowing them to sell things to people that will sometimes make them worse off."

24   Others worry, however, that the widening income gap between the wealthy and the less fortunate is being exacerbated by the spread of high-interest, high-fee financing. "People are being encouraged to live beyond their means by companies that are preying on low-income consumers," says Jacob S. Hacker, a political scientist at Yale.

25   Higher rates aren't deterring low-income borrowers. Payday lenders, which provide expensive cash advances due on the customer's next payday, have multiplied from 300 in the early 1990s to more than 25,000. Savvy financiers are rolling up payday businesses and pawn shops to form large chains. The stocks of five of these companies now trade publicly on the New York Stock Exchange (NYX) and NASDAQ (NDAQ). The investment bank Stephens Inc. estimates that the volume of "alternative financial services" provided by these sorts of businesses totals more than $250 billion a year.

26   Mainstream financial institutions are helping to fuel this explosion in subprime lending to the working poor. Wells Fargo & Co. (WFC) and U.S. Bancorp (USB) now offer their own versions of payday loans, charging $2 for every $20 borrowed. Based on a 30-day repayment period, that's an annual interest rate of 120 percent. (Wells Fargo says the loans are designed for emergencies not long-term financial needs.) Bank of America's revolving credit line to Byrider provides up to $110 million. Merrill Lynch & Co. (MER) works with CompuCredit to package credit-card receivables as securities, which are bought by hedge funds and other big investors.

27   Once, major banks and companies avoided the poor side of town. "The mentality was: low income means low revenue, so let's not locate there," says Matt Fellowes, a researcher at the Brookings Institution in Washington, D.C. Now, he says, a growing number of sizable corporations are realizing that viewed in the aggregate, the working poor are a choice target. Income for the 40 million U.S. households earning $30,000 or less totaled $650 billion in 2004, according to Federal Reserve data.

28   John T. Hewitt a pioneer in the tax-software industry, recognized the opportunity. The founder of Jackson Hewitt Tax Service Inc. (JTX) says that as his company grew in the 1980s, "we focused on the low-hanging fruit: the less affluent people who wanted their money quick."

29   In the 1990s, Jackson Hewitt franchises blanketed lower-income neighborhoods around the country. They soaked up fees not just by preparing returns but also by loaning money to taxpayers too impatient or too desperate to wait for the government to send them their checks. During this period, Congress expanded the Earned-Income Tax Credit, a program that guarantees refunds to the working poor. Jackson Hewitt and rival tax-prep firms inserted themselves into this wealth-transfer system and became "the new welfare office," observes Kathryn Edin, a visiting professor at Harvard University's John F. Kennedy School of Government. Today, recipients of the tax credit are Jackson Hewitt's prime customers.

30   "Money Now," as Jackson Hewitt markets its refund-anticipation loans, comes at a steep price. Lakissisha M. Thomas learned that the hard way. For years, Thomas, 29, has bounced between government assistance and low-paying jobs catering to the wealthy of Hilton Head Island, South Carolina. She worked most recently as a cahier at a jewelry store, earning $8.50 an hour, until she was laid off in April. The single mother lives with her five children in a dimly lit four-bedroom apartment in a public project a few hundred yards from the manicured entrance of Indigo Run, a resort where homes sell for more than $1 million.

31   Thomas finances much of what she buys, but admits she usually doesn't understand the terms. "What do you call it—interest?" she asks, sounding confused. Two years ago she borrowed $400 for and food from Advance America Cash Advance Centers Inc. (AEA), a payday chain. She renewed the loan every two weeks until last November, paying more than $2,500 in fees.

32   This January, eager for a $4,351 earned-income credit, she took out a refund-anticipation loan from Jackson Hewitt. She used the money to pay overdue rent and utility bills, she says. "I thought it would help me get back on my feet."

33   A public housing administrator who reviews tenants' tax returns pointed out to Thomas that Jackson Hewitt had pared $453, or 10.4 percent in tax-prep fees and interest from Thomas' anticipated refund. Only then did she discover that various services for low-income consumers prepare taxes for free and promise returns in as little as a week. "Why should I pay somebody else, some big company, when I could go to the free service?" she asks.

34   The lack of sophistication of borrowers like Thomas helps ensure that the Money Now loan and similar offerings remain big sellers. "I don't know whether I was more bothered by the ignorance of the customers or by the company taking advantage of the ignorance of the customers," says Kehinde Powell, who worked during 2005 as a preparer at a Jackson Hewitt office in Columbus, Ohio. She changed jobs voluntarily.

35   State and federal law enforcers lately have objected to some of Jackson Hewitt's practices. In a settlement in January of a suit brought by the California Attorney General's Office, the company, which is based in Parsippany, New Jersey, agreed to pay $5 million, including $4 million in consumer restitution. The state alleged Jackson Hewitt had pressured customers to take out expensive loans rather than encourage them to wait a week or two to get refunds for free. The company denied liability. In a separate series of suits filed in April, the U.S. Justice Department alleged that more than 125 Jackson Hewitt outlets in Chicago, Atlanta, Detroit, and the Raleigh-Durham (North Carolina) area had defrauded the Treasury by seeking undeserved refunds.

36   Jackson Hewitt stressed that the federal suits targeted a single franchisee. The company announced an internal investigation and stopped selling one type of refund-anticipation loan, known as a preseason loan. The bulk of refund loans are unaffected. More broadly, the company said in a written statement prepared for *BusinessWeek* that customers are "made aware of all options available," including direct electronic filing with the IRS. Refund loan applicants, the company said, receive "a variety of both verbal and written disclosures" that include cost comparisons. Jackson Hewitt added that it provides a valuable service for people who "have a need for quick access to funds to meet a timely expense." The two

franchises that served Thomas declined to comment or didn't return calls.

37   Vincent Humphries, 61, has watched the evolution of low-end lending with a rueful eye. Raised in Detroit and now living in Atlanta, he never got past high school. He started work in the early 1960s at Ford Motor Co.'s hulking Rouge plant outside Detroit for a little over $2 an hour. Later he did construction, rarely earning more than $25,000 a year while supporting five children from two marriages. A masonry business he financed on credit cards collapsed. None of his children have attended college, and all hold what he calls "dead-end jobs."

38   Over the years he has "paid through the nose" for used cars, furniture, and appliances, he says. He has borrowed from short-term, high-interest lenders and once worked as a deliveryman for a rent-to-own store in Atlanta that allowed buyers to pay for televisions over time but ended up charging much more than a conventional retailer. "You would have paid for it three times," he says. As for himself, he adds: "I've had plenty of accounts that have gone into collection. I hope I can pay them before I die." His biggest debts now are medical bills related to a heart condition. He lives on $875 a month from Social Security.

39   Around the time his heath problems ended his work as a bricklayer eight years ago, Humphries picked up a new hobby, computer programming. The shelves of the tidy two-room apartment where he lives alone, in a high-rise on Atlanta's crime-ridden South Side, are crammed with books on programming languages Java, C++, and HTML. He spends most days at his PC on a wooden desk nestled in the corner.

40   When his computer broke down in 2005, Humphries fretted that he would never be able to afford a new one. A solution appeared one night in a TV ad for a company with a catchy name. BlueHippo offered "top-of-the-line" PCs, no credit check necessary. He telephoned the next day.

41   He remembers the woman on the other end describing the computer in vague terms, but she was emphatic about getting his checking account information. She said BlueHippo would debit the account for $124, and Humphries then would owe 17 payments of $71.98 every other week. At the time, $800 would have bought a faster computer at Circuit City Stores (CC), but he didn't have the cash.

42   It wasn't until a week after placing his order that he realized that BlueHippo's terms meant he would pay $1,347.66 over nine months, Humphries says. He called to cancel. The company told him that would take as many as 10 days, he says. When he called again, a week later a customer-service representative said cancellation would take an additional 15 days. "I sensed then that I had my hand in the lion's mouth," Humphries says. During his next call, a phone rep told him BlueHippo had a no-refund policy. He would lose his $124, even though he had never received a computer.

43   Humphries takes some responsibility for this frustrating encounter. "I should have done my homework" before ordering, he says. But he also believes he was "strong armed" out of

$124. He was angry enough to send a detailed complaint to the attorney general of Maryland, where BlueHippo is based. That led to his becoming a lead plaintiff in a private class action pending in California against the company. The suit alleges that scores of customers were similarly duped. Blue-Hippo denies the allegation and says it treats all customers fairly.

44   The attorneys general of New York and West Virginia are investigating the company, and the Illinois attorney general has filed a consumer-protection suit in that state. In response to a Freedom of information Act request by *Business Week*, the Federal Trade Commission says it has accumulated 8,000 pages of consumer complaints about BlueHippo. The FTC is investigating whether the company has engaged in deceptive practices.

45   Chief Executive Joseph K. Rensin started BlueHippo four years ago at the same Baltimore address where he had operated a company called Creditrust Corp. Creditrust, which bought other companies' bad customer debts, enjoyed some success but ultimately slid into Chapter 11 bankruptcy proceedings. In 2005, Rensin and his insurer agreed to pay $7.5 million to settle shareholder allegations that he made misleading statements in an attempt to inflate Creditrust's stock. Rensin and the company denied acting improperly.

46   Rensin established himself anew with BlueHippo, whose cartoon mascot adorns a sign in the lobby of its Baltimore building. Most of the 200 employees inside answer phones. Call-center training materials reviewed by *Business Week* refer to BlueHippo's prime prospects as families, "typically $25k/yr income & less" who "have had trouble getting credit."

47   BlueHippo sells well-known brands such as Apple Inc. (AAPL) computers and Sony Corp. (SNE) televisions. Gateway Inc. (GTW) became a major supplier in December 2003. "We've clearly been aware of their business model from the get-go," says Gateway spokesman David Hallisey. More recently, Gateway became troubled by customer complaints and decided earlier this year to sever ties with BlueHippo. Given its knowledge all along about BlueHippo's methods, why did the separation occur only this year? Hallisey explains: "We're publicly traded and trying to make a profit, so that's a consideration."

48   Three former workers say BlueHippo typically tries to commit consumers to regular electronic debits, then, as in the Humphries case, stalls when they cancel orders or ask about receiving shipment. Many customers give up, according to these employees. Refusing refunds, the company keeps whatever money it receives, whether or not it ships a computer, the trio of form her employees say. "We knew we were misleading people. They weren't getting their computers," says Quinn Smith, a former call-center salesman who says he was fired last December after complaining about these practices. Smith has provided information to the plaintiffs in the California class action but isn't party to the suit.

49   Rensin declined to comment. In a written statement, the company denied any impropriety. It said it ships purchases when promised, though it acknowledged that consumers who can purchase products outright "are better off" doing so, rather than using its "hybrid" layaway and installment financing. The company confirmed that it refuses refunds but said customers may "use any funds paid to purchase other items form BlueHippo." It added that its prices are relatively high because of the "added risk of dealing with customers who have poor credit." In contrast to its training materials, the company said its typical customer earns more than $40,000 a year.

50   A few months after his BlueHippo experience, Humphries did buy a new computer. He borrowed $400 from a friend and bought a General Quality PC from Fry's Electronics, a retail chain. The loan covered the purchase of a 17-inch flat-screen monitor, a DVD burner, and a desktop computer with a 40-gigabyte hard drive. Humphries tightened his belt and paid his friend back in $100 installments over four months, interest-free.

51   Just like everyone else, the working poor find their mailboxes stuffed with "pre-approved" credit card offers. Luisa and Rose Ajuria have trouble saying no. The Ajuria sisters live in a brown-brick bungalow on Chicago's financially pressed South Side. They care for a niece named Caroline and five cats. Neither sister studied past high school or married. "Momma said I wasn't college material," says Luisa, 57. She and Rose, 54, lived most of their lives under the strict supervision of their father, Manuel, who died in 1993. A Mexican immigrant and former sheet-metal press operator, he dutifully paid all the bills. Every week, Lusia handed him her paycheck from Warshawsky & Co., an auto-parts seller where she worked as a supervisor.

52   The sisters now manage their finances themselves—by their own admission, badly. Their father had paid off the $60,000 mortgage. But twice in the past six years, Luisa refinanced the cluttered bungalow, using the money to pay bills and repair aging fixtures in two bathrooms and the kitchen of the 75-year-old house. Now there's a new $140,000 mortgage, with Wells Fargo charging 8 percent interest. The $1,130 monthly payments eat up more than half of Luisa's paycheck from her current job as a secretary at the IRS. If she also made full payments on a $9,000 home-equity line of credit from HSBC Finance Corp. (HBC) and a half-dozen credit-card accounts, they would consume the rest. In total, Luisa owes creditors $169,585. "I don't read things. I just sign them," she says.

53   The debt has forced the Ajurias to consider selling their house and moving to an apartment. But it hasn't stopped companies from offering more credit. Last year, Rose received a come-on for a Tribute MasterCard. She was surprised a company would offer her credit, since she brings in only about $7,500 a year in disability benefits and wages as a part-time worker at an adult day care center. She signed up for the card.

54   Caroline, the 32-year-old niece, who is agoraphobic and rarely leaves the house, quickly ran up $1,268 in charges on the Tribute card, shopping online for Christmas and birthday gifts. Of her newest card, Rose says: "I regret this one. Truly, I do."

55   Terms of the Tribute MasterCard are a world away from the money-back and frequent-flier offers familiar to more prosperous cardholders. Marketed by Atlanta-based CompuCredit, a giant in the subprime card business, Tribute MasterCard offers no such fringe benefits. Rose Ajuria's card carries an interest rate of 28 percent, compared with about 10 percent on a typical card. Since she's paying only a nominal $10 a month, the debt her niece incurred is growing swiftly. "I think we've painted ourselves into a corner," Rose says. Many Tribute MasterCard customers pay a lower 20 percent interest, but CompuCredit typically charges them a $150 annual fee, a separate $6 monthly fee, and a one-time payment of $20 required before using the card.

56   This is the sort of choppy water where many of Compu-Credit's customers paddle—and where the company manages to find profits. CompuCredit was co-founded 11 years ago by David G. Hanna, scion of a family that made a fortune in debt collection. Its 55-member analytics team has devised models to assess more than 200 categories of customer data, from the duration of past credit-card accounts to the number of bad debts. The algorithms apparently work: last year CompuCredit reported earnings of $107 million on $1.3 billion in revenue.

57   Whether the company will make money on Rose Ajuria's account is uncertain at this point. CompuCredit says that customers offered the Tribute MasterCard at 28 percent generally have middling credit histories and that it is willing to work with those who have trouble paying their bills.

58   Executives say the company clearly discloses interest rates and imposes fees up front so consumers won't be surprised later. But in February 2007, CompuCredit disclosed that the FTC and the FDIC had launched separate civil investigations into the marketing of one of its other credit cards. The company denies any wrongdoing. As a goodwill gesture, it says it has stopped charging late fees and interest on accounts more than 90 days past due.

59   On its Web sites and in its marketing brochures, Compu-Credit says it helps customers "rebuild credit" by reporting all of their loan payments to credit bureaus, unlike traditional payday lenders. Not that altruism drives the operation, says co-founder Hanna. "We're not going to chase somebody where we can't make money."

60   Even for those who climb above the lowest rungs of the economic ladder, a legacy of debt can threaten to undercut progress. Connie McBride, a 44-year-old computer programmer who lives near Tacoma, Washington, grew up in foster homes and has led an adult life notably lacking in stability. She has held decent jobs but sometimes has subsisted on food stamps. She earns $47,000 a year as a freelance programmer, working from the weather-beaten aluminum trailer she rents for $590 a month. Wind whistles through small holes in the walls, and she keeps warm in the winter by feeding a wood-fired stove on a cracked cement foundation.

61   McBride showed an early aptitude for math and received a GED at age 16. In the late 1980s, she studied computer science at Washington State University, sometimes arriving for class with her three young children. "Taking those classes, given my life, I felt this was the only way out," she says.

62   She graduated in 1992, owing $45,000 on student loans. That debt became her main financial burden, she says. The 9.5 percent interest rate isn't particularly steep, but she tended to view the payments as less pressing than putting food on the table or paying rent. Late fees piled up. Today she owes $159,991, up from $117,000 only 18 months ago. When dunning notices arrive, she tosses them in the stove.

63   Personal bankruptcy proceedings in 2003 dissolved dozens of McBride's liabilities. But by law her debt to student lender SLM Corp. (SLM), better known as Sallie Mae, wasn't affected. Every month, $450 is garnisheed from her wages, reducing her take-home pay to $1,338. The garnishment doesn't even cover interest and penalties, let alone the principal. Says McBride: "There's no way this thing will ever be paid off."

64   New obligations are piling up. She pays $385 a month on a 21 percent car loan. And now she's buying baby supplies. McBride says her adult son can't deal with his four-month-old daughter, who has medical problems. McBride can't bear the thought of her granddaughter going to a foster home. So she is postponing nonessential expenditures such as fixing a badly chipped front tooth.

65   McBride acknowledges her mistakes. "My life is full of bad decisions," she says. But if she had started out with the funds for college, she wonders whether she would at least be able to afford an apartment and a trip to the dentist. "If you have money to begin with, you don't have these issues or these kinds of bills," she says. "You don't have to worry about the rent or pay double for a car."

Source: Reprinted with special permission from Brian Grow and Keith Epstein, "The Poverty Business: Inside U.S. Companies' Audacious Drive to Extract More Profits from the Nation's Working Poor," *BusinessWeek Online*, May 11, 2007. Copyright © 2007 The McGraw-Hill Companies.

DISCUSSION QUESTIONS

1. What is the responsibility of for-profit companies to attempt to help customers like Roxanne Tsosie see the dangers of indebtedness?

2. Assuming that Byrider is acting legally, is it acting ethically?

3. Under what conditions must customers take responsibility for their decisions?

4. Do you believe that customers who are poor credit risks deserve to be charged higher interest rates? If you say yes, are you not taking advantage of customers who can least afford to pay extra for the things that they buy?

5. Do you believe that every consumer pays hidden or unanticipated charges for the things that they buy? High interest rates on unpaid balances? Annual membership fees? Service charges? Are such charges ethical? Do you want to work for companies that make such charges?

Chapter **Four**

The External Environment

After reading and studying this chapter, you should be able to

1. Describe the three tiers of environmental factors that affect the performance of a firm.

2. List and explain the five factors in the remote environment.

3. Give examples of the economic, social, political, technological, and ecological influences on a business.

4. Explain the five forces model of industry analysis and give examples of each force.

5. Give examples of the influences of entry barriers, supplier power, buyer power, substitute availability, and competitive rivalry on a business.

6. List and explain the five factors in the operating environment.

7. Give examples of the influences of competitors, creditors, customers, labor, and direct suppliers on a business.

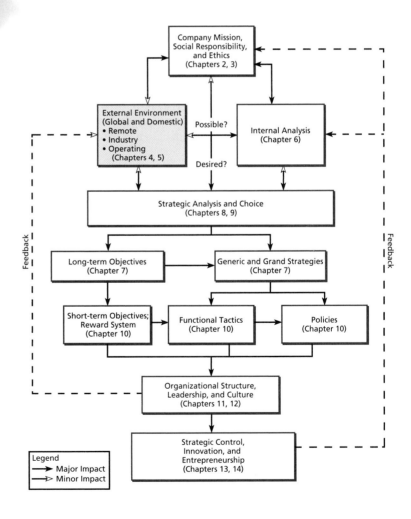

EXHIBIT 4.1
**The Firm's External
Environment**

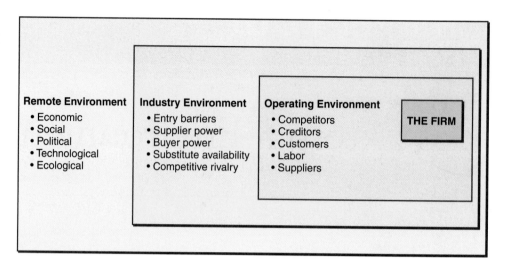

THE FIRM'S EXTERNAL ENVIRONMENT

**external
environment**
The factors beyond the
control of the firm that
influence its choice of
direction and action,
organizational structure,
and internal processes.

A host of external factors influence a firm's choice of direction and action and, ultimately, its organizational structure and internal processes. These factors, which constitute the **external environment,** can be divided into three interrelated subcategories: factors in the remote environment, factors in the industry environment, and factors in the operating environment. This chapter describes the complex necessities involved in formulating strategies that optimize a firm's market opportunities. Exhibit 4.1 suggests the interrelationship between the firm and its remote, its industry, and its operating environments. In combination, these factors form the basis of the opportunities and threats that a firm faces in its competitive environment.

REMOTE ENVIRONMENT

**remote
environment**
Economic, social,
political, technological,
and ecological factors
that originate beyond,
and usually irrespective
of, any single firm's
operating situation.

The **remote environment** comprises factors that originate beyond, and usually irrespective of, any single firm's operating situation: (1) economic, (2) social, (3) political, (4) technological, and (5) ecological factors. That environment presents firms with opportunities, threats, and constraints, but rarely does a single firm exert any meaningful reciprocal influence. For example, when the economy slows and construction starts to decrease, an individual contractor is likely to suffer a decline in business, but that contractor's efforts in stimulating local construction activities would be unable to reverse the overall decrease in construction starts. The trade agreements that resulted from improved relations between the United States and China and the United States and Russia are examples of political factors that impact individual firms. The agreements provided individual U.S. manufacturers with opportunities to broaden their international operations.

Economic Factors

Economic factors concern the nature and direction of the economy in which a firm operates. Because consumption patterns are affected by the relative affluence of various market segments, each firm must consider economic trends in the segments that affect its industry. On both the national and international level, managers must consider the general availability of credit, the level of disposable income, and the propensity of people to spend. Prime interest rates, inflation rates, and trends in the growth of the gross national product are other economic factors they should monitor.

Top Strategist
Harold Messmer, CEO of Robert Half International

Exhibit
4.2

Robert Half CEO Harold Messmer has been around long enough to know how to ride a wave. And he has surfed the tightening of labor markets like an old pro. The jobless rate for professionals has been low, especially in the company's sweet spot: placing accountants, marketing specialists, attorneys, and programmers. Messmer excels by targeting small and midsize companies. Smaller clients are less likely to seek discounts and don't mind paying a higher price for top-caliber personnel. In 2006, most of its units grew 20 percent or more, and the one that places permanent accountants saw revenue jump 53 percent. Messmer also has pushed deeper into the international arena, breaking ground in both Germany and Spain, where the market for temporary staffing is less developed than in the United States. And he set up his temp business for the first time in Asia by taking advantage of existing office space in Robert Half units already operating there.

Source: Reprinted with special permission from The *BusinessWeek* 50—The Best Performers, *BusinessWeek*, March 26, 2007. Copyright © 2007 The McGraw-Hill Companies.

For example, in 2003, the depressed economy hit Crown Cork & Seal Co. especially hard because it had $2 billion in debt due in the year and no way to raise the money to pay it. The down market had caused its stock price to be too low to raise cash as it normally would. Therefore, Crown Cork managers turned to issuing bonds to refinance its debt. With the slow market, investors were taking advantage of such bonds because they could safely gain higher returns over stocks. Not only were investors getting a deal, but Crown Cork and other companies were seeing the lowest interest rates on bonds in years and by issuing bonds could reorganize their balance sheets.

Closely monitoring the economic conditions that affect growth in the financial services industry has been a key to the success of Robert Half International. Its CEO adjusts the company's business strategy to maximize opportunities that arise during changing employment cycles, as described in, Exhibit 4.2, Top Strategist.

The emergence of new international power brokers has changed the focus of economic environmental forecasting. Among the most prominent of these power brokers are the European Economic Community (EEC, or Common Market), the Organization of Petroleum Exporting Countries (OPEC), and coalitions of developing countries.

The EEC, whose members include most of the West European countries, eliminated quotas and established a tariff-free trade area for industrial products among its members. By fostering intra-European economic cooperation, it has helped its member countries compete more effectively in non-European international markets.

Social Factors

The social factors that affect a firm involve the beliefs, values, attitudes, opinions, and lifestyles of persons in the firm's external environment, as developed from cultural, ecological, demographic, religious, educational, and ethnic conditioning. As social attitudes change, so

Tapping a Market That Is Hot, Hot, Hot

BusinessWeek

When National City Corp. bank decided to roll out 78 new branches in Chicago two years ago, it went in knowing its market. With Hispanics expected to account for virtually all of the city's population growth over the next decade, the bank hired dozens of Spanish-speaking staffers and printed thousands of glossy pamphlets, hawking savings accounts to new immigrants and explaining the benefits of IRAs to more established Latinos. This year, the nation's 10th-largest bank will double its Hispanic marketing budget, targeting middle-class Latinos with direct mail offering mortgage financing and money-market accounts, all written *en español.*

The growing economic clout of the Hispanic community is well known. So what's driving the banking push? For starters, it's the fact that relatively few Latinos have any kind of banking accounts. Fully 56 percent of the nation's 40 million Hispanics have never held a bank account, according to market researcher Simmons Inc.

That's a rich vein for banks to tap. With Hispanics' wealth and population rising three times faster than the U.S. average, the FDIC [Federal Deposit Insurance Corporation] predicts that they will account for more than 50 percent of U.S. retail banking growth over the next decade. That amounts to more than $200 billion in new business, since U.S. retail banking revenues are projected to increase 44 percent, to $963 billion over the decade, according to Economy.com.

At Bank of America, Spanish-language advertising brought in 1 million new checking accounts from Hispanics last year—fully 25 percent of the new accounts opened. And Banco Popular, a fast-growing bank based in Puerto Rico, now sends trucks that are outfitted with teller booths to U.S. construction sites so Latino laborers can deposit their checks directly into banking accounts. Wherever Latinos live and work, banks are not far behind.

Source: Reprinted with special permission from Brian Grow, "Tapping a Market That Is Hot, Hot, Hot," *BusinessWeek,* January 17, 2005. Copyright © 2005 The McGraw-Hill Companies.

too does the demand for various types of clothing, books, leisure activities, and so on. Like other forces in the remote external environment, social forces are dynamic, with constant change resulting from the efforts of individuals to satisfy their desires and needs by controlling and adapting to environmental factors. Teresa Iglesias-Soloman hopes to benefit from social changes with *Niños,* a children's catalog written in both English and Spanish. The catalog features books, videos, and Spanish cultural offerings for English-speaking children who want to learn Spanish and for Spanish-speaking children who want to learn English. *Niños'* target market includes middle- to upper-income Hispanic parents, consumers, educators, bilingual schools, libraries, and purchasing agents. Iglesias-Solomon has reason to be optimistic about the future of *Niños,* because the Hispanic population is growing five times faster than the general U.S. population and ranks as the nation's largest minority.

The increasing awareness of the market power of Hispanics in the U.S. has reached almost every business sector. Exhibit 4.3, Strategy in Action, provides a few of the details that drive many businesses' interest in attracting Hispanics as customers.

One of the most profound social changes in recent years has been the entry of large numbers of women into the labor market. This has not only affected the hiring and compensation policies and the resource capabilities of their employers; it has also created or greatly expanded the demand for a wide range of products and services necessitated by their absence from the home. Firms that anticipated or reacted quickly to this social change offered such products and services as convenience foods, microwave ovens, and day care centers.

A second profound social change has been the accelerating interest of consumers and employees in quality-of-life issues. Evidence of this change is seen in recent contract negotiations. In addition to the traditional demand for increased salaries, workers demand such benefits as sabbaticals, flexible hours or four-day workweeks, lump-sum vacation plans, and opportunities for advanced training.

A third profound social change has been the shift in the age distribution of the population. Changing social values and a growing acceptance of improved birth control methods are expected to raise the mean age of the U.S. population, which was 27.9 in 1970, and 34.9 in the year 2000. This trend will have an increasingly unfavorable effect on most producers of predominantly youth-oriented goods and will necessitate a shift in their long-range marketing strategies. Producers of hair and skin care preparations already have begun to adjust their research and development to reflect anticipated changes in demand.

A consequence of the changing age distribution of the population has been a sharp increase in the demands made by a growing number of senior citizens. Constrained by fixed incomes, these citizens have demanded that arbitrary and rigid policies on retirement age be modified and have successfully lobbied for tax exemptions and increases in Social Security benefits. Such changes have significantly altered the opportunity-risk equations of many firms—often to the benefit of firms that anticipated the changes.

Cutting across these issues is concern for individual health. The fast-food industry has been the target of a great deal of public concern. A great deal of popular press attention has been directed toward Americans' concern over the relationship between obesity and health. As documented by the hit movie *Supersize Me,* McDonald's was caught in the middle of this new social concern because its menu consisted principally of high-calorie, artery-clogging foods. Health experts blamed the fast-food industry for the rise in obesity, claiming that companies like McDonald's created an environment that encouraged overeating and discouraged physical activity. Specifically, McDonald's was charged with taking advantage of the fact that kids and adults were watching more TV, by targeting certain program slots to increase sales.

McDonald's responded aggressively and successfully. The company's strategists soon established McDonald's Corp. as an innovator in healthy food options. By 2005, the world's largest fast-food chain launched a new promotional campaign touting healthy lifestyles, including fruit and milk in Happy Meals, activity programs in schools, and a new partnership with the International Olympic Committee. At the time of the announcement, McDonald's was enjoying its longest ever period of same-store sales growth in 25 years, with 24 consecutive months of improved global sales resulting from new healthy menu options, later hours, and better customer service, such as cashless payment options. McDonald's healthy options included a fruit and walnut salad, Paul Newman's brand lowfat Italian dressing, and premium chicken sandwiches in the United States and chicken flatbread and fruit smoothies in Europe.

Translating social change into forecasts of business effects is a difficult process, at best. Nevertheless, informed estimates of the impact of such alterations as geographic shifts in populations and changing work values, ethical standards, and religious orientation can only help a strategizing firm in its attempts to prosper.

Political Factors

The direction and stability of political factors are a major consideration for managers on formulating company strategy. Political factors define the legal and regulatory parameters within which firms must operate. Political constraints are placed on firms through fair-trade decisions, antitrust laws, tax programs, minimum wage legislation, pollution and pricing policies, administrative jawboning, and many other actions aimed at protecting employees, consumers, the general public, and the environment. Because such laws and regulations are most commonly restrictive, they tend to reduce the potential profits of firms. However, some political actions are designed to benefit and protect firms. Such actions include patent laws, government subsidies, and product research grants. Thus, political factors either may limit or benefit the firms they influence. For example, in a pair of surprising decisions in 2003, the Federal Communications Commission (FCC) ruled that local phone companies had to continue to lease their lines to the long-distance carriers at what the locals said was below cost. At the same time, the FCC ruled that the local companies were not required to lease their broadband lines to the national carriers. These decisions were good and bad for the local companies because, although they would lose money by leasing to the long-distance carriers, they could regain some of that loss with their broadband services that did not have to be leased.

The decisions did not mean that the local carriers had to remove existing lines and replace them with broadband lines. Instead, the local carriers would have to run two networks to areas where they want to incorporate broadband because the long-distance carriers had a right to the conventional lines as ruled in the decision. These regulations caused the local carriers to alter their strategies. For example, they often chose to reduce capital investments on new broadband lines because they had to maintain old lines as well. The reduction in capital investments was used to offset the losses they incurred in subsidizing their current lines to the long-distance carriers.

The direction and stability of political factors are a major consideration when evaluating the remote environment. Consider piracy. Microsoft's performance in the Chinese market is greatly affected by the lack of legal enforcement of piracy and also by the policies of the Chinese government. Likewise, the government's actions in support of its competitor, Linux, have limited Microsoft's ability to penetrate the Chinese market.

Political activity also has a significant impact on two governmental functions that influence the remote environment of firms: the supplier function and the customer function.

Supplier Function

Government decisions regarding the accessibility of private businesses to government-owned natural resources and national stockpiles of agricultural products will affect profoundly the viability of the strategies of some firms.

Customer Function

Government demand for products and services can create, sustain, enhance, or eliminate many market opportunities. For example, the Kennedy administration's emphasis on landing a man on the moon spawned a demand for thousands of new products; the Carter administration's emphasis on developing synthetic fuels created a demand for new skills, technologies, and products; the Reagan administration's strategic defense initiative (the "Star Wars" defense) sharply accelerated the development of laser technologies; Clinton's federal block grants to the states for welfare reform led to office rental and lease opportunities; and the war against terrorism during the Bush administration created enormous investment in aviation.

Technological Factors

The fourth set of factors in the remote environment involves technological change. To avoid obsolescence and promote innovation, a firm must be aware of technological changes that might influence its industry. Creative technological adaptations can suggest possibilities for new products or for improvements in existing products or in manufacturing and marketing techniques.

technological forecasting
The quasi-science of anticipating environmental and competitive changes and estimating their importance to an organization's operations.

A technological breakthrough can have a sudden and dramatic effect on a firm's environment. It may spawn sophisticated new markets and products or significantly shorten the anticipated life of a manufacturing facility. Thus, all firms, and most particularly those in turbulent growth industries, must strive for an understanding both of the existing technological advances and the probable future advances that can affect their products and services. This quasi-science of attempting to foresee advancements and estimate their impact on an organization's operations is known as **technological forecasting.**

Technological forecasting can help protect and improve the profitability of firms in growing industries. It alerts strategic managers to both impending challenges and promising opportunities. As examples: (1) Advances in xerography were a key to Xerox's success but caused major difficulties for carbon paper manufacturers, and (2) the perfection of transistors changed the nature of competition in the radio and television industry, helping such giants as RCA while seriously weakening smaller firms whose resource commitments required that they continue to base their products on vacuum tubes.

The key to beneficial forecasting of technological advancement lies in accurately predicting future technological capabilities and their probable impacts. A comprehensive analysis of the effect of technological change involves study of the expected effect of new technologies on the remote environment, on the competitive business situation, and on the business-society interface. In recent years, forecasting in the last area has warranted particular attention. For example, as a consequence of increased concern over the environment, firms must carefully investigate the probable effect of technological advances on quality-of-life factors, such as ecology and public safety.

For example, by combining the powers of Internet technologies with the capability of downloading music in a digital format, Bertelsmann has found a creative technological adaptation for distributing music online to millions of consumers whenever or wherever they might be. Bertelsmann, AOL Time Warner, and EMI formed a joint venture called Musicnet. The ease and wide availability of Internet technologies is increasing the marketplace for online e-tailers. Bertelsmann's response to the shifts in technological factors enables it to distribute music more rapidly through Musicnet to a growing consumer base.

Ecological Factors

ecology
The relationships among human beings and other living things and the air, soil, and water that supports them.

pollution
Threats to life-supporting ecology caused principally by human activities in an industrial society.

The most prominent factor in the remote environment is often the reciprocal relationship between business and the ecology. The term **ecology** refers to the relationships among human beings and other living things and the air, soil, and water that support them. Threats to our life-supporting ecology caused principally by human activities in an industrial society are commonly referred to as **pollution.** Specific concerns include global warming, loss of habitat and biodiversity, as well as air, water, and land pollution.

The global climate has been changing for ages; however, it is now evident that humanity's activities are accelerating this tremendously. A change in atmospheric radiation, due in part to ozone depletion, causes global warming. Solar radiation that is normally absorbed into the atmosphere reaches the earth's surface, heating the soil, water, and air.

Another area of great importance is the loss of habitat and biodiversity. Ecologists agree that the extinction of important flora and fauna is occurring at a rapid rate and, if this pace is continued, could constitute a global extinction on the scale of those found in fossil records. The earth's life-forms depend on a well-functioning ecosystem. In addition, immeasurable advances in disease treatment can be attributed to research involving substances found in plants. As species become extinct, the life support system is irreparably harmed. The primary cause of extinction on this scale is a disturbance of natural habitat. For example, current data suggest that the earth's primary tropical forests, a prime source of oxygen and potential plant "cure," could be destroyed in only five decades.

Air pollution is created by dust particles and gaseous discharges that contaminate the air. Acid rain, or rain contaminated by sulfur dioxide, which can destroy aquatic and plant life, is believed to result from coal-burning factories in 70 percent of all cases. A health-threatening "thermal blanket" is created when the atmosphere traps carbon dioxide emitted from smokestacks in factories burning fossil fuels. This "greenhouse effect" can have disastrous consequences, making the climate unpredictable and raising temperatures.

Water pollution occurs principally when industrial toxic wastes are dumped or leak into the nation's waterways. Because fewer than 50 percent of all municipal sewer systems are in compliance with Environmental Protection Agency requirements for water safety, contaminated waters represent a substantial present threat to public welfare. Efforts to keep from contaminating the water supply are a major challenge to even the most conscientious of manufacturing firms.

Land pollution is caused by the need to dispose of ever-increasing amounts of waste. Routine, everyday packaging is a major contributor to this problem. Land pollution is more dauntingly caused by the disposal of industrial toxic wastes in underground sites. With approximately 90 percent of the annual U.S. output of 500 million metric tons of hazardous industrial wastes being placed in underground dumps, it is evident that land pollution and its resulting endangerment of the ecology have become a major item on the political agenda.

As a major contributor to ecological pollution, business now is being held responsible for eliminating the toxic by-products of its current manufacturing processes and for cleaning up the environmental damage that it did previously. Increasingly, managers are being required by the government or are being expected by the public to incorporate ecological concerns into their decision making. For example, between 1975 and 1992, 3M cut its pollution in half by reformulating products, modifying processes, redesigning production equipment, and recycling by-products. Similarly, steel companies and public utilities have invested billions of dollars in costlier but cleaner-burning fuels and pollution control equipment. The automobile industry has been required to install expensive emission controls in cars. The gasoline industry has been forced to formulate new low-lead and no-lead products. And thousands of companies have found it necessary to direct their R&D resources into the search for ecologically superior products, such as Sears's phosphate-free laundry detergent and Pepsi-Cola's biodegradable plastic soft-drink bottle.

Environmental legislation impacts corporate strategies worldwide. Many companies fear the consequences of highly restrictive and costly environmental regulations. However, some manufacturers view these new controls as an opportunity, capturing markets with products that help customers satisfy their own regulatory standards. Other manufacturers contend that the costs of environmental spending inhibit the growth and productivity of their operations.

Despite cleanup efforts to date, the job of protecting the ecology will continue to be a top strategic priority—usually because corporate stockholders and executives choose it, increasingly because the public and the government require it. As evidenced by Exhibit 4.4, the government has made numerous interventions into the conduct of business for the purpose of bettering the ecology.

Benefits of Eco-Efficiency

Many of the world's largest corporations are realizing that business activities must no longer ignore environmental concerns. Every activity is linked to thousands of other transactions and their environmental impact; therefore, corporate environmental responsibility must be taken seriously and environmental policy must be implemented to ensure a comprehensive organizational strategy. Because of increases in government regulations and consumer environmental concerns, the implementation of environmental policy has become a point of competitive advantage. Therefore, the rational goal of business should be to limit its impact on the environment, thus ensuring long-run benefits to both the firm and society. To neglect this responsibility is to ensure the demise of both the firm and our ecosystem.

Responding to this need, General Electric unveiled plans in 2005 to double its research funds for technologies that reduce energy use, pollution, and emissions tied to global warming. GE said it would focus even more on solar and wind power as well as other environmental technologies it is involved with, such as diesel-electric locomotives, lower emission aircraft engines, more efficient lighting, and water purification. The company's "ecomagination" plans for 2010 include investing $1.5 billion annually in cleaner technologies research, up from $700 million in 2004; and doubling revenues to $20 billion from environmentally friendly products and services.

EXHIBIT 4.4
Federal Ecological Legislation

National Environmental Policy Act, 1969 Established Environmental Protection Agency; consolidated federal environmental activities under it. Established Council on Environmental Quality to advise president on environmental policy and to review environmental impact statements.

Air Pollution:

Clean Air Act, 1963 Authorized assistance to state and local governments in formulating control programs. Authorized limited federal action in correcting specific pollution problems.
Clean Air Act, Amendments (Motor Vehicle Air Pollution Control Act), 1965 Authorized federal standards for auto exhaust emission. Standards first set for 1968 models.
Air Quality Act, 1967 Authorized federal government to establish air quality control regions and to set maximum permissible pollution levels. Required states and localities to carry out approved control programs or else give way to federal controls.
Clean Air Act Amendments, 1970 Authorized EPA to establish nationwide air pollution standards and to limit the discharge of six principal pollutants into the lower atmosphere. Authorized citizens to take legal action to require EPA to implement its standards against undiscovered offenders.
Clean Air Act Amendments, 1977 Postponed auto emission requirements. Required use of scrubbers in new coal-fired power plants. Directed EPA to establish a system to prevent deterioration of air quality in clean areas.

Solid Waste Pollution:

Solid Waste Disposal Act, 1965 Authorized research and assistance to state and local control programs.
Resource Recovery Act, 1970 Subsidized construction of pilot recycling plants; authorized development of nationwide control programs.
Resource Conservation and Recovery Act, 1976 Directed EPA to regulate hazardous waste management, from generation through disposal.
Surface Mining and Reclamation Act, 1976 Controlled strip mining and restoration of reclaimed land.

Water Pollution:

Refuse Act, 1899 Prohibited dumping of debris into navigable waters without a permit. Extended by court decision to industrial discharges.
Federal Water Pollution Control Act, 1956 Authorized grants to states for water pollution control. Gave federal government limited authority to correct specific pollution problems.
Water Quality Act, 1965 Provided for adoption of water quality standards by states, subject to federal approval.
Water Quality Improvement Act, 1970 Provided for federal cleanup of oil spills. Strengthened federal authority over water pollution control.
Federal Water Pollution Control Act Amendments, 1972 Authorized EPA to set water quality and effluent standards; provided for enforcement and research.
Safe Drinking Water Act, 1974 Set standards for drinking water quality.
Clean Water Act, 1977 Ordered control of toxic pollutants by 1984 with best available technology economically feasible.

eco-efficiency
Company actions that produce more useful goods and services while continuously reducing resource consumption and pollution.

Stephen Schmidheiny, chairman of the Business Council for Sustainable Development, has coined the term **eco-efficiency** to describe corporations that produce more-useful goods and services while continuously reducing resource consumption and pollution. He cites a number of reasons for corporations to implement environmental policy: customers demand cleaner products, environmental regulations are increasingly more stringent, employees prefer to work for environmentally conscious firms, and financing is more readily available for eco-efficient firms. In addition, the government provides incentives for environmentally responsible companies.

Setting priorities, developing corporate standards, controlling property acquisition and use to preserve habitats, implementing energy-conserving activities, and redesigning products (e.g., minimizing packaging) are a number of measures the firm can implement to enhance an eco-efficient strategy. One of the most important steps a firm can take in achieving a competitive position with regard to the eco-efficient strategy is to fully capitalize on technological developments as a method of gaining efficiency.

There are four key characteristics of eco-efficient corporations:

- Eco-efficient firms are proactive, not reactive. Policy is initiated and promoted by business because it is in their own interests and the interest of their customers, not because it is imposed by one or more external forces.
- Eco-efficiency is designed in, not added on. This characteristic implies that the optimization of eco-efficiency requires every business effort regarding the product and process to internalize the strategy.
- Flexibility is imperative for eco-efficient strategy implementation. Continuous attention must be paid to technological innovation and market evolution.
- Eco-efficiency is encompassing, not insular. In the modern global business environment, efforts must cross not only industrial sectors but national and cultural boundaries as well.

International Environment

Monitoring the international environment, perhaps better thought of as the international dimension of the global environment, involves assessing each nondomestic market on the same factors that are used in a domestic assessment. While the importance of factors will differ, the same set of considerations can be used for each country. For example, Exhibit 4.5, Global Strategy in Action, lists economic, political, legal, and social factors used to assess international environments. However, there is one complication to this process, namely, that the interplay among international markets must be considered. For example, in recent years, conflicts in the Middle East have made collaborative business strategies among firms in traditionally antagonistic countries especially difficult to implement.

INDUSTRY ENVIRONMENT

industry environment
The general conditions for competition that influence all businesses that provide similar products and services.

Harvard professor Michael E. Porter propelled the concept of **industry environment** into the foreground of strategic thought and business planning. The cornerstone of his work first appeared in the *Harvard Business Review,* in which Porter explains the five forces that shape competition in an industry. His well-defined analytic framework helps strategic managers to link remote factors to their effects on a firm's operating environment.

With the special permission of Professor Porter and the *Harvard Business Review,* we present in this section of the chapter the major portion of his seminal article on the industry environment and its impact on strategic management.[1]

HOW COMPETITIVE FORCES SHAPE STRATEGY

The essence of strategy formulation is coping with competition. Yet it is easy to view competition too narrowly and too pessimistically. While we sometimes hear executives complaining to the contrary, intense competition in an industry is neither coincidence nor bad luck.

[1] M. E. Porter, "How Competitive Forces Shape Strategy," *Harvard Business Review,* March–April 1979, pp. 137–45. Copyright © 1979 by the Harvard Business School Publishing Corporation; all rights reserved.

ECONOMIC ENVIRONMENT
- Level of economic development
- Population
- Gross national product
- Per capita income
- Literacy level
- Social infrastructure
- Natural resources
- Climate
- Membership in regional economic blocs (EU, NAFTA, LAFTA)
- Monetary and fiscal policies
- Wage and salary levels
- Nature of competition
- Currency convertibility
- Inflation
- Taxation system
- Interest rates

LEGAL ENVIRONMENT
- Legal tradition
- Effectiveness of legal system
- Treaties with foreign nations
- Patent trademark laws
- Laws affecting business firms

POLITICAL SYSTEM
- Form of government
- Political ideology
- Stability of government
- Strength of opposition parties and groups
- Social unrest
- Political strife and insurgency
- Governmental attitude towards foreign firms
- Foreign policy

CULTURAL ENVIRONMENT
- Customs, norms, values, beliefs
- Language
- Attitudes
- Motivations
- Social institutions
- Status symbols
- Religious beliefs

Source: Arvind V. Phatak, *International Management* (Cincinnati, OH: South-Western College Publishing, 1997), p. 6. Reprinted with permission of the author.

Moreover, in the fight for market share, competition is not manifested only in the other players. Rather, competition in an industry is rooted in its underlying economics, and competitive forces exist that go well beyond the established combatants in a particular industry. Customers, suppliers, potential entrants, and substitute products are all competitors that may be more or less prominent or active depending on the industry.

The state of competition in an industry depends on five basic forces, which are diagrammed in Exhibit 4.6. The collective strength of these forces determines the ultimate profit potential of an industry. It ranges from intense in industries like tires, metal cans, and steel, where no company earns spectacular returns on investment, to mild in industries like oil-field services and equipment, soft drinks, and toiletries, where there is room for quite high returns.

In the economists' "perfectly competitive" industry, jockeying for position is unbridled and entry to the industry very easy. This kind of industry structure, of course, offers the worst prospect for long-run profitability. The weaker the forces collectively, however, the greater the opportunity for superior performance.

Whatever their collective strength, the corporate strategist's goal is to find a position in the industry where his or her company can best defend itself against these forces or can influence them in its favor. The collective strength of the forces may be painfully apparent to all the antagonists; but to cope with them, the strategist must delve below the surface and analyze the sources of competition. For example, what makes the industry vulnerable to entry? What determines the bargaining power of suppliers?

EXHIBIT 4.6 **Forces Driving Industry Competition**

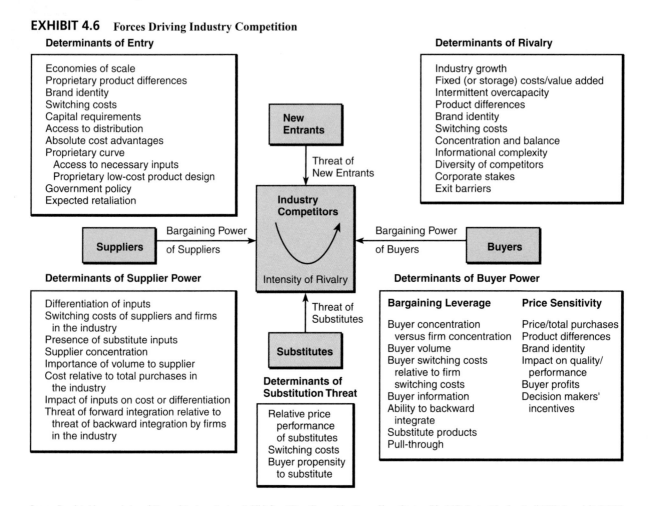

Determinants of Entry

Economies of scale
Proprietary product differences
Brand identity
Switching costs
Capital requirements
Access to distribution
Absolute cost advantages
Proprietary curve
    Access to necessary inputs
    Proprietary low-cost product design
Government policy
Expected retaliation

Determinants of Rivalry

Industry growth
Fixed (or storage) costs/value added
Intermittent overcapacity
Product differences
Brand identity
Switching costs
Concentration and balance
Informational complexity
Diversity of competitors
Corporate stakes
Exit barriers

New Entrants

Threat of New Entrants

Industry Competitors

Intensity of Rivalry

Bargaining Power of Suppliers

Suppliers

Bargaining Power of Buyers

Buyers

Threat of Substitutes

Substitutes

Determinants of Supplier Power

Differentiation of inputs
Switching costs of suppliers and firms
    in the industry
Presence of substitute inputs
Supplier concentration
Importance of volume to supplier
Cost relative to total purchases in
    the industry
Impact of inputs on cost or differentiation
Threat of forward integration relative to
    threat of backward integration by firms
    in the industry

Determinants of Substitution Threat

Relative price
    performance
    of substitutes
Switching costs
Buyer propensity
    to substitute

Determinants of Buyer Power

Bargaining Leverage	Price Sensitivity
Buyer concentration versus firm concentration	Price/total purchases
	Product differences
Buyer volume	Brand identity
Buyer switching costs relative to firm switching costs	Impact on quality/ performance
	Buyer profits
Buyer information	Decision makers' incentives
Ability to backward integrate	
Substitute products	
Pull-through	

Knowledge of these underlying sources of competitive pressure provides the groundwork for a strategic agenda of action. They highlight the critical strengths and weaknesses of the company, animate the positioning of the company in its industry, clarify the areas where strategic changes may yield the greatest payoff, and highlight the places where industry trends promise to hold the greatest significance as either opportunities or threats.

Understanding these sources also proves to be of help in considering areas for diversification.

CONTENDING FORCES

The strongest competitive force or forces determine the profitability of an industry and so are of greatest importance in strategy formulation. For example, even a company with a strong position in an industry unthreatened by potential entrants will earn low returns if it faces a superior or a lower-cost substitute product—as the leading manufacturers of vacuum tubes and coffee percolators have learned to their sorrow. In such a situation, coping with the substitute product becomes the number one strategic priority.

Different forces take on prominence, of course, in shaping competition in each industry. In the ocean-going tanker industry, the key force is probably the buyers (the major oil companies),

Kodak's Moment of Truth

BusinessWeek

Antonio M. Perez left the consumer inkjet printer business after he lost out to Carly Fiorina for the top slot at Hewlett-Packard. But it has never been far from his mind. That's why, a few weeks after he joined a struggling Eastman Kodak Co. as president, he was peering into a microscope in a lab on Kodak's sprawling Rochester (New York) campus. Ever since then, Perez and Kodak have been working on a top-secret plan, code-named Goya, to make a big entrance into the consumer inkjet printer business.

The Kodak printers are designed, first and foremost, to print high-quality photos: the ink is formulated so prints will stay vibrant for 100 years rather than 15. Most impressive of all, replacement ink cartridges will cost half of what consumers are used to paying. The new printers arrived in stores in March 2007, priced at $149 to $299. Black ink cartridges cost $9.99, color $14.99. If consumers buy Kodak's economical Photo Value Pack, which combines paper and ink, the cost per print is about 10 cents, versus 24 cents for HP's comparable package.

If Kodak pulls this off—and that's a big if, considering the forces it's up against—it could pose a huge challenge to the $50 billion printer industry. Those companies now rely on a razor-and-blades strategy, often discounting machines and making most of their profits on replacement cartridges. In particular, Kodak's strategy is an assault on the profit engine of industry leader HP. Printing supplied 60 percent of HP's $6.56 billion in operating earnings in 2006.

Perez predicts the inkjet printers will become a multibillion-dollar product line. He'd better be right. Kodak has struggled for years to find a replacement for its rapidly declining photo-film business. If he doesn't show growth soon, investors could bail out.

Analysts who have seen Kodak's printers have come away impressed. "The print quality is really good. They're at least as good as everybody else," says Larry Jamieson, director of industry-watcher Lyra Research Inc.

But Perez and Kodak are challenging a giant competitor that has a 33 percent worldwide market share and a sterling reputation among PC and digital-camera users. HP not only gets prime merchandising spots for its printers and ink in stores, but also gets to display its printers in the computer sections, because it bundles printers with its PCs. "HP has a lot of customer loyalty. They build a great product. The printers don't break," says analyst Alyson Frasco of market researcher Interactive Data Corp.

Source: Reprinted with special permission from Steve Hamm, "Kodak's Moment of Truth," *BusinessWeek*, February 19, 2007. Copyright © 2007 The McGraw-Hill Companies.

while in tires it is powerful OEM buyers coupled with tough competitors. In the steel industry the key forces are foreign competitors and substitute materials.

Every industry has an underlying structure, or a set of fundamental economic and technical characteristics, that gives rise to these competitive forces. The strategist, wanting to position his or her company to cope best with its industry environment or to influence that environment in the company's favor, must learn what makes the environment tick.

This view of competition pertains equally to industries dealing in services and to those selling products. To avoid monotony, I refer to both products and services as *products*. The same general principles apply to all types of business.

A few characteristics are critical to the strength of each competitive force. They will be discussed in this section.

Threat of Entry

New entrants to an industry bring new capacity, the desire to gain market share, and often substantial resources. Kodak's entry into the consumer inkjet printer business, described in Exhibit 4.7, Strategy in Action, presented a classic threat to the competitive dynamics in the industry. Similarly, companies diversifying through acquisition into the industry from other markets often leverage their resources to cause a shake-up, as Philip Morris did with Miller beer.

The seriousness of the threat of entry depends on the barriers present and on the reaction from existing competitors that the entrant can expect. If barriers to entry are high and a newcomer can expect sharp retaliation from the entrenched competitors, he or she obviously will not pose a serious threat of entering.

There are six major sources of barriers to entry:

Economies of Scale

These economies deter entry by forcing the aspirant either to come in on a large scale or to accept a cost disadvantage. Scale economies in production, research, marketing, and service are probably the key barriers to entry in the mainframe computer industry, as Xerox and GE sadly discovered. **Economies of scale** also can act as hurdles in distribution, utilization of the sales force, financing, and nearly any other part of a business.

economies of scale
The savings that companies achieve because of increased volume.

Economies of scale refer to the savings that companies within an industry achieve due to increased volume. Simply put, when the volume of production increases, the long-range average cost of a unit produced will decline.

Economies of scale result from technological and nontechnological sources. The technological sources of these economies are higher levels of mechanization or automation and a greater modernization of plant and facilities The nontechnological sources include better managerial coordination of production functions and processes, long-term contractual agreements with suppliers, and enhanced employee performance arising from specialization.

Economies of scale are an important determinant of the intensity of competition in an industry. Firms that enjoy such economies can charge lower prices than their competitors. They also can create barriers to entry by reducing their prices temporarily, or permanently, to deter new firms from entering the industry.

Product Differentiation

product differentiation
The extent to which customers perceive differences among products and services.

Product differentiation, or brand identification, creates a barrier by forcing entrants to spend heavily to overcome customer loyalty. Advertising, customer service, being first in the industry, and product differences are among the factors fostering brand identification. It is perhaps the most important entry barrier in soft drinks, over-the-counter drugs, cosmetics, investment banking, and public accounting. To create high fences around their business, brewers couple brand identification with economies of scale in production, distribution, and marketing.

Capital Requirements

The need to invest large financial resources to compete creates a barrier to entry, particularly if the capital is required for unrecoverable expenditures in upfront advertising or R&D. Capital is necessary not only for fixed facilities but also for customer credit, inventories, and absorbing start-up losses. While major corporations have the financial resources to invade almost any industry, the huge capital requirements in certain fields, such as computer manufacturing and mineral extraction, limit the pool of likely entrants.

Cost Disadvantages Independent of Size

Entrenched companies may have cost advantages not available to potential rivals, no matter what their size and attainable economies of scale. These advantages can stem from the effects of the learning curve (and of its first cousin, the experience curve), proprietary technology, access to the best raw materials sources, assets purchased at preinflation prices, government subsidies, or favorable locations. Sometimes cost advantages are enforceable

The Experience Curve as an Entry Barrier

In recent years, the experience curve has become widely discussed as a key element of industry structure. According to this concept, unit costs in many manufacturing industries (some dogmatic adherents say in all manufacturing industries) as well as in some service industries decline with "experience," or a particular company's cumulative volume of production. (The experience curve, which encompasses many factors, is a broader concept than the better-known learning curve, which refers to the efficiency achieved over time by workers through much repetition.)

The causes of the decline in unit costs are a combination of elements, including economies of scale, the learning curve for labor, and capital-labor substitution. The cost decline creates a barrier to entry because new competitors with no "experience" face higher costs than established ones, particularly the producer with the largest market share, and have difficulty catching up with the entrenched competitors.

Adherents of the experience curve concept stress the importance of achieving market leadership to maximize this barrier to entry, and they recommend aggressive action to achieve it, such as price cutting in anticipation of falling costs in order to build volume. For the combatant that cannot achieve a healthy market share, the prescription is usually, "Get out."

Is the experience curve an entry barrier on which strategies should be built? The answer is, not in every industry. In fact, in some industries, building a strategy on the experience curve can be potentially disastrous.

That costs decline with experience in some industries is not news to corporate executives. The significance of the experience curve for strategy depends on what factors are causing the decline.

A new entrant may well be more efficient than the more experienced competitors: if it has built the newest plant, it will face no disadvantage in having to catch up. The strategic prescription, "You must have the largest, most efficient plant," is a lot different from "You must produce the greatest cumulative output of the item to get your costs down."

Whether a drop in costs with cumulative (not absolute) volume erects an entry barrier also depends on the sources of the decline. If costs go down because of technical advances known generally in the industry or because of the development of improved equipment that can be copied or purchased from equipment suppliers, the experience curve is not an entry barrier at all—in fact, new or less-experienced competitors may actually enjoy a cost advantage over the leaders. Free of the legacy of heavy past investments, the newcomer or less-experienced competitor can purchase or copy the newest and lowest cost equipment and technology.

If, however, experience can be kept proprietary, the leaders will maintain a cost advantage. But new entrants may require less experience to reduce their costs than the leaders needed. All this suggests that the experience curve can be a shaky entry barrier on which to build a strategy.

legally, as they are through patents. (For analysis of the much-discussed experience curve as a barrier to entry, see Exhibit 4.8, Strategy in Action.)

Access to Distribution Channels

The new boy or girl on the block must, of course, secure distribution of his or her product or service. A new food product, for example, must displace others from the supermarket shelf via price breaks, promotions, intense selling efforts, or some other means. The more limited the wholesale or retail channels are and the more that existing competitors have these tied up, obviously the tougher that entry into the industry will be. Sometimes this barrier is so high that, to surmount it, a new contestant must create its own distribution channels, as Timex did in the watch industry.

Government Policy

The government can limit or even foreclose entry to industries, with such controls as license requirements, limits on access to raw materials, and tax incentives. Regulated industries like trucking, liquor retailing, and freight forwarding are noticeable examples; more subtle government restrictions operate in fields like ski-area development and coal mining. The government also can play a major indirect role by affecting entry barriers through such controls as air and water pollution standards and safety regulations.

The potential rival's expectations about the reaction of existing competitors also will influence its decision on whether to enter. The company is likely to have second thoughts if incumbents have previously lashed out at new entrants, or if

> The incumbents possess substantial resources to fight back, including excess cash and unused borrowing power, productive capacity, or clout with distribution channels and customers.

> The incumbents seem likely to cut prices because of a desire to keep market shares or because of industrywide excess capacity.

> Industry growth is slow, affecting its ability to absorb the new arrival and probably causing the financial performance of all the parties involved to decline.

Powerful Suppliers

Suppliers can exert bargaining power on participants in an industry by raising prices or reducing the quality of purchased goods and services. Powerful suppliers, thereby, can squeeze profitability out of an industry unable to recover cost increases in its own prices. By raising their prices, soft-drink concentrate producers have contributed to the erosion of profitability of bottling companies because the bottlers—facing intense competition from powdered mixes, fruit drinks, and other beverages—have limited freedom to raise their prices accordingly.

The power of each important supplier (or buyer) group depends on a number of characteristics of its market situation and on the relative importance of its sales or purchases to the industry compared with its overall business.

A *supplier* group is powerful if

1. It is dominated by a few companies and is more concentrated than the industry it sells.

2. Its product is unique or at least differentiated, or if it has built-up switching costs. Switching costs are fixed costs that buyers face in changing suppliers. These arise because, among other things, a buyer's product specifications tie it to particular suppliers, it has invested heavily in specialized ancillary equipment or in learning how to operate a supplier's equipment (as in computer software), or its production lines are connected to the supplier's manufacturing facilities (as in some manufacturing of beverage containers).

3. It is not obliged to contend with other products for sale to the industry. For instance, the competition between the steel companies and the aluminum companies to sell to the can industry checks the power of each supplier.

4. It poses a credible threat of integrating forward into the industry's business. This provides a check against the industry's ability to improve the terms on which it purchases.

5. The industry is not an important customer of the supplier group. If the industry is an important customer, suppliers' fortunes will be tied closely to the industry, and they will want to protect the industry through reasonable pricing and assistance in activities like R&D and lobbying.

Powerful Buyers

Customers likewise can force down prices, demand higher quality or more service, and play competitors off against each other—all at the expense of industry profits.

A *buyer* group is powerful if

1. It is concentrated or purchases in large volumes. Large-volume buyers are particularly potent forces if heavy fixed costs characterize the industry—as they do in metal containers,

corn refining, and bulk chemicals, for example—which raise the stakes to keep capacity filled.

2. The products it purchases from the industry are standard or undifferentiated. The buyers, sure that they always can find alternative suppliers, may play one company against another, as they do in aluminum extrusion.

3. The products it purchases from the industry form a component of its product and represent a significant fraction of its cost. The buyers are likely to shop for a favorable price and purchase selectively. Where the product sold by the industry in question is a small fraction of buyers' costs, buyers are usually much less price sensitive.

4. It earns low profits, which create great incentive to lower its purchasing costs. Highly profitable buyers, however, are generally less price sensitive (i.e., of course, if the item does not represent a large fraction of their costs).

5. The industry's product is unimportant to the quality of the buyers' products or services. Where the quality of the buyers' products is very much affected by the industry's product, buyers are generally less price sensitive. Industries in which this situation exists include oil field equipment, where a malfunction can lead to large losses, and enclosures for electronic medical and test instruments, where the quality of the enclosure can influence the user's impression about the quality of the equipment inside.

6. The industry's product does not save the buyer money. Where the industry's product or service can pay for itself many times over, the buyer is rarely price sensitive; rather, he or she is interested in quality. This is true in services like investment banking and public accounting, where errors in judgment can be costly and embarrassing, and in businesses like the mapping of oil wells, where an accurate survey can save thousands of dollars in drilling costs.

7. The buyers pose a credible threat of integrating backward to make the industry's product. The Big Three auto producers and major buyers of cars often have used the threat of self-manufacture as a bargaining lever. But sometimes an industry so engenders a threat to buyers that its members may integrate forward.

Most of these sources of buyer power can be attributed to consumers as a group as well as to industrial and commercial buyers; only a modification of the frame of reference is necessary. Consumers tend to be more price sensitive if they are purchasing products that are undifferentiated, expensive relative to their incomes, and of a sort where quality is not particularly important.

The buying power of retailers is determined by the same rules, with one important addition. Retailers can gain significant bargaining power over manufacturers when they can influence consumers' purchasing decisions, as they do in audio components, jewelry, appliances, sporting goods, and other goods.

Substitute Products

By placing a ceiling on the prices it can charge, substitute products or services limit the potential of an industry. Unless it can upgrade the quality of the product or differentiate it somehow (as via marketing), the industry will suffer in earnings and possibly in growth.

Manifestly, the more attractive the price-performance trade-off offered by substitute products, the firmer the lid placed on the industry's profit potential. Sugar producers confronted with the large-scale commercialization of high-fructose corn syrup, a sugar substitute, learned this lesson.

Substitutes not only limit profits in normal times but also reduce the bonanza an industry can reap in boom times. The producers of fiberglass insulation enjoyed unprecedented demand as a result of high energy costs and severe winter weather. But the industry's ability to raise prices was tempered by the plethora of insulation substitutes, including cellulose, rock wool, and Styrofoam. These substitutes are bound to become an even stronger force once the current round of plant additions by fiberglass insulation producers has boosted capacity enough to meet demand (and then some).

Substitute products that deserve the most attention strategically are those that *(a)* are subject to trends improving their price-performance trade-off with the industry's product or *(b)* are produced by industries earning high profits. Substitutes often come rapidly into play if some development increases competition in their industries and causes price reduction or performance improvement.

Jockeying for Position

Rivalry among existing competitors takes the familiar form of jockeying for position—using tactics like price competition, product introduction, and advertising slug fests. This type of intense rivalry is related to the presence of a number of factors:

1. Competitors are numerous or are roughly equal in size and power. In many U.S. industries in recent years, foreign contenders, of course, have become part of the competitive picture.

2. Industry growth is slow, precipitating fights for market share that involve expansion-minded members.

3. The product or service lacks differentiation or switching costs, which lock in buyers and protect one combatant from raids on its customers by another.

4. Fixed costs are high or the product is perishable, creating strong temptation to cut prices. Many basic materials businesses, like paper and aluminum, suffer from this problem when demand slackens.

5. Capacity normally is augmented in large increments. Such additions, as in the chlorine and vinyl chloride businesses, disrupt the industry's supply–demand balance and often lead to periods of overcapacity and price cutting.

6. Exit barriers are high. Exit barriers, like very specialized assets or management's loyalty to a particular business, keep companies competing even though they may be earning low or even negative returns on investment. Excess capacity remains functioning, and the profitability of the healthy competitors suffers as the sick ones hang on. If the entire industry suffers from overcapacity, it may seek government help—particularly if foreign competition is present.

7. The rivals are diverse in strategies, origins, and "personalities." They have different ideas about how to compete and continually run head-on into each other in the process.

As an industry matures, its growth rate changes, resulting in declining profits and (often) a shakeout. In the booming recreational vehicle industry of the early 1970s, nearly every producer did well; but slow growth since then has eliminated the high returns, except for the strongest members, not to mention many of the weaker companies. The same profit story has been played out in industry after industry—snowmobiles, aerosol packaging, and sports equipment are just a few examples. Exhibit 4.9, Strategy in Action, describes some of the competitive dynamics in the flat-panel television industry and details several strategic responses of the companies involved.

An acquisition can introduce a very different personality to an industry, as has been the case with Black & Decker's takeover of McCullough, the producer of chain saws. Technological innovation can boost the level of fixed costs in the production process, as it did in the shift from batch to continuous-line photo finishing.

While a company must live with many of these factors—because they are built into the industry economics—it may have some latitude for improving matters through strategic shifts. For example, it may try to raise buyers' switching costs or increase product

Flat Panels, Thin Margins

BusinessWeek

Like just about everyone else checking out the flat-panel TVs at Best Buy in Manhattan, graphic designer Roy Gantt came in coveting a Philips, Sony, or Panasonic. But after seeing the price tags, he figured a Westinghouse might be a better buy. At $800, the Westinghouse 32-inch set seems like a steal compared with $950 to $1,400 for better-known brands.

Thanks to the likes of Westinghouse, which undercut the prices of premier brands by 20 percent to 40 percent, LCDs are no longer a luxury item. Nearly one-third of the 30 million TVs sold in North America in 2006 had LCDs, and in 2007 they accounted for half of all TV sales. The average 27-inch LCD set now retails for less than $650, compared with $1,000 in early 2006, says iSuppli, while 40-inch models have plunged to about $1,600, down from $3,000 during the same period.

For many in the industry, though, the competition is brutal. Prices for LCD sets are falling so rapidly that retailers who place orders too far in advance risk getting stuck with expensive inventory. Circuit City Stores Inc. cited plummeting prices in its February 8, 2007, announcement that it will shutter nearly 70 outlets. The Asian companies that make the LCD panels that go into the TVs are getting slammed, too. Korea's LG.Philips LCD Co. attributed a $186 million loss in the fourth quarter to the 40 percent drop in display prices last year. With panel prices falling 20 percent in 2007, the world's dozen or so makers of displays are scrambling to sell at almost any price just to generate the cash to survive.

Chalk it up to the new dynamics of TV manufacturing in the age of globalization. The wide availability of standardized digital components from Asian suppliers has ushered in virtual manufacturers such as Westinghouse Digital, Vizio, and Syntax-Brillian. With annual sales of $650 million and just 120 employees, Westinghouse Digital typifies the model.

Westinghouse rival Vizio Inc. is even more spartan. The brand didn't exist three years ago, but now it's no. 6 overall in LCD sets, iSupply says, with 7 percent of the North American market. Vizio has a mere 55 full-time employees, but saw sales of $700 million last year. The private company claims its overhead costs are just 0.7 percent of sales, compared with 10 to 20 percent for big, diversified electronics conglomerates, and that it gets by on profit margins of just 2 percent.

With LCD prices falling by 3 to 5 percent a month, Vizio's biggest challenge is making sure it doesn't pay too much for orders placed months in advance. The company negotiates flexible terms with suppliers and manages to keep only two weeks of inventory on hand by constantly monitoring retailers' shelves. That's a big challenge given that Vizio says it has enough orders from retailers to sell nearly 3 million TVs this year, which would triple its revenues.

Source: Reprinted with special permission from Pete Engardio, "Flat Panels, Thin Margins: Rugged Competition from Smaller Brands Has Made the TV Sets Cheaper Than Ever," *BusinessWeek,* February 26, 2007. Copyright © 2007 The McGraw-Hill Companies.

differentiation. A focus on selling efforts in the fastest growing segments of the industry or on market areas with the lowest fixed costs can reduce the impact of industry rivalry. If it is feasible, a company can try to avoid confrontation with competitors having high exit barriers and, thus, can sidestep involvement in bitter price cutting.

INDUSTRY ANALYSIS AND COMPETITIVE ANALYSIS

Designing viable strategies for a firm requires a thorough understanding of the firm's industry and competition. The firm's executives need to address four questions: (1) What are the boundaries of the industry? (2) What is the structure of the industry? (3) Which firms are our competitors? (4) What are the major determinants of competition? The answers to these questions provide a basis for thinking about the appropriate strategies that are open to the firm.

Industry Boundaries

industry
A group of companies that provide similar products and services.

An **industry** is a collection of firms that offer similar products or services. By "similar products," we mean products that customers perceive to be substitutable for one another. Consider, for example, the brands of personal computers (PCs) that are now being marketed. The firms that produce these PCs, such as Hewlett-Packard, IBM, Apple, and Dell, form the nucleus of the microcomputer industry.

Suppose a firm competes in the microcomputer industry. Where do the boundaries of this industry begin and end? Does the industry include desktops? Laptops? These are the kinds of questions that executives face in defining industry boundaries.

Why is a definition of industry boundaries important? First, it helps executives determine the arena in which their firm is competing. A firm competing in the microcomputer industry participates in an environment very different from that of the broader electronics business. The microcomputer industry comprises several related product families, including personal computers, inexpensive computers for home use, and workstations. The unifying characteristic of these product families is the use of a central processing unit (CPU) in a microchip. On the other hand, the electronics industry is far more extensive; it includes computers, radios, supercomputers, superconductors, and many other products.

The microcomputer and electronics industries differ in their volume of sales, their scope (some would consider microcomputers a segment of the electronics industry), their rate of growth, and their competitive makeup. The dominant issues faced by the two industries also are different. Witness, for example, the raging public debate being waged on the future of the "high-definition TV." U.S. policy makers are attempting to ensure domestic control of that segment of the electronics industry. They also are considering ways to stimulate "cutting-edge" research in superconductivity. These efforts are likely to spur innovation and stimulate progress in the electronics industry.

Second, a definition of industry boundaries focuses attention on the firm's competitors. Defining industry boundaries enables the firm to identify its competitors and producers of substitute products. This is critically important to the firm's design of its competitive strategy.

Third, a definition of industry boundaries helps executives determine key factors for success. Survival in the premier segment of the microcomputer industry requires skills that are considerably different from those required in the lower end of the industry. Firms that compete in the premier segment need to be on the cutting edge of technological development and to provide extensive customer support and education. On the other hand, firms that compete in the lower end need to excel in imitating the products introduced by the premier segment, to focus on customer convenience, and to maintain operational efficiency that permits them to charge the lowest market price. Defining industry boundaries enables executives to ask these questions: Do we have the skills it takes to succeed here? If not, what must we do to develop these skills?

Finally, a definition of industry boundaries gives executives another basis on which to evaluate their firm's goals. Executives use that definition to forecast demand for their firm's products and services. Armed with that forecast, they can determine whether those goals are realistic.

Problems in Defining Industry Boundaries

Defining industry boundaries requires both caution and imagination. Caution is necessary because there are no precise rules for this task and because a poor definition will lead to poor planning. Imagination is necessary because industries are dynamic—in every industry, important changes are under way in such key factors as competition, technology, and consumer demand.

Defining industry boundaries is a very difficult task. The difficulty stems from three sources:

1. The evolution of industries over time creates new opportunities and threats. Compare the financial services industry as we know it today with that of the 1990s, and then try to imagine how different the industry will be in the year 2020.

2. Industrial evolution creates industries within industries. The electronics industry of the 1960s has been transformed into many "industries"—TV sets, transistor radios, micro and macrocomputers, supercomputers, superconductors, and so on. Such transformation allows some firms to specialize and others to compete in different, related industries.

3. Industries are becoming global in scope. Consider the civilian aircraft manufacturing industry. For nearly three decades, U.S. firms dominated world production in that industry. But small and large competitors were challenging their dominance by 1990. At that time, Airbus Industries (a consortium of European firms) and Brazilian, Korean, and Japanese firms were actively competing in the industry.

Developing a Realistic Industry Definition

Given the difficulties just outlined, how do executives draw accurate boundaries for an industry? The starting point is a definition of the industry in global terms; that is, in terms that consider the industry's international components as well as its domestic components.

Having developed a preliminary concept of the industry (e.g., computers), executives flesh out its current components. This can be done by defining its product segments. Executives need to select the scope of their firm's potential market from among these related but distinct areas.

To understand the makeup of the industry, executives adopt a longitudinal perspective. They examine the emergence and evolution of product families. Why did these product families arise? How and why did they change? The answers to such questions provide executives with clues about the factors that drive competition in the industry.

Executives also examine the companies that offer different product families, the overlapping or distinctiveness of customer segments, and the rate of substitutability among product families.

To realistically define their industry, executives need to examine five issues:

1. Which part of the industry corresponds to our firm's goals?
2. What are the key ingredients of success in that part of the industry?
3. Does our firm have the skills needed to compete in that part of the industry? If not, can we build those skills?
4. Will the skills enable us to seize emerging opportunities and deal with future threats?
5. Is our definition of the industry flexible enough to allow necessary adjustments to our business concept as the industry grows?

Industry Structure

structural attributes
The enduring characteristics that give an industry its distinctive character.

Defining an industry's boundaries is incomplete without an understanding of its structural attributes. **Structural attributes** are the enduring characteristics that give an industry its distinctive character. Consider the cable television and financial services industries. Both industries are competitive, and both are important for our quality of life. But these industries have very different requirements for success. To succeed in the cable television industry, firms require vertical integration, which helps them lower their operating costs and ensures their access to quality programs; technological innovation, to enlarge the scope of their services and deliver them in new ways; and extensive marketing, using appropriate segmentation techniques to locate potentially viable niches. To succeed in the financial services industry, firms need to meet very different requirements, among which are extensive orientation of customers and an extensive capital base.

How can we explain such variations among industries? The answer lies in examining the four variables that industry comprises: (1) concentration, (2) economies of scale (discussed earlier), (3) product differentiation, and (4) barriers to entry.

Concentration

concentration
The extent to which industry sales are dominated by a few firms.

Concentration refers to the extent to which industry sales are dominated by only a few firms. In a highly concentrated industry (i.e., an industry whose sales are dominated by a handful of companies), the intensity of competition declines over time. High concentration serves as a barrier to entry into an industry because it enables the firms that hold large market shares to achieve significant economies of scale (e.g., savings in production costs due to increased production quantities) and, thus, to lower their prices to stymie attempts of new firms to enter the market.

The U.S. aircraft manufacturing industry is highly concentrated. Its concentration ratio—the percent of market share held by the top four firms in the industry—is 67 percent. Competition in the industry has not been vigorous. Firms in the industry have been able to deter entry through proprietary technologies and the formation of strategic alliances (e.g., joint ventures).

Product Differentiation

This variable refers to the extent to which customers perceive products or services offered by firms in the industry as different.

The differentiation of products can be real or perceived. The differentiation between Apple's Macintosh and IBM's PS/2 Personal Computer was a prime example of real differentiation. These products differed significantly in their technology and performance. Similarly, the civilian aircraft models produced by Boeing differed markedly from those produced by Airbus. The differences resulted from the use of different design principles and different construction technologies. For example, the newer Airbus planes followed the principle of "fly by wire," whereas Boeing planes utilized the laws of hydraulics. Thus, in Boeing planes, wings were activated by mechanical handling of different parts of the plane, whereas in the Airbus planes, this was done almost automatically.

Perceived differentiation results from the way in which firms position their products and from their success in persuading customers that their products differ significantly from competing products. Marketing strategies provide the vehicles through which this is done. Witness, for example, the extensive advertising campaigns of the automakers, each of which attempts to convey an image of distinctiveness. BMW ads highlight the excellent engineering of the BMW and its symbolic value as a sign of achievement. Some automakers focus on roominess and durability, which are desirable attributes for the family segment of the automobile market.

Real and perceived differentiations often intensify competition among existing firms. On the other hand, successful differentiation poses a competitive disadvantage for firms that attempt to enter an industry.

Barriers to Entry

barriers to entry
The conditions that a firm must satisfy to enter an industry.

Barriers to entry are the obstacles that a firm must overcome to enter an industry. The barriers can be tangible or intangible. The tangible barriers include capital requirements, technological know-how, resources, and the laws regulating entry into an industry. The intangible barriers include the reputation of existing firms, the loyalty of consumers to existing brands, and access to the managerial skills required for successful operation in an industry.

Entry barriers both increase and reflect the level of concentration, economies of scale, and product differentiation in an industry, and such increases make it more difficult for new firms to enter the industry. Therefore, when high barriers exist in an industry, competition in that industry declines over time.

In summary, analysis of concentration, economies of scale, product differentiation, and barriers to entry in an industry enable a firm's executives to understand the forces that determine competition in an industry and set the stage for identifying the firm's competitors and how they position themselves in the marketplace.

Industry regulations are a key element of industry structure and can constitute a significant barrier to entry for corporations. Escalating regulatory standards costs have been a serious concern for corporations for years. As legislative bodies continue their stronghold on corporate activities, businesses feel the impact on their bottom line. In-house counsel departments have been perhaps the most significant additions to corporate structure in the past decade. Legal fees have skyrocketed and managers have learned the hard way about the importance of adhering to regulatory standards.

Competitive Analysis

How to Identify Competitors

In identifying their firm's current and potential competitors, executives consider several important variables:

1. How do other firms define the scope of their market? The more similar the definitions of firms, the more likely the firms will view each other as competitors.

2. How similar are the benefits the customers derive from the products and services that other firms offer? The more similar the benefits of products or services, the higher the level of substitutability between them. High substitutability levels force firms to compete fiercely for customers.

3. How committed are other firms to the industry? Although this question may appear to be far removed from the identification of competitors, it is in fact one of the most important questions that competitive analysis must address, because it sheds light on the long-term intentions and goals. To size up the commitment of potential competitors to the industry, reliable intelligence data are needed. Such data may relate to potential resource commitments (e.g., planned facility expansions).

Common Mistakes in Identifying Competitors

Identifying competitors is a milestone in the development of strategy. But it is a process laden with uncertainty and risk, a process in which executives sometimes make costly mistakes. Examples of these mistakes are:

1. Overemphasizing current and known competitors while giving inadequate attention to potential entrants.

2. Overemphasizing large competitors while ignoring small competitors.

3. Overlooking potential international competitors.

4. Assuming that competitors will continue to behave in the same way they have behaved in the past.

5. Misreading signals that may indicate a shift in the focus of competitors or a refinement of their present strategies or tactics.

6. Overemphasizing competitors' financial resources, market position, and strategies while ignoring their intangible assets, such as a top management team.

7. Assuming that all of the firms in the industry are subject to the same constraints or are open to the same opportunities.

8. Believing that the purpose of strategy is to outsmart the competition, rather than to satisfy customer needs and expectations.

OPERATING ENVIRONMENT

operating environment
Factors in the immediate competitive situation that affect a firm's success in acquiring needed resources.

The **operating environment,** also called the *competitive* or *task environment,* comprises factors in the competitive situation that affect a firm's success in acquiring needed resources or in profitably marketing its goods and services. Among the most important of these factors are the firm's competitive position, the composition of its customers, its reputation among suppliers and creditors, and its ability to attract capable employees. The operating environment is typically much more subject to the firm's influence or control than the remote environment. Thus, firms can be much more proactive (as opposed to reactive) in dealing with the operating environment than in dealing with the remote environment.

Competitive Position

Assessing its competitive position improves a firm's chances of designing strategies that optimize its environmental opportunities. Development of competitor profiles enables a firm to more accurately forecast both its short- and long-term growth and its profit potentials. Although the exact criteria used in constructing a competitor's profile are largely determined by situational factors, the following criteria are often included:

1. Market share.
2. Breadth of product line.
3. Effectiveness of sales distribution.
4. Proprietary and key account advantages.
5. Price competitiveness.
6. Advertising and promotion effectiveness.
7. Location and age of facility.
8. Capacity and productivity.
9. Experience.
10. Raw materials costs.
11. Financial position.
12. Relative product quality.
13. R&D advantages position.
14. Caliber of personnel.
15. General images.
16. Customer profile.
17. Patents and copyrights.
18. Union relations.
19. Technological position.
20. Community reputation.

Once appropriate criteria have been selected, they are weighted to reflect their importance to a firm's success. Then the competitor being evaluated is rated on the criteria, the ratings are multiplied by the weight, and the weighted scores are summed to yield a numerical profile of the competitor, as shown in Exhibit 4.10.

This type of competitor profile is limited by the subjectivity of its criteria selection, weighting, and evaluation approaches. Nevertheless, the process of developing such profiles is of considerable help to a firm in defining its perception of its competitive position. Moreover, comparing the firm's profile with those of its competitors can aid its managers in identifying factors that might make the competitors vulnerable to the strategies the firm might choose to implement.

Customer Profiles

Perhaps the most vulnerable result of analyzing the operating environment is the understanding of a firm's customers that this provides. Developing a profile of a firm's present and prospective customers improves the ability of its managers to plan strategic operations,

EXHIBIT 4.10
Competitor Profile

Key Success Factors	Weight	Rating*	Weighted Score
Market share	0.30	4	1.20
Price competitiveness	0.20	3	0.60
Facilities location	0.20	5	1.00
Raw materials costs	0.10	3	0.30
Caliber of personnel	0.20	1	0.20
	1.00†		3.30

*The rating scale suggested is as follows: very strong competitive position (5 points), strong (4), average (3), weak (2), very weak (1).
†The total of the weights must always equal 1.00.

to anticipate changes in the size of markets, and to reallocate resources so as to support forecast shifts in demand patterns. The traditional approach to segmenting customers is based on customer profiles constructed from geographic, demographic, psychographic, and buyer behavior information.

Enterprising companies have quickly learned the importance of identifying target segments. In recent years, market research has increased tremendously as companies realize the benefits of demographic and psychographic segmentation. Research by American Express (AMEX) showed that competitors were stealing a prime segment of the company's business, affluent business travelers. AMEX's competing companies, including Visa and Mastercard, began offering high-spending business travelers frequent flier programs and other rewards including discounts on new cars. In turn, AMEX began to invest heavily in rewards programs, while also focusing on its strongest capabilities, assets, and competitive advantage. Unlike most credit card companies, AMEX cannot rely on charging interest to make money because its customers pay in full each month. Therefore, the company charges higher transaction fees to its merchants. In this way, increases in spending by AMEX customers who pay off their balances each month are more profitable to AMEX than to competing credit card companies.

Assessing consumer behavior is a key element in the process of satisfying your target market needs. Many firms lose market share as a result of assumptions made about target segments. Market research and industry surveys can help to reduce a firm's chances of relying on illusive assumptions. Firms most vulnerable are those that have had success with one or more products in the marketplace and as a result try to base consumer behavior on past data and trends.

Geographic

It is important to define the geographic area from which customers do or could come. Almost every product or service has some quality that makes it variably attractive to buyers from different locations. Obviously, a Wisconsin manufacturer of snow skis should think twice about investing in a wholesale distribution center in South Carolina. On the other hand, advertising in the *Milwaukee Journal-Sentinel* could significantly expand the geographically defined customer market of a major Myrtle Beach hotel in South Carolina.

Demographic

Demographic variables most commonly are used to differentiate groups of present or potential customers. Demographic information (e.g., information on sex, age, marital status, income, and occupation) is comparatively easy to collect, quantify, and use in strategic forecasting, and such information is the minimum basis for a customer profile.

Psychographic

Personality and lifestyle variables often are better predictors of customer purchasing behavior than geographic or demographic variables. In such situations, a psychographic study is an important component of the customer profile. Advertising campaigns by soft-drink producers—Pepsi-Cola ("the Pepsi generation"), Coca-Cola ("the real thing"), and 7UP ("America's turning 7UP")—reflect strategic management's attention to the psychographic characteristics of their largest customer segment—physically active, group-oriented non-professionals.

Buyer Behavior

Buyer behavior data also can be a component of the customer profile. Such data are used to explain or predict some aspect of customer behavior with regard to a product or service. Information on buyer behavior (e.g., usage rate, benefits sought, and brand loyalty) can provide significant aid in the design of more accurate and profitable strategies.

Suppliers

Dependable relationships between a firm and its suppliers are essential to the firm's long-term survival and growth. A firm regularly relies on its suppliers for financial support, services, materials, and equipment. In addition, it occasionally is forced to make special requests for such favors as quick delivery, liberal credit terms, or broken-lot orders. Particularly at such times, it is essential for a firm to have had an ongoing relationship with its suppliers.

In the assessment of a firm's relationships with its suppliers, several factors, other than the strength of that relationship, should be considered. With regard to its competitive position with its suppliers, the firm should address the following questions:

Are the suppliers' prices competitive? Do the suppliers offer attractive quantity discounts?

How costly are their shipping charges? Are the suppliers competitive in terms of production standards?

In terms of deficiency rates, are the suppliers' abilities, reputations, and services competitive?

Are the suppliers reciprocally dependent on the firm?

Creditors

Because the quantity, quality, price, and accessibility of financial, human, and material resources are rarely ideal, assessment of suppliers and creditors is critical to an accurate evaluation of a firm's operating environment. With regard to its competitive position with its creditors, among the most important questions that the firm should address are the following:

Do the creditors fairly value and willingly accept the firm's stock as collateral?

Do the creditors perceive the firm as having an acceptable record of past payment? A strong working capital position? Little or no leverage?

Are the creditors' loan terms compatible with the firm's profitability objectives?

Are the creditors able to extend the necessary lines of credit?

The answers to these and related questions help a firm forecast the availability of the resources it will need to implement and sustain its competitive strategies.

Human Resources: Nature of the Labor Market

A firm's ability to attract and hold capable employees is essential to its success. However, a firm's personnel recruitment and selection alternatives often are influenced by the nature of its operating environment. A firm's access to needed personnel is affected primarily by four factors: the firm's reputation as an employer, local employment rates, the ready availability of people with the needed skills, and its relationship with labor unions.

Reputation

A firm's reputation within its operating environment is a major element of its ability to satisfy its personnel needs. A firm is more likely to attract and retain valuable employees if it is seen as permanent in the community, competitive in its compensation package, and concerned with the welfare of its employees, and if it is respected for its product or service and appreciated for its overall contribution to the general welfare.

Employment Rates

The readily available supply of skilled and experienced personnel may vary considerably with the stage of a community's growth. A new manufacturing firm would find it far more difficult to obtain skilled employees in a vigorous industrialized community than in an economically depressed community in which similar firms had recently cut back operations.

Availability

The skills of some people are so specialized that relocation may be necessary to secure the jobs and the compensation that those skills commonly command. People with such skills include oil drillers, chefs, technical specialists, and industry executives. A firm that seeks to hire such a person is said to have broad labor market boundaries; that is, the geographic area within which the firm might reasonably expect to attract qualified candidates is quite large. On the other hand, people with more common skills are less likely to relocate from a considerable distance to achieve modest economic or career advancements. Thus, the labor market boundaries are fairly limited for such occupational groups as unskilled laborers, clerical personnel, and retail clerks.

Many manufacturers in the United States attempt to minimize the labor cost disadvantage they face in competing with overseas producers by outsourcing to lower-cost foreign locations or by hiring immigrant workers. Similarly, companies in construction and other labor-intensive industries try to provide themselves with a cost advantage by hiring temporary, often migrant, workers. An example of the sophistication of such worker location efforts is described in Exhibit 4.11, Strategy in Action.

Labor Unions

Approximately 12 percent of all workers in the United States belong to a labor union; the percentages are higher in Japan and western Europe at about 25 and 40 percent, respectively, and extremely low in developing nations. Unions represent the workers in their negotiations with employers through the process of collective bargaining. When managers' relationships with their employees are complicated by the involvement of a union, the company's ability to manage and motivate the people that it needs can be compromised.

EMPHASIS ON ENVIRONMENTAL FACTORS

This chapter has described the remote, industry, and operating environments as encompassing five components each. While that description is generally accurate, it may give the false impression that the components are easily identified, mutually exclusive, and equally applicable in all situations. In fact, the forces in the external environment are so dynamic and interactive that the impact of any single element cannot be wholly disassociated from the effect of other elements. For example, are increases in OPEC oil prices the result of economic, political, social, or technological changes? Or are a manufacturer's surprisingly good relations with suppliers a result of competitors', customers', or creditors' activities or

Click for Foreign Labor:
Companies Are Using Online Middlemen to Find Legal Workers

BusinessWeek

When she could not find enough workers for the construction firm owned by her son Thomas, Ann Carroll decided to go online. After typing in such search terms as "construction laborer" and "Mexican workers," she landed on the Web site for Labormex Foreign Labor Solutions. Within days she had a quote: $100 each for 11 Mexican workers and $1,340 to cover the visas. In October, Carroll Construction Co.'s recruits began laying sewer pipes in Ocean Springs, Mississippi, where the company is located. "I don't know what we would've done if we didn't go this route," says Carroll. "We're very happy with the workers."

Amid a federal crackdown on illegal immigration—including the December 2006 arrest of 1,282 Swift & Co. meatpacking workers—and a roiling political debate over expanding guest-worker programs, companies are turning to online middlemen to find legitimate foreign laborers. Job sites such as Monster.com and CareerBuilder.com have been helping companies scour the globe for white-collar talent since the late 1990s. Now unskilled workers, too, are a few clicks away, a boon for such chronically labor-starved industries as construction, agriculture, and catering.

Labormex was founded in 2002 by Seymour Taylor, an entrepreneur descended from a family of American settlers in Mexico. Business took off when he set up a Web site about a year ago and began advertising on Yahoo! and Google. The site boasts of "hardworking people acclimated to tough physical labor and who have worked under severe warm-weather conditions"—guys like Andreas Alcala Martinez, 29, who works for Carroll Construction. "Little money, but not hard work," says Martinez. He makes $9 an hour and arrived on an H-2B visa, of which the United States. issues 66,000 annually for low-skilled work. He can work for Carroll for 10 months, with the option of renewal.

Next to the big job sites, Labormex is a minnow. Taylor says he placed about 200 people in 2006 and expects to triple that in 2007. But the company, which has offices in New York and Monterrey, Mexico, has reeled in big clients, including Super 8 Motels and the Sonic Drive-Ins fast-food chain.

The U.S. Department of Labor lists hundreds of officially sanctioned recruiting agencies on its Web site. The online recruiters are already providing ammunition for immigration critics. "They're getting employers addicted to a supply of cheap labor and lowering incentives for them to look for domestic workers," says Jessica M. Vaughn, a senior policy analyst at the Center for Immigration Studies, which opposes expanding guest-worker programs. But with many Americans unwilling to mow lawns, build houses, and wait tables, many companies see online recruiters as a necessary way to tap a labor pool that is increasingly global.

Source: Reprinted with special permission from Moira Herbst, "Click for Foreign Labor," *BusinessWeek,* January 15, 2007. Copyright © 2007 The McGraw-Hill Companies.

of the supplier's own activities? The answer to both questions is probably that a number of forces in the external environment have combined to create the situation. Such is the case in most studies of the environment.

Strategic managers are frequently frustrated in their attempts to anticipate the environment's changing influences. Different external elements affect different strategies at different times and with varying strengths. The only certainty is that the effect of the remote and operating environments will be uncertain until a strategy is implemented. This leads many managers, particularly in less powerful or smaller firms to minimize long-term planning, which requires a commitment of resources. Instead, they favor allowing managers to adapt to new pressures from the environment. While such a decision has considerable merit for many firms, there is an associated trade-off, namely that absence of a strong resource and psychological commitment to a proactive strategy effectively bars a firm from assuming a leadership role in its competitive environment.

There is yet another difficulty in assessing the probable impact of remote, industry, and operating environments on the effectiveness of alternative strategies. Assessment of this kind involves collecting information that can be analyzed to disclose predictable effects.

EXHIBIT 4.12
Strategic Forecasting
Issues

Key Issues in the Remote Environment Economy

What are the probable future directions of the economies in the firm's regional, national, and international market? What changes in economic growth, inflation, interest rates, capital availability, credit availability, and consumer purchasing power can be expected? What income differences can be expected between the wealthy upper middle class, the working class, and the underclass in various regions? What shifts in relative demand for different categories of goods and services can be expected?

Society and demographics

What effects will changes in social values and attitudes regarding childbearing, marriage, lifestyle, work, ethics, sex roles, racial equality, education, retirement, pollution, and energy have on the firm's development? What effects will population changes have on major social and political expectations—at home and abroad? What constraints or opportunities will develop? What pressure groups will increase in power?

Ecology

What natural or pollution-caused disasters threaten the firm's employees, customers, or facilities? How rigorously will existing environment legislature be enforced? What new federal, state, and local laws will affect the firm, and in what ways?

Politics

What changes in government policy can be expected with regard to industry cooperation, antitrust activities, foreign trade, taxation, depreciation, environmental protection, deregulation, defense, foreign trade barriers, and other important parameters? What success will a new administration have in achieving its stated goals? What effect will that success have on the firm? Will specific international climates be hostile or favorable? Is there a tendency toward instability, corruption, or violence? What is the level of political risk in each foreign market? What other political or legal constraints or supports can be expected in international business (e.g., trade barriers, equity requirements, nationalism, patent protection)?

Technology

What is the current state of the art? How will it change? What pertinent new products or services are likely to become technically feasible in the foreseeable future? What future impact can be expected from technological breakthroughs in related product areas? How will those breakthroughs interface with the other remote considerations, such as economic issues, social values, public safety, regulations, and court interpretations?

Key Issues in the Industry Environment

New entrants

Will new technologies or market demands enable competitors to minimize the impact of traditional economies of scale in the industry? Will consumers accept our claims of product or service differentiation? Will potential new entrants be able to match the capital requirements that currently exist? How permanent are the cost disadvantages (independent of size) in our industry? Will conditions change so that all competitors have equal access to marketing channels? Is government policy toward competition in our industry likely to change?

Bargaining power of suppliers

How stable are the size and composition of our supplier group? Are any suppliers likely to attempt forward integration into our business level? How dependent will our suppliers be in the future? Are substitute suppliers likely to become available? Could we become our own supplier?

EXHIBIT 4.12
(continued)

Substitute products or services

Are new substitutes likely? Will they be price competitive? Could we fight off substitutes by price competition? By advertising to sharpen product differentiation? What actions could we take to reduce the potential for having alternative products seen as legitimate substitutes?

Bargaining power of buyers

Can we break free of overcommitment to a few large buyers? How would our buyers react to attempts by us to differentiate our products? What possibilities exist that our buyers might vertically integrate backward? Should we consider forward integration? How can we make the value of our components greater in the products of our buyers?

Rivalry among existing firms

Are major competitors likely to undo the established balance of power in our industry? Is growth in our industry slowing such that competition will become fiercer? What excess capacity exists in our industry? How capable are our major competitors of withstanding intensified price competition? How unique are the objectives and strategies of our major competitors?

Key Issues in the Operating Environment

Competitive position

What strategic moves are expected by existing rivals—inside and outside the United States? What competitive advantage is necessary in selected foreign markets? What will be our competitors' priorities and ability to change? Is the behavior of our competitors predictable?

Customer profiles and market changes

What will our customer regard as needed value? Is marketing research done, or do managers talk to each other to discover what the customer wants? Which customer needs are not being met by existing products? Why? Are R&D activities under way to develop means for fulfilling these needs? What is the status of these activities? What marketing and distribution channels should we use? What do demographic and population changes portend for the size and sales potential of our market? What new market segments or products might develop as a result of these changes? What will be the buying power of our customer groups?

Supplier relationships

What is the likelihood of major cost increases because of dwindling supplies of a needed natural resource? Will sources of supply, especially of energy, be reliable? Are there reasons to expect major changes in the cost or availability of inputs as a result of money, people, or subassembly problems? Which suppliers can be expected to respond to emergency requests?

Creditors

What lines of credit are available to help finance our growth? What changes may occur in our creditworthiness? Are creditors likely to feel comfortable with our strategic plan and performance? What is the stock market likely to feel about our firm? What flexibility would our creditors show toward us during a downturn? Do we have sufficient cash reserves to protect our creditors and our credit rating?

Labor market

Are potential employees with desired skills and abilities available in the geographic areas in which our facilities are located? Are colleges and vocational/technical schools that can aid in meeting our training needs located near our plant or store sites? Are labor relations in our industry conducive to meeting our expanding needs for employees? Are workers whose skills we need shifting toward or away from the geographic location of our facilities?

Except in rare instances, however, it is virtually impossible for any single firm to anticipate the consequences of a change in the environment; for example, what is the precise effect on alternative strategies of a 2 percent increase in the national inflation rate, a 1 percent decrease in statewide unemployment, or the entry of a new competitor in a regional market?

Still, assessing the potential impact of changes in the external environment offers a real advantage. It enables decision makers to narrow the range of the available options and to eliminate options that are clearly inconsistent with the forecast opportunities. Environmental assessment seldom identifies the best strategy, but it generally leads to the elimination of all but the most promising options.

Exhibit 4.12 provides a set of key strategic forecasting issues for each level of environmental assessment—remote, industry, and operating. While the issues that are presented are not inclusive of all of the questions that are important, they provide an excellent set of questions with which to begin. Chapter 4 Appendix, Sources for Environmental Forecasting, is provided to help identify valuable sources of data and information from which answers and subsequent forecasts can be constructed. It lists governmental and private marketplace intelligence that can be used by a firm to gain a foothold in undertaking a strategic assessment of any level of the competitive environment.

Summary

A firm's external environment consists of three interrelated sets of factors that play a principal role in determining the opportunities, threats, and constraints that the firm faces. The remote environment comprises factors originating beyond, and usually irrespective of, any single firm's operating situation—economic, social, political, technological, and ecological factors. Factors that more directly influence a firm's prospects originate in the environment of its industry, including entry barriers, competitor rivalry, the availability of substitutes, and the bargaining power of buyers and suppliers. The operating environment comprises factors that influence a firm's immediate competitive situation—competitive position, customer profiles, suppliers, creditors, and the labor market. These three sets of factors provide many of the challenges that a particular firm faces in its attempts to attract or acquire needed resources and to profitably market its goods and services. Environmental assessment is more complicated for multinational corporations (MNCs) than for domestic firms because multinationals must evaluate several environments simultaneously.

Thus, the design of business strategies is based on the conviction that a firm able to anticipate future business conditions will improve its performance and profitability. Despite the uncertainty and dynamic nature of the business environment, an assessment process that narrows, even if it does not precisely define, future expectations is of substantial value to strategic managers.

Key Terms

barriers to entry, *p. 114*
concentration, *p. 114*
eco-efficiency, *p. 101*
ecology, *p. 99*
economies of scale, *p. 106*

external environment, *p. 94*
industry, *p. 112*
industry environment, *p. 102*
operating environment, *p. 116*
pollution, *p. 99*

product differentiation, *p. 106*
remote environment, *p. 94*
structural attributes, *p. 113*
technological
forecasting, *p. 98*

Questions for Discussion

1. Briefly describe two important recent changes in the remote environment of U.S. business in each of the following areas:
   a. Economic.
   b. Social.
   c. Political.
   d. Technological.
   e. Ecological.

2. Describe two major environmental changes that you expect to have a major impact on the wholesale food industry in the next 10 years.
3. Develop a competitor profile for your college and for the college geographically closest to yours. Next, prepare a brief strategic plan to improve the competitive position of the weaker of the two colleges.
4. Assume the invention of a competitively priced synthetic fuel that could supply 25 percent of U.S. energy needs within 20 years. In what major ways might this change the external environment of U.S. business?
5. With your instructor's help, identify a local firm that has enjoyed great growth in recent years. To what degree and in what ways do you think this firm's success resulted from taking advantage of favorable conditions in its remote, industry, and operating environments?
6. Choose a specific industry and, relying solely on your impressions, evaluate the impact of the five forces that drive competition in that industry.
7. Choose an industry in which you would like to compete. Use the five-forces method of analysis to explain why you find that industry attractive.
8. Many firms neglect industry analysis. When does this hurt them? When does it not?
9. The model below depicts industry analysis as a funnel that focuses on remote-factor analysis to better understand the impact of factors in the operating environment. Do you find this model satisfactory? If not, how would you improve it?

10. Who in a firm should be responsible for industry analysis? Assume that the firm does not have a strategic planning department.

Chapter 4 Discussion Case

Siemens' Culture Clash

BusinessWeek

1 If things had turned out a little differently, Siemens Chief Executive Klaus Kleinfeld might already be on his way to executive stardom, like his role model Jack Welch. Just two years after Kleinfeld took over the Munich electronics and engineering behemoth, Siemens is on track to hit its aggressive internal earnings targets for the first time since 2000. In fact, it is expanding both sales and profits faster than Welch's former fiefdom, General Electric Co. What's more, the company has a larger presence than GE in rapid-growth markets such as India.

2 But instead of literary agents breaking down his door in pursuit of a tome of management wisdom, Kleinfeld has angry employees demonstrating outside his window. He has gotten little applause for boosting 2006 sales by 16 percent and profits by 35 percent, and he faces questions about a bribery scandal that has sapped his authority even though he is not personally implicated.

3 Transforming Siemens was never going to be easy. With branches in 190 countries and $114 billion in sales last year, the company has long been respected for its engineering prowess but derided for its sluggishness. And Germany Inc., with its long-standing tradition of labor harmony and powerful workers' councils, is highly resistant to the kind of change Kleinfeld has tried to implement. That's one reason Siemens lags seriously in overall profits, with a margin of 3.5 percent compared with 12.6 percent for GE. Kleinfeld concedes that some people doubt Siemens can change its ways, but he counters: "It took less time than we originally planned to get that growth momentum started."

4 Against the odds, in just two years Kleinfeld has managed a mighty restructuring. He has quoted the management precepts of Welch and has drawn on the GE playbook to realign Siemens as the world's leading provider of such infrastructure as airports, power plants, and medical equipment. He has pushed Siemens' 475,000 employees to make decisions faster and focus as much on customers as on technology. He spun off underperforming telecommunications-gear businesses and simplified the company's structure. And when one group of managers failed to deliver, he broke up an entire division.

RESPECT AND RESENTMENT

5 Although restructuring has dominated his tenure, Kleinfeld isn't just a cost-cutter. If you want to make his eyes light up, say "megatrends." The 49-year-old believes Siemens is perfectly positioned to profit from huge global shifts in population and wealth, and he spent $8.6 billion last year on acquisitions in areas such as medical diagnostics and wind power. As people in the developing world get richer, he says, Siemens will supply CT and MRI scanners to diagnose their ills. It will build switching systems and engines for their trains and subways. And it will sell them water-purification equipment, power plants, and machines to run mines and factories. Barely a day goes by without Siemens announcing orders to modernize a steel mill in Russia, build a cement plant in Yemen, or set up a desalination operation in Pakistan. Says Kleinfeld: "This company is solving the biggest issues this planet has."

6 Investors have warmed to Kleinfeld's vision. Siemens shares have risen 26 percent in the two years since he took over versus 6 percent for GE. But his tactics have made him a target for German resentment of globalization and the perceived heartlessness of U.S.-style management methods. When, in an attempt at openness, Kleinfeld invited workers to respond to his blog, they did—in spades. "I used to feel good in the Siemens family," one employee wrote. "But there's not much of that feeling left."

7 More alarming, Siemens is the target of an expanding investigation by Munich prosecutors. In the probe of alleged bribes to foreign officials to win telecommunications contracts, authorities briefly jailed a former member of Siemens' executive board and many lower-ranking managers. Siemens admits that as much as $546 million may have been misused. Kleinfeld, who was stationed in the United States during much of the time the alleged misconduct took place, has not been identified as a target of the investigation and has taken measures to prevent future scandals. He has hired a former senior German prosecutor to serve as compliance officer and retained an outside law firm to conduct an independent inquiry. Munich prosecutors say Siemens is cooperating in the bribery probe. That hasn't stopped some shareholder activists from criticizing Kleinfeld's handling of the crisis, and he is sure to come under fire when the company holds its annual meeting in Munich on January 25, 2007. Shareholder groups have already filed motions to withhold approval of the Siemens management board, normally a formality in Germany.

8 The pressure is apt to grow. Siemens says it expects the U.S. Securities & Exchange Commission to investigate, potentially exposing the company to hundreds of millions of dollars in fines. But unless new and far more damaging revelations arise, Kleinfeld is unlikely to be forced out. Still, the crisis has become a distraction. "Yes, it is taking part of my time," says Kleinfeld, who has offloaded some responsibilities to other members of the management board as a result.

9 If Kleinfeld is worried, though, he isn't showing it. A few weeks after Munich prosecutors seized documents from 30 Siemens locations—including his office—Kleinfeld seems relaxed and self-assured. Never mind that in a waiting room a few feet from his door, headlines on a stack of newspapers arrayed neatly on a table blare the latest news on the scandal. He yawns occasionally, the only sign of fatigue.

10 Provided Kleinfeld weathers all the turbulence, he still has the potential to emerge as one of Europe's most dynamic chief executives. With an eye to his German critics, Kleinfeld these days deflects comparisons to Welch. But it's hard not to see some of the former GE chief's energy and competitive spirit—not to mention impatience—in Kleinfeld. He rises before dawn to jog and often barrages subordinates with phone calls and e-mails late into the night. "If you turn off your phone, he calls your wife," says one manager who counts himself a Kleinfeld admirer. Siemens executives know that an e-mail ending with the word bitte ("please") means get it done now—or else. "I wonder when that guy sleeps," says Hermann Requardt, Siemens' chief of research and development.

HAPPY IN THE HEARTLAND

11 Kleinfeld downplays the influence of his three years in the United States, a stint ordinary Germans view as a blot on his résumé. There's no question, though, that he counts those years among his best. "I liked it over there," says Kleinfeld, who served as CEO of Siemens' U.S. operations in 2002 and 2003. "Wherever I went, I made friends." And to this day, Kleinfeld's style is decidedly less German-centric than that of his predecessor, Heinrich von Pierer. Von Pierer played tennis with the Chancellor. Kleinfeld runs the New York Marathon. Von Pierer served on a half-dozen boards of German companies. Kleinfeld does so for Citigroup, Alcoa, and the New York Metropolitan Opera. Von Pierer speaks English well but prefers German. Kleinfeld is totally fluent in English.

12 His affection for the United States comes naturally, perhaps because Kleinfeld personifies the American ideal of the self-made man. He was 10 when his father died, and by the age of 12 he was working in a supermarket and taking on other part-time jobs to help make ends meet. Later, while working full-time at Siemens, he completed his doctoral work on corporate communications strategy, which was published as a book.

13 Today, Kleinfeld is as comfortable hobnobbing with global leaders as he is chatting with entry-level employees.

September 2006 found him speaking about climate change at the Clinton Global Initiative in New York, then meeting workers in a nearby suburb.

14   He also knows how to enjoy himself. In December 2006, Kleinfeld danced the night away at a Christmas party for U.S. employees at New York's B.B. King Blues Club. He even plays a decent blues harmonica, though never in public.

15   One of Kleinfeld's problems is that few inside Siemens can match his energy. The Old Guard tend to grumble that Kleinfeld is too impatient and demanding. Soon after taking office in January 2005, he vowed that Siemens would finally achieve ambitious profit-margin goals established in 2000 for each unit. The targets range from 6 percent for auto parts to 13 percent for the top-performing medical-equipment division. Kleinfeld staked his job on the company hitting those numbers by April 2007—which now looks likely, analysts say. His message: everyone, including the boss, is accountable. "We commit to something, and we deliver," Kleinfeld says. "That is the culture we want to form."

16   Communicating that culture change across such a sprawling enterprise is a massive challenge. The company's 11 main business units operate almost as separate entities, with their own boards and distinct corporate cultures, making it hard for directives from the top to filter down to the troops. One executive says Kleinfeld's biggest impact so far has been increased pressure to speak English throughout the company—hardly an earth-shattering reform. And while Siemens excels at technological breakthroughs, such as mobile phones with built-in music players, they have often failed because of poor marketing and a lack of focus on the consumers who use the products. So how do you persuade Siemens' vaunted engineers to pay more attention to customers? Kleinfeld declared that he would personally visit Siemens' 100 biggest clients in his first 100 days in office. He wound up meeting more than 300 of them.

17   Kleinfeld isn't shy about administering harsh medicine when he feels it's needed. That's something new at the 159-year-old company. At the end of 2005, it became clear that the Logistics & Assembly Systems Division, which made products such as sorting equipment used by the U.S. Postal Service, would deliver only a 2 percent profit margin. Most unpardonable in Kleinfeld's eyes was that the unit's managers waited too long to alert him to the problem. So Kleinfeld transferred the most profitable parts of the division, such as baggage-handling systems for airports, to other parts of Siemens. The rest was sold. Within weeks, an entire Siemens division with $1.9 billion in annual sales was vaporized. Around Siemens, there was a collective gasp.

TOSSING OUT TELECOM

18   He has been equally tough on some sacred pieces of the Siemens empire. Founder Werner von Siemens made his name laying intercontinental telegraph lines in the mid-1800s, but that didn't stop Kleinfeld from getting rid of communications businesses. He paid Taiwan's BenQ Corp. to take the money-losing mobile-phone division off his hands at a total cost to Siemens of $1.4 billion. And he put most of Siemens' telecommunications-equipment business into a joint venture run by Finland's Nokia Corp. But the Nokia deal has been delayed until questions about the bribery scandal are cleared up. In September 2006, BenQ declared the German handset unit insolvent. Although Kleinfeld insists he thought it had a future under BenQ, workers have charged that he should have foreseen the disaster. In the face of pressure from labor leaders and German politicians, Siemens ultimately coughed up $46 million to aid workers who lost their jobs.

19   Some Siemens watchers say Kleinfeld has become more cautious following the bribery investigation and the uproar over his restructuring moves. Those controversies clearly rob him of political capital, and plenty of people both inside and outside Siemens would surely love to see Kleinfeld fail. Says a consultant who has worked closely with Siemens: "Some people are betting that he doesn't survive and that they can go on in the normal way."

20   Kleinfeld, though, has no plans to give up, and he is pressing to reshape the "normal" ways in which the giant company operates even as the investigations continue. Says Kleinfeld: "We are fitter than ever."

DISCUSSION QUESTIONS

1. What are the industry forces that dominate Siemens' industries?

2. What are the different types of responsibility that Kleinfeld shoulders in his job as CEO? Do you consider them to be strategic responsibilities?

3. Do you think that the level of strategic turbulence and restructuring that Kleinfeld faces is common in business? Do you believe that Kleinfeld helps to create this turmoil?

4. How do you see the U.S. and German business environments as different?

5. To what degree do you believe Kleinfeld must simply react to his environments as opposed to "creating" them?

Chapter 4 Appendix

Sources for Environmental Forecasting

Remote and Industry Environments

A. Economic considerations:
1. *Predicasts* (most complete and up-to-date review of forecasts)
2. National Bureau of Economic Research
3. *Handbook of Basic Economic Statistics*
4. *Statistical Abstract of the United States* (also includes industrial, social, and political statistics)
5. Publications by Department of Commerce agencies:
   a. Office of Business Economics (e.g., *Survey of Business*)
   b. Bureau of Economic Analysis (e.g., *Business Conditions Digest*)
   c. Bureau of the Census (e.g., *Survey of Manufacturers* and various reports on population, housing, and industries)
   d. Business and Defense Services Administration (e.g., *United States Industrial Outlook*)
6. Securities and Exchange Commission (various quarterly reports on plant and equipment, financial reports, working capital of corporations)
7. The Conference Board
8. *Survey of Buying Power*
9. *Marketing Economic Guide*
10. *Industrial Arts Index*
11. U.S. and national chambers of commerce
12. American Manufacturers Association
13. *Federal Reserve Bulletin*
14. *Economic Indicators,* annual report
15. *Kiplinger Newsletter*
16. International economic sources:
    a. *Worldcasts*
    b. Master key index for business international publications
    c. Department of Commerce
       (1) Overseas business reports
       (2) Industry and Trade Administration
       (3) Bureau of the Census—*Guide to Foreign Trade Statistics*
17. *Business Periodicals Index*

B. Social considerations:
1. Public opinion polls
2. Surveys such as *Social Indicators and Social Reporting,* the annals of the American Academy of Political and Social Sciences
3. Current controls: Social and behavioral sciences
4. Abstract services and indexes for articles in sociological, psychological, and political journals

5. Indexes for *The Wall Street Journal, New York Times,* and other newspapers
6. Bureau of the Census reports on population, housing, manufacturers, selected services, construction, retail trade, wholesale trade, and enterprise statistics
7. Various reports from such groups as the Brookings Institution and the Ford Foundation
8. World Bank Atlas (population growth and GNP data)
9. World Bank–World Development Report

C. Political considerations:
1. *Public Affairs Information Services Bulletin*
2. CIS Index (Congressional Information Index)
3. Business periodicals
4. Funk & Scott (regulations by product breakdown)
5. Weekly compilation of presidential documents
6. *Monthly Catalog of Government Publications*
7. *Federal Register* (daily announcements of pending regulations)
8. *Code of Federal Regulations* (final listing of regulations)
9. Business International Master Key Index (regulations, tariffs)
10. Various state publications
11. Various information services (Bureau of National Affairs, Commerce Clearing House, Prentice Hall)

D. Technological considerations:
1. *Applied Science and Technology Index*
2. *Statistical Abstract of the United States*
3. Scientific and Technical Information Service
4. University reports, congressional reports
5. Department of Defense and military purchasing publishers
6. Trade journals and industrial reports
7. Industry contacts, professional meetings
8. Computer-assisted information searches
9. National Science Foundation annual report
10. *Research and Development Directory* patent records

E. Industry considerations:
1. *Concentration Ratios in Manufacturing* (Bureau of the Census)
2. *Input-Output Survey* (productivity ratios)
3. *Monthly Labor Review* (productivity ratios)
4. *Quarterly Failure Report* (Dun & Bradstreet)
5. *Federal Reserve Bulletin* (capacity utilization)

6. *Report on Industrial Concentration and Product Diversification in the 1,000 Largest Manufacturing Companies* (Federal Trade Commission)
7. Industry trade publications
8. Bureau of Economic Analysis, Department of Commerce (specialization ratios)

Industry and Operating Environments

A. Competition and supplier considerations:
   1. Target Group Index
   2. U.S. Industrial Outlook
   3. Robert Morris annual statement studies
   4. Troy, Leo *Almanac of Business & Industrial Financial Ratios*
   5. *Census of Enterprise Statistics*
   6. Securities and Exchange Commission (10-K reports)
   7. Annual reports of specific companies
   8. *Fortune 500 Directory, The Wall Street Journal, Barron's, Forbes, Dun's Review*
   9. Investment services and directories: Moody's, Dun & Bradstreet, Standard & Poor's, Starch Marketing, Funk & Scott Index
   10. Trade association surveys
   11. Industry surveys
   12. Market research surveys
   13. *Country Business Patterns*
   14. *Country and City Data Book*
   15. Industry contacts, professional meetings, salespeople
   16. *NFIB Quarterly Economic Report for Small Business*

B. Customer profile:
   1. *Statistical Abstract of the United States,* first source of statistics
   2. *Statistical Sources* by Paul Wasserman (a subject guide to data—both domestic and international)
   3. *American Statistics Index* (Congressional Information Service Guide to statistical publications of U.S. government—monthly)
   4. Office of the Department of Commerce:
      a. Bureau of the Census reports on population, housing, and industries
      b. *U.S. Census of Manufacturers* (statistics by industry, area, and products)
      c. *Survey of Current Business* (analysis of business trends, especially February and July issues)

5. Market research studies (*A Basic Bibliography on Market Review,* compiled by Robert Ferber et al., American Marketing Association)
6. *Current Sources of Marketing Information: A Bibliography of Primary Marketing Data* by Gunther & Goldstein, AMA
7. *Guide to Consumer Markets,* The Conference Board (provides statistical information with demographic, social, and economic data—annual)
8. *Survey of Buying Power*
9. *Predicasts* (abstracts of publishing forecasts of all industries, detailed products, and end-use data)
10. *Predicasts Basebook* (historical data from 1960 to present, covering subjects ranging from population and GNP to specific products and services; series are coded by Standard Industrial Classifications)
11. *Market Guide* (individual market surveys of over 1,500 U.S. and Canadian cities; includes population, location, trade areas, banks, principal industries, colleges and universities, department and chain stores, newspapers, retail outlets, and sales)
12. *Country and City Data Book* (includes bank deposits, birth and death rates, business firms, education, employment, income of families, manufacturers, population, savings, and wholesale and retail trade)
13. *Yearbook of International Trade Statistics* (UN)
14. *Yearbook of National Accounts Statistics* (UN)
15. *Statistical Yearbook* (UN—covers population, national income, agricultural and industrial production, energy, external trade, and transport)
16. *Statistics of (Continents): Sources for Market Research* (includes separate books on Africa, America, Europe)

C. Key natural resources:
   1. *Minerals Yearbook, Geological Survey* (Bureau of Mines, Department of the Interior)
   2. *Agricultural Abstract* (Department of Agriculture)
   3. Statistics of electric utilities and gas pipeline companies (Federal Power Commission)
   4. Publications of various institutions: American Petroleum Institute, Atomic Energy Commission, Coal Mining Institute of America, American Steel Institute, and Brookings Institution

The Global Environment

After reading and studying this chapter, you should be able to

1. Explain the importance of a company's decision to globalize.

2. Describe the four main strategic orientations of global firms.

3. Understand the complexity of the global environment and the control problems that are faced by global firms.

4. Discuss major issues in global strategic planning, including the differences for multinational and global firms.

5. Describe the market requirements and product characteristics in global competition.

6. Evaluate the competitive strategies for firms in foreign markets, including niche market exporting, licensing and contract manufacturing, franchising, joint ventures, foreign branching, private equity, and wholly owned subsidiaries.

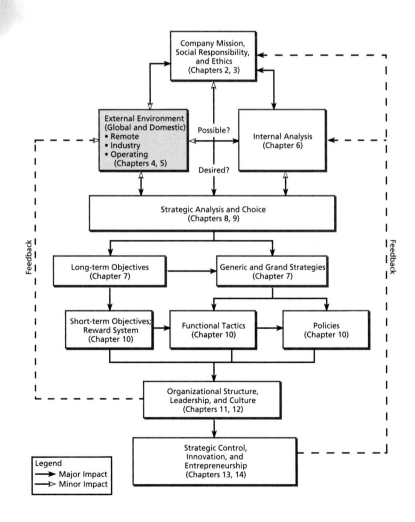

Company Mission, Social Responsibility, and Ethics (Chapters 2, 3)

External Environment (Global and Domestic)
• Remote
• Industry
• Operating
(Chapters 4, 5)

Possible?

Desired?

Internal Analysis (Chapter 6)

Strategic Analysis and Choice (Chapters 8, 9)

Long-term Objectives (Chapter 7)

Generic and Grand Strategies (Chapter 7)

Short-term Objectives; Reward System (Chapter 10)

Functional Tactics (Chapter 10)

Policies (Chapter 10)

Organizational Structure, Leadership, and Culture (Chapters 11, 12)

Strategic Control, Innovation, and Entrepreneurship (Chapters 13, 14)

Feedback

Legend
→ Major Impact
⇒ Minor Impact

GLOBALIZATION

globalization
The strategy of approaching worldwide markets with standardized products.

Special complications confront a firm involved in the globalization of its operations. **Globalization** refers to the strategy of approaching worldwide markets with standardized products. Such markets are most commonly created by end consumers that prefer lower-priced, standardized products over higher-priced, customized products and by global corporations that use their worldwide operations to compete in local markets. Global corporations headquartered in one country with subsidiaries in other countries experience difficulties that are understandably associated with operating in several distinctly different competitive arenas.

Awareness of the strategic opportunities faced by global corporations and of the threats posed to them is important to planners in almost every domestic U.S. industry. Among corporations headquartered in the United States that receive more than 50 percent of their annual profits from foreign operations are Citicorp, Coca-Cola, ExxonMobil, Gillette, IBM, Otis Elevator, and Texas Instruments. In fact, the 100 largest U.S. globals earn an average of 37 percent of their operating profits abroad. Equally impressive is the effect of foreign-based globals that operate in the United States. Their "direct foreign investment" in the United States now exceeds $90 billion, with Japanese, German, and French firms leading the way.

Understanding the myriad and sometimes subtle nuances of competing in global markets or against global corporations is rapidly becoming a required competence of strategic managers. For example, experts in the advertising community contend that Korean companies only recently recognized the importance of making their names known abroad. In the 1980s, there was very little advertising of Korean brands, and the country had very few recognizable brands abroad. Korean companies tended to emphasize sales and production more than marketing. The opening of the Korean advertising market in the 1990s indicated that Korean firms had acquired a new appreciation for the strategic competencies that are needed to compete globally and created an influx of global firms like Saatchi and Saatchi, J. W. Thompson, Ogilvy and Mather, and Bozell. Many of them established joint ventures or partnerships with Korean agencies. An excellent example of such a strategic approach to globalization by Philip Morris's KGFI is described in Exhibit 5.1, Global Strategy in Action. The opportunities for corporate growth often seem brightest in global markets. Exhibit 5.2 reports on the growth in national shares of the world's outputs and growth in national economies to the year 2020. While the United States had a commanding lead in the size of its economy in 1992, it was caught by China in the year 2000 and will be far surpassed by 2020. Overall, in less than 20 years, rich industrial countries will be overshadowed by developing countries in their produced share of the world's output.

Because the growth in the number of global firms continues to overshadow other changes in the competitive environment, this section will focus on the nature, outlook, and operations of global corporations.

DEVELOPMENT OF A GLOBAL CORPORATION

The evolution of a global corporation often entails progressively involved strategy levels. The first level, which often entails export-import activity, has minimal effect on the existing management orientation or on existing product lines. The second level, which can involve foreign licensing and technology transfer, requires little change in management or operation. The third level typically is characterized by direct investment in overseas operations, including manufacturing plants. This level requires large capital outlays and the development of global management skills. Although the domestic operations of a firm at this level

Outside of its core Western markets, Kraft General Foods International's (KGFI) food products have a growing presence in one of the most dynamic business environments in the world—the Asia-Pacific region. Its operations there are expanding rapidly, often aided by links with local manufacturers and distributors.

Japan and Korea are important examples. In both countries, local alliances can be crucial to market entry and success. Realizing this fact in the early 1970s, General Foods established joint ventures in both Japan and Korea. These joint ventures, combined with Kraft General Foods International's (KGFI) stand-alone operations, generate more than $1 billion in revenues. In the aggregate, their combined food operations in Japan and Korea are larger than many *Fortune* 500 companies.

Whereas soluble coffee accounts for just over 25 percent of the coffee consumed in U.S. homes, it fills more than 70 percent of the cups consumed in the homes of convenience-minded Japan. Additionally, Japan is the origin of a unique form of packaged coffee—liquid—and a unique channel of distribution—vending machines. Japanese consumers have purchased packaged liquid coffee for years, and it amounts to a $5 billion category. Some 2 million vending machines dispense 9 billion cans of liquid coffee annually—an average of 75 cans per person.

Japan offers a culturally unique distribution channel for coffee products—the gift-set market. Many Japanese exchange specially packaged food or beverage assortments at least twice a year to commemorate holidays as well as special personal or business occasions. The gift-set business has helped Maxim products reinforce their quality image; it also will be a launching pad and support vehicle for Carte Noire coffees.

Outside the Ajinomoto General Foods joint venture, KGFI is developing a freestanding food business under the name Kraft Japan. It is building a cheese business with imported Philadelphia Brand cream cheese,

the leading cream cheese in the Tokyo metropolitan market, as well as locally manufactured and licensed Kraft Milk Farm cheese slices. The cheese market is expected to grow approximately 5 percent per year. This is a rapid growth rate for a large food category. In addition to cheese, KGFI also imports Oscar Mayer prepared meats and Jocobs Suchard chocolates.

KGFI's joint venture in Korea, Doug Suh Foods Corporation, is one of the top 10 food companies in the country. Doug Suh manufactures coffees and cereals and has its own distribution network. One of Doug Suh's other businesses in Korea, Post Cereals, is also a strong number two, with a 42 percent category share.

Korea's $400 million coffee market is the fastest-growing major coffee market in the world, expanding at an average annual rate of 14 percent. Growing with the market, Maxim and Maxwell soluble coffees, in both traditional "agglomerate" and freeze-dried forms, account for more than 70 percent of the country's soluble coffee sales. The strength of these brands also brings the company a strong number one position in coffee mix, a mixture of soluble coffee, creamer, and sugar. In addition, its Frima brand leads the market in the nondairy creamer segment.

Beyond Japan and Korea, KGFI is targeting many other countries for geographic expansion. In Indonesia, for instance, KGFI has established a rapidly growing cheese business through a licensee and introduced other KGFI products. In Taiwan, the joint venture company, PremierFoods Corporation, holds a 34 percent share of the soluble coffee market and is aggressively developing a Kraft cheese and Jocobs Suchard import business. KGFI Philippines, a wholly owned subsidiary, has a leading position in the cheese and powdered soft-drink markets in its country. In the People's Republic of China, the company produces and markets Maxwell House coffees and Tang powdered soft drinks through two successful and rapidly growing joint ventures.

continue to dominate its policy, such a firm is commonly categorized as a true multinational corporation (MNC). The most involved strategy level is characterized by a substantial increase in foreign investment, with foreign assets comprising a significant portion of total assets. At this level, the firm begins to emerge as a global enterprise with global approaches to production, sales, finance, and control.

To get a more complete understanding of the many elements of a multinational environment that need to be considered by strategic planners, study Appendix 5-A. It contains lists of important competitive issues that will help you to see the complexity of the multinational landscape and to better appreciate the complicated and sophisticated nature of strategic planning.

EXHIBIT 5.2   **Projected Economic Growth**

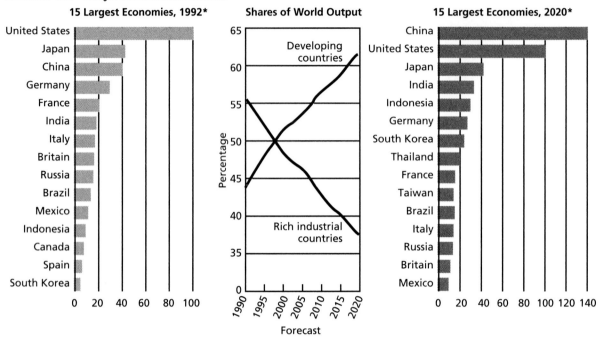

Source: World Bank, *Global Economic Prospects and the Developing Countries.*

Some firms downplay their global nature (to never appear distracted from their domestic operations), whereas others highlight it. For example, General Electric's formal statement of mission and business philosophy includes the following commitment:

> To carry out a diversified, growing, and profitable worldwide manufacturing business in electrical apparatus, appliances, and supplies, and in related materials, products, systems, and services for industry, commerce, agriculture, government, the community, and the home.

A similar global orientation is evident at IBM, which operates in 125 countries, conducts business in 30 languages and more than 100 currencies, and has 23 major manufacturing facilities in 14 countries.

WHY FIRMS GLOBALIZE

The technological advantage once enjoyed by the United States has declined dramatically during the past 30 years. In the late 1950s, more than 80 percent of the world's major technological innovations were first introduced in the United States. By 1990, the figure had declined to less than 50 percent. In contrast, France is making impressive advances in electric traction, nuclear power, and aviation. Germany leads in chemicals and pharmaceuticals, precision and heavy machinery, heavy electrical goods, metallurgy, and surface transport equipment. Japan leads in optics, solid-state physics, engineering, chemistry, and process metallurgy. Eastern Europe and the former Soviet Union, the so-called COMECON (Council for Mutual Economic Assistance) countries, generate 30 percent of annual worldwide patent applications. However, the United States has regained some of its lost technological advantage. Through globalization, U.S. firms often can reap benefits from industries and technologies developed abroad. Even a relatively small service firm that possesses a distinct competitive advantage can capitalize on large overseas operations.

Diebold Inc. once operated solely in the United States, selling automated teller machines (ATMs), bank vaults, and security systems to financial institutions. However, with the U.S. market saturated, Diebold needed to expand internationally to continue its growth. The firm's globalization efforts led to both the development of new technologies in emerging markets and opportunistic entry into entirely new industries that significantly improved Diebold's sales.

In many situations, global development makes sense as a competitive weapon. Direct penetration of foreign markets can drain vital cash flows from a foreign competitor's domestic operations. The resulting lost opportunities, reduced income, and limited production can impair the competitor's ability to invade U.S. markets. A case in point is IBM's move to establish a position of strength in the Japanese mainframe computer industry before two key competitors, Fiyitsue and Hitachi, could dominate it. Once IBM had achieved a substantial share of the Japanese market, it worked to deny its Japanese competitors the vital cash and production experience they needed to invade the U.S. market.

Firms that operate principally in the domestic environment have an important decision to make with regard to their globalization: Should they act before being forced to do so by competitive pressures or after? Should they (1) be proactive by entering global markets in advance of other firms and thereby enjoy the first-mover advantages often accruing to risk-taker firms that introduce new products or services or (2) be reactive by taking the more conservative approach and following other companies into global markets once customer demand has been proven and the high costs of new-product or new-service introductions have been absorbed by competitors? Although the answers to these questions are determined by the specifics of the company and the context, the issues raised in Exhibit 5.3 are helpful to strategic decision makers faced with the dilemma.

Strategic Orientations of Global Firms

Multinational corporations typically display one of four orientations toward their overseas activities. They have a certain set of beliefs about how the management of foreign operations should be handled. A company with an **ethnocentric orientation** believes that the values and priorities of the parent organization should guide the strategic decision making of all its operations. If a corporation has a **polycentric orientation,** then the culture of the country in which a strategy is to be implemented is allowed to dominate the decision-making process. In contrast, a **regiocentric orientation** exists when the parent attempts to blend its own predispositions with those of the region under consideration, thereby arriving at a region-sensitive compromise. Finally, a corporation with a **geocentric orientation** adopts a global systems approach to strategic decision making, thereby emphasizing global integration.

American firms often adopt a regiocentric orientation for pursing strategies in Europe. U.S. e-tailers have attempted to blend their own corporate structure and expertise with that of European corporations. For example, Amazon has been able to leverage its experience in the United States while developing regionally and culturally specific strategies overseas. By purchasing European franchises that have had regional success, E*Trade is pursuing a foreign strategy in which they insert their European units into corporate structure. This strategy requires the combination and use of culturally different management styles and involves major challenges for upper management.

Exhibit 5.4 shows the effects of each of the four orientations on key activities of the firm. It is clear from the figure that the strategic orientation of a global firm plays a major role in determining the locus of control and corporate priorities of the firm's decision makers.

---

ethnocentric orientation

When the values and priorities of the parent organization guide the strategic decision making of all its international operations.

polycentric orientation

When the culture of the country in which the strategy is to be implemented is allowed to dominate a company's international decision-making process.

regiocentric orientation

When a parent company blends its own predisposition with those of its international units to develop region-sensitive strategies.

geocentric orientation

When an international firm adopts a systems approach to strategic decision making that emphasizes global integration.

EXHIBIT 5.3
Reasons for Going Global

Proactive	
Advantage/Opportunity	**Explanation of Action**
Additional resources	Various inputs—including natural resources, technologies, skilled personnel, and materials—may be obtained more readily outside the home country.
Lowered costs	Various costs—including labor, materials, transportation, and financing—may be lower outside the home country.
Incentives	Various incentives may be available from the host government or the home government to encourage foreign investment in specific locations.
New, expanded markets	New and different markets may be available outside the home country; excess resources—including management, skills, machinery, and money—can be utilized in foreign locations.
Exploitation of firm-specific advantages	Technologies, brands, and recognized names can all provide opportunities in foreign locations.
Taxes	Differing corporate tax rates and tax systems in different locations provide opportunities for companies to maximize their after-tax worldwide profits.
Economies of scale	National markets may be too small to support efficient production, while sales from several combined allow for larger-scale production.
Synergy	Operations in more than one national environment provide opportunities to combine benefits from one location with another, which is impossible without both of them.
Power and prestige	The image of being international may increase a company's power and prestige and improve its domestic sales and relations with various stakeholder groups.
Protect home market through offense in competitor's home	A strong offense in a competitor's market can put pressure on the competitor that results in a pull-back from foreign activities to protect itself at home.

Reactive	
Outside Occurrence	**Explanation of Reaction**
Trade barriers	Tariffs, quotas, buy-local policies, and other restrictive trade practices can make exports to foreign markets less attractive; local operations in foreign locations thus become attractive.
International customers	If a company's customer base becomes international, and the company wants to continue to serve it, then local operations in foreign locations may be necessary.
International competition	If a company's competitors become international, and the company wants to remain competitive, foreign operations may be necessary.
Regulations	Regulations and restrictions imposed by the home government may increase the cost of operating at home; it may be possible to avoid these costs by establishing foreign operations.
Chance	Chance occurrence results in a company deciding to enter foreign locations.

EXHIBIT 5.4   Orientation of a Global Firm

	Ethnocentric	Polycentric	Regiocentric	Geocentric
	Orientation of the Firm			
Mission	Profitability (viability)	Public acceptance (legitimacy)	Profitability and public acceptance (viability and legitimacy)	Same as regiocentric
Governance	Top-down	Bottom-up (each subsidiary decides on local objectives)	Mutually negotiated between region and its subsidiaries	Mutually negotiated at all levels of the corporation
Strategy	Global integration	National responsiveness	Regional integration and national responsiveness	Global integration and national responsiveness
Structure	Hierarchical product divisions	Hierarchical area divisions, with autonomous national units	Product and regional organization tied through a matrix	A network of organizations (including some competitors)
Culture	Home country	Host country	Regional	Global
Technology	Mass production	Batch production	Flexible manufacturing	Flexible manufacturing
Marketing	Product development determined by the needs of home country	Local product development based on local needs	Standardize within region but not across regions	Global product, with local variations
Finance	Repatriation of profits to home country	Retention of profits in host country	Redistribution within region	Redistribution globally
Personnel practices	People of home country developed for key positions in the world	People of local nationality developed for key positions in their own country	Regional people developed for key positions anywhere in the region	Global personnel development and placement

Source: Reprinted from *Columbia Journal of World Business,* Summer 1985, Balaji S. Chakravarthy and Howard V. Perlmutter. "Strategic Planning for a Global Business," p. 506. Copyright © 1985 with permission from Elsevier.

AT THE START OF GLOBALIZATION

External and internal assessments are conducted before a firm enters global markets. For example, Japanese investors conduct extensive assessments and analyses before selecting a U.S. site for a Japanese-owned firm. They prefer states with strong markets, low unionization rates, and low taxes. In addition, Japanese manufacturing plants prefer counties characterized by manufacturing conglomeration; low unemployment and poverty rates; and concentrations of educated, productive workers.

External assessment involves careful examination of critical features of the global environment, particular attention being paid to the status of the host nations in such areas as economic progress, political control, and nationalism. Expansion of industrial facilities, favorable balances of payments, and improvements in technological capabilities over the past decade are gauges of the host nation's economic progress. Political status can be gauged by the host nation's power in and impact on global affairs.

Internal assessment involves identification of the basic strengths of a firm's operations. These strengths are particularly important in global operations, because they are often the characteristics of a firm that the host nation values most and, thus, offer significant

The following considerations were drawn from an 88-point checklist developed by Business International Corporation.

Economic Factors:
1. Size of GNP and projected rate of growth
2. Foreign exchange position
3. Size of market for the firm's products; rate of growth

Political Factors:
4. Form and stability of government
5. Attitude toward private and foreign investment by government, customers, and competition
6. Degree of antiforeign discrimination

Geographic Factors:
7. Proximity of site to export markets
8. Availability of local raw materials
9. Availability of power, water, gas

Labor Factors:
10. Availability of managerial, technical, and office personnel able to speak the language of the parent company
11. Degree of skill and discipline at all levels
12. Degree and nature of labor voice in management

Tax Factors:
13. Tax-rate trends
14. Joint tax treaties with home country and others
15. Availability of tariff protection

Capital Source Factors:
16. Cost of local borrowing
17. Modern banking systems
18. Government credit aids to new businesses

Business Factors:
19. State of marketing and distribution system
20. Normal profit margins in the firm's industry
21. Competitive situation in the firm's industry: do cartels exist?

bargaining leverage. The firm's resource strengths and global capabilities must be analyzed. The resources that should be analyzed include, in particular, technical and managerial skills, capital, labor, and raw materials. The global capabilities that should be analyzed include the firm's product delivery and financial management systems.

A firm that gives serious consideration to internal and external assessment is Business International Corporation, which recommends that seven broad categories of factors be considered. As shown in Exhibit 5.5, Global Strategy in Action, these categories include economic, political, geographic, labor, tax, capital source, and business factors.

COMPLEXITY OF THE GLOBAL ENVIRONMENT

By 2003, Coke was finally achieving a goal that it had set a decade earlier when it went to India. That goal was to take the market away from Pepsi and local beverage companies. However, when it arrived, Coke found that the Indian market was extremely complex and smaller than it had estimated. Coke also encountered cultural problems, in part because the chief of Coke India was an expatriate. The key to overcoming this cultural problem was promoting an Indian to operations chief. Coke also changed its marketing strategy by pushing their "Thums Up" products, a local brand owned by Coke. Then, they began to focus their efforts on creating new products for rural areas and lowering the prices of their existing products to increase sales. Once Coke had new products in the market, they focused on a new advertising campaign to better relate to Indian consumers.

A Milestone for Human Rights

BusinessWeek

In the mid-1990s, reports emerged out of Burma that villagers in the remote Yadana region had been forced by the military to clear jungle for the construction of a $1.2 billion natural gas pipeline. The allegations were horrendous: to round up workers for the project, the Burmese military had resorted to torture, rape, and murder to enslave villagers, even throwing one woman's baby in a fire after killing her husband. Before long, U.S. human rights groups had filed suit against Unocal Corp., based in El Segundo, California, one of the four pipeline partners, on behalf of 15 unnamed Burmese villagers.

Now, after years of courtroom sparring, Unocal has quietly agreed to settle the suits, one filed in California state court and another in the U.S. District Court in Los Angeles. Insiders say that Unocal will pay about $30 million in damages to settle the cases. The award will include money for the 15 plaintiffs and for a fund to improve living conditions, health care, and education in the pipeline region.

The settlement may mark a milestone in human rights advocates' struggle to use U.S. courts to force American multinationals to protect their workers against abuse by repressive regimes. The Unocal case "shows that corporations have both direct and indirect human rights responsibilities," says Susan Aaronson, director of globalization studies at the Kennan Institute, a Washington think tank.

Unocal is the first of a series of U.S. multinationals to face allegations that they acquiesced in or benefited from human rights violations, committed mostly by authoritarian governments. Other defendants include ExxonMobil, Coca-Cola, Drummond, Occidental Petroleum, and Del Monte Foods. The companies are all fighting the suits.

Source: Reprinted with special permission from Paul Magnusson, "A Milestone for Human Rights," *BusinessWeek*, January 24, 2005. Copyright © 2005 The McGraw-Hill Companies.

Coke's experience highlights the fact that global strategic planning is more complex than purely domestic planning. There are at least five factors that contribute to this increase in complexity:

1. Globals face multiple political, economic, legal, social, and cultural environments as well as various rates of changes within each of them. Occasionally, foreign governments work in concert with their militaries to advance economic aims even at the expense of human rights. International firms must resist the temptation to benefit financially from such immoral opportunities. Specifics of just one abusive situation are presented in Exhibit 5.6, Strategy in Action.

2. Interactions between the national and foreign environments are complex, because of national sovereignty issues and widely differing economic and social conditions.

3. Geographic separation, cultural and national differences, and variations in business practices all tend to make communication and control efforts between headquarters and the overseas affiliates difficult.

4. Globals face extreme competition, because of differences in industry structures within countries.

5. Globals are restricted in their selection of competitive strategies by various regional blocs and economic integrations, such as the European Economic Community, the European Free Trade Area, and the Latin American Free Trade Area.

CONTROL PROBLEMS OF THE GLOBAL FIRM

An inherent complicating factor for many global firms is that their financial policies typically are designed to further the goals of the parent company and pay minimal attention to

Top Strategist
Francisco D'Souza, CEO of Cognizant Technology Solutions

Exhibit
5.7

Even in the fast-growing outsourcing industry, Cognizant is a standout. Propelled by the increased outsourcing of health care data processing and by a growing number of European clients, Cognizant's 2006 sales jumped 61 percent. Its bread and butter, though, remains managing financial and information-tech services for U.S. clients; companies such as Wells Fargo, Citigroup, and Aetna account for 86 percent of its sales. To keep growth humming, CEO Francisco D'Souza plans to hew to the company's policy of investing aggressively in operations and staff, adding 16,000 workers, mostly in India and China. And he plans to spend $200 million on more office space and infrastructure in India, where Cognizant has 70 percent of its operations. The outlay comes at the cost of margins lower than Indian rivals Wipro and Infosys Technologies, but so far these bets have paid off in growth.

the goals of the host countries. This built-in bias creates conflict between the different parts of the global firm, between the whole firm and its home and host countries, and between the home country and host country themselves. The conflict is accentuated by the use of various schemes to shift earnings from one country to another in order to avoid taxes, minimize risk, or achieve other objectives.

Moreover, different financial environments make normal standards of company behavior concerning the disposition of earnings, sources of finance, and the structure of capital more problematic. Thus, it becomes increasingly difficult to measure the performance of international divisions.

In addition, important differences in measurement and control systems often exist. Fundamental to the concept of planning is a well-conceived, future-oriented approach to decision making that is based on accepted procedures and methods of analysis. Consistent approaches to planning throughout a firm are needed for effective review and evaluation by corporate headquarters. In the global firm, planning is complicated by differences in national attitudes toward work measurement, and by differences in government requirements about disclosure of information.

Although such problems are an aspect of the global environment, rather than a consequence of poor management, they are often most effectively reduced through increased attention to strategic planning. Such planning will aid in coordinating and integrating the firm's direction, objectives, and policies around the world. It enables the firm to anticipate and prepare for change. It facilitates the creation of programs to deal with worldwide development. Finally, it helps the management of overseas affiliates become more actively involved in setting goals and in developing means to more effectively utilize the firm's total resources. A strategic manager who shares this view is Francisco D'Souza, the CEO of Cognizant Technology Solutions. Some of his company's recent global strategic initiatives are discussed in Exhibit 5.7, Top Strategist.

An example of the need for coordination in global ventures and evidence that firms can successfully plan for global collaboration (e.g., through rationalized production) is the Ford Escort (Europe), the best-selling automobile in the world, which has a component manufacturing network that consists of plants in 15 countries.

GLOBAL STRATEGIC PLANNING

It should be evident from the previous sections that the strategic decisions of a firm competing in the global marketplace become increasingly complex. In such a firm, managers cannot view global operations as a set of independent decisions. These managers are faced with trade-off decisions in which multiple products, country environments, resource sourcing options, corporate and subsidiary capabilities, and strategic options must be considered.

stakeholder activism
Demands placed on a global firm by the stakeholders in the environments in which it operates.

A recent trend toward increased activism of stakeholders has added to the complexity of strategic planning for the global firm. **Stakeholder activism** refers to demands placed on the global firm by the foreign environments in which it operates, principally by foreign governments. This section provides a basic framework for the analysis of strategic decisions in this complex setting.

Multidomestic Industries and Global Industries

Multidomestic Industries

International industries can be ranked along a continuum that ranges from multidomestic to global.

multidomestic industry
An industry in which competition is segmented from country to country.

A **multidomestic industry** is one in which competition is essentially segmented from country to country. Thus, even if global corporations are in the industry, competition in one country is independent of competition in other countries. Examples of such industries include retailing, insurance, and consumer finance.

In a multidomestic industry, a global corporation's subsidiaries should be managed as distinct entities; that is, each subsidiary should be rather autonomous, having the authority to make independent decisions in response to local market conditions. Thus, the global strategy of such an industry is the sum of the strategies developed by subsidiaries operating in different countries. The primary difference between a domestic firm and a global firm competing in a multidomestic industry is that the latter makes decisions related to the countries in which it competes and to how it conducts business abroad.

Factors that increase the degree to which an industry is multidomestic include[1]

- The need for customized products to meet the tastes or preferences of local customers.
- Fragmentation of the industry, with many competitors in each national market.
- A lack of economies of scale in the functional activities of firms in the industry.
- Distribution channels unique to each country.
- A low technological dependence of subsidiaries on R&D provided by the global firm.

An interesting example of a multidomestic strategy is the one designed by Renault-Nissan for the low-cost automobile industry. As described in Exhibit 5.8, Strategy in Action, Renault's strategy involves designing cars to fit the budgets of buyers in different countries, rather than being restricted to the production of cars that meet the safety and emission standards of countries in Western Europe and the United States or by their consumer preferences for technological advancements and stylish appointments.

---

[1] Y. Doz and C. K. Prahalad, "Patterns of Strategic Control within Multinational Corporations," *Journal of International Business Studies,* Fall 1984, pp. 55–72.

The Race to Build Really Cheap Cars

BusinessWeek

How cheap is cheap? Renault-Nissan Chief Executive Carlos Ghosn is betting that for autos, the magic number is under $3,000. At a plant-opening ceremony in India in 2007, he was already talking up the industry's next challenge: a future model that would sport a sticker price as low as $2,500—about 40 percent less than the least expensive subcompact currently on the market.

Renault already has a runaway hit with its bare-bones Logan sedan. The automaker began offering the roomy Logan in Europe for just $7,200 in 2004—some 40 percent less than rival sedans—and has since sold 450,000 of the cars in 51 countries. A $3,000 car for Asian markets, built in low-cost India with a local partner, is the next logical step.

That realization is now dawning on the industry's giants. When Tata made its vow to build a $2,500 car, many Western auto executives ridiculed the project, dubbing it a four-wheel bicycle. They aren't laughing anymore. Tata's model is a real car with four doors, a 33-horsepower engine, and a top speed of around 80 mph. The automaker claims it will even pass a crash test. The key is India's low-cost engineers and their prodigious ability to trim needless spending to the bone, a skill developed by years of selling to the bottom of the pyramid.

By 2012, the market for vehicles priced under $10,000 is likely to reach 18 million cars, or a fifth of world auto sales, according to Roland Berger Strategy Consultants. That's up from 12 million in 2007.

Car manufacturers, of course, have always sought to cut costs and pack more value into each new-model generation to stay competitive. But now, emerging markets like India offer cheap engineering, inexpensive parts-sourcing, and low-cost manufacturing. For its new car, for example, Tata should be able to slash the cost of the engine to about $700, or 50 percent lower than a Western-developed equivalent, says one consultant close to the company.

To make a success of the Logan, Renault manufactured in low-cost Romania. It developed a design that reduced the total number of parts and made assembly a cinch. It stripped out sophisticated electronics, dispensed with high-tech curved windshields, and even saved $3 per vehicle by using identical rear-view mirrors on each side. The biggest breakthrough: Renault was able to eliminate expensive prototypes and the pricey tooling involved in building them, an innovation that saved the French car company $40 million.

The majority of low-cost cars will range from $5,000 to $10,000, depending on size and features. Analysts say adding equipment required for safety and emissions control in Western markets would automatically bring the price of a cheap Chinese or Indian car up to $6,000 to $7,000.

Source: Reprinted with special permission from Gail Edmondson, "The Race to Build Really Cheap Cars," *BusinessWeek*, April 23, 2007. Copyright © 2007 The McGraw-Hill Companies.

Global Industries

global industry
An industry in which competition crosses national borders on a worldwide basis.

A **global industry** is one in which competition crosses national borders. In fact, it occurs on a worldwide basis. In a global industry, a firm's strategic moves in one country can be significantly affected by its competitive position in another country. The very rapidly expanding list of global industries includes commercial aircraft, automobiles, mainframe computers, and electronic consumer equipment. Many authorities are convinced that almost all product-oriented industries soon will be global. As a result, strategic management planning must be global for at least six reasons:

1. *The increased scope of the global management task.* Growth in the size and complexity of global firms made management virtually impossible without a coordinated plan of action detailing what is expected of whom during a given period. The common practice of management by exception is impossible without such a plan.

2. *The increased globalization of firms.* Three aspects of global business make global planning necessary: (*a*) differences among the environmental forces in different countries, (*b*) greater distances, and (*c*) the interrelationships of global operations.

3. *The information explosion.* It has been estimated that the world's stock of knowledge is doubling every 10 years. Without the aid of a formal plan, executives can no longer know all that they must know to solve the complex problems they face. A global planning process provides an ordered means for assembling, analyzing, and distilling the information required for sound decisions.

4. *The increase in global competition.* Because of the rapid increase in global competition, firms must constantly adjust to changing conditions or lose markets to competitors. The increase in global competition also spurs managements to search for methods of increasing efficiency and economy.

5. *The rapid development of technology.* Rapid technological development has shortened product life cycles. Strategic management planning is necessary to ensure the replacement of products that are moving into the maturity stage, with fewer sales and declining profits. Planning gives management greater control of all aspects of new-product introduction.

6. *Strategic management planning breeds managerial confidence.* Like the motorist with a road map, managers with a plan for reaching their objectives know where they are going. Such a plan breeds confidence, because it spells out every step along the way and assigns responsibility for every task. The plan simplifies the managerial job.

A firm in a global industry must maximize its capabilities through a worldwide strategy. Such a strategy necessitates a high degree of centralized decision making in corporate headquarters so as to permit trade-off decisions across subsidiaries.

Among the factors that make for the creation of a global industry are

- Economies of scale in the functional activities of firms in the industry.
- A high level of R&D expenditures on products that require more than one market to recover development costs.
- The presence in the industry of predominantly global firms that expect consistency of products and services across markets.
- The presence of homogeneous product needs across markets, which reduces the requirement of customizing the product for each market. The presence of a small group of global competitors.
- A low level of trade regulation and of regulation regarding foreign direction investment.[2]

Six factors that drive the success of global companies are listed in Exhibit 5.9, Strategy in Action. They address key aspects of globalizing a business's operations and provide a framework within which companies can effectively pursue the global marketplace.

The Global Challenge

Although industries can be characterized as global or multidomestic, few "pure" cases of either type exist. A global firm competing in a global industry must be responsive, to some degree, to local market conditions. Similarly, a global firm competing in a multidomestic industry cannot totally ignore opportunities to utilize intracorporate resources in competitive positioning. Thus, each global firm must decide which of its corporate functional activities should be performed where and what degree of coordination should exist among them.

[2] G. Harveland and C. K. Prahalad, "Managing Strategic Responsibility in the MNC," *Strategic Management Journal*, October–December 1983, pp. 341–51.

Factors That Drive Global Companies

1. Global Management Team
Possesses global vision and culture.

Includes foreign nationals.

Leaves management of subsidiaries to foreign nationals.

Frequently travels internationally.

Has cross-cultural training.

2. Global Strategy
Implement strategy as opposed to independent country strategies.

Develop significant cross-country alliances.

Select country targets strategically rather than opportunistically.

Perform business functions where most efficient—no home-country bias.

Emphasize participation in the triad—North America, Europe, and Japan.

3. Global Operations and Products
Use common core operating processes worldwide to ensure quantity and uniformity.

Product globally to obtain best cost and market advantage.

4. Global Technology and R&D
Design global products but take regional differences into account.

Manage development work centrally but carry out globally.

Do not duplicate R&D and product development; gain economies of scale.

5. Global Financing
Finance globally to obtain lowest cost.

Hedge when necessary to protect currency risk.

Price in local currencies.

List shares on foreign exchanges.

6. Global Marketing
Market global products but provide regional discretion if economies of scale are not affected.

Develop global brands.

Use core global marketing practices and themes.

Simultaneously introduce new global products worldwide.

Source: Reprinted from *Business Horizons*, Volume 37, Robert N. Lussier, Robert W. Baeder and Joel Corman, "Measuring Global Practices: Global Strategic Planning through Company Situational Analysis," p. 57. Copyright © 1994, with permission from Elsevier.

Location and Coordination of Functional Activities

Typical functional activities of a firm include purchases of input resources, operations, research and development, marketing and sales, and after-sales service. A multinational corporation has a wide range of possible location options for each of these activities and must decide which sets of activities will be performed in how many and which locations. A multinational corporation may have each location perform each activity, or it may center an activity in one location to serve the organization worldwide. For example, research and development centered in one facility may serve the entire organization.

A multinational corporation also must determine the degree to which functional activities are to be coordinated across locations. Such coordination can be extremely low, allowing each location to perform each activity autonomously, or extremely high, tightly linking the functional activities of different locations. Coca-Cola tightly links its R&D and marketing functions worldwide to offer a standardized brand name, concentrate formula, market positioning, and advertising theme. However, its operations function is more autonomous, with the artificial sweetener and packaging differing across locations.

Location and Coordination Issues

Exhibit 5.10 presents some of the issues related to the critical dimensions of location and coordination in multinational strategic planning. It also shows the functional activities that

EXHIBIT 5.10
Location and Coordination Issues of Functional Activities

Functional Activity	Location Issues	Coordination Issues
Operations	Location of production facilities for components.	Networking of international plants.
Marketing	Product line selection. Country (market) selection.	Commonality of brand name worldwide. Coordination of sales to multinational accounts. Similarity of channels and product positioning worldwide. Coordination of pricing in different countries
Service	Location of service organization.	Similarity of service standards and procedures worldwide.
Research and development	Number and location of R&D centers.	Interchange among dispersed R&D centers. Developing products responsive to market needs in many countries. Sequence of product introductions around the world.
Purchasing	Location of the purchasing function.	Managing suppliers located in different countries. Transferring market knowledge. Coordinating purchases of common items.

Source: From Michael E. Porter, "Changing Patterns of International Competition," *California Management Review,* Winter 1986. Copyright © 1986, by The Regents of the University of California. Reprinted from the California Management review, Vol. 28, No. 2. By permission of The Regents.

the firm performs with regard to each of these dimensions. For example, in connection with the service function, a firm must decide where to perform after-sale service and whether to standardize such service.

How a particular firm should address location and coordination issues depends on the nature of its industry and on the type of international strategy that the firm is pursuing. As discussed earlier, an industry can be ranked along a continuum that ranges between multidomestic at one extreme and global at the other. Little coordination of functional activities across countries may be necessary in a multidomestic industry, since competition occurs within each country in such an industry. However, as its industry becomes increasingly global, a firm must begin to coordinate an increasing number of functional activities to effectively compete across countries.

Going global impacts every aspect of a company's operations and structure. As firms redefine themselves as global competitors, workforces are becoming increasingly diversified. The most significant challenge for firms, therefore, is the ability to adjust to a workforce of varied cultures and lifestyles and the capacity to incorporate cultural differences to the benefit of the company's mission.

Market Requirements and Product Characteristics

Businesses have discovered that being successful in foreign markets often demands much more than simply shipping their well-received domestic products overseas. Firms must

Rate of Change of Product

Fast

Maintain differentiation	**Operate an ever-changing "global warehouse"**
Computer chips	Consumer Watch cases
Automotive electronics	electronics Dolls
Color film	Automobiles
Pharmaceutical	Trucks
Chemicals	
Telecommunications	
Network equipment	Toothpaste Industrial
	Shampoo machinery

Standardized in All Markets — — — — — — — — — — — — — — — — — — **Customized Market-by-Market**

Minimize Delivered Cost	**Practice** Toilets
Steel	**Opportunistic** Chocolate
Petrochemicals (e.g.,	**Niche** bars
polyethylene)	**Exploration**
Cola beverages	
Fabric for	
men's shirts	

Slow

Source: Lawrence H. Wortzel, *1989 International Business Book* (Strategic Direction Publishers, 1989).

assess two key dimensions of customer demand: customers' acceptance of standardized products and the rate of product innovation desired. As shown in Exhibit 5.11, Global Strategy in Action, all markets can be arrayed along a continuum from markets in which products are standardized to markets in which products must be customized for customers from market to market. Standardized products in all markets include color film and petrochemicals, while dolls and toilets are good examples of customized products.

Similarly, products can be arrayed along a continuum from products that are not subject to frequent product innovations to products that are often upgraded. Products with a fast rate of change include computer chips and industrial machinery, while steel and chocolate bars are products that fit in the slow rate of change category.

Exhibit 5.11 shows that the two dimensions can be combined to enable companies to simultaneously assess both customer need for product standardization and rate of product innovation. The examples listed demonstrate the usefulness of the model in helping firms to determine the degree of customization that they must be willing to accept to become engaged in transnational operations.

International Strategy Options

Exhibit 5.12, Global Strategy in Action, presents the basic multinational strategy options that have been derived from a consideration of the location and coordination dimensions. Low coordination and geographic dispersion of functional activities are implied if a firm is operating in a multidomestic industry and has chosen a country-centered strategy. This allows each subsidiary to closely monitor the local market conditions it faces and to respond freely to these conditions.

High coordination and geographic concentration of functional activities result from the choice of a pure global strategy. Although some functional activities, such as after-sale

International Strategy Options

	Geographically Dispersed	Geographically Concentrated
High	High foreign investment with extensive coordination among subsidiaries	Global strategy
Low	Country-centered strategy by multinationals with a number of domestic firms operating in only one country	Export-based strategy with decentralized marketing

Coordination of Activities (vertical axis: High / Low)

Location of Activities (horizontal axis: Geographically Dispersed / Geographically Concentrated)

Source: From Michael E. Porter, "Changing Patterns of International Competition," *California Management Review*, Winter 1986. Copyright © 1986, by The Regents of the University of California. Reprinted from the *California Management Review*, Vol. 28, No. 2. By permission of The Regents.

service, may need to be located in each market, tight control of those activities is necessary to ensure standardized performance worldwide. For example, IBM expects the same high level of marketing support and service for all of its customers, regardless of their location.

Two other strategy options are shown in Exhibit 5.12. High foreign investment with extensive coordination among subsidiaries would describe the choice of remaining at a particular growth stage, such as that of an exporter. An export-based strategy with decentralized marketing would describe the choice of moving toward globalization, which a multinational firm might make.

COMPETITIVE STRATEGIES FOR FIRMS IN FOREIGN MARKETS

Strategies for firms that are attempting to move toward globalization can be categorized by the degree of complexity of each foreign market being considered and by the diversity in a company's product line (see Exhibit 5.13, Global Strategy in Action). *Complexity* refers to the number of critical success factors that are required to prosper in a given competitive arena. When a firm must consider many such factors, the requirements of success increase in complexity. *Diversity,* the second variable, refers to the breadth of a firm's business lines. When a company offers many product lines, diversity is high.

Together, the complexity and diversity dimensions form a continuum of possible strategic choices. Combining these two dimensions highlights many possible actions.

Niche Market Exporting

The primary niche market approach for the company that wants to export is to modify select product performance or measurement characteristics to meet special foreign demands.

Escalating Commitments to International Markets

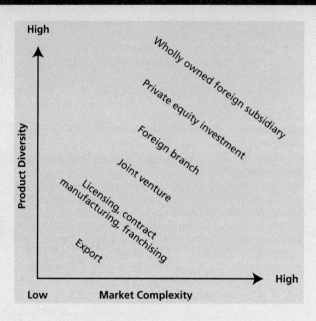

Combining product criteria from both the U.S. and the foreign markets can be slow and tedious. There are, however, a number of expansion techniques that provide the U.S. firm with the know-how to exploit opportunities in the new environment. For example, copying product innovations in countries where patent protection is not emphasized and utilizing nonequity contractual arrangements with a foreign partner can assist in rapid product innovation. N. V. Philips and various Japanese competitors, such as Sony and Matsushita, now are working together for common global product standards within their markets. Siemens, with a centralized R&D in electronics, also has been very successful with this approach.

The Taiwanese company, Gigabyte, researched the U.S. market and found that a sizable number of computer buyers wanted a PC that could complete the basic tasks provided by domestic desktops, but that would be considerably smaller. Gigabyte decided to serve this niche market by exporting their mini-PCs into the United States with a price tag of $200 to $300. This price was considerably less than the closest U.S. manufacturer, Dell, whose minicomputer was still larger and cost $766.

Exporting usually requires minimal capital investment. The organization maintains its quality control standards over production processes and finished goods inventory, and risk to the survival of the firm is typically minimal. Additionally, the U.S. Commerce Department through its Export Now Program and related government agencies lowers the risks to smaller companies by providing export information and marketing advice.

Licensing and Contract Manufacturing

Establishing a contractual arrangement is the next step for U.S. companies that want to venture beyond exporting but are not ready for an equity position on foreign soil. Licensing involves the transfer of some industrial property right from the U.S. licensor to a motivated licensee. Most tend to be patents, trademarks, or technical know-how that are granted to the licensee for a specified time in return for a royalty and for avoiding tariffs or import quotas. Bell South and U.S. West, with various marketing and service competitive advantages valuable to Europe, have extended a number of licenses to create personal computer networks in the United Kingdom.

Another licensing strategy open to U.S. firms is to contract the manufacturing of its product line to a foreign company to exploit local comparative advantages in technology, materials, or labor.

U.S. firms that use either licensing option will benefit from lowering the risk of entry into the foreign markets. Clearly, alliances of this type are not for everyone. They are used best in companies large enough to have a combination of international strategic activities and for firms with standardized products in narrow margin industries.

Two major problems exist with licensing. One is the possibility that the foreign partner will gain the experience and evolve into a major competitor after the contract expires. The experience of some U.S. electronics firms with Japanese companies shows that licensees gain the potential to become powerful rivals. The other potential problem stems from the control that the licensor forfeits on production, marketing, and general distribution of its products. This loss of control minimizes a company's degrees of freedom as it reevaluates its future options.

Franchising

A special form of licensing is franchising, which allows the franchisee to sell a highly publicized product or service, using the parent's brand name or trademark, carefully developed procedures, and marketing strategies. In exchange, the franchisee pays a fee to the parent company, typically based on the volume of sales of the franchisor in its defined market area. The franchise is operated by the local investor who must adhere to the strict policies of the parent.

Franchising is so popular that an estimated 500 U.S. businesses now franchise to over 50,000 local owners in foreign countries. Among the most active franchisees are Avis, Burger King, Canada Dry, Coca-Cola, Hilton, Kentucky Fried Chicken, Manpower, Marriott, Midas, Muzak, Pepsi, and ServiceMaster. However, the acknowledged global champion of franchising is McDonald's, which has 70 percent of its company-owned stores as franchisees in foreign nations.

Joint Ventures

As the multinational strategies of U.S. firms mature, most will include some form of joint venture (JV) with a target nation firm. AT&T followed this option in its strategy to produce its own personal computer by entering into several joint ventures with European producers to acquire the required technology and position itself for European expansion. Because JVs begin with a mutually agreeable pooling of capital, production or marketing equipment, patents, trademarks, or management expertise, they offer more permanent cooperative relationships than export or contract manufacturing.

Compared with full ownership of the foreign entity, JVs provide a variety of benefits to each partner. U.S. firms without the managerial or financial assets to make a profitable independent impact on the integrated foreign markets can share management tasks and cash requirements often at exchange rates that favor the dollar. The coordination of manufacturing and marketing allows ready access to new markets, intelligence data, and reciprocal flows of technical information.

For example, Siemens, the German electronics firm, has a wide range of strategic alliances throughout Europe to share technology and research developments. For years, Siemens grew by acquisitions, but now, to support its horizontal expansion objectives,

Wrapping the Globe in Tortillas

BusinessWeek

Tortillas are a hot topic in Mexico these days. Since December 2006, prices for the staple disks of corn have shot up 67 percent, spurring the government to impose price controls on both finished tortillas and the flour used to make them. In theory, that should be devastating for a company such as Gruma, Mexico's leading flour producer. But that's not so. While Gruma's earnings in Mexico will likely take a hit due to the controls, it is the world's no. 1 tortilla maker, and more than two-thirds of its $3 billion-plus in sales this year will come from outside its home country.

That's because Gruma has spent years building a global market for its quintessentially Mexican comestibles. In September 2006, Gruma opened a new factory in Shanghai that will churn out tens of millions of tortillas annually for KFC restaurants and other customers in China. All told, the company now produces tortillas and chips in 89 factories from Australia to Britain.

But Gruma's global expansion is now speeding up, thanks to CEO Jairo Senise. After getting the top job last year, he took a month-long trip with stops in cities from Manila to Moscow, sampling food in local markets with an eye toward producing tortillas that might fit the local fare. "We're able to think globally but respect the tastes and preferences of each country where we operate," Senise says.

The Shanghai plant is a key part of Gruma's global expansion. The company built the facility at the request of KFC, which had been importing frozen Gruma tortillas from California for the chicken wrap sandwiches it offers in more than 1,800 restaurants in China.

The company's international operations seem to be running more smoothly than those at home. That's because of the price controls, which the government introduced on January 18, 2007, after the cost of imported corn soared. Gruma, which supplies 75 percent of Mexico's corn flour for tortillas, had to agree to keep a lid on its prices. As a result, Merrill Lynch & Co. predicts Gruma will earn $111 million on $3.1 billion in sales in 2007, versus estimated profits of $145 million and revenues of $2.85 billion in 2006.

Senise is now eyeing opportunities in South Africa, Morocco, Egypt, and India. And he'd like to move into industrial tortilla production at home, where mom-and-pop tortillerias dominate the market and Gruma mainly sells flour. That could be tough. Today, Gruma makes tortillas only in a few cities, and Mexico's anti-monopoly watchdog may not allow it to expand.

Source: Reprinted with special permission from Geri Smith, "Wrapping the Globe in Tortillas," *BusinessWeek*, February 26, 2007. Copyright © 2007 The McGraw-Hill Companies.

it is engaged in joint ventures with companies like Groupe Bull of France, International Computers of Britain, General Electric Company of Britain, IBM, Intel, Philips, and Rolm. Another example is Airbus Industries, which produces wide-body passenger planes for the world market as a direct result of JVs among many companies in Britain, France, Spain, and Germany.

JVs speed up the efforts of U.S. firms to integrate into the political, corporate, and cultural infrastructure of the foreign environment, often with a lower financial commitment than acquiring a foreign subsidiary. General Electric's (GE) 3 percent share in the European lighting market was very weak and below expectations. Significant increases in competition throughout many of their American markets by the European giant, Philips Lighting, forced GE to retaliate by expanding in Europe. GE's first strategy was an attempted joint venture with the Siemens lighting subsidiary, Osram, and with the British electronics firm, Thorn EMI. Negotiations failed over control issues. When recent events in Eastern Europe opened the opportunity for a JV with the Hungarian lighting manufacturer, Tungsram, which was receiving 70 percent of revenues from the West, GE capitalized on it.

Although joint ventures can address many of the requirements of complex markets and diverse product lines, U.S. firms considering either equity- or non-equity-based JVs face many challenges. For example, making full use of the native firm's comparative advantage

Russians Have Driven a Ford Lately

BusinessWeek

In 2006, New York Motors, on a commercial strip in southwest Moscow, sold more Fords than any other dealership in the world. All told, salesmen in the crowded showroom moved 10,060 vehicles, helping Ford race past rivals Hyundai, Toyota, and Chevrolet to become the top-selling auto nameplate in Russia.

The brand's success in Russia stands in striking contrast to Ford Motor Co.'s flagging fortunes elsewhere. The automaker clocked a global loss of $12.7 billion in 2006, but sales of Ford-branded vehicles in Russia soared 92 percent, to 115,985 cars and trucks, for some $2 billion in revenues. That's partly due to Russia's thriving economy, which has stoked strong demand for foreign models. In 2006, foreign brands outsold domestic nameplates for the first time, topping 1 million—a 65 percent increase from 2005 and 20 times the level in 2000, according to the Association of European Businesses in Moscow.

In 1999, Ford made a big bet on Russia, spending $150 million on a plant near St. Petersburg—the country's first foreign-owned auto factory. The facility opened in 2002, and in 2006 production climbed to 62,400 Focus sedans, hatchbacks, and wagons.

Competition is heating up as rivals copy Ford's strategy of local production. Volkswagen, Toyota, Nissan, GM, and Fiat have all announced plans to build plants in Russia.

Still, local production has helped Ford keep prices down. Although about 80 percent of the parts used in the Focus are imported, the company sells the cars for as little as $13,000, or about $3,000 less than similarly equipped imports, which are subject to a 25 percent duty. While that's not exactly pocket change in Russia, it's low enough for a growing number of middle-class consumers. Sure, the cheapest Focus is nearly $4,000 more than a Russian-made Lada or low-cost foreign cars such as the Renault Logan and Daewoo Nexia.

Source: Reprinted with special permission from Jason Bush, "They've Driven a Ford Lately: Russians Are Snapping Up Its Locally Made Models in Record Numbers," *BusinessWeek*, February 26, 2007. Copyright © 2007 The McGraw-Hill Companies.

---

may involve managerial relationships where no single authority exists to make strategic decisions or solve conflicts. Additionally, dealing with host-company management requires the disclosure of proprietary information and the potential loss of control over production and marketing quality standards. Addressing such challenges with well-defined covenants agreeable to all parties is difficult. Equally important is the compatibility of partners and their enduring commitments to mutually supportive goals. Without this compatibility and commitment, a joint venture is critically endangered.

Foreign Branching

A foreign branch is an extension of the company in its foreign market—a separately located strategic business unit directly responsible for fulfilling the operational duties assigned to it by corporate management, including sales, customer service, and physical distribution. Host countries may require that the branch be "domesticated," that is, have some local managers in middle and upper-level positions. The branch most likely will be outside any U.S. legal jurisdiction, liabilities may not be restricted to the assets of the given branch, and business licenses for operations may be of short duration, requiring the company to renew them during changing business regulations. Gruma, Mexico's leading flour producer and the world's leading tortillas manufacturer has manufacturing branches in 89 foreign countries. The story of Gruma's success is presented in Exhibit 5.14, Strategy in Action.

Equity Investment

Small and medium-size enterprises with strong growth potential frequently have the need for additional funds to be able to grow further before deciding to trade their stock publicly

private equity
Money from private sources that is invested by a venture capital or private equity company in start-ups and other risky—but potentially very profitable—small and medium-size enterprises.

in the marketplace. These firms often enlist the support of a venture capital firm or **private equity** company that invests its shareholders' money in start-ups and other risky but potentially very profitable small and medium-size enterprises. In exchange for a private equity stake, which is sometimes a majority or controlling position, the Venture Capital (VC) or private equity company provides investment capital and a range of business services, including management expertise.

Wholly Owned Subsidiaries

Wholly owned foreign subsidiaries are considered by companies that are willing and able to make the highest investment commitment to the foreign market. These companies insist on full ownership for reasons of control and managerial efficiency. Policy decisions about local product lines, expansion, profits, and dividends typically remain with the U.S. senior managers. An excellent example of a wholly owned subsidiary is the manufacturing and sales organization of Ford Motor in Russia, as described in Exhibit 5.15, Strategy in Action.

Fully owned subsidiaries can be started either from scratch or by acquiring established firms in the host country. U.S. firms can benefit significantly if the acquired company has complementary product lines or an established distribution or service network.

U.S. firms seeking to improve their competitive postures through a foreign subsidiary face a number of risks to their normal mode of operations. First, if the high capital investment is to be rewarded, managers must attain extensive knowledge of the market, the host nation's language, and its business culture. Second, the host country expects both a long-term commitment from the U.S. enterprise and a portion of their nationals to be employed in positions of management or operations. Fortunately, hiring or training foreign managers for leadership positions is commonly a good policy, because they are close to both the market and contacts. This is especially important for smaller firms when markets are regional. Third, changing standards mandated by foreign regulations may eliminate a company's protected market niche. Product design and worker protection liabilities also may extend back to the home office.

The strategies shown in Exhibit 5.13 are not exhaustive. For example, a firm may engage in any number of joint ventures while maintaining an export business. Additionally, there are a number of other strategies that a firm should consider before deciding on its long-term approach to foreign markets. These will be discussed in detail in Chapter 6 under the topic of grand strategies. However, the strategies discussed in this chapter provide the most popular starting points for planning the globalization of a firm.

Summary

To understand the strategic planning options available to a corporation, its managers need to recognize that different types of industry-based competition exist. Specifically, they must identify the position of their industry along the global versus multidomestic continuum and then consider the implications of that position for their firm.

The differences between global and multidomestic industries about the location and coordination of functional corporate activities necessitate differences in strategic emphasis. As an industry becomes global, managers of firms within that industry must increase the coordination and concentration of functional activities.

The Appendix at the end of this chapter lists many components of the environment with which global corporations must contend. This list is useful in understanding the issues that confront global corporations and in evaluating the thoroughness of global corporation strategies.

As a starting point for global expansion, the firm's mission statement needs to be reviewed and revised. As global operations fundamentally alter the direction and strategic capabilities of a firm, its mission statement, if originally developed from a domestic perspective, must be globalized.

The globalized mission statement provides the firm with a unity of direction that transcends the divergent perspectives of geographically dispersed managers. It provides a basis for strategic decisions in situations where strategic alternatives may appear to conflict. It promotes corporate values and commitments that extend beyond single cultures and satisfies the demands of the firm's internal and external claimants in different countries. Finally, it ensures the survival of the global corporation by asserting the global corporation's legitimacy with respect to support coalitions in a variety of operating environments.

Movement of a firm toward globalization often follows a systematic pattern of development. Commonly, businesses begin their foreign nation involvements progressively through niche market exporting, license-contract manufacturing, franchising, joint ventures, foreign branching, and foreign subsidiaries.

Key Terms

ethnocentric orientation, *p. 133*

geocentric orientation, *p. 133*

global industry, *p. 140*

globalization, *p. 130*

multidomestic industry, *p. 139*

polycentric orientation, *p. 133*

private equity, *p. 150*

regiocentric orientation, *p. 133*

stakeholder activism, *p. 139*

Questions for Discussion

1. How does environmental analysis at the domestic level differ from global analysis?
2. Which factors complicate environmental analysis at the global level? Which factors are making such analysis easier?
3. Do you agree with the suggestion that soon all industries will need to evaluate global environments?
4. Which industries operate almost devoid of global competition? Which inherent immunities do they enjoy?
5. Explain when and why it is important for a company to globalize.
6. Describe the four main strategic orientations of global firms.
7. Explain the control problems that are faced by global firms.
8. Describe the differences between multinational and global firms.
9. Describe the market requirements and product characteristics in global competition.
10. Evaluate the competitive strategies for firms in foreign markets:
    a. Niche market exporting
    b. Licensing and contract manufacturing
    c. Franchising
    d. Joint ventures
    e. Foreign branching
    f. Private equity investment
    g. Wholly owned subsidiaries

Chapter 5 Discussion Case

China Mobile's Hot Signal

1   Dagoucun feels like the kind of place that progress missed entirely in its sweep through China. Nestled at 10,000 feet in the pine-studded foothills of the Tibetan plateau, the village is little more than a few dozen stone houses and a Buddhist shrine. Getting there from the nearest big city, Chengdu, takes five hours by car, much of it on a muddy, rutted road.

2   But given the electronic trills emanating from the fields of barley, potatoes, and corn, it's clear that the twenty-first century has finally made it to Dagoucun. Last year, the village got cell-phone service, dramatically transforming the way its residents live and work. With better information about crop prices delivered to their phones, farmers have started planting more marketable crops such as Chinese cabbage and herbs for traditional medicines. And they no longer have to truck their produce to distant cities in hopes of finding buyers. "Before, we had to travel 20 kilometers to make a phone call," says village chief Xie Sufang, a 65-year-old mother of seven. "Now we contact the buyers, and they come to us."

3   The company responsible for bringing change to this rural outpost: China Mobile Ltd. Since it was spun off from fixed-line operator China Telecom Corp. in 2000, China Mobile has grown into the world's biggest cellular carrier. The company is signing up nearly 5 million new customers a month and recently topped the 300 million mark—more than the entire population of the United States. In 2006, revenues grew 21 percent, to $37.8 billion, and net income 23 percent, to $8.7 billion, estimates Deutsche Bank. And its Hong Kong–traded shares more than doubled in the past year, giving China Mobile a market capitalization of $198 billion and making it the most valuable cellular carrier on earth. The company also has global ambitions: on January 22, 2007, it announced it was buying 89 percent of Paktel Ltd., Pakistan's fifth-largest cellular carrier.

4   China Mobile built its early success on urban China. Problem is, just about everyone in mainland cities who can afford cellular service already has it. Mobile-phone penetration in Beijing, Shanghai, and Shenzhen is approaching 100 percent. So to keep growing, China Mobile is plunging ever deeper into the interior, building cell towers from the deserts of Inner Mongolia to the mountains of Tibet. In rural China, home to 700 million, just over 1 in 10 people has a cell phone. "It is a market with huge potential," says China Mobile Chairman Wang Jianzhou.

5   China Mobile's torrid growth hasn't escaped the attention of Western companies seeking to tap the potential of China, both urban and rural. The carrier has inked agreements with Vodafone Group, News Corp., Viacom's MTV Networks, and the National Basketball Association. Last summer, China Mobile launched a music-download service called M.Music in partnership with Sony bmg, Universal Music Group, emi,

and Warner Music. And on January, 4, 2007, Google Inc. announced that its search engine would be featured on China Mobile's Monternet mobile phone portal.

6   What's behind the flurry of deals? "We want to make the cell phone into a new medium," says Wang. The company is aggressively pushing extras such as ringtones and music downloads. Demand for such services is expected to surge with the launch of third-generation (3G) mobile technology in time for the Beijing Olympics in 2008. Beijing telecom consultancy BDA China estimates revenues from such services will jump from $10.4 billion last year to $28.6 billion by 2010. Wang believes his company's continued dominance of China's cell-phone market will depend on the news, entertainment, and music it can beam to subscribers. So in June, China Mobile plunked down $166 million for a 19.9 percent stake in Phoenix Satellite Television Holdings, the mainland's most popular cable news and entertainment channel.

7   China Mobile is also turning its sights overseas. Its $284 million purchase of Paktel, likely to conclude in late February, 2007, will be the company's first overseas acquisition, though early last year it bought Hong Kong's No. 4 mobile company, People's Telephone, with 1.1 million subscribers. Last summer, China Mobile made a $5 billion-plus play for Luxembourg's Millicom International Cellular—Paktel's parent—which has mobile networks in Africa and Latin America as well as Asia. But negotiations broke down due to concerns about the big price tag, analysts say. While Wang declined to comment on the collapse of the Millicom talks, he says China Mobile is interested in acquisitions in other developing countries: "We are familiar with emerging markets. Their experiences may be very similar to ours."

8   Wang has plenty to keep him busy at home as the government turns up the competitive heat on the cell-phone industry. Until now, China Mobile has had to contend with just one rival: China Unicom Ltd. Like China Mobile, Unicom is listed in Hong Kong and is state-controlled. With 143 million subscribers, though, Unicom is a distant no. 2, which some attribute to the complications it faces in maintaining a network that uses two mobile standards. China Mobile, by contrast, can operate more efficiently using a single technology, the gsm standard developed in Europe. Sometime this year, Beijing is expected to award 3G licenses to both current carriers and also possibly to two new rivals, most likely China's state-owned fixed-line operators, China Netcom Group and China Telecom.

PROFIT PUSH

9   China's leadership could complicate life for Wang & Co. in other ways, too. In an effort to boost its international prestige,

Beijing is pushing the development of a homegrown 3G standard not used elsewhere. China Mobile, China Netcom, and China Telecom are all currently running trials of the new technology. But analysts expect China Mobile to win the dubious honor of leading the rollout, which could be a costly distraction that will almost certainly be more complex than introducing one of the 3G standards already deployed in other countries. Being forced to build a network using China's technology "definitely is a liability," says Zhang Dongming, director of research at consultancy BDA.

10 Even with a smooth rollout of 3G, China Mobile could have a tough time keeping revenue and earnings growing at double-digit rates. As it pushes ever deeper into the interior, the company faces the same dilemma as the likes of Procter & Gamble Co. and General Motors Corp.: how to win new customers without sacrificing profit margins. Incomes in rural China average just over $400 per year, or less than one-third what city dwellers earn. To drum up business in places such as Dagoucun, China Mobile is cutting prices, and the amount of money it gets from each subscriber has declined modestly in the past year, to about $11. "The key is to maintain profitability even while penetrating rural areas," says Steve Zhang, CEO of Beijing's AsiaInfo Holdings Inc., a telecom software and services company that works with China Mobile.

11 Wang insists he's not jeopardizing earnings. One reason, he says, is that China Mobile runs a much leaner operation in the countryside. It has largely dispensed with stores and is instead relying on village chiefs such as Xie to persuade neighbors to buy handsets and prepaid cards. China Mobile offers cell-phone plans tailored for farmers that include information such as crop prices and tips on duck breeding delivered via text message, the Internet, and a call-in phone service. The plan costs a nominal 25 cents a month, but users must pay extra to place calls and send text messages. Since its launch in October, 2006, the service has been rolled out to 12 provinces in western China and is expected to go nationwide later this year. "Our main purpose now is to provide farmers with information that benefits them," says Qin Dabin, vice general manager of China Mobile's operations in the western city of Chongqing. Although it will take some time before the initiative turns a profit, Qin says it's helping to attract subscribers.

12 China Mobile isn't abandoning cities, either. Far from it. The company has an upscale service called Go-Tone for businesspeople. The $6.40 basic monthly fee (phone and message charges are extra) includes reduced membership rates at golf courses and access to VIP waiting rooms at many Chinese airports. And a $2-a-month plan called M-Zone is aimed at music-mad teenagers and twentysomethings. China Mobile puts on special events for M-Zone members, such as appearances by the likes of Chinese-American pop star Pan Weibo.

13 Meanwhile, back in the mountains of Sichuan, villagers are figuring out more ways to wring money from their new phones. Cabbages from Dagoucun now travel all the way to the southern cities of Guangzhou and Shenzhen as it's easier to reach buyers across the country. Villagers have sold a rare caterpillar fungus—prized in Asia for its antiviral attributes—to customers in Singapore who were contacted via cell phone. And residents are building a three-story lodge for mountain climbers and anglers in a bid to transform their remote village into a flourishing center for ecotourism. "With our mobile phones, potential tourists can contact us and learn more about our village," says village chief Xie. "We can increase our incomes in many ways."

Telecom Titans: The World's Biggest Cellular Companies

Operator	Subscriber Accounts (millions)	Average Revenue per User
China Mobile	300	$11.19
China Unicom	143	6.80
Cingular	60	49.76
Verizon Wireless	59	50.59
Sprint USA	54	52.25

Source: Reprinted with special permission from Dexter Roberts, "China Mobile's Hot Signal: It's Already the World's Biggest Cellular Carrier. Now It's Planning to Get Even Bigger," *BusinessWeek*, February 2007. Copyright © 2007 The McGraw-Hill Companies.

DISCUSSION QUESTIONS

1. How do you believe that the mobile phone industry in China differs form the one in the United States?

2. Do you think that the investment opportunity in China's mobile phone industry is attractive?

3. What difficulties do you expect China's mobile phone industry to encounter as it tries to expand?

4. Can you detect any patterns or rules of development from the China mobile phone industry that could be applied to the development of the mobile phone industry in other countries?

5. Do you agree that "globalization is the strategy of approaching worldwide markets with standardized products?" Are mobile phones an example?

Chapter 5 Appendix

Components of the Multinational Environment

Multinational firms must operate within an environment that has numerous components. These components include the following:

1. Government, laws, regulations, and policies of home country (United States, for example)

   a. Monetary and fiscal policies and their effect on price trends, interest rates, economic growth, and stability
   b. Balance-of-payments policies
   c. Mandatory controls on direct investment
   d. Interest equalization tax and other policies
   e. Commercial policies, especially tariffs, quantitative import restrictions, and voluntary import controls
   f. Export controls and other restrictions on trade
   g. Tax policies and their impact on overseas business
   h. Antitrust regulations, their administration, and their impact on international business
   i. Investment guarantees, investment surveys, and other programs to encourage private investments in less-developed countries
   j. Export-import and government export expansion programs
   k. Other changes in government policy that affect international business

2. Key political and legal parameters in foreign countries and their projection

   a. Type of political and economic system, political philosophy, national ideology
   b. Major political parties, their philosophies, and their policies
   c. Stability of the government
      (1) Changes in political parties
      (2) Changes in governments
   d. Assessment of nationalism and its possible impact on political environment and legislation
   e. Assessment of political vulnerability
      (1) Possibilities of expropriation
      (2) Unfavorable and discriminatory national legislation and tax laws
      (3) Labor laws and problems
   f. Favorable political aspects
      (1) Tax and other concessions to encourage foreign investments
      (2) Credit and other guarantees
   g. Differences in legal system and commercial law
   h. Jurisdiction in legal disputes
   i. Antitrust laws and rules of competition
   j. Arbitration clauses and their enforcement

   k. Protection of patents, trademarks, brand names, and other industrial property rights

3. Key economic parameters and their projection

   a. Population and its distribution by age groups, density, annual percentage increase, percentage of working age, percentage of total in agriculture, and percentage in urban centers
   b. Level of economic development and industrialization
   c. Gross national product, gross domestic product, or national income in real terms and also on a per capita basis in recent years and projections over future planning period
   d. Distribution of personal income
   e. Measures of price stability and inflation, wholesale price index, consumer price index, other price indexes
   f. Supply of labor, wage rates
   g. Balance-of-payments equilibrium or disequilibrium, level of international monetary reserves, and balance-of-payments policies
   h. Trends in exchange rates, currency stability, evaluation of possibility of depreciation of currency
   i. Tariffs, quantitative restrictions, export controls, border taxes, exchange controls, state trading, and other entry barriers to foreign trade
   j. Monetary, fiscal, and tax policies
   k. Exchange controls and other restrictions on capital movements, repatriation of capital, and remission of earnings

4. Business system and structure

   a. Prevailing business philosophy: mixed capitalism, planned economy, state socialism
   b. Major types of industry and economic activities
   c. Numbers, size, and types of firms, including legal forms of business
   d. Organization: proprietorships, partnerships, limited companies, corporations, cooperatives, state enterprises
   e. Local ownership patterns: public and privately held corporations, family-owned enterprises
   f. Domestic and foreign patterns of ownership in major industries
   g. Business managers available: their education, training, experience, career patterns, attitudes, and reputations
   h. Business associations and chambers of commerce and their influence
   i. Business codes, both formal and informal
   j. Marketing institutions: distributors, agents, wholesalers, retailers, advertising agencies, advertising media, marketing research, and other consultants

k. Financial and other business institutions: commercial and investment banks, other financial institutions, capital markets, money markets, foreign exchange dealers, insurance firms, engineering companies

l. Managerial processes and practices with respect to planning, administration, operations, accounting, budgeting, and control

5. Social and cultural parameters and their projections

  a. Literacy and educational levels

b. Business, economic, technical, and other specialized education available

c. Language and cultural characteristics

d. Class structure and mobility

e. Religious, racial, and national characteristics

f. Degree of urbanization and rural-urban shifts

g. Strength of nationalistic sentiment

h. Rate of social change

i. Impact of nationalism on social and institutional change

Internal Analysis

After reading and studying this chapter, you should be able to

1. Understand how to conduct a SWOT analysis, and be able to summarize its limitations.

2. Understand value chain analysis and how to use it to disaggregate a firm's activities and determine which are most critical to generating competitive advantage.

3. Understand the resource-based view of a firm and how to use it to disaggregate a firm's activities and resources to determine which resources are best used to build competitive advantage.

4. Apply four different perspectives for making meaningful comparisons to assess a firm's internal strengths and weaknesses.

5. Refamiliarize yourself with ratio analysis and basic techniques of financial analysis to assist you in doing internal analysis to identify a firm's strengths and weaknesses.

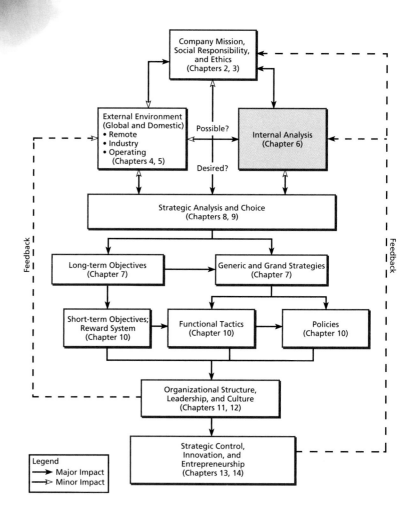

The late R. David Thomas was once ridiculed by many restaurant industry veterans and analysts as he set about building "yet another" hamburger chain named after his young daughter, Wendy. While they thought the name was fine, critics argued that North America was already saturated with hamburger outlets such as McDonald's, Burger King, Hardees, Dairy Queen, White Castle, and others. Yet, as things turned out, Wendy's became the fastest growing restaurant chain in the history of the world, having replaced Burger King as the second largest chain. Cisco, the global leader in networking equipment and switching devices linking wired and wireless computer systems worldwide, twice entered and tried to dominate the home-networking market. It failed each time, wasting more than $250 million in the process. Finally, just a few years ago, it acquired Link-Sys, the market leader, with the promise it would never try to bring Link-Sys into the normal Cisco company structure for fear of destroying the extraordinary success Link-Sys had achieved—not the least of which was vanquishing the much more powerful and wealthy Cisco twice in the last decade. Apple Computer was being written off in the increasingly competitive personal computer industry when it introduced, to a lukewarm reception, its new iPod device and iTunes service. Written off by many as a cute fad, that modest start pioneered a vast new global industry—much like Apple's original personal computer did three decades earlier.

Common to each of these diverse settings were insightful managers and business leaders who based their firm's pursuit of market opportunities not only on the existence of external opportunities but also on a very sound awareness of their firm's competitive advantages arising from the firm's internal resources, capabilities, and skills. A *sound, realistic awareness and appreciation of their firm's internally generated advantages* brought Wendy's, Apple, and Link-Sys immense success while its absence brought much the opposite to Cisco's home-networking ventures and to the competitors and critics of R. David Thomas and Steven Jobs. This chapter, then, focuses on how managers identify the key resources and capabilities around which to build successful strategies.

Managers often do this subjectively, based on intuition and "gut feel." Years of seasoned industry experience positions managers to make sound subjective judgments. But just as often, or more often, this may not be the case. In fast-changing environments, reliance on past experiences can cause management myopia—or a tendency to accept the status quo and disregard signals that change is needed. And with managers new to strategic decision making, subjective decisions are particularly suspect. A lack of experience is easily replaced by emotion, narrow functional expertise, and the opinions of others, thus creating the foundation on which newer managers build strategic recommendations. So it is that new managers' subjective assessments often come back to haunt them.

John W. Henry broke the most fabled curse in sports when his Boston Red Sox won their first World Championship since 1918. Most sports analysts, sports business managers, and regular fans (if they are honest now) would have bet a small fortune, based on their own subjective assessment, that there was no way the Boston Red Sox, having already lost three games, would win four straight games to beat the New York Yankees and then go on to win the World Series. That subjective assessment or "feel" would have led them to believe there were just too many reasons to bet the Red Sox could pull it out. At the same time, a seasoned global futures market trader, John W. Henry, relied on applying his systematic global futures market approach to baseball player selection along with selected other resources and capabilities unique to the Boston area and situation in his bet that the Red Sox could win it all. His very systematic approach to internal analysis of the Boston Red Sox sports enterprise and the leveraging of his/their strengths led to the World Series championship and perhaps many more, as described in Exhibit 6.1, Top Strategist.

Managers often start their internal analysis with questions like, How well is the current strategy working? What is our current situation? Or what are our strengths and weaknesses? The chapter begins with a review of a long-standing, traditional approach managers have

Top Strategist
John W. Henry, CEO of the Boston Red Sox

Exhibit
6.1

John W. Henry, CEO of the Boston
Red Sox, and Slugger David Ortiz

John W. Henry long ago earned his fortune—and a reputation as one of the nation's premier players in the global futures markets. But in 2004 and 2007, Henry may have achieved immortality by leading the Boston Red Sox to their first two World Championships since 1918, reversing the most fabled curse in sports. This triumph was due to more than inspired play of a team that rallied from 0–3 in the American League Championship Series to beat the New York Yankees.

Henry set the stage for victory by applying the same statistical acumen that made him a fortune in the futures market. He also boosted revenue by making the most of Fenway park, the oldest stadium in Major League Baseball, by squeezing in more seats and then charging the highest prices for home games, all of which sold out. At the same time, they started broadcasting home games in high definition on their 80 percent–owned cable sports network, New England Sports Network—helping it routinely win in regional prime-time ratings.

All of this turned the Red Sox into baseball's second-most-lucrative franchise and gave it the financial muscle to take on the Yankees, who consistently open every season with a league-leading record payroll. The Sox are now consistently second in payroll, thanks to Henry.

Henry—a numbers genius, whose proprietary futures-trading system consistently produces double-digit returns—closed the gap with sabermetrics. That's a system for mining baseball stats to find undervalued players while avoiding long contracts for aging stars—such as pitcher Pedro Martinez—whose performance is likely to decline. Henry built baseball's most effective team but won't settle for one championship. After ending an 86-year drought, he's aiming for a dynasty.

Sources: Reprinted with special permission from "Who Needs Johnny Damon," *BusinessWeek*, March 20, 2006; and "John Henry: Boston Red Sox," *BusinessWeek*, January 10, 2005, p. 61. Copyright © 2006 The McGraw-Hill Companies.

frequently used to answer these questions, SWOT analysis. This approach is a logical framework intended to help managers thoughtfully consider their company's internal capabilities and use the results to shape strategic options. Its value and continued use is found in its simplicity. At the same time, SWOT analysis has limitations that have led strategists to seek more comprehensive frameworks for conducting internal analysis.

Value chain analysis is one such framework. Value chain analysis views a firm as a "chain" or sequential process of value-creating activities. The sum of all of these activities represents the "value" the firm exists to provide its customers. So undertaking an internal analysis that breaks down the firm into these distinct value activities allows for a detailed, interrelated evaluation of a firm's internal strengths and weaknesses that improves upon what strategists can create using only SWOT analysis.

The resource-based view (RBV) of a firm is another important framework for conducting internal analysis. This approach improves upon SWOT analysis by examining a variety of different yet specific types of resources and capabilities any firm possesses and then evaluating the degree to which they become the basis for sustained competitive advantage based on industry and competitive considerations. In so doing, it provides a disciplined approach to internal analysis.

Common to all the approaches to internal analysis is the use of meaningful standards for comparison in internal analysis. We conclude this chapter by examining how managers use past performance, comparison with competitors or other "benchmarks," industry norms, and traditional financial analysis to make meaningful comparisons.

SWOT ANALYSIS: A TRADITIONAL APPROACH TO INTERNAL ANALYSIS

SWOT analysis
SWOT is an acronym for the internal Strengths and Weaknesses of a firm, and the environmental Opportunities and Threats facing that firm. SWOT analysis is a technique through which managers create a quick overview of a company's strategic situation.

SWOT is an acronym for the internal **S**trengths and **W**eaknesses of a firm and the environmental **O**pportunities and **T**hreats facing that firm. **SWOT analysis** is a historically popular technique through which managers create a quick overview of a company's strategic situation. It is based on the assumption that an effective strategy derives from a sound "fit" between a firm's internal resources (strengths and weaknesses) and its external situation (opportunities and threats). A good fit maximizes a firm's strengths and opportunities and minimizes its weaknesses and threats. Accurately applied, this simple assumption has sound, insightful implications for the design of a successful strategy.

Environmental and industry analysis in Chapters 3 and 4 provides the information needed to identify opportunities and threats in a firm's environment, the first fundamental focus in SWOT analysis.

Opportunities

opportunity
A major favorable situation in a firm's environment.

An **opportunity** is a major favorable situation in a firm's environment. Key trends are one source of opportunities. Identification of a previously overlooked market segment, changes in competitive or regulatory circumstances, technological changes, and improved buyer or supplier relationships could represent opportunities for the firm. Sustained, growing interest in organic foods has created an opportunity that is a critical factor shaping strategic decisions at groceries and restaurants worldwide.

Threats

threat
A major unfavorable situation in a firm's environment.

A **threat** is a major unfavorable situation in a firm's environment. Threats are key impediments to the firm's current or desired position. The entrance of new competitors, slow market growth, increased bargaining power of key buyers or suppliers, technological changes, and new or revised regulations could represent threats to a firm's success.

Large national residential home builders have seen rising interest rates start to slow demand for single-family housing developments nationwide. These same residential home builders have had to face an increasing threat of rapidly accelerating energy and materials costs brought on both by their collective, fast-paced development activities, further exacerbated by the exploding demand for these same building supplies in the Chinese marketplace. So these large national home builders had to craft strategies built around these major threats to survive and eventually grow.

Once managers agree on key opportunities and threats facing their firm, they have a frame of reference or context from which to evaluate their firm's ability to take advantage of opportunities and minimize the effect of key threats. And vice versa: Once managers agree on their firm's core strengths and weaknesses, they can logically move to consider opportunities that best leverage their firm's strengths while minimizing the effect certain weaknesses may present until remedied.

strength
A resource advantage relative to competitors and the needs of the markets a firm serves or expects to serve.

Strengths

A **strength** is a resource or capability controlled by or available to a firm that gives it an advantage relative to its competitors in meeting the needs of the customers it serves.

Strengths arise from the resources and competencies available to the firm. Southland Log Homes' southeastern plant locations (Virginia, South Carolina, and Mississippi) provide both transportation and raw material cost advantages along with ideal proximity to the United States' most rapidly growing second-home markets. Southland has leveraged these strengths to take advantage of the moderate interest rates and rapidly growing baby boomer second-home demand trend to become the largest log home company in North America.

Weaknesses

weakness
A limitation or deficiency in one or more resources or competencies relative to competitors that impedes a firm's effective performance.

A **weakness** is a limitation or deficiency in one or more of a firm's resources or capabilities relative to its competitors that create a disadvantage in effectively meeting customer needs. Limited financial capacity was a weakness recognized by Southwest Airlines, which charted a selective route expansion strategy to build the best profit record in a deregulated airline industry.

Using SWOT Analysis in Strategic Analysis

The most common use of SWOT analysis is as a logical framework guiding discussion and reflection about a firm's situation and basic alternatives. This often takes place as a series of managerial group discussions. What one manager sees as an opportunity, another may see as a potential threat. Likewise, a strength to one manager may be a weakness to another. The SWOT framework provides an organized basis for insightful discussion and information sharing, which may improve the quality of choices and decisions managers subsequently make. Consider what initial discussions among Apple Computer's management team might have been that led to the decision to pursue the rapid development and introduction of the iPod. A brief SWOT analysis of their situation might have identified:

Strengths

Sizable miniature storage expertise

User-friendly engineering skill

Reputation and image with youthful consumers

Brand name

Web-savvy organization and people

Jobs's Pixar experience

Weaknesses

Economies of scale versus computer rivals

Maturing computer markets

Limited financial resources

Limited music industry expertise

Opportunities

Confused online music situation

Emerging file-sharing restrictions

Few core computer-related opportunities

Digitalization of movies and music

Threats

Growing global computer companies

Major computer competitors

EXHIBIT 6.2
SWOT Analysis
Diagram

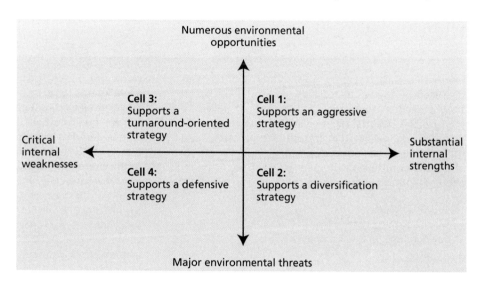

It is logical to envision Apple managers' discussions evolving to a consensus that the combination of Apple's storage and digitalization strengths along with their strong brand franchise with "hip" consumers, when combined with the opportunity potentially arising out of the need for a simple way to legally buy and download music on the Web would be the basis for a compelling strategy for Apple to become a first mover in the emerging downloadable music industry.

Exhibit 6.2 illustrates how SWOT analysis might take managerial planning discussions into a slightly more structured approach to aid strategic analysis. The objective is identification of one of four distinct patterns in the match between a firm's internal resources and external situation. Cell 1 is the most favorable situation; the firm faces several environmental opportunities and has numerous strengths that encourage pursuit of those opportunities. This situation suggests growth-oriented strategies to exploit the favorable match. Our example of Apple Computer's intensive market development strategy in the online music services and the iPod is the result of a favorable match of its strong technical expertise, early entry, and reputation resources with an opportunity for impressive market growth as millions of people sought a legally viable, convenient way to obtain, download, store, and use their own customized music choices.

Sun Microsystems applied SWOT analysis, creating an advertisement responding to the Hewlett-Packard (HP) board of directors' ongoing search for a new CEO after their dismissal of celebrity CEO Carly Fiorina. The ad shows Sun Microsystems attempting a Cell 1 strategic response pursuing a key opportunity made available by the uncertainty for HP corporate clients during this time (see Exhibit 6.3, Strategy in Action). In the ad, as you can see, Sun simply attempts to state—in very direct terms—what it believes its strengths might be for interested and frustrated HP clients (and, subtly, IBM's customers) in the face of this opportunity created for Sun by HP's strategic confusion.

Cell 4 is the least favorable situation, with the firm facing major environmental threats from a weak resource position. This situation clearly calls for strategies that reduce or redirect involvement in the products or markets examined by means of SWOT analysis. Texas Instruments offers a good example of a cell 4 firm. It was a sprawling maker of chips, calculators, laptop PCs, military electronics, and engineering software on a sickening slide toward oblivion just 10 years ago. Its young CEO, Tom Engibous, reinvigorated the ailing electronics giant and turned it into one of the hottest plays in semiconductors by betting the company on an emerging class of chips known

Sun Microsystems Uses a SWOT Analysis to Target Frustrated HP Customers in 2005

BusinessWeek

Hewlett-Packard celebrity CEO Carly Fiorina was dismissed by the HP board, five years after her hard-fought decision to merge Compaq and HP failed to produce the payoffs she predicted. Sun Microsystems placed the following ad in *The Wall Street Journal* and other business periodicals, aimed at disgruntled HP and Compaq business customers (a SWOT opportunity) and highlighting key strengths at Sun Microsystems:

To: HP Customers
From: Sun Microsystems Inc.
Subject: Time for one last change?
Cc: IBM

Odds are, you're an HP customer because you believed in the HP way. You believed in the DEC strategy. The Compaq strategy. The PA-RISC/HP-UX strategy. The Tru64 strategy. The Itanium strategy. But time after time, you've been disappointed.

We at Sun have taken a different tack: there's enough change in the world. Focus. Innovate. Grow customers 1 by 1. And stay consistent to your mission, even when the pundits and competitors say otherwise.

We've had a consistent vision for 24 years: The Network is the Computer™. More true today than 10 years ago.

We've had a consistent vision of how the network should be programmed: Java™. More true today than 10 years ago.

We've had a consistent vision of how operating systems should be built: to military-grade security,

carrier-grade scale, and open to the world: Solaris™ 10. More true today than 10 years ago.

We've had a consistent view that servers and storage should be: built to scale, built to last, built with best-in-class innovation. That's why SPARC® is the #1 64-bit microprocessor out there, and our AMD Opteron™ processor-based systems now claim seven new performance world records, and we've got the most compelling storage product in the industry (the Sun StorEdge™ 6920). More true today than 10 years ago.

We've had a consistent view that innovation matters—from Linux and the open source world, to Microsoft interoperability. More true today than 10 years ago.

And most of all, we've had a consistent view that simplicity is our single biggest competitive advantage. $1/cpu-hr is a simpler grid offering than forcing customers to buy consultants "on demand." More true today than 10 years ago.

So if you'd like to experience a partner driven to focus while you try to drive change–versus the opposite–call us. (800) SUN-0404. Or go to www.sun.com/welcome_2_Sun to learn about our special HP migration programs.

Sources: Reprinted with special permission from "Sun's Rebound," *BusinessWeek Online*, September 13, 2006; and "A New Dawn for Sun Microsystems," *BusinessWeek*, May 9, 2005. Copyright © 2006 The McGraw-Hill Companies.

as digital signal processors (DSPs). The chips crunch vast streams of data for an array of digital gadgets, including modems and cellular phones. Engibous shed billions of dollars worth of assets to focus on DSPs, which he calls "the most important silicon technology of the next decade." TI now commands half of the $8 billion global market for the most advanced DSPs, and it is the No. 1 chip supplier to the digital wireless phone market.

In cell 2, a firm that has identified several key strengths faces an unfavorable environment. In this situation, strategies would seek to redeploy those strong resources and competencies to build long-term opportunities in more opportunistic product markets. IBM, a dominant manufacturer of mainframes, servers, and PCs worldwide, has nurtured many strengths in computer-related and software-related markets for many years. Increasingly, however, it has had to address major threats that include product commoditization, pricing pressures, accelerated pace of innovation, and the like. IBM's decision to sell its PC business to the Chinese firm Lenovo and focus instead on continued development of ISSC, better known now as IBM Global Services, has allowed IBM to build a long-term opportunity in the (hopefully) more profitable, growing markets of the next decade. In the past 10 years, Global

Services has become the fastest-growing division of the company, its largest employer, and the keystone of IBM's strategic future. The group does everything from running a customer's IT (information technology) department to consulting on legacy system upgrades to building custom supply-chain management applications. As IBM's hardware divisions struggle against price wars and commoditization and its software units fight to gain share beyond mainframes, it is Global Services that drives the company's growth.

A firm in cell 3 faces impressive market opportunity but is constrained by weak internal resources. The focus of strategy for such a firm is eliminating the internal weaknesses so as to more effectively pursue the market opportunity. Microsoft has big problems with computer viruses. Alleviating such problems, or weaknesses, is driving massive changes in how Microsoft writes software—to make it more secure before it reaches the market rather than fix it later with patches. Microsoft is also shaking up the security software industry by acquiring several smaller companies to accelerate its own efforts to create specialized software that detects, finds, and removes malicious code.[1]

Limitations of SWOT Analysis

SWOT analysis has been a framework of choice among many managers for a long time because of its simplicity and its portrayal of the essence of sound strategy formulation—matching a firm's opportunities and threats with its strengths and weaknesses. But SWOT analysis is a broad conceptual approach, making it susceptible to some key limitations.

1. A SWOT analysis can overemphasize internal strengths and downplay external threats. Strategists in every company have to remain vigilant against building strategies around what the firm does well now (its strengths) without due consideration of the external environment's impact on those strengths. Apple's success with the iPod and its iTunes downloadable music Web site provides a good example of strategists who placed a major emphasis on external considerations—the legal requirements for downloading and subsequently using individual songs, what music to make available, and the evolution of the use of the Web to download music—as a guide to shaping Apple's eventual strategy. What would Apple's success have been like if its strategy had been built substantially with a focus on its technology in making the iPod device and offering it in the consumer marketplace—without bothering with the development and creation of iTunes?

2. A SWOT analysis can be static and can risk ignoring changing circumstances. A frequent admonition about the downfall of planning processes says that plans are one-time events to be completed, typed, and relegated to their spot on a manager's shelf while s/he goes about the actual work of the firm. So it is not surprising that critics of SWOT analysis, with good reason, warn that it is a one-time view of a changing, or moving, situation. Major U.S. airlines pursued strategies built around strengths that were suddenly much less important when airline deregulation took place. Likewise, those airlines built huge competitive advantages around "hub and spoke" systems for bringing small-town flyers to key hubs to be redistributed to flights elsewhere and yet allow for centralized maintenance and economies of scale. The change brought about by discount airlines that "cherry-picked" key routes, and eventual outsourcing of routine maintenance to Latin America and the Caribbean, did great harm to those strategies. Bottom line: SWOT analysis, along with most planning techniques, must avoid being static and ignoring change.

3. A SWOT analysis can overemphasize a single strength or element of strategy. Dell Computer's long-dominant strength based on a highly automated, Internet, or phone-based direct sales model gave Dell, according to chairman and founder Michael Dell, "a competitive advantage [strength] as wide as the Grand Canyon." He viewed it as being

---

[1] "Aiming to Fix Flaws, Microsoft Buys Another Antivirus Firm," *The Wall Street Journal,* February 9, 2005, p. B1.

prohibitively expensive for any rival to copy this source of strength. Unfortunately for Dell shareholders, Dell's reliance on that "key" strength proved to be an oversimplified basis around which to sustain the company's strategy for continued dominance and growth in the global PC industry. HP's size alone, with its reemphasis on printing and technical skills, and Lenovo's home base in the fast-growing Asian market seemingly have overcome Dell's dominance in the global PC industry.

4. A strength is not necessarily a source of competitive advantage. Cisco Systems Inc. has been a dominant player in providing switching equipment and other key networking infrastructure items around which the global computer communications system has been able to proliferate. It has substantial financial, technological, and branding expertise. Cisco Systems twice attempted to use its vast strengths in these areas as the basis to enter and remain in the market for home computer networks and wireless home-networking devices. It failed both times and lost hundreds of millions of dollars in the process. It possesses several compelling strengths, but none were sources of sustainable competitive advantage in the home-computer-networking industry. After leaving that industry for several years, it recently chose to reenter it by acquiring Link-Sys, an early pioneer in that industry. Cisco management acknowledged that it was doing so precisely because it did not possess those sources of competitive advantage and that, furthermore, it would avoid any interference with that business lest it disrupt the advantage around which Link-Sys's success has been built.

In summary, SWOT analysis is a longtime, traditional approach to internal analysis among many strategists. It offers a generalized effort to examine internal capabilities in light of external factors, most notably key opportunities and threats. It has limitations that must be considered if SWOT analysis is to be the basis for any firm's strategic decision-making process. Another approach to internal analysis that emerged, in part, to add more rigor and depth in the identification of competitive advantages around which a firm might build a successful strategy is value chain analysis. We examine it next.

VALUE CHAIN ANALYSIS

value chain
A perspective in which business is seen as a chain of activities that transforms inputs into outputs that customers value.

The term **value chain** describes a way of looking at a business as a chain of activities that transform inputs into outputs that customers value. Customer value derives from three basic sources: activities that differentiate the product, activities that lower its cost, and activities that meet the customer's need quickly. **Value chain analysis** (VCA) attempts to understand how a business creates customer value by examining the contributions of different activities within the business to that value.

value chain analysis
An analysis that attempts to understand how a business creates customer value by examining the contributions of different activities within the business to that value.

VCA takes a process point of view: It divides (sometimes called disaggregates) the business into sets of activities that occur *within the business,* starting with the inputs a firm receives and finishing with the firm's products (or services) and after-sales service to customers. VCA attempts to look at its costs across the series of activities the business performs to determine where low-cost advantages or cost disadvantages exist. It looks at the attributes of each of these different activities to determine in what ways each activity that occurs between purchasing inputs and after-sales service helps differentiate the company's products and services. Proponents of VCA believe it allows managers to better identify their firm's competitive advantages by looking at the business as a process—a chain of activities—of what actually happens in the business rather than simply looking at it based on arbitrary organizational dividing lines or historical accounting protocol.

Exhibit 6.4 shows a typical value chain framework. It divides activities within the firm into two broad categories: primary activities and support activities. **Primary activities** (sometimes called *line functions*) are those involved in the physical creation of the product, marketing and transfer to the buyer, and after-sale support. **Support activities** (sometimes

EXHIBIT 6.4
The Value Chain

Source: Based on Michael Porter. *On Competition,* 1998. Harvard Business School Press.

The Value Chain

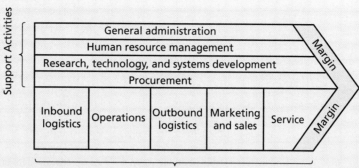

primary activities
The activities in a firm of those involved in the physical creation of the product, marketing and transfer to the buyer, and after-sale support.

support activities
The activities in a firm that assist the firm as a whole by providing infrastructure or inputs that allow the primary activities to take place on an ongoing basis.

Primary Activities

- **Inbound logistics**—Activities, costs, and assets associated with obtaining fuel, energy, raw materials, parts components, merchandise, and consumable items from vendors; receiving, storing, and disseminating inputs from suppliers; inspection; and inventory management.
- **Operations**—Activities, costs, and assets associated with converting inputs into final product form (production, assembly, packaging, equipment maintenance, facilities, operations, quality assurance, environmental protection).
- **Outbound logistics**—Activities, costs, and assets dealing with physically distributing the product to buyers (finished goods warehousing, order processing, order picking and packing, shipping, delivery vehicle operations).
- **Marketing and sales**—Activities, costs, and assets related to sales force efforts, advertising and promotion, market research and planning, and dealer/distributor support.
- **Service**—Activities, costs, and assets associated with providing assistance to buyers, such as installation, spare parts delivery, maintenance and repair, technical assistance, buyer inquiries, and complaints.

Support Activities

- **General administration**—Activities, costs, and assets relating to general management, accounting and finance, legal and regulatory affairs, safety and security, management information systems, and other "overhead" functions.
- **Human resources management**—Activities, costs, and assets associated with the recruitment, hiring, training, development, and compensation of all types of personnel; labor relations activities; development of knowledge-based skills.
- **Research, technology, and systems development**—Activities, costs, and assets relating to product R&D, process R&D, process design improvement, equipment design, computer software development, telecommunications systems, computer-assisted design and engineering, new database capabilities, and development of computerized support systems.
- **Procurement**—Activities, costs, and assets associated with purchasing and providing raw materials, supplies, services, and outsourcing necessary to support the firm and its activities. Sometimes this activity is assigned as part of a firm's inbound logistic purchasing activities.

Value Chain Analysis "Morphs" Federal Express into an Information Company

BusinessWeek

Founder Fred Smith and executives running companies controlled by FedEx sought a monumental shift in the FedEx mission. They accelerated plans to focus on information systems that track and coordinate packages. They sought to "morph" from being a transportation company into an information company.

FedEx had one of the most heavily used Web sites on the Internet. Company management claimed to have 1,500 in-house programmers writing more software code than almost any other nonsoftware company. To complement package delivery, FedEx designs and operates high-tech warehouses and distribution systems for big manufacturers and retailers around the world. For almost two decades, FedEx steadily invested massive amounts to develop software and create a giant digital network. FedEx has built corporate technology campuses around the world, and its electronic systems are directly linked via the Internet or otherwise to millions of customers worldwide. That system allows FedEx to track packages on an hourly basis, and it also allows FedEx to predict future flows of goods and then rapidly refigure the information and logistical network to handle those flows.

"Moving an item from point A to point B is no longer a big deal," says James Barksdale, early architect of FedEx's information strategies. "Having the information about that item, and where it is, and the best way to use it . . . That is value. The companies that will be big winners will be the ones who can best maximize the value of these information systems." Where FedEx's value has long been built on giant airplanes and big trucks, founder Smith envisioned a time when it will be built on information, computers, and the allure of the FedEx brand name. These days FedEx is a linchpin of the just-in-time deliveries revolution—its planes and trucks serve as mobile warehouses—that has helped companies around the globe cut costs and boost their productivity. FedEx's logistics info services now contribute the lion's share—92 percent—of FedEx's annual revenue. FedEx's value chain has shrunk in areas involved with inbound and outbound operations—taking off and landing on the tarmac—and expanded in areas involved with zapping around the pristine and pilot-free world of cyberspace to manage a client's supply chain and its distribution network.

Sources: Reprinted with special permission from "FedEx Delivers a Boost," *BusinessWeek,* November 7, 2006; and Dean Foust, "Fred Smith on the Birth of FedEx," *BusinessWeek,* September 20, 2004. Copyright © 2006 The McGraw-Hill Companies.

called *staff* or *overhead functions*) assist the firm as a whole by providing infrastructure or inputs that allow the primary activities to take place on an ongoing basis. The value chain includes a profit margin because a markup above the cost of providing a firm's value-adding activities is normally part of the price paid by the buyer—creating value that exceeds cost so as to generate a return for the effort.[2]

Judgment is required across individual firms and different industries because what may be seen as a support activity in one firm or industry may be a primary activity in another. Computer operations might typically be seen as infrastructure support, for example, but may be seen as a primary activity in airlines, newspapers, or banks. Exhibit 6.5, Strategy in Action, describes how Federal Express reconceptualized its company using a value chain analysis that ultimately saw its information support become its primary activity and source of customer value.

Conducting a Value Chain Analysis

Identify Activities

The initial step in value chain analysis is to divide a company's operations into specific activities or business processes, usually grouping them similarly to the primary and support activity categories shown earlier in Exhibit 6.4. Within each category, a firm typically performs a number of discrete activities that may be key to the firm's success. Service

---

[2] Different "value chain" or value activities may become the focus of value chain analysis. For example, companies using Hammer's *Reengineering the Corporation* might use (1) order procurement, (2) order fulfillment, (3) customer service, (4) product design, and (5) strategic planning plus support activities.

EXHIBIT 6.6   **The Difference between Traditional Cost Accounting and Activity-Based Cost Accounting**

Traditional Cost Accounting in a Purchasing Department		Activity-Based Cost Accounting in the Same Purchasing Department for Its "Procurement" Activities	
Wages and salaries	$175,000	Evaluate supplier capabilities	$ 67,875
Employee benefits	57,500	Process purchase orders	41,050
Supplies	3,250	Expedite supplier deliveries	11,750
Travel	1,200	Expedite internal processing	7,920
Depreciation	8,500	Check quality of items purchased	47,150
Other fixed charges	62,000	Check incoming deliveries against	
Miscellaneous operating expenses	12,625	purchase orders	24,225
	$320,075	Resolve problems	55,000
		Internal administration	65,105
			$320,075

activities, for example, may include such discrete activities as installation, repair, parts distribution, and upgrading—any of which could be a major source of competitive advantage or disadvantage. The manager's challenge at this point is to be very detailed attempting to "disaggregate" what actually goes on into numerous distinct, analyzable activities rather than settling for a broad, general categorization.

Allocate Costs

The next step is to attempt to attach costs to each discrete activity. Each activity in the value chain incurs costs and ties up time and assets. Value chain analysis requires managers to assign costs and assets to each activity, thereby providing a very different way of viewing costs than traditional cost accounting methods would produce. Exhibit 6.6 helps illustrate this distinction. Both approaches in Exhibit 6.6 tell us that the purchasing department (procurement activities) cost $320,075. The traditional method lets us see that payroll expenses are 73 percent [($175 + $57.5)/$320] of our costs with "other fixed charges" the second largest cost, 19 percent [$62/$320] of the total procurement costs. VCA proponents would argue that the benefit of this information is limited. Their argument might be the following:

> With this information we could compare our procurement costs to key competitors, budgets, or industry averages and conclude that we are better, worse, or equal. We could then ascertain that our "people" costs and "other fixed charges" cost are advantages, disadvantages, or "in line" with competitors. Managers could then argue to cut people, add people, or debate fixed overhead charges. However, they would get lost in what is really a budgetary debate without ever examining what it is those people do in accomplishing the procurement function, what value that provides, and how cost effective each activity is.

VCA proponents hold that the activity-based VCA approach would provide a more meaningful analysis of the procurement function's costs and consequent value added. The activity-based side of Exhibit 6.6 shows that approximately 21 percent of the procurement cost or value added involves evaluating supplier capabilities. A rather sizable cost, 20 percent, involves internal administration, with an additional 17 percent spent resolving problems and almost 15 percent spent on quality control efforts. VCA advocates see this information as being much more useful than traditional cost accounting information, especially when compared with the cost information of key competitors or other "benchmark" companies. VCA supporters assert the following argument that the benefit of this activity-based information is substantial:

> Rather than analyzing just "people" and "other charges," we are now looking at meaningful categorizations of the work that procurement actually does. We see, for example, that a key value-added activity (and cost) involves "evaluating supplier capabilities." The amount spent on "internal administration" and "resolving problems" seems high and may indicate a weakness or area for improvement if the other activities' costs are in line and outcomes favorable. The bottom line is that this approach lets us look at what we actually "do" in the business—the specific activities—to create customer value, and that in turn allows more specific internal analysis than traditional, accounting-based cost categories.

Recognizing the Difficulty in Activity-Based Cost Accounting

It is important to note that existing financial management and accounting systems in many firms are not set up to easily provide activity-based cost breakdowns. Likewise, in virtually all firms, the information requirements to support activity-based cost accounting can create redundant work because of the financial reporting requirements that may force firms to retain the traditional approach for financial statement purposes. The time and energy to change to an activity-based approach can be formidable and still typically involve arbitrary cost allocation decisions—trying to allocate selected asset or people costs across multiple activities in which they are involved. Challenges dealing with a cost-based use of VCA have not deterred use of the framework to identify sources of differentiation. Indeed, conducting a VCA to analyze competitive advantages that differentiate the firm is compatible with the resource-based view's examination of intangible assets and capabilities as sources of distinctive competence.

Identify the Activities That Differentiate the Firm

Scrutinizing a firm's value chain may not only reveal cost advantages or disadvantages, it may also bring attention to several sources of differentiation advantage relative to competitors. Google considers its Internet-based search algorithms (activities) to be far superior to any competitor's. Google knows it has a cost advantage because of the time and expense replicating this activity would take. But Google considers it an even more important source of value to the customer because of the importance customers place on this activity, which differentiates Google from many would-be competitors. Likewise, Federal Express, as we noted in Exhibit 6.5, considers its information management skills to have become the core competence and essence of the company because of the value these skills allow FedEx to provide its customers and the importance they in turn place on such skills. Exhibit 6.7 suggests some factors for assessing primary and support activities' differentiation and contribution.

Examine the Value Chain

Once the value chain has been documented, managers need to identify the activities that are critical to buyer satisfaction and market success. It is those activities that deserve major scrutiny in an internal analysis. Three considerations are essential at this stage in the value chain analysis. First, the company's basic mission needs to influence managers' choice of activities to be examined in detail. If the company is focused on being a low-cost provider, then management attention to lower costs should be very visible, and missions built around commitment to differentiation should find managers spending more on activities that are differentiation cornerstones. Retailer Wal-Mart focuses intensely on costs related to inbound logistics, advertising, and loyalty to build its competitive advantage (see Exhibit 6.10, page 176), while Nordstrom builds its distinct position in retailing by emphasizing sales and support activities on which they spend twice the retail industry average.

Second, the nature of value chains and the relative importance of the activities within them vary by industry. Lodging firms like Holiday Inn have major costs and concerns that

EXHIBIT 6.7 Possible Factors for Assessing Sources of Differentiation in Primary and Support Activities

General Administration
- Capability to identify new-product market opportunities and potential environmental threats
- Quality of the strategic planning system to achieve corporate objectives
- Coordination and integration of all value chain activities among organizational subunits
- Ability to obtain relatively low-cost funds for capital expenditures and working capital
- Level of information systems support in making strategic and routine decisions
- Timely and accurate management information on general and competitive environments
- Relationships with public policymakers and interest groups
- Public image and corporate citizenship

Human Resource Management
- Effectiveness of procedures for recruiting, training, and promoting all levels of employees
- Appropriateness of reward systems for motivating and challenging employees
- A work environment that minimizes absenteeism and keeps turnover at desirable levels
- Relations with trade unions
- Active participation by managers and technical personnel in professional organizations
- Levels of employee motivation and job satisfaction

Technology Development
- Success of research and development activities in leading to product and process innovations
- Quality of working relationships between R&D personnel and other departments
- Timeliness of technology development activities in meeting critical deadlines
- Quality of laboratories and other facilities
- Qualification and experience of laboratory technicians and scientists
- Ability of work environment to encourage creativity and innovation

Procurement
- Development of alternate sources for inputs to minimize dependence on a single supplier
- Procurement of raw materials (1) on a timely basis, (2) at lowest possible cost, (3) at acceptable levels of quality
- Procedures for procurement of plant, machinery, and buildings
- Development of criteria for lease-versus-purchase decisions
- Good, long-term relationships with reliable suppliers

Support Activities · *Profit Margin*

Inbound Logistics	Operations	Outbound Logistics	Marketing and Sales	Service
■ Soundness of material and inventory control systems	■ Productivity of equipment compared to that of key competitors	■ Timeliness and efficiency of delivery of finished goods and services	■ Effectiveness of market research to identify customer segments and needs	■ Means to solicit customer input for product improvements
■ Efficiency of raw material warehousing activities	■ Appropriate automation of production processes	■ Efficiency of finished goods warehousing activities	■ Innovation in sales promotion and advertising	■ Promptness of attention to customer complaints
	■ Effectiveness of production control systems to improve quality and reduce costs		■ Evaluation of alternate distribution channels	■ Appropriateness of warranty and guarantee policies
	■ Efficiency of plant layout and work-flow design		■ Motivation and competence of sales force	■ Quality of customer education and training
			■ Development of an image of quality and a favorable reputation	■ Ability to provide replacement parts and repair services
			■ Extent of brand loyalty among customers	
			■ Extent of market dominance within the market segment or overall market	

Profit Margin

Primary Activities

Source: Based on Michael Porter, *On Competition,* 1998, Harvard Business School Press.

involve operational activities—it provides its service instantaneously at each location—and marketing activities, while having minimal concern for outbound logistics. Yet for a distributor, such as the food distributor PYA, inbound and outbound logistics are the most critical area. Major retailers like Wal-Mart have built value advantages focusing on purchasing and inbound logistics, while the most successful personal computer companies have built via sales, outbound logistics, and service through the mail-order process.

Third, the relative importance of value activities can vary by a company's position in a broader value system that includes the value chains of its upstream suppliers and downstream customers or partners involved in providing products or services to end users. A producer of roofing shingles depends heavily on the downstream activities of wholesale distributors and building supply retailers to reach roofing contractors and do-it-yourselfers. Maytag manufactures its own appliances, sells them through independent distributors, and provides warranty service to the buyer. Sears outsources the manufacture of its appliances while it promotes its brand name—Kenmore—and handles all sales and service.

As these examples suggest, it is important that managers take into account their level of vertical integration when comparing their cost structure for activities on their value chain to those of key competitors. Comparing a fully integrated rival with a partially integrated one requires adjusting for the scope of activities performed to achieve meaningful comparison. It also suggests the need for examining costs associated with activities provided by upstream or downstream companies; these activities ultimately determine comparable, final costs to end users. Said another way, one company's comparative cost disadvantage (or advantage) may emanate more from activities undertaken by upstream or downstream "partners" than from activities under the direct control of that company—therefore suggesting less of a relative advantage or disadvantage within the company's direct value chain.

RESOURCE-BASED VIEW OF THE FIRM

Toyota versus GM is a competitive situation virtually all of us recognize. Stock analysts look at the two and conclude that Toyota is the clear leader. They cite Toyota's superiority in tangible assets (newer factories worldwide, R&D facilities, computerization, cash, etc.) and intangible assets (reputation, brand name awareness, quality-control culture, global business system, etc.). They also mention that Toyota leads GM in several capabilities to make use of these assets effectively—managing distribution globally, influencing labor and supplier relations, managing franchise relations, marketing savvy, and speed of decision making to take quick advantage of changing global conditions are just a few that are frequently mentioned. The combination of capabilities and assets, most analysts conclude, creates several competencies that give Toyota key competitive advantages over GM that are durable and not easily imitated.

resource-based view
A method of analyzing and identifying a firm's strategic advantages based on examining its distinct combination of assets, skills, capabilities, and intangibles as an organization.

The Toyota–GM situation provides a useful illustration for understanding several concepts central to the **resource-based view** (RBV) of the firm. The RBV is a method of analyzing and identifying a firm's strategic advantages based on examining its distinct combination of assets, skills, capabilities, and intangibles as an organization. The RBV's underlying premise is that firms differ in fundamental ways because each firm possesses a unique "bundle" of resources—tangible and intangible assets and organizational capabilities to make use of those assets. Each firm develops competencies from these resources, and, when developed especially well, these become the source of the firm's competitive advantages. Toyota's decision to enter global markets locally and regularly invest in or build newer factory locations in those global markets has given Toyota a competitive advantage analysts estimate GM has lost and will take at least 20 years or longer, if ever, to match. Toyota's strategy for the last 15 years was based in part on the identification of these resources and the development of them into a distinctive competence—a sustained competitive advantage.

Core Competencies

core competence
A capability or skill that a firm emphasizes and excels in doing while in pursuit of its overall mission.

Executives charting the strategy of their business have more recently concentrated their thinking on the notion of a "core competence." A **core competence** is a capability or skill that a firm emphasizes and excels in doing while in pursuit of its overall mission. Core competencies that differ from those found in competing firms would be considered *distinctive competencies*. Apple's competencies in pulling together available technologies and others' software and combining this with their own product design skills and new-product introduction prowess result in an innovation competence that is different and distinct from any firm against which Apple competes. Toyota's pervasive organizationwide pursuit of quality; Wendy's systemwide emphasis on and ability to provide fresh meat daily; and the University of Phoenix's ability to provide comprehensive educational options for working adults worldwide are all examples of competencies that are unique to these firms and distinctive when compared to their competitors.

Distinctive competencies that are identified and nurtured throughout the firm, allowing it to execute effectively so as to provide products or services to customers that are superior to competitor's offerings, become the basis for a lasting *competitive advantage*. Executives, enthusiastic about the notion that their job as strategists was to identify and leverage core competencies into distinctive ones that create sustainable competitive advantage, encountered difficulty applying the concept because of the generality of its level of analysis. The RBV emerged as a way to make the core competency notion and thought process more focused and measurable—creating a very important, and more meaningful, tool for internal analysis. Let's look at the basic concepts underlying the RBV.

Three Basic Resources: Tangible Assets, Intangible Assets, and Organizational Capabilities

tangible assets
The most easily identified assets, often found on a firm's balance sheet. They include production facilities, raw materials, financial resources, real estate, and computers.

The RBV's ability to create a more focused, measurable approach to internal analysis starts with its delineation of three basic types of resources, some of which may become the building blocks for distinctive competencies. These resources are defined below and illustrated in Exhibit 6.8.

Tangible assets are the easiest "resources" to identify and are often found on a firm's balance sheet. They include production facilities, raw materials, financial resources, real estate, and computers. Tangible assets are the physical and financial means a company uses to provide value to its customers.

intangible assets
A firm's assets that you cannot touch or see but that are very often critical in creating competitive advantage: brand names, company reputation, organizational morale, technical knowledge, patents and trademarks, and accumulated experience within an organization.

Intangible assets are "resources" such as brand names, company reputation, organizational morale, technical knowledge, patents and trademarks, and accumulated experience within an organization. While they are not assets that you can touch or see, they are very often critical in creating competitive advantage.

organizational capabilities
Skills (the ability and ways of combining assets, people, and processes) that a company uses to transform inputs into outputs.

Organizational capabilities are not specific "inputs" like tangible or intangible assets; rather, they are the skills—the ability and ways of combining assets, people, and processes—that a company uses to transform inputs into outputs. Apple pioneered and has subsequently leveraged its iPod and iTunes success into a major leadership position in digitalized music, entertainment, and communication on a global basis for individual consumers. Microsoft and others have attempted to copy Dell, but remain far behind Apple's diverse organizational capabilities. Apple has subsequently revolutionized its own iPod, using it to automate and customize a whole new level of entertainment capability that combines assets, people and processes throughout and beyond the Apple organization. Finely developed capabilities, such as Apple's Internet-based, customer-friendly iPod/iTunes

EXHIBIT 6.8
Examples of Different "Resources"

Source: From R.M. Grant, *Contemporary Strategy Analysis,* Blackwell Publishing, 2001, p. 140. Reprinted with permission of Wiley-Blackwell.

Tangible Assets	Intangible Assets	Organizational Capabilities
Hampton Inn's reservation system	Budweiser's brand name	Travelocity's customer service P&G's management training program
Toyota Motor Company's cash reserves	Apple's reputation	Wal-Mart's purchasing and inbound logistics
Georgia Pacific's land holdings	Nike's advertising with LeBron James	Google's product-development processes
FedEx's plane fleet	Katie Couric as CBS's *Evening News* anchor	Coke's global distribution coordination
Coca-Cola's Coke formula	eBay's management team Goldman Sach's culture	3M's innovation process

Classifying and Assessing the Firm's Resources

Resource	Relevant Characteristics	Key Indicators
Tangible Resources		
Financial resources	The firm's borrowing capacity and its internal funds generation determine its resilience and capacity for investment.	• Debt/equity ratio • Operating cash flow/free cash flow • Credit rating
Physical resources	Physical resources constrain the firm's set of production possibilities and impact its cost position. Key characteristics include • The size, location, technical sophistication, and flexibility of plant and equipment • Location and alternative uses for land and buildings • Reserves of raw materials	• Market values of fixed assets • Vintage of capital equipment • Scale of plants • Flexibility of fixed assets
Intangible Resources		
Technological resources	Intellectual property: patent portfolio, copyright, trade secrets Resources for innovation: research facilities, technical and scientific employees	• Number and significance of patents • Revenue from licensing patents and copyrights • R&D staff as a percent of total employment • Number and location of research facilities
Reputation	Reputation with customers through the ownership of brands and trademarks; established relationships with customers; the reputation of the firm's products and services for quality and reliability. The reputation of the company with suppliers (including component suppliers, banks and financiers, employees and potential employees), with government and government agencies, and with the community.	• Brand recognition • Brand equity • Percent of repeat buying • Objective measures of comparative product performance (e.g., Consumers' Association ratings, J. D. Power ratings) • Surveys of corporate reputation (e.g., *BusinessWeek*)

system, can be a source of sustained competitive advantage. They enable a firm to take the same input factors as rivals (such as Microsoft, HP, or Dell) and convert them into products and services, either with greater efficiency in the process or greater quality in the output, or both.

What Makes a Resource Valuable?

Once managers identify their firm's tangible assets, intangible assets, and organizational capabilities, the RBV applies a set of guidelines to determine which of those resources represent strengths or weaknesses—which resources generate core competencies that are sources of sustained competitive advantage. These RBV guidelines derive from the idea that resources are more valuable when they

1. Are *critical to* being able to *meet a customer's need* better than other alternatives.
2. Are *scarce*—few others if any possess that resource or skill to the degree you do.
3. *Drive* a key portion of overall *profits,* in a manner controlled by your firm.
4. Are *durable* or sustainable over time.

   Before proceeding to explain each basis for making resources valuable, we suggest that you keep in mind a simple, useful idea: Resources are most valuable when they meet all four of these guidelines. We will return to this point after we explain each guideline more thoroughly.

RBV Guideline 1: Is the resource or skill critical to fulfilling a customer's need better than that of the firm's competitors?

Two restaurants offer similar food, at similar prices, but one has a location much more convenient to downtown offices than the other. The tangible asset, location, helps fulfill daytime workers' lunch-eating needs better than its competitor, resulting in greater profitability and sales volume for the conveniently located restaurant. Wal-Mart redefined discount retailing and outperformed the industry in profitability by 4.5 percent of sales—a 200 percent improvement. Four resources—store locations, brand recognition, employee loyalty, and sophisticated inbound logistics—allowed Wal-Mart to fulfill customer needs much better and more cost effectively than Kmart and other discount retailers (see Exhibit 6.10, page 176). In both of these examples, *it is important to recognize that only resources that contributed to competitive superiority were valuable.* At the same time, other resources such as the restaurant's menu and specific products or parking space at Wal-Mart were essential to doing business but contributed little to competitive advantage because they did not help fulfill customer needs better than those of the firm's key competitors.

RBV Guideline 2: Is the resource scarce? Is it in short supply or not easily substituted for or imitated?

Short Supply   When a resource is scarce, it is more valuable. When a firm possesses a resource and few if any others do, and it is central to fulfilling customers' needs, then it can become the basis of a competitive advantage for the firm. Literal physical scarcity is perhaps the most obvious way a resource might meet this guideline. Very limited natural resources, a unique location, skills that are truly rare—all represent obvious types of scarce resource situations.

Availability of Substitutes   We discussed the threat of substitute products in Chapter 3 as part of the five forces model for examining industry profitability. This basic idea can be taken further and used to gauge the scarcity-based value of particular resources. Whole Foods has been an exciting growth company for several years, focused exclusively on selling wholesome, organic food. The basic idea was to offer food grown organically, without pesticides or manipulation, in a convenient grocery atmosphere. Investors were excited about this concept because of the processed, nonorganic foods offered by virtually every existing grocery chain. Unfortunately for their more recent investors, substitutes for Whole Foods's offerings are becoming easily available from several grocery chains and regional organic chains. Publix, Harris-Teeter, and even Wal-Mart are easily adapting their grocery operations to offer organic fare. With little change to their existing facilities and operational resources, these companies are quickly creating alternatives to Whole Foods's offerings if not offering some of the same items, cheaper. So some worry about the long-term impact on Whole Foods. Investors have seen the value of their Whole Foods's stock decline as substitute resources and capabilities are readily created by existing and new entrants into the organic grocery sectors.

Imitation A resource that competitors can readily copy can only generate temporary value. It is "scarce" for only a short time. It cannot generate a long-term competitive advantage. When Wendy's first emerged, it was the only major hamburger chain with a drive-through window. This unique organizational capability was part of a "bundle" of resources that allowed Wendy's to provide unique value to its target customers: young adults seeking convenient food service. But once this resource, or organizational capability, proved valuable to fast-food customers, every fast-food chain copied the feature. Then Wendy's continued success was built on other resources that generated other distinctive competencies.

The scarcity that comes with an absence of imitation seldom lasts forever, as the Wendy's example illustrates. Competitors will match or better any resource as soon as they can. It should be obvious, then, that the firm's ability to forestall this eventuality is very important. So how does a firm create resource scarcity by making resources hard to imitate? The RBV identifies four characteristics, called **isolating mechanisms,** that make resources difficult to imitate:

- *Physically unique resources* are virtually impossible to imitate. A one-of-a-kind real estate location, mineral rights, and patents are examples of resources that cannot be imitated. Disney's Mickey Mouse copyright or Winter Park, Colorado's Iron Horse resort possess physical uniqueness. While many strategists claim that resources are physically unique, this is seldom true. Rather, other characteristics are typically what make most resources difficult to imitate.

- *"Path-dependent" resources* are very difficult to imitate because of the difficult "path" another firm must follow to create the resource. These are resources that cannot be instantaneously acquired but rather must be created over time in a manner that is frequently very expensive and always difficult to accelerate. When Michael Dell once said that "Anyone who tries to go direct now will find it very difficult—like trying to jump over the Grand Canyon," he was asserting that Dell's system of selling customized PCs direct via the Internet and Dell's unmatched customer service is, in effect, a path-dependent organizational capability. It would take any competitor years to develop the expertise, infrastructure, reputation, and capabilities necessary to compete effectively with Dell, which HP eventually accomplished after 10 years and considerable effort. Coca-Cola's brand name, Gerber Baby Food's reputation for quality, and Steinway's expertise in piano manufacture would take competitors many years and millions of dollars to match. Consumers' many years of experience drinking Coke or using Gerber or playing a Steinway would also need to be matched.

- *Causal ambiguity* is a third way resources can be very difficult to imitate. This refers to situations in which it is difficult for competitors to understand exactly how a firm has created the advantage it enjoys. Competitors can't figure out exactly what the uniquely valuable resource is or how resources are combined to create the competitive advantage. Causally ambiguous resources are often organizational capabilities that arise from

isolating mechanisms
Characteristics that make resources difficult to imitate. In the RBV context these are physically unique resources, path-dependent resources, causal ambiguity, and economic deterrence.

EXHIBIT 6.9
Resource Imitation

Source: From David J.
Collins and Cynthia A.
Montgomery, *Corporate
Strategy: A Resource-Based
Approach*, McGraw-Hill/Irwin,
2005, p. 39. Copyright © 2005
The McGraw-Hill Companies,
Inc. Reprinted with permission.

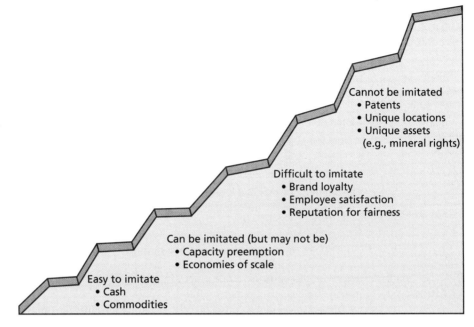

subtle combinations of tangible and intangible assets and culture, processes, and organizational attributes the firm possesses. Southwest Airlines has regularly faced competition from major and regional airlines, with some like United and Continental eschewing their traditional approach and attempting to compete by using their own version of the Southwest approach—same planes, routes, gate procedures, number of attendants, and so on. They have yet to succeed. The most difficult thing to replicate is Southwest's "personality," or culture of fun, family, and frugal yet focused services and attitude. Just how that works is hard for United and Continental to figure out.

• *Economic deterrence* is a fourth source of inimitability. This usually involves large capital investments in capacity to provide products or services in a given market that are scale sensitive. It occurs when a competitor understands the resources that provide a competitive advantage and may even have the capacity to imitate, but chooses not to because of the limited market size that realistically would not support two players the size of the first mover.

While we may be inclined to think of the ability to imitate a resource as a yes-or-no situation, imitation is more accurately measured on a continuum that reflects difficulty and time. Exhibit 6.9 illustrates such a continuum. Some resources may have multiple imitation deterrents. For example, 3M's reputation for innovativeness may involve path dependencies and causal ambiguity.

RBV Guideline 3: Appropriability: Who actually gets the profit created by a resource?

Warren Buffett is known worldwide as one of the most successful investors of the last 25 years. One of his legendary investments was the Walt Disney Company, which he once said he liked "because the Mouse does not have an agent."[3] What he was really saying was that Disney owned the Mickey Mouse copyright, and all profits from that valuable resource went directly to Disney. Other competitors in the "entertainment" industry generated similar profits from their competing offerings, for example, movies, but they often "captured" substantially less of those profits because of the amounts that had to be paid to well-known

[3] *The Harbus*, March 25, 1996, p. 12.

EXHIBIT 6.10
Wal-Mart's Resource-Based Competitive Advantage

Source: Pankaj Ghemawat, "Wal-Mart Stores' Discount Operations," Harvard Business School Case Number 9-387-018.

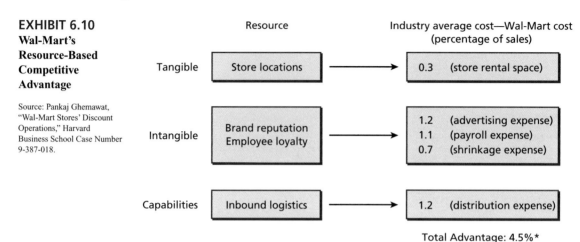

	Resource	Industry average cost—Wal-Mart cost (percentage of sales)
Tangible	Store locations	0.3 (store rental space)
Intangible	Brand reputation Employee loyalty	1.2 (advertising expense) 1.1 (payroll expense) 0.7 (shrinkage expense)
Capabilities	Inbound logistics	1.2 (distribution expense)

Total Advantage: 4.5%*

* Wal-Mart's cost advantage as a percent of sales. Each percentage point advantage is worth well over $500 million in net income to Wal-Mart.

actors or directors or other entertainment contributors seen as the real creators of the movie's value.

Disney's eventual acquisition of Pixar illustrates just the opposite situation for the home of the Mouse. Pixar's expertise in digital animation had proven key to the impressive success of several major animation films released by Disney in the past several years. While Disney apparently thought its name and distribution clout justified its sizable share of the profits this five-year joint venture generated, Steve Jobs and his Pixar team felt otherwise. Pixar's assessment was that their capabilities were key drivers of the huge profits by *Ants* and *Finding Nemo,* leading them not to renew their Disney partnership. Pixar's unmatched digitalization animation expertise quickly "appropriated" the profits generated by this key competitive advantage, and Disney Studios struggled to catch up. Disney eventually solved the dilemma by acquiring Pixar at a handsome premium. The movie *Cars* soon followed.[4]

Sports teams, investment services, and consulting businesses are other examples of companies that generate sizable profits based on resources (e.g., key people, skills, contacts) that are not inextricably linked to the company and therefore do not allow the company to easily capture the profits. Superstar sports players can move from one team to another or command excessively high salaries, and this circumstance could arise in other personal services business situations. It could also occur when one firm joint ventures with another, sharing resources and capabilities and the profits that result. Sometimes restaurants or lodging facilities that are franchisees of a national organization are frustrated by the fees they pay the franchisor each month and decide to leave the organization and go "independent." They often find, to their dismay, that the business declines significantly. The value of the franchise name, reservation system, and brand recognition is critical in generating the profits of the business.

Wal-Mart's success in appropriating profits associated with five key resources or capabilities (see Exhibit 6.10) has, for many years, meant an additional 4.5 cents out of every sales dollar more than its average competitor accrues to Wal-Mart (Wal-Mart "appropriates it") and that money in turn flows to its bottom line. The discount retailing industry is extremely competitive, and this historically allowed Wal-Mart's profitability to reach two to three times the industry average—a sizable competitive advantage for Wal-Mart that was durable and largely under Wal-Mart's control (for the past 20 years). Interestingly, as you will see later in Exhibit 6.13 (page 181), competitors like Target and Kroger have worked intently over the past 10 years to reduce Wal-Mart's intangible and capabilities resource

[4] "Disney Buys Pixar," *Money.CNN.com,* January 1, 2006.

advantages in a way that is beginning to create a new resource-based source of competitive advantage for them.

RBV Guideline 4: Durability: How rapidly will the resource depreciate?

The slower a resource depreciates, the more valuable it is. Tangible assets, such as commodities or capital, can have their depletion measured. Intangible resources, such as brand names or organizational capabilities, present a much more difficult depreciation challenge. The Coca-Cola brand has continued to appreciate, whereas technical know-how in various computer technologies depreciates rapidly. In the increasingly hypercompetitive global economy of the twenty-first century, distinctive competencies and competitive advantages can fade quickly, making the notion of durability a critical test of the value of key resources and capabilities. Some believe that this reality makes well-articulated visions and associated cultures within organizations potentially the most important contributor to long-term survival.[5]

Using the Resource-Based View in Internal Analysis

To use the RBV in internal analysis, a firm must first identify and evaluate its resources to find those that provide the basis for future competitive advantage. This process involves defining the various resources the firm possesses and examining them based on the preceding discussion to gauge which resources truly have strategic value. It is usually helpful in this undertaking to

• *Disaggregate resources*—break them down into more specific competencies—rather than stay with broad categorizations. Saying that Domino's Pizza has better marketing skills than Pizza Hut conveys little information. But dividing that into subcategories such as advertising that, in turn, can be divided into national advertising, local promotions, and coupons allows for a more measurable assessment. Exhibit 6.11 provides a useful illustration of this at the United Kingdom's largest full-service restaurant operator—Whitbread's Restaurant.

• *Utilize a functional perspective.* Looking at different functional areas of the firm, disaggregating tangible and intangible assets as well as organizational capabilities that are present, can begin to uncover important value-building resources and activities that deserve further analysis. Appendix 6A lists a variety of functional area resources and activities that deserve consideration.

• *Look at organizational processes* and combinations of resources and not only at isolated assets or capabilities. While disaggregation is critical, you must also take a creative, gestalt look at what competencies the firm possesses or has the potential to possess that might generate competitive advantage.

• *Use the value chain approach* to uncover organizational capabilities, activities, and processes that are valuable potential sources of competitive advantage.

Once the resources are identified, managers apply the four RBV guidelines for uncovering "valuable" resources. The objective for managers at this point is to identify resources and capabilities that are valuable for most if not all of the reasons our guidelines suggest a resource can be valuable.

If a resource creates the ability to meet a unique customer need, it has value. But if it is not scarce, or if it is easily imitated, it would be unwise to build a firm's strategy on that resource or capability unless that strategy included plans to build scarcity or inimitability into it. If a resource provided the basis for meeting a unique need, was scarce, was not

[5] James C. Collins, *Good to Great: Why Some Companies Make the Leap . . . and Others Don't* (New York: HarperCollins, 2001).

EXHIBIT 6.11
Disaggregating Whitbread Restaurant's Customer Service Resource

Source: Andrew Campbell and Kathleen Sommers-Luchs, *Core Competency-Based Strategy* (London: International Thomson, 1997).

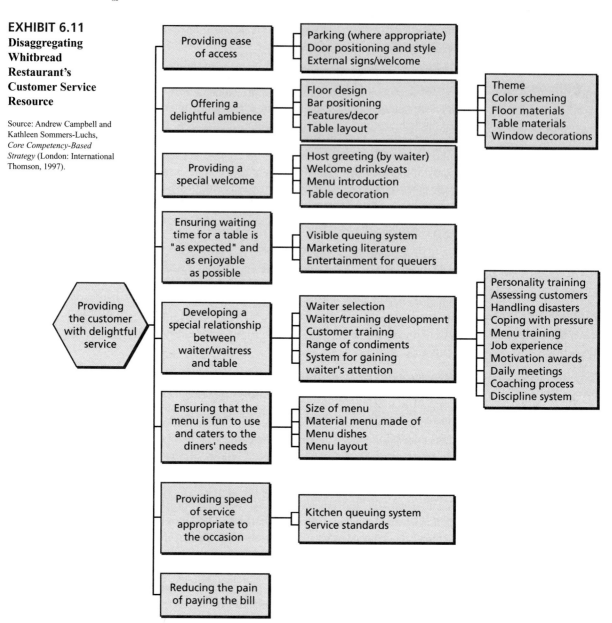

easily imitated, and was easily sustainable over time, managers would be attracted to build a strategy on it more than likely. Our example of Pixar's relationship with Disney earlier in this chapter would seem to suggest this was Pixar's position early in its joint venture with Disney. Yet even with all of those sources confirming a very high value in its digital animation expertise and intellectual property resources, Pixar was not "appropriating" the share of the animation movie profits that were attributable to those resources. Pixar was fortunate: it had the choice not to renew its five-year contract with Disney, and so it did. That eventually led Disney to pay a premium price to acquire Pixar, to regain the strategic value of Pixar's unique resources.

The key point here is that applying RBV analysis should focus on identifying resources that contain all sources of value identified in our four guidelines. Consider the diagram in

EXHIBIT 6.12
Applying the Resource-Based View to Identify the Best Sources of Competitive Advantage

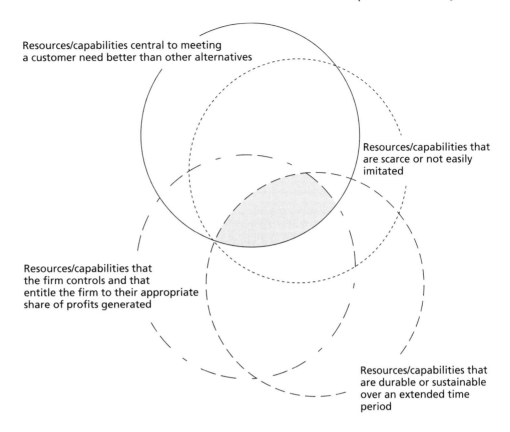

Resources/capabilities central to meeting a customer need better than other alternatives

Resources/capabilities that are scarce or not easily imitated

Resources/capabilities that the firm controls and that entitle the firm to their appropriate share of profits generated

Resources/capabilities that are durable or sustainable over an extended time period

Exhibit 6.12. Each circle in that diagram represents one way resources have value. The area where all circles intersect or overlap would represent resources that derive value in all four ways. Such resources are the ones managers applying the RBV should seek to identify. They are powerful sources around which to build competitive advantage and craft successful strategies. And resources that possess some but not all sources of value become points of emphasis by a management team able to identify ways to build the missing source of value into that resource over time much like Pixar did in its relationship with Disney.

By using RBV, value chain analysis, and SWOT analysis, firms are virtually certain to improve the quality of internal analysis undertaken to help craft a company's competitive strategy. Central to the success of each technique is the strategists' ability to make meaningful comparisons. The next section examines how meaningful comparisons can be made.

INTERNAL ANALYSIS: MAKING MEANINGFUL COMPARISONS

Managers need objective standards to use when examining internal resources and value-building activities. Whether applying the SWOT approach, VCA, or the RBV, strategists rely on three basic perspectives to evaluate how their firms stack up on internal capabilities. These three perspectives are discussed in this section.

Comparison with Past Performance

Strategists use the firm's historical experience as a basis for evaluating internal factors. Managers are most familiar with the internal capabilities and problems of their firms because they have been immersed in the financial, marketing, production, and R&D activities. Not surprisingly, a manager's assessment of whether a certain internal factor—such as production facilities, sales organization, financial capacity, control systems, or key personnel—is a strength or a weakness will be strongly influenced by his or her experience in connection with that factor. In the capital-intensive package delivery industry, for example, operating margin is a strategic internal factor affecting a firm's flexibility to add capacity. UPS managers view UPS's declining operating margins (down from 16 percent to 13.9 percent in 2007) as a potential weakness, limiting its flexibility to aggressively continue to expand its overnight air fleet. FedEx managers view its considerably lower 2007 operating margin of 9.3 percent as a growing strength because it has almost doubled from its 5.0 percent level five years earlier.

Although historical experience can provide a relevant evaluation framework, strategists must avoid tunnel vision in making use of it. NEC, Japan's IBM, initially dominated Japan's PC market with a 70 percent market share by using a proprietary hardware system, much higher screen resolution, powerful distribution channels, and a large software library from third-party vendors. Far from worried, Hajime Ikeda, manager of NEC's planning division at the time, was quoted as saying, "We don't hear complaints from our users." Soon, IBM, Apple, and HP filled the shelves in Japan's famous consumer electronics district, Akihabara. Hiroki Kamata, president of a Japanese computer research firm, reported that Japan's PC market, worth more than $35 billion, saw Apple, Dell, IBM, and HP with more market share than NEC because of better technology, software, and the restrictions created by NEC's proprietary technology. As NEC eventually learned, using only historical experience as a basis for identifying strengths and weaknesses can prove dangerously inaccurate.

Benchmarking: Comparison with Competitors

A major focus in determining a firm's resources and competencies is comparison with existing (and potential) competitors. Firms in the same industry often have different marketing skills, financial resources, operating facilities and locations, technical know-how, brand images, levels of integration, managerial talent, and so on. These different internal resources can become relative strengths (or weaknesses) depending on the strategy a firm chooses. In choosing a strategy, managers should compare the firm's key internal capabilities with those of its rivals, thereby isolating its key strengths and weaknesses.

In the U.S. home appliance industry, for example, Sears and General Electric have been major rivals. Sears's principal strength is its retail network. For GE, distribution—through independent franchised dealers—has traditionally been a relative weakness. GE's possession of the financial resources needed to support modernized mass production has enabled it to maintain both cost and technological advantages over its rivals, particularly Sears. This major strength for GE is a relative weakness for Sears, which depends solely on subcontracting to produce its Kenmore appliances. On the other hand, maintenance and repair service are important in the appliance industry. Historically, Sears has had strength in this area because it maintains fully staffed service components and spreads the costs of components over numerous departments at each retail location. GE, on the other hand, has had to depend on regional service centers and on local contracting with independent service firms by its independent local dealers. Among the internal factors that Sears and GE must consider in developing a strategy are distribution networks, technological capabilities, operating costs, and service facilities. For example, GE's major move creating alliances with Home Depot and Lowe's to sell appliances has been a major factor in turning what has been a relative weakness into what now appears to be a major strength. Managers in both Sears and GE have built successful strategies, yet those strategies are quite different. Benchmarking each other, they have identified ways to build on relative strengths while avoiding dependence on capabilities at which the other firm excels.

Wal-Mart's Midlife Crisis: Falling Behind Its Rivals in Key Success Factors

BusinessWeek

For nearly five decades, Wal-Mart's signature "everyday low prices" and their enabler—low costs—defined not only its business model but also the distinctive personality of this proud, insular company that emerged from the Ozarks backwoods to dominate retailing. Over the past year and a half, though, Wal-Mart's growth formula has stopped working. In 2006 its U.S. division eked out a 1.9 percent gain in same-store sales—its worst performance ever—and this year has begun no better. By this key measure, such competitors as Target, Costco, Kroger, Safeway, Walgreen's, CVS, and Best Buy now are all growing two to five times faster than Wal-Mart.

One can argue that the deceleration of Wal-Mart's organic growth is a function of the aging of its outlets, given that same-store sales rates slow as stores mature. Outlets five years or older accounted for 17 percent of all U.S. Supercenters in 2000 and 44 percent in 2006, and will top 60 percent in 2010. Meanwhile, the underlying economics of expansion have turned against Wal-Mart, even as it relies increasingly on store-building to compensate for sagging same-store sales. On balance, the new Supercenters are just not pulling in enough sales to offset fully the sharply escalating costs of building them.

Part of the problem is that many new stores are located so close to existing ones that Wal-Mart ends up competing with itself. All in all, the retailer's pretax return on fixed assets, which includes things such as computers and trucks as well as stores, has plunged 40 percent since 2000. Wal-Mart disclosed a year and a half ago that same-store sales were rising 10 times, or 1,000 percent, faster at the 800 best-managed outlets than at the 800 worst-run ones. Equally shocking was its admission that 25 percent of its stores failed to meet minimum expectations of cleanliness, product availability, checkout times, and so on.

Over the past decade, top competitors in most every retailing specialty have succeeded in narrowing their cost gap with Wal-Mart by restructuring their operations. They eliminated jobs, remodeled stores, and replaced warehouses, investing heavily in new technology to tie it all together. Unionized supermarkets even managed to chip away at Wal-Mart's nonunion-labor cost advantage, signaling their resolve by taking a long strike in Southern California in 2003–2004. The end result: rival chains gradually were able to bring their prices down closer to Wal-Mart's and again make good money.

Consider the return to form of Kroger Co., the largest and oldest U.S. supermarket chain. Cincinnati-based Kroger competes against more Wal-Mart Supercenters—1,000 at last count—than any other grocer. Which is why until recently the only real interest Wall Street took in the old-line giant was measuring it for a coffin. Today, though, a rejuvenated Kroger is gaining share faster in the 32 markets where it competes with Wal-Mart than in the 12 where it does not.

A recent Bank of America survey of three such markets—Atlanta, Houston, and Nashville—found that Kroger's prices were 7.5 percent higher on average than Wal-Mart's, compared with 20 to 25 percent five years ago. This margin is thin enough to allow Kroger to again bring to bear such "core competencies" as service, quality, and convenience, says BofA's Scott A. Mushkin, who recently switched his Kroger rating to buy from sell. "We're saying the game has changed, and it looks like it has changed substantially in Kroger's favor," he says.

Source: Reprinted with special permission from "Wal-Mart's Midlife Crisis," *BusinessWeek,* April 30, 2007. Copyright © 2007 The McGraw-Hill Companies.

benchmarking
Evaluating the sustainability of advantages against key competitors. Comparing the way a company performs a specific activity with a competitor or other company doing the same thing.

Benchmarking, or comparing the way "our" company performs a specific activity with a competitor or other company doing the same thing, has become a central concern of managers in quality commitment companies worldwide. Particularly as the value chain framework has taken hold in structuring internal analysis, managers seek to systematically benchmark the costs and results of the smallest value activities against relevant competitors or other useful standards because it has proven to be an effective way to continuously improve that activity. The ultimate objective in benchmarking is to identify the "best practices" in performing an activity and to learn how lower costs, fewer defects, or other outcomes linked to excellence are achieved. Companies committed to benchmarking attempt to isolate and identify where their costs or outcomes are out of line with what the best practices of a particular activity experience (competitors and noncompetitors) and then attempt to change their activities to achieve the new best practices standard. General Electric sends managers to benchmark FedEx's customer service practices, seeking to compare and improve on its own practices within a diverse set of businesses none of which compete directly with FedEx. It earlier did the same thing with Motorola, leading it to embrace Motorola's Six Sigma program for quality control and continuous improvement.

Comparison with Success Factors in the Industry

Industry analysis (see Chapter 4) involves identifying the factors associated with successful participation in a given industry. As was true for the evaluation methods discussed earlier, the key determinants of success in an industry may be used to identify a firm's internal strengths and weaknesses. By scrutinizing industry competitors as well as customer needs, vertical industry structure, channels of distribution, costs, barriers to entry, availability of substitutes, and suppliers, a strategist seeks to determine whether a firm's current internal capabilities represent strengths or weaknesses in new competitive arenas. The discussion in Chapter 4 provides a useful framework—five industry forces—against which to examine a firm's potential strengths and weaknesses. General Cinema Corporation, the largest U.S. movie theater operator, determined that its internal skills in marketing, site analysis, creative financing, and management of geographically dispersed operations were key strengths relative to major success factors in the soft-drink bottling industry. This assessment proved accurate. Within 10 years after it entered the soft-drink bottling industry, General Cinema became the largest franchised bottler of soft drinks in the United States, handling Pepsi, 7UP, Dr Pepper, and Sunkist. Exhibit 6.13, Strategy in Action, describes the dilemma facing once-mighty Wal-Mart as it falls precipitously behind key rivals on two critical success factors in discount retailing: same-store sales growth and age/quality of 60 percent of its U.S. stores. These two critical success factors drive and indicate the relative health of large discount retail firms. Firms with solid same-store sales growth indicate wise choices in location, attractiveness of their stores, and the merchandise inside them. Likewise, aging and probably substandard store facilities are typically not as efficient as newer ones, nor are they as inviting to shoppers. So Wal-Mart, Target, and other discount retailers conduct internal analyses in part by comparing themselves on these two (and surely others) critical success factors to interpret their strength or weakness relative to factors that drive industry success.

product life cycle (PLC)
A concept that describes a product's sales, profitability, and competencies that are key drivers of the success of that product as it moves through a sequence of stages from development, introduction to growth, maturity, decline, and eventual removal from a market.

Product Life Cycle

Product life cycle (PLC) is one way to identify success factors against which executives can evaluate their firm's competencies relative to its key product or products. The **product life cycle** is a concept that describes a product's sales, profitability, and competencies that are key drivers of the success of that product as it moves through a sequence of stages from development, introduction to growth, maturity, decline, and eventual removal from a market. Exhibit 6.14 illustrates the "typical" product life cycle.

EXHIBIT 6.14
Illustration of the Product Life Cycle

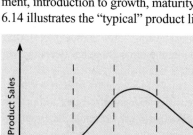

Core competencies associated with success are thought to vary across different stages of the product life cycle. Those competencies might include the following:

Introduction Stage

During this stage the firm needs competence in building product awareness and market development along with the resources to support initial losses:

- Ability to create product awareness.
- Good channel relationships in ways to get the product introduced quickly, gaining a first-mover advantage.
- Premium pricing to "skim" profitability if few competitors exist.
- Solid relationships with and access to trend-setting early adopters.
- Financial resources to absorb an initial cash drain and lack of profitability.

Growth

During this stage market growth accelerates rapidly, with the firm seeking to build brand awareness and establish/increase market share:

- Brand awareness and ability to build brand.
- Advertising skills and resources to back them.
- Product features that differentiate versus increased competitive offerings.
- Establishing and stabilizing market shares.
- Access to multiple distribution channels.
- Ability to add additional features.

Maturity

This stage sees growth in sales slow significantly, along with increased competition and similar product offerings leading the firm to need competencies that allow it to defend its market share while maximizing profit:

- Sustained brand awareness.
- Ability to differentiate products and features.
- Resources to initiate or sustain price wars.
- Operating advantages to improve slimming margins.
- Judgment to know whether to stay in or exit saturated market segments.

Decline

At this point the product and its competitors start to experience declining sales and increased pressure on margins. Competencies needed are:

- Ability to withstand intense price-cutting.
- Brand strength to allow reduced marketing.
- Cost cutting capacity and slack to allow it.
- Good supplier relationships to gain cost concessions.
- Innovation skills to create new products or "re-create" existing ones.

The PLC is an interesting concept or framework against which executives might gauge the strength of relevant competencies. Caution is necessary in its use beyond that purpose, however. In reality, very few products follow exactly the cycle portrayed in the PLC model. The length in each stage can vary, the length and nature of the PLC for any particular product can vary dramatically, and it is not easy to tell exactly what stage a product might be in at any given time. Not all products go through each stage. Some, for example, go from introduction to decline. And movement from one stage to the next can be accelerated by strategies or tactics executives emphasize. For example, price-cutting can accelerate the movement from maturity to decline.

Product life cycles can describe a single product, a category of products, or an industry segment. Applying the basic idea to an industry segment (category of products) rather than a specific product has been a more beneficial adaptation of the PLC concept, providing executives with a conceptual tool to aid them in strategic analysis and choice in the context of the evolution of an industry segment in which their firm competes. So we will examine the concept of stages of evolution of an industry segment or category of products as a tool of strategic analysis and choice in Chapter 8.

Summary

This chapter looked at several ways managers achieve greater objectivity and rigor as they analyze their company's internal resources and capabilities. Managers often start their internal analysis with questions like, How well is the current strategy working? What is our current situation? What are our strengths and weaknesses? SWOT analysis is a traditional approach that has been in use for decades to help structure managers' pursuit of answers to these questions. A logical approach still used by many managers today, SWOT analysis has limitations linked to the depth of its analysis and the risk of overlooking key considerations.

Two techniques for internal analysis have emerged that overcome some of the limitations of SWOT analysis, offering more comprehensive approaches that can help managers identify and assess their firm's internal resources and capabilities in a more systematic, objective, and measurable manner. Value chain analysis has managers look at and disaggregate their business as a chain of activities that occur in a sequential manner to create the products or services they sell. The value chain approach breaks down the firm's activities into primary and support categories of activities, then breaks these down further into specific types of activities with the objective to disaggregate activity into as many meaningful subdivisions as possible. Once done, managers attempt to attribute costs to each. Doing this gives managers very distinct ways of isolating the things they do well and not so well, and it isolates activities that are truly key in meeting customer needs—true potential sources of competitive advantage.

The third approach covered in this chapter was the resource-based view (RBV). RBV is based on the premise that firms build competitive advantage based on the unique resources, skills, and capabilities they control or develop, which can become the basis of unique, sustainable competitive advantages that allow them to craft successful competitive strategies. The RBV provides a useful conceptual frame to first inventory a firm's potential competitive advantages among its tangible assets, intangible assets, and its organizational capabilities. Once inventoried, the RBV provides four fundamental guidelines that managers can use to "value" these resources and capabilities. Those with major value, defined as ones that are valuable for several reasons, become the bases for building strategies linked to sustainable competitive advantages.

Finally, this chapter covered three ways objectivity and realism are enhanced when managers use meaningful standards for comparison regardless of the particular analytical framework they employ in internal analysis. This chapter is followed by two appendixes. The first provides a useful inventory of the types of activities in different functional areas of a firm that can be sources of competitive advantage. The second appendix covers traditional financial analysis to serve as a refresher and reminder about this basic internal analysis tool.

When matched with management's environmental analyses and mission priorities, the process of internal analysis provides the critical foundation for strategy formulation. Armed with an accurate, thorough, and timely internal analysis, managers are in a better position to formulate effective strategies. The next chapter describes basic strategy alternatives that any firm may consider.

Key Terms

benchmarking, *p. 181*
core competence, *p. 171*
intangible assets, *p. 171*
isolating mechanisms, *p. 174*
opportunity, *p. 159*
organizational capabilities, *p. 171*

primary activities, *p. 165*
product life cycle (PLC), *p. 182*
resource-based view, *p. 170*
strength, *p. 159*
SWOT analysis, *p. 159*
support activities, *p. 165*

tangible assets, *p. 171*
threat, *p. 159*
value chain, *p. 164*
value chain analysis, *p. 164*
weakness, *p. 160*

Questions for Discussion

1. Describe SWOT analysis as a way to guide internal analysis. How does this approach reflect the basic strategic management process?
2. What are potential weaknesses of SWOT analysis?
3. Describe the difference between primary and support activities using value chain analysis.
4. How is VCA different from SWOT analysis?
5. What is the resource-based view? Give examples of three different types of resources.
6. What are three ways resources become more valuable? Provide an example of each.
7. Explain how you might use VCA, RBV, and SWOT analysis to get a better sense of what might be a firm's key building blocks for a successful strategy.
8. Attempt to apply SWOT, VCA, and RBV to yourself and your career aspirations. What are your major strengths and weaknesses? How might you use your knowledge of these strengths and weaknesses to develop your future career plans?

Chapter 6 Discussion Case

BusinessWeek

Apple's Blueprint for Genius

DESIGNED BY APPLE IN CALIFORNIA

1 The words are printed in such small type on the back of Apple's tiny iPod Nano MP3 player that you have to squint to read them. But they speak volumes about why Apple is standing so far out from the crowd these days. At a time when rivals are outsourcing as much design as possible to cut costs, Apple remains at its core a product company—one that would never give up control of how those products are created.

2 In this age of commodity tech products, design, after all, is what makes Apple Apple. This focus is apparent to anyone who has used one of its trailblazing products. While the Silicon Valley pioneer sells only a few dozen models, compared to the hundreds offered by many of its rivals, many of those "designed in California" products are startling departures from the norm—and they often set the directions for the rest of the industry. Examples abound, from the iPhone to Apple TV to the iPod, the Airport Extreme, or the simple smallness of the new Mac mini PC.

3 What's the secret? The precise details are almost impossible to get, because Apple treats its product-development processes like state secrets—going so far as to string black drapes around the production lines at the factories of the contract manufacturers it hires to assemble its products. In one case, says a source who once worked on an Apple project, the outfit even insisted that its wares be built only on the midnight shift, when fewer prying eyes might be around.

INSANELY GREAT

4 But the general themes are clear. Most CEOs are focused on achieving their financial and operational goals, and on executing a strategy. But Apple's Steve Jobs believes his company's ultimate advantage comes from its ability to make unique, or as he calls them, "insanely great" products. Introducing the iPhone in 2007, Jobs simply said, "We reinvented the phone."

5 Jobs's entire company is focused on that task. That means while rival computer, phone, and digital media product makers increasingly rely on so-called outsourced design manufacturers (ODMs) for key design decisions, Jobs keeps most of those tasks in-house. Sure, he relies on ODMs to manufacture his products, but the big decisions on Apple products are made in Silicon Valley.

6 Jobs himself is a crucial part of the formula. He's unique among big-time hardware CEOs for his hands-on involvement in the design process. Even product-design experts marvel at the power of the Jobs factor.

FIRST, AN IDEA

7 "I've been thinking hard about the Apple product-development process since I left," says design guru Donald Norman, co-founder of the design consultants Nielsen Norman Group, who left Apple in 1997. "If you follow my [guidelines], it will guarantee good design. But Steve Jobs doesn't want good design. He wants great design, and my method will never give you that. That takes a rare leader, who can bring both the cohesion and commitment and style. And Steve has it."

8 Many executives believe that outsourcing design allows them to lower the salaries they must pay and lets them have engineers working on the products across all time zones. Jobs thinks that's short-sighted. He argues that the cost-savings aren't worth what you give up in terms of teamwork, communication, and the ability to get groups of people working together to bring a new idea to life. Indeed, with top-notch mechanical, electrical, software, and industrial designers all housed at Apple's Infinite Loop campus in Cupertino, Calif., the company's design capability is more vertically integrated than almost any other tech outfit.

9 Typically, a new Apple product starts with a big idea for an unmet customer need. For the original iPod, it was for an MP3 player that, unlike earlier models, could hold and easily manage your entire music collection. Then, Apple's product architects and industrial designers figure out what that product should look like and what features it should have—and, importantly, not have. "Apple has a much more holistic view of product design," says David Carey, president of design consulting firm Portelligent. "Good product design starts from the outside, and works its way inside."

HALF MEASURE

10 Already, that's different from the process by which the bulk of tech products are made. Increasingly, tech companies meet with ODMs to see what designs they have cooked up. Then, the ODMs are asked to tweak those basic blueprints to add a few features and to match the look and feel of the company's other products.

11 That's where the "design" input might end for most companies. But since it's almost always trying to create one-of-a-kind products, Apple has to ask its own engineers to do the critical electrical and mechanical work to bring products to life.

12 In the iPod Shuffle, for example, designers cut a circuit card in two and stacked the pieces, bunk-bed style, to make use of the empty air space created by the height of the battery in the device. "They realized they could erase the height penalty [of the battery] to help them win the battle of the bulge," says Carey, whose company did a detailed engineering analysis of the iPod Nano.

SCREW-FREE

13 Even more important, Apple's products are designed to run a particular set of programs or services. By contrast, a Dell or HP device must be ready for whatever new features Microsoft comes out with or whatever Windows program a customer opts to install.

14 But Apple makes much of its own software, from the MAS OSX operating system to applications such as iPhoto and iTunes. "That's Apple's trump card," says one Apple rival. "The ODMs just don't have the world-class industrial design, the style, or the ability to make easy-to-use software—or the ability to integrate it all. They may some day, but they don't have it now."

15 Of course, Apple also sets itself apart by designing machines that are also little works of art—even if it means making life difficult for manufacturers contracted to build those designs. During a trip to visit ODMs in Asia, one executive told securities analyst Jim Grossman of Thrivent Investment Management about Steve Jobs's insistence that no screws be visible on the laptop his company was manufacturing for Apple. The executive said his company had no idea how to handle the job and had to invent a new tooling process for the job. "They had to learn new ways to do things just to meet Apple's design," says Grossman.

TOUGH CUSTOMER

16 That's not to say Apple is completely bucking the outsourcing trend. All its products are manufactured by ODMs in Asia. Just as it buys chips and disk drives from other suppliers, sources say Apple lets ODMs take some role in garden-variety engineering work—but not much. "This is an issue for Apple, because the A-team engineers [at the ODMs] don't like working with Apple. It's like when you were a kid, all your dad let you do was hold the flashlight, rather than let you try to fix the car yourself," says an executive at a rival MP3 maker.

17 In fairness, Apple's reliance on a smaller number of products than its rivals and go-it-alone design means it's always a dud or two from disaster. But at the moment, it's proving that "made in Cupertino" is a trademark for success.

VOICES OF INNOVATION

An Interview with Steve Jobs, Chairman and CEO of Apple

BusinessWeek: What can we learn from Apple's struggle to innovate during the decade before your return in 1997?

Steve Jobs: "You need a very product-oriented culture. Apple had a monopoly on the graphical user interface for almost 10 years. How are monopolies lost? Some very good product people invent some very good products, and the company achieves a monopoly. [But] what's the point of focusing on making the product even better when the only company you can take business from is yourself? So a different group of people starts to move up. And who usually ends up running the show?

The sales guy. Then one day the monopoly expires, for whatever reason . . . but by then, the best product people have left or they are no longer listened to. And so the company goes through this tumultuous time, and it either survives or it doesn't.

BusinessWeek: How do you systematize innovation?

Steve Jobs: You don't. You hire good people who will challenge each other every day to make the best products possible. That's why you don't see any big posters on the walls around here, stating our mission statement. Our corporate culture is simple.

BusinessWeek: So the key is to have good people with a passion for excellence.

Steve Jobs: When I got back, Apple had forgotten who we were. Remember that "Think Different" ad campaign we ran? It was certainly for customers, but it was even more for Apple. That ad was to remind us of who our heroes are and who we are. Companies sometimes do forget. Fortunately, we woke up. And Apple is doing the best work in its history.

DISCUSSION QUESTIONS

1. Apply the three internal analysis frameworks—SWOT analysis, value chain analysis, and the resource-based view—as a way to explain and evaluate aspects of Apple's internal environment highlighted in the Chapter Case about Apple and the interview with Steve Jobs.

   a. What are Apple's strengths and weaknesses, opportunities and threats?

   b. Roughly what would Apple's value chain look like, and how might it differ from other companies mentioned in this case?

   c. What are Apple's key resources and capabilities? Which are most valuable? Why?

2. Which is the most meaningful type of comparison you make use of in conducting each approach to internal analysis at Apple?

3. Which approach to internal analysis works best in your internal analysis of the aspects about Apple covered in this case? Why?

4. In your opinion, would it be best to use that approach (your answer to question 3) alone or to use it along with the other two approaches if you were a manager responsible for conducting an internal analysis of your company as part of its strategic management process?

Sources: Reprinted with special permission from "The Future of Apple," *BusinessWeek*, January 10, 2007, "Apple's Blueprint for Genius," *BusinessWeek Online Extra*, March 23, 2005; and "Steven Jobs on Apple Innovation," *BusinessWeek*, October 4, 2005. Copyright © 2007 The McGraw-Hill Companies.

Chapter 6 Appendix A

Key Resources across Functional Areas

MARKETING

Firm's products-services: breadth of product line
Concentration of sales in a few products or to a few customers
Ability to gather needed information about markets
Market share or submarket shares
Product-service mix and expansion potential: life cycle of key products; profit-sales balance in product-service
Channels of distribution: number, coverage, and control
Effective sales organization: knowledge of customer needs
Internet usage; Web presence
Product-service image, reputation, and quality
Imaginativeness, efficiency, and effectiveness of sales promotion and advertising
Pricing strategy and pricing flexibility
Procedures for digesting market feedback and developing new products, services, or markets
After-sale service and follow-up
Goodwill—brand loyalty

FINANCIAL AND ACCOUNTING

Ability to raise short-term capital
Ability to raise long-term capital; debt-equity
Corporate-level resources (multibusiness firm)
Cost of capital relative to that of industry and competitors
Tax considerations
Relations with owners, investors, and stockholders
Leverage position; capacity to utilize alternative financial strategies, such as lease or sale and leaseback
Cost of entry and barriers to entry
Price-earnings ratio
Working capital; flexibility of capital structure
Effective cost control; ability to reduce cost
Financial size
Efficiency and effectiveness of accounting system for cost, budget, and profit planning

PRODUCTION, OPERATIONS, TECHNICAL

Raw materials' cost and availability, supplier relationships
Inventory control systems; inventory turnover
Location of facilities; layout and utilization of facilities
Economies of scale
Technical efficiency of facilities and utilization of capacity
Effectiveness of subcontracting use
Degree of vertical integration; value added and profit margin
Efficiency and cost-benefit of equipment

Effectiveness of operation control procedures: design, scheduling, purchasing, quality control, and efficiency
Costs and technological competencies relative to those of industry and competitors
Research and development—technology—innovation
Patents, trademarks, and similar legal protection

PERSONNEL

Management personnel
Employees' skill and morale
Labor relations costs compared with those of industry and competitors
Efficiency and effectiveness of personnel policies
Effectiveness of incentives used to motivate performance
Ability to level peaks and valleys of employment
Employee turnover and absenteeism
Specialized skills
Experience

QUALITY MANAGEMENT

Relationship with suppliers, customers
Internal practices to enhance quality of products and services
Procedures for monitoring quality

INFORMATION SYSTEMS

Timeliness and accuracy of information about sales, operations, cash, and suppliers
Relevance of information for tactical decisions
Information to manage quality issues: customer service
Ability of people to use the information that is provided
Linkages to suppliers and customers

ORGANIZATION AND GENERAL MANAGEMENT

Organizational structure
Firm's image and prestige
Firm's record in achieving objectives
Organization of communication system
Overall organizational control system (effectiveness and utilization)
Organizational climate; organizational culture
Use of systematic procedures and techniques in decision making
Top-management skill, capabilities, and interest
Strategic planning system
Intraorganizational synergy (multibusiness firms)

Using Financial Analysis

One of the most important tools for assessing the strength of an organization within its industry is financial analysis. Managers, investors, and creditors all employ some form of this analysis as the beginning point for their financial decision making. Investors use financial analyses in making decisions about whether to buy or sell stock, and creditors use them in deciding whether or not to lend. They provide managers with a measurement of how the company is doing in comparison with its performance in past years and with the performance of competitors in the industry.

Although financial analysis is useful for decision making, some weaknesses should be noted. Any picture that it provides of the company is based on past data. Although trends may be noteworthy, this picture should not automatically be assumed to be applicable to the future. In addition, the analysis is only as good as the accounting procedures that have provided the information. When making comparisons between companies, one should keep in mind the variability of accounting procedures from firm to firm.

There are four basic groups of financial ratios: liquidity, leverage, activity, and profitability.

Depicted in Exhibit 6.B1 are the specific ratios calculated for each of the basic groups. Liquidity and leverage ratios represent an assessment of the risk of the firm. Activity and profitability ratios are measures of the return generated by the assets of the firm. The interaction between certain groups of ratios is indicated by arrows.

Typically, two common financial statements are used in financial analyses: the balance sheet and the income statement. Exhibit 6.B2 is a balance sheet and Exhibit 6.B3 an income statement for the ABC Company. These statements will be used to illustrate the financial analyses.

LIQUIDITY RATIOS

Liquidity ratios are used as indicators of a firm's ability to meet its short-term obligations. These obligations include any current liabilities, including currently maturing long-term debt. Current assets move through a normal cash cycle of inventories—sales—accounts receivable—cash. The firm then uses cash to pay off or reduce its current liabilities. The best-known liquidity ratio is the current ratio: current assets divided by current liabilities. For the ABC Company, the current ratio is calculated as follows:

$$\frac{\text{Current assets}}{\text{Current liabilities}} = \frac{\$4,125,000}{\$2,512,500} = 1.64 \, (2011)$$

$$= \frac{\$3,618,000}{\$2,242,250} = 1.161 \, (2010)$$

Most analysts suggest a current ratio of 2 to 3. A large current ratio is not necessarily a good sign; it may mean that an organization is not making the most efficient use of its assets. The optimum current ratio will vary from industry to industry, with the more volatile industries requiring higher ratios.

Because slow-moving or obsolescent inventories could overstate a firm's ability to meet short-term demands, the quick ratio is sometimes preferred to assess a firm's liquidity. The quick ratio is current assets minus inventories, divided by current liabilities. The quick ratio for the ABC Company is calculated as follows:

$$\frac{\text{Current assets} - \text{Inventories}}{\text{Current liabilities}} = \frac{\$1,950,000}{\$2,512,500} = 0.78 \, (2011)$$

$$= \frac{\$1,618,000}{\$2,242,250} = 0.72 \, (2010)$$

A quick ratio of approximately 1 would be typical for American industries. Although there is less variability in the quick ratio than in the current ratio, stable industries would be able to operate safely with a lower ratio.

LEVERAGE RATIOS

Leverage ratios identify the source of a firm's capital—owners or outside creditors. The term *leverage* refers to the fact that using capital with a fixed interest charge will "amplify" either profits or losses in relation to the equity of holders of common stock. The most commonly used ratio is total debt divided by total assets. Total debt includes current liabilities and long-term liabilities. This ratio is a measure of the percentage of total funds provided by debt. A total debt–total assets ratio higher than 0.5 is usually considered safe only for firms in stable industries.

$$\frac{\text{Total debt}}{\text{Total assets}} = \frac{\$3,862,500}{\$7,105,000} = 0.54 \, (2011)$$

$$= \frac{\$3,667,250}{\$6,393,000} = 0.57 \, (2010)$$

The ratio of long-term debt to equity is a measure of the extent to which sources of long-term financing are provided by creditors. It is computed by dividing long-term debt by the stockholders' equity:

$$\frac{\text{Long-term debt}}{\text{Equity}} = \frac{\$1,350,000}{\$3,242,500} = 0.42 \, (2011)$$

$$= \frac{\$1,425,000}{\$2,725,750} = 0.52 \, (2010)$$

EXHIBIT 6.B1 **Financial Ratios**

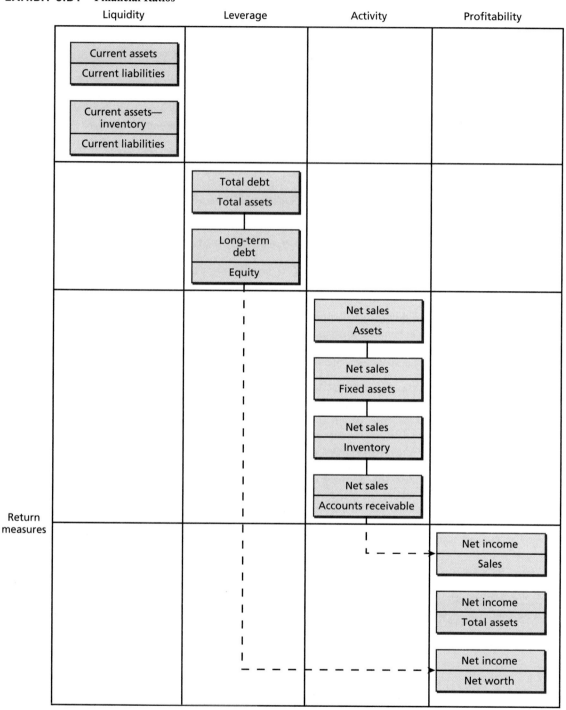

EXHIBIT 6.B2   ABC Company Balance Sheet as of December 31, 2010, and 2011

	2011		2010
Assets			
Current assets:			
Cash		$ 140,000	$ 115,00
Accounts receivable		1,760,000	1,440,000
Inventory		2,175,000	2,000,000
Prepaid expenses		50,000	63,000
Total current assets		4,125,000	3,618,000
Fixed assets:			
Long-term receivable		1,255,000	1,090,000
Property and plant	$2,037,000		$2,015,000
Less: Accumulated depreciation	862,000		860,000
Net property and plant		1,175,000	1,155,000
Other fixed assets		550,000	530,000
Total fixed assets		2,980,000	2,775,000
Total assets		$7,105,000	$6,393,000
Liabilities and Stockholders' Equity			
Current liabilities:			
Accounts payable		$1,325,000	$1,225,000
Bank loans payable		475,000	550,000
Accrued federal taxes		675,000	425,000
Current maturities (long-term debt)		17,500	26,000
Dividends payable		20,000	16,250
Total current liabilities		2,512,500	2,242,250
Long-term liabilities		1,350,000	1,425,000
Total liabilities		3,862,000	3,667,250
Stockholders' equity:			
Common stock			
(104,046 shares outstanding in 2005;			
101,204 shares outstanding in 2004)		44,500	43,300
Additional paid-in-capital		568,000	372,450
Retained earnings		2,630,000	2,310,000
Total stockholders' equity		3,242,500	2,725,750
Total liabilities and stockholders' equity		$7,105,000	$6,393,000

EXHIBIT 6.B3   ABC Company Income Statement for the years ending December 31, 2010, and 2011

	2011		2010
Net sales		$8,250,000	$8,000,000
Cost of goods sold	$5,100,000		$5,000,000
Administrative expenses	1,750,000		1,680,000
Other expenses	420,000		390,000
Total		7,270,000	7,070,000
Earnings before interest and taxes		980,000	930,000
Less: Interest expense		210,000	210,000
Earnings before taxes		770,000	720,000
Less: Federal income taxes		360,000	325,000
Earnings after taxes (net income)		$ 410,000	$ 395,000
Common stock cash dividends		$ 90,000	$ 84,000
Addition to retained earnings		$ 320,000	$ 311,000
Earnings per common share		$ 3.940	$ 3.90
Dividends per common share		$ 0.865	$ 0.83

ACTIVITY RATIOS

Activity ratios indicate how effectively a firm is using its resources. By comparing revenues with the resources used to generate them, it is possible to establish an efficiency of operation. The asset turnover ratio indicates how efficiently management is employing total assets. Asset turnover is calculated by dividing sales by total assets. For the ABC Company, asset turnover is calculated as follows:

$$\text{Asset turnover} = \frac{\text{Sales}}{\text{Total assets}} = \frac{\$8,250,000}{\$7,105,000} = 1.16 \ (2011)$$

$$= \frac{\$8,000,0000}{\$6,393,000} = 1.25 \ (2010)$$

The ratio of sales to fixed assets is a measure of the turnover on plant and equipment. It is calculated by dividing sales by net fixed assets.

$$\frac{\text{Fixed asset}}{\text{turnover}} = \frac{\text{Sales}}{\text{Net fixed assets}} = \frac{\$8,250,000}{\$2,980,000} = 2.77 \ (2011)$$

$$= \frac{\$8,000,000}{\$2,775,000} = 2.88 \ (2010)$$

Industry figures for asset turnover will vary with capital-intensive industries, and those requiring large inventories will have much smaller ratios.

Another activity ratio is inventory turnover, estimated by dividing sales by average inventory. The norm for U.S. industries is 9, but whether the ratio for a particular firm is higher or lower normally depends on the product sold. Small, inexpensive items usually turn over at a much higher rate than larger, expensive ones. Because inventories normally are carried at cost, it would be more accurate to use the cost of goods sold in place of sales in the numerator of this ratio. Established compilers of industry ratios, such as Dun & Bradstreet, however, use the ratio of sales to inventory.

$$\frac{\text{Inventory}}{\text{turnover}} = \frac{\text{Sales}}{\text{Inventory}} = \frac{\$8,250,000}{\$2,175,000} = 3.79 \ (2011)$$

$$= \frac{\$8,000,000}{\$2,000,000} = 4.00 \ (2010)$$

The accounts receivable turnover is a measure of the average collection period on sales. If the average number of days varies widely from the industry norm, it may be an indication of poor management. A too-low ratio could indicate the loss of sales because of a too-restrictive credit policy. If the ratio is too high, too much capital is being tied up in accounts receivable, and management may be increasing the chance of bad debts. Because of varying industry credit policies, a comparison for the firm over time or within an industry is the only useful analysis. Because information on credit sales for other firms generally is unavailable, total sales must be used. Because not all firms have the same percentage of credit sales, there is only approximate comparability among firms:

$$\frac{\text{Accounts}}{\text{receivable}} = \frac{\text{Sales}}{\text{Accounts receivable}} = \frac{\$8,250,000}{\$1,760,000} = 4.69 \ (2011)$$

$$= \frac{\$8,000,000}{\$1,440,000} = 5.56 \ (2010)$$

$$\text{Average collection period} = \frac{360}{\text{Accounts receivable turnover}}$$

$$= \frac{360}{4.69} = 77 \text{ days } (2011)$$

$$= \frac{360}{5.56} = 65 \text{ days } (2010)$$

PROFITABILITY RATIOS

Profitability is the net result of a large number of policies and decisions chosen by an organization's management. Profitability ratios indicate how effectively the total firm is being managed. The profit margin for a firm is calculated by dividing net earnings by sales. This ratio is often called *return on sales* (ROS). There is wide variation among industries, but the average for U.S. firms is approximately 5 percent.

$$\frac{\text{Net earnings}}{\text{Sales}} = \frac{\$410,000}{\$8,250,000} = 0.0497 \ (2011)$$

$$= \frac{\$395,000}{\$8,000,000} = 0.0494 \ (2010)$$

A second useful ratio for evaluating profitability is the *return on investment*—or ROI, as it is frequently called— found by dividing net earnings by total assets. The ABC Company's ROI is calculated as follows:

$$\frac{\text{Net earnings}}{\text{Total assets}} = \frac{\$410,000}{\$7,105,000} = 0.0577 \ (2011)$$

$$= \frac{\$395,000}{\$6,393,000} = 0.0618 \ (2010)$$

The ratio of net earnings to net worth is a measure of the rate of return or profitability of the stockholders' investment. It is calculated by dividing net earnings by net worth, the common stock equity and retained earnings account. ABC Company's *return on net worth* or *return on equity,* also called ROE, is calculated as follows:

$$\frac{\text{Net earnings}}{\text{Net worth}} = \frac{\$410,000}{\$3,242,500} = 0.1264 \ (2011)$$

$$= \frac{\$395,000}{\$2,725,750} = 0.1449 \ (2010)$$

It is often difficult to determine causes for lack of profitability. The Du Pont system of financial analysis provides

EXHIBIT 6.B4   Du Pont's Financial Analysis

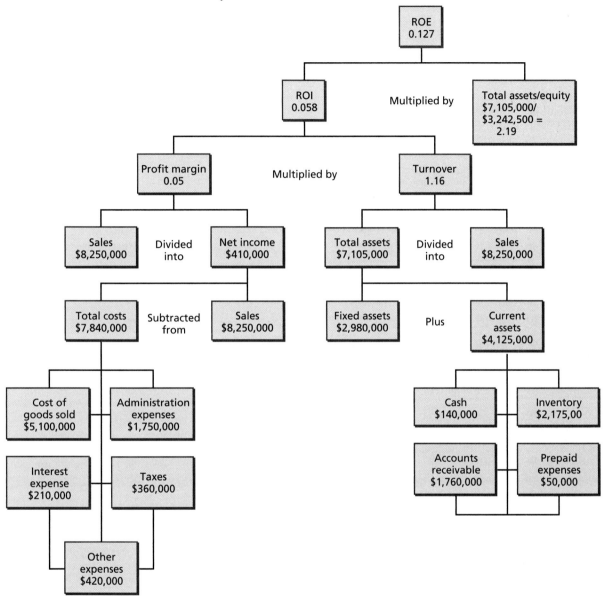

management with clues to the lack of success of a firm. This financial tool brings together activity, profitability, and leverage measures and shows how these ratios interact to determine the overall profitability of the firm. A depiction of the system is set forth in Exhibit 6.B4.

The right side of the exhibit develops the turnover ratio. This section breaks down total assets into current assets (cash, marketable securities, accounts receivable, and inventories) and fixed assets. Sales divided by these total assets gives the turnover on assets.

The left side of the exhibit develops the profit margin on sales. The individual expense items plus income taxes are subtracted from sales to produce net profits after taxes. Net profits divided by sales gives the profit margin on sales. When the asset turnover ratio on the right side of Exhibit 6.B4 is multiplied by the profit margin on sales developed on the left side of the exhibit, the product is the return on assets (ROI) for the firm. This can be shown by the following formula:

$$\frac{\text{Sales}}{\text{Total assets}} \times \frac{\text{Net earnings}}{\text{Sales}} = \frac{\text{Net earnings}}{\text{Total assets}} = \text{ROI}$$

The last step in the Du Pont analysis is to multiply the rate of return on assets (ROI) by the equity multiplier, which is the ratio of assets to common equity, to obtain the rate of return on equity (ROE). This percentage rate of return, of course, could be calculated directly by dividing net income by common equity. However, the Du Pont analysis demonstrates how the return on assets and the use of debt interact to determine the return on equity.

The Du Pont system can be used to analyze and improve the performance of a firm. On the left, or profit, side of the exhibit, attempts to increase profits and sales could be investigated. The possibilities of raising prices to improve profits (or lowering prices to improve volume) or seeking new products or markets, for example, could be studied. Cost accountants and production engineers could investigate ways to reduce costs. On the right, or turnover, side, financial officers could analyze the effect of reducing investment in various assets as well as the effect of using alternative financial structures.

There are two basic approaches to using financial ratios. One approach is to evaluate the corporation's performance over several years. Financial ratios are computed for different years, and then an assessment is made about whether there has been an improvement or deterioration over time. Financial ratios also can be computed for projected, pro forma, statements and compared with present and past ratios.

The other approach is to evaluate a firm's financial condition and compare it with the financial conditions of similar firms or with industry averages in the same period. Such a comparison gives insight into the firm's relative financial condition and performance. Financial ratios for industries are provided by Robert Morris Associates, Dun & Bradstreet, Prentice Hall, and various trade association publications. (Associations and their addresses are listed in the *Encyclopedia of Associations* and in the *Directory of National Trade Associations.*) Information about individual firms is available through *Moody's Manual,* Standard & Poor's manuals and surveys, annual reports to stockholders, and the major brokerage houses.

To the extent possible, accounting data from different companies must be so standardized that companies can be compared or so a specific company can be compared with an industry average. It is important to read any footnotes of financial statements, because various accounting or management practices can have an effect on the financial picture of the company. For example, firms using sale-leaseback methods may have leverage pictures quite different from what is shown as debts or assets on the balance sheet.

ANALYSIS OF THE SOURCES AND USES OF FUNDS

The purpose of this analysis is to determine how the company is using its financial resources from year to year. By comparing balance sheets from one year to the next, we can determine how funds were obtained and how these funds were employed during the year.

To prepare a statement of the sources and uses of funds, it is necessary to (1) classify balance sheet changes that increase and decrease cash, (2) classify from the income statement those factors that increase or decrease cash, and (3) consolidate this information on a sources and uses of funds statement form.

Sources of Funds That Increase Cash

1. A net decrease in any other asset than a depreciable fixed asset.
2. A gross decrease in a depreciable fixed asset.
3. A net increase in any liability.
4. Proceeds from the sale of stock.
5. The operation of the company (net income, and depreciation if the company is profitable).

Uses of Funds

1. A net increase in any other asset than a depreciable fixed asset.
2. A gross increase in depreciable fixed assets.
3. A net decrease in any liability.
4. A retirement or purchase of stock.
5. Payment of cash dividends.

We compute gross changes to depreciable fixed assets by adding depreciation from the income statement for the period to net fixed assets at the end of the period and then subtracting from the total net fixed assets at the beginning of the period. The residual represents the change in depreciable fixed assets for the period.

For the ABC Company, the following change would be calculated:

Net property and plant (2011)	$1,175,000
Depreciation for 2011	+ 80,000
	$1,255,000
Net property and plant (2010)	−1,155,000
	$ 100,000

To avoid double counting, the change in retained earnings is not shown directly in the funds statement. When the funds statement is prepared, this account is replaced by the earnings after taxes, or net income, as a source of funds, and dividends paid during the year as a use of funds. The difference between net income and the change in the retained earnings account will equal the amount of dividends paid during the year. The accompanying sources and uses of funds statement was prepared for the ABC Company.

A funds analysis is useful for determining trends in working-capital positions and for demonstrating how the firm has acquired and employed its funds during some period.

ABC Company Sources and Uses of Funds Statement for 2011

Sources		Uses	
Prepaid expenses	$ 13,000	Cash	$ 25,000
Accounts payable	100,000	Accounts receivable	320,000
Accrued federal taxes	250,000	Inventory	175,000
Dividends payable	3,750	Long-term receivables	165,000
Common stock	1,200	Property and plant	100,000
Additional paid-in capital	195,000	Other fixed assets	20,000
Earnings after taxes (net income)	410,000	Bank loans payable	75,000
Depreciation	80,000	Current maturities of long-term debt	8,500
Total sources	$1,053,500	Long-term liabilities	75,000
		Dividends paid	90,000
		Total uses	$1,053,500

Conclusion

It is recommended that you prepare a chart, such as that shown in Exhibit 6.B5, so you can develop a useful portrayal of these financial analyses. The chart allows a display of the ratios over time. The "Trend" column could be used to indicate your evaluation of the ratios over time (e.g., "favorable," "neutral," or "unfavorable"). The "Industry Average" column could include recent industry averages on these ratios or those of key competitors. These would provide information to aid interpretation of the analyses. The "Interpretation" column could be used to describe your interpretation of the ratios for this firm. Overall, this chart gives a basic display of the ratios that provides a convenient format for examining the firm's financial condition.

Finally, Exhibit 6.B6 is included to provide a quick reference summary of the calculations and meanings of the ratios discussed earlier.

EXHIBIT 6.B5   **A Summary of the Financial Position of a Firm**

Ratios and Working Capital	2007	2008	2009	2010	2011	Trend	Industry Average	Interpre- tation
Liquidity: Current								
Quick								
Leverage: Debt-assets								
Debt-equity								
Activity: Asset turnover								
Fixed asset ratio								
Inventory turnover								
Accounts receivable turnover								
Average collection period								
Profitability: ROS								
ROI								
ROE								
Working-capital position								

EXHIBIT 6.B6 **A Summary of Key Financial Ratios**

Ratio	Calculation	Meaning
Liquidity Ratios:		
Current ratio	$\dfrac{\text{Current assets}}{\text{Current liabilities}}$	The extent to which a firm can meet its short-term obligations.
Quick ratio	$\dfrac{\text{Current assets} - \text{Inventory}}{\text{Current liabilities}}$	The extent to which a firm can meet its short-term obligations without relying on the sale of inventories.
Leverage Ratios:		
Debt-to-total-assets ratio	$\dfrac{\text{Total debt}}{\text{Total assets}}$	The percentage of total funds that are provided by creditors.
Debt-to-equity ratio	$\dfrac{\text{Total debt}}{\text{Total stockholders' equity}}$	The percentage of total funds provided by creditors versus the percentage provided by owners.
Long-term-debt-to-equity ratio	$\dfrac{\text{Long-term debt}}{\text{Total stockholders' equity}}$	The balance between debt and equity in a firm's long-term capital structure.
Times-interest-earned ratio	$\dfrac{\text{Profits before interest and taxes}}{\text{Total interest charges}}$	The extent to which earnings can decline without the firm becoming unable to meet its annual interest costs.
Activity Ratios:		
Inventory turnover	$\dfrac{\text{Sales}}{\text{Inventory of finished goods}}$	Whether a firm holds excessive stocks of inventories and whether a firm is selling its inventories slowly compared to the industry average.
Fixed assets turnover	$\dfrac{\text{Sales}}{\text{Fixed assets}}$	Sales productivity and plant equipment utilization.
Total assets turnover	$\dfrac{\text{Sales}}{\text{Total assets}}$	Whether a firm is generating a sufficient volume of business for the size of its assets investment.
Accounts receivable turnover	$\dfrac{\text{Annual credit sales}}{\text{Account receivable}}$	In percentage terms, the average length of time it takes a firm to collect on credit sales.
Average collection period	$\dfrac{\text{Account receivable}}{\text{Total sales}/365 \text{ days}}$	In days, the average length of time it takes a firm to collect on credit sales.
Profitability Ratios:		
Gross profit margin	$\dfrac{\text{Sales} - \text{Cost of goods sold}}{\text{Sales}}$	The total margin available to cover operating expenses and yield a profit.
Operating profit margin	$\dfrac{\text{Earning before interest and taxes (EBIT)}}{\text{Sales}}$	Profitability without concern for taxes and interest.
Net profit margin	$\dfrac{\text{Net income}}{\text{Sales}}$	After-tax profits per dollar of sales.
Return on total assets (ROA)	$\dfrac{\text{Net income}}{\text{Total assets}}$	After-tax profits per dollar of assets; this ratio is also called *return on investment* (ROI).

EXHIBIT 6.B6 *(continued)*

Ratio	Calculation	Meaning
Return on stockholders' equity (ROE)	$$\frac{\text{Net income}}{\text{Total Stockholders' equity}}$$	After-tax profits per dollar of stockholders investment in the firm.
Earnings per share (EPS)	$$\frac{\text{Net income}}{\text{Number of shares of common stock outstanding}}$$	Earnings available to the owners of common stock.
Growth Ratios:		
Sales	Annual percentage growth in total sales	Firm's growth rate in sales.
Income	Annual percentage growth in profits	Firm's growth rate in profits.
Earnings per share	Annual percentage growth in EPS	Firm's growth rate in EPS.
Dividends per share	Annual percentage growth in dividends per share	Firm's growth rate in dividends per share.
Price-earnings ratio	$$\frac{\text{Market price per share}}{\text{Earnings per share}}$$	Faster-growing and less risky firms tend to have higher price-earnings ratios.

Long-Term Objectives
and Strategies

After reading and studying this chapter, you should be able to

1. Discuss seven different topics for long-term corporate objectives.

2. Describe the five qualities of long-term corporate objectives that make them especially useful to strategic managers.

3. Explain the generic strategies of low-cost leadership, differentiation, and focus.

4. Discuss the importance of the value disciplines.

5. List, describe, evaluate, and give examples of the 15 grand strategies that decision makers use as building blocks in forming their company's competitive plan.

6. Understand the creation of sets of long-term objectives and grand strategies options.

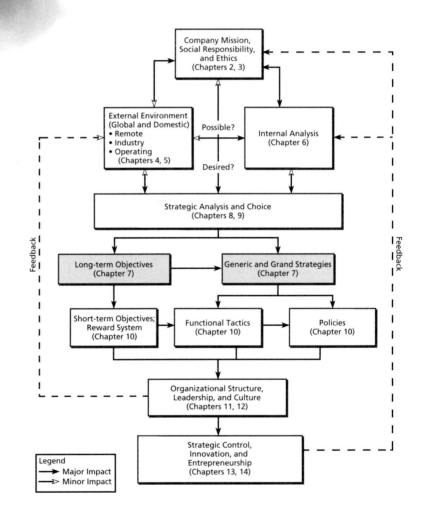

The company mission was described in Chapter 2 as encompassing the broad aims of the firm. The most specific statement of aims presented in that chapter appeared as the goals of the firm. However, these goals, which commonly dealt with profitability, growth, and survival, were stated without specific targets or time frames. They were always to be pursued but could never be fully attained. They gave a general sense of direction but were not intended to provide specific benchmarks for evaluating the firm's progress in achieving its aims. Providing such benchmarks is the function of objectives.[1]

The first part of this chapter will focus on long-term objectives. These are statements of the results a firm seeks to achieve over a specified period, typically three to five years. The second part will focus on the formulation of grand strategies. In combination, these two components of long-term planning provide a comprehensive general approach in guiding major actions designed to accomplish the firm's long-term objectives.

The chapter has two major aims: (1) to discuss in detail the concept of long-term objectives, the topics they cover, and the qualities they should exhibit; and (2) to discuss the concept of grand strategies and to describe the 15 principal grand strategy options that are available to firms singly or in combination, including three newly popularized options that are being used to provide the basis for global competitiveness.

LONG-TERM OBJECTIVES

Strategic managers recognize that short-run profit maximization is rarely the best approach to achieving sustained corporate growth and profitability. An often repeated adage states that if impoverished people are given food, they will eat it and remain impoverished; however, if they are given seeds and tools and shown how to grow crops, they will be able to improve their condition permanently. A parallel choice confronts strategic decision makers:

1. Should they eat the seeds to improve the near-term profit picture and make large dividend payments through cost-saving measures such as laying off workers during periods of slack demand, selling off inventories, or cutting back on research and development?

2. Or should they sow the seeds in the effort to reap long-term rewards by reinvesting profits in growth opportunities, committing resources to employee training, or increasing advertising expenditures?

For most strategic managers, the solution is clear—distribute a small amount of profit now but sow most of it to increase the likelihood of a long-term supply. This is the most frequently used rationale in selecting objectives.

To achieve long-term prosperity, strategic planners commonly establish long-term objectives in seven areas:

Profitability The ability of any firm to operate in the long run depends on attaining an acceptable level of profits. Strategically managed firms characteristically have a profit objective, usually expressed in earnings per share or return on equity.

Productivity Strategic managers constantly try to increase the productivity of their systems. Firms that can improve the input-output relationship normally increase profitability. Thus, firms almost always state an objective for productivity. Commonly used productivity objectives are the number of items produced or the number of services rendered per unit of input. However, productivity objectives sometimes are stated in terms of desired cost decreases. For example, objectives may be set for reducing defective items, customer

---

[1] The terms *goals* and *objectives* are each used to convey a special meaning, with goals being the less specific and more encompassing concept. Most authors follow this usage; however, some use the two words interchangeably, while others reverse the usage.

complaints leading to litigation, or overtime. Achieving such objectives increases profitability if unit output is maintained.

Competitive Position One measure of corporate success is relative dominance in the marketplace. Larger firms commonly establish an objective in terms of competitive position, often using total sales or market share as measures of their competitive position. An objective with regard to competitive position may indicate a firm's long-term priorities. For example, Gulf Oil set a five-year objective of moving from third to second place as a producer of high-density polypropylene. Total sales were the measure.

Employee Development Employees value education and training, in part because they lead to increased compensation and job security. Providing such opportunities often increases productivity and decreases turnover. Therefore, strategic decision makers frequently include an employee development objective in their long-range plans. For example, PPG has declared an objective of developing highly skilled and flexible employees and, thus, providing steady employment for a reduced number of workers.

Employee Relations Whether or not they are bound by union contracts, firms actively seek good employee relations. In fact, proactive steps in anticipation of employee needs and expectations are characteristic of strategic managers. Strategic managers believe that productivity is linked to employee loyalty and to appreciation of managers' interest in employee welfare. They, therefore, set objectives to improve employee relations. Among the outgrowths of such objectives are safety programs, worker representation on management committees, and employee stock option plans.

Technological Leadership Firms must decide whether to lead or follow in the marketplace. Either approach can be successful, but each requires a different strategic posture. Therefore, many firms state an objective with regard to technological leadership. For example, Caterpillar Tractor Company established its early reputation and dominant position in its industry by being in the forefront of technological innovation in the manufacture of large earthmovers. E-commerce technology officers will have more of a strategic role in the management hierarchy of the future, demonstrating that the Internet has become an integral aspect of corporate long-term objective setting. In offering an e-technology manager higher-level responsibilities, a firm is pursuing a leadership position in terms of innovation in computer networks and systems. Officers of e-commerce technology at GE and Delta Air have shown their ability to increase profits by driving down transaction-related costs with Web-based technologies that seamlessly integrate their firms' supply chains. These technologies have the potential to "lock in" certain suppliers and customers and heighten competitive position through supply chain efficiency.

Public Responsibility Managers recognize their responsibilities to their customers and to society at large. In fact, many firms seek to exceed government requirements. They work not only to develop reputations for fairly priced products and services but also to establish themselves as responsible corporate citizens. For example, they may establish objectives for charitable and educational contributions, minority training, public or political activity, community welfare, or urban revitalization. In an attempt to exhibit their public responsibility in the United States, Japanese companies, such as Toyota, Hitachi, and Matsushita, contribute more than $500 million annually to American educational projects, charities, and nonprofit organizations.

Qualities of Long-Term Objectives

What distinguishes a good objective from a bad one? What qualities of an objective improve its chances of being attained? These questions are best answered in relation to five criteria that should be used in preparing long-term objectives: flexible, measurable over time, motivating, suitable, and understandable.

Flexible Objectives should be adaptable to unforeseen or extraordinary changes in the firm's competitive or environmental forecasts. Unfortunately, such flexibility usually is increased at the expense of specificity. One way of providing flexibility while minimizing its negative effects is to allow for adjustments in the level, rather than in the nature, of objectives. For example, the personnel department objective of providing managerial development training for 15 supervisors per year over the next five-year period might be adjusted by changing the number of people to be trained. In contrast, changing the personnel department's objective of "assisting production supervisors in reducing job-related injuries by 10 percent per year" after three months had gone by would understandably create dissatisfaction.

Measurable Objectives must clearly and concretely state what will be achieved and when it will be achieved. Thus, objectives should be measurable over time. For example, the objective of "substantially improving our return on investment" would be better stated as "increasing the return on investment on our line of paper products by a minimum of 1 percent a year and a total of 5 percent over the next three years."

Motivating People are most productive when objectives are set at a motivating level—one high enough to challenge but not so high as to frustrate or so low as to be easily attained. The problem is that individuals and groups differ in their perceptions of what is high enough. A broad objective that challenges one group frustrates another and minimally interests a third. One valuable recommendation is that objectives be tailored to specific groups. Developing such objectives requires time and effort, but objectives of this kind are more likely to motivate.

Objectives must also be achievable. This is easier said than done. Turbulence in the remote and operating environments affects a firm's internal operations, creating uncertainty and limiting the accuracy of the objectives set by strategic management. To illustrate, the rapidly declining U.S. economy in 2000–2003 made objective setting extremely difficult, particularly in such areas as sales projections. Motorola provides a good example of well-constructed company objectives. Motorola saw its market share of the mobile telephone market shrink from 26 to 14 percent between 1996 and 2001, while its main rival Nokia captured all of Motorola's lost share and more. As a key part of a plan to recapture its market position, Motorola's CEO challenged his company with the following long-term objectives:

1. Cut sales, marketing, and administrative expenses from $2.4 billion to $1.6 billion in the next fiscal year.
2. Increase gross markings from 20 to 27 percent by 2002.
3. Reduce the number of Motorola telephone styles by 84 percent to 20 and the number of silicon components by 82 percent to 100 by 2003.

Suitable Objectives must be suited to the broad aims of the firm, which are expressed in its mission statement. Each objective should be a step toward the attainment of overall goals. In fact, objectives that are inconsistent with the company mission can subvert the firm's aims. For example, if the mission is growth oriented, the objective of reducing the debt-to-equity ratio to 1.00 would probably be unsuitable and counterproductive.

Understandable Strategic managers at all levels must understand what is to be achieved. They also must understand the major criteria by which their performance will be evaluated. Thus, objectives must be so stated that they are as understandable to the recipient as they are to the giver. Consider the misunderstandings that might arise over the objective of "increasing the productivity of the credit card department by 20 percent within two years." What does this objective mean? Increase the number of outstanding cards? Increase the use of outstanding cards? Increase the employee workload? Make productivity gains each year? Or hope that the new computer-assisted system, which should improve productivity, is approved by year 2? As this simple example illustrates, objectives must be clear, meaningful, and unambiguous.

The Balanced Scorecard

balanced scorecard
A set of four measures directly linked to a company's strategy: financial performance, customer knowledge, internal business processes, and learning and growth.

The **balanced scorecard** is a set of measures that are directly linked to the company's strategy. Developed by Robert S. Kaplan and David P. Norton, it directs a company to link its own long-term strategy with tangible goals and actions. The scorecard allows managers to evaluate the company from four perspectives: financial performance, customer knowledge, internal business processes, and learning and growth.

The balanced scorecard, as shown in Exhibit 7.1, contains a concise definition of the company's vision and strategy. Surrounding the vision and strategy are four additional boxes; each box contains the objectives, measures, targets, and initiatives for one of the four perspectives:

- The box at the top of Exhibit 7.1 represents the financial perspective and answers the question "To succeed financially, how should we appear to our shareholders?"
- The box to the right represents the internal business process perspective and addresses the question "To satisfy our shareholders and customers, what business processes must we excel at?"

Exhibit 7.1   **The Balanced Scorecard**
The balanced scorecard provides a framework to translate a strategy into operational terms

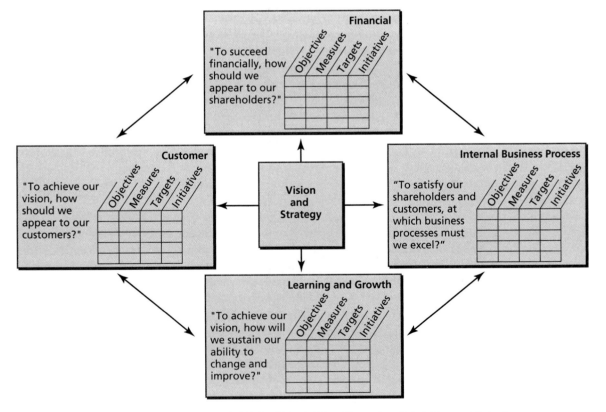

Source: Reprinted by permission of *Harvard Business Review*. Exhibit from "Using the Balanced Scorecard as a Strategic Management System," by Robert S. Kaplan and David P. Norton, January–February 1996. Copyright © 1996 by the Harvard Business School Publishing Corporation; all rights reserved.

- The learning and growth box at the bottom of Exhibit 7.1 answers the question "To achieve our vision, how will we sustain our ability to change and improve?"
- The box at the left reflects the customer perspective and responds to the question "To achieve our vision, how should we appear to our customers?"

All of the boxes are connected by arrows to illustrate that the objectives and measures of the four perspectives are linked by cause-and-effect relationships that lead to the successful implementation of the strategy. Achieving one perspective's targets should lead to desired improvements in the next perspective, and so on, until the company's performance increases overall.

A properly constructed scorecard is balanced between short- and long-term measures, financial and nonfinancial measures, and internal and external performance perspectives.

The balanced scorecard is a management system that can be used as the central organizing framework for key managerial processes. Chemical Bank, Mobil Corporation's US Marketing and Refining Division, and CIGNA Property and Casualty Insurance have used the Balanced Scorecard approach to assist in individual and team goal setting, compensation, resource allocation, budgeting and planning, and strategic feedback and learning.

GENERIC STRATEGIES

Many planning experts believe that the general philosophy of doing business declared by the firm in the mission statement must be translated into a holistic statement of the firm's strategic orientation before it can be further defined in terms of a specific long-term strategy. In other words, a long-term or grand strategy must be based on a core idea about how the firm can best compete in the marketplace.

generic strategy
A core idea about how a firm can best compete in the marketplace.

The popular term for this core idea is **generic strategy.** From a scheme developed by Michael Porter, many planners believe that any long-term strategy should derive from a firm's attempt to seek a competitive advantage based on one of three generic strategies:

1. Striving for overall *low-cost leadership* in the industry.
2. Striving to create and market unique products for varied customer groups through *differentiation.*
3. Striving to have special appeal to one or more groups of consumer or industrial buyers, *focusing* on their cost or differentiation concerns.

Advocates of generic strategies believe that each of these options can produce above average returns for a firm in an industry. However, they are successful for very different reasons.

Low-Cost Leadership

Low-cost leaders depend on some fairly unique capabilities to achieve and sustain their low-cost position. Examples of such capabilities are having secured suppliers of scarce raw materials, being in a dominant market share position, or having a high degree of capitalization. Low-cost producers usually excel at cost reductions and efficiencies. They maximize economies of scale, implement cost-cutting technologies, stress reductions in overhead and in administrative expenses, and use volume sales techniques to propel themselves up the earning curve. The commonly accepted requirements for successful implementation of the low-cost and the other two generic strategies are overviewed in Exhibit 7.2.

A low-cost leader is able to use its cost advantage to charge lower prices or to enjoy higher profit margins. By so doing, the firm effectively can defend itself in price wars, attack competitors on price to gain market share, or, if already dominant in the industry,

EXHIBIT 7.2
Requirements for Generic Competitive Strategies

Generic Strategy	Commonly Required Skills and Resources	Common Organizational Requirements
Overall cost leadership	Sustained capital investment and access to capital. Process engineering skills. Intense supervision of labor. Products designed for ease in manufacture. Low-cost distribution system.	Tight cost control. Frequent, detailed control reports. Structured organization and responsibilities. Incentives based on meeting strict quantitative targets.
Differentiation	Strong marketing abilities. Product engineering. Creative flare. Strong capability in basic research. Corporate reputation for quality or technological leadership. Long tradition in the industry or unique combination of skills drawn from other businesses. Strong cooperation from channels.	Strong coordination among functions in R&D, product development, and marketing. Subjective measurement and incentives instead of quantitative measures. Amenities to attract highly skilled labor, scientists, or creative people.
Focus	Combination of the above policies directed at the particular strategic target.	Combination of the above policies directed at the regular strategic target.

simply benefit from exceptional returns. As an extreme case, it has been argued that National Can Company, a corporation in an essentially stagnant industry, is able to generate attractive and improving profits by being the low-cost producer.

In the wake of the tremendous successes of such low-cost leaders as Wal-Mart and Target, only a rare few companies can ignore the mandate to reduce cost. Yet, doing so without compromising the key attributes of a company's products or services is a difficult challenge. One company that has succeeded in its efforts to become a low-cost leader while maintaining quality standards is Nucor. The company's Top Strategist, Daniel Dimicco, is profiled in Exhibit 7.3.

Differentiation

Strategies dependent on differentiation are designed to appeal to customers with a special sensitivity for a particular product attribute. By stressing the attribute above other product qualities, the firm attempts to build customer loyalty. Often such loyalty translates into a firm's ability to charge a premium price for its product. Cross-brand pens, Brooks Brothers suits, Porsche automobiles, and Chivas Regal Scotch whiskey are all examples.

The product attribute also can be the marketing channels through which it is delivered, its image for excellence, the features it includes, and the service network that supports it. As a result of the importance of these attributes, competitors often face "perceptual" barriers to entry when customers of a successfully differentiated firm fail to see largely identical products as being interchangeable. For example, General Motors hopes that customers will accept "only genuine GM replacement parts."

Because advertising plays a major role in a company's development and differentiation of it brand, many strategists use celebrity spokespeople to represent their companies. These spokespeople, most often actors, models, and athletes, help give the company's products and services a popular, successful, trendy, modern, cache. An example of such a celebrity

Top Strategist
Daniel Dimicco, CEO of Nucor

Exhibit
7.3

Nucor has long been known as the best operator in the steel business and is especially famous for its enlightened workforce relations and commitment to new technologies. It pays line workers according to their productivity and listens to, and implements, their ideas to make the process better. Responsibility is pushed as close to the front line as possible. For most of its history, Nucor only grew organically, but under CEO Daniel Dimicco the company has found it's often cheaper to buy than build. Now executives export the Nucor way to a series of acquired plants: in the past year, it has bought Connecticut Steel, Harris Steel Group, and the assets of Verco Manufacturing. Acquisitions such as Verco, a maker of steel floors and roof decks, help broaden Nucor's product line and support its migration into higher-margin products.

Source: Reprinted with special permission from "The *BusinessWeek* 50—The Best Performers," *BusinessWeek,* March 26, 2007. Copyright © 2007 The McGraw-Hill Companies.

endorser is Dwyane Wade of the Miami Heat, who is discussed in Exhibit 7.4, Strategy in Action.

Focus

A focus strategy, whether anchored in a low-cost base or a differentiation base, attempts to attend to the needs of a particular market segment. Likely segments are those that are ignored by marketing appeals to easily accessible markets, to the "typical" customer, or to customers with common applications for the product. A firm pursuing a focus strategy is willing to service isolated geographic areas; to satisfy the needs of customers with special financing, inventory, or servicing problems; or to tailor the product to the somewhat unique demands of the small- to medium-sized customer. The focusing firms profit from their willingness to serve otherwise ignored or underappreciated customer segments. The classic example is cable television. An entire industry was born because of a willingness of cable firms to serve isolated rural locations that were ignored by traditional television services. Brick producers that typically service a radius of less than 100 miles and commuter airlines that serve regional geographic areas are other examples of industries where a focus strategy frequently yields above-average industry profits.

A well-known brand that is enjoying tremendous success with a focus strategy is the automobile manufacturer Lamborghini. Its financial turnaround, which is based on controlled growth, is described in Exhibit 7.5, Strategy in Action.

While each of the generic strategies enables a firm to maximize certain competitive advantages, each one also exposes the firm to a number of competitive risks. For example, a low-cost leader fears a new low-cost technology that is being developed by a competitor; a differentiating firm fears imitators; and a focused firm fears invasion by a firm that largely targets customers. As Exhibit 7.6 suggests, each generic strategy presents the firm with a number of risks.

Building a Megabrand Named Dwyane

BusinessWeek

Practice is over at American Airlines Arena, and Dwyane Wade takes a minute to explain how he's putting his touch on a new mobile phone. The All-Star guard for the Miami Heat and a self-proclaimed budding businessman is helping wireless carrier T-Mobile USA Inc. design a limited-edition Sidekick, the texting device/cell phone beloved by 20-somethings.

Wade is changing the marketing landscape in ways other phenoms can learn from. He isn't simply endorsing products, he's partnering with major brands to design items other than sports equipment and apparel. On February 17, 2007, the weekend of the NBA All-Star Game, the D Wade Sidekick—the T-Mobile device he co-designed—was introduced with much fanfare.

Team Wade, led by agent Henry Thomas, aims to transform its young client into one of the top 10 brands in sports. The idea, says marketing strategist Andrew Stroth of Chicago's CSMG Sports Ltd., is to create a global brand that transcends sports. "Forget his peers in the NBA," he says. "We want people to think of Dwyane Wade the same way they think of [David] Beckham, Jordan, and Tiger."

Wade's original Converse contract was worth $500,000 a year. But after Wade showed his mettle in the 2005 playoffs, the Converse contract was renegotiated to about $10 million a year. As part of the deal, Converse agreed to make not only Wade basketball shoes but also casual and active attire. He'll receive incentives based on the success

of these breakout categories, says Ric Wilson, sports marketing chief at Converse. "Converse is backed by the Nike engine, and it gives us the opportunity to reinvent Converse with Wade as the face."

But the most innovative aspect of the Wade branding campaign may be its Web strategy—which was born from a moment of serendipity in the sky. Team Wade had already launched a Web site but knew they needed to leverage the Internet more effectively to engage his young fans. On October, 17, 2006, on a flight from New York to Chicago, Stroth sat next to a Google executive. They agreed the two camps should meet. The next week, in Chicago, Google reps preached moving beyond "independent sites" such as Wade's. Those sites, along with charity appearances, TV ads, and video games, make for an "episodic" relationship between the athlete and fans. But digital media allow for brands to be built daily or hourly—what Google calls "dialogue" marketing.

So Team Wade gave Google the go-ahead to develop a plan that would make Dwyanewade.com an integral part of fans' daily digital lives. The goal? A fully interactive site built by Google with Google Search functions embedded. Fans would get a customized mix of e-mail, sports news feeds, flash games, and promotional messages.

Source: Reprinted with special permission from Roger O. Crockett, "Building a Megabrand Named Dwyane," *BusinessWeek*, February 12, 2007. Copyright © 2007 The McGraw-Hill Companies.

THE VALUE DISCIPLINES

International management consultants Michael Treacy and Fred Wiersema propose an alternative approach to generic strategy that they call the value disciplines.[2] They believe that strategies must center on delivering superior customer value through one of three value disciplines: operational excellence, customer intimacy, or product leadership.

Operational excellence refers to providing customers with convenient and reliable products or services at competitive prices. Customer intimacy involves offerings tailored to match the demands of identified niches. Product leadership, the third discipline, involves offering customers leading-edge products and services that make rivals' goods obsolete.

Companies that specialize in one of these disciplines, while simultaneously meeting industry standards in the other two, gain a sustainable lead in their markets. This lead is derived from the firm's focus on one discipline, aligning all aspects of operations with it. Having decided on the value that must be conveyed to customers, firms understand more clearly what must be done to attain the desired results. After transforming their

[2] The ideas and examples in this section are drawn from Michael Treacy and Fred Wiersema, "Customer Intimacy and Other Value Disciplines," *Harvard Business Review* 71, no. 1 (1993), pp. 84–94.

A Burst of Speed at Lamborghini

BusinessWeek

After years of restructuring, the sports car maker is finally a serious rival to Ferrari.

Lamborghini has long held mythic sway over car aficionados. Its exotic flying-saucer design, its horse-power on steroids, and its deafening engines have been a powerful draw for fans such as comedian Jay Leno and actor Jamie Foxx. But for years, Lamborghini suffered from financial woes and quality problems. The Italian super-sports-car maker went through six owners in 16 years and spent 1978–1981 in bankruptcy. So for most of Lamborghini's 44-year history, it has been a mere speck in Ferrari's rearview mirror, selling just about 250 cars a year at $274,000 for a Gallardo Spyder and $354,000 for a Murcielago roadster.

Now an infusion of German cash is helping Lamborghini burn rubber. In 1998, automaker Audi bought the company. After spending some $500 million revamping production and developing models, Lamborghini has the scale to mount a real challenge to Ferrari. In 2006, Lamborghini says it sold more than 2,000 cars, and sales in the U.S. shot up 48 percent in the first 10 months alone. The company today has about 100 showrooms worldwide, up from only 45 in 1998, although Ferrari still has roughly twice as many dealers.

Besieged with orders, Lamborghini's factory in Sant'Agata Bolognese, near Modena, is running full tilt, turning out 10 cars daily. That's brisk, considering it takes a worker an entire day just to cut and hand-stitch one leather seat. Still, it's not fast enough for all the Lamborghini lovers getting in line. Both the 640-hp Murcielago and the 520-hp Gallardo have one-year waiting lists.

With sales finally soaring, Lamborghini is on a stronger financial footing, too. Cost-cutting helped boost 2006 operating margins to nearly 4 percent, up from 1.8 percent in 2005, Morgan Stanley estimates. The brokerage predicts pretax profit could more than double in 2007, to $14 million, as revenues increase 30 percent to $400 million. That's still small compared with Ferrari's expected 2006 sales of $1.9 billion and 5,400 cars. But by tapping into Audi's engineering expertise, purchasing power, and supplier relationships, Lamborghini could eventually match Ferrari's sales—and surpass its 12 percent operating margin.

To preserve its super-luxury image, Lamborghini will take a page from Ferrari and pursue profits over growth. In 2007, it expects to expand sales less than 10 percent. "We are a niche of a niche," says chief executive Stephan Winkelmann. The former Fiat executive wants to boost earnings with limited-edition models packed with pricey options. Another untapped vein for Lamborghini is clothing and other gear emblazoned with its raging-bull logo. The company is starting to license merchandise, a business that generates some $200 million a year each for Ferrari and Porsche.

Source: Reprinted with special permission from Gail Edmondson, "A Burst of Speed at Lamborghini," *BusinessWeek*, January 15, 2007. Copyright © 2007 The McGraw-Hill Companies.

organizations to focus on one discipline, companies can concentrate on smaller adjustments to produce incremental value. To match this advantage, less focused companies require larger changes than the tweaking that discipline leaders need.

Operational Excellence

Operational excellence is a specific strategic approach to the production and delivery of products and services. A company that follows this strategy attempts to lead its industry in price and convenience by pursuing a focus on lean and efficient operations. Companies that employ operational excellence work to minimize costs by reducing overhead, eliminating intermediate production steps, reducing transaction costs, and optimizing business processes across functional and organizational boundaries. The focus is on delivering products or services to customers at competitive prices with minimal inconvenience. Exhibit 7.7, Strategy in Action, provides an example of successful operational excellence in the personal computer (PC) industry.

Operational excellence is also the strategic focus of General Electric's large appliance business. Historically, the distribution strategy for large appliances was based on

EXHIBIT 7.6
Risks of the Generic Strategies

Source: Adapted with the permission of The Free Press, a division of Simon & Schuster Adult Publishing Group, from *Competitive Strategy: Techniques for Analyzing Industries and Competitors* by Michael E. Porter. Copyright © 1980, 1998 by The Free Press. All rights reserved.

Risks of Cost Leadership	Risks of Differentiation	Risks of Focus
Cost of leadership is not sustained: • Competitors imitate. • Technology changes. • Other bases for cost leadership erode.	Differentiation is not sustained: • Competitors imitate. • Bases for differentiation become less important to buyers.	The focus strategy is imitated. The target segment becomes structurally unattractive: • Structure erodes. • Demand disappears.
Proximity in differentiation is lost.	Cost proximity is lost.	Broadly targeted competitors overwhelm the segment: • The segment's differences from other segments narrow. • The advantages of a broad line increase.
Cost focusers achieve even lower cost in segments.	Differentiation focusers achieve even greater differentiation in segments.	New focusers subsegment the industry.

requiring that dealers maintain large inventories. Price breaks for dealers were based on order quantities. However, as the marketplace became more competitive, principally as a result of competition for multibrand dealers like Sears, GE recognized the need to adjust its production and distribution plans.

The GE system addresses the delivery of products. As a step toward organizational excellence, GE created a computer-based logistics system to replace its in-store inventories model. Retailers use this software to access a 24-hour online order processing system that guarantees GE's best price. This system allows dealers to better meet customer needs, with instantaneous access to a warehouse of goods and accurate shipping and production information. GE benefits from the deal as well. Efficiency is increased since manufacturing now occurs in response to customer sales. Additionally, warehousing and distribution systems have been streamlined to create the capability of delivering to 90 percent of destinations in the continental United States within one business day.

Firms that implement the strategy of operational excellence typically restructure their delivery processes to focus on efficiency and reliability, and use state-of-the art information systems that emphasize integration and low-cost transactions.

Customer Intimacy

Companies that implement a strategy of customer intimacy continually tailor and shape products and services to fit an increasingly refined definition of the customer. Companies excelling in customer intimacy combine detailed customer knowledge with operational flexibility. They respond quickly to almost any need, from customizing a product to fulfilling special requests to create customer loyalty.

Customer-intimate companies are willing to spend money now to build customer loyalty for the long term, considering each customer's lifetime value to the company, not the profit of any single transaction. Consequently, employees in customer-intimate companies go to great lengths to ensure customer satisfaction with low regard for initial cost.

Home Depot implements the discipline of customer intimacy. Home Depot clerks spend the necessary time with customers to determine the product that best suits their needs,

A Racer Called Acer

It's a good thing Gianfranco Lanci likes coffee. He shuttles between his home in Milan and job in Taiwan as president of computer maker Acer Inc. "You cannot waste time, since you spend so much time already on the plane," says Lanci, 52. "The coffee," he adds, "also helps."

Acer seems to be on a caffeine kick of its own. Americans who know the brand likely recall it hit the big time in the 1990s, then quickly fell into obscurity. While Acer remains weak in the United States, globally it's no. 4 in PCs overall, behind Hewlett-Packard, Dell, and Lenovo. In 2006, Acer boosted its share by 1.2 percentage points, to 5.9 percent, according to IDC Corp. That puts Acer just behind Lenovo, which rose to no. 3 when it bought IBM PC division two years ago. Lenovo is "successful in China, [but] we are growing everywhere," says Acer CEO J. T. Wang.

The battle to overtake Lenovo is about more than just bragging rights. The PC industry has shrunk to a handful of players, and more consolidation is likely. For Acer, getting bigger is "a survival issue," says Kevin Chang, an analyst in Taipei with Credit Suisse Group. "You need to be a top-three player to make a sustainable profit." Acer had sales of $11.1 billion in 2006 and profits of $338 million, estimates Credit Suisse.

Acer has been gaining ground thanks to low-cost machines and unconventional distribution. It shuns direct sales, instead selling only through distributors and outsourcing all production to factories in China. Acer has also been the driving force in price wars that have taken a toll on former no. 1 Dell Inc. Although Acer has some premium offerings, such as its Ferrari line of sleek machines in red racing stripes, it typically underprices competitors by 5 to 10 percent. Even so, Acer usually offers retailers a bigger chunk of the selling price than rivals do.

The strategy is working: Sales have more than doubled since 2003, although it has cut Acer's profit margin to about 2 percent, or less than half that of HP or Dell.

To keep the momentum going, Acer must expand beyond its stronghold in Europe. There, it's the market leader in laptops and no. 3 overall, thanks to Lanci. Now Acer is taking the fight directly to China, where it is no. 9. In 2005, Acer revamped its operation on the mainland, halving head count to 200 and outsourcing distribution.

Acer also hopes to improve its position in the United States, where it has just 1.8 percent of the market. Acer has raised its profile with U.S. consumers over the past two years through deals to sell its wares at Wal-Mart, CompUSA, and Circuit City—which could ultimately pay off with big companies, says U.S. sales chief Mark Hill.

because the company's business strategy is built around selling information and service in addition to home-repair and improvement items. Consequently, consumers concerned solely with price fall outside Home Depot's core market.

Companies engaged in customer intimacy understand the difference between the profitability of a single transaction and the profitability of a lifetime relationship with a single customer. The company's profitability depends in part on its maintaining a system that differentiates quickly and accurately the degree of service that customers require and the revenues their patronage is likely to generate. Firms using this approach recognize that not every customer is equally profitable. For example, a financial services company installed a telephone-computer system capable of recognizing individual clients by their telephone numbers when they call. The system routes customers with large accounts and frequent transactions to their own senior account representative. Other customers may be routed to a trainee or junior representative. In any case, the customer's file appears on the representative's screen before the phone is answered.

The new system allows the firm to segment its services with great efficiency. If the company has clients who are interested in trading in a particular financial instrument, it can group them under the one account representative who specializes in that instrument.

This saves the firm the expense of training every representative in every facet of financial services. Additionally, the company can direct certain value-added services or products to a specific group of clients that would have interest in them.

Businesses that select a customer intimacy strategy have decided to stress flexibility and responsiveness. They collect and analyze data from many sources. Their organizational structure emphasizes empowerment of employees close to customers. Additionally, hiring and training programs stress the creative decision-making skills required to meet individual customer needs. Management systems recognize and utilize such concepts as customer life-time value, and norms among employees are consistent with a "have it your way" mind set.

Product Leadership

Companies that pursue the discipline of product leadership strive to produce a continuous stream of state-of-the-art products and services. Three challenges must be met to attain that goal. Creativity is the first challenge. Creativity is recognizing and embracing ideas usually originating outside the company. Second, innovative companies must commercialize ideas quickly. Thus, their business and management processes need to be engineered for speed. Product leaders relentlessly pursue new solutions to problems. Finally, firms utilizing this discipline prefer to release their own improvements rather than wait for competitors to enter. Consequently, product leaders do not stop for self-congratulation; they focus on continual improvement.

For example, Johnson & Johnson's organizational design brings good ideas in, develops them quickly, and looks for ways to improve them. In 1983, the president of J&J's Vistakon Inc., a maker of specialty contact lenses, received a tip concerning an ophthalmologist who had conceived of a method to manufacture disposable contact lenses inexpensively. Vistakon's president received this tip from a J&J employee from a different subsidiary whom he had never met. Rather than dismiss the tip, the executives purchased the rights to the technology, assembled a management team to oversee the product's development team to oversee the product's development, and built a state-of-the-art facility in Florida to manu-facture disposable contact lenses called Acuvue. Vistakon and its parent, J&J, were willing to incur high manufacturing and inventory costs before a single lens was sold. A high-speed production facility helped give Vistakon a six-month head start over the competition that, taken off guard, never caught up.

Like other product leaders, J&J creates and maintains an environment that encourages employees to share ideas. Additionally, product leaders continually scan the environment for new-product or service possibilities and rush to capitalize them. Product leaders also avoid bureaucracy because it slows commercialization of their ideas. In a product leader-ship company, a wrong decision often is less damaging than one made late. As a result, managers make decisions quickly, their companies encouraging them to decide today and implement tomorrow. Product leaders continually look for new methods to shorten their cycle times.

The strength of product leaders lies in reacting to situations as they occur. Shorter reac-tion times serve as an advantage in dealings with the unknown. For example, when com-petitors challenged the safety of Acuvue lenses, the firm responded quickly and distributed data combating the charges to eye care professionals. This reaction created goodwill in the marketplace.

Product leaders act as their own competition. These firms continually make the products and services they have created obsolete. Product leaders believe that if they do not develop a successor, a competitor will. So, although Acuvue is successful in the marketplace, Vistakon continues to investigate new material that will extend the wearability of contact lenses and technologies that will make current lenses obsolete. J&J and other innovators recognize that the long-run profitability of an existing product or service is less important to the company's future than maintaining its product leadership edge and momentum.

GRAND STRATEGIES

grand strategy
A master long-term plan that provides basic direction for major actions directed toward achieving long-term business objectives.

While the need for firms to develop generic strategies remains an unresolved debate, designers of planning systems agree about the critical role of grand strategies. **Grand strategies,** often called master or business strategies, provide basic direction for strategic actions. They are the basis of coordinated and sustained efforts directed toward achieving long-term business objectives.

The purpose of this section is twofold: (1) to list, describe, and discuss 15 grand strategies that strategic managers should consider and (2) to present approaches to the selection of an optimal grand strategy from the available alternatives.

Grand strategies indicate the time period over which long-range objectives are to be achieved. Thus, a grand strategy can be defined as a comprehensive general approach that guides a firm's major actions.

The 15 principal grand strategies are concentrated growth, market development, product development, innovation, horizontal integration, vertical integration, concentric diversification, conglomerate diversification, turnaround, divestiture, liquidation, bankruptcy, joint ventures, strategic alliances, and consortia. Any one of these strategies could serve as the basis for achieving the major long-term objectives of a single firm. But a firm involved with multiple industries, businesses, product lines, or customer groups—as many firms are—usually combines several grand strategies. For clarity, however, each of the principal grand strategies is described independently in this section, with examples to indicate some of its relative strengths and weaknesses.

Concentrated Growth

Many of the firms that fell victim to merger mania were once mistakenly convinced that the best way to achieve their objectives was to pursue unrelated diversification in the search for financial opportunity and synergy. By rejecting that "conventional wisdom," such firms as Martin-Marietta, KFC, Compaq, Avon, Hyatt Legal Services, and Tenant have demonstrated the advantages of what is increasingly proving to be sound business strategy. A firm that has enjoyed special success through a strategic emphasis on increasing market share through concentration is Chemlawn. With headquarters in Columbus, Ohio, Chemlawn is the North American leader in professional lawn care. Like others in the lawn care industry, Chemlawn is experiencing a steadily declining customer base. Market analysis shows that the decline is fueled by negative environmental publicity, perceptions of poor customer service, and concern about the price versus the value of the company's services, given the wide array of do-it-yourself alternatives. Chemlawn's approach to increasing market share hinges on addressing quality, price, and value issues; discontinuing products that the public or environmental authorities perceive as unsafe; and improving the quality of its workforce.

concentrated growth
A grand strategy in which a firm directs its resources to the profitable growth of a single product, in a single market, with a single dominant technology.

These firms are just a few of the majority of businesses worldwide firms that pursue a concentrated growth strategy by focusing on a dominant product-and-market combination. **Concentrated growth** is the strategy of the firm that directs its resources to the profitable growth of a dominant product, in a dominant market, with a dominant technology. The main rationale for this approach, sometimes called a market penetration strategy, is that by thoroughly developing and exploiting its expertise in a narrowly defined competitive arena, the company achieves superiority over competitors that try to master a greater number of product and market combinations.

Rationale for Superior Performance

Concentrated growth strategies lead to enhanced performance. The ability to assess market needs, knowledge of buyer behavior, customer price sensitivity, and effectiveness of promotion are characteristics of a concentrated growth strategy. Such core capabilities are a more important determinant of competitive market success than are the environmental forces faced by the firm. The high success rates of new products also are tied to avoiding situations that require undeveloped skills, such as serving new customers and markets, acquiring new technology, building new channels, developing new promotional abilities, and facing new competition.

A major misconception about the concentrated growth strategy is that the firm practicing it will settle for little or no growth. This is certainly not true for a firm that correctly utilizes the strategy. A firm employing concentrated growth grows by building on its competencies, and it achieves a competitive edge by concentrating in the product-market segment it knows best. A firm employing this strategy is aiming for the growth that results from increased productivity, better coverage of its actual product-market segment, and more efficient use of its technology.

Conditions That Favor Concentrated Growth

Specific conditions in the firm's environment are favorable to the concentrated growth strategy. The first is a condition in which the firm's industry is resistant to major technological advancements. This is usually the case in the late growth and maturity stages of the product life cycle and in product markets where product demand is stable and industry barriers, such as capitalization, are high. Machinery for the paper manufacturing industry, in which the basic technology has not changed for more than a century, is a good example.

An especially favorable condition is one in which the firm's targeted markets are not product saturated. Markets with competitive gaps leave the firm with alternatives for growth, other than taking market share away from competitors. The successful introduction of traveler services by Allstate and Amoco demonstrates that even an organization as entrenched and powerful as the AAA could not build a defensible presence in all segments of the automobile club market.

A third condition that favors concentrated growth exists when the firm's product markets are sufficiently distinctive to dissuade competitors in adjacent product markets from trying to invade the firm's segment. John Deere scrapped its plans for growth in the construction machinery business when mighty Caterpillar threatened to enter Deere's mainstay, the farm machinery business, in retaliation. Rather than risk a costly price war on its own turf, Deere scrapped these plans.

A fourth favorable condition exists when the firm's inputs are stable in price and quantity and are available in the amounts and at the times needed. Maryland-based Giant Foods is able to concentrate in the grocery business largely due to its stable long-term arrangements with suppliers of its private-label products. Most of these suppliers are makers of the national brands that compete against the Giant labels. With a high market share and aggressive retail distribution, Giant controls the access of these brands to the consumer. Consequently, its suppliers have considerable incentive to honor verbal agreements, called bookings, in which they commit themselves for a one-year period with regard to the price, quality, and timing of their shipments to Giant.

The pursuit of concentrated growth also is favored by a stable market—a market without the seasonal or cyclical swings that would encourage a firm to diversify. Night Owl Security, the District of Columbia market leader in home security services, commits its customers to initial four-year contracts. In a city where affluent consumers tend to be quite transient, the length of this relationship is remarkable. Night Owl's concentrated growth strategy has been reinforced by its success in getting subsequent owners of its customers' homes to extend and renew the security service contracts. In a similar way, Lands' End reinforced its growth strategy by asking customers for names and addresses of friends and relatives living overseas who would like to receive Lands' End catalogs.

A firm also can grow while concentrating, if it enjoys competitive advantages based on efficient production or distribution channels. These advantages enable the firm to formulate advantageous pricing policies. More efficient production methods and better handling of distribution also enable the firm to achieve greater economies of scale or, in conjunction with marketing, result in a product that is differentiated in the mind of the consumer. Graniteville Company, a large South Carolina textile manufacturer, enjoyed decades of growth and profitability by adopting a "follower" tactic as part of its concentrated growth strategy. By producing fabrics only after market demand had been well established, and by featuring products that reflected its expertise in adopting manufacturing innovations and in maintaining highly efficient long production runs, Graniteville prospered through concentrated growth.

Finally, the success of market generalists creates conditions favorable to concentrated growth. When generalists succeed by using universal appeals, they avoid making special appeals to particular groups of customers. The net result is that many small pockets are left open in the markets dominated by generalists, and that specialists emerge and thrive in these pockets. For example, hardware store chains, such as Home Depot, focus primarily on routine household repair problems and offer solutions that can be easily sold on a self-service, do-it-yourself basis. This approach leaves gaps at both the "semiprofessional" and "neophyte" ends of the market—in terms of the purchaser's skill at household repairs and the extent to which available merchandise matches the requirements of individual homeowners.

Risk and Rewards of Concentrated Growth

Under stable conditions, concentrated growth poses lower risk than any other grand strategy; but, in a changing environment, a firm committed to concentrated growth faces high risks. The greatest risk is that concentrating in a single product market makes a firm particularly vulnerable to changes in that segment. Slowed growth in the segment would jeopardize the firm because its investment, competitive edge, and technology are deeply entrenched in a specific offering. It is difficult for the firm to attempt sudden changes if its product is threatened by near-term obsolescence, a faltering market, new substitutes, or changes in technology or customer needs. For example, the manufacturers of IBM clones faced such a problem when IBM adopted the OS/2 operating system for its personal computer line. That change made existing clones out of date.

The concentrating firm's entrenchment in a specific industry makes it particularly susceptible to changes in the economic environment of that industry. For example, Mack Truck, the second-largest truck maker in America, lost $20 million as a result of an 18-month slump in the truck industry.

Entrenchment in a specific product market tends to make a concentrating firm more adept than competitors at detecting new trends. However, any failure of such a firm to properly forecast major changes in its industry can result in extraordinary losses. Numerous makers of inexpensive digital watches were forced to declare bankruptcy because they failed to anticipate the competition posed by Swatch, Guess, and other trendy watches that emerged from the fashion industry.

A firm pursuing a concentrated growth strategy is vulnerable also to the high opportunity costs that result from remaining in a specific product market and ignoring other options that could employ the firm's resources more profitably. Overcommitment to a specific technology and product market can hinder a firm's ability to enter a new or growing product market that offers more attractive cost-benefit trade-offs. Had Apple Computers maintained its policy of making equipment that did not interface with IBM equipment, it would have missed out on what have proved to be its most profitable strategic options.

Concentrated Growth Is Often the Most Viable Option

Examples abound of firms that have enjoyed exceptional returns on the concentrated growth strategy. Such firms as McDonald's, Goodyear, and Apple Computers have used firsthand knowledge and deep involvement with specific product segments to become powerful competitors in their markets. The strategy is associated even more often with successful smaller firms that have steadily and doggedly improved their market position.

The limited additional resources necessary to implement concentrated growth, coupled with the limited risk involved, also make this strategy desirable for a firm with limited funds. For example, through a carefully devised concentrated growth strategy, medium-sized John Deere & Company was able to become a major force in the agricultural machinery business even when competing with such firms as Ford Motor Company. While other firms were trying to exit or diversify from the farm machinery business, Deere spent $2 billion in upgrading its machinery, boosting its efficiency, and engaging in a program to strengthen its dealership system. This concentrated growth strategy enabled it to become the leader in the farm machinery business despite the fact that Ford was more than 10 times its size.

The firm that chooses a concentrated growth strategy directs its resources to the profitable growth of a narrowly defined product and market, focusing on a dominant technology. Firms that remain within their chosen product market are able to extract the most from their technology and market knowledge and, thus, are able to minimize the risk associated with unrelated diversification. The success of a concentration strategy is founded on the firm's use of superior insights into its technology, product, and customer to obtain a sustainable competitive advantage. Superior performance on these aspects of corporate strategy has been shown to have a substantial positive effect on market success.

A grand strategy of concentrated growth allows for a considerable range of action. Broadly speaking, the firm can attempt to capture a larger market share by increasing the usage rates of present customers, by attracting competitors' customers, or by selling to nonusers. In turn, each of these options suggests more specific options, some of which are listed in the top section of Exhibit 7.8.

When strategic managers forecast that their current products and their markets will not provide the basis for achieving the company mission, they have two options that involve moderate costs and risk: market development and product development.

Market Development

market development
A grand strategy of marketing present products, often with only cosmetic modification, to customers in related marketing areas.

Market development commonly ranks second only to concentration as the least costly and least risky of the 15 grand strategies. It consists of marketing present products, often with only cosmetic modifications, to customers in related market areas by adding channels of distribution or by changing the content of advertising or promotion. Several specific market development approaches are listed in Exhibit 7.8. Thus, as suggested by the figure, firms that open branch offices in new cities, states, or countries are practicing market development. Likewise, firms are practicing market development if they switch from advertising in trade publications to advertising in newspapers or if they add jobbers to supplement their mail-order sales efforts.

Market development allows firms to leverage some of their traditional strengths by identifying new uses for existing products and new demographically, psychographically, or geographically defined markets. Frequently, changes in media selection, promotional appeals, and distribution signal the implementation of this strategy. Du Pont used market development when it found a new application for Kevlar, an organic material that police,

EXHIBIT 7.8
Specific Options under the Grand Strategies of Concentration, Market Development, and Product Development

Source: Adapted from Philip Kotler and Kevin Keller, *Marketing Management,* 12th ed., 2006. Reprinted by permission of Pearson Education, Upper Saddle River, NJ.

Concentration (increasing use of present products in present markets):

1. Increasing present customers' rate of use:
   a. Increasing the size of purchase.
   b. Increasing the rate of product obsolescence.
   c. Advertising other uses.
   d. Giving price incentives for increased use.
2. Attracting competitors' customers:
   a. Establishing sharper brand differentiation.
   b. Increasing promotional effort.
   c. Initiating price cuts.
3. Attracting nonusers to buy the product:
   a. Inducing trial use through sampling, price incentives, and so on.
   b. Pricing up or down.
   c. Advertising new uses.

Market development (selling present products in new markets):

1. Opening additional geographic markets:
   a. Regional expansion.
   b. National expansion.
   c. International expansion.
2. Attracting other market segments:
   a. Developing product versions to appeal to other segments.
   b. Entering other channels of distribution.
   c. Advertising in other media.

Product development (developing new products for present markets):

1. Developing new-product features:
   a. Adapt (to other ideas, developments).
   b. Modify (change color, motion, sound, odor, form, shape).
   c. Magnify (stronger, longer, thicker, extra value).
   d. Minify (smaller, shorter, lighter).
   e. Substitute (other ingredients, process, power).
   f. Rearrange (other patterns, layout, sequence, components).
   g. Reverse (inside out).
   h. Combine (blend, alloy, assortment, ensemble; combine units, purposes, appeals, ideas).
2. Developing quality variations.
3. Developing additional models and sizes (product proliferation).

security, and military personnel had used primarily for bulletproofing. Kevlar now is being used to refit and maintain wooden-hulled boats, since it is lighter and stronger than glass fibers and has 11 times the strength of steel.

The medical industry provides other examples of new markets for existing products. The National Institutes of Health's report of a study showing that the use of aspirin may lower the incidence of heart attacks was expected to boost sales in the $2.2 billion analgesic market. It was predicted that the expansion of this market would lower the market share of nonaspirin brands, such as industry leaders Tylenol and Advil. Product extensions currently planned include Bayer Calendar Pack, 28-day packaging to fit the once-a-day prescription for the prevention of a second heart attack.

Another example is Cheesebrough-Ponds, a major producer of health and beauty aids, which decided several years ago to expand its market by repacking its Vaseline Petroleum Jelly in pocket-size squeeze tubes as Vaseline "Lip Therapy." The corporation decided to place a strategic emphasis on market development, because it knew from market studies that its petroleum-jelly customers already were using the product to prevent chapped lips. Company leaders reasoned that their market could be expanded significantly if the product were repackaged to fit conveniently in consumers' pockets and purses.

Product Development

product development
A grand strategy that involves the substantial modification of existing products that can be marketed to current customers.

Product development involves the substantial modification of existing products or the creation of new but related products that can be marketed to current customers through established channels. The product development strategy often is adopted either to prolong the life cycle of current products or to take advantage of a favorite reputation or brand name. The idea is to attract satisfied customers to new products as a result of their positive experience with the firm's initial offering. The bottom section in Exhibit 7.8 lists some of the options available to firms undertaking product development. A revised edition of a college textbook, a new car style, and a second formula of shampoo for oily hair are examples of the product development strategy.

Similarly, Pepsi changed its strategy on beverage products by creating new products to follow the industry movement away from mass branding. This new movement was designed to attract a younger, hipper customer segment. Pepsi's new products include a version of Mountain Dew, called Code Red, and new Pepsi brands, called Pepsi Twist and Pepsi Blue.

The product development strategy is based on the penetration of existing markets by incorporating product modifications into existing items or by developing new products with a clear connection to the existing product line. The telecommunications industry provides an example of product extension based on product modification. To increase its estimated 8 to 10 percent share of the $5 to $6 billion corporate user market, MCI Communication Corporation extended its direct-dial service to 146 countries, the same as those serviced by AT&T, at lower average rates than those of AT&T. MCI's addition of 79 countries to its network underscores its belief in this market, which it expects to grow 15 to 20 percent annually. Another example of expansions linked to existing lines is Gerber's decision to engage in general merchandise marketing. Gerber's recent introduction included 52 items that ranged from feeding accessories to toys and children's wear. Likewise, Nabisco Brands seeks competitive advantage by placing its strategic emphasis on product development. With headquarters in Parsippany, New Jersey, the company is one of three operating units of RJR Nabisco. It is the leading producer of biscuits, confections, snacks, shredded cereals, and processed fruits and vegetables. To maintain its position as leader, Nabisco pursues a strategy of developing and introducing new products and expanding its existing product line. Spoon Size Shredded Wheat and Ritz Bits crackers are two examples of new products that are variations on existing products.

The development of new products is so critical to companies in many industries that a cottage industry has sprung up to help provide them. To read about one of the firms that specialize in idea creation, see Exhibit 7.9, Strategy in Action.

Innovation

innovation
A grand strategy that seeks to reap the premium margins associated with creation and customer acceptance of a new product or service.

In many industries, it has become increasingly risky not to innovate. Both consumer and industrial markets have come to expect periodic changes and improvements in the products offered. As a result, some firms find it profitable to make **innovation** their grand strategy. They seek to reap the initially high profits associated with customer acceptance of a new or greatly improved product. Then, rather than face stiffening competition as the basis of profitability shifts from innovation to production or marketing competence, they search for other original or novel ideas. The underlying rationale of the grand strategy of innovation is to create a new product life cycle and thereby make similar existing products obsolete. Thus, this strategy differs from the product development strategy of extending an existing

Inside a White-Hot Idea Factory

BusinessWeek

Some big names are turning to upstart Fahrenheit 212 to dream up new products.

For several years, spirits giant Diageo rode high on the popularity of its Smirnoff Ice beverage. Then consumers got bored, and the party was over. Try as it might, the no. 1 global liquor company couldn't reignite sales of Ice—a crucial part of its Smirnoff brand. So Diageo turned to Fahrenheit 212, a tiny New York outfit that promises to help clients dream up hit products and services. Fahrenheit listened, then disappeared.

The firm reemerged with some startling advice: forget the Smirnoff Ice brand for now. Instead, Diageo should use its malt technology to create wildly different Smirnoff drinks. Among Fahrenheit's 10 or so fully realized products: Smirnoff Raw Tea, which appeared in August, and Smirnoff Source, an alcoholic water expected to launch this spring.

Fahrenheit 212 specializes in a new approach to product development. With little to no inside knowledge of its clients, the company dives into their problems and within months cooks up a portfolio of products it thinks will solve them. One part management consultant, one part advertising agency, and one part design house, Fahrenheit 212 attempts to deliver ready-to-go answers, including everything from an analysis of each potential market down to the design and packaging of the product itself. As companies seek to maximize efficiency by outsourcing just about everything, Fahrenheit 212 promises to serve up something most chief executives dream about: new products created from existing assets that will earn sizable revenue from untapped markets.

Spun off from advertising agency Saatchi & Saatchi in November 2006, Fahrenheit 212 expects to generate only about $8 million in revenues in 2007. But it has signed up an impressive roster of clients. It won't disclose specifics, but Fahrenheit has come up with new applications for Samsung's LCD panels, cooked up new products for Hershey as the company moves beyond candy, and is helping NBC Universal identify new sources of revenue in the digital world.

Clients think of the firm as a way to make long-shot bets without having to use their own research and development resources. "Samsung is a lean organization. We can't afford to have people coming up with ideas that don't work," says chief marketing officer Gregory Lee. "The people at Fahrenheit are very helpful because they are working on ideas that can fail—it allows you to experiment a bit." What's more, Fahrenheit ties much of its compensation to the success of the product, making it an even safer bet.

product's life cycle. For example, Intel, a leader in the semiconductor industry, pursues expansion through a strategic emphasis on innovation. With headquarters in California, the company is a designer and manufacturer of semiconductor components and related computers, of microcomputer systems, and of software. Its Pentium microprocessor gives a desktop computer the capability of a mainframe. Exhibit 7.10, Strategy in Action, makes an important point. Companies under pressure to innovate often supplement their own R&D efforts by partnering with other firms in their industry that have complementary needs.

While most growth-oriented firms appreciate the need to be innovative, a few firms use it as their fundamental way of relating to their markets. An outstanding example is Polaroid, which heavily promotes each of its new cameras until competitors are able to match its technological innovation; by this time, Polaroid normally is prepared to introduce a dramatically new or improved product. For example, it introduced consumers in quick succession to the Swinger, the SX-70, the One Step, and the Sun Camera 660.

Few innovative ideas prove profitable because the research, development, and premarketing costs of converting a promising idea into a profitable product are extremely high. A study by the Booz Allen & Hamilton management research department provides some understanding of the risks. As shown in Exhibit 7.11, Booz Allen & Hamilton found that less than 2 percent of the innovative projects initially considered by 51 companies

The Power of the Pipeline for Bristol-Myers Squibb

BusinessWeek

As interim CEO James M. Cornelius tries to steady Bristol's wobbly finances—the New York drug maker, Bristol-Myers Squibb just recorded its first quarterly loss since 1995—the one part of the company he's barely touching is Dr. Elliot Sigal's. Bristol has launched eight new drugs since Sigal became head of development in 2002, has three cancer drugs in late-stage development, and has more than a dozen compounds in its pipeline to treat diseases ranging from diabetes to depression. With many growth-starved Big Pharma companies desperate for new potential blockbusters, and a verdict due soon in the Plavix trial, a Bristol acquisition, predicts Morgan Stanley analyst Jami Rubin, "is not a question of if. It's a question of when."

Sigal has turned around Bristol's unproductive research labs using a combination of hard and soft incentives. He has fine-tuned a compensation plan that ties scientists' bonuses to the drugs they discover, awarding the highest premiums to the compounds that reach late-stage clinical trials. Sigal keeps his troops motivated by introducing them to patients who have been treated with Bristol's drugs, most recently bringing in a cancer patient who has benefited from Bristol's new product, Sprycel.

Another way Sigal has managed to pump up Bristol's pipeline is through what he calls the globalization of the research process. While developing Sprycel, for example, the company recruited 911 trial patients in 33 countries. Because the drug treats a rare form of leukemia, it would have taken several months to find enough patients just in the United States.

Bristol has also become more selective in choosing its partners, seeking deals that will fill holes in its strategy of developing drugs to address large, unmet medical needs without stretching its resources too thin. In January 2007, Bristol structured a smart deal with London-based drug giant AstraZeneca PLC to develop two diabetes drugs.

Investors and potential acquirers will be watching closely for the verdict in the Plavix patent trial. Bristol is expected to prevail and regain its exclusive hold on the market until 2011. But the damage has already been done: Bristol's generic rival, Weston (Ontario)-based Apotex Inc., flooded distribution channels with six months' worth of its version of Plavix before a judge ordered it to stop selling the drug last August.

The Plavix debacle only underscores the urgency of Sigal's quest to generate a variety of new drug candidates that will mitigate the risk of future patent losses.

Source: Reprinted with special permission from Arlene Weintraub, "The Power of the Pipeline: Bristol-Myers Squibb is Beset with Troubles, But Its New-Drug Potential Makes It a Target," *BusinessWeek,* February 26, 2007. Copyright © 2007 The McGraw-Hill Companies.

eventually reached the marketplace. Specifically, out of every 58 new product ideas, only 12 pass an initial screening test that finds them compatible with the firm's mission and long-term objectives, only 7 remain after an evaluation of their potential, and only 3 survive development attempts. Of the three survivors, two appear to have profit potential after test marketing and only one is commercially successful.

Horizontal Integration

horizontal integration
A grand strategy based on growth through the acquisition of similar firms operating at the same stage of the production-marketing chain.

When a firm's long-term strategy is based on growth through the acquisition of one or more similar firms operating at the same stage of the production-marketing chain, its grand strategy is called **horizontal integration**. Such acquisitions eliminate competitors and provide the acquiring firm with access to new markets. One example is Warner-Lambert's acquisition of Parke Davis, which reduced competition in the ethical drugs field for Chilcott Laboratories, a firm that Warner-Lambert previously had acquired. Another example is the long-range acquisition pattern of White Consolidated Industries, which expanded in the refrigerator and freezer market through a grand strategy of horizontal integration, by acquiring Kelvinator Appliance, the Refrigerator Products Division of Bendix Westinghouse Automotive Air Brake, and Frigidaire Appliance from General Motors.

Exhibit 7.11
**Decay of New
Product Ideas
(51 Companies)**

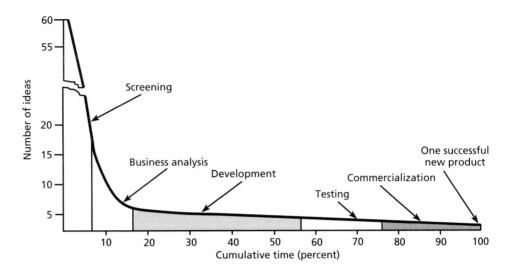

Nike's acquisition in the dress shoes business and N. V. Homes's purchase of Ryan Homes have vividly exemplified the success that horizontal integration strategies can bring.

The attractions of a horizontal acquisition strategy are many and varied.[3] However every benefit provides the parent firm with critical resources that it needs to improve overall profitability. For example, the acquiring firm that uses a horizontal acquisition can quickly expand its operations geographically, increase its market share, improve its production capabilities and economies of scale, gain control of knowledge-based resources, broaden its product line, and increase its efficient use of capital. An added attraction of horizontal acquisition is that these benefits are achieved with only moderately increased risk, because the success of the expansion is principally dependent on proven abilities.

A horizontal merger can provide the firm with an opportunity to offer its customers a broader product line. This motivation has sparked a series of acquisitions in the security software industry. Because Entrust purchased Business Signatures, the consolidated company is able to offer banks a full suite of antifraud products. Similarly, Verisign's acquisitions of m-Qube and Snapcentric, enabled Verisign to expand its cross-marketing options by offering password-generating software, transaction monitoring software, and identity protection. RSA Security's horizontal acquisitions started with the purchase of PassMark, which reduced competitors in the authentication software space. RSA Security then acquired Cyota to provide its customers with both transaction monitoring and authentication software. As a final example, Symantec bought both Veritas Software and WholeSecurity to provide its customers of storage with additional features, such as antivirus software.

The motivation to gain market share has prompted the financial industry to feature horizontal merger strategies. The acquisition of First Coastal Bank by Citizens Business Bank provided new bases of operation in Los Angeles and Manhattan for Citizen Business Bank. The merger of Raincross Credit Union with Visterra Credit Union enabled these credit unions to achieve the size to justify the expansion of services their customers were demanding.

Some horizontal mergers are motivated by the opportunity to combine resources as a means to improve operational efficiency. In the energy industry, for example, there were eight announced horizontal acquisitions with a combined value of $64 billion between January 2004 and January 2007. In each case, increased operational efficiencies resulted

---

[3] This section was drawn from John A. Pearce II and D. Keith Robbins, "Strategic Transformation as the Essential Last Step in the Process of Business Turnaround," *Business Horizons* 50, no. 5 (2008).

from the elimination of duplicated costs. In 2005, Duke Energy acquired Cinergy Corp. for $14.1 billion. The friendly takeover worked well because Duke's Energy North America division was a great match with Cinergy's energy trading operation and provided economies of scale and scope. The combined company lowered costs by an estimated $400 million per year by using a broad platform to serve both electricity and natural gas customers.[4]

A second example of an efficiency-driven merger is one between Constellation and FPL, which saves between $1.5 and $2.1 billion by eliminating overlapping operations.[5] Another example is the acquisition of Green Mountain Power by Gaz Metro, a subsidiary of Northern New England Energy Power for $187 million. The merger was prompted by Green Mountain Power's expiring supplier contracts that threatened it with high costs of going to suppliers who were out of its geographic region—but within the region of Gaz Metro. The horizontal acquisition enabled Green Mountain Power to avail itself of Gaz Metro's suppliers.

Deutsche Telekom's growth strategy was horizontal acquisition. Deutsche Telekom was a dominant player in the European wireless services market, but without a presence in the fast-growing U.S. market in 2000. To correct this limitation, Deutsche Telekom horizontally integrated by purchasing the American firm Voice-Stream Wireless, a company that was growing faster than most domestic rivals and that owned spectrum licenses providing access to 220 million potential customers.

Vertical Integration

vertical integration
A grand strategy based on the acquisition of firms that supply the acquiring firm with inputs or new customers for its outputs.

When a firm's grand strategy is to acquire firms that supply it with inputs (such as raw materials) or are customers for its outputs (such as warehousers for finished products), **vertical integration** is involved. To illustrate, if a shirt manufacturer acquires a textile producer—by purchasing its common stock, buying its assets, or exchanging ownership interests—the strategy is vertical integration. In this case, it is *backward* vertical integration, because the acquired firm operates at an earlier stage of the production-marketing process. If the shirt manufacturer had merged with a clothing store, it would have been *forward* vertical integration—the acquisition of a firm nearer to the ultimate consumer.

Amoco emerged as North America's leader in natural gas reserves and products as a result of its acquisition of Dome Petroleum. This backward integration by Amoco was made in support of its downstream businesses in refining and in gas stations, whose profits made the acquisition possible.

Exhibit 7.12 depicts both horizontal and vertical integration. The principal attractions of a horizontal integration grand strategy are readily apparent. The acquiring firm is able to greatly expand its operations, thereby achieving greater market share, improving economies of scale, and increasing the efficiency of capital use. In addition, these benefits are achieved with only moderately increased risk, because the success of the expansion is principally dependent on proven abilities.

The reasons for choosing a vertical integration grand strategy are more varied and sometimes less obvious. The main reason for backward integration is the desire to increase the dependability of the supply or quality of the raw materials used as production inputs. That desire is particularly great when the number of suppliers is small and the number of competitors is large. In this situation, the vertically integrating firm can better control its costs and, thereby, improve the profit margin of the expanded production-marketing system. Forward integration is a preferred grand strategy if great advantages accrue to stable production. A firm can increase the predictability of demand for its output through forward integration; that is, through ownership of the next stage of its production-marketing chain.

[4] G. Terzo, "Duke and Cinergy Spur Utility M&A, "*The Investment Dealer's Digest IDD,* January 16, 2006, p. 1.
[5] J. Fontana, "A New Wave of Consolidation in the Utility Industry," *Electric Light and Power,* 84, no. 4 (July/August 2006), pp. 36–38.

Exhibit 7.12
**Vertical and
Horizontal
Integrations**

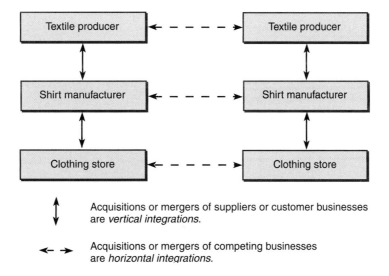

Acquisitions or mergers of suppliers or customer businesses are *vertical integrations*.

Acquisitions or mergers of competing businesses are *horizontal integrations*.

Some increased risks are associated with both types of integration. For horizontally integrated firms, the risks stem from increased commitment to one type of business. For vertically integrated firms, the risks result from the firm's expansion into areas requiring strategic managers to broaden the base of their competencies and to assume additional responsibilities.

Concentric Diversification

**concentric
diversification**
A grand strategy that
involves the operation of
a second business that
benefits from access
to the first firm's core
competencies.

Concentric diversification involves the acquisition of businesses that are related to the acquiring firm in terms of technology, markets, or products. With this grand strategy, the selected new businesses possess a high degree of compatibility with the firm's current businesses. The ideal concentric diversification occurs when the combined company profits increase the strengths and opportunities and decrease the weaknesses and exposure to risk. Thus, the acquiring firm searches for new businesses whose products, markets, distribution channels, technologies, and resource requirements are similar to but not identical with its own, whose acquisition results in synergies but not complete interdependence.

Abbott Laboratories pursues an aggressive concentric growth strategy. As described in Exhibit 7.13, Strategy in Action, Abbott seeks to acquire a wide range of businesses that have some important connection to its basic business. In recent years, this strategy has led the company to acquire pharmaceuticals, a diagnostic business, and a medical device manufacturer.

Conglomerate Diversification

**conglomerate
diversification**
A grand strategy that
involves the acquisition
of a business because
it presents the most
promising investment
opportunity available.

Occasionally a firm, particularly a very large one, plans to acquire a business because it represents the most promising investment opportunity available. This grand strategy is commonly known as **conglomerate diversification**. The principal concern, and often the sole concern, of the acquiring firm is the profit pattern of the venture. Unlike concentric diversification, conglomerate diversification gives little concern to creating product-market synergy with existing businesses. What such conglomerate diversifiers as ITT, Textron, American Brands, Litton, U.S. Industries, Fuqua, and I. C. Industries seek is financial synergy. For example, they may seek a balance in their portfolios between current businesses with cyclical sales and acquired businesses with countercyclical sales, between high-cash/low-opportunity and low-cash/high-opportunity businesses, or between debt-free and highly leveraged businesses.

Over nine months, Abbott Laboratories has dished out $10.1 billion for acquisitions, including $3.7 billion for cholesterol drug specialists Kos Pharmaceuticals Inc. In 2006, many analysts figured, chairman and chief executive Miles D. White would take a breather to allow the company to absorb its newest assets or lighten its $7 billion debt load. They figured wrong.

Just a month after closing the deal for Kos, Abbott was set to announce on January 18, 2007, that it was selling about two-thirds of its $4 billion diagnostics business to General Electric Co. for $8.1 billion in cash. While emphasizing that he's not going to rush into doing deals, White says he'll likely use the money to buy more medical products outfits to help boost overall sales and profits by at least 10 percent a year into the next decade. When it comes to acquisitions, White says, "you can never afford to rest."

White, 51, has been wheeling and dealing almost since the day in 1999 that he was promoted to CEO, after earlier heading Abbott's diagnostics operations. He began with a bang, paying $7.2 billion in cash for the Knoll Pharmaceuticals Co. subsidiary of Germany's BASF in 2001. Among other deals, White bought TheraSense Inc., an Alameda (California) maker of devices that monitor blood glucose, for $1.2 billion in cash in 2004.

While many big drug companies have come to rue their growth-by-acquisition strategies, analysts say Abbott has done well. The Knoll purchase, for example,

yielded Humira, a drug for rheumatoid arthritis that topped $2 billion in sales in 2006. And a $4.1 billion takeover of Guidant Corp.'s stent operations in early 2006 gave Abbott a drug-coated stent, branded Xience. If it passes final clinical trials, it could hit the U.S. market by year-end; it's projected to reach $1.5 billion in sales in 2008. Abbott hasn't overpaid and has been adroit in integrating personnel and facilities, often putting managers of acquired entities in charge of similar Abbott units.

White's dealmaking has lifted Abbott's top and bottom lines. In 2006, Abbott earned $3.8 billion on sales of $22.5 billion, with gross margins nearing 59 percent, says Glenn J. Novarro of Banc of America Securities in New York. That's up roughly 10 percent annually from $2.4 billion in net income on $13.2 billion in sales in 1999, when gross margins were 54.5 percent, and puts Abbott ahead of Merck, Bristol-Myers Squibb, and Eli Lilly in sales and earnings growth.

Abbott has a 20-person business development team that works full-time with chiefs of Abbott units to find and evaluate deals. "We make sure we're up-to-date on our homework so that if we want to get into a new segment, we can," White says. "We won't be doing nothing."

The principal difference between the two types of diversification is that concentric diversification emphasizes some commonality in markets, products, or technology, whereas conglomerate diversification is based principally on profit considerations.

Several of the grand strategies discussed above, including concentric and conglomerate diversification and horizontal and vertical integration, often involve the purchase or acquisition of one firm by another. It is important to know that the majority of such acquisitions fail to produce the desired results for the companies involved. Exhibit 7.14, Strategy in Action, provides seven guidelines that can improve a company's chances of a successful acquisition.

Motivation for Diversification

Grand strategies involving either concentric or conglomerate diversification represent distinctive departures from a firm's existing base of operations, typically the acquisition or internal generation (spin-off) of a separate business with synergistic possibilities counterbalancing the strengths and weaknesses of the two businesses. For example, Head Ski sought to diversify into summer sporting goods and clothing to offset the seasonality of its "snow" business. Additionally, diversifications occasionally are undertaken as unrelated

Seven Deadly Sins of Strategy Acquisition

1. The wrong target.

The first step to avoid such a mistake is for the acquirer and its financial advisors to determine the strategic goals and identify the mission. The product of this strategic review will be specifically identified criteria for the target.

The second step required to identify the right target is to design and carry out an effective due diligence process to ascertain whether the target indeed has the identified set of qualities selected in the strategic review.

2. The wrong price.

The key to avoiding this problem lies in the acquirer's valuation model. The model will incorporate assumptions concerning industry trends and growth patterns developed in the strategic review.

3. The wrong structure.

The two principal aspects of the acquisition process that can prevent this problem are a comprehensive regulatory compliance review and tax and legal analysis.

4. The lost deal.

The letter of intent must spell out not only the price to be paid but also many of the relational aspects that will make the strategic acquisition successful. Although an acquirer may justifiably focus on expenses, indemnification, and other logical concerns in the letter of intent, relationship and operational concerns are also important.

5. Management difficulties.

The remedy for this problem must be extracted from the initial strategic review. The management compensation structure must be designed with legal and business advisors to help achieve those goals. The financial rewards to management must depend upon the financial and strategic success of the combined entity.

6. The closing crisis.

Closing crises may stem from unavoidable changed conditions, but most often they result from poor communication. Negotiators sometimes believe that problems swept under the table maintain a deal's momentum and ultimately allow for its consummation. They are sometimes right—and often wrong. Charting a course through an acquisition requires carefully developed skills for every kind of professional—business, accounting, and legal.

7. The operating transition crisis.

Even the best conceived and executed acquisition will prevent significant transition and postclosing operation issues. Strategic goals cannot be achieved by quick asset sales or other accelerated exit strategies. Management time and energy must be spent to ensure that the benefits identified in the strategic review are achieved.

Source: From Academy of Management Review by D.A. Tanner. Copyright © 1991 by Academy of Management. Reproduced with permission of Academy of Management via Copyright Clearance Center.

investments, because of their high profit potential and their otherwise minimal resource demands.

Regardless of the approach taken, the motivations of the acquiring firms are the same:

- Increase the firm's stock value. In the past, mergers often have led to increases in the stock price or the price-earnings ratio.
- Increase the growth rate of the firm.
- Make an investment that represents better use of funds than plowing them into internal growth.
- Improve the stability of earnings and sales by acquiring firms whose earnings and sales complement the firm's peaks and valleys.
- Balance or fill out the product line.
- Diversify the product line when the life cycle of current products has peaked.
- Acquire a needed resource quickly (e.g., high-quality technology or highly innovative management).

- Achieve tax savings by purchasing a firm whose tax losses will offset current or future earnings.
- Increase efficiency and profitability, especially if there is synergy between the acquiring firm and the acquired firm.[6]

Turnaround

turnaround
A grand strategy of cost reduction and asset reduction by a company to survive and recover from declining profits.

For any one of a large number of reasons, a firm can find itself with declining profits. Among these reasons are economic recessions, production inefficiencies, and innovative breakthroughs by competitors. In many cases, strategic managers believe that such a firm can survive and eventually recover if a concerted effort is made over a period of a few years to fortify its distinctive competencies. This grand strategy is known as **turnaround.** It typically is begun through one of two forms of retrenchment, employed singly or in combination:

1. *Cost reduction.* Examples include decreasing the workforce through employee attrition, leasing rather than purchasing equipment, extending the life of machinery, eliminating elaborate promotional activities, laying off employees, dropping items from a production line, and discontinuing low-margin customers.
2. *Asset reduction.* Examples include the sale of land, buildings, and equipment not essential to the basic activity of the firm and the elimination of "perks," such as the company airplane and executives' cars.

Interestingly, the turnaround most commonly associated with this approach is in management positions. In a study of 58 large firms, researchers Shendel, Patton, and Riggs found that turnaround almost always was associated with changes in top management.[7] Bringing in new managers was believed to introduce needed new perspectives on the firm's situation, to raise employee morale, and to facilitate drastic actions, such as deep budgetary cuts in established programs.

Strategic management research provides evidence that the firms that have used a *turnaround strategy* have successfully confronted decline. The research findings have been assimilated and used as the building blocks for a model of the turnaround process shown in Exhibit 7.15, Strategy in Action.

The model begins with a depiction of external and internal factors as causes of a firm's performance downturn. When these factors continue to detrimentally impact the firm, its financial health is threatened. Unchecked decline places the firm in a turnaround situation.

A *turnaround situation* represents absolute and relative-to-industry declining performance of a sufficient magnitude to warrant explicit turnaround actions. Turnaround situations may be the result of years of gradual slowdown or months of sharp decline. In either case, the recovery phase of the turnaround process is likely to be more successful in accomplishing turnaround when it is preceded by planned retrenchment that results in the achievement of near-term financial stabilization. For a declining firm, stabilizing operations and restoring profitability almost always entail strict cost reduction followed by a shrinking back to those segments of the business that have the best prospects of attractive profit margins. The need for retrenchment was reflected in unemployment figures during the 2000–2003 recession. More layoffs of American workers were announced in 2001 than in any of the previous eight

---

[6] Godfrey Devlin and Mark Bleackley, "Strategic Alliances—Guidelines for Success," *Long Range Planning,* October 1988, pp. 18–23.

[7] Other forms of joint ventures (such as leasing, contract manufacturing, and management contracting) offer valuable support strategies. They are not included in the categorization, however, because they seldom are employed as grand strategies.

A Model of the Turnaround Process

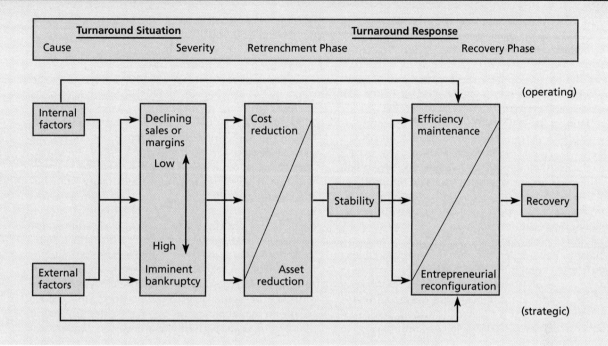

years when U.S. companies announced nearly 2 million layoffs as the economy sunk into its first recession in a decade.

The immediacy of the resulting threat to company survival posed by the turnaround situation is known as *situation severity.* Severity is the governing factor in estimating the speed with which the retrenchment response will be formulated and activated. When severity is low, a firm has some financial cushion. Stability may be achieved through cost retrenchment alone. When turnaround situation severity is high, a firm must immediately stabilize the decline or bankruptcy is imminent. Cost reductions must be supplemented with more drastic asset reduction measures. Assets targeted for divestiture are those determined to be underproductive. In contrast, more productive resources are protected from cuts and represent critical elements of the future core business plan of the company (i.e., the intended recovery response).

Turnaround responses among successful firms typically include two stages of strategic activities: retrenchment and the recovery response. *Retrenchment* consists of cost-cutting and asset-reducing activities. The primary objective of the retrenchment phase is to stabilize the firm's financial condition. Situation severity has been associated with retrenchment responses among successful turnaround firms. Firms in danger of bankruptcy or failure (i.e., severe situations) attempt to halt decline through cost and asset reductions. Firms in less severe situations have achieved stability merely through cost retrenchment. However, in either case, for firms facing declining financial performance, the key to successful turnaround rests in the effective and efficient management of the retrenchment process.

The primary causes of the turnaround situation have been associated with the second phase of the turnaround process, the *recovery response.* For firms that declined primarily

It Just Got Hotter in Kraft's Kitchen

BusinessWeek

As Kraft Foods Inc. used to remind consumers, America spells cheese k-r-a-f-t. Lately, those letters have been spelling something else: frustration. Since Altria Group Inc. spun off a minority interest in Kraft in mid-2001, the stock price of the packaged-food giant has risen just 12.6 percent, lagging its peer group, the Standard & Poor's 500-stock index, and even bank certificates of deposit.

On January 31, 2007, Altria said it will distribute its remaining 88.6 percent stake in Kraft to shareholders on March 30. Altria may have been OK with an underachiever; if nothing else, Kraft's steadiness helped balance the uncertainties of Altria's cigarette business.

In the short term, in fact, Kraft's results may suffer. Analysts say Rosenfeld will have to hike outlays on marketing, R&D, and information technology to make up for inadequate spending in the past. Kraft also will have to pay 4.9 percent more for raw ingredients in 2007, after benefiting from a small cost decline in 2006, figures analyst Edgar Roesch of Banc of America Securities. In addition, the overnight release of nearly 1.5 billion Kraft shares is expected to swamp demand.

Higher expenses in 2007 should keep returns close to flat. David Nelson, an analyst with Credit Suisse, predicts Kraft will net $3.1 billion, or $1.90 a share, in 2007 on sales of $35.1 billion. Nelson's target price for Kraft stock over the next 12 months: $31 a share, the same price it opened at in its initial public offering 5½ years ago.

Kraft has a lot going for it, of course. The Northfield (Illinois) company is the nation's biggest maker of packaged foods and second worldwide only to Nestlé of Switzerland. Look through the kitchens of 200 U.S. households and you'll find a Kraft product in all but one of them. Its brands include Oscar Mayer, Post, and Nabisco. A half-dozen boast sales of more than $1 billion a year, while 50 top $100 million. And the company has also had some new successes. Sales of its South Beach Diet line of products, introduced in early 2005, rose to $350 million last year, estimates analyst Roesch. Its California Pizza Kitchen frozen pizzas are selling well, too.

Problem is, other old brands like Velveeta, Maxwell House, and Jell-O are sinking. Like its rivals, Kraft has extended product lines to get the most from its blockbusters. But the strategy may be played out. The company already markets 14 varieties of Oreo cookies, for instance.

Under Altria, management used acquisitions, such as the $18.9 billion takeover of Nabisco in 2000, to overcome slow internal growth. Rosenfeld says that now Kraft will be better able to use its stock, worth $57.8 billion, to make more buys. She has started unloading noncore or underperforming brands; on January 23, 2007, Kraft sold it slow-growth Cream of Wheat brand for $200 million. Others sales could include Oscar Mayer, Planters nuts, and Grey Poupon mustard.

Source: Reprinted with special permission from Michael Arndt, "It Just Got Hotter in Kraft's Kitchen," *BusinessWeek*, February 12, 2007. Copyright © 2007 The McGraw-Hill Companies.

as a result of external problems, turnaround most often has been achieved through creative new entrepreneurial strategies. For firms that declined primarily as a result of internal problems, turnaround has been most frequently achieved through efficiency strategies. *Recovery* is achieved when economic measures indicate that the firm has regained its predownturn levels of performance.

Divestiture

divestiture strategy
A grand strategy that involves the sale of a firm or a major unit of a firm as a going concern.

A **divestiture strategy** involves the sale of a firm or a major component of a firm. Sara Lee Corp. (SLE) provides a good example. It sells everything from Wonderbras and Kiwi shoe polish to Endust furniture polish and Chock Full o'Nuts coffee. The company used a conglomerate diversification strategy to build Sara Lee into a huge portfolio of disparate brands. A new president, C. Steven McMillan, faced stagnant revenues and earnings. So he consolidated, streamlined, and focused the company on its core categories—food, underwear, and household products. He divested 15 businesses, including Coach leather goods, which together equaled more than 20 percent of the company's revenue, and laid off 13,200 employees, nearly 10 percent of the workforce. McMillan used the cash from asset sales to snap up brands that enhanced Sara Lee's clout in key categories, like the $2.8 billion purchase of St. Louis–based breadmaker Earthgrains Co. to quadruple Sara Lee's bakery operations. In another case of divestitures, Kraft Foods found that it could improve its overall operations by selling some of its best-known brands, as discussed in Exhibit 7.16, Strategy in Action.

When retrenchment fails to accomplish the desired turnaround, as in the Goodyear situation, or when a nonintegrated business activity achieves an unusually high market value, strategic managers often decide to sell the firm. However, because the intent is to find a buyer willing to pay a premium above the value of a going concern's fixed assets, the term *marketing for sale* is often more appropriate. Prospective buyers must be convinced that because of their skills and resources or because of the firm's synergy with their existing businesses, they will be able to profit from the acquisition.

Corning undertook a turnaround that followed retrenchment with divestitures. In 2001, Corning found itself in a declining market for its core product of fiber-optic cable. The company needed to develop a strategy that would allow it to turn around its falling sales and begin to grow once more. It began with retrenchment. Corning laid off 12,000 workers in 2001 and another 4,000 in 2002. Corning also began the divestiture of its noncore assets, such as its nontelecom businesses and its money-losing photonics operation, to stabilize its financial situation so that it could begin its recovery.

The reasons for divestiture vary. They often arise because of partial mismatches between the acquired firm and the parent corporation. Some of the mismatched parts cannot be integrated into the corporation's mainstream activities and, thus, must be spun off. A second reason is corporate financial needs. Sometimes the cash flow or financial stability of the corporation as a whole can be greatly improved if businesses with high market value can be sacrificed. The result can be a balancing of equity with long-term risks or of long-term debt payments to optimize the cost of capital. A third, less frequent reason for divestiture is government antitrust action when a firm is believed to monopolize or unfairly dominate a particular market.

Although examples of the divestiture grand strategy are numerous, CBS Inc. provides an outstanding example. In a two-year period, the once diverse entertainment and publishing giant sold its Records Division to Sony, its magazine publishing business to Diamandis Communications, its book publishing operations to Harcourt Brace Jovanovich, and its music publishing operations to SBK Entertainment World. Other firms that have pursued this type of grand strategy include Esmark, which divested Swift & Company, and White Motors, which divested White Farm.

Liquidation

liquidation
A grand strategy that involves the sale of the assets of the business for their salvage value.

When **liquidation** is the grand strategy, the firm typically is sold in parts, only occasionally as a whole—but for its tangible asset value and not as a going concern. In selecting liquidation, the owners and strategic managers of a firm are admitting failure and recognize that this action is likely to result in great hardships to themselves and their employees. For these reasons, liquidation usually is seen as the least attractive of the grand strategies. As a long-term strategy, however, it minimizes the losses of all the firm's stockholders. Faced with bankruptcy, the liquidating firm usually tries to develop a planned and orderly system that will result in the greatest possible return and cash conversion as the firm slowly relinquishes its market share.

Planned liquidation can be worthwhile. For example, Columbia Corporation, a $130 million diversified firm, liquidated its assets for more cash per share than the market value of its stock.

Bankruptcy

bankruptcy
When a company is unable to pay its debts as they become due, or has more debts than assets.

Business failures are playing an increasingly important role in the American economy. In an average week, more than 300 companies fail and file for **bankruptcy**. More than 75 percent of these financially desperate firms file for a *liquidation bankruptcy*—they agree to a complete distribution of their assets to creditors, most of whom receive a small fraction of the amount they are owed. Liquidation is what the layperson views as bankruptcy: the business cannot pay its debts, so it must close its doors. Investors lose their money, employees lose their jobs, and managers lose their credibility. In owner-managed firms, company and personal bankruptcy commonly go hand in hand.

The other 25 percent of these firms refuse to surrender until one final option is exhausted. Choosing a strategy to recapture its viability, such a company asks the courts for a *reorganization bankruptcy*. The firm attempts to persuade its creditors to temporarily freeze their claims while it undertakes to reorganize and rebuild the company's operations more profitably. The appeal of a reorganization bankruptcy is based on the company's ability to convince creditors that it can succeed in the marketplace by implementing a new strategic plan, and that when the plan produces profits, the firm will be able to repay its creditors, perhaps in full. In other words, the company offers its creditors a carefully designed alternative to forcing an immediate, but fractional, repayment of its financial obligations. The option of reorganization bankruptcy offers maximum repayment of debt at some specified future time if a new strategic plan is successful.

The Bankruptcy Situation

Imagine that your firm's financial reports have shown an unabated decline in revenue for seven quarters. Expenses have increased rapidly, and it is becoming difficult, and at times not possible, to pay bills as they become due. Suppliers are concerned about shipping goods without first receiving payment, and some have refused to ship without advanced payment in cash. Customers are requiring assurances that future orders will be delivered and some are beginning to buy from competitors. Employees are listening seriously to rumors of financial problems and a higher than normal number have accepted other employment. What can be done? What strategy can be initiated to protect the company and resolve the financial problems in the short term?

Chapter 7: The Harshest Resolution

If the judgment of the owners of a business is that its decline cannot be reversed, and the business cannot be sold as a going concern, then the alternative that is in the best interest of all may be a liquidation bankruptcy, also known as Chapter 7 of the Bankruptcy Code. The court appoints a trustee, who collects the property of the company, reduces it to cash, and distributes the proceeds proportionally to creditors on a pro rata basis as expeditiously as possible. Because all assets are sold to pay outstanding debt, a liquidation bankruptcy terminates a business. This type of filing is critically important to sole proprietors or partnerships. Their owners are personally liable for all business debts not covered by the sale of the business assets unless they can secure a Chapter 7 bankruptcy, which will allow them to cancel any debt in excess of exempt assets. Although they will be left with little personal property, the liquidated debtor is discharged from paying the remaining debt.

The shareholders of corporations are not liable for corporate debt and any debt existing after corporate assets are liquidated is absorbed by creditors. Corporate shareholders may simply terminate operations and walk away without liability to remaining creditors. However, filing a Chapter 7 proceeding will provide for an orderly and fair distribution of assets to creditors and thereby may reduce the negative impact of the business failure.

Chapter 11: A Conditional Second Chance

A proactive alternative for the endangered company is reorganization bankruptcy. Chosen for the right reasons, and implemented in the right way, reorganization bankruptcy can provide a financially, strategically, and ethically sound basis on which to advance the interests of all of the firm's stakeholders.

A thorough and objective analysis of the company may support the idea of its continuing operations if excessive debt can be reduced and new strategic initiatives can be undertaken. If the realistic possibility of long-term survival exists, a reorganization under Chapter 11 of the Bankruptcy Code can provide the opportunity. Reorganization allows a business debtor to restructure its debts and, with the agreement of creditors and approval of the court, to continue as a viable business. Creditors involved in Chapter 11 actions often receive less than the total debt due to them but far more than would be available from liquidation.

A Chapter 11 bankruptcy can provide time and protection to the debtor firm (which we will call the *Company*) to reorganize and use future earnings to pay creditors. The Company may restructure debts, close unprofitable divisions or stores, renegotiate labor contracts, reduce its workforce, or propose other actions that could create a profitable business. If the plan is accepted by creditors, the Company will be given another chance to avoid liquidation and emerge from the bankruptcy proceedings rehabilitated.

Seeking Protection of the Bankruptcy Court

If creditors file lawsuits or schedule judicial sales to enforce liens, the Company will need to seek the protection of the Bankruptcy Court. Filing a bankruptcy petition will invoke the protection of the court to provide sufficient time to work out a reorganization that was not achievable voluntarily. If reorganization is not possible, a Chapter 7 proceeding will allow for the fair and orderly dissolution of the business.

If a Chapter 11 proceeding is the required course of action, the Company must determine what the reorganized business will look like, if such a structure can be achieved, and how it will be accomplished while maintaining operations during the bankruptcy proceeding. Will sufficient cash be available to pay for the proceedings and reorganization? Will customers continue to do business with the Company or seek other more secure businesses with which to deal? Will key personnel stay on or look for more secure employment? Which operations should be discontinued or reduced?

Emerging from Bankruptcy

Bankruptcy is only the first step toward recovery for a firm. Many questions should be answered: How did the business get to the point at which the extreme action of bankruptcy was necessary? Were warning signs overlooked? Was the competitive environment understood? Did pride or fear prevent objective analysis? Did the business have the people and resources to succeed? Was the strategic plan well designed and implemented? Did financial problems result from unforeseen and unforeseeable problems or from bad management decisions?

Commitments to "try harder," "listen more carefully to the customer," and "be more efficient" are important but insufficient grounds to inspire stakeholder confidence. A recovery strategy must be developed to delineate how the company will compete more successfully in the future.

An assessment of the bankruptcy situation requires executives to consider the causes of the Company's decline and the severity of the problem it now faces. Investors must decide whether the management team that governed the company's operations during the downturn can return the firm to a position of success. Creditors must believe that the company's managers have learned how to prevent a recurrence of the observed and similar problems. Alternatively, they must have faith that the company's competencies can be sufficiently augmented by key substitutions to the management team, with strong support in decision making from a board of directors and consultants, to restore the firm's competitive strength.

The 12 grand strategies discussed earlier, used singly and much more often in combinations, represent the traditional alternatives used by firms in the United States. Recently, three new grand types have gained in popularity (thus totaling the 15 grand strategies we said we would discuss); all fit under the broad category of corporate combinations. Although they do not fit the criterion by which executives retain a high degree of control over their operations, these grand strategies deserve special attention and consideration especially by companies that operate in global, dynamic, and technologically driven industries. These three newly popularized grand strategies are joint ventures, strategic alliances, and consortia.

Joint Ventures

joint venture
A grand strategy in which companies create a co-owned business that operates for their mutual benefit.

Occasionally two or more capable firms lack a necessary component for success in a particular competitive environment. For example, no single petroleum firm controlled sufficient resources to construct the Alaskan pipeline. Nor was any single firm capable of processing and marketing all of the oil that would flow through the pipeline. The solution was a set of **joint ventures**, which are commercial companies (children) created and operated for the benefit of the co-owners (parents). These cooperative arrangements provided both the funds needed to build the pipeline and the processing and marketing capacities needed to profitably handle the oil flow.

The particular form of joint ventures discussed above is *joint ownership.* In recent years, it has become increasingly appealing for domestic firms to join foreign firms by means of this form. For example, Diamond-Star Motors is the result of a joint venture between a U.S. company, Chrysler Corporation, and Japan's Mitsubishi Motors corporation. Located in Normal, Illinois, Diamond-Star was launched because it offered Chrysler and Mitsubishi a chance to expand on their long-standing relationship in which subcompact cars (as well as Mitsubishi engines and other automotive parts) are imported to the United States and sold under the Dodge and Plymouth names.

The joint venture extends the supplier-consumer relationship and has strategic advantages for both partners. For Chrysler, it presents an opportunity to produce a high-quality car using expertise brought to the venture by Mitsubishi. It also gives Chrysler the chance to try new production techniques and to realize efficiencies by using the workforce that was not included under Chrysler's collective bargaining agreement with the United Auto Workers. The agreement offers Mitsubishi the opportunity to produce cars for sale in the United States without being subjected to the tariffs and restrictions placed on Japanese imports.

As a second example, Bethlehem Steel acquired an interest in a Brazilian mining venture to secure a raw material source. The stimulus for this joint ownership venture was grand strategy, but such is not always the case. Certain countries virtually mandate that foreign firms entering their markets do so on a joint ownership basis. India and Mexico are good examples. The rationale of these countries is that joint ventures minimize the threat of foreign domination and enhance the skills, employment, growth, and profits of local firms.

It should be noted that strategic managers understandably are wary of joint ventures. Admittedly, joint ventures present new opportunities with risks that can be shared. On the other hand, joint ventures often limit the discretion, control, and profit potential of partners, while demanding managerial attention and other resources that might be directed toward the firm's mainstream activities. Nevertheless, increasing globalization in many industries may require greater consideration of the joint venture approach, if historically national firms are to remain viable.

Collaborative Growth in China through Joint Ventures[8]

A prime example of the value of joint ventures is seen in their use by foreign businesses that seek to do business in China. Until very recently, China enthusiastically invited foreign

---

[8] This section was drawn from Pearce II and Robbins, "Strategic Transformation as the Essential Last Step in the Process of Business Turnaround."

investment to help in the development of its economy. However, in the early 2000s, China increased its regulations on foreign investment to moderate its economic growth and to ensure that Chinese businesses would not be at a competitive disadvantage when competing for domestic markets. The new restrictions require local companies to retain control of Chinese trademarks and brands, prevent foreign investors from buying property that is not for their own use, limit the size of foreign-owned retail chains, and restrict foreign investment in selected industries.[9] With these increasing regulations, investment in China through joint ventures with Chinese companies has become a prominent strategy for foreign investors who hope to circumvent some of the limitations on their strategies, therefore more fully capitalizing on China's economic growth.

In China, a host country partner can greatly facilitate the acceptance of a foreign investor and help minimize the costs of doing business in an unknown nation. Typically, the foreign partner contributes financing and technology, while the Chinese partner provides the land, physical facilities, workers, local connections, and knowledge of the country.[10] In a wholly owned venture, the foreign company is forced to acquire the land, build the workspace, and hire and train the employees, all of which are especially expensive propositions in a country in which the foreign company lacks guanxi.[11] Additionally, because China restricts direct foreign investment in the life insurance, energy, construction of transportation facilities, higher education, and health care industries, asset or equity joint ventures are sometimes the only option for foreign firms.

Foreign partners in equity joint ventures benefit from speed of entry to the Chinese market, tax incentives, motivational and competitive advantages of a mutual long-term commitment, and access to the resources of its Chinese partner. In 2006, two large joint ventures in the media industry were created when Canada's AGA Resources partnered with Beijing Tangde International Film and Culture Co and when the United States' Sequoia Capital formed a joint venture with Hunan Greatdreams Cartoon Media.[12] Joint ventures in China's asset management industry include the 2006 partnerships between Italy's Banca Lombarda, the United States' Lord Abbett, and Chinese companies.

Similar opportunities exist for international joint ventures in the construction and operation of oil refineries, in the building of the nation's railroad transportation system, and in the development of specific geographic areas. In special economic zones, foreign firms operate businesses with Chinese joint venture partners. The foreign companies receive tax incentives in the form of rates that are lower than the standard 30 percent corporate tax rate. For example, in the Shanghai Pudong New Area, a 15 percent tax rate applies.[13]

The number of international joint ventures is increasing because of China's admission to the World Trade Organization (WTO). Under the conditions of its membership, China is expanding the list of industries that permit foreign investment.[14] As of 2007, for example, foreign investors that participate with Chinese partners in joint ventures are permitted to hold an increased share of JVs in several major industries: banks (up to 20 percent), investment funds (33 percent), life insurance (50 percent), and telecommunications (25 percent).

[9] E. Kurtenbach, "China Raising Stakes for Foreign Investment," *Philadelphia Inquirer*, September 24, 2006.

[10] Ying Qui, "Problems of Managing Joint Ventures in China's Interior: Evidence from Shaanxi," *Advanced Management Journal* 70, no. 3 (2005), pp. 46–57.

[11] J. A. Pearce II and R. B. Robinson Jr., "Cultivating Guanxi as a Corporate Foreign-Investor Strategy," *Business Horizons* 43, no. 1 (2000), pp. 31–38.

[12] Andrew Bagnell, "China Business," *China Business Review* 33, no. 5 (2006), pp. 88–92.

[13] N. P. Chopey, "China Still Beckons Petrochemical Investments," *Chemical Engineering* 133, no. 8 (2006) pp. 19–23.

[14] "China's WTO Scorecard: Selected Year-Three Service Commitments," *The US-China Business Council* (2005), pp. 1–2.

Yahoo!'s Unlikely Amigos

BusinessWeek

Evidently the newspapers are going to try to partner their way out of it. In this case, "it" is whatever disadvantages the medium faces in the online world. And sliding revenues, reported by major newspaper companies in the last half of 2006. And those companies' steep stock price declines. A nine-company consortium representing more than 215 U.S. dailies has already signed on with Yahoo!—itself no stranger to share price slippage of late—to partner with Yahoo! HotJobs in an online classifieds venture. This consortium, including the likes of E. W. Scripps (which is mulling what it may do with its newspapers), Hearst Newspapers, and MediaNews Group, is in a 90-day exclusive negotiating period with the online giant over at least five key areas to broaden the partnership. And the three companies behind the online help-wanted classifieds site careerbuilder.com—Gannett, McClatchy, and Tribune—are discussing an alliance to create an online ad network.

Both groups welcome other partners, but the Yahoo! partnership has had better luck in scoring them so far. Morris Communications and Media General have signed on since the HotJobs deal was announced. New York Times Co. and the newspaper division of Advance Publications (which also owns the glossy magazine world's Conde Nast Publications) are discussing joining up as well, say executives familiar with the matter.

The Yahoo! partnership has a weakness for wacky monikers. The online giant and its "Nine Amigos" have assigned at least five "tiger teams" to explore relationships with Yahoo!. Among them: extending distribution of Amigos news stories with Yahoo! including spotlighting them in search results; turning over Amigos site-search engines to Yahoo! and creating co-branded search toolbars; finding ways to integrate Yahoo!'s local search with newspapers' data; having newspaper sales staffs sell Yahoo! ads to local advertisers and having Yahoo! staff sell national ads for the Amigos sites; and allowing the Amigos Web sites to use Yahoo!'s ad technology.

You can argue that newspapers are dealing with a sworn enemy here, but the reality is more nuanced. The big online players have a horrible record in tailoring products to local markets.

Yahoo! seeks a fix appropriate to its content-centric ways. The world's no. 1 portal is betting that, like Microsoft, it can't do local by itself. It's also betting there is huge upside in the local space for the kinds of display ads in which it still outshines Google. And it's a nod to the reality that advertisers remain more comfortable having their ads around tamer and more traditional media rather than, say, user-generated videos. As for the newspapers, nuances aside, they are dealing with the kind of company—online, and measuring profit by the billion—that they once feared. But these days, they fear reality more.

Source: Reprinted with special permission from Jon Fine, "Yahoo!'s Unlikely Amigos," *BusinessWeek*, January 29, 2007. Copyright © 2007 The McGraw-Hill Companies.

Strategic Alliances

strategic alliances
Contractual partnerships because the companies involved do not take an equity position in one another

Strategic alliances are distinguishable from joint ventures because the companies involved do not take an equity position in one another. In many instances, strategic alliances are *partnerships* that exist for a defined period during which partners contribute their skills and expertise to a cooperative project. For example, one partner provides manufacturing capabilities while a second partner provides marketing expertise. In other situations, a strategic alliance can enable similar companies to combine their capabilities to counter the threats of a much larger or new type of competitor. Exhibit 7.17, Strategy in Action, provides an example of a strategic alliance that provides "strength in numbers."

Strategic alliances are sometimes undertaken because the partners want to develop in-house capabilities to supplant the partner when the contractual arrangement between them reaches its termination date. Such relationships are tricky because, in a sense, the partners are attempting to "steal" each other's know-how. Exhibit 7.18, Global Strategy in Action, lists some important questions about their learning intentions that prospective partners should ask themselves before entering into a strategic alliance.

In other instances, strategic alliances are synonymous with *licensing agreements*. Licensing involves the transfer of some industrial property right from the U.S. licensor to a motivated licensee in a foreign country. Most tend to be patents, trademarks, or technical

Key Issues in Strategic Alliance Learning

Objective	Major Questions
1. Assess and value partner knowledge.	• What were the strategic objectives in forming the alliance? • What are the core competencies of our alliance partner? • What specific knowledge does the partner have that could enhance our competitive strategy?
2. Determine knowledge accessibility.	• How have key alliance responsibilities been allocated to the partners? • Which partner controls key managerial responsibilities? • Does the alliance agreement specify restrictions on our access to the alliance operations?
3. Evaluate knowledge tacitness and ease of transfer.	• Is our learning objective focused on explicit operational knowledge? • Where in the alliance does the knowledge reside? • What are we trying to learn and how can we use the knowledge?
4. Establish knowledge connections between the alliance and the partner.	• Are parent managers in regular contact with senior alliance managers? • Has the alliance been incorporated into parent strategic plans? • What is the level of trust between parent and alliance managers?
5. Draw on existing knowledge to facilitate learning.	• In the learning process, have efforts been made to involve managers with prior experience in either/both alliance management and partner ties? • Are experiences with other alliances being used as the basis for managing the current alliance?
6. Ensure that partner and alliance managerial cultures are in alignment.	• Is the alliance viewed as a threat or an asset by parent managers? • In the parent, is there agreement on the strategic rationale for the alliance? • In the alliance, do managers understand the importance of the parent's learning objective?

know-how that are granted to the licensee for a specified time in return for a royalty and for avoiding tariffs or import quotas. Bell South and U.S. West, with various marketing and service competitive advantages valuable to Europe, have extended a number of licenses to create personal computers networks in the United Kingdom. Another example of licensing is discussed in Exhibit 7.19, Strategy in Action, which describes UTEK Corporation's successful strategy for licensing discoveries resulting from research efforts at universities.

Another licensing strategy is to contract the manufacturing of its product line to a foreign company to exploit local comparative advantages in technology, materials, or labor. MIPS Computer Systems has licensed Digital Equipment Corporation, Texas Instruments, Cypress Semiconductor, and Bipolar Integrated Technology in the United States and Fujitsu, NEC, and Kubota in Japan to market computers based on its designs in the partner's country.

A Matchmaker for Inventors

BusinessWeek

For George E. Inglett, a researcher with the U.S. Department of Agriculture, the eureka moment came in 1995. Searching for a use for oat hulls, he shoveled a couple of pounds into a high-speed centrifuge in his lab in Peoria, Illinois. What emerged was a white gel with no taste or calories. Adding it to food cut the fat and calories dramatically but the gel had no impact on taste or texture. Inglett had discovered nutrition's Holy Grail: an all-natural fat substitute.

Inglett's discovery might have been for naught without UTEK Corp., which ultimately found a small company to commercialize his product: ZTrim in Mundelein, Illinois. UTEK, a technology matchmaker with an unusual business model, gives researchers like Inglett an outlet for their ideas, and it gives companies like ZTrim a way to outsource innovation by providing access to a database of more than 35,000 discoveries that would otherwise go unnoticed.

For university and government researchers struggling to license their discoveries, UTEK can make all the difference. Many universities have technology-transfer offices that are understaffed and underfunded. And many risk-averse companies are unwilling to take a flyer on an interesting idea with uncertain commercial potential. The result: only about 30 percent of the 18,000 discoveries made by university and government researchers each year ever see the light of day as commercial products.

North Carolina A&T State University's experience is instructive. When a researcher there stumbled on a way to detect microscopic cracks in an airplane fuselage, the discovery, while promising, turned out to be nearly impossible to sell. The technology-transfer office spent two years scouring North America and Europe for a buyer.

Then UTEK showed up, with Material Technologies Inc. in tow. Unlike other technology-transfer companies, which license technologies they've acquired or charge fees to broker deals, UTEK pays the research lab for licensing rights to its discovery. It then sells those rights to the client company for shares of stock, which UTEK agrees to hold for one year. UTEK might pay $500,000 for the discovery and receive stock worth $2.5 million. A lot can happen in a year—UTEK's stake in ZTrim, for example, ballooned to $6 million.

UTEK has had more hits than misses, including deals involving technologies for fertilizer production, pollution monitoring, even land mine detection. Since 2003 the number of tech-transfer deals UTEK has brokered has quadrupled, despite robust competition, which includes 10 publicly traded tech-transfer companies. UTEK, which went public in 2000, now holds equity stakes in 55 companies, for a portfolio valued at $60 million. And each year it adds several thousand discoveries to its database.

Source: Reprinted with special permission from Louis Lavelle, "A Matchmaker for Investors; UTEK is Earning Big Bucks by Pairing Brainstorms with Businesses," *BusinessWeek*, February 26, 2007. Copyright © 2007 The McGraw-Hill Companies.

Service and franchise-based firms—including Anheuser-Busch, Avis, Coca-Cola, Hilton, Hyatt, Holiday Inns, Kentucky Fried Chicken, McDonald's, and Pepsi—have long engaged in licensing arrangements with foreign distributors as a way to enter new markets with standardized products that can benefit from marketing economies.

Outsourcing is a basic approach to strategic alliances that enables firms to gain a competitive advantage. Significant changes within many segments of American business continue to encourage the use of outsourcing practices. Within the health care arena, an industry survey recorded 67 percent of hospitals using provider outsourcing for at least one department within their organization. Services such as information systems, reimbursement, and risk and physician practice management are outsourced by 51 percent of the hospitals that use outsourcing.

Another successful application of outsourcing is found in human resources. A survey of human resource executives revealed 85 percent have personal experience leading an outsourcing effort within their organization. In addition, it was found that two-thirds of pension departments have outsourced at least one human resource function. Within customer service and sales departments, outsourcing increases productivity in such areas as product information, sales and order taking, sample fulfillment, and complaint handling. For an interesting example of the use of outsourcing to save money in the retail sector, see Exhibit 7.20, Strategy in Action.

What Happens to That Scarf You Really Hated?

BusinessWeek

Shoppers, on average, return about 6 percent of everything they buy. That proportion spikes in January to nearly 10 percent. This used to be a sore point for retailers. Rather than try to make sense of a hodgepodge of generally used, sometimes broken goods with packaging shredded or instructions missing, stores tended just to write the lot off as a loss. But over the past decade, an opportunistic industry has sprung up to give the reject pile a new lease on life.

Most big-box retailers—Sears, Target, Best Buy, Kohl's, and many others—now outsource the handling of returns to companies that specialize in so-called reverse logistics. These third parties' job, basically, is to pick up a store's returns and figure out what to do with them—restock an item, sell it somewhere else, like in Peru or at a flea market, or throw it in the trash.

For retailers, it's a way to squeeze money from what previously was a cost center, because they get a cut of any eventual sales. Genco, the biggest such service provider, charges stores a management fee to collect and sort the products at its 33 return centers. If it's able to sell a returned item to a secondary market, the proceeds are split with the retailer. Newgistics, an Austin (Texas) company, handles returns specifically for online sales—where return rates can surge up to 20 percent—for Amazon.com, J. Crew, and Nordstrom, among others, charging by package. Other companies, such as Liquidity Services, don't charge a fee, only taking a cut from auctions of the goods.

The best gift you can give a returns processor is to bring back something for no other reason than you just changed your mind. If that item gets back to a Genco center, for example, the manufacturer may give the retailer a credit for the return (free money). Then Genco will send the defect-free, originally wrapped product back to the retailer to be sold again (more money).

Pittsburgh-based, privately held Genco helped develop this niche in 1993 when, as a $34 million-a-year company, it started handling returns for Wal-Mart Stores Inc. By 2006, Genco had $570 million in revenue. Now it does logistics work for more than 100 clients.

The trick for logistics companies is to find other places for returned merchandise. Much of what Genco sells goes to closeout retailers or dollar stores. If something is defective, it goes back to the manufacturer, or if that's not possible, Genco will try to fix it. It even puts products up on eBay. Each retailer has its own restrictions about its returned goods' eventual home. About 40 percent of Genco's $1 billion in turnover comes from goods it sells in secondary markets overseas. Some retailers require Genco to scrub the product of logos; some just want the highest bid.

Source: Reprinted with special permission from Brian Hindo, "What Happens to that Scarf You Really Hated?" *BusinessWeek*, January 15, 2007. Copyright © 2007 The McGraw-Hill Companies.

Consortia, *Keiretsus*, and *Chaebols*

consortia
Large interlocking relationships between businesses of an industry.

Consortia are defined as large interlocking relationships between businesses of an industry. In Japan such consortia are known as *keiretsus;* in South Korea as *chaebols.*

In Europe, consortia projects are increasing in number and in success rates. Examples include the Junior Engineers' and Scientists' Summer Institute, which underwrites cooperative learning and research; the European Strategic Program for Research and Development in Information Technologies, which seeks to enhance European competitiveness in fields related to computer electronics and component manufacturing; and EUREKA, which is a joint program involving scientists and engineers from several European countries to coordinate joint research projects.

keiretsus
A Japanese consortia of businesses that is coordinated by a large trading company to gain a strategic advantage.

A Japanese *keiretsu* is an undertaking involving up to 50 different firms that are joined around a large trading company or bank and are coordinated through interlocking directories and stock exchanges. It is designed to use industry coordination to minimize risks of competition, in part through cost sharing and increased economies of scale. Examples include Sumitomo, Mitsubishi, Mitsui, and Sanwa.

chaebol
A Korean consortia financed through government banking groups to gain a strategic advantage.

A South Korean chaebol resembles a consortium or keiretsu except that they are typically financed through government banking groups and are largely run by professional managers trained by participating firms expressly for the job.

A Profile of Strategic Choice Options

	Six Strategic Choice Options					
	1	**2**	**3**	**4**	**5**	**6**
Interactive opportunities	West Coast markets present little competition		Current markets sensitive to price competition		Current industry product lines offer too narrow a range of markets	
Appropriate long-range objectives (limited sample): Average 5-year ROI.	15%	19%	13%	17%	23%	15%
Company sales by year 5.	+ 50%	+ 40%	+ 20%	+ 0%	+ 35%	+ 25%
Risk of negative profits.	.30	.25	.10	.15	.20	.05
Grand strategies	Horizontal integration	Market development	Concentration	Selective retrenchment	Product development	Concentration

SELECTION OF LONG-TERM OBJECTIVES AND GRAND STRATEGY SETS

At first glance, the strategic management model, which provides the framework for study throughout this book, seems to suggest that strategic choice decision making leads to the sequential selection of long-term objectives and grand strategies. In fact, however, strategic choice is the simultaneous selection of long-range objectives and grand strategies. When strategic planners study their opportunities, they try to determine which are most likely to result in achieving various long-range objectives. Almost simultaneously, they try to forecast whether an available grand strategy can take advantage of preferred opportunities so the tentative objectives can be met. In essence, then, three distinct but highly interdependent choices are being made at one time. Several triads, or sets, of possible decisions are usually considered.

A simplified example of this process is shown in Exhibit 7.21, Strategy in Action. In this example, the firm has determined that six strategic choice options are available. These options stem from three interactive opportunities (e.g., West Coast markets that present little competition). Because each of these interactive opportunities can be approached through different grand strategies—for options 1 and 2, the grand strategies are horizontal integration and market development—each offers the potential for achieving long-range objectives to varying degrees. Thus, a firm rarely can make a strategic choice only on the basis of its preferred opportunities, long-range objectives, or grand strategy. Instead, these three elements must be considered simultaneously, because only in combination do they constitute a strategic choice.

In an actual decision situation, the strategic choice would be complicated by a wider variety of interactive opportunities, feasible company objectives, promising grand strategy options, and evaluative criteria. Nevertheless, Exhibit 7.21 does partially reflect the nature and complexity of the process by which long-term objectives and grand strategies are selected.

In the next chapter, the strategic choice process will be fully explained. However, knowledge of long-term objectives and grand strategies is essential to understanding that process.

SEQUENCE OF OBJECTIVES AND STRATEGY SELECTION

The selection of long-range objectives and grand strategies involves simultaneous, rather than sequential, decisions. While it is true that objectives are needed to prevent the firm's direction and progress from being determined by random forces, it is equally true that objectives can be achieved only if strategies are implemented. In fact, long-term objectives and grand strategies are so interdependent that some business consultants do not distinguish between them. Long-term objectives and grand strategies are still combined under the heading of company strategy in most of the popular business literature and in the thinking of most practicing executives.

However, the distinction has merit. Objectives indicate what strategic managers want but provide few insights about how they will be achieved. Conversely, strategies indicate what types of actions will be taken but do not define what ends will be pursued or what criteria will serve as constraints in refining the strategic plan.

Does it matter whether strategic decisions are made to achieve objectives or to satisfy constraints? No, because constraints are themselves objectives. The constraint of increased inventory capacity is a desire (an objective), not a certainty. Likewise, the constraint of an increase in the sales force does not ensure that the increase will be achieved, given such factors as other company priorities, labor market conditions, and the firm's profit performance.

DESIGNING A PROFITABLE BUSINESS MODEL

business model
A clear understanding of how the firm will generate profits and the strategic actions it must take to succeed over the long term.

The process of combining long-term objectives and grand strategies produces a **business model**. Creating an effective model requires a clear understanding of how the firm will generate profits and the strategic action it must take to succeed over the long term.

Adrian Slywotzky and David Morrison identified 22 business models—designs that generate profits in a unique way.[15] They present these models as examples, believing that others do or can exist. The authors also believe that in some instances profitability depends on the interplay of two or more business models. Their study demonstrates that the mechanisms of profitability can be very different but that a focus on the customer is the key to the effectiveness of each model.

Slywotzky and Morrison suggest that the two most productive questions asked of executives are these:

1. What is our business model?
2. How do we make a profit?

The classic strategy rule suggested, "Gain market share and profits will follow." This approach once worked for some industries. However, because of competitive turbulence

---

[15] This section is excerpted from A. J. Slywotzky, D. J. Morrison, and B. Andelman, *The Profit Zone; How Strategic Business Design Will Lead You To Tomorrow's Profits* (New York: Times Books, 1997).

caused by globalization and rapid technological advancements, the once-popular belief in a strong correlation between market share and profitability has collapsed in many industries.

How can businesses earn sustainable profits? The answer is found by analyzing the following questions: Where will the firm make a profit in this industry? How should the business model be designed so that the firm will be profitable? Slywotzky and Morrison describe the following profitability business models as ways to answer those questions.

1. *Customer development customer solutions profit model.* Companies that use this business model make money by finding ways to improve their customers' economics and investing in ways for customers to improve their processes.

2. *Product pyramid profit model.* This model is effective in markets where customers have strong preferences for product characteristics, including variety, style, color, and price. By offering a number of variations, companies can build so-called product pyramids. At the base are low-priced, high-volume products, and at the top are high-priced, low-volume products. Profit is concentrated at the top of the pyramid, but the base is the strategic firewall (i.e., a strong, low-priced brand that deters competitor entry), thereby protecting the margins at the top. Consumer goods companies and automobile companies use this model.

3. *Multicomponent system profit model.* Some businesses are characterized by a production/marketing system that consists of components that generate substantially different levels of profitability. In hotels, for example, there is a substantial difference between the profitability of room rentals and that of bar operations. In such instances, it often is useful to maximize the use of the highest-profit components to maximize the profitability of the whole system.

4. *Switchboard profit model.* Some markets function by connecting multiple sellers to multiple buyers. The switchboard profit model creates a high-value intermediary that concentrates these multiple communication pathways through one point or "switchboard" and thereby reduces costs for both parties in exchange for a fee. As volume increases, so too do profits.

5. *Time profit model.* Sometimes, speed is the key to profitability. This business model takes advantage of first-mover advantage. To sustain this model, constant innovation is essential.

6. *Blockbuster profit model.* In some industries, profitability is driven by a few great product successes. This business model is representative of movie studios, pharmaceutical firms, and software companies, which have high R&D and launch costs and finite product cycles. In this type of environment, it pays to concentrate resource investments in a few projects rather than to take positions in a variety of products.

7. *Profit multiplier model.* This business model reaps gains, repeatedly, from the same product, character, trademark capability, or service. Think of the value that Michael Jordan Inc. creates with the image of the great basketball legend. This model can be a powerful engine for businesses with strong consumer brands.

8. *Entrepreneurial profit model.* Small can be beautiful. This business model stresses that diseconomies of scale can exist in companies. They attack companies that have become comfortable with their profit levels with formal, bureaucratic systems that are remote from customers. As their expenses grow and customer relevance declines, such companies are vulnerable to entrepreneurs who are in direct contact with their customers.

Where Dell Went Wrong

BusinessWeek

At Dell, how it all began is never forgotten. Even on January 31, 2007, as founder Michael S. Dell returned to the role of CEO after 18 months of bad news and faltering financials, the press release trumpeted how, 23 years ago, Dell launched what would become a $56 billion business with just $1,000 and a simple idea.

Like many long-forgotten former champions, Dell succumbed to complacency in the belief that its business model would always keep it far ahead of the pack. While Dell broadened its product line, it never dealt with the vast improvement in the competition or used its lead in direct sales and the cash generated to invest in new business lines, talent, or innovation that could provide another competitive edge. "Dell is a textbook example of single-formula growth: 'We make PCs cheap. This is what we do, and we do it a lot,'" says Jim Mackey, managing director at the Billion Dollar Growth Network. "You can grow very fast when you're on a single formula, but when you get to a certain point, you don't have the ability to create new growth."

"When it's all you can do to keep up with the growth your current business model is providing, you just don't feel that urgency," says Harvard Business School professor Clayton Christensen. "It's hard to get worried." He visited Dell's Round Rock (Texas) offices in 1998 and again in 2000, and warned Dell and then-CEO Kevin Rollins that they needed to focus on growth five to eight years out, on the model that would augment their built-to-order machines. Instead, Dell pushed its model into new types of hardware, such as storage, printers, and TVs, in the hopes of making easy profits by selling products made by other companies.

Hubris crept in. In 1999, Dell bought a start-up called ConvergeNet, which had a sophisticated storage product that turned out to be not ready for prime time. Dubbing rival EMC Corp. the "Excessive Margin Company," Dell seemed to expect storage to follow the same pattern PCs had, moving from pricey, feature-laden models into a standards-based commodity. Dell underestimated the competition and is an also-ran in the segment. By 2005, PC rivals, particularly HP, which has taken the market-share lead from Dell, had closed the efficiency gap and were enjoying resurgent sales at retail stores.

Dell's loyalty to its business model could make it difficult to recapture growth. Dell has suggested a new offensive to enlarge its computer services business, which so far has focused largely on repair and upgrading of Dell's hardware. Dell has struggled to find other growth areas large enough to matter. After a promising start in printers, moving quickly to no. 3, the most recent quarterly data from research firm IDC shows Dell's market share at 3.6 percent, down from 6.2 percent the previous year. Its once-promising move into networking gear has fizzled, and its share in the storage systems market is flat compared with a year ago.

9. *Specialization profit model.* This business model stresses growth through sequenced specialization. Consulting companies have used this design successfully.

10. *Installed base profit model.* A company that pursues this model profits because its established user base subsequently buys the company's brand of consumables or follow-on products. Installed base profits provide a protected annuity stream. Examples include razors and blades, software and upgrades, copiers and toner cartridges, and cameras and film.

11. *De facto standard profit model.* A variant of the installed base profit model, this model is appropriate when the installed base model becomes the de facto standard that governs competitive behavior in the industry.

Exhibit 7.22, Strategy in Action, discusses the business model of Dell. Once praised as innovative, it is now criticized as overly narrow, blind to opportunities, and insufficiently ambitious.

Summary

Before we learn how strategic decisions are made, it is important to understand the two principal components of any strategic choice; namely, long-term objectives and the grand strategy. The purpose of this chapter was to convey that understanding.

Long-term objectives were defined as the results a firm seeks to achieve over a specified period, typically five years. Seven common long-term objectives were discussed: profitability, productivity, competitive position, employee development, employee relations, technological leadership, and public responsibility. These, or any other long-term objectives, should be flexible, measurable over time, motivating, suitable, and understandable.

Grand strategies were defined as comprehensive approaches guiding the major actions designed to achieve long-term objectives. Fifteen grand strategy options were discussed: concentrated growth, market development, product development, innovation, horizontal integration, vertical integration, concentric diversification, conglomerate diversification, turnaround, divestiture, liquidation, bankruptcy, joint ventures, strategic alliances, and consortia.

Key Terms

balanced scorecard, *p. 202*
bankruptcy, *p. 227*
business model, *p. 237*
chaebol, *p. 235*
concentrated growth, *p. 211*
concentric diversification, *p. 221*
conglomerate diversification, *p. 221*

consortia, *p. 235*
divestiture strategy, *p. 226*
generic strategy, *p. 203*
grand strategy, *p. 211*
horizontal integration, *p. 218*
innovation, *p. 216*
joint venture, *p. 230*

keiretsus, *p. 235*
liquidation, *p. 227*
market development, *p. 214*
product development, *p. 216*
strategic alliances, *p. 232*
turnaround strategy, *p. 224*
vertical integration, *p. 220*

Questions for Discussion

1. Identify firms in the business community nearest to your college or university that you believe are using each of the 15 grand strategies discussed in this chapter.
2. Identify firms in your business community that appear to rely principally on 1 of the 15 grand strategies. What kind of information did you use to classify the firms?
3. Write a long-term objective for your school of business that exhibits the seven qualities of long-term objectives described in this chapter.
4. Distinguish between the following pairs of grand strategies:

   a. Horizontal and vertical integration.
   b. Conglomerate and concentric diversification.
   c. Product development and innovation.
   d. Joint venture and strategic alliance.

5. Rank each of the 15 grand strategy options discussed in this chapter on the following three scales:

High	Low
	Cost

High	Low
	Risk of failure

High	Low
	Potential for exceptional growth

6. Identify firms that use the eight specific options shown in Exhibit 7.8 under the grand strategies of concentration, market development, and product development.

Chapter 7 Discussion Case

BusinessWeek

VW's New Strategic Plan for the United States—Part 1: *Crispin Porter + Bogusky's Plan to Rekindle Our Love Affair with VW*

1 Remember the Volkswagen Rabbit? The boxy, fuel-efficient hatchback was launched in 1974 to replace the legendary Beetle as the company's big seller and was the first VW made in the United States. It also became known for catching fire and breaking down, and thus became the symbol of VW's collapse in America through the 1980s. At the insistence of VW's German parent, the Rabbit name was killed in 1985, and the Westmoreland (Pennsylvania) assembly plant was shuttered soon after.

2 So it was audacious indeed when Alex Bogusky, chief creative officer of Crispin Porter + Bogusky, which took over the VW advertising account last December, suggested resurrecting the Rabbit name. In a March 20,2006, meeting at the Auburn Hills (Michigan) headquarters of VW of America, with company brass and two members of its dealer council, Bogusky reasoned that the redesigned Golf launching in the United States this year had already been selling in Europe for two years, so auto writers probably wouldn't pay much attention to the stateside debut. "So let's change the story," offered the 42-year-old ad director before the assembled group. Nervous laughter followed. VW supervisory board chairman Ferdinand K. Piech, known for his bad temper and for insisting that VW have global model names, was certain to disapprove. But VW's U.S. chief, Adrian M. Hallmark, bought in and took the idea to the carmaker's German headquarters in Wolfsburg on March 25, 2006. Worldwide brand chief Wolfgang Bernhard said yes and ordered new signs, photography, and press releases to be rushed for the New York International Auto Show on April 12, despite whispers that Piech, already gunning for Bernhard's boss, management board chairman Bernd Pischetsrieder, was unhappy.

HATE MAIL

3 Many love the Rabbit idea, but plenty hate it. That's just the kind of strong, polarized reaction Bogusky and his partners like to provoke. VW's U.S. dealer council supports the move. But consider some of the hostile reaction: Peter M. DeLorenzo, founder and publisher of influential Webzine Autoextremist.com Inc., called the decision to return to the Rabbit name "pure, unadulterated lunacy," and wrote that if U.S. VW marketing chief Kerri Martin and her agency weren't stopped, they would "destroy the brand in the U.S. once and for all." Steven Wilhite, former VW marketing chief and current global chief marketing officer at Nissan Motor Co., pronounced the idea "brain-dead." Rance E. Crain, editor-in-chief of *Advertising Age*, editorialized that Crispin's first

work for VW has been "so horrendously awful that [it] smoothes the way for [VW's] quick and complete withdrawal [from the American market]." Says a habitually cool Bogusky, wearing a Kiss T-shirt and stabbing his fork in the air as he scarfed banana pancakes at Greenstreet's, a cafe near his Miami office: "I like that they are talking about the work. If they aren't talking, then your brand is dead."

4 Indeed, Volkswagen is trying to avoid the kind of near-death experience it had in the early 1990s, when sales sank so low that German managers seriously pondered pulling up U.S. stakes altogether. At 224,000 cars sold last year, VW is a long way from the nadir of 49,000 in 1992. But to insiders who have watched the numbers drop by 131,000 sales per year since a peak of 355,648 in 2001, this period has felt eerily like the dark days a decade ago, before the New Beetle lifted the entire brand out of quicksand. Internal research shows a lasting loss of confidence in the brand after costly, repetitive quality problems: VW's U.S. division has lost more than $1 billion in each of the past two years, and this year could be nearly as bad. On May 2, 2006, Pischetsrieder had his contract renewed for six years, but only after intense pressure by the supervisory board to deliver better results with fewer job cuts than the 20,000 he wants. "No question about it, it's a five-alarm fire," says Crispin president Jeff Hicks.

5 Enter Crispin Porter + Bogusky, the eccentric ad shop in Miami that's known for using viral marketing and creating nutty characters like the Subservient Chicken for Burger King Holdings Inc.'s ailing franchises. VW had been through three years of coolly received ad efforts as it juggled a failed luxury sedan (the tony Phaeton, priced at more than $75,000) and the $50,000 Touareg SUV, alongside $20,000 Golfs and Jettas. Former agency Arnold Worldwide, saddled with temporary VW ad directors before marketing chief Kerri Martin arrived, struggled to make sense of it all. A year ago, Martin got the heady title of director of brand innovation, having been the celebrated marketing whiz at MINI USA and Harley-Davidson Inc. Crispin worked with her at MINI to create the kind of B-school case-study advertising excitement for which VW used to be known.

6 As Crispin tries to douse the flames engulfing the VW brand, it has to prove that it won the VW assignment on merit, not just as Martin's pet agency. Situated 1,300 miles south of Madison Avenue's groupthink, Crispin stands apart. Whether it was running MINI Cooper hatchbacks around cities atop Ford Excursion SUVs or getting teens to dump some 1,200 faux body bags at the door of a tobacco company for an antismoking campaign, Crispin has been changing the industry's playbook. It famously helped solve Burger King's irrelevancy problem, especially with consumers aged 14 to 25, with the Subservient Chicken Web site, where a visitor could make a chicken do almost anything on command—dust furniture or play air guitar.

7   That simple, inexpensive, wacky idea has generated a staggering 460 million-plus hits in two years and helped Burger King post its first string of positive growth quarters in a decade. The agency's relaunch of the MINI brand helped the unit of BMW surpass sales targets by 80 percent. Crispin's success has fueled growth in its own staff from 105 in 2000 to 438. As it transforms marketing messages into entertainment time and again, "the agency has been redefining what consumers even recognize as advertising," says rival and admirer Jeff Goodby, co-chairman of Goodby, Silverstein & Partners in San Francisco.

8   It's early days, but it looks as if Crispin's style of marketing is working once more. Since its ads started running, VW sales are up, dealers are enthusiastic, Internet chatter about VW is as high as it has been since the public relations bonanza around the New Beetle in 1998. Just about every aspect of Crispin's work in its first five months on the job has been covered in major media outlets. As the agency and Martin have challenged many of VW's old ways and ignored some of the company's internal political trip-wires, the brand is being talked about again around the water cooler, a must for any consumer company today that hopes to not just survive but thrive.

WEB ALLURE

9   Volkswagen, of course, has its own special place in advertising history. Two separate agencies defined themselves, and advertising as a whole, in two different decades working for VW. In the 1960s it was Doyle Dane Bernbach, which created the headlines "Think Small" and "Lemon," pioneering the use of self-deprecating humor and wit to sell cars. "It was the first time ever that people talked about ads at cocktail parties and at work," says Andrew Langer, vice chairman of Lowe & Partners Worldwide, who worked at DDB then. In the 1990s, VW and Boston's Arnold Fortuna Lawner & Cabot, before it was Arnold Worldwide, ignited a new genre of storytelling mixed with independent rock music: the "Da Da Da" ad, playing the German song of the same title while two slackers drove around town in their Golf. "It fits your life," went the ad's voiceover, "or your complete lack thereof." Now it's Crispin's turn to make history—or humiliate itself trying—by taking on America's favorite advertising account for yet another comeback.

10   It certainly didn't take long for Crispin to get people talking again. In place of a subservient chicken, Crispin invented a German-accented, dominatrix-type blonde bombshell named Helga. She appears in ads with an effete German engineer named Wolfgang, whose message to introduce the GTI hatchback is "Unpimp Your Auto," a swipe at the over-accessorized, high-performance small Japanese cars often dubbed "rice rockets." Billboards for the GTI read "Auf Wiedersehen, sucka" and "Fast as Schnell."

Schnell, and then some. Day One on the account, December 11 6, 2005 the agency began to perform triage on the ailing carmaker. Bogusky, a Miami native who dropped out of art school though both parents are graphic artists, met with creative director Andrew Keller, 35, and more than 40 writers, art directors, and researchers in the agency's big conference room. The brief for the GTI read: "How does GTI regain its position as the original hot hatch?" By the way, Keller told the crowd, "we have to figure this out and execute a plan in time to launch during the Winter Olympics [on] February 6." That gave the team fewer than 60 days, with a Christmas holiday in the middle.

Crispin's cognitive anthropologists went to work. Two- 12 hour in-home interviews with two dozen GTI buyers, all men 18 to 30, were done in five cities. The researchers sent the subjects an assignment in advance of visits: Make a collage with magazine pictures to illustrate how they felt about Japanese "tuner" cars, like Honda Civics, on which owners tack thousands of dollars in speed-enhancing and cosmetic accessories. Then cut out pictures representing the European tuner cars like GTI and BMW M cars that are accessorized at the German factories. One GTI fan contrasted cutouts of Tweety Bird and a tuner "dude" wearing a chrome dollar-sign necklace to represent the Asian tuner "posers" with images of a black wolf and Ninja warrior depicting the "more authentic and serious" Euro tuner crowd.

Crispin's researchers then asked them to write epitaphs on 13 paper tombstones after the phrase "Here Lies the Japanese Hot Hatch," and recipes that begin with, "My perfect recipe for driving is . . ." One recipe reads: "One S-curve, a pinch of fishtail, two parts turbo toast, an ounce of hard rock music. Combine and bring to a boil." The strategy drawn from all this was to flog the GTI as tuned in Germany by speed-happy engineers rather than at some U.S. neighborhood retail joint.

In launching the GTI and reviving the Volkswagen brand 14 in general, Crispin faced two challenges. First, since the debut of the New Beetle, the VW brand has become feminized, says Keller. Loyal young males who were hanging on to VW by a thread needed to be reassured. Too many men had come to view VW as a "chick's brand." Worse, women were turning away from VW because of quality issues. Second, VW loyalists had become baffled about the pricey Phaeton and Touareg and loaded Jettas with price tags topping $30,000. A decade into the popularity of small SUVs priced under $25,000, VW has none. "Affordable German engineering is a huge part of VW's DNA, and these decisions really confused customers," says Tom Birk, Crispin vice president for research and planning.

Crispin's employee handbook says advertising is "anything 15 that makes our clients famous." So for the GTI, Bogusky and Keller are pulling no punches. This is a car built for driving fast and having fun. And for men, that inevitably leads to a certain amount of sex, they reckoned. That led to Helga, an over-the-top parody of a German nightclubbing valkyrie. She is in ads—and stars in VW's GTI Web site. Anyone configuring a GTI, choosing interior, wheels, engine, and the like, can take a virtual test drive with the boot-wearing siren, who comments about each driver's selections. "I see from your paddle shifters, you're ready to go." And, "I luf leather." There are some 500 variations of GTI, and Helga can talk you through them all.

16   Helga and Wolfgang, says Hicks, are an example of taking an audience to a place they didn't know they wanted to go. "A lot of advertisers try and mirror what the research tells them. What we do is try and make the brand part of the pop culture." Ads featuring Helga and Wolfgang ran on TV in March and April 2006, but now enthusiasts all over the Net are downloading them. In one, engineer Wolfgang is consulting a young owner with an oversized intake port on his hood that sucks air into the engine compartment. Says Helga: "It's definitely sucking." Thanks to the Internet, VW has been fielding requests for copies of these ads from media outlets and VW clubs as far away as India.

17   A spike in Net chatter will go only so far. Although VW ranked third from the bottom in J. D. Power & Associates' 2005 Initial Quality Survey, it improved from the year before—by 10 percent fewer glitches per 100 cars. VW's quality woes have spread around the Net as fast as Helga's double entendres. This month, says VW, it will post another big improvement, while dealers are reporting half as many warranty repairs on new models as they did in 2004.

SEXY SYMBOL

18   Despite its hasty execution, the campaign has already achieved what Martin hoped it would. "We needed to ignite a new conversation with owners," she says. The viral dimension has worked well. For about two weeks, VW ads were the top download from video-sharing site YouTube.com. Wolfgang and Helga have become part of the new VW story. They have sites on MySpace.com, where more than 7,500 fans have signed up as Helga's "friends" and are downloading a printable life-size Helga. "Bachelor parties, maybe," quips Keller.

19   Can Crispin's edgy playfulness go over the line? With the suggestive content, charges of sexism have followed. TV ads for the Winter Olympics depicted young men so into their GTIs that one refused to roll up the window to shield his girlfriend's wind-blown hair and told her to stop "yackin" so he could enjoy the engine's growl. Another refused to take his girlfriend on an errand in his GTI because her weight would slow him down. Ouch. Nissan's Wilhite says he's all for shaking up VW's message, "but I can't go along with ads that marginalize women like beer commercials often do." Suzanne Farley, a Boston education consultant and owner of a 1999 VW Passat, agrees, saying the ads "made me feel weird, like they were talking right past me." But the agency just introduced its first work for Miller Lite and junked the predictable frat-boy approach. Instead, icons like Burt Reynolds and Pittsburgh Steelers running back Jerome Bettis thoughtfully discuss "man laws," like how long to wait before dating a buddy's ex-girlfriend.

20   There's no doubt that Crispin and Volkswagen's Martin are out to take some risks, and that for now at least they have a long leash from management, which is doing its part to supply the right products. VW is moving fast under Pischetsrieder and Bernhard to bring out several new models in the next 20 months, including a minivan, two light SUVS, and two sports cars—the Eos convertible and a new interpretation of the 1970s and 1980s VW Scirocco—all priced under $30,000. A pricier sedan larger than the Passat is due, too, to try to hold on to aging boomer fans. It's the fastest product proliferation in VW history, and Crispin had better get a coherent strategy to reposition the entire brand before the new models arrive. "We are on a whole new timetable for getting this brand right and will move faster than people around here thought we could," says Bernhard.

21   In an industry that celebrates the slogan, that magical line of ad copy that crystallizes a brand's essence, Crispin hasn't yet hit on one for VW. It did, however, kill off VW's 10-year-old "Drivers wanted" line. "A slogan or tag line is not important if the messaging is right," says Bogusky. Still, Crispin likes the VW logo so much that it came up with a gimmick in the GTI ads in which Wolfgang forms the V and W with his interlocked fingers. That's already sticking online. People selling VWs on eBay, for example, have turned up in pictures in their cars making the hand sign.

22   Crispin may offer a new slogan sometime in 2007. For now, it's giving each model its own campaign. It just relaunched the Jetta with ads that are far from funky or sexy. In an about-face from its usual humorous tack, Crispin spotlights the car's top side-impact safety ratings. And like almost everything else the agency does, even these sober-as-a-judge ads have stirred conversation. In one, two couples are chatting as they drive away from a movie house. The driver is distracted and gets creamed by an SUV in real time. The effect on the TV viewer is jolting. The ad moves from the crash to the people standing by, shaky but unharmed, looking at the crushed car. A survivor says, "Holy . . ." and the ad cuts to a video frame that says "Safe Happens." Requests for Jetta brochures went up 30 percent after the ads' debut. And dozens of newspapers and NBC's *The Today Show* have reported on their jarring quality. "When [*Today Show* host] Matt Lauer talks for seven minutes about our ads, I know it's right," says Santa Monica (California) VW dealer Mike Sullivan. GTI sales are at 20-year highs, and VW sales overall are up 20 percent this year since Crispin's ads began.

Source: Reprinted with special permission from David Kiley, "The Craziest Ad Guys in America," *BusinessWeek*, May 22, 2006. Copyright © 2007 The McGraw-Hill Companies.

DISCUSSION QUESTIONS

1. How would you describe VW's new intended business strategy?

2. How would you describe VW's new advertising strategy?

3. Explain how effective you believe that the advertising strategy will be in helping to achieve the business strategy of VW in the long term.

4. Do you agree with Martin (paragraph 18) when he concludes that the advertising campaign achieved its goal of "igniting a new conversation with owners"?

5. If ad copy "crystallizes a brand's essence," what is the essence of VW? If it can be easily changed with a new ad campaign, what do we know about VW's business strategy?

VW's New Strategic Plan for the United States—Part 2

1 Volkswagen's experience in the United States has always been one of highs and lows. But rarely have its fortunes sunk so low as now. Less than a decade ago, the quirky reinvented Beetle helped VW come roaring back from a previous crisis. But for the past three years, its U.S. operations have lost close to $1 billion annually.

2 Now it's trying again to save the brand in the United States. To head U.S. operations, it's bringing in Stefan Jacoby, a German with close ties to VW chairman Martin Winterkorn and supervisory board chairman Ferdinand K. Piech, who took control of the company this year after a shakeup that left Porsche as VW's controlling shareholder. Jacoby, 49, an accountant by training, made his mark as head of VW's global sales and marketing. Since Jacoby took charge, the company boosted its European market share to 20.3 percent from 18.1 percent, helping keep it solidly in place as the Continent's leading brand. With its U.S. fortunes in long-term decline, Jacoby is facing his biggest challenge yet. His mission: to meet Winterkorn's target of breaking even in the United States by 2009.

3 Only a year ago, VW was gearing up a huge marketing campaign to relaunch a revamped Rabbit and Jetta in a bid to recapture its niche as the affordable, stylish European car of choice for younger buyers. VW hired former MINI USA marketing chief Kerri Martin, who recruited super-hot U.S. ad agency Crispin Porter + Bogusky. The plan, as chronicled in Part 1 of this case study, was to create a VW renaissance.

4 It didn't work out that way. A string of attention-grabbing adds—one campaign showed people surviving crashes unscathed and another starred a German dominatrix named Helga—did little to juice sales of VW's two most important models, the Jetta and the Passat. "I've never seen a brand struggle so hard to understand the U.S. market and fail so miserably," says Rebecca Lindland, a director at consulting firm Global Insight Inc. VW's sales slid to 235,000 last year, from 338,000 in 2002. Martin left in December 2006, part of a shakeup when Porsche took over.

5 Making matters worse is the perception in the United States that VW's quality lags versus its Japanese rivals. VW's interiors, for example, don't stand up to the kind of abuse they get from U.S. drivers, who do a lot more eating, drinking coffee, and applying makeup in their cars than Europeans do. That's one factor in J. D. Power & Associates Inc. ranking VW in the bottom 20 percent for reliability, quality, and service. "That really hurts VW when its young customer base does so much online comparative shopping," says Power Information Network analyst Tom Libby.

6 To turn operations around, Jacoby has to battle the punishingly high euro and VW's limited manufacturing presence in North America. Even more important, the company needs to introduce new models that build on its long tradition of quirkiness and connect with U.S. consumers. Instead, the carmaker's more recent offerings feel bland. Dealers think VW blew a golden opportunity when it chose not to introduce an updated version of the wildly popular Microbus from the 1960s and 1970s. Instead, the company is launching a repackaged, Volkswagen-branded, Chrysler minivan. Casey Gunther, VW's top-selling U.S. dealer, in Coconut Creek, Florida, is worried. "We're missing the funkiness" that U.S. buyers expect from VW, he says. "The Germans don't understand." And unlike in Europe, affluent buyers don't see VW as an aspirational brand.

7 Winterkorn vows the turnaround of the U.S. business is his "no. 1 priority." But there's only so long any management can put up with nearly $1 billion annual losses. Says one executive close to VW: "For the first time in some time, the phrase 'If we are to stay in the U.S.' precedes a lot of conversations at VW."

Source: Reprinted with special permission from David Kiley and Gail Edmondson, "Can VW Finally Find Its Way In America? A Last-Ditch Drive Must Correct Disastrous Turns to Make the U.S. Profitable Again," *BusinessWeek*, July 23, 2007. Copyright © 2007 The McGraw-Hill Companies.

DISCUSSION QUESTIONS

1. Does the trouble at VW suggest that VW executives confused business strategy with advertising (a non-strategic marketing activity)?

2. What are three essential elements that you would prefer to see in an ad campaign which would parallel the message in VW's business strategy?

3. To help answer the question of whether VW should plan to stay in the U.S., what information would executives need to consider?

4. How do you explain the relative success of VW in Europe (paragraph 2) given its failure in the U.S.?

5. Does this case teach us something about the classic debate over "style versus substance"? If it does, how does what you learned apply generally to formulating a business strategy?

Chapter **Eight**

Business Strategy

After reading and studying this chapter, you should be able to

1. Determine why a business would choose a low-cost, differentiation, or speed-based strategy.

2. Explain the nature and value of a market focus strategy.

3. Illustrate how a firm can pursue both low-cost and differentiation strategies.

4. Identify requirements for business success at different stages of industry evolution.

5. Determine good business strategies in fragmented and global industries.

6. Decide when a business should diversify.

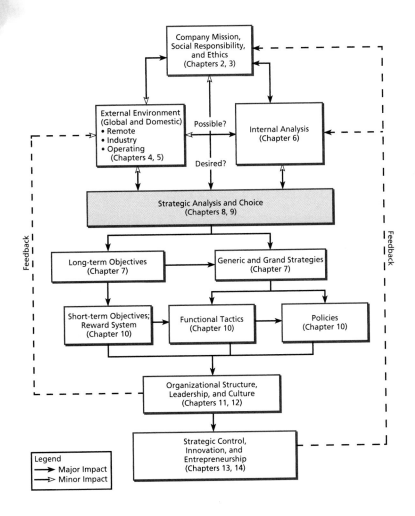

Strategic analysis and choice is the phase of the strategic management process in which business managers examine and choose a business strategy that allows their business to maintain or create a sustainable competitive advantage. Their starting point is to evaluate and determine which competitive advantages provide the basis for distinguishing the firm in the customer's mind from other reasonable alternatives. Businesses with a dominant product or service line must also choose among alternate grand strategies to guide the firm's activities, particularly when they are trying to decide about broadening the scope of the firm's activities beyond its core business. This chapter examines strategic analysis and choice in single- or dominant-product/service businesses by addressing two basic issues:

1. **What strategies are most effective at building sustainable competitive advantages for single business units?** What competitive strategy positions a business most effectively in its industry? For example, Scania, the most productive truck manufacturer in the world, joins its major rival Volvo as two anchors of Sweden's economy. Scania's return on sales of 9.9 percent far exceeds Mercedes (2.6 percent) and Volvo (2.5 percent), a level it has achieved most of the last 60 years. Scania has built a sustainable competitive advantage with a strategy of focusing solely on heavy transport vehicles in three geographic markets—Europe, Latin America, and Asia—by providing vehicles customized to specific tasks yet built using modularized components (20,000 components per vehicle versus 25,000 for Volvo and 40,000 for Mercedes). Scania is a low-cost producer of a differentiated heavy transport vehicle that can be custom-manufactured quickly and sold to a regionally focused market.

2. **Should dominant-product/service businesses diversify to build value and competitive advantage?** For example, Dell and Coca-Cola managers have examined the question of diversification and apparently concluded that continued concentration on their core products and services and development of new markets for those same core products and services are best. IBM and Pepsi examined the same question and concluded that concentric diversification and vertical integration were best. Why?

EVALUATING AND CHOOSING BUSINESS STRATEGIES: SEEKING SUSTAINED COMPETITIVE ADVANTAGE

Business managers evaluate and choose strategies that they think will make their business successful. Businesses become successful because they possess some advantage relative to their competitors. The two most prominent sources of competitive advantage can be found in the business's cost structure and its ability to differentiate the business from competitors. DisneyWorld in Orlando offers theme park patrons several unique, distinct features that differentiate it from other entertainment options. Costco offers retail customers the lowest prices on popular consumer items because they have created a low-cost structure that results in a competitive advantage over most competitors.

Businesses that create competitive advantages from one or both of these sources usually experience above-average profitability within their industry. Businesses that lack a cost or differentiation advantage usually experience average or below-average profitability. Two well-recognized studies found that businesses that do not have either form of competitive advantage perform the poorest among their peers, while businesses that possess both forms of competitive advantage enjoy the highest levels of profitability within their industry.[1]

---

[1] G. G. Dess and G. T. Lumpkin, "Emerging Issues in Strategy Process Research," in *Handbook of Strategic Management,* M. A. Hitt, R. E. Freeman, and J. S. Harrison (eds) (Oxford: Blackwell, 2001), pp. 3–34; and R. B. Robinson and J. A. Pearce, "Planned Patterns of Strategic Behavior and Their Relationship to Business Unit Performance," *Strategic Management Journal* 9, no. 1 (1988), pp. 43–60.

The average return on investment for more than 2,500 businesses across seven industries looked like this:

Differentiation Advantage	Cost Advantage	Overall Average ROI across Seven Industries
High	High	35.0%
Low	High	26.0
High	Low	22.0
Low	Low	9.5

Initially, managers were advised to evaluate and choose strategies that emphasized one type of competitive advantage. Often referred to as generic strategies, firms were encouraged to become either a differentiation-oriented or low-cost-oriented company. In so doing, it was logical that organizational members would develop a clear understanding of company priorities and, as these studies suggest, likely experience profitability superior to competitors without either a differentiation or low-cost orientation.

The studies mentioned here, and the experience of many other businesses, indicate that the highest profitability levels are found in businesses that possess both types of competitive advantage at the same time. In other words, businesses that have one or more resources/capabilities that truly differentiate them from key competitors and also have resources/capabilities that let them operate at a lower cost will consistently outperform their rivals that don't. So the challenge for today's business managers is to evaluate and choose business strategies based on core competencies and value chain activities that sustain both types of competitive advantage simultaneously. Exhibit 8.1, Strategy in Action, shows Honda Motor Company attempting to do just this in Europe.

Evaluating Cost Leadership Opportunities

Business success built on cost leadership requires the business to be able to provide its product or service at a cost below what its competitors can achieve. And it must be a sustainable cost advantage. Through the skills and resources identified in Exhibit 8.2, a business must be able to accomplish one or more activities in its value chain activities—procuring materials, processing them into products, marketing the products, and distributing the products or support activities—in a more cost-effective manner than that of its competitors or it must be able to reconfigure its value chain so as to achieve a cost advantage. Exhibit 8.2 provides examples of such **low-cost strategies.**

low-cost strategies
Business strategies that seek to establish long-term competitive advantages by emphasizing and perfecting value chain activities that can be achieved at costs substantially below what competitors are able to match on a sustained basis. This allows the firm, in turn, to compete primarily by charging a price lower than competitors can match and still stay in business.

Strategists examining their business's value chain for low-cost leadership advantages evaluate the sustainability of those advantages by benchmarking (refer to Chapter 6 for a discussion of this comparison technique) their business against key competitors and by considering the effect of any cost advantage on the five forces in their business's competitive environment. Low-cost activities that are sustainable and that provide one or more of these advantages relative to key industry forces should become a key basis for the business's competitive strategy:

Low-cost advantages that reduce the likelihood of pricing pressure from buyers
When key competitors cannot match prices from the low-cost leader, customers pressuring the leader risk establishing a price level that drives alternate sources out of business.

Truly sustained low-cost advantages may push rivals into other areas, lessening price competition Intense, continued price competition may be ruinous for all rivals, as seen occasionally in the airline industry.

Strategy in Action

Exhibit 8.1

Honda Pursues Young Buyers via Low-Cost Leadership and Differentiation Strategies

BusinessWeek

Honda is hot. In the United States, the Tokyo company can barely keep up with demand for models like the Acura MDX sport utility vehicle and the Odyssey minivan. North American sales have grown 60 percent in the last decade and its cost leadership is legendary: Honda earned $1,581 on every car sold in North America last year, versus $701 for General Motors.

But the road is not entirely smooth for the Japanese car maker. Honda Motor Co. has suffered a serious breakdown in Europe.

So Honda managers have gone into overdrive to repair the European business. Their game plan includes cost leadership initiatives: boosting capacity at two plants in Britain, heeding European calls for cars with diesel engines, and implementing a hard-nosed cost-cutting program that targets parts suppliers . . . and differentiation opportunities: launching an all-new car for the subcompact market.

The European problem, even against the background of record results in the United States, underscores Honda's fragility. Although less than 10 percent of Honda's global volume—and far less revenue—comes from Europe, the region has outsized importance to Honda executives. Why? Because Honda has no safe harbor if its sales in the United States begin to flag. The company earns some 90 percent of its profits in America, a far higher percentage than other Japanese car makers. "Honda is the least globally diverse Japanese automobile manufacturer," says Chris Redl, director of equity research at UBS Warburg's office in Tokyo. "It's a minor problem for now, but with the U.S. market heading down, it could become a major problem." So a closer look at the cost leadership and differentiation approach at Honda Europe, their confident answer, is as follows:

COST LEADERSHIP

Honda's struggles in Europe are partly the result of a key strategic error it made when it started making cars in Britain 10 years ago. Company officials didn't foresee the huge runup in the value of the British pound against Europe's single currency, the euro, which made its cars more expensive than competing models manufactured on the Continent. Subpar sales cut output in Britain last year to levels near 50 percent of capacity: it's impossible to make money at that production level. "Europe is definitely an Achilles' heel for Honda," says Toru Shimano, an analyst at Okasan Securities Co. in Tokyo.

So Honda is increasing purchases of cheaper parts from suppliers outside Britain and moving swiftly to freshen its lineup. Earlier in 2005, a remodeled and roomier five-door Civic hatchback with improved fuel efficiency rolled off production lines in Britain. To goose output at its British operations, Honda started exporting perky three-door Civic sedans built at its newest plant to the United States and Japan in 2005 and in 2007 began to export its British-made CR-V compact SUV to America to augment the Japan-made CR-Vs now being sold there.

DIFFERENTIATION

All of that will help, but Honda's big issue is the hole in its lineup: subcompacts. While one-liter-engine cars sell poorly in the United States, Europeans and Japanese can't get enough of them. "Honda does not have a product for Europe yet," says UBS Warburg's Redl. It missed out with its one-liter Logo. "It didn't stand out from the crowd," Honda executives admit.

So the Logo is history, and Honda's initial solution in Europe was a five-door hatchback called the Fit. At 1.3 liters, its engine outpowers Toyota's competing Vitz-class line of cars. Honda says the sporty Fit also boasts a number of nifty features, including that owners are able to flatten all four seats, including the driver's, at the flick of a switch—a selling point for youths keen to load bikes or sleep in it on long road trips. It recently added a compact hybrid Sports Concept car to target young European buyers interested in safe, sporty driving.

Sources: Reprinted with special permission from "Honda's Sporty Hybrid," *BusinessWeek*, March 14, 2007; and David Welch, "Honda's Drive for Young Buyers," *BusinessWeek*, February 21, 2005. Copyright © 2007 The McGraw-Hill Companies

New entrants competing on price must face an entrenched cost leader without the experience to replicate every cost advantage   EasyJet, a British start-up with a Southwest Airlines copycat strategy, entered the European airline market with much fanfare and low-priced, city-to-city, no-frills flights.

Analysts have cautioned for some time that British Airways, KLM's no-frills off-shoot (Buzz), and Virgin Express will simply match fares on easyJet's key routes and let high

Exhibit 8.2
Evaluating a
Business's Cost
Leadership
Opportunities

Source: Based on Michael Porter, *On Competition,* 1998, Harvard Business School Press.

A. Skills and Resources That Foster Cost Leadership

Sustained capital investment and access to capital
Process engineering skills
Intense supervision of labor or core technical operations
Products or services designed for ease of manufacture or delivery
Low-cost distribution system

B. Organizational Requirements to Support and Sustain Cost Leadership Activities

Tight cost control
Frequent, detailed control reports
Continuous improvement and benchmarking orientation
Structured organization and responsibilities
Incentives based on meeting strict, usually quantitative targets

C. Examples of Ways Businesses Achieve Competitive Advantage via Cost Leadership

Technology Development	Process innovations lower production costs	Product redesign reduces the number of components
Human Resource Management	Safety training for all employees reduces absenteeism, downtime, and accidents	
General Administration	Reduced levels of management cut corporate overhead	Computerized, integrated information system reduces errors and administrative costs
Procurement	Favorable long-term contracts; captive suppliers or key customer for supplier.	

Global, online suppliers provide automatic restocking of orders based on our sales.	Economy of scale in plant reduces equipment costs and depreciation.	Computerized routing lowers transportation expense.	Cooperative advertising with distributors creates local cost advantage in buying media space and time.	Subcontracted service technicians repair product correctly the first time or they bear all costs.
Inbound logistics	Operations	Outbound logistics	Marketing and Sales	Service

(Profit Margin)

landing fees and flight delays take their toll on the British upstart. Yet first-mover easyJet has survived and solidified its leadership position in the European airline industry's low-cost segment.[2]

Low-cost advantages should lessen the attractiveness of substitute products A serious concern of any business is the threat of a substitute product in which buyers can meet their original need. Low-cost advantages allow the holder to resist this happening because it allows them to remain competitive even against desirable substitutes, and it allows them to lessen concerns about price facing an inferior, lower-priced substitute.

Higher margins allow low-cost producers to withstand supplier cost increases and often gain supplier loyalty over time Sudden, particularly uncontrollable increases in the costs suppliers face can be more easily absorbed by low-cost, higher-margin producers. Severe

[2] "EasyJet Expands as Profits Soar," *BBC News,* November 14, 2006; and "Demand Boost Cuts easyJet Losses," *BBC News,* May 9, 2007.

droughts in California quadrupled the price of lettuce—a key restaurant demand. Some chains absorbed the cost; others had to confuse customers with a "lettuce tax." Furthermore, chains that worked well with produce suppliers gained a loyal, cooperative "partner" for possible assistance in a future, competitive situation.

Once managers identify opportunities to create cost advantage–based strategies, they must consider whether key risks inherent in cost leadership are present in a way that may mediate sustained success. The key risks with which they must be concerned are discussed next.

Many cost-saving activities are easily duplicated Computerizing certain order entry functions among hazardous waste companies gave early adopters lower sales costs and better customer service for a brief time. Rivals quickly adapted, adding similar capabilities with similar effects on their costs.

Exclusive cost leadership can become a trap Firms that emphasize lowest price and can offer it via cost advantages where product differentiation is increasingly not considered must truly be convinced of the sustainability of those advantages. Particularly with commodity-type products, the low-cost leader seeking to sustain a margin superior to lesser rivals may encounter increasing customer pressure for lower prices with great damage to both leader and lesser players.

Obsessive cost cutting can shrink other competitive advantages involving key product attributes Intense cost scrutiny can build margin, but it can reduce opportunities for or investment in innovation, processes, and products. Similarly, such scrutiny can lead to the use of inferior raw materials, processes, or activities that were previously viewed by customers as a key attribute of the original products. Some mail-order computer companies that sought to maintain or enhance cost advantages found reductions in telephone service personnel and automation of that function backfiring with a drop in demand for their products even though their low prices were maintained.

Cost differences often decline over time As products age, competitors learn how to match cost advantages. Absolute volumes sold often decline. Market channels and suppliers mature. Buyers become more knowledgeable. All of these factors present opportunities to lessen the value or presence of earlier cost advantages. Said another way, cost advantages that are not sustainable over a period of time are risky.

Once business managers have evaluated the cost structure of their value chain, determined activities that provide competitive cost advantages, and considered their inherent risks, they start choosing the business's strategy. Those managers concerned with differentiation-based strategies, or those seeking optimum performance incorporating both sources of competitive advantage, move to evaluating their business's sources of differentiation.

Evaluating Differentiation Opportunities

differentiation
A business strategy that seeks to build competitive advantage with its product or service by having it be "different" from other available competitive products based on features, performance, or other factors not directly related to cost and price. The difference would be one that would be hard to create and/or difficult to copy or imitate.

Differentiation requires that the business have sustainable advantages that allow it to provide buyers with something uniquely valuable to them. A successful differentiation strategy allows the business to provide a product or service of perceived higher value to buyers at a "differentiation cost" below the "value premium" to the buyers. In other words, the buyer feels the additional cost to buy the product or service is well below what the product or service is worth compared with other available alternatives.

Differentiation usually arises from one or more activities in the value chain that create a unique value important to buyers. Perrier's control of a carbonated water spring in France, Stouffer's frozen food packaging and sauce technology, Apple's control of iTunes download software that worked solely with iPods at first, American Greeting Card's automated

Exhibit 8.3

Evaluating a Business's Differentiation Opportunities

Source: Based on Michael Porter, *On Competition,* 1998, Harvard Business School Press.

A. Skills and Resources That Foster Differentiation

Strong marketing abilities
Product engineering
Creative talent and flair
Strong capabilities in basic research
Corporate reputation for quality or technical leadership
Long tradition in an industry or unique combination of skills drawn from other businesses
Strong cooperation from channels
Strong cooperation from suppliers of major components of the product or service

B. Organizational Requirements to Support and Sustain Differentiation Activities
Strong coordination among functions in R&D, product development, and marketing
Subjective measurement and incentives instead of quantitative measures
Amenities to attract highly skilled labor, scientists, and creative people
Tradition of closeness to key customers
Some personnel skilled in sales and operations—technical and marketing

C. Examples of Ways Businesses Achieve Competitive Advantage via Differentiation

Technology Development	Use cutting-edge production technology and product features to maintain a "distinct" image and actual product.
Human Resource Management	Develop programs to ensure technical competence of sales staff and a marketing orientation of service personnel.
General Administration	Develop comprehensive, personalized database to build knowledge of groups of customers and individual buyers to be used in "customizing" how products are sold, serviced, and replaced.
Procurement	Maintain quality control presence at key supplier facilities; work with suppliers' new-product development activities.

Purchase superior quality, well-known components, raising the quality and image of final products.	Carefully inspect products at each step in production to improve product performance and lower defect rate.	Coordinate JIT with buyers; use own or captive transportation service to ensure timeliness.	Build brand image with expensive, informative advertising and promotion.	Allow service personnel considerable discretion to credit customers for repairs.
Inbound logistics	Operations	Outbound logistics	Marketing and Sales	Service

Profit Margin

inventory system for retailers, and Federal Express's customer service capabilities are all examples of sustainable advantages around which successful differentiation strategies have been built. A business can achieve differentiation by performing its existing value activities or reconfiguring in some unique way. And the sustainability of that differentiation will depend on two things: a continuation of its high perceived value to buyers and a lack of imitation by competitors.

Exhibit 8.3 provides examples of the types of key skills and resources on which managers seeking to build differentiation-based strategies would base their underlying, sustainable competitive advantages. Examples of value chain activities that provide a differentiation advantage are also provided.

Strategists examining their business's resources and capabilities for differentiation advantages evaluate the sustainability of those advantages by benchmarking (refer to Chapter 6 for a discussion of this comparison technique) their business against key competitors and by considering the effect of any differentiation advantage on the five forces in their business's competitive environment. Sustainable activities that provide one or more of the following opportunities relative to key industry forces should become the basis for differentiation aspects of the business's competitive strategy:

Rivalry is reduced when a business successfully differentiates itself BMW's Z4, made in Greer, South Carolina, does not compete with Saturns made in central Tennessee. A Harvard education does not compete with an education from a local technical school. Both situations involve the same basic needs—transportation or education. However, one rival has clearly differentiated itself from others in the minds of certain buyers. In so doing, they do not have to respond competitively to that competitor.

Buyers are less sensitive to prices for effectively differentiated products The Highlands Inn in Carmel, California, and the Ventana Inn along the Big Sur charge a minimum of $600 and $900, respectively, per night for a room with a kitchen, fireplace, hot tub, and view. Other places are available along this beautiful stretch of California's spectacular coastline, but occupancy rates at these two locations remain over 90 percent. Why? You can't get a better view and a more relaxed, spectacular setting to spend a few days on the Pacific Coast. Similarly, buyers of differentiated products tolerate price increases low-cost-oriented buyers would not accept. The former become very loyal to certain brands. Harley Davidson motorcycles continue to rise in price, and its buyer base continues to expand worldwide, even though many motorcycle alternatives more reasonably priced are easily available.

Brand loyalty is hard for new entrants to overcome Many new beers are brought to market in the United States, but Budweiser continues to gain market share. Why? Brand loyalty is hard to overcome! And Anheuser-Busch has been clever to extend its brand loyalty from its core brand into newer niches, such as nonalcohol brews, that other potential entrants have pioneered.

Managers examining differentiation-based advantages must take potential risks into account as they commit their business to these advantages. Some of the more common ways risks arise are discussed next.

Imitation narrows perceived differentiation, rendering differentiation meaningless AMC pioneered the Jeep passenger version of a truck 40 years ago. Ford created the Explorer, or luxury utility vehicle, in 1990. It took luxury car features and put them inside a jeep. Ford's payoff was substantial. The Explorer became Ford's most popular domestic vehicle. However, virtually every vehicle manufacturer offered a luxury utility in 2006, with customers beginning to be hard pressed to identify clear distinctions between lead models. Ford's Explorer managers have sought to shape a new business strategy for the next decade that relies both on new sources of differentiation and placing greater emphasis on low-cost components in their value chain.

Technological changes that nullify past investments or learning The Swiss controlled more than 95 percent of the world's watch market into the 1970s. The bulk of the craftspeople, technology, and infrastructure resided in Switzerland. U.S.-based Texas Instruments decided to experiment with the use of its digital technology in watches. Swiss producers were not interested, but Japan's SEIKO and others were. In 2009, the Swiss will make less than 3 percent of the world's watches.

The cost difference between low-cost competitors and the differentiated business becomes too great for differentiation to hold brand loyalty Buyers may begin to choose to sacrifice some of the features, services, or image possessed by the differentiated business for large cost savings. The rising cost of a college education, particularly at several "premier" institutions, has caused many students to opt for lower-cost destinations that offer very similar courses without image, frills, and professors who seldom teach undergraduate students anyway.

Evaluating Speed as a Competitive Advantage

The cool design of the iPod is often cited as prima facie evidence of the product's greatness. But what you hear less about are the scores of little strategic decisions that were equally important in its speed-related tactics that ultimately made it a phenomenon. For instance, Apple licensed key technologies for the gadget's guts to accelerate its readiness for proto-type availability; it acquired, rather than wrote, the software that became iTunes for the same reason; and chief executive Steve Jobs set a demanding nine-month time line to get the first version done, which focused internal attention throughout the organization on the device and ensured speed to market. Altogether, those steps systematically "de-risked" the iPod launch by placing a key emphasis on *speed* and enabled the phenomenal success of Apple's $100 million bet.[3]

speed-based strategies
Business strategies built around functional capabilities and activities that allow the company to meet customer needs directly or indirectly more rapidly than its main competitors.

Speed-based strategies, or rapid responses to customer requests or market and technological changes, have become a major source of competitive advantage for numerous firms in today's intensely competitive global economy. Speed is certainly a form of differentiation, but it is more than that. Speed involves the *availability of a rapid response* to a customer by providing current products quicker, accelerating new-product development or improvement, quickly adjusting production processes, and making decisions quickly. While low cost and differentiation may provide important competitive advantages, managers in tomorrow's successful companies will base their strategies on creating speed-based competitive advantages. Exhibit 8.4 describes and illustrates key skills and organizational requirements that are associated with speed-based competitive advantage. Jack Welch, the now-retired CEO who transformed General Electric from a fading company into one of Wall Street's best performers over the past 25 years, had this to say about speed:

> Speed is really the driving force that everyone is after. Faster products, faster product cycles to market. Better response time to customers. . . . Satisfying customers, getting faster communications, moving with more agility, all these things are easier when one is small. And these are all characteristics one needs in a fast-moving global environment.[4]

Speed-based competitive advantages can be created around several activities:

Customer Responsiveness   All consumers have encountered hassles, delays, and frustration dealing with various businesses from time to time. The same holds true when dealing business to business. Quick response with answers, information, and solutions to mistakes can become the basis for competitive advantage—one that builds customer loyalty quickly.

Product Development Cycles   Japanese automakers have focused intensely on the time it takes to create a new model because several experienced disappointing sales growth in the last decade in Europe and North America competing against new vehicles like Ford's Explorer and Renault's Megane. VW had recently conceived, prototyped, produced, and marketed a totally new 4-wheel-drive car in Europe within 12 months. Honda, Toyota, and Nissan lowered their product development cycle from 24 months to 9 months from conception to production. This capability is old hat to 3M Corporation, which is so successful at speedy product development that one-fourth of its sales and profits each year are from products that didn't exist five years earlier.

Product or Service Improvements   Like development time, companies that can rapidly adapt their products or services and do so in a way that benefits their customers or creates new customers have a major competitive advantage over rivals that cannot do this.

Speed in Delivery or Distribution   Firms that can get you what you need when you need it, even when that is tomorrow, realize that buyers have come to expect that level of

---

[3] "Don't Worry, Be Ready," *BusinessWeek,* May 28, 2007.
[4] "Jack Welch: A CEO Who Can't Be Cloned," *BusinessWeek,* September 17, 2001.

Exhibit 8.4 **Evaluating a Business's Rapid Response (Speed) Opportunities**

A. Skills and Resources That Foster Speed

Process engineering skills
Excellent inbound and outbound logistics
Technical people in sales and customer service
High levels of automation
Corporate reputation for quality or technical leadership
Flexible manufacturing capabilities
Strong downstream partners
Strong cooperation from suppliers of major components of the product or service

B. Organizational Requirements to Support and Sustain Rapid Response Activities

Strong coordination among functions in R&D, product development, and marketing.
Major emphasis on customer satisfaction in incentive programs
Strong delegation to operating personnel
Tradition of closeness to key customers
Some personnel skilled in sales and operations—technical and marketing
Empowered customer service personnel

C. Examples of Ways Businesses Achieve Competitive Advantage via Speed

Technology Development	Use companywide technology sharing activities and autonomous product development teams to speed new-product development.				
Human Resource Management	Develop self-managed work teams and decision making at the lowest levels to increase responsiveness.				
General Administration	Develop highly automated and integrated information processing system. Include major buyers in the "system" on a real-time basis.				
Procurement	Integrate preapproved online suppliers into production.				
	Work very closely with suppliers to include their choice of warehouse location to minimize delivery time.	Standardize dies, components, and production equipment to allow quick changeover to new or special orders.	Ensure very rapid delivery with JIT delivery plus partnering with express mail services.	Use of laptops linked directly to operations to speed the order process and shorten the sales cycle.	Locate service technicians at customer facilities that are geographically close.
	Inbound logistics	Operations	Outbound logistics	Marketing and Sales	Service

Profit Margin

responsiveness. Federal Express's success reflects the importance customers place on speed in inbound and outbound logistics.

Information Sharing and Technology Speed in sharing information that becomes the basis for decisions, actions, or other important activities taken by a customer, supplier, or partner has become a major source of competitive advantage for many businesses. Telecommunications, the Internet, and networks are but a part of a vast infrastructure that is being used by knowledgeable managers to rebuild or create value in their businesses via information sharing.

These rapid response capabilities create competitive advantages in several ways. They create a way to lessen rivalry because they have *availability* of something that a rival may not have. It can allow the business to charge buyers more, engender loyalty, or otherwise enhance the business's position relative to its buyers. Particularly where impressive customer response is involved, businesses can generate supplier cooperation and concessions because their business ultimately benefits from increased revenue. Finally, substitute products and new entrants find themselves trying to keep up with the rapid changes rather than introducing them. Exhibit 8.5, Strategy in Action, provides examples of how "speed" can become a source of competitive advantage for your business or your customer.

While the notion of speed-based competitive advantage is exciting, it has risks managers must consider. First, speeding up activities that haven't been conducted in a fashion that prioritizes rapid response should only be done after considerable attention to training, reorganization, and/or reengineering. Second, some industries—stable, mature ones that have very minimal levels of change—may not offer much advantage to the firm that introduces some forms of rapid response. Customers in such settings may prefer the slower pace or the lower costs currently available, or they may have long time frames in purchasing such that speed is not that important to them.

Evaluating Market Focus as a Way to Competitive Advantage

market focus

This is a generic strategy that applies a differentiation strategy approach, or a low-cost strategy approach, or a combination—and does so solely in a narrow (or "focused") market niche rather than trying to do so across the broader market. The narrow focus may be geographically defined or defined by product type features, or target customer type, or some combination of these.

Small companies, at least the better ones, usually thrive because they serve narrow market niches. This is usually called **market focus,** the extent to which a business concentrates on a narrowly defined market. Take the example of Soho Beverages, a business former Pepsi manager Tom Cox bought from Seagram after Seagram had acquired it and was unable to make it thrive. The tiny brand, once a healthy niche product in New York and a few other East Coast locations, languished within Seagrams because its sales force was unused to selling in delis. Cox was able to double sales in one year. He did this on a lean marketing budget that didn't include advertising or database marketing. He hired Korean- and Arabic-speaking college students and had his people walk into practically every deli in Manhattan in order to reacquaint owners with the brand, spot consumption trends, and take orders. He provided rapid stocking services to all Manhattan-area delis, regardless of size. The business has continued sales growth at more than 50 percent per year. Why? Cox says, "It is attributable to focusing on a niche market, delis; differentiating the product and its sales force; achieving low costs in promotion and delivery; and making rapid, immediate response to any deli owner request its normal practice."[5]

Two things are important in this example. First, this business focused on a narrow niche market in which to build a strong competitive advantage. But focus alone was not enough to build competitive advantage. Rather, Cox created several capabilities, resources, and value chain activities that achieved differentiation, low-cost, and rapid response competitive advantages within this niche market that would be hard for other firms, particularly mass market–oriented firms, to replicate.

Market focus allows some businesses to compete on the basis of low cost, differentiation, and rapid response against much larger businesses with greater resources. Focus lets a business "learn" its target customers—their needs, special considerations they want accommodated—and establish personal relationships in ways that "differentiate" the smaller firm or make it more valuable to the target customer. Low costs can also be achieved, filling niche needs in a buyer's operations that larger rivals either do not want to bother with or cannot do as cost effectively. Cost advantage often centers around the high level of customized service the focused, smaller business can provide. And perhaps the greatest competitive weapon that can arise is rapid response. With enhanced knowledge of its customers and intricacies of their operations, the small, focused company builds up organizational knowledge about timing-sensitive ways to work with a customer. Often the needs of that narrow

[5] Michael Porter, *On Competition* (Boston: Harvard Business School Press, 1998), p. 57.

The Pitch for Speed

BusinessWeek

Time is money, sure. But customers are increasingly more interested in saving time than they are in saving money. Incorporating one or more of the six benefits below in what you sell, or what your customer seeks to sell, is a potential source of competitive advantage for one or both of you.

1. **Faster to Market.** If you can show how your offering will help your customer get a new product or service ready to sell faster than competitive offerings, you will be giving them a competitive advantage. Don't forget that you may be competing against their in-house resources, too. Portal Player helped accelerate the launch of the iPod and iTunes by selling Apple its software to manage music via the net. Portal Player helped Apple gain competitive advantage. Apple's programmers may have had better ideas, but time to market was the key consideration.

2. **Faster Results.** Customers want instant results. Perhaps you can show them how they can measure the results of a marketing campaign or manufacturing process faster than before by using your offering. You can explain that by speeding up the process, they can make corrections sooner, which decreases error rates and waste. Many online advertisers sell this benefit, but you can apply it to almost any process. Many a kiosk was bought by an airline, a bank, or other users because it offered them the benefit of offering their customer faster results.

3. **Faster to Operate.** If you sell equipment that can produce more widgets per hour, offer it as a valuable benefit to your customer. Find out if your customers need more production power at certain peak times, such as over holidays or during the summer months. You could offer to save them costly overtime or outsourcing expenses.

4. **Faster to Train.** If your customer's business has high employee turnover, sell the offering based on its learning curve and ease of use. After all, if your customers have to wait to train their employees, they're losing precious efficiency and productivity. For an offering that takes more time to learn to use, offer a training DVD or a Webinar employees can watch any time. It may be enough to win the order for you.

5. **Faster to Modify, Upgrade, or Customize.** Customers know their needs will change over time, but they want to get the longest useful life out of their purchases. If you sell accounting software, for example, show your customers how easy it is to upgrade when tax rates or withholding tables change. Apply the same idea to all types of equipment.

6. **Faster to Deliver or Install.** Sometimes, the first seller to be able to deliver wins the order. I've bought expensive items simply because they were in stock, and you probably have, too. If your customer can begin saving money or earning more revenue very soon after they buy from you, use this benefit to close them.

Source: Reprinted with special permission from "The Pitch for Speed," *BusinessWeek*, May 7, 2007. Copyright © 2007 The McGraw-Hill Companies.

set of customers represent a large part of the small, focused business's revenues. Exhibit 8.6, Top Strategist, illustrates how Ireland's Ryanair has become the European leader in discount air travel via the focused application of low cost, differentiation, and speed.

The risk of focus is that you attract major competitors who have waited for your business to "prove" the market. Domino's proved that a huge market for pizza delivery existed and now faces serious challenges. Likewise, publicly traded companies built around focus strategies become takeover targets for large firms seeking to fill out a product portfolio. And perhaps the greatest risk of all is slipping into the illusion that it is focus itself, and not some special form of low cost, differentiation, or rapid response, that is creating the business's success.

Managers evaluating opportunities to build competitive advantage should link strategies to resources, capabilities, and value chain activities that exploit low cost, differentiation, and rapid response competitive advantages. When advantageous, they should consider ways to use focus to leverage these advantages. One way business managers can enhance their likelihood of identifying these opportunities is to consider several different "generic" industry environments from the perspective of the typical value chain activities most often linked to sustained competitive advantages in those unique industry situations. The next section discusses key generic industry environments and the value chain activities most associated with success.

Stages of Industry Evolution and Business Strategy Choices

The requirements for success in industry segments change over time. Strategists can use these changing requirements, which are associated with different stages of industry evolution, as a way to isolate key competitive advantages and shape strategic choices around them. Exhibit 8.7 depicts four stages of industry evolution and the typical functional capabilities that are often associated with business success at each of these stages.

Competitive Advantage and Strategic Choices in Emerging Industries

emerging industry
An industry that has growing sales across all the companies in the industry based on growing demand for the relatively new products, technologies, and/or services made available by the firms participating in this industry.

Emerging industries are newly formed or re-formed industries that typically are created by technological innovation, newly emerging customer needs, or other economic or sociological changes. **Emerging industries** of the last decade have been the Internet social networking, satellite radio, surgical robotics, and online services industries.

From the standpoint of strategy formulation, the essential characteristic of an emerging industry is that there are no "rules of the game." The absence of rules presents both a risk and an opportunity—a wise strategy positions the firm to favorably shape the emerging industry's rules.

Business strategies must be shaped to accommodate the following characteristics of markets in emerging industries:

- Technologies that are mostly proprietary to the pioneering firms and technological uncertainty about how product standardization will unfold.
- Competitor uncertainty because of inadequate information about competitors, buyers, and the timing of demand.
- High initial costs but steep cost declines as the experience curve takes effect.
- Few entry barriers, which often spurs the formation of many new firms.
- First-time buyers requiring initial inducement to purchase and customers confused by the availability of a number of nonstandard products.
- Inability to obtain raw materials and components until suppliers gear up to meet the industry's needs.
- Need for high-risk capital because of the industry's uncertainty prospects.

For success in this industry setting, business strategies require one or more of these features:

1. The ability to *shape the industry's structure* based on the timing of entry, reputation, success in related industries or technologies, and role in industry associations.
2. The ability to *rapidly improve product quality* and performance features.
3. *Advantageous relationships* with key suppliers and promising distribution channels.
4. The ability to *establish the firm's technology as the dominant one* before technological uncertainty decreases.
5. The early acquisition of *a core group of loyal customers* and then the expansion of that customer base through model changes, alternative pricing, and advertising.
6. The ability to *forecast future competitors* and the strategies they are likely to employ.

A firm that has had repeated successes with business in emerging industries is 3M Corporation. In each of the past 20 years, more than 25 percent of 3M's annual sales have come

Top Strategist
Michael O'Leary, CEO of Ryanair

Exhibit
8.6

Michael O'Leary, CEO of Ryanair

It was vintage Michael O'Leary. Outfitting his staff in full combat gear, O'Leary drove an old World War II tank to England's Luton airport and demanded access to the base of archrival easyJet Airline Co. With military theme music blaring, O'Leary declared he was "liberating the public from easyJet's high fares." When security—surprise!—refused to let the Ryanair armor roll in, O'Leary led the troops in his own rendition of a platoon march song: "I've been told and it's no lie. easyJet's fares are way too high!"

Buffoonery? Of course. But "O'Leary and his management team are absolutely the best at adopting a focus strategy and sticking to it relentlessly," said Ryanair's chairman David Bonderman.

Ryanair's focus strategy has key differentiation, low cost, and speed elements allowing it to far out-pace European airline competitors. They are as follows:

DIFFERENTIATION

Ryanair flies to small, secondary airports outside major European cities. Often former military bases are attractive access points to European tourists, which the airports and small towns encourage. Virtually all of its rivals, including discount rival easyJet, focus on business travelers and major international airports in Europe's largest cities. Its fares average 30 percent less than rival easyJet and are far lower than major European airlines. And Ryanair, one of Europe's leading e-tailers, Ryanair.com, sells more than 95 percent of its tickets online and has hooked

(continued)

from products that did not exist five years earlier. Start-up companies enhance their success by having experienced entrepreneurs at the helm, a knowledgeable management team and board of directors, and patient sources of venture capital. Steven Jobs's dramatic unveiling of Apple's iPod came to be seen by many as the catalyst for the emergence of a new personalized digital music industry. Jobs and Apple certainly took advantage by building a strategy that shaped the industry's structure, established the firm's technology as a dominant one, endeared themselves to a core group of loyal customers, and rapidly improved the product quality and Internet-based music service.

Competitive Advantages and Strategic Choices in Growing Industries

growth industry strategies
Business strategies that may be more advantageous for firms participating in rapidly growing industries and markets.

Rapid growth brings new competitors into the industry. Oftentimes, those new entrants are large competitors with substantial resources who have waited for the market to "prove" itself before they committed significant resources. At this stage, **growth industry strategies** that emphasize brand recognition, product differentiation, and the financial resources to support both heavy marketing expenses and the effect of price competition on cash flow can be key strengths. Accelerating demand means scaling up production or service capacity to meet the growing demand. Doing so may place a premium on being able to adapt product design and production facilities to meet rapidly increasing demand effectively. Increased investment in plant and equipment, in research and development (R&D), and especially marketing efforts to target specific customer groups along with developing strong distribution capabilities place a demand on the firm's capital resources.

Exhibit 8.6 cont.

up with hotel chains, car rentals, life insurers, and mobile phone companies to offer one-stop shopping to the European leisure traveler.

LOW COST

Ryanair bought 100 new Boeing 737-800s less than a year after placing an order for 150 next-generation 737s. Boeing offered Ryanair 40 percent off list price, significantly lowering Ryanair's cost of capital, maintenance costs, and operating expenses. Ryanair's differentiation choice of flying mainly to small, secondary airports outside major European cities has led to sweetheart deals on everything from landing and handling fees to marketing support. Less congestion lets Ryanair significantly lower personnel costs and the time a plane stays on the ground compared with rivals. Ryanair sells snacks and rents the back of seats and overhead storage to advertisers.

SPEED

Ryanair's Ryanair.com sells more than 95 percent of its tickets quickly and conveniently for customers seeking simplicity, speed, and convenience. Its large purchases from Boeing allow it to grow to additional airports at a rate of about 30 percent annually. Its use of less congested airports allows Ryanair to get its planes back in the air in 25 minutes—half the time it takes competitors at major airports. This lets Ryanair provide significantly more frequent flights, which simplifies and adds time-saving convenience for the leisure traveler and business traveler.

FOCUS

O'Leary continues to focus like a light beam on small outlying airports and leisure travelers with speedy, low-cost services. "I've always been a transport innovator," he jokes. Millions of Europeans flying Ryanair planes would agree.

Sources: Reprinted with special permission from "Wal-Mart With Wings," *BusinessWeek,* November 27, 2006; "Ryanair Down Amid Dispute with Pilots," *BusinessWeek,* March 30, 2005; Stanley Holmes, "An Updraft for Boeing and Airbus," *BusinessWeek,* October 20, 2004 and Kerry Capell, "Ryanair Rising," *BusinessWeek,* June 2, 2003. Copyright © 2006 The McGraw-Hill Companies.

For success in this industry setting, business strategies require one or more of these features:

1. The ability to *establish strong brand recognition* through promotional resources and skills that increase selective demand.
2. The ability and resources to *scale up to meet increasing demand,* which may involve production facilities, service capabilities, and the training and logistics associated with that capacity.
3. *Strong product design skills* to be able to adapt products and services to scaled operations and emerging market niches.
4. The ability to *differentiate the firm's product[s]* from competitors entering the market.
5. *R&D resources and skills* to create product variations and advantages.
6. The ability to *build repeat buying from established customers* and attract new customers.
7. Strong capabilities in *sales and marketing.*

IBM entered the personal computer market—which Apple pioneered in the growth stage—and was able to rapidly become the market leader with a strategy based on its key strengths in brand awareness and possession of the financial resources needed to support consumer advertising. Many large technology companies today prefer exactly this approach: to await proof of an industry or product market and then to acquire small pioneer firms with first-mover advantage as a means to obtain an increasingly known

EXHIBIT 8.7   Sources of Distinctive Competence at Different Stages of Industry Evolution

Functional Area	Introduction	Growth	Maturity	Decline
Marketing	Resources/skills to create widespread awareness and find acceptance from customers; advantageous access to distribution	Ability to establish brand recognition, find niche, reduce price, solidify strong distribution relations, and develop new channels	Skills in aggressively promoting products to new markets and holding existing markets; pricing flexibility; skills in differentiating products and holding customer loyalty	Cost-effective means of efficient access to selected channels and markets; strong customer loyalty or dependence; strong company image
Production operations	Ability to expand capacity effectively, limit number of designs, develop standards	Ability to add product variants, centralize production, or otherwise lower costs; ability to improve product quality; seasonal subcontracting capacity	Ability to improve product and reduce costs; ability to share or reduce capacity; advantageous supplier relationships; subcontracting	Ability to prune product line; cost advantage in production, location or distribution; simplified inventory control; subcontracting or long production runs

Unit sales

Profit (dollars)

Growth rate ≤ 0

brand, or to acquire technical know-how and experience behind which the firms can put its resources and distribution strength to build brand identify and loyalty. In 2005 as the PC market matured, IBM sold its PC division to a Chinese company and now outsources its PCs.

Competitive Advantages and Strategic Choices in Mature Industry Environments

As an industry evolves, its rate of growth eventually declines. This "transition to maturity" is accompanied by several changes in its competitive environment: Competition for market share becomes more intense as firms in the industry are forced to achieve sales growth at one another's expense. Firms working with the **mature industry strategies** sell increasingly to experienced, repeat buyers who are now making choices among known alternatives. Competition becomes more oriented to cost and service as knowledgeable buyers expect similar price and product features. Industry capacity "tops out" as sales growth ceases to cover up poorly planned expansions. New products and new applications are harder to come by. International competition increases as cost pressures lead to overseas production advantages. Profitability falls, often permanently, as a result of pressure to lower prices and the increased costs of holding or building market share. Exhibit 8.8, Strategy in Action, looks at how American Patricia Russo is trying to craft a turnaround

mature industry strategies
Strategies used by firms competing in markets where the growth rate of that market from year to year has reached or is close to zero.

EXHIBIT 8.7 *(continued)*

Functional Area	Introduction	Growth	Maturity	Decline
Finance	Resources to support high net cash overflow and initial losses; ability to use leverage effectively	Ability to finance rapid expansion, to have net cash outflows but increasing profits; resources to support product improvements	Ability to generate and redistribute increasing net cash inflows; effective cost control systems	Ability to reuse or liquidate unneeded equipment; advantage in cost of facilities; control system accuracy; stream-lined management control
Personnel	Flexibility in staffing and training new management; existence of employees with key skills in new products or markets	Existence of an ability to add skilled personnel; motivated and loyal workforce	Ability to cost effec-tively, reduce workforce, increase efficiency	Capacity to reduce and reallocate personnel; cost advantage
Engineering and research and development	Ability to make engi-neering changes, have technical bugs in product and process resolved	Skill in quality and new feature develop-ment; ability to start developing successor product	Ability to reduce costs, develop variants, differentiate products	Ability to support other grown areas or to apply product to unique customer needs
Key functional area and strategy focus	Engineering: market penetration	Sales: consumer loyalty; market share	Production efficiency; successor products	Finance; maximum investment recovery

strategy for French-based Alcatel-Lucent in the maturing global telecommunications equipment industry.

These changes necessitate a fundamental strategic reassessment. Strategy elements of successful firms in maturing industries often include the following:

1. *Product line* pruning, or dropping unprofitable product models, sizes, and options from the firm's product mix.
2. *Emphasis on process innovation* that permits low-cost product design, manufacturing methods, and distribution synergy.
3. *Emphasis on cost reduction* through exerting pressure on suppliers for lower prices, switching to cheaper components, introducing operational efficiencies, and lowering administrative and sales overhead.
4. *Careful buyer selection* to focus on buyers who are less aggressive, more closely tied to the firm, and able to buy more from the firm.
5. *Horizontal integration* to acquire rival firms whose weaknesses can be used to gain a bargain price and that are correctable by the acquiring firms.
6. *International expansion* to markets where attractive growth and limited competition still exist and the opportunity for lower-cost manufacturing can influence both domestic and international costs.

Hard Times at Alcatel-Lucent

Alcatel-Lucent Chief Executive Patricia Russo is running out of time. Less than a year after the American woman took the top job at the Paris telecom equipment maker, she leads and Alcatel that is in free fall. Five years after the global telecom meltdown and in a maturing telecom equipment industry, news from Alcatel just keeps getting worse, and Alcatel's board called an emergency meeting to ask Russo to present a turnaround plan within 30 days.

Can Russo, the U.S.-born former boss of Lucent, pull the merged company out of this tailspin? Can she even hold onto her job? What are key elements of their strategy in a maturing industry that might work, or that may not?

HORIZONTAL INTEGRATION AND INTERNATIONAL EXPANSION

French Alcatel and U.S.-based Lucent agreed to merge a few years ago as a mutual horizontal integration strategy seeking to become more competitive in a maturing industry. Second, each represented a chance to reach international markets already served by the other partner. Five years later, the combined company has yet to see the benefits hoped for in this original combination. A decision made on Russo's watch—the recent acquisition of Nortel's next-generation wireless business—has compounded the problems in Europe, because integrating the new business has hampered Alcatel-Lucent's ability to fight off aggressive competitors.

COST REDUCTION

Russo has embarked on a cost-cutting plan to save $2.5 billion over the next three years. Only a day before the recent profit warning, the company concluded negotiations with French unions to cut more than 1,400 jobs. But cost-cutting won't remedy the worsening problem of its wireless business, whose troubles first emerged after the acquisition of the additional wireless business.

PRODUCT LINE PRUNING

Already, some industry watchers are talking about jettisoning big parts of the company—and Russo herself. "There are serious questions about Pat's viability as CEO," says Richard Windsor, a London-based analyst. There's growing consensus that the company will have to sell off its wireless business, including European operations formerly held by Alcatel, and U.S. holdings that once belonged to Lucent. Some analysts are calling for even more drastic steps. Per Lindberg, a London analyst, says the company should sell Bell Labs—which it inherited from Lucent—while eliminating 30,000 jobs, more than twice the 12,000 layoffs that the company has already forecast.

Business strategists in maturing industries must avoid several pitfalls. First, they must make a clear choice among the three generic strategies and avoid a middle-ground approach, which would confuse both knowledgeable buyers and the firm's personnel. Second, they must avoid sacrificing market share too quickly for short-term profit. Finally, they must avoid waiting too long to respond to price reductions, retaining unneeded excess capacity, engaging in sporadic or irrational efforts to boost sales, and placing their hopes on "new" products, rather than aggressively selling existing products.

Competitive Advantages and Strategic Choices in Declining Industries

declining industry
An industry in which the trend of total sales as an indicator of total demand for an industry's products or services among all the participants in the industry have started to drop from the last several years with the likelihood being that such a trend will continue indefinitely.

Declining industries are those that make products or services for which demand is growing slower than demand in the economy as a whole or is actually declining. This slow growth or decline in demand is caused by technological substitution (such as the substitution of electronic calculators for slide rules), demographic shifts (such as the increase in the number of older people and the decrease in the number of children), and shifts in needs (such as the decreased need for red meat).

Firms in a declining industry should choose strategies that emphasize one or more of the following themes:

1. *Focus* on segments within the industry that offer a chance for higher growth or a higher return.
2. *Emphasize product innovation and quality improvement,* where this can be done cost effectively, to differentiate the firm from rivals and to spur growth.
3. *Emphasize production and distribution efficiency* by streamlining production, closing marginal production facilities and costly distribution outlets, and adding effective new facilities and outlets.
4. *Gradually harvest the business*—generate cash by cutting down on maintenance, reducing models, and shrinking channels and make no new investment.

Strategists who incorporate one or more of these themes into the strategy of their business can anticipate relative success, particularly where the industry's decline is slow and smooth and some profitable niches remain. Penn Tennis, the nation's no. 1 maker of tennis balls, watched industrywide sales steadily decline over the last decade. In response it started marketing tennis balls as "dog toys" in the rapidly growing pet products industry. It secondly made Penn balls the official ball at major tournaments. Third, it created three different quality levels; then, as sales revived, Penn Sports sold its tennis ball business to Head Sports.

Competitive Advantage in Fragmented Industries

fragmented industry
An industry in which there are numerous competitors (providers of the same or similar products or services the industry involves) such that no single firm or small group of firms controls any significant share of the overall industry sales.

Fragmented industries are another setting in which identifiable types of competitive advantages and the strategic choices suggested by those advantages can be identified. A **fragmented industry** is one in which no firm has a significant market share and can strongly influence industry outcomes. Fragmented industries are found in many areas of the economy and are common in such areas as professional services, retailing, distribution, wood and metal fabrication, and agricultural products. The funeral industry is an example of a highly fragmented industry. Business strategists in fragmented industries pursue low-cost or differentiation strategies or focus competitive advantages in one of five ways:

Tightly Managed Decentralization   Fragmented industries are characterized by a need for intense local coordination, a local management orientation, high personal service, and local autonomy. Recently, however, successful firms in such industries have introduced a high degree of professionalism into the operations of local managers.

"Formula" Facilities   This alternative, related to the previous one, introduces standardized, efficient, low-cost facilities at multiple locations. Thus, the firm gradually builds a low-cost advantage over localized competitors. Fast-food and motel chains have applied this approach with considerable success.

Increased Value Added   The products or services of some fragmented industries are difficult to differentiate. In this case, an effective strategy may be to add value by providing more service with the sale or by engaging in some product assembly that is of additional value to the customer.

Specialization   Focus strategies that creatively segment the market can enable firms to cope with fragmentation. Specialization can be pursued by

1. *Product type.* The firm builds expertise focusing on a narrow range of products or services.
2. *Customer type.* The firm becomes intimately familiar with and serves the needs of a narrow customer segment.

3. *Type of order.* The firm handles only certain kinds of orders, such as small orders, custom orders, or quick turnaround orders.
4. *Geographic area.* The firm blankets or concentrates on a single area.

Although specialization in one or more of these ways can be the basis for a sound focus strategy in a fragmented industry, each of these types of specialization risks limiting the firm's potential sales volume.

Bare Bones/No Frills Given the intense competition and low margins in fragmented industries, a "bare bones" posture—low overhead, minimum wage employees, tight cost control—may build a sustainable cost advantage in such industries.

Competitive Advantage in Global Industries

Global industries present a final setting in which success is often associated with identifiable sources of competitive advantage. A **global industry** is one that comprises firms whose competitive positions in major geographic or national markets are fundamentally affected by their overall global competitive positions. To avoid strategic disadvantages, firms in global industries are virtually required to compete on a worldwide basis. Oil, steel, automobiles, apparel, motorcycles, televisions, and computers are examples of global industries.

global industry
Industry in which competition crosses national borders.

Global industries have four unique strategy-shaping features:

- Differences in prices and costs from country to country due to currency exchange fluctuations, differences in wage and inflation rates, and other economic factors.
- Differences in buyer needs across different countries.
- Differences in competitors and ways of competing from country to country.
- Differences in trade rules and governmental regulations across different countries.

These unique features and the global competition of global industries require that two fundamental components be addressed in the business strategy: (1) the approach used to gain global market coverage and (2) the generic competitive strategy. Three basic options can be used to pursue global market coverage:

1. *License* foreign firms to produce and distribute the firm's products.
2. *Maintain a domestic production base* and export products to foreign countries.
3. *Establish foreign-based plants and distribution* to compete directly in the markets of one or more foreign countries.

Along with the market coverage decision, strategists must scrutinize the condition of the global industry features identified earlier to choose among four generic global competitive strategies:

1. *Broad-line global competition*—directed at competing worldwide in the full product line of the industry, often with plants in many countries, to achieve differentiation or an overall low-cost position.
2. *Global focus* strategy—targeting a particular segment of the industry for competition on a worldwide basis.
3. *National focus* strategy—taking advantage of differences in national markets that give the firm an edge over global competitors on a nation-by-nation basis.
4. *Protected niche* strategy—seeking out countries in which governmental restraints exclude or inhibit global competitors or allow concessions, or both, that are advantageous to localized firms.

Old World French Steelmaker Vallourec Crafts a New Global Focus Strategy

BusinessWeek

With sky-high labor costs, a 35-hour workweek, and a surging currency, France hardly seems the kind of place where an export-focused manufacturer might prosper. Yet specialty steelmaker Vallourec, based just outside Paris, is not only beating the odds, it's performing so well that it landed the top spot on the European BW50 list.

Vallourec, which traces its roots to nineteenth-century mill towns in Burgundy and northern France, illustrates how some of Europe's quintessentially old economy companies are learning to compete in the new, globalized world. Until the 1990s, Vallourec was a hodgepodge of businesses ranging from construction and engineering to metallurgy and steelmaking, and its growth was anemic. Since then, it has shed peripheral operations to focus on its most profitable products: steel pipes used in oil drilling and electric power plants. "We have oriented ourselves to the high end of the market," says Pierre Verluca, chairman of Vallourec's management board.

Vallourec has also gone global. Seven years ago, all its factories were in Europe. But it now makes some 35 percent of its pipes in Texas and in Brazil and is expanding operations in China and India. That offers it a crucial hedge against the strong euro because about 60 percent of its sales are outside of Europe.

The result: earnings last year rose 58 percent, to $1.36 billion, on sales that were up 29 percent, to $7.5 billion. That has helped boost shares more than sixfold over the past two years, to 280 from 38. Recent rumors that Vallourec could be a takeover target for newly merged Arcelor Mittal have added bounce to its share price, although neither company has confirmed talks.

Of course, Vallourec has profited from high oil prices that fueled a boom in oil exploration. But it is also offering new services such as pipe installation and maintenance. Innovation is another key to Vallourec's success. The company has invested millions to develop high-pressure piping for the next generation of power plants. Expanding this business, which now accounts for 16 percent of sales, hedges against the possibility of an oil and gas slump.

Still, Vallourec can't afford to rest. It is keeping a close eye on China, where a quickly modernizing steel industry could provide a low-cost challenge. For now, though, oil companies are willing to pay extra for Vallourec's quality and reliability. "The cost of the pipe, even though it's expensive, is a fraction of the cost of a failure" in the oil field. So, an Old World company that makes steel pipes. It may not sound that exciting—unless, that is, you're a Vallourec investor who has ridden its success to riches.

Source: Reprinted with special permission from Carol Matlack, "Steel Beats the Odds," *BusinessWeek, Europe,* May 3, 2007. Copyright © 2007 The McGraw-Hill Companies.

Competing in a global context has become a reality for most businesses in virtually every economy around the world. So most firms must consider among the global competitive strategies identified above. Exhibit 8.9, Strategy in Action, describes how an "Old World" French steelmaker did just this to craft a global focus strategy selling steel pipe worldwide and in the process increase its market value sevenfold in five short years.

DOMINANT PRODUCT/SERVICE BUSINESSES: EVALUATING AND CHOOSING TO DIVERSIFY TO BUILD VALUE

McDonald's has frequently looked at numerous opportunities to diversify into related businesses or to acquire key suppliers. Its decision has consistently been to focus on its core business using the grand strategies of concentration, market development, and product development. Rival Yum Brands, on the other hand, has chosen to diversify into related businesses and vertical integration as the best grand strategies for it to build long-term value. Both firms experienced unprecedented success during the last 20 years.

Many dominant product businesses face this question as their core business proves successful: What grand strategies are best suited to continue to build value? Under what circumstances should they choose an expanded focus (diversification, vertical integration); steady

Exhibit 8.10   **Grand Strategy Selection Matrix**

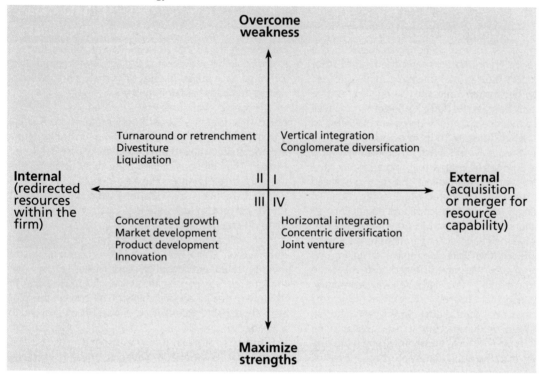

---

grand strategy selection matrix
A four-cell guide to strategies based upon whether the business is (1) operating from a position of strength or weakness and (2) rely on its own resources versus having to acquire resources via merger or acquisition.

vertical integration
Acquisition of firms that supply inputs such as raw materials, or customers for its outputs, such as warehouses for finished products.

conglomerate diversification
Acquiring or entering businesses unrelated to a firm's current technologies, markets, or products.

continued focus (concentration, market or product development); or a narrowed focus (turnaround or divestiture)? This section examines two ways you can analyze a dominant product company's situation and choose among 12 grand strategies identified in Chapter 7.

Grand Strategy Selection Matrix

One valuable guide to the selection of a promising grand strategy is the **grand strategy selection matrix** shown in Exhibit 8.10. The basic idea underlying the matrix is that two variables are of central concern in the selection process: (1) the principal purpose of the grand strategy and (2) the choice of an internal or external emphasis for growth or profitability.

In the past, planners were advised to follow certain rules or prescriptions in their choice of strategies. Now, most experts agree that strategy selection is better guided by the conditions of the planning period and by the company strengths and weaknesses. It should be noted, however, that even the early approaches to strategy selection sought to match a concern over internal versus external growth with a desire to overcome weaknesses or maximize strengths.

The same considerations led to the development of the grand strategy selection matrix. A firm in quadrant I, with "all its eggs in one basket," often views itself as over-committed to a particular business with limited growth opportunities or high risks. One reasonable solution is **vertical integration,** which enables the firm to reduce risk by reducing uncertainty about inputs or access to customers. Another is **conglomerate diversification,** which provides a profitable investment alternative with diverting management attention from the original business. However, the external approaches to overcoming weaknesses usually result in the most costly grand strategies. Acquiring a second business demands large investments of time and sizable financial resources. Thus, strategic managers considering these approaches must guard against exchanging one set of weaknesses for another.

More conservative approaches to overcoming weaknesses are found in quadrant II. Firms often choose to redirect resources from one internal business activity to another. This approach maintains the firm's commitment to its basic mission, rewards success, and enables further development of proven competitive advantages. The least disruptive of the quadrant II strategies is **retrenchment,** pruning the current activities of a business. If the weaknesses of the business arose from inefficiencies, retrenchment can actually serve as a *turnaround* strategy—that is, the business gains new strength from the streamlining of its operations and the elimination of waste. However, if those weaknesses are a major obstruction to success in the industry and the costs of overcoming them are unaffordable or are not justified by a cost-benefit analysis, then eliminating the business must be considered. **Divestiture** offers the best possibility for recouping the firm's investment, but even **liquidation** can be an attractive option if the alternatives are bankruptcy or an unwarranted drain on the firm's resources.

A common business adage states that a firm should build from strength. The premise of this adage is that growth and survival depend on an ability to capture a market share that is large enough for essential economies of scale. If a firm believes that this approach will be profitable and prefers an internal emphasis for maximizing strengths, four grand strategies hold considerable promise. As shown in quadrant III, the most common approach is **concentrated growth,** that is, market penetration. The firm that selects this strategy is strongly committed to its current products and markets. It strives to solidify its position by reinvesting resources to fortify its strengths.

Two alternative approaches are **market development** and **product development.** With these strategies, the firm attempts to broaden its operations. Market development is chosen if the firm's strategic managers feel that its existing products would be well received by new customer groups. Product development is chosen if they feel that the firm's existing customers would be interested in products related to its current lines. Product development also may be based on technological or other competitive advantages. The final alternative for quadrant III firms is **innovation.** When the firm's strengths are in creative product design or unique production technologies, sales can be stimulated by accelerating perceived obsolescence. This is the principle underlying the innovative grand strategy.

Maximizing a firm's strengths by aggressively expanding its base of operations usually requires an external emphasis. The preferred options in such cases are shown in quadrant IV. **Horizontal integration** is attractive because it makes possible a quick increase in output capability. Moreover, in horizontal integration, the skills of the managers of the original business often are critical in converting newly acquired facilities into profitable contributors to the parent firm; this expands a fundamental competitive advantage of the firm—its management.

Concentric diversification is a good second choice for similar reasons. Because the original and newly acquired businesses are related, the distinctive competencies of the diversifying firm are likely to facilitate a smooth, synergistic, and profitable expansion.

The final alternative for increasing resource capability through external emphasis is a **joint venture** or **strategic alliance.** This alternative allows a firm to extend its strengths into competitive arenas that it would be hesitant to enter alone. A partner's production, technological, financial, or marketing capabilities can reduce the firm's financial investment significantly and increase its probability of success.

Model of Grand Strategy Clusters

A second guide to selecting a promising strategy is the **grand strategy cluster** shown in Exhibit 8.11. The figure is based on the idea that the situation of a business is defined

---

retrenchment
Cutting back on products, markets, operations because the firm's overall competitive and financial situation cannot support commitments needed to sustain or build its operations.

divestiture
The sale of a firm or a major component.

liquidation
Closing down the operations of a business and selling its assets and operations to pay its debts and distribute any gains to stockholders.

concentrated growth
Aggressive market penetration where a firm's strong position and favorable market growth allow it to "control" resources and effort for focused growth.

market development
Selling present products, often with only cosmetic modification, to customers in related marketing areas by adding channels of distribution or by changing the content of advertising or promotion.

Exhibit 8.11   **Model of Grand Strategy Clusters**

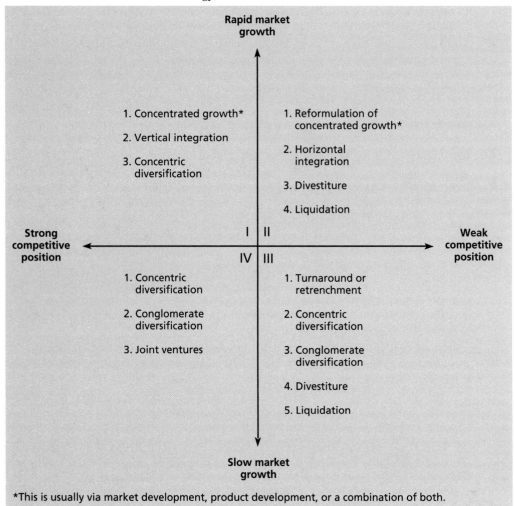

*This is usually via market development, product development, or a combination of both.

product development

The substantial modification of existing products or the creation of new but related products that can be marketed to current customers through established channels.

in terms of the growth rate of the general market and the firm's competitive position in that market. When these factors are considered simultaneously, a business can be broadly categorized in one of four quadrants: (I) strong competitive position in a rapidly growing market, (II) weak position in a rapidly growing market, (III) weak position in a slow-growth market, or (IV) strong position in a slow-growth market. Each of these quadrants suggests a set of promising possibilities for the selection of a grand strategy.

Firms in quadrant I are in an excellent strategic position. One obvious grand strategy for such firms is continued concentration on their current business as it is currently defined. Because consumers seem satisfied with the firm's current strategy, shifting notably from it would endanger the firm's established competitive advantages. McDonald's Corporation has followed this approach for 25 years. However, if the firm has resources that exceed the demands of a concentrated growth strategy, it should consider vertical integration. Either forward or backward integration helps a firm protect its profit margins and market share by ensuring better access to consumers or material inputs. Finally, to diminish the risks associated with a narrow product or service line, a quadrant I firm might be wise to consider concentric diversification; with this strategy, the firm continues to invest heavily in its basic area of proven ability.

innovation
A strategy that seeks to reap the initially high profits associated with customer acceptance of a new or greatly improved product.

horizontal integration
Growth through the acquisition of one or more similar firms operating at the same stage of the production-marketing chain.

concentric diversification
Acquisition of businesses that are related to the acquiring firm in terms of technology, markets, or products.

joint ventures
Commercial companies created and operated for the benefit of the co-owners; usually two or more separate companies that form the venture.

strategic alliances
Partnerships that are distinguished from joint ventures because the companies involved do not take an equity position in one another.

grand strategy clusters
Strategies that may be more advantageous for firms to choose under one of four sets of conditions defined by market growth rate and the strength of the firm's competitive position.

Firms in quadrant II must seriously evaluate their present approach to the marketplace. If a firm has competed long enough to accurately assess the merits of its current grand strategy, it must determine (1) why that strategy is ineffectual and (2) whether it is capable of competing effectively. Depending on the answers to these questions, the firm should choose one of four grand strategy options: formulation or reformulation of a concentrated growth strategy, horizontal integration, divestiture, or liquidation.

In a rapidly growing market, even a small or relatively weak business often is able to find a profitable niche. Thus, formulation or reformulation of a concentrated growth strategy is usually the first option that should be considered. However, if the firm lacks either a critical competitive element or sufficient economies of scale to achieve competitive cost efficiencies, then a grand strategy that directs its efforts toward horizontal integration is often a desirable alternative. A final pair of options involves deciding to stop competing in the market or product area of the business. A multiproduct firm may conclude that it is most likely to achieve the goals of its mission if the business is dropped through divestiture. This grand strategy not only eliminates a drain on resources but also may provide funds to promote other business activities. As an option of last resort, a firm may decide to liquidate the business. This means that the business cannot be sold as a going concern and is at best worth only the value of its tangible assets. The decision to liquidate is an undeniable admission of failure by a firm's strategic management and, thus, often is delayed—to the further detriment of the firm.

Strategic managers tend to resist divestiture because it is likely to jeopardize their control of the firm and perhaps even their jobs. Thus, by the time the desirability of divestiture is acknowledged, businesses often deteriorate to the point of failing to attract potential buyers. The consequences of such delays are financially disastrous for firm owners because the value of a going concern is many times greater than the value of its assets.

Strategic managers who have a business in quadrant III and expect a continuation of slow market growth and a relatively weak competitive position will usually attempt to decrease their resource commitment to that business. Minimal withdrawal is accomplished through retrenchment; this strategy has the side benefits of making resources available for other investments and of motivating employees to increase their operating efficiency. An alternative approach is to divert resources for expansion through investment in other businesses. This approach typically involves either concentric or conglomerate diversification because the firm usually wants to enter more promising arenas of competition than integration or concentrated growth strategies would allow. The final options for quadrant III businesses are divestiture, if an optimistic buyer can be found, and liquidation.

Quadrant IV businesses (strong competitive position in a slow-growth market) have a basis of strength from which to diversify into more promising growth areas. These businesses have characteristically high cash flow levels and limited internal growth needs. Thus, they are in an excellent position for concentric diversification into ventures that utilize their proven acumen. A previous example in this chapter described how the no. 1 tennis ball maker, Penn Racquet Sports, chose concentric diversification from humans to dogs as their best option. A second option is conglomerate diversification, which spreads investment risk and does not divert managerial attention from the present business. The final option is joint ventures, which are especially attractive to multinational firms. Through joint ventures, a domestic business can gain competitive advantages in promising new fields while exposing itself to limited risks.

Opportunities for Building Value as a Basis for Choosing Diversification or Integration

The grand strategy selection matrix and model of grand strategy clusters are useful tools to help dominant product company managers evaluate and narrow their choices among alternative grand strategies. When considering grand strategies that would broaden the scope of their company's business activities through integration, diversification, or joint venture strategies, managers must examine whether opportunities to build value are present. Opportunities to build value via diversification, integration, or joint venture strategies are usually found in market-related, operating-related, and management activities. Such opportunities center around reducing costs, improving margins, or providing access to new revenue sources more cost effectively than traditional internal growth options via concentration, market development, or product development. Major opportunities for sharing and value building as well as ways to capitalize on core competencies are outlined in the next chapter, which covers strategic analysis and choice in diversified companies.

Dominant product company managers who choose diversification or integration eventually create another management challenge. That challenge is charting the future of a company that becomes a collection of several distinct businesses. These distinct businesses often encounter different competitive environments, challenges, and opportunities. The next chapter examines ways managers of such diversified companies attempt to evaluate and choose corporate strategy. Central to their challenge is the continued desire to build value, particularly shareholder value.

Summary

This chapter examined how managers in businesses that have a single or dominant product or service evaluate and choose their company's strategy. Two critical areas deserve their attention: (1) their business's value chain, and (2) the appropriateness of 12 different grand strategies based on matching environmental factors with internal capabilities.

Managers in single-product-line business units examine their business's value chain to identify existing or potential activities around which they can create sustainable competitive advantages. As managers scrutinize their value chain activities, they are looking for three sources of competitive advantage: low cost, differentiation, and rapid response capabilities. They also examine whether focusing on a narrow market niche provides a more effective, sustainable way to build or leverage these three sources of competitive advantage.

Managers in single- or dominant-product/service businesses face two interrelated issues: (1) They must choose which grand strategies make best use of their competitive advantages. (2) They must ultimately decide whether to diversify their business activity. Twelve grand strategies were identified in this chapter along with three frameworks that aid managers in choosing which grand strategies should work best and when diversification or integration should be the best strategy for the business. The next chapter expands the coverage of diversification to look at how multibusiness companies evaluate continued diversification and how they construct corporate strategy.

Key Terms

concentrated growth, *p. 267*
concentric diversification, *p. 269*
conglomerate diversification, *p. 266*
declining industry, *p. 262*
differentiation, *p. 250*
divestiture, *p. 267*
emerging industry, *p. 257*
fragmented industry, *p. 263*

global industry, *p. 264*
grand strategy cluster, *p. 269*
grand strategy selection matrix, *p. 266*
growth industry strategies, *p. 258*
horizontal integration, *p. 269*
innovation, *p. 269*
joint ventures, *p. 269*
liquidation, *p. 267*

low-cost strategies, *p. 247*
market development, *p. 267*
market focus, *p. 255*
mature industry strategies, *p. 260*
product development, *p. 268*
retrenchment, *p. 267*
speed-based strategies, *p. 253*
strategic alliances, *p. 269*
vertical integration, *p. 266*

Questions for Discussion

1. What are three activities or capabilities a firm should possess to support a low-cost leadership strategy? Use Exhibit 8.2 to help you answer this question. Can you give an example of a company that has done this?
2. What are three activities or capabilities a firm should possess to support a differentiation-based strategy? Use Exhibit 8.3 to help you answer this question. Can you give an example of a company that has done this?
3. What are three ways a firm can incorporate the advantage of speed in its business? Use Exhibit 8.4 to help you answer this question. Can you give an example of a company that has done this?
4. Do you think it is better to concentrate on one source of competitive advantage (cost versus differentiation versus speed) or to nurture all three in a firm's operation?
5. How does market focus help a business create competitive advantage? What risks accompany such a posture?
6. Using Exhibits 8.10 and 8.11, describe situations or conditions under which horizontal integration and concentric diversification would be preferred strategic choices.

Chapter 8 Discussion Case

DHL's American Strategy

BusinessWeek

1 No question, those cheeky DHL ads seemed to be everywhere, from the New York City subways to the World Series. In one TV pitch, a FedEx worker goes on holiday, enjoying parasailing and golf—only to see DHL trucks speeding parcels to their destinations. Then there was the bus stop poster that took a swipe at UPS: "Yellow. It's the new Brown." And a print ad proclaimed what DHL hopes is inevitable: "The Roman empire, the British empire, the FedEx empire. Nothing lasts forever."

2   In short, it was war, as DHL, the $35 billion delivery and logistics company started in San Francisco and acquired in 2002 by Deutsche Post World Net—the privatized German postal service—fought to become a credible alternative in the United States to FedEx Corp. and United Parcel Service Inc. DHL is the largest express carrier in Europe with a 40 percent share, and the largest international express carrier in Asia, also with 40 percent. Now DHL, whose U.S. base is in Plantation, Florida, is seeking to build its presence by expanding its trucking routes, creating air hubs, and advertising heavily to raise awareness of its brand in a country where it has only 7 percent of the air and ground parcel market.

3   With North American express traffic accounting for nearly half the worldwide total, no carrier with global ambitions can afford to ignore it. And DHL has set its sights on the small- and medium-size U.S. businesses that are increasingly involved in foreign trade. "It's a global economy now," says Hans Hickler, CEO of DHL-USA Inc. "You have to be everywhere."

4   But taking on FedEx and UPS, which together command 78 percent of the U.S. parcel market, is a daunting task. For example, it took more than two years before the company won a bruising legal battle, when regulators turned aside

challenges by FedEx and UPS that the planes DHL contracted to use here constituted illegal foreign control of an airline. Completing the integration of Airborne Inc., the Seattle carrier that merged with DHL, was a massive job. And DHL's limited ground network has hurt its ability to attract domestic customers who want to cut costs by sending parcels overland rather than by air. In fact, until 2005, DHL had almost no ground network in much of the Midwest and Rocky Mountain states.

5   The result: DHL, with $8 billion in American revenues, projects it will break even with its U.S. operations in 2009. Even after reaching profitability, Hickler says that DHL's return on investment is unlikely to top 4 percent for the next few years.

Can DHL Deliver?
It aims to be a strong No. 3 among U.S. couriers.
How it plans to get there:

Get Better Known
DHL has spent $150 million annually on an ad campaign that tweaks UPS and FedEx

Improve the Infrastructure
Build stronger trucking network in Rocky Mountain and Midwest regions; open West Coast air hub

Target the Little Guy
Focus on midmarket and smaller businesses by offering more personal service

Boost Market Share
In five years, DHL wants 12 percent to 14 percent of the market, up from 7 percent in 2005.

CROWN JEWELS

6   It's clearly going to take a lot more than a snappy ad campaign to turn DHL into a winner. Analysts have raised substantial doubts about whether DHL can be a viable no. 3 in the United States. Since the mid-1990s, Deutsche Post has acquired over 100 logistics, transport, and freight-forwarding services, and expertly integrated them to build its worldwide business. DHL and Airborne were to be the crown jewels, the acquisitions that extended its grasp into the world's richest economy. But Deutsche Post "underestimated the challenges," said Raimund Saxinger, a fund manager at Frankfurt Trust in Frankfurt.

7   Chief among those challenges has been the lack of ground transport capability. DHL had virtually none when it was acquired by Deutsche Post, while Airborne was just getting started. Now, with high fuel prices boosting the cost of air shipment, the parcel market in the United States is shifting toward ground transport, which is DHL's weakest link. So DHL is investing $1.2 billion over the next three years in sorting centers, drop-off points, and other network improvements. Nationally, for instance, DHL has only 16,000 drop-off points—about one-third FedEx's number. "It takes a lot of money and a lot of talent to build a high-quality network. That's a big hurdle," says Kurt Kuehn, senior vice president of worldwide sales and marketing for UPS.

8   But DHL is determined to build out its network. "If we did not have an efficient pickup and delivery system in the U.S., it would be very tough for us to hold on to our no. 1 position in Europe and Asia," says Klaus Zumwinkel, chief executive of parent Deutsche Post and the mastermind behind its global strategy.

9   DHL is better situated in terms of air transport. In the past five years, it and Airborne have collectively invested $1.9 billion in the United States and Canada, much of it on projects such as the consolidation of air operations at its Wilmington (Ohio) hub and its four strategically located gateways in New York, Miami, Los Angeles, and San Francisco. But those outlays only begin to get DHL into the game. "It does not close the gap," said Satish Jindel, president of transportation consultant SJ Consulting Group Inc. Over the same period, FedEx and UPS each spent more than $6 billion in North America.

10   While investing $1.9 billion to increase infrastructure along with a $150 million media campaign is part of DHL's strategy to compete with UPS and FedEx, rolling out a strategy to differentiate itself from these key competitors is the other. DHL is counting on improved customer service to build its U.S.-based business. While the company knows that it won't be easy to separate customers from their UPS drivers, it's trying to mold a more customer-friendly workforce. Analysts say that task was neglected by Airborne. And in one survey, DHL rated even lower than Airborne did on customer satisfaction.

11   For DHL, that has meant changing the way customers perceive DHL. Hans Hickler created the "Customer Service Initiative," a strategy to solidify among both customers and employees just who DHL is and what values the company represents. He identified 82 customer "touch points" within DHL to systematically evaluate, change, and monitor changes to solidify the customer-centric DHL difference. "Customers don't just do business with you for one year in this business," Hickler said. "They're buying in to your strategy, especially in the shipping business, which is a very global and international business. People don't switch easily, and so they need to understand that what you stand for is there."

12   Personalized service can be a winning pitch for some customers. Shoemaker Skechers USA Inc. already has shifted about a third of the business from its Manhattan Beach (California) headquarters from FedEx to DHL, which it also uses for international shipments. "I've been responsible for shipping and receiving for 13 years, and it wasn't until this past year that I met my FedEx rep. DHL is constantly out here," says Michael Cardenas, Skechers' office services manager. He also praises DHL's hustle. "UPS and FedEx are more reluctant to go to remote locations. DHL will just do it. If their driver has to sit in the parking lot and fill out the air bills, he'll do it."

13   For now, DHL has modest goals in the United States. The company aims just to raise market share to between 12 percent and 14 percent—a statement that draws derision from competitors. "I don't think that customers will turn over their mission-critical operations to a fledgling operation whose stated goal is to become the No. 3 player," said the vice president for investor relations at FedEx. Even if DHL doesn't break even in the United States by 2009, don't expect it to stop trying. With a deep-pocketed corporate parent, it can keep plugging away for years. "They can afford a U.S. problem," says analyst Markus Hesse at HVB Group in Munich. Good thing, because it looks like a problem that's not going to go away soon.

Sources: Reprinted with special permission from Mark Scott, "Brand Builder," *Smart Business*, Cleveland, OH, February 2007; "DHL: Delivering the Goods," *BusinessWeek*, August 11, 2006; Jack Ewing and Dean Foust, "DHL's American Adventure," *BusinessWeek*, November 29, 2004; and Jack Ewing "A Mercedes in the Parcel Industry," *BusinessWeek*, November 29, 2004. Copyright © 2007 The McGraw-Hill Companies.

AN INTERVIEW WITH DR. KLAUS ZUMWINKEL, CHAIRMAN, DEUTSCHE POST

DHL, a unit of Germany's Deutsche Post, is the dominant express and parcel company in Europe and also the leader in crossborder air express in Asia. In the United States, though, DHL is still tiny compared with market leaders UPS and FedEx. Deutsche Post chairman Klaus Zumwinkel is trying to change that, in part by acquiring Airborne and merging it with

DHL. Mr. Zumwinkel aims to be the transportation services "Mercedes" in the U.S. market.

But gaining ground in the United States is proving tougher than expected. DHL announced that it won't break even in the United States until 2009, instead of 2006 as planned. This is partly because DHL was held up by a regulatory battle after rivals complained that the air fleet used under contract by the German outfit constituted illegal foreign control of an airline. DHL prevailed in the dispute earlier this year. Still, many analysts doubt whether even the revised profit goal is realistic.

Zumwinkel, who has overseen transformation of the German postal service into a global express-courier and logistics company, remains determined. He spoke recently with *BusinessWeek* about how DHL will prove the doubters wrong.

Question: Why is the U.S. worth investing [$1.9] billion in?

Zumwinkel: In an industry like ours, the network has to be complete. Customers inside the U.S. and outside are welcoming an increase in our U.S. presence. If we didn't have an efficient pickup and delivery system in the U.S., it would be very tough for us to hold onto our no. 1 position in Europe and Asia.

Question: Has the U.S. been more difficult than you expected? Have there been any surprises?

Zumwinkel: In the beginning we had a long battle with our competitors because of [regulatory issues regarding] the air fleet used by DHL. . . . We lost some time in streamlining and integrating and restructuring the whole thing. But with all of our acquisitions, we're now experts in integration. We have integrated more than 100 companies.

Question: How big a priority is DHL in the U.S. for you?

Zumwinkel: In such a big group we have several priorities. We had the IPO of Postbank [Deutsche Post's retail banking unit in Germany], and Asia is a very attractive and strong growth area. In Europe, we're integrating heavily in several key countries like Italy, the U.K., [and] France. The U.S. is one of these priorities, it's in this class.

Question: So it's not keeping you up at night?

Zumwinkel: No [laughs].

Question: The U.S. market is moving toward a ground network. Does that increase the amount of investment you have to put into the U.S.?

Zumwinkel: Yes. . . . Airborne had already established a ground-based network. Like everybody else in this industry, Airborne found that if you have a good ground network, why should the customer pay so much for air products?

This is a secular trend. We want to provide the same kind of quality our customers are used to in other parts of the world. We want to be the Mercedes in our industry.

Question: What are your profit goals for DHL in the U.S.? Will you be satisfied to break even?

Zumwinkel: Naturally, management is concentrating on [breaking even] [by 2009] [and on the goals] to restructure [the U.S. business], to integrate two companies, to integrate into the worldwide network, [and] to build a ground network. That will keep everybody busy for the next [few] years. [If we broke even,] we would have 500 million [euros or $750 million] more profit, we would have 500 million [euros] losses less. That is only 10 percent of our whole group profit. That's the main objective. After that, we will see.

Question: Can you foresee that the U.S. will become a major profit center?

Zumwinkel: Sure. We have invested a lot of money in the U.S. Our competitors are earning nice profit rates, double-digit margins—something we're not used to in Europe. We won't get these margins for a while because our competitors have larger economies of scale, but with our economies of scale worldwide, I think we can [realize these margins in the long term].

Question: Is this like the Japanese carmakers coming into the U.S. decades ago where you're willing to invest for a long time in order to get a permanent foothold in the market?

Zumwinkel: I don't compare myself with Japanese carmakers. Here the game is very simple. The express game is an international game. To be international, one has to cover the largest economy in the world—the U.S. Otherwise, one is not thoroughly competitive in Asia or Europe.

We're in the U.S. for the long term. I think the globalization trend will strengthen in the next 10 years. World trade has to be transported, and we're here to provide the transport.

DISCUSSION QUESTIONS

1. What aspects of DHL's strategy for entering the United States reflect a low-cost strategy? A differentiation strategy?

2. Are there any aspects that appear to reflect a focus strategy?

3. How has DHL incorporated "speed" into its overall strategy?

4. What appear to be DHL's most important competitive advantages? Are they best suited to a mature industry or a growth industry? Which way would you characterize the U.S. parcel market and the global parcel market?

5. What appears to be the likelihood that DHL will succeed? What key factors will determine that?

6. DHL comes to you for advice on whether they should continue a global focus on parcels and express mail or diversify their business activities into other types of businesses. What would you advise and why?

Chapter Nine

Multibusiness Strategy

After reading and studying this chapter, you should be able to

1. Understand the portfolio approach to strategic analysis and choice in multibusiness companies.

2. Understand and use three different portfolio approaches to conduct strategic analysis and choice in multibusiness companies.

3. Identify the limitations and weaknesses of the various portfolio approaches.

4. Understand the synergy approach to strategic analysis and choice in multibusiness companies.

5. Evaluate the parent company role in strategic analysis and choice to determine whether and how it adds tangible value in a multibusiness company.

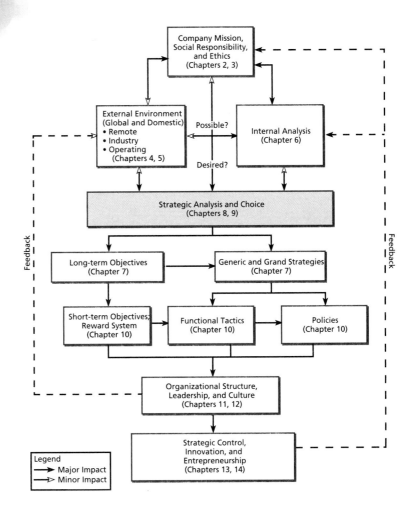

275

Jeff Immelt, successor to the globally admired Jack Welch as chairman and CEO of General Electric, said in response to a question about GE's future that his greatest fear for GE was that it would become boring and his top managers would become cowards. His real concern was how to determine what businesses GE should build its future around, and which businesses it should not. Should GE stay in appliances, in lighting, in television with its NBC network, or should it sell some of these businesses? Should he take a risk and move GE into renewable energy equipment, or water, or security, or biomedicine, or making movies? How much of the company should any of these dramatic new businesses represent? So, if you were about to finish this semester and Immelt came to talk at your school, and if he posed this fundamental concern today, singled you out to give him advice, what would you say? What should he do?

General Motors, for so long the world's oldest and largest car company, faces a real dilemma. Does it intentionally and aggressively shrink its number of car brands, its overall car businesses, and reduce its involvement in other businesses such as consumer finance services so that a profitable but much smaller version of its old self becomes the new GM? Or does it seek to build many if not all of it venerable brand names? What would you advise GM's CEO Rick Wagoner? Likewise, rumors abounded just last year that Microsoft and Yahoo! should merge to create a meaningful competitor to all-powerful Google. Suppose any of these executives came to your strategy class to speak and asked each class team to tell him which was the best way to go and why. What would you say?

Strategic analysis and choice is complicated for corporate-level managers because they must create a strategy to guide a company that contains numerous businesses. They must examine and choose which businesses to own and which ones to forgo or divest. They must consider business managers' plans to capture and exploit competitive advantage in each business, and then decide how to allocate resources among those businesses. This chapter covers ways managers in multibusiness companies analyze and choose what businesses to be in and how to allocate resources across those businesses.

The portfolio approach was one of the early approaches for charting strategy and allocating resources in multibusiness companies. It was particularly popular in the 1960s and 1970s, after which corporate managers, concerned with some shortcomings in this type of approach, welcomed new options. Yet while many companies have moved on to use other approaches, the portfolio approach remains a useful technique for some. Indeed, after GE pioneered one form of the approach and subsequently abandoned it under Jack Welch, GE's new leader Jeff Immelt has brought it back and made it the central theme in his corporate strategic decision making and development. Immelt's recent comment to GE shareholders after his first five years leading GE were as follows:

> *I would ask investors to think about the progress we have made with our portfolio [of businesses] over the last five years. In 2001, one-third of our earnings were generated by businesses that could not consistently hit our 10 percent earnings growth and 20 percent return goals. Since then, we have executed a disciplined portfolio strategy to create a sustainable competitive advantage based on technology, brand and a valuable installed base. GE now has a portfolio of six strong businesses aligned to grow with the market trends of today and tomorrow. This is not by chance. It is the result of considered, strategic investment in each business over time—and ahead of external realities.*[1]

Perhaps, as they say, history repeats itself—or what goes around comes around. Exhibit 9.1, Strategy in Action, provides a more in-depth description of the manifestations of a return to a portfolio approach at General Electric under Immelt's watch.

---

[1] "Letter to Shareholders," *2006 G.E. Annual Report.*

Strategy in Action

Hum? Is it Back to the Future—GE Returns to the Portfolio Approach

Shuffling the Portfolio
Immelt has spent more than $75 billion to bolster GE's mix of businesses. Some new capabilities:

Media Content	Biosciences	Security	Water	Renewable Energy
Buying Universal gave GE a rich library, film studio, cable networks, and theme parks. Bravo and Telemundo help, too.	With Amersham, GE can bring diagnostics down to the cellular level and be a leader in personalized medicine.	GE bought its way into fire safety and industrial security with Edwards Systems. Ion Track and InVision gave it entrée into homeland security, from bomb detection to screening for narcotics.	Buying Ionics and Osmonics gets GE into desalination, fluid filtration, and other water processing services. The goal: to increase the availability of clean water around the world.	GE moved into solar and wind power and biogas with acquisitions such as Enron Wind.

To lay the groundwork for an organization that grows through innovation, Immelt took steps early on to rejigger the GE portfolio. He sold several profitable businesses such as insurance and GE Plastics while shelling out more than $75 billion in acquisitions to dive into hot areas such as bioscience, cable and film entertainment, security, water processing, and wind power that have better growth prospects. In doing so, he pared the low-margin, slower-growth businesses like appliances or lighting, which he diplomatically calls "cash generators" instead of "losers," down to 10 percent of the portfolio, from 33 percent in 2000. Nicole M. Parent of Credit Suisse First Boston is impressed with "the way they have been able to evolve the portfolio in such a short time" and with so little disruption. "This is a company where managers will do anything to achieve their goals."

That in itself may be a stretch of the imagination for now, but Immelt is trying to recast the company for decades to come. He's spending big bucks to create the kind of infrastructure that can equip and foster an army of dreamers. That means beefing up GE's research facilities, creating something akin to a global brain trust that GE can tap to spur innovation. He has sunk $100 million into overhauling the company's research center in Niskayuna, New York, and forked out for cutting-edge centers in Bangalore, Shanghai, and Munich.

Now that Immelt has repositioned the portfolio and added resources, his main objective is to get more immediate growth out of the businesses he already has. That's where the Imagination Breakthroughs come in. over the past five years, Immelt has invested more than $15 billion in 80 projects that range from creating microjet engines to overhauling the brand image of 3,000 consumer-finance locations. The hope is that the first lot will generate $40 billion in revenue by 2009—cheap, if it works, when you consider what it would cost to acquire something from the outside with that level of sales. In the next year or two, Immelt expects to have 400 such projects under way.

Sources: Reprinted with special permission from "GE and the Global Economy," *BusinessWeek*, April 13, 2007; "The Secret to GE's Success," *BusinessWeek*, January 29, 2007; and "Shuffling the Portfolio," *BusinessWeek*, March 28, 2005. Copyright © 2007 The McGraw-Hill Companies.

Improvement on the portfolio approach focused on ways to broaden the rationale behind pursuit of diversification strategies. This approach centered on the idea that at the heart of effective diversification is the identification of core competencies in a business or set of businesses to then leverage as the basis for competitive advantage in the growth of those businesses and the entry in or divestiture of other businesses. This notion of leveraging core competencies as a basis for strategic choice in multibusiness companies has been a popular one for the past 20 years.

Recent evolution of strategic analysis and choice in this setting has expanded on the core competency notion to focus on a series of fundamental questions that multibusiness companies should address in order to make diversification work. With both the accelerated rates of change in most global markets and trying economic conditions, multibusiness companies have adapted the fundamental questions into an approach called "patching" to map and remap their business units swiftly against changing market opportunities. Finally, as companies have embraced lean organizational structures, strategic analysis in multibusiness companies has included careful assessment of the corporate parent, its role, and value or lack thereof in contributing to the stand-alone performance of their business units. This chapter will examine each of these approaches to shaping multibusiness corporate strategy.

THE PORTFOLIO APPROACH: A HISTORICAL STARTING POINT

portfolio techniques
An approach pioneered by the Boston Consulting Group that attempted to help managers "balance" the flow of cash resources among their various businesses while also identifying their basic strategic purpose within the overall portfolio.

The past 30 years we have seen a virtual explosion in the extent to which single-business companies seek to acquire other businesses to grow and to diversify. There are many reasons for this emergence of multibusiness companies: Companies can enter businesses with greater growth potential; enter businesses with different cyclical considerations; diversify inherent risks; increase vertical integration, and thereby reduce costs; capture value added; and instantly have a market presence rather than slower internal growth. As businesses jumped on the diversification bandwagon, their managers soon found a challenge in managing the resource needs of diverse businesses and their respective strategic missions, particularly in times of limited resources. Responding to this challenge, the Boston Consulting Group (BCG) pioneered an approach called **portfolio techniques** that attempted to help managers "balance" the flow of cash resources among their various businesses while also identifying their basic strategic purpose within the overall portfolio. Three of these techniques are reviewed here. Once reviewed, we will identify some of the problems with the portfolio approach that you should keep in mind when considering its use.

The BCG Growth-Share Matrix

market growth rate
The projected rate of sales growth for the market being served by a particular business.

relative competitive position
The market share of a business divided by the market share of its largest competitor.

stars
Businesses in rapidly growing markets with large market shares.

cash cows
Businesses with a high market share in low-growth markets or industries.

Managers using the BCG matrix plotted each of the company's businesses according to market growth rate and relative competitive position. **Market growth rate** is the projected rate of sales growth for the market being served by a particular business. Usually measured as the percentage increase in a market's sales or unit volume over the two most recent years, this rate serves as an indicator of the relative attractiveness of the markets served by each business in the firm's portfolio of businesses. **Relative competitive position** usually is expressed as the market share of a business divided by the market share of its largest competitor. Thus, relative competitive position provides a basis for comparing the relative strengths of the businesses in the firm's portfolio in terms of their positions in their respective markets. Exhibit 9.2 illustrates the growth-share matrix.

The **stars** are businesses in rapidly growing markets with large market shares. These businesses represent the best long-run opportunities (growth and profitability) in the firm's portfolio. They require substantial investment to maintain (and expand) their dominant position in a growing market. This investment requirement is often in excess of the funds that they can generate internally. Therefore, these businesses are often short-term, priority consumers of corporate resources.

Cash cows are businesses with a high market share in low-growth markets or industries. Because of their strong competitive positions and their minimal reinvestment requirements, these businesses often generate cash in excess of their needs. Therefore, they are selectively "milked" as a source of corporate resources for deployment elsewhere (to stars and question marks). Cash cows are yesterday's stars and the current foundation of corporate portfolios. They provide the

EXHIBIT 9.2
The BCG Growth-Share Matrix

Source: The growth-share matrix was originally developed by the Boston Consulting Group.

Description of Dimensions

Market share: Sales relative to those of other competitors in the market (dividing point is usually selected to have only the two to three largest competitors in any market fall into the high market share region)

Growth rate: Industry growth rate in constant dollars (dividing point is typically the GNP's growth rate)

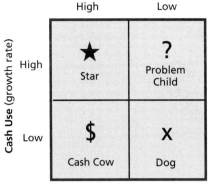

Cash Generation (market share)

cash needed to pay corporate overhead and dividends and provide debt capacity. They are managed to maintain their strong market share while generating excess resources for corporatewide use. Look back at Exhibit 9.1, which summarizes GE chairman/CEO Jeff Immelt's assessment of GE "cash cows" and "cash generators" to target businesses from which he will generate resources to invest in GE's portfolio of new "start" businesses.

dogs
Low market share and low market growth businesses.

Low market share and low market growth businesses are the **dogs** in the firm's portfolio. Facing mature markets with intense competition and low profit margins, they are managed for short-term cash flow (e.g., through ruthless cost cutting) to supplement corporate-level resource needs. According to the original BCG prescription, they are divested or liquidated once this short-term harvesting has been maximized.

question marks
Businesses whose high growth rate gives them considerable appeal but whose low market share makes their profit potential uncertain.

Question marks are businesses whose high growth rate gives them considerable appeal but whose low market share makes their profit potential uncertain. Question marks are cash guzzlers because their rapid growth results in high cash needs, while their small market share results in low cash generation. At the corporate level, the concern is to identify the question marks that would increase their market share and move into the star group if extra corporate resources were devoted to them. Where this long-run shift from question mark to star is unlikely, the BCG matrix suggests divesting the question mark and repositioning its resources more effectively in the remainder of the corporate portfolio.

The Industry Attractiveness–Business Strength Matrix

Corporate strategists found the growth-share matrix's singular axes limiting in their ability to reflect the complexity of a business's situation. Therefore, some companies adopted a matrix with a much broader focus. This matrix, developed by McKinsey & Company at General Electric, is called the industry attractiveness–business strength matrix. This matrix uses multiple factors to assess industry attractiveness and business strength rather than the single measures (market share and market growth, respectively) employed in the BCG matrix. It also has nine cells as opposed to four—replacing the high/low axes with high/medium/low axes to make finer distinctions among business portfolio positions.

The company's businesses are rated on multiple strategic factors within each axis, such as the factors described in Exhibit 9.3. The position of a business is then calculated by "subjectively" quantifying its rating along the two dimensions of the matrix. Depending on the location of a business within the matrix as shown in Exhibit 9.4, one of the following strategic approaches is suggested: (1) invest to grow, (2) invest selectively and manage for earnings, or (3) harvest or divest for resources. The resource allocation decisions remain quite similar to those of the BCG approach.

EXHIBIT 9.3
Factors Considered in Constructing an Industry Attractiveness–Business Strength Matrix

Industry Attractiveness

Nature of Competitive Rivalry

Number of competitors
Size of competitors
Strength of competitors' corporate parents
Price wars
Competition on multiple dimensions

Bargaining Power of Suppliers/Customers

Relative size of typical players
Numbers of each
Importance of purchases from or sales to
Ability to vertically integrate

Threat of Substitute Products/New Entrants

Technological maturity/stability
Diversity of the market
Barriers to entry
Flexibility of distribution system

Economic Factors

Sales volatility
Cyclicality of demand
Market growth
Capital intensity

Financial Norms

Average profitability
Typical leverage
Credit practices

Sociopolitical Considerations

Government regulation
Community support
Ethical standards

Business Strength

Cost Position

Economies of scale
Manufacturing costs
Overhead scrap/waste/rework
Experience effects
Labor rates
Proprietary processes

Level of Differentiation

Promotion effectiveness
Product quality
Company image
Patented products
Brand awareness

Response Time

Manufacturing flexibility
Time needed to introduce new products
Delivery times
Organizational flexibility

Financial Strength

Solvency
Liquidity
Break-even point
Cash flows
Profitability
Growth in revenues

Human Assets

Turnover
Skill level
Relative wage/salary
Morale
Managerial commitment
Unionization

Public Approval

Goodwill
Reputation
Image

Although the strategic recommendations generated by the industry attractiveness–business strength matrix are similar to those generated by the BCG matrix, the industry attractiveness–business strength matrix improves on the BCG matrix in three fundamental ways:

1. The terminology associated with the industry attractiveness–business strength matrix is preferable because it is less offensive and more understandable.

2. The multiple measures associated with each dimension of the business strength matrix tap many factors relevant to business strength and market attractiveness besides market share and market growth.

EXHIBIT 9.4 **The Industry Attractiveness–Business Strength Matrix**

		Business Strength		
		Strong	**Average**	**Weak**
Industry Attractiveness	**High**	**Premium—invest for growth:** • Provide maximum investment • Diversify worldwide • Consolidate position • Accept moderate near-term profits • Seek to dominate	**Selective—invest for growth** • Invest heavily in selected segments • Share ceiling • Seek attractive new segments to apply strengths	**Protect/refocus—selectively invest for earnings:** • Defend strengths • Refocus to attractive segments • Evaluate industry revitalization • Monitor for harvest or divestment timing • Consider acquisitions
	Medium	**Challenge—invest for growth:** • Build selectively on strengths • Define implications of leadership challenge • Avoid vulnerability—fill weaknesses	**Prime—selectively invest for earnings:** • Segment market • Make contingency plans for vulnerability	**Restructure—harvest or divest:** • Provide no unessential commitment • Position for divestment or • Shift to more attractive segment
	Low	**Opportunistic—selectively invest for earnings:** • Ride market and maintain overall position • Seek niches, specialization • Seek opportunity to increase strength (for example through acquisition) • Invest at maintenance levels	**Opportunistic—preserve for harvest:** • Act to preserve or boost cash flow • Seek opportunistic sale or • Seek opportunistic rationalization to increase strengths • Prune product lines • Minimize investment	**Harvest or divest:** • Exit from market or prune product line • Determine timing so as to maximize present value • Concentrate on competitor's cash generators

Source: From N. Paley, *The Manager's Guide to Competitive Marketing Strategies*, 2/e, CRC Press, 1999, p. 155. Copyright © Taylor & Francis Group, Ltd. Via Copyright Clearance Center.

3. In turn, this makes for broader assessment during the planning process, bringing to light considerations of importance in both strategy formulation and strategy implementation.

Exhibit 9.1 (see page 277) shows GE chairman and CEO Jeff Immelt's surprising return to the use of a portfolio approach in 2006 as he charts GE's future.

BCG's Strategic Environments Matrix

BCG's latest matrix offering (see Exhibit 9.5) took a different approach, using the idea that it was the nature of competitive advantage in an industry that determined the strategies available to a company's businesses, which in turn determined the structure of the industry. Their idea was that such a framework could help ensure that individual businesses' strategies were consistent with strategies appropriate to their strategic environment. Furthermore,

EXHIBIT 9.5
BCG's Strategic
Environments Matrix

Source: R. M. Grant, *Contemporary Strategy Analysis*, 2001, p. 327. Reprinted with permission of Blackwell Publishing.

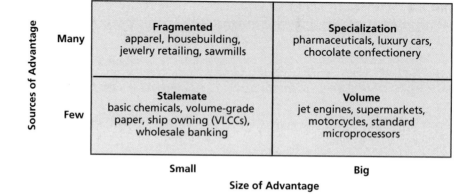

volume businesses
Businesses that have few sources of advantage, but the size is large—typically the result of scale economies.

stalemate businesses
Businesses with few sources of advantage, most of them small. Skills in operational efficiency, low overhead, and cost management are critical to profitability.

fragmented businesses
Businesses with many sources of advantage, but they are all small. They typically involve differentiated products with low brand loyalty, easily replicated technology, and minimal scale economies.

specialization businesses
Businesses with many sources of advantage. Skills in achieving differentiation (product design, branding expertise, innovation, and perhaps scale) characterize winning specialization businesses.

for corporate managers in multiple-business companies, this matrix offered one way to rationalize which businesses they are in—businesses that share core competencies and associated competitive advantages because of similar strategic environments.

The matrix has two dimensions. The number of sources of competitive advantage could be many with complex products and services (e.g., automobiles, financial services) and few with commodities (chemicals, microprocessors). Complex products offer multiple opportunities for differentiation as well as cost, while commodities must seek opportunities for cost advantages to survive.

The second dimension is size of competitive advantage. How big is the advantage available to the industry leader? The two dimensions then define four industry environments as follows:

- **Volume businesses** are those that have few sources of advantage, but the size is large—typically the result of scale economies. Advantages established in one such business may be transferable to another as Honda has done with its scale and expertise with small gasoline engines.

- **Stalemate businesses** have few sources of advantage, with most of those small. This results in very competitive situations. Skills in operational efficiency, low overhead, and cost management are critical to profitability.

- **Fragmented businesses** have many sources of advantage, but they are all small. This typically involves differentiated products with low brand loyalty, easily replicated technology, and minimal scale economies. Skills in focused market segments, typically geographic, the ability to respond quickly to changes, and low costs are critical in this environment.

- **Specialization businesses** have many sources of advantage and find those advantages potentially sizable. Skills in achieving differentiation—product design, branding expertise, innovation, first-mover, and perhaps scale—characterize winners here.

BCG viewed this matrix as providing guidance to multibusiness managers to determine whether they possessed the sources and size of advantage associated with the type of industry facing each business and allowed them a framework to realistically explore the nature of the strategic environments in which they competed or were interested in entering.

Limitations of Portfolio Approaches

Portfolio approaches made several contributions to strategic analysis by corporate managers convinced of their ability to transfer the competitive advantage of professional management across a broad array of businesses. They helped convey large amounts of information about diverse business units and corporate plans in a greatly simplified format. They illuminated similarities and differences between business units and helped convey the logic behind corporate strategies for each business with a common vocabulary. They simplified priorities for sharing corporate resources across diverse business units that generated and used those resources. They provided a simple prescription that gave corporate managers a sense of what they should accomplish—a balanced portfolio of businesses—and a way to control and allocate resources among them. While these approaches offered meaningful contributions, they had several critical limitations and shortcomings:

- A key problem with the portfolio matrix was that it did not address how value was being created across business units—the only relationship between them was cash. Addressing each business unit as a stand-alone entity ignores common core competencies and internal synergies among operating units.

- Truly accurate measurement for matrix classification was not as easy as the matrices portrayed. Identifying individual businesses, or distinct markets, was not often as precise as underlying assumptions required. Comparing business units on only two fundamental dimensions can lead to the conclusion that these are the only factors that really matter and that every unit can be compared fairly on those bases.

- The underlying assumption about the relationship between market share and profitability—the experience curve effect—varied across different industries and market segments. Some have no such link. Some find that firms with low market share can generate superior profitability with differentiation advantages.

- The limited strategic options, intended to describe the flow of resources in a company, came to be seen more as basic strategic missions, which creates a false sense of what each business's strategy actually entails. What do we actually "do" if we're a star? A cash cow? This becomes even more problematic when attempting to use the matrices to conceive strategies for average businesses in average-growth markets.

- The portfolio approach portrayed the notion that firms needed to be self-sufficient in capital. This ignored capital raised in capital markets.

- The portfolio approach typically failed to compare the competitive advantage a business received from being owned by a particular company with the costs of owning it. The 1980s saw many companies build enormous corporate infrastructures that created only small gains at the business level. The reengineering and deconstruction of numerous global conglomerates in the past 10 years reflects this important omission. We will examine this consideration in greater detail later in this chapter.

- Recent research by well-known consulting firm Booz-Allen-Hamilton suggests that "conventional wisdom is wrong. Corporate managers often rely on accounting metrics [based on past performance] to make business decisions." They go on to argue that "past performance is a poor predictor of the future. When performance is assessed over time, greater shareholder value can be created by improving the operations of the company's worst-performing businesses." "The way to thrive," they say, "is to love your dogs." Their point, backed up by impressive research, is that a corporate manager can learn to identify "value assets," hold and nurture them, and produce superior performance ultimately leading to increased shareholder value more so than can be achieved by acquiring and trying to add value to an overvalued "star."[2]

---

[2] A comprehensive discussion of these ideas to include their research examining the performance of "falling stars" and "rising dogs" can be found at Harry Quaris, Thomas Pernsteiner, and Kasturi Rangan, "Love your 'Dogs,'" *Strategy+Business Magazine,* Booz Allen Hamilton, www.strategy-business.com/resiliencereport/resilience/rr00030, 2007.

EXHIBIT 9.6 **Value Building in Multibusiness Companies**

Opportunities to Build Value or Sharing	Potential Competitive Advantage	Impediments to Achieving Enhanced Value
Market-Related Opportunities		
Shared salesforce activities, shared sales office, or both	Lower selling costs Better market coverage Stronger technical advice to buyers Enhanced convenience for buyers (can buy from single source) Improved access to buyers (have more products to sell)	• Buyers have different purchasing habits toward the products. • Different salespersons are more effective in representing the product. • Some products get more attention than others. • Buyers prefer to multiple-source rather than single-source their purchases.
Shared after-sale service and repair work	Lower servicing costs Better utilization of service personnel (less idle time) Faster servicing of customer calls	• Different equipment or different labor skills, or both, are needed to handle repairs. • Buyers may do some in-house repairs.
Shared brand name	Stronger brand image and company reputation Increased buyer confidence in the brand	• Company reputation is hurt if quality of one product is lower.
Shared advertising and promotional activities	Lower costs Greater clout in purchasing ads	• Appropriate forms of messages are different. • Appropriate timing of promotions is different.
Common distribution channels	Lower distribution costs Enhanced bargaining power with distributors and retailers to gain shelf space, shelf positioning, stronger push and more dealer attention, and better profit margins	• Dealers resist being dominated by a single supplier and turn to multiple sources and lines. • Heavy use of the shared channel erodes willingness of other channels to carry or push the firm's products.
Shared order processing	Lower order processing costs One-stop shopping for buyer to enhance service and, thus, differentiation	• Differences in ordering cycles disrupt order-processing economies.
Operating Opportunities		
Joint procurement of purchased inputs.	Lower input costs Improved input quality Improved service from suppliers	• Input needs are different in terms of quality or other specifications. • Inputs are needed at different plant locations, and centralized purchasing is not responsive to separate needs of each plant.
Shared manufacturing and assembly facilities	Lower manufacturing/assembly costs Better capacity utilization, because peak demand for one product correlates with valley demand for the other Bigger scale of operation to improve access to better technology, resulting in better quality	• Higher changeover costs in shifting from one product to another. • High-cost special tooling or equipment is required to accommodate quality differences or design differences.

EXHIBIT 9.6 (*continued*)

Opportunities to Build Value or Sharing	Potential Competitive Advantage	Impediments to Achieving Enhanced Value
Operating Opportunities (cont.)		
Shared inbound or outbound shipping and materials handling	Lower freight and handling costs Better delivery reliability More frequent deliveries, such that inventory costs are reduced	• Input sources or plant locations, or both, are in different geographic areas. • Needs for frequency and reliability of inbound/outbound delivery differ among the business units.
Shared product and process technologies, technology development, or both.	Lower product or process design costs, or both, because of shorter design times and transfers of knowledge from area to area More innovative ability, owing to scale of effort and attraction of better R&D personnel	• Technologies are the same, but the applications in different business units are different enough to prevent much sharing of real value.
Shared administrative support activities	Lower administrative and operating overhead costs	• Support activities are not a large proportion of cost, and sharing has little cost impact (and virtually no differentiation impact).
Management Opportunities		
Shared management know-how, operating skills, and proprietary information	Efficient transfer of a distinctive competence—can create cost savings or enhance differentiation More effective management as concerns strategy formulation, strategy implementation, and understanding of key success factors	• Actual transfer of know-how is costly or stretches the key skill personnel too thinly, or both. • Increased risks that proprietary information will leak out.

Source: Based on Michael Porter, *On Competition*, Harvard Business School Press.

Constructing business portfolio matrices must be undertaken with these limitations in mind. Perhaps it is best to say that they provide one form of input to corporate managers seeking to balance financial resources. While limitations have meant portfolio approaches are seen as mere historical concepts, seldom recommended, it is interesting that the new chairman of the company that pioneered and subsequently abandoned the portfolio has come full circle in 2006, embracing the concept as a key basis for helping the post-Welch GE rationalize a dramatically new approach to the twenty-first century at GE (see Exhibit 9.1). Perhaps this foretells a continued use of the portfolio approach, recognizing its limitations, to provide a picture of the "balance" of resource generators and users, to test underlying assumptions about these issues in more involved corporate planning efforts, and to leverage core competencies to build sustained competitive advantages. Indeed, the next major approach in the evolution of multibusiness strategic analysis is to leverage shared capabilities and core competencies.

THE SYNERGY APPROACH: LEVERAGING CORE COMPETENCIES

Opportunities to build value via diversification, integration, or joint venture strategies are usually found in market-related, operations-related, and management activities. Each business's basic value chain activities or infrastructure become a source of potential synergy and competitive advantage for another business in the corporate portfolio. Morrison's Cafeterias, once a mainstay of the food-service industry in malls across much of the United States, accelerated its diversification into other restaurant concepts such as Ruby Tuesday's, followed by L&N Seafood Grill, Silver Spoon Café, Mozzarella's, and Tia's Tex-Mex. It also acquired three other food-contract firms. Numerous opportunities for shared operating capabilities and management capabilities drove this decision and, upon repeated strategic analysis, accelerated corporate managers' decision to move Morrison's totally out of the cafeteria segment a few years later. Some of the more common opportunities to share value chain activities and build value are identified in Exhibit 9.6.

Strategic analysis is concerned with whether or not the potential competitive advantages expected to arise from each value opportunity have materialized. Where advantage has not materialized, corporate strategists must take care to scrutinize possible impediments to achieving the synergy or competitive advantage. We have identified in Exhibit 9.6 several impediments associated with each opportunity, which strategists are well advised to examine. Good strategists assure themselves that their organization has ways to avoid or minimize the effects of any impediments, or they recommend against further integration or diversification and consider divestiture options.

Two elements are critical in meaningful shared opportunities:

1. The shared opportunities must be a significant portion of the value chain of the businesses involved. Returning to Morrison's Cafeteria, its purchasing and inbound logistics infrastructure give Ruby Tuesday's operators an immediate cost-effective purchasing and inventory management capability that lowered its cost in a significant cost activity.

2. The businesses involved must truly have shared needs—need for the same activity—or there is no basis for synergy in the first place. Novell, the U.S.-based networking software giant, paid $900 million for WordPerfect, envisioning numerous synergies serving offices globally, not to mention 15 million WordPerfect users. Little more than a year later, Novell would sell WordPerfect for less than $300 million, because, as CEO Bob Frankenberg said, "It is not because WordPerfect is not a business without a future, but for Novell it represented a distraction from our strategy."

Corporate strategies have repeatedly rushed into diversification only to find perceived opportunities for sharing were nonexistent because the businesses did not really have shared needs.

The most compelling reason companies should diversify can be found in situations where core competencies—key value-building skills—can be leveraged with other products or into markets that are not a part of where they were created. Where this works well, extraordinary value can be built. Managers undertaking diversification strategies should dedicate a significant portion of their strategic analysis to this question.

General Cinema was a company that grew from drive-in theaters to eventually dominate the multicinema, movie exhibition industry. Next, they entered soft-drink bottling and became the largest bottler of soft drinks (Pepsi) in North America. Their stock value rose 2,000 percent in 10 years. They found that core competencies in movie exhibition—managing many small, localized businesses; dealing with a few large suppliers; applying central marketing skills locally; and acquiring or crafting a "franchise"—were virtually the same in soft-drink bottling. IBM CEO Sam Palmisano and his management team have done an extraordinary job of creating a virtually new IBM by adapting a multibusiness strategy

IBM Gets a Second Life . . . and Its CEO an Avatar

BusinessWeek

Big Blue's consumer-related business is growing fast thanks to the migration of its technologies from enterprise computing to consumer applications.

IBM may be one of the last tech outfits to come to mind when you think about consumer products. After all, the company severed its direct sales link with consumers when it sold its PC division to Lenovo Group two years ago. Among the glitzy, tricked-out Consumer Electronics Show booths for Sony (SNE), Samsung, and XM Satellite Radio (XMSR), IBM has set up a sprawling showcase for its technologies and services.

No, Big Blue isn't getting into the gadget business. Instead, it makes a host of technologies that go inside other companies' products—whether it's video game consoles, TVs, or even virtual worlds such as Second Life. "There are a lot of ways we can play (in consumer markets) but not necessarily be the game console maker or the YouTube," said IBM chief executive Samuel Palmisano.

Most of IBM's revenue comes from selling powerful computers, software, and services to large corporations, but one of the fastest-growing pieces of its business is the consumer sphere.

ENTERPRISE INVESTMENT, CONSUMER BENEFITS

Some of IBM's competitors belittle its consumer aspirations. Microsoft CEO Steven Ballmer said he doesn't even consider IBM to be a broad-based technology company anymore, because it focuses so much on the enterprise.

Still, analysts credit IBM with crafting a smart and successful corporate strategy designed to leverage and share core competencies across a diverse set of businesses. "A few years ago, nobody would have dreamed that IBM would score the top three game consoles," says analyst Rick Doherty of market researcher Envisioneering Group. "Now there's an opportunity for IBM to do similar things in the digital living room and portable devices. And this isn't just about hardware. They can manage content and security for the entertainment industry."

IBM has found a way to make many of its research investments in enterprise computing also pay off in the consumer realm, and vice versa. The Cell microprocessor, which it co-developed with partners Sony and Toshiba, is being employed by Mercury Computer in so-called blade servers that are used for medical imaging, defense electronics, and, you guessed it, video gaming.

SECOND LIFE—Sam Palmisano, IBM Chairman and CEO
On November 14, Sam Palmisano's avatar made an appearance on the IBM island in Second Life to announce that the computer giant is investing $100 million in a new business unit to explore the potential of new technologies like virtual worlds in commerce, e-learning, and customer services.

SEVERAL DIVISIONS INVOLVED

On the software side, programs designed to manage and safeguard corporate data can be used for movies and music. "You have a convergence between the computer world and the consumer world," says Adalio Sanchez, general manager of IBM's Technology Collaboration Solutions business unit, one of its emerging businesses, which targets the consumer sphere. "In the past, discoveries in the computer world fed the consumer space. That's flipping today."

Other parts of IBM are also instrumental in its consumer play. IBM Research labs provided the real-time speech translation technology being used by the U.S. Army in Iraq and now being targeted by IBM at consumer uses. Its engineering services division helps consumer companies design whole new products and services, including the Joysound Karaoke service being sold by Xing to bars in Japan.

Sources: Reprinted with special permission from Steve Hamm, "IBM at CES: Right at Home," *BusinessWeek*, May 11, 2007; and Steve Hamm, "Palmisano Gets a Second Life," *BusinessWeek*, November 20, 2006. Copyright © 2007 The McGraw-Hill Companies.

centered around finding, sharing, and leveraging core competencies across a seemingly diverse set of businesses and markets. Not only have they done so with existing competencies, but their organization has proven remarkably adept at leveraging newly found technologies and capabilities within each business across other businesses—enterprise focused business competencies deployed in consumer product offerings and vice versa as described in Exhibit 9.7, Strategy in Action.

Each Core Competency Should Provide a Relevant Competitive Advantage to the Intended Businesses

The core competency must assist the intended business in creating strength relative to key competition. This could occur at any step in the business's value chain. But it must represent a major source of value to be a basis for competitive advantage—and the core competence must be transferable. Honda of Japan viewed itself as having a core competence in manufacturing small, internal combustion engines. It diversified into small garden tools, perceiving that traditional electric tools would be much more attractive if powered by a lightweight, mobile, gas combustion motor. Their core competency created a major competitive advantage in a market void of gas-driven hand tools. When Coca-Cola added bottled water to its portfolio of products, it expected its extraordinary core competencies in marketing and distribution to rapidly build value in this business. Ten years later, Coke sold its water assets, concluding that the product did not have enough margin to interest its franchised bottlers and that marketing was not a significant value-building activity among many small suppliers competing primarily on the cost of "producing" and shipping water. In the last few years, however, Coke has reversed its decision and added the Dasani water brand because a rapidly increasing consumer demand has made the value of its extensive distribution network a relevant competitive advantage to the Dasani water product line.

Businesses in the Portfolio Should Be Related in Ways That Make the Company's Core Competencies Beneficial

Related versus unrelated diversification is an important distinction to understand as you evaluate the diversification question. "Related" businesses are those that rely on the same or similar capabilities to be successful and attain competitive advantage in their respective product markets. Earlier, we described General Cinema's spectacular success in both movie exhibition and soft-drink bottling. Seemingly unrelated, they were actually very related businesses in terms of key core competencies that shaped success—managing a network of diverse business locations, localized competition, reliance on a few large suppliers, and centralized marketing advantages. Thus, the products of various businesses do not necessarily have to be similar to leverage core competencies. While their products may not be related, it is essential that some activities in their value chains require similar skills to create competitive advantage if the company is going to leverage its core competence(s) in a value-creating way. Exhibit 9.7 offered an example of IBM's remarkable effectiveness in doing just this the last five years. In fact, their CEO now even has an Avatar on Second Life to build an understanding of ways IBM's core competencies could be related to and leveraged in the emerging virtual world on the Web.

Situations that involve "unrelated" diversification occur when no real overlapping capabilities or products exist other than financial resources. We refer to this as *conglomerate diversification* in Chapter 7. Recent research indicates that the most profitable firms are those that have diversified around a set of resources and capabilities that are specialized enough to confer a meaningful competitive advantage in an attractive industry, yet adaptable enough to be advantageously applied across several others. The least profitable are broadly diversified firms whose strategies are built around very general resources

Strategy in Action

Exhibit 9.8

Six Critical Questions for Diversification

WHAT CAN OUR COMPANY DO BETTER THAN ANY OF ITS COMPETITORS IN ITS CURRENT MARKET(S)?

Managers often diversify on the basis of vague definitions of their business rather than on a systematic analysis of what sets their company apart from its competitors. By determining what they can do better than their existing competitors, companies will have a better chance of succeeding in new markets.

WHAT CORE COMPETENCIES DO WE NEED IN ORDER TO SUCCEED IN THE NEW MARKET?

Excelling in one market does not guarantee success in a new and related one. Managers considering diversification must ask whether their company has every core competency necessary to establish a competitive advantage in the territory it hopes to conquer.

CAN WE CATCH UP TO OR LEAPFROG COMPETITORS AT THEIR OWN GAME?

All is not necessarily lost if managers find that they lack a critical core competency. There is always the potential to buy what is missing, develop it in-house, or render it unnecessary by changing the competitive rules of the game.

WILL DIVERSIFICATION BREAK UP CORE COMPETENCIES THAT NEED TO BE KEPT TOGETHER?

Many companies introduce their time-tested core competencies and capabilities in a new market and still fail. That is because they have separated core competencies and capabilities that rely on one another for their effectiveness and hence are not able to function alone.

WILL WE SIMPLY BE A PLAYER IN THE NEW MARKET OR WILL WE EMERGE AS A WINNER?

Diversifying companies are often quickly outmaneuvered by their new competitors. Why? In many cases, they have failed to consider whether their strategic assets can be easily imitated, purchased on the open market, or replaced.

WHAT CAN OUR COMPANY LEARN BY DIVERSIFYING, AND ARE WE SUFFICIENTLY ORGANIZED TO LEARN IT?

Savvy companies know how to make diversification a learning experience. They see how new businesses can help improve existing ones, act as stepping-stones to industries previously out of reach, or improve organizational efficiency.

Source: Reprinted by permission of *Harvard Business Review*. Exhibit from "To Diversify or Not to Diversify," by C. C. Markides, November–December 1997. Copyright © 1997 by the Harvard Business School Publishing Corporation; all rights reserved.

(e.g., money) that are applied in a wide variety of industries, but that are seldom instrumental to competitive advantage in those settings.[3]

Any Combination of Competencies Must Be Unique or Difficult to Recreate

Skills that corporate strategists expect to transfer from one business to another, or from corporate to various businesses, may be transferable. They may also be easily replicated by competitors. When this is the case, no sustainable competitive advantage is created. Sometimes strategists look for a combination of competencies, a package of various interrelated skills, as another way to create a situation where seemingly easily replicated competencies become unique, sustainable competitive advantages. 3M Corporation has the enviable record of having 25 percent of its earnings always coming from products introduced within the last five years. 3M has been able to "bundle" the skills necessary to

[3] David J. Collis and Cynthia A. Montgomery, *Corporate Strategy* (Chicago: McGraw-Hill/Irwin, 2005), p. 88; "Why Mergers Fail," *McKinsey Quarterly Report,* 2001, vol. 4; and "Deals That Create Value," *McKinsey Quarterly Report,* 2001, vol. 1.

accelerate the introduction of new products so that it consistently extracts early life-cycle value from adhesive-related products that hundreds of competitors with similar technical or marketing competencies cannot touch.

All too often companies envision a combination of competencies that make sense conceptually. This vision of synergy develops an energy of its own, leading CEOs to relentlessly push the merger of the firms involved. But what makes sense conceptually and is seen as difficult for competitors to recreate often proves difficult if not impossible to create in the first place. Exhibit 9.8, Strategy in Action, summarizes six key questions managers should answer to identify the strategic risks and opportunities that diversification presents.

THE CORPORATE PARENT ROLE: CAN IT ADD TANGIBLE VALUE?

Realizing synergies from shared capabilities and core competencies is a key way value is added in multibusiness companies. Research suggests that figuring out if the synergies are real and, if so, how to capture those synergies is most effectively accomplished by business unit managers, not the corporate parent.[4] How then can the corporate parent add value to its businesses in a multibusiness company? We want to acquaint you with two perspectives to use in attempting to answer this question: the parenting framework and the patching approach.

The Parenting Framework

parenting framework
The perspective that the role of corporate headquarters (the "parent") in multibusiness (the "children") companies is that of a parent sharing wisdom, insight, and guidance to help develop its various businesses to excel.

The **parenting framework** perspective sees multibusiness companies as creating value by influencing—or parenting—the businesses they own. The best parent companies create more value than any of their rivals do or would if they owned the same businesses. To add value, a parent must improve its businesses. Obviously there must be room for improvement. Advocates of this perspective call the potential for improvement within a business "a parenting opportunity." They identify 10 places to look for parenting opportunities, which then become the focus of strategic analysis and choice across multiple businesses and their interface with the parent organization.[5] Let's look at each briefly.

Size and Age

Old, large, successful businesses frequently engender entrenched bureaucracies and overhead structures that are hard to dismantle from inside the business. Doing so may add value, and getting it done may be best done by an external catalyst, the parent. Small, young businesses may lack some key functional skills, or outgrow their top managers' capabilities, or lack capital to deal with a temporary downturn or accelerated growth opportunity. Where these are relevant issues within one or more businesses, a parenting opportunity to add value may exist.

Management

Does the business employ managers superior in comparison with its competitors? Is the business's success dependent on attracting and keeping people with specialized skills?

---

[4] Michael Goold, Andrew Campbell, and Marcus Alexander, "The Quest for Parenting Advantage," *Harvard Business Review*, March–April 1995; Michael Goold, Andrew Campbell, and Marcus Alexander, "How Corporate Parents Add Value to the Stand-Alone Performance of Their Businesses," *Business Strategy Review*, Winter 1994.

[5] Ibid, p. 126. These 10 areas of opportunity are taken from an insert entitled "Ten Places to Look for Parenting Opportunities" on this page of the *Harvard Business Review* article.

Are key managers focused on the right objectives? Ensuring that these issues are addressed and objectively assessed and assisting in any resolution may be a parenting opportunity that could add value.

Business Definition

Business unit managers may have a myopic or erroneous vision of what their business should be, which, in turn, has them targeting a market that is too narrow or broad. They may employ too much vertical integration or not enough. Accelerated trends toward out-sourcing and strategic alliances are changing the definitions of many businesses. All of this creates a parenting opportunity to help redefine a business unit in a way that creates greater value.

Predictable Errors

The nature of a business and its unique situation can lead managers to make predictable mistakes. Managers responsible for previous strategic decisions are vested in the success of those decisions, which may prevent openness to new alternatives. Older, mature businesses often accumulate a variety of products and markets, which becomes excessive diversification within a particular business. Cyclical markets can lead to underinvestment during downturns and overinvestment during the upswing. Lengthy product life cycles can lead to overreliance on old products. All of these are predictable errors a parent can monitor and attempt to avoid, creating, in turn, added value.

Linkages

Business units may be able to improve market position or efficiency by linking with other businesses that are not readily apparent to the management of the business unit in question. Whether apparent or not, linkages among business units within or outside the parent company may be complex or difficult to establish without parent company help. In either case, an opportunity to add value may exist.

Common Capabilities

Fundamental to successful diversification, as we have discussed earlier, is the notion of sharing capabilities and competencies needed by multiple business units. Parenting opportunities to add value may arise from time to time through regular scrutiny of opportunities to share capabilities or add shared capabilities that would otherwise go unnoticed by business unit managers closer to daily business operations.

Specialized Expertise

There may be situations in which the parent company possesses specialized or rare expertise that may benefit a business unit and add value in the process. Unique legal, technical, or administrative expertise critical in a particular situation or decision point, which is quickly and easily available, can prove very valuable.

External Relations

Does the business have external stakeholders—governments, regulators, unions, suppliers, shareholders—the parent company could manage more effectively than individual business units? If so, a natural parenting opportunity exists that should add value.

Major Decisions

A business unit may face difficult decisions in areas for which it lacks expertise—for example, making an acquisition, entering China, a major capacity expansion, divesting and outsourcing a major part of the business's operations. Obtaining capital externally to fund a major investment may be much more difficult than doing so through the parent

Top Strategist
Indra Nooyi, CEO of PepsiCo

Exhibit
9.9

Keep an eye on Indra Nooyi. Analysts expect this daughter of Chennai, India, to accelerate the beverage and snack giant's efforts to broaden its portfolio and globalize its brands as PepsiCo chairperson and CEO.

At PepsiCo Inc., Indra Nooyi has long been known for two things: a prescient business sense and an irreverent personal style. The combination became obvious soon after she joined the company as its chief strategist 13 years ago. She pushed chief executive Roger Enrico to spin off Taco Bell, Pizza Hut, and KFC in 1997 because she didn't feel PepsiCo could add enough value to the fast-food business. She later was instrumental in the purchase of Tropicana, the spinoff of Pepsi's bottling business, and the $13 billion merger with Quaker Oats Co. Each of these moves has paid off.

All the while, Nooyi has proved comfortable enough with her leadership presence to patrol the office barefoot at times and even sing in the halls, perhaps a holdover from her teen days in an all-girl rock band in her hometown of Chennai, India. She gave Enrico a karaoke machine before he left in 2001 and hired a live "Jam-eoke" band to help senior executives belt out tunes at a management conference earlier this year.

"Indra can drive as deep and hard as anyone I've ever met," Enrico says, "but she can do it with a sense of heart and fun." Enrico praises Nooyi for her practicality, vision, and courage—"This was a woman who was well-known for walking around barefoot and singing songs," he laughs. "She is a mature and seasoned executive, but she hasn't lost her spontaneity and sense of humor."

Nooyi learned early on to embrace rather than hide her differences in the corporate world. Nooyi wore a sari to an interview at Boston Consulting Group and was offered the job. She later held corporate strategy posts at Motorola Inc. and what is now ABB Group. What drew her to PepsiCo was the chance to make a difference in a company that was struggling.

Over the past decade, she says, "PepsiCo has transformed itself to become among the best food companies and one of the better corporations in the world." Since 2000, when she became chief financial officer, the company's annual revenues have risen 72 percent, while net profit more than doubled, to $5.6 billion last year. As chairman and CEO, Nooyi promotes the concept of "performance with purpose," trying to make PepsiCo a ground-breaker in areas like selling healthy food and diversifying its workforce.

With her passion for globalization and sharp eye for acquisitions, Nooyi has been a major force in shaping the direction of PepsiCo for some time now. She brings a rich understanding of emerging markets at a time when they have become critical growth areas for PepsiCo. It was her idea to move south of the border and buy Mexican subsidiary Sabritas, bringing their products into the United States and selling them through smaller mom-&-pop retail outlets in Mexican-dominated areas. It was an immediate hit with the 50 million Hispanic population in the United States.

By defining its mission as serving the customer, a global customer, rather than protecting its venerable brands, PepsiCo under Nooyi's leadership appears to be leveraging its central, corporate parent capabilities in support of opportunities for product and market growth and improvement driven from the consumer end, not the corporate end. And she is doing so on a global scale.

Source: Reprinted with special permission from Diane Brady, "Indra Nooyi: Keeping Cool in Hot Water," *Business-Week*, June 11, 2007. Copyright © 2007 The McGraw-Hill Companies.

company—GE proved this could be a major parenting advantage in the way it developed GE Capital into a major source of capital for its other business units as well as to finance major capital purchases by customers of its own business units.

Major Changes

Sometimes a business needs to make major changes in ways critical to the business's future success yet which involve areas or considerations in which the business unit's management has little or no experience. A complete revamping of a business unit's information management process, outsourcing all that capability to India, or shifting all of a business unit's production operations to another business unit in another part of the world—these are just a few examples of major changes in which the parent may have extensive experience with what feels like unknown territory to the business's management team.

Overlap in some of these 10 sources of parenting opportunities may exist. For example, specialized expertise in China and a major decision to locate or outsource operations there may be the same source of added value. And that decision would involve a major change. The fact that overlap, or redundancy may exist in classifying sources of parenting opportunity is a minor consideration, however, relative to the value of the parenting framework for strategic analysis in multibusiness companies. The portfolio approaches focus on how businesses' cash, profit, and growth potential create a balance within the portfolio. The core competence approach concentrates on how business units are related and can share technical and operating know-how and capacity. The parenting framework adds to these approaches and the strategic analysis in a multibusiness company because it focuses on competencies of the parent organization and on the value created from the relationship between the parent and its businesses. Exhibit 9.9, Top Strategist, shows how PepsiCo's chairwoman and CEO Indra Nooyi has created a significant corporate parenting role as she fosters innovations, acquires new brands, divests certain businesses, all the time building organizational linkages and sharing core competencies across several PepsiCo business units and brands, both domestically and globally.

The Patching Approach

patching
The process by which corporate executives routinely "remap" their businesses to match rapidly changing market opportunities—adding, splitting, transferring, exiting, or combining chunks of businesses.

strategic processes
Decision making, operational activities, and sales activities that are critical business processes.

strategic positioning
The way a business is designed and positioned to serve target markets.

Another approach that focuses on the role and ability of corporate managers to create value in the management of multibusiness companies is called "patching."[6] **Patching** is the process by which corporate executives routinely remap businesses to match rapidly changing market opportunities. It can take the form of adding, splitting, transferring, exiting, or combining chunks of businesses. Patching is not seen as critical in stable, unchanging markets. When markets are turbulent and rapidly changing, patching is seen as critical to the creation of economic value in a multibusiness company.

Proponents of this perspective on the strategic decision-making function of corporate executives say it is the critical, and arguably only, way corporate executives can add value beyond the sum of the businesses within the company. They view traditional corporate strategy as creating defensible strategic positions for business units by acquiring or building valuable assets, wisely allocating resources to them, and weaving synergies among them. In volatile markets, they argue, this traditional approach results in business units with strategies that are quickly outdated and competitive advantages rarely sustained beyond a few years.[7] As a result, they say, strategic analysis should center on **strategic processes** more than **strategic positioning.** In these volatile markets, patchers' strategic analysis focuses on making quick, small, frequent changes in parts of businesses and organizational processes that enable dynamic strategic repositioning rather than building long-term defensible positions. Exhibit 9.10 compares differences between traditional approaches to shaping corporate strategy with the patching approach.

[6] Kathleen M. Eisenhardt and Shona L. Brown, "Patching: Restitching Business Portfolios in Dynamic Markets," *Harvard Business Review,* May–June 1999, pp. 72–82.

[7] Ibid, p. 76; and K. M. Eisenhardt and D. N. Sull, "Strategy as Simple Rules," *Harvard Business Review,* January 2001.

EXHIBIT 9.10 Three Approaches to Strategy

Managers competing in business can choose among three distinct ways to fight. They can build a fortress and defend it; they can nurture and leverage unique resources; or they can flexibly pursue fleeting opportunities within simple rules. Each approach requires different skill sets and works best under different circumstances.

	Position	**Resources**	**Patching [Simple Rules]**
Strategic logic	Establish position	Leverage resources	Pursue opportunities
Strategic steps	Identify an attractive market	Establish a vision Build resources	Jump into the confusion Keep moving
	Locate a defensible position	Leverage across markets	Seize opportunities Finish strong
	Fortify and defend		
Strategic question	Where should we be?	What should we be?	How should we proceed?
Source of advantage	Unique, valuable position with tightly integrated activity system	Unique, valuable, inimitable resources	Key processes and unique simple rules
Works best in	Slowly changing, well-structured markets	Moderately changing, well-structured markets	Rapidly changing, ambiguous markets
Duration of advantage	Sustained	Sustained	Unpredictable
Risk	Too difficult to alter position as conditions change	Too slow to build new resources as conditions change	Too tentative in executing promising opportunities
Performance goal	Profitability	Long-term dominance	Growth

Source: Reprinted by permission of *Harvard Business Review*. Exhibit from "Strategy as Simple Rules," by K. M. Eisenhardt and D. N. Sull, January 2001. Copyright © 2001 by the Harvard Business School Publishing Corporation; all rights reserved.

To be successful with a patching approach to corporate strategic analysis and choice in turbulent markets, Eisenhardt and Sull suggest that managers should flexibly seize opportunities—as long as that flexibility is disciplined. Effective corporate strategists, they argue, focus on key processes and *simple rules*. The following example at Miramax helps illustrate the notion of strategy as simple rules:

> Miramax—well known for artistically innovative movies such as *The Crying Game, Life is Beautiful*, and *Pulp Fiction*—has boundary rules that guide the all-important movie-picking process: First, every movie must revolve around a central human condition, such as love *(The Crying Game)* or envy *(The Talented Mr. Ripley)*. Second, a movie's main character must be appealing but deeply flawed—the hero of *Shakespeare in Love* is gifted and charming but steals ideas from friends and betrays his wife. Third, movies must have a very clear story line with a beginning, middle, and end (although in *Pulp Fiction* the end comes first). Finally, there is a firm cap on production costs. Within the rules, there is flexibility to move quickly when a writer or director shows up with a great script. The result is an enormously creative and even surprising flow of movies and enough discipline to produce superior, consistent financial results. *The English Patient*, for example, cost $27 million to make, grossed more than $200 million, and grabbed nine Oscars.[8]

[8] Ibid, Eisenhardt and Sull, p. 111.

EXHIBIT 9.11   Simple Rules, Summarized

In turbulent markets, managers should flexibly seize opportunities—but flexibility must be disciplined. Smart companies focus on key processes and simple rules. Different types of rules help executives manage different aspects of seizing opportunities.

Type	Purpose	Example
How-to rules	Spell out key features of how a process is executed—"What makes our process unique?"	Akami's rules for the customer service process: Staff must consist of technical gurus, every question must be answered on the first call or e-mail, and R&D staff must rotate through customer service.
Boundary rules	Focus on which opportunities can be pursued and which are outside the pale.	Cisco's early acquisitions rule: Companies to be acquired must have no more than 75 employees, 75 percent of whom are engineers.
Priority rules	Help managers rank the accepted opportunities.	Intel's rule for allocating manufacturing capacity: Allocation is based on a product's gross margin.
Timing rules	Synchronize managers with the pace of emerging opportunities and other parts of the company.	Nortel's rules for product development: Project teams must know when a product has to be delivered to the customer to win, and product development time must be less than 18 months.
Exit rules	Help managers decide when to pull out of yesterday's opportunities.	Oticon's rule for pulling the plug on projects in development: If a key team member—manager or not—chooses to leave the project for another within the company, the project is killed.

Source: Reprinted by permission of *Harvard Business Review.* Exhibit from "Strategy as Simple Rules," by K. M. Eisenhardt and D. N. Sull, January 2001. Copyright © 2001 by the Harvard Business School Publishing Corporation; all rights reserved.

Different types of rules help managers and strategists manage different aspects of seizing opportunities. Exhibit 9.11 explains and illustrates five such types of rules. These rules are called "simple" rules because they need to be brief, be axiomatic, and convey fundamental guidelines to decisions or actions. They need to provide just enough structure to allow managers to move quickly to capture opportunities with confidence that the judgments and commitments they make are consistent with corporate intent. At the same time, while they set parameters on actions and decisions, they are not thick manuals or rules and policies that managers in turbulent environments may find paralyze any efforts to quickly capitalize on opportunities. Exhibit 9.12, Strategy in Action, helps explain the simple rules idea behind the patching approach to corporate strategic decision making by explaining what simple rules are not.

The patching approach then relies on simple rules unique to a particular parent company that exist to guide managers in the corporate organization and its business units in making rapid decisions about quickly reshaping parts of the company and allocating time as well as money to capitalize on rapidly shifting market opportunities. The fundamental argument of this approach is that no one can predict how long a competitive advantage will last, particularly in turbulent, rapidly changing markets. While managers in stable markets may be able to rely on complex strategies built on detailed predictions of future trends, managers in complex, fast-moving markets—where significant growth and wealth creation may occur—face constant unpredictability; hence, strategy must be simple, responsive, and dynamic to encourage success.

What Simple Rules Are Not

It is impossible to dictate exactly what a company's simple rules should be. It is possible, however, to say what they should *not* be.

BROAD

Managers often confuse a company's guiding principles with simple rules. The celebrated "HP way," for example, consists of principles like "we focus on a high level of achievement and contribution" and "we encourage flexibility and innovation." The principles are designed to apply to every activity within the company, from purchasing to product innovation. They may create a productive culture, but they provide little concrete guidance for employees trying to evaluate a partner or decide whether to enter a new market. The most effective simple rules, in contrast, are tailored to a single process.

VAGUE

Some rules cover a single process but are too vague to provide real guidance. One Western bank operating in Russia, for example, provided the following guideline for screening investment proposals: all investments must be currently undervalued and have potential for long-term capital appreciation. Imagine the plight of a newly hired associate who turns to that rule for guidance!

A simple screen can help managers test whether their rules are too vague. Ask: could any reasonable person argue the exact opposite of the rule? In the case of the bank in Russia, it is hard to imagine anyone suggesting that the company target overvalued companies with no potential for long-term capital appreciation. If your rules flunk this test, they are not effective.

MINDLESS

Companies whose simple rules have remained implicit may find upon examining them that these rules destroy rather than create value. In one company, managers listed their recent partnership relationships and then tried to figure out what rules could have produced the list. To their chagrin, they found that one rule seemed to be: always form partnerships with small, weak companies that we can control. Another was: always form partnerships with companies that are not as successful as they once were. Again, use a simple test; reverse-engineer your processes to determine your implicit simple rules. Throw out the ones that are embarrassing.

STALE

In high-velocity markets, rules can linger beyond their sell-by dates. Consider Banc One. The Columbus, Ohio–based bank grew to be the seventh-largest bank in the United States by acquiring more than 100 regional banks. Banc One's acquisitions followed a set of simple rules that were based on experience: Banc One must never pay so much that earnings are diluted, it must only buy successful banks with established management teams, it must never acquire a bank with assets greater than one-third of Banc One's, and it must allow acquired banks to run as autonomous affiliates. The rules worked well until others in the banking industry consolidated operations to lower their costs substantially. Then Banc One's loose confederation of banks was burdened with redundant operations, and it got clobbered by efficient competitors.

How do you figure out if your rules are stale? Slowing growth is a good indicator. Stock price is even better. Investors obsess about the future, while your own financials report the past. So if your share price is dropping relative to your competitors' share prices, or if your percentage of the industry's market value is declining, or if growth is slipping, your rules may need to be refreshed.

Source: Reprinted by permission of *Harvard Business Review.* Exhibit from "Strategy as Simple Rules," by K. M. Eisenhardt and D. N. Sull, January 2001. Copyright © 2001 by the Harvard Business School Publishing Corporation; all rights reserved.

Summary

This chapter examined how managers make strategic decisions in multibusiness companies. One of the earliest approaches was to look at the company as a portfolio of businesses. This portfolio was then examined and evaluated based on each business's growth potential, market position, and need for and ability to generate cash. Corporate strategists then allocated resources, divested, and acquired businesses based on the balance across this portfolio of businesses or possible businesses.

The notion of synergy across business units—sharing capabilities and leveraging core competencies—has been another very widely adopted approach to making strategic decisions in multibusiness companies. Sharing capabilities allows for greater efficiencies, enhanced expertise, and competitive advantage. Core competencies that generate competitive advantage can often be leveraged across multiple businesses, thereby expanding the impact and value added from that competitive advantage.

Globalization, rapid change, outsourcing, and other major forces shaping today's economic landscape have ushered in multibusiness strategic decision making that also focuses on the role and value-added contributions, if any, of the parent company itself. Does the parent company add or could it add value beyond the sum of the businesses it owns? Two perspectives that have gained popularity in multibusiness companies' strategic decision making are the parenting framework and the patching approach. The parenting framework focuses on 10 areas of opportunity managers should carefully explore to find ways the parent organization might add value to one or more businesses and the overall company. The patching approach concentrates on multibusiness companies in turbulent markets of the twenty-first century, where managers need to make quick, small shifts and adjustments in processes, markets, and products, and offers five types of "simple rules" that managers use as guidelines to structure quick decisions throughout a multibusiness company on a continuous basis.

Key Terms	cash cows, *p. 278*	portfolio techniques, *p. 278*	stalemate businesses, *p. 282*
	dogs, *p. 279*	relative competitive	stars, *p. 278*
	fragmented businesses, *p. 282*	position, *p. 278*	strategic positioning, *p. 293*
	market growth rate, *p. 278*	question marks, *p. 279*	strategic processes, *p. 293*
	parenting framework, *p. 290*	specialization	volume businesses, *p. 282*
	patching, *p. 293*	businesses, *p. 282*	

Questions for Discussion

1. How does strategic analysis at the corporate level differ from strategic analysis at the business unit level? How are they related?
2. When would multibusiness companies find the portfolio approach to strategic analysis and choice useful?
3. What are three types of opportunities for sharing that form a sound basis for diversification or vertical integration? Give an example of each from companies you have read about.
4. Describe three types of opportunities through which a corporate parent could add value beyond the sum of its separate businesses.
5. What does "patching" refer to? Describe and illustrate two rules that might guide managers to build value in their businesses.

Chapter 9 Discussion Case

eBay's Changing Identity: *Best known for online auctions, the PayPal parent is building a diversified portfolio of Internet businesses. So why aren't investors happier?*

Meg Whitman, CEO, eBay

1   In its television ads, eBay describes itself as the place to get "it," whatever it may be. The company deliberately leaves "it" undefined to emphasize the immense variety of goods available for auction on its site. "It" is anything a consumer can imagine. But as eBay expands into myriad new businesses—from telecommunications to social networking—some investors are puzzling over what it (eBay) is becoming.

2   Since shelling out $1.5 billion in 2002 to acquire online payment processor PayPal, eBay has aggressively expanded into areas well beyond its core business of charging people fees to auction off goods via the Internet. Over the last five years, a spate of acquisitions—some of which are just now generating significant profits—has made the company into something of an enigma. EBay is a Web auctioneer. It's an online payment processor and bank of sorts (PayPal). It's a ticket seller (StubHub). It's a global Internet telephone service (Skype). It's a classified ad service (Kijiji).

3   Now eBay is said to be moving into the social search business. Tech industry blogs such as GigaOm and TechCrunch are buzzing that eBay is in talks to acquire StumbleUpon, a popular site that lets users find other Web sites based on their interests and the recommendations of others. Both eBay and StumbleUpon declined comment.

CORE CONCERNS

4   The difficulty of defining eBay and how its businesses fit together partially explains the subdued reaction to the company's 2007 earnings, a 52 percent increase over the prior year. Much of the growth stemmed from eBay's new businesses: "Our diverse portfolio of businesses that we began to build a few years ago is showing sustainable traction. We're extremely pleased with their results this quarter," eBay chief executive Meg Whitman told analysts during a conference call.

5   Such growth would typically impress investors. Particularly when Wall Street was predicting lower growth than the revenues eBay reported. But investors didn't show much enthusiasm. The stock declined slightly after the announcement.

6   What's troubling investors is a slowdown in the company's "core" auction business, even as other businesses post gains. EBay's auction business accounts for 69 percent of its revenue. That business grew 23 percent, but investors have been used to growth rates of 40 percent. Active auction users grew 10 percent—a significant drop considering the category grew 25 percent during 2006 compared to the prior year. "Our concern is the core eBay business has been in a pretty steady downward spiral for several years now and it doesn't seem to be reversing itself," says Derek Brown, an analyst at Cantor Fitzgerald. Brown is recommending investors shed the stock.

7   The trouble with that view, say some analysts, is that it fails to see what eBay is evolving into. Tim Boyd, an analyst at American Technology Research who correctly anticipated eBay's revenues would beat the Street's expectations, sees eBay as an e-commerce and online advertising company that uses each business to fuel the other. "It doesn't make sense to look at this thing as solely an auction company anymore," says Boyd.

POSITIVE PRUNING?

8   Whitman attributed the year, in part, to more product listings turning into actual sales on eBay's site. The company's core auction business had suffered last year from sellers dumping slow-selling and patently unwanted merchandise in their eBay stores, as well as pricing some items too high for eBay's bargain-hunting audience. The result was a poorer experience for buyers and inventory that sat on the site far longer than desired, Whitman explained.

9   Last spring and summer, eBay raised fees by roughly 6 percent in order to encourage merchants to sell items people want and to price them to move. So far, the plan seems to be working. The site saw declines in the inventory that languished in eBay stores before selling or that didn't sell at all. "We are moving toward a better eBay marketplace," Whitman said during the call, cautioning that there was still work to do this year. Company CFO Bob Swan said that conversion rates have yet to reach their 2005 levels, but that they markedly improved since 2006.

10 In a note to investors, Goldman Sachs analyst Anthony Noto indicated he was pleased with eBay's efforts to "prune" low-quality listings. "EBay's focus on successful listings, as opposed to listings at any cost, is the key focus and driver of growth for eBay at this juncture," he wrote, adding "improved revenue-per-listing trends reinforce our view that eBay is at the early stages of a multi-quarter period of stabilizing-to-accelerating growth."

A PAL THAT PAYS

11 Indeed, eBay sees itself as a portfolio of companies that encompasses all the activities people perform on the Internet: trade, communicate, shop, search, and entertain. The eBay bulls see it as a diversified company with a hand in each one of the Internet's cash pots.

12 The newer members of eBay's portfolio are gaining momentum. PayPal revenue grew 31 percent in 2007. Its user base expanded 36 percent, to 143 million accounts. For eBay, an initial attraction of PayPal was its potential to enable sellers and buyers to share one trusted payment service instead of registering and working with multiple merchant bank cards. Facilitating transactions is important for eBay, which makes most of its money from taking a cut of sales.

13 PayPal's largest growth, however, has come from outside eBay. In the first quarter of 2007, it processed roughly $11.4 billion in transactions—about $4.4 billion was on non-eBay sites. That amount was a 51 percent increase from the prior year. For PayPal users, the service functions as something of an online bank, delivering interest, processing transactions, and even wiring money to friends through eBay's Internet phone service Skype. "The company [PayPal] has a lot of potential," says Matthew Kelmon, a portfolio manager at Kelmoore Investment, which owns eBay shares.

14 The big surprise of the season, however, was the strength of Pay Pal's services, which were supposed to be suffering at the hands of Google. PayPal posted revenues of $417 million, a 37 percent growth rate compared with 2005's fourth quarter. The payment-service company handled a record $11 billion in transactions, up 57 percent.

15 In fact, Whitman said that all the hype over Google Checkout actually boosted sales for market-leading PayPal, which reaped publicity amid the coverage of Google's foray. "I think we have disproportionately benefited from news in this category," Whitman said. She added that PayPal has an advantage over Google Checkout in that it's not just "a wrapper for Visa and Mastercard" but functions as an independent payment service.

16 Scott Devitt, an analyst at Stifel, Nicolaus & Company, says that acquiring PayPal was one of eBay's best moves. EBay purchased the payment company for $1.5 billion in 2002. "PayPal has just been phenomenal," says Devitt. "It is one of the best acquisitions in the history of the Internet in terms of the returns."

BRANCHING OUT

17 EBay jumped into the communications business by acquiring Skype in September 2005, for $2.6 billion plus stock. The service posted its first profitable quarter in 2007, growing 123 percent, to sales of $79 million, and adding 101 million new users. (Skype now has nearly 250 million customers.) EBay uses Skype to lubricate transactions by making it easier for consumers to talk to sellers, ask questions, and build trust. Skype also is a leader in the market for Web phones.

18 Despite the positive glow overall, the jury is still out on the eBay acquisition of Skype. While many analysts agree that the service has potential, they worry about eBay's ability to make money off of Skype's growing number of users. One positive sign: Google is working with Skype in developing click-to-call ads, says Devitt. The move may show that Google isn't so confident about being able to effectively challenge Skype for pay-per-call ads with its own competing service.

19 In the future, eBay could merge Skype with its classified advertising businesses to serve click-to-call ads, tapping into the market for local advertising. EBay is currently exploring such a service with Google and Yahoo! separately. Market researcher Borrell Associates estimates that about $8.6 billion will be spent on local Web ads in 2010.

20 EBay's advertising business and other small services also posted significant growth, swelling 65 percent to $60 million. This business is perhaps the most complicated of all because it is not confined to simply one kind of advertising. EBay has been serving classified ads through a network of foreign ad sites, such as Kijiji and Marketplaats, as well as via its 25 percent stake in Craigslist. It shares advertising revenue with Google, which serves search-related text ads on its non-U.S. auction pages. The company also has a wide-ranging advertising deal with Yahoo! By 2010, Internet advertising is expected to become a $27.8 billion market in the United States and a $29.5 billion market outside the United States, according to a January Oppenheimer & Co. report.

STUBHUB

21 In terms of acquisitions, Devitt also believes eBay picked a winner, for $310 million, in ticket reseller StubHub. EBay expects that the site will bring in between $105 and $120 million in 2007. That would help boost the company's overall revenues this year. During the call, eBay raised its revenue estimates for 2007 to between $7.05 and $7.3 billion for the full year. It predicts earnings-per-share growth of between 20 and 23 percent in the range of $1.25 to $1.29.

22 "StubHub has been extremely successful in the online tickets segment, and it's a perfect complement to eBay's tickets business," said Bill Cobb, president, eBay North America Marketplaces. "Together we can strengthen both businesses and provide fans with more choice and better service."

23 Standard & Poor's equity analyst Scott Kessler says Whitman is buying smart, for a price valuing StubHub at around three times what he estimates were its 2006 revenues. "We think this is a sound strategic move for eBay, which already has what we view as a strong tickets category," Kessler said in a research note. "We foresee notable business opportunities where StubHub would work with eBay, as well as PayPal, Shopping.com, and even Skype."

24 "StubHub's business model is an excellent fit with eBay, a company we've admired for a long time," StubHub CEO Jeff Fluhr said in the press release. "StubHub exists to serve passionate fans—and we feel great knowing our customers will benefit from the power of eBay and its community of users."

25 The 30-something Fluhr co-founded StubHub in March 2000, after getting the idea at Stanford Business School to resell hard-to-find tickets online for everything from concerts to sporting events. When asked in 2005 how he felt about going up against an 800-pound gorilla like eBay, he said he wouldn't underestimate them. But he also pointed out that his company has things like guaranteed fulfillment and integration with FedEx.

STUMBLING UPON NEW OPPORTUNITIES

26 With such large markets available for eBay's new businesses, it is not difficult to imagine a future in which eBay's auction business no longer dominates the company. EBay sees that long-term potential, though company executives underscore that a chief objective is to "reinvigorate" the core business. An acquisition such as StumbleUpon could help eBay's auction business by leveraging its recommendation technology to suggest other specific items related to goods sellers are bidding on or have bought. Currently, eBay recommends related categories of products.

27 Of course, eBay also could integrate Skype with StumbleUpon, using the call features to strengthen the networking aspects of both. It could potentially integrate the service with its classified ad business, using it to recommend ads related to products people are looking for.

28 Share gains aside, eBay thinks the stock merits a higher value and announced a plan to repurchase $2 billion in stock over the next two years. The plan shows the company's confidence in its ability to grow, says Devitt. He adds that he thinks the company will show mid- to upper-teens growth on a three-year basis.

29 With the variety of businesses that are now part of the company, what is eBay? More than just auctions—that's for sure.

Sources: Reprinted with special permission from Catherine Holahan, "eBay's Changing Identity," *BusinessWeek*, April 23, 2007; Catherine Holahan, "eBay Holds Its Turf Against Google," *BusinessWeek*, January 25, 2007; and "Is StubHub the Ticket for eBay?" *BusinessWeek*, January 11, 2007. Copyright © 2007 The McGraw-Hill Companies.

DISCUSSION QUESTIONS

1. What does eBay's corporate or multibusiness strategy for the twenty-first century appear to be?
2. List the businesses eBay is emphasizing and deemphasizing.
3. Which framework in this chapter—portfolio approach, leveraging core competencies, or parenting/patching—best helps explain what eBay is doing today in its corporate strategy? Why?
4. What appears to be the major advantage of this new eBay strategy and the major disadvantage or risk?
5. What would you advise Meg Whitman to do differently, and why?
6. Do you agree with her/eBay's approach and the logic of eBay moving from being an online auction–based company to being a broader, Internet services–based company? Why?

Part **Three**

Strategy Implementation, Control, and Innovation

The last section of this book examines what is often called the action phase of the strategic management process: implementation of the chosen strategy. Up to this point, three phases of that process have been covered—strategy formulation, analysis of alternative strategies, and strategic choice. Although important, these phases alone cannot ensure success.

To ensure success, the strategy must be translated into carefully implemented action. This means that

1. The strategy must be translated into guidelines for the daily activities of the firm's members.
2. The strategy and the firm must become one—that is, the strategy must be reflected in
   a. The way the firm organizes its activities.
   b. The key organization leaders.
   c. The culture of the organization.
3. The company's managers must put into place "steering" controls that provide strategic control and the ability to adjust strategies, commitments, and objectives in response to ever-changing future conditions.
4. Increasingly, organizations must make a serious commitment to be innovative and must consider bringing the entrepreneurship process into their company to survive, grow, and prosper in a vastly more competitive and rapidly changing global business arena.

Chapter 10 explains how organizational action is successfully initiated in four interrelated steps:

1. Creation of clear *short-term objectives* and *action plans*.
2. Development of specific *functional tactics*, to include *outsourcing*, that create competitive advantage.
3. Empowerment of operating personnel through *policies* to guide decisions.
4. Implementation of effective *reward systems*.

Short-term objectives and action plans guide implementation by converting long-term objectives into short-term actions and targets. Functional tactics, whether done internally or outsourced to other partners, translate the business strategy into activities that build advantage. Policies empower operating personnel by defining guidelines for making decisions. Reward systems encourage effective results.

Today's competitive environment requires careful analysis in designing the organizational structure most suitable to build and sustain competitive advantage. Chapter 11 examines traditional organizational structures—their pros and cons. It looks at the pervasive trend toward outsourcing, along with outsourcing's pros and cons. It concludes with examination of the latest developments in creating ambidextrous, virtual, boundaryless organizations designed to adapt in a highly interconnected, lightning-speed, global business environment.

There can be no doubt that effective organizational leadership and the consistency of a strong organizational culture reinforcing norms and behaviors best suited to the organization's mission are two central ingredients in enabling successful execution of a firm's strategies and objectives. Chapter 12 examines leadership, the critical things good leaders do, and how to nurture effective operating managers as they become outstanding future organizational leaders. Chapter 12 then examines the organizational culture, how it is shaped, and creative ways of managing the strategy-culture relationship.

Because the firm's strategy is implemented in a changing environment, successful implementation requires strategic control—an ability to "steer" the firm through an extended future time period when premises, sudden events, internal implementation efforts, and general economic and societal developments will be sources of change not anticipated or predicted when the strategy was conceived and initiated. Chapter 13 examines how to set up strategic controls to deal with the important steering function during the implementation process. The chapter also examines operational control functions and the balanced scorecard approach to integrating strategic and operational control.

The overriding concerns in executing strategies and leading a company are survival, growth, and prosperity. In a global economy that allows everyone everywhere instant information and instant connectivity, change often occurs at lightning speed. Thus, leaders are increasingly encouraging their firms to embrace innovation and entrepreneurship as key ways to respond to such overwhelming uncertainty. Chapter 14 examines innovation in general, different types of innovation, and the best ways to bring more innovative activity into a firm. It examines the entrepreneurship process as another way to build innovative responsiveness and opportunity recognition into a firm, both in new-venture settings and in large business organizations.

Implementation is "where the action is." It is the arena that most students enter at the start of their business careers. It is the strategic phase in which staying close to the customer, achieving competitive advantage, and pursuing excellence become realities. These five chapters in Part Three will help you understand how this is done and how to prepare to take your place as a future leader of successful, innovative business organizations.

Chapter **Ten**

Implementation

After reading and studying this chapter, you should be able to

1. Understand how short-term objectives are used in strategy implementation.

2. Identify and apply the qualities of good short-term objectives to your own experiences.

3. Illustrate what is meant by functional tactics and understand how they are used in strategy implementation.

4. Gain a general sense of what outsourcing is and how it becomes a choice in functional tactics decisions for strategy implementation.

5. Understand what policies are and how to use policies to empower operating personnel in implementing business strategies and functional tactics.

6. Understand the use of financial reward in executive compensation.

7. Identify different types of executive compensation and when to use each in strategy implementation.

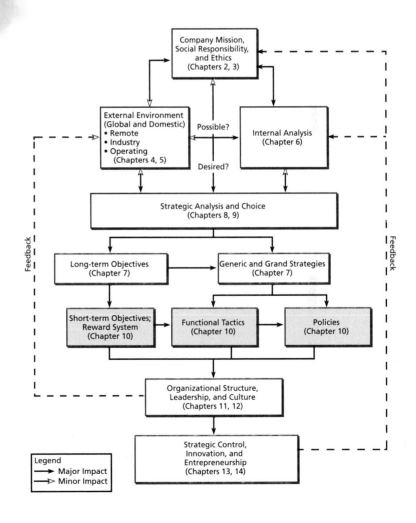

Xerox and Hewlett-Packard faced difficult times as this decade began. For Xerox, bankruptcy was a real possibility given its $14 billion debt and its serious problems with the U.S. Securities and Exchange Commission. Hewlett-Packard was falling behind in the computer business while living solely on profits from its printer division. Anne Mulcahy became Xerox CEO during this time. Carly Fiorina became HP's CEO. Five years later, Anne Mulcahy was celebrated for the success of her strategy at Xerox while Carly Fiorina was dismissed for the failure of the path she chose. Two legendary technology companies and two celebrated CEOs who shattered the "glass ceiling" in being selected to lead two legendary companies back to glory: why did one succeed and the other fail?

Analysts suggest that the "devil is in the detail." Fiorina's strategy was to acquire Compaq, build the size of HP's PC business, and use profits from HP's venerable printer business to sustain a reorganization of the combined companies. Mark Anderson, an investment analyst who has followed HP for more than 20 years, said this about Carly Fiorina's strategy:

> I would say it stinks, but it isn't even a strategy. A few bullet points don't make a strategy. Such an approach lacks the technical and market understanding necessary to drive HP.[1]

In other words, Carly Fiorina's strategy was a glitzy combination of two large computer companies, but it was less clear exactly what key actions and tactics would bring about a reinvented, "new," profitable HP.

Anne Mulcahy took a different approach, in part reflecting her 28 years inside Xerox. She set about to "reinvent" Xerox as well, but made four functional tactics and their respective short-term objectives very clear building blocks for reinventing Xerox: (1) She prioritized aggressive cost cutting—30 percent—throughout the company to restore profitability. (2) She emphasized a productivity increase in each Xerox division. (3) She quickly settled Xerox's SEC litigation about its accounting practices, and she refinanced Xerox's massive debt. (4) She made a major point of continued heavy R&D funding even as every other part of Xerox suffered through severe cost cutting. This, she felt, sent a message of belief in Xerox's future. It clearly established her priorities.

Mulcahy's articulation of specific tactical efforts, and the short-term objectives they were intended to achieve, turned Xerox around in three short years. As she proudly pointed out:

> Probably one of the hardest things was to continue investing in the future, in growth. One of the most controversial decisions we made was to continue our R&D investment. When you're drastically restructuring in other areas, that's a tough decision. It makes it harder for the other businesses to some extent. But it was important for the Xerox people to believe we were investing in the future. Now two-thirds of our revenue is coming from products and services introduced in the last two years.[2]

The reason Anne Mulcahy succeeded while Carly Fiorina did not, the focus of this chapter, involves translating strategic thought into organizational action. In the words of two well-worn phrases, they move from "planning their work" to "working their plan." Anne Mulcahy successfully made this shift at Xerox when she did these five things well:

1. Identify short-term objectives.
2. Initiate specific functional tactics.
3. Outsource nonessential functions.
4. Communicate policies that empower people in the organization.
5. Design effective rewards.

---

[1] "The Only HP Way Worth Trying," Viewpoint, *BusinessWeek,* March 9, 2005.
[2] "She Put the Bounce Back in Xerox," *BusinessWeek,* January 10, 2005.

Short-term objectives translate long-range aspirations into this year's targets for action. If well developed, these objectives provide clarity, a powerful motivator and facilitator of effective strategy implementation.

Functional tactics translate business strategy into daily activities people need to execute. Functional managers participate in the development of these tactics, and their participation, in turn, helps clarify what their units are expected to do in implementing the business's strategy.

Outsourcing nonessential functions normally performed in-house frees up resources and the time of key people to concentrate on leveraging the functions and activities critical to the core competitive advantages around which the firm's long range strategy is built.

Policies are empowerment tools that simplify decision making by empowering operating managers and their subordinates. Policies can empower the "doers" in an organization by reducing the time required to decide and act.

Rewards that align manager and employee priorities with organizational objectives and shareholder value provide very effective direction in strategy implementation.

SHORT-TERM OBJECTIVES

short-term objective
Measurable outcomes achievable or intended to be achieved in one year or less.

Chapter 7 described business strategies, grand strategies, and long-term objectives that are critically important in crafting a successful future. To make them become a reality, however, the people in an organization who actually "do the work" of the business need guidance in exactly what they need to do. Short-term objectives help do this. **Short-term objectives** are measurable outcomes achievable or intended to be achieved in one year or less. They are specific, usually quantitative, results operating managers set out to achieve in the immediate future.

Short-term objectives help implement strategy in at least three ways:

1. Short-term objectives "operationalize" long-term objectives. If we commit to a 20 percent gain in revenue over five years, what is our specific target or objective in revenue during the current year, month, or week to indicate we are making appropriate progress?

2. Discussion about and agreement on short-term objectives help raise issues and potential conflicts within an organization that usually require coordination to avoid otherwise dysfunctional consequences. Exhibit 10.1 illustrates how objectives within marketing, manufacturing, and accounting units within the same firm can be very different even when created to pursue the same firm objective (e.g., increased sales, lower costs).

3. Finally, short-term objectives assist strategy implementation by identifying measurable outcomes of action plans or functional activities, which can be used to make feedback, correction, and evaluation more relevant and acceptable.

Short-term objectives are usually accompanied by action plans, which enhance these objectives in three ways. First, action plans usually identify functional tactics and activities that will be undertaken in the next week, month, or quarter as part of the business's effort to build competitive advantage. The important point here is *specificity*—what exactly is to be done. We will examine functional tactics in a subsequent section of this chapter. The second element of an action plan is a clear *time frame for completion*—when the effort will begin and when its results will be accomplished. A third element action plans contain is identification of *who is responsible* for each action in the plan. This accountability is very important to ensure action plans are acted upon.

Because of the particular importance of short-term objectives in strategy implementation, the next section addresses how to develop meaningful short-term objectives. Exhibit 10.2, Top Strategist, provides a *BusinessWeek* interview with Symantec CEO John Thompson about the nature and importance of short-term objectives to Symantec's success.

EXHIBIT 10.1
Potential Conflicting Objectives and Priorities

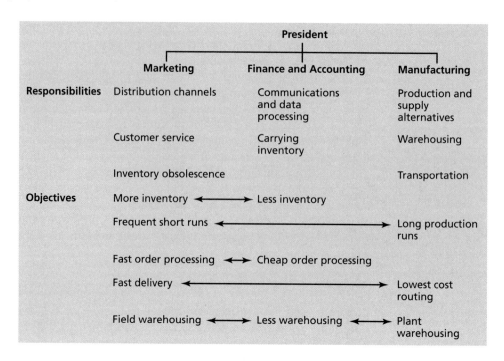

Qualities of Effective Short-Term Objectives
Measurable

Short-term objectives are more consistent when they clearly state *what* is to be accomplished, *when* it will be accomplished, and *how* its accomplishment will be *measured*. Such objectives can be used to monitor both the effectiveness of each activity and the collective progress across several interrelated activities. Exhibit 10.3 illustrates several effective and ineffective short-term objectives. Measurable objectives make misunderstanding less likely among interdependent managers who must implement action plans. It is far easier to quantify the objectives of *line* units (e.g., production) than of certain *staff* areas (e.g., personnel). Difficulties in quantifying objectives often can be overcome by initially focusing on *measurable activity* and then identifying *measurable outcomes*.

Priorities

Although all annual objectives are important, some deserve priority because of a timing consideration or their particular impact on a strategy's success. If such priorities are not established, conflicting assumptions about the relative importance of annual objectives may inhibit progress toward strategic effectiveness. Anne Mulcahy's turnaround of Xerox described at the beginning of this chapter emphasized several important short-term objectives. But it was clear throughout Xerox that her highest priority in the first two years was to dramatically lower overhead and production costs so as to satisfy the difficult challenge of continuing to invest heavily in R&D while also restoring profitability.

Priorities are established in various ways. A simple ranking may be based on discussion and negotiation during the planning process. However, this does not necessarily communicate the real difference in the importance of objectives, so such terms as primary, top, and secondary may be used to indicate priority. Some firms assign weights (e.g., 0 to 100 percent) to establish and communicate the relative priority of objectives. Whatever the method, recognizing priorities is an important dimension in the implementation value of short-term objectives.

Top Strategist
John Thompson, Chairman and CEO of Symantec

Exhibit 10.2

John Thompson, Chairman and CEO of Symantec

"If you could only monitor five objectives to run/steer your business, what would they be and why?" is a question *BusinessWeek* posed to John Thompson, chairman and CEO of Symantec, a Cupertino (California)-based Internet security outfit that makes antivirus and firewall technology as it implemented a merger with Veritas in 2005. Since Thompson joined Symantec as top exec, revenues have grown eightfold, from $632 million to more than $5.3 billion in 2007.

Q: So what would be your critical objectives, and why?

A: Let's define what objectives are: They are vectors for how you are performing now, but also indicators for how you will do in the future. Here are five critical objectives I use to manage Symantec. Our most critical objectives are customer satisfaction and market share.

CUSTOMER SATISFACTION
We use an outside firm to poll customers on a continuous basis to determine their satisfaction with our products and services. This needs to be an anonymous relationship—a conversation between our pollster and our customers. Polling is done by product area: firewall, antivirus, services, and other product lines.

MARKET SHARE
There are a couple of ways we look at this. We have our own views based on relevant markets. Then we use industry analysts such as Gartner, IDC, and Giga as benchmarks for annualized results on market share. On a quarterly basis, we look at our revenue performance and growth rates, and that of our competitors. We compare against actual realized growth rates, as compared to growth rates of relevant competitors in similar segments.

The purpose is to get trending data. That gives us a sense of market changes and market growth. We also use a blended (rating) of analyst companies in the same space. Each industry-analyst firm counts things a bit differently, based on its methodology. The numbers don't have to be spot on or Six Sigma precise.

REVENUE GROWTH
You have to consider if revenue is growing at a rate equal to or greater than the market rate. If you look at the antivirus market, for example, industry analysts projected growth in the high teens while our enterprise antivirus sector grew at a rate of 32 percent. This indicates that we are gaining market share faster than the market growth rate for the industry.

We can then assess how we had planned to grow. Did we plan to grow at 32 percent or less—or more? You have to gauge your growth relative to the market for your product or service and your own internal expectations of your performance.

EXPENSES
It is important to always plan for how much money will have to be spent to generate a certain level of revenue. This enables you to monitor funds flow in the company. Did I plan to spend $10 or $12, and what did I get for that expense in return? The purpose is to keep expenses in equilibrium to revenue generation.

EARNINGS
Two keys to watch here—operating margins and earnings per share (EPS). A business running efficiently is improving its operating margins. If you are efficient in your operating margins, this should produce a strong EPS, which is a strong objective that Wall Street looks at all the time.

Q: What problems do tracking objectives solve for a corporation? How does maintaining objectives help you manage and steer the direction of the corporation?

A: I am a little old-fashioned—I don't believe you can manage what you don't measure. The importance of objectives becomes more important as the enterprise grows in size and scale. Objectives also serve as an indication for

(continued)

Exhibit 10.2 cont.

the team about what you are paying attention to. If employees know you are measuring market growth and customer satisfaction, they will pay attention to those considerations and will behave based on indicators that you, as the leader, provide to the organization. Objectives helps the team focus on what's important for an organization.

Q: How should companies consider industry-specific objectives versus broad financial objectives: P/E [price to earnings] ratio, etc?

A: This is an issue for all of us. I am on the board of a utility company. The company has achieved modest single-digit revenue growth. They are quite proud of that, while I would be quite concerned if that were to be the growth rate for a software firm. For example: An important consideration may be what you are spending in R&D in comparison to your peer group. Or, for a software firm, what is the license revenue mix?

I couldn't care less about the performance of Symantec relative to that of a financial-services company. But I would care about the performance of Symantec in comparison with an enterprise software company or with another securities software firm. Whatever measures you choose should give you the ability to measure your performance against like-industry companies.

Q: What do new managers need to keep in mind as they consider/reevaluate the use of objectives for their companies?

A: Live by the adage that you can't manage what you can't measure. The best objectives are simple to understand, simple to communicate, and relatively easy for everyone to get access to the data that represents the results. That makes your objectives an effective management tool. If you make your objectives difficult to gather, manage, or communicate, they won't be effective. Simplicity is key.

My experience has proven to me the importance of picking the few objectives that are the most critical for the running of the business. Stick with them—and communicate them to both internal and external audiences.

Cascading: From Long-Term Objectives to Short-Term Objectives

The link between short-term and long-term objectives should resemble cascades through the firm from basic long-term objectives to specific short-term objectives in key operation areas. The cascading effect has the added advantage of providing a clear reference for communication and negotiation, which may be necessary to integrate and coordinate objectives and activities at the operating level.

3M's recent refocus on growth, particularly in international markets, provides a good example of cascading objectives. 3M's CEO, George Buckley, has had to aggressively seek to turn around the company's declining performance by accelerating sales growth while financing the growth internally by improving cash flow and profitability. Currently, 60 percent of 3M's sales come from outside the United States and Buckley expects that to rise to 75 percent in two years. At the same time, only 35 percent of their manufacturing and distribution facilities are located outside the United States. To achieve 3M's sales goals, and growth abroad, operating managers have set an objective of 18 new plants or major expansions online within the next two years, with 11 new plants being outside the United States and four of those in China alone. Managers of 3M's logistic chain have identified lowering the number of "days 3M products spend traveling through its supply lines" as a critical objective to increase cash flow, which in turn helps free up cash to build these new plants. Currently, a typical product might be extruded in Canada, machined in France, packaged

EXHIBIT 10.3
Creating Measurable
Objectives

Examples of Deficient Objectives	Examples of Objectives with Measurable Criteria for Performance
To improve morale in the division (plant, department, etc.)	To reduce turnover (absenteeism, number of rejects, etc.) among sales managers by 10 percent by January 1, 2008. *Assumption:* Morale is related to measurable outcomes (i.e., high and low morale are associated with different results).
To improve support of the sales effort	To reduce the time lapse between order data and delivery by 8 percent (two days) by June 1, 2008. To reduce the cost of goods produced by 6 percent to support a product price decrease of 2 percent by December 1, 2008. To increase the rate of before- or on-schedule delivery by 5 percent by June 1, 2008.
To improve the firm's image	To conduct a public opinion poll using random samples in the five largest U.S. metropolitan markets to determine average scores on 10 dimensions of corporate responsibility by May 15, 2008. To increase our score on those dimensions by an average of 7.5 percent by May 1, 2008.

in Mexico, and sold in Japan—tying up a sizable inventory around the world just sitting on boats, in trucks, and in warehouses—currently averaging 100 days. Supply chain managers have the objective of freeing up $1 billion in working capital, and $200 million in cost savings annually from a more efficient supply chain. Buckley will be monitoring working capital as a percent of sales which, as it declines, provides the needed internal cash flow to achieve the overall goal of international plant and facilities expansion.[3]

FUNCTIONAL TACTICS THAT IMPLEMENT BUSINESS STRATEGIES

functional tactics
Detailed statements of the "means" or activities that will be used by a company to achieve short-term objectives and establish competitive advantage.

Functional tactics are the key, routine activities that must be undertaken in each functional area—marketing, finance, production/operations, R&D, and human resource management—to provide the business's products and services. In a sense, functional tactics translate thought (grand strategy) into action designed to accomplish specific short-term objectives. Every value chain activity in a company executes functional tactics that support the business's strategy and help accomplish strategic objectives.

Exhibit 10.5 Strategy in Action, illustrates the difference between functional tactics and business strategy. It also shows that functional tactics are essential to implement business strategy. It explains the situation at California Pizza Kitchen, where consultants were brought in to identify specific tactical things employees needed to do or deal with to implement an overall business strategy to differentiate the growing pizza chain from many other restaurant competitors. The business strategy outlined the competitive posture of its operations in the restaurant industry. To increase the likelihood that these strategies would be successful, specific functional tactics were needed for the firm's operating components. These functional tactics clarified the business strategy, giving specific,

[3] Brian Hindo, "3M Chief Plants a Money Tree," *BusinessWeek Online,* June 11, 2007.

EXHIBIT 10.4
The Value-Added Benefit of Short-Term Objectives and Action Plans

Source: Reprinted with special permission from Brian Hindo, "3M Chief Plants a Money Tree," *BusinessWeek Online,* June 11, 2007. Copyright © 2007 The McGraw-Hill Companies.

- They give operating personnel a better understanding of their role in the firm's mission.
- The process of developing them becomes a forum for raising and resolving conflicts between strategic intent and operational reality.
- They provide a basis for developing budgets, schedules, trigger points, and other sources of strategic control.
- They can be powerful motivators, especially when connected to the reward system.

short-term guidance to operating managers and employees in the areas of marketing, operations, and finance.

Differences between Business Strategies and Functional Tactics

Functional tactics are different from business or corporate strategies in three fundamental ways:

1. Time horizon.
2. Specificity.
3. Participants who develop them.

Time Horizon

Functional tactics identify activities to be undertaken "now" or in the immediate future. Business strategies focus on the firm's posture three to five years out. Exhibit 10.6, Strategy in Action, shows functional tactics turnaround CEO Alan Mulally seeks to implement in five strategic areas of concern at Ford Motor Company.

The shorter time horizon of functional tactics is critical to the successful implementation of a business strategy for two reasons. First, it focuses the attention of functional managers on what needs to be done *now* to make the business strategy work. Second, it allows functional managers like those at 3M to adjust to changing current conditions.

Specificity

Functional tactics are more specific than business strategies. Business strategies provide general direction. Functional tactics identify the specific activities that are to be undertaken in each functional area and thus allow operating managers to work out *how* their unit is expected to pursue short-term objectives. Exhibit 10.5, Strategy in Action, illustrated the nature and value of specificity in functional tactics versus business strategy at California Pizza Kitchen.

Specificity in functional tactics contributes to successful implementation by

- Helping ensure that functional managers know what needs to be done and can focus on accomplishing results.
- Clarifying for top management how functional managers intend to accomplish the business strategy, which increases top management's confidence in and sense of control over the business strategy.
- Facilitating coordination among operating units within the firm by clarifying areas of interdependence and potential conflict.

Participants

Different people participate in strategy development at the functional and business levels. Business strategy is the responsibility of the general manager of a business unit. That manager typically delegates the development of functional tactics to subordinates charged with running the operating areas of the business. The manager of a business unit must

The Nature and Value of Specificity in Functional Tactics versus Business Strategy

BusinessWeek

A restaurant business was encountering problems. Although its management had agreed unanimously that it was committed to a business strategy to differentiate itself from other competitors based on concept and customer service rather than price, California Pizza Kitchen continued to encounter inconsistencies across different store locations in how well it did this. Consultants indicated that the customer experience varied greatly from store to store. The conclusion was that while the management understood the "busi-

ness strategy," and the employees did too in general terms, the implementation was inadequate because of a lack of specificity in the functional tactics—what everyone should do every day in the restaurant—to make the vision a reality in terms of the customers' dining experience. The following breakdown of part of their business strategy into specific functional tactics just in the area of customer service helps illustrate the value specificity in functional tactics brings to strategy implementation.

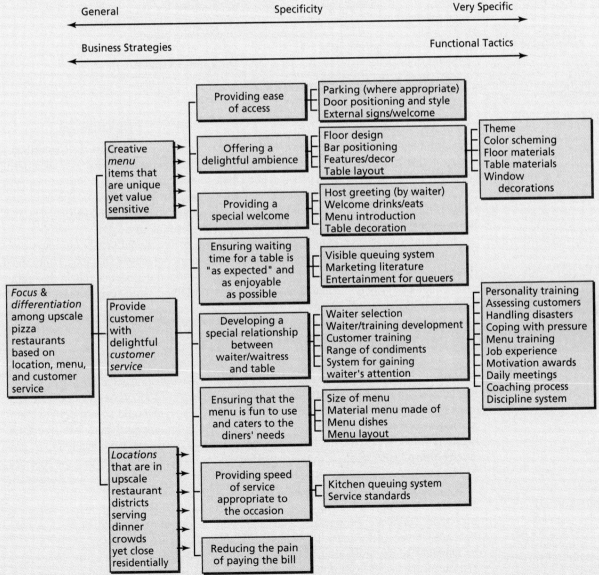

Sources: Adapted from Dennis Milton, "California Pizza Kitchen: Say Cheese!," *BusinessWeek*, July 15, 2003; and A. Campbell and K. Luchs, Eds., *Core Competency – Based Strategy* (London: Thompson, 1997).

The Mulally Difference in Key Tactics to Save
Ford Motor Company

BusinessWeek

How Things Are Changing at Ford Now That the New Boss Has Arrived

	Before	After
Organization	Regional fiefdoms. Every global market has had its own strategy and products.	Mulally wants to break down geographic hierarchies and create a single worldwide organization.
Division chief meetings	Held monthly. Lots of happy talk. Little information sharing.	Held weekly. Discussing problems is encouraged. Goal is to spot red flags early.
Product mix	Emphasis on trucks, SUVs, niche sports cars.	Focus is shifting to passenger cars and or crossovers.
Brand vision	To diversify away from ford brand. The company acquired dysfunctional luxury brands.	Strengthen the traditional blue oval Ford brand. Sell off or close poor-performing brands.
Promotions	Managers changed jobs frequently to develop their skills.	Executives stay in place, winning only promotions that are deserved.

Source: Reprinted with special permission from "The Mulally Difference," *BusinessWeek*, June 7, 2007. Copyright © 2007 The McGraw-Hill Companies.

establish long-term objectives and a strategy that corporate management feels contributes to corporate-level goals. Similarly, key operating managers must establish short-term objectives and operating strategies that contribute to business-level goals. Just as business strategies and objectives are approved through negotiation between corporate managers and business managers, so, too, are short-term objectives and functional tactics approved through negotiation between business managers and operating managers.

Involving operating managers in the development of functional tactics improves their understanding of what must be done to achieve long-term objectives and, thus, contributes to successful implementation. It also helps ensure that functional tactics reflect the reality of the day-to-day operating situation. And perhaps most important, it can increase the commitment of operating managers to the strategies developed.

OUTSOURCING FUNCTIONAL ACTIVITIES

A generation ago, it was conventional wisdom that a business has a better chance of success if it controls the doing of everything necessary to produce its products or services. Referring back to Chapter 6's value chain approach, the "wise" manager would have sought to maintain control of virtually all the "primary" activities and the "support" activities associated with the firm's work. Not any longer. Starting for most firms with the outsourcing of producing payroll each week, companies worldwide are embracing the idea that the best way to implement their strategies is to retain responsibility for executing some functions while seeking outside people and companies to do key support and key primary activities where they can do so more effectively and more inexpensively. **Outsourcing,** then, is acquiring an activity, service, or product necessary to provide a company's products or services from "outside" the people or operations controlled by that acquiring company.

DuPont Co. has always run corporate training and development out of its Wilmington (Delaware) head office. But these days, Boston-based Forum Corp. handles it instead. In Somers, New York, PepsiCo Inc. employees, long used to receiving personal financial

outsourcing
Obtaining work previously done by employees inside the companies from sources outside the company.

planning from their employer, now get that service from KPMG Peat Marwick. Denver's TeleTech Holdings Inc. is taking customer-service calls from AT&T customers and books seat reservations for Continental Airlines.

Wyck Hay's first entrepreneurial effort was a smashing success: The co-founder of herbal tea maker Celestial Seasonings helped sell the company to Kraft Foods for $40 million in 1984. But Hay found managing 300 employees a headache. So when he launched Woodside (California)-based Kaboom Beverages a few years ago, he kept a decidedly small payroll: himself. In lieu of a workforce, Hay assembled a team of contractors to perform every task at his $2 million business—from label design to manufacturing of his "power juice" drinks. Hay said outsourcing saves him at least 30 percent, while minimizing his daily distractions. "I don't know that I ever plan to hire any employees," he mused.[4]

Relentless cost cutting is the main force behind the trend. BellSouth Corp., which shed 13,200 employees over two years, outsourced about $60 million in services to replace them. Companies are parceling out everything from mailroom management to customer service, from pieces of human resources departments to manufacturing and distribution. "We're at the beginning of an explosion," predicts Scott Hartz, managing partner of PricewaterhouseCoopers consulting group. "Many of the firms doing more outsourcing aren't troubled corporations trying to save a nickel. They are often the corporate leaders." All major corporations now outsource at least some services.[5] Exhibit 10.7 provides a summary of the increase in outsourcing.

It's hardly just rote work that's being outsourced—even such key functions as marketing are now up for bidding. "Some CEOs say they'd rather focus on operations and finance," says Dave Camp, the director of creative services at Bellevue (Washington)-based Outsource Marketing. The 12-person company originally provided basic marketing support to small clients. Today, it acts as the full marketing department for some clients.[6]

The hype over outsourcing's benefits, however, disguises numerous problems. General Electric Co. stubbed its toe when the introduction of a new washing machine was delayed by production problems at a contractor to whom it had farmed out key work. GE only lost three weeks as a result of the glitches, but it could have been worse. Southern Pacific Rail Corp. suffered through myriad computer breakdowns and delays after outsourcing its internal computer network to IBM.

The important point to recognize at this point is that functional activities long associated with doing the work of any business organization are increasingly subject to be outsourced if they can be done more cost effectively by other providers. So it becomes critical for managers implementing strategic plans to focus company activities on functions deemed central to the company's competitive advantage and to seek others outside the firm's structure to provide the functions that are necessary, but not within the scope of the firm's core competencies. And, increasingly, this decision considers every organizational activity fair game—even marketing, product design, innovation. We will explore this in greater detail in Chapter 11.

EMPOWERING OPERATING PERSONNEL: THE ROLE OF POLICIES

Specific functional tactics provide guidance and initiate action implementing a business's strategy, but more is needed. Supervisors and personnel in the field have been charged in today's competitive environment with being responsible for customer value—for being

---

[4] Dean Foust, et al., "The Outsourcing Food Chain," *BusinessWeek Online,* March 11, 2004.

[5] Steven Goldman, "Dynamism as the Norm," *BusinessWeek Online,* April 18, 2005.

[6] Ibid.

EXHIBIT 10.7
Outsourcing Is Increasing

Source: Estimated based on various articles in *BusinessWeek* on outsourcing.

ORDERING OUT... Companies That Say They Outsource Some Functional Activity		
	Yes	No
2008	98%	2%
2000	75	25
1995	52	48
1990	23	77

. . . FOR EVERYTHING Functional Activities Most Frequently Outsourced	
Payroll	75%
Manufacturing	72
Maintenance	68
Warehousing/transportation/distribution	62
Information technology	52
Travel	48
Temporary service	48
HR activities (varied)	40
Product design	35
R&D	25
Marketing	22

the "front line" of the company's effort to truly meet customers' needs. Meeting customer needs is a buzzword regularly cited as a key priority by most business organizations. Efforts to do so often fail because employees that are the real contact point between the business and its customers are not empowered to make decisions or act to fulfill customer needs. One solution has been to empower operating personnel by pushing down decision making to their level. General Electric allows appliance repair personnel to decide about warranty credits on the spot, a decision that used to take several days and multiple organizational levels. American Air Lines allows customer service personnel and their supervisors wide range in resolving customer ticket pricing decisions. Federal Express couriers make decisions and handle package routing information that involves five management levels in the U.S. Postal Service.

empowerment
The act of allowing an individual or team the right and flexibility to make decisions and initiate action.

Empowerment is the act of allowing an individual or team the right and flexibility to make decisions and initiate action. It is being expanded and widely advocated in many organizations today. Training, self-managed work groups, eliminating whole levels of management in organizations, and aggressive use of automation are some of the ways and ramifications of this fundamental change in the way business organizations function. At the heart of the effort is the need to ensure that decision making is consistent with the mission, strategy, and tactics of the business while at the same time allowing considerable latitude to operating personnel. One way operating managers do this is through the use of policies.

policies
Broad, precedent-setting decisions that guide or substitute for repetitive or time-sensitive managerial decision making.

Policies are directives designed to guide the thinking, decisions, and actions of managers and their subordinates in implementing a firm's strategy. Sometimes called *standard operating procedures,* policies increase managerial effectiveness by standardizing many routine decisions and clarifying the discretion managers and subordinates can exercise in implementing functional tactics. Logically, policies should be derived from functional

Selected Policies That Aid Strategy Implementation

3M Corporation has a *personnel policy,* called the *15 percent rule,* that allows virtually any employee to spend up to 15 percent of the workweek on anything that he or she wants to, as long as it's product related. (This policy supports 3M's corporate strategy of being a highly innovative manufacturer, with each division required to have a quarter of its annual sales come from products introduced within the past five years.)

Wendy's has a *purchasing policy* that gives local store managers the authority to buy fresh meat and produce locally, rather than from regionally designated or company-owned sources. (This policy supports Wendy's functional strategy of having fresh, unfrozen hamburgers daily.)

General Cinema has a *financial policy* that requires annual capital investment in movie theaters not to exceed annual depreciation. (By seeing that capital investment is no greater than depreciation, this policy supports General Cinema's financial strategy of maximizing cash flow—in this case, all profit—to its growth areas. The policy also reinforces General Cinema's financial strategy of leasing as much as possible.)

Crown, Cork, and Seal Company has an *R&D policy* of not investing any financial or people resources in basic research. (This policy supports Crown, Cork, and Seal's functional strategy, which emphasizes customer services, not technical leadership.)

Bank of America has an *operating policy* that requires annual renewal of the financial statement of all personal borrowers. (This policy supports Bank of America's financial strategy, which seeks to maintain a loan-to-loss ratio below the industry norm.)

tactics (and, in some instances, from corporate or business strategies) with the key purpose of aiding strategy execution.[7] Exhibit 10.8, Strategy in Action, illustrates selected policies of several well-known firms.

Creating Policies That Empower

Policies communicate guidelines to decisions. They are designed to control decisions while defining allowable discretion within which operational personnel can execute business activities. They do this in several ways:

1. *Policies establish indirect control over independent action* by clearly stating how things are to be done *now.* By defining discretion, policies in effect control decisions yet empower employees to conduct activities without direct intervention by top management.

2. *Policies promote uniform handling of similar activities.* This facilitates the coordination of work tasks and helps reduce friction arising from favoritism, discrimination, and the disparate handling of common functions—something that often hampers operating personnel.

[7] The term *policy* has various definitions in management literature. Some authors and practitioners equate policy with strategy. Others do this inadvertently by using "policy" as a synonym for company mission, purpose, or culture. Still other authors and practitioners differentiate policy in terms of "levels" associated, respectively, with purpose, mission, and strategy. "Our policy is to make a positive contribution to the communities and societies we live in" and "Our policy is not to diversify out of the hamburger business" are two examples of the breadth of what some call policies. This book defines *policy* much more narrowly as specific guides to managerial action and decisions in the implementation of strategy. This definition permits a sharper distinction between the formulation and implementation of functional strategies. And, of even greater importance, it focuses the tangible value of the policy concept where it can be most useful—as a key administrative tool to enhance effective implementation and execution of strategy.

3. *Policies ensure quicker decisions* by standardizing answers to previously answered questions that otherwise would recur and be pushed up the management hierarchy again and again—something that requires unnecessary levels of management between senior decision makers and field personnel.

4. *Policies institutionalize basic aspects of organization behavior.* This minimizes conflicting practices and establishes consistent patterns of action in attempts to make the strategy work—again, freeing operating personnel to act.

5. *Policies reduce uncertainty in repetitive and day-to-day decision making,* thereby providing a necessary foundation for coordinated, efficient efforts and freeing operating personnel to act.

6. *Policies counteract resistance to or rejection of chosen strategies by organization members.* When major strategic change is undertaken, unambiguous operating policies clarify what is expected and facilitate acceptance, particularly when operating managers participate in policy development.

7. *Policies offer predetermined answers to routine problems.* This greatly expedites dealing with both ordinary and extraordinary problems—with the former, by referring to these answers; with the latter, by giving operating personnel more time to cope with them.

8. *Policies afford managers a mechanism for avoiding hasty and ill-conceived decisions in changing operations.* Prevailing policy can always be used as a reason for not yielding to emotion-based, expedient, or temporarily valid arguments for altering procedures and practices.

Policies may be written and formal or unwritten and informal. Informal, unwritten policies are usually associated with a strategic need for competitive secrecy. Some policies of this kind, such as promotion from within, are widely known (or expected) by employees and implicitly sanctioned by management. Managers and employees often like the latitude granted by unwritten and informal policies. However, such policies may detract from the long-term success of a strategy. Formal, written policies have at least seven advantages:

1. They require managers to think through the policy's meaning, content, and intended use.
2. They reduce misunderstanding.
3. They make equitable and consistent treatment of problems more likely.
4. They ensure unalterable transmission of policies.
5. They communicate the authorization or sanction of policies more clearly.
6. They supply a convenient and authoritative reference.
7. They systematically enhance indirect control and organizationwide coordination of the key purposes of policies.

The strategic significance of policies can vary. At one extreme are such policies as travel reimbursement procedures, which are really work rules and may not have an obvious link to the implementation of a strategy. Exhibit 10.9, Strategy in Action, provides an interesting example of how the link between a simple policy and strategy implementation regarding customer service can have serious negative consequences when it is neither obvious to operating personnel nor well thought out by bank managers. At the other extreme are organizationwide policies that are virtually functional strategies, such as Wendy's requirement that every location invest 1 percent of its gross revenue in local advertising.

Make Sure Policies Aren't Used to Drive Away Customers

Every year *Inc.* magazine sponsors a conference for the 500 fastest growing companies in the United States to share ideas, hear speakers, and network. A recent conference included a talk by Martha Rogers, co-author of *The One to One Future.* Here is an interesting anecdote about policies she used in her talk:

> The story was about a distinguished-looking gentleman in blue jeans who walked into a bank and asked a teller to complete a transaction. The teller said she was sorry, but the person responsible was out for the day. The man would have to come

back. He then asked to have his parking receipt validated. Again, she said she was sorry, but under bank policy she could not validate a parking receipt unless the customer completed a transaction. The man pressed her. She did not waver. "That's our policy," she said.

So the man completed a transaction. He withdrew all $1.5 million from his account. It turned out he was John Akers, then chairman of IBM.

The moral: Give employees information about the value of customers, not mindless policies.

Policies can be externally imposed or internally derived. Policies regarding equal employment practices are often developed in compliance with external (government) requirements, and policies regarding leasing or depreciation may be strongly influenced by current tax regulations.

Regardless of the origin, formality, and nature of policies, the key point to bear in mind is that they can play an important role in strategy implementation. Communicating specific policies will help overcome resistance to strategic change, empower people to act, and foster commitment to successful strategy implementation.

Policies empower people to act. Compensation, at least theoretically, rewards their action. The last decade has seen many firms realize that the link between compensation, particularly executive management compensation, and value-building strategic outcomes within their firms was uncertain. The recognition of this uncertainty has brought about increased recognition of the need to link management compensation with the successful implementation of strategies that build long-term shareholder value. The next section examines this development and major types of executive bonus compensation plans.

BONUS COMPENSATION PLANS[8]

Major Plan Types

Company shareholders typically believe that the goal of a bonus compensation plan is to motivate executives and key employees to achieve maximization of shareholder wealth. Because shareholders are both owners and investors of the firm, they desire a reasonable return on their investment. Because they are absentee landlords, shareholders expect their board of directors to ensure that the decision-making logic of their firm's executives to be concurrent with their own primary motivation.

However, the goal of shareholder wealth maximization is not the only goal that executives may pursue. Alternatively, executives may choose actions that increase their personal compensation, power, and control. Therefore, an executive compensation plan that contains

---

[8] We wish to thank Roy Hossler for his assistance on this section.

EXHIBIT 10.10 **Types of Executive Bonus Compensation**

Bonus Type	Description	Rationale	Shortcomings
Stock option grants	Right to purchase stock in the future at a price set now. Compensation is determined by "spread" between option price and exercise price.	Provides incentive for executive to create wealth for shareholders as measured by increase in firm's share price.	Movement in share price does not explain all dimensions of managerial performance.
Restricted stock plan	Shares given to executive who is prohibited from selling them for a specific time period. May also include performance restrictions.	Promotes longer executive tenure than other forms of compensation.	No downside risk to executive, who always profits unlike other shareholders.
Golden handcuffs	Bonus income deferred in a series of annual installments. Deferred amounts not yet paid are forfeited with executive resignation.	Offers an incentive for executive to remain with the firm.	May promote risk-averse decision making due to downside risk borne by executive.
Golden parachute	Executives have right to collect the bonus if they lose position due to takeover, firing, retirement, or resignation.	Offers an incentive for executive to remain with the firm.	Compensation is achieved whether or not wealth is created for shareholders. Rewards either success or failure.
Cash based on internal business performance using financial measures	Bonus compensation based on accounting performance measures such as return on equity.	Offsets the limitations of focusing on market-based measures of performance.	Weak correlation between earnings measures and shareholder wealth creation. Annual earnings do not capture future impact of current decisions.

a bonus component can be used to orient management's decision making toward the owners' goals. The success of bonus compensation as an incentive hinges on a proper match between an executive bonus plan and the firm's strategic objectives. As one author has written, "Companies can succeed by clarifying their business vision or strategy and aligning company pay programs with its strategic direction."[9] Exhibit 10.10 summarizes five types of executive compensation plans we will now explore in more detail.

Stock Options

A common measure of shareholder wealth creation is appreciation of company stock price. Therefore, a popular form of bonus compensation is stock options. Stock options have typically represented more than 50 percent of a chief executive officer's average pay

---

[9] James E. Nelson, "Linking Compensation to Business Strategy," *The Journal of Business Strategy* 19, no. 2 (1998), pp. 25–27.

stock options
The right, or "option," to purchase company stock at a fixed price at some future date.

package.[10] **Stock options** provide the executive with the right to purchase company stock at a fixed price in the future. The precise amount of compensation is based on the difference, or "spread," between the option's initial price and its selling, or exercised, price. As a result, the executive receives a bonus only if the firm's share price appreciates. If the share price drops below the option price, the options become worthless.

Stock options were the source of extraordinary wealth creation for executives, managers, and rank-and-file employees in the technology boom of the last decade. Behind using options as compensation incentives was the notion that they were essentially free. Although they dilute shareholders' equity when they're exercised, taking the cost of stock options as an expense against earnings was not required. That, in turn, helped keep earnings higher than actual costs to the company and its shareholders. The bear market and corporate scandals of the last few years brought increased scrutiny on the use of and accounting for stock options. Recent changes in SEC guidelines have encouraged expensing stock options to more accurately reflect company performance. The following table shows the effect expensing stocks options would have on the net earnings of Standard & Poor's (S&P) 500 firms in recent years. "Stock options were a free resource, and because of that, they were used freely," said BankOne CEO James Dimon, who voluntarily began to expense stock options in 2003. "But now," he said, "when you have to expense options, you start to think, 'Is it an effective cost? Is there a better way?'" The Financial Accounting Standards Board issued a new ruling in 2004 that required expensing of stock options beginning in 2006.[11]

A Big Hit to Earnings

If options had been expensed the past 10 years, earnings would have been whacked as their popularity grew as shown below:

Options Expense as a Percent of Net Earnings for S&P 500 Companies				
1996	**1998**	**2000**	**2002**	**2005**
2%	5%	8%	23%	22%

Source: *The Analysis Accounting Observer,* R. G. Associates Inc.

Microsoft shocked the business world in 2003 by announcing it would discontinue stock options, eliminating a form of pay that made thousands of Microsoft employees millionaires and helped define the culture of the tech industry. Starting in September 2003, the company began paying its 54,000 employees with restricted stock, a move that will let employees make money even if the company's share price declines. Like options, the restricted stock will vest gradually over a five-year period, and grants of restricted stock are counted as expenses and charged against earnings. Said CEO Steven Ballmer, "We asked: Is there a smarter way to compensate our people, a way that would make them feel even more excited about their financial deal at Microsoft and at the same time be something that was at least as good for the shareholders as today's compensation package?" At the time of Ballmer's announcement, more than 20,000 employees who had joined Microsoft in the past three years held millions of stock options that were "under water," meaning the market value of Microsoft stock was far below the stock price of their stock options.

Restricted stock has the advantage of offering employees more certainty, even if there is less potential for a big win. It also means shareholders don't have to worry about massive

[10] Louis Lavelle, Frederick Jespersen, and Spencer Ante, "Executive Pay," *BusinessWeek,* April 21, 2003.
[11] U.S. GAAP (generally accepted accounting principles) required expensing of stock options using one of two acceptable valuation methods starting in the first fiscal year after June 15, 2005. (www.wikipedia.org/wiki/employee_stock_options)

dilution after employees exercise big stock gains, as happened in the 1990s. Another advantage is that grants of restricted stock are much easier to value than options because restricted stock is equivalent to a stock transfer at the market price. That improves the transparency of corporate accounting.[12]

Research suggests that stock option plans lack the benefits of plans that include true stock ownership. Stock option plans provide unlimited upside potential for executives, but limited downside risk because executives incur only opportunity costs. Because of the tremendous advantages to the executive of stock price appreciation, there is an incentive for the executive to take undue risk. Thus, supporters of stock ownership plans argue that direct ownership instills a much stronger behavioral commitment, even when the stock price falls, because it binds executives to their firms more than do options.[13] Additionally, "Executive stock options may be an efficient means to induce management to undertake more risky projects."[14]

Options may have been overused and indeed abused in the last two bull markets,[15] but evidence suggests that the smart use of options and other incentive compensation does boost performance. Companies that spread ownership throughout a large portion of their workforce deliver higher returns than similar companies with more concentrated ownership. If options seemed for a time to be the route that enriched CEOs, employees, and investors alike, it still appears they will be used, although with less emphasis than a mix of options, restricted stock, and cash bonuses. Whatever the exact mix, they are likely to be more closely tied to achieving specific operating goals. The next section examines restricted stock and cash bonuses in greater detail.

Restricted Stock

restricted stock
Stock given to an employee who is prohibited or "restricted" from selling the stock for a certain time period and not at all if they leave the company before that time period.

A **restricted stock** plan is designed to provide benefits of direct executive stock ownership. In a typical restricted stock plan, an executive is given a specific number of company stock shares. The executive is prohibited from selling the shares for a specified time period. Should the executive leave the firm voluntarily before the restricted period ends, the shares are forfeited. Therefore, restricted stock plans are a form of deferred compensation that promotes longer executive tenure than other types of plans.

In addition to being contingent on a vesting period, restricted stock plans may also require the achievement of predetermined performance goals. Price-vesting restricted stock plans tie vesting to the firm's stock price in comparison to an index or to reaching a predetermined goal or annual growth rate. If the executive falls short on some of the restrictions, a certain amount of shares are forfeited. The design of these plans motivates the executive to increase shareholder wealth while promoting a long-term commitment to stay with the firm.

If the restricted stock plan lacks performance goal provisions, the executive needs only to remain employed with the firm over the vesting period to cash in on the stock. Performance provisions make sure executives are not compensated without achieving some

---

[12] Many argue that stock options are critical to start-up firms as a way to motivate and retain talented employees with the promise of getting rich should the new venture succeed. Among them appear to be FASB chairman Robert Herz, who favors sentiment to make special exceptions in the expensing of options in pre-IPO firms.

[13] Jeffrey Pfeffer, "Seven Practices of Successful Organizations," *California Management Review,* Winter 1998.

[14] Richard A. DeFusco, Robert R. Johnson, and Thomas S. Zorn, "The Effect of Executive Stock Option Plans on Stockholders and Bondholders," *Journal of Finance* 45, no. 2 (1990), pp. 617–35.

[15] Erik Lie and Randall A. Heron, "Does Backdating Explain the Stock Price Pattern Around Stock Option Grants," *Journal of Financial Economics* 83, (2007) pp. 271–95. Lie and Heron found 30 percent of all U.S. publicly traded firms apparently manipulated (backdated) stock option grants to increase the payoff to executives receiving the grants. See the Chapter 10 Discussion Case Part II for more details.

level of shareholder wealth creation. Like stock options, restricted stock plans offer no downside risk to executives because the shares were initially gifted to the executive. Unlike options, the stock retains value tied to its market value once ownership is fully vested. Shareholders, on the other hand, do suffer a loss in personal wealth resulting from a share price drop.

Golden Handcuffs

golden handcuffs
A form of executive compensation where compensation is deferred (either a restricted stock plan or bonus income deferred in a series of annual installments).

The rationale behind plans that defer compensation forms the basis for another type of executive compensation called golden handcuffs. **Golden handcuffs** refer to either a restricted stock plan, where the stock compensation is deferred until vesting time provisions are met, or to bonus income deferred in a series of annual installments. This type of plan may also involve compensating an executive a significant amount upon retirement or at some predetermined age. In most cases, compensation is forfeited if the executive voluntarily resigns or is discharged before certain time restrictions.

Many boards consider their executives' skills and talents to be their firm's most valuable assets. These "assets" create and sustain the professional relationships that generate revenue and control expenses for the firm. Research suggests that the departure of key executives is unsettling for companies and often disrupts long-range plans when new key executives adopt a different management strategy.[16] Thus, the golden handcuffs approach to executive compensation is more congruent with long-term strategies than short-term performance plans, which offer little staying-power incentive.

Firms may turn to golden handcuffs if they believe stability of management is critical to sustained growth. Jupiter Asset Management recently tied 10 fund managers to the firm with golden handcuffs. The compensation scheme calls for a cash payment in addition to base salaries if the managers remain at the firm for five years. In the first year of the plan, the firm's pretax profits more than doubled, and their assets under management increased 85 percent. The firm's chairman has also signed a new incentive deal that will keep him at Jupiter for four years.

Deferred compensation is worrisome to some executives. In cases where the compensation is payable when the executives are retired and no longer in control, as when the firm is acquired by another firm or a new management hierarchy is installed, the golden handcuff plans are considerably less attractive to executives.

Golden handcuffs may promote risk averseness in executive decision making due to the huge downside risk borne by executives. This risk averseness could lead to mediocre performance results from executives' decisions. When executives lose deferred compensation if the firm discharges them voluntarily or involuntarily, the executive is less likely to make bold and aggressive decisions. Rather, the executive will choose safe, conservative decisions.

Golden Parachutes

golden parachute
A form of bonus compensation that guarantees a substantial cash payment if the executive quits, is fired, or simply retires.

Golden parachutes are a form of bonus compensation that guarantees a substantial cash payment to an executive if the executive quits, is fired, or simply retires. In addition, the golden parachute may also contain covenants that allow the executive to cash in on noninvested stock compensation.

The popularity of golden parachutes grew with the increased popularity of takeovers, which often led to the ouster of the acquired firm's top executives. In these cases, the golden parachutes encouraged executives to take an objective look at takeover offers. The executives could decide which move was in the best interests of the shareholders, having been personally protected in the event of a merger. The "parachute" helps soften the fall

---

[16] William E. Hall, Brian J. Lake, Charles T. Morse, and Charles T. Morse, Jr., "More Than Golden Handcuffs," *Journal of Accountancy* 184, no. 5 (1997), pp. 37–42.

of the ousted executive. It is "golden" because the size of the cash payment often varies from several to tens of millions of dollars.

AMP Incorporated, the world's largest producer of electronic connectors, had golden parachutes for several executives. When Allied Signal proclaimed itself an unsolicited suitor for AMP, the action focused attention on the AMP parachutes for its three top executives. Robert Ripp became AMP's chief executive officer during this time. If Allied Signal ousted him, he stood to receive a cash payment of three times the amount of his salary as well as his highest annual bonus from the previous three years. His salary at the time was $600,000 and his previous year's bonus was $200,000. The cash payment to Ripp would therefore exceed $2 million. Parachutes would also open for the former chief executive officer and the former chairman who were slated to officially retire a year later. They stood to receive their parachutes if they were ousted before their respective retirement dates with each parachute valued at more than $1 million.

In addition to cash payments, these three executives' parachutes also protect existing blocks of restricted stock grants and nonvested stock options. The restricted stock grants were scheduled to become available within three years. Should the takeover come to fruition, the executives would receive the total value of the restricted stock even if it was not yet vested. The stock options would also become available immediately. Some of the restricted stock was performance restricted. Under normal conditions this stock would not be available without the firm reaching certain performance levels. However, the golden parachutes allow the executives to receive double the value of the performance-restricted stock.

Golden parachutes are designed in part to anticipate hostile takeovers like this. In AMP's case, Ripp's position is to lead the firm's board of directors in deciding if Allied Signal's offer is in the long-term interests of shareholders. Because Ripp is compensated heavily whether AMP is taken over or not, the golden parachute has helped remove the temptation that Ripp could have of not acting in the best interests of shareholders.

By design, golden parachutes benefit top executives whether or not there is evidence that value is created for shareholders. In fact, research has suggested that since high-performing firms are rarely taken over, golden parachutes often compensate top executives for abysmal performance.[17] Recent stockholder reactions to excessive executive compensation regardless of company performance are seen in Exhibit 10.11, Strategy in Action.

Cash

Executive bonus compensation plans that focus on accounting measures of performance are designed to offset the limitations of market-based measures of performance. This type of plan is most usually associated with the payment of periodic (quarterly or annual) cash bonuses. Market factors beyond the control of management, such as pending legislation, can keep a firm's share price repressed even though a top executive is exceeding the performance expectations of the board. In this situation, a highly performing executive loses bonus compensation due to the undervalued stock. However, accounting measures of performance correct for this problem by tying executive bonuses to improvements in internally measured performance.

Traditional accounting measures, such as net income, earnings per share, return on equity, and return on assets, are used because they are easily understood, are familiar to senior management, and are already tracked by firm data systems.[18] Sears bases annual

---

[17] Graef S. Crystal, *In Search of Excess* (New York: W. W. Norton & Company, 1991).

[18] Francine C. McKenzie and Matthew D. Shilling, "Avoiding Performance Measurement Traps: Ensuring Effective Incentive Design and Implementation," *Compensation and Benefits Review,* July–August 1998, pp. 57–65.

Shareholder Reaction to Executive Compensation Plans

BusinessWeek

BACK-DATED OPTIONS

Iowa professor Erik Lie found that more than 30 percent of all U.S. public corporations—2,000 companies—routinely manipulated stock option accounting rules to increase executive pay.

FED-UP SHAREHOLDERS

Unions and public pension funds have racked up more than two dozen majority votes for shareholder resolutions opposing high executive pay.

GOLDEN PARACHUTES

At Alcoa, 65 percent of shareholders voted for a union resolution calling for stockholder approval of lavish executive severance packages. Similar proposals won majorities at Delta and Raytheon.

CUSHY RETIREMENT DEALS

A proposal at U.S. Bancorp seeking shareholder votes on special executive pension benefits passed by 52 percent. Labor pulled resolutions at GE, Coke, and Exelon after they agreed to reforms.

EXPENSING STOCK OPTIONS

Labor resolutions demanding that companies deduct option costs from earnings have garnered majorities at 15 companies, including Apple and Capital One.

Sources: Reprinted with special permission from "He's Making Hay As CEOs Squirm," *BusinessWeek*, January 15, 2007; and Amy Borrus, "Executive Pay: Labor Strikes Back," *BusinessWeek*, May 26, 2003. Copyright © 2007 The McGraw-Hill Companies.

bonus payments on such performance criteria, given an executive's business unit and level with the firm. The measures used by Sears include return on equity, revenue growth, net sales growth, and profit growth.

Critics argue that because of inherent flaws in accounting systems, basing compensation on these figures may not result in an accurate gauge of managerial performance. Return on equity estimates, for example, are skewed by inflation distortions and arbitrary cost allocations. Accounting measures are also subject to manipulation by firm personnel to artificially inflate key performance figures. Firm performance schemes, critics believe, need to be based on a financial measure that has a true link to shareholder value creation.[19] This issue led to the creation of the Balanced Scorecard, which emphasizes not only financial measures, but also such measures as new-product development, market share, and safety as discussed in Chapter 12.

Matching Bonus Plans and Corporate Goals

Exhibit 10.12 provides a summary of the five types of executive bonus compensation plans. The figure includes a brief description, a rationale for implementation, and the identification of possible shortcomings for each of the compensation plans. Not only do compensation plans differ in the method through which compensation is rewarded to the executive, but they also provide the executive with different incentives.

Exhibit 10.12 matches a company's strategic goal with the most likely compensation plan. On the vertical axis are common strategic goals. The horizontal axis lists the main compensation types that serve as incentives for executives to reach the firm's goals. A rationale is provided to explain the logic behind the connection between the firm's goal and the suggested method of executive compensation.

Researchers emphasize that fundamental to these relationships is the importance of incorporating the level of strategic risk of the firm into the design of the executive's

[19] William Franklin, "Making the Fat Cats Earn Their Cream," *Accountancy,* July 1998, pp. 38–39.

EXHIBIT 10.12   **Compensation Plan Selection Matrix**

Strategic Goal	Cash	Golden Handcuffs	Golden Parachutes	Restricted Stock Plans	Stock Options	Rationale
Achieve corporate turnaround					X	Executive profits only if turnaround is successful in returning wealth to shareholders.
Create and support growth opportunities					X	Risk associated with growth strategies warrants the use of this high-reward incentive.
Defend against unfriendly takeover			X			Parachute helps takeover remove temptation for executive to evaluate takeover based on personal benefits.
Evaluate suitors objectively			X			Parachute compensates executive if job is lost due to a merger favorable to the firm.
Globalize operations					X	Risk of expanding overseas requires a plan that compensates only for achieved success.
Grow share price incrementally	X					Accounting measures can identify periodic performance benchmarks.
Improve operational efficiency	X					Accounting measures represent observable and agreed-upon measures of performance.
Increase assets under management				X		Executive profits proportionally as asset growth leads to long-term growth in share price.
Reduce executive turnover		X				Handcuffs provide executive tenure incentive.
Restructure organization					X	Risk associated with major change in firm's assets warrants the use of this high-reward incentive.
Streamline operations				X		Rewards long-term focus on efficiency and cost control.

Table header spanning "Type of Bonus Compensation" over Cash, Golden Handcuffs, Golden Parachutes, Restricted Stock Plans, Stock Options.

compensation plan. Incorporating an appropriate level of executive risk can create a desired behavioral change commensurate with the risk level of strategies shareholders and their firms want.[20] To help motivate an executive to pursue goals of a certain risk-return level, the compensation plan can quantify that risk-return level and reward the executive accordingly.

[20] Lavelle, Jespersen, and Ante, "Executive Pay."

The links we show between bonus compensation plans and strategic goals were derived from the results of prior research. The basic principle underlying Exhibit 10.12 is that different types of bonus compensation plans are intended to accomplish different purposes; one element may serve to attract and retain executives; another may serve as an incentive to encourage behavior that accomplishes firm goals.[21] Although every strategy option has probably been linked to each compensation plan at some time, experience shows that there may be scenarios where a plan type best fits a strategy option. Exhibit 10.12 attempts to display the "best matches."

Once the firm has identified strategic goals that will best serve shareholders' interests, an executive bonus compensation plan can be structured in such a way as to provide the executive with an incentive to work toward achieving these goals.

Summary

The first concern in the implementation of business strategy is to translate that strategy into action throughout the organization. This chapter discussed five considerations for accomplishing this.

Short-term objectives are derived from long-term objectives, which are then translated into current actions and targets. They differ from long-term objectives in time frame, specificity, and measurement. To be effective in strategy implementation, they must be integrated and coordinated. They also must be consistent, measurable, and prioritized.

Functional tactics are derived from the business strategy. They identify the specific, immediate actions that must be taken in key functional areas to implement the business strategy.

Outsourcing of selected functional activities has become a central tactical agenda for virtually every business firm in today's global economy. Can we get that activity done more effectively—and more inexpensively—outside our company? This question has become a regular one managers ask as they seek to make their business strategies work.

Employee empowerment through policies provides another means for guiding behavior, decisions, and actions at the firm's operating levels in a manner consistent with its business and functional strategies. Policies empower operating personnel to make decisions and take action quickly.

Compensation rewards action and results. Once the firm has identified strategic objectives that will best serve stockholder interests, there are five bonus compensation plans that can be structured to provide the executive with an incentive to work toward achieving those goals.

Objectives, functional tactics, policies, and compensation represent only the start of the strategy implementation. The strategy must be institutionalized—it must permeate the firm. The next chapter examines this phase of strategy implementation.

[21] Nelson, "Linking Compensation to Business Strategy."

Key Terms

empowerment, *p.314*	golden parachute, *p.321*	restricted stock, *p. 320*
functional tactics, *p. 309*	outsourcing, *p.312*	short-term objective, *p. 305*
golden handcuffs, *p. 321*	policies, *p. 314*	stock options, *p. 319*

Questions for Discussion

1. How does the concept "translate thought into action" bear on the relationship between business strategy and operating strategy? Between long-term and short-term objectives?
2. How do functional tactics differ from corporate and business strategies?
3. What key concerns must functional tactics address in marketing? finance? production/operations management? personnel?
4. What is "outsourcing?" Why has it become a key element in shaping functional tactics within most business firms today?
5. How do policies aid strategy implementation? Illustrate your answer.
6. Use Exhibits 10.9 and 10.11 to explain five executive bonus compensation plans.
7. Illustrate a policy, an objective, and a functional tactic in your personal career strategy.
8. Why are short-term objectives needed when long-term objectives are already available?

Chapter 10 Discussion Case 1

BusinessWeek

A Better Look at the Boss's Pay

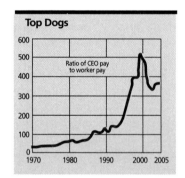

Top Dogs

Ratio of CEO pay to worker pay

Since 1993, CEO pay has increased faster than the cost of gasoline, Ivy League tuition, residential real estate prices, and a whole lot else. Your boss may have an inflated ego, but it's probably not nearly as inflated as his paycheck. In 1993, chief executives' salaries averaged $2.6 million, and by 2005 they had skyrocketed to $10.5 million—a 304 percent increase over 12 years.

1 No topic inflames the passions of business leaders and shareholders like executive pay. Companies and compensation consultants argue that, in a free market, they'd be foolish not to pay the going rate for top talent. Investors demand that compensation be tied to performance and complain loudly when pay rises while share prices don't.

2 The perennial battle is about to reach a new level of contentiousness. The proxy season, just getting started, will be the first under new Securities and Exchange Commission reporting rules that force companies to disclose more about executive pay than ever before—from the hundreds of millions some executives stand to gain in severance, pensions, and deferred pay, to any perk worth more than $10,000. Golden parachutes and sybaritic benefits such as club memberships and personal use of company jets won't score many

points against a backdrop of the options-backdating scandal and increasingly empowered activist investors.

Thanks to recent blowups like that at Home Depot, **3** shareholder-rights groups hold a distinct advantage in the public-relations war. Former Chief Executive Robert L. Nardelli walked away from Home Depot Inc. in early January with a $210 million severance package, shocking shareholders unhappy with the company's flagging stock. And the timing couldn't have been worse for companies nervously preparing to reveal their own pay practices. "Home Depot is a preview of things to come," says Michael S. Melbinger, a compensation lawyer with Winston & Strawn in Chicago. "It's the perfect example of the rich payout that would have been buried before, but which everyone now must disclose."

Governance advocates and politicians gain even more **4** public support when they point out that in 2005 the average CEO in the Standard & Poor's 500-stock index took home 369 times the pay of the average worker, up from 28 times the average in 1970. The counterargument, that the ratio is down from the 514 multiple in 2000, doesn't get much traction.

THE LITTLE THINGS

Some boards have been looking hard at executive contracts **5** and even tried to renegotiate them. Such minor perks as the personal driver and financial planning services are often on the table. But most boards plan to do little more.

In many cases, they can't. Almost all CEOs have contracts **6** guaranteeing their big payouts. And the fear of angering a CEO over a pay issue has made directors reluctant to push harder. "No one wants to be responsible for seeing the CEO walk," says Jannice L. Koors, a managing director of pay consultants Pearl Meyer & Partners. In a survey of 110 companies at year-end, Mercer Human Resource Consulting found that 70 percent planned only minimal changes to their executive compensation programs as a result of the new SEC rules; just 15 percent said the impact would be more substantial. Cutbacks in executives' packages are "just not terribly widespread," says Mark A. Borges, a former SEC official who is a principal at Mercer. Chicago lawyer Melbinger, who has sat in on recent board meetings, echoes Borges' view: "Yes, there's pressure to get rid of these deals, but I have not seen a single situation where an executive was willing to give one up."

7   To avoid provoking shareholders, companies are most commonly shifting pay out of categories that raise questions. Late last year aerospace giant Lockheed Martin Corp. said it would stop paying for a car and driver as well as club dues for CEO Robert J. Stevens. Instead, it hiked his $1.48 million salary $40,000. A spokesman says ending perks was in the company's best interests.

8   Some items, however, are too large to move or obscure. The biggest fights are likely to be over multimillion-dollar deferred pay and retirement accounts, as well as guaranteed payments for executives who are fired or who leave when the company is acquired. Such items have been focal points of recent firestorms, from the Nardelli flap to the $82 million pension Pfizer Inc. paid outgoing CEO Hank McKinnell last year.

9   The surprise this proxy season, predicts Shekhar Purohit, a principal of pay consultants James F. Reda & Associates, will be just how common, and lucrative, these severance packages are. Typically they include a payment of three times salary and bonus, immediate vesting of options and restricted stock awards, and, in many cases, payment of taxes owed. Purohit says dozens of executives could have payouts of $100 million or more.

10   Revelations of extra-sweet deferred-compensation deals are sure to raise eyebrows, too. Such plans usually allow executives to sock away money tax-free, often with a company match—much like 401(k) accounts, only with no limit on the contributions. And some companies guarantee better-than-market interest for executives. American Express Co. gave CEO Kenneth I. Chenault $1.1 million in above-market returns on his deferred compensation account in 2005. The company won't divulge the rate it gave that year, but in 2006 it paid 13 percent on executives' deferred balances. In late January, AmEx said it would continue to pay 13 percent to 16 percent on money they set aside between 1994 and 2004 if the company meets or beats financial targets, and will pay 9 percent to 11 percent on money deferred after 2005. A spokesman says the plan is consistent with industry practice.

RICH RETIREES

11   Pension plans will likely draw attention, too. Whereas regular workers typically retire on one-half to two-thirds of their average salary in their last three to five years, some CEOs get far more. Pfizer's deal with McKinnell was unusually

rich: in calculating his final pay, Pfizer counted not only salary and bonus, but stock awards that vested through 2004. That notched his annual pension up from roughly $3.5 million to $6.6 million. The company says it stopped including new stock awards in pension calculations in 2001, but earlier grants were grandfathered in. Huge bonuses issued just before retirement can also pump up pensions. "It's the gift that keeps on giving," says Kevin J. Murphy, a professor at the University of Southern California's Marshall School of Business.

12   Governance activists are already targeting such practices. The United Brotherhood of Carpenters has identified 14 companies, including AT&T and Johnson & Johnson, where it believes the inclusion of large incentive bonuses in pension calculations has led to excessive benefits. So far, the union can claim one small victory. In January, American Express also announced further limits on retirement benefits. Rather than basing them on total salary and bonus—which for Chenault were $1.1 million and $6 million, respectively, in 2005—earnings used in calculating retirement will be capped at twice the annual salary. The AmEx spokesman says the changes, long in the works, stem from the shift away from traditional defined benefit pensions to 401(k)-type defined contribution plans.

13   As for the smaller perks, companies maintain that some are born of legitimate need. For example, many argue that use of a company jet even for personal flights is a must in the post-9/11 era. Ditto home alarm systems and other security measures. The practice isn't universal. Intel Corp. and Goldman Sachs & Co. both forbid personal use of company jets.

14   Even so, in a study of 2005 proxies filed by the 100 largest U.S. companies, compensation research firm Equilar Inc. found that the median value of personal travel on corporate jets rose 21.7 percent, to $109,000, while execs got roughly $37,000 to safeguard themselves, up 69 percent. The numbers for individuals can fly much higher. United Technologies Corp. chief George David ran up a $581,396 tab for "personal use of the corporate aircraft for security reasons," according to SEC filings. The company declined to comment. FedEx Corp. gave CEO Frederick W. Smith $833,000 in jet use and security services on top of his $1.3 million salary in fiscal 2006. FedEx, which requires the CEO to use the jet for all travel, says an independent security consultant determined the need for the benefits.

15   Still, jet travel irks some. Richard C. Breeden, a former SEC chairman who runs a hedge fund, criticized restaurant chain Applebee's International Inc. over the issue. He found that, over a 10-month period, Applebee's jet made 29 trips to Galveston, Texas, where Lloyd Hill, who stepped down as CEO in September but remains chairman, has a beach house. A spokeswoman for Applebee's, which said on February 13 it will explore a sale, says its plane policy is disclosed.

16   One thing is clear: it is increasingly tough for boards to keep everyone happy. Retired General Hugh Shelton, the former chairman of the U.S. Joint Chiefs of Staff who heads the compensation committee of software maker Red Hat Inc., says boards are focused more on finding the right balance between shareholder demands to link pay to performance and the company's need to ensure good executives have the right incentives. "You try to be fair, and give appropriate rewards for performance," he says. But ultimately, "you compensate them so that they're not desperate to go to work for someone else."

Source: Reprinted with special permission from "A Better Look at the Boss's Pay," *BusinessWeek*, February 26, 2007. Copyright © 2007 The McGraw-Hill Companies.

Discussion Case 2

BusinessWeek

He's Making Hay as CEOs Squirm: *Erik Lie Uncovered*
Widespread Backdating of Stock Options. Now He's Reaping Rewards

17 Erik Lie loves academic life. The University of Iowa associate finance professor is free to research whatever topic intrigues him, and his $160,000-plus income goes a nice long way in Iowa City. Summers off means that Lie (rhymes with "key"), his wife, and two kids can travel back to his parents' vacation home in Norway. During the rest of the year, he's free to take off after class for a run or some cross-country skiing. "Life as a professor is good," says the lanky 38-year-old.

18   It's particularly good now that Lie's research is having a major impact on Corporate America. His mid-2005 research first suggested that hundreds of companies may have routinely manipulated stock-option accounting rules to sweeten top executives' paydays. A later study done with his research partner, Indiana University associate professor Randall Heron, puts the number at 2,000, or 29 percent of all public corporations. Five executives face criminal indictments for such alleged backdating, more than 100 companies face civil charges and shareholder suits, and hundreds more are neck-deep in comprehensive investigations of their books to try to make sure the Feds don't add them to the list.

19   The scandal is creating a financial windfall for Lie. He and Heron have created a limited partnership now that the initial crush of calls from reporters has given way to people willing to actually pay for their insights. Lie says he has earned around $100,000 from hedge funds and other investors, who pay him to handicap whether a company's options irregularities are harmless paperwork errors or the kinds of fraud that lead to CEO ousters and big civil penalties. He'll probably draw $400 an hour or more doing consulting work for law firms, and still more as an expert witness. He's now a senior adviser at the Brattle Group, a consultancy in Washington. All told, Lie figures he could make $250,000 before the options scandal fades from memory.

20   Lie may be underestimating his prospects. An elite business professor can make tens of thousands for a one-day consulting gig. Notre Dame University professor Paul H. Schultz, who in the mid-1990s discovered that NASDAQ market makers were skimming pennies from investors on stock trades, says he earned $250,000 over three years, charging $250 an hour to work with plaintiffs' attorneys. "But Erik can do quite a bit better, if he wants to," Schultz says. "There are more lawsuits, and he should be charging a higher rate."

LUCKY TIMING?

Rarely has an academic had such an outsize, real-time impact on **21** the business world. Academics had long known that companies tended to grant options with remarkable acuity—just before big rises that gave those options immediate value, at least on paper. But Lie and Heron were first to suggest that this could only have happened with the help of hindsight. That's because those favorable trading patterns appeared only in cases where companies had delayed their options paperwork for months, giving them the ability to look back and cherry-pick the most lucrative grant dates. That's a violation of federal law—and of many corporate options plans—if not properly disclosed.

Lie helped make sure the scandal exploded, notifying the **22** Securities and Exchange Commission of his work and showing *The Wall Street Journal* how to interpret a particular company's options records, although he insists he never identified companies himself. He's clearly proud of his work's resonance but insists the attendant financial opportunities are a low priority. He limits his consulting time, he says, to less than one day a week. "I did not start this line of research for the money, and I am still not in this for the money," Lie says.

Now he's turning away many opportunities, he says— **23** particularly from plaintiffs' lawyers who would like to tailor his findings to suit their cases. But he is helping "less pushy" plaintiffs' attorneys prepare potential cases against three dozen companies, diving into details of specific transactions. Indeed, he says he'll probably take the stand as an expert witness in some high-profile cases. He won't name any names, in part because it's too early to know which companies will settle rather than make it into court, but does say that he "may become involved in litigations" against Apple Computer.

Lie is also open to working with defendants facing **24** options-related allegations, although none have taken him up on the offer. "People tend to think I'm against all companies," he says, "but I think some of the companies identified in the media are innocent"—perhaps a dozen or so of the 200 companies that have announced options irregularities. He says some guiltless CEOs are likely to lose their jobs simply because they were at the helm when mistakes were made by others. Still, "it's one of those necessary evils; a small price to pay to get more transparency into the system. How much is good governance worth to the economy? I don't know, but it's billions and billions."

25   Lie grew up the son of left-leaning parents in southern Norway. His father, Rolf, a retired construction engineer, thinks Lie is imbued with the economic egalitarianism they taught him. "Erik doesn't like that people have gotten money they didn't deserve," says the elder Lie. The son briefly considered a career in law but later caught the academic bug while doing a finance research project at the University of Oregon.

SERENDIPITY

26   When he began researching stock options as a young professor in 2002, it wasn't to find a scandal. "Shareholders were giving executives options so they'd work harder to change corporate behavior," he says. "I just wanted to see how it manifested itself"—say, by companies repurchasing more shares. Even after Lie began to suspect backdating, it took a while for anyone to listen. An initial paper in 2004 was slammed by a reviewer who said that Lie was "overreaching" and that his conclusions "made little economic sense." After Sarbanes-Oxley regulations were imposed, however, all option grants had to be reported to the SEC within two days. By comparing the new grants with pre-Sarbanes-Oxley grants, Lie and Heron were able to document a disappearance of the windfall obtained by execs at companies that had taken months to file in the past.

    Defense lawyers dismiss Lie's analysis because it doesn't **27** consider legitimate explanations for how options may have been granted at low stock prices. For example, CEOs during the boom routinely granted options on days when their stocks were down because of unfounded rumors. That way, they could provide some extra incentive to employees before cranking up their investor relations efforts to refute the rumor. "His analysis is simplistic," says Richard Marmaro of Skadden, Arps, Slate, Meagher & Flom, who is representing indicted former Brocade Communications Systems CEO Greg Reyes. "There are people whose job it is to grant options, who are expert in understanding what they perceived to be low prices."

    Lie says he's going into this next phase of the scandal **28** with his eyes wide open, expecting to have his motives criticized, and ready for persuasive arguments about why a specific company, board, or executive did nothing wrong. He figures that the bulk of backdaters have yet to be identified, and that just 10 percent will ever be punished in any way. "I don't anticipate I'll be able to create something of this magnitude again," he says. "But it's not necessary for me that there is a consequence for every single firm. My research has already helped curb this behavior. That's the most important thing."

Source: Reprinted with special permission from "He's Making Hay as CEOs Squirm," *BusinessWeek,* January 15, 2007. Copyright © 2007 The McGraw-Hill Companies.

Discussion Case 3

BusinessWeek

Google Gives Employees Another Option: *The Search Giant's Innovative Program Offers Workers Another Way to Realize the Value of Their Stock Options*

29 In a bid to breathe new life into scandal-tainted stock options, Google plans to give employees a novel method of cashing in their options starting next April. The search giant will let employees sell their vested stock options, which give the holder the right to reap the difference between the initial price and the current price, to selected financial institutions in an auction marketplace it's setting up with Morgan Stanley.

30   The program is a unique stab at unlocking for employees the underlying value of these securities that have been a favored method of luring and keeping employees, particularly among technology companies. In the past year or so, as rules requiring the expensing of stock options kicked in, employers have been cutting back on the number of options they grant, or doling out new incentives such as restricted stock, in a bid to avoid a hit to reported profits.

31   That has some observers worrying about the possible demise of a classic performance incentive tool. While options continue to be granted by many companies, some 30 percent

have cut back their options grants, and 25 percent of employees who once received options and other equity awards now do not, according to the National Center for Employee Ownership, a nonprofit research group in Oakland, California. And for those getting grants, the value of their options is about a third lower than it used to be.

HOW IT WORKS

Under Google's Transferable Stock Option program, **32** employees could sell their stock options on the semi-private marketplace much the way public options are sold today. That would let employees potentially reap more than if they merely exercised and then sold the securities. Say an employee holds an option with a strike price of $400, meaning it can be purchased for $400 and then resold at a higher price. If Google's stock is trading at $500, an investor might pay $150 for that option, betting that the stock will rise well past $500 during the life of the option. The employee selling the option could net an immediate $150. An employee exercising and then selling the same option would net only $100, the difference between the strike price and the current price.

33   The impetus for the new approach is Google's volatile stock, which can change substantially in the space of a month or even days. Google's stock has been on a long if volatile rise since the company's initial public offering in 2004 at $85 a share. Just since September 1, 2006, the shares have risen 27 percent, to $481.78 on December 12, after rising above $500 in November.

34   As a result, many recent and incoming employees may feel the options don't have much value, given how high Google's stock already is. Moreover, an employee who joins one week ultimately may end up having very different compensation than another hired a few weeks later. That difference can raise pay equity issues and potentially reduce the incentive for employees to stick around. "This goes a long way toward solving recruiting and retention issues," says Dave Rolefson, Google's equity and executive compensation manager.

"VERY INNOVATIVE"

35   If Google's plan works—an open question at this point—other companies once again might find options an attractive offering for hiring and keeping talent. "I think it's a very good idea," says James Glassman, resident fellow at the American Enterprise Institute, who was briefed on the plan. "It achieves Google's goal of making the value of options more apparent to people who get them."

36   There could also be some unpredictable consequences to the plan. Investors buying these options no doubt will want to hedge their bets, possibly through a short sale—a bet that Google's stock will fall. That's not usually something companies like to see. But Google believes the overall impact of the program on the company will be positive. Former Securities and Exchange Commission chairman Arthur Levitt, now a senior advisor to the Carlyle Group, says he's not sure what all the implications will be. "But on balance, it's a very innovative program," he says.

37   The plan is only for employees, not executives, who Google says are already adequately compensated. So on its face the plan doesn't address some of the recent problems surrounding stock options, including manipulation of the date on which the securities are granted, so-called backdating, that have landed companies other than Google in legal hot water. But it does offer a different—and possibly more accurate—way to value stock options, an area of great debate even now, nearly a year after options were required to be logged as expenses on a company's books.

NO BENEFIT TO THE BOTTOM LINE

38   Google's program isn't aimed at minimizing the impact to its bottom line, however. Indeed, the company expects to incur a larger expense on its books as the plan rolls out. That's because the fair market value of the options will be greater under the new plan than the current one. The reason: the options, which are estimated to have a four-year average life before employees exercise them, will convert to two-year options when they're sold to investors. So their expected life will be essentially extended by two years—making them more valuable because investors will have two more years for Google's stock potentially to rise, and thus more of an impact on Google's bottom line.

39   If Google's stock doesn't rise, or even falls, the options may well still have value, because investors may assume that over a two-year period the stock has a good chance to rise again. So employees may be able to sell even underwater options—those whose strike price is higher than the current stock price—and reap gains. "Underwater options lose their value as retention tools," notes Levitt. Even under Google's new plan, however, if its stock price drops well below options' strike prices, investors may not want to pay for them, and the options will still be worthless.

40   Google said it's not implementing the new plan because it's having problems attracting and retaining employees—at least not yet. "We're not having any problem recruiting people to work at Google," says Rolefson. "Attrition rates are very low." The idea, in an increasingly competitive business, is to keep it that way.

Source: Reprinted with special permission from "Google Gives Employees Another Option," *BusinessWeek,* December 13, 2006. Copyright © 2006 The McGraw-Hill Companies.

DISCUSSION QUESTIONS

1. What has been the compensation of CEOs relative to their "line" workers the past few years?

2. Do you think it is deserved? Why?

3. Do executives and related compensation/incentives appear key to effective implementation, or unrelated?

4. Regarding Case 2, does it seem reasonable for executives and employees to "backdate" stock option grants so that their grants are priced at the lowest daily stock price within a two- to four-month time period? Why?

5. Regarding Case 3, does it appear Google has found a way to add liquidity and simplicity to employee stock options designed to reward effective implementation and performance? Why?

Chapter 10 Appendix

Functional Tactics

FUNCTIONAL TACTICS THAT IMPLEMENT BUSINESS STRATEGIES

Functional tactics are the key, routine activities that must be undertaken in each functional area—marketing, finance, production/operations, R&D, and human resource management—to provide the business's products and services. In a sense, functional tactics translate thought (grand strategy) into action designed to accomplish specific short-term objectives. Every value chain activity in a company executes functional tactics that support the business's strategy and help accomplish strategic objectives.

The next several sections will highlight key tactics around which managers can build competitive advantage and add value in each of the various functional areas.

FUNCTIONAL TACTICS IN PRODUCTION/OPERATIONS

Basic Issues

Production/operations management (POM) is the core function of any organization. That function converts inputs (raw materials, supplies, machines, and people) into value-enhanced output. The POM function is most easily associated with manufacturing firms, but it also applies to all other types of businesses (e.g., service and retail firms). POM tactics must guide decisions regarding (1) the basic nature of the firm's POM system, seeking an optimum balance between investment input and production/operations output, and (2) location, facilities design, and process planning on a short-term basis. Exhibit 10.A1 highlights key decision areas in which the POM tactics should provide guidance to functional personnel.

POM facility and equipment tactics involve decisions regarding plant location, size, equipment replacement, and facilities utilization that should be consistent with grand strategy and other operating strategies. In the mobile home industry, for example, the facilities and equipment tactic of Winnebago was to locate one large centralized, highly integrated production center (in Iowa) near its raw materials. On the other extreme, Fleetwood Inc., a California-based competitor, located dispersed, decentralized production facilities near markets and emphasized maximum equipment life and less-integrated, labor-intensive production processes. Both firms are leaders in the mobile home industry, but have taken very different tactical approaches.

The interplay between computers and rapid technological advancement has made flexible manufacturing systems (FMS) a major consideration for today's POM tacticians. FMS allows managers to automatically and rapidly shift production systems to retool for different products or other steps

EXHIBIT 10.A1 Key Functional Tactics in POM

Functional Tactic	Typical Questions That the Functional Tactic Should Answer
Facilities and equipment	How centralized should the facilities be? (One big facility or several small facilities?)
	How integrated should the separate processes be?
	To what extent should further mechanization or automation be pursued?
	Should size and capacity be oriented toward peak or normal operating levels?
Sourcing	How many sources are needed?
	How should suppliers be selected, and how should relationships with suppliers be managed over time?
	What level of forward buying (hedging) is appropriate?
Operations planning and control	Should work be scheduled to order or to stock?
	What level of inventory is appropriate?
	How should inventory be used, controlled, and replenished?
	What are the key foci for control efforts (quality, labor cost, downtime, product use, other)?
	Should maintenance efforts be oriented to prevention or to breakdown?
	What emphasis should be placed on job specialization? Plant safety? The use of standards?

in a manufacturing process. Changes that previously took hours or days can be done in minutes. The result is decreased labor cost, greater efficiency, and increased quality associated with computer-based precision.

Sourcing has become an increasingly important component in the POM area. Many companies now accord sourcing a separate status like any other functional area. Sourcing tactics provide guidelines about questions such as, Are the cost advantages of using only a few suppliers outweighed by the risk of overdependence? What criteria (e.g., payment requirements) should be used in selecting vendors? Which vendors can provide "just-in-time" inventory, and how can the business provide it to our customers? How can operations be supported by the volume and delivery requirements of purchases?

POM planning and control tactics involve approaches to the management of ongoing production operations and are intended to match production/operations resources with longer-range, overall demand. These tactical decisions usually determine whether production/operations will be demand oriented, inventory oriented, or outsourcing oriented to seek a balance between the two extremes. Tactics in this component also address how issues such as maintenance, safety, and work organization are handled. Quality control procedures are yet another focus of tactical priorities in this area.

Just-in-time (JIT) delivery, outsourcing, and statistical process control (SPC) have become prominent aspects of the way today's POM managers create tactics that build greater value and quality in their POM system. JIT delivery was initially a way to coordinate with suppliers to reduce inventory carrying costs of items needed to make products. It also became a quality control tactic because smaller inventories made quality checking easier on smaller, frequent deliveries. It has become an important aspect of supplier-customer relationships in today's best businesses.

Outsourcing, or the use of a source other than internal capacity to accomplish some task or process, has become a major operational tactic in today's downsizing-oriented firms. Outsourcing is based on the notion that strategies should be built around the core competencies that add the most value in the value chain and that functions or activities that add little value or that cannot be done cost effectively should be done outside the firm—outsourced. When done well, the firm gains a supplier that provides superior quality at lower cost than it could provide itself. JIT and outsourcing have increased the strategic importance of the purchasing function. Outsourcing must include intense quality control by the buyer. ValuJet's tragic 1996 crash in the Everglades was caused by poor quality control over its outsourced maintenance providers.

The Internet and e-commerce have begun to revolutionize functional tactics in operations and marketing. How we sell, where we make things, how we logistically coordinate what we do—all of these basic business functions and questions have new perspectives and ways of being addressed because of the technological effect of the globally emerging ways we link together electronically, quickly, and accurately.

FUNCTIONAL TACTICS IN MARKETING

The role of the marketing function is to achieve the firm's objectives by bringing about the profitable sale of the business's products/services in target markets. Marketing tactics should guide sales and marketing managers in determining who will sell what, where, to whom, in what quantity, and how. Marketing tactics at a minimum should address four fundamental areas: products, price, place, and promotion. Exhibit 10.A2 highlights typical questions marketing tactics should address.

In addition to the basic issues raised in Exhibit 10.A2, marketing tactics today must guide managers addressing the effect of the communication revolution and the increased diversity among market niches worldwide. The Internet and the accelerating blend of computers and telecommunications has facilitated instantaneous access to several places around the world. A producer of plastic kayaks in Easley, South Carolina, receives orders from somewhere in the world about every 30 minutes over the Internet without any traditional distribution structure or global advertising. It fills the order within five days without any transportation capability. Speed linked to the ability to communicate instantaneously is causing marketing tacticians to radically rethink what they need to do to remain competitive and maximize value.

Diversity has accelerated because of communication technology, logistical capability worldwide, and advancements in flexible manufacturing systems. The diversity that has resulted is a virtual explosion of market niches—adaptations of products to serve hundreds of distinct and diverse customer segments that would previously have been served with more mass-market, generic products or services. Where firms used to rely on volume associated with mass markets to lower costs, they now encounter smaller niche players carving out subsegments they can serve more timely *and* more cost effectively. These new, smaller players lack the bureaucracy and committee approach that burdens the larger firms. They make decisions, outsource, incorporate product modifications, and make other agile adjustments to niche market needs before their larger competitors get through the first phase of committee-based decision making.

FUNCTIONAL TACTICS IN ACCOUNTING AND FINANCE

While most functional tactics guide implementation in the immediate future, the time frame for functional tactics in the area of finance varies because these tactics direct the use of financial resources in support of the business strategy, long-term goals, and annual objectives. Financial tactics with longer time perspectives guide financial managers in long-term capital investment, debt financing, dividend allocation, and leveraging. Financial tactics designed to manage working

EXHIBIT 10.A2 **Key Functional Tactics in Marketing**

Functional Tactic	Typical Questions That the Functional Tactic Should Answer
Product (or service)	Which products do we emphasize? Which products/services contribute most to profitability? What product/service image do we seek to project? What consumer needs does the product/service seek to meet? What changes should be influencing our customer orientation?
Price	Are we competing primarily on price? Can we offer discounts on other pricing modifications? Are our pricing policies standard nationally, or is there regional control? What price segments are we targeting (high, medium, low, and so on)? What is the gross profit margin? Do we emphasize cost/demand or competition-oriented pricing?
Place	What level of market coverage is necessary? Are there priority geographic areas? What are the key channels of distribution? What are the channel objectives, structure, and management? Should the marketing managers change their degree of reliance on distributors, sales reps, and direct selling? What sales organization do we want? Is the salesforce organized around territory, market, or product?
Promotion	What are the key promotion priorities and approaches? Which advertising/communication priorities and approaches are linked to different products, markets, and territories? Which media would be most consistent with the total marketing strategy?

EXHIBIT 10.A3 **Key Functional Tactics in Finance and Accounting**

Functional Tactic	Typical Questions That the Functional Tactics Should Answer
Capital acquisition	What is an acceptable cost of capital? What is the desired proportion of short- and long-term debt? Preferred and common equity? What balance is desired between internal and external funding? What risk and ownership restrictions are appropriate? What level and forms of leasing should be used?
Capital allocation	What are the priorities for capital allocation projects? On what basis should the final selection of projects be made? What level of capital allocation can be made by operating managers without higher approval?
Dividend and working capital management	What portion of earnings should be paid out as dividends? How important is dividend stability? Are things other than cash appropriate as dividends? What are the cash flow requirements? The minimum and maximum cash balances? How liberal/conservative should the credit policies be? What limits, payment terms, and collection procedures are necessary? What payment timing and procedure should be followed?

capital and short-term assets have a more immediate focus. Exhibit 10.A3 highlights some key questions that financial tactics must answer.

Accounting managers have seen their need to contribute value increasingly scrutinized. Traditional expectations centered around financial accounting; reporting requirements from bank and SEC entities and tax law compliance remain areas in which actions are dictated by outside governance. Managerial accounting, where managers are responsible for keeping records of costs and the use of funds within their company, has taken on increased strategic significance in the last decade. This change has

involved two tactical areas: (1) how to account for costs of creating and providing their business's products and services and (2) valuing the business, particularly among publicly traded companies.

Managerial cost accounting has traditionally provided information for managers using cost categories like those shown on the left side of the following table. However, value chain advocates have been increasingly successful getting managers to seek activity-based cost accounting information like that shown on the right side. In so doing, accounting is becoming a more critical, relevant source of information that truly benefits strategic management.

Traditional Cost Accounting in a Purchasing Department		Activity-Based Cost Accounting in the Same Purchasing Department	
Wages and salaries	$350,000	Evaluate supplier capabilities	$135,750
Employee benefits	115,000	Process purchase orders	82,100
Supplies	6,500	Expedite supplier deliveries	23,500
Travel	2,400	Expedite internal processing	15,840
Depreciation	17,000	Check quality of items purchased	94,300
Other fixed charges	124,000	Check incoming deliveries against purchase orders	48,450
Miscellaneous operating expenses	25,250		
	$640,150	Resolve problems	110,000
		Internal administration	130,210
			$640,150

Source: From Terence P. Pare, "A New Tool for Managing Costs," *Fortune*, June 14, 1993, pp. 124–29. Copyright, © 1993, Time, Inc. All rights reserved.

FUNCTIONAL TACTICS IN RESEARCH AND DEVELOPMENT

With the increasing rate of technological change in most competitive industries, research and development has assumed a key strategic role in many firms. In the technology-intensive computer and pharmaceutical industries, for example, firms typically spend between 4 and 6 percent, respectively, of their sales dollars on R&D. In other industries, such as the hotel/motel and construction industries, R&D spending is less than 1 percent of sales. Thus, functional R&D tactics may be more critical instruments of the business strategy in some industries than in others.

Exhibit 10.A4 illustrates the types of questions addressed by R&D tactics. First, R&D tactics should clarify whether basic research or product development research will be emphasized. Several major oil companies now have solar energy subsidiaries in which basic research is emphasized, while the smaller oil companies emphasize product development research.

The choice of emphasis between basic research and product development also involves the time horizon for R&D efforts. Should these efforts be focused on the near term or

the long term? The solar energy subsidiaries of the major oil companies have long-term perspectives, while the smaller oil companies focus on creating products now in order to establish a competitive niche in the growing solar industry.

R&D tactics also involve organization of the R&D function. For example, should R&D work be conducted solely within the firm, or should portions of that work be contracted out? A closely related issue is whether R&D should be centralized or decentralized. What emphasis should be placed on process R&D versus product R&D?

Decisions on all of these questions are influenced by the firm's R&D posture, which can be offensive or defensive, or both. If that posture is offensive, as is true for small high-technology firms, the firm will emphasize technological innovation and new-product development as the basis for its future success. This orientation entails high risks (and high payoffs) and demands considerable technological skill, forecasting expertise, and the ability to quickly transform innovations into commercial products.

A defensive R&D posture emphasizes product modification and the ability to copy or acquire new technology. Converse Shoes is a good example of a firm with such an R&D posture. Faced with the massive R&D budgets of Nike and Reebok, Converse placed R&D emphasis on

EXHIBIT 10.A4 **Key Functional Tactics in R&D**

R&D Decision Area	Typical Questions That the Functional Tactics Should Answer
Basic research versus product and process development	To what extent should innovation and breakthrough research be emphasized? In relation to the emphasis on product development, refinement, and modification? What critical operating processes need R&D attention? What new projects are necessary to support growth?
Time horizon	Is the emphasis short term or long term? Which orientation best supports the business strategy? The marketing and production strategy?
Organizational fit	Should R&D be done in-house or contracted out? Should R&D be centralized or decentralized? What should be the relationship between the R&D units and product managers? Marketing managers? Production managers?
Basic R&D posture	Should the firm maintain an offensive posture, seeking to lead innovation in its industry? Should the firm adopt a defensive posture, responding to the innovations of its competitors?

EXHIBIT 10.A5 **Key Functional Tactics in HRM**

Functional Tactic	Typical Questions That HRM Tactics Should Answer
Recruitment, selection, and orientation	What key human resources are needed to support the chosen strategy? How do we recruit these human resources? How sophisticated should our selection process be? How should we introduce new employees to the organization?
Career development and training	What are our future human resource needs? How can we prepare our people to meet these needs? How can we help our people develop?
Compensation	What levels of pay are appropriate for the tasks we require? How can we motivate and retain good people? How should we interpret our payment, incentive, benefit, and seniority policies?
Evaluation, discipline, and control	How often should we evaluate our people? Formally or informally? What disciplinary steps should we take to deal with poor performance or inappropriate behavior? In what ways should we "control" individual and group performance?
Labor relations and equal opportunity requirements	How can we maximize labor-management cooperation? How do our personnel practices affect women/minorities? Should we have hiring policies?

bolstering the product life cycle of its prime products (particularly canvas shoes).

Large companies with some degree of technological leadership often use a combination of offensive and defensive R&D strategy. GE in the electrical industry, IBM in the computer industry, and Du Pont in the chemical industry all have a defensive R&D posture for currently available products *and* an offensive R&D posture in basic, long-term research.

FUNCTIONAL TACTICS IN HUMAN RESOURCE MANAGEMENT

The strategic importance of human resource management (HRM) tactics received widespread endorsement in the 1990s. HRM tactics aid long-term success in the development of managerial talent and competent employees, the creation of systems to manage compensation or regulatory concerns, and guiding the effective utilization of human resources to achieve both the firm's short-term objectives and employees' satisfaction and development. HRM tactics are helpful in the areas shown in Exhibit 10.A5. The recruitment, selection, and orientation should establish the basic parameters for bringing new people into a firm and adapting them to "the way things are done" in the firm. The career development and training component should guide the action that personnel take to meet the future human resources needs of the overall business strategy. Merrill Lynch, a major brokerage firm whose long-term corporate strategy is to become a diversified financial service institution, has moved into such areas as investment banking, consumer credit, and venture capital. In support of its long-term objectives, it has incorporated extensive early-career training and ongoing career development programs to meet its expanding need for personnel with multiple competencies. Larger organizations need HRM tactics that guide decisions regarding labor relations; Equal Employment Opportunity Commission requirements; and employee compensation, discipline, and control.

Current trends in HRM parallel the reorientation of managerial accounting by looking at their cost structure anew. HRM's "paradigm shift" involves looking at people expense as an investment in human capital. This involves looking at the business's value chain and the "value" of human resource components along the various links in that chain. One of the results of this shift in perspective has been the downsizing and outsourcing phenomena of the last quarter century. While this has been traumatic for millions of employees in companies worldwide, its underlying basis involves an effort to examine the use of "human capital" to create value in ways that maximize the human contribution. This scrutiny continues to challenge the HRM area to include recent major trends to outsource some or all HRM activities not regarded as part of a firm's core competence. The emerging implications for human resource management tactics may be a value-oriented perspective on the role of human resources in a business's value chain as suggested here:

Traditional HRM Ideas	Emerging HRM Ideas
Emphasis solely on physical skills	Emphasis on total contribution to the firm
Expectation of predictable, repetitive behavior	Expectation of innovative and creative behavior
Comfort with stability and conformity	Tolerance of ambiguity and change
Avoidance of responsibility and decision making	Accepting responsibility for making decisions
Training covering only specific tasks	Open-ended commitment; broad continuous development
Emphasis placed on outcomes and results	Emphasis placed on processes and means
High concern for quantity and throughput	High concern for total customer value
Concern for individual efficiency	Concern for overall effectiveness
Functional and subfunctional specialization	Cross-functional integration
Labor force seen as unnecessary expense	Labor force seen as critical investment
Workforce is management's adversary	Management and workforce are partners

Source: From A. Miller and G. Dess, *Strategic Management,* 2002, p. 400. Copyright © 2002 The McGraw-Hill Companies, Inc. Reprinted with permission.

To summarize, functional tactics reflect how each major activity of a firm contributes to the implementation of the business strategy. The specificity of functional tactics and the involvement of operating managers in their development help ensure understanding of and commitment to the chosen strategy. A related step in implementation is the development of policies that empower operating managers and their subordinates to make decisions and to act autonomously.

Chapter **Eleven**

Organizational Structure

After reading and studying this chapter, you should be able to

1. Identify five traditional organizational structures and the pros and cons of each.

2. Describe the product-team structure and explain why it is a prototype for a more open, agile organizational structure.

3. Explain five ways improvements have been sought in traditional organizational structures.

4. Describe what is meant by agile, virtual organizations.

5. Explain how outsourcing can create agile, virtual organizations, along with its pros and cons.

6. Describe boundaryless organizations and why they are important.

7. Explain why organizations of the future need to be ambidextrous learning organizations.

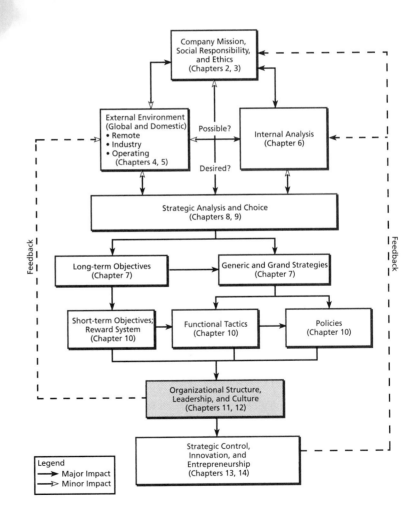

Legend
→ Major Impact
⇢ Minor Impact

Until this point in the strategic management process, managers have maintained a decidedly market-oriented focus as they formulate strategies and begin implementation through action plans detailing the tactics and actions that will be taken in each functional activity. Now the process takes an organizational focus—getting the work of the business done efficiently and effectively so as to make the strategy work. What is the best way to organize people and tasks to execute the strategy effectively? What should be done "in-house" and what activities should be "outsourced" for others to do?

What has happened at Hewlett-Packard over the course of this decade? It began with new CEO Carly Fiorina taking over HP in the midst of a global recession. The unfortunate reality for her: HP's lumbering organization was losing touch with its global customers. Her response: as illustrated in Exhibit 11.1, Strategy in Action, Fiorina immediately dismantled the decentralized structure honed throughout HP's 64-year history. Pre-Fiorina, HP was a collection of 83 independently run units, each focused on a product such as scanners or security software. Fiorina collapsed those into four sprawling organizations. One so-called back-end unit developed and built computers; another focused on printers and imaging equipment. The back-end divisions were to hand products off to the two "front-end" sales and marketing groups to peddle the wares—one to consumers, the other to corporations. The theory: the new structure would boost collaboration, giving sales and marketing execs a direct pipeline to engineers so products were developed from the ground up to solve customer problems. This was the first time a company with thousands of product lines and scores of businesses attempted a front-back approach, a structure that requires laser focus and superb coordination.

Fiorina believed she had little choice lest the company experience a near-death experience like Xerox or, 10 years earlier, IBM. The conundrum: how could HP put the full force of the company behind winning in its immediate fiercely competitive technology business when they must also cook up brand-new megamarkets? It's a riddle Fiorina said she could solve only by sweeping structural change that would ready HP for the next stage of the technology revolution, when companies latch on to the Internet to transform their operations. At its core lay a conviction that HP must become "ambidextrous and boundaryless," excelling at short-term execution while pursuing long-term visions that create new markets.

Did it work? No. After five years, Fiorina was dismissed. The chairman of the HP board of directors, Patricia Dunn, said at that time that the board did not intend to change HP's strategy. She indicated that the board was confident in HP's overall strategy even though, she acknowledged, several analysts and stockholders disagreed with the board on this. Confident that the strategy was correct, she indicated that the HP board concluded it had been execution of that strategy, particularly with regard to the "new" HP organizational structure, that the board felt was a major contributor to the lack of success at HP. So, Dunn said, the board wanted a new CEO who would simply execute better. Two months later, Mark Hurd, a 25-year veteran of NCR's sprawling portfolio of businesses, became HP's new chief executive.

Hurd had distinguished himself turning around NCR over the previous two years by cutting costs and tightening marketing and increasing accountability. His NCR turnaround produced eight consecutive profitable quarters at NCR. His organizational structure preference—smaller independently run units, each with a narrow product focus—allowed a clear sense of responsibilities, measurable accountability, tight spending controls, and the ability to execute by controlling their units production-to-sales activities.

The result: HP's return to smaller, semi-autonomous units led to exceptional success at HP culminating in it recently eclipsing Dell as the world's largest computer company, while remaining a global leader and highly profitable printer company. The HP saga is a useful one for you to keep in mind because it shows you a well-known, major, global technology company trying to find an organizational structure to help if be more competitive in the twenty-first century. And it highlights the need for more openness in an organizational structure—a "boundaryless" organization, as management icon Jack Welch called his approach—but also

Fiorina Gives Way to Hurd at Hewlett-Packard

When Carly Fiorina arrived at HP, the company was a confederation of 83 autonomous product units reporting through four groups. She radically revamped the structure into two "back-end" divisions—one developing printers, scanners, and the like, and the other computers. These report to "front-end" groups that market and sell HP's wares. Here's how the overhaul went:

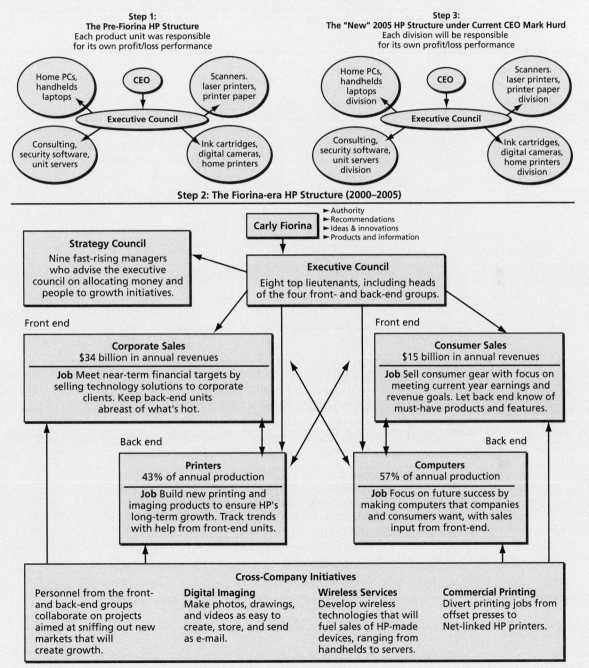

Step 1:
The Pre-Fiorina HP Structure
Each product unit was responsible for its own profit/loss performance

Home PCs, handhelds laptops

CEO

Scanners. laser printers, printer paper

Executive Council

Consulting, security software, unit servers

Ink cartridges, digital cameras, home printers

Step 3:
The "New" 2005 HP Structure under Current CEO Mark Hurd
Each division will be responsible for its own profit/loss performance

Home PCs, handhelds laptops division

CEO

Scanners. laser printers, printer paper division

Executive Council

Consulting, security software, unit servers division

Ink cartridges, digital cameras, home printers division

Step 2: The Fiorina-era HP Structure (2000–2005)

Carly Fiorina
▶ Authority
▶ Recommendations
▶ Ideas & innovations
▶ Products and information

Strategy Council
Nine fast-rising managers who advise the executive council on allocating money and people to growth initiatives.

Executive Council
Eight top lieutenants, including heads of the four front- and back-end groups.

Front end

Front end

Corporate Sales
$34 billion in annual revenues

Job Meet near-term financial targets by selling technology solutions to corporate clients. Keep back-end units abreast of what's hot.

Consumer Sales
$15 billion in annual revenues

Job Sell consumer gear with focus on meeting current year earnings and revenue goals. Let back end know of must-have products and features.

Back end

Back end

Printers
43% of annual production

Job Build new printing and imaging products to ensure HP's long-term growth. Track trends with help from front-end units.

Computers
57% of annual production

Job Focus on future success by making computers that companies and consumers want, with sales input from front-end.

Cross-Company Initiatives

Personnel from the front- and back-end groups collaborate on projects aimed at sniffing out new markets that will create growth.

Digital Imaging
Make photos, drawings, and videos as easy to create, store, and send as e-mail.

Wireless Services
Develop wireless technologies that will fuel sales of HP-made devices, ranging from handhelds to servers.

Commercial Printing
Divert printing jobs from offset presses to Net-linked HP printers.

(continued)

Exhibit 11.1 cont.

Fiorina's Expectations The Assessment	What Actually Happened over Fiorina's 5 Years The Assessment
Happier Customers Clients should find HP easier to deal with, since they'll work with just one account team.	**Overwhelmed with Duties** With so many products being made and sold by just four units, HP execs have more on their plates and could miss the details that keep products competitive.
Sales Boost HP should maximize its selling opportunities because account reps will sell all HP products, not just those from one division.	**Poorer Execution** When product managers oversaw everything from manufacturing to sales, they could respond quickly to changes. That will be harder with front- and back-end groups synching their plans only every few weeks.
Real Solutions HP can sell its products in combination as "solutions"—instead of just PCs or printers—to companies facing e-business problems.	**Less Accountability** Profit-and-loss responsibility is shared between the front- and back-end groups so no one person is on the hot seat. Finger-pointing and foot-dragging could replace HP's collegial cooperation.
Financial Flexibility With all corporate sales under one roof, HP can measure the total value of a customer, allowing reps to discount some products and still maximize profits on the overall contract.	**Fewer Spending Controls** With powerful division chiefs keeping a tight rein on the purse strings, spending rarely got out of hand in the old HP. In the fourth quarter, expenses soared as those lines of command broke down.

the importance of coordination and control of the organization's performance and execution of strategy through its structure. In some ways Fiorina's structure more reflected the way twenty-first-century organizations are seeking to organize themselves, while Hurd's approach is a return to a more traditional organization. Hurd's approach has found success in part because it is an attempt to combine attributes of traditional organizational structures and those of newer, boundaryless or virtual organization approaches in an effort to balance a need for control, coordination, openness, and innovation in implementing a strategy best suited to HP's situation.

Today's fast-changing, global economy demands ever-increasing productivity, speed, and flexibility from companies that seek to survive, perhaps thrive. To do so, companies must change their organizational structures dramatically, retaining the best of their traditional (hierarchical) structures while embracing radically new structures that leverage the value of the people who generate ideas, collaborate with colleagues and customers, innovate and therein generate future value for the company. So this chapter seeks to familiarize you with both perspectives on organizational structure and the major trends in structuring business organizations today. Let's start by looking at what have been traditional ways to organize, along with the advantages and disadvantages of each organizational structure.

TRADITIONAL ORGANIZATIONAL STRUCTURES AND THEIR STRATEGY-RELATED PROS AND CONS

You may be one of several students who choose to start your own business rather than take a job with an established company when you finish your current degree program.

Or perhaps you are currently in a full-time job position but soon plan to leave that job and start your own company. Like millions of others who have done or will soon do the same thing, usually with a few other "partners," your group will be faced with the question of how to organize your work and the activities and tasks necessary to do the work of your new company. What you are looking for is an organizational structure. We do not mean, here, the "legal" structure of your company such as a proprietorship, corporation, limited liability corporation, or limited partnership to mention a few. **Organizational structure** refers to the formalized arrangement of interaction between and responsibility for the tasks, people, and resources in an organization. It is most often seen as a chart, often a pyramidal chart, with positions or titles and roles in cascading fashion. The organizational structure you and your partners would have in this start-up of which you are a part would most likely be a "simple" organization.

Simple Organizational Structure

In the smallest business enterprise, a simple structure usually prevails. A **simple organizational structure** is one where there is an owner and, usually, a few employees and where the arrangement of tasks, responsibilities, and communication is highly informal and accomplished through direct supervision. All strategic and operating decisions are made by the owner, or a small owner-partner team. Because the scope of the firm's activities are modest, there is little need to formalize roles, communication, and procedures. With the strategic concern primarily being survival, and the likelihood that one bad decision could seriously threaten continued existence, this structure maximizes the owner's control. It can also allow rapid response to product/market shifts and the ability to accommodate unique customer demands without major coordination difficulties. This is in part because the owner is directly involved with customers on a regular basis. Simple structures encourage employees to multitask, and they are efficacious in businesses that serve a simple, local product/market or narrow niche.

The simple structure can be very demanding on the owner-manager. If it is successful, and starts to grow, this can cause the owner-manager to give increased attention to day-to-day concerns, which may come at the expense of time invested in stepping back and examining strategic questions about the company's future. At the same time, the company's reliance on the owner as the central point for all decisions can limit the development of future managers capable of assuming duties that allow the owner time to be a strategist. And, this structure usually requires a multitalented, resourceful owner, good at producing and selling a product or service—and at controlling scarce funds.

Most businesses in this country and around the world are of this type. Many survive for a period of time, then go out of business because of financial, owner, or market conditions. Some grow, having been built on an idea or capability that taps a great need for what the company does. As they grow, the need to "get organized" is increasingly heard among owners and a growing number of employees in the growing company. That fortunate circumstance historically led to the need for a functional organizational structure.

Functional Organizational Structure

Continuing our example, you and your partners, no doubt being among the successful ones, find increased demand for your product or service. Your sales have grown substantially—and so have the number of people you employ to do the work of your business. Once you reach 15 to 25 people in the organization, you will experience a need to have some people handle sales, some operations, a financial accounting person or two—that is, you will need to have different people focus on different functions within the business to become better organized and efficient, and to achieve control and coordination.

organizational structure
Refers to the formalized arrangements of interaction between and responsibility for the tasks, people, and resources in an organization.

simple organizational structure
Structure in which there is an owner and a few employees and where the arrangement of tasks, responsibilities, and communication is highly informal and accomplished through direct supervision.

functional organizational structure
Structure in which the tasks, people, and technologies necessary to do the work of the business are divided into separate "functional" groups (e.g., marketing, operations, finance) with increasingly formal procedures for coordinating and integrating their activities to provide the business's products and services.

A **functional organizational structure** is one in which the tasks, people, and technologies necessary to do the work of the business are divided into separate "functional" groups (such as marketing, operations, finance) with increasingly formal procedures for coordinating and integrating their activities to provide the business's products and services.

Functional structures predominate in firms with a single or narrow product focus and that have experienced success in their marketplace, leading to increased sales and an increased number of people needed to do the work behind those sales. Such firms require well-defined skills and areas of specialization to build competitive advantages in providing their products or services. Dividing tasks into functional specialties enables the personnel of these firms to concentrate on only one aspect of the necessary work. This allows use of the latest technical skills and develops a high level of efficiency.

Product, customer, or technology considerations determine the identity of the parts in a functional structure. A hotel business might be organized around housekeeping (maids), the front desk, maintenance, restaurant operations, reservations and sales, accounting, and personnel. An equipment manufacturer might be organized around production, engineering/quality control, purchasing, marketing, personnel, and finance/accounting. Two examples of functional organizations are illustrated in Exhibit 11.2.

The strategic challenge presented by the functional structure is effective coordination of the functional units. The narrow technical expertise achieved through specialization can lead to limited perspectives and to differences in the priorities of the functional units. Specialists may see the firm's strategic issues primarily as "marketing" problems or "production" problems. The potential conflict among functional units makes the coordinating role of the chief executive critical. Integrating devices (such as project teams or planning committees) are frequently used in functionally organized firms to enhance coordination and to facilitate understanding across functional areas.

Divisional Structure

When a firm diversifies its product/service lines, covers broad geographic areas, utilizes unrelated market channels, or begins to serve heterogeneous customer groups, a functional structure rapidly becomes inadequate. If a functional structure is retained under these circumstances, production managers may have to oversee the production of numerous and varied products or services, marketing managers may have to create sales programs for vastly different products or sell through vastly different distribution channels, and top management may be confronted with excessive coordination demands. A new organizational structure is often necessary to meet the increased coordination and decision-making requirements that result from increased diversity and size, and the divisional structure is the form often chosen.

divisional organizational structure
Structure in which a set of relatively autonomous units, or divisions, are governed by a central corporate office but where each operating division has its own functional specialists who provide products or services different from those of other divisions.

A **divisional organizational structure** is one in which a set of relatively autonomous units, or divisions, are governed by a central corporate office but where each operating division has its own functional specialists who provide products or services different from those of other divisions. For many years, global automobile companies have used divisional structures organized by product groups. Manufacturers often organize sales into divisions based on differences in distribution channels.

A divisional structure allows corporate management to delegate authority for the strategic management of distinct business entities—the division. This expedites decision making in response to varied competitive environments and enables corporate management to concentrate on corporate-level strategic decisions. The division usually is given profit responsibility, which facilitates accurate assessment of profit and loss. Exhibit 11.3 illustrates a divisional organizational structure and specifies the strategic advantages and disadvantages of such structures.

EXHIBIT 11.2
Functional
Organization
Structures

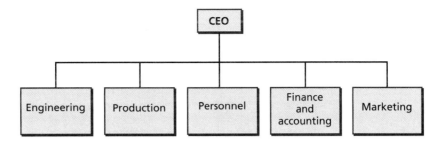

A process-oriented functional structure (an electronics distributor):

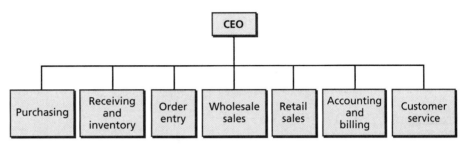

Strategic Advantages	Strategic Disadvantages
1. Achieves efficiency through specialization	1. Promotes narrow specialization and functional rivalry or conflict
2. Develops functional expertise	2. Creates difficulties in functional coordination and interfunctional decision making
3. Differentiates and delegates day-to-day operating decisions	3. Limits development of general managers
4. Retains centralized control of strategic decisions	4. Has a strong potential for interfunctional conflict—priority placed on functional areas, not the entire business
5. Tightly links structure to strategy by designating key activities as separate units	5. May cost more to do a function than it does "outside" the company, unless outsourced

Strategic Business Unit

strategic business unit
An adaptation of the divisional structure in which various divisions or parts of divisions are grouped together based on some common strategic elements, usually linked to distinct product/market differences.

Some firms encounter difficulty in controlling their divisional operations as the diversity, size, and number of these units continues to increase. Corporate management may encounter difficulty in evaluating and controlling its numerous, often multi-industry divisions. Under these conditions, it may become necessary to add another layer of management in order to improve implementation, promote synergy and gain greater control over the diverse business interests. The **strategic business unit** (SBU) is an adaptation of the divisional structure whereby various divisions or parts of divisions are grouped together based on some common strategic elements, usually linked to distinct product/market differences. General Foods, after originally organizing itself along product lines (which served overlapping markets), created an SBU organization along menu lines with SBUs for breakfast foods, beverages, main meals, desserts, and pet foods. This change allowed General Foods to adapt a vast divisional organization into five strategic business areas with a distinct market focus for each unit and the divisions each contained.

EXHIBIT 11.3
Divisional
Organizational
Structure

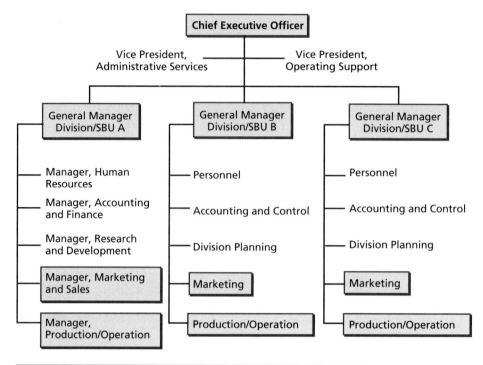

Strategic Advantages	Strategic Disadvantages
1. Forces coordination and necessary authority down to the appropriate level for rapid response	1. Fosters potentially dysfunctional competition for corporate-level resources
2. Places strategy development and implementation in closer proximity to the unique environments of the division	2. Presents the problem of determining how much authority should be given to division managers
3. Frees chief executive officer for broader strategic decision making	3. Creates a potential for policy inconsistencies among divisions
4. Sharply focuses accountability for performance	4. Presents the problem of distributing corporate overhead costs in a way that's acceptable to division managers with profit responsibility
5. Retains functional specialization within each division	5. Increases costs incurred through duplication functions
6. Provides good training ground for strategic managers	6. Creates difficulty maintaining overall corporate image
7. Increases focus on products, markets, and quick response to change	

The advantages and disadvantages of the SBU form are very similar to those identified for divisional structures in Exhibit 11.3. Added to its potential disadvantages would be the increased costs of coordination with another "pricy" level of management.

Holding Company

A final form of the divisional organization is the **holding company structure,** where the corporate entity is a broad collection of often unrelated businesses and divisions such

holding company structure
Structure in which the corporate entity is a broad collection of often unrelated businesses and divisions such that it (the corporate entity) acts as financial overseer "holding" the ownership interest in the various parts of the company, but has little direct managerial involvement.

that it (the corporate entity) acts as financial overseer "holding" the ownership interest in the various parts of the company but has little direct managerial involvement. Berkshire Hathaway owns a wide variety of businesses in full or in part. Essentially, at the corporate level, it provides financial support and manages each of these businesses, or divisions, through financial goals and annual review of performance, investment needs, etc. Otherwise, strategic and operating decisions are made in each separate company or division, which operates autonomously. The corporate office acts simply as a holding company.

This approach can provide a cost savings over the more active SBU approach since the additional level of "pricy" management is not that much. The negative, of course, becomes the degree to which the corporate office is dependent on each business unit's management team and the lack of control over the decisions those managers make in terms of being able to make timely adjustments or corrections.

Matrix Organizational Structure

In large companies, increased diversity leads to numerous product and project efforts of major strategic significance. The result is a need for an organizational form that provides skills and resources where and when they are most vital. For example, a product development project needs a market research specialist for two months and a financial analyst one day per week. A customer site application needs a software engineer for one month and a customer service trainer one day per month for six weeks. Each of these situations is an example of a matrix organization that has been used to temporarily put people and resources where they are most needed. Citicorp, Matsushita, Microsoft, Dow Chemical, and Accenture are firms that now use some form of matrix organization.

matrix organizational structure
The matrix organization is a structure in which functional and staff personnel are assigned to both a basic functional area and to a project or product manager. It provides dual channels of authority, performance responsibility, evaluation, and control.

The **matrix organizational structure** is one in which functional and staff personnel are assigned to both a basic functional area and to a project or product manager. It provides dual channels of authority, performance responsibility, evaluation, and control, as shown in Exhibit 11.4. The matrix form is intended to make the best use of talented people within a firm by combining the advantages of functional specialization and product-project specialization.

The matrix structure also increases the number of middle managers who exercise general management responsibilities (through the project manager role) and, thus, broaden their exposure to organizationwide strategic concerns. In this way, the matrix structure overcomes a key deficiency of functional organizations while retaining the advantages of functional specialization.

Although the matrix structure is easy to design, it is difficult to implement. Dual chains of command challenge fundamental organizational orientations. Negotiating shared responsibilities, the use of resources, and priorities can create misunderstanding or confusion among subordinates. These problems are heightened in an international context with the complications introduced by distance, language, time, and culture.

product-team structure
Assigns functional managers and specialists to a new product, project, or process team that is empowered to make major decisions about their product. Team members are assigned permanently in most cases.

Product-Team Structure

To avoid the deficiencies that might arise from a permanent matrix structure, some firms are accomplishing particular strategic tasks, by means of a "temporary" or "flexible" *overlay structure*. This approach, used recently by such firms as Motorola, Matsushita, Philips, and Unilever, is meant to take *temporary* advantage of a matrix-type team while preserving an underlying divisional structure. This adaptation of the matrix approach has become known as the "product-team structure." The **product-team structure** seeks to simplify and amplify the focus of resources on a narrow but strategically important product, project, market, customer, or innovation. Exhibit 11.5 illustrates how the product-team structure looks.

EXHIBIT 11.4
Matrix
Organizational
Structure

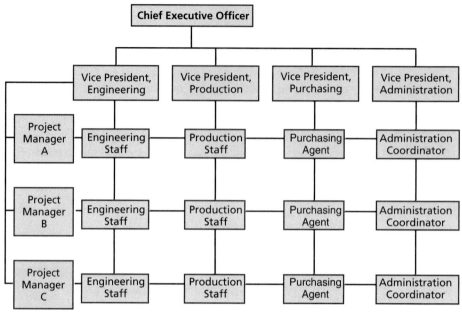

Strategic Advantages	Strategic Disadvantages
1. Accommodates a wide variety of project-oriented business activities	1. May result in confusion and contradictory policies
2. Provides good training ground for strategic managers	2. Necessitates tremendous horizontal and vertical coordination
3. Maximizes efficient use of functional managers	3. Can proliferate information logjams and excess reporting
4. Fosters creativity and multiple sources of diversity	4. Can trigger turf battles and loss of accountability
5. Gives middle management broader exposure to strategic issues	

The product-team structure assigns functional managers and specialists (e.g., engineering, marketing, financial, R&D, operations) to a new product, project, or process team that is empowered to make major decisions about their product. The team is usually created at the inception of the new-product idea, and they stay with it indefinitely if it becomes a viable business. Instead of being assigned on a temporary basis, as in the matrix structure, team members are assigned permanently to that team in most cases. This results in much lower coordination costs and, because every function is represented, usually reduces the number of management levels above the team level needed to approve team decisions.

It appears that product teams formed at the beginning of product-development processes generate cross-functional understanding that irons out early product or process design problems. They also reduce costs associated with design, manufacturing, and marketing, while typically speeding up innovation and customer responsiveness because authority rests with the team allowing decisions to be made more quickly. That ability to make speedier, cost-saving decisions has the added advantage of eliminating the need for one or more management layers above the team level, which would traditionally have been in place to review and control these types of decisions. While seemingly obvious, it has only recently become apparent that those additional management layers were also making these decisions with

EXHIBIT 11.5
The Product-Team
Structure

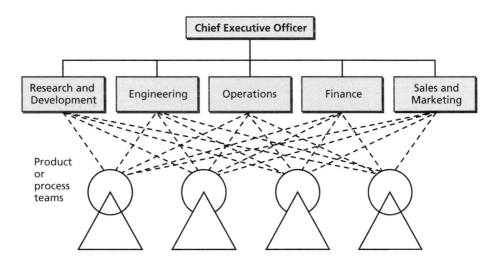

less firsthand understanding of the issues involved than the cross-functional team members brought to the product or process in the first place. Exhibit 11.6, Strategy in Action, gives examples of a product-team approach at several well-known companies and some of the advantages that appear to have accrued.

WHAT A DIFFERENCE A CENTURY MAKES

Exhibit 11.7 offers a useful perspective for designing effective organizational structures in tomorrow's global economy. In contrasting twentieth- and twenty-first-century corporations on different characteristics, it offers a historical or evolutionary perspective on organizational attributes associated with successful strategy execution today and just a few years ago. Successful organizations once required an internal focus, structured interaction, self-sufficiency, a top-down approach. Today and tomorrow, organizational structure reflects an external focus, flexible interaction, interdependency, and a bottom-up approach, just to mention a few characteristics associated with strategy execution and success. Three fundamental trends are driving decisions about effective organizational structures in the twenty-first century: globalization, the Internet, and speed of decision making.

Globalization

Pulitzer Prize–winning author Thomas Friedman[1] described the first 10 years of the twenty-first century as "Globalization 3.0." This, he says, is a whole new era in which the world is shrinking from a size "small" to a size "tiny" and flattening the global playing field for everyone at the same time. He describes it as follows:

> Globalization 1.0 was countries globalizing;
> Globalization 2.0 was companies globalizing;
> Globalization 3.0 is the newfound power for *individuals*
> To collaborate and compete globally, instantly;
> Individuals from every corner of the flat world are
> Being empowered to enter a wide open, global marketplace.[2]

---

[1] Thomas L. Friedman, *The World Is Flat* (New York: Farrar, Straus and Giroux, 2005).
[2] Ibid, p. 10.

Cross-Functional Teams

"I work for Unilever as a brand developer for the beauty brand Dove Soap. I am currently working on the initial stages of a new-product concept that will enter several foreign markets in a few years. That means that I work on everything from developing a product and packaging it to creating a retail marketing strategy with the help of a cross-functional team made up of international, regional, and local R&D, market research, promotions, finance, legal, supply chain and sales people. These members of my team have other responsibilities in their specialty, but they are responsible to me in helping develop this concept into a profitable new addition to Unilever's Dove brand of products." . . . Jason Levin, MBA graduate, Georgetown University.

"At Electronic Arts, innovations happen from small, cross-functional teams of programmers, designers, artists, development and marketing people. And we have found that the best way to avoid the usual conflict between development/programming [our "operations"] and marketing is to have a cross-functional team leader with experience in both camps. The next best is a leader with great empathy for the other function. In the video game business, that means that marketing leaders should be awesome game-players, and game-makers should be awesome tv-commercial makers." . . . Bing Gordon, CEO, Electronic Arts.

"I'm a Workplace Solutions Domain Engineer at IBM in Cambridge, Mass. As part of a cross-functional, software product development team, I manage product requirements by working with clients, analysts, and experts to adapt the product and strengthen its position and differentiation. As the external communicator for my team, I talk with customers, press, analysts and deliver product demonstration talks to audiences worldwide. Almost every day I turn on Sametime, our internal chat program, and have regular meetings and conversations with my cross-functional team members which includes people in Massachusetts, North Carolina and many in China. Questions, requests, and can-you-join-a-conference-call-right-now are normal pings." . . . Sally McSwiney, MBA graduate, Bentley College.

In his 20-year career at BMW, CEO Norbert Reithofer has worked his way up from maintenance planner to head of production and, by 2007, CEO. Along the way, he has built an informal network of associates across the company. Five years ago, he and Development Chief Burkhard Goeschel wanted to halve the time it took to reach full production on a next generation 3 series. They reached deep into the organization to assemble a cross-functional team of R&D and production aces who then worked for three years to reach their goal. The car was introduced in March, with full production of 800 cars daily in June. The cross-functional team had defied the skeptics. . . . Norbert Reithofer, Head of Production and now CEO, BMW, Germany.

This means that companies in virtually every industry either operate globally (e.g., computers, aerospace) or will soon do so. In the past 10 years, the percentage of sales from outside the home market for these five companies grew dramatically:

	1995	2000	2005	2010 est.
General Electric	16%	35%	41%	55%
Wal-Mart	0	18	32	43
McDonald's	46	65	71	79
Nokia	85	98	99	99+
Toyota	44	53	61	78

The need for global coordination and innovation is forcing constant experimentation and adjustment to get the right mix of local initiative, information flow, leadership, and corporate culture. At Swedish-based Ericsson, top managers scrutinize compensation schemes to make managers pay attention to global performance and avoid turf battles, while also

EXHIBIT 11.7
What a Difference a Century Can Make

Source: Reprinted with special permission from "21st Century Corporation," *BusinessWeek,* August 28, 2000. Copyright © 2000 The McGraw-Hill Companies.

Contrasting Views of the Corporation:		
Characteristic	**20th Century**	**21st Century**
Organization	The pyramid	The Web or network
Focus	Internal	External
Style	Structured	Flexible
Source of strength	Stability	Change
Structure	Self-sufficiency	Interdependencies
Resources	Atoms—physical assets	Bits—information
Operations	Vertical integration	Virtual integration
Products	Mass production	Mass customization
Reach	Domestic	Global
Financials	Quarterly	Real time
Inventories	Months	Hours
Strategy	Top-down	Bottom-up
Leadership	Dogmatic	Inspirational
Workers	Employees	Employees and free agents
Job expectations	Security	Personal growth
Motivation	To compete	To build
Improvements	Incremental	Revolutionary
Quality	Affordable best	No compromise

attending to their local operations. Companies such as Dutch electronics giant Philips regularly move headquarters for different businesses to the hottest regions for new trends—the "high voltage" markets. Its digital set-top box is now in California; its audio business moved from Europe to Hong Kong.[3]

Global once meant selling goods in overseas markets. Next was locating operations in numerous countries. Today companies will call on talents and resources wherever they can be found around the globe, just as they now sell worldwide. Such companies may be based in the United States, do their software programming in New Delhi, their engineering in Germany, and their manufacturing in Indonesia. The ramifications for organizational structures are revolutionary.

The Internet

The Net gives everyone in the organization, or working with it—from the lowest clerk to the CEO to any supplier or customer—the ability to access a vast array of information—instantaneously, from anywhere. Ideas, requests, and instructions zap around the globe in the blink of an eye. The Net allows the global enterprise with different functions, offices, and activities dispersed around the world to be seamlessly connected so that far-flung customers, employees, and suppliers can work together in real time. The result—coordination, communication, and decision-making functions are accomplished quickly and easily, making traditional organizational structures look slow, inefficient, and noncompetitive.

Speed

Technology, or digitization, means removing human minds and hands from an organization's most routine tasks and replacing them with computers and networks. Digitizing everything from employee benefits to accounts receivable to product design cuts cost, time, and payroll, resulting in cost savings and vast improvements in speed. "Combined with the Internet,

[3] Wendy Zellner, "See the World, Erase Its Borders," *BusinessWeek,* August 28, 2000.

the speed of actions, deliberations, and information will increase dramatically," says Intel's Andy Grove. "You are going to see unbelievable speed and efficiencies," says Cisco's John Chambers, "with many companies about to increase productivity 20 percent to 40 percent per year." Leading-edge technologies will enable employees throughout the organization to seize opportunity as it arises. These technologies will allow employees, suppliers, and freelancers anywhere in the world to converse in numerous languages online without need for a translator to develop markets, new products, new processes. Again, the ramifications for organizational structures are revolutionary.

Whether technology assisted or not, globalization of business activity creates a potential velocity of decision making that challenges traditional hierarchical organizational structures. A company like Cisco, for example, may be negotiating 50 to 60 alliances at one time due to the nature of its diverse operations. The speed at which these negotiations must be conducted and decisions made requires a simple and accommodating organizational structure lest the opportunities may be lost. Consider these recent observations by *BusinessWeek* editors at the end of a year-long research effort asking just the same question:

> The management of multinationals used to be a neat discipline with comforting rules and knowable best practices. But globalization and the arrival of the information economy have rapidly demolished all the old precepts. The management of global companies, which must innovate simultaneously and speed information through horizontal, global-spanning networks, has become a daunting challenge. Old, rigid hierarchies are out—and flat, speedy, virtual organizations are in. Teamwork is a must and compensation schemes have to be redesigned to reward team players. But aside from that bit of wisdom, you can throw out the textbooks.
>
> CEOs will have to custom-design their organizations based on their industry, their own corporate legacy, and their key global customers—and they may have to revamp more than once to get it right. Highly admired companies such as General Electric, Hewlett-Packard, ABB Ltd., and Ericsson have already been through several organizational reincarnations in the past decade to boost global competitiveness.[4]

Faced with these and other major trends, what are managers doing to structure effective organizations? Let's examine this question two ways. First, we will summarize some key ways managers are changing traditional organizational structures to make them more responsive to this new reality. Second, we will examine current ideas for creating agile, virtual organizations.

INITIAL EFFORTS TO IMPROVE THE EFFECTIVENESS OF TRADITIONAL ORGANIZATIONAL STRUCTURES

Major efforts to improve traditional organizational structures seek to reduce unnecessary control and focus on enhancing core competencies, reducing costs, and opening organizations more fully to outside involvement and influence. One key emphasis in large organizations has been corporate headquarters.

Redefine the Role of Corporate Headquarters from Control to Support and Coordination

The role of corporate management in multibusiness and multinational companies increasingly face a common dilemma: How can the resource advantages of a large company be exploited, while ensuring the responsiveness and creativity found in the small companies

---

[4] John Byrne, "The 21st Century Corporation," *BusinessWeek,* August 28, 2000.

against which each of their businesses compete? This dilemma constantly presents managers with conflicting priorities or adjustments as corporate managers:[5]

- Rigorous financial controls and reporting enable cost efficiency, resource deployment, and autonomy across different units; flexible controls are conducive to responsiveness, innovation and "boundary spanning."

- Multibusiness companies historically gain advantage by exploiting resources and capabilities across different businesses and markets, yet competitive advantage in the future increasingly depends on the creation of new resources and capabilities.

- Aggressive portfolio management seeking maximum shareholder value is often best achieved through independent businesses; the creation of competitive advantage increasingly requires the management—recognition and coordination—of business interdependencies.

Increasingly, globally engaged, multibusiness companies are changing the role of corporate headquarters from one of control, resource allocation, and performance monitoring to one of coordinator of linkages across multiple businesses, supporter, and enabler of innovation and synergy. One way this has been done is to create an executive council comprised of top managers from each business, usually including four to five of their key managers, with the council then serving as the critical forum for corporate decision, discussions, and analysis. IBM's Sam Palmisano uses this approach today at IBM to cross-fertilize ideas and opportunities across its software, enterprise services, chip design, and now virtual world business activities. These councils replace the traditional corporate staff function of overseeing and evaluating various business units, replacing it instead with a forum to share business unit plans, to discuss problems and issues, to seek assistance and expertise, and to foster cooperation and innovation.

Jack Welch's experience at GE provides a useful example. Upon becoming chairman, he viewed GE headquarters as interfering too much in GE's various businesses, generating too much paperwork, and offering minimal value added. He sought to "turn their role 180 degrees from checker, inquisitor, and authority figure to facilitator, helper, and supporter of GE's 13 businesses." He said, "What we do here at headquarters . . . is to multiply the resources we have, the human resources, the financial resources, and the best practices . . . Our job is to help, it's to assist, it's to make these businesses stronger, to help them grow and be more powerful." GE's Corporate Executive Council was reconstituted from predominantly a corporate level group of sector managers (which was eliminated) into a group comprised of the leaders of GE's 13 businesses and a few corporate executives. They met formally two days each quarter to discuss problems and issues and to enable cooperation and resource sharing. This has expanded to other councils throughout GE intent on greater coordination, synergy, and idea sharing.

Balance the Demands for Control/Differentiation with the Need for Coordination/Integration

Specialization of work and effort allows a unit to develop greater expertise, focus, and efficiency. So it is that some organizations adopt functional, or similar, structures. Their strategy depends on dividing different activities within the firm into logical, common groupings—sales, operations, administration, or geography—so that each set of activities can be done most efficiently. Control of sets of activities is at a premium. Dividing activities in this manner, sometimes called "differentiation," is an important structural decision. At the same time, these separate activities, however they are differentiated, need to be coordinated and integrated back together as a whole so the business functions effectively.

---

[5] Robert M. Grant, *Contemporary Strategy Analysis* (Oxford: Blackwell, 2001), p. 503.

Demands for control and the coordination needs differ across different types of businesses and strategic situations.

The rise of a consumer culture around the world has led brand marketers to realize they need to take a multidomestic approach to be more responsive to local preferences. Coca-Cola, for example, used to control its products rigidly from its Atlanta headquarters. But managers have found in some markets consumers thirst for more than Coke, Diet Coke, and Sprite. So Coke has altered its structure to reduce the need for control in favor of greater coordination/integration in local markets where local managers independently launch new flavored drinks. At the same time, GE, the paragon of new-age organization, had altered its GE Medical Systems organization structure to allow local product managers to handle everything from product design to marketing. This emphasis on local coordination and reduced central control of product design led managers obsessed with local rivalries to design and manufacture similar products for different markets—a costly and wasteful duplication of effort. So GE reintroduced centralized control of product design, with input from a worldwide base of global managers and their customers, resulting in the design of several single global products produced quite cost competitively to sell worldwide. GE's need for control of product design out-weighed the coordination needs of locally focused product managers.[6] At the same time, GE obtained input from virtually every customer or potential customer worldwide before finalizing the product design of several initial products, suggesting that it rebalanced in favor of more control, but organizationally coordinated input from global managers and customers so as to ensure a better potential series of medical scanner for hospitals worldwide. Virtually all companies serving global markets face a similar organizational puzzle—how does the company integrate itself with diverse markets yet ensure adequate control and differentiation of internal units so that it executes profitably and effectively? We will examine some ways to do so later in this chapter.

Restructure to Emphasize and Support Strategically Critical Activities

restructuring
Redesigning an organizational structure with the intent of emphasizing and enabling activities most critical to a firm's strategy to function at maximum effectiveness.

Restructuring is redesigning an organizational structure with the intent of emphasizing and enabling activities most critical to the firm's strategy to function at maximum effectiveness. At the heart of the restructuring trend is the notion that some activities within a business's value chain are more critical to the success of the business's strategy than others. Wal-Mart's organizational structure is designed to ensure that its impressive logistics and purchasing competitive advantages operate flawlessly. Coordinating daily logistical and purchasing efficiencies among separate stores lets Wal-Mart lead the industry in profitability yet sell retail for less than many competitors buy the same merchandise at wholesale. Motorola's organizational structure is designed to protect and nurture its legendary R&D and new-product development capabilities—spending over twice the industry average in R&D alone each year. Motorola's R&D emphasis continually spawns proprietary technologies that support its technology-based competitive advantage. Coca-Cola emphasizes the importance of distribution activities, advertising, and retail support to its bottlers in its organizational structure. All three of these companies emphasize very different parts of the value chain process, but they are extraordinarily successful in part because they have designed their organizational structures to emphasize and support strategically critical activities. Two developments that have become key ways many of these firms have sought to improve their emphasis and support of strategic activities are business process reengineering and downsizing/self-management.

---

[6] Zellner, "See the World, Erase Its Borders."

business process reengineering
A customer-centric restructuring approach. It involves fundamental rethinking and radical redesigning of a business process so that a company can best create value for the customer by eliminating barriers that create distance between employees and customers.

Business process reengineering (BPR) was originally advocated by consultants Michael Hammer and James Champy[7] as a "customer-centric" restructuring approach. BPR is intended to place the decision-making authority that is most relevant to the customer closer to the customer, in order to make the firm more responsive to the needs of the customer. This is accomplished through a form of empowerment, facilitated by revamping organizational structure.

Business reengineering reduces fragmentation by crossing traditional departmental lines and reducing overhead to compress formerly separate steps and tasks that are strategically intertwined in the process of meeting customer needs. This "process orientation," rather than a traditional functional orientation, becomes the perspective around which various activities and tasks are then grouped to create the building blocks of the organization's structure. This is usually accomplished by assembling a multifunctional, multilevel team (the product-team approach discussed earlier) that begins by identifying customer needs and how the customer wants to deal with the firm. Customer focus must permeate all phases. Companies that have successfully reengineered their operations around strategically critical business processes have pursued the following steps[8]

• Develop a flowchart of the total business process, including its interfaces with other value chain activities.

• Try to simplify the process first, eliminating tasks and steps where possible and analyzing how to streamline the performance of what remains.

• Determine which parts of the process can be automated (usually those that are repetitive, time-consuming, and require little thought or decision); consider introducing advanced technologies that can be upgraded to achieve next-generation capability and provide a basis for further productivity gains down the road.

• Evaluate each activity in the process to determine whether it is strategy-critical or not. Strategy-critical activities are candidates for benchmarking to achieve best-in-industry or best-in-world performance status—and ones to emphasize in reengineered organizational structures.

• Weigh the pros and cons of outsourcing activities that are noncritical or that contribute little to organizational capabilities and core competencies.

• Design a structure for performing the activities that remain; reorganize the personnel and groups who perform these activities into the new structure.

When asked about his BPR-derived networking-oriented structure that helped revitalize IBM, former IBM CEO Gerstner responded: "It's called *reengineering*. It's called *getting competitive*. It's called *reducing cycle time and cost, flattening organizations, increasing customer responsiveness*. All of these require a collaboration with the customer and with suppliers and with vendors."[9] Ten years later IBM is still at it as we see in Exhibit 11.8, Strategy in Action, about which current CEO Sam Palmisano said:

> IBM has developed a system that lets it shift work to the areas with available skills at the lowest-available costs. The goal is to deliver higher-quality services at competitive prices. Clearly one opportunity associated with globalization is costs. You have access to expertise wherever it is in the world—if you have the infrastructure and the relationships to take advantage of it.[10]

---

[7] Michael Hammer, *The Agenda* (New York: Random House, 2001); and Michael Hammer and James Champy, *Reengineering the Corporation* (New York: HarperBusiness, 1993).

[8] Judy Wade, "How to Make Reengineering Really Work," *Harvard Business Review* 71, no. 6 (November–December 1993), pp. 119–31.

[9] Ira Sager, "How IBM Became a Growth Company Again," *BusinessWeek Online*, Dec. 9, 1996.

[10] Steve Hamm, "Big Blue Wields the Knife Again," *BusinessWeek*, May 30, 2007.

IBM Continuously Reengineers Its BPO Business

BusinessWeek

Job reductions are nothing new for IBM's huge global-IT services business, still the No. 1 tech services company in the world. The cuts started when IBM, shocked by very poor results two years ago, began a major restructuring in Europe and the United States that eliminated 15,000 jobs in a matter of months. Ever since then, every few months, a new batch of jobs is trimmed from high-cost countries, including 700 in the first quarter of this year.

The trend is likely to continue. In the first quarter, the largest chunk of the services business, called Global Technology Services, grew a relatively healthy 7 percent, but its operating margin narrowed, shrinking by 2.5 points to just 7.8 percent. In comparison, the top Indian services outfits have operating profits of between 25 percent and 30 percent.

To improve its efficiency, IBM has adopted the business process reengineering approach called the "Lean Operations discipline" developed by Toyota Motor for manufacturing cars. It's adapting Lean so it applies to a global service organization, something the top Indian companies began two years ago. The basic principle of Lean Operations is that a company should be making continuous, incremental improvements in its business processes. That's one of the ways IBM figures out where it can eliminate work. The company also keeps a master database, nicknamed "Blue Monster," of all of its services employees. Supervisors use the information to track who is working on what project and when they'll be available for another

assignment. In this way, the company hopes to minimize the amount of time people are between assignments.

All of this cost-cutting is the task of Robert Moffat, senior vice president for integrated operations. His goal is to make the Global Technology Services workforce 10 to 15 percent more efficient each year. The key for him is to take costs out of the equation through a combination of workforce globalization, process improvements, and replacing manual labor with software. In a little more than six months, Moffat said at the May 17, 2007, analysts' meeting, he has rolled out the new formula for 22 of IBM's largest clients in seven countries. In some cases, he said, the clients have seen up to a 50 percent improvement in productivity. Now, Moffat is extending the new system to 600 more accounts.

All of this huffing and puffing over efficiency won't calm the frazzled nerves of IBM's 155,000-strong services workforce. True, there are still abundant employment opportunities in the company. About 30 percent of the people whose jobs are eliminated find other jobs within the behemoth, and, in the first four months of this year alone, IBM hired more than 19,000 people. But a lot of those hires were made in India. For the U.S. workforce, there is always fear that jobs will be lost to foreigners.

Source: Reprinted with special permission from Steve Hamm, "Big Blue Wields the Knife Again," *BusinessWeek*, May 30, 2007. Copyright © 2007 The McGraw-Hill Companies.

downsizing
Eliminating the number of employees, particularly middle management, in a company.

self-management
Allowing work groups or work teams to supervise and administer their work as a group or team without a direct supervisor exercising the supervisory role. These teams set parameters of their work, make decisions about work-related matters, and perform most of the managerial functions previously done by their direct supervisor.

Downsizing and self-management at operating levels are additional ways companies restructure critical activities. **Downsizing** is eliminating the number of employees, particularly middle management, in a company. The arrival of a global marketplace, information technology, and intense competition caused many companies to reevaluate middle management activities to determine just what value was really being added to the company's products and services. The result of this scrutiny, along with continuous improvements in information processing technology, has been widespread downsizing of the number of management personnel in thousands of companies worldwide. *BusinessWeek*'s survey of companies worldwide that have been actively downsizing are shown in Exhibit 11.9, Strategy in Action.

One of the outcomes of downsizing was increased **self-management** at operating levels of the company. Cutbacks in the number of management people left those who remained with more work to do. The result was that remaining managers had to give up a good measure of control to operating personnel. Spans of control, traditionally thought to maximize under 10 people, have become much larger due to information technology, running "lean and mean," and delegation to lower levels. Ameritech, one of the Baby Bells, has seen its spans of control rise to as much as 30 to 1 in some divisions because most of the people who did staff work—financial analysts, assistant managers, and so on—have disappeared.

How Lean Is Your Company?

BusinessWeek

Company Characteristic	Analysis
1. Layers of management between CEO and the shop floor	Some companies, such as Ameritech, now have as few as 4 or 5 where as many as 12 had been common. More than 6 is most likely too many.
2. Number of employees managed by the typical executive	At lean companies, spans of control range up to 1 manager to 30 staffers. A ratio lower than 1:10 is a warning of arterial sclerosis.
3. Amount of work cut out by your downsizing	Eliminating jobs without cutting out work can bring disaster. A downsizing should be accompanied by at least a 25 percent reduction in the number of tasks performed. Some lean companies have hit 50 percent.
4. Skill levels of the surviving management group	Managers must learn to accept more responsibility and to eliminate unneeded work. Have you taught them how?
5. Size of your largest profit center by number of employees	Break down large operating units into smaller profit centers—less than 500 employees is a popular cutoff—to gain the economies of entrepreneurship and offset the burdens of scale.
6. Post-downsizing size of staff at corporate headquarters	The largest layoffs, on a percentage basis, should be at corporate headquarters. It is often the most over-staffed—and the most removed from customers.

Source: Reprinted with special permission from John Byrne, "The 21st Century Corporation," *BusinessWeek,* August 28, 2000. Copyright © 2000 The McGraw-Hill Companies.

This delegation, also known as *empowerment,* is accomplished through concepts such as self-managed work groups, reengineering, and automation. It is also seen through efforts to create distinct businesses within a business—conceiving a business as a confederation of many "small" businesses, rather than one large, interconnected business. Whatever the terminology, the idea is to push decision making down in the organization by allowing major management decisions to be made at operating levels. The result is often the elimination of up to half the levels of management previously existing in an organizational structure.

CREATING AGILE, VIRTUAL ORGANIZATIONS

virtual organization
A temporary network of independent companies—suppliers, customers, subcontractors, and even competitors—linked primarily by information technology to share skills, access to markets, and costs.

Corporations today are increasingly seeing their "structure" become an elaborate network of external and internal relationships. This organizational phenomenon has been termed the **virtual organization,** which is defined as a temporary network of independent companies—suppliers, customers, subcontractors, even competitors—linked primarily by information technology to share skills, access to markets, and costs.[11] An **agile organization** is one that identifies a set of business capabilities central to high-profitability operations and then builds a virtual organization around those capabilities, allowing the agile firm to build its business around the core, high-profitability information, services, and products. Creating an agile, virtual organization structure involves outsourcing, strategic alliances, a boundaryless structure,

[11] W. H. Davidow and M. S. Malone, *The Virtual Corporation* (New York: Harper, 1992); and Steven Goldman, *Agile Competitors and Virtual Organizations* (New York: Van Nostrand Reinhold, 1995).

agile organization
A firm that identifies a set of business capabilities central to high-profitability operations and then builds a virtual organization around those capabilities.

outsourcing
Obtaining work previously done by employees inside the companies from sources outside the company.

an ambidextrous learning approach, and Web-based organization. Let's examine each of the approaches to creating a virtual organization in more detail.

Outsourcing—Creating a Modular Organization

Outsourcing was an early driving force for the virtual organization trend. Dell does not make PCs. Cisco doesn't make its world renowned routers. Motorola doesn't make cell phones. Sony makes Apple's low-end PowerBook computers. **Outsourcing** is simply obtaining work previously done by employees inside the companies from sources outside the company. Managers have found that as they attempt to restructure their organizations, particularly if they do so from a business process orientation, numerous activities can often be found in their company that are not "strategically critical activities." This has particularly been the case of numerous staff activities and administrative control processes previously the domain of various middle management levels in an organization. But it can also refer to primary activities that are steps in their business's value chain—purchasing, shipping, manufacturing, and so on. Further scrutiny has led managers to conclude that these activities either add little or no value to the product or services, or that they can be done much more cost effectively (and competently) by other businesses specializing in these activities. If this is so, then the business can enhance its competitive advantage by outsourcing the activities.

modular organization
An organization structured via outsourcing where the organization's final product or service is based on the combination of several companies' self-contained skills and business capabilities.

Choosing to outsource activities has been likened to creating a "modular" organization. A **modular organization** provides products or services using different, self-contained specialists or companies brought together—outsourced—to contribute their primary or support activity to result in a successful outcome. Dell is a "modular" organization because it uses outsourced manufacturers and assemblers to provide parts and assemble its computers. It also uses outsourced customer service providers in different parts of the world to provide most of its customer service and support activities. These outsourced providers are independent companies, many of which offer similar services to other companies including, in some cases, Dell's competitors. Dell remains the umbrella organization and controlling organization in fact and certainly in the customers' mind, yet it is able to do so based on putting together a variety of "modules" or parts because of its ability to provide computers and related services through extensive dependence on outsourcing.

Many organizations long ago started outsourcing functions like payroll and benefits administration—routine administrative functions more easily and cost effectively done by a firm specializing in that activity. But outsourcing today has moved into virtually every aspect of what a business does to provide the products and services it exists to provide. Exhibit 11.10, Top Strategist, shows the biggest sectors for outsourcing so far. And not only large companies are involved. Veteran entrepreneur and co-founder of Celestial Seasonings, Wyck Hay, has returned from retirement to build a new company, Kaboom Beverages, in California. What is interesting is that Hay, like many entrepreneurs today, is building a totally modular organization. Every function in Kaboom Beverages is outsourced to a variety of specialists and specialized companies. Indeed, one of the drivers for outsourcing to create a modular organization is to be able to combine world-class talent, wherever it resides, into a company's ability to deliver the best product and service it can.

Boeing opened its own engineering center in Moscow, where it employs 1,100 skilled but relatively inexpensive aerospace engineers to design parts of the 787 Dreamliner. It also has Japanese, Korean, and European companies making various parts of that critical new plane. Chicago-based law firm Baker and Mckenzie has its own English-speaking team in Manila that drafts documents and does market research. Bank of America (BOA) has its own India subsidiary, but also teamed up with InfoSys and Tata Consultancies—BOA estimates that

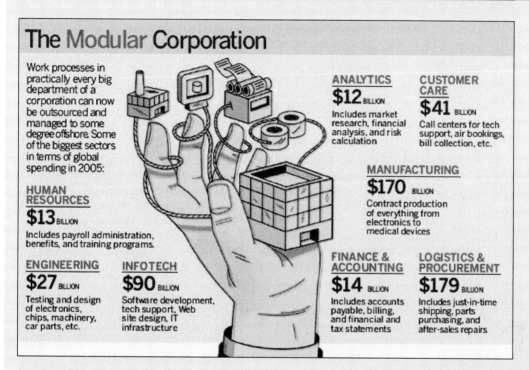

The Modular Corporation

Work processes in practically every big department of a corporation can now be outsourced and managed to some degree offshore. Some of the biggest sectors in terms of global spending in 2005:

HUMAN RESOURCES
$13 BILLION
Includes payroll administration, benefits, and training programs.

ENGINEERING
$27 BILLION
Testing and design of electronics, chips, machinery, car parts, etc.

INFOTECH
$90 BILLION
Software development, tech support, Web site design, IT infrastructure

ANALYTICS
$12 BILLION
Includes market research, financial analysis, and risk calculation

CUSTOMER CARE
$41 BILLION
Call centers for tech support, air bookings, bill collection, etc.

MANUFACTURING
$170 BILLION
Contract production of everything from electronics to medical devices

FINANCE & ACCOUNTING
$14 BILLION
Includes accounts payable, billing, and financial and tax statements

LOGISTICS & PROCUREMENT
$179 BILLION
Includes just-in-time shipping, parts purchasing, and after-sales repairs

Source: Reprinted with special permission from "The Modular Corporation," *BusinessWeek,* January 30, 2006. Copyright © 2006 The McGraw-Hill Companies.

business process outsourcing
Having an outside company manage numerous routine business management activities previously done by employees inside the company such as HR, supply procurement, finance and accounting, customer care, supply-chain logistics, engineering, R&D, sales and marketing, facilities management, and management/development.

it has saved almost $200 million in IT work the last two years, while improving product quality at the same time.

Outsourcing IT services, call center services, and routine computer programming services—and managing a company's IT systems—have become major industries unto themselves. IT outsourcing to companies in India alone reached $20 billion in 2005 and is projected to top $50 billion by 2008. India's Infosys and Wipro (India's GE) are multi-billion-dollar revenue providers of IT outsourced services.

Business process outsourcing (BPO) is the most rapidly growing segment of the outsourcing services industry worldwide, and it is expected to reach more than $200 billion in revenues in 2008. BPO includes a broad array of administrative functions—HR, supply procurement, finance and accounting, customer care, supply-chain logistics, engineering, research and development, sales and marketing, facilities management and even management training and development.[12] IBM strategist Bruce Harreld estimates that the world's companies spend about $19 trillion each year on sales, general, and administrative expenses. Only $14 trillion-worth of this, he estimates, has been outsourced to other firms. He further expects that many of the advantages in scale, wage rates, and productivity found when manufacturing was outsourced will quickly emerge driving a rapid increase in BPO over the next 10 years.[13] Many big companies estimate they could outsource half or more

[12] Pete Engardio and Bruce Einhorn, "Outsourcing Innovation," *BusinessWeek,* March 21, 2005.
[13] "A World of Work," *The Economist,* November 11, 2004.

of this work currently done in-house. Similarly, banking services currently deliver less than 1 percent of their services remotely—a major global outsourcing opportunity.[14]

Perhaps the more controversial outsourcing trends involve product design and even innovation activities. Particularly in consumer electronics markets, companies such as Dell, Motorola, and Philips are buying complete designs of some digital devices from Asian developers, tweaking them to their own specifications, and just adding their brand name before selling or having a more effective sales channel sell the product for them. This trend seems to be spreading. Boeing works with an Indian software company to develop its software for landing gear, navigation systems, and cockpit controls in its newest planes. Procter & Gamble, the consummate innovator, wants half of its new-product ideas by 2010 to come from outside the company—outsourced R&D or innovation—versus 20 percent right now. Eli Lilly has outsourced selected biotech research for new drugs to an Asian biotech research firm. Consider this comment in a recent *BusinessWeek* article:

> The result is a rethinking of the structure of the modern corporation. What, specifically, has to be done in-house anymore? At a minimum, most leading Western companies are turning toward a new model of innovation, one that employs global networks of partners. These can include U.S. chipmakers, Taiwanese engineers, Indian software developers, and Chinese factories. IBM is even offering the smarts of its famed research labs and a new global team of 1,200 engineers to help customers develop future products using next-generation technologies. When the whole chain works in sync, there can be a dramatic leap in the speed and efficiency of product development.[15]

Outsourcing as a means to create an agile, virtual organization has many potential advantages:

1. *It can lower costs incurred when the activity outsourced is done in-house.*

An accountant with a masters degree from UGA working for Ernst & Young in Atlanta, George, costs E&Y $75,000 annually. Her colleague with the same education returning to her native Philippines to live, works on a similar E&Y audit team in Southeast Asia and via the Internet in the United States—$7,000 annual salary.

2. *It can reduce the amount of capital a firm must invest in production or service capacity.*

Lenovo will cover the capital expenditure for its new Chinese PC manufacturing facilities; IBM will not. IBM will sell Lenovo its existing PC manufacturing facilities around the world, freeing up that capital for investment in IBM's development of its own core competencies, and just buy PCs very cheaply from Lenovo as it needs them. It will include a markup in doing so to pass along to its IT management services clients.

3. *The firm's managers and personnel can concentrate on mission-critical activities.*

As noted in the preceding example, not only does IBM free up capital, but it frees up its people and remaining capital to focus more intensely on its new emphasis on IT systems, BPO, and consulting.

4. *This concentration and focus allow the firm to control and enhance the source of its core competitive advantage.*

Dell outsources the manufacture of its computers. It carefully controls and continuously improves its Web-based direct sales capability so that it increasingly distances itself from the closest competitors. It is able to build such a strong direct sales capability because that is virtually all it concentrates on, even though it is a computer company.

---

[14] "Time to Bring It Back," *The Economist,* March 3, 2005.

[15] Engardio and Einhorn, "Outsourcing Innovation."

5. *Careful selection of outsourced partners allows the firm to potentially learn and develop its abilities through ideas and capabilities that emerge from the growing expertise and scope of work done by the outsource partner for several firms.*

Outsourced cell phone manufacturers in Korea and Taiwan have become large providers to several large, global cell phone companies. Their product design prototypes and improvements for one client quickly find their way to the attention of other clients. Their improvement in logistics with some firms becomes knowledge incorporated in their dealings with another client.

Outsourcing is not without its "cons," however. There are several:

1. *Outsourcing involves loss of some control and reliance on "outsiders."*

By definition, outsourcing places control of that function or activity "outside" the requesting firm. This loss of control can result in many future problems such as delays, quality issues, customer complaints, and loss of competitor-sensitive information. Recent thefts of personal ID information from U.S.-based bank clients using major information management outsourcing services from Indian companies have caused major problems for the banks obtaining these services.

2. *Outsourcing can create future competitors.*

Companies that supply the firm with basic IT services or software programming assistance or product design services may one day move "up the chain" to undertake the higher level work the firm was attempting to reserve for itself. IBM has outsourced considerable work to Indian companies related to its "value-added" IT system management services—its strategic future. It now is experiencing competition from some of these former suppliers of programming support that have become multi-billion-dollar software and IT service providers in their own right.

3. *Skills important to a product or service are "lost."*

While things a company does may not be considered essential to its core competency, they still may be quite important. And as it continues over time to outsource that activity, it loses any capacity in the firm of being able to do it effectively. That, potentially, leaves the company vulnerable.

4. *Outsourcing may cause negative reaction from the public and investors.*

Outsourcing manufacturing, tech support, and back-office work may make sense to investors, but product design and innovation? Asking what value the company is providing and protecting will be an obvious potential reaction. Publicly, the loss of jobs from home country to low-cost alternative locations represents difficult job losses and transitions for people who bring political heat.

5. *Crafting good legal agreements, especially for services, is difficult.*

When outsourced manufacturers send product, you take delivery, inspect, and pay. When service providers supply a service, it is a continuous process. Bottom line: It takes considerable trust and cross-cultural understanding to work.

6. *The company may get locked into long-term contracts at costs that are no longer competitive.*

Multiyear IT management contracts can be both complex and based on costs that are soon noncompetitive because of other sources providing much more cost-effective solutions.

7. *Cost aren't everything: What if my supplier underbids?*

EDS (Dallas, Texas) has a multiyear contract as an outsource provider to the U.S. Navy to provide IT services and consolidate 70,000 different IT systems. Two years into the contract, in 2005, it was $1.5 billion in the red. It hopes to make that heavy loss up over the life of the contract. But what if it was a smaller company and couldn't afford to carry a loss for a contract it poorly bid?

8. *Outsourcing can lead to increasingly fragmented work cultures where low-paid workers get the work done with little initiative or enthusiasm.*

"A mercenary may shoot a gun the same as a soldier, but he will not create a revolution, build a new society, or die for the homeland," says a Silicon Valley manager who objects to his company's turning to contract workers for services.[16]

Its potential disadvantages not withstanding, outsourcing has become a key, standard means by which agile, virtual organization structures are built. It has become an essential building block; most firms in any market anywhere in the world structure some of their business activities to allow them to remain cost competitive, dynamic, and able to develop their future core competencies. As outsourcing moves from sourcing manufacturing and IT management to all business management processes, careful attention and efforts to build trust and cross-cultural understanding will be important as will effective contractual arrangements to govern multiyear, ongoing relationships.

Strategic Alliances

strategic alliances
Alliances with suppliers, partners, contractors, and other providers that allow partners in the alliance to focus on what they do best, farm out everything else, and quickly provide value to the customer.

Strategic alliances are arrangements between two or more companies in which they both contribute capabilities, resources, or expertise to a joint undertaking, usually with an identity of its own, with each firm giving up overall control in return for the potential to participate in and benefit from the joint venture relationship. They are different from outsourcing relationships because the requesting company usually retains control when outsourcing, whereas strategic alliances involve firms giving up overall control to the joint entity, or alliance, in which they become a partner. Texas-based EDS was awaiting word at the time of this writing on whether the "Atlas Consortium" would be awarded a 10-year, $7.6 billion contract to manage 150,000 computers and networking software for British military personnel. The Atlas Consortium is a strategic alliance, formed by EDS as the "lead" firm with the Dutch firm LogicaCMG and a British subsidiary of the defense company, EADS, as full partners. While EDS is the "lead" member of the alliance, final control of the alliance rests not in EDS but in the governance that all three partners have the right to influence and shape.

This is a good example of a strategic alliance—three different firms all with other major business commitments and activities. They have joined together, investing time, analysis resources, and negotiations so as to be in a position to bid as a team (or alliance) on a major 10-year contract. In a few weeks they will know. If they get the contract, then their alliance will have a lengthy commitment to the British military and their firms to the Atlas Consortium. If they don't, then they may or may not work together to pursue other deals. But this relationship allowed each firm to seek work it could not have otherwise pursued independently because of restrictions imposed by the British government, the limitations of each firm individually, or both. It expanded the exposure of each firm to the other, to selected markets, to the building of relationships that may be usefully leveraged in each company's interests in the future.

Strategic alliances can be for long-term or for very short periods. Engaging in alliances, whether long-term or one time, lets each participant take advantage of fleeting opportunities quickly, usually without tying up vast amounts of capital. Strategic alliances allow companies with world-class capabilities to partner together in a way that combines different core competencies so that within the alliance each can focus on what they do best, but the alliance can pull together what is necessary to quickly provide superior value to the customer. FedEx and the U.S. Postal Service have formed an alliance—FedEx planes carry USPS

---

[16] "Time to Bring It Back," *The Economist,* March 3, 2005.

EXHIBIT 11.11
General Motors:
Alliances with
Competitors

Source: General Motors
Corporation annual reports;
"Carmakers Take Two Routes
to Global Growth," *Financial
Times* (July 11, 2000), p. 19.

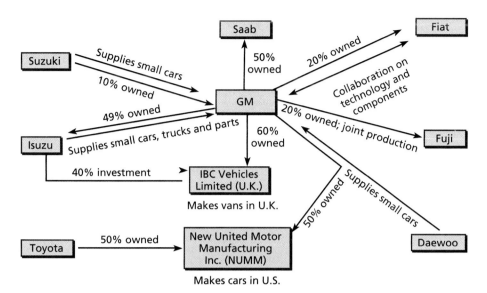

next-day letters and USPS delivers FedEx ground packages—to allow both to challenge their common rival, UPS.

Strategic alliances sometimes put competitors together as partners in some settings while they remain competitors in others. EDS competes with LogicaCMG in some situations, but they are close partners in the Atlas Consortium. Exhibit 11.11 shows how General Motors, in its effort to become more competitive globally, entered into numerous alliances with competitors.

Strategic alliances have the following pros and cons for firms seeking agile, responsive organizational structures:

Advantages

1. *Leverages several firms' core competencies.*

This allows alliance members to be more competitive in seeking certain project work or input.

2. *Limits capital investment.*

One partner firm does not have to have all the resources necessary to do the work of the alliance.

3. *Is flexible.*

Alliances allow a firm to be involved yet continue to pursue its other, "regular" business opportunities.

4. *Leads to networking and relationship building.*

Alliances get companies together, sometimes even competitors. They allow key players to build relationships that are valuable, even if the present alliance doesn't "pan out." Alliance partners learn more about each others' capabilities and gain advantage or benefit from referrals and other similar behaviors, creating win–win situations.

Disadvantages

1. *Can result in loss of control.*

A firm in an alliance by definition cedes ultimate control to the broader alliance for the undertaking for which the alliance is formed. This can prove problematic if the alliance doesn't work out as planned—or is not well planned.

2. *Can be hard to establish good management control of the project—loss of operational control.*

Where multiple firms have interrelated responsibilities for a sizable joint project, it should not be difficult to imagine problems arising as the players go about implementing a major project as in the example of EDS and its Dutch and British partners in the Atlas Consortium. It requires good up-front planning and use of intercompany project team groups early on in the bidding process.

3. *Can distract a participating company's management and key players.*

One strategic alliance can consume the majority attention of key players essential to the overall success of the "home" company. Whether because of their technical skills, managerial skills, key roles, or all three, the potential for lost focus or time to devote to key responsibilities exists.

4. *Raises issues of control of proprietary information and intellectual property.*

Where technology development is the focus of the alliance, or maybe part of it, firms partnered together may also compete in other circumstances. Or they may have the potential to do so. So partnering together gives each the opportunity to learn much more about the other, their contacts, capabilities, and unique skills or trade secrets.

Strategic alliances have proven a very popular mechanism for many companies seeking to become more agile competitors in today's dynamic global economy. They have proven a major way for small companies to become involved with large players to the benefit of both—allowing the smaller player to grow in a way that builds its future survival possibilities and the larger player to tap expertise and knowledge it can no longer afford to retain or develop in-house.

Toward Boundaryless Structures

boundaryless organization
Organizational structure that allows people to interface with others throughout the organization without need to wait for a hierarchy to regulate that interface across functional, business, and geographic boundaries.

Management icon Jack Welch coined the term **boundaryless organization** to characterize his vision of what he wanted GE to become: to be able to generate knowledge, share knowledge, and get knowledge to the places it could be best used to provide superior value. A key component of this concept was erasing internal divisions so the people in GE could work across functional, business, and geographic boundaries to achieve an integrated diversity—the ability to transfer the best ideas, the most developed knowledge, and the most valuable people quickly, easily, and freely throughout GE. Here is his description:

> Boundaryless behavior is the soul of today's GE … Simply put, people seem compelled to build layers and walls between themselves and others, and that human tendency tends to be magnified in large, old institutions like ours. These walls cramp people, inhibit creativity, waste time, restrict vision, smother dreams and above all, slow things down . . . Boundaryless behavior shows up in actions of a woman from our Appliances Business in Hong Kong helping NBC with contacts needed to develop satellite television service in Asia . . . And finally, boundaryless behavior means exploiting one of the unmatchable advantages a multibusiness GE has over almost any other company in the world. Boundaryless behavior combines 12 huge global businesses—each number one or number two in its markets—into a vast laboratory whose principal product is new ideas, coupled with a common commitment to spread them throughout the Company.
>
> *—Letter to Shareholders, Jack Welch,*
> *chairman, General Electric Company, 1981–2001*

horizontal boundaries
Rules of communication, access, and protocol for dealing with different departments or functions or processes within an organization.

Boundaries, or borders, arise in four "directions" based on the ways we traditionally structure and run organizations:

1. **Horizontal boundaries**—between different departments or functions in a firm. Salespeople are different from administrative people or operating people or engineering people. One division is separate from another.

vertical boundaries
Limitations on interaction, contact, and access between operations and management personnel; between different levels of management; and between different organizational parts like corporate versus divisional units.

geographic boundaries
Limitations on interaction and contact between people in a company based on being at different physical locations domestically and globally.

external interface boundaries
Formal and informal rules, locations, and protocol that separate and/or dictate the interaction between members of an organization and those outside the organization—customers, suppliers, partners, regulators, associations, and even competitors.

2. **Vertical boundaries**—between operations and management, and levels of management; between "corporate" and "division," in virtually every organization.

3. **Geographic boundaries**—between different physical locations; between different countries or regions of the world (or even within a country) and between cultures.

4. **External interface boundaries**—between a company and its customers, suppliers, partners, regulators, and, indeed, its competitors.

Outsourcing, strategic alliances, product-team structures, reengineering, restructuring—all are ways to move toward boundaryless organization. Culture and shared values across an organization that value boundaryless behavior and cooperation help enable these efforts to work.

As we noted at the beginning of this section, globalization has accelerated many changes in the way organizations are structured, and that is certainly driving the recognition by many organizations of their need to become more boundaryless, to become an agile, virtual organization. Technology, particularly driven by the Internet, has and will be a major driver of the boundaryless organization. Commenting on technology's effect on Cisco, John Chambers observed that with all its outsourcing and strategic alliances, roughly 90 percent of all orders come into Cisco without ever being touched by human hands. "To my customers, it looks like one big virtual plant where my suppliers and inventory systems are directly tied into our virtual organization," he said. "That will be the norm in the future. Everything will be completely connected, both within a company and between companies. We will become boundaryless. The people who get that will have a huge competitive advantage."[17]

The Web's contribution electronically has simultaneously become the best analogy in explaining the future boundaryless organization. And it is not just the Web as in the Internet, but a weblike shape of successful organizational structures in the future. If there are a pair of images that symbolize the vast changes at work, they are the pyramid and the web. The organizational chart of large-scale enterprise had long been defined as a pyramid of ever-shrinking layers leading to an omnipotent CEO at its apex. The twenty-first-century corporation, in contrast, is far more likely to look like a web: a flat, intricately woven form that links partners, employees, external contractors, suppliers, and customers in various collaborations. The players will grow more and more interdependent. Fewer companies will try to master all the disciplines necessary to produce and market their goods but will instead outsource skills—from research and development to manufacturing—to outsiders who can perform those functions with greater efficiency.[18]

Exhibit 11.12 illustrates this evolution in organization structure to what it calls the B-Web, a truly Internet-driven form of organization designed to deliver speedy, customized, service-enhanced products to savvy customers from an integrated boundaryless B-Web organization, pulling together abundant, world-class resources digitally. Take Colgate-Palmolive. The company needed a more efficient method for getting its toothpaste into the tube—a seemingly straightforward problem. When its internal R&D team came up empty-handed, the company posted the specs on InnoCentive, one of many new marketplaces that link problems with problem-solvers. A Canadian engineer named Ed Melcarek proposed putting a positive charge on fluoride powder, then grounding the tube. It was an effective application of elementary physics, but not one that Colgate-Palmolive's team of chemists had ever contemplated. Melcarek was duly rewarded with $25,000 for a few hours' work. Today, some 120,000 scientists like Melcarek have registered with InnoCentive and hundreds of companies pay annual fees of roughly $80,000 to tap the talents of a global

[17] Peter Burrows, "Can Cisco Shift into Higher Gear?" *BusinessWeek Online*, October 4, 2004.
[18] Byrne, "The 21st Century Organization."

EXHIBIT 11.12
From Traditional Structure to B-Web Structure

Source: Reprinted by permission of Harvard Business School Press. From *Digital Capital: Harnessing the Power of Business Webs* by Don Tapscott, David Ticoll, and Alex Lowy, Boston, MA, 1993, p. 19. Copyright © 1993 by the Harvard Business School Publishing Corporation; all rights reserved.

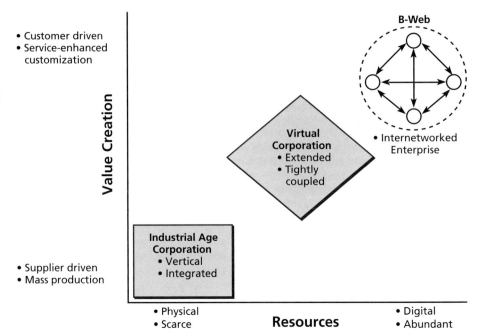

scientific community. Launched as an e-business venture by U.S. pharmaceutical giant Eli Lilly in 2001, the company now provides on-demand solutions to innovation-hungry titans such as Boeing, Dow, DuPont, P&G, and Novartis.[19]

Managing this intricate network of partners, spin-off enterprises, contractors, and free-lancers will be as important as managing internal operations. Indeed, it will be hard to tell the difference. All of these constituents will be directly linked in ways that will make it nearly impossible for outsiders to know where an individual firm begins and where it ends. "Companies will be much more molecular and fluid," predicts Don Tapscott, co-author of *Digital Capital*. "They will be autonomous business units connected not necessarily by a big building but across geographies all based on networks. The boundaries of the firm will be not only fluid or blurred but in some cases hard to define.[20]

learning organization
Organization structured around the idea that it should be set up to enable learning, to share knowledge, to seek knowledge, and to create opportunities to create new knowledge. It would move into new markets to learn about those markets rather than simply to bring a brand to it, or find resources to exploit in it.

Ambidextrous Learning Organizations

The evolution of the virtual organizational structure as an integral mechanism managers use to implement strategy has brought with it recognition of the central role knowledge plays in this process. *Knowledge* may be in terms of operating know-how, relationships with and knowledge of customer networks, technical knowledge upon which products or processes are based or will be, relationships with key people or a certain person that can get things done quickly, and so forth. Exhibit 11.13, Strategy in Action, shares how McKinsey organizational expert Lowell Bryan sees this shaping future organizational structure with managers becoming knowledge "nodes" through which intricate networks of personal relationships—inside and outside the formal organization—are constantly coordinated to bring together relevant know-how and successful action.

A shift from what Subramanian Rangan calls *exploitation to exploration* indicates the growing importance of organizational structures that enable a **learning organization** to

[19] Don Tapscott and Anthony Williams, "Ideagora, a Marketplace for Minds," *BusinessWeek*, February 15, 2007.
[20] Ibid.

Strategy in Action

Q&A with McKinsey's Lowell Bryan about Organizational Structures

Lowell Bryan, a senior partner and director at consultancy McKinsey & Co., leads McKinsey's global industries practice and is the author of *Race for the World: Strategies to Build a Great Global Firm* and *Market Unbound: Unleashing Global Capitalism.*

Q: How will global companies be managed in the twenty-first century?

A: Describing it is hard because the language of management is based on command-and-control structures and "who reports to whom." Now, the manager is more of a network operator. He is part of a country team and part of a business unit. Some companies don't even have country managers anymore.

Q: What is the toughest challenge in managing global companies today?

A: Management structures are now three-dimensional. You have to manage by geography, products, and global customers. The real issue is building networked structures between those three dimensions. That is the state of the art. It's getting away from classic power issues. Managers are becoming nodes, which are part of geographical structures and part of a business unit.

Q: What are the telltale questions that reflect whether a company is truly global?

A: CEOs should ask themselves four questions: First, how do people interact with each other—do employees around the world know each other and communicate regularly? Second, do management processes reflect a network or an old-style hierarchy? Third, is information provided to everyone simultaneously? And fourth, is the company led from the bottom up, not the top down?

Q: Why do multinationals that have operated for decades in foreign markets need to overhaul their management structures?

A: The sheer velocity of decisions that must be made is impossible in a company depending on an old-style vertical hierarchy. Think of a company [like] Cisco that is negotiating 50 to 60 alliances at one time. The old corporate structures [can't] integrate these

decisions fast enough. The CEO used to be involved in every acquisition, every alliance. Now, the role of the corporate center is different. Real business decisions move down to the level of business units.

Q: If there is not clear hierarchy, and managers have conflicting opinions, how does top management know when to make a decision? Doesn't that raise the risk of delay and inaction?

A: In the old centralized model, there was no communication. If you have multiple minds at work on a problem, the feedback is much quicker. If five managers or "nodes" in the network say something is not working right, management better sit up and take notice.

Q: Are there any secrets to designing a new management architecture?

A: Many structures will work. [H]aving the talent and capabilities you need to make a more fluid structure work [is key]. [But] it's much harder to do. The key is to create horizontal flow across silos to meet customers' needs. The question is how you network across these silos. [G]etting people to work together [is paramount]. That's the revolution that is going on now.

Q: What is the role of the CEO?

A: The CEO is the architect. He puts in place the conditions to let the organization innovate. No one is smart enough to do it alone anymore. Corporate restructuring should liberate the company from the past. As you break down old formal structures, knowledge workers are the nodes or the glue that hold different parts of the company together. They are the network. Nodes are what it is all about.

Q: How do you evaluate performance in such a squishy system?

A: The role of the corporate center is to worry about talent and how people do relative to each other. Workers build a set of intangibles around who they are. If they are not compensated for their value-added, they will go somewhere else.

Source: Reprinted with special permission from John Byrne, "The 21st Century Corporation," *BusinessWeek,* August 28, 2000. Copyright © 2000 The McGraw-Hill Companies.

ambidextrous organization
Organization structure most notable for its lack of structure wherein knowledge and getting it to the right place quickly are the key reasons for organization. Managers become knowledge "nodes" through which intricate networks of personal relationships—inside and outside the formal organization—are constantly, and often informally, coordinated to bring together relevant know-how and successful action.

allow global companies the chance to build competitive advantage.[21] Rather than going to markets to exploit brands or for inexpensive resources, in Rangan's view, the smart ones are going global to learn. This shift in the intent of the structure, then, is to seek information, to create new competences. Demand in another part of the world could be a new-product trendsetter at home. So a firm's structure needs to be organized to enable learning, to share knowledge, to create opportunities to create it. Others look to companies like 3M or Procter & Gamble that allow slack time, new-product champions, manager mentors—all put in place in the structure to provide resources, support, and advocacy for cross-functional collaboration leading to innovation in new-product development, and the generation and use of new ideas. This perspective is similar to the boundaryless notion—accommodate the speed of change and therefore opportunity by freeing up historical constraints found in traditional organizational approaches. So having structures that emphasize coordination over control, that allow flexibility (are **ambidextrous**), that emphasize the value and importance of informal relationships and interaction over formal systems, techniques, and controls are all characteristics associated with what are seen as effective structures for the twenty-first century.

Summary

This chapter has examined ways organizations are structured and ways to make those structures most effective. It described five traditional organizational structures–simple organization, functional structure, divisional structure, matrix structure, and product-team structure. Simple structures are often found in small companies, where tight control is essential to survival. Functional structures take advantage of the specialization of work by structuring the organization into interconnected units like sales, operations, and accounting/finance. This approach generates more efficiency, enhances functional skills over time, and is perhaps the most pervasive organizational structure. Coordination and conflict across functional units are the perpetual challenge in functional structures.

As companies grow they add products, services, and geographic locations, which leads to the need for divisional structures which divide the organization into units along one or more of these three lines. This division of the business into units with common settings increases focus and allows each division to operate more like an independent business itself. That in turn can generate competition for corporate level resources and potentially loose consistency and image corporatewide. Companies that work intensely with certain clients or projects created the matrix organization structure to temporarily assign functional specialists to those activities while having them remain accountable to their "home" functional unit. The product-team structure has evolved from the matrix approach, where functional specialists' assignments can be for an extended time and usually center around creating a functionally balanced team to take charge of a new-product idea from generation to production, sales, and market expansion. This approach has been found to create special synergy, teamwork, and cooperation since these specialists are together building a new revenue stream from its inception through its success and expansion.

The twenty-first century has seen an accelerating move away from traditional organizational structures toward hybrid adaptations that emphasize an external focus, flexible interaction, interdependency, and a bottom-up approach. Organizations have sought to adapt their traditional structures in this direction by redefining the role of corporate headquarters, rebalancing the need for control versus coordination, adjusting and reengineering the structure to emphasize strategic activities, downsizing and moving toward self-managing operational activities.

[21] Subramanian Rangan, *A Prism on Globalization* (Fountainebleau, France: INSEAD, 1999).

More successful organizations are becoming agile, virtual organizations—temporary networks of independent companies linked by information technology to share skills, markets, and costs. Outsourcing has been a major way organizations have done this. They retain certain functions, while having other companies take full responsibility for accomplishing other functions necessary to provide the product or services of this host organization. Strategic alliances are arrangements between two or more companies who typically contribute resources or skills to a joint undertaking where the joint entity is a separate, distinct organization itself and usually created to seek a particular contract or activities that represent too great an undertaking for any one player in the alliance.

Twenty-first century leaders have increasingly spoken about making their organizations boundaryless, by which they mean the absence of internal and external "boundaries" between units, levels, and locations that lessen their company's ability to generate knowledge, share knowledge, and get knowledge to the places it can be best used to create value. Forward thinkers describe ambidextrous learning organizations as ones that innately share knowledge, enable learning within and across organizations, and nurture informal relationships within and outside organizations to foster opportunities to be at the forefront of creating new knowledge.

Key Terms

agile organization, *p. 356*

ambidextrous organization, *p. 366*

boundaryless organization, *p. 362*

business process outsourcing, *p. 357*

business process reengineering, *p. 353*

divisional organizational structure, *p. 342*

downsizing, *p. 354*

external interface boundaries, *p. 363*

functional organizational structure, *p. 342*

geographic boundaries, *p. 363*

holding company structure, *p. 345*

horizontal boundaries, *p. 362*

learning organization, *p. 364*

matrix organizational structure, *p. 345*

modular organization, *p. 356*

organizational structure, *p.341*

outsourcing, *p. 356*

product-team structure, *p. 345*

restructuring, *p. 352*

self-management, *p. 354*

simple organizational structure, *p. 341*

strategic alliances, *p. 360*

strategic business unit, *p. 343*

vertical boundaries, *p. 363*

virtual organization, *p. 355*

Questions for Discussion

1. Explain each traditional organizational structure.
2. Select a company you have worked for or research one in the business press that uses one of these traditional structures. How well suited is the structure to the needs and strategy of the organization? What seems to work well, and what doesn't?
3. What organizations do you think are most likely to use product-team structures? Why?
4. Identify an organization that operated like a twentieth-century organization but has now adopted a structure that manifests twenty-first-century characteristics. Explain how you see or detect the differences.
5. How would you use one or more of the ways to improve traditional structures to improve the company you last worked in? Explain what might result.
6. What organization are you familiar with that you would consider the most agile, virtual organization? Why?
7. What situation have you personally seen outsourcing benefit?
8. What "boundary" would you first eliminate or change in an organization you are familiar with? Explain what you would do to eliminate it or change it and how that should make it more effective.

Chapter 11 Discussion Case

BusinessWeek

The Secret of BMW's Success: *BMW's Success Can*
Be Traced to Its Speed, Organizational Agility, and
Lateral Management Techniques

1 At 4:00 p.m. on a Friday afternoon, when most German workers have long departed for the weekend, the mini-cafés sprinkled throughout BMW's sprawling R&D center in Munich are jammed with engineers, designers, and marketing managers deliberating so intently it's hard to hear above the din. Even the cappuccino machine is running on empty. It's an atmosphere far more Silicon Valley than Detroit.

2 "At lunch and breaks everyone is discussing ideas and projects all the time. It's somewhat manic. But it makes things move faster," says BMW chief designer Adrian van Hooydonk.

3 The intense employee buzz at BMW is hot management theory in action. Top consultants and academics say the kind of informal networks that flourish at BMW and the noise and borderline chaos they engender in big organizations are vital for innovation—especially in companies where knowledge sits in the brains of tens of thousands of workers and not in a computer server. Melding that brain power, they say, is essential to unleashing the best ideas.

HANDS ACROSS DIVISIONS

4 "Cross-functional teams look messy and inefficient, but they are more effective at problem solving," says James M. Manyika, a partner at McKinsey & Co. in San Francisco who has studied the effectiveness of such networks. Companies such as BMW that leverage workers' tacit knowledge through such networks "are widely ahead of their competitors," Manyika adds.

5 BMW is one of a handful of global companies including Nokia and Raytheon that have turned to networks to manage day-to-day operations, superseding classic hierarchies. Those pioneering companies still turn to management hierarchies to set strategic goals, but workers have the freedom to forge teams across divisions and achieve targets in the best way possible—even if that way is unconventional.

6 And they are encouraged to build ties across divisions to speed change. "Good companies have this lateral ability to communicate across divisions and silos, not just up and down the hierarchy. That's what makes BMW tick," says chief financial officer Stefan Krause.

LIGHTNING-FAST CHANGES

7 Speed and organizational agility is increasingly vital to the auto industry, since electronics now make up some 20 percent of a car's value—and that level is rising. BMW figures some 90 percent of the innovations in its new models are electronics-driven. That requires once-slow-moving automakers to adapt to the lightning pace of innovation and change driving the semiconductor and software industries. Gone is the era of the 10-year model cycle.

8 Now automakers must ram innovation into high gear to avoid being overtaken by the competition. That's especially true in the luxury-auto leagues, where market leaders must pulse new innovations constantly onto the market, from podcasting for cars to infrared night vision systems.

9 By shifting effective management of day-to-day operations to such human networks, which speed knowledge laterally through companies faster and better than old hierarchies can, BMW has become as entrepreneurial as a tech start-up, consultants say. "Not many large companies take on lateral communications the way BMW does. It's a knocking down of barriers, like Jack Welch did at General Electric to make a boundaryless corporation," says Jay Galbraith, a Breckenridge (Colorado)-based management consultant.

Deep-six the egos Rigorously screen new hires for their ability to thrive as part of a team. Promote young talent but hold back perks until they've shown their stuff.

Build a share mythology New hires learn about 1959, when BMW nearly went bankrupt. Its recovery remains the centerpiece of company lore, inspiring a deep commitment to innovation.

Worship the network Teams from across the company work elbow to elbow in open, airy spaces, helping them to create informal networks where they hatch ideas quickly and resolve disagreements.

Work outside the system The sleek Z4 coupe exists because a young designer's doodle inspired a team to push his concept even though management had already killed the program.

Keep the door open From the factory floor to the executive suite, everyone is encouraged to speak out. Ideas bubble up freely, and even the craziest proposals will get a hearing.

MOBILE-PHONE MESSAGES

10 BMW's ability to drive innovation even pervades its marketing division. "People talk about innovation in products, but what's underestimated is innovation in processes and organization," says Ernst Baumann, head of personnel at BMW, which has its share of radical new ideas.

11 To reach a younger crowd of potential buyers for its new 1 Series launch in 2004, BMW used mobile-phone messages as the main source of buzz, directing interested people to signups on BMW's Web site for pre-launch test drives in August that year—something unheard of in the industry at the time. The experimental tactic worked: BMW sparked responses from 150,000 potential customers—and sales of the 1 Series took off when it was launched in September, 2004.

12 In 2001, BMW stunned the advertising world by investing ad spending normally set aside for Super Bowl spots in short films that had nothing to do with telling consumers about its cars. The slick, professionally made films were pure entertainment, like its series of short films, *The Hire,* starring Clive Owens, and they cost a bundle: $25 million.

BALANCING ACT

13 The risky bet triggered serious consternation at BMW's Munich headquarters. "You have to worry when your marketing team goes into the business of making films," says Krause, who noted that Internet-driven businesses were imploding left and right in 2001. Given those conditions, "Who cares how many clicks you get."

14 Few large companies are willing to embrace the lack of organizational clarity and nebulous structures that drive innovative ideas. At most companies, headquarters would have put the kibosh on the short-film idea, which has since been widely imitated. Researchers say most experiment with networks on a small scale and very few use the practice to full effect since doing so means an uncomfortable balancing act between hierarchy and discipline on one hand, and free-wheeling networks that can veer toward near-chaos.

15 But for innovation-driven companies, networks that enable entrepreneurial risk-taking are a silver bullet. "The ideas are richer, they implement more effectively, and there is less resistance to change," says Rob Cross, assistant professor of management at the University of Virginia.

IDEAS FIRST

16 How does BMW manage discipline with creativity and keep the anarchy of networks from careening out of control? Workers at the Bavarian automaker are encouraged from their first day on the job to build a network or web of personal ties to speed problem-solving and innovation, be it in R&D, design, production, or marketing. Those ties run across divisions and up and down the chain of command.

17 When it comes to driving innovation, forget formal meetings, hierarchy, and stamps of approval. Each worker learns quickly that pushing fresh ideas is paramount. "It's easier to ask forgiveness for breaking the rules than to seek permission," says Richard Gaul, a 33-year veteran at BMW and former head of communications at the $60 billion automaker.

18 BMW's complex customized production system, the polar opposite of Toyota's standardized lines, is easier to manage if workers feel empowered to drive change. Like Dell Computer, BMW configures its cars to customers' orders, so each auto moving down the production line is different.

FORGET OLD-SCHOOL RIGIDITY

19 Making sure the system works without a hitch requires savvy workers who continually suggest how to optimize processes. "Networks can do things that hierarchies cannot, because hierarchies lack the freedom. With a network you get the powerful ability to leverage knowledge quickly to bear on solving problems," says Karen Stephenson, management consultant and Harvard professor. "A network is the only way to effectively manage BMW's kind of complexity."

20 By contrast, companies that don't have lateral nimbleness are crippled in fast-moving technology-driven industries. Rigid hierarchies that stifle fresh ideas and slow reaction times are one problem facing General Motors and Ford Motor.

21 Once giants like GM were king, dominating the market with their huge volume and purchasing muscle. Big is no longer the ticket to success, and the slow-moving bureaucracies that big companies are saddled with are now a major handicap. "Lean is passé. What is in is lean and agile: the ability to shift and adjust as circumstances in the market change," says David Cole, partner at the Center for Automotive Research in Ann Arbor, Michigan.

KNOW THY CONSUMER

22 BMW managers, by contrast, even talk about the "physics of chaos" and how to constantly nurture innovation and creativity by operating on the very edge of chaos without getting out of control. "Discipline and creativity are not a paradox, there is a borderline case of self-controlling systems," says Gaul. "Where you break rules you have to be very disciplined." That's the industry's next *kaizen*—the art automakers will be forced to master in the twenty-first century.

23 The novel advertising scheme developed back in 2001 is a good example. Jim McDowell, then U.S. vice president of marketing, was confident the project, dubbed "Big Idea," and kept under tight security in "War Room" No. 6 at BMW USA's Woodlake (New Jersey) headquarters, would create just the kind of consumer buzz that BMW wanted—and would ultimately be more cost-effective for BMW than Super Bowl advertising. The idea was to give film directors a BMW car around which a compelling short film was to be made. Many of the tales centered on life-and-death chase scenes, but several were humorous or even melancholy.

24 McDowell figured if *The Hire* took off and the films were downloaded from BMW's Web site by more than 2 million viewers, BMW would chalk up the same number of eyeballs as a snappy advertising campaign aired during the Super Bowl, but would reach a higher percentage of BMW-type customers, progressives with a nose for cinema, technology, and high bandwidth. "If you really understand your consumer, you can be very clever about how to communicate. You can change the whole paradigm," says McDowell, who is now executive vice president at Mini.

SNOWBALL EFFECT

25 McDowell didn't take any half-measures. He went after talented directors such as John Frankenheimer (*The French Connection*) and Ang Lee (*Crouching Tiger, Hidden Dragon*), and signed up stars such as Madonna, Clive Owens, and Gary Oldman—giving them complete artistic freedom, aside from the BMW model that starred in each film. No advance advertising heralded the Internet launch of the films.

26 The buzz started slowly with the first film but grew to avalanche proportions by the time Madonna's short comedy film about a cranky diva was released, overwhelming BMW's expectations and forcing the automaker to add servers as fast as it could.

27 But it didn't stop there. As the short-film gambit rocketed around the blogosphere, national TV broadcasters flooded McDowell's office with requests for interviews on CBS, *Entertainment Tonight*, and Fox News. The novelty of an automaker producing films fanned public interest and stoked downloads.

"EXPERIMENTAL ENVIRONMENT"

28 After one year, the number of viewers who had visited BMW's Web site to download *The Hire* shot to more than 21 million, and with three more films added in 2002, it rocketed to 100 million, sparking a Harvard Business School case study. One million enthusiasts ordered a DVD with all eight films.

29 McKinsey's Manyika, who has studied networks extensively, says knowledge forced through a company top-down drives "conformity, consistency, and efficiency." That's better suited to companies that make a standardized widget than a complex, electronics-driven product that requires constant innovation.

30 Companies such as BMW have to tap into tacit knowledge to spark fresh ideas. "It's more of a learning and experimental environment. It's building on what people know. It's learning instead of instruction," says Manyika.

HOW IDEAS TRAVEL

31 For academics and consultants studying the phenomenon of corporate networks, the most fascinating element is the "node" or the broker individual who can join two separate clusters with different pools of knowledge. Such a broker may have once worked in purchasing but now sits in R&D. As such, he or she can bridge the two worlds by "reaching across the white space of disconnected people," says Ronald S. Burt, a sociologist at the University of Chicago, who is studying the impact corporate networks have on performance.

32 That linkage speeds learning throughout companies—a vital tool to industries that should continually innovate. "People exposed to a diversity of information are at higher risk of seeing a new angle, a better way to frame ideas," says Burt. And companies that recognize and tap such social capital "have better growth rates and better patent rates. Formal structures decide whom to blame. Informal structures decide how to get things done," he says.

Extra: An Interview with Helmut Panke, newly retired CEO, who talks about why BMW is the world's greatest automobile company

33 Helmut Panke became chief executive at BMW in 2001 as the company was recovering from the failed 1994 acquisition of Rover. He has since powered the German automaker through the fastest model expansion in its history. Panke recently turned 60, the mandatory retirement age at BMW, handing over the job as CEO to production chief Norbert Reithofer. His legacy is a company that churns out top profits but nonetheless continues to question its own success—and innovate at a breakneck pace.

34 Panke, a PhD-holding physicist who did brief stints as a physics professor and a consultant at McKinsey before joining BMW, epitomized the automaker's bottom-up culture throughout his 24-year career. His easy-going, walk-around management style encouraged staffers to express opinions, challenge the views of associates or superiors, and even engage in debate with Panke himself.

35 Unlike the Sun King CEOs who dominate many large corporations with their oversize egos, Panke loves to engage in arguments that test his preconceptions and make him see things differently. "I hate to admit it, but you're right," says Panke, when he's won over—according to managers who work closely with him.

PERFORMANCE CLASS

36 The trim, energetic, detail-obsessed manager constantly set an example for breaking down silos to speed the transfer of knowledge throughout the company—one of the secrets of BMW's success.

37 Like many archetype BMW chiefs, Panke, who sits on Microsoft's board of directors, gathered his own intelligence about the $60 billion automaker by showing up in factories, sales offices, company cafeterias, research labs, and test tracks to ask a lot of questions. His personal knowledge about everything from new engine technology to electronics software and market trends runs deep. His favorite tactic in the boardroom was throwing out intelligence he gathered from "the machinery room," a German idiom meaning the

deepest levels of the company's operations—his own secret sources—and sparking debate.

38   Even as a member of Germany's industrial elite, Panke remained a low-key manager who avoided hobnobbing with politicians, preferring to spar with his own employees, test-drive the company's cars, or escape the official routine to do his own market sleuthing in Asia. A top priority for Panke is spending one day a month behind the wheel of new BMW prototypes or rivals' cars, together with the entire management board, scrutinizing everything from handling to interiors to design.

Question: *How does the BMW organization balance creative freedom with the discipline needed for building high-performance cars?*

Helmut Panke: Our philosophy is to get recommendations and then take decisions on the level where the competence lies, which by definition is not always at the top of the company. If expertise sits at the level of a department manager, he or she should decide—whether you are an engineer for R&D, or marketing expert, or technical planner—the archetype BMW associate has more freedom and authority to decide what he or she does than in most companies.

    Despite our focus on innovation, on technology, and on marketing, we have a culture of strong cost controls, and we are driven by cost targets, even in the early stages of developing a car. Still, the individual has more room to decide how he or she will reach the targets that have been agreed on.

Question: *Can you give an example?*

Helmut Panke: The freedom BMW associates have can be exemplified by major capital investment decisions that don't reach the board of management but are decided one or two levels lower in the organization. Projects with a value of up to several hundred million dollars don't need 10 stamps of approval. In other organizations they would go to the board.

Question: *So where are the controls?*

Helmut Panke: No individual is in a position to decide alone. We have the four-eye principle. Contracts with binding agreements must be approved and signed by at least two people.

Question: *BMW has been a pioneer in implementing new management concepts and organizational models. You were very quick, for example, to jump on the idea of creating a "skunkworks" to spur innovation outside the corporate organization. How*

did a German-based company decide in the early 1980s to be among the first to test a newfangled approach to innovation?

Helmut Panke: BMW was among the first companies to create its own skunkworks. We heard that Lockheed took engineers out of the regular organization to work on special projects. We thought the approach interesting and created BMW Technik GmbH—which was designed to bring together engineers with different technological backgrounds.

    Their work was not specifically project-based or budget-based. They could play. Out of playing around, they created the Z1 concept car, with downward moving doors. They explored the possibilities of working with different materials and engines. [Today's Aston Martin CEO] Ulrich Bez ran it in the beginning. We set up the company in a different building [in Munich] and created an entirely different HR and compensation system. BMW's contracts and work-time limits didn't apply. To give an example, employees were allowed to work at night if they wanted to.

Question: *How would you describe BMW's management structure?*

Helmut Panke: It is a much more informal, open, nonhierarchical way to work. I get e-mails from associates deep down in the organization with creative proposals or simple comments. My door is open. It's not uncommon to have managers below my immediate reports to call me [directly]. There is no structured hierarchical process communication. We have become more open. In 1982, it was a no-no to call another division. You wrote memos that went up and down the chain of command.

Question: *BMW encourages employees to speak out and defend their ideas—even to the point of prompting open conflicts. How do you manage that process effectively?*

Helmut Panke: It's a positive handling of different opinions and judgments. One good example is the process of tangible discussions, step-by-step, in designing a new model. Design starts at the beginning of the concept phase. You start by defining proportions, such as the front overhang, the rear overhang, the height, the width, the length. We look at proportions independent from what an engineer might say about whether it can or can't be done.

The participants in the discussions can't just say they don't like it. They have to argue and explain. We debate and express differences. Maybe the amount of metal compared to glass is too much. Maybe the design is too round, too smooth, or has too many lines. You express, argue, and explain as you go from six to seven versions to two to three models. The differences in opinion are expressed and backed up by clear argumentation. We don't move forward until it's clear there is mutual agreement. Yet, we have a culture of conflict. But if something is easy, it becomes routine. It's part of BMW's culture to push the limits. The challenge is to make a best seller even better.

Question: *BMW is big on encouraging informal networks of employees to work across divisions, spurring innovative ideas and solving problems. And you spend a fair amount of time soliciting ideas and input from all ranks at the company. Do you have your own personal network that you use in managing BMW?*

Helmut Panke: Yes, I like to go into the belly of the organization. One interest of mine is to stay informed through my network of former colleagues. Two weeks ago I met someone I knew in my first job at BMW as product planner and chatted with him. I still have a network, and I get information from it. I don't just talk to board members. It's fun to talk with department managers. The information is much less filtered, cleansed, or politicized.

Sources: Reprinted with special permission from Gail Edmondson, "The Secret of BMW's Success," *BusinessWeek,* October 16, 2006; and "Danke Panke," *BusinessWeek,* October 16, 2006. Copyright © 2006 The McGraw-Hill Companies.

DISCUSSION QUESTIONS

1. How does BMW use cross-functional teams?
2. What role does "speed" play in BMW's structure?
3. How has the role of electronics in cars influenced the way BMW's organization works?
4. What appear to be the strengths, and weaknesses, of BMW's approach?
5. Does outsourcing play a role at BMW?
6. How is BMW an ambidextrous organization?

Chapter **Twelve**

Leadership and Culture

After reading and studying this chapter, you should be able to

1. Describe what good organizational leadership involves.

2. Explain how vision and performance help leaders clarify strategic intent.

3. Explain the value of passion and selection/development of new leaders in shaping an organization's culture.

4. Briefly explain seven sources of power and influence available to every manager.

5. Define and explain what is meant by organizational culture, and how it is created, influenced, and changed.

6. Describe four ways leaders influence culture.

7. Explain four strategy-culture situations.

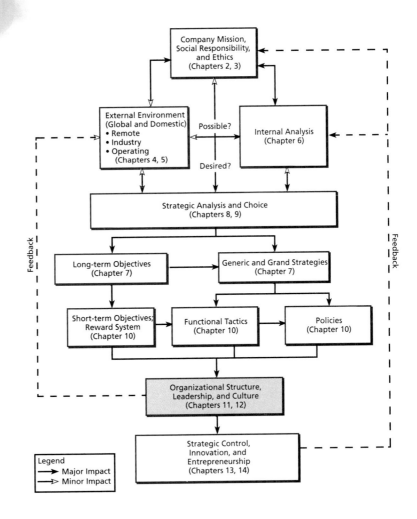

Company Mission, Social Responsibility, and Ethics (Chapters 2, 3)

External Environment (Global and Domestic)
• Remote
• Industry
• Operating
(Chapters 4, 5)

Possible?

Desired?

Internal Analysis (Chapter 6)

Strategic Analysis and Choice (Chapters 8, 9)

Long-term Objectives (Chapter 7)

Generic and Grand Strategies (Chapter 7)

Short-term Objectives; Reward System (Chapter 10)

Functional Tactics (Chapter 10)

Policies (Chapter 10)

Organizational Structure, Leadership, and Culture (Chapters 11, 12)

Strategic Control, Innovation, and Entrepreneurship (Chapters 13, 14)

Feedback

Feedback

Legend
→ Major Impact
⇢ Minor Impact

The job of leading a company has never been more demanding, and it will only get more challenging amidst the global dynamism businesses face today. The CEO will retain ultimate authority, but the corporation will depend increasingly on the skills of the CEO and a host of subordinate leaders to lead, coordinate, make decisions, and act quickly. The accelerated pace and complexity of business will continue to force corporations to push authority down through increasingly horizontal, flattened management structures. As we saw in the last chapter, these organizations will also need to be more and more open, agile, and boundaryless. This will require all the more emphasis on able leadership and a strong culture to shape decisions that must be made quickly, even when the stakes are big. In the future, every line manager will have to exercise leadership's prerogatives—and bear its burdens—to an extent unthinkable 20 years ago.[1]

John Kotter, a widely recognized leadership expert, predicted this evolving role of leadership in an organization when he distinguished between management and leadership:

> Management is about coping with complexity. Its practices and procedures are largely a response to one of the most significant developments of the twentieth century: the emergence of large organizations. Without good management, complex enterprises tend to become chaotic in ways that threaten their very existence. Good management brings a degree of order and consistency to key dimensions like the quality and profitability of products.
>
> Leadership, by contrast, is about coping with change. Part of the reason it has become so important in recent years is that the business world has become more competitive and more volatile. . . . The net result is that doing what was done yesterday, or doing it 5 percent better, is no longer a formula for success. Major changes are more and more necessary to survive and compete effectively in this new environment. More change always demands more leadership.[2]

organizational leadership
The process and practice by key executives of guiding and shepherding people in an organization toward a vision over time and developing that organization's future leadership and organization culture.

Organizational leadership, then, involves action on two fronts. The first is in guiding the organization to deal with constant change. This requires CEOs who embrace change, and who do so by clarifying strategic intent, who build their organization and shape their culture to fit with opportunities and challenges change affords. The second front is in providing the management skill to cope with the ramifications of constant change. This means identifying and supplying the organization with operating managers prepared to provide operational leadership and vision as never before. Thus, organizational leadership is guiding and shepherding toward a vision over time and developing that organization's future leadership and organizational culture.

Consider the challenge currently facing Ford Motor Company CEO Alan Mulally as he seeks to transform Ford's culture and return the company to profitability after years of accelerating decline. He was brought in by CEO Bill Ford, great-grandson of the founder, who finally threw up his arms in frustration and concluded that an insider could no longer fix Ford. Mulally was not Bill Ford's first choice, but Ford concluded Mulally was someone who knows how to shake the company to its foundations.

Mulally inherited virtually all the managers he must work through. Ford was losing from $3,000 to $5,000 on most every car it sold. There is a legacy within the company of placing a premium on personal ties to the Ford family, sometimes trumping actual performance in promotion decisions. Mulally had no experience in the automobile industry and was viewed with suspicion as an outsider in a town that places a premium on lifelong association with the industry. On Mulally's first meeting with his inherited management team, one manager asked early on: "How are you going to tackle something as complex and unfamiliar as the auto business when we are in such tough financial shape?"

---

[1] Larry Bossidy, "What Your Leader Expects of You," *Harvard Business Review,* June 2007; and Anthony Bianco, "The New Leadership," *BusinessWeek,* August 28, 2000.

[2] John P. Kotter, "What Leaders Really Do," *Harvard Business Review* (May–June 1990), p. 104.

Wall Street was skeptical early on. Of 15 analysts surveyed by Bloomberg.com, only two rated it a buy. The other 13's opinion: fixing Ford will require much more than simply whacking expenses and replacing a few key people. The company will have to figure out how to produce more vehicles consumers actually want. And doing that requires addressing the most fundamental problem of all: Ford's dysfunctional, often defeatist, culture. Once a model of efficiency, it has degenerated into a symbol of inefficiency, and its managers seem comfortable with the idea of losing money.

If you were Alan Mulally, how would you lead the dramatic change that appears to be needed at Ford Motor Company? How would you seek to move Ford's 300,000-plus employees and managers in a direction that abandons ingrained, and to some "sacred," cultural and leadership norms, quickly.

Consider another example. Jeff Immelt took the reins of leadership of GE from Jack Welch, recognized worldwide as one of the truly great business leaders of the twentieth century and faced a leadership and organizational culture challenge quite different in some ways from what Alan Mulally is addressing. GE under Welch built more value for its stockholders than any other company in the history of global commerce. That legacy alone would be pressure enough on a new leader, wouldn't you think?

Fortunately, some would quickly answer, Immelt had trained for many years under and in Welch's shadow. He was Welch's choice as successor. He was deeply schooled in the GE way and the Jack Welch leadership approach, as were all the other 300,000 GE employees over the prior 20 years. That Welch/GE way valued, above all, executives who could cut costs, cut deals, and generate continuous improvement in their business units. They were evaluated personally by Welch on an annual basis, in front of each other at the GE School.

But a storm was brewing. Shortly after Immelt became CEO, the 9/11 tragedy unfolded. A major recession and stock market drop soon followed. The option to continue mega deal making was slowing down with fewer candidates. The ability to generate GE-caliber earnings growth via sales growth combined with relentless efficiency was slowing down. So Immelt concluded that he could not continue with the old strategy. Rather, he would have to embark on virtually a new direction at GE that would dramatically change what he needed GE executives as leaders to prioritize and become. Instead of being experts in deal making and continuous improvement, they needed, in Immelt's vision, to become creative, innovators of internal growth generated by identifying new markets and technologies and needs as yet unknown.

With a slower-growing domestic economy, less tolerance among investors for buying your way to growth, and more global competitors, Immelt, like many of his peers, is being forced to shift the emphasis from deals and cost-cutting to new products, services, and markets. "It's a different world," says Immelt, than the one Welch knew. And so, he inherited one of the world's greatest companies yet faced a situation he concluded required dramatic changes in the way GE would be led, in the nature of the culture it needed, and in the fundamental priorities its managers would build GE's future.

If you were Jeff Immelt, how would you lead such a change? How would you seek to move GE's 300,000 people in a direction that abandons "sacred" cultural and leadership norms that were well used and entrenched under Welch's watch to make GE great? How would you quickly and convincingly lead those people to accept massive change throughout this special company and very quickly have that uncertain change produce the growth and profitability investors understandably expect?

The challenges Immelt and Mulally faced were different, but both were nothing short of a revolution. Indeed, the case at the end of this chapter will examine how Mulally is attempting to revolutionize Ford Motor Company. The bottom line is that Immelt and Mulally as well as all good executives, focus intensely and aggressively on the organizational leadership and organizational culture elements we will now examine.

STRATEGIC LEADERSHIP: EMBRACING CHANGE

The blending of telecommunications, computers, the Internet, and one global marketplace has increased the pace of change exponentially during the past 10 years. All business organizations are affected. Change has become an integral part of what leaders and managers deal with daily. The opening example about Jeff Immelt shows a manager normally able to celebrate 20 years of historically unmatched accomplishment, only to face the need for dramatic change at a GE employees and investors had come to believe was infallible.

The leadership challenge is to galvanize commitment among people within an organization as well as stakeholders outside the organization to embrace change and implement strategies intended to position the organization to succeed in a vastly different future. Leaders galvanize commitment to embrace change through three interrelated activities: clarifying strategic intent, building an organization, and shaping organizational culture.

Clarifying Strategic Intent

strategic intent
Leaders' clear sense of where they want to lead their company and what results they expect to achieve.

Leaders help their company embrace change by setting forth their **strategic intent**—a clear sense of where they want to lead the company and what results they expect to achieve. They do this by concentrating simultaneously and very clearly on two very different issues: vision and performance.

Vision

leader's vision
An articulation of a simple criterion or characterization of what a leader sees the company must become in order to establish and sustain global leadership.

A leader needs to communicate clearly and directly a fundamental vision of what the business needs to become. Traditionally, the concept of vision has been a description or picture of what the company could be that accommodates the needs of all its stakeholders. The intensely competitive, rapidly changing global marketplace has refined this to be targeting a very narrowly defined **leader's vision**—an articulation of a simple criterion or characterization of what the leader sees the company must become to establish and sustain global leadership. Former IBM CEO Lou Gerstner is a good example of a leader in the middle of trying to shape strategic intent when he began to try to change IBM from a computer company to a business solutions management company. He said at the time: "One of the great things about this industry is that every decade or so, you get a chance to redefine the playing field." He further commented, "We're in that phase of redefinition right now, and winners or losers are going to emerge from it. We've got to become the leader in 'network-centric computing.' It's a shift brought about by telecommunications-based change that is changing IBM more than semiconductors did in the last decade." Said Gerstner, "I sensed there were too many people inside IBM who wanted to fight the war we lost," referring to PCs and PC software, so he aggressively instilled network-centric computing as the strategic intent for IBM in the next decade. It is a comment on his sense of vision that his successor, Sam Palmisano, sold IBM's PC business to China's Lenovo, creating the world's third-largest PC company, and is aggressively pushing his IBMers to concentrate on newer IBM businesses in IT services, software, and servers—and seriously examining IBM's future in the online digital world, the 3D Internet.

Keep the Vision Simple   The late Sam Walton's vision for Wal-Mart, *value to the consumer*, lives on in that amazing global company, guiding its development in a vastly changed world. Meg Whitman's leadership of eBay has produced explosive growth, keeping everyone committed to a vision that eBay simply exists to help you buy or sell anything, anywhere, anytime. Coca-Cola's legendary former CEO and chairman Roberto Goizueta said, "Our company is a global business system for which we raise capital to make concentrate and sell it at an operating profit. Then we pay the cost of that capital. Shareholders pocket the difference." Coke averaged 27 percent annual return on stockholder equity for 18 years under his leadership. Exhibit 12.1, Top Strategist, shows how Mayor Michael Bloomberg articulated a radical yet simple vision of New York City that has resonated with New York's famously cynical citizenry, who give him a 75 percent approval rating. All four of these organizations are very different, but their leaders were each effective in shaping and communicating a vision that clarified strategic intent in a way that helped everyone understand, or at least have a sense of, where the organization needed to go and, as a result, created a better sense of the rationale behind any new, and often radically changing, strategy. When you read the discussion case at the end of the chapter about Mulally at Ford, examine this issue and whether Mulally communicates a clear vision for a new Ford Motor Company.

Performance

Clarifying strategic intent must also ensure the survival of the enterprise as it pursues a well-articulated vision, and after it reaches the vision. So a key element of good organizational leadership is to make clear the performance expectations a leader has for the organization, and managers in it, as they seek to move toward that vision.

Oftentimes this can create a bit of a paradox, because the vision is a future picture and performance is now and tomorrow and next quarter and this year. Steven Reinemund, former CEO of PepsiCo and responsible for its impressive performance the last several years, offered an insightful way to think about this role of a good leader in clarifying strategic intent. "As I am looking to select other leaders, it's important to remember that results count. If you can't get the results over the goal line, are you really a leader?" The job of a good leader, in clarifying strategic intent, is to do so by painting a picture of that intent in future terms, and in setting sound performance expectations while moving toward that vision and as the vision becomes a reality.[3]

Jim McNerney, Boeing CEO and GE alumnus, described how he handles this paradox at Boeing and 3M as a contrast between an encouraging style (visioning) and setting expectations (performance).

> I think the harder you push people, the more you have to encourage them. Some people feel you either have a demanding, command-and-control management style or you have a nurturing, encouraging management style. I believe you have to have both. If you're only demanding, without encouraging, eventually that runs out of gas. And if you're only encouraging, without setting high expectations, you're not getting as much out of people. It's not either/or. You can't have one without the other.[4]

A real challenge for Alan Mulally at Ford is changing managers' mindsets about being profitable. When he was reviewing Ford's 2008 product line as the new CEO, he was told that Ford loses close to $3,000 every time a customer buys a Focus compact. "Why haven't you figured out a way to make a profit?" he asked. Executives explained that Ford needed the high sales volume to maintain the company's CAFÉ, or corporate average fuel economy, rating and that the plant that makes the car is a high-cost UAW factory in Michigan. "That's not what I asked," he shot back. "I want to know why no one figured out a way to build this car at a profit, whether it has to be built in Michigan or China or India, if that's what it takes." Nobody had a good answer.[5]

Building an Organization

The previous chapter examined alternative structures to use in designing the organization necessary to implement strategy. Leaders spend considerable time shaping and refining

[3] Diane Brady, "The Six "Ps" of PepsiCo's Chief," *BusinessWeek Online,* January 10, 2005.
[4] Michael Arndt, "The Hard Work in Leadership," *BusinessWeek Online,* April 12, 2004.
[5] David Kiley, "New Heat on Ford," *BusinessWeek,* June 4, 2007.

Top Strategist
Mike Bloomberg, The CEO Mayor

Exhibit
12.1

Applying lessons from an early career on Wall Street and from two decades building his eponymous financial information and media empire, New York City Mayor Michael R. Bloomberg is using technology, marketing, data analysis, and results-driven incentives to manage what is often seen as an unmanageable city of 8 million.

Bloomberg sees New York City as a corporation; its citizens as customers; its sanitation workers, police officers, clerks, and deputy commissioners as talent. He is the chief executive. Call him a technocrat all you want; he's O.K. with that. "I hear a disparaging tone, like there's something wrong with accountability and results," he says. "What was I hired for?"

Yet his checklist-obsessed operating style has resonated with New York's famously cynical citizenry—75 percent approval ratings attest to that—and well beyond Gotham. "People see that this can be done in a place like New York, effectively managing something so large and complex," says Time Warner CEO Richard D. Parsons, a Bloomberg friend and someone mentioned as a possible mayoral candidate himself. "And they think, 'Hey, this can be done elsewhere.'"

THE CITY IS A BRAND

Put yourself in Bloomberg's size 9½ loafers on January 1, 2002, the day he was sworn in as New York's 108th mayor. The city was grappling with the psychological and financial impact of the terrorist attacks. It faced a budget gap of nearly $6 billion. On Wall Street, there was talk of abandoning Manhattan for the safer precincts of New Jersey or Connecticut.

Bloomberg had three options: cut services, raise taxes, or both. He did what no mayor had dared to do in more than a decade: he jacked up property taxes. And he didn't agonize over the decision a bit. "It [was] easy to make that choice," he recalls.

Some of his aides tried to talk him out of it, fearing the move amounted to political suicide. And by the following summer, Bloomberg's approval ratings had plunged, to 31 percent. But the novice mayor was undeterred. Where most politicians would have seen only a fiscal solution to the budget gap, he spotted a marketing opportunity. He was protecting the New York City "brand." Bloomberg saw a low crime rate, good public transportation, and clean streets as indispensable to selling New York. Cutting back on services, he felt, would send the wrong message to the business community and the outside world.

At the same time, Bloomberg boosted New York's promotional efforts. First, he consolidated three existing operations under a not-for-profit entity called NYC & Co. He tripled the city's contribution to the annual marketing budget, to $22 million. Then he went out and hired as CEO a veteran ad man, George Fertitta, whose branding and marketing firm had handled the likes of Coca-Cola, Perry Ellis, and Disney. All cities have marketing arms. But Fertitta's operation is essentially an advertising agency with an in-house creative services unit that uses various media, from bus shelters to the city's cable channel, to help sell the Big Apple.

Ever the metric junkie, Bloomberg set a goal for NYC & Co.: lure 50 million visitors a year by 2015. And knowing that foreign tourists spend three times as much as U.S. visitors, he ordered Fertitta to open more branch offices around the world. Today, NYC & Co. has a presence in 14 cities, with new offices set to open in Seoul, Tokyo, and Shanghai in coming months.

Since 2003, New York says it has added 151,100 new private sector jobs, boosting the economy and fueling a construction boom. And last year [2006], partly owing to a weak U.S. dollar, the city reports attracting 44 million visitors, up from 35 million in 2002. As for that 18.5 percent property tax hike, it got a whole lot easier to swallow when the average value of a single family home surged by 55 percent. Now, with the city in surplus, Bloomberg plans to hand out $1.3 billion in tax cuts not only to homeowners but also to businesses and shoppers.

THE VOTERS ARE CUSTOMERS

Bloomberg the executive was obsessive about catering to his customers, establishing 24-hour call lines,

(continued)

Exhibit 12.1 cont.

collecting data to help develop new products, and sending his executives out into the field to solicit feedback directly from clients. "Good companies listen to their customers, No. 1," he says. "Then they try to satisfy their needs, No. 2. But don't let [them] drive the internal decisions of the company."

As daunting as it may sound in a city never shy about complaining, Bloomberg decided New York needed its own 24-hour customer-service line. Yes, other cities had deployed 311 numbers, but never on such a grand scale. The benefit, beyond giving the public a new outlet to vent, would be making city government more efficient.

One month after being sworn in, Bloomberg proposed a 311 line that would allow New Yorkers to report everything from noise pollution to downed power lines. More important, 311 would give the mayor unprecedented access to what was on his constituents' minds. Bloomberg sees the weekly reports and gets a sense of the citizenry's angst—and whether problems are getting solved and how quickly.

Since it launched in March 2003, at a start-up cost of $25 million, 311 has received 49 million calls. The service employs 370 round-the-clock call takers. And New York has done an impressive job of data-mining the calls and quickly responding, says Stephen Goldsmith, the former mayor of Indianapolis and now a professor at Harvard's Kennedy School of Government. "Something special is going on in New York," he says. As far as the mayor is concerned, the numbers tell the story. Emergency 911 traffic is down by 1 million calls since 311's inception, meaning first responders are being called to fewer nonemergencies. The Buildings Department uses 311 to streamline the permit process and the review of plans by inspectors. The average wait time for an appointment with a building inspector has dropped from 40 days to less than a week. Two years after 311 launched, inspections for excessive noise were up 94 percent; rodent exterminations, 36 percent.

Heather Schwartz, a 30-year-old graduate student, is a regular user of the 311 line and says she became a big fan last year when she called about graffiti in a northern Manhattan subway station. Within days, the walls were painted over. Each time the graffiti artists returned, the city would paint over their handiwork. Finally the vandals gave up. Now Schwartz calls 311 for everything from elevator inspections to trash in the streets. "I am thrilled with it," she says. "It professionalizes the city."

THE MORE LIGHT, THE BETTER

Earlier this year, during a morning meeting with top staffers, Bloomberg noticed the large doors to the ornate conference room in City Hall. They were wooden. How could that be? Bloomberg thought he'd made City Hall "see-through." All meeting rooms had glass windows, so you could look inside. His desk and those of his staff were clustered in a room without walls to facilitate better and faster communication. By week's end the room had glass doors.

Bloomberg has tried to make the government and its agencies more open, too. In a task that previously fell to city budget directors, Bloomberg himself each year makes three budget presentations in the same day: one to city council, another for other elected officials, and one to the press. He uses easy-to-follow charts and tables, much like a CEO's Power-Point presentation to analysts. His hope is that, by explaining the forces shaping the city's economy, a better understanding of his tax and spending priorities will emerge. The approach has not only helped him in budget negotiations with city council but also fostered a smoother relationship with civic and advocacy groups, says Mitchell Moss, an urban policy and planning professor at New York University.

What's more, citizens can get a closer look at their city government than ever before. The semiannual mayor's management report once exceeded 1,000 pages in three printed volumes. Today, the report—which reviews the delivery of city services—is 186 pages, is available online, and includes many more features than before, including neighborhood data and five-year trends that allow New Yorkers to compare past and present. In addition, the city plans and budget, once convoluted fiscal documents with only summaries available online, are now fully accessible on the city's Web site. Before, a New Yorker could never see a specific agency's overhead costs—its pensions and legal claims, say. The costs were pooled as a single number. Now each agency breaks them out.

HIRE SMART AND DELEGATE

The first thing most politicians do upon winning office is fill top jobs with people to whom they owe their support or who have long-standing ties

(continued)

Exhibit 12.1 cont.

to the political establishment. Bloomberg arrived at City Hall with no such debts. That's partly because he financed his own campaign. But even if he hadn't, Bloomberg says, he still would have recruited his lieutenants based on their ability to set targets and hit them. One of them was Katherine Oliver. Bloomberg had a turnaround mission in mind for her at the city's Office of Film, Theatre & Broadcasting. Oliver was working in London, overseeing Bloomberg global radio and television operations, when she got the call. Her marching orders from the mayor were simple: build a customer-service organization. She wasn't prepared for how much the film office needed modernizing and refocusing. Toronto and Louisiana, among other places, were stealing business from New York. Production companies were required to visit the office and fill out permit applications on paper. And to Oliver's astonishment, the agency had only one computer. Most staff were tapping away on electric typewriters.

Within a month of her arrival, her 22 employees had new Dell flat-screens, and production companies were able to file for permits online. Approvals have since surged to 200 a day, up from 200 a week in 2002. Oliver also put a photo library on the Web site, letting producers scout locations from their desks. She began offering a combined 15 percent tax credit to film and TV productions that complete at least 75 percent of their stage work in the city. Oliver says the program has generated $2.4 billion in new business and 10,000 new jobs since 2005. She offered filmmakers free advertising space on public property. And she set up a dedicated team of 33 police officers to ease shoots in the city.

"We tried to look at this as B to B," says Oliver. "This is a microcosm of what Michael wanted to do for the entire city."

BE BOLD, BE FEARLESS

"A major part of the CEO's responsibilities is to be the ultimate risk-taker and decision-maker. Truman ('The buck stops here') had it right." So wrote Bloomberg in his 1997 autobiography *Bloomberg By Bloomberg*. The mayor has embraced risk with an almost reckless disregard for political repercussions. Sometimes it has worked out: His controversial smoking ban in bars and restaurants is being replicated in other cities. Sometimes it hasn't: in a crushing defeat, he lost the 2012 Olympics bid to London.

Bloomberg recently reflected on the rare setback. "In business, you reward people for taking risks. When it doesn't work out, you promote them because they were willing to try new things. If people come back and tell me they skied all day and never fell down, I tell them to try a different mountain." He adds: "I have always joked that [the difference between] having the courage of your convictions and being pigheaded is in the results."

What has Bloomberg learned as mayor? "The real world, whether in business or government, requires that you don't jump to the endgame [or] to success right away," he says. "You do it piece by piece. Some people get immobilized when they come to a roadblock. My answer is, 'you know, it's a shame it's there, but now where else can we go? Let's just do it.'"

Source: Reprinted with special permission from Tom Lowry, "The CEO Mayor," *BusinessWeek*, June 25, 2007. Copyright © 2007 The McGraw-Hill Companies.

their organizational structure and making it function effectively to accomplish strategic intent. Because leaders are attempting to embrace change, they are often rebuilding or remaking their organization to align it with the ever-changing environment and needs of a new strategy. And because embracing change often involves overcoming resistance to change, leaders find themselves addressing problems such as the following as they attempt to build or rebuild their organization:

- Ensuring a common understanding about organizational priorities.
- Clarifying responsibilities among managers and organizational units.
- Empowering newer managers and pushing authority lower in the organization.

- Uncovering and remedying problems in coordination and communication across the organization and across boundaries inside and outside the organization.
- Gaining the personal commitment to a shared vision from managers throughout the organization.
- Keeping closely connected with what's going on inside and outside the organization and with its customers.

There are three ways good leaders go about building the organization they want and dealing with problems and issues like those listed: education, principles, and perseverance.

Education and **leadership development** is the effort to familiarize future leaders with the skills important to the company and to develop exceptional leaders among the managers you employ. Jack Welch was legendary for the GE education center in Croton-on-Hudson, New York, and its role in allowing the GE leader to educate current and future GE managers on the ways of GE and the vision of its future. It allowed a leader to shape future leaders, thereby building an organization. His successor, Jeff Immelt, uses the same facility to interact with and discuss GE's future with a new crop of future leaders.

Leaders do this in many ways. Larry Bossidy, former chairman of Honeywell and co-author of the best seller, *Execution,* spent 50 percent of his time each year flying to Allied Signal's various operations around the world, meeting with managers and discussing decisions, results, and progress. Bill Gates at Microsoft reportedly spent two hours each day reading and sending e-mail to any of Microsoft's 36,000 employees who want to contact him. All managers adapt structures, create teams, implement systems, and otherwise generate ways to coordinate, integrate, and share information about what their organization is doing and might do. Once again, here is what Jim McNerney had to say:

> It comes down to personal engagement. I spend a lot of time out with our people. I probably do 30 major events a year with 100 people or more, where I spend time debating things and pushing my ideas, telling them what I am thinking and soliciting feedback. Most CEOs are smart enough to figure out where to go with a company. The hard work is engaging everyone in doing it. That's the hard work in leadership.[6]

Others create customer advisory groups, supplier partnerships, R&D joint ventures, and other adjustments to build an adaptable, learning organization that buys into the leader's vision and strategic intent and the change driving the future opportunities facing the business. These, in addition to the fundamental structural guidelines described in the previous chapter for restructuring to support strategically critical activities, are key ways leaders constantly attempt to educate and build a supportive organization.

Principles are your fundamental personal standards that guide your sense of honesty, integrity, and ethical behavior. If you have a clear moral compass guiding your priorities and those you set for the company, you will be a more effective leader. This observation is repeatedly one of the first thing effective leaders interviewed by researchers, business writers, and students mention when they answer a question about what they think is most important in explaining their success as leaders and the success of leaders they admire. Steven Reinemund, PepsiCo's very successful (former) CEO, said it this way:

> It starts with basic beliefs and values. It's important to make clear to the people in the organization what those are, so you're transparent. They have to be consistent with the values of the organization, or there will be a problem. If you look at all the issues that have happened in the corporate world of the last few years, . . . it all boils down to a basic lack of a moral compass and checks and balances among leaders. We as leaders have to check each other. We're going to make mistakes. If we don't check each other on them, you

leadership development
The effort to familiarize future leaders with the skills important to the company and to develop exceptional leaders among the managers employed.

principles (of a leader)
A leader's fundamental personal standards that guide her sense of honesty, integrity and ethical behavior.

[6] Ibid.

get in trouble. Most of the companies that got into trouble had a set of stated principles, but the leaders didn't check each other on those principles.[7]

Principle boils down to a personal philosophy we all deal with at an individual level—choices involving honesty, integrity, ethical behavior. Indeed Exhibit 12.2, Strategy in Action, gives you the chance to "test" *your* personal principles in comparison with the actions of some of your business school peers at Duke university's MBA program, and *BusinessWeek*'s thoughts too. The key thing to remember as a future leader is that your personal philosophies, or choices, manifest themselves exponentially for you or any key leaders of any organization. The people who do the work of any organization watch their leaders and what their leaders do, sanction, or stand for. So do people outside that organization who deal with it. These people then reflect those principles in what they do or come to believe is the way to do things in or with that organization. An effective organization is better built—is stronger—when its leaders show by example what they want their people to do and the principles they want their people to operate by on a day-to-day basis and in making decisions shaped by values and principles—a clear sense of right or wrong. "Values," "Lead by example," "Do as I say AND as I do"—these are very basic notions that good leaders find great strength in using. *BusinessWeek*'s "The Ethics Guy" says simply that principles should boil down to "five easy principles," which are:[8]

1. Do no harm
2. Make things better
3. Respect others
4. Be fair
5. Be compassionate

The value of that kind of clarity, and transparency, as PepsiCo's Reinemund described it, can become a major force by which a leader will shape and move his or her organization.

perseverance (of a leader)

The capacity to see a commitment through to completion long after most people would have stopped trying.

Perseverance is the capacity to see a commitment through to completion long after most people would have stopped trying. The opening example about Jeff Immelt conjures up images of some people in GE being hesitant to follow him because of their longtime loyalty to Jack Welch and his ways. Immelt will need to have patience and perseverance to deal with these people, to help them gradually shift their loyalty and accept the new. The example also conjures up another image, one of people excited to embrace Immelt's effort to take GE in a new direction—just because of the excitement of the moment along with some sense that a change is needed. But imagine that the first signs are not good, that it is unclear whether the radical new approach will work or not. It is relatively easy to then imagine a significant negative shift in the enthusiasm and faith of this group—again, Immelt must call on considerable perseverance to simply continue to bring them along and build their commitment over the long term.

PepsiCo's Reinemund talked about perseverance and says it is "sticking with it through the good and the bad times, mostly the bad." He goes on to credit his predecessor with having the perseverance at PepsiCo to stick with a vision that didn't "take" right away but that has proven to be exactly the vision PepsiCo needed to pursue to create a favorable future.

Shaping Organizational Culture

Leaders know well that the values and beliefs shared throughout their organization will shape how the work of the organization is done. And when attempting to embrace

---

[7] Brady, "The Six Ps."

[8] Bruce Weinstein, "Five Easy Principles," *BusinessWeek,* January 10, 2007.

On April 27, 2007, the dean of Duke's business school had the unfortunate task of announcing that nearly 10 percent of the Class of 2008 had been caught cheating on a take-home final exam. The scandal, which has cast yet another pall over the leafy, Gothic campus, is already going down as the biggest episode of alleged student deception in the business school's history.

Almost immediately, the questions started swirling. The accused MBAs were, on average, 29 years old. They were the cut-and-paste generation, the champions of Linux. Before going to business school, they worked in corporations for an average of six years. They did so at a time when their bosses were trumpeting the brave new world of open source, where one's ability to aggregate (or rip off) other people's intellectual property was touted as a crucial competitive advantage.

It's easy to imagine the explanations these MBAs, who are mulling an appeal, might come up with. Teaming up on a take-home exam: that's not academic fraud, it's postmodern learning, wiki style. Text-messaging exam answers or downloading essays onto iPods: that's simply a wise use of technology.

One can understand the confusion. This is a generation that came of age nabbing music off Napster and watching bootlegged Hollywood blockbusters in their dorm rooms. "What do you mean?" you can almost hear them saying. "We're not supposed to share?"

GO ALONG OR GO SOLO

That's not to say that university administrators should ignore unethical behavior, if it in fact occurred. But in this wired world, maybe the very notion of what constitutes cheating has to be reevaluated. The scandal at Duke points to how much the world has changed, and how academia and corporations are confused about it all, sending split messages.

We're told it's all about teamwork and shared information. But then we're graded and ranked as individuals. We assess everybody as single entities. But then we plop them into an interdependent world and tell them their success hinges on creative collaboration.

The new culture of shared information is vastly different from the old, where hoarding information was power. But professors—and bosses, for that matter—need to be able to test individual ability. For all the talk about workforce teamwork, there are plenty of times when a person is on his or her own, arguing a case, preparing a profit and loss statement, or writing a research report.

Still, many believe that a rethinking of the assessment process is in store. The Stanford University Design School, for example, is so collaborative that "it would be impossible to cheat," says design school professor Robert I. Sutton. "If you found somebody to help you write a group project, in our view that's a sign of an inventive team member who gets stuff done. If you found someone to do work for free who was committed to open source, we'd say, 'Wow, that was smart.' One group of students got the police to help them with a school project to build a roundabout where there were a lot of bike accidents. Is that cheating?"

That's food for thought at a time when learning is becoming more and more of a social process embedded in a larger network. This is in no way a pass on those who consciously break the rules. With countries aping American business practices, a backlash against an ethically rudderless culture can't happen soon enough. But the saga at Duke raises an interesting question: In the age of Twitter, a social network that keeps users in constant streaming contact with one another, what is cheating?

So, what do you think? Is what the Duke MBAs did "cheating," or is it simply collaborative learning as *BusinessWeek* posits?

accelerated change, reshaping their organization's culture is an activity that occupies considerable time for most leaders. Elements of good leadership—vision, performance, principles, perseverance, which have just been described—are important ways leaders shape organizational culture as well. Leaders shape organizational culture through their passion for the enterprise and the selection/development of talented managers to be future leaders. We will examine these two ideas and then cover the notion of organizational culture in greater detail.

**passion
(of a leader)**
A highly motivated sense of commitment to what you do and want to do.

Passion, in a leadership sense, is a highly motivated sense of commitment to what you do and want to do. PepsiCo's Reinemund described it this way:

> I remember when I was a kid, Kennedy made the announcement that he wanted to put a man on the moon and bring him back safely to earth. That was so motivating and passionate. Nobody believed it could happen, but he inspired them to do it with his passion.[9]

Like many other traits of good leaders, passion is best seen through the leaders' intermittent behaviors while in the throws of the challenging times of the organizations they lead. They must use special moments to convey a sincere passion for and delight in the work of the company they lead. These observations by and about Ryanair CEO Michael O'Leary about competing in the increasingly competitive European airline industry and archrival easyJet provide a useful example:

> It was vintage Michael O'Leary. On May 13, the 42-year-old CEO of Dublin-based discount airline Ryanair outfitted his staff in full combat gear, drove an old World War II tank to England's Luton airport, an hour north of London, then demanded access to the base of archrival easyJet Airline Co. With the theme to the old television series *The A-Team* blaring, O'Leary declared he was "liberating the public from easyJet's high fares." When security—surprise!—refused to let the Ryanair armor roll in, O'Leary led the troops in his own rendition of a platoon march song: "I've been told and it's no lie. EasyJet's fares are way too high!" So it is that there are new rivals for O'Leary to conquer. "When we were a much smaller company, we compared ourselves to British Airways. But they are such a mess, most people just feel sorry for them," O'Leary says. "Now we're turning the guns on easyJet."[10]

It was readily apparent to anyone on this scene that O'Leary was passionate about Ryanair, and that example sent a clear message that he wanted an organizational culture that was aggressive, competitive, and somewhat free-wheeling in order to take advantage of change in the European airline industry. He did this by passionate example, by expectations felt by his managers, and in the way decision making is approached within Ryanair.

Sam Walton used to lead cheers at every Wal-Mart store he visited each year before and long after Wal-Mart was an overwhelming success. Kathy Mulhany at Xerox, a 28-year company veteran when she assumed the presidency with Xerox close to bankruptcy, started and continues to travel to every Xerox location worldwide twice annually just to convey her passion for Xerox as a way of rallying veteran Xerox employees to continue to buy into her vision and continue its extraordinary turnaround. GE's Jeff Immelt is described by a board member as a natural salesman who still happily recounts the days when he drove around his territory in a Ford Taurus while at GE Plastics. "He knows the world looks to GE as a harbinger of future trends," says Ogilvy & Mather Worldwide CEO Rochelle Lazarus, who sits on the board. "He really feels GE has a responsibility to the world to get out in front and play a leadership role." Immelt, it would seem, is passionate about GE and its future opportunities. Indeed, at the most recent gathering of GE's top 650 executives, amidst a situation where GE stock price is down 20 percent from last year, Immelt insisted that "there's never been a better day, a better time, or a better place to be," meaning than GE. That's passion.

Leaders also use reward systems, symbols, and structure among other means to shape the organization's culture. Travelers' Insurance Co.'s notable turnaround was accomplished in part by changing its "hidebound" culture through a change in its agent reward system. Employees previously on salary with occasional bonuses were given rewards that involved substantial cash bonuses and stock options. A major Travelers' customer and risk management director at drug-maker Becton Dickinson said: "They're hungrier now. They want to make deals. They're different than the old, hidebound Travelers' culture." Jeff Immelt is doing something similar to reshape the ingrained GE culture—tying executive compensation

---

[9] Ibid.

[10] "Ryanair Rising," *BusinessWeek*, June 2, 2003.

to their ability to come up with new ideas that show improved customer service, generate cash growth, and boost sales instead of simply meeting bottom-line targets.[11]

As leaders clarify strategic intent, build an organization, and shape their organization's culture, they look to one key element to help—their management team throughout their organization. As Honeywell's chairman Larry Bossidy candidly observed when asked about how after 42 years at General Electric, Allied Signal, and now Honeywell, with seemingly drab businesses, he could expect exciting growth: "There's no such thing as a mature market. What we need is mature executives who can find ways to grow."[12] Leaders look to managers they need to execute strategy as another source of leadership to accept risk and cope with the complexity that change brings about. So selection and development of key managers become major leadership roles.

Recruiting and Developing Talented Operational Leadership

As we noted at the beginning of this section on organizational leadership, the accelerated pace and complexity of business will increase pressure on corporations to push authority down in their organizations, ultimately meaning that every line manager will have to exercise leadership's prerogatives to an extent unthinkable a generation earlier. We also defined one of the key roles of good organizational leadership as building the organization by educating and developing new leaders. They will each be global managers, change agents, strategists, motivators, strategic decision makers, innovators, and collaborators if the business is to survive and prosper. So we want to examine this more completely by looking at key competencies these future managers need to possess or develop. Exhibit 12.3, Strategy in Action, provides an interesting perspective on this reality showing IBM's use of Internet-based, three-dimensional (3D) games to train and develop future global leaders in today's fast-paced, global marketplace.

Today's need for fluid learning organizations capable of rapid response, sharing, and cross-cultural synergy place incredible demands on young managers to bring important competencies to the organization. Exhibit 12.4 describes the needs organizations look to managers to meet and then identifies the corresponding competencies managers would need to do so. Ruth Williams and Joseph Cothrel drew this conclusion in their research about competencies needed from managers in today's fast-changing business environment.

> Today's competitive environment requires a different set of management competencies than we traditionally associate with the role. The balance has clearly shifted from attributes traditionally thought of as masculine (strong decision making, leading the troops, driving strategy, waging competitive battle) to more feminine qualities (listening, relationship-building, and nurturing). The model today is not so much "take it on your shoulders" as it is to "create the environment that will enable others to carry part of the burden." The focus is on unlocking the organization's human asset potential.[13]

Researcher David Goleman addressed the question of what types of personality attributes generate the type of competencies described in Exhibit 12.4. His research suggested that a set of four characteristics commonly referred to as emotional intelligence play a key role in bringing the competencies needed from today's desirable manager:[14]

- *Self-awareness* in terms of the ability to read and understand one's emotions and assess one's strengths and weaknesses, underlain by the confidence that stems from positive self-worth.

- *Self-management* in terms of control, integrity, conscientiousness, initiative, and achievement orientation.

---

[11] Howard Gleckman, "A Golden Opportunity," *BusinessWeek Online,* March 29, 2003.

[12] Diane Brady, "The Immelt Revolution," *BusinessWeek Online,* October 18, 2005.

[13] Ruth Williams and Joseph Cothrel, *Current Trends in Strategic Management* (New York: Blackwell Publishing, 2007).

[14] D. Goleman "What Makes a Leader?" *Harvard Business Review* (November–December 1998), pp. 93–102.

IBM's Management Games

BusinessWeek

Thunder crashes, lightning flashes, and a camera zooms in on a shadowy, futuristic-looking, gray-and-black office. The camera follows a female avatar in slacks and a button-down shirt as she jogs from one cubicle to the next, up a spiral staircase, and across a high gangplank as dramatic classical music plays in the background. This YouTube trailer could easily be a plug for a new shoot-'em-up video game, or a slasher flick. Instead, it's promoting a video game called Innov8, which IBM will start selling in September 2007.

Yes, IBM. The computer giant says it received dozens of calls from potential customers after showing the video clip at a recent conference for clients. Designed to help tech managers better understand the roles of businesspeople, and vice versa, players go into a virtual business unit to test their hand at ventures such as redesigning a call center, opening a brokerage account, or processing an insurance claim.

WAR OF THE WORLDS

The game will be available free of charge to universities around the world. No price has been set yet for corporate customers because it will depend on how much IBM has to change the game to accommodate a particular business process a client might want to improve. The game will be available online and will also be able to run on standalone PCs.

Innov8 is only one of several initiatives afoot at Big Blue to incorporate features of online games into business. IBM recently launched an internal competition,

dubbed "War of the Worlds," to encourage employees to, for instance, start virtual businesses or meet with real clients through a slew of online games. Each member of the winning team will receive a Nintendo Wii. The company hopes to use the exercise to determine which virtual ventures are best for specific business tasks or processes.

Why is one of the world's most buttoned-down organizations encouraging its people—and customers—to play games? IBM says that the skills honed playing massive multiplayer dragon-slaying games like "World of Warcraft" can be useful when managing modern multinationals. The company says its research supports that claim and it will release its findings the same day as its War of the Worlds contest.

DEVELOPING LEADERSHIP

While IBM's research may be aimed at helping to build its own consulting business, it comes at a time when there's a flurry of corporate experimentation in games. McKinsey & Co. is using video games to test recruits for leadership potential and assess their team-building style. Royal Philips Electronics and Johnson & Johnson, meanwhile, are using multiplayer games to improve collaboration between far-flung divisions, as well as between managers and their overseas underlings.

What distinguishes the latest corporate forays into the gaming world is the degree to which companies are tapping virtual environments to hone the leadership skills of their workers. By 2011, 80 percent

---

position power
The ability and right to influence and direct others based on the power associated with your formal position in the organization.

reward power
The ability to influence and direct others that comes from being able to confer rewards in return for desired actions or outcomes.

- *Social awareness* in relation to sensing others' emotions (empathy), reading the organization (organizational awareness), and recognizing customers' needs (service orientation).
- *Social skills* in relation to influencing and inspiring others; communicating, collaborating, and building relationships with others; and managing change and conflict.

A key way these characteristics manifest themselves in a manager's routine activities is found in the way they seek to get the work of their unit or group done over time. How do they use power and influence to get others to get things done? Effective leaders seek to develop managers who understand they have many sources of power and influence, and that relying on the power associated with their position in an organization is often the least effective means to influence people to do what is needed. Managers have available seven sources of power and influence (see Exhibit 12.5).

Organizational sources of power are derived from a manager's role in the organization. **Position power** is formally established based on the manager's position in the organization. By virtue of holding that position, certain decision-making authorities and responsibilities of Internet users will have avatars, or digital versions of themselves, for work and play, according to market researcher Gartner. By the end of 2012, half of all U.S. companies will also have digital offices or "networked virtual environments," adds Gartner. The online game world will become an important place to hold meetings, orient new hires, and communicate across the globe.

For IBM's new research, the computer giant tracked the leadership qualities of gamers with the help of Seriosity (a company that develops enterprise software inspired by multiplayer games), Stanford, and the Massachusetts Institute of Technology (MIT). IBM also surveyed more than 200 game-playing managers at the company over a seven-month period. Besides IBM, there are several others, such as Joi Ito, a tech entrepreneur, looking at how managing fast-expanding "guilds," or teams, in multiplayer games provides a forum for trying out different corporate management styles.

MANAGEMENT FLIGHT SIMULATORS

The IBM researchers found that those who are deeply immersed in online worlds that link millions of players, such as "World of Warcraft," were ideally suited to manage in the new millennium. They were particularly savvy at gathering information from far-flung sources, determining strategic risks, failing fast, and moving on to the next challenge quickly. "If you want to see what business leadership will look like in three to five years, look at what's happening in online games," says Byron

Reeves, a Stanford University communications professor and co-founder of Seriosity.

One of the key findings from the research, says Thomas Malone, an MIT professor of management and Seriosity board member, is that companies need to create more opportunities for flexible, project-oriented leadership. In fast-paced games, people can jump in to manage a team for as little as 10 minutes, if they have the needed skills for the task at hand. "Games make leaders from lemmings," says Tony O'Driscoll, an IBM learning strategist and one of the authors of the study. "Since leadership happens quickly and easily in online games, otherwise reserved players are more likely to try on leadership roles."

The study points out that games can become "management flight simulators" of sorts, letting employees manage a global workforce in cyberspace before they do so in the real world. More than half of the managers surveyed say playing massive multiplayer games had helped them lead at work. Three-quarters of those surveyed believed that specific game tools, such as expressive avatars that can communicate via body language, as well as by voice and typing, would help manage remote employees in the real world.

Source: Reprinted with special permission from Ali McCannon, "IBM's Management Games," *BusinessWeek*, June 14, 2007. Copyright © 2007 The McGraw-Hill Companies.

information power
The ability to influence others based on your access to information and your control of dissemination of information that is important to subordinates and others yet not otherwise easily obtained.

punitive power
Ability to direct and influence others based on your ability to coerce and deliver punishment for mistakes or undesired actions by others, particularly subordinates.

are conferred that the manager is entitled to use to get things done. It is the source of power many new managers expect to be able to rely on, but often the least useful. **Reward power** is available when the manager confers rewards in return for desired actions and outcomes. This is often a power source. **Information power** can be particularly effective and is derived from a manager's access to and control over the dissemination of information that is important to subordinates yet not easily available in the organization. **Punitive power** is the power exercised via coercion or fear of punishment for mistakes or undesired actions by a manager's subordinates.

Leaders today increasingly rely on their personal ability to influence others perhaps as much, if not more so, than organizational sources of power. Personal influence, a form of "power," comes mainly from three sources. **Expert influence** is derived from a leader's knowledge and expertise in a particular area or situation. This can be a very important source of power in influencing others. **Referent influence** comes from having others want to identify with the leader. We have all seen or worked for leaders who have major influence over others based simply on their charisma, personality, empathy, and other personal

EXHIBIT 12.4
What Competencies Should Managers Possess?

Source: Ruth L. Williams and Joseph P. Cothrel, "Building Tomorrow's Leaders Today," *Strategy and Leadership* 26, October 1997. Reprinted with permission of Emerald Group Publishing Limited.

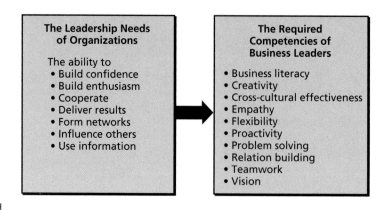

The Leadership Needs of Organizations

The ability to
- Build confidence
- Build enthusiasm
- Cooperate
- Deliver results
- Form networks
- Influence others
- Use information

The Required Competencies of Business Leaders
- Business literacy
- Creativity
- Cross-cultural effectiveness
- Empathy
- Flexibility
- Proactivity
- Problem solving
- Relation building
- Teamwork
- Vision

expert influence
The ability to direct and influence others because they defer to you based on your expertise or specialized knowledge that is related to the task, undertaking, or assignment in which they are involved.

referent influence
The ability to influence others derived from their strong desire to be associated with you, usually because they admire you, gain prestige or a sense of purpose by that association, or believe in your motivations.

peer influence
The ability to influence individual behavior among members of a group based on group norms, a group sense of what is the right thing or right way to do things, and the need to be valued and accepted by the group.

attributes. And finally, **peer influence** can be a very effective way for leaders to influence the behavior of others. Most people in organizations and across an organization find themselves put in groups to solve problems, serve customers, develop innovations, and perform a host of other tasks. Leaders can use the assignment of team members and the charge to the team as a way to enable peer-based influence to work on key managers and the outcomes they produce.

Effective leaders make use of all seven sources of power and influence, very often in combination, to deal with the myriad situations they face and need others to handle. The exact best source(s) of power and influence are often shaped by the nature of the task, project, urgency of an assignment, or the unique characteristics of specific personnel, among myriad factors. Organizational leaders such as Jeff Immelt at GE draw on all these sources and, equally important, seek to develop their organizations around subordinate leaders and managers who insightfully and effectively make use of all their sources of power and influence.

One final perspective on the role of organizational leadership and management selection is found in the work of Bartlett and Ghoshal. Their study of several of the most successful global companies in the last decade suggests that combining flexible responsiveness with integration and innovation requires rethinking the management role and the distribution of management roles within a twenty-first-century company. They see three critical management roles: the *entrepreneurial process* (decisions about opportunities to pursue and resource deployment), the *integration process* (building and deploying organizational capabilities), and the *renewal process* (shaping organizational purpose and enabling change). Traditionally viewed as the domain of top management, their research suggests that these functions need to be shared and distributed across three management levels as suggested in Exhibit 12.6.[15]

ORGANIZATIONAL CULTURE

organizational culture
The set of important assumptions and beliefs (often unstated) that members of an organization share in common.

Organizational culture is the set of important assumptions (often unstated) that members of an organization share in common. Every organization has its own culture. An organization's culture is similar to an individual's personality—an intangible yet ever-present theme that provides meaning, direction, and the basis for action. In much the same way as personality influences the behavior of an individual, the shared assumptions

---

[15] C. A. Barlett and S. Ghoshal, "The Myth of the General Manager: New Personal Competencies for New Management Roles," *California Management Review* 40 (Fall 1997), pp. 92–116; "Beyond Structure to Process," *Harvard Business Review* (January–February 1995).

EXHIBIT 12.5
Sources of Power and Influence

Organizational Power	Personal Influence
Position power	Expert influence
Reward power	Referent influence
Information power	Peer influence
Punitive power	

(beliefs and values) among a firm's members influence opinions and actions within that firm. Exhibit 12.7, Strategy in Action, shows the results of a *BusinessWeek* survey conducted by Staffing.org to identify how employees view their company's culture in the context of various TV shows or cartoon characters.

A member of an organization can simply be aware of the organization's beliefs and values without sharing them in a personally significant way. Those beliefs and values have more personal meaning if the member views them as a guide to appropriate behavior in the organization and, therefore, complies with them. The member becomes fundamentally committed to the beliefs and values when he or she internalizes them; that is, comes to hold them as personal beliefs and values. In this case, the corresponding behavior is *intrinsically rewarding* for the member—the member derives personal satisfaction from his or her actions in the organization because those actions are congruent with corresponding personal beliefs and values. *Assumptions become shared assumptions through internalization among an organization's individual members.* And those shared, internalized beliefs and values shape the content and account for the strength of an organization's culture.

The Role of the Organizational Leader in Organizational Culture

The previous section of this chapter covered organizational leadership in detail. Part of that coverage discussed the role of the organizational leader in shaping organizational culture. Several points in that discussion apply here. We will not repeat them, but it is important to emphasize that the leader and the culture of the organization s/he leads are inextricably intertwined. The leader is the standard bearer, the personification, the ongoing embodiment of the culture (Steve Jobs, Jeff Immelt) or the new example (Alan Mulally, Mike Bloomberg) of what it should become. As such, several of the aspects of what a leader does or should do represent influences on the organization's culture, either to reinforce it or to exemplify the standards and nature of what it needs to become. How the leader behaves and emphasizes those aspects of being a leader become what all the organization sees are "the important things to do and value."

Build Time in the Organization

Some leaders have been with the organization for a long time. If they have been in the leader role for an extended time, then their association with the organization is usually strongly entrenched. They continue to reinforce the current culture, are empowered by it, and understandably go to considerable lengths to reinforce it as a key element in sustaining continued success. The problematic long-time leaders are those who have built a successful enterprise that also sustains a culture that appears unethical or worse. Exhibit 12.8, Strategy in Action, describes just such a situation at AIG. Either type of long-time leader is often a widely known figure in today's media-intense business world. And in their setting, while the culture may be exceptionally strong, their role in creating it usually means they seemingly hold sway over the culture rather than the other way around.

Many leaders in recent years, and inevitably in any organization, are new to the top post of the organization. Their relationship with the organization's culture is perhaps more complex. Those who built a management career within that culture—Jeff Immelt at GE, Anne Mulcahy at Xerox, Alan Lafley at P&G—have the benefit of knowledge of the culture and credibility

EXHIBIT 12.6

Management Processes and Levels of Management

Sources: C. A. Bartlett and S. Ghoshal, "The Myth of the General Manager: New Personal Competencies for New Management Roles," *California Management Review* 40 (Fall, 1997); R. M. Grant, *Contemporary Strategy Analysis* (Oxford: Blackwell, 2001), p. 529.

Front-Line Management	Middle Management	Top Management
Attracting resources and capabilities and developing the business	**RENEWAL PROCESS** Developing operating managers and supporting their activities; maintaining organizational trust	Providing institutional leadership through shaping and embedding corporate purpose and challenging embedded assumptions
Managing operational interdependencies and personal networks	**INTEGRATION PROCESS** Linking skills, knowledge, and resources across units; reconciling short-term performance and long-term ambition	Creating corporate direction; developing and nurturing organizational values
Creating and pursuing opportunities; managing continuous performance improvement	**ENTREPRENEURIAL PROCESS** Reviewing, developing, and supporting initiatives	Establishing performance standards

as an "initiated" member of that culture. This may be quite useful in helping engender confidence as they take on the task of leader of that culture or, perhaps more difficult (as with these three), as change agent for parts of that culture as the company moves forward.

In the other situation, a new leader who is not an "initiated" member of the culture or tribe faces a much more challenging task. Quite logically, they must earn credibility with the "tribe," which is usually somewhat resistant to change. And, very often, they are being brought in with a board of directors desiring change in the strategy, company, and usually culture. That becomes a substantial challenge for these new leaders to face. Some make it happen, others find the strength of the organization's culture far more powerful than their ability to change it.

Exhibit 12.9, Strategy in Action, provides an interesting example of these two perspectives as viewed through the experience of the same founder/CEO of successful companies with two very different cultures. It explains how Netflix founder and CEO Reed Hastings sought to dramatically change the culture and way of doing things at Netflix, his second company, after his experience with the nature of the culture that his first start-up, Pure Software, grew into as it became a part of IBM through a series of acquisitions and mergers. Hastings said of Pure, "We got more bureaucratic as we grew," and that it went from being a place that was fast-paced and the "where-everybody-wanted-to-be" place to a "dronish, when-does-the-day-end" software factory. After leaving Pure, Hastings spent about two years thinking about how to build a culture in his next start-up that would not have "big company creep."

At Netflix, Hastings has instilled a very unique "freedom and responsibility" culture that seeks to revolutionize both the way people rent movies and, perhaps more important to Hastings, how his managers work. In the face of Blockbuster, Wal-Mart, Amazon, the cable companies, and Apple, Hastings is attempting to create a culture so unique at Netflix that it is an "A" talent magnet, ensuring the best players in the business line up to help Netflix outsmart these very sizable competitors. And in doing so, Hastings is a "new" leader of a new company with a different business model that is trying to outlast and outcompete other, well established, major players in selling movie rentals. So in a sense, Hastings is a new leader, but with solid experience as a successful entrepreneur and innovator in similarly competitive, large, firmly entrenched, industry niches.

It may suggest that one way new leaders coming to established cultures can improve their chances of succeeding (where changing that culture is desired) is if they bring a similar background such that they establish credibility quicker, lower resistance easier, or simply

What Is Your Workplace Culture Most Like?

THE BIG PICTURE

THINK YOUR WORKPLACE is like a sitcom? In an online survey, Staffing.org, a performance research firm, asked 300 people to describe their company's culture using one of four fictional touchstones. The results:

"A lot like *The Office*" 57%	"More like *Dilbert* than I'd like to admit" 24%	"*M*A*S*H*, on a good day" 14%	"Like *Leave It to Beaver*" 5%

Source: Reprinted with special permission from "The Big Picture," *BusinessWeek*, May 25, 2007. Copyright © 2007 The McGraw-Hill Companies.

have a better basis for understanding the situation. At the same time, examples such as former R. J. Reynolds executive Lou Gerstner, who took over and pulled a declining IBM from the ashes, suggest that it can also be done if you come from an entirely different industry. So it may be that the skills of the leader and other relevant experience in the strategic dynamics at previous assignments are both critical to new leaders facing established cultures they must change.

ethical standards
A person's basis for differentiating right from wrong.

Ethical standards are a person's basis for differentiating right from wrong. An earlier section of this chapter emphasized the importance of "principles" in defining what a leader needs to incorporate in his or her recipe to become an effective leader. We need not repeat those points in the context of being a leader, but it is critical to recognize that the culture of an organization, and particularly the link between the leader and the culture's very nature, is inextricably tied to the ethical standards of behavior, actions, decisions, and norms that leader personifies. Enron, WorldCom, Qwest, Computer Associates, Ken Lay, Jeff Skillings, Sanjay Kumar, Joseph Nacchio, Bernie Ebbers, and Martha Stewart are companies, people, and situations we discussed in Chapter 3—they are all imprinted in each of our minds (see Exhibit 12.10, Strategy in Action). They speak volumes about this very point: Leaders, and their key associates, play a key role in shaping and defining the ethical standards that become absorbed into and shape the culture of the organizations they lead. Those ethical standards then become powerful, informal guidelines for the behaviors, decisions, and dealings of members of that culture or tribe. Exhibit 12.8 provided an example of where ethical standards shape culture and the challenges they present to insurance giant AIG's new CEO, Martin Sullivan, when the culture was led by a leader whose standards were rather unethical. An interesting question to ask yourself when you read the Exhibit 12.8 example is whether or not Martin Sullivan, in your opinion, is the right person to lead AIG toward a new culture and, if so, what the best relationship between AIG and Mr. Greenberg should be.

Searching for a New Culture, Even Though Business Is Great!

BusinessWeek

Wall Street cheered Martin Sullivan in late 2007: "AIG has emerged from a tumultuous period as a stronger, more disciplined, and more transparent company," Bank of America analyst Tamara Kravec said in a research note. "With the issue of regulatory settlement behind the company, we believe investors can now focus on improving fundamentals across AIG's businesses, particularly in its foreign life operations." Kravec made AIG Bank of America's top pick in financial services for 2007. Just a few years ago, Sullivan's cheers were few. The company he assumed leadership of had to change. And the problem wasn't its profitable, core business.

Instead, the problem was the archaic style and opaque business practices of Sullivan's former boss, the legendary Maurice R. "Hank" Greenberg, who resigned under pressure. For almost 40 years, no one challenged Greenberg's iron rule. While the 79-year-old chairman, president, and CEO delivered great results, he was frequently bellicose, known to yell at staffers with such intensity that at least one insider jokingly compared his tenure to a reign of terror. More significant, he was slow to embrace efforts to improve corporate governance, even characterizing the expenses of the Sarbanes-Oxley law as "an enormous burden."

Sullivan, 50, a witty charmer who eschews his predecessor's confrontational style, promised to cooperate fully with regulators. While the findings of the latest investigation were yet to be determined, they raised concerns about whether AIG may have used techniques to elevate results in the past, especially given its record of consistently outperforming industry peers.

A far harder job for Sullivan: yanking this mystery-shrouded organization's culture into the twenty-first century by pushing for greater transparency and a stronger board. About half of the AIG board was independent, and the company strengthened that contingent with the addition of former Merrill Lynch executive Stephen L. Hammerman. But investors like the AFL-CIO preferred to see a two-thirds majority of truly independent directors.

One item that Sullivan was expected to place high on his agenda: breaking down two little-known Byzantine private entities, Starr International and C.V. Starr & Co. These companies, which held shares in AIG, seemed to do little more than grossly enrich senior executives. Starr International, in which Greenberg still held a directorship, was much like a private partnership used to compensate senior managers. Getting a stake equates with winning entrance to an elite club. C.V. Starr & Co. was essentially a broker that did business with AIG. Several of its board members were also senior AIG executives, including Greenberg and Sullivan. Both entities stayed largely immune from public scrutiny but had drawn the ire of shareholders and regulators alike.

Last but not least: Sullivan was encouraged to speed up the exit of Greenberg, who sought to stay on as nonexecutive chairman and, within the private entities, exert enormous control. Having him hang around would make it tougher to speed through reform and restore the confidence of investors.

Sullivan inherited a strong global franchise, but he also headed a company that bears the stamp of Greenberg, a brilliant but tone-deaf autocrat who continued to complain about increased regulation even as AIG was immersed in scandal. Says Patrick McGurn, of Institutional Shareholder Services: "Was there a reform he ever put in place that he liked?" Investors' hope that Sullivan would embrace the reforms needed to bring AIG and its culture into the twenty-first century was eventually rewarded, and AIG is now in Wall Street's good graces.

Sources: Reprinted with special permission from "Investors Cheer AIG Results," *BusinessWeek*, March 2, 2007; and Diane Brady, "AIG Needs New Policies," *BusinessWeek*, March 17, 2005. Copyright © 2005 The McGraw-Hill Companies.

Leaders use every means available to them as an organizational leader to influence an organization's culture and their relationship with it. It bears repeating in this regard that reward systems, assignment of new managers from within versus outside the organization, composition of the firm's board of directors, reporting relationships, and organizational structure—each of these fundamental elements of executing a company's vision and strategy are also a leader's key "levers" for attempting to shape organizational culture in a direction she or he sees it needing to go. Because we have already discussed these levers, we move on to other ways leaders have sought to shape and reinforce their organization's culture.

Netflix Builds a Revolutionary, Unique Culture

BusinessWeek

I had the great fortune of doing a mediocre job at my first company," says Netflix Inc. founder Reed Hastings. He's talking about his 1990s start-up Pure Software, a wildly successful maker of debugging programs that, through a series of mergers, became part of IBM. Hastings says Pure, like many other outfits, went from being a heat-filled, everybody-wants-to-be-here place to a dronish, when-does-the-day-end sausage factory. "We got more bureaucratic as we grew," says Hastings.

After Pure, the Stanford-trained engineer spent two years thinking about how to ensure his next endeavor wouldn't suffer the same big-company creep.

The resulting sequel is Netflix, where Hastings is trying to revolutionize not only the way people rent movies but also how his managers work. Hastings pays his people lavishly, gives them unlimited vacations, and lets them structure their own compensation packages. In return, he expects ultra-high performance. His 400 salaried employees are expected to do the jobs of three or four people. Netflix is no frat party with beer bashes and foosball tables. Nor does the company want to play cruise director to its employees. Rather, Netflix is a tough, fulfilling, "fully formed adult" culture, says marketing manager Heather McIlhany. "There's no place to hide at Netflix."

Hastings calls his approach "freedom and responsibility." And as one might expect, employees get all cinematic when describing the vibe. Netflix is the workplace equivalent of *Ocean's 11*, says Todd S. Yellin, hired to perfect the site's movie-rating system. Hastings is Danny Ocean, the bright, charismatic leader who recruits the best in class, gives them a generous cut, and provides the flexibility to do what they *do best*, all while uniting them on a focused goal. The near-impossible mission, in this case, is trying to outmaneuver Blockbuster, Amazon, the cable companies, and Apple in the race to become the leading purveyor of online movies.

The tension has never been higher. Last quarter, for the first time in Netflix's history, the company lost customers in its bloody, fight-to-the-death battle with Blockbuster Inc. Netflix shares cratered and have yet to recover. Some analysts are talking doom.

Netflix executives like to point out, though, that the company has been pronounced dead more than once before. When Wal-Mart started offering online movie rentals in 2002, for example, analysts started referring to Netflix as *The Last Picture Show*. But by 2005, Wal-Mart had closed shop. It referred all its customers to Netflix.

Today, Netflix is embroiled in an even tougher, two-front war: competing with Blockbuster for online supremacy in DVD rentals while also inaugurating a digital streaming service to compete with the likes of Apple. That's one mighty gang of entrenched competitors. "There's usually room in a marketplace for more than one," says Wedbush Morgan Securities analyst Michael Pachter. "But in this case there really isn't."

Hastings is betting on Netflix's *culture* to get the company out of this corner. The plan includes continuing to increase what Hastings calls "talent density." Most companies go to great scientific lengths to ensure they are paying just enough to attract talent but not a dollar more than they need to. Netflix, which hands out salaries that are typically much higher than what is customary in Silicon Valley, is unabashed in its we-pay-above-market swagger. "We're unafraid to pay high," says Hastings.

To ensure that the company is constantly nabbing A players, company talent hunters are told that money is no object. Each business group has what amounts to an internal boutique headhunting firm. Employees often recommend people they bonded with at work before (that *Ocean's 11* effect again).

Gibson Biddle, who runs the Web site, knew that Yellin, who had both deep tech and film expertise, was the perfect guy to help Netflix improve how it recommends movies to customers on its site. Yellin had worked for Biddle at a family entertainment site during the boom. The snag was that Yellin, also a filmmaker, was finishing up his first feature film, *Brother's Shadow,* in Los Angeles. He also was allergic to anything corporate or publicly traded.

Impossible sell, right? But Netflix threw so much cash and flexibility at Yellin that he couldn't turn it down. During his first three months he flew back and forth between L.A. and San Francisco doing his Netflix job and finishing his movie. "This company is *über*-flexible," says Yellin. "I'm given the freedom to do what I do well without being micromanaged."

NO GOLDEN HANDCUFFS

Pay is not tied to performance reviews, nor to some predetermined raise pool, but to the job market. Netflix bosses are constantly gleaning market compensation data from new hires and then amping up salaries when needed. And what happens when someone doesn't live up to expectations? "At most companies, average

(continued)

Exhibit 12.9 cont.

BusinessWeek

performers get an average raise," says Hastings. "At Netflix, they get a generous severance package." Why? Because Hastings believes that otherwise managers feel too guilty to let someone go.

When it comes to paychecks, Netflix is arguably going where no public company has gone before. Employees are free to choose annually how much of their compensation they want in cash versus stock. Unlike the case at most companies, options vest immediately. Netflix doesn't want golden-handcuffs types. One engineer got so excited that he told human resources head Patty McCord to give him half his pay in stock. When McCord saw him drive away in an old minivan, she wasn't surprised when he popped into her office the next day and told her he wanted to make it more cash: 80–20.

Good thing for him. With great choice comes great risk. Netflix employees who loaded up on stock this year have gotten hammered, leaving some to pine for the paternalism that has long shielded employees from the vagaries of stock market volatility. But great risk also means great freedom, as in: "Take as much vacation as you want." Last year, engineering manager Aroon Ramadoss took off five weeks to go to Europe with his girlfriend. He plans on taking another extended vacation next year in Brazil. "I like to travel in bigger chunks rather than take five days off and rush right back," says Ramadoss.

Source: Reprinted with special permission from "Netflix Flees to the Max," *BusinessWeek*, September 24, 2007. Copyright © 2007 The McGraw-Hill Companies.

Emphasize Key Themes or Dominant Values

Businesses build strategies around distinct competitive advantages they possess or seek. Quality, differentiation, cost advantages, and speed are four key sources of competitive advantage. Insightful leaders nurture key themes or dominant values within their organization that reinforce competitive advantages they seek to maintain or build. Key themes or dominant values may center around wording in an advertisement. They are often found in internal company communications. They are most often found as a new vocabulary used by company personnel to explain "who we are." At Xerox, the key themes include respect for the individual and services to the customer. At Procter & Gamble (P&G), the overarching value is product quality; McDonald's uncompromising emphasis on QSCV—quality, service, cleanliness, and value—through meticulous attention to detail is legendary; Southwest Airlines is driven by the "family feeling" theme, which builds a team spirit and nurtures each employee's cooperative attitude toward others, cheerful outlook toward life, and pride in a job well done. Du Pont's safety orientation—a report of every accident must be on the chairman's desk within 24 hours—has resulted in a safety record that was 27 times better than the chemical industry average and 68 times better than the all-manufacturing average.

Encourage Dissemination of Stories and Legends about Core Values

Companies with strong cultures are enthusiastic collectors and tellers of stories, anecdotes, and legends in support of basic beliefs. Frito-Lay's zealous emphasis on customer service is reflected in frequent stories about potato chip route salespeople who have slogged through sleet, mud, hail, snow, and rain to uphold the 99.5 percent service level to customers in which the entire company takes great pride. Milliken (a textile leader) holds "sharing" rallies once every quarter at which teams from all over the company swap success stories and ideas. Typically, more than 100 teams make five-minute presentations over a two-day period. Every rally is designed around a major theme, such as quality, cost reduction, or customer service. No criticisms are allowed, and awards are given to reinforce this

CEOs as Founders, Felons, Convicted of Fraud, Conspiracy, and Securities Violations

BusinessWeek

The "I-knew-nothing-about-the-books" defense failed to persuade juries. "This is absolutely going to raise the level of expectation that CEOs should know everything that's going on inside their companies, because they will be held responsible for it," says Dan Reingold, a CSFB analyst. The collapse of WorldCom, Enron, and significant damage to Qwest, Computer Associates, and Martha Stewart OmniMedia have profoundly affected the business climate in the United States. They were major reasons lawmakers passed the Sarbanes-Oxley Act. Five important lessons can be gleaned from the testimony in their trials for investors, business school students, and aspiring execs alike:

1. **Beware of companies with cult-like corporate cultures.**

   From the start, most of these companies functioned more like a tribe than a business. Their operations centered around a charismatic leader, who also had a close relationship with the company's chief financial officer. Together, they exercised unquestioned authority and demanded unquestioned loyalty from employees.

   Company stock was imbued with enormous symbolism. Each employee received a grant of stock, a form of initiation into the tribe. But the culture created by these key leaders often prevented them from selling the stock, lest the employees be ostracized from the group.

2. **Beware of too much corporate reliance on Washington.**

   WorldCom, Qwest, Enron, and other companies, spent an enormous amount of time and energy lobbying regulators and elected officials. The telecom boom led by WorldCom was driven mostly by the government-ordered breakup of AT&T in 1984 and the Telecom Act of 1996. WorldCom, Qwest, and Enron benefited from rules that helped it compete. But when the rules unexpectedly changed, it found itself in trouble, ultimately pulling out of the consumer market.

3. **Beware of companies that rely too heavily on mergers and acquisitions.**

   There's no question that M&A is a legitimate means of growth for many companies. But when a corporation bases its business plan on aggressively acquiring companies (e.g., WorldCom did nearly 70 deals in less than five years), that's a flashing yellow light. It's a strong signal that the other engines of growth, such as product development, sales, and marketing, aren't very strong. The constant write-offs of good will, which reflects the premium that an acquiring company pays on a purchase, distorts quarterly earnings and can lead to confusion. If it is too good, it just may be.

4. **Beware of close personal ties between management and the board.**

   Most of the directors in these companies had been with the company for years. Many of them invested in the company at the founding, or led companies that were subsequently acquired. All of them received significant amounts of stock and in some cases enjoyed perks like the use of corporate jets. Yes, their share values dropped, too, like everyone else's, when the companies hit the skids, and there's no suggestion that any were aware of fraud. Still, close ties didn't help those boards when it came to asking tough questions about their company's accounting, or probing the wisdom of a CEO's strategy, or offering hundreds of millions of dollars in loans to CEOs who are also their personal benefactors.

5. **The biggest lesson.**

   The most haunting of them all, is the image of each executive sitting in an old courtroom, stoically contemplating his or her fate before the jury returned its verdict. It's no place you want to be!

Sources: Reprinted with special permission from "Cornered in the Corner Office," *BusinessWeek*, June 25, 2007; "Corporate Justice," December 18, 2006; and Steven Rosenbush, "Five Lessons of the WorldCom Debacle," *BusinessWeek Online*, March 16, 2005. Copyright © 2007 The McGraw-Hill Companies.

institutionalized approach to storytelling. L. L. Bean tells customer service stories; 3M tells innovation stories; P&G, Johnson & Johnson, IBM, and Maytag tell quality and innovation stories. These stories are very important in developing an organizational culture, because organization members identify strongly with them and come to share the beliefs and values they support.

Institutionalize Practices That Systematically Reinforce Desired Beliefs and Values

Companies with strong cultures are clear on what their beliefs and values need to be and take the process of shaping those beliefs and values very seriously. Most important, the values espoused by these companies underlay the strategies they employ. For example, McDonald's has a yearly contest to determine the best hamburger cooker in its chain. First, there is a competition to determine the best hamburger cooker in each store; next, the store winners compete in regional championships; finally, the regional winners compete in the "All-American" contest. The winners, who are widely publicized throughout the company, get trophies and All-American patches to wear on their McDonald's uniforms.

Adapt Some Very Common Themes in Their Own Unique Ways

The most typical beliefs that shape organizational culture include (1) a belief in being the best (or, as at GE, "better than the best"); (2) a belief in superior quality and service; (3) a belief in the importance of people as individuals and a faith in their ability to make a strong contribution; (4) a belief in the importance of the details of execution, the nuts and bolts of doing the job well; (5) a belief that customers should reign supreme; (6) a belief in inspiring people to do their best, whatever their ability; (7) a belief in the importance of informal communication; and (8) a belief that growth and profits are essential to a company's well-being. Every company implements these beliefs differently (to fit its particular situation), and every company's values are the handiwork of one or two legendary figures in leadership positions. Accordingly, every company has a distinct culture that it believes no other company can copy successfully. And in companies with strong cultures, managers and workers either accept the norms of the culture or opt out from the culture and leave the company.

The stronger a company's culture and the more that culture is directed toward customers and markets, the less the company uses policy manuals, organization charts, and detailed rules and procedures to enforce discipline and norms. The reason is that the guiding values inherent in the culture convey in crystal-clear fashion what everybody is supposed to do in most situations. Poorly performing companies often have strong cultures. However, their cultures are dysfunctional, being focused on internal politics or operating by the numbers as opposed to emphasizing customers and the people who make and sell the product.

Manage Organizational Culture in a Global Organization[16]

The reality of today's global organizations is that organizational culture must recognize cultural diversity. *Social norms* create differences across national boundaries that influence how people interact, read personal cues, and otherwise interrelate socially. *Values* and *attitudes* about similar circumstances also vary from country to country. Where individualism is central to a North American's value structure, the needs of the group dominate the value structure of their Japanese counterparts. *Religion* is yet another source of cultural differences. Holidays, practices, and belief structures differ in very fundamental ways that must be taken into account as one attempts to shape organizational culture in a global setting. Finally, *education,* or ways people are accustomed to learning, differs across national borders. Formal classroom learning in the United States may teach things that are only learned via apprenticeship in other cultures. Because the process of shaping an organizational

---

[16] Differing backgrounds, often referred to as *cultural diversity,* is something that most managers will certainly see more of, both because of the growing cultural diversity domestically and the obvious diversification of cultural backgrounds that result from global acquisitions and mergers. For example, Harold Epps, manager of a computer keyboard plant in Boston, manages 350 employees representing 44 countries of origin and 19 languages.

culture often involves considerable "education," leaders should be sensitive to global differences in approaches to education to make sure their cultural education efforts are effective. Henning Kagermann, CEO of German-based global software company SAP, spoke to this issue recently when he said: "If you are a big company, you need to tap into the global talent pool. It's foolish to believe the smartest people are in one nation. In Germany, we now have this big public debate about there being a shortage of engineers in the country. Well, I don't care, or at least not as CEO of SAP. We are a collection of talented engineers in Germany, India, China, the U.S., Israel, Brazil, and the diversity therein represented enriches the culture, creativity, and market responsiveness of SAP."[17] Kagermann seeks significant representation of cultures and communities worldwide so that SAP truly reflects the vast global settings in which it does business.

Manage the Strategy-Culture Relationship

Managers find it difficult to think through the relationship between a firm's culture and the critical factors on which strategy depends. They quickly recognize, however, that key components of the firm—structure, staff, systems, people, style—influence the ways in which key managerial tasks are executed and how critical management relationships are formed. And implementation of a new strategy is largely concerned with adjustments in these components to accommodate the perceived needs of the strategy. Consequently, managing the strategy-culture relationship requires sensitivity to the interaction between the changes necessary to implement the new strategy and the compatibility or "fit" between those changes and the firm's culture. Exhibit 12.11 provides a simple framework for managing the strategy-culture relationship by identifying four basic situations a firm might face.

Link to Mission

A firm in cell 1 is faced with a situation in which implementing a new strategy requires several changes in structure, systems, managerial assignments, operating procedures, or other fundamental aspects of the firm. However, most of the changes are potentially compatible with the existing organizational culture. Firms in this situation usually have a tradition of effective performance and are either seeking to take advantage of a major opportunity or are attempting to redirect major product-market operations consistent with proven core capabilities. Such firms are in a very promising position: They can pursue a strategy requiring major changes but still benefit from the power of cultural reinforcement.

Four basic considerations should be emphasized by firms seeking to manage a strategy-culture relationship in this context:

1. *Key changes should be visibly linked to the basic company mission.* Because the company mission provides a broad official foundation for the organizational culture, top executives should use all available internal and external forums to reinforce the message that the changes are inextricably linked to it.

2. *Emphasis should be placed on the use of existing personnel* where possible to fill positions created to implement the new strategy. Existing personnel embody the shared values and norms that help ensure cultural compatibility as major changes are implemented.

3. *Care should be taken if adjustments in the reward system are needed.* These adjustments should be consistent with the current reward system. If, for example, a new product-market thrust requires significant changes in the way sales are made, and, therefore, in incentive compensation, common themes (e.g., incentive oriented) should be emphasized. In this way, current and future reward approaches are related, and the changes in the reward system are justified (encourage development of less familiar markets).

[17] "Tapping Global Talent in Software," *BusinessWeek*, June 9, 2007.

EXHIBIT 12.11
Managing the Strategy-Culture Relationship

Changes in key organizational factors that are necessary to implement the new strategy

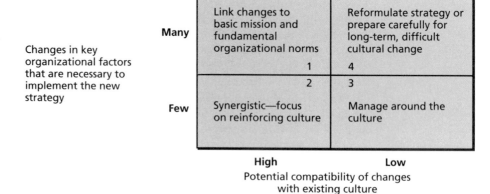

	High	Low
Many	Link changes to basic mission and fundamental organizational norms 1	Reformulate strategy or prepare carefully for long-term, difficult cultural change 4
Few	2 Synergistic—focus on reinforcing culture	3 Manage around the culture

High   Low

Potential compatibility of changes
with existing culture

4. *Key attention should be paid to the changes that are least compatible with the current culture,* so current norms are not disrupted. For example, a firm may choose to subcontract an important step in a production process because that step would be incompatible with the current culture.

P&G's new innovation approach under Alan Lafley, described in Exhibit 12.12, Strategy in Action, offers an excellent example of a company in this situation. P&G's long-standing mission as a consumer products company had been one of innovative product design and development. Alan Lafley was very careful to push for a more open culture in terms of who would help P&G innovate more effectively, but he was also emphatic about linking these new efforts at changing how the "great innovator" innovated with the core notion that P&G people, and P&G's 100-year-old tradition or mission was still *THE* global consumer products innovator. He linked changes to the basic P&G mission. Lafley next emphasized speaking positively about P&G people and getting them to buy in to the changes he sought. He placed emphasis on existing personnel. Third, he included new rewards to encourage acceptance of the different way of doing things. And fourth, he made sure on changes that were "stretching people too much" to use what he called an accelerator and a throttle approach. He identified himself as the accelerator, pushing aggressively for change. And he assigned his managers as his throttle, to regularly meet and discuss and perhaps alter the pace of change, depending on their assessment of whether the changes were taking or whether people were being pushed to change too quickly. So in this way Lafley made sure to monitor changes least compatible with P&G's current culture.

Maximize Synergy

A firm in cell 2 needs only a few organizational changes to implement its new strategy, and those changes are potentially quite compatible with its current culture. A firm in this situation should emphasize two broad themes:

1. *Take advantage of the situation to reinforce and solidify the current culture.*
2. *Use this time of relative stability to remove organizational roadblocks to the desired culture.*

3M's current effort to reacquire its culture of innovation illustrates this situation. Earlier this decade, James McNerney became the first outsider to lead 3M in its 100-year history. He had barely stepped off the plane before he announced he would change the DNA of the place. His playbook was classic pursuit of efficiency: he axed 8,000 workers (about 11 percent of the workforce), intensified the performance-review process, tightened the purse strings, and implemented a Six Sigma program to decrease production defects and increase efficiency. Five years later, McNerney abruptly left for a bigger opportunity—Boeing. His successor, George Buckley, faced a challenging question: whether the relentless emphasis on efficiency had made 3M a less creative company. That's a vitally important issue for a company whose very identity is built on innovation—the company that has always prided itself on drawing at least one-third of sales from products released in the past five years; today that fraction has slipped to only one-quarter.

Those results are not coincidental. Efficiency programs such as Six Sigma are designed to identify problems in work processes—and then use rigorous measurement to reduce variation and eliminate defects. When these types of initiatives become ingrained in a company's culture, as they did at 3M, creativity can easily get squelched. After all, a break-through innovation is something that challenges existing procedures and norms. "Invention is by its very nature a disorderly process," says CEO Buckley, who has dialed some key McNerney's initiatives as he attempts to return 3M to its roots and its culture of innovation. "You can't put a Six Sigma process into that area and say, well, I'm getting behind on inven-tion, so I'm going to schedule myself for three good ideas on Wednesday and two on Friday. That's not how creativity works." While process excellence demands precision, consistency, and repetition, innovation calls for variation, failure, and serendipity.[18] Buckley is taking advantage of this difficult situation to reinforce and solidify 3M's "re"-embrace of its former, innovation culture by bringing back flexible funding for innovative ideas among other traditions. At the same time, he is using the general embrace of a return to its old cul-ture to make some key changes in manufacturing practices and plant locations outside the United States to make 3M more cost effective and competitive in a global economy.

Manage around the Culture

A firm in cell 3 must make a few major organizational changes to implement its new strategy, but these changes are potentially inconsistent with the firm's current organiza-tional culture. The critical question for a firm in this situation is whether it can make the changes with a reasonable chance of success.

A firm can manage around the culture in various ways: create a separate firm or divi-sion; use task forces, teams, or program coordinators; subcontract; bring in an outsider; or sell out. These are a few of the available options, but the key idea is to create a method of achieving the change desired that avoids confronting the incompatible cultural norms. As cultural resistance diminishes, the change may be absorbed into the firm.

IBM's recent sale of its PC business to China's Lenovo, creating the third-largest global PC firm behind Dell and HP, was a strategic decision it took three years to conclude. IBM management became increasingly concerned with the problem that the PC business, and the culture surrounding it, were incompatible with the culture and direction IBM's core business had been taking for some time. The conflict, and the inability to reconcile different cultural needs, led IBM executives to explore the sale of the PC division almost three years ago to Lenovo. At the time IBM's PC division was in disarray and losing $400 million annu-ally. Lenovo's reaction was to send IBM packing out of China with a sense they had tried to take Lenovo's executives for fools who would buy a "pig in a poke." But IBM executives, still desperately concerned about the fundamental and cultural difference between the PC business and the rest of IBM set about an intense 18-month effort to wring costs out of the PC's supply chain, bring it back to profitability, and then go to call on Lenovo again. They achieved both in 18 months and, in their next business, found a more receptive Lenovo management team—ultimately concluding the deal a few months later. In so doing, IBM worked feverishly even to include creating a profitable global PC business only to then sell it quickly and cheaply so that it could "manage around a culture" in the sense of allowing IBM to unify around a different business model and remove the business it was most known

---

[18] "At 3M, a Struggle Between Efficiency and Creativity," *BusinessWeek,* June 11, 2007.

Recreating P&G and Its 170-Year-Old Culture

BusinessWeek

Lafley is changing Procter & Gamble. He's undertaking the company's most sweeping remake since it was founded in 1837. Nothing is sacred any longer at the Cincinnati-based maker of Tide, Pampers, and Crest. And in the process, he has made P&G one of the world's top five innovation companies in 2007.

Lafley has inverted the invent-it-here mentality by turning outward for innovation. He's broadening P&G's definition of brands and how it prices goods. He's moving P&G deep into the beauty-care business with several large acquisitions over five years. And he's redefining P&G's core business by outsourcing operations—like information technology and bar-soap manufacturing.

What's surprising is that at the start, Lafley was perceived as a tame pair of hands—far from a person who would conduct a radical makeover. He followed a forceful change agent, Durk Jager, who had tried to jump-start internal innovation, launching a host of new brands. Jager also criticized P&G's insular culture, which he sought to shake up. In the end, though, he overreached, as P&G missed earnings forecasts and employees bucked under his leadership.

Lafley answered some questions recently about his views on leading change at P&G:

Q: When you started, you weren't perceived as a forceful change agent like your predecessor. Yet you're making more dramatic changes. Can you discuss that?

A: Durk and I had believed very strongly that the company had to change and make fundamental changes in a lot of the same directions. There are two simple differences: One is I'm very externally focused. I expressed the change in the context of how we're going to serve consumers better,

how we're going to win with the retailer, and how we're going to defeat the competitor in the marketplace.

The most important thing—I didn't attack. I avoided saying P&G people are bad. I thought that was a big mistake [on Jager's part]. The difference is, I preserved the core of the culture and pulled people where I wanted to go. I enrolled them in change. I didn't tell them.

Q: Why did you both see a need for change?

A: We were looking at slow growth. An inability to move quickly, to commercialize on innovation and get full advantage out of it. We were looking at new technologies that were changing competition in our industry, retailers, and the supply base. We were looking at a world that all of a sudden was going to go 24/7, and we weren't ready for that kind of world.

Q: Was the view on the need for change widely held within P&G?

A: It depends on who you ask. Without a doubt, Durk and I and a few others were in the camp of "We need a much bigger change."

Q: Jager says he tried to change P&G too fast. What do you think about that?

A: I think he's right.

Q: Are you concerned about the same thing?

A: I'm worried that I will ask the organization to change ahead of its understanding, capability, and commitment, because that's a problem. I have been a catalyst of change and encourager of change and a coach of change management.

for, the IBM-PC business, from its organization along with the cultural incompatibility it represented.

Reformulate the Strategy or Culture

A firm in cell 4 faces the most difficult challenge in managing the strategy-culture relationship. To implement its new strategy, such a firm must make organizational changes that are incompatible with its current, usually entrenched, values and norms. A firm in this situation faces the complex, expensive, and often long-term challenge of changing its culture; it is a challenge that borders on impossible.

When a strategy requires massive organizational change and engenders cultural resistance, a firm should determine whether reformulation of the strategy is appropriate.

And I've tried not to drive change for the sake of change.

Q: How do you pace change?

A: I have tremendous trust in my management team. I let them be the brake. I am the accelerator. I help with direction and let them make the business strategic choices.

Q: Did the fact that P&G was in crisis when you came in help you implement change?

A: It was easier. I was lucky. When you have a mess, you have a chance to make more changes.

Q: Jager tried to drive innovation from within. You would like P&G to ultimately get 50 percent of its ideas from outside. Why?

A: Durk and I both wanted more innovation. We both felt we absolutely, positively had to get more innovation. We had to get more innovation commercialized and more innovation globalized. So we were totally together.

He tried to drive it all internally. He tried to rev the R&D organization, supercharge them, and hoped that enough would come out of there that we would achieve the goals of commercializing more of it and globalizing more of it. We got in trouble 'cause we pulled stuff out that was half-baked or that was never going to be successful. We hadn't developed it far enough.

The difference is that my hypothesis is that innovation and discovery are likely to come from anywhere. What P&G is really good at is developing innovations and commercializing them. So what I said is, "We need an open marketplace."

We're probably as good as the next guy at inventing. But we are not absolutely and positively better than everybody else at inventing. There are a lot of good inventors out there.

Q: How hard will it be to shift P&G's R&D focus outwards, given that it has historically focused inwards?

A: It will be a challenge, but I think we'll get there. It's like a flywheel. That first turn is really difficult. Then the second turn is a little bit easier. This has been like turning a flywheel. We will have failures. We will have to celebrate that failure.

Q: When you couple your outward focus on innovation with your moves toward outsourcing, it seems you're making P&G a less vertically integrated company.

A: I don't believe in vertical integration. I think it's a trap. I believe in horizontal networked organizations.

Our core capability is to develop and commercialize. Branding is a core capability. Customer business development is a core capability. We concluded in a lot of areas that manufacturing isn't. Therefore, I let the businesses go do more outsourcing. We concluded that running a back room wasn't a core capability. You do what you do best and can do world-class.

Sources: Reprinted with special permission from Jean McGregor, "P&G Asks: What's the Big Idea," *BusinessWeek*, May 4, 2007; and Jay Greene and Mike France, "P&G: New & Improved," *BusinessWeek*, July 7, 2003. Copyright © 2007 The McGraw-Hill Companies.

Are all of the organizational changes really necessary? Is there any real expectation that the changes will be acceptable and successful? If these answers are yes, then massive changes are often necessary. When you study the chapter case about Alan Mulally's actions at Ford over the last few years you will see him making major changes in an attempt to change Ford's culture to suit its new strategy: bringing outsiders in as top execs, changing long-standing executive compensation programs, emphasizing sales and marketing over the traditional, patronage-based culture as, sadly, Ford's most "prized" cultural element. These are elements through which Ford, under Mulally, is undergoing massive change as he tries to build a different culture compatible with a new vision and strategy.

Merrill Lynch faced the challenge of strategy-culture incompatibility in the last decade. Seeking to remain no. 1 in the newly deregulated financial services industry, it chose to pursue a product development strategy in its brokerage business. Under this strategy, Merrill Lynch would sell a broader range of investment products to a more diverse customer base and would integrate other financial services, such as real estate sales, into the Merrill Lynch organization. The new strategy could succeed only if Merrill Lynch's traditionally service-oriented brokerage network became sales and marketing oriented. Initial efforts to implement the strategy generated substantial resistance from Merrill Lynch's highly successful brokerage network. The strategy was fundamentally inconsistent with long-standing cultural norms at Merrill Lynch that emphasized personalized service and very close broker-client relationships. Merrill Lynch ultimately divested its real estate operation, reintroduced specialists who supported broker/retailers, and refocused its brokers more narrowly on basic client investment needs.

Summary

This chapter has examined organizational leadership and organization culture—two factors essential to the successful implementation and execution of a company's strategic plan. Organizational leadership is guiding and shepherding an organization over time and developing that organization's future leadership and its organization culture.

We saw that good organizational leadership involves three considerations: clarifying strategic intent, building an organization, and shaping the organization's culture. Strategic intent is clarified through the leader's vision, a broad picture of where he or she is leading the firm, and candid attention to and clear expectations about performance.

Leaders use education, principles, and perseverance to build their organization. Education involves familiarizing managers and future leaders with an effective understanding of the business and the skills they need to develop. Principles are the leader's personal standards that guide her or his sense of honesty, integrity and ethical behavior. They are more essential than ever in today's world as key building blocks for the type of organization for which a leader's principles reflect and are watched with great interest by every manager, employee, customer, and supplier of the organization. Perseverance, the ability to stick to the challenge when most others falter, is an unquestionable tool for leaders to instill faith in the vision they seek when times are hard.

Leaders start to shape organizational culture by the passion they bring to their role, and their choice and development of young manager and future leaders. Passion, a highly motivated sense of commitment to what you do and want to do, is a force that permeates attitudes throughout an organization and helps them buy into your cultural aspirations. Combining those with the skills, aspirations, and inclinations you seek to make the vision a reality—and then helping them develop—is a key way to build a culture over the long term. One of the key skills of these rising leaders is to learn how to motivate, lead, and get others to do what they need.

Understanding seven sources of power and influence, rather than just the power of position and punishment, is a critical skill for effective future leaders to grasp.

Organizational culture is the set of important assumptions, values, beliefs, and norms that members of an organization share in common. The organizational leader plays a critical role in developing, sustaining, and changing organizational culture. Ethical standards, the leader's basis for differentiating right from wrong, quickly spread as a centerpiece between the leader and the organization's culture. Leaders use many means to reinforce and develop their organization's culture—from rewards and appointments to story telling and rituals. Managing the strategy-culture relationship requires different approaches, depending on the match between the demands of the new strategy and the compatibility of the culture with that strategy. This chapter examined four different scenarios.

Key Terms

ethical standards, *p. 391*
expert influence, *p. 388*
information power, *p. 387*
leadership development, *p. 381*
leader's vision, *p. 376*
organizational culture, *p. 388*

organizational leadership, *p. 374*
passion (of a leader), *p. 384*
peer influence, *p. 388*
perseverance (of a leader), *p. 382*
position power, *p. 386*
principles (of a leader), *p. 381*

punitive power, *p. 387*
referent influence, *p. 388*
reward power, *p. 386*
strategic intent, *p. 376*

Questions for Discussion

1. Think about any two leaders you have known, preferably one good and one weak. They can be businesspersons, coaches, someone you work(ed) with, and so forth. Make a list of five traits, practices, or characteristics that cause you to consider one good and the other weak. Compare the things you chose with the seven factors used to differentiate effective organizational leadership in the first half of this chapter.

2. This chapter describes seven attributes that enable good leadership—vision, performance, principles, education of subordinates, perseverance, passion, and leader selection/development. Which one have you found to be the most meaningful to you in the leaders you respond to the best?

3. Consider the following situation and determine whether the VC group is engaging in something that would violate your principles, or be totally acceptable to you. Explain why.

   Who likes those ubiquitous online pop-up ads planted by intrusive spyware? Technology Crossover Ventures is betting few do. The Silicon Valley venture-capital firm helped to finance the anti-spyware company Webroot Software. But it appears to hedge that bet with a sizable investment in Claria, a company vilified for spreading spyware.

   More than 40 million Web surfers viewed Claria ads. TCV pumped at least $13 million into Claria, but it has removed the company from a list of investments on its Web site.

   Critics wonder why TCV would make dual investments. "Users are rubbed the wrong way by even the suggestion that the same companies that made this mess are now profiting from helping to clean it up," says Harvard University researcher and spyware expert Ben Edelman. TCV declined to comment. There is a similar element in both ventures: the potential to make money.

4. Read Exhibit 12.2. What would you do if you were asked to serve as an Ethics Review Arbitrator and render a decision on what should happen to the Duke MBA students? Summarize the key reasons supporting your ruling.

5. Do you think Martin Sullivan is a good CEO candidate for AIG right now? See Exhibit 12.8.

6. Do you think Alan Lafley is a good organizational leader? What is his most important contribution to his organizational culture in your opinion?

7. What three sources of power and influence are best suited to you as a manager?

8. Describe two organizations you have been a part of based on differences in their organizational cultures.

9. What key things is Alan Mulally doing at Ford (see the following case) as an organizational leader to shape Ford's organizational culture? Do you think he will succeed? Why?

Chapter 12 Discussion Case

The New Heat on Ford

The Mulally Difference: **How things are changing at Ford now that the new boss has arrived**

	Before	After
Organization	Regional fiefdoms. Every global market has had its own strategy and products.	Mulally wants to break down geographic hierarchies and create a single worldwide organization.
Division chief meetings	Held monthly. Lots of happy talk. Little information sharing.	Held weekly. Discussing problems is encouraged. Goal is to spot red flags early.

(continued)

The Mulally Difference: How things are changing at Ford now that the new boss has arrived   *cont.*

	Before	After
Production mix	Emphasis on trucks, SUVs, niche sports cars.	Focus is shifting to passenger cars and crossovers.
Brand vision	To diversify away from Ford brand, the company acquired dysfunctional luxury brands.	Strengthen the traditional blue oval Ford brand. Sell off or close poor-performing brands.
Promotions	Managers changed jobs frequently to develop their skills.	Executives stay in place, winning only promotions that are deserved.

1   On a chilly morning in February, the new chief executive of Ford Motor Co., Alan R. Mulally, boarded one of the company's Falcon twin-turbo jets and flew to *Consumer Reports* magazine's automobile testing facility in East Haddam, Connecticut. He was joined by two senior engineers. Their mission: to spend half a day with the publication's staff getting detailed evaluations of every model made by Ford, Lincoln, and Mercury.

2   It wasn't a fun trip, according to a source close to the company. At one point, the *Consumer Reports* team criticized the new Ford Edge crossover SUV for lacking an electric opener triggered by the key fob—or at least a handle on the rear hatch. Both are standard equipment on many of its rivals. A woman on the magazine's staff demonstrated how she, at five feet tall, struggled to open the rear of the SUV as she carried two bags of groceries. Had it been a rainy day, she would have had to set her purchases down on the wet pavement and then muscle up the hatch. Once she'd done that, she'd face another hurdle: she was too short to shut it.

3   After a couple of hours on the firing line, Ford's engineers got defensive. Interrupting the testers, they started airing their side of the story in front of the new boss. Sensing that the meeting was deteriorating, Mulally says he handed each one a pad and pen. "You know what? Let's just listen and take notes," he said. The episode was a perfect illustration of what Mulally considers one of Ford's major problems: the tendency of employees to rationalize mistakes instead of fixing them. "We seek to be understood more than we seek to understand," he observes.

4   It's no secret Ford is fighting for its life. After losing $12.7 billion last year, it had to endure the indignity of pledging its factories, headquarters, and the rights to the iconic blue oval logo to the banks and bondholders just to get enough money to finance its turnaround plan. Those were all tough steps. But these are tough times for the U.S. auto industry. With Cerberus Capital Management taking over at Chrysler, the status quo is no longer an option in Detroit, a town infamous for incremental change.

5   For Mulally to have any chance of making Ford profitable by 2009, he'll have to strike a tough deal with the United Auto Workers (UAW) this summer [2007]. He will also likely ditch a struggling brand such as Jaguar or Mercury. But fixing Ford will require more than simply whacking expenses. One way or another, the company will also have to figure out how to produce more vehicles that consumers actually want. And doing that will require addressing the most fundamental problem of all: Ford's dysfunctional, often defeatist culture.

6   Although Ford once exemplified corporate efficiency—it is the birthplace of the assembly line and home of the celebrated Whiz Kids, who pioneered many modern management techniques in the 1960s—it has degenerated into a symbol of inefficiency. Weary corporate lifers have become all too comfortable with the idea of losing money. Mediocrity is acceptable. The company's complacency shows up in the very language it uses internally to rate its own models. It uses the designations "L" for Leader, "AL" for Among Leaders, and "C" for Competitive. Too many executives simply strive for Cs, says William C. "Bill" Ford Jr., executive chairman of the board. When asked about the grading system, the great-grandson of Henry Ford mimes putting a gun to his head and pulling the trigger. "We still do that?" he asks in disbelief. "I don't know where that came from."

FEET TO THE FIRE

7   Last September, the 50-year-old family scion, who had served as chief executive for nearly five years, threw up his arms in frustration and concluded that an insider could no longer fix Ford. The job required the emotional detachment of an outsider. While Mulally was not his first choice, the former chief of Boeing Co.'s commercial airlines division had impressive turnaround credentials. He helped the aerospace giant bounce back from the September 11, 2001, terrorist attacks by axing 27,000 workers, cutting jet production in half, repairing the company's antiquated production lines, and making a courageous bet on the 787 Dreamliner. That remarkable performance earned the 61-year-old ex-engineer recognition as one of *BusinessWeek*'s top managers of the year in 2005. The hard-nosed Mulally is somebody, Ford promises, "who knows how to shake the company to its foundations."

8   Just eight months into the job, Mulally is working hard to change institutional work habits that took years to develop. He wants managers to think more about customers than their own careers. He has made it a top priority to encourage his team to admit mistakes, to share more information, and to cooperate across divisions. He's holding everybody's feet to the fire

Ford: A Brief History of Management Evolution

Henry Ford era: 1902–1940	The company founder invented modern manufacturing. He was innovative and dictatorial.
Whiz Kids era: 1940s–1950s	Home to some of the most creative business thinkers in the postwar era. Ford evolved into a management lab.
"Hank the Deuce" era: 1960–1980	The imperious Henry Ford II pitted managers against one another. He often clashed with the Whiz Kids.
OPEC era: 1970s	Ford became more political under the autocratic Lee Iacocca, president from 1970 to 1978.
Global competition era: 1980s–1990s	While Ford had some huge hits, its passenger car business foundered and it lost ground to foreign rivals.
"Way forward" era: 2001-Present	Henry's great-grandson, Bill Ford, failed to transform the culture. He recruited Alan Mulally to instill discipline.

with tough operational oversight and harsh warnings about Ford's predicament. "We have been going out of business for 40 years," Mulally told a group of 100 information technology staffers at a "town meeting" in February. He has repeated the message to every employee group that he has addressed.

9 It is far from guaranteed, of course, that any of his cultural reforms will be enough to rescue Ford. Far-reaching as they are, they may not go far enough to do the job. And now that Cerberus is in the process of buying Chrysler, Mulally can no longer claim the title of most feared outsider in town. He may very well have to develop an even more radical rebuilding plan to stay ahead of his crosstown rival.

10 Mulally has yet to convince Wall Street that he can reach his goal of profitability by 2009. Of 15 analysts surveyed by Bloomberg.com News recently, only two rate the stock a buy. "They're in a precarious situation," says John Novak, an analyst with Morningstar Investment Service Inc. in Chicago. "Mulally's honeymoon period isn't going to last."

11 History provides ample basis for such skepticism. Ford is a place that's notorious for destroying auto industry outsiders—and Mulally is admittedly no car guy. Despite Bill Ford's strong backing, Mulally has run into plenty of internal resistance. Nearly all of his managers have been inherited, and some of them snickered when he received a $28 million paycheck for his first four months' work. On Mulally's first meeting with his inherited team, one manager asked: "How are you going to tackle something as complex and unfamiliar as the auto business when we are in such tough financial shape?"

12 The questioner discovered that the wiry former Boy Scout from Lawrence, Kansas, a veteran of many bruising political battles at Boeing, is hard to intimidate. Unfazed by the challenge, he looked the questioner directly in the eye and said: "An automobile has about 10,000 moving parts, right? An airplane has 2 million, and it has to stay up in the air."

GLADIATOR ARENA

13 Although Mulally lacks in-depth auto industry knowledge, he is also free of many of the intellectual biases and habits that have gotten Detroit into so much trouble. "He doesn't know what he doesn't know," says Ford Americas President Mark Fields. When Mulally was reviewing the company's 2008 product line last September, for example, he was told that Ford loses close to $3,000 every time a customer buys a Focus compact, according to one executive. "Why haven't you figured out a way to make a profit?" he asked. Executives explained that Ford needed the high sales volume to maintain the company's CAFE, or corporate average fuel economy, rating and that the plant that makes the car is a high-cost UAW factory in Michigan. "That's not what I asked," he shot back. "I want to know why no one figured out a way to build this car at a profit, whether it has to be built in Michigan or China or India, if that's what it takes." Nobody had a good answer.

14 How did Ford evolve from one of the most admired companies in the world into one where losing money has seemingly lost nearly all of its stigma? Until the mid-1960s, it was considered a management shrine. Under U.S. Defense Secretary Robert S. McNamara, one of a celebrated group of military veterans at the company dubbed the Whiz Kids, Ford developed scientific consumer research techniques that are now commonplace throughout the business world. It was one of the first auto companies to create products that were based on hard data rather than the personal tastes of executives.

15 But after McNamara exited in 1961, Henry Ford II (Bill's uncle) gradually assumed a bigger role in management. He built a high-testosterone culture where rising stars like successive Ford Presidents Lee Iacocca and Semon "Bunkie" Knudson were often pitted against one another like gladiators to prove themselves. As the auto industry's postwar growth slowed, limiting opportunities for a swelling cadre of managers, executives turned on one another. They also became more cautious. "The bureaucracy at Ford grew, and managers took refuge in the structure when things got tough rather than innovate or try new ideas that seemed risky," says Allan Gilmour, a retired chief financial officer at Ford who has met twice with Mulally, at Bill Ford's behest, to offer historical perspective on the company's woes.

16 Personal ties with the Ford family, always important at the company, sometimes trumped genuine performance in promotion decisions. So ambitious managers focused increasingly on kissing the right rings instead of racking up results. It became "something of a palace atmosphere," says Gerald C. Meyers, a professor at the University of Michigan School of Business. Some critics also blame the family, which has many members who depend on dividends as their main source of income, for encouraging a focus on current profits rather than long-term planning over the decades.

17 In the royal hierarchy at Ford, an elaborate system of employment grades clearly established an employee's rank in the pecking order. The grades also had the unintentional effect of quashing ideas and keeping information tightly controlled. When Fields, now president of Ford Americas, first arrived at the company from IBM in 1989, he couldn't make a lunch date with an executive who held a higher grade. People asked him what his grade was "as a condition of including me or socializing with me," Fields recalls. And he was discouraged from airing problems at meetings unless his boss approved first.

TOO MANY FIEFDOMS

18 The company's unusual approach to grooming leaders also discouraged collaboration. Ford has a long tradition of rapidly cycling executives through new posts every two years or so. In fact, managers refer to their posts as "assignments" rather than jobs. But one consequence of employees' need to make their mark in such a short time was to discourage cooperation with other divisions and regions, whose products were often on a different timetable. And no engineer ever got noticed by carrying over his predecessor's design or idea—even if it saved big money. Mulally, who is moving to lengthen job tenures, finds this system appalling. "I had the same job at Boeing for seven years," he says. "You can't hold somebody accountable for a job they've held for nine months."

19 Thus did Ford become what it is today: a balkanized mess. It has four parallel operating units worldwide, each with its own costly bureaucracy, factories, and product development staff. According to a Mulally audit designed to uncover cost-cutting opportunities, no two vehicles in Ford's lineup share the same mirrors, headlamps, or even such mundane pieces as the springs and hinges for the hood. And that's just taking into account the Ford brand. Add Volvo, Jaguar, and Land Rover to the mix, and the company has more than 30 engineering platforms worldwide. That leaves Ford at a big cost disadvantage in engineering and parts compared with General Motors, Chrysler, Toyota, and Honda. Mulally wants to get that number down to five or six platforms, similar to Honda. "There's no global company I know of that can succeed with the level of complexity we have at Ford," he says.

20 Examples of Ford losing opportunities because of its byzantine corporate structure abound. A recent example involves Sync, a system that allows voice-command control of a cell phone and MP3 player. It was a big success at last January's North American International Auto Show. Ford developed it with Microsoft Corp. last year and will start rolling it out this fall. Although Volvo and Land Rover are also dying to offer Sync, neither will get the system because the electrical architectures of the Swedish and British cars are incompatible with Ford's. Mulally finds that incomprehensible, considering that Ford has owned the European brands for nearly a decade.

21 To try to eliminate all of Ford's unnecessary duplication, Mulally is asserting more control over the product line. Now he personally approves every new vehicle worldwide. Production is now coordinated by Derrick M. Kuzak, Ford's first-ever chief of global product development.

22 Kuzak's team is already hard at work designing cars that can be easily adapted to appeal to worldwide markets. They've developed a global small car that Ford will build in two or three plants starting in 2010, and which will sell in the United States for $10,000 to $12,000. It will differ only slightly from the version that will sell in South America, Europe, and Asia. Another key goal in the near future is to create a midsize sedan that could serve both North America and Europe. Today, for example, the European Mondeo sedan and the North American Fusion are built independently of one another. Kuzak is overseeing an attempt to coordinate the future designs of those vehicles.

23 But Mulally knows that changing the organizational chart won't cure Ford. The company's deeply ingrained hierarchical culture needs to be blown up. So for the first time ever he's forcing every operating group to share all its financial data with every other group. That information used to be closely guarded. Shortly after he ordered the change, three separate executives called him to make sure they had heard right. Says Mulally: "You can't manage a secret."

24 To spread his new religion, Mulally has turned the traditional monthly meeting of divisional chiefs into a weekly affair. Every executive has to attend in person or by video-conference. No subordinates can be sent. To ensure focus, the BlackBerrys that used to be common at these meetings are now banned. So are side conversations when someone is talking, even if by video link. But the most radical change is that operating chiefs are now encouraged to bring a different subordinate to every meeting—a big step at a company where underlings formerly were not privy to sensitive data. Mulally wants staffers to start buzzing about his ideas through unofficial e-mail, blog, and watercooler channels.

HEALTH CARE MINEFIELD

25 He is also taking symbolic steps to treat white-collar and blue-collar employees more equitably. This year many workers on the shop floor will receive bonuses of $300 to $800, based on a new formula that is also being applied to executives. Of course, his popularity with union workers will depend a lot on this summer's contract negotiations with the UAW. The new deal will give Mulally an opportunity to cut his workforce's costly health benefits. That's expected to lead to divisiveness.

The arrival at Chrysler of Cerberus, though it increases the competitive pressure on Mulally, may turn out to be a blessing in this arena. Cerberus has sent a message to labor leaders that the old ways of doing business are no longer acceptable. Partially for that reason, the Cerberus deal "is good for us," Mulally says.

26   Ford's new CEO is fond of talking about how he is breaking long-standing company taboos, such as the one about never admitting when you don't know something. At a meeting last fall, one of Mulally's operating chiefs chattered on for several minutes trying to answer a question to which he clearly did not have the answer. After the meeting, Mulally asked Fields why the executive droned on for so long. "Because 'I don't know' isn't in Ford's vocabulary," Fields explained.

27   Now it is. To reinforce the point, Mulally has actually banned the thick background binders executives used to bring to the weekly meetings. That means they sometimes can't immediately summon the necessary details to answer Mulally's questions. That's fine with him: "I know that if they don't have the answer one week, they'll have it next week," he says.

28   As a longtime observer of the auto industry, David E. Cole, chairman of the Center for Automotive Research in Ann Arbor, Michigan, is not sure that Mulally will succeed in his mission. But he has concluded that Ford's culture is beyond fixing by anyone who has spent a long time inside the company, or any of the "usual candidates" at other automakers. "Ford employees feel very paternalistic toward Ford," says Cole, "and the only way Bill was going to convince them that the company was truly at risk was by bringing in someone they'd never heard of to break the cycle."

Sources: Reprinted with special permission from "The New Heat on Ford," *BusinessWeek,* June 7, 2007; and "The Mulally Difference," *BusinessWeek,* June 24, 2007. Copyright © 2007 The McGraw-Hill Companies.

DISCUSSION QUESTIONS

1. What attributes of good organizational leadership do you see Alan Mulally display?

2. What changes is he making in rewards, skills, and selection of key leaders that are most different from Ford's past?

3. Do you think they will be embraced? And work?

4. How is he changing the Ford culture?

5. What will be his hardest task?

6. Do you sense he operates at the margin, ethically speaking, or that his principles are transparent? Why?

Strategic Control

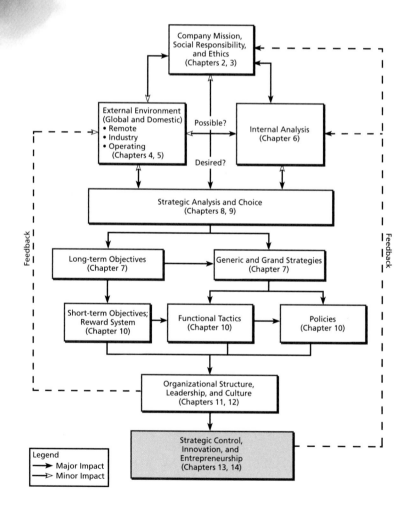

Company Mission, Social Responsibility, and Ethics (Chapters 2, 3)

External Environment (Global and Domestic)
• Remote
• Industry
• Operating (Chapters 4, 5)

Possible?

Internal Analysis (Chapter 6)

Desired?

Strategic Analysis and Choice (Chapters 8, 9)

Long-term Objectives (Chapter 7)

Generic and Grand Strategies (Chapter 7)

Short-term Objectives; Reward System (Chapter 10)

Functional Tactics (Chapter 10)

Policies (Chapter 10)

Organizational Structure, Leadership, and Culture (Chapters 11, 12)

Strategic Control, Innovation, and Entrepreneurship (Chapters 13, 14)

Feedback

Legend
→ Major Impact
⇢ Minor Impact

STRATEGIC CONTROL

Strategies are forward looking, designed to be accomplished several years into the future. They are based on management assumptions about numerous events that have not yet occurred. How should executives "control" a strategy, and its execution?

Consider the recent experiences of Motorola and Dell Computer. Motorola's CEO Ed Zander looked like a genius in early 2007, executing his strategy of cranking out "wow" products like the Razr phone and delivering them via an even-more-efficient supply chain. Then, quickly, Motorola ran into a cell-phone price war, and its profit margins sank dramatically, revealing an outsourced manufacturing process that was much less efficient and more costly than rival Nokia's in-house operations were steadily delivering. Motorola's stock quickly dropped almost 50 percent in value, and CEO Zander faced some serious challenges to his leadership and the efficacy of the Motorola strategy.

Dell Computer saw its rival Hewlett-Packard struggle with a poorly integrated acquisition of Compaq and a confusing reorganization of HP a few years ago. IBM sold its PC business to China's Lenovo, admitting it couldn't compete with the Dell approach. Dell was a world leader in PCs and was broadening its offerings into printers and other electronic devices. But within two years, HP's new CEO Mark Hurd had HP much more focused, and it soon eclipsed Dell as the world's largest seller of PCs. Lenovo was gaining strength in the Asia-Pacific area. And Dell found itself losing market share and experiencing declining profitability, excess inventory, and problems with its outsourced customer service. Founder Michael Dell has recently returned to the CEO role after firing his handpicked former successor, Ken Rollins, and is attempting to rebuild Dell and its strategy.

So we see two great companies with seemingly solid strategies that deteriorated very quickly. What could they have done or done better? How could Motorola and Dell have adjusted their strategies and actions when key premises, technology, competitors, or sudden events changed everything for them? How could they have established better "strategic control" and reduced the impact of negative events or taken advantage of new opportunities?

strategic control
Management efforts to track a strategy as it is being implemented, detect problems or changes in its underlying premises, and make necessary adjustments.

Strategic control is concerned with tracking a strategy as it is being implemented, detecting problems or changes in its underlying premises, and making necessary adjustments. In contrast to postaction control, strategic control is concerned with guiding action on behalf of the strategy as that action is taking place and when the end result is still several years off. Managers responsible for the success of a strategy typically are concerned with two sets of questions:

1. Are we moving in the proper direction? Are key things falling into place? Are our assumptions about major trends and changes correct? Are we doing the critical things that need to be done? Should we adjust or abort the strategy?

2. How are we performing? Are objectives and schedules being met? Are costs, revenues, and cash flows matching projections? Do we need to make operational changes?

The rapidly accelerating level of change in the global marketplace has made the need for strategic control key in managing a company. This chapter examines strategic control.

ESTABLISHING STRATEGIC CONTROLS

The control of strategy can be characterized as a form of "steering control." As time elapses between the initial implementation of a strategy and achievement of its intended results, investments are made and numerous projects and actions are undertaken to implement the strategy. Also, during that time, changes are taking place in both the environmental situation and the firm's internal situation. Strategic controls are necessary to steer the firm through these events. They must provide the basis for adapting the firm's strategic actions and directions in response to these developments and changes. The four basic types of strategic control summarized in Exhibit 13.1 are

1. Premise control.
2. Strategic surveillance.
3. Special alert control.
4. Implementation control.

Premise Control

premise control
Management process of systematically and continuously checking to determine whether premises upon which the strategy is based are still valid.

Every strategy is based on certain planning premises—assumptions or predictions. **Premise control** is designed to check systematically and continuously whether the premises on which the strategy is based are still valid. If a vital premise is no longer valid, the strategy may have to be changed. The sooner an invalid premise can be recognized and rejected, the better are the chances that an acceptable shift in the strategy can be devised. Planning premises are primarily concerned with environmental and industry factors.

Environmental Factors

Although a firm has little or no control over environmental factors, these factors exercise considerable influence over the success of its strategy, and strategies usually are based on key premises about them. Inflation, technology, interest rates, regulation, and demographic/social changes are examples of such factors.

The second generation Internet, known as Web 2.0, and its intersection with rapid globalization, is spawning a global youth culture that presents both a challenge to the old ways of doing business and an opportunity to gain tremendous leverage via the right goods and services. "Flying blind" is how some executives describe their effort to adapt to it: the tens of millions of digital elite who are the vanguard of a fast-emerging global culture based on smartphones, blogs, instant messaging, Flickr, MySpace, Skype, YouTube, dig, and de.lic.ious, to mention a few. These highly influential young people are sharing ideas and information across borders that will drive products, employment, services, food, fashion, and ideas—rapidly. Savvy companies are recognizing this phenomenon as perhaps the most critical environmental factor/phenomenon they need to monitor and understand.[1]

Industry Factors

The performance of the firms in a given industry is affected by industry factors. Competitors, suppliers, product substitutes, and barriers to entry are a few of the industry factors about which strategic assumptions are made.

Rubbermaid has long been held up as a model of predictable growth, creative management, and rapid innovation in the plastic housewares and toy industry. Its premise in its most recent strategic plan was that large retail chains would continue to prefer its products over competitors' because of this core competence. This premise included continued receptivity to regular price increases when necessitated by raw materials costs. Retailers, most notably Wal-Mart, recently balked at Rubbermaid's attempt to raise prices to offset the doubling of petroleum-based resin costs. Furthermore, traditionally overlooked competitors have begun to make inroads with computerized stocking services. Rubbermaid is moving aggressively to adjust its strategy because of the response of Wal-Mart and other key retailers.

Strategies are often based on numerous premises, some major and some minor, about environmental and industry variables. Tracking all of these premises is unnecessarily

[1] Steve Hamm, "Children of the Web," *BusinessWeek*, July 2, 2007.

EXHIBIT 13.1 Four Types of Strategic Control

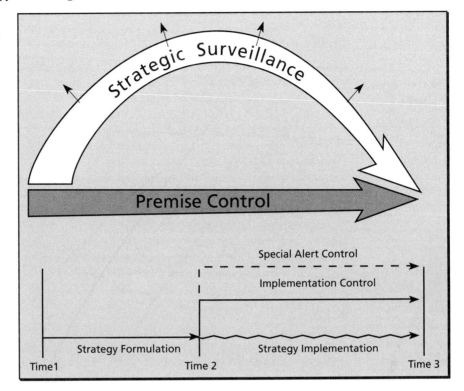

Characteristics of the Four Types of Strategic Control

	Types of Strategic Control			
Basic Characteristics	**Premise Control**	**Implementation Control**	**Strategic Surveillance**	**Special Alert Control**
Objects of control	Planning premises and projections	Key strategic thrusts and milestones	Potential threats and opportunities related to the strategy	Occurrence of recognizable but unlikely events
Degree of focusing	High	High	Low	High
Data acquisition:				
Formalization	Medium	High	Low	High
Centralization	Low	Medium	Low	High
Use with:				
Environmental factors	Yes	Seldom	Yes	Yes
Industry factors	Yes	Seldom	Yes	Yes
Strategy-specific factors	No	Yes	Seldom	Yes
Company-specific factors	No	Yes	Seldom	Seldom

expensive and time consuming. Managers must select premises whose change (1) is likely and (2) would have a major impact on the firm and its strategy.

Strategic Surveillance

strategic surveillance
Management efforts to monitor a broad range of events inside and more often outside the firm that are likely to affect the course of its strategy over time.

By their nature, premise controls are focused controls; strategic surveillance, however, is unfocused. **Strategic surveillance** is designed to monitor a broad range of events inside and outside the firm that are likely to affect the course of its strategy.[2] The basic idea behind strategic surveillance is that important yet unanticipated information may be uncovered by a general monitoring of multiple information sources.

Strategic surveillance must be kept as unfocused as possible. It should be a loose "environmental scanning" activity. Trade magazines, *The Wall Street Journal,* trade conferences, conversations, and intended and unintended observations are all subjects of strategic surveillance. Despite its looseness, strategic surveillance provides an ongoing, broad-based vigilance in all daily operations that may uncover information relevant to the firm's strategy. P&G has used strategic surveillance of Europe's private label trend to shape an aggressive response minimizing any effect on its European sales compared with the dramatically negative effect the trend has had by blindsiding many European consumer products giants like Nestlé, Unilever, and L'Oreal, as discussed in Exhibit 13.2, Strategy in Action.

Special Alert Control

special alert control
Management actions undertaken to thoroughly, and often very rapidly, reconsider a firm's strategy because of a sudden, unexpected event.

Another type of strategic control, really a subset of the other three, is special alert control. A **special alert control** is the thorough, and often rapid, reconsideration of the firm's strategy because of a sudden, unexpected event. The tragic events of September 11, 2001; an outside firm's sudden acquisition of a leading competitor; an unexpected product difficulty, like the fingertip in a bowl of Wendy's chili—events of these kinds can drastically alter the firm's strategy.

Such an event should trigger an immediate and intense reassessment of the firm's strategy and its current strategic situation. In many firms, crisis teams handle the firm's initial response to unforeseen events that may have an immediate effect on its strategy. IBM's shock at the precipitous decline in the sales growth and profitability of its core IT services business in 2005 resulted in a special alert and ongoing focus on this business's strategy as summarized in Exhibit 13.2. Increasingly, firms have developed contingency plans along with crisis teams to respond to circumstances such as United Airlines did on September 11, 2001, and JetBlue did after its snow-storm fiasco at New York's JFK International Airport in the winter of 2007.

Implementation Control

implementation control
Management efforts designed to assess whether the overall strategy should be changed in light of results associated with the incremental actions that implement the overall strategy. These are usually associated with specific strategic thrusts or projects and with predetermined milestone reviews.

Strategy implementation takes place as a series of steps, programs, investments, and moves that occur over an extended time. Special programs are undertaken. Functional areas initiate strategy-related activities. Key people are added or reassigned. Resources are mobilized. In other words, managers implement strategy by converting broad plans into the concrete, incremental actions and results of specific units and individuals.

Implementation control is the type of strategic control that must be exercised as those events unfold. **Implementation control** is designed to assess whether the overall strategy should be changed in light of the results associated with the incremental actions that implement the overall strategy. The two basic types of implementation control are (1) monitoring strategic thrusts and (2) milestone reviews.

[2] G. Schreyogg and H. Steinmann, "Strategic Control: A New Perspective," *Academy of Management Review* 12, no. 1 (1987), p. 101.

PREMISE CONTROL AT BANK OF AMERICA

Bank of America, and other financial service companies, recently lobbied aggressively in Washington, D.C., opposing Wal-Mart's application for a bank charter. Most were surprised and somewhat blindsided by Wal-Mart's sudden attempt to add financial services—and particularly, banking—for its retail customers at its thousands of locations throughout the U.S.

Wal-Mart has come back with an announcement that it will not be a bank but that it will offer a host of financial services at more than 1,000 stores by 2008, which will include check cashing, bill payments, international money transfers, and a pre-paid Wal-Mart Money Card. Bank of America is examining Wal-Mart's move into limited financial services and reworking key premises that underlie its current strategic plan. One key premise is whether or not there is a whole generation of consumers—Gen Y in particular—who are going to form their opinions of what bank to use based on where they shop now. Some experts argue that banks have focused on longstanding customers, "seniors and boomers," and not so much on younger patrons or potential patrons. So Bank of America is much more closely monitoring its premises based on Wal-Mart's moves.

IMPLEMENTATION CONTROL AT BOEING

All eyes are on Boeing as it begins the final assembly of the first 787 Dreamliner. Rollout for the first jet is slated for July 8, 2007, and the first flight is scheduled for mid-August, provided the plane is ready to fly. Boeing's first customer, All Nippon Airways, should receive its first Dreamliner in May 2008. Meeting those deadlines is key, as delivery is when Boeing collects most of its money, and faces penalties if delayed. "Today, we begin assembling the first airplane of a new generation, and a new way of building airplanes," boasted Scott Strode, 787 VP of airline production. The actual snapping together of enormous composite parts built by different companies in Asia, Europe, and North America is the first milestone of this new airplane, and Boeing's strategy that is built on the concept of outsourcing components and even sections of the fuselage worldwide—a revolutionary new approach to building airplanes.

STRATEGIC SURVEILLANCE AT P&G

It was not long ago that big global brands among consumer products companies did not lose sleep over private labels. Indeed retail's worst-kept secret is that house brands in many grocery stores are often produced by Nestlé, Cadbury Schweppes, and H. J. Heinz. But over the last few years, Europe's private-label business has taken off due to the rapid growth of discounters such as Germany's Aldi and France's Leader Price. Their no-frills stores, which stock almost entirely private labels that usually cost consumers up to 40 percent less than comparable global brands, have lured customers away from established retailers. Some of Europe's big names—Nestlé, L'Oreal, and Unilever—have been getting clobbered. Not Procter & Gamble. It picked up on this trend in the course of its ongoing strategic surveillance in the European publications looking at consumer lifestyles. As a result, P&G says sales are growing as planned. P&G flexed its pricing muscle causing a British private-label competitor to write off a $1.5 billion invested in Ontex, a disposable diaper, after P&G clobbered Ontex by slashing prices on Pampers in selected markets. P&G's European CEO said, "We have surveyed this general trend in Europe for some time and concluded that discounters don't need to be a threat, rather, they can be an opportunity!"

SPECIAL ALERT CONTROL AT IBM

The $48-billion-a-year information technology services business that saved IBM from ruin in the 1990s is becoming a slow-growing, low-margin drag on the rest of the company. The special alert control attention to the IT services business and its strategy started in 2005, when IBM was shocked by the poor profit results in the first quarter of that year. IBM's growth and profit margin both declined substantially during that time, due in large part to the accelerated growth and success of India's Tata Consultancy Services and Infosys, which have seen steady 30 percent growth with profit margins three to four times what IBM achieves. IBM's reaction was to cut 15,000 jobs in Europe and the United States in a matter of months of that first shocking result. Even though IBM remains the No. 1 tech services company in the world, with 7.2 percent market share in 2007, it has a regular special alert review of its sales growth and profit levels in the IT services business each quarter, which has resulted in the elimination of approximately 700 to 1,500 jobs in North America and Europe each quarter since that initial shock as it attempts to reorganize this business and the nature of the way it does work around the globe.

Sources: Reprinted with special permission from Steve Hamm, "Big Blue Wields the Knife Again," *BusinessWeek*, May 30, 2007; Stanley Holmes, "Crunch Time for Boeing," *BusinessWeek*, May 22, 2007; "How P&G Skips the Middle Man," *BusinessWeek*, January 8, 2007; and Pallavi Gogoi, "Why Wal-Mart Will Help Finance Customers," *BusinessWeek*, June 20, 2007. Copyright © 2007 The McGraw-Hill Companies.

Monitoring Strategic Thrusts or Projects

strategic thrusts or projects
Special efforts that are early steps in executing a broader strategy, usually involving significant resource commitments yet where predetermined feedback will help management determine whether continuing to pursue the strategy is appropriate or whether it needs adjustment or major change.

As a means of implementing broad strategies, narrow strategic projects often are undertaken—projects that represent part of what needs to be done if the overall strategy is to be accomplished. These **strategic thrusts** provide managers with information that helps them determine whether the overall strategy is progressing as planned or needs to be adjusted.

Although the utility of strategic thrusts seems readily apparent, it is not always easy to use them for control purposes. It may be difficult to interpret early experience or to evaluate the overall strategy in light of such experience. One approach is to agree early in the planning process on which thrusts or which phases of thrusts are critical factors in the success of the strategy. Managers responsible for these implementation controls will single them out from other activities and observe them frequently. Another approach is to use stop/go assessments that are linked to a series of meaningful thresholds (time, costs, research and development, success, and so forth) associated with particular thrusts. Exhibit 13.2 describes Boeing's current effort to do this as it coordinates globally diverse outsourcing partners' production of various parts of the revolutionary new 787 Dreamliner fuselage and its components.

Milestone Reviews

milestone reviews
Points in time, or at the completion of major parts of a bigger strategy, where managers have predetermined they will undertake a go–no go type of review regarding the underlying strategy associated with the bigger strategy.

Managers often attempt to identify significant milestones that will be reached during strategy implementation. These milestones may be critical events, major resource allocations, or simply the passage of a certain amount of time. The **milestone reviews** that then take place usually involve a full-scale reassessment of the strategy and of the advisability of continuing or refocusing the firm's direction.

A useful example of implementation control based on milestone review is offered by an earlier Boeing's product-development strategy of entering the supersonic transport (SST) airplane market. Boeing had invested millions of dollars and years of scarce engineering talent during the first phase of its SST venture, and competition from the British/French Concorde effort was intense. Because the next phase represented a billion-dollar decision, Boeing's management established the initiation of the phase as a milestone. The milestone reviews greatly increased the estimates of production costs; predicted relatively few passengers and rising fuel costs, thus raising the estimated operating costs; and noted that the Concorde, unlike Boeing, had the benefit of massive government subsidies. These factors led Boeing's management to scrap its SST strategy in spite of high sunk costs, pride, and patriotism. Only an objective, full-scale strategy reassessment could have led to such a decision. A similar decision by Boeing regarding its current strategic "bet" on the new 787 Dreamliner is very unlikely as it nears final assembly and initial test flights of this revolutionary, next-generation, composite airplane (see Exhibit 13.2).

In the SST example, a milestone review occurred at a major resource allocation decision point. Milestone reviews may also occur concurrently when a major step in a strategy's implementation is being taken or when a key uncertainty is resolved. Managers even may set an arbitrary period, say, two years, as a milestone review point. Whatever the basis for selecting that point, the critical purpose of a milestone review is to thoroughly scrutinize the firm's strategy so as to control the strategy's future.

Implementation control is also enabled through operational control systems like budgets, schedules, and key success factors. While strategic controls attempt to steer the company over an extended period (usually five years or more), operational controls provide postaction evaluation and control over short periods—usually from one month to one year. To be effective, operational control systems must take four steps common to all postaction controls:

1. Set standards of performance.
2. Measure actual performance.

EXHIBIT 13.3   **Monitoring and Evaluating Performance Deviations**

Key Success Factors	Objective, Assumption, or Budget	Forecast Performance at This Time	Current Performance	Current Deviation	Analysis
Cost control: Ratio of indirect overhead cost to direct field and labor costs	10%	15%	12%	+3 (ahead)	Are we moving too fast, or is there more unnecessary overhead than was originally thought?
Gross profit	39%	40%	40%	0%	
Customer service: Installation cycle in days	2.5 days	3.2 days	2.7 days	+0.5 (ahead)	Can this progress be maintained?
Ratio of service to sales personnel	3.2	2.7	2.1	−0.6 (behind)	Why are we behind here? How can we maintain the installation-cycle progress?
Product quality: Percentage of products returned	1.0%	2.0%	2.1%	−0.1% (behind)	Why are we behind here? What are the ramifications for other operations?
Product performance versus specification	100%	92%	80%	−12% (behind)	
Marketing: Monthly sales per employee	$12,500	$11,500	$12,100	+$600 (ahead)	Good progress. Is it creating any problems to support?
Expansion of product line	6	3	5	+2 products (ahead)	Are the products ready? Are the perfect standards met?
Employee morale in service area: Absenteeism rate	2.5%	3.0%	3.0%	(on target)	Looks like a problem!
Turnover rate	5%	10 %	15%	−8% (behind)	Why are we so far behind?
Competition: New-product introductions (average number)	6	3	6	−3 (behind)	Did we underestimate timing? What are the implications for our basic assumptions?

3. Identify deviations from standards set.
4. Initiate corrective action.

Exhibit 13.3 illustrates a typical operational control system. These indicators represent progress after two years of a five-year strategy intended to differentiate the firm as a customer-service–oriented provider of high-quality products. Management's concern is to compare *progress to date* with *expected progress*. The *current deviation* is of particular interest because it provides a basis for examining *suggested actions* (usually suggested by subordinate managers) and for finalizing decisions on changes or adjustments in the firm's operations.

From Exhibit 13.3, it appears that the firm is maintaining control of its cost structure. Indeed, it is ahead of schedule on reducing overhead. The firm is well ahead of its delivery cycle target, while slightly below its target service-to-sales personnel ratio.

Its product returns look OK, although product performance versus specification is below standard. Sales per employee and expansion of the product line are ahead of schedule. The absenteeism rate in the service area is on target, but the turnover rate is higher than that targeted. Competitors appear to be introducing products more rapidly than expected.

After deviations and their causes have been identified, the implications of the deviations for the ultimate success of the strategy must be considered. For example, the rapid product-line expansion indicated in Exhibit 13.3 may have been a response to the increased rate of competitors' product expansion. At the same time, product performance is still low, and, while the installation cycle is slightly above standard (improving customer service), the ratio of service to sales personnel is below the targeted ratio. Contributing to this substandard ratio (and perhaps reflecting a lack of organizational commitment to customer service) is the exceptionally high turnover in customer service personnel. The rapid reduction in indirect overhead costs might mean that administrative integration of customer service and product development requirements have been cut back too quickly.

This information presents operations managers with several options. They may attribute the deviations primarily to internal discrepancies. In that case, they can scale priorities up or down. For example, they might place more emphasis on retaining customer service personnel and less emphasis on overhead reduction and new-product development. On the other hand, they might decide to continue as planned in the face of increasing competition and to accept or gradually improve the customer service situation. Another possibility is reformulating the strategy or a component of the strategy in the face of rapidly increasing competition. For example, the firm might decide to emphasize more standardized or lower-priced products to overcome customer service problems and take advantage of an apparently ambitious salesforce.

This is but one of many possible interpretations of Exhibit 13.3. The important point here is the critical need to monitor progress against standards and to give serious in-depth attention to both the causes of observed deviations and the most appropriate responses to them. After the deviations have been evaluated, slight adjustments may be made to keep progress, expenditure, or other factors in line with the strategy's programmed needs. In the unusual event of extreme deviations—generally because of unforeseen changes—management is alerted to the possible need for revising the budget, reconsidering certain functional plans related to budgeted expenditures, or examining the units concerned and the effectiveness of their managers.

balanced scorecard
A management control system that enables companies to clarify their strategies, translate them into action, and provide quantitative feedback as to whether the strategy is creating value, leveraging core competencies, satisfying the company's customers, and generating a financial reward to its shareholders.

The Balanced Scorecard Methodology

An alternative approach linking operational and strategic control, developed by Harvard Business School professors Robert Kaplan and David Norton, is a system they named the **balanced scorecard.** Recognizing some of the weaknesses and vagueness of previous implementation and control approaches, the balanced scorecard approach was intended to provide a clear prescription as to what companies should measure in order to "balance" the financial perspective in implementation and control of strategic plans.[3]

The balanced scorecard is a management system (not only a measurement system) that enables companies to clarify their strategies, translate them into action, and provide

[3] This methodology is covered in great detail in a number of books and articles by R. S. Kaplan and D. P. Norton. It is also the subject of frequent special publications by the *Harvard Business Review* that provided updated treatment of uses and improvements in the balanced scorecard methodology. Some useful books include *Balanced Scorecard: Translating Strategies into Action* (Boston: Harvard Business School Press, 1996); *The Strategy-Focused Organization* (Boston: Harvard Business School Press, 2001). HBR offers "Using the Balanced Scorecard as a Strategic Management System," *Harvard Business Review,* January–February 1996. Numerous useful Web sites also exist such as www.bscol.com.

meaningful feedback. It provides feedback around both the internal business processes and external outcomes in order to continuously improve strategic performance and results. When fully deployed, the balanced scorecard is intended to transform strategic planning from a separate top management exercise into the nerve center of an enterprise. Kaplan and Norton describe the innovation of the balanced scorecard as follows:

> The balanced scorecard retains traditional financial measures. But financial measures tell the story of past events, an adequate story for industrial age companies for which investments in long-term capabilities and customer relationships were not critical for success. These financial measures are inadequate, however, for guiding and evaluating the journey that information age companies must make to create future value through investment in customers, suppliers, employees, processes, technology, and innovation.[4]

The balanced scorecard methodology adapts the total quality management (TQM) ideas of customer-defined quality, continuous improvement, employee empowerment, and measurement-based management/feedback into an expanded methodology that includes traditional financial data and results. The balanced scorecard incorporates feedback around internal business process *outputs,* as in TQM, but also adds a feedback loop around the *outcomes* of business strategies. This creates a "double-loop feedback" process in the balanced scorecard. In doing so, it links together two areas of concern in strategy execution—quality operations and financial outcomes—that are typically addressed separately yet are obviously critically intertwined as any company executes its strategy. A system that links shareholder interests in return on capital with a system of performance management that is linked to ongoing, operational activities and processes within the company is what the balanced scorecard attempts to achieve.

Exhibit 13.4 illustrates the balanced scorecard approach drawing on the traditional Du Pont formula discussed in Chapter 5 and historically used to examine drivers of stockholder-related financial performance across different company activities. The balanced scorecard seeks to "balance" shareholder goals with customer goals and operational performance goals, and Exhibit 13.4 shows that they are interconnected: shareholder value creation is linked to divisional concerns for return on capital employed, which, in turn, is driven by functional outcomes in sales, inventory, capacity utilization, that, in turn, come about through the results of departments' and teams' daily activities throughout the company. The balanced scorecard suggests that we view the organization from four perspectives and to develop metrics, collect data, and analyze it relative to each of these perspectives:

1. *The learning and growth perspective: How well are we continuously improving and creating value?* The scorecard insists on measures related to innovation and organizational learning to gauge performance on this dimension—technological leadership, product development cycle times, operational process improvement, and so on.

2. *The business process perspective: What are our core competencies and areas of operational excellence?* Internal business processes and their effective execution as measured by productivity, cycle time, quality measures, downtime, and various cost measures, among others, provide scorecard input here.

3. *The customer perspective: How satisfied are our customers?* A customer satisfaction perspective typically adds measures related to defect levels, on-time delivery, warranty

---

[4] Another useful treatment of various aspects of the balanced scoreboard that includes further learning opportunities you may wish to explore, especially with regard to the use of this approach with governmental organizations, may be found at www.balancedscorecard.org. Chapter 7 in this book describes how the balanced scorecard approach is used to help create measurable objectives linked directly to the company's strategy.

EXHIBIT 13.4
Integrating Shareholder Value and Organizational Activities across Organizational Levels

Source: From R. M. Grant, *Contemporary Strategy Analysis*, 2001, p. 56. Reprinted with permission of Wiley-Blackwell.

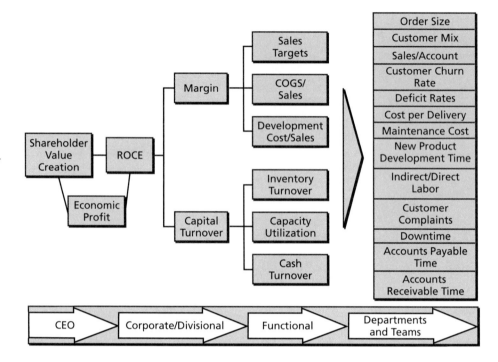

support and product development, among others, that come from direct customer input and are linked to specific company activities.

4. *The financial perspective: How are we doing for our shareholders?* A financial perspective typically uses measures like cash flow, return on equity, sales, and income growth.

Through the integration of goals from each of these four perspectives, the balanced scorecard approach enables the strategy of the business to be linked with shareholder value creation while providing several measurable short-term outcomes that guide and monitor strategy implementation. The integrating power of the balanced scorecard can be seen at Mobil Corporation's North American Marketing and Refining business (NAM&R). NAM&R's scorecard is shown in Exhibit 13.5. Assisted by Kaplan and Norton, an unprofitable NAM&R adopted the scorecard methodology to better link its strategy with financial objectives and to translate these into operating performance targets tailored to outcomes in each business unit, functional departments and operating process within them. They included measures developed with key customers from their perspective. The result was an integrated system in which scorecards provided measurable outcomes through which the performance of each department and operating unit, team, or activity within NAM&R was monitored, adjusted, and used to determine performance-related pay bonuses.[5]

dashboard
A user interface that organizes and presents information from multiple digital sources simultaneously in a user-designed format on the computer screen.

Executives and CEOs are increasingly monitoring specific measurable outcomes related to the execution of their strategies. Now, thanks to the Internet and new Web-based software tools known as **dashboards,** accessing this type of specific information is as easy as clicking a mouse. Exhibit 13.6, Top Strategists, shows how a few well-known CEOs embrace the dashboard as a key management tool for timely strategic and operational control. So, for example, an executive at Mobil Corporation might now use a dashboard to monitor updated information on where the company stands on some of the key measures

---

[5] "How Mobil Became a Strategy-Focused Organization," Chapter 2 in R. Kaplan and D. Norton, *The Strategy-Focused Organization* (Boston: Harvard Business School Press, 2001). For an online version of the Mobil NAM&R case study, see www.bscol.com.

EXHIBIT 13.5
Balanced Scorecard
for Mobil
Corporation's
NAM&R

Source: Reprinted by
permission of *Harvard
Business Review.* Exhibit
from "Putting the Balanced
Scorecard to Work," by
R. Kaplan and D. Norton,
September–October 1993.
Copyright © 1993 by the
Harvard Business School
Publishing Corporation; all
rights reserved.

		Strategic Objectives	Strategic Measures
Financially Strong	Financial	F1 Return on Capital Employed F2 Cash Flow F3 Profitability F4 Lowest Cost F5 Profitable Growth F6 Manage Risk	• ROCE • Cash Flow • Net Margin • Full cost per gallon delivered to customer • Volume growth rate vs. industry • Risk index
Delight the Consumer **Win–Win Relationship**	Customer	C1 Continually delight the targeted consumer C2 Improve dealer/distributor profitability	• Share of segment in key markets • Mystery shopper rating • Dealer/distributor margin on gasoline • Dealer/distributor survey

Safe and Reliable
 	
Competitive Supplier
 	
Good Neighbor
 	
On Spec On Time
	Internal	I1 Marketing
		  1. Innovative products and services
		  2. Dealer/distributor quality
		
		I2 Manufacturing
		  1. Lower manufacturing costs
		  2. Improve hardware and performance
		
		I3 Supply, Trading, Logistics
		  1. Reducing delivered cost
		  2. Trading organization
		  3. Inventory management
		
		I4 Improve health, safety, and environmental performance
		I5 Quality
			• Non-gasoline revenue and margin per square foot
			• Dealer/distributor acceptance rate of new programs
			• Dealer/distributor quality ratings
			• ROCE on refinery
			• Total expenses (per gallon) vs. competition
			• Profitability index
			• Yield index
			Delivered cost per gallon vs. competitors
			• Trading margin
			• Inventory level compared to plan and to output rate
			• Number of incidents
			• Days away from work
			• Quality index

Motivated and Prepared	Learning and growth	L1 Organization involvement L2 Core competencies and skills L3 Access to strategic information	• Employee survey • Strategic competitive availability • Strategic information availability

generated through their balanced scorecard process as shown in Exhibit 13.5. The opportunity to react, take action, ask questions, and so forth approaches real time with the advent of the dashboard software options. That is, of course, when there is a high level of confidence in the reliability of the data that appear—both for the CEO and the managers who might expect a question or expression of concern. The variety of ways the four executives in Exhibit 13.6 report they use their dashboards gives an interesting look at the different

Top Strategists
Using a Dashboard for Strategic Control

Exhibit
13.6

STEVE BALLMER, MICROSOFT

Ballmer requires his top officers to bring their dashboards with them into one-on-one meetings. Ballmer zeroes in on such metrics as sales, customer satisfaction, and status of key products under development.

JEFF IMMELT, GENERAL ELECTRIC

Many GE executives use dashboards to run their day-to-day operations, monitoring profits per product line and fill rates for orders. Immelt occasionally looks at a dashboard. But he relies on his managers to run the businesses so he can focus on the big picture.

IVAN SEIDENBERG, VERIZON

Seidenberg and others can choose from more than 300 metrics to put on their dashboards, from broadband sales to wireless defections. Managers pick the metrics they want to track, and the dashboard flips the pages 24 hours a day.

LARRY ELLISON, ORACLE

A fan of dashboards, Ellison uses them to track sales activity at the end of a quarter, the ratio of sales divided by customer service requests, and the number of hours that technicians spend on the phone solving customer problems.

ways they might use them, and the different types of information they would choose as key indicators about the unfolding success of their strategies.

Strategic controls and comprehensive control programs like the balanced scorecard bring the entire management task into focus. Organizational leaders can adjust or radically change their firm's strategy based on feedback from a balanced scorecard approach as well as other strategic controls. Other, similar approaches like Six Sigma, which is described in Chapter 14, can also be sources of information and specific measurable outcomes useful in strategic and operational control efforts. The overriding goal is to enable the survival and long-term success of the business. In addition to using controls, leaders are increasingly embracing innovation and entrepreneurship as a way to accomplish this overriding goal in rapidly changing environments. They look to young business graduates, like you, to bring a fresh sense of innovativeness and entrepreneurship with you as you join their companies. We will examine innovation and entrepreneurship in the next chapter.

Summary

Strategies are forward looking, usually designed to be accomplished over several years into the future. They are often based in part on management assumptions about numerous events and factors that have not yet occurred. Strategic controls are intended to steer a company toward its long-term strategic goals under uncertain, often changing, circumstances.

Premise controls, strategic surveillance, special alert controls, and implementation controls are four types of strategic controls. All four types are designed to meet top management's needs to track a strategy as it is being implemented; to detect underlying problems, circumstances, or assumptions surrounding that strategy; and to make necessary adjustments. These strategic controls are linked to environmental assumptions and the key operating requirements necessary for successful strategy implementation. Ever-present forces of change fuel the need for and focus of strategic control.

Operational control systems require systematic evaluation of performance against predetermined standards and targets. A critical concern here is identification and evaluation of performance deviations, with careful attention paid to determining the underlying reasons for and strategic implications of observed deviations before management reacts. Approaches like the balanced scorecard and Six Sigma (discussed in the next chapter) have emerged as comprehensive control systems that integrate strategic goals, operating outcomes, customer satisfaction, and continuous improvement into an ongoing strategic management system.

The emergence of the Internet has led to innovative software that further assists executives in more closely and carefully monitoring outcomes in real time as a strategy is being implemented. This allows executives and managers to have *dashboards* on their computers, laptops, or mobile devices that further enhance their ability to control and adjust strategies as they are being executed.

A central goal with any strategy is the survival, growth, and improved competitive position of the company in the face of ever-accelerating rates of change. Executives, as they seek to control the execution of their strategy, are also increasingly aware of the need for innovation and entrepreneurial thinking as a companion to their emphasis on control as a means to accomplish these key goals in the face of rapid global change. The next chapter will examine innovation and entrepreneurship.

Key Terms

balanced scorecard, *p. 416*
dashboard, *p. 418*
implementation control, *p. 412*

milestone reviews, *p. 414*
premise control, *p. 410*
special alert control, *p. 412*

strategic control, *p. 409*
strategic surveillance, *p. 412*
strategic thrusts or projects, *p. 414*

Questions for Discussion

1. Distinguish between strategic control and operating control. Give an example of each.
2. Select a business whose strategy is familiar to you. Identify what you think are the key premises of the strategy. Then select the key indicators that you would use to monitor each of these premises.
3. Explain the differences between implementation controls, strategic surveillance, and special alert controls. Give an example of each.
4. Why are budgets, schedules, and key success factors essential to operations control and evaluation?
5. What are the key considerations in monitoring deviations from performance standards?
6. How is the balanced scorecard related to strategic and operational control?
7. Read the first chapter discussion case. How would strategic controls be used to help those three situations?
8. What is a dashboard?

Chapter 13 Discussion Cases

BusinessWeek

Case 13-1: Big Blue Wields the Knife Again: *To Wrest Profits from Its Ailing IT Services Business, IBM Is Slashing Its North American Workforce and Finding Efficiencies Overseas*

1 On the surface, IBM seems to be cruising. Its stock is trading near a six-year high, at almost $106, and its overall financial performance has been improving steadily for more than a year. The company raised this year's per-share earnings forecast after stepping up a stock repurchase plan.

2 Yet the company is battling a bugbear that keeps it from breaking out and prevents the stock from really soaring. Ironically, its problem is with the $48 billion-a-year business that saved it from ruin in the 1990s: IT services. What was once IBM's growth engine seems to be turning into a chronically slow-growing, low-margin drag on the rest of the company.

3 Fresh evidence of IBM's trouble with services came May 30, when the company revealed that it had just eliminated 1,573 services jobs, mostly in North America, bringing to 3,023 the total jobs cut in the high-cost region this quarter alone. That's a small percentage of the company's total workforce of more than 355,000. Yet when weighed against rapid growth in low-cost India, where the staff topped 53,000 at the beginning of the year, the cuts underscore the biggest challenge facing Big Blue: the Indian tech industry.

INDIAN RIVALS FORCE CHANGE

4 IBM remains the No. 1 tech services company in the world, with 7.2 percent of the market last year, but its share slipped from 7.5 percent in 2005. India's tech services exports grew 32 percent, to $31 billion last fiscal year, ended in March, and are expected by analysts to top $60 billion by 2010. With a combination of low labor costs, high quality, and efficiency in how it handles jobs, the Indian companies have forced IBM and other Western services giants to fundamentally restructure the way they do business and massively shift work offshore. "The Indians are doing to the world's IT processes what the Japanese did to manufacturing," says analyst John McCarthy of Forrester Research.

5 IBM's answer isn't as simple as moving more jobs offshore. The company has developed a system that lets it shift work to the areas with available skills at the lowest available costs. The goal is to deliver higher-quality services at competitive prices. "Clearly one opportunity associated with globalization is costs," IBM chief executive Samuel Palmisano told a gathering of stock analysts on May 17, 2007. "You have access to expertise wherever it is in the world—if you have the infrastructure and the relationships to take advantage of it."

CONTINUING TREND

6 Job reductions are nothing new for IBM's huge global-services workforce, which has been under the knife continuously in the past two years. The cuts started when IBM, shocked by very poor results for the first quarter of 2005, began a major restructuring in Europe and the United States that eliminated 15,000 jobs in a matter of months. Ever since then, every few months, a new batch of jobs is trimmed from high-cost countries, including 700 in the first quarter of this year.

7 The trend is likely to continue. In the first quarter, the largest chunk of the services business, called Global Technology Services, grew a relatively healthy 7 percent, but its operating margin narrowed, shrinking by 2.5 points to just 7.8 percent. In comparison, the top Indian services outfits have operating profits of between 25 and 30 percent.

8 And their quarterly revenues are growing 30 to 40 percent year over year. IBM "is in a transition," says S. Padmanabhan, an executive vice president at Tata Consultancy Services, India's largest IT services firm. "We have been doing this for over 35 years, and it has taken a lot of intellectual capital to fine-tune the process. It's taking these companies time to reach our level of maturity."

LEANER AND LEANER

9 Meanwhile, the Indians are taking on larger and larger contracts and doing evermore sophisticated work. Even IBM's seemingly most solid relationships can become unstuck. For instance, when China's Lenovo Group bought IBM's personal computer business two years ago, IBM became a major supplier of services for Lenovo's operations. Yet Lenovo is now undertaking a massive cost-cutting campaign, and, according to a source familiar with the situation, the company has opened up bidding on its effort to integrate all of its operations using run-the-business software from SAP.

10 Why are the Indian companies able to underprice IBM and still make a much better profit? Partly—geography. The Indians typically employ about 80 percent of their staffs in low-cost countries and place the remaining 20 percent near their clients in the United States and Europe.

11 To improve its efficiency, IBM has adopted the so-called Lean Operations discipline developed by Toyota Motor for manufacturing cars. It's adapting Lean so it applies to a global service organization, something the top Indian companies began two years ago. The basic principle of Lean Operations is that a company should be making continuous, incremental improvements in its business processes. That's one of the ways IBM figures out where it can eliminate work. The company also keeps a master database, nicknamed "Blue Monster," of all of its services employees. Supervisors use

the information to track who is working on what project and when they'll be available for another assignment. In this way, the company hopes to minimize the amount of time people are between assignments.

MOFFAT'S MISSION

12 All of this cost-cutting is the task of Robert Moffat, senior vice president for integrated operations. His goal is to make the Global Technology Services workforce 10 to 15 percent more efficient each year. The key for him is to take costs out of the equation through a combination of workforce globalization, process improvements, and replacing manual labor with software. In a little more than six months, Moffat said at the May 17, 2007, analysts' meeting, he has rolled out the new formula for 22 of IBM's largest clients in seven countries. In some cases, he said, the clients have seen up to a 50 percent improvement in productivity. Now, Moffat is extending the new system to 600 more accounts.

13 All of this huffing and puffing over efficiency won't calm the frazzled nerves of IBM's 155,000-strong services workforce. True, there are still abundant employment opportunities in the company. About 30 percent of the people whose jobs are eliminated find other jobs within the behemoth, and, in the first four months of this year alone, IBM hired more than 19,000 people. But a lot of those hires were made in India. For the U.S. workforce, there is always fear that jobs will be lost to foreigners.

14 For investors, the fear is just the opposite—that IBM won't make the shift quickly enough. Only then will its massive services business be healthy again.

Source: Reprinted with special permission from Steve Hamm, "Big Blue Wields the Knife Again," *BusinessWeek*, May 30, 2007. Copyright © 2007 The McGraw-Hill Companies.

CASE 13-2: Crunch Time for Boeing: *As an August Deadline Looms for the 787 Dreamliner, Company Executives Insist It's on Target, Despite Supplier Delays*

1 All eyes are on Boeing as it begins the final assembly of the first 787 Dreamliner.

2 Even Washington Governor Christine Gregoire joined the official ceremony that kicked off the process on May 21, 2007, at the company's sprawling new state-of-the-art aircraft plant in Everett, Washington. A lot is at stake, of course, for all interested parties, including the state. The Dreamliner has notched 568 firm orders from 44 airlines, making it the fastest selling new airplane in aviation history, and it is partly responsible for reviving the once fading fortunes of Boeing's commercial airplane division.

3 But now Boeing actually has to begin building the complicated composite jets and still faces the crucial test: seeing if it can make the plane fly. "If there are going to be problems—and every new airplane program has some—it's going to start appearing now and over the next 9 to 12 months," says Richard Aboulafia, aerospace analyst for the Teal Group. "So far, so good. But you can bet that few senior Boeing executives are going to be sleeping well over the next few months."

EXECUTIVE ENTHUSIASM

4 Rollout for the first jet is slated for July 8, 2007, and the first flight is scheduled for mid-August, provided the airplane is ready to fly. Boeing's first customer, All Nippon Airways, should receive its first Dreamliner in May 2008. Meeting those deadlines is key, as delivery is when Boeing collects most of its money.

5 Boeing executives, as expected, put on a brave face May 21, 2007, and gushed enthusiastically about progress so far. The large composite fuselage sections, the first set of carbon-fiber wings, and the horizontal stabilizer have all been delivered safely to the staging area at Boeing's stripped-down assembly space. Boeing is transporting the big airplane component parts to Everett on modified 747s, called Dreamlifters, from factories in Japan, Italy, South Carolina, and Kansas.

6 "Today, we begin assembling the first airplane of a new generation," boasted Scott Strode, 787 vice president of airplane production. "The 787 not only will revolutionize air travel, it represents a new way of building airplanes."

CONTINGENCY PLAN

7 As final assembly has drawn closer, people inside Boeing say some challenges are emerging. The actual snapping together of enormous composite parts built by different companies in Asia, Europe, and North America is the first test of this new system. Boeing's supplier partners did not install many of the electronic and hydraulic systems into their respective fuselage sections as planned. Boeing is shifting workers—known as "travelers" in airplane production argot—from other airplane programs, such as the 777 Jetliner, to make up for the unfinished work. That is sure to boost overtime pay, push workers harder, and create havoc as employees frantically try to catch up on the unfinished work.

8 But on May 21, Strode downplayed some of the production challenges, saying they were typical of a new airplane program. He said suppliers did not integrate the systems in the first fuselage sections as they focused on producing their first composite structures. He said the company has it under

control. In the future, however, fuselage sections will come stuffed with the electronics and hydraulic systems, so that Boeing workers will just have to connect the wiring and piping to the other sections and then snap the plane together.

9   Strode said one challenge is that fuselage sections are currently being held together by temporary fasteners. The cause, he said, is a global shortage of fasteners—the bolts that hold the airplane together—as a result of the boost in jet production at Boeing and Airbus. Mike Bair, Boeing vice president of the 787, had said earlier during a conference call with reporters that "the fastener industry is stretched tighter than a rubber band."

SUPPLIER DELAYS

10   The other continuing challenge has been production delays from Italy. Alenia Aeronautica, which builds the 62-foot composite horizontal stabilizer and the center fuselage, had fallen behind on creating its first barrel section. This caused concern for people in the 787 program. Although Alenia Aeronautica delivered its horizontal stabilizer early, the quality of the part had many defects that Strode said were caused by the early manufacturing challenges Alenia faced. He says the Italians now have a handle on the production issue and expects to see much improved stabilizers in the near future. But such design and manufacturing fixes cost more money.

11   In an earlier quarterly financial call with analysts, Boeing executives said the company is spending an additional $1 billion to cover contingencies that could occur as production of the 787 gears up. Some of that money is earmarked for the development of the 747-8 Intercontinental.

12   Still, the making of the 787 represents a new way to produce commercial jetliners, and the changes could be positive for Boeing, if not the entire industry.

PRODUCTION LINE

13   The biggest change is the outsourcing of much of the manufacturing work to global suppliers. The Japanese are making the composite wings and wing box. Dallas-based Vought Aircraft Industries and Spirit AeroSystems of Wichita, Kansas, are making fuselage and nose sections. Italy's Alenia is making the center fuselage and the horizontal stabilizer.

14   The 787 production system has been designed using lean manufacturing techniques honed on other Boeing airplane programs, resulting in a simplified final assembly process. A huge advantage of using composites on the airframe is that Boeing and its suppliers build the wing or the nose section in just one unified piece. This means the final assembly workers will only have to fasten together six major items—the forward, center, and aft fuselage sections, the wings, the horizontal stabilizer, and the vertical fin, Boeing officials say. That drastically cuts production time compared to other current programs, where workers have to attach many more component parts to the different aircraft sections.

15   Portable tools, designed with ergonomics in mind, move the assemblies into place. No overhead cranes are used to move the different airplane structures. Although the first airplane will take about seven weeks to assemble, executives say production flow time will increase to where mechanics in final assembly are producing a Dreamliner in six days. Ultimately, the goal is to roll out a 787 every three days.

Source: Reprinted with special permission from Stanley Holmes, "Crunch Time for Boeing," *BusinessWeek*, May 22, 2007. Copyright © 2007 The McGraw-Hill Companies.

Case 13-3: Unproductive Uncle Sam: *To Boost Performance, Government Needs to Measure and Set Targets for Its Programs*

1   The past decade has been one of America's finest in terms of productivity growth. Yet a crucial 20 percent of our economy appears to have been left behind: government. Despite numerous attempts at management reform and a panoply of opportunities to transfer best practices between the private and public sectors, government seems to have missed out on the productivity boom seen in the private sector. That's a shame, because while there are important differences between the public and private sectors, government does an abundance of grant making, procurement, property management, customer service, and other jobs ripe for productivity improvement.

2   So just how far behind is government? We can't say with any certainty because the Bureau of Labor Statistics, which used to measure its productivity, stopped in 1996. Our analysis shows that government kept up with the private sector until 1987, when a gap emerged. It went on widening until 1994, when the data ran out. We believe it has widened further still.

3   This public productivity deficit couldn't come at a worse moment. Americans today say they want to limit the cost of government, but they also want more homeland security, better-managed borders, more disaster readiness, extra help in the face of global trade, cheaper health care, and better public schools. These demands sit uncomfortably with our budget deficit and our natural desire not to pay more taxes. In short, we are stuck in a productivity bind: we want more output but no more input.

4   In a white paper our firm, McKinsey & Co., published this week, "How Can American Government Meet Its Productivity Challenge?", we map out an agenda inspired by lessons from the private sector. Having studied productivity growth around the world for more than 15 years, the McKinsey Global

Institute has shown that competitive intensity at the industry sector level is the prime catalyst for productivity growth. It forces managers to improve performance and allows innovation to diffuse quickly across the sector.

5 Make no mistake, government is a sector—structured and regulated in ways that can foster or stunt productivity growth at its "firms" (agencies). And while it may not be possible to use competition in government to exert pressure to perform, Congress and the White House or state legislators and governors have plenty of tools to improve public agencies.

6 The most natural tool is the budget process, but the reality in Washington and many state capitals is that performance remains a secondary factor in budget decision making. Congressmen fight for their district or their passions, and accordingly, agencies privately admit that you budget for what you can get, not what you need or deserve. Yet when government performance, or the lack thereof, is highly visible (witness the response after Katrina), everyone takes action.

7 That's why we think a radical new approach to transparency of how government programs are performing is required. Only this will push Congress to exert performance pressure on government agencies. First, government should measure public productivity again and set national targets for productivity growth against which everyone can be held accountable. Next, political leaders should create a body we call "Gov-Star," modeled after fund-rating agency Morningstar Inc., to provide completely independent measurement of government program performance; to develop comparable program data over time—between programs, between governments, and with the private sector; and to make the data and their implications clear to appropriators and citizens.

8 But in government, pressure without support can yield demoralization and underperformance. So we also need to adopt key transformation initiatives: incentives that allow agencies to reinvest savings to the top line of programs; the introduction of chief operating officers at public agencies, to be appointed based on management experience in government or leading corporations; and a SWAT team of management experts at the Office of Management and Budget to help lagging agencies.

9 It's a long list. But if we want our government to do more and do better, we must take public management and productivity more seriously. Otherwise, citizen demands for effective government in the future will go unheeded.

Source: Reprinted with special permission from Nancy Killefer and Lenny Mendonca, "Unproductive Uncle Sam," *BusinessWeek*, August 14, 2007. Copyright © 2007 The McGraw-Hill Companies. Nancy Killefer, a senior partner at McKinsey & Co., is former Assistant Treasury Secretary for Management. Lenny Mendonca is a senior partner and chairman of the McKinsey Global Institute.

Questions for Discussion

Case 13-1: IBM

1. What is the strategy IBM is monitoring and controlling within its IT business?

2. What implementation controls (measures) and industry comparison measures does IBM appear to be using to evaluate and control its ongoing implementation and execution?

Case 13-2: Boeing

1. How is Boeing using milestones and other implementation measures to gauge its 787 Dreamliner strategy's successful implementation?

2. How could a dashboard approach help the vice president for Dreamliner production control strategy execution?

3. What complications do so many outsourced partners create for Boeing?

Case 13-3: Uncle Sam

1. How might strategic and operational controls help increase implementation effectiveness among government programs?

2. Is it realistic to expect that doing so is feasible?

3. How would you apply strategic control or operational control to a specific government program?

Innovation and Entrepreneurship

After reading and studying this chapter, you should be able to

1. Summarize the difference between incremental and breakthrough innovation.

2. Explain what is meant by continuous improvement and how it contributes to incremental innovation.

3. Summarize the risks associated with an incremental versus a breakthrough approach to innovation.

4. Describe the three key elements of the entrepreneurship process.

5. Explain intrapreneurship and how to enable it to thrive.

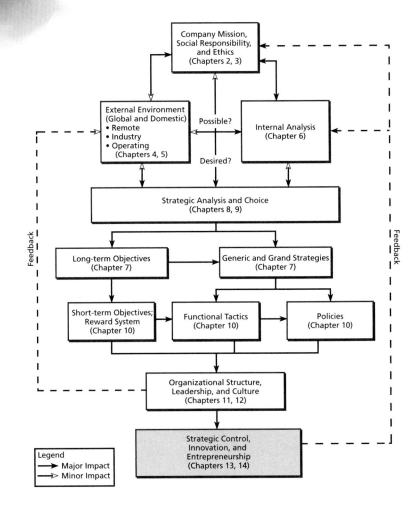

Company Mission, Social Responsibility, and Ethics (Chapters 2, 3)

External Environment (Global and Domestic)
• Remote
• Industry
• Operating
(Chapters 4, 5)

Possible?

Internal Analysis (Chapter 6)

Desired?

Strategic Analysis and Choice (Chapters 8, 9)

Long-term Objectives (Chapter 7)

Generic and Grand Strategies (Chapter 7)

Short-term Objectives; Reward System (Chapter 10)

Functional Tactics (Chapter 10)

Policies (Chapter 10)

Organizational Structure, Leadership, and Culture (Chapters 11, 12)

Strategic Control, Innovation, and Entrepreneurship (Chapters 13, 14)

Feedback

Feedback

Legend
→ Major Impact
⇾ Minor Impact

Survival and long-term success in a business enterprise eventually come down to two outcomes: sales growth or lower costs, and hopefully both. Rapid change, globalization, and connectivity in the global economy have led to impressive growth across many sectors of the global economy. Most companies have spent the last decade or two putting continuous pressure on their organizations to drive out excessive costs and inefficiencies so as to compete in this increasingly price sensitive global arena. Increasingly, executives in these same companies see growth, particularly growth via innovation, as the key priority to their firm's long-term survival and prosperity.

Recent studies by four prominent consulting organizations have documented the critical importance of innovation for CEOs of companies large and small around the globe as these CEOs seek to chart the destinies of their companies into the next decade. IBM's study of almost 800 CEOs found innovation in three ways to be the central focus among today's CEOs:—product/service/market innovation, business model innovation, and operational innovation.[1] Accenture and the Center for Strategy Research surveyed executives in the *Fortune* 1000 companies and found innovation to be very important to 95 percent of the firms represented, with innovation being most important when it results in improvements to existing products or services, decreases in costs, or improvements in meeting customer needs.[2] The Boston Consulting Group surveyed senior executives from 500 companies in 47 countries and found that almost 75 percent of those companies would increase their spending on innovation the next few years an average of 15 percent each year; more than 90 percent of these companies said that generating growth through innovation had become essential for success in their industry.[3]

The other interesting finding in the study was that fewer than half of these executives were satisfied with the returns on their investments to date in innovation. "Unless companies improve their approach to innovation," BCG Senior Vice President Jim Andrew said, "increased investment may in fact lead to increased disappointment." These executives indicated their three biggest problems with innovation were

1. Moving quickly from the idea generation to initial sales.
2. Leveraging suppliers for new ideas.
3. Appropriately balancing risks, timeframes, and returns.

Yet these executives were anxious to become more innovative. After identifying Apple, 3M, GE, Microsoft, and Sony as the innovators they most admire—the "most innovative" companies worldwide, 80 percent of these executives indicated that they anticipated even higher innovation spending by 2007.[4]

WHAT IS INNOVATION?

invention
The creation of new products or processes through the development of new knowledge or from new combinations of knowledge.

Common to the vocabulary of most business executives is a distinction between *invention* and *innovation*. We define the two using this common perspective:

Invention is the creation of new products or processes through the development of new knowledge or from new combinations of existing knowledge. The jet engine was patented in 1930, yet the first commercial jet airplane did not fly until 1957. Computers were based on three different sets of knowledge created decades before the first computer.

---

[1] *IBM Global CEO Study,* IBM Global Business Services, www-935.ibm.com/services, 2007.

[2] Toni Langlinais and Bruce Bendix, "Moving from Strategy to Execution to High Performance," *Accenture Outlook,* No. 2, (October 2006).

[3] "Global Firms Will Increase Their Spending on Innovation," *PRNewswire,* December 8, 2004.

[4] Ibid.

innovation
The initial commercialization of invention by producing and selling a new product, service, or process.

Innovation is the initial commercialization of invention by producing and selling a new product, service, or process. As executives across each of the surveys summarized earlier typically put it, "Innovation is turning ideas into profits."[5]

Apple's iPod was a *product innovation* that applied Apple's chip storage technology with sleek device styling to create an innovation within six months in 2001 at Apple. Steven Jobs then worked intensely for almost two years negotiating digital music rights with a recalcitrant music industry, culminating in the launching of iTunes in 2003—a music download *service innovation* with 200,000 digital songs to choose from for your iPod. That quickly became more than 1 million songs, and Apple had a $1 billion revenue stream added to its business. Starbucks added the simple service of wireless access free to its customers at most of its 8,000 stores in what turned out to be a highly successful *service innovation* that resulted in customers using the service staying nine times longer than regular customers, and doing so during off-peak hours.

While these two leading innovators are creating profitable product and service innovations, Toyota is perhaps the most envied business *process innovator* worldwide due to its meticulous attention to business and operating processes. Several years ago, Toyota made one change to its production lines, using a single brace to hold auto frames together instead of the 50 it previously took. While a minute part of Toyota's overall production process, this "global body line" system slashed 75 percent off the cost of refitting a production line. It is the reason behind Toyota's ability to make different models on a single production line, estimated to save Toyota more than $2.6 billion in 2005 alone.

To some business managers, "innovation seems as predictable as a rainbow and as manageable as a butterfly. Penicillin, Teflon, Post-it-notes—they sprang from such accidents as moldy Petri dishes, a failed coolant, and a mediocre glue." Not surprisingly, many managers forgo trying to harness innovation systematically. "Our approach has always been very simple, which is to try not to manage innovation," says Michael Moritz, a partner with world-renowned venture capital firm Sequoia Capital. "We prefer to just let the market manage it."[6] Exhibit 14.1 outlines a typical innovation process. For those managers who try to manage innovation, it is important to distinguish two types of innovations: incremental innovation and breakthrough innovation.

incremental innovation
Simple changes or adjustments in existing products, services, or processes.

continuous improvement
The process of relentlessly trying to find ways to improve and enhance a company's products and processes from design through assembly, sales, and service. It is called *kaizen* in Japanese. It is usually associated with incremental innovation.

Incremental Innovation

Incremental innovation refers to simple changes or adjustments in existing products, services, or processes. There is growing evidence that companies seeking to increase the payoff from innovation investments best do so by focusing on incremental innovations. We will examine the payoff research more completely in a subsequent section on risks associated with innovation. First, however, we need to examine how companies are seeking incremental innovation. A major driver of incremental innovation in many companies the last several years has come from programs aimed at continuous improvement, cost reduction and quality management.

Continuous improvement, what in Japanese is called *kaizen,* is the process of relentlessly trying to find ways to improve and enhance a company's products and processes from design through assembly, sales, and service. This approach, or really an operating philosophy, seeks to always find slight improvements or refinements in every aspect of what

[5] Ibid.

[6] Robert Hof, Steve Hamm, Diane Brady, and Ian Rowley, "Building an Idea Factory," *BusinessWeek,* October 11, 2004.

EXHIBIT 14.1 **Genesis of an Innovation**

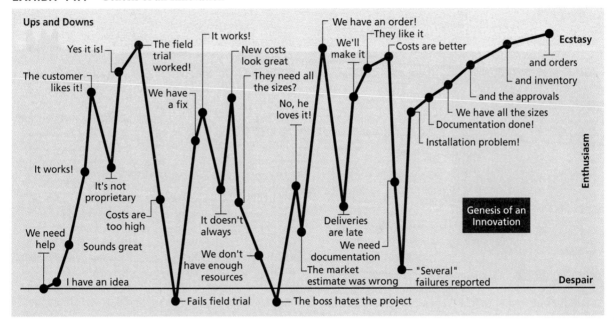

a company does so that it will result in lower costs, higher quality and speed, or more rapid response to customer needs.[7]

Toyota's extraordinary success the last five years is one good example of a cost-oriented continuous improvement effort (see Exhibit 14.2, Top Strategist). Named **CCC21** (Construction of Cost Competitiveness for the 21st Century), Toyota embarked on this intense scrutiny of every product it purchases or builds to include in the assembly of its automobiles in response to growing concern about the relative cost advantage to be derived from a surge in global automobile company mergers starting with Daimler-Chrysler. The result: a stunning $10 billion in cost savings over the past five years in the parts it buys, while also improving quality significantly. Taking the Japanese perspective, 1001 small innovations or improvements together have become something transformative. A good example would be Toyota engineers disassembling the horns made by a Japanese supplier and finding ways to eliminate 6 of 28 horn components, saving 40 percent in costs and improving quality. Or, interior assist grips above each door—once there were 35 different grips but now, across 90 different Toyota models, there are only 3. Toyota engineers call this process *kawaita zokin wo shiboru,* or "wringing drops from a dry towel," which means an excruciating, unending process essential to Toyota's continuous improvement success.

Six Sigma is another continuous improvement approach widely used by many companies worldwide to spur incremental innovation in their businesses. Six Sigma is a rigorous and analytical approach to quality and continuous improvement with an objective to improve profits through defect reduction, yield improvement, improved consumer satisfaction, and best-in-class performance. Six Sigma complements TQM philosophies such as

CCC21

A world-famous, cost-oriented continuous improvement program at Toyota (Construction of Cost Competitiveness for the 21st Century).

Six Sigma

A continuous improvement program adopted by many companies in the last two decades that takes a very rigorous and analytical approach to quality and continuous improvement with an objective to improve profits through defect reduction, yield improvement, improved customer satisfaction, and best-in-class performance.

[7] TQM, total quality management, is the initial continuous improvement philosophy used worldwide to focus managers and employees on customer defined quality since starting in Japan in the 1970s.

Top Strategist
Katsuaki Watanabe, President, Toyota Motor Corp.

Exhibit
14.2

There are milestones—and then there are ground-shifting, era-smashing milestones, like word that Toyota dislodged General Motors as the world's biggest seller of cars and trucks for the first time ever in 2007.

A FANATICAL ATTENTION TO DETAIL

Even more daunting, though, is Toyota's deeply ingrained commitment to manufacturing excellence that runs throughout this sprawling global operation. That work ethic seems to reside in the collective gene pool of company executives decade after decade, and dates back to founder Kiichiro Toyoda, who launched the company some 70 years ago.

Toyota's Katsuaki Watanabe may be self-effacing to the extreme—ever-smiling and somewhat colorless—but his sole focus in good years and so-so ones is that Toyota never lose its fanatical attention to detail, corrective adjustment, frugality, process redesign, and market adaptation.

Watanabe, and every 20-something-year-old factory hand and designer, are mindful of the heritage bestowed upon them by Taiichi Ohno, a leader still revered inside the company as the father of the fabled Toyota production system. Decades ago, Ohno established a set of in-house precepts on efficient and lean manufacturing that evolved to include just-in-time delivery; continuous improvement (*kaizen*); mistake proofing (*pokayoke*); and *obeya,* or face-to-face brainstorming sessions among engineers, designers, marketing pros, and suppliers. Toyota didn't just revolutionize car making—but pretty much global manufacturing as well.

Visit any Toyota plant in Japan, and you will see a high-tech ballet of a half dozen separate car models—from the Corolla compact to the youth-oriented models like the Scion xB—gliding along a single production line in any of a half-dozen colors. Overhead, car doors flow by on a conveyor belt that descends to floor level and drops off the right door in the correct color for each vehicle.

AVOIDING BIG-COMPANY DISEASE

The same exacting efficiency and quality standards are expected at Toyota plants anywhere in the world. Toyota's best workers are trained by in-house quality gurus at their local plant—or flown off to Japan to learn the Toyota way of double- and triple checking parts and processes for trouble and immediately signaling to superiors when things go wrong.

Above all, Toyota workers value frugality—whether it's turning down the heat at company-owned dormitories during working hours back in Japan or spending weeks jawboning with suppliers to figure out ways to redesign a key component and shave another 10 percent from production costs.

Toyota is scarcely a flawless organization, but it has managed, so far, to avoid what Watanabe and others have called the "big-company disease"—and by that what they really mean (though will never say it) is the GM disease. "The scariest symptom," Watanabe said in an interview with *BusinessWeek,* "is that complacency will breed in the company. To be satisfied with becoming the top runner, and to become arrogant, is the path we must be most fearful of." If Toyota can manage to keep that sentiment in mind, it's going to be leading the global industry for a very long time to come.

Source: Reprinted with special permission from Brian Bremmer, "Toyota: A Carmaker Wired to Win," *BusinessWeek,* April 24, 2007. Copyright © 2007 The McGraw-Hill Companies.

management leadership, continuous education and customer focus while deploying a disciplined and structured approach of hard-nosed statistics.[8]

Companies such as Honeywell, Motorola, BMW, GE, Polaroid, SAP, IBM, and Texas Instruments have adopted the Six Sigma discipline as a major business initiative. Many of these companies invested heavily in and pursued this model initially to create products and services that were of equal and higher quality than those of its competitors and to improve relationships with customers. A Six Sigma program at many organizations simply means a measure of quality that strives for near perfection in every facet of the business including every product, process, and transaction:

How the Six Sigma Statistical Concept Works

Six Sigma means a failure rate of 3.4 parts per million or 99.9997 percent. At the sixth standard deviation from the mean under a normal distribution, 99.9996 percent of the population is under the curve with not more than 3.4 parts per million defective. The higher the sigma value, the less likely a process will produce defects as excellence is approached.

If you played 100 rounds of golf per year and played at:
2 Sigma: You'd miss 6 putts per round.
3 Sigma: You'd miss 1 putt per round.
4 Sigma: You'd miss 1 putt every 9 rounds.
5 Sigma: You'd miss 1 putt every 2.33 years.
6 Sigma: You'd miss 1 putt every 163 years!

Source: From John Petty, "When Near Enough Is Not Good Enough," *Australian CPA* (May 2000), pp. 34–35.

Many frameworks, management philosophies, and specific statistical tools exist for implementing the Six Sigma methodology and its objective to create a near-perfect process or service. One such method for improving a system for existing processes falling below specification while looking for incremental improvement is the DMAIC process (define, measure, analyze, improve, control) shown in Exhibit 14.3.

Incremental innovation via continuous improvement programs is viewed by most proponents as virtually a new organizational culture and way of thinking. It is built around an intense focus on customer satisfaction; on accurate measurement of every critical variable in a business's operation; on continuous improvement of products, services, and processes; and on work relationships based on trust and teamwork. One useful explanation of the continuous improvement philosophy suggests 10 essential elements that lead to meaningful incremental innovation:

1. *Define quality and customer value.* Rather than be left to individual interpretation, company personnel should have a clear definition of what *quality* means in the job, department, and throughout the company. It should be developed from your customer's perspective and communicated as a written policy. Thinking in terms of customer value broadens the definition of *quality* to include efficiency and responsiveness. Said another way, quality to your customer often means that the product performs well; that it is priced competitively (efficiency); and that you provide it quickly and adapt it when needed (responsiveness). Customer value is found in the combination of all three—quality, price, and speed.

2. *Develop a customer orientation.* Customer value is what the customer says it is. Don't rely on secondary information—talk to your customers directly. Also recognize your "internal" customers. Usually less than 20 percent of company employees come into

---

[8] ISO certification, from the International Standards Organization, is another widely used means of encouraging rigorous and analytically based assessment and confirmation of meeting quality and building continuous improvement into the way the organization functions.

EXHIBIT 14.3   The DMAIC Six Sigma Approach

Define

- Project definition
- Project charter
- Gathering voice of the customer
- Translating customer needs into specific requirements

Measure

- Process mapping (as-is process)
- Data attributes (continuous vs. discrete)
- Measurement system analysis
- Gauge repeatability and reproducibility
- Measuring process capability
- Calculating process sigma level
- Visually displaying baseline performance

Analyze

- Visually displaying data (histogram, run chart, pareto chart, scatter diagram)
- Value-added analysis

- Cause-and-effect analysis (a.k.a. Fishbone, Ishikawa)
- Verification of root causes
- Determining opportunity (defects and financial) for improvement
- Project charter review and revision

Improve

- Brainstorming
- Quality function deployment (house of quality)
- Failure modes and effects analysis (FMEA)
- Piloting your solution
- Implementation planning
- Culture modification planning for your organization

Control

- Statistical process control (SPC) overview
- Developing a process control plan
- Documenting the process

contact with external customers, while the other 80 percent serve internal customers—other units with real performance expectations—in a process that looks like this:

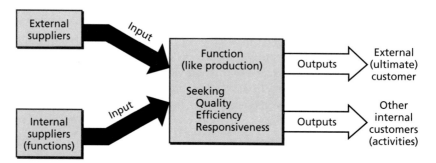

3. *Focus on the company's business processes.* Break down every minute step in the process of providing the company's product or service, and look at ways to improve it, rather than focusing simply on the finished product or service. Each process contributes value in some way, which can be improved or adapted to help other processes (internal customers) improve. Here are several examples of ways customer value is enhanced across business processes in several functions:

	Quality	Efficiency	Responsiveness
Marketing	Provides accurate assessment of customer's product preferences to R&D	Targets advertising campaign at customers, using cost-effective medium	Quickly uncovers and reacts to changing market trends
Operations	Consistently produces goods matching engineering design	Minimizes scrap and rework through high-production yield	Quickly adapts to latest demands with production flexibility

(continued)

	Quality	Efficiency	Responsiveness
Research and development	Designs products that combine customer demand and production capabilities	Uses computers to test feasibility of idea before going to more expensive full-scale prototype	Carries out parallel product/process designs to speed up overall innovation
Accounting	Provides the information that managers in other functions need to make decisions	Simplifies and computerizes to decrease the cost of gathering information	Provides information in "real time" (as the events described are still happening)
Purchasing	Selects vendors for their ability to join in an effective "partnership"	Given the required vendor quality, negotiates prices to provide good value	Schedules inbound deliveries efficiently, avoiding both extensive inventories and stock-outs
Personnel	Trains workforce to perform required tasks	Minimizes employee turnover, reducing hiring and training expenses	In response to strong growth in sales, finds large numbers of employees and quickly teaches needed skills

4. *Develop customer and supplier partnerships.* Organizations have a destructive tendency to view suppliers and even customers adversarily. It is better to understand the horizontal flow of a business—outside suppliers to internal suppliers/customers (a company's various departments) to external customers. This view suggests suppliers are partners in meeting customer needs, and customers are partners by providing input so the company and suppliers can meet and exceed those expectations.

Ford Motor Company's Dearborn, Michigan, plant is linked electronically with supplier Allied Signal's Kansas City, Missouri, plant. A Ford computer recently sent the design for a car's connecting rod to an Allied Signal factory computer, which transformed the design into instructions that it fed to a machine tool on the shop floor. The result: quality, efficiency, and responsiveness.

5. *Take a preventive approach.* Many organizations reward "fire fighters" not "fire preventers" and identify errors after the work is done. Management, instead, should be rewarded for being prevention oriented and seeking to eliminate non-value-added work as CCC21 does quite well at Toyota.

6. *Adopt an error-free attitude.* Instill an attitude that "good enough" is not good enough anymore. "Error free" should become each individual's performance standard, with managers taking every opportunity to demonstrate and communicate the importance of this Six Sigma–type imperative.

7. *Get the facts first.* Continuous improvement–oriented companies make decisions based on facts, not on opinions. Accurate measurement, often using readily available statistical techniques, of every critical variable in a business's operation—and using those measurements to trace problems to their roots and eliminate their causes—is a better way.

8. *Encourage every manager and employee to participate.* Employee participation, empowerment, participative decision making, and extensive training in quality techniques, statistical techniques, and measurement tools are the ingredients continuous improvement companies employ to support and instill a commitment to customer value.

9. *Create an atmosphere of total involvement.* Quality management cannot be the job of a few managers or of one department. Maximum customer value cannot be achieved unless all areas of the organization apply quality concepts simultaneously.

10. *Strive for continuous improvement.* Stephen Yearout, director of Ernst & Young's Quality Management Center, recently observed that "Historically, meeting your customers' expectations would distinguish you from your competitors. The twenty-first century will require that you anticipate customer expectations and deliver quality service faster than the competition."

Quality, efficiency, and responsiveness are not one-time programs of competitive response because they create a new standard to measure up to. Organizations quickly find that continually improving quality, efficiency, and responsiveness in their processes, products, and services is not just good business; it's an excellent means to identify incremental innovations that become foundations for long-term survival.

Disciplines like Six Sigma are systematic ways to improve customer service and quality; the added benefit that emerged has been its effectiveness in cutting costs and improving profitability. That has made it a powerful tool, but the notion that Six Sigma is a survival cure-all is subsiding. Once a company has created incremental innovations that maximize profitability, some argue that "kick-starting the top line" becomes paramount, which in turn means acquisition or dramatic, revenue-generating product or service innovations. And that, they argue, calls less for Six Sigma's "define, measure, analyze, improve, control" regiment and more for a "fuzzier" front-end, creative-idea-generation type of orientation.[9] That calls for a more disruptive form of innovation, which we call *breakthrough innovation.*

Breakthrough Innovation

Clayton Christensen of Harvard Business School makes the distinction between "sustaining" technologies, which are incremental innovations that improve product or process performance, and "disruptive" technologies, which revolutionize industries and create new ones.[10] Rather than an innovation that reduces the cost of a mirror on a car by 40 percent, Christensen is focusing when speaking of disruptive technologies on the product idea that works 10 times better than existing ones or costs less than half what the existing ones do to make—a breakthrough innovation. A **breakthrough innovation**, then, is an innovation in a product, process, technology, or the cost associated with it that represents a quantum leap forward in one or more of those ways.

Apple's innovation with iPod and iTunes is a breakthrough innovation. It was not an incremental improvement in Apple's computer offerings. It was an application of the microprocessor technology associated with Apple's computers, applied in a totally different industry. Apple, which only has a 2 percent market share in the personal computer industry, now has positioned itself as a dominant force in the emerging digital music and entertainment industries based on this breakthrough innovation.

Breakthrough innovations, which Christensen calls "disruptive," often shake up the industries with which they are associated, even though many times they may come from totally different origins or industry settings than the industry to start with. Apple seems to make a habit of creating new industries; Apple's original innovation 20 years earlier in Jobs's and Wozniak's garage that created the first Apple computer was viewed as a toy by most players in the computer industry at the time, but it quickly tore the mainstream computer industry apart and almost brought down the mighty IBM. Texas Instrument's digital watch resulted in the virtual destruction of the dominant Swiss watch industry. Breakthrough innovations can also be appreciated by some fringe (often new) customer group for features such as being cheap, simple, easy to use, or smaller, which is seen as underperforming the

breakthrough innovation
An innovation in a product, process, technology, or the cost associated with it that represents a quantum leap forward in one or more of these ways.

[9] Brian Hindo and Brian Grow, "Six Sigma: So Yesterday?" *BusinessWeek,* June 11, 2007.
[10] Clayton M. Christensen, *The Innovator's Dilemma* (Boston: HBS Press, 1997).

EXHIBIT 14.4
**From Idea to
Profitable Reality**

Source: Industrial Research
Institute, Washington, D.C.

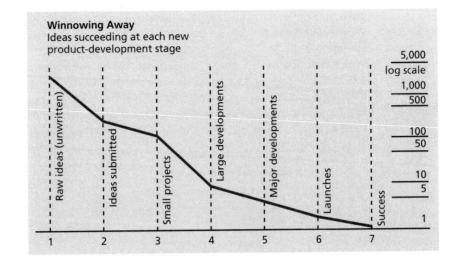

mainstream products. Sony's Walkman, Wal-Mart's discount retailing, and health insurance industry HMOs are all examples of breakthrough innovations that ultimately caused the demise of or significant reduction in key industry participants. Former Digital Equipment Company CEO Ken Olsen, a leading industry figure and a leading computer manufacturer at the time, said of Apple and the idea of a personal computer in your home when the early Apple computers were being sold: "I can think of no reason why an individual should wish to have a computer in his own home."[11]

Breakthrough approaches to innovation are inherently more risky than incremental innovation approaches. The reason can be seen in Exhibit 14.4, which is provided by the Industrial Research Institute in Washington, D.C. Their conclusion is that firms committed to breakthrough innovation must first have the ability to explain clearly to all employees, at every level, just how critical the breakthrough project is to the company's future. The second is to set next-to-impossible goals for those involved. The third is to target only "rich domains"—areas of investigation where plenty of answers are still waiting to be found. The fourth, and maybe the most important, is to move people regularly between laboratories and business units, to ensure that researchers fully understand the needs of the marketplace. These thoughts, of course, apply more to larger firms and particularly ones where breakthrough efforts are concentrated in laboratories and other separate R&D units.

Smaller firms are often sources for breakthrough innovation because they have less invested in serving a large, established customer base and gradually improving on the products, services, or processes used to serve them. We will explore these differences more completely in the section on entrepreneurship. Regardless of the size of a firm, it is important to consider risks associated with incremental versus breakthrough innovation.

Risks Associated with Innovation[12]

Innovation involves creating something that doesn't now exist. It may be a minor creation or something monumental. In either case, there is risk associated with it. Exhibit 14.4 shows the conclusions of the Industrial Research Institute's examination of breakthrough

[11] Robert M. Grant, *Contemporary Strategic Analysis* (Oxford: Blackwell, 2002), p. 330.

[12] See Morten Hansen and Julian Birkinshaw, "The Innovation Value Chain," *Harvard Business Review,* June 2007, for an interesting use of a value chain "breakdown" of innovation to use in assessing risks and sources of problems in innovation efforts.

innovation outcomes, which suggests that you need to start with 3,000 "bright" ideas, which are winnowed down to four product launches, then one major success emerges. Long odds for sure.

A recent study of 197 product innovations, 111 of which were successes and 86 failures, sought to compare the two groups in order to see what might explain differences between innovation success and innovation failure. They first sought to examine what was common to successful innovations and what was common to failing innovations First, they found that successful innovations had some, or all, of the following five characteristics:[13]

- Moderately new to the marketplace.
- Based on tried and tested technology.
- Saved money for users of the innovation.
- Reportedly met customer needs.
- Supported existing practices.

In contrast, product innovations that failed were based on cutting-edge or untested technology, followed a "me-too" approach, or were created with no clearly defined problem or solution in mind.

The second set of findings from this study emerged from the researchers' examination of what they called "idea factors." Idea factors were concerned with how the idea for the innovation originated. They identified six idea factors:

- *Need spotting*—actively looking for an answer to a known problem.
- *Solution spotting*—finding a new way of using an existing technology.
- *Mental inventions*—things dreamed up in the head with little reference to the outside world.
- *Random events*—serendipitous moments when innovators stumbled on something they were not looking for but immediately recognized its significance.
- *Market research*—traditional market research techniques to find ideas.
- *Trend following*—following demographic and other broad trends and trying to develop ideas that may be relevant and useful.

The researchers then compared the "success-to-failure" ratio of these six idea factors to see which idea factors were more often associated with success or failure of the related innovation. The two most failure-prone idea factors were trend following and mental inventions, both producing three times as many failures as successes. Need spotting produced twice as many successes as failures. Market research produced four times as many, and solution spotting seven times more successes than failures. Taking advantage of random events was the clear winner, generating 13 times more successes than failures. Their conclusion: focus on eliminating bad ideas early in the process, emphasize market research and technology application/solution spotting efforts, while being open to serendipitous outcomes in the process.

Inherent in their analysis is the presence of two key risks associated with innovation—market risks and technology risks. Market risks come from uncertainty with regard to the presence of a market, its size, and its growth rate for the product or service in question: do customers exist and will they buy it? Technology risks derive from uncertainty about how the technology will evolve and the complexity through which technical standards and dominant designs or approaches emerge: will it work?

Research by Michael Treacy of GEN3 Partners reported in the *Harvard Business Review* suggests that incremental innovation is far more effective than breakthrough innovation in managing the market and technology risk associated with innovation. Exhibit 14.5 provides

[13] "Expect the Unexpected," *The Economist,* September 4, 2004.

EXHIBIT 14.5 Risks Associated with Innovation

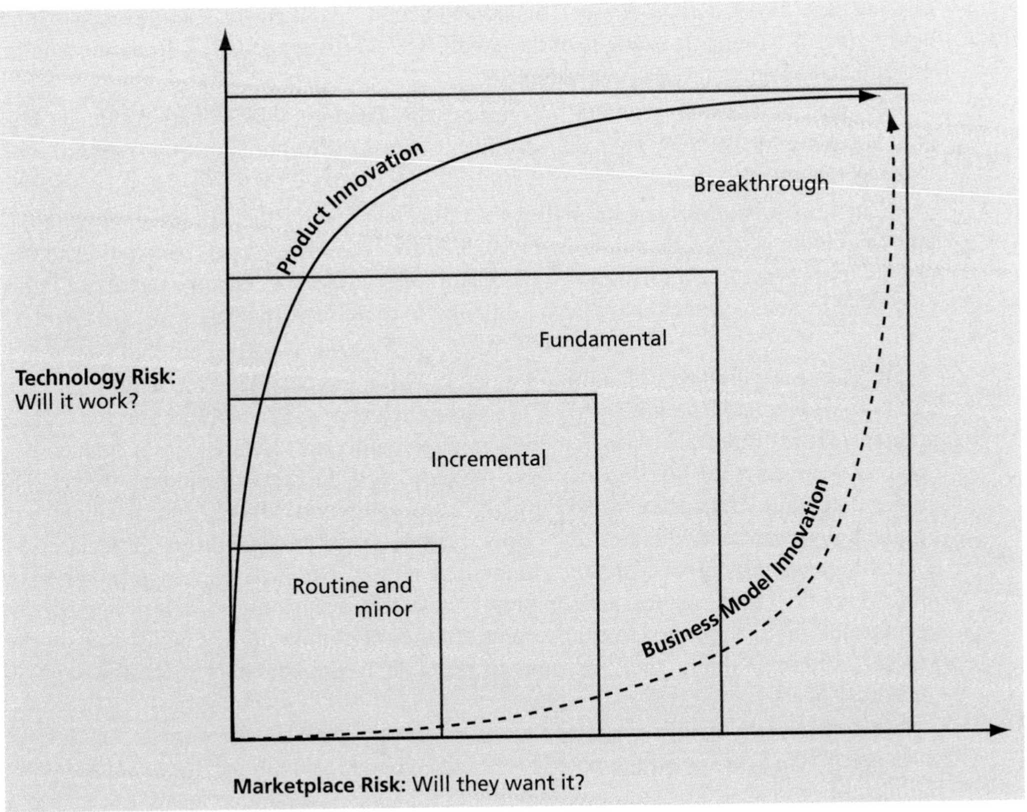

Source: Reprinted by permission of *Harvard Business Review*, Exhibit from "Innovation as a Last Resort," by Michael Treacy, July 1, 2004. Copyright © 2004 by the Harvard Business School Publishing Corporation; all rights reserved.

a visual portrayal of his research.[14] In it he suggests that technology risk is primary and marketplace risk secondary in product innovations; the reverse is true for business model or process innovations.

The point that emerges from this graph is that breakthrough innovation, while glamourous and exciting, is very risky compared with incremental innovation. Breakthrough innovations, according to Treacy's examination of much of the research to date on innovation, usually get beaten down or outperformed by the slow and steady approach of incremental innovation. He makes several useful points about managing the resulting risks:

• Remember, *the point of innovation is growth.* So ask the question, Can I increase revenue without innovation? Retain existing customers and improve targeted coverage of existing and similar new customers, where innovation isn't necessary to keep existing customers.

• *Get the most out of minimum innovation.* Tweaking a business process doesn't incur much technology risk. Incremental product or service innovation does not incur nearly the market risk that a radical one would. So emphasize an incremental approach to most innovation efforts.

• Incremental product innovations can be particularly good at *locking in existing customers.* Every saved customer is an additional source of revenue.

[14] Michael Treacy, "Innovation as a Last Resort," *Harvard Business Review,* July 1, 2004.

- Incremental business process innovations can *generate more revenue gain or cost savings with less risk* than radical ones. The earlier example about Toyota's single brace to hold auto frames is a dramatic example of the payoff—$2.6 billion annually—from one simple, incremental business process innovation.

- Radical innovations are often *too radical for existing markets,* and customers will balk at paying for that new approach, product, process, or technology. So it will fail with existing customers.

- The time to launch breakthrough innovations is not when they are necessary, important, or of interest to your business, but *when they are essential to the marketplace.* And that usually takes time, like the 10 years it has taken for car buyers to become interested in the electric/hybrid vehicles that have been available for more than 10 years.

The case for incremental innovation as a less risky approach than breakthrough innovation is widely advocated. Clayton Christensen offers a word of caution in this regard, arguing that as important as incremental improvements are, steady improvements to a company's product do not conquer new markets. Nor do they guarantee survival. He argues that while **disruptive** (breakthrough) **innovations** may underperform established products in mainstream markets, they often offer features or capabilities appreciated by some fringe (usually new) customer group—like being easier to use, cheaper, smaller, or more versatile. Often, his research suggests, those fringe customers swell in numbers to become the mainstream market, absorbing the newly informed old mainstream in the process. And in so doing, they "disrupt" or bring about the downfall of leading existing industry players.

Not surprisingly, many companies are experimenting with new ways to lower risks and improve chances for failure regardless of the innovation approach they use. For years the idea of product teams and cross-functional groups within the company has played a major role in trying to improve the odds that innovations will succeed, or that bad ideas are eliminated much earlier in the innovation management process. This approach broadens to include several more:

disruptive innovation
A term to characterize breakthrough innovation popularized by Harvard Professor Clayton Christensen; usually shakes up or revolutionizes industries with which they are associated even though they often come from totally different origins or industry settings than the industry they "disrupt."

- *Joint ventures* with other firms that have an interest in the possible innovation share the costs and risks associated with the effort. Toyota is now negotiating with General Motors to share its hybrid vehicle technology and jointly build a manufacturing facility in the United States to lower both companies' risk associated with this innovation.

- *Cooperation with lead users* is increasingly used in both types of innovation. Nike tests new shoes with inner-city street gangs; software companies beta-test their new software with loyal users; GE works with railroad companies to create a new, ecofriendly locomotive.

- *"Do it yourself"* innovation allows a company to work directly with key existing or expected customers, further allowing these customers to play a lead role in developing a product, service, or process—not just get a sense of their reaction to developments. This approach allows a company to go beyond the traditional market research model or simply cooperating with lead users. Instead, it has customers actually conceptualize or make design proposals which become the starting point for developing a new innovation. BMW sent 1,000 customers a "toolkit" that let them develop ideas, showing how the firm could take advantage of telematics and in-car online services. BMW chose 15 submissions, brought them to Germany from all over the world, and worked further with them to flesh out those ideas. Four ideas are now in prototype stage, and BMW anticipates several will emerge in new models along with an increased use of this new customer-innovation effort.

Microsoft's Last Best Hope in Search

BusinessWeek

Microsoft executives like to say they're still in the early stages of the lucrative business of Internet search, contending that as wide as Google's lead may seem now, it's not insurmountable. But for all of Microsoft's protestations, only 8.4 percent of all searches among U.S. Web surfers went through Microsoft compared with Google's 56.3 percent share in 2007.

Microsoft isn't going to give up the fight any time soon. Rather, Microsoft has been spending money to boost its efforts in what's known as vertical search, those niche markets where Netizens go when they're looking for specialized information.

Microsoft's vertical search acquisitions aren't that well known, but they may form the foundation of a different way to keep Google in check. Microsoft bought MotionBridge, a Paris-based provider of search technology for mobile phones. A few weeks later, Microsoft picked up Medstory, a small Foster City (California) start-up focused on dishing up health care information. And then Microsoft announced it bought voice-recognition leader Tellme Networks, whose technology could help Microsoft bake voice recognition into its mobile search efforts. Finally, a $6 billion acquisition of Web advertising giant aQuantive confirms Microsoft's taste for buying search innovations rather than doing it in-house to survive or thrive in search, which ultimately means finding a chink in Google's seemingly impenetrable armor.

That's why analysts think that if Google is vulnerable it may be in those specialized areas where there isn't an established leader. And despite Microsoft's best efforts to compete in generic search, vertical search may prove more strategic. "You've got to find a way to change the rules of the game," says Eric Enge, founder of Stone Temple Consulting, a search engine optimization business in Southborough, Massachusetts.

Source: Reprinted with special permission from Jay Greene, "Microsoft's Last, Best Hope in Search," *BusinessWeek*, June 26, 2007. Copyright © 2007 The McGraw-Hill Companies.

• *Acquiring innovation* has become a major way larger companies bring innovation into their firm while mitigating the risk/reward trade-off in the process. Exhibit 14.6, Strategy in Action, describes Microsoft's recent use of this approach as its "last, best hope" to compete with Google in the Internet search business. CISCO has built itself into a dominant player in the computer and networking equipment industries in large part by buying smaller companies that had developed and tentatively proven new market niches but who needed capital and distribution to rapidly exploit the new technological advantage. CISCO acquired these companies for a premium using stock, but it invested little or nothing in the early development of the technology. Thus, the smaller firm bore all the early risk of failure, and those that succeeded were rewarded in the price of the sale of their company, but CISCO got to avoid the losses associated with the majority of the innovations attempted but not successful.

• *Outsourcing innovation,* particularly product design, has become a major part of the "modular" organizational structure of today's global technology companies. Nokia, Samsung, and Motorola—cell phone giants—get proposed new-product design prototypes from HTC, Flextronics and Cellon—unknown global, billion-dollar-plus companies that create new designs and sell them to cell phone and other electronics brand-name companies annually at the biggest trade shows around the world. To Nokia and it competitors, this shifts the risk of product design innovation to these emerging technology outsourcing powerhouses.

Procter & Gamble, under Alan Lafley, has radically changed that company's culture so that it accepts as a matter of corporate strategy that 50 percent of its consumer product innovations will come from outside P&G. The resulting growth and profitability due to

ideagoras

Web-enabled, virtual marketplaces which connect people with unique ideas, talents, resources, or capabilities with companies seeking to address problems or potential innovations in a quick, competent manner.

new-product innovations at P&G over the last five years have made it the new model of open source product/service/market innovation worldwide.[15]

Ideagoras, defined as places where millions of ideas and solutions change hands in something akin to an eBay for innovation, reflects one of the newest approaches to open innovation, which leverages the value of the Internet to access talent worldwide, instantly. Companies seeking solutions to seemingly insoluble problems can tap the insights of hundreds of thousands of enterprising scientists without having to employ any of them full time. Take, for example, Colgate-Palmolive, which needed a more efficient method for getting its toothpaste into the tube—a seemingly straightforward problem. When its internal R&D team came up empty-handed, the company posted the specs on InnoCentive, one of many ideagoras or marketplaces that link problems with problem solvers. A Canadian engineer named Ed Melcarek proposed putting a positive charge on fluoride powder, then grounding the tube. It was an effective solution, an application of elementary physics, but not one that Colgate-Palmolive's team of chemists had ever contemplated.[16] Melcarek earned $25,000 for a few hours work, and a timely innovation from outside the company accrued to another client company.

Today more than 150,000 scientists like Melcarek have registered with InnoCentive, and hundreds of companies pay annual fees of roughly $80,000 to tap the talents of this global scientific community. Launched as a e-business by Eli Lilly in 2001, the company now provides solutions to some of the world's most well-known and innovation-hungry companies. The reason? Mature companies cannot keep up with the speed of innovation nor the demands for growth by relying on internal capabilities alone. This approach creates a much more flexible, free-market mechanism; secondly, it taps a vastly changing global landscape where the talent to generate disruptive or path-breaking innovation will increasingly reside in China, India, Brazil, Eastern Europe, or Russia. P&G figures that for every one of its 9,000 top-notch scientists, there are another 200 outside who are just as good. That's a total of 1.8 million talented people it could potentially tap, using ideagoras to seek out ideas, innovations, and uniquely qualified minds on a global scale quickly, efficiently, and productively.[17]

Such openness in seeking new, key innovations that determine a company's future survival and growth—as opposed to doing innovation on a closely guarded, internal basis—is viewed with skepticism and as a risk that cuts at the very core of what a company essentially exists to do. Product design, major innovations, even incremental innovations, have long been viewed as key, secret core competencies and competitive advantages that generate the long-term success of the company that possesses them. Outsourcing these activities, or doing so via ideagoras, puts the whole firm at risk in the minds of observers opposed to this open type of innovation. That said, the example of Canada's Goldcorp and Switzerland's Novartis in Exhibit 14.7, Strategy in Action, seems to be reflective of a broadening embrace of Web-enabled, wide-open collaboration in breakthrough innovation.

Another way of looking at the notion of innovation, and an organization's ability to manage it effectively, is found in the argument that innovation is associated with entrepreneurial behavior. And so, to be more innovative, a firm has to become more entrepreneurial.

---

[15] "P&G: What's the Big Idea," *BusinessWeek,* May 4, 2007.

[16] Don Tapscott and Anthony D. Williams, "Ideagora, a Marketplace for Minds," *BusinessWeek,* February 15, 2007.

[17] Ibid. See also "Innovation in the Age of Mass Collaboration," *BusinessWeek,* February 1, 2007; "The New Science of Sharing," *BusinessWeek,* March 2, 2007; *Wikinomics,* by Don Tapscott and Anthony Williams; and Satish Nambisan and M. Sawhney, "A Buyer's Guide to the Innovation Bazaar," *Harvard Business Review,* June 2007, p. 109.

A few years back, Toronto-based gold mining company Goldcorp was in trouble. Besieged by strikes, lingering debts, and an exceedingly high cost of production, the company had terminated mining operations. Without evidence of substantial new gold deposits, Goldcorp was likely to fold. Chief executive officer Rob McEwen needed a miracle. Frustrated that his in-house geologists couldn't reliably estimate the value and location of the gold on his property, McEwen did something unheard of in his industry: he published his geological data on the Web for all to see and challenged the world to do the prospecting. The "Goldcorp Challenge" made a total of $575,000 in prize money available to participants who submitted the best methods and estimates. Every scrap of information (some 400 megabytes worth) about the 55,000-acre property was revealed on Goldcorp's Web site. News of the contest spread quickly around the Internet, and more than 1,000 virtual prospectors from 50 countries got busy crunching the data.

Mining is one of the world's oldest industries, and it's governed by some pretty conventional thinking. Take Industry Rule No. 1: don't share your proprietary data. The fact that McEwen went open-source was a stunning gamble.

Within weeks, submissions from around the world were flooding into Goldcorp headquarters. There were entries from graduate students, management consultants, mathematicians, military officers, and a virtual army of geologists. "We had applied math, advanced physics, intelligent systems, computer graphics, and organic solutions to inorganic problems. There were capabilities I had never seen before in the industry," says McEwen. "When I saw the computer graphics, I almost fell out of my chair."

The contestants identified 110 targets on the Red Lake property, more than 80 percent of which yielded substantial quantities of gold. In fact, since the challenge was initiated, an astounding 8 million ounces of gold have been found—worth well over $3 billion. Not a bad return on a half-million-dollar investment.

Today, Goldcorp is reaping the fruits of its radical approach to exploration. McEwen's willingness to open-source the prospecting process not only yielded copious quantities of gold, it introduced Goldcorp to state-of-the-art technologies and exploration methodologies, including new drilling techniques, data collection procedures, and more advanced approaches to geological modeling. This catapulted his underperforming $100 million company into a $9 billion juggernaut while transforming a backward mining site in Northern Ontario into one of the most innovative and profitable properties in the industry. McEwen and his shareholders are happy miners—$100 invested in the company in 1993 is worth more than $3,000 today.

Swiss drugmaker Novartis recently did something similar—again, almost unheard of in the high-stakes, highly competitive world of Big Pharma. After investing millions trying to unlock the genetic basis of type 2 diabetes, the company released all of its raw data on the Internet. This means anyone (or any company) with the inclination is free to use the data—no strings attached.

Type 2 diabetes and related cardiovascular risk factors—including obesity, high blood pressure, and high cholesterol—are among the most common and most costly public health challenges in the industrialized world. Pinpointing their precise genetic origins could unlock a treasure trove of new medicines and result in a major windfall for Novartis shareholders.

So why the giveaway? "These discoveries are but a first step," says Mark Fishman, president of the Novartis Institute for BioMedical Research. "To translate this study's provocative identification of diabetes-related genes into the invention of new medicines will require a global effort."

In other words, the research conducted by Novartis and its university partners at the Massachusetts Institute of Technology and Lund University in Sweden merely sets the stage for the more complex and costly drug identification and development process. According to researchers, there are far more leads than any one lab could possibly follow up alone. So by placing its data in the public domain, Novartis hopes to leverage the talents and insights of a global research community to dramatically scale and speed up its early-stage R&D activities.

EXHIBIT 14.8
Who Is the
Entrepreneur?

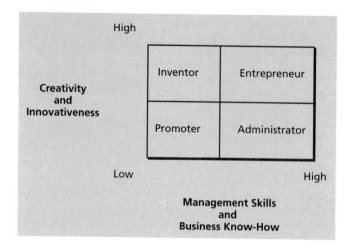

The example of CISCO and the acquiring innovation approach is one way smart companies have targeted the reality that breakthrough innovation occurs very often in the smallest of firms, where focus, intensity, and total survival depend on that innovation succeeding. Advocates of this perspective make the point that many industry-creating and paradigm-changing breakthrough innovations (e.g., personal computers; digital file sharing), as well as seemingly obvious incremental innovations ignored by large industry players (e.g., Paychex serving small businesses), came from start-up or small companies—entrepreneurs—that have since become major industry leaders.

Taking this perspective has led some other forward-thinking large companies to seek ways to make themselves more entrepreneurial and to enable their "entrepreneurs within" to emerge and succeed in building new businesses around innovative ideas. Such people, termed "intrapreneurs" in the business and academic press, have proven to be effective champions of innovation-based growth in many companies that have sincerely encouraged their emergence. But whether it is through the entrepreneurs within, or becoming or teaming with independent entrepreneurs, ensuring the presence of entrepreneurship in an organization is central to innovation, long-term survival, and renewal.

WHAT IS ENTREPRENEURSHIP?

entrepreneurship
The process of bringing together the creative and innovative ideas and actions with the management and organizational skills necessary to mobilize the appropriate people, money, and operating resources to meet an identifiable need and create wealth in the process.

The Global Entrepreneurship Monitor estimates that 11 percent of all working adults are self-employed, a number they project is steadily growing.[18] New entrepreneurial ventures are recognized globally as key drivers of economic development, job creation, and innovation. So what is entrepreneurship? What does it involve?

Entrepreneurship is the process of bringing together creative and innovative ideas and actions with the management and organizational skills necessary to mobilize the appropriate people, money, and operating resources to meet an identifiable need and create wealth in the process. Whether the process is undertaken by a single individual or a team of individuals, there is mounting evidence that growth-minded entrepreneurs possess not only a creative and innovative flair but also solid management skills and business know-how—or they ensure the presence of both in the fledgling organizations they start. Exhibit 14.8

[18] The Global Entrepreneurship Monitor is a not-for-profit research consortium that is the largest single study of entrepreneurial activity in the world. Initiated in 1999 by Babson College and London Business School, it now involves research teams at universities and other organizations worldwide. It provides annual and quarterly GEM updates at www.gemconsortium.org.

Frederick W. Smith: No Overnight Success

BusinessWeek

Frederick W. Smith, founder of FedEx Corp., has transportation in his blood. His grandfather was a steamboat captain, and his father built from scratch a regional bus line that became the Southern backbone of the Greyhound Bus system. Smith learned to fly as a teenager, a skill he turned to cash by working weekends as a charter pilot while a student at Yale University in the 1960s. While flying students and other passengers around, Smith had the insight that led him to revolutionize the delivery business. He noticed that he was also frequently ferrying spare parts for computer companies such as IBM that didn't want to wait for the passenger airlines to get critical components to customers.

Smith, an economics major, first broached his idea for an express delivery service in what became one of the most infamous term papers in Corporate America. Lore has it that he received a modest C, though Smith doesn't think that was the case. Whatever the grade, he wasn't deterred. "I knew the idea was profound," he said.

After a hitch with the Marines in Vietnam, Smith set up Federal Express Corp. in 1971 and guaranteed overnight delivery of critical goods between any two points in an 11-city network. Hardly an overnight success, Smith secured just seven packages for the first night's run.

Sparse initial volume wasn't the only headache. Until the late 1970s, the postal monopoly stopped FedEx from delivering documents. By 1973, Smith was so desperate for cash that he flew to Las Vegas to play the blackjack tables. He wired the $27,000 he won back to FedEx. Smith's persistence paid off. By the late 1970s, America came to rely on FedEx's ability to deliver goods overnight. Merrill Lynch & Co. execs even discovered employees were using FedEx to deliver documents between floors of its Manhattan headquarters building because it was faster and more reliable than the interoffice mail. These days, FedEx is a linchpin of the just-in-time deliveries revolution—its planes and trucks serving as mobile warehouses—that has helped companies around the globe cut costs and boost their productivity.

Its fleet of 675 aircraft and 72,000 trucks carry an average of 6.5 million shipments in 220 countries each day. And all because a college kid could see a market that others couldn't.

Sources: Reprinted with special permission from "FedEx Delivers," *BusinessWeek*, June 20, 2007; and Dean Foust, "Frederick Smith: No Overnight Success," *BusinessWeek*, September 20, 2004. Copyright © 2007 The McGraw-Hill Companies.

illustrates the fundamental skills associated with being entrepreneurial versus those suitable for promoters, managers, and inventors.

Inventors are exceptional for their technical talents, insights, and creativity. But their creations and inventions often are unsuccessful in becoming commercial or organizational realities because their interests and skills are lacking in terms of reading a market and bringing products or services to creation and then marketing and selling them effectively. *Promoters* are in some way just the opposite—clever at devising schemes or programs to push a product or service, but aimed more at a quick payoff than a profitable, business-building endeavor for the longer term.

Administrators, the good ones, develop strong management skills, specific business know-how, and the ability to organize people. They usually take pride in overseeing the smooth, efficient functioning of operations largely as they are. Their administrative talents are focused on creating and maintaining efficient routines and organization—creative and innovative behavior may actually be counterproductive within the organizations they operate.

The ideal *entrepreneur* has that unusual combination of talent: strength in both creativity and management. In a new venture, these strengths enable the entrepreneur to conceive and launch a new business as well as make it grow and succeed. In a large organization, these talents enable strong players to emerge and build new ideas into impressive new revenue streams and profitability for a larger company. Because these strengths so rarely coexist in one individual, entrepreneurship is increasingly found to involve teams of people that combine their strengths to build the business they envision. Exhibit 14.9, Strategy in Action, tells the story of just such a rare entrepreneur, Fred Smith, founder and chairman of Federal Express.

New ventures and small, growth-oriented business entrepreneurs are able to achieve success from effectively managing three elements central to the entrepreneurial process in creating and sustaining new ventures. Those three elements are opportunity, the entrepreneurial team, and resources:

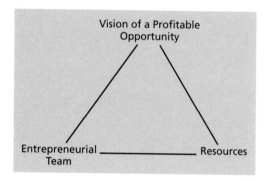

Opportunity

The most frequent cause of failure of new ventures, as reported by Dun & Bradstreet (D&B) in its yearly failure record, is lack of sales; the second is competitive weakness. Both causes stem from the lack of appreciation of the necessity for a market orientation as the basis of any new venture. In other words, failure among new ventures, is heavily linked to ventures started because someone had the idea for such a business but did not identify a concrete market opportunity.

Entrepreneurs doomed to learn from their all too frequent failure conceive an idea for a product or service and immediately become enamored of it. They invest time, money, and energy in developing the idea into a commercial reality. And, tragically, they make only a minimum investment in identifying the customers, the customers' needs, and their willingness to buy the product or service as an answer to those needs. Such entrepreneurs are focused inward, perhaps satisfying their own personal ego needs. The result is often a product or service that few customers will buy. The customers are seeking to buy benefits, and the ineffective entrepreneur is consumed with selling his/her product.

The effective entrepreneur is more likely to assume a marketing orientation and look outward at a target market to identify or confirm the presence of a specific need or desired solution. Here the entrepreneur is focused on potential customers and on seeking to understand their need. The effective entrepreneur seeks to confirm an opportunity defined by what the customer wants and is willing to pay. It is interesting that the most effective approach in the way firms seek to innovate is to bring customers into the innovation process to help shape the solution they seek. In essence, customers define what they want. The design of an effective entrepreneur's product or service comes in response to an opportunity, not the other way around.

Another way to determine if an entrepreneur is focused on simply an idea or a good opportunity is to apply the same criteria venture capitalists use to evaluate new venture investment opportunities. It is important to recognize that these criteria are applied by investors interested primarily in high-growth ventures. The criteria for smaller ventures would be less demanding in scope (e.g., a minimum $200 million market) but similar in the types of concerns that should be addressed in an effort to determine whether the opportunity is a good one. Let's look at each criterion individually:

1. *The venture team can clearly identify its customers and the market segment(s) it plans to capture.* Exactly who are the target customers? Who makes the buying decision?

Does the entrepreneur have evidence that these customers are enthusiastic about the product or service and will act favorably (e.g., pay in advance) on that enthusiasm? Firm purchase orders or other tangible purchase commitments help confirm the timing is right.

2. *A minimum market as large as $200 million.* A market this size suggests that the firms can achieve significant sales without having to attain a dominant share of its market. That, in turn, means the new venture can grow without attracting much competitive reaction. It is important to recognize that this threshold pertains to high-growth opportunities, not smaller, lifestyle ventures.

3. *A market growing at a rate of 30 to 50 percent.* This is another indicator that the timing is right to act on an opportunity; it means new entrants can enter the fray without evoking defensive reactions from established competitors. On the other hand, if the market is static or growing only marginally, then either the opportunity must offer a realistic chance of revolutionizing the industry—a rare occurrence—or the timing is bad.

4. *High gross margins (selling price less direct, variable costs) that are durable.* When entrepreneurs can sell their product or service at gross margins in the 50+ percent range, there is an attractive cushion built in that covers the mistakes they are likely to make while developing a new enterprise. When margins are small, the margin for error is too.

5. *There is no dominant competitor in the market segments representing the venture opportunity.* A market share of 40 to 60 percent usually translates into significant power over suppliers, customers, pricing, and costs. The absence of such a competitor means more room for the newcomer to maneuver, without fear of serious retaliation.

6. *A significant response time, or lead time, in terms of technical superiority, proprietary protection, distribution, or capacity.* When a new venture possesses this type of legitimate "unfair advantage," the new firm should be able to create barriers to entry or expansion by others who are aware of the profitable opportunity. When an entrepreneur can take advantage of this sort of proprietary edge, and the edge will last, the timing is right.

7. *An experienced entrepreneur or team capable of enthusiastically and professionally building a company to exploit the profitable opportunity.* Venture capitalists universally identify this as an essential ingredient for the timing to be right to invest in a proposed venture. Aspiring entrepreneurs should likewise use it as a criterion for whether it is wise to pursue the new venture opportunity they are considering. Let's examine this last point more fully.

Entrepreneurial Teams

Successful entrepreneurs and entrepreneurial teams bring several competencies and characteristics to their new ventures. Let's examine both.

- *Technical competence.* The entrepreneur or team must possess the knowledge and skill necessary to create the products or services the new venture will provide. It may be that some of those competencies exist outside the entrepreneur or team, in which case meaningful arrangements to outsource them become part of the technical competence equation. But know-how and capability are essential to success.

- *Business management skills.* The survival and growth of a technically viable new venture depend on the ability of the entrepreneur to understand and manage the economics of the business. Financial and accounting know-how in areas of cash flow, liquidity, costs and contributions, record keeping, pricing, structuring debt, and asset acquisition are essential. People management skills, marketing, organizational skills, sales, computer literacy, and planning skills are just some of those essential to success.

Technical and business skills being critical, they alone are not enough. Observers identify several behavioral and psychological characteristics that are usually associated with successful entrepreneurs:

- *Endless commitment and determination.* Ask any number of entrepreneurs the secret of their success, and they inevitably cite this one. Entrepreneurs' level of commitment can usually be gauged by their willingness to jeopardize personal economic well-being, to tolerate a lower standard of living than they would otherwise enjoy early in the enterprise, and even to sacrifice time with their family.

- *A strong desire to achieve.* Need to achieve is a strong entrepreneurial motivator. Money is a way to keep score, but outdoing their own expectations is an almost universal driver.

- *Orientation toward opportunities and goals.* Good entrepreneurs always like to talk about their customers and their customers' needs. They can readily respond when asked what their goals are for this week, month, and year.

- *An internal locus of control.* Successful entrepreneurs are self-confident. They believe they control their own destiny. To use a sports analogy, they want the ball for the critical last-second shot.

- *Tolerance for ambiguity and stress.* Start-up entrepreneurs face the need to meet payroll when revenue has yet to be received, jobs are constantly changing, customers are ever new, and setbacks and surprises are inevitable.

- *Skills in taking calculated risks.* Entrepreneurs are like pilots: they take calculated risks. They do everything possible to reduce or share risks. They prepare or anticipate problems; confirm the opportunity and what is necessary for success; create ways to share risk with suppliers, investors, customers, and partners; and are typically obsessed with controlling key roles in the execution of the firm's operations.

- *Little need for status and power.* Power accrues to good entrepreneurs, but their focus is on opportunities, customers, markets, and competition. They may use that power in these settings, but they do not often seek status for the sake of having it.

- *Problem solvers.* Good entrepreneurs seek out problems that may affect their success and methodically go about overcoming them. Not intimidated by difficult situations, they are usually decisive and capable of enormous patience.

- *A high need for feedback.* "How are we doing?" The question is ever-present in an entrepreneur's mind. They seek feedback. They nurture mentors to learn from and expand their network of contacts.

- *Ability to deal with failure.* Entrepreneurs love to win, but they accept failure and aggressively learn from it as a way to better manage their next venture.

- *Boundless energy, good health, and emotional stability.* Their challenges are many, so good entrepreneurs seem to embrace their arena and pursue good health to build their stamina and emotional well-being.

- *Creativity and innovativeness.* New ways of looking at things, tinkering, staying late to talk with a customer or employee—all these are typical of entrepreneurs' obsession with doing things better, more efficiently, and so forth. They see an opportunity instead of a problem, a solution instead of a dilemma.

- *High intelligence and conceptual ability.* Good entrepreneurs have "street smarts," a special sense for business, and the ability to see the big picture. They are good strategic thinkers.

- *Vision and the capacity to inspire.* The capacity to shape and communicate a vision in a way that inspires others is a valuable skill entrepreneurs need in themselves or from someone in their core team.

Resources

The third element in new venture entrepreneurship involves *resources*—money and time. Let's summarize money first. A vital ingredient for any business venture is the capital necessary to acquire equipment, facilities, people, and capabilities to pursue the targeted opportunity. New ventures do this in two ways. **Debt financing** is money provided to the venture that must be repaid at some point in time. The obligation to pay is usually secured by property or equipment bought by the business, or by the entrepreneur's personal assets. **Equity financing** is money provided to the venture that entitles the provider to rights or ownership in the venture and which is not expected to be repaid. It entitles the source to some form of ownership in the venture, for which the source usually expects some future return or gain on that investment.

Debt financing is generally obtained from a commercial bank to pay for property, equipment, and maybe provide working capital—all available only after there is proven revenue coming into the business. Family and friends are debt sources, as are leasing companies, suppliers, and companies that lend against accounts receivable. Entrepreneurs benefit when using debt capital because they retain ownership and increase the return on their investment if things go as planned. If not, debt financing can be a real problem for new ventures because rapid growth requires steady cash flow (to pay salaries, bills, interest), which creates a real dilemma if interest rates rise and sales slow down. Most new ventures find early debt capital hard to get anyway, so gradually nurturing a relationship with a commercial lender, letting them get to know the entrepreneur and the business, is a wise approach for the new entrepreneur.

Equity financing is usually obtained from one or more of three sources: friendly sources, informal venture investors, or professional venture capitalists. In each case, it is often referred to as "patient money," meaning it does not have to be paid back immediately or on any particular schedule. *Friendly sources* are prevalent early in many new ventures—friends, family, wealthy individuals who know the entrepreneur. *Informal venture investors,* usually wealthy individuals, or what are now called "angel" investors (for obvious reasons), are increasingly active and accessible as possible equity investors. *Professional venture capitalists* seek investment in the truly high-growth potential ventures. They have stringent criteria as we have seen, and expect a return of five times their money in three to five years! A fourth source of equity capital, *public stock offerings,* is available for a very select few new ventures. They are usually firms that have gone through the other three sources first.

Regardless of the source, equity capital is money that does not have to be repaid on an immediate, regular basis as debt capital requires. So when a firm is rapidly growing and needs to use all its cash flow to grow, not having to repay makes equity more attractive than debt. The unattractive aspect of equity financing for some people is that it constitutes selling part of the ownership of the business and, with it, a say in the decisions directing the venture.

The other resource is time—time of the entrepreneur(s) and key players in the business venture's chance for success. The entrepreneur is the catalyst, the glue that holds the fledgling business together and oftentimes the critical source of energy to make success happen. As we noted earlier, determination is a key characteristic of entrepreneurs. And time is the most critical resource, combined with determination, to virtually "will" the new venture's success at numerous junctures in its early development.

Successful entrepreneurs are impressive growth and value building innovators. Their success often comes at the expense of large firms with which they compete, do business, obtain supplies, and such. Their success in commercializing new ideas has drawn the attention of many larger companies leading to the question, Can a big firm be more entrepreneurial? The conclusion has been a tentative yes, that larger firms can increase their level of innovation and subsequent commercialization success if they encourage

---

debt financing
Money "loaned" to an entrepreneur or business venture that must be repaid at some point in time.

equity financing
Money provided to a business venture that entitles the provider to rights or ownership in the venture and which is not expected to be repaid.

entrepreneurship and entrepreneurs within their organizations. Understanding and encouraging entrepreneurship in large organizations to improve future survival and growth has become a major agenda in thousands of large companies today. The ideas behind these efforts, which have been called *intrapreneurship,* are examined in the next section.

Intrapreneurship

intrapreneurship
A term associated with entrepreneurship in large, established companies; the process of attempting to identify, encourage, enable, and assist entrepreneurship within a large, established company so as to create new products, processes, services, or improvements that become major new revenue streams and/or sources of cost savings for the company.

intrapreneurship freedom factors
Ten characteristics identified by Dr. Gordon Pinchot and elaborated upon by others that need to be present in large companies seeking to encourage and increase the level of intrapreneurship within their company.

Intrapreneurship, or entrepreneurship in large companies, is the process of attempting to identify, encourage, enable, and assist entrepreneurship within a large, established company so as to create new products, processes, or services that become major new revenue streams and sources of cost savings for the company. Gordon Pinchot, founder of a school for intrapreneurs and creator of the phrase itself, suggests 10 **freedom factors** that need to be present in large companies seeking to encourage intrapreneurship:

1. *Self-selection.* Companies should give innovators the opportunity to bring forth their ideas, rather than making the generation of new ideas the designated responsibility of a few individuals or groups.

2. *No hand-offs.* Once ideas surface, managers should allow the person generating the idea to pursue it rather than instructing him or her to turn it over ("hand it off") to someone else.

3. *The doer decides.* Giving the originator of an idea some freedom to make decisions about its further development and implementation, rather than relying on multiple levels of approval for even the most minor decision, enhances intrapreneurship.

4. *Corporate "slack."* Firms that set aside money and time ("slack") facilitate innovation.

5. *End the "home run" philosophy.* Some company cultures foster an interest in innovative ideas only when they represent major breakthroughs. Intrapreneurship is restricted in that type of culture.

6. *Tolerance of risk, failure, and mistakes.* Where risks and failure are damaging to their careers, managers carefully avoid them. But innovations inherently involve risks, so calculated risks and some failures should be tolerated and chalked up to experience.

7. *Patient money.* The pressure for quarterly profits in many U.S. companies stifles innovative behavior. Investment in intrapreneurial activity may take time to bear fruit.

8. *Freedom from turfness.* In any organization, people stake out turf. Boundaries go up. Intrapreneurship is stifled by this phenomenon because cross-fertilization is often central to innovation and successful entrepreneurial teams.

9. *Cross-functional teams.* Organizations inhibit cross-functional interaction by insisting that communication flow upward. That inhibits sales from learning from operations and company people from interacting with relevant outsiders.

10. *Multiple options.* When an individual with an idea has only one person to consult or one channel to inquire into for developing the idea, innovation can be stifled. Intrapreneurship is encouraged when people have many options for discussing or pursuing innovative ideas.

When you read Pinchot's 10 freedom factors, they sound very much like characteristics associated with entrepreneurs or the nature of the types of resources—money and time—that we identified as being central to the entrepreneurship process. And that, obviously, is exactly what intrapreneurship is trying to do—replicate the presence of entrepreneurs (small undertakings) inside a large enterprise that offers the potential advantage of easier money, expertise, facilities, distribution, and so forth. Exhibit 14.10, Strategy in Action, describes how Yahoo! is trying to launch its own intrapreneurs in just this manner at a facility it calls

Yahoo!'s Intrapreneurs

Yahoo!'s mash-up service, Pipes, was the first product to come out of "Brickhouse," Yahoo!'s answer to the tiny, nimble shops that have nipped at its heels and chewed away at its revenues in recent years. Brickhouse marks a dramatic break from the old ways of doing things at Yahoo!. It's designed to feel completely different from its established—and yes, older—online parent. The 14,000-square-foot offices are located in the hip South of Market neighborhood in San Francisco, 40 miles away from Yahoo! headquarters in strip-mall-laden Sunnyvale. The facility is bereft of Yahoo! logos. Purple, the company's signature color, is noticeably absent.

The staff is made up of Yahoo! employees with the kind of ideas that, in theory at least, would have venture capitalists whipping out their checkbooks. Teams are built around ideas. And the whole effort is led by a genuine star of the Web 2.0 movement, Caterina Fake, who co-founded the innovative photo-sharing site Flickr, which Yahoo! acquired two years ago. The idea is that Brickhouse will give Yahoo! a way to push the envelope and develop brand-new projects, while employees have the chance to experiment with ideas far from their day-to-day jobs.

Brickhouse was born out of the notion that Yahoo!'s employees come up with ideas for new ventures, but they haven't had an effective way to execute them. Bradley Horowitz, vice-president for product strategy, points to a recent experience stemming from Yahoo!'s Hack Day, a two-day event held the last weekend of September 2006, during which all Yahoo! employees were given the ability to hack into the company's programs to develop new features and applications. One employee designed a tool that would leave behind users' fingerprints, in the form of their image or profile, when they visited a page. Yahoo! executives realized the program could be useful to publishers and warrant development. However, the employee had another assignment and there wasn't a good way, at the time, to allow him to easily leave his current project to work on the idea.

Yahoo!'s brand is another challenge. People associate the company and its trademark yodel with one of the Web's prime destinations for mail, news, entertainment, and search. But Yahoo!'s status as an established, family-oriented, commercial brand can turn away some cutting-edge users. That's why, with Brickhouse, Yahoo! is going to launch many more products off-brand than it has done in the past. That he says will let the company float new, edgier ideas without having an adverse impact on the Yahoo! brand, and it may attract users who have negative associations with Yahoo!'s brand.

OUTLET FOR CREATIVE EMPLOYEES

Yahoo! is treating the site as an outlet of sorts for entrepreneurial and creative employees. It wants them to have the ability, as they would if they started their own company, to give things their best shot and then, if they don't really work, walk away.

In this way, Horowitz and others hope Brickhouse serves to help retain employees who otherwise would go off on their own in search of funding. Brickhouse developers whose ideas succeed would receive additional financial compensation for their work. He said the figure would be somewhere between a pat on the back and an acquisition-size bonus. "The idea is they would enjoy some upside," he says.

Whether Brickhouse will succeed remains to be seen. But the scope of Yahoo!'s ambition is clear. Sometimes to think big, you have to act small.

Source: Reprinted with special permission from Catherine Holahan, "Yahoo! Taps Its Inner Startup," *BusinessWeek,* February 9, 2007. Copyright © 2007 The McGraw-Hill Companies.

"Brickhouse." Even with all the advantages noted earlier, it is still a challenge for larger organizations to attract, allow, and retain true entrepreneurial behavior within their midst, as Yahoo! readily acknowledges even as it attempts to enhance innovation via intrapreneurship in its Brickhouse.[19] Nine specific ways companies are attempting to enable intrapreneurs and intrapreneurship to flourish in their companies are given here:[20]

[19] Catherine Holahan, "Yahoo! Taps Its Inner Startup," *BusinessWeek,* February 9, 2007.

[20] For elaboration on these and other ideas, see "Lessons from Apple," *The Economist,* June 7, 2007; "Remember to Forget, Borrow, and Learn," *BusinessWeek,* March 28, 2007; "Clayton Christensen's Innovation Brain," *BusinessWeek,* June 15, 2007; and www.Businessweek.com/innovation.

- *Designate intrapreneurship "sponsors."* Formally identify several people with credibility and influence in the company to serve as facilitators of new ideas. These "sponsors" usually have discretionary funds to allocate on the spot to help innovators develop their ideas.

- *Allow innovation time.* 3M was know for its "15 percent rule," which means that members of its engineering group can spend 15 percent of their time tinkering with whatever idea they think has market potential. Google gives employees one day a week to work on their own projects.

- *Accommodate intrapreneurial teams.* 3M calls it "tin cupping." American Cement calls it "innovation volunteers." P&G sets up teams across product divisions to intentionally cross-pollinate new business. The idea is for companies to give managers interdepartmental or unit flexibility to let informal idea-development teams (a marketing person, an engineer, and an operations person) interact about promising ideas and develop them as though they were an independent business.

- *Provide intrapreneurial forums.* Owens Corning calls them "skunkworks, innovation boards, and innovation fairs." 3M has "technical forums," annual "technical review fairs," and "sales clubs." P&G, eBay, and Amazon bring in outsiders, customers especially, to help form the basis for interaction about new ideas where ones that gain traction can quickly move to more serious pursuit using other specific ways described here.

- *Use intrapreneurial controls.* Quarterly profit contribution does not work with intrapreneurial ventures at their early stages. Milestone reviews like we discussed earlier in this chapter—key timetables, resource requirements—provide a type of control more suited to early, innovative activity.

- *Provide intrapreneurial rewards.* Recognition for success, financial bonuses if successful, and most importantly the opportunity to "do it again," with even greater freedom in developing and implementing the next idea are extremely important to this type of venture.

- *Articulate specific innovation objectives.* Clearly setting forth organizational objectives that legitimize and indeed call for intrapreneurship and innovation helps encourage an organizational culture to support this activity. 3M is the "granddaddy" of this approach, having long held to a corporate objective, which they have hit every year since 1970, that "25 percent of annual sales each year will come from products introduced within the last five years." P&G has a corporate goal that 50 percent of its innovations originate outside the company to encourage collaborative, "open," innovative behavior.

- *Create a culture of intrapreneurship.* Jeff Bezos of Amazon.com calls it a "culture of divine discontent," in which everyone itches to improve things. P&G calls it letting outsiders into P&G to innovate, and CEO Lafley is working to ensure that more than half of P&G new products will come from outsiders teamed with inside intrapreneurs. GE's Immelt hires successful intrapreneurs from other companies to become leaders in a usually insider-promoted organization, both to get the intrapreneur involved and even more importantly to send a message of fundamental cultural change toward intrapreneurship. Other firms create internal "banks" to invest in new internal start-ups. Intel has its own venture capital arm investing aggressively in entrepreneurial ventures inside and outside the company, often spinning them off.

- *Encourage innovation from without as well as within.* Apple is widely assumed to be an innovator "within." In fact, its real skill lies in stitching together its own ideas with technologies from outside and then wrapping the results in elegant software and simple, stylish designs.

Innovation and entrepreneurship are intertwined phenomena and processes. Organizations seeking to control their destiny, which most all seek to do, increasingly "get it" that even having a destiny may be the issue. And to have that opportunity or chance, organizations need leaders who embrace the importance of being innovative and entrepreneurial to give their companies the chance to find ways to adapt, be relevant, to position themselves in a future that, to use a trite phrase, has but one real constant—change.

Summary

A central goal with any strategy is the survival, growth, and improved competitive position of the company in the future. Executives seek ways to make their organizations innovative and entrepreneurial because these are increasingly seen as essential capabilities for survival, growth, and relevance. Incremental innovation—where companies increasingly, in concert with their customers, seek to steadily refine and improve their products, services, and processes—has proven to be a very effective approach to innovation. The continuous improvement philosophy, and programs such as CCC21 and Six Sigma, are key ways firms make incremental innovation a central part of their organization's ongoing work activities.

Breakthrough innovation involves far more risk than the incremental approach yet brings high reward when successful. Firms with this approach need a total commitment and are often going against mainstream markets in the process. Large, well-known global companies are increasingly embracing "open" approaches to innovation, including breakthrough innovation, in ways that would have been unthinkable 20 years ago. They have embraced the outsourcing of much product design innovation in recent years and are rapidly adopting Web-enabled forums for tapping expertise located around the globe to gain assistance and collaboration in generating breakthrough innovation. They also increasingly look to innovate by acquiring small, entrepreneurial firms that often generate breakthrough innovations because they have a narrow focus, tolerate risks, have a passion for what they are doing, and benefit greatly if they succeed.

Entrepreneurship is central to making businesses innovative and fresh. New-venture entrepreneurship is the source of much innovation, and it is really a process involving opportunity, resources, and key people. Opportunity is focusing intensely on solving problems and benefits to customers rather than product or service ideas someone just dreams up. Resources involve money and time. Key people, the entrepreneurial team, need to bring technical skill, business skill, and key characteristics to the new venture endeavor for it to succeed.

Intrapreneurship is entrepreneurship in large organizations. Many firms now claim that they seek to encourage intrapreneurship. For intrapreneurship to work, individual intrapreneurs need freedom and support to pursue perceived opportunities, be allowed to fail, and do more of the same more easily if they succeed.

Key Terms

breakthrough innovation, *p. 434*
CCC21, *p. 429*
continuous improvement, *p. 428*
debt financing, *p. 447*
disruptive innovation, *p. 438*

entrepreneurship, *p. 442*
equity financing, *p. 447*
ideagoras, *p. 440*
incremental innovation, *p. 428*
innovation, *p. 428*

intrapreneurship, *p. 448*
intrapreneurship freedom
factors, *p. 448*
invention, *p. 427*
Six Sigma, *p. 429*

Questions for Discussion

1. What is the difference between incremental and breakthrough innovation? What risks are associated with each approach?
2. Why is continuous improvement, and programs such as CCC21 and Six Sigma, a good way to develop incremental innovation?
3. What is an ideagora?
4. How are big, global companies looking "outward" to accelerate their innovativeness and break-through innovations?
5. Why do most breakthrough innovations occur in smaller firms?
6. What are the three key elements in the entrepreneurship process in new ventures?
7. What is intrapreneurship, and how is it best enabled?

Chapter 14 Discussion Case

At 3M, a Struggle between Efficiency and Creativity

3M and Innovation: George Buckley, 3M's chief executive, wants to jump-start sales growth with breakthrough products and return the company to its risk-taking roots

- 3M has built a reputation for being an outstanding corporate innovator over its 100-plus-year history. In looking back at some of the company's "greatest hits," it's striking how serendipity played a big role in the birth of the breakthrough ideas. For a long while, it was a matter of 3M corporate policy to encourage risk-taking and to tolerate failure.
- By the late 1990s, though, the company had become bloated and sluggish. Profits were erratic, and its stock price languished. In December 2000, CEO Jim McNerney brought much-needed managerial discipline to the company before leaving to take the CEO job at Boeing in 2005. Some critics, however, argue that the Six Sigma mindset he inculcated had an unintended side-effect: crowding out the creative culture needed to innovate. Current CEO George Buckley has shifted the corporate mandate back to sales growth, eased up on Six Sigma, and is looking for more innovative breakthroughs on his watch.

1 Not too many years ago, the temple of management was General Electric. Former CEO Jack Welch was the high priest, and his disciples spread the word to executive suites throughout the land. One of his most highly regarded followers, James McNerney, was quickly snatched up by 3M after falling short in the closely watched race to succeed Welch. 3M's board considered McNerney a huge prize, and the company's stock jumped nearly 20 percent in the days after December 5, 2000, when his selection as CEO was announced. The mere mention of his name made everyone richer.

2   McNerney was the first outsider to lead the insular St. Paul (Minnesota) company in its 100-year history. He had barely stepped off the plane before he announced he would change the DNA of the place. His playbook was vintage GE. McNerney axed 8,000 workers (about 11 percent of the workforce), intensified the performance-review process, and tightened the purse strings at a company that had become a profligate spender. He also imported GE's vaunted Six Sigma program—a series of management techniques designed to decrease production defects and increase efficiency. Thousands of staffers became trained as Six Sigma "black belts." The plan appeared to work: McNerney jolted 3M's moribund stock back to life and won accolades for bringing discipline to an organization that had become unwieldy, erratic, and sluggish.

3   Then, four and a half years after arriving, McNerney abruptly left for a bigger opportunity, the top job at Boeing. Now his successors face a challenging question: whether the relentless emphasis on efficiency had made 3M a less creative company. That's a vitally important issue for a company whose very identity is built on innovation. After all, 3M is the birthplace of masking tape, Thinsulate, and the Post-it note. It is the invention machine whose methods were consecrated in the influential 1994 best-seller *Built to Last* by Jim Collins and Jerry I. Porras. But those old hits have become distant memories. It has been a long time since the debut of 3M's last game-changing technology: the multilayered optical films that coat liquid-crystal display screens. At the company that has always prided itself on drawing at least one-third of sales from products released in the past five years, today that fraction has slipped to only one-quarter.

4   Those results are not coincidental. Efficiency programs such as Six Sigma are designed to identify problems in work

processes—and then use rigorous measurement to reduce variation and eliminate defects. When these types of initiatives become ingrained in a company's culture, as they did at 3M, creativity can easily get squelched. After all, a breakthrough innovation is something that challenges existing procedures and norms. "Invention is by its very nature a disorderly process," says current CEO George Buckley, who has dialed back many of McNerney's initiatives. "You can't put a Six Sigma process into that area and say, well, I'm getting behind on invention, so I'm going to schedule myself for three good ideas on Wednesday and two on Friday. That's not how creativity works." McNerney declined to comment for this story.

PROUD CREATIVE CULTURE

5   The tension that Buckley is trying to manage—between innovation and efficiency—is one that's bedeviling CEOs everywhere. There is no doubt that the application of lean and mean work processes at thousands of companies, often through programs with obscure-sounding names such as ISO 9000 and total quality management, has been one of the most important business trends of past decades. But as once-bloated U.S. manufacturers have shaped up and become profitable global competitors, the onus shifts to growth and innovation, especially in today's idea-based, design-obsessed economy. While process excellence demands precision, consistency, and repetition, innovation calls for variation, failure, and serendipity.

6   Indeed, the very factors that make Six Sigma effective in one context can make it ineffective in another. Traditionally, it uses rigorous statistical analysis to produce unambiguous data that help produce better quality, lower costs, and more efficiency. That all sounds great when you know what outcomes you'd like to control. But what about when there are few facts to go on—or you don't even know the nature of the problem you're trying to define? "New things look very bad on this scale," says MIT Sloan School of Management professor Eric von Hippel, who has worked with 3M on innovation projects that he says "took a backseat" once Six Sigma settled in. "The more you hardwire a company on total quality management, [the more] it is going to hurt breakthrough innovation," adds Vijay Govindarajan, a management professor at Dartmouth's Tuck School of Business. "The mindset that is needed, the capabilities that are needed, the metrics that are needed, the whole culture that is needed for discontinuous innovation, are fundamentally different."

7   The exigencies of Wall Street are another matter. Investors liked McNerney's approach to boosting earnings, which may have sacrificed creativity but made up for it in consistency. Profits grew, on average, 22 percent a year. In Buckley's first year, sales approached $23 billion and profits totaled $1.4 billion, but two quarterly earnings misses and a languishing stock made it a rocky ride. In 2007, Buckley seems to have satisfied many skeptics on the Street, convincing them he can ignite top-line growth without killing the McNerney-led productivity improvements. Shares are up 12 percent since January.

Buckley's street cred was hard-won. He's nowhere near the management rock star his predecessor was. McNerney could play the President on TV. He's tall and athletic, with charisma to spare. Buckley is of average height, with a slight middle-age paunch, an informal demeanor, and a scientist's natural curiosity. In the office he prefers checked shirts and khakis to suits and ties. He's bookish and puckish, in the way of a tenured professor.   8

Buckley, in short, is just the kind of guy who has traditionally thrived at 3M. It was one of the pillars of the "3M Way" that workers could seek out funding from a number of company sources to get their pet projects off the ground. Official company policy allowed employees to use 15 percent of their time to pursue independent projects. The company explicitly encouraged risk and tolerated failure. 3M's creative culture foreshadowed the one that is currently celebrated unanimously at Google.   9

Perhaps all of that made it particularly painful for 3M's proud workforce to deal with the hard reality the company faced by the late 1990s. Profit and sales growth were wildly erratic. It bungled operations in Asia amid the 1998 financial crisis there. The stock sat out the entire late 1990s boom, budging less than 1 percent from September 1997, to September 2000. The flexibility and lack of structure, which had enabled the company's success, had also by then produced a bloated staff and inefficient workflow. So McNerney had plenty of cause to whip things into shape.   10

GREEN-BELT TRAINING REGIMEN

One of his main tools was Six Sigma, which originated at Motorola in 1986 and became a staple of corporate life in the 1990s after it was embraced by GE. The term is now so widely and divergently applied that it's hard to pin down what it actually means. At some companies, Six Sigma is plainly a euphemism for cost-cutting. Others explain it as a tool for analyzing a problem (e.g., high shipping costs) and then using data to solve each component of it. But on a basic level, Six Sigma seeks to remove variability from a process. In that way you avoid errors, or defects, and increase predictability (technically speaking, Six Sigma quality has come to be accepted as no more than 3.4 defects per million).   11

At 3M, McNerney introduced the two main Six Sigma tools. The first and more traditional version is an acronym known as DMAIC (pronounced "dee-may-ic"), which stands for define, measure, analyze, improve, control. These five steps are the essence of the Six Sigma approach to problem solving. The other flavor is called Design for Six Sigma, or DFSS, which purports to systematize a new-product development process so that something can be made to Six Sigma quality from the start.   12

Thousands of 3Mers were trained as black belts, an honorific awarded to experts who often act as internal consultants for their companies. Nearly every employee participated in a several-day "green-belt" training regimen, which explained DMAIC and DFSS, familiarized workers with statistics, and   13 showed them how to track data and create charts and tables on a computer program called Minitab. The black belts fanned out and led bigger-scale "black-belt projects," such as increasing production speed 40 percent by reducing variations and removing wasted steps from manufacturing. They also often oversaw smaller "green-belt projects," such as improving the order fulfillment process. This Six Sigma drive undoubtedly contributed to 3M's astronomical profitability improvements under McNerney; operating margins went from 17 percent in 2001 to 23 percent in 2005.

14   While Six Sigma was invented as a way to improve quality, its main value to corporations now clearly is its ability to save time and money. McNerney arrived at a company that had been criticized for throwing cash at problems. In his first full year, he slashed capital expenditures 22 percent, from $980 million to $763 million, and 11 percent more to a trough of $677 million in 2003. As a percentage of sales, capital expenditures dropped from 6.1 percent in 2001 to just 3.7 percent in 2003. McNerney also held R&D funding constant from 2001 to 2005, hovering over $1 billion a year. "If you take over a company that's been living on innovation, clearly you can squeeze costs out," says Charles O'Reilly, a Stanford Graduate School of Business management professor. "The question is, what's the long-term damage to the company?"

15   Under McNerney, the R&D function at 3M was systematized in ways that were unheard of and downright heretical in St. Paul, even though the guidelines would have looked familiar at many other conglomerates. Some employees found the constant analysis stifling. Steven Boyd, a PhD who had worked as a researcher at 3M for 32 years before his job was eliminated in 2004, was one of them. After a couple of months on a research project, he would have to fill in a "red book" with scores of pages worth of charts and tables, analyzing everything from the potential commercial application, to the size of the market, to possible manufacturing concerns.

16   Traditionally, 3M had been a place where researchers had been given wide latitude to pursue research down whatever alleys they wished. After the arrival of the new boss, the DMAIC process was laid over a phase-review process for innovations—a novelty at 3M. The goal was to speed up and systematize the progress of inventions into the new-product pipeline. The DMAIC questions "are all wonderful considerations, but are they appropriate for somebody who's just trying to . . . develop some ideas?" asks Boyd. The impact of the Six Sigma regime, according to Boyd and other former 3Mers, was that more predictable, incremental work took precedence over blue-sky research. "You're supposed to be having something that was going to be producing a profit, if not next quarter, it better be the quarter after that," Boyd says.

17   For a long time, 3M had allowed researchers to spend years testing products. Consider, for example, the Post-it note. Its inventor, Art Fry, a 3M scientist who's now retired, and others fiddled with the idea for several years before the product went into full production in 1980. Early during the Six Sigma effort, after a meeting at which technical employees were briefed on

the new process, "we all came to the conclusion that there was no way in the world that anything like a Post-it note would ever emerge from this new system," says Michael Mucci, who worked at 3M for 27 years before his dismissal in 2004. (Mucci has alleged in a class action that 3M engaged in age discrimination; the company says the claims are without merit.)

18   There has been little formal research on whether the tension between Six Sigma and innovation is inevitable. But the most notable attempt yet, by Wharton School professor Mary Benner and Harvard Business School professor Michael L. Tushman, suggests that Six Sigma will lead to more incremental innovation at the expense of more blue-sky work. The two professors analyzed the types of patents granted to paint and photography companies over a 20-year period, before and after a quality improvement drive. Their work shows that, after the quality push, patents issued based primarily on prior work made up a dramatically larger share of the total, while those not based on prior work dwindled.

19   Defenders of Six Sigma at 3M claim that a more systematic new-product introduction process allows innovations to get to market faster. But Fry, the Post-it note inventor, disagrees. In fact, he places the blame for 3M's recent lack of innovative sizzle squarely on Six Sigma's application in 3M's research labs. Innovation, he says, is "a numbers game. You have to go through 5,000 to 6,000 raw ideas to find one successful business." Six Sigma would ask, why not eliminate all that waste and just come up with the right idea the first time? That way of thinking, says Fry, can have serious side effects. "What's remarkable is how fast a culture can be torn apart," says Fry, who lives in Maplewood, Minnesota, just a few minutes south of the corporate campus and pops into the office regularly to help with colleagues' projects. "[McNerney] didn't kill it, because he wasn't here long enough. But if he had been here much longer, I think he could have."

REINVIGORATED WORKFORCE

20   Buckley, a PhD chemical engineer by training, seems to recognize the cultural ramifications of a process-focused program on an organization whose fate and history is so bound up in inventing new stuff. "You cannot create in that atmosphere of confinement or sameness," Buckley says. "Perhaps one of the mistakes that we made as a company—it's one of the dangers of Six Sigma—is that when you value sameness more than you value creativity, I think you potentially undermine the heart and soul of a company like 3M."

21   In recent years, the company's reputation as an innovator has been sliding. In 2004, 3M was ranked No. 1 on Boston Consulting Group's Most Innovative Companies list (now the *BusinessWeek*/BCG list). It dropped to No. 2 in 2005, to No. 3 in 2006, and down to No. 7 this year. "People have kind of forgotten about these guys," says Dev Patnaik, managing associate of innovation consultancy Jump Associates. "When was the last time you saw something innovative or experimental coming out of there?"

Control and Release: The contrasting styles and strategies of Jim McNerney and George Buckley

McNerney		Buckley
Huge. Renowned as a GE Ober-manager. Was runner-up to Jeff Immelt in the bake-off to succeed Jack Welch.	Reputation upon Arrival	Almost nonexistent. Cut his managerial teeth at Emerson Electric and revived boatmaker Brunswick.
Increase profitability at a company that had become a sluggish performer and a disappointment to investors.	Mandate	Bring back the legendary creative oomph, while preserving the operating efficiencies McNerney won.
To remake the culture of 3M, instigated one of the most ambitious Six Sigma drives in corporate history.	Attitude toward Six Sigma	Dialed back on Six Sigma regime, especially in the research labs, while preserving it in manufacturing.
Clamped down on profligate spending to goose cash flow and improve operating margins.	Capital Spending	Worried about underinvestment, plowed $1.5 billion into 18 new plants or major expansions.
Held R&D spending constant and allocated funds to promising new markets such as pharmaceuticals.	Research Priorities	Boosted R&D budget. Refocused on "core" research and away from ancillary businesses like pharma.
Instilled a GE-like managerial sensibility.	Culture	Reignited the innovation machine by encouraging risk-taking.
From central casting. Former college baseball player is tall, athletic, and charismatic.	Appearance	From the research lab. Bespectacled and unassuming, has an informal "call me George" demeanor.

22   Buckley has loosened the reins a bit by removing 3M research scientists' obligation to hew to Six Sigma objectives. There was perhaps a one-size-fits-all approach to the application of Six Sigma as the initial implementation got under way, says Dr. Larry Wendling, a vice president who directs the "R" in 3M's R&D operation. "Since [McNerney] was driving it to the organization, you know, there were metrics established across the organization and quite frankly, some of them did not make as much sense for the lab as they did other parts of the organization," Wendling says. What sort of metrics? Keeping track of how many black-belt and green-belt projects were completed, for one.

23   In fact, it's not uncommon for Six Sigma to become an end unto itself. That may be appropriate in an operations context—at the end of the year, it's easy enough for a line manager to count up all the money he's saved by doing green-belt projects. But what 3Mers came to realize is that these financially definitive outcomes were much more elusive in the context of a research lab. "In some cases in the lab it made sense, but in other cases, people were going around dreaming up green-belt programs to fill their quota of green-belt programs for that time period," says Wendling. "We were letting, I think, the process get in the way of doing the actual invention."

24   To help get the creative juices flowing, Buckley is opening the money spigot—hiking spending on R&D, acquisitions, and capital expenditures. The overall R&D budget will grow 20 percent this year, to $1.5 billion. Even more significant than the increase in money is Buckley's reallocation of those funds. He's funneling cash into what he calls "core" areas of 3M technology, 45 in all, from abrasives to nanotechnology to flexible electronics. That is another departure from McNerney's priorities; he told *BusinessWeek* in 2004 that the 3M product with the most promise was skin-care cream Aldara, the centerpiece to a burgeoning pharmaceuticals business. In January, Buckley sold the pharma business for $2 billion.

25   Quietly, the McNerney legacy is being revised at 3M. While there is no doubt the former CEO brought some positive change to the company, many workers say they are reinvigorated now that the corporate emphasis has shifted from profitability and process discipline to growth and innovation. Timm Hammond, the director of strategic business development, says "[Buckley] has brought back a spark around creativity." Adds Bob Anderson, a business director in 3M's radio frequency identification division: "We feel like we can dream again."

26   That move already may have had a psychic payoff, as workers at the science-centric company seem newly energized about Buckley's more flexible growth agenda.

27   The big risk comes in the more tangible measurements, such as profit margins. Buckley knows he can't simply undo the profitability and productivity improvements that McNerney won. His challenge is to figure out how to loosen up the organization, but still keep costs under control. How's he going to do it? "Did Jim take all the money trees?" Buckley asks. His answer, clearly, is no. The big money tree Buckley is eyeing is the company's convoluted supply chain, where he hopes to wring wasted money out of the system.

EXPANSION AND CONTRACTION

28 Buckley plans to spend $1.5 billion on 18 new plants or major expansions around the world, including 11 outside the United States, with four new factories in China alone. The thinking is that the new factories will add much needed capacity—especially abroad, where 3M pulls in more than 60 percent of its revenues, and where it expects to get up to 75 percent over the next several years.

29 Despite a vast, complicated network of 64 international subsidiary companies, just 35 percent of 3M's manufacturing capacity is overseas. In Buckley's view, the plant expansions won't just add capacity—they are an opportunity to make the whole logistics chain more efficient by shortening supply lines and bringing production closer to local markets.

30 How did things get that way at 3M? For a long time, one of the tenets of the 3M catechism was "make a little, sell a little." Once a project was green-lighted, it might receive funding, but the developer or scientist would have to make small quantities of the product in an ad hoc manner by using idle spots of time at factories throughout the 3M system. It was a way to minimize the financial risk of a new product, and it served the company quite well—when its infrastructure and sales were centered mainly in the United States.

KEEPING INVENTORY MOVING

31 Now, "make a little, sell a little" means that a typical product might be extruded in Canada, machined in France, packaged in Mexico, and sold in Japan. That's costly, and it means that half of 3M products spend 100 days traveling through the supply line, according to Buckley, even before it has to jump any local bureaucratic hurdles.

32 The net result is that 3M has a lot of money tied up in inventory around the world that's just sitting on boats, in trucks, and in warehouses. In the fourth quarter of 2006, for instance, sales rose about $500 million. But working capital went up $450 million and receivables increased $250 million, Buckley says. If that trend continues, "You'd be borrowing money to grow," he says.

33 Buckley expects over the next two years to free $1 billion in working capital and to achieve another "hundreds of millions" in cost savings from the more efficient supply chain. "Working capital as a percent of sales is a big metric for CEOs these days," says Jack Kelly, an analyst at Goldman Sachs, "because if you can reduce working capital, you can increase your cash flow." As Buckley explains, "This is the money tree."

Sources: Reprinted with special permission from Brian Hindo, "At 3M, a Struggle Between Efficiency and Creativity," *BusinessWeek*, June 11, 2007; "3M Chief Plants a Money Tree," *BusinessWeek*, June 11, 2007. Copyright © 2007 The McGraw-Hill Companies.

DISCUSSION QUESTIONS

1. Describe the nature of incremental innovations derived at 3M through the adoption of the Six Sigma discipline earlier in the decade under the leadership of James McNerney.

2. How is the approach of George Buckley different? Is it more of a breakthrough type approach to innovation?

3. Does Buckley's approach involve any outside involvement or openness to outside ideas or outside ventures and acquisitions?

4. Are elements of entrepreneurship present under either leader's approach?

5. Which approach to innovation do you think would be best at 3M?

6. Is it seemingly wise to try to have both Six Sigma and incremental innovation alongside a more open, creative breakthrough innovation approach? What challenges may emerge at 3M in attempting to do this?

7. Go to http://images.businessweek.com/ss/07/05/0530_3m_products/index_01.htm for an interesting slide presentation of 3M's innovations and history of innovation.

Part **Four**

Cases

Guide to Strategic Management Case Analysis

THE CASE METHOD

Case analysis is a proven educational method that is especially effective in a strategic management course. The case method complements and enhances the text material and your professor's lectures by focusing attention on what a firm has done or should do in an actual business situation. Use of the case method in a strategic management course offers you an opportunity to develop and refine analytical skills. It also can provide exciting experience by allowing you to assume the role of the key decision maker for the organizations you will study.

When assuming the role of the general manager of the organization being studied, you will need to consider all aspects of the business. In addition to drawing on your knowledge of marketing, finance, management, production, and economics, you will be applying the strategic management concepts taught in this course.

The cases in this book are accounts of real business situations involving a variety of firms in a variety of industries. To make these opportunities as realistic as possible, the cases include a variety of quantitative and qualitative information in both the presentation of the situation and the exhibits. As the key decision maker, you will need to determine which information is important, given the circumstances described in the case. Keep in mind that the results of analyzing one firm will not necessarily be appropriate for another since every firm is faced with a different set of circumstances.

PREPARING FOR CASE DISCUSSION

The case method requires an approach to class preparation that differs from the typical lecture course. In the typical lecture course, you can still benefit from each class session even if you did not prepare, by listening carefully to the professor's lecture. This approach will not work in a course using the case method. For a case course, proper preparation is essential.

Suggestions for Effective Preparation

1. *Allow adequate time in preparing a case.* Many of the cases in this text involve complex issues that are often not apparent without careful reading and purposeful reflection on the information in the cases.

2. *Read each case twice.* Because many of these cases involve complex decision making, you should read each case at least twice. Your first reading should give you an overview of the firm's unique circumstances and the issues confronting the firm. Your second reading allows you to concentrate on what you feel are the most critical issues and to understand what information in the case is most important. Make limited notes identifying key points during your first reading. During your second reading, you can add details to your original notes and revise them as necessary.

3. *Focus on the key strategic issue in each case.* Each time you read a case you should concentrate on identifying the key issue. In some cases, the key issue will be identified by the case writer in the introduction. In other cases, you might not grasp the key strategic issue until you have read the case several times. (Remember that not every piece of information in a case is equally important.)

4. *Do not overlook exhibits.* The exhibits in these cases should be considered an integral part of the information for the case. They are not just "window dressing." In fact, for many cases you will need to analyze financial statements, evaluate organizational charts, and understand the firm's products, all of which are presented in the form of exhibits.

5. *Adopt the appropriate time frame.* It is critical that you assume the appropriate time frame for each case you read. If the case ends in 2005, that year should become the present for you as you work on that case. Making a decision for a case that ends in 2005 by using data you could not have had until 2007 defeats the purpose of the case method. For the same reason, although it is recommended that you do outside reading on each firm and industry, you should not read material written after the case ended unless your professor instructs you to do so.

6. *Draw on all of your knowledge of business.* As the key decision maker for the organization being studied, you will need to consider all aspects of the business and industry. Do not confine yourself to strategic management concepts presented in this course. You will need to determine if the key strategic issue revolves around a theory you have learned in a functional area, such as marketing, production, finance, or economics, or in the strategic management course.

USING THE INTERNET IN CASE RESEARCH

The proliferation of information available on the Internet has direct implications for business research. The Internet has become a viable source of company and industry data to assist those involved in case study analysis. Principal sources of useful data include company Web sites, U.S. government Web sites, search engines, investment research sites, and online data services. This section will describe the principal Internet sources of case study data and offer means of retrieving that data.

Company Web Sites

Virtually every public and private firm has a Web site that any Internet user can visit. Accessing a firm's Web site is easy. Many firms advertise their Web address through both TV and print advertisements. To access a site when the address is known, enter the address into the address line on any Internet service provider's homepage. When the address is not known, use of a search engine will be necessary. The use of a search engine will be described later. Often, but not always, a firm's Web address is identical to its name, or is at least an abbreviated form of its name.

Company Web sites contain data that are helpful in case study analysis. A firm's Web site may contain descriptions of company products and services, recent company accomplishments and press releases, financial and stock performance highlights, and an overview of a firm's history and strategic objectives. A company's Web site may also contain links to relevant industry Web sites that contain industry statistics as well as current and future industry trends. The breadth of data available on a particular firm's Web site will vary but in general larger, global corporations tend to have more complete and sophisticated Web sites than do smaller, regional firms.

U.S. Government Web Sites

The U.S. government allows the public to access virtually all of the information that it collects. Most of this information is available online to Internet users. The government collects a great range of data types, from firm-specific data the government mandates all publicly traded firms to supply to highly regarded economic indicators. The usefulness of many U.S. government Web sites depends on the fit between the case you are studying and the data located on the Web site. For example, a study of an accounting firm may be supplemented with data supplied by the Internal Revenue Service Web site, but not the Environmental Protection Agency Web site. A sampling of prominent government Web sites and their addresses is shown here:

Environmental Protection Agency: www.epa.gov

General Printing Office: www.gpo.gov

Internal Revenue Service: www.irs.ustreas.gov

Libraries of Congress: www.loc.gov

National Aeronautics and Space Administration: www.hq.nasa.gov

SEC's Edgar Database: www.sec.gov/edgarhp.htm

Small Business Administration: www.sba.gov

STAT-USA: www.stat-usa.gov

U.S. Department of Commerce: www.doc.gov

U.S. Patent and Trademark Office: uspto.gov

U.S. Department of Treasury: www.ustreas.gov

One of the most useful sites for company case study analysis is the Securities and Exchange Commission's EDGAR database. The EDGAR database contains the documents that the government mandates all publicly traded firms to file including 10-Ks and 8-Ks. A form 10-K is the annual report that provides a comprehensive overview of a firm's financials in addition to discussions regarding industry and product background. Form 8-K reports the occurrence of any material events or corporate changes that may be of importance to investors. Examples of reported occurrences include key management personnel changes, corporate restructures, and new debt or equity issuance. This site is very user friendly and requires the researcher to provide only the company name in order to produce a listing of all available reports.

Search Engines

Search engines allow a researcher to locate information on a company or industry without prior knowledge of a specific Internet address. Generally, to execute a search the search engine requires the entering of a keyword, for example, a company name. However, each search engine differs slightly in its search capabilities. For example, to narrow a search on one search engine may be accomplished differently than narrowing a search on another.

The information retrieved by search engines typically includes articles and other information that contain the entered keyword or words. Because the search engine has retrieved data that contain keywords does not necessarily mean that the information is useful. Internet data are unfiltered, meaning they may not be checked for accuracy before the data are posted online. However, data copyrighted or published by a reputable source may greatly increase the chance that the data are indeed accurate. A list of popular Internet search engines is shown here:

Alta Vista: www.altavista.digital.com

DogPile: www.dogpile.com

Google: www.google.com

HotBot: www.hotbot.lycos.com

InfoSeek: www.infoseek.com

Lycos: www.lycos.com

Metacrawler: www.metacrawler.com

WebCrawler: www.webcrawler.com

Yahoo!: www.yahoo.com

Investment Research Sites

Investment research sites provide company stock performance data including key financial ratios, competitor identification, industry data, and links to research reports and SEC filings. These sites provide support for the financial analysis portion of a case study, but only for publicly traded businesses. Most investment research sites also contain macro market data that may not be company specific, but may still affect many investors of equities.

Investment research sites usually contain a search mechanism if a desired stock's ticker symbol is not known. In this case, the company name is entered to enable the site to find the corresponding equity. Because these sites are geared toward traders who want recent stock prices and data, searching for data relevant to a case may require more elaborate investigations at multiple sites. The following list includes many popular investment research sites:

American Stock Exchange: www.amex.com

CBS Market Watch: cbsmarketwatch.com

CNN FinancialNews: money.cnn.com

DBC Online: www.esignal.com

Hoover's Online: www.hoovers.com

InvestorGuide: www.investorguide.com

Wall Street Research Net: www.wsrn.com

Market Guide: www.marketguide.com

Money Search: www.moneysearch.com

MSN Money: moneycentral.msn.com

NASDAQ: www.nasdaq.com

New York Stock Exchange: www.nyse.com

PC Financial Network: www.csfbdirect.com

Quote.Com: finance.lycos.com

Stock Smart: www.stocksmart.com

Yahoo.com/finance

Wright Investors' Service on the World Wide Web: www.wisi.com

The Wall Street Journal Online: online.wsj.com/public/us

Zacks Investment Research: my.zacks.com

One site that conveniently contains firm, industry, and competitor data is Hoover's Online. Hoover's also provides financials, stock charts, current and archived news stories, and links to research reports and SEC filings. Yahoo!'s "Finance" option is another excellent resource for company-related research. Some of these data, most notably the lengthy research reports produced by analysts, are fee-based and must be ordered.

Online Data Sources

Online data sources provide wide access to a huge volume of business reference material. Information retrieved from these sites typically includes descriptive profiles, stock price performance, SEC filings, and newspaper, magazine, and journal articles related to a particular company, industry, or product. Online data services are popular with educational and financial institutions. While some services are free to all users, to utilize the entire array of these sites' services, a fee-based subscription is usually necessary.

Accessing these sites requires only the source's address, or the use of a search engine to find the address. The source's homepage will clearly indicate the nature of the information available and describe how to search for and access the data. Most sites have help screens to assist in locating the desired information.

One of the most useful online sources for business research is the Lexis-Nexis Universe. This source provides a wide array of news, business, legal, and reference information. The information is categorized into dozens of topics including general news; company and industry news; company financials that include SEC filings; government and political news; accounting, auditing, and tax data; and legal research. One particularly impressive service is a search mechanism that allows a user to locate a particular article when the specific citation is known. A list of several notable online data sources is shown here:

ABI/Inform (Proquest Direct): www.il.proquest.com/proquest

American Express: americanexpress.com

Bloomberg Financial News Services: www.bloomberg.com

BusinessWeek Online: businessweek.com

Dow Jones News Retrieval: http://bis.dowjones.com

EconLit: www.econlit.org

Lexis-Nexis Universe: www.lexis-nexis.com

PARTICIPATING IN CLASS

Because the strategic management course uses the case method, the success and value of the course depend on class discussion. The success and value of the class discussion, in turn, rely on the roles both you and your professor perform. Following are aspects of your role and your professor's that, if kept in mind, will enhance the value and excitement of this course.

Students as Active Learners

The case method requires your active participation. This means your role is no longer one of sitting and listening.

1. *Attend class regularly.* Not only is your grade likely to depend on your involvement in class discussions, but the benefit you derive from this course is directly related to your involvement in and understanding of the discussions.

2. *Be prepared for class.* The need for adequate preparation already has been discussed. You will benefit more from the discussions, will understand and participate in the exchange of ideas, and will avoid the embarrassment of being called on when not prepared. By all means, bring your book to class. Not only is there a good chance you will need to refer to a specific exhibit or passage from the case, you may need to refresh your memory of the case (particularly if you made notes in the margins while reading).

3. *Participate in the discussion.* Attending class and being prepared are not enough; you need to express your views in class. You can participate in a number of ways: by addressing a question asked by your professor, by disagreeing with your professor or your classmates (by all means, be tactful), by building on an idea expressed by a classmate, or by simply asking a relevant question.

4. *Participate wisely.* Although you do not want to be one of those students who never raises his or her hand, you also should be sensitive to the fact that others in your class will want to express themselves. You have probably already had experience with a student who attempts to dominate each class discussion. A student who invariably tries to dominate the class discussion breeds resentment.

5. *Keep a broad perspective.* By definition, the strategic management course deals with the issues facing general managers or business owners. As already mentioned, you need to consider all aspects of the business, not just one particular functional area.

6. *Pay attention to the topic being discussed.* Focus your attention on the topic being discussed. When a new topic is introduced, do not attempt to immediately introduce another topic for discussion. Do not feel you have to have something to say on every topic covered.

Your Professor as Discussion Leader

Your professor is a discussion leader. As such, he or she will attempt to stimulate the class as a whole to share insights, observations, and thoughts about the case. Your professor will not necessarily respond to every comment you or your classmates make. Part of the value of the case method is to get you and your classmates to assume this role as the course progresses.

The professor in a strategic management case course performs several roles:

1. *Maintaining focus.* Because multiple complex issues need to be explored, your professor may want to maintain the focus of the class discussion on one issue at a time. He or she may ask you to hold your comment on another issue until a previous issue is exhausted. Do not interpret this response to mean your point is unimportant; your professor is simply indicating there will be a more appropriate time to pursue that particular comment.

2. *Getting students involved.* Do not be surprised if your professor asks for input from volunteers and nonvolunteers alike. The value of the class discussion increases as more people share their comments.

3. *Facilitating comprehension of strategic management concepts.* Some professors prefer to lecture on strategic management concepts on a "need-to-know" basis. In this scenario, a lecture on a particular topic will be followed by an assignment to work on a case that deals with that particular topic. Other professors will have the class work through a case or two before lecturing on a topic to give the class a feel for the value of the topic being covered and for the type of information needed to work on cases. Still other professors prefer to cover all of the theory in the beginning of the course, thereby allowing uninterrupted case discussion in the remaining weeks of the term. All three of these approaches are valued.

4. *Playing devil's advocate.* At times your professor may appear to be contradicting many of the comments or observations being made. At other times your professor may

adopt a position that does not immediately make sense, given the circumstances of the case. At other times your professor may seem to be equivocating. These are all examples of how your professor might be playing devil's advocate. Sometimes the professor's goal is to expose alternative viewpoints. Sometimes he or she may be testing your resolve on a particular point. Be prepared to support your position with evidence from the case.

ASSIGNMENTS

Written Assignments

Written analyses are a critical part of most strategic management courses. Each professor has a preferred format for these written analyses, but a number of general guidelines will prove helpful to you in your written assignments.

1. *Analyze.* Avoid merely repeating the facts presented in the case. Analyze the issues involved in the case and build logically toward your recommendations.

2. *Use headings or labels.* Using headings or labels throughout your written analysis will help your reader follow your analysis and recommendations. For example, when you are analyzing the weaknesses of the firm in the case, include the heading Weaknesses. Note the headings in the cases that follow.

3. *Discuss alternatives.* Follow the proper strategic management sequence by (*a*) identifying alternatives, (*b*) evaluating each alternative, and (*c*) recommending the alternative you think is best.

4. *Use topic sentences.* You can help your reader more easily evaluate your analysis by putting the topic sentence first in each paragraph and following with statements directly supporting the topic sentence.

5. *Be specific in your recommendations.* Develop specific recommendations logically and be sure your recommendations are well defended by your analysis. Avoid using generalizations, clichés, and ambiguous statements. Remember that any number of answers are possible and so your professor is most concerned about how your reasoning led to your recommendations and how well you develop and support your ideas.

6. *Do not overlook implementation.* Many good analyses receive poor evaluations because they do not include a discussion of implementation. Your analysis will be much stronger when you discuss how your recommendation can be implemented. Include some of the specific actions needed to achieve the objectives you are proposing.

7. *Specifically state your assumptions.* Cases, like all real business situations, involve incomplete information. Therefore, it is important that you clearly state any assumptions you make in your analysis. Do not assume your professor will be able to fill in the missing points.

Oral Presentations

Your professor is likely to ask you and your classmates to make oral presentations on a particular case. Oral presentations usually are done by groups of students. In these groups, each member will typically be responsible for one aspect of the overall case. Keep the following suggestions in mind when you are faced with an oral presentation:

1. *Use your own words.* Avoid memorizing a presentation. The best approach is to prepare an outline of the key points you want to cover. Do not be afraid to have the outline in front of you during your presentation, but do not just read the outline.

2. *Rehearse your presentation.* Do not assume you can simply read the outline you have prepared or that the right words will come to you when you are in front of the class making

your presentation. Take the time to practice your speech, and be sure to rehearse the entire presentation with your group.

3. *Use visual aids.* The adage "a picture is worth a thousand words" contains quite a bit of truth. The people in your audience will more quickly and thoroughly understand your key points—and will retain them longer—if you use visual aids. Think of ways you and your team members can use the blackboard in the classroom; a graph, chart, or exhibit on a large posterboard; or, if you will have a number of these visual aids, a flip chart.

4. *Be prepared to handle questions.* You probably will be asked questions by your classmates. If questions are asked during your presentation, try to address those that require clarification. Tactfully postpone more elaborate questions until you have completed the formal phase of your presentation. During your rehearsal, try to anticipate the types of questions that you might be asked.

Working as a Team Member

Many professors assign students to groups or teams for analyzing cases. This adds more realism to the course, since most strategic decisions in business are addressed by a group of key managers. If you are a member of a group assigned to analyze a case, keep in mind that your performance is tied to the performance of the other group members, and vice versa. The following are some suggestions to help you be an effective team member:

1. *Be sure the division of labor is equitable.* It is not always easy to decide how the workload can be divided equitably, since it is not always obvious how much work needs to be done. Try breaking down the case into the distinct parts that need to be analyzed to determine if having a different person assume responsibility for each part is equitable. All team members should read and analyze the entire case, but different team members can be assigned primary responsibility for each major aspect of the analysis. Each team member with primary responsibility for a major aspect of the analysis also will be the logical choice to write that portion of the written analysis or to present it orally in class.

2. *Communicate with other team members.* This is particularly important if you encounter problems with your portion of the analysis. Because, by definition, the team members are dependent on each other, it is critical that you communicate openly and honestly with each other. Therefore, it is essential that your team members discuss problems, such as some members not doing their fair share of work or members insisting that their point of view dominate the team's report.

3. *Work as a team.* A group's output should reflect a combined effort, so the whole group should be involved in each part of the analysis, even if different individuals assume primary responsibility for different parts of the analysis. Avoid having the marketing major do the marketing portion of the analysis, the production major handle the production issues, and so forth. This will both hamper the group's aggregate analysis and do all of the team members a disservice by not giving each member exposure to decision making involving the other functional areas. The strategic management course provides an opportunity to look at all aspects of the business situation, to develop the ability to see the big picture, and to integrate the various functional areas.

4. *Plan and structure team meetings.* When you are working with a group on case analysis, it is impossible to achieve the team's goals and objectives without meeting outside of class. As soon as the team is formed, establish mutually convenient times for regular meetings, and be sure to keep this time available each week. Be punctual in going to the meetings, and manage the meetings so they end at a predetermined time. Plan several shorter meetings, as opposed to one longer session right before the case is due. (This, by the way, is another way realism is introduced in the strategic management course. Planning and

managing your time is essential in business, and working with others to achieve a common set of goals is a critical part of life in the business world.)

SUMMARY

The strategic management course is your opportunity to assume the role of a key decision maker in a business organization. The case method is an excellent way to add excitement and realism to the course. To get the most out of the course and the case method, you need to be an active participant in the entire process.

The case method offers you the opportunity to develop your analytical skills and to understand the interrelationships of the various functional areas of business; it also enables you to develop valuable skills in time management, group problem solving, creativity, organization of thoughts and ideas, and human interaction.

Planet Apple

1 Steve Jobs had plenty of problems to contend with as he sauntered onstage for his first speech after returning to the top of Apple in 1997. He faced a shrinking market for his Mac computers, bloated costs, and a severe shortage of cash. But on that day, Jobs chose to talk to the Mac faithful mostly about another problem: Apple's growing isolation. Despite the company's reputation for making the world's finest PCs, very little software or add-on gear worked with the Mac. "Apple lives in an ecosystem, and it needs help from other partners," said Jobs. "And it needs to help other partners."

2 Jobs then did the unthinkable, inviting arch-nemesis Bill Gates to join him on stage via videoconference to announce details of a deal to forget any patent claims in exchange for $150 million, and a promise by Microsoft Corp. to continue making a Mac-compatible version of its ubiquitous Office software.

3 Today, that Apple Inc. ecosystem has morphed from a sad little high-tech shtetl into a global empire. Once known for defining the digital future but never fully capitalizing on it, Apple has been transformed into tech's most influential hit-maker. More than 200,000 companies have signed on in the past year to create Apple-compatible products, a 26% increase from the year before. That includes software makers such as gamemaker Electronic Arts Inc. and corporate supplier VMware, drawn by Mac sales that are growing three times faster than the overall PC market. A cottage industry of iPod accessories continues to blossom into something far more substantial. Consider that this year, some 70% of new U.S.-model cars have iPod connectors built in, and about 100,000 airline seats will have the same. And Apple's online iTunes Music Store has become the world's third-largest music retailer after Wal-Mart Stores Inc. and Best Buy Co.

JOINING THE JOBS CLUB

4 With the June 29 debut of the iPhone, Apple seems poised to extend its reach even further. A new flock of partners, from AT&T Corp. to Salesforce.com Inc., is set to jump on the bandwagon for the slick phone/Web browser/music player/camera. Sure, the hype prior to iPhone's launch bordered on ridiculous (Comedy Central Stephen Colbert joked that the iPhone launch is the second most important event in human history, after the birth of Christ). But phonemakers such as Nokia and Motorola, and carriers like Verizon, are waiting nervously to see if Apple can remake the U.S. cellular business by determining what services consumers get and leaving the carriers out of the loop.

5 As long as Apple stays on its game, leading providers of everything from silicon chips to Hollywood flicks will feel pressure to strike deals to Jobs' liking. Apple can confer brand hipness on its partners. And its ascendence in markets like cell phones and who knows what else in the future may impose a new focus on more consumer-friendly parts, software, and

services. But to be part of the Jobs club, you give up a certain amount of independence on everything from design to identity to pricing.

6   Jobs is upending two decades of conventional wisdom about the nature of competition in digital markets. Since the rise of Microsoft and Intel's "Wintel" PC standard in the 1980s, the assumption has been that markets would be dominated by those that could set technical standards—say, Microsoft in operating systems or Intel in microprocessors—and then benefit as thousands of others competed to build products on top of these "platforms."

7   But Apple's strategy is far simpler: Focus on making the best product, and rewards will follow. In fact, Apple's new partners are signing up in spite of, rather than because of, Jobs' rules of engagement. Apple makes little pretense of building a level playing field, but routinely picks favorites—such as Google for building mapping and video applications for the iPhone. And rather than aim for the most partners, Apple focuses on attracting the best ones. As a result, the Mac and iPod feel more like a gated, elitist community, with Apple keeping close watch over who gets in. "The notion of a platform is a very PC-oriented way of looking at the world," says Silicon Valley financier Roger McNamee. "Consumers just want a great experience. They don't buy platforms."

8   Consider how Apple changed expectations about portable music devices. There were plenty of MP3 players around before the iPod arrived in 2001. Now, if the iPhone works as advertised, it could similarly redefine the mobile-phone experience. As any BlackBerry or Treo owner knows, all of the 25 million smartphones sold last year offer similar capabilities, such as Web browsing and e-mail. But none has captured the heart of the mainstream consumer. And on paper, at least, the iPhone erases myriad frustrations faced by hundreds of millions of phone users—from maddeningly complex menus, to the inability to find a contact while on a call.

9   Spin it out a few years, and it's not hard to see why many companies want to be on Apple's side. iPhone buyers now sign up for an AT&T cellular package via iTunes. In the future, maybe they'll also be able to sign up for all the broadband and data services needed to power their Macs, iPods, and future Apple products (can you say: "I want my Apple iHomeTheater"?) and make them work together. That would play to Apple's strength—making the complex simple. "What you end up with is a kind of Apple archipelago—this cluster of islands in this big digital sea that are great places to hang out," says Silicon Valley futurist and consultant Paul Saffo.

10   Of course, Apple's products have to continue to delight—a real question for the iPhone, which doesn't even have a physical keyboard. But if Apple succeeds, it could raise itself and its ecosystem above the cacophony of industry giants now battling to "own" the digital consumer. The telephone and cable companies try to take advantage of their control of customers' access to video, data, and voice content. Google Inc. and Yahoo! Inc. want to leverage their power as online concierge for millions of consumers. Apple comes at it from the device perspective: If it can control the gadget you use to connect with all those other platforms, it increases its control over what you do, and how much you pay (99 cents a song, for example).

11   There are lots of phone carriers and cable companies, each with fairly similar offerings. Google and Yahoo! are powerful in their own right, but they can't totally control their destiny since Web users are a click away from using another search engine or portal. For now, though, Apple is head and shoulders above others in making the actual machines you use to pull up Web pages, music, TV shows, movies, and soon, perhaps, phone conversations. Says David Sanderson, head of Bain & Co.'s global media practice: "We're moving from a distributor-driven paradigm to a consumer-driven paradigm—and Apple gets consumers."

12   And not just any consumers, but those who will pay a premium. The Mac is gaining share despite an average price tag of $1,400, nearly twice that of the typical PC. iPod shoppers still paid an average price of $181 in May, 15% above other music players. The iPhone is

even more audaciously priced. The $499 base price compares with an average $66 for a regular phone, or $160 for a smartphone such as a BlackBerry or Treo, says NPD Group Inc. analyst Stephen Baker.

THE COMPATIBILITY FACTOR

13 None of this would have come about if Jobs hadn't had his epiphany about reaching out beyond the insular world of the Mac. The Office deal was a symbolic first step, but the real wake-up call came with the 2003 decision to do a Windows-compatible version of iTunes. Rather than hurt Mac sales, as some feared, this opened the floodgates on iPod sales by making the device usable by the 98% of computer users who ran Windows. Another milestone came when the company switched from PowerPC processors made by IBM to Intel's far more popular chips. This made it possible for Macs to run Windows (an important insurance policy to many Mac newbies) and made it far easier for software developers to adapt their programs for Apple's products.

14 Consider the perspective of one big video-game producer, Electronic Arts. In the early 1980s, about half of the people working at EA's Redwood City (Calif.) campus were Apple alumni. Yet EA stopped making Mac-compatible games later in the decade, when Apple turned its attention to corporate markets. EA co-founder Bing Gordon recalls his shock when Apple's then-CEO John Sculley said in 1987 that "there is no home-computer market." Says Gordon: "They were working so hard to get respect, the last thing they wanted was for people who wore suits to think of the Mac as a toy." Predictably, game sales on the Mac plummeted, making it even less worthwhile for EA to make the big investments to adapt its PC games to run on the Mac's unique innards.

15 But because today's Intel-based Macs don't look much different from any Windows PC from EA's perspective, Gordon says it should be cheaper to churn out Mac games than, say, adapting them to game consoles like the Sony PlayStation or Nintendo Wii. With the Mac rapidly gaining share with younger shoppers, EA has announced plans to release its new *Harry Potter* game and three other titles on the Mac this summer.

16 Another rarely mentioned advantage is Apple's so-called developer program. Once iPod sales began skyrocketing in 2003, the company worked with makers of portable speakers, music-player cases, and other add-on gadgets. And Apple is working on the most mobile platform of all. Since BMW first added an optional iPod connector in the glove compartment of many of its 2004 models, carmakers including Chrysler, Ford, and Honda have followed suit. General Motors Corp.'s 2008 Cadillac CTS will come with a center console that features the iPod's "rotate and click" interface, not only for pulling music off an iPod but also for playing the radio or listening to CDs or satellite radio. "It's about getting to your music, not having to learn a new set of tricks for each service," says James Grace, the 27-year-old GM manager who leads the project.

17 With the iPhone, Apple seems ready to open up opportunities for software developers who were mostly shut out from the iPod. On June 11, it announced that any Web 2.0 program designed to work with Apple's Safari browser would work on the iPhone. That means such popular sites as MySpace, Digg, or Amazon.com will be able to adapt their services to take advantage of the device—say, by adding a virtual button on their sites so that iPhone users could actually place a phone call with a fellow Netizen, rather than just trade e-mails or post messages.

18 To be sure, many developers gripe that this approach is a far cry from letting them create applications designed from the ground up to work directly with the iPhone. That's a privilege Apple has conferred on only a few partners, such as Google. But "it's a good first step," says Digg Chairman Jay Adelson, who expects Apple to become more inclusive as

time goes by. "For now, it's a very strange kind of controlled system—because they have these insanely high bars [for reliability and user experience] that they want to hit."

19   Many partners won't wait for a formal invite. Despite doubts about the iPhone's usefulness to serious businesspeople, Salesforce.com is working on an iPhone version of its sales management software. "It's not just about market share, it's about showing what is possible and what is cool," says CEO Marc Benioff. And more than 150 developers have registered to attend an ad hoc "iPhone Developers Camp" in San Francisco on July 6, to trade ideas and create new applications.

20   But if the Apple orchard is growing, it is still no Eden. For those partners that make the cut, Apple enforces a brutal perfectionism. "The stereotype is that they're this loosey-goosey California company, but nothing could be further from the truth," says Gary Johnson, the former CEO of chipmaker PortalPlayer Inc., which roared to prosperity by providing the electronic brains of the first generations of iPods. Johnson says that whenever a project fell off track or a part fell short of Apple's needs, its engineers were demanding "root cause analysis" and explanations within 12 hours. "You could pacify other customers by putting 10 engineers on a plane to see them. Not Apple."

"AN UNREASONABLENESS"

21   Working with Apple can be exhausting. Johnson says the company almost never issued documents outlining its technical requirements, preferring to keep things oral to avoid a paper trail that might be leaked. And no supplier was given a full picture of what exactly Apple was working on: Everything was on a "need to know" basis. "There's an unreasonableness," says Johnson. "It's as though your entire reason for being is to serve them." Yet he adds he has no hard feelings: "It wasn't a malicious thing. It's almost machine-like. You may have friendships or business relationships, but they don't really count." Johnson found that out on an April morning in 2006, when he learned Apple had decided not to use a chip that had been under development for more than a year and was expected to bring in half of PortalPlayer's sales. The company's stock crashed 50% when Johnson told Wall Street a few days later. Seven months later, it was purchased by Nvidia Corp. for $357 million—half of its peak market cap.

22   Suppliers of TV shows, movies, and other video content have their own reasons for being wary of joining the Apple ecosystem. They know what happened in the music industry. Jobs created a kind of reverse razor-and-blades model with the iPod, where Apple sells lucrative razors (music players) and the studios are stuck selling cheapo blades (music). Hollywood has resisted Jobs' vision for placing movies on the iPod and iPhone. Only movies from Walt Disney Co. (where Jobs is the largest individual shareholder) and Paramount Pictures have licensed movies to iTunes. The 52 million TV shows and movies sold so far by Apple amounts to fewer than two videos per iPod.

23   This makes Apple's newest partnership with AT&T for iPhone service all the more intriguing. Since the iPhone was announced in January, many observers have wondered if Jobs pulled another fast one, using his consumer cred to win unprecedented influence over the $140 billion cellular-phone business. Normally, carriers in the U.S. control how cellphones are priced and marketed, right down to deciding whether they will turn on capabilities built into the phones, such as wireless music downloading. But that's not how Apple rolls. Apple defined the 16 services that are highlighted on the iPhone homepage, and users sign up for them via iTunes, not on AT&T's homepage or in its stores.

24   Has AT&T set itself up to be marginalized? The carrier stands to steal subscribers from its rivals; CEO Randall L. Stephenson said on June 19 that of the 1.1 million people who had inquired about the iPhone, 40% were not currently signed up with AT&T. But analysts

MIRKO ILIC

The Apple Ecosystem

Its lineup of digital music players, computers, and phones places Apple in the center of an expanding world of suppliers, accessory producers, and content providers. Here's a look.

SUPPLIERS

Apple has the two things suppliers look for: big orders today and momentum. For example, Apple will buy 19% of all the NAND flash memory chips (a key component in the iPod Nano and in the iPhone) produced worldwide this year. Now it's making a big bet on touch-screens. And hundreds of thousands of new software developers are creating programs for Apple products.

Data: Apple Inc., NPD Group Inc., iSuppli Corp.

ACCESSORIES

A $1 billion-plus industry of independently sold iPod accessories has sprung up, everything from toilet-paper-holder docking stations to shoulder-bag boom boxes. Apple says 70% of all 2007 U.S. car models are offering iPod connectivity. It is teaming up with four airlines to let passengers charge iPods and watch video on seat backs. And already, more than 1,000 iPhone products are being advertised.

CONTENT

Major TV networks, from Warner Bros. to CBS, Fox, and MTV, have sold about 50 million shows through Apple's iTunes software in the past two years, for total sales of about $100 million. Also, some 2 million movies have sold in the past year. Apple has sold about 2.5 billion songs from labels including EMI, Universal, and Sony. It sells an estimated 70% of all digital music and ranks as the third-largest seller of music in the U.S., in any format.

say Apple will earn a luxurious 35% gross margin on each of the $500 devices. AT&T is offering a $59 base plan for phone and data services—roughly $20 less than the cost for corporate e-mail devices like Treo. Besides potentially taking a bite out of AT&T's margins, this could cause its other handset makers to demand sweeter deals, too.

25   But the real test will be whether Jobs can change the way consumers think about a phone. This is Apple's first entry into a preexisting mass market, and those other phone manufacturers can't afford to let Jobs rewire things to suit Apple's strengths. Some already have rolled out cheaper products that, if not exactly as capable as the iPhone, may be close enough. Will most consumers eventually choose to save money, even at the expense of a bit of elegance? History says they will, according to Harvard Business School professor Clayton M. Christensen: "The world always ends up thanking innovators for their cool products—but won't pay for them. There are forces of gravity at work."

26   Now there's a matchup worth watching: Steve Jobs vs. gravity.

Case 2

BusinessWeek

Saving Starbucks' Soul: *Chairman Howard Schultz Is on a Mission to Take His Company Back to Its Roots. Oh, Yeah—He Also Wants to Triple Sales in Five Years*

> *"A heady aroma of coffee reached out and drew me in. I stepped inside and saw what looked like a temple for the worship of coffee. . . . It was my Mecca. I had arrived."*
>
> —*Howard Schultz on his first visit to Starbucks in 1981*

From: Howard Schultz
Sent: Wednesday, February 14, 2007 10:39 AM Pacific Standard Time
To: Jim Donald
Cc: Anne Saunders; Dave Pace; Dorothy Kim; Gerry Lopez; Jim Alling; Ken Lombard; Martin Coles; Michael Casey; Michelle Gass; Paula Boggs; Sandra Taylor

Subject: The Commoditization of the Starbucks Experience

As you prepare for the FY 08 strategic planning process, I want to share some of my thoughts with you.

Over the past ten years, in order to achieve the growth, development, and scale necessary to go from less than 1,000 stores to 13,000 stores and beyond, we have had to make a series of decisions that, in retrospect, have led to the watering down of the Starbucks experience, and, what some might call the commoditization of our brand.

Many of these decisions were probably right at the time, and on their own merit would not have created the dilution of the experience; but in this case, the sum is much greater and, unfortunately, much more damaging than the individual pieces. For example, when we went to automatic espresso machines, we solved a major problem in terms of speed of service and efficiency. At the same time, we overlooked the fact that we would remove much of the romance and theatre that was in play with the use of the La Marzocca machines. This specific decision became even more damaging when the height of the machines, which are now in thousands of stores, blocked the visual sight line the customer previously had to watch the drink being made, and for the intimate experience with the barista. This, coupled with the need for fresh roasted coffee in every North America city and every international market, moved us toward the decision and the need for flavor locked packaging. Again, the right decision at the right time, and once again I believe we overlooked the cause and the affect of flavor lock in our stores. We achieved fresh roasted bagged coffee, but at what cost? The loss of aroma—perhaps the most powerful non-verbal signal we had in our stores; the loss of our people scooping fresh coffee from the bins and grinding it fresh in front of the customer, and once again stripping the store of tradition and our heritage? Then we moved to store design. Clearly we have had to streamline store design to gain efficiencies of scale and to make sure we had the ROI on sales to investment ratios that would satisfy the financial side of our business. However, one of the results has been stores that no longer have the soul of the past and reflect a chain of stores vs. the warm feeling of a neighborhood store. Some people even call our stores sterile, cookie cutter, no longer reflecting the passion our partners feel about our coffee. In fact, I am not sure people today even know we are roasting coffee. You certainly can't get the message from being in our stores. The merchandise, more art than science, is far removed from being the merchant that I believe we can be and certainly at a minimum should support the foundation of our coffee heritage. Some stores don't have coffee grinders, French presses from Bodum, or even coffee filters.

Now that I have provided you with a list of some of the underlying issues that I believe we need to solve, let me say at the outset that we have all been part of these decisions. I take full responsibility myself, but we desperately need to look into the mirror and realize it's time to get back to the core and make the changes necessary to evoke the heritage, the tradition, and the passion that we all have for the true Starbucks experience. While the current state of affairs for the most part is self induced, that has lead to competitors of all kinds, small and large coffee companies, fast-food operators, and mom and pops, to position themselves in a way that creates awareness, trial and loyalty of people who previously have been Starbucks customers. This must be eradicated.

I have said for 20 years that our success is not an entitlement and now it's proving to be a reality. Let's be smarter about how we are spending our time, money and resources. Let's get back to the core. Push for innovation and do the things necessary to once again differentiate Starbucks from all others. We source and buy the highest quality coffee. We have built the most trusted brand in coffee in the world, and we have an enormous responsibility to both the people who have come before us and the 150,000 partners and their families who are relying on our stewardship.

Finally, I would like to acknowledge all that you do for Starbucks. Without your passion and commitment, we would not be where we are today.

Onward . . .

1   On Apr. 3, Starbucks launches a pair of confections called Dulce de Leche Latte and Dulce de Leche Frappuccino. A 16-oz. Grande latte has a robust 440 calories (about the same as two packages of M&M's) and costs about $4.50 in New York City—or about three times as much as McDonald's most expensive premium coffee. Starbucks Corp. describes its latest concoctions, which took 18 months to perfect, this way: "Topped with whipped cream and a dusting of toffee sprinkles, Starbucks' version of this traditional delicacy is a luxurious tasty treat."

2   If you find yourself at Starbucks in the next few weeks, letting a Dulce de Leche Latte slide over your taste buds, you might wonder how this drink came to be. It's a tale worth hearing. On the surface it's a story about how the Starbucks marketing machine conjures and sells café romance to millions of people around the world. On a deeper level it's a story about how a company, along with its messianic leader, is struggling to hold on to its soul.

3   Ask Schultz for the key to Starbucks and he'll tell you it's all about storytelling. Starbucks is centered on two oft-repeated tales: Schultz' trip to Seattle in 1981, where he first enjoyed gourmet coffee, and a 1983 trip to Milan, where he discovered espresso bar culture. Not only are these journeys useful touchstones for recruits, they also provide the original marketing story for a company that prides itself on giving customers an authentic experience. "The one common thread to the success of these stories and the company itself," says Schultz, "is that they have to be true—and they have to be authentic."

TRUE BELIEVERS

4   Stories alone aren't enough, though, to fuel Starbucks' other obsession: to grow really, really big. By 2012, Schultz aims to nearly triple annual sales, to $23.3 billion. The company also plans to have 40,000 stores worldwide, up from 13,500 today, not long after that. To hit its profit targets, Starbucks has become expert at something that's decidedly unromantic—streamlining operations. Over the past 10 years the company has redesigned the space behind the counter to boost barista efficiency. Automatic espresso machines speed the time it takes to serve up a shot. Coffee is vacuum-sealed, making it easier to ship over long distances. To boost sales, the company sells everything from breath mints to CDs to notebooks. Add it up and you have an experience that's nothing like the worn wooden counters of the first store in Pike Place Market or an Italian espresso bar.

5   Somewhere along the way that disconnect began to gnaw at Schultz. Most recently it manifested itself in a note he wrote to his senior team. The Valentine's Day memo, which leaked to the Web, cut to the heart of what he sees as the company's dilemma. "We have had to make a series of decisions," Schultz wrote, "that, in retrospect, have led to the watering down of the Starbucks experience, and what some might call the commoditization of our brand."

6   Now, Schultz is asking his lieutenants to redouble their efforts to return to their roots. "We're constantly—I don't want to say battling—but we don't want to be that big company that's corporate and slick," says Michelle Gass, senior vice-president and chief merchant for global products. "We don't. We still think about ourselves as a small entrepreneurial company." That's a tricky business when you have 150,000 employees in 39 countries. But keeping that coffee joie de vivre alive inside Starbucks is crucial to Schultz' entire philosophy. Who better to sell something than a true believer?

7   In 2004, Starbucks introduced something called the Coffee Master program for its employees. It's a kind of extra-credit course that teaches the staff how to discern the subtleties of regional flavor. Graduates (there are now 25,000) earn a special black apron and an insignia on their business cards. The highlight is the "cupping ceremony," a tasting ritual traditionally used by coffee traders. After the grounds have steeped in boiling water, tasters "crest" the mixture, penetrating the crust on top with a spoon and inhaling the aroma. As employees slurp the brew, a Starbucks Coffee Educator encourages them to taste a Kenyan coffee's "citrusy" notes or the "mushroomy" flavor of a Sumatran blend.

8   If the ritual reminds you of a wine tasting, that's intentional. Schultz has long wanted to emulate the wine business. Winemakers, after all, command a premium by focusing on provenance: the region of origin, the vineyard, and, of course, the grape that gives the wine its particular notes—a story, in other words. Bringing wine's cachet to coffee would help take the brand upmarket and allow Starbucks to sell premium beans.

9   The product and marketing people call the strategy "Geography is a Flavor." And in 2005 they began selling this new story with whole-bean coffee. The company reorganized the menu behind the counter, grouping coffees by geography instead of by "smooth" or "bold." It replaced the colorful Starbucks coffee bags with clean white packages emblazoned with colored bands representing the region of origin. Later, for those connoisseurs willing to pay $28 a pound, Starbucks introduced single-origin beans called "Black Apron Exclusives."

10   The next step was to reach the masses who buy drinks in the stores. The team decided to launch a series of in-store promotions, each with a new set of drinks, that would communicate regional idiosyncrasies to customers. The first promotion, the team decided, would highlight Central and South America, where Starbucks buys more than 70% of its beans.

11   The sort of authenticity Schultz loves to talk about is hard to pull off when you're the size of Starbucks. Telling a story to a mass audience sometimes requires smoothing over inconvenient cultural nuances. Plus, the marketing folks have to work quickly to stay abreast of beverage trends, not to mention ahead of such rivals as Dunkin' Donuts and McDonald's. Diving deep is not an option.

12   A year ago, 10 Starbucks marketers and designers got on a plane and went looking for inspiration in Costa Rica. "It's being able to say: 'This is how and why this [drink] is made,'" says Angie McKenzie, who runs new-product design. "Not because someone told us or we read it somewhere." The Starbucks team spent five days in Costa Rica, traveling on a minivan owned by TAM Tours. Later, a smaller group toured Mexico City and Oaxaca as well.

MADE IN CHINA

13   The mission was to find products that would evoke an authentic vibe in the U.S. That's harder than it sounds. Philip Clark, a merchandising executive, wanted to sell traditional

Costa Rican mugs. But the ones typically used to drink coffee were drab and brown; they wouldn't pop on store shelves. Plus, they broke easily. Then he found Cecilia de Figueres, who handpaints ceramic mugs in a mountainside studio an hour from the capital, San Jose. The artist favors bright floral patterns; they would pop nicely. Starbucks paid de Figueres a flat fee for her designs. Each mug will have a tag bearing her name and likeness; on the bottom it will say "Made in China."

14 Starbucks will weave artisans and other Costa Ricans into the in-store promotional campaign. Painter Eloy Zuñiga Guevara will appear on a poster with a decidedly homespun Latin aesthetic. (And if customers want some authenticity to take home with them, they can buy one of five paintings of Costa Rican farmers that Guevara produced for Starbucks. They will sell for $25 apiece.) A second poster will feature Costa Rican coffee farmers from whom Starbucks buys beans. A third will show a grandmotherly figure cooking up dulce de leche on a gas stove. (She's a paid model from Seattle.) Each poster will feature the tagline "I am Starbucks."

15 Having devised a story, Starbucks needed a drink that would say "Latin America." Beverage brainstorming takes place in the Liquid Lab, an airy space painted in Starbucks' familiar blue, green, and orange hues. The room features huge bulletin boards plastered with the latest beverage trends. In this case it didn't take an anthropologist to figure out which drink Starbucks should use to promote its Latin American theme.

16 Dulce de leche is a caramel-and-milk dessert enjoyed throughout much of the region. What's more, Häagen-Dazs introduced dulce de leche ice cream in 1998, and Starbucks followed suit with its own ice cream in 1999. So Americans are familiar with the flavor, says McKenzie, but "it still has a nice exotic edge to it." Besides, she adds, caramel and milk go great with coffee.

17 Even so, concocting a drink is never simple at Starbucks. The research-and-development department routinely tackles 70 beverage projects a year, with 8 of them leading to new drinks. A drink must not only appeal to a broad swath of coffee drinkers but also be easy for a barista to make quickly so as to maximize sales per store (hello, Wall Street). "The store . . . is a little manufacturing plant," says Gass, and yet it must seem as though the drink is being handcrafted specially for the customer (hello, Howard Schultz).

18 Creating the Dulce de Leche Latte and Frappuccino fell to Debbie Ismon, a 26-year-old beverage developer who holds a degree in food science and has worked at Starbucks for 2½ years. In late June, 2006, the design team brought her a small sample they'd whipped up that they felt embodied the right tastes, plus a written description of the characteristics they hoped to see. For the next four months, Ismon fiddled with various ratios of caramel, cooked milk, and sweetness "notes." After the design group decided which version tasted most "in-concept," Ismon mixed up three different flavors for the big taste test. One hundred or so random Starbucks employees filed in, sampled the drinks, and rated them on computer screens. The process was repeated two more times for each drink. Finally, 18 months after starting the process, Starbucks had its two latest premium beverages.

19 If previous drinks, such as Caramel Macchiato, are any guide, Starbucks' Dulce de Leche drinks will sell briskly. That should please Wall Street and perhaps even help perk up the stock, which is down 20% from its May, 2006, high on worries that operating margins are falling and that Starbucks could miss its ambitious growth targets.

20 And as you wait in line for your Dulce de Leche Latte, you might ask yourself: Are you paying $4.50 for a caffeine jolt and caramel topping? Or have you simply been dazzled by Howard Schultz' storytelling magic?

Source: Reprinted with special permission from "Saving Starbucks' Soul," *BusinessWeek,* July 9, 2007. Copyright © 2007 The McGraw-Hill Companies.

Case 3

Facebook Faces Up

1 Facebook has had a rough ride of late. Users complain about the site's frequent shutdowns, with some observers seeing the malfunction as a possible troubling security breach.

2 And though the news media continue to talk about the network's rapid growth and market dominance, commentators have expressed misgivings about Facebook's ability to sustain and monetize that expansion.

3 Now, with founder Mark Zuckerberg heading back to court Aug. 8 to defend himself against accusations that he stole the site's concept from ConnectU, another collegiate social network with its roots at Harvard, the vultures are on the sidelines, flapping their wings.

STAYING IN SCHOOL

4 Not least among them are those looking to fill the void they claim Facebook has left behind by deserting its core audience, college students. According to ComScore, 71% of users are now outside the college age-bracket. As of May, anyone could join the network, whereas users once needed a.edu e-mail address (as proof of college affiliation) to join.

5 But the demand for student-only online spaces—the very thing that made Facebook take off in the first place—remains. And that's where three ventures by young alumni—CollegeOTR.com, CollegeTonight.com, and CollegeWikis.com—hope to come in. Their success and strategy depend on staying loyal to that college niche, and they're looking to find ways to complement rather than compete with the networks students already use.

6 Niche marketing has been the strategy of choice for many new networks in the last year. Users have responded well to being a part of a distinct community, whether grouped by profession, ethnicity, or school. And advertisers like that specificity too.

COLLEGE-SPECIFIC BLOGS

7 Furthermore, research done this April by iProspect shows that among the younger age group, the top social networks have overlapping user-bases. For each of the eight social sites in the report, 30% to 40% of 18- to 24-year-olds surveyed reported some involvement, which means most respondents are frequenting more than one of the sites. According to iProspect, the likely overlap is three to five networks per average student user. If that's true, the niche model just got a whole lot more interesting to mainstream business.

8 College campuses provide an ideal niche case, not only because they are self-contained, but because they are communities with ample social needs and active online populations. "[They] are probably the best example we've seen of communities that can be easily activated by online media," says Columbia alumnus Doug Imbruce. This September, Imbruce is launching a series of college-specific blogs called CollegeOTR.com, where students can post information about their schools, their peers, and their professors and administrators, while using a pseudonym.

9 Content will be managed by student-editors reporting to an editor-in-chief in CollegeOTR.com's New York offices. Though the controlled structure and pseudonyms may seem impersonal, Imbruce promises that editors will be chiefly concerned with controlling logistics, technology, and privacy. He predicts a site culture in which students collectively feel free to post the truth of college life as they see it. By virtue of its selectivity—students

can only contribute to their own college's page—Imbruce believes Off The Record is "more intimate" than a larger network or more public blog.

PEP SQUAD

10   Given the specificity of the information that will be contained within each blog thread, Imbruce also promises the sites will remain exclusive to each college. "We're looking to create college sites," he says. "We may add more content, sports scores, and news, but we will stay vertical within these communities."

11   Student-exclusive networks provide users with a sense of importance: It's easy to become a big fish in a small, students-only pond. Emory University alumus Zach Suchin hopes to capitalize on this desire. His venture, CollegeTonight.com, will establish distinct networks for each U.S. college, where students can post information about parties, concerts, and social events, download contact lists to their mobile phones, and make plans to meet up. In September, CollegeTonight will launch a nine-month nightlife tour of 129 sponsored events at colleges across the country. Business partners already include car manufacturer Subaru and CBS, which will sponsor the concerts and parties on the tour in the hope of reaching Suchin's user base.

12   Suchin proposes the site as a tool chiefly for "the trendsetters and the tastemakers" and, notably, wealthy students with disposable income (the tour begins at Ivy League schools Yale and Brown). And it's actively promoting a sense of exclusivity and privacy. Former FBI profiler John Douglas crafted the site's privacy settings and users must have a .edu e-mail to join. "That will never change," Suchin says. "We're trying to create the sense of community that Facebook abandoned."

WEANING AWAY FROM FACEBOOK

13   As it turns out, for now at least, students are loath to leave the network that still dominates online socializing. "Facebook has such a strong hold on the college social networking market that people are [still] interested in developing things for Facebook," explains Joe DiPasquale, founder of CollegeWikis.com. He hopes to strike a balance by creating college-specific sites with a widget that links to Facebook.

14   On CollegeWikis.com, students can e-mail questions about local restaurants, classes, and dorm life. Each question and e-mailed response from other students becomes instant content on the Wikipedia-style Web site, a viral format that DiPasquale believes students are more likely to use than mass administrative e-mails, which most students simply delete. Since its launch in April, CollegeWikis has expanded to 60 schools nationwide and achieved 15% penetration at some campuses.

15   Meanwhile, on CollegeWikis.com's sponsored Facebook application, SuperWall, users post college-specific information that is instantly communicated to the virtual message walls of other registered users at their college. SuperWall is currently one of Facebook's 10 most popular applications.

ROOM FOR EVERYONE

16   Again, the appeal of CollegeWikis.com is its specificity. A site is created for any college if a student submits a request to the central wiki page. Within that wiki, users can join or create lists for their major, their class, and their dorm. Already the average college wiki page has 216 more-specific lists. Says DiPasquale, "When we did focus groups, we found people wanted the sites as specific as they could be."

17   DiPasquale's dual approach to advertising and site sponsorship—be authentic, be transparent—epitomizes these niche networks' business model. Young consumers are expert multi-taskers so there is room for multiple offerings within their expanding online life. These three young entrepreneurs hope their offerings will complement one another and Facebook, creating more business for all of them. Says CollegeOTR.com's Imbruce, "Media in this group [are] additive and not really competitive." Though he's talking about college students, the insight applies to online business overall, and even "old fogeys."

FOGEYS FLOCK TO FACEBOOK

18   Facebook, the online hangout for college kids and recent graduates, is growing up. The site has amassed an audience of 33 million Web users, initially by catering to well-scrubbed kids who use the social network to nudge their friends, share photos, and swap music tips—all while consuming ads from Gen Y brands like Apple, Jeep, and Red Bull.

19   Lately, an influx of older users—professionals in their 30s and 40s, many in high-tech—is changing the face of Facebook. Among Silicon Valley executives, journalists, and publicists, Facebook has become the place to see and be seen. And it's not just tech. Consulting company Ernst & Young's Facebook network boasts 16,000 members, Citigroup's claims nearly 8,500.

20   Factor in plans by Microsoft, Facebook's biggest business partner, to help turn the site into a tool for making professional connections, and the Palo Alto (Calif.) Internet company could be on the cusp of expanding its already impressive advertising roster, increasing its value as a buyout target or initial public offering candidate, and challenging professional-networking site LinkedIn as the go-to nexus for recruiters and investors.

CHANGING TRAFFIC PATTERNS

21   "People in the Valley definitely search professionally on Facebook first," says Keith Rabois, vice-president of strategy and business development at Slide.com, which makes photo-sharing applications that can be used on other sites, including Facebook. Rabois was an executive at LinkedIn until May.

22   But older users are behind the recent traffic surge at Facebook, which says it signs up 150,000 new users a day. In June, 11.5 million of the individual visitors to the site were 35 or older, more than double the number a year before, according to market researcher ComScore Media Metrix. The 35-and-up crowd now accounts for more than 41% of all Facebook visitors. Among the fogeys with profiles: Internet pioneer and Google executive Vinton Cerf, venture capitalist Vinod Khosla, and Salesforce.com CEO Marc Benioff. Jeff Pulver, a telecom entrepreneur and blogger, famously said in a recent post that he was forsaking LinkedIn for Facebook as his main professional hub.

23   Even Facebook's competitors acknowledge change is afoot. "Clearly, Facebook has lots of traffic and a lot of that traffic is from the same group of users as on LinkedIn," says David Cowan, a managing partner at Bessemer Venture Partners, a LinkedIn investor. Yet during Facebook's most recent growth spurt—it has added 1.3 million visitors since May, according to ComScore—LinkedIn's audience hasn't declined, Cowan says.

"A LOT MORE BUZZ"

24   So the question now for Facebook, marketers looking to advertise there, companies that want to own it, and investors who eventually may buy its shares is whether 23-year-old CEO

Mark Zuckerberg and his deputies can keep attracting the long-in-the-tooth crowd while preserving the site's spring-break atmosphere of beer-drinking photos and innuendo.

25   Since its start in 2004, Facebook has attracted a more upscale young audience than News Corp.'s MySpace, while avoiding the button-down feel of LinkedIn. "In some ways, LinkedIn feels more like a Chamber of Commerce mixer," says Barry Parr, a media analyst at JupiterResearch. "Facebook clearly has a lot more buzz." More than 48% of Facebook visitors in June came from households with incomes over $75,000, rivaling 55% for LinkedIn, and well above MySpace's 39% figure, according to ComScore.

26   Advertisers have taken notice. Coca-Cola has been running promotions on MySpace the past two years for brands including Cherry Coke and Fanta, and has promoted Diet Coke and other drinks on Google's YouTube. The company has yet to advertise with more than simple banners on Facebook but is weighing its first large-scale promotion there. "We see a lot of opportunity there," says Coke spokeswoman Susan Stribling. Procter & Gamble has advertised Crest toothpaste, Secret deodorant, and Noxema skin-care products on Facebook, and more campaigns are coming in the fall, a spokeswoman says without elaborating.

27   Most of Facebook's revenue comes from banner ads placed by Microsoft as part of a 2006 deal between the companies. Facebook also directly sells more interactive campaigns, including sponsored profiles and "stories" that appear in users' constantly updated news feed on the site, advertising such things as Hewlett-Packard computers and PNC Bank financial services. As the site lures more professionals, it could attract more brand advertisers that want to aim word-of-mouth campaigns at an upscale audience, says Parr. "Facebook is obviously a wonderful environment to reach people in a way that's personal, but not too invasive," he says.

GREASING THE WHEELS

28   Today, Facebook's main professional value is "building social capital" among business contacts, says co-founder and vice-president of product engineering, Dustin Moskovitz. He's referring to the informal banter, such as through status updates and games with industry friends on the site, that can grease the wheels for interaction when work needs to get done. Is anyone using Facebook to add new contacts to their Rolodex? "They're certainly doing it with us," says Moskovitz, who says his Facebook inbox is starting to function a lot like traditional e-mail.

29   Informal interaction could be just step one in Facebook's plans to burnish its professional credentials. Microsoft is helping the company with technology that could turn Facebook's trove of data on members' names, ages, connections, and tastes into directories of users accessible by business software programs. "They may very well be building one of the next interesting collaborative platforms, and it may have business applications as well," says Dan'l Lewin, a corporate vice-president at Microsoft. "They're learning in real time, and the audience is speaking."

30   In May, Facebook announced that it would let third-party software developers tap into its user data to build miniature software programs that could make the site more useful. So far, the results have been mostly programs such as iLike, which lets users share music preferences, or SuperPoke, whereby users can virtually slap, spank, or pinch pals. Microsoft envisions more sober applications: It recently released design software that can let nontechnical users combine Facebook data with elements of other Web sites and blogs like Microsoft's Virtual Earth and Yahoo!'s Flickr to create new programs.

IN THE DRIVER'S SEAT

31   Facebook's expanding scope could also increase its market value. Bear Stearns analyst Robert Peck estimated in an Aug. 1 report that Facebook could fetch $4.9 billion in an

acquisition; he argued that Yahoo! should buy it or another social site to capture Internet ad revenue flowing to such networks. Facebook's revenue could more than double, to $358 million, in 2008 from $140 million in 2007, Peck said.

32   Facebook has turned down an acquisition offer from Yahoo!, and according to reports it also rebuffed Google, Microsoft, and Viacom. Now, those snubs could look shrewd. In other signs the company is girding for expansion, if not an IPO. In July it hired a new chief financial officer, Gideon Yu, who was CFO at YouTube before the company sold itself to Google. The same month, Facebook hired Chamath Palihapitiya, an investor at venture capital firm Mayfield Fund as vice-president of product marketing and operations.

33   On July 19, Facebook made its first-ever acquisition, snaring two creators of the open-source Firefox Web browser. Facebook director and early investor Peter Theil said in a recent interview with *The Deal* that an IPO wouldn't come until 2009 at the earliest. Facebook "is focused on being an independent company," says a spokeswoman, who declined to comment on the prospect of an IPO or make Zuckerberg available for an interview.

SPEED BUMPS ALONG THE WAY

34   To be sure, Facebook has experienced growing pains. High-profile users say they're starting to get unwanted requests from strangers who try to horn in on their network to ask for favors. Some college-age kids see the influx of users old enough to be their parents as an affront. And a couple of Zuckerberg's old Harvard University classmates sued the company in July for allegedly stealing their ideas. In 2006 the company had to quell complaints from users who said Facebook's broadcast of their every move on the site violated their privacy.

35   What's more, Facebook's world of pokes, spanks, and party photos can't hold a candle to LinkedIn's more professional milieu for executives who want to make connections, says Reid Hoffman, LinkedIn's co-founder, chairman, and president. "Many of the bloggers don't really understand the use case for LinkedIn," he says.

36   Still, Hoffman admits that people are "piling on and taking a look around" Facebook. "If you're going to recruit college students, heck, I'd go to Facebook," he says. Given the flock of older professionals joining the Facebook crowd, before long it won't just be headhunters who have business to do there.

Sources: Reprinted with special permission from "Facebook Faces Up," *BusinessWeek,* August 8, 2007, and "Fogeys Flock to Facebook," *BusinessWeek,* August 6, 2007. Copyright © 2007 The McGraw-Hill Companies.

Case 4 BusinessWeek

MySpace Goes Hollywood: *The Social Networking Web Site Will Distribute Videos from Big-Time Producers in an Effort to Counter Rival Facebook*

Ronald Grover

1   Tired of watching skateboarding dogs and exploding diet cola bottles? MySpace.com, in a race to keep users from sampling such consumer-generated videos on YouTube and other sites, is going Hollywood. The online social network owned by News Corp. has been taking meetings, holding power lunches, and returning calls from well-placed agents to lengthen a growing lineup of professionally produced videos for its large (and increasingly over-30) audience.

2   The most recent case in point comes Sept. 13, when MySpace will announce it has signed with Marshall Herskovitz and Edward Zwick, producers of the Leonardo DiCaprio film *Blood Diamond* and the 1980s TV show *thirtysomething*, to distribute via MySpace a series of 8-minute videos called *quarterlife*.

3   The series, which tells the story of twentysomething writers, actresses, and dancers trying to break into show business, is being trumpeted as the first "network quality" show to be produced specifically for the Web. By that, the producers mean it won't be cheap to make—far more than the estimated $5,000 a pop it cost to produce Michael Eisner's *Prom Queen*, itself considered higher in quality than much online fare.

HIGH PRODUCTION VALUES

4   How much more? The production tab will probably run higher than $80,000 an installment, based on Herskovitz' estimate that each 48-minute episode will cost somewhere north of $500,000. Each episode will then be divided into six installments to be distributed online.

5   The *quarterlife* deal comes two days after MySpace's agreement to team up with newly launched independent Web producer My Damn Channel, which has signed on well-known talent like sitcom writer and comedian Harry Shearer and Rolling Stones music producer Don Was to create their own videos.

6   MySpace has also inked other high-end content deals lately, including getting short "minisode" versions of classic TV shows such as *The Jeffersons* from Sony and programming from sports leagues like the National Basketball Association. In July, the social network also signed Dark Horse Comics to create its own channel of online comic books.

MYSPACE'S BIG AD STRATEGY

7   "At the outset, MySpace was a blank canvas for our users," says MySpaceTV.com General Manager Jeff Berman. "What we're doing now is giving some of the best creative folks we can find a blank canvas to create the kinds of content that a MySpace user wants." Herskovitz and Zwick, Berman points out, "have Emmys on their desk."

8   Getting some of those people on board has forced MySpace to make concessions. Herskovitz says the News Corp. unit was initially uneasy about his company's plan to have its own social networking site, quarterlife.com. The potential competitor could lure folks from MySpace to a separate site where Herskovitz and Zwick will have links to classes and other tools to help young artists break into show business. "I'm sure they didn't want folks

to leave, but we eventually found a compromise where they'd have their own *quarterlife* site and we'd have ours," Herskovitz says. "And the viewers will go where the viewers want to go." In addition, MySpace won't own the content, and it will be exclusive for only a day before it can be shown on quarterlife.com, says Herskovitz.

9   What MySpace folks are counting on, however, is keeping folks on their site long enough to sell plenty of ads. Those folks currently stick around an average of more than three hours a month, about 20 minutes more than Facebook. Moreover, News Corp. Chairman Rupert Murdoch has big plans for MySpace as an advertising vehicle, and has said that the unit that owns MySpace will be profitable this year and generate more than $1 billion in revenue next year with "margins well above 20%."

COUNTERING FACEBOOK'S GROWTH SPURT

10   That's one reason the site will soon begin offering truly professional content: prime-time TV programs from a new service called Hulu, backed by NBC and News Corp.'s Fox network. MySpace expects to get other content from traditional outlets like networks, but Berman refused to name them. MySpace is also keen to further distinguish itself from rival Facebook, a social networking site that's undergoing a growth surge after making it easier for software developers to build all manner of games, tools, and information that users can attach to their pages.

11   These may just be the opening scenes of Hollywood's romance with MySpace. There's a huge amount of freedom in programming for the Web, says My Damn Channel President and founder Rob Barnett, formerly CBS Radio's president of programming. "No one sent me any notes on what they'd like me to change," he says.

12   And MySpace will almost certainly get calls from agents for other high-powered creative types, figures Herskovitz, who says consolidation in the old media world means that traditional TV networks today produce their own shows and rarely turn to outsiders. "A few years ago there were 40 independent TV companies in Hollywood; now there are zero," says Herskovitz. "MySpace is a distribution platform with no controls. We just produce, and it gets a huge audience." Meanwhile, it has created a hubbub over Hulu.

THE HUBBUB OVER HULU

13   In March, News Corp. and NBC Universal made an announcement akin to an end-of-season cliffhanger. The media titans were teaming up to bring the best of prime-time TV and other high-quality programming to a new Web site they would develop together. The site didn't have a name. The shows it would feature were not yet known. The launch date was to be determined. But, if all went according to plan, executives promised the site would change the online video landscape. Just stay tuned, they said.

14   Five months later, the companies are finally revealing key details about the joint venture: The site's name is Hulu. And on Aug. 29, the Hulu team began accepting requests for inclusion in an invitation-only test, scheduled to begin in October with a few hundred people. "Our hope is that Hulu will embody our (admittedly ambitious) never-ending mission, which is to help you find and enjoy the world's premier content when, where, and how you want it," Hulu CEO Jason Kilar said in a statement.

A FEW DETAILS ON PROGRAMMING

15   Other than the name, which the company says was chosen for its fun factor and because it's easy to pronounce, the team would reveal little else about the much-hyped project. The

home page features promotional shots from some of NBC's and News Corp.'s most popular shows: *Heroes*, *Family Guy*, *The Simpsons*, *24*, and *Friday Night Lights*, to name a few. Yet it is unclear whether single episodes, entire seasons, or only clips of those shows and others will be available on the site. "We are still continuing to figure out the programming we will have at launch," company spokesperson Christina Lee says.

16   Others familiar with the site say all NBC programming currently available online will appear on Hulu and on sites owned by its distribution partners, which include Microsoft and Time Warner's AOL. The site will also have content from Comcast, including shows on the Style and Golf channels, as well as shows from small networks including the Oxygen network, Sundance Channel, TV Guide, and National Geographic. Other major networks such as CBS, Disney ABC, and Viacom have not signed on.

17   The Hulu team also would not confirm a *New York Times* report that it turned to a Rhode Island investment firm, Providence Equity Partners, for $100 million in cash—despite having two of the most deep-pocketed parents in the business.

READY TO COMPETE WITH GOOGLE?

18   All the mystery has some wondering whether Hulu stands a chance of challenging Google's YouTube, Joost, or the host of other video sites competing for user attention and advertiser dollars. Tech blogger Michael Arrington wrote in a March blog post that Google executives "have been referring to the project as Clown Co. privately" and that their YouTube business "doesn't look to be in any trouble."

19   In addition to competing with other networks' sites and those that rely on video generated by users, Hulu will also vie for attention with the properties owned by News Corp's Fox and NBC. As NBC sees it, that's not such a bad thing. Some viewers will choose to watch its content on Hulu, where they can also watch shows from competing networks, and some will opt to watch on NBC.com. The point is, they'll be watching. "At the end of the day, we believe premium professional content wins," says George Kliavkoff, NBC Universal's Chief Digital Officer. "We believe there is power in aggregating that content, and we believe in ubiquitous distribution."

20   Still, whether the Hulu site will really draw in audiences depends largely on what it has to offer, says Paul Verna, senior analyst at research firm eMarketer. If it has a trove of easily accessible content that people want, along with, perhaps, some of the social features that people like so much on YouTube, it will grab an audience, says Verna. If it doesn't, people will just stay with what's familiar. "I think people do eventually reach a point where they just want to go to the sites they are familiar with," says Verna.

BLINKX AIMS FOR "UBIQUITOUS DISTRIBUTION"

21   So far, it seems that Hulu's offering won't have content from CBS and other major networks. That could change if Hulu gets a huge audience. Right now, however, CBS and others are focusing on distributing their content as widely as possible to the places where people are already watching. "CBS's strategy is to pursue open, multi-partner, nonexclusive relationships with established video destinations, widgets, and application vendor companies, as well as regular syndicators," says Quincy Smith, president of CBS Interactive. In short, says Smith, the company wants to "take it to where the eyeballs are."

22   That's on the social networks. Networks such as CBS and Fox see the potential to distribute their content, via shareable "widget" video players, on those sites. Hulu also plans to distribute its content, via a player, on all manner of sites.

23   Part of the wide distribution philosophy comes from the marketing value of having television shows near one another, instead of on unique silos around the Web. The wisdom is that, if a person is already watching—say, Fox's Simpsons—online they can easily be convinced to tune into Viacom's *The Daily Show* or NBC's comedy *30 Rock*. That's why deals are being struck left and right to bring content together.

24   On Aug. 30, video search engine blinkx announced a partnership with Michael Eisner's new media studio Vuguru to bring the Web drama *Prom Queen* to its site. Already, blinkx brings together clips of premium content from around the Web via its video search engine, before directing users to where they can watch the full shows. "Ubiquitous distribution is primarily about marketing and building an audience around a product," says blinkx founder Suranga Chandratillake.

25   The point of spreading content around is that it also spreads around the ads, generating more revenue from additional viewers. Of course, that revenue is only extra if those viewers are not existing fans who would otherwise visit the network site but instead watch on a site where the ad sales must be split between a variety of partners. Hulu's owners will welcome the viewership however it comes. Now they need to ensure there's plenty to watch once there.

Sources: Reprinted with special permission from "MySpace Goes Hollywood," *BusinessWeek*, September 13, 2007, and "The Hubbub Over Hulu," *BusinessWeek*, August 30, 2007. Copyright © 2007 The McGraw-Hill Companies.

Case 5 BusinessWeek

AT&T Rebrands. Again

1 The wireless giant's revenues are surging, but it's still struggling to make the most of its new corporate identity. The country's largest wireless company, San Antonio-based AT&T, announced on Sept. 11 that it would reshuffle some key elements of its corporate identity, revealing a communications giant still grappling to find its voice in the rapidly evolving cellular market.

2 AT&T said Tuesday it will further incorporate the signature Cingular orange hue into its branding, including online, on billing statements, and in its 1,900 U.S. stores. At the same time, the company will launch splashy new television and Internet marketing campaigns, including six nationally broadcast TV spots directed by Wes Anderson, whose films, including *Rushmore* and *The Royal Tenenbaums*, have attracted a stylish, hipster following. AT&T, working with agencies BBDO Worldwide, Rich Media, and Big Icon U.S., would not disclose how much it's spending to make the branding changes.

3 AT&T is still attempting to figure out a coherent brand proposition following its titanic $86 billion merger with one of Cingular's former parents, BellSouth, finalized last year. The union presented the company with an opportunity to transform itself from an old-world telecom into a cutting-edge wireless player. But many consumers still associate AT&T with old-fashioned landlines and 10-lb. phone books amid a world of high-speed digital networks and Web-based personal networking. Cingular, meanwhile, the roguish cellular upstart created by SBC and BellSouth seven years ago, had a more modern look that didn't jibe with AT&T's monolithic feel. Reconciling the two has provided a branding conundrum, and it's by no means clear that this latest round of redesigns has solved the company's identity issues.

IDENTITY CRISIS?

4 The new proposition sees the company heading back to basics in an attempt to convey the seamless blend of both merged companies. And, in a move that suggests executives may regret having been so quick to ditch all things Brand Cingular (its quirky but memorable "Jack" logo, often shown bouncing around the screen in ads, was officially retired in May) the wireless company's characteristic effervescent orange will now get more prominent play throughout AT&T's wireless operations. Monthly billing statements adopted the new color in July, and everything from signs to marketing materials within AT&T's retail outlets should be complete by the end of next month. The company's Web site will be upgraded to reflect the new color while other updated elements such as building signs, awnings, and product packaging, will also roll out in the next few months.

5 The company's commitment to the new identity scheme may be reflected in its decision to make over its brick-and-mortar outlets. "Capital investment in the stores is usually a sign of a long-term brand investment, which is written off over a period of three to maybe five years," says Bill Gardner of the Wichita-based brand and design firm, Gardner Design. Gardner also runs the logo design Web site, Logolounge.com.

6 But, some branding experts are skeptical about how much effect adopting more of Cingular's orange can really have on AT&T's image. "Simply adding more color isn't going to change people's view of AT&T," says Tom Geismar, co-founder of the New York-based firm Chermayeff & Geismar, which has designed iconic corporate logos for companies including ExxonMobil, Public Broadcasting Service, NBC, and Intel. "Cingular's whole look and presentation was just much fresher."

7   "They may have underestimated how much equity was in the Cingular brand and are now trying to bring it back," says Rob Giampietro, one of the founders of the New York-based design studio, Giampietro+Smith. Simply attempting to blend the two further could confuse customers more, not less. "It suggests some lack of brand leadership," he warns. "What you could end up with is a 'bizzaro' version of what they think their customers' vision of the brand is." And that, as all branding experts preach, is a surefire way to appeal to no one in an attempt to attract everyone.

BOTTOM LINE

8   Even as the company feels its way through the transition, it has managed to strengthen its bottom line. In the second quarter of 2007, AT&T nearly doubled revenues, to $26.8 billion from the $14 billion of the same quarter the year before. The company's bottom-line growth also shot to $2.9 billion, from $1.8 billion. Of course, this year's figures include the bonuses of the merger, but even excluding boosts associated with mergers, revenues were up 2%.

9   And yet, since February, the company's stock has underperformed compared to the S&P 500 telecom and IT sector, which, on average, grew by more than 20%, while its share price remained relatively stagnant. To pull off the transformation, generate investor buzz, and continue stoking growth, AT&T is going to have to make itself relevant by proving it is a viable mobile brand.

POSITIVE PARTNER, CONFUSING CAMPAIGN?

10   One almost purely positive step for AT&T has been the partnership with Apple to launch the iPhone, likely the most hotly anticipated consumer communications device in decades. The move has been effective in drawing younger customers and raising brand awareness. A quarter of iPhone buyers in July switched to AT&T's service from another carrier and 57% were 35 or younger, according to the El Segundo (Calif.)-based research firm iSuppli. Wendy Clark, AT&T's senior vice-president of advertising, says the massively scrutinized product launch allowed consumer awareness of AT&T as a wireless brand to finally surpass that of Cingular.

11   But partnerships and individual products can only do so much for AT&T's brand. A mounting chorus of grumbles about outlandish international bills and spotty service, not to mention the incensed outcry raised by Apple's $200 price drop just 66 days after the iPhone's launch, could potentially taint the product's distributed brand sheen. And, the iPhone remains an Apple product—the two companies' exclusivity deal reportedly runs out in 2012. Gene Munster, a senior analyst with the Minneapolis-based securities firm Piper Jaffray, estimates that Apple's own stores could be selling as many iPhones each day as AT&T stores do each week, suggesting the product is more associated with Apple than AT&T in the minds of consumers.

12   As for the new ad campaign itself, the TV spots feature mobile professionals and young people in front of quickly rotating backdrops intended to illustrate the "seamless world" of the company's mobile services. One of the ads features three locations in which a professional might live, work, and play: China, London, and Moscow. The conclusion: that "AT&T works in more places like Chilondoscow," an amalgamation of the names of those locations.

13   In trying to combine a handful of different places and ideas, the spots could potentially confuse more than clarify, though the company alleges that customers responded positively to the ads in market testing. It remains to be seen whether consumers will connect with the quirky, difficult-to-pronounce names like New Sanfrakota (New York, San Francisco, South Dakota) and Newbosmento (New York, Boston, Sacramento). Or if they'll respond to this "new" wireless brand that, it seems, is still living somewhere between the old Cingular and the new AT&T.

Source: Reprinted with special permission from "AT&T Rebrands Again," *BusinessWeek,* September 11, 2007. Copyright © 2007 The McGraw-Hill Companies.

Case 6

Ice Cream Wars: Nestlé vs. Unilever

1   The $59 billion industry is dominated by two global giants looking to expand in Asia and Latin America—European Giants Nestlé and Unilever.

2   Witness the lines of tourists snaking their way toward the famous Berthillon ice cream counter on the Ile Saint-Louis in Paris, and you know that in the dog days of summer, nothing beats the heat better than a refreshing scoop of ice cream. From rich, super-premium flavors such as Ben & Jerry's Chunky Monkey, to reduced-fat offerings from Dreyer's, to Berthillon's to-die-for pear sorbet, sellers have blanketed the market with confections to suit every taste and budget.

3   What many consumers may not realize, though, is just how big a business ice cream has become around the world. The days of mom-and-pop parlors and local brands are fading fast. Today, the $59 billion ice cream industry is dominated by two global giants: Switzerland's Nestlé and Anglo-Dutch conglomerate Unilever. Together, they control more than one-third of the worldwide market—and half of ice cream sales in the U.S.—and they're looking to expand as they move into developing regions in Asia and Latin America.

4   It's a high-stakes battle in a growing and profitable business. Researcher Euromonitor figures that global ice cream sales are rising 2.5% annually and will hit $65 billion in 2010. Western Europe, the world's largest market, gobbled up $21.5 billion worth of ice cream and other frozen desserts last year, while North Americans devoured $16.3 billion worth. The most promising markets for growth are in emerging economies such as China and Brazil, where annual sales are soaring 8.5% and 8%, respectively.

RICH PRETAX MARGINS

5   Neither Nestlé nor Unilever had nearly so much presence in ice cream two decades ago. But starting in the 1990s, both began aggressive acquisition campaigns. Nestlé snapped up Häagen-Dazs, Dreyer's, and Swiss brand Mövenpick. Unilever bought Breyers Ice Cream and Ben & Jerry's. Today, Nestlé boasts a 17.5% share of the world market, while Unilever is close behind with 16%.

6   The rest of the market is highly fragmented: The No. 3 maker in the U.S., Wells' Dairy, has just 5% share. Other marques of note around the world are Baskin-Robbins (a unit of Dunkin' Brands) and Japan's Lotte, which remains No. 1 at home. China's top maker, Inner Mongolian Yili Industrial Group, has 17% domestic market share and will be the sole dairy sponsor for the 2008 Beijing Summer Olympics.

7   The decision to target ice cream has paid off handsomely for both Nestlé and Unilever. The Swiss company got nearly 20% of its $42 billion in first-half 2007 revenues from its milk products and ice cream division. With pretax margins of 10.5%, the unit kicked in nearly $900 million in profits, up more than in any other part of the company. Unilever's ice cream and beverages division supplied just over 20% of its $26.7 billion in first-half revenues. Analyst Ian Kellett with brokerage Numis Securities figures ice cream alone accounted for 10% of Unilever's $3 billion of first-half profits.

8   To stoke growth, both companies have relied on getting consumers to pay more for frozen treats. With their tit-for-tat acquisitions of American icons Häagen-Dazs and Ben & Jerry's—now distributed around the world—the food giants have helped lead a consumer trend away from down-market, mass-produced brands to more profitable superpremium

products. "By focusing on superpremium brands, both companies have increased the value of their products," says Euromonitor packaged food analyst Francisco Redruello.

RESPONDING TO HEALTH CONCERNS

9   Rising economies around the world should further the trend, as people have more money in their pockets to spend on goods such as up-market ice cream. "The focus on quality, indulgence brands has been integral to our growth," says Jean-Marie Gurné, head of Nestlé's ice cream strategic business unit. Gurné predicts Nestlé's worldwide ice cream sales should increase by 3% next year.

10   At the same time, both Nestlé and Unilever have been alert to growing health consciousness, particularly in Western Europe and North America. The industry has responded by rolling out lower-fat, lower-calorie products. Nestlé's $2.5 billion takeover of Dreyer's Grand Ice Cream in 2002 helped it secure the lion's share of this increasingly important market in North America. Dreyer's low-fat "Slow Churned" line, with 50% less fat and 30% fewer calories, has proved a runaway success, even forcing Unilever to roll out similar products under its Ben & Jerry's marque.

11   "Better-for-you ice creams have been a real boost," says Carl Short, an analyst with Standard & Poor's, which like *BusinessWeek* is a unit of The McGraw-Hill Companies. "Nestlé and Unilever are both focusing on this growth market in an attempt to attract new customers."

TARGETING STREET SALES IN ASIA

12   While such healthier options have helped boost sales in developed markets, the biggest growth prospects lie in Asia, where the ice cream business is set to increase by double digits over the next five years. Total revenue from the Asia Pacific region reached $11.6 billion last year, with $3.7 billion in China alone.

13   For now, market penetration remains low, although both Unilever and Nestlé are gearing up in countries such as the Philippines and Indonesia in hopes of attracting increasingly affluent consumers. Because many homes in developing countries don't have freezers, the companies are focused on selling single-serving portions through street vendors. That should help expand their markets in countries where refrigeration remains an out-of-reach luxury.

14   As of now, Nestlé and Unilever appear evenly matched, though analysts say Nestlé has shown a greater willingness to innovate in local markets than its Anglo-Dutch rival. Either way, the increasing globalization of the ice cream industry makes it hard for local makers to take on the big boys. With their massive distribution networks and rich marketing budgets, Nestlé and Unilever have an edge. And both have said they may make more acquisitions, particularly in Asia, in the future.

15   No question, the days of the local ice cream shop have passed. But as long as the European food giants provide a tasty treat to help people cool off in the summer heat, no one particularly seems to mind.

Case 7

Getting Inside Google's gPhone

1   The search giant's mobile offensive, like the iPhone, may force new cracks in the way the wireless industry operates. Some would say it is simply serving notice to the wireless industry without seriously considering having its own iPhone. Still coming to terms with Apple's iPhone invasion, the cellular industry now finds itself bracing for yet another intrusion by a mighty outsider bent on altering the way wireless does business. This time it's Google.

2   New signals and speculation about Google's mobile initiatives emerge daily, but with no clear proclamations as yet from the Web search leader. One day there's buzz that Google will follow Apple's lead by introducing its own mobile device, the gPhone. Next comes word the company has developed its own mobile operating system or Web browser. Against this uncertain backdrop, providers of wireless service, handsets, and software have been left to guess anxiously at Google's true intentions, not unlike children gathered about a campfire, scanning for monsters in the shadowy forest.

GOOGLE PLATFORM?

3   So what's really lurking behind those trees? A source familiar with the situation tells BusinessWeek.com that Google may be preparing a new mobile platform, a would-be rival to the Nokia-dominated Symbian OS, Microsoft's Windows Mobile, mobile Linux, Palm, and other operating systems.

4   The new operating system, which may be named gPhone, was developed in part with know-how Google acquired with a startup named Android in 2005. The platform is designed to enable lower-priced "smartphones" featuring more robust Web browsing and multimedia applications. Most importantly for Google, it will work hand in glove with the company's mobile search engine and other Google applications that are already popular on personal computers. And it would allow Google to bring new applications to the wireless market faster. Google declined to confirm or deny this information.

5   A number of handset makers have already created prototypes of lower-cost phones based on the Google platform, the source says. These handsets, expected to sell for about $100, are being shopped around to carriers worldwide, including those in the U.S. On top of the lower price tag, Google also hopes to attract customers with the promise of lower monthly cell bills. But in Google style, that means users will have to agree to receive ads on their mobile phones, an approach that's enjoyed some limited success in certain trials by other companies with far less clout than Google. In effect, Google will attempt to introduce not just a new platform, but also a new business model for the wireless-services industry.

YAHOO!'S MOBILE SEARCH SUCCESS

6   This project marks just one of the many ambitious mobile initiatives Google has undertaken. The search giant has indicated it would likely bid in a federal auction to use new swaths of the public airwaves for wireless services. The plan would be to either build its own cellular network or to partner with another company to do so. All the while, Google keeps beefing up its arsenal of mobile applications. On Aug. 30, the U.S. Patent Office published a patent filed by a Google inventor for a mobile payment system designed to allow people to pay for goods and services via text messages. Consider also that Google currently has 67 openings

on its Web site for mobile-related positions, mostly in wireless software development, and it becomes clear that something big is afoot.

7   It's easy to see why Google is turning so much energy toward wireless. The company generated nearly all of last year's $10.6 billion in revenue from online search advertising. But while it dominates that arena with a 62.7% market share, according to research by the consultancy Compete, the company is lagging Microsoft and Yahoo! in mobile search and other applications for the cell phone. More than 20 million devices will ship this year with either Mobile Windows or other Microsoft software on them, according to the Yankee Group. But Google—despite deals with handset makers including Motorola and LG and carriers such as Sprint Nextel—won't come anywhere near to that sort of distribution, figures John Jackson, an analyst at Yankee.

8   Yahoo! has also enjoyed more success in its wireless endeavors. Thanks to its new mobile search engine, oneSearch, Yahoo! has actually stolen some business away from Google. In January, Opera replaced Google with oneSearch as the default search engine on its browser for mobile devices. Though Opera's share of the mobile browser isn't huge, such developments could spell trouble if, as some experts expect, Web searches on mobile devices begin to exceed those on PCs. To protect its core business, then, Google needs to carve its spot in the cell market now.

A SLICE OF APPLE'S APPROACH

9   This might have been easier to accomplish had Google not forged a somewhat acrimonious relationship with big cellular carriers such as AT&T and Verizon Wireless. Even before Google revealed its plan to compete directly with them in the wireless auction, the company rankled the cellular establishment with its decision to build a Wi-Fi broadband network in Mountain View, Calif., and join EarthLink in constructing a Wi-Fi network in San Francisco (a plan that's since unraveled).

10   Now, as it charts more of an independent course, Google may even use the gPhone as Apple has the iPhone, stoking discontent with the current state of mobile Web access. Today's cellular providers, to prevent their customers from wandering the Internet freely on phones as they do on computers, herd users to their own branded mobile portals and a limited selection of approved partner sites—a model reminiscent of the "walled garden" that AOL thrived on a decade ago until customers rebelled. Thanks to such obstacles, while 15% of U.S. wireless users have browsed Web pages on their mobile phones, only 3% have used a mobile search engine, according to JupiterResearch.

11   Though its brand doesn't generate the same passions among consumers as Apple's, Google may hope its new platform will present an irresistible attraction to handset makers and carriers seeking the next "it" phone, replicating at least some of the success the iPhone has managed since its U.S. launch through AT&T.

12   Google's new, ad-supported business model may ultimately appeal to the carriers as they struggle to boost revenues in markets where the price competition is fierce and first-time users are becoming scarce. "The addition of new business models simply creates more opportunities for all companies in the industry to sell more products," says John Starkweather, general manager of mobile communications at Microsoft.

BOOST TO WIRELESS BROADBAND?

13   While analysts have long frowned on the idea of mobile ads, Virgin Mobile recently reported that 330,000 of its 4.8 million subscribers have agreed to view ads in exchange for free calling minutes. When a small carrier named Revel recently gave 5,000 subscribers a

one-time $10 discount for agreeing to receive ads on their phones for a 12-week trial, "the satisfaction levels were off the charts," says Jon Jackson, CEO of Mobile Posse, the ad technology provider in the trial. In fact, Mobile Posse's research shows that marketing on mobile phones can generate up to $40 in ad revenue per month—which isn't very far from the $50-plus that carriers generate from monthly service plans. Mobile Posse says it's now conducting trials with two other larger carriers, offering free text-messaging and mobile data access to users who'll accept ads.

14   Meanwhile, if Google succeeds in bringing a lower-priced yet more robust phone to the market, the gPhone could have some broader impact than the iPhone, which still costs $400 after a recent price cut. "Today, the overall mobile experience, candidly, is not great," says Shawn Freeman, chief technology officer at Handango, a provider of mobile content and applications. With better Web-surfing and search capabilities, such a handset could fill a void in developing markets where many people can't afford computers. Elsewhere, by increasing interest in mobile Web access, Google also might speed consumer adoption of wireless broadband. "If they produce something that's a good experience, the whole market will rise," says Barry West, chief technology officer at Sprint. "Google is a big name on the Internet. This reaffirms that the Internet is going mobile."

15   But the main goal for Google is to provide mobile phone users with devices that smoothly integrate all Google applications so that, at a push of a button, they can launch a search or use the mobile payment service. Today, carriers like AT&T and Verizon Wireless only provide access to a smattering of Google applications, such as Google Maps and YouTube video, and not on all phones.

WIRELESS PLAYERS GEARING UP

16   Yet by launching its own operating system, Google faces a disadvantage in terms of the limited number of applications that will be available for that platform. It will take time to build the sort of ecosystem that surrounds Symbian and Windows Mobile, where there are thousands of third-party applications to choose from and more being written by software developers every day. "If you have a smaller platform, it's harder to get people to develop for it," says Julie Ask, an analyst at JupiterResearch.

17   It is possible to build a mobile platform from scratch without having a ubiquitous operating system like Windows as your foundation. Symbian says it now commands a 72% share of the smartphone market. But it has taken 10 years and more than $750 million in investment to get there. "It's fairly easy for someone to trivialize creating a feature-rich operating system, but there's a lot of man-years involved," says Jerry Panagrossi, vice-president of U.S. operations at Symbian.

18   Despite such hurdles, there's no doubt that major wireless players are factoring in the potential game-changing tactics of Google and Apple as they compete with their traditional rivals. On Aug. 29, Nokia unveiled a new suite of mobile Internet services called Ovi. And at a recent investment conference, a Microsoft executive hinted that his company may be working on a phone version of its Zune music player. "Competition breeds innovation," says Rich Nespola, founder of consultancy TMNG. "If Google is planning on entering this business, everyone gets prepared."

19   It's important to remember Google's end goal, though: changing the wireless business. "They want the carriers to open up," says Handango's Freeman. "This is another way to drive the market in the direction they want to go."

Source: Reprinted with special permission from "Getting Inside Google's gPhone," *BusinessWeek*, September 9, 2007. Copyright © 2007 The McGraw-Hill Companies.

Case 8

BusinessWeek

Microsoft in Europe: The Real Stakes

1   Nothing less than the future of government regulation in the tech industry is riding on a key antitrust ruling in Europe. Microsoft's legal battle with Europe's competition regulator will reach a climax on Sept. 17, when Europe's second-highest court, the Luxembourg-based Court of First Instance, hands down a judgment that could determine the future of antitrust policy in the technology sector, as well as the commercial and legal strategy of the U.S software behemoth.

2   The immediate issue before the court is whether to uphold the European Commission's landmark 2004 antitrust decision against Microsoft or to side with Microsoft in its appeal. But the stakes are much higher than just one case. If the Luxembourg court validates the Commission's order, Microsoft could face a future in which its product design decisions and licensing policies are subject to scrutiny by governments around the world. If the court sides with Microsoft, it could signal the death knell for any serious attempt by policymakers anywhere to rein in the software giant.

3   The issue is of vital importance in Europe and beyond. Even as both sides have waited for a ruling from the appeals court, a group representing Microsoft rivals, including IBM, Oracle, and Nokia, filed yet another complaint against Microsoft with the Commission last year. They argue that with the new Vista version of Windows and Office 2007, Microsoft is trying to extend its dominance into even more areas of the market—and threatening the open nature of the Internet.

4   If the court overturns the Commission's 2004 decision, it would eviscerate Europe's antitrust effort—and likely stop movement on the new complaint. But if the justices affirm that Microsoft employed unlawful business tactics in the past, "the Commission will be empowered to prohibit their use in the future," says Thomas Vinje, a partner at the law firm Clifford Chance in Brussels who represents a coalition of tech companies behind the latest complaint. Microsoft almost certainly will press on, even if it loses: The company is expected to appeal a negative ruling to the European Court of Justice, the highest body in the bloc and final arbiter.

MOMENT OF TRUTH

5   Microsoft has been in the crosshairs of European antitrust officials since 1998. In March, 2004, the EU's Competition Directorate, under the leadership of Mario Monti, ordered the company to offer a version of Windows without a built-in, or "bundled," digital Media Player. Microsoft also had to share proprietary technical information to help rival software products communicate better with Windows desktops and servers. And the EC ordered the company to pay a $613 million fine, imposing an additional $390 million penalty in July, 2006, for Microsoft's failure to comply with the technical disclosure remedy.

6   Microsoft appealed, and now, at last, the moment of truth has arrived. Legal experts familiar with the Microsoft case—as well as with the Court of First Instance and Europe's skimpy collection of antitrust precedents—are deeply divided on the likely outcome. Some predict a split decision, with Microsoft winning on the media player (bundling) component of the case but losing on the interoperability (disclosure) part. One way or another, the Sept. 17 ruling will determine how effectively the European Commission can go forward with legal challenges to companies such as Microsoft and Intel.

7   That's critical because even while waiting for the appeal ruling, the Commission has launched an antitrust investigation against Intel. On July 27, it issued a "statement of objections" that alleges Intel broke European Union law with the aim of excluding its main rival, AMD, from the market for the widely used x86 computer chip.

SLOW-MOVING REGULATORS

8   In recent years, the European Union increasingly has taken on the role of global regulator for the tech industry, filling the vacuum left behind as the U.S. Justice Dept., under the Bush Administration, took a much less active role in pursuing antitrust cases. The EU push continues under Competition Commissioner Neelie Kroes, who replaced Monti in 2004. Analysts say the outcome of this case will determine if the Commission's Competition Directorate has the legal toolkit to enforce antitrust law in the complex and fast-changing technology business.

9   Indeed, many observers complain that regulators and courts are far too slow ever to be effective at shaping tech competition. During the years Microsoft has squared off with the EU, its market share in server operating software has grown to more than 70%, while Windows still holds a 93% share of desktop operating systems and Microsoft Office commands a 97% share of personal productivity applications.

10   That's why rivals are prodding the EC to go after Microsoft again. They argue that Vista and Office 2007 demonstrate a longstanding strategy by Microsoft to eliminate alternative platforms that threaten its market control. "Microsoft continues to protect and extend its monopolies through bundling and selective denial of interoperability information," says attorney Vinje, who represents the group of tech companies going after the software giant in the latest protest. Besides IBM, Oracle, and Nokia, the coalition, which filed its complaint as the European Committee for Interoperable Systems, or ECIS, includes Sun Microsystems, Adobe Systems, RealNetworks, and open-source software maker Red Hat.

ANTITRUST DECISION'S WEAKNESSES

11   The ECIS argues that the European Commission should take action to restore competition in the server market and preserve the open-source operating system Linux and the Internet as alternative computing platforms. If it doesn't, the risk is that much of the world will be locked into using Microsoft software for the next 10 years, says Carlo Piana, a partner at Milan law firm Tamos Piana & Partners who represents the Free Software Foundation Europe, an industry group that champions open-source software.

12   Brussels antitrust lawyers say it is possible the new complaint will go forward even if the Commission loses on several counts on Sept. 17. The EC's 2004 decision does have some potential weaknesses, say antitrust lawyers. The remedy to fix Microsoft's Media Player monopoly failed miserably, for instance: The EC forced Microsoft to sell a version of its Windows operating system without Media Player software bundled in—but only a few thousand copies of the stripped-down version were ever sold. And RealNetworks, despite the ruling, became irrelevant in the media player market.

13   Another problem is Microsoft has negotiated private settlements with five of the major rivals who supported the original European case: Time Warner, Sun Microsystems, Novell, the Computer & Communications Industry Assn., and RealNetworks. That means all the evidence submitted by companies such as RealNetworks was stripped from the record before being submitted to the Court of First Instance.

APPEAL POSSIBLE FROM EITHER SIDE

14   The court could, in fact, rule against the Commission on procedure, fact, or remedy. What is essential for the Commission is that the legal grounds for its decision are upheld. Without that, it may lack the legal precedent—and gumption—to proceed with new cases.

15   Microsoft is hoping for victory, of course, though it couches its ambitions in diplomatic language. "This isn't really a question of win or lose," says spokesman Tom Brookes. "Microsoft hopes it will get clarity on some of the big questions regarding what its responsibilities are, and hopes that will form a basis for a constructive conversation with the regulators and with the industry so we can all move forward."

16   Either side has two months and 10 days to appeal the judgment of the Court of First Instance to the European Court of Justice. If that happens, it is likely to take at least another 18 months for a final decision to be reached.

Case 9

BusinessWeek

Philips Maps Out a New Direction

1 Chief Executive Kleisterlee is refocusing the company on three primary markets, with new product lines and executive changes. Not long ago, Royal Philips Electronics was nowhere in the Chinese television market. But as liquid-crystal display technologies have taken hold, the Dutch conglomerate's flat-screen TV unit has shot up to the No. 2 spot in one of the world's fastest-growing economies. Markets change, says chief executive Gerard Kleisterlee, and so can Philips.

2 The affable but intense CEO, who took office in 2001, looks to have accomplished the impossible: turning around the once-lumbering electronics giant and putting it back on a growth track. Now, he has laid out his plan for the next step in Philips' long revival. At an Amsterdam press conference on Sept. 10, Kleisterlee unveiled a reorganization that will streamline the company into just three major units—and promises to double operating profits by 2010. Philips shares jumped 3.1% in Amsterdam trading on the news and closed up 4% in New York.

A MAKEOVER IN THE MAKING

3 Kleisterlee's makeover has indeed been impressive. When he took over, Philips had more than a half-dozen divisions that barely communicated—and often worked at cross-purposes. Its products spanned toasters, low-margin electronic components, and semiconductors. Kleisterlee launched a multiyear divestiture program, culminating with last year's successful spinout of the volatile chip unit for $10 billion to a group of private equity investors. Meanwhile, he has shelled out more than $6.6 billion during the past two years buying companies to fill out Philips' portfolio.

4 The result is a much more focused company that is now staking its future on three primary markets: health care, lighting, and consumer "lifestyle" products, such as small domestic appliances and consumer electronics. The simplification—and a high-profile marketing campaign—also has helped increase Philips' brand recognition. The company has jumped 23 notches since 2004 in the annual *BusinessWeek*/Interbrand global rankings, from No. 65 three years ago to No. 42 this year, while the value of its brand has soared 75%, to $7.7 billion, over the same period.

5 Kleisterlee also has emphasized market-driven innovation, with a particular focus on making Philips' myriad products easier to use. In *BusinessWeek*'s annual ranking of the world's most innovative companies, Philips jumped from No. 67 in 2006 to No. 38 this year. "Our focus on brand and innovation is paying off," Kleisterlee says.

BOTTOM-LINE (AND OTHER) IMPROVEMENTS

6 Yet for all his progress—including stemming a tide of red ink—the 61-year-old Kleisterlee hasn't been able to drive Philips' revenues through the €30 billion ($41.3 billion) mark, where they have stagnated for years, while also delivering the earnings growth demanded by investors. The reorganization, plus a continuation of Philips' aggressive acquisition strategy and a continued push into emerging markets, is designed to drive that growth. The CEO now says Philips will show at least 6% comparable annual sales growth for 2008–10, on average.

7   He's also looking for bottom-line improvements. Cost efficiencies from the simplified organization should save €150 million to €200 million ($207 million to $276 million). Add to that better margin management, increased profit contribution from recent acquisitions, and improvement in the product mix, and Kleisterlee figures pretax margins for the company's current businesses should exceed 10% by 2010. "This is one more big step—I'd like to think a giant step—in a long journey of transformation," he says.

8   The reorganization will create three core business sectors with a CEO in charge of each. As of Jan. 1, 2008, the existing Consumer Electronics unit will be merged with the Domestic Appliances & Personal Care unit into a new group called the Consumer Lifestyle sector. The main rationale for merging the two is to save on logistical and back-office costs, Philips says, while better meeting the demands of retailers that often sell products from both units.

9   The new group will be run by Andrea Ragnetti, an Italian marketing whiz recruited by Kleisterlee who has led the company's successful rebranding campaign over the last five years. Ragnetti is currently chief of the Domestic Appliances & Personal Care division, as well as chief marketing officer for Philips as a whole. It's not clear whether he'll retain the latter title when he takes charge of the new Consumer Lifestyle unit.

NEW DIVISIONS

10   Thanks to the introduction of new LCD TVs and related product lines, Philips should see good growth this year in consumer electronics, says investment bank Kempen & Co. That, plus the introduction of new domestic appliances such as shavers and an oral-care line, should drive 5% to 6% revenue growth for the combined unit.

11   The second major new division, called Philips Healthcare, will be formed from the merger of Philips' professionally-oriented Medical Systems unit and the former Consumer Healthcare Solutions, now redubbed Home Healthcare Solutions. The business, which should turn in 6% growth this year, will be run by Stephen Rusckowski, currently the CEO of Philips Medical Systems. Medical has been the big star for Philips in recent years, as it rides demographic trends and the increasing role of electronics in health care.

12   The third leg of the stool is Philips' huge lighting division, which produces everything from consumer bulbs to complex displays such as the hourly light show on the Eiffel Tower. Rudy Provoost, now CEO of the Consumer Electronics division, will move to the Philips Lighting sector, taking over from Theo van Deursen, who is set to retire on Apr. 1, 2008.

13   Far from the sleepy business it might appear, lighting is enmeshed in critical changes, such as the evolution from incandescent bulbs to light-emitting diodes. To attack the challenges, Philips acquired American solid-state lighting company Color Kinetics for $793.5 million last June. Overall, the lighting unit is expected to grow 6% this year.

REORGANIZATION OUTCOME?

14   Will the reorganization help Philips achieve its growth goals? Jan Willem Berghuis, a financial analyst at Kempen & Co., says he is convinced Philips can do it. The company has a debt-free balance sheet, so it could double earnings through acquisitions or share buybacks. Instead, it has said it plans to grow its operational margin from 7.5% to 10% organically by 2010. "That is quite a strong target," says Berghuis, "but they have more or less reached all their targets over the last three years, particularly in the medical field, and their track record is very good."

15   Others aren't as convinced. Paul O'Donovan, a consumer electronics analyst in the London office of technology consultancy Gartner, wonders whether Philips can meet its targets. "I can't point to something they have done recently that convinces me that they are on this path to success," O'Donovan says. He considers Philips "a very clever, very innovative company with lots of good products," but calls it slow, "not fleet of foot like a Samsung."

16   The company still has branding challenges to overcome, as well. In the U.S., some people still think Philips makes Milk of Magnesia or screwdrivers. Complicating matters, Philips products in North America are marketed under a range of names, including Norelco razors, Sonicare toothbrushes, and Magnavox audio and video systems.

17   Counting on emerging markets for growth isn't a sure bet either, says Donovan. In China, for instance, Philips' recent triumph in LCD TVs could be short-lived if Chinese makers increase their local capacity and take back the market. Kleisterlee aims to stay ahead by developing brand loyalty and aspirational products. But as he well knows, though market change is good, it's also a double-edged sword.

Source: Reprinted with special permission from "Philips Maps Out a New Direction," *BusinessWeek*, September 10, 2007. Copyright © 2007 The McGraw-Hill Companies.

Case 10

Wal-Mart's Midlife Crisis: *Declining Growth, Increasing Competition, and Not an Easy Fix in Sight*

1   John E. Fleming, Wal-Mart's newly appointed chief merchandising officer, is staring hard at a display of $14 women's T-shirts in a Supercenter a few miles from the retailer's Bentonville (Ark.) headquarters. The bright-hued stretch T's carry Wal-Mart's own George label and are of a quality and stylishness not commonly associated with America's *über*-discounter. What vexes Fleming is that numerous sizes are out of stock in about half of the 12 colors, including frozen kiwi and black soot.

2   Fleming may be America's most powerful merchant, but a timely solution is beyond him even so. Wal-Mart failed to order enough of these China-made T-shirts last year, and so they and other George-brand basics will remain in short supply in most of its 3,443 U.S. stores until 2007's second half, depriving the retailer of tens of millions of dollars a week it sorely needs. "The issue with apparel is long lead times," says the quietly intense Fleming, who spent 20 years at Target Corp. before joining Wal-Mart Stores Inc. "We will get it fixed."

3   For nearly five decades, Wal-Mart's signature "everyday low prices" and their enabler— low costs—defined not only its business model but also the distinctive personality of this proud, insular company that emerged from the Ozarks backwoods to dominate retailing. Over the past year and a half, though, Wal-Mart's growth formula has stopped working. In 2006 its U.S. division eked out a 1.9% gain in same-store sales—its worst performance ever—and this year has begun no better. By this key measure, such competitors as Target, Costco, Kroger, Safeway, Walgreen's, CVS, and Best Buy now are all growing two to five times faster than Wal-Mart.

4   Wal-Mart's botched entry into cheap-chic apparel is emblematic of the quandary it faces. Is its alarming loss of momentum the temporary result of disruptions caused by transitory errors like the T-shirt screwup and by overdue improvements such as the store remodeling program launched last year? Or is Wal-Mart doing lasting damage to its low-budget franchise by trying to compete with much hipper, nimbler rivals for the middle-income dollar? Should the retailer redouble its efforts to out-Target Target, or would it be better off going back to basics?

5   If Wal-Mart seems short of answers at the moment, it might well be because there aren't any good ones. Increasingly, it appears that America's largest corporation has steered itself into a slow-growth cul de sac from which there is no escape. "There are a lot of issues here, but what they add up to is the end of the age of Wal-Mart," contends Richard Hastings, a senior analyst for the retail rating agency Bernard Sands. "The glory days are over."

6   Simple mathematics suggest that a 45-year-old company in an industry growing no faster than the economy as a whole will struggle to sustain the speedy growth rates of its youth. In Wal-Mart's case, this difficulty is exacerbated by its great size and extreme dominance of large swaths of the U.S. retail market. Wal-Mart already controls 20% of dry grocery, 29% of nonfood grocery, 30% of health and beauty aids, and 45% of general merchandise sales, according to ACNielsen.

7   However, the expansion impulse is as deeply embedded in Wal-Mart's DNA as its allegiance to cut-rate pricing. Wal-Mart was able to boost total U.S. revenues by 7.2% last year by opening new stores at the prodigious rate of nearly one a day. According to Wal-Mart CEO H. Lee Scott Jr., the company plans to sustain this pace for at least the next five years. In fact, he is on record saying that room remains in the U.S. for Wal-Mart to add 4,000 Supercenters—the largest of its store formats by far—to the 2,000 it now operates.

8   Does Scott, 58, recognize any limits whatsoever to Wal-Mart's growth potential in the U.S., which accounted for 78% of its $345 billion in sales last year? "Actually, and I know it's going to sound naive to you, I don't," he replies. "The real issue is, are [we] going to be good enough to take advantage of the opportunities that exist?"

TOO CLOSE FOR COMFORT

9   Wall Street does not share Scott's bullishness, to put it mildly. Wal-Mart shares are trading well below their 2004 high and have dropped 30% in total since Scott was named CEO in 2000, even as the Morgan Stanley retail index has risen 180%. "The stock has been dead money for a long time," says Charles Grom, a JPMorgan Chase & Co. analyst.

10   Even money managers who own Wal-Mart's shares tend to see the retailer as a beaten-down value play, not a growth company. "I'd be surprised if true growth-oriented investors were involved at this point," says Walter T. McCormick, manager of the $1.2 billion Ever-green Fundamental Large Cap Fund, which began buying the stock a year ago. "The issue the Street has is market saturation: We may be in the seventh inning of a nine-inning game."

11   One can argue that the deceleration of Wal-Mart's organic growth is a function of the aging of its outlets, given that same-store sales rates slow as stores mature. Outlets five years or older accounted for 17% of all U.S. Supercenters in 2000 and 44% in 2006, and will top 60% in 2010, according to HSBC analyst Mark Husson. "There's an inevitability of bad middle age," he says.

12   Meanwhile, the underlying economics of expansion have turned against Wal-Mart, even as it relies increasingly on store-building to compensate for sagging same-store sales. On balance, the new Supercenters are just not pulling in enough sales to offset fully the sharply escalating costs of building them. Part of the problem is that many new stores are located so close to existing ones that Wal-Mart ends up competing with itself. All in all, the retailer's pretax return on fixed assets, which includes things such as computers and trucks as well as stores, has plunged 40% since 2000.

13   Even many analysts with a buy on Wal-Mart want it to follow the lead of McDonald's Corp. and cut way back on new-store building to concentrate instead on extracting more value from existing stores, which vary wildly in their performance. Wal-Mart disclosed a year and a half ago that same-store sales were rising 10 times, or 1,000%, faster at the 800 best-managed outlets than at the 800 worst-run ones. Equally shocking was its admission that 25% of its stores failed to meet minimum expectations of cleanliness, product availability, checkout times, and so on.

14   Scott is acutely aware of the Street's discontent. "We have to find a way to give our shareholders back the returns that they need through some mechanism," he acknowledges. In March, Wal-Mart boosted its dividend 31%. Apparently, the board also is considering spinning off Sam's Club, the warehouse club division that is a perennial also-ran to Costco.

15   Wal-Mart announced late last year that it would trim its customary 8% annual addition to U.S. square footage to 7% in 2007. At the moment, though, slamming on the brakes is out of the question. Says Scott: "If you stop the growth at Wal-Mart, you'd be silly to think that [alone] means you're going to have better stores."

16   Wal-Mart's "home office" has taken a series of steps to improve the performance of its far-flung store network. Last year it implemented a whole new supervisory structure that required many of its 27 regional administrators to move out of Bentonville and live in the districts they manage. In April, Scott removed the executive in charge of U.S. store operations and put her in charge of corporate personnel instead.

17   The number of stores falling below the threshold of minimum customer expectations has declined but remains "more than would be acceptable," says Scott, who is surprisingly

philosophical about the persistence of mediocrity. Asked why it has been so difficult to fix bad stores, he replies: "That's a very good question. It's a question I ask all the time."

18   The polite, self-deprecating Scott is no Robert L. Nardelli, whose ouster as Home Depot Inc.'s chief had as much to do with his abrasive personality as the chain's business problems. That said, Wal-Mart's stock has performed worse under Scott than Home Depot's did under Nardelli. "The Street is going to look to the back half of 2007 for evidence of improvement," says an adviser to a large, longtime Wal-Mart shareholder. "If that doesn't happen, you're going to see a tremendous amount of pressure."

19   Scott & Co. already are struggling to cope with mounting sociopolitical backlash to Wal-Mart's size and aggressive business practices. Over the past decade, dozens of lawsuits were brought by employees claiming to be overworked and underpaid, including the mother of all sex discrimination class actions. Organized labor set up two Washington-based organizations to oppose the antiunion employer at every turn. And hundreds of municipalities across the country erected legal obstacles of one kind or another.

20   Wal-Mart's initial reaction to the gathering storm of opposition was to ignore it and maintain the defiant insularity that is a legacy of its Ozarks origins. "The best thing we ever did was hide back there in the hills," Sam Walton, the company's legendary founder, declared shortly before his death in 1992.

21   In the past few years, Scott has reluctantly brought Wal-Mart out from behind its Bentonville barricades. Virtually from scratch, this famously conservative company has built a large public and government relations apparatus headed by Leslie A. Dach, a veteran Washington political operative of pronounced liberal bent. Few CEOs have embraced environmental sustainability as avidly as has Scott, who also broke with the Republican orthodoxy of his predecessors by advocating a hike in the federal minimum wage.

22   It's not just rhetoric: Wal-Mart has indeed made substantive reforms in some areas. It has struck up effective working relationships with many of the very environmental groups it once disdained. No less dramatically, the company has added three women (one is Hispanic) and two African American directors to its board and also tied all executive bonuses to diversity goals.

23   It turns out, though, that there is a dark, paranoid underside to Wal-Mart's visible campaign of outreach. What began as an attempt by Wal-Mart's Threat Research and Assessment Group to detect theft and pro-union sympathies among store workers grew into surveillance of certain outside critics, consultants, stockholders, and even Wal-Mart's board. Bruce Gabbard, a security technician fired for allegedly unauthorized wiretapping of a *New York Times* reporter, has described himself as "the guy listening to the board of directors when Lee Scott is excused from the room."

24   Wal-Mart's spreading Spygate scandal is perhaps the most damaging in a long sequence of PR disasters, including last year's conviction of former No. 2 executive Thomas M. Coughlin on fraud and tax evasion charges stemming from embezzlement of company funds. Coughlin, a Walton protégé who had been Scott's leading rival for the CEO post, is serving a sentence of 27 months of house arrest.

25   There is no way of measuring how much business Wal-Mart is losing to competitors with more benign reputations. According to a recent survey conducted by Wal-Mart itself, though, 14% of Americans living within range of one of its stores—which takes in 90% of the population—are so skeptical of the company as to qualify as "conscientious objectors."

26   But the Arkansas giant's fundamental business problem is that selling for less no longer confers the overwhelming business advantage it once did. Low prices still define the chain's appeal to its best customers, the 45 million mostly low-income Americans who shop its stores frequently and broadly. But the collective purchasing power of these "loyalists," as Wal-Mart calls them, has shriveled in recent years as hourly wages have stagnated and the cost of housing and energy have soared.

27   More affluent shoppers also walk Wal-Mart's aisles in great numbers, but they tend to buy sparingly, loading up on toothpaste, detergent, and other "consumables" priced barely above cost while shunning higher-margin items such as clothes and furniture. To the selective middle-income shopper, quality, style, service, and even store aesthetics increasingly matter as much as price alone. "Here's the big thought Wal-Mart missed: Price is not enough anymore," says Todd S. Slater, an analyst at Lazard Capital Markets.

BACKWOODS KNOWHOW

28   At first, Wal-Mart management blamed its loss of momentum mostly on rising gasoline prices—a theory undercut when same-store sales kept falling even as the cost of gas receded during the latter half of 2006. Today, Wal-Mart executives are more willing to acknowledge the X factor of intensified competition. Says Fleming: "We're now up against world-class competitors that are each taking a slice of our business."

29   Wal-Mart not only was slow to recognize this threat but also responded haphazardly once it did. The nub of the problem was that the discounter had relied for so long on selling for less that it did not know any other way to sell. Wal-Mart did not begin to build a marketing department worthy of the name until Fleming was named to the new position of chief marketing officer in spring, 2005, an appointment Scott hailed as "an extraordinary move for us."

30   Founded in 1962, Wal-Mart rose to dominance on the strength of its mastery of retailing's "back-end" mechanics. Forced by the isolation of the Ozarks to do for itself what most retailers relied on others to do for them, Wal-Mart built a cutting-edge distribution system capable of moving goods from factory loading dock to store cash register faster and cheaper by far than any competitor. It added to its cost advantage by refusing to acquiesce to routine increases in wholesale prices, continually pressing suppliers to charge less.

31   Walton, who was both a gifted merchant and a born tightwad, also pinched pennies in every other facet of business, from wages and perks (there were none) to fixtures and furnishings. Aesthetics counted for so little that when the retailer finally put down carpet in its stores it took care to choose a color that matched the sludgy gray-brown produced by mixing dirt, motor oil, and the other contaminants most commonly tracked across its floors. To Wal-Mart, the beauty of its hideous carpet was that it rarely needed cleaning.

32   Low costs begat low prices. Instead of relying on promotional gimmickry, Wal-Mart sold at a perpetual discount calculated to make up for in volume what it lost in margin. Walton's philosophy was price it low, pile it high, and watch it fly. His belief in everyday low prices made him a populist hero even as he built America's largest fortune. (His descendants still own 40% of Wal-Mart's shares, a stake worth $80 billion.) Regulators forced "Mr. Sam" to modify his slogan of "Always the lowest price" to the hedged "Always low prices!" But hundreds of retailers went broke trying to compete with Wal-Mart on price just the same.

33   In many ways, Wal-Mart has remained reflexively tight-fisted under Scott, a 28-year company veteran who trained at Walton's knee and rose to the top through trucking and logistics. Last year, Wal-Mart began remodeling the apparel, home, and electronics sections in 1,800 stores, replacing miles of that stain-colored carpeting with vinyl that looks like wood. To Fleming, the new "simulated wood" floor is all about aesthetic improvement. His boss takes the classical Wal-Mart view. "The truth is that vinyl costs less," Scott says. "And the maintenance on the vinyl costs less than the maintenance on the carpet."

34   Yet Wal-Mart is neither as low-cost nor as low-price a retailer as it was in Walton's day, or even when Scott moved up to CEO. Most dramatically, overhead costs jumped 14.8% in 2006 alone and now amount to 18.6% of sales, compared with 16.4% in Scott's first year—a momentous rise in a business that counts profit in pennies on the dollar.

35   The imperatives of reputational damage control have prompted Bentonville to add hundreds of staff jobs in public relations, corporate affairs, and other areas that the company happily ignored when it was shielded by the force field of Walton's folksy charisma. And as the nation's largest electricity consumer and owner of its second-largest private truck fleet, Wal-Mart was hit doubly hard by the explosion of energy costs.

36   Wal-Mart also has purposefully, if not entirely voluntarily, inflated its cost base in expanding far beyond its original rural Southern stronghold. It is far more expensive to buy land and to build, staff, and operate stores in the large cities that are the final frontier of Wal-Mart's expansion than in the farm towns where it began. Then, too, the company is encountering mounting resistance as it pushes deeper into the Northeast, Upper Midwest, and West Coast, requiring it to retain legions of lawyers and lobbyists to fight its way into town.

NARROWING THE GAP

37   Under Scott, Wal-Mart even blunted its seminal edge in distribution by letting billions of dollars in excess inventories accumulate at mismanaged stores. A dubious milestone was reached in 2005 as inventories rose even faster than sales. "You'd see these big storage containers behind stores, but what was more amazing was that [local] managers were going outside Wal-Mart's distribution network to subcontract their own warehouse space," says Bill Dreher, a U.S. retailing analyst for Deutsche Bank.

38   Over the past decade, top competitors in most every retailing specialty have succeeded in narrowing their cost gap with Wal-Mart by restructuring their operations. They eliminated jobs, remodeled stores, and replaced warehouses, investing heavily in new technology to tie it all together. Unionized supermarkets even managed to chip away at Wal-Mart's nonunion-labor cost advantage, signaling their resolve by taking a long strike in Southern California in 2003–04. The end result: Rival chains gradually were able to bring their prices down closer to Wal-Mart's and again make good money.

39   Consider the return to form of Kroger Co., the largest and oldest U.S. supermarket chain. Cincinnati-based Kroger competes against more Wal-Mart Supercenters—1,000 at last count—than any other grocer. Which is why until recently the only real interest Wall Street took in the old-line giant was measuring it for a coffin. Today, though, a rejuvenated Kroger is gaining share faster in the 32 markets where it competes with Wal-Mart than in the 12 where it does not.

40   A recent Bank of America survey of three such markets—Atlanta, Houston, and Nashville—found that Kroger's prices were 7.5% higher on average than Wal-Mart's, compared with 20% to 25% five years ago. This margin is thin enough to allow Kroger to again bring to bear such "core competencies" as service, quality, and convenience, says BofA's Scott A. Mushkin, who recently switched his Kroger rating to buy from sell. "We're saying the game has changed, and it looks like it has changed substantially in Kroger's favor," he says.

41   While Wal-Mart vies with a plethora of born-again rivals for the trade of middle-income Americans, it also must contend on the low end of the income spectrum with convenience and dollar-store chains and with such "hard discounters" as Germany's Aldi Group. These no-frills rivals are challenging Wal-Mart's hold over budget-minded shoppers by underpricing it on many staples.

42   To right Wal-Mart's listing U.S. flagship division, Scott installed Eduardo Castro-Wright as its president and CEO in fall, 2005. The Ecuador-born, U.S.-educated Castro-Wright, now 51, worked for RJR Nabisco and Honeywell International Inc. before joining Wal-Mart in 2001. In Castro-Wright's three years as CEO of Wal-Mart Mexico, revenues soared 50%, powered by sparkling same-store sales growth of 10% a year.

43   To date, Castro-Wright has fallen so far short of replicating the miracle of Mexico that in January he had to publicly deny rumors that he was about to be transferred back to

international. Instead, Scott shifted the vice-chairman over Castro-Wright to new duties. That the U.S. chief now reports directly to Scott both solidifies Castro-Wright's status and ups the pressure on him to show results.

44   Castro-Wright can point to progress on the cost side of the ledger. By tightening controls over the stores, headquarters has halved the growth rate of inventories to 5.6% from 11.5% two years ago. Wal-Mart also has squeezed more productivity out of its 1.3 million store employees for eight consecutive quarters. This was done by capping wages for most hourly positions, converting full-time jobs to part-time ones, and installing a sophisticated scheduling system to adjust staffing levels to fluctuations in customer traffic.

45   Wal-Mart has found other new ways to economize, notably by cutting out middlemen to do more contract manufacturing overseas. The company's much publicized green initiatives have tempered criticism from some left-leaning opponents but are perhaps best understood as a politically fashionable manifestation of its traditional cost-control imperative.

46   By any conventional measure, Wal-Mart remains a solidly profitable company. Rising overhead costs have cut into net income, which in 2006 rose a middling 6.7%, a far cry from the double-digit increases of the 1990s. Return on equity continues to top 20%, however, and U.S. operating margins actually have widened a bit under Castro-Wright, as costs have risen a bit slower than Wal-Mart's average selling price.

47   Evidently, though, it is going to take a lot more than Castro-Wright's workmanlike adjustments to revive Wal-Mart's moribund stock. In the end, Scott's aversion to a McDonald's-style strategic about-face leaves Wal-Mart no alternative but to try to grow its way back into Wall Street's good graces. But if opening a new Wal-Mart or Sam's Club almost every day can't move the dial, what will?

48   Foreign markets present an intriguing mix of potential and peril for Wal-Mart, which first ventured abroad in 1992. Although the company now owns stores in 13 countries, the lion's share of those revenues comes from Mexico, Canada, and Britain. In 2006 international revenues rose 30%, to $77 billion. At the same time, though, Wal-Mart's long-standing struggles to adapt its quintessentially American low-cost, low-price business model to foreign cultures was underscored by the $863 million loss it took in exiting Germany.

49   Wal-Mart is the rare U.S. company that is more politically constrained at home than abroad in angling for outsize growth opportunities. In March it withdrew its application for a Utah bank charter just before a congressional committee was set to convene hearings. The retreat marks an apparent end to its decade-long campaign to diversify into consumer banking.

50   Although Wal-Mart regularly makes sizable acquisitions abroad, it is in no position to respond in kind to such domestic dagger thrusts as CVS's $26.5 billion acquisition of pharmacy benefits manager Caremark Rx. "That deal is a real threat, but Wal-Mart would have huge antitrust problems if it made an acquisition of any size," says a top mergers-and-acquisitions banker. "They are kind of stuck."

51   In the end, Wal-Mart seems unlikely to regain its stride unless it can solve what might be the diciest conundrum in retailing today. That is, can it seduce tens of millions of middle-income shoppers into stepping up their purchases in a major way without alienating its low-income legions in the process?

52   Largely because of the pressing need to differentiate itself from Wal-Mart, Target began grappling with this very puzzle more than a decade ago and gradually solved it with the cheap-chic panache that transformed it into "Tar-zhay." Says the president of a leading apparel maker: "Target has an awareness of what's happening in fashion equal to a luxury player, maybe greater. They have set the bar very high."

53   Scott acknowledged as much in making former Target exec Fleming chief marketing officer, reporting to Castro-Wright. Fleming, who had been CEO of Wal-Mart.com, went outside to fill every key slot in building a 40-person marketing group from scratch. He supported Wal-Mart's move into higher-priced, more fashionable apparel and home furnishings

with the splashiest marketing the retailer had ever done, buying ad spreads in *Vogue* and sponsoring an open-air fashion show in Times Square.

54   Wal-Mart's top management all the way up to and including Scott presumed that Wal-Mart could run like Tar-zhay before it had learned to walk. "What Wal-Mart tried to do smacks of a kind of arrogant attitude toward fashion—that you can just order it, put it down, and people will buy it," says Eric Beder, a specialty retailing analyst at Brean Murray, Carret & Co.

CRASH COURSE

55   Wal-Mart did everything at once and precipitously, introducing ads even as it was flooding stores with new merchandise and before it could complete its store remodeling program. Bentonville was learning marketing on the fly and did not even attempt to adopt the sort of formal, centralized merchandise planning at which Target and many big department-store chains excel. Instead, Wal-Mart relied on dozens of individual buyers to make critical decisions as it pushed hard into unfamiliar product areas.

56   How else to explain why a retailer whose typical female customer is thought to be a size 14 loaded up on skinny-leg jeans? Or why Wal-Mart's cheap-chic Metro7 line got off to a flying start in 350 stores only to crash and burn as it was rolled out to 1,150 more? Or why Wal-Mart not only severely misread demand for George-brand basics but also is unable to replenish its stocks for months on end while "fast-fashion" chains such as H&M easily turn over entire collections every six weeks?

57   Scott loved Wal-Mart's bold new direction until he hated it, his enthusiasm diminishing in sync with same-store sales throughout much of 2006. "We are going to sell for less," Scott says now, emphasizing a return to Wal-Mart's first principles. "I believe that long after we are gone, the person who sells for less will do more business than the person who doesn't."

58   Yet Scott also signaled his continuing commitment to the pursuit of the middle-income shopper by promoting Fleming to yet another new post, chief merchandising officer, as part of a January shakeup of the senior ranks. Although Wal-Mart no doubt has sponsored its last glitzy runway show, Fleming insists that the company is sticking with its underlying strategy of "customer relevance"—that is, of moving beyond a monolithic focus on price to try to boost sales by targeting particular customers in new ways. "We're not going to back off," he vows. "We've learned certain lessons. Some things we'll build on, some things we won't."

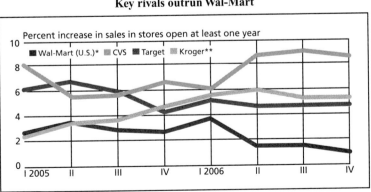

Key rivals outrun Wal-Mart

*Does not include Sam's Club
**Not including fuel sales

Source: Company reports, JPMorgan Chase & Co., Bank of America.

59   While the look of its stores is primarily a function of how much Wal-Mart chooses to spend on them, the retailer is unlikely ever to come up with an ambience conducive to separating the affluent from their money without changing its whole approach to labor. The chain's dismal scores on customer satisfaction surveys imply that it is understaffing stores to the point where many of them struggle merely to meet the demands of its self-service format.

60   It is entirely possible even so that Wal-Mart in time will figure out how to sell vast quantities of dress-for-success blazers, 400-thread-count sheets, laptop computers, and even prepackaged sushi. But as Wal-Mart closes in on $400 billion in annual revenues, it is going to have to overachieve just to get same-store sales rising again at 3% to 5% a year.

61   The odds are that Scott, or his successor, will have to choose between continuing to disappoint Wall Street or milking the U.S. operation for profits better reinvested overseas. Only by hitting the business development equivalent of the lottery in countries like China, India, or Brazil can the world's largest retailer hope to restore the robust growth that once seemed like a birthright.

Case 11

VW's Plan to Triple U.S. Sales

1   Volkswagen of America's Stefan Jacoby predicts that a new home and new models will save the struggling automaker. Newly installed Volkswagen of America Chief Executive Stefan Jacoby made quite an impression on just his sixth day on the job. He announced a shift of the company's headquarters from Michigan to Virginia and the cutting of around 400 jobs. That's the bad news for VW's workforce. The more promising news, though, is that he has an audacious plan to triple Volkswagen's North American sales in the next five to eight years.

2   Such projected growth seems as unlikely to some analysts and critics of Volkswagen as it is surprising from a company that lately has seemed much more interested in growing sales in developing markets such as Russia, China, and Brazil than slugging it out in the U.S. with models that go head-to-head with growing Asian brands such as Toyota Motor, Honda Motor, and Hyundai.

U.S. WORKERS BLAME GERMANY

3   Volkswagen sales, on track to reach about 235,000 this year, are flat from last year, but even that is misleading. Sales are actually off by more than 100,000 units a year from 2003. Sales of the Jetta are off 8.5% this year, and Passat sales are off 31%. Touareg sales are down 24%. The New Beetle is down 20%. Incentive spending on those four models by Volkswagen exceeds the average spending for each of those segments, according to Edmunds.com. That's anathema to Volkswagen, which has historically discouraged incentive spending to maintain brand integrity and resale values.

4   Volkswagen employees, who were given the news of the job cuts Sept. 6 in a town-hall meeting, have complained that the biggest problem dogging VW the last decade has been the micromanaging of the U.S. operation from Germany, which has deprived its American unit of the right mix of products it needs to compete. VW, for example, won't launch its first sport-utility vehicle priced under $30,000, the Tiguan, until next year, even though that has been the fastest-growing category since 2000. The German management did, however, force an $80,000 sedan, the Phaeton, on the U.S. that flopped. Jacoby said he did not disagree with the complaint. "We have not done a good job of creating the right product mix for America, but that is going to change, and it is already underway," he said.

5   Jacoby said VW's product plan for the U.S. calls for four core, high-volume products, each of which will generate between 135,000 and 150,000 sales per year in North America. Those products, he says, would include a midsize sedan, probably the next Jetta design, to compete against the Honda Accord and Toyota's Camry. He also says he envisions a smaller sedan/hatchback that would compete against the Toyota Corolla. And he is thinking of selling two crossover SUVs, the Tiguan and one other. He says that a small car priced below $15,000 is in the plans, and that he would even like to introduce a small city car, like Mercedes-Benz's Smart, to the U.S.

BATTLING THE EXCHANGE RATE

6   It is a surprisingly ambitious plan that will demand that VW build a new North American manufacturing facility. "We are looking at making the business case for this plan now," says Jacoby. Jacoby's master plan would result in VW hitting about 700,000 sales a year in North

America, a very tall order considering the strength of Asian automakers and the weakness of VW's brand and its reputation for poor quality.

7   Volkswagen is bedeviled by the lopsided currency exchange between the euro and the greenback, which has hovered between $1.30 and $1.40 for the last few years. Volkswagen of America has lost $2 billion in the last two years alone. "The currency exchange is like trying to run a marathon when you start 10 miles behind the starting line," he says. Jacoby says the decision to build a plant in the U.S. has not been made. But it's clear that he wants to make the case to Volkswagen's board in Germany. "You can reduce head count and slash marketing budgets, but you still can't reverse the losses unless you are building your high-volume models in the local market."

8   Volkswagen Chairman Martin Winterkorn set a goal for VW's American unit to break even by 2009. Jacoby says that unless exchange rates substantially worsen, he can achieve black ink with new products and the job cuts.

9   Jacoby, 49, worked at Volkswagen of America for one year as a management trainee in the late 1980s, and was tasked, ironically, with helping to wind down the only U.S. manufacturing plant Volkswagen ever had, in Westmoreland, Pa. There, Volkswagen built Rabbits and small pickup trucks. He was also part of the group that decided that Volkswagen products for the U.S. would be designed and developed in Europe, and that unique American design elements would take a backseat to German design leadership.

NEW MODELS TAILORED TO A U.S. MARKET

10   Twenty years later, though, Jacoby says he believes the only way VW will come back to profitability is by developing unique, high-volume models for the U.S. The next Jetta design, for example, is being designed specifically for the U.S. market. The current model, he says, was built for the U.S. and Europe, and was too dependent on being built off the Golf/Rabbit engineering platform. Critics of the design say it lacks Volkswagen's brand identity and is too close to the blandness of most Asian passenger cars. Caset Gunther, the biggest Volkswagen dealer in the U.S., based in Coconut Creek, Fla., says, "VW's have to have a lot of emotion and fun in the design or they don't sell."

11   Jacoby takes over Volkswagen's American unit following a management upheaval in Germany that saw its chairman, Bernd Pischetsrieder, ousted in favor of former Audi chief Winterkorn. VW has also seen the reassertion of Supervisory Board Chairman Ferdinand Piech's will into the long-term strategy of the company and the recent moves of Porsche to buy a controlling stake in Volkswagen. Piech's family controls the voting stock of Porsche. And German press reports say that Porsche is preparing to buy 51% of VW.

12   Jacoby, who engineered successful turnarounds of Volkswagen's Japan and German operations, as well as of Mitsubishi Motors of Europe during a stint at the Japanese carmaker, is the first Volkswagen of America chief who has reported directly to the sitting Volkswagen chairman. Jacoby says the fact the he is "wired into Volkswagen's top management, engineering, and product development staffs" gives him the best chance of anyone who has run the company to put VW on the best competitive footing against rivals such as Toyota and Honda.

13   An accountant by training, Jacoby has personally tracked marketing wherever he has worked. And he considers fixing Volkswagen's image through smarter marketing in the U.S. to be a priority. His priority is to find a chief marketing officer in the next few months. "We need to put some of the funkiness back in the brand, because that is our strength." To that end, he says he is "fighting like crazy" to get a plan approved for a new version of the New Beetle. The car went on sale in 1999 and did much to boost Volkswagen's sagging fortunes then. But a decade later, the car still hasn't been retooled. "It is a big opportunity that we have let go by," says Jacoby.

NEW DIRECTIONS IN ADVERTISING

14   Volkswagen's advertising, long part of the brand's legacy in the U.S., has been confused the last five years. Ad agency Crispin, Porter & Bogusky was handed the ad assignment in late 2005. And while the agency has created some memorable ad campaigns, such as one for the GTI featuring an engineer named Wolfgang and a dominatrix named Helga, the overall effort has wandered. The much-lauded ad agency has been seen to be on the hot seat. "I have a lot of homework to do about the advertising, but one thing I know is that an ad agency can't be expected to guide the brand if we don't know where we are going."

15   One place the new CEO knows he is going as of April, 2008, is Fairfax County, Va.—"out of the shadow of the Big Three," he says. The move to Virginia for Volkswagen, says Jacoby, is meant to spark a new beginning and a change of direction. He admits it's a "symbolic" move he feels will benefit VW's corporate culture, refit VW's organization, open it up to different talent, and move employees closer to the heart of VW's customer base in the mid-Atlantic region of the country.

16   Says Jacoby, "It's not the whole solution, but I feel strongly it is part of what we need to do to fix the company and the brand for the long term."

Case 12

BusinessWeek

Volvo Wants Rugged—and Safe

1 Struggling Volvo shifts its branding strategy to convince buyers it's more than just a Swedish "minivan." In a new ad for the Volvo V70/XC70 crossover sport-utility vehicle (psssst . . . it's really a wagon), a couple that look as though they strolled out of a backpack ad in *Outdoor Life* drive the vehicle over mountain roads and down a hill off-road to an adapted song based on the kid's tune *Wheels on the Bus*. In another TV ad, for the S80 sedan, we see a riff on a Pierce Brosnan James Bond movie action sequence.

2 If the ads, from Volvo's new ad agency Arnold Worldwide, seem disjointed and unconnected, they're not. What the Swedish carmaker is after in the new brand positioning and ad campaign is to add some ruggedness and a bit of adventure to Volvo's well-established reputation for building vehicles that are extremely safe to drive. If the new Volvo image desired by the company and the agency were manifested in a single couple and family, it would be, I think, Brad Pitt and Angelina Jolie, iPods set to Natalie Merchant, walking with their children to the set of a romantic action movie they are shooting in the Himalayas. The word "soulful" must have come up a lot in Arnold's PowerPoint presentation to Volvo.

VIEWED AS A MINIVAN BRAND

3 Volvo for years has been a problem brand for its Swedish management and American owner Ford Motor. It has an almost indelible brand image with car buyers in the U.S. and Europe as a vehicle you buy after you have kids. Whether the current vehicles are substantially safer than Hyundai, Mercedes-Benz, Chevrolet, or Ford is open to debate. But the fact remains if you ask consumers to associate a brand with trust and safety, Volvo handily wins that battle.

4 Every car company strives for clarity of brand like Volvo's. So what's the problem? For one, tougher safety regulations and the proliferation of air-bag technology in most vehicles have watered down Volvo's advantage in the minds of many when it comes to safety. And even though Volvo does not sell a minivan, in the minds of many, especially men, Volvo is a minivan brand. And for many, the minivan is a badge not of soccer-mom honor, but of sacrificial parenthood. In other words, "I really can't have it all if I have to drive a minivan, or a . . . Volvo." This is the mindset Volvo and Arnold are combating.

5 Another problem for Volvo is it is neither a mass-market nor luxury brand. It's premium. "Premium" in the car business means I have to pay more than I would for a mass brand, but not to enjoy the status of luxury. It's tough being in the middle. Volvo is also amid a launch of the C30, a sporty hatchback, to draw in single people, younger buyers, and Volvo devotees who need a second car not quite as utilitarian as the wagons or XC90 SUV.

BETWEEN PROFIT AND LOSS

6 Indeed, Volvo sales have been unremarkable. In the U.S., sales are down 9.5% this year despite the new S80's launch. Since Ford acquired the Swedish car company (Ford does not own Volvo heavy trucks) in 1999, the division has wavered between acceptable profitability and loss. Who needs that financial performance when Ford has Lincoln to perform in mediocre fashion? In fact, Ford is currently studying whether to sell Volvo to another carmaker or to a private equity firm to see if someone else can make a buck from a company based in Sweden and a culture where no one ever gets laid off no matter how business is doing, and people eat shark meat at family celebrations. The likelihood is Volvo will be sold.

7   Despite rhetoric from Ford the past several years about engineering synergies between Ford, Lincoln, and Volvo (vehicles such as the current Ford Taurus, Taurus X, and forth-coming Flex crossover are built off the old S80 engineering platform), the truth is Volvo's engineering culture and apparatus is incredibly difficult to integrate with Ford's, and using Volvo engineering platforms at Ford has saved the company very little.

8   The new TV ads, then, come at a time when other carmakers and financiers are literally kicking the tires on the whole company. The TV ad set to *Wheels on the Bus* is a good example of how Arnold is out to strike the balance between safety, adventure, ruggedness, and kids. It's also a terrific case study in how to incorporate actual product benefits into an ad that is entertaining to watch. The couple picks up a fellow hiker and pushes the button for the power liftgate. The song lyric becomes "The power tailgate goes up and down, up and down, up and down . . ." They drive gently down a steep hill under total control with no wheel skid, and the lyric shifts to "The hill descent control goes nice and slow, nice and slow, nice and slow . . ."

NOT FOR A FOOTBALL AUDIENCE

9   None of the men in these ads look as if they are apt to be watching *Monday Night Football* with their pals over a six-pack of Molson. They all seem too pretty attentive to their wives for that. And I suppose that's the way it's meant to be in a Volvo ad. These ads are aimed at making Volvos seem very un-minivan-like to both men and women, but they are especially designed, it seems, for men to feel like they might be more attractive to their wives if they were the kind of men who could be happy in a Volvo with them out on a picnic or a rugged trek to the top of a mountain instead of driving a Lamborghini to watch the game on Monday night.

10   Whether the new positioning takes hold and increases sales and consideration will take at least two years to determine, though I doubt Volvo's owners—Ford or a new company—will wait that long to try and find out. One thing is for sure. The depth of Volvo's brand image is incredibly valuable. The company just has to get the attention of more people who like what it stands for.

Case 13

BusinessWeek

Getty Images' Future?

1   Getty Images revolutionized the stock image business. Now the industry is shifting again, is the giant's future in jeopardy?

2   Say you work at Design Army, in Washington, D.C., and you need a photo. If you asked your co-workers for help, they'd probably trill, "Just Getty it." "Same as when some people say, 'Just Google it,'" explains Pum Lefebure, the design firm's co-owner. "We use the photos, but we also browse Getty for inspiration." When Design Army needed photos of bamboo shoots for a Ringling Bros. installation, Getty had more high-quality images than anywhere else. If the firm is hunting for images that inspire the tone for a piece of branding, Getty has the richest cache of pictures, all a single keyword away on one of the industry's most comprehensive, user-friendly websites. When it comes to visuals, Getty is Wal-Mart and the New York Public Library rolled into one.

3   Lefebure's remark sums up the trend among many design firms like hers. Over the past few years, Getty has gobbled up so many smaller stock houses that it now owns 40 percent of the market, large enough to have become the subject of the kind of regulatory, pre-merger antitrust investigations usually associated with banks and airlines. In recent months, the U.S. Department of Justice finished its review of Getty's proposed buyout of MediaVast, which owns the party-picture agency WireImage. Stock has become big business in a remarkably short time. But that status seems precarious—and Getty and its photographers are straining to adapt.

4   Getty was founded in 1993 by two investment bankers: Jonathan Klein and Mark Getty, an heir to the Getty oil fortune. At that time, the stock photo market overflowed with small agencies—a classic opportunity for an industry "roll up," in business school parlance. Getty Images was formed to buy up those mom-and-pop companies and digitize all their collections.

5   It's a story that has unfolded again and again in other fields: Some emerging player, on the wings of a new technology or business practice, becomes dominant by scooping up small enterprises. Size pays: Photographers who might once have gained better fees in a more competitive marketplace now find themselves with limited leverage against a monolithic negotiating partner.

6   It's no wonder that photographers and stock buyers gripe that Getty grabs profits where it can, leaving everyone else a skinny slice. A number of art directors and stock buyers contacted for this article—many of whom asked to remain anonymous—pointed out that Getty has much more rigid pricing than its predecessors. Says a former Getty agent who now works at a smaller photo agency, "[Getty is] very strict with licenses. I left because my relationships with clients became just processing orders." Carol, an art buyer for an established New York firm, bears witness to that shift: "Agents used to take into account the little details about how you were using an image, but not Getty."

7   Photographers have felt Getty's influence in the way they work and in how much money they take home. "There are a lot of strong-arm tactics involved in getting lower fees from photographers," says Lucy, a photo producer who works alongside her husband, a veteran stock photographer. Partly as a result of Getty's increased bargaining power, the money photographers make from rights-managed photographs—which give a buyer exclusive image rights—has dwindled. "The industry standard cut for photographers used to be 50 percent," Lucy adds. "It's now 20 to 40 percent. People sign with market leaders like Getty to make it up in volume." For rights-managed images, the average commission at Getty is now closer to 33 percent, according to the company's latest annual report.

8   Not surprisingly, Getty resists being characterized as an industry heavy that slashes fees at will. "There is a misconception that Getty Images controls the stock industry," says Andrew Saunders, Getty's vice president of imagery. "We are the market leader, but there are far bigger forces at play. With digital photography, it's now possible for many more photographers to get involved in selling stock images, making the industry far more competitive."

9   Stock was once a reliable sideline for many photographers subsidizing their commissioned work, but Getty's cutthroat marketplace doesn't favor part-timers. "Getty has been getting much more selective, focusing on the most productive relationships that provide the greatest return," says Betsy Reid, executive director of Stock Artists Alliance, a nonprofit group that represents stock photographers. And yet even for committed shooters, the company's mammoth database makes for daunting competition. "There are so many pictures that your work becomes a needle in a haystack," says one longtime photographer for Getty's 2005 acquisition, Photonica. Jim Pickerell, publisher of the trade magazine *Selling Stock*, adds, "The collections will likely grow larger and larger, so the odds of any images being licensed have become less and less."

10   That process is self-perpetuating: Fresh photos that appear in the first pages of search results on Getty's site become all-important, and photographers must shoot new images to stay visible. Though many buyers and photographers (even among those not enamored of the company) note that Getty's keyword system is useful and fast—the site is searchable both by content and by conceptual themes tagged by editors—the flood of images has meant that the useful life of stock images has declined drastically. Pickerell gives the example of a stock photographer he knows who made more than $200,000 in 2005 through Getty. In 2006, says Pickerell, "He added 400 new pictures, at great cost, and almost doubled his collection. But his income stayed the same."

11   As it becomes harder for photographers to make a living, the industry's vitality may be sapped. "We see seasoned photographers leaving stock because of reduced opportunity, but also because of reduced enthusiasm. They're unlikely to be replaced by a new generation of pros, nor will their level of imagery be replicated by amateurs," says Reid. "Those photographers who stay had better be delivering high-value imagery." David Walker, who has covered Getty extensively for *Photo District News*, concurs: "Getty's about volume and efficiency. That naturally drives their collection toward images that are going to sell the best."

12   It's debatable whether this state of affairs necessarily leads to blandness in photos' style and subject matter, though it's a belief a few hold dear. "There was a time in the '80s and '90s when there were lots of young, new stock agencies interested in unconventional stock," notes Stephen Frailey, chair of the photography department at New York's School of Visual Arts. "Some people think those have been consolidated and diluted." Among those critics is Joe Marianek, a New York-based graphic designer whose former job at a large design firm often entailed visits to the Getty website. "With Getty I'd tend to find a certain tone of voice," he says. "There's a *Pleasantville* aspect. If you look for a young group, it'll be biracial, and they'll be kind of doing something together and laughing about it and they'll all be beautiful. You can almost see the big-idea tagline. Getty caters to an American East Coast design culture that's attempting to describe the world for a lot of national corporations." Getty's Andrew Saunders thinks that logic is a bit too simple. "I think it's fair to say we've worked hard to avoid homogenization," he says. "Perhaps demand for pre-shot imagery has at times outpaced the producers' ability to innovate. Trying to persuade photographers to evolve when they've had financial success is difficult. It's our biggest challenge. Getty Images has always championed—and, I would argue, enhanced—the creative direction of the agencies and collections it has acquired."

13   Photographers and art buyers who don't agree are finding increasingly varied ways to avoid working with Getty. Says Reid, "A lot of photographers have gone back to marketing themselves directly, discovering other ways to put their images onto the market." One such option is Digital Railroad, a website founded four years ago that allows agencies and photographers to self-publish work. It returns 80 percent of sales to the photographer. "We're not an agency, we're a marketplace. We let anyone publish, and the best get voted to the top," says Evan Nisselson, the company's founder. "The holy grail is a community that'll replace the need for gatekeepers. They [are the ones who] keep the best images from being seen by buyers."

14   The creation of alternative photography venues coincides with a transition in the types of projects art directors are working on. Web projects can support stock that would never be viable for print: low-res, relatively small, and sometimes free, non-copyrighted images often suffice. And since users of those sites, and of cell phones and other portable small screens, are already accustomed to such pictures, an upswing in demand for more polished (and more expensive) photos seems unlikely. "Getty was founded to sell images for print, but buyers are using images in different ways, figuring out new sources, and expecting to pay less," says *PDN*'s Walker. As video takes over the web, buyers may even start turning away from still images altogether.

15   While Getty appears to be unshakable, its future may well be at the mercy of such changes in the business. Perhaps the most significant threat the company faces is the rise of so-called microstock agencies, like BigStockPhoto and Shutterstock, which accept images from nearly anyone and sell them for as little as $1. As one industry veteran puts it, "Just like if you put 100 monkeys in a room with a hundred typewriters and one would eventually type Shakespeare, some of these photos are decent based on sheer volume." Getty reacted by buying iStockphoto, an industry pioneer, in 2006; Corbis, Getty's much smaller rival, announced last June that it would create its own microstock site. Those are flank-protecting moves. "If someone's going to cannibalize your business, better it be one of your other businesses," said Getty's Jonathan Klein last year. It's still a potentially dire situation for both agencies. Even Design Army's Pum Lefebure notes that she prefers the steep discounts offered by iStockphoto and others: "If we want an image of sky or grass, I'd rather spend $10 than $350."

16   That said, Getty's understanding of its foes and its own shortcomings puts it in a formidable position—one that it is defending through expansion into new territory. In June, Getty bought Pump Audio, which licenses independent music for commercial clients. After the move, Klein sounded a familiar note: "Today there is wide agreement in the music industry that the market for commercial music licensing is fragmented, inefficient and confusing, just as the imagery market once was." Klein sounds ready to Getty it.

SAP's Very Big Small Biz Challenge

1   The German business-software giant wants to extend its global reach and reach out to small and medium-sized companies with new products. It's amazing second in command is amazingly candid about the challenge such a focus presents a large global company.

2   The man is a true linguistic marvel. Léo Apotheker switches effortlessly between German and French, converses in Hebrew and gives presentations in fluent English.

3   But now this cosmopolitan executive faces a true trial by fire. "I have to learn the language of small to medium-sized businesses," he says. This is no easy task for someone running a global company.

4   Léo Apotheker has been the second-in-command at software giant SAP since March, and he is widely touted as being destined for the top spot at SAP when the contract of its current CEO, Henning Kagermann, expires in 2009.

5   Apotheker, 53, spent 19 years in his Paris office helping to make a global player out of the company, based in the southwestern German town of Walldorf. His efforts have clearly paid off: Today SAP is the global market leader in the business software industry, employing almost 42,000 people in 50 countries.

6   A born salesman, Apotheker has been a member of the SAP board of directors since 2002. He is intimately familiar with most of the world's major corporations, including companies like Volkswagen, Aventis Pharma, Siemens and Deutsche Bank.

7   But now Apotheker will have to learn to think on a small scale, putting himself in the shoes of German ball bearing manufacturers, Indian textile producers and French purveyors of luxury foods. "We must develop solutions for the problems that keep owners of small and medium-sized businesses awake at night," he says.

8   It's an enormous task, and for SAP it means nothing less than completely reinventing itself: its technology, it distribution channels, its marketing and its consulting. Hardly any aspect of SAP's business with major companies is relevant to smaller businesses with 50 or so employees.

9   These sorts of companies don't need fine-tuned, customized products, but a reliable, easy-to-use and inexpensive program. SAP has already developed a uniform and robust platform for these new customers. Starting with this platform, the customer can develop special programs specific to his industry. "This is essentially a major step toward the industrialization of software," says Apotheker.

10   The new product is so different, so foreign, that although it was developed within SAP, a separate subsidiary was set up specifically for it. This approach is meant to prevent a potential dilution of SAP's traditional values. "We are still practically religious when it comes to quality and reliability," says Apotheker.

11   The new software for mid-sized companies, which is currently known by its working name, A1S, and which SAP will unveil in New York on Sept. 19, undoubtedly marks the most radical shift in the company's 35-year history. Unlike SAP's corporate software packages, which are sold under license and modified by SAP consultants, a process that sometimes takes years, the new product will be available for download by mid-sized companies in early 2008. The company is pursuing an "on-demand" model in which the product is leased instead of purchased and where software can be updated, modified and maintained online. "It has to be as easy as downloading music from Apple's iTunes," says Apotheker. "I want to create a cool platform for companies."

12   Cool? SAP? Until now the Walldorf-based software company was notorious for its complicated products, which caused endless headaches for company's IT departments. And now SAP wants to become another Apple?

13   "We are undergoing an image evolution," says Apotheker. The company needs to take a different, more mass-market approach to its communication strategy if it wants to appeal to smaller businesses. This is where the marketing experts come in. SAP is running TV advertising for the first time, a series of self-mocking spots in which small business owners express their surprise at the fact that they can now simply buy SAP software.

14   Coming up with a name for the new baby, which will be announced in New York, was a long and complicated process. SAP's marketing strategists spent three months racking their brains, testing and trying out possible names. Some of the names they came up with—and discarded—like R/3, simply aren't sexy enough for the mass market.

15   "Sexy software?" Henning Kagermann asks, clearly irritated, as he sits in the lobby of the Hyatt New Delhi, where he is staying on a short trip to India. The 60-year-old, who has been sole chairman of SAP's executive board and CEO since 2003, is by profession a physicist. Kagermann is also a problem-solver and strategist and is writing a book about corporate transformation in his free time. He is clearly not a marketing man. "We don't talk big. It would only hurt our image," says Kagermann. "You would expect that from some competitors, but not from us," he adds, in a cutting reference to his archrival Larry Ellison, the big-mouthed CEO of California-based Oracle.

16   Ellison has always been a thorn in SAP's side, constantly announcing his intention to overtake SAP in the business world—and its founder, Hasso Plattner, in the sport of sailing. But he continues to fall short of the mark, at least when it comes to business. With its 25-percent market share, SAP remains the market leader in the corporate software sector, even after Oracle spent roughly $20 billion to acquire 30 competitors in 2004. "Ellison has to buy his customers," says Kagermann, "but we grow organically. We are the market leader because we innovate from within. That's something you can't just buy."

17   Indeed, it's not necessary to buy expertise—sometimes theft is also an option. Ellison recently caught SAP trying to steal Oracle software in the United States. In November, an SAP subsidiary downloaded far more software than would be considered normal from an Oracle customer Web site.

18   Ellison claims SAP stole from Oracle and is suing the German company for damages. With great reluctance, Kagermann was forced to admit that the accusations were true. The two rivals were due to meet in court in San Francisco this week—a deeply humiliating situation for down-to-earth SAP—but the hearing has now been postponed to Sept. 25.

19   What irks Kagermann even more is the fact that Wall Street has reacted much more positively to Ellison's shopping spree than to SAP's strategy of sustainable growth. But he doesn't let this stand in his way. "Sometimes you also have to take risks, even when the market would rather wait," he says.

20   But this approach is also risky. A share price that is too low attracts takeover candidates. Investors, concerned that SAP's stock has been hovering near the bottom of the DAX for so long, initially reacted cautiously to the company's enormous €400 million investment in A1S.

21   Kagermann went on the offensive in mid-2007 when he presented an ambitious growth plan, which envisages increasing the number of SAP customers from 40,000 to 100,000 by 2010. The effects of the program are already evident. In the last quarter, SAP surprised the markets with a 10-percent rise in sales. The markets responded by pushing the company's share price up to over €42.

22   Investors now appear to have found confidence in SAP's change in strategy, having forgotten Plattner's now-discredited conviction that companies would never download their software from the Internet. They have also forgotten the period when SAP took their eye off the ball and completely missed out on the Internet's opportunities.

23   In retrospect, some experts even believe that being a latecomer to the Internet has ultimately helped the company. While many other companies plunged headlong into the Internet—and into financial ruin due to the whole e-business hype—SAP was able to calmly study the Web's real opportunities after the bubble burst, without inflicting significant damage on itself. SAP essentially prepared its entry into the Internet on the ashes of the New Economy.

24   Kagermann decided to embark on the A1S program in 2003. His strategy was clear: Business was likely to stagnate in the big customer sector for the foreseeable future. For SAP to continue achieving double-digit growth figures, it would have to acquire new customers: small and mid-sized businesses. In this market, only one third of companies had already purchased SAP's "old" software packages, Business One and All-in-One. Kagermann hopes that the new technology will enable the company "to gain a large share of this new market segment."

25   His decision also spelled radical transformation for the entire corporation. "The old SAP no longer exists," says Léo Apotheker.

A PAINFUL METAMORPHOSIS

26   For decades, SAP was controlled from its Walldorf headquarters, where the R&D work was done and where all major decisions were made. Looking to California's Silicon Valley, management hit upon the idea that its programming could be done much more cheaply in India. SAP was still running all of its operations from its headquarters in a small southern German village next to asparagus fields. But when the company decided to move into the global village, everything changed rapidly. "In the past, Walldorf was the sun, and everything revolved around it. Today we have a global network," Apotheker explains.

27   Since then SAP's decision centers have migrated to where the greatest competency can be found. Its creative drive comes from Palo Alto, Israel supplies ideas and complex programming problems are solved in Walldorf. The Indians are at the forefront in industrial design, with China following close behind.

28   Most of SAP's employees still work in Walldorf, where about 11,000 software developers are crowded into a space that has always been too small. The Silicon Valley facility has 7,000 employees, while another 4,200 work in SAP's Indian plant in Bangalore.

29   SAP's metamorphosis into a global company has not been entirely painless. Employees at the Walldorf headquarters suffer from a loss of status and are concerned about low-wage competition from Asia. They have even formed a works council, despite considerable opposition within the company. Kagermann has trouble understanding their fears. "I always tell them: You are among the best, and as long as you make this clear, it's really a no-brainer."

30   But are German software developers still the cream of the crop? Kagermann admits they are no longer automatically always the best. Sixty percent of the world's population lives in Asia, so that sheer numbers alone make the potential talent pool that much bigger.

31   Two weeks ago, SAP's entire senior management traveled to Bangalore to formally open the company's new campus. In a ceremony accompanied by Indian music, Kagermann lit a number of candles at an altar of flowers, and then an architect wearing a turban gave the SAP executives a tour through the new facility's spacious buildings and offices. Bubbling fountains surround the open-air cafeteria, and gardens line the paths between the glass-enclosed buildings.

32   The campus is designed to provide a pleasant working environment in India's high-tech metropolis, where the demand for competent personnel is as high as the turnover. SAP manages to retain its employees here for three years on average. Salaries here are seeing double digit growth; as they rise, so do expectations. Companies hoping to attract the top echelon of Bangalore's talent must offer more than just good salaries and perks such as transportation in air-conditioned buses and health insurance plans that even include benefits for employees' parents: Indian's highly qualified professionals now also want to have a say in the company.

33   This shift in attitudes meant that German developers have now been reporting to their Indian colleagues for the first time, because the Indians had been placed in charge of developing the A1S user interface. With this new level of autonomy, SAP's overseas operations have even become career stepping stones, so much so that employees from the company's Walldorf headquarters are now applying in droves for positions in Bangalore, Israel and China. The competition is enormous, partly because SAP provides support to university computer science programs in an effort to recruit future employees early on. SAP donates free software to 15 universities in India alone, and to more than 700 worldwide.

34   And the company needs its international personnel—after all, SAP earns 80 percent of its revenues abroad. "The customer, wherever he may be, demands qualified local support," says Kagermann. "We have to be a global company, but one with strong local competence."

35   People from more than 100 countries work together under one roof at SAP—but not entirely without friction. Stabs at multiculturalism such as offering "Chinese food week" in the cafeteria and playing Mexican salsa music on the company's phone answering system are no longer enough. SAP now offers diversity management courses to integrate the various cultures. There is even a Web site where employees can test their cultural awareness.

36   The case of Shai Agassi, the former chief developer in Palo Alto, shows just how difficult navigating among the many cultures is. Agassi, an Israeli, was Hasso Plattner's favorite. As president of SAP's Product and Technology Group, he guided the company into the Internet and was slated to become Kagermann's successor. But the man, who speaks very little German, was unpopular among the employees in Walldorf. They found his behavior, which included an appearance in a Superman costume, perplexing and were opposed to his willingness to take risks. The employees derisively dubbed Agassi's Walldorf residence "Shai's house." When the CEO-to-be announced his intention to run SAP from California, his popularity ratings plunged permanently.

37   The supervisory board extended Kagermann's contract until 2009. The plan was to allow Agassi and old-timer Apotheker to run the company after that. But this dream came to an end on March 28, when Agassi resigned. What happened? One rumor circulating at company headquarters is that he was tired of waiting for the top job—but at the age of 39? Another persistent rumor is that he was forced out.

38   Will a foreigner ever run SAP? Kagermann says that he could certainly see this happening, because nationality is less and less important in a global company.

39   But roots remain important. Even if the programming is done in China, SAP ultimately relies on its reputation for high-quality German engineering. German conscientiousness is undoubtedly one of the company's recipes for success.

40   The Walldorf employees were greatly relieved to learn about Apotheker's promotion. They feel that Apotheker, a native of the western German city of Aachen, is one of them, despite the fact that he grew up in Antwerp, studied economics in Jerusalem, has lived in Paris for the last 20 years and worked in the United States.

41   Apotheker's nickname among employees is the "grand old gentleman," because of his goatee, his baroque appearance, and his love of good food, red wine, the theater and chess.

42   Apotheker has also sufficiently demonstrated that he is a doer. He successfully ran SAP France, the European division, and in 2002 he restructured the US division, sending Oracle CEO Ellison into a state of agitation. This alone is enough for most SAP employees to forgive him for being the first sales executive—someone who can't even write code, a real faux pas in this techie company—to rise to the top. Another sign of change is the fact that salesmen are playing an increasingly important role in the new mass-market business.

43   But Apotheker did manage to endear himself to the Walldorf staff by taking an apartment in Heidelberg, not far from SAP headquarters, despite the fact that his family lives in Paris and that he is on the road 170 days a year.

44   The power he now enjoys as the number two man at the world's third-largest software company hasn't gone to his head. But he is acutely aware of the responsibility that comes from being in such a senior position in a company that Apotheker believes facilitates, in one way or another, more than half the world's trade. " I certainly don't want to be the one who wakes up one day and says: Now I've ruined the world."

Case 15

Mittal & Son

1   Deep inside the Beaux Arts Palace in Luxembourg that serves as headquarters of steel giant Arcelor Mittal, a half-dozen men in their forties and fifties listen intently as plant managers from around the world file in to make presentations. This is no bunch of lightweights: Almost everyone at the table has decades of experience in the steel industry. The lone exception is 31-year-old Aditya Mittal, the baby-faced chief financial officer and son of the founder and chief executive, Lakshmi N. Mittal. But in this room full of veterans, he's the one who's really calling the shots. When Louis Schorsch, who heads the company's operations in the Americas, brings up the delicate topic of personnel problems at one important plant, it's Aditya Mittal who responds. "Feel free," Mittal says impassively, "to change the management."

2   Tough words, chilly delivery. This kid doesn't fool around. Aditya's father isn't at the meeting, yet everyone knows the trim, serious son has Lakshmi Mittal's full backing. That's nothing new. Despite Aditya's tender years, he has worked with his father for a decade and is his closest confidant. The pair is today the most powerful father-son duo on the global business stage. Together, the Mittals have come to dominate one of the oldest, most elemental businesses on earth. In the process, they've helped revive a flagging industry—and created staggering wealth. The Mittals' 45% stake in Arcelor Mittal is worth $33 billion, ranking them among the world's richest families.

3   You may well know Lakshmi Mittal. His company is responsible for 10% of world steel output. He lives in a 12-bedroom London mansion with butlers on call and a Picasso on the wall. And he famously dropped $55 million on his daughter's wedding, which included a party at Versailles. Few outside the steel industry, though, know much about Aditya and the outsize role he plays in his father's success. Where the 56-year-old Lakshmi is the steel industry visionary, Aditya is the financial dealmaker. The smooth, Wharton-educated son pushed for the $38 billion takeover of Arcelor, the giant European steel company, then helped hammer out every aspect of the deal that closed last June.

A RARE CASE

4   At the heart of their success is the Mittals' powerful bond. In many a family dynasty, sons and daughters are either desperately trying to win their father's approval or deviously plotting to overthrow the old man. But the Mittal team seems to be a rare case of inter-generational respect and shared power. Lakshmi has given his son the running room he needs to build and shape the company. Aditya, in turn, is smart enough and confident enough to learn from his dad at every turn. "A father and son in business is usually a pretty tricky, complex relationship," says Mittal board member Wilbur Ross, who sold his American company, International Steel Group, to the Mittals in 2004 and who has $250 million invested in Arcelor Mittal. "But in this case, it seems to work just fine."

5   One reason it does may be that the Mittals are in many ways very different. The son of a traveling salesman, Lakshmi lived in a poor and remote Indian village without running water until the age of five. His father later started a small steel mill, giving young Lakshmi a taste for the business. Lakshmi, in turn, went on to found his own steel company, developing the instincts of a from-the-gut manager. Aditya grew up as the cherished only son of a rising entrepreneur, then was dispatched by his father to the U.S. to acquire the financial skills that can only be had in the West.

6   Rough-hewn father, polished son: The two are part of a larger theme in India Inc., even though the Mittals now operate from London. One Indian family after another—the Ambanis of Reliance, the Premjis of Wipro—has strengthened itself by dispatching its children to Britain and the U.S. for schooling. Lakshmi is comfortable chatting up line workers and still knows how to operate the electric arc furnaces used to turn scrap into molten metal. Aditya feels more at home with a Wall Street crowd, enjoys scuba diving and skiing, and has become a master dealmaker.

7   They're also free of many of the social and cultural constraints that so often hamstring business in both Europe and India. The Mittals are Marwaris, a group from the Indian state of Rajasthan known for producing shrewd merchants. But Lakshmi built his business first from Indonesia and then from London and is seen as something of an outsider in his homeland. As a result, he has become a kind of world citizen without roots.

8   Both father and son can be equal parts cunning, tenacious, and tough—if not downright ruthless—pushing aside anyone in their way. They are legendary for their long meetings, fueled by little more than green tea and sandwiches. The Mittals have cajoled, sweet-talked, or outwitted legions of steel executives from every corner of the planet. When they decide they want something, they don't give up. "You can't say no to that man," one steel executive says of Lakshmi. The Mittals, for instance, negotiated through three years of shifting political winds before winning a steel plant in Romania.

9   The question is whether the son is pushing the father too far. There's no doubt that Lakshmi Mittal embraces risk: He built his empire by taking over fading steel mills that no one else wanted. But with Aditya in charge of mergers and acquisitions, the Mittals have shifted their business away from snapping up rust-bucket plants on the cheap. Instead, they're now paying top dollar for some of the best mills in the industry. The Arcelor deal meant loading up the company with debt, now totaling about $20 billion. Any slump in demand combined with a surge of steel exports from China could make it hard to pay that off.

10   The Mittals argue that they have made their business more stable by increasing its geographical breadth. Despite a recent slump in U.S. prices, Arcelor Mittal is throwing off cash by the ton. It reported operating income of $11.8 billion on sales of $88.5 billion last year. And investors don't seem too worried about the debt load: The stock has surged from the low 30s to 54 since the two companies began working together in August.

11   Over the decades, the Mittal strategy has been nothing if not consistent. The story starts back in 1978, when Mittal opened his first mill in Surabaya, Indonesia. Although demand was slack in the U.S. and Europe, the industry was booming in Asia. Lakshmi came to believe that steel companies could churn out heavyweight profits if they grew big enough to negotiate on an equal footing with suppliers of iron ore and coal and with customers such as automakers. That has been Mittal's organizing principle straight through to the Arcelor deal. Now the Mittals have the power to ramp up or slow down production depending on local demand. In the long run Lakshmi's vision is an industry dominated by a handful of powerful companies, strong enough to cut output rather than prices in a downturn.

12   Aditya's dealmaking is helping turn his father's vision into reality as the pair play a key role in rehabilitating the steel business, not long ago the troubled stepchild of global industry. Hungry predators are now paying enormous prices for once-scorned companies such as Britain's Corus Group, which India's Tata Steel bought for $12 billion on Apr. 2. "The Mittals have made steel a more stable business that is accessible to investors," says Dalton G. Dwyer, managing director of Industry Corporate Finance Ltd., which specializes in industrial M&A.

13   While his father zips around the globe in his Gulfstream G550, dining with presidents and potentates, Aditya bears down on the nitty-gritty details. He's in charge of forging one company from the lean-and-mean Mittal Steel Co. and Arcelor, an amalgamation of three

Men of Steel: The Mittals have created an empire, one step at a time

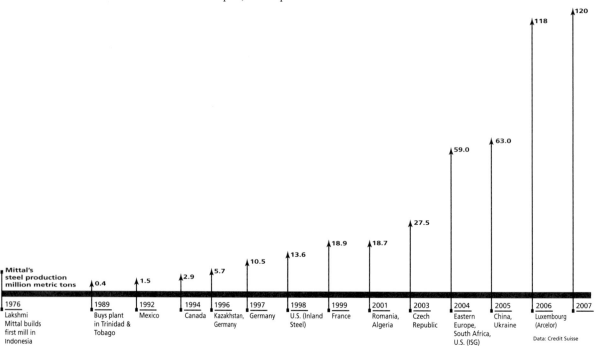

Mittal's steel production million metric tons

Year	Value	Event
1976	0.4	Lakshmi Mittal builds first mill in Indonesia
1989	1.5	Buys plant in Trinidad & Tobago
1992	2.9	Mexico
1994	5.7	Canada
1996	10.5	Kazakhstan, Germany
1997	13.6	Germany
1998	18.9	U.S. (Inland Steel)
1999	18.7	France
2001	27.5	Romania, Algeria
2003	59.0	Czech Republic
2004	63.0	Eastern Europe, South Africa, U.S. (ISG)
2005	118	China, Ukraine
2006	120	Luxembourg (Arcelor)

Data: Credit Suisse

long-coddled European enterprises. His No. 1 job is squeezing a promised $5.3 billion in savings and revenue gains from the new company by 2008. Since August he has also been the board member overseeing most operations in the Americas: four plants in the U.S., as well as mills in Canada, Mexico, Chile, Argentina, and Brazil.

14   Although he's young—and looks even younger—Aditya is no newcomer to steel. He has been on the job since he was 21 and, in fact, got his start much earlier. Aditya was born in Kolkata in 1976 but while still an infant he moved with his family to Indonesia, where he attended the 110-student Surabaya International School. "It was a very simple life," he says. With little other amusement available, as a teenager he often tagged along on his father's troubleshooting missions at the plant, where he loved to watch the furnace swallow scrap metal with a roar like rolling thunder. "I used to spend Saturday nights at the melt shop," a cavernous space with giant ladles full of molten steel, he recalls.

15   The Mittals now have a rule, not always obeyed, of not talking about work at home. Yet when Aditya was growing up it was all business, all the time, allowing the son to soak up both his father's love of the industry and his acute sense of strategy and timing. "He would tell me about his travels, what companies he had bought," Aditya remembers. "I would go to his office, hang around, and talk to the people there."

16   As a result, Aditya has steel in his blood. Just about anyone in their empire can recount tales of visits from the Mittals, who often remember individual workers from tours even years earlier. They ask pointed questions about operations and inquire whether requested improvements were made. "They are in love with steel just like we are," says Gonzalo Urquijo, Arcelor's former CFO and now a member of the combined company's board. But they're also demanding. U.S. employees recall meeting a 90-day deadline for relining a blast furnace, despite losing more than two weeks to a mechanical problem. Lakshmi's reaction? "So next time you can do it in 72 days."

NUMBERS MAN

17   When Aditya set off for Wharton in 1993, he had no intention of immediately joining the family business, hoping instead to work in finance. There, he met his future bride, Megha, who for months refused to give Aditya the time of day. Yet again, his tenacity worked to his advantage. "I made sure I had a lot of opportunity to spend time with her," Aditya says. "Eventually all my hard work and persistence paid off." The two were wed in 1998, and last summer, just days after the Arcelor deal closed, the couple had a baby girl.

18   His time outside the family business was brief. After graduating magna cum laude, Aditya joined a training program at Credit Suisse First Boston. But he stayed less than a year. He left to help his father create a public company called Ispat International from many of the steel assets Mittal had been buying. "I always believed [a stock offering] would open up more opportunities," Aditya says.

19   He quickly found his role. Aditya showed a mastery of numbers and had a nose for sniffing out targets, so in 2000 Lakshmi put him in charge of M&A. It was a tough time, though, for Aditya to cut his teeth. A brutal steel slump that led to a wave of bankruptcies had sent Ispat's shares plummeting from an IPO price of 27 in 1997 to just 1.50 in late 2001, and the company's $2 billion Mexican operation was teetering on the edge of default.

20   But the Mittals turned the crisis to their advantage. They snatched up plants in Eastern Europe and Algeria at rock-bottom prices. Capitalizing on the desire of many governments to shed money-losing assets, and backed by favorable financing from the World Bank and the European Bank for Reconstruction & Development, the Mittals doubled their annual production capacity to 30 million tons over just two years. "Everywhere there was something for sale," says Aditya.

21   The Mittals' double-or-nothing bet, though, didn't sit well with some Ispat shareholders. Some of the acquisitions were made privately by the Mittals despite assurances in the IPO prospectus that they would only buy steel plants through the listed company. That left investors complaining that the family was privately snapping up quality mills while leaving less attractive assets in the public company. The Mittals counter that purchases in emerging markets at a troubled time for the industry would have been too risky for public shareholders.

22   Then, in 2004, Aditya helped plug a hole in the portfolio with a big U.S. deal. The company agreed to acquire International Steel Group—which included assets of the old Bethlehem Steel—for $4.5 billion from Ross, turning the Mittals overnight into top players in the U.S. industry. They used the transaction to clean up their messy public-private structure. Ispat acquired their private company, LNM Holdings, for $13 billion to create Mittal Steel Co. Lakshmi paid himself a $2 billion dividend.

23   When Aditya first hit on the notion of going after Arcelor, his father was less than enthusiastic. Says Lakshmi: "I felt it was a far-fetched idea." While on a ski vacation at the family's house in Saint Moritz, Switzerland, in December, 2005, Aditya made his case. Arcelor was also buying up steel plants, and both companies had bid for a mill just two months earlier in Ukraine. Although Mittal had prevailed, Aditya figured Arcelor's challenge had pushed the price up by nearly 40%, to $4.8 billion. That helped convince his father. "They were bidding against us on every purchase," Lakshmi says.

24   The Mittals first tried a friendly approach. Aditya invited Arcelor CEO Guy Dollé to dinner in the London mansion. A large painting of a Mogul ruler cradling a falcon presided over the scene; the wine flowed. At one point, Dollé boasted how well Arcelor was doing, further whetting the Mittals' appetite. But after a three-hour meal, Dollé shrugged off any suggestions of a deal.

A CRACK IN THE DEFENSE

25   After Dollé ducked further meetings, Aditya took the gloves off. An investment banker hastily summoned to work on the bid said the deal was classic Mittal. Their own business was performing well, giving them the nerve to go after the biggest target around. Still, the team wasn't nearly as prepared as their bankers would have liked. For one thing, the regulatory climate of Luxembourg, where Arcelor was headquartered, was unknown territory. "No other corporate entity would have done this," the banker said.

26   A bitter five-month battle ensued. The Mittals thought they were cooked when at the end of May Arcelor accepted a rival offer. Dollé agreed to sell a 32% stake in the company to Russian oligarch Alexey Mordashov in exchange for a controlling interest in steelmaker Severstal. "We were all struggling to find a crack in the Arcelor defense," says Shahriar Tadjbakhsh, an investment banker from Goldman Sachs & Co. who worked on the deal. The opening appeared when members of Arcelor's board grew uncomfortable with what they saw as the company's extreme defense tactics and its general refusal to deal with the Mittals.

27   In June, against Goldman's advice, the Mittals sent a letter to Arcelor. That broke the ice, and Aditya began a series of quiet meetings, paving the way for a deal. Aditya "was the person who probably had the best mastery of key elements of the transactions," Tadjbakhsh says. Adds Jeremy Fletcher, a banker at Credit Suisse in London who also participated: "Arcelor was conceptually very much Aditya's deal."

28   Such clout is testimony to his father's confidence in Aditya. The two have an easy rapport, often finishing each other's sentences. When they're in London, the Mittals typically lunch together, with the meal delivered from Lakshmi's mansion. When in different cities, they're on the phone with one another at least twice a day. "There are very few things that we don't talk to each other about," says Aditya, who always refers to his father as "Mr. Mittal" in front of outsiders. That respect is returned. "I don't see him as young," says Lakshmi. "I admire him for his intellect and for his ideas, suggestions, and convictions."

29   The knock-down fight for Arcelor put to rest any doubts others might have had about Aditya. He took a beating when Dollé made an issue of nepotism. And Dollé still questions the wisdom of the deal. "Before judging any merger, you have to wait a long time—four or five years," he says. But Aditya sure looks like a winner for now. He tells of touring, like a conqueror, the city of Luxembourg, taking in the opera house and other landmarks. His guide: None other than the Prime Minister. And to seal the deal, the Mittals had promised that an Arcelor executive would hold the CEO post at the combined company, naming Arcelor executive vice-president Roland Junck to the job. But three months later, Junck stepped aside. Lakshmi is now CEO, and Aditya is overseeing the integration. His younger sister, Vanisha, also works in the company and serves on the board. Arcelor Mittal's headquarters may be in Luxembourg, Aditya says, but the "power is in London."

30   The Mittals, like most billionaires, live differently from the rest of us. Lakshmi is chauffeured around in a Maybach limousine and logs countless hours on his Gulfstream. Aditya, too, can use the jet at will, often arriving at the airport by helicopter. Yet, for all their gilt edges, the Mittals are surprisingly down-to-earth. Sure, they may splurge on a big family event like the wedding, but they're more formal than flashy. And they are intensely private, focusing what little downtime they have on the family's inner circle.

31   Mostly, though, their lives are about work. As part of a broad shakeup in the U.S., Aditya has brought in new management to run a huge mill in Burns Harbor, Ind., on the southern shore of Lake Michigan. He wants the new team to crank up production by 25%, which would make it the most profitable plant in the U.S. That's where Arcelor comes in. Unlike the rattle-trap facilities in developing markets that Lakshmi made his fortune buying, Arcelor isn't a collection of dinosaurs. While the two companies were roughly the same size, Arcelor annually spent more than 10 times what Mittal did on research and development. The best Arcelor plants outperform Mittal mills in efficiency, reliability, and quality of steel.

32   To tap into that expertise, Burns Harbor recently dispatched a team of engineers to Sidmar, Arcelor's crown jewel, in Ghent, Belgium. The idea was to figure out why, with the exact same inputs, the Europeans were able to squeeze about 7% more steel out of their mills than the U.S. plants could. The Americans relished the candlelight dinners in the old quarter of Ghent, but they were even more wowed by the advanced technology and shop-floor know-how they saw in Belgium. Now, they're gearing up to use a Sidmar device called a bomb that can be plunged into molten steel to sample its chemical properties and detect imperfections early on. The Mittals are pushing for just that sort of knowledge exchange across the company's global network, from Brazil to Kazakhstan. The many cultures now under the Arcelor Mittal flag provide "an inexhaustible source of competitive advantage," says Greg Ludkovsky, the company's chief technology officer for the Americas.

STRETCHED THIN

33   There's still a huge amount of work to do integrating Arcelor, which is not as sharp commercially as it is on technology. Competitors say Mittal had its hands full even before the megadeal, and the company's U.S. executives acknowledge they're stretched. They have yet to install common computer systems, for instance. That loss of focus has enabled others to grab business, says Daniel R. DiMicco, CEO of Charlotte (N.C.)-based Nucor Corp. "We've probably gained customers" since the Mittals bought ISG in 2004, he says.

34   The Mittals, though, are already looking ahead to the next deal. They just bought another Mexico plant, they're building a new steel pipe plant in Saudi Arabia, and they may next go after Vallourec, a big French maker of pipes for the oil industry. The big hole is Asia, where state-owned steel plants and national champions have made it tough to buy assets. Some even think the Mittals could make a run at South Korea's giant Posco. They already own 33% of Hunan Valin, a Chinese producer, and they have also agreed to build a $9 billion plant in the Indian state of Orissa. "If they had Asia exposure, they would have the world sewn up," says Michael Shillaker, an analyst at Credit Suisse in London.

35   The Mittals have time on their side. Aditya still has many years ahead of him, and so, too, does his father. Will the two always be together? Aditya isn't so sure. "I don't know if I am going to be here for the long run," he says. "It depends on the opportunities and the requirements of the company."

36   Most give the Mittal father-son act at least another decade. It's when fathers hit their 70s and sons their 40s that such unions start to unravel, as the younger generation itches to take control, says Randel S. Carlock, a professor at the INSEAD business school's Singapore campus. But for now, at least, the Mittal team looks rock-solid. "The father is an entrepreneurial icon, one of the great business leaders of the 21st century. The son is obviously a very capable young man," says Carlock. "That's the best situation you can have."

Case 16

The Last Rajah: *India's Ratan Tata Aims to Transform His Once-Stodgy Conglomerate into a Global Powerhouse. But Can It Thrive after He Steps Down?*

1 Among Asia's business titans, Ratan N. Tata stands out for his modesty. The chairman of the Tata Group—India's biggest conglomerate, with businesses ranging from software, cars, and steel to phone service, tea bags, and wristwatches—usually drives himself to the office in his $12,500 Tata Indigo Marina wagon. He prefers to spend weekends in solitude with his two dogs at a beachfront home he designed himself. And disdainful of pretense, he travels alone even on long business trips, eschewing the retinues of aides who typically coddle corporate chieftains.

2 But the 69-year-old Tata also has a daredevil streak. An avid aviator, he often flies a corporate Falcon 2000 jet around India. And in February he caused a sensation at the Aero India 2007 air show by co-piloting Lockheed F-16 and Boeing F-18 fighter jets.

3 Tata's business dealings reflect the bolder side of his personality. In the past four years he has embarked on an investment binge that is building his group from a once-stodgy regional player into a global heavyweight. Since 2003, Tata has bought the truck unit of South Korea's Daewoo Motors, a stake in one of Indonesia's biggest coal mines, and steel mills in Singapore, Thailand, and Vietnam. It has taken over a slew of tony hotels including New York's Pierre, the Ritz-Carlton in Boston, and San Francisco's Camden Place. The 2004 purchase of Tyco International's undersea telecom cables for $130 million, a price that in hindsight looks like a steal, turned Tata into the world's biggest carrier of international phone calls. With its $91 million buyout of British engineering firm Incat International, Tata Technologies now is a major supplier of outsourced industrial design for American auto and aerospace companies, with 3,300 engineers in India, the U.S., and Europe.

Go-Go Tata

Since beginning a global push four years ago, India's once-plodding Tata Group has expanded aggressively at home and abroad in a wide range of industries.

Tata Motors	2007 REVENUES	2007 PROFITS
Building a new car plant and sharply boosting output of its small truck, the Ace. A new venture with Fiat will co-produce 150,000 cars and 250,000 trucks annually. The biggest gamble: a $2,500 people's car to be launched in 2008.	$7.2 Billion (+36%)	$490 Million (+26%)
Tata Steel		
Bought mills in Singapore, Thailand, and Vietnam, and is now expanding in India. With its $13 billion purchase of Corus, Europe's No. 2 steelmaker, capacity should reach 50 million tons by 2010, behind only Arcelor Mittal.	$6.6 Billion (+99%)	$923 Million (+33%)
Tata Consultancy Services		
Riding the software and tech services outsourcing boom, TCS has grown explosively in the past five years. Now it's developing its own software for transportation, retail, finance, and other industries.	$4.2 Billion (+41%)	$930 Million (+43%)

All figures for fiscal year ended Mar. 31, 2007

4   The crowning deal to date has been Tata Steel's $13 billion takeover in April of Dutch-British steel giant Corus Group, a target that would have been unthinkable just a few years ago. In one swoop, the move greatly expands Tata Steel's range of finished products, secures access to automakers across the U.S. and Europe, and boosts its capacity fivefold, with mills added in Pennsylvania and Ohio.

5   Now, a new gambit may catapult Tata into the big leagues of global auto manufacturing: The company is said to be weighing a bid for Jaguar Cars and Land Rover, which Ford Motor Co. wants to sell. On top of all this, the group plans $28 billion in capital investments at home over the next five years in steel, autos, telecom, power, chemicals, and more. "We rescaled our thinking in terms of growth," Tata says over tea at Bombay House, the group's headquarters since 1926, a tranquil oasis with well-worn marble floors, a vast collection of modern Indian art, and staffers who circulate with bowls of vanilla ice cream every day at 3 p.m. "We just forced and cajoled our businesses to make this happen."

SPIRITUAL CEMENT

6   The forcing and cajoling has worked brilliantly. The market value of the 18 listed Tata companies has swelled to $62 billion, from $12 billion, since 2003. Group sales and profits have doubled, to $29 billion and $2.8 billion, respectively. The three big companies that account for 75% of sales—Tata Steel, Tata Motors, and Tata Consultancy Services—are enjoying some of their best years ever. And in May, Tata Tea netted $523 million in profit when Coca-Cola Co. paid $1.2 billion for its 30% stake in Energy Brands Inc., the maker of Glacéau Vitamin Water. Not bad for a purchase made just nine months earlier. "This is a transformed Tata," says Rajeev Gupta, managing director of private equity shop Carlyle Advisory Partners.

7   The global push began four years ago. After a rocky first decade as chairman, Tata commissioned a sweeping review to plot strategy, including a study comparing India with China. He was struck by the sheer audacity of Chinese projects. "Whether they built a port or a highway, they did it big, the kind of scale that caused skeptics to say, My God, this is over the top,'" he says. "But China always grew into it." India, he concluded, should also think big—and so should Tata Group. By leveraging India's vast potential, he thought, the company could shift into turbocharged expansion to become a global heavyweight.

8   Tata is arguably the most important among a new pack of multinationals charging out of big developing nations such as China, Brazil, and Russia. These emerging giants can tap into abundant low-cost labor, tech talent, and mineral resources, while cutting their teeth in the world's biggest growth markets. Brimming with cash and confidence, they also are starting to export innovative business models honed in some of the planet's most challenging places to operate.

9   Building an organization with a coherent vision and capable of succeeding in so many industries and so many markets, though, is a daunting task. Asia has witnessed the rise of many soup-to-nuts behemoths that thrived when economic tides were high, such as Korea's Daewoo, Thailand's Charoen Pokphand, and Indonesia's Salim Group. Most eventually fell apart. The real test for Tata, too, is likely to come when India's boom abates and battles for talent and market share involving both aggressive Indian rivals and deep-pocketed multinationals intensify. But unlike most other Asian groups, "Tata already has proved it can survive turmoil and constantly reinvent itself," says Harvard Business School professor Tarun Khanna, who has closely studied the group for a decade.

10   At the center of the empire is Tata himself. An architecture graduate from Cornell University in 1962, he serves as the group's chief dealmaker, visionary, and spiritual cement.

He joined the company after college, then steadily rose through the ranks. He took over 16 years ago—after the death of his gregarious uncle, J.R.D. Tata—just as India began dismantling decades of socialist-style business controls. Tata has overseen sharp downsizing, risky plunges into auto manufacturing and telecom, and a transformation of the conglomerate's insular and lethargic management culture. Now he wants to prove Tata companies can compete in the rich West as well as in the unpredictable but hugely promising markets of the developing world. What's more, Tata wants to set the group solidly on a path to achieving all this before he retires.

11   The barrel-chested tycoon hasn't named a successor or said when he plans to step down. He'll turn 70 in December, but he still has a vice-like handshake, and associates are amazed at his command of numbers and technical details of the various Tata companies. That makes his failure to designate a successor all the more disconcerting. Some even question whether his departure might spur the group's breakup. "Who will be the glue?" worries one veteran insider. "Will there even be a central leader?"

12   Ratan could even be the last Tata to oversee the group. The Tata family tree, on display at a company museum, stretches back 800 years through generations of Parsi priests, an Indian minority descended from Persians. It ends with Ratan—single and childless—and his siblings. Younger brother Jimmy and three half-sisters aren't involved in Tata businesses. His reclusive half-brother, Noel, runs a Tata-owned retail chain, but it's unclear whether he's tycoon timber. Succession "is a problem," Ratan acknowledges. "I am involved in more issues than I think I should be."

13   When he does step down, Ratan Tata will leave a big void. Even though he and other family members own just 3% of shares in Tata Sons, the private holding company with controlling stakes in its businesses, Tata himself chairs key units including Tata Motors and Tata Steel. He is intimately involved in all major deals and pushed for acquisitions such as Corus. The ventures into passenger cars and telecom are his babies. And Tata is instrumental in hatching new businesses, bouncing ideas gleaned from his travels to managers for follow-up.

14   Ratan Tata serves another vital function: While at ease with lawyers and investment bankers, he remains firmly planted in the developing world. He is a passionate promoter of corporate social responsibility, a mission that dates to the group's founding in the 1870s by Tata's great-grandfather, Jamsetji Tata. The founder was a pioneering industrialist, philanthropist, and fervent nationalist who traveled to the U.S. with a swami, meeting the tycoons of the day. He opened India's first textile mill, in large part to wean Indians from their industrial dependence on Britain, which until then had milled much of the subcontinent's cotton and then shipped the high-cost cloth back to the colonies. Tata offered worker benefits such as child care and pensions long before most companies in the West, and later one of Jamsetji's sons helped bankroll a young Mahatma Gandhi while he agitated in South Africa for the rights of immigrant Indians.

15   To this day, the Tata Group remains devoted to good works: Charitable trusts own 66% of the shares in parent Tata Sons, and many of its companies fund grassroots anti-poverty projects that seem far removed from their core businesses. Ask the chairman to name the group's biggest challenges and he quickly cites two: "Talent, and retaining our value system as we get bigger and more diverse. We have to increase the management bandwidth, and with the same ethical standards."

16   He also concedes that the group is much less focused than he envisioned back in 1991, when he pledged to pare it from scores of companies to just a dozen or so. Tata did dump marginal businesses—cosmetics, paints, and cement—but entered retail, telecom, biotech, and others. Today, Tata Group comprises nearly 100 companies with 300 subsidiaries in 40 businesses. Slimming the group down "is one area where I have not succeeded in what I set out to do," he admits.

"I'M NOT MOVING"

17 His hope is that Tata's unorthodox structure will give individual companies the agility to respond to new opportunities and threats. "The organization is a lot lighter than a Western conglomerate," says Alan Rosling, a Briton who spearheads international expansion for Tata. "There is no central strategy. We don't even have consolidated financial statements." The group is bound together by the small staffs of Tata Sons and another holding company, Tata Industries. These two, chaired by Ratan, provide strategic vision, control the Tata brand, and lend a hand on big deals. And Tata Sons can raise cash to launch new businesses or help fund purchases such as Corus. In 2004 it pulled in $1.3 billion by floating a 10% share in Tata Consultancy Services.

18 Bombay House also exerts influence through the Group Corporate Office, another Ratan invention. The nine senior executives in this unit sit on the boards of Tata companies and act as "stewards," mentoring managers and promoting corporate responsibility values. For example, former Tata Tea and Indian Hotels chief R. K. Krishna Kumar helped incubate Ginger Hotels, a new chain of budget inns offering free Internet and cable TV for about $25 in India's most expensive business hubs—one-tenth of what most business hotels charge. R.Gopalakrishnan, who retired from Unilever's Indian affiliate in 1998, is chairman of a new Tata drug-research company and has advised fertilizer maker Tata Chemicals on an ambitious new strategy to market everything from seeds to low-cost insurance by setting up a network of stores and working with poor farmers to improve crop yields. Bombay House "offers guidance and sets perspective," says Satish Pradhan, who heads the Tata Group's sprawling management training center in Pune. "We hand-hold the businesses in a nonintrusive manner."

19 The chief steward, though, clearly is Ratan Tata. He negotiates major deals and steeps himself in the details of automaking, telecom, or steel. "He has a tremendous technological brain," says Tata Steel Managing Director B. Muthuraman. He's also not afraid of a fight. During a strike at Tata Motors' Pune plant, militant unionists assaulted Tata managers and occupied a section of the city. "If you put a gun to my head," Tata declared, "you had better take the gun away or pull the trigger, because I'm not moving." Tata signed a deal with a rival union and broke the strike after a confrontation between police and the militants. "While he doesn't look it," says Muthuraman, "he's one of the toughest people I've ever known."

20 The transformation of Tata Steel illustrates his impact. In the early '90s, when India started opening to global competition, the 100-year-old company was saddled with antiquated plants, a bloated payroll, and "no market orientation . . . we were a good study in demise," recalls Muthuraman. Over the years, Tata cut the workforce from 78,000 to 38,000 and spent $2.5 billion on modernization. A decade later, Tata Steel had become one of the world's most efficient and profitable producers and began to acquire rivals. "Ratan was the chief architect" of the Corus deal, says Muthuraman. "I was worried about the magnitude and the amount of money. But he instilled confidence." The strategy: Because Tata is one of the few big steelmakers with its own abundant coal and iron ore reserves, it can produce raw steel at low cost in India, then ship it to Corus' first-rate mills in the West to make finished products.

21 But Tata Steel highlights the challenges of balancing Old World ways with New Economy realities. Jamshedpur, the company's home base in northern India, resembles a time capsule of a more paternalistic industrial age, a leafy city of genteel colonial-era structures and wide boulevards hacked from the jungle in 1908. Tata spends some $40 million a year supplying all civic services and schools, even though it employs just 20,000 of Jamshedpur's 700,000 residents. And in its downsizing program, workers who agreed to early retirement got full pay until age 60 and lifelong health care.

22   Tata Steel also spends millions annually on education, health, and agricultural development projects in 800 nearby villages. In Sidhma Kudhar, for instance, a dusty outpost of whitewashed stone houses with thatched roofs, the 32 families until two years ago subsisted on a single crop of low-grade rice and the $1 a day they could earn by stripping branches from nearby hills. Thanks to funds from Tata, they now have irrigation systems that allow them to grow rice crops and a variety of vegetables. The hillsides are now covered with thousands of mahogany and teak seedlings for future income, as well as jatropha bushes, whose seeds can be used for biofuel. Most children now attend classes in the refurbished school, and the village has three televisions, powered by Tata solar units that also supply enough juice for electric lights and clocks.

23   Such generosity will be put to the test now that Tata owns struggling Corus. The deal loads the Indian steelmaker with $7.4 billion in debt, and absorbing Corus' higher-cost operations will weaken margins. One key question is what to do with Corus mills such as the one at Port Talbot in Wales, which employs 3,000 workers. Tata says it will proceed with Corus' plans for the mill. But the union representing most Corus workers wants Tata Steel to invest an additional $600 million in Port Talbot to assure it will remain competitive so it won't have to cut jobs. A delegation of 20 Corus labor reps visited Jamshedpur in April to meet the mill's new owners, but Tata executives declined to give guarantees. "We were extremely impressed by their workforce and commitment to social responsibility," says labor leader Michael Leahy. "But how will they be able to translate those principles into the British and European context? They couldn't answer that."

24   A bid for Jaguar and Land Rover might present an even more daunting challenge. The Ford assets would give Tata a luxury brand and a big boost in SUVs, but it would be an uphill climb to restore Jaguar's luxury cachet, which was damaged by sharing basic designs with Ford. Tata executives, who won't confirm their interest in Jaguar and Land Rover, have downplayed auto ambitions in the U.S., citing the high cost of entry and their commitments in emerging markets. And an attempt to sell small cars under the Rover name in Britain lasted just two years amid complaints about quality. Tata Motors, which once made only trucks, surprised skeptics with the success of the Indica, an affordable passenger car developed from scratch and rolled out in the 1990s. The Indica is now India's No. 2 car and is selling well in South Africa, Spain, and Italy. Tata also will soon start exporting cars and trucks through a venture with Fiat and is eyeing a similar project in South America. The company had another big hit in 2006 with the Ace, a bare-bones truck for less than $6,000. Tata already is boosting its output from 75,000 minitrucks to 250,000.

INEVITABLE STUMBLES

25   Ratan's big passion, though, is the "one lakh" car. (One lakh is 100,000. And that many rupees equals about $2,500.) Since the mid-'90s, he has wanted to develop reliable but supercheap vehicles, a project he believes could ultimately revolutionize the auto industry and make India a major economic power. Tata personally supervised the project and traveled frequently to Tata Motors' development center in Pune to check on progress. Originally he envisioned a fundamentally new kind of vehicle—one made of plastics, for example, that didn't even resemble what we think of today as a car. He concedes that the spartan, oval-shaped model to be launched in early 2008 doesn't meet his lofty aims. It's made of steel. And it looks like, well, a car. To get the price to $2,500, engineers shrunk the size and stripped out frills such as reclining seats and a radio. "There is not a lot of innovation," he says. "We didn't reinvent the business."

26   Tata has similar ambitions to reinvent solar energy. Tata BP Solar Ltd., a $260 million venture with British energy giant BP, supplies buildings in Germany with rooftop

solar-electric systems. But in developing nations, the company sees a vast market in bringing affordable power to villages that are off the power grid. The company has introduced low-cost, solar-powered water pumps, refrigerators, and $30 lanterns that burn for two hours on a day's charge. And it has fitted 50,000 homes with $300 systems that can power two lights, a hot plate, a fan, and a 14-inch TV. "But this is a drop in the ocean," says Tata BP Solar CEO K. Subramanya. "We ought to be touching millions."

27   There is little question that the opportunities for Tata in India and abroad are staggering. But can the group succeed on all these fronts simultaneously? The interesting dilemmas will come when the Indian economy slows and some Tata affiliates inevitably stumble. Future managers could look at expensive burdens such as Jamshedpur and rural-development projects as tempting targets for cuts when times get tight. Tata companies could lose interest in low-cost goods for the masses without a passionate promoter as group chairman. And the group could take a tougher look at businesses to spin off.

28   For the foreseeable future, though, these are nonissues. Though Tata vows that he "won't carry this on endlessly," he says he will stay on at least two years beyond when he chooses a successor. So he seems likely to fulfill the last big item on his agenda: building a network of companies capable of thriving in 21st century global competition while still adhering to traditional values long after the departure of Ratan Tata.

Case 17

Nokia Aims Way Beyond Handsets: *It Will Offer Multiplayer Games, Maps, New Ways to Swap Music and Photos, and More*

1   For the last several years, Finnish handset giant Nokia has been on a furious shopping spree. It spent $60 million on a rival to Apple () iTunes called Loudeye, the largest independent music distributor on the Net, and followed that up by acquiring navigation software maker gate5 and media-sharing site Twango.

2   Now it's clear what the buying binge was all about. At an Aug. 29 London press conference, Nokia unveiled plans to launch a slew of services for mobile users, starting later this year in Europe and Asia. The scheme includes an online music store aimed at the 200 million music-capable Nokia mobile phones already on the market, an interactive multiplayer game service, and a new venue for Nokia handset users to swap photos, videos, and music. Put all the pieces together and it's the most ambitious bid by a phonemaker to spin profits out of content and services. "Devices alone are not enough anymore," says Nokia Chief Executive Olli-Pekka Kallasvuo. "Consumers want a complete experience."

3   Europe's mobile operators shunned Nokia's earlier efforts to break into services. This time they're listening because their own efforts to create music stores and other destinations have failed. Without such offerings, there's no way mobile subscribers are going to run up the kinds of high monthly data charges companies are counting on. "Mobile operators around the world have invested a fortune in networks, services, and marketing—and it has been a gigantic disaster," says John Strand, CEO of Copenhagen mobile consultancy Strand Consult. For example, instead of downloading music over the airwaves as operators had hoped, most Europeans "sideload" music to phones from their computers.

4   Britain's Vodafone Group, the world's largest global service provider, is one company that spent big for naught. It sunk a total of $38 billion into third-generation mobile licenses, hoping to spur customers to use data services such as mobile music. But as of last spring, only 32 million of its 206 million subscribers used its Vodafone Live! content portal.

5   Nokia says its move beyond hardware can help the carriers. Take Nokia Maps, the service it launched earlier this year, which now comes preloaded on the high-end Nokia N95 phone sold by many of the world's operators. Users choose nearby points of interest on their screens, such as a coffeehouse, and the service shoots back directions or a map. Operators have the option of handling the billing for this in exchange for a cut of Nokia's content revenues. Its new music, photo, and game services probably will be handled the same way.

6   Arrangements like this should appeal to smaller mobile operators. But analysts expect some resistance from large players such as Vodafone and Orange, which may balk at the

Services That Go Ka-Ching   Nokia is launching a Web gateway called Ovi to deliver digital content via carriers or direct to consumers.

Music:	Games:	Maps:
Taking on Apple's iTunes, Nokia will offer millions of songs over the air or via the Web	A community for mobile gamers offers downloads, previews, tips– and a place to brag	Working with GPS, Nokia Maps helps you find a local pub or get home if you're lost

Source: Nokia.

idea of replacing their own music services with Nokia's. And while Nokia claims it has had "very positive discussions" with most wireless carriers, few have been willing to comment publicly on the initiative.

7   Nokia's service push also puts it in competition with Google and Yahoo!. But while those Internet companies have strong brands, they don't have control over the phone's screen. Nokia, on the other hand, can bundle imaginative services with specially tailored, user-friendly hardware. With close to a billion customers and longstanding relationships with hundreds of mobile operators around the world, Nokia looks to have a head start on marrying the Web with the wireless world.

NOKIA BARGES INTO MOBILE SERVICES

8   Ever since the mobile-phone powerhouse started the ringtone fad, it has been seeking a way to extend its reach. The new Ovi service is a marketplace of content.

9   Long before Apple introduced iTunes or dreamed up the iPhone, Nokia created a Web portal to let owners of its phones download snippets of music known as ringtones. It was the year 2000, and Nokia could see that selling content and services along with its hardware would be a smart extension of its business. But the gambit, called Club Nokia, irritated mobile operators, who wanted to run such services themselves—and who were also Nokia's biggest clients.

10   The Finnish company backed down, but never quite gave up. On Aug. 29, at a London press conference in a converted fish market alongside the Thames, Nokia's chief executive Olli-Pekka Kallasvuo unveiled plans to launch a slew of services for mobile users—initially in Europe and Asia, and perhaps later in the U.S. Called Ovi (Finnish for "door") the gateway to music, photos, maps, and other content will be available starting later this year.

11   This time around, mobile operators may be willing to join in. The scheme includes an online music store rivaling Apple's iTunes, aimed primarily, but not exclusively, at the 200 million music-capable Nokia mobile phones already on the market. It also features an interactive multiplayer game service accessible to the 40 million Nokia Nseries phones now in use. And early next year, Nokia will add a service that lets consumers swap personal photos, videos, and audio.

DEVICES ARE NOT ENOUGH

12   The road map announced in London is an effort to weave all of Nokia's software and services into a seamless package. Researchers have been toiling for years in Nokia's labs on such technology, and more recently the company has been on a furious shopping spree to beef up its portfolio. In October, 2006, for instance, it bought an iTunes rival called Loudeye, the largest independent music distribution platform, for $60 million.

13   The same month it snapped up gate5, a maker of navigation software for mobile phones, and in July of this year, it bought media-sharing site Twango—both for undisclosed prices. No other handset maker has made a comparable effort to profit in mobile communications by distributing content, not just hardware. "Devices alone are not enough anymore," says Kallasvuo. "Consumers want a complete experience."

14   Europe's mobile operators are paying close attention because their own efforts to launch digital music stores and other data services have largely failed. Yet without such offerings, there's no way subscribers are going to run up monthly data charges as high as the operators are counting on. "Mobile operators around the world have invested a fortune on networks, services, and marketing, and it has been a gigantic disaster," says John Strand, head of Copenhagen-based mobile consultancy Strand Consult. "Not a single one has succeeded with a 'walled-garden' strategy," which directs users to a closed set of services rather than to the wide-open Internet.

HELP FOR OPERATORS

15   So where do Europe's mobile-phone surfers spend their time? Surveys show they visit the same sites popular on the Internet: Rather than flocking to offerings created by mobile operators for news, finance, or search, they go to trusted brands such as Google or Yahoo!, says Mark Newman, chief research officer at Informa Telecoms & Media, a London technology consultancy. And they rarely download music over the airwaves, as operators had hoped. Most prefer to "sideload" music to their phones from their computers.

16   Britain-based Vodafone Group, the world's largest global service provider, provides a cautionary example. The company has sunk a total of $37.91 billion into third-generation mobile licenses, hoping to spur customers to use data services such as mobile music. But as of spring 2007, only 32.3 million of its 206.4 million subscribers used its Vodafone Live! portal. That leaves Vodafone and other mobile operators in danger of becoming "dumb pipes," or providers of generic wireless data access, unable to differentiate themselves from competitors or to profit by selling content.

17   Nokia says there are several ways it can help operators generate more revenues from mobile data. One is a location-based service it launched earlier this year, Nokia Maps, which comes preloaded on the high-end Nokia N95 phone sold by many of the world's operators. Users choose nearby points of interest on their screens, such as a coffeehouse, and the service gives back the address or a map. Operators have the option of handling the billing for this service in exchange for a cut of Nokia's content revenues. Nokia's new music, photo, and game services likely will be handled the same way.

CONTROLLING THE SCREEN

18   While mobile operators have every incentive to sign on to Nokia's services offerings, analysts still expect some resistance. Some of the bigger operators, like Vodafone and Orange, for example, are expected to balk at the idea of replacing their own music service with Nokia's. And although Nokia claims it has had "very positive discussions" with most operators, few are willing to comment on the new initiative.

19   Nokia's service push also puts it into more direct competition with Google and Yahoo!. But while the Internet companies have strong brands, they don't have control over the phone's screen. Nokia, on the other hand, can bundle great services with specially tailored, user-friendly hardware. With close to a billion customers and its established relationships with hundreds of mobile operators around the world, Nokia looks to have a head start on marrying the Web world with the wireless world.

Case 18

Nintendo's Quirky Hit Game: *Mario May Still Hog the Limelight, But Is It Wario Who's Really Pushing Nintendo Forward?*

1   If you ever want to convince yourself that the entertainment industry is doomed, why not grab a sheet of paper and spend the afternoon trying to define exactly what "fun" is. This, after all, is what game companies in particular are meant to make their money selling to us. But what is it? What are its characteristics and components? Why do some find it in manipulating every heavily researched lever and dial of a submarine simulator, while others seek it in the pure abstraction of Rez or Tetris?

2   Just as it seems that "fun" must be hopelessly subjective, another difficult word to add to the list next to big hitters like "art" and "love," along comes a game with almost universal appeal, a game so disarming and ridiculous, so seemingly slight, that you'd be forgiven for assuming it didn't contain any insights into anything at all. But Made In Wario is a rare beast: fun that practically everybody agrees about.

3   At first glance, that might seem surprising. Nearing release, Made In Wario looked so willfully niche not even hardcore Nintendo fans were sure what they'd make of it. Hundreds of individual games? Five-second playing times? One-word instructions? How could it work?

4   In fact, it works almost flawlessly. Wario reduces four decades of videogaming to first principles, cutting away the clutter and dilution, the apocalyptic storylines, the bulk and bloat that have weighed so many titles down. All that's left is the simple notion of pressing a button and making something happen, that vital piece of DNA that has powered every game since Spacewar.

5   Although it's overflowing with ideas, Wario has embraced the lost art of brevity, cramming heroics, sports, car chases, fireworks, humor and surprise into the length of time it takes most people to tie their shoelaces. It's a game about games, reveling in every limitation of the form and parodying Nintendo's own back catalogue.

6   It's about history, too, a title that could only be produced when gaming had achieved a kind of critical mass of nostalgia and established conventions. It's a game that you may feel you've been spending your whole life practicing for, and yet non-gamers can take to it as easily as Minesweeper.

7   Early reviews were positive but often slightly baffled, lauding it for its humor but regularly missing the wider significance. After all, important games are meant to feel important when you first play them: most titles announce their own magnitude with all the subtlety of Wagner presiding over global thermonuclear war.

8   Although most reviewers put a brave face on it, confusion reigned. Most disconcerting, and a sign that the industry may have steadily been losing its way all these years, is that the greatest hurdle Made In Wario had to overcome was that it initially seemed too entertaining. It wasn't just fun—it was too much fun to be respectable, too much fun to be taken seriously.

9   That hasn't stopped it from bringing serious change to the industry, however. That laughable oddball turned out to be the defining battle in a very Nintendo-styled war. This, it seems, was the real revolution, and its novel approach—bite-sized, gimmick gaming to fit in around your normal life—has been massively influential.

10   How much of Nintendo's new strategy—the success of the DS and Wii, and even, to a certain extent, the industry-wide craze for casual gaming—can be traced back to this starting point? Mario may still be the company mascot, but it might be Wario who's worth more in the long run, as his catalogue of new moves like prodding, poking and sneezing start to really rival jumping and running in gamers' affections.

11   Obvious in hindsight, it was still a gamble. The danger of taking 40 years of gaming conventions apart in as swift and clear-eyed a manner as Nintendo did is that you run the risk you'll be left with nothing but a handful of useless nuts and bolts that may not fit back together again.

12   Reducing games to mere button presses, a space-chimp's educational diet of simple cause and effect, might have easily become a thoroughly depressing exercise. Dodge, jump, match, aim: summer holidays spent indoors with the curtains drawn, friendships sacrificed, fortunes squandered on the latest hardware, and all for this?

13   But, of course, the final product is anything but depressing. Made In Wario is not a joyless videogame deconstruction, but rather a powerful affirmation of the skills that transform such cause and effect into something far more involving. Even as it hits you that many of the microgames use exactly the same mechanics over and over again, you marvel at how a reworked presentation—from clip-art to lush anime, abstract shapes to Polaroid photography—can make the same experience feel so utterly different each time.

14   Made In Wario serves to illustrate exactly why you can never define a game by its control scheme alone—they're much more complex machines, with scenario, art style, feedback and timing all playing their roles.

15   Few games have shown such willingness to continuously shed their skins, abandoning all established rules on presentation. An antidote to endless corridors and the same old warehouses and crates, every five seconds Made In Wario takes you somewhere utterly different: underwater, back to school, off to the races. It's a greedy approach delicately weighted to appeal to as wide a variety of gamers as possible—quick paced and mindless for those who want nothing more than a series of colorful surprises, but deep enough and shot through with score targets and unlockables for players who need something to master.

16   Alongside variety, Made In Wario uses another weapon few other games bother with: familiarity. Bringing gaming into the kitchen, the bathroom and the office, no aspect of real life is out of bounds. Welcoming to non-gamers, the results also ensure a strange kind of intimacy: whether it's catching toast or getting a haircut, Made In Wario plays out on a uniquely personal level.

17   Yet if it was simply force of numbers and quirky real-world subject matter that made it work, Made in Wario would be easy to copy. However, it's failure that seems to await every company tempted by that deceptively handmade look. One of Wario's least charming legacies is the endless minigame compilations that swarm and multiply in its wake, eroding goodwill and drowning the Wii in particular in the worst kind of shovelware.

18   Although everyone seems to be trying, no one can quite recreate the magic formula. Titles like Rayman: Raving Rabbids and Hot PXL, though well-intentioned, copy the mechanics but miss the joy, their quirkiness becoming hollow and then shrill, like a comic who picks on the audience when his material dies.

19   One of the crucial things separating Made In Wario from its competitors is that simple five-second rule at its heart. Sometimes, as Rayman in particular discovered, even 30 seconds can be too long to stretch a mechanic built for the blink of an eye. Equally, rivals often miss the bigger picture, failing to spot the way the individual games work as a whole, setting up routines and then riffing, sharing textures and echoing earlier designs, parodying and subverting the rules as they go along.

20   It's this deep self-involvement that gives Wario's games their consistency: there's a simple but effective internal rhythm at work, using repetition and deviation to make you by turns both satisfied and surprised. While each game follows a simple personal path of rising speed and complexity, there's no guessing how a later variant will twist its basic premise, luring you in and then making you jump, reversing pivotal roles, or suddenly turning a game that used to be about administering eye-drops into a game about explosive laser vision.

21   So while no single videogame will ever be capable of completely demystifying fun, Made In Wario is at least able to fill in some of the blanks. Flighty yet deep, it's certainly chosen to cover its bases, but there are universal elements at work too—pattern recognition, brevity, carefully placed twists—all of which perform on a level that bypasses mere taste and preference.

22   Eventually, though, there's a point at which simple analysis comes up short. Choose a favorite: the family avoiding the giant glass tumbler, the paper plane endlessly spiraling downstairs, the dog that wants you to shake its hand—could you really put your finger on exactly why it appeals to you?

23   That's a thought that should keep Nintendo's competitors awake at night. And here's another: while the trends it helped set in motion are quietly disrupting the balance of the current hardware generation, and the formula that made its success so effortless continues to elude all imitators, perhaps the most intimidating aspect of Made In Wario is its breezy self-assurance.

24   What at first may have seemed like carelessness is actually a potently youthful self-confidence, seen best in the way the game flippantly toys with Nintendo's own closely guarded crown jewels. That a title this brashly exuberant, a game so seemingly ad-libbed and explosive, should come from a company which might rightfully be settling into creaking middle age should give pause to the entire industry. Made In Wario may seem easy, and even childish, but it isn't. That's because, ultimately, fun is a very serious business.

Case 19

BusinessWeek

The Pet Economy: *Americans Spend an Astonishing $41 Billion a Year on Their Furry Friends*

1   If there's still any doubt whether the pampering of pets is getting out of hand, the debate should be settled once and for all by Neuticles, a patented testicular implant that sells for up to $919 a pair. The idea, says inventor Gregg A. Miller, is to "let people restore their pets to anatomical preciseness" after neutering, thereby allowing them to retain their natural look and self-esteem. "People thought I was crazy when I started 13 years ago," says the Oak Grove (Mo.) entrepreneur. But he has since sold more than 240,000 pairs (a few of which went on prairie dogs, water buffalo, and monkeys). "Neutering is creepy. But with Neuticles, it's like nothing has changed." Nothing, except there's a fake body part where a real one used to be.

2   Americans now spend $41 billion a year on their pets—more than the gross domestic product of all but 64 countries in the world. That's double the amount shelled out on pets a decade ago, with annual spending expected to hit $52 billion in the next two years, according to Packaged Facts, a consumer research company based in Rockville, Md. That puts the yearly cost of buying, feeding, and caring for pets in excess of what Americans spend on the movies ($10.8 billion), playing video games ($11.6 billion), and listening to recorded music ($10.6 billion) combined. "People are no longer satisfied to reward their pet in pet terms," argues Bob Vetere, president of the American Pet Products Manufacturers Assn. (APPMA). "They want to reward their pet in human terms." That means hotels instead of kennels, braces to fix crooked teeth, and frilly canine ball gowns. Pet owners are becoming increasingly demanding consumers who won't put up with substandard products, unstimulating environments, or shoddy service for their animals. But the escalating volume and cost of services, especially in the realm of animal medicine, raises ethical issues about how far all this loving should go.

Reigning Cats and Dogs: Where the Money Goes

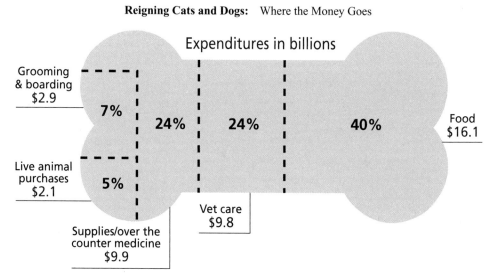

Source: American Pet Products Manufacturers Association.

3   It wasn't so very long ago that the phrase "a dog's life" meant sleeping outside, enduring the elements, living with aches, and sitting by the dinner table, waiting for a few scraps to land on the floor. Today's dog has it much better. APPMA reports that 42% of dogs now sleep in the same bed as their owners, up from 34% in 1998. Their menu reflects every fad in human food—from locally sourced organic meat and vegan snacks to gourmet meals bolstered by, say, glucosamine to ward off stiff joints. Half of all dog owners say they consider their pet's comfort when buying a car, and almost a third buy gifts for their dogs' birthdays. Richard G. Wolford, chairman and CEO of Del Monte Foods Co., refuses even to use the word "owner." "Anyone who has a pet understands who owns whom," says Wolford, who is owned by two Jack Russell terriers. His company's pet business has gone from nothing to 40% of overall sales through acquisitions of brands such as Meow Mix and Milk-Bone in the past five years.

4   The rising status of pets has started an unprecedented wave of entrepreneurship in an industry once epitomized by felt mice and rubber balls. There are now $430 indoor potties, $30-an-ounce perfume, and $225 trench coats aimed solely at four-footed consumers and their wallet-toting companions. Even those who shun animal couture are increasingly willing to spend thousands on drugs for depression or anxiety in pets, as well as psychotherapy, high-tech cancer surgery, cosmetic procedures, and end-of-life care. About 77% of dogs and 52% of cats have been medicated in the past year, according to APPMA, an increase of about 20 percentage points from 1996. Some spending can be spurred by vets who find such services more lucrative than giving shots or ending a pet's life when it contracts a painful or terminal disease.

GRAVY TRAIN

5   Once acquired as sidekicks for kids, animal companions are more popular now with empty-nesters, single professionals, and couples who delay having children. What unites these disparate demographic groups is a tendency to have time and resources to spare. With more people working from home or living away from their families, pets also play a bigger role in allaying the isolation of modern life. About 63% of U.S. households, or 71 million homes, now own at least one pet, up from 64 million just five years ago. And science is starting to validate all those warm feelings with research that documents the depth of the human-animal bond.

6   It doesn't take a scientist to figure out that there's money to be made in this environment. Companies from Procter & Gamble and Nestlé to fashion brands including Polo Ralph Lauren and thousands of small entrepreneurs are sniffing around for new opportunities in the pet sector. After consumer electronics, pet care is the fastest-growing category in retail, expanding about 6% a year. More new pet products were launched in the first six months of last year than in all of 2005. And that doesn't account for the ways existing products are being recast to woo pet lovers. Del Monte has refocused staples to look more like human snacks—from Snausages breakfast treats shaped like bacon and eggs to Pup-Peroni rib snacks so appetizing that Wolford had to stop a TV anchor from popping one into his mouth on air. Even Meow Mix now comes in plastic cups rather than cans.

7   The typical target of such products is a pet lover like Graham Gemoets, a caterer in Houston, who showers luxuries on his beloved "chi weenie" (Chihuahua/dachshund mix), Bradford. "He's my best friend and my best-accessorized friend," says Gemoets, whose splurges for Bradford include a $1,200 Hermès collar and leash, as well as $500 Chanel pearls for parties. "I know it's crazy, but I've had him for five years, and if you priced it out per month, it's like a phone bill."

8   Thanks to passionate consumers like that, the quality gap between two-legged and four-legged mammals is rapidly disappearing in such industries as food, clothing, health care, and services. The race now is to provide animals with products and services more closely modeled after the ones sold to humans. Most of the pet business world's attention is directed at the country's 88 million cats and 75 million dogs. The reason is simple. As Philip L. Francis, CEO of PetSmart Inc., the world's largest pet specialty retailer, explains: "You can't train a fish or groom a snake."

9   PetSmart, for one, has shifted its mission from being the top seller of pet food to helping consumers become better "pet parents." Along with making his 928 retail locations homier and hosting pet parties, Francis is rolling out blue-shingled "pet hotels" (kennels) in his stores. They feature private suites with raised platform beds and TVs airing shows from Animal Planet for $31 a night, as well as "bone booths," where pets can take calls from their owners, and porous pebble floors where dogs can pee. Cats get live fish tanks to watch in their rooms and separate air filtration systems so their scents don't drive the dogs crazy. The hotels, along with services such as grooming, training, and in-store hospitals, have helped PetSmart expand its service business from essentially nothing in 2000 to $450 million, or 10% of overall sales, this year. Pet owners are now less driven by price than "emotion and passion," says Francis, who shares a bed with his wife and their mutt, Bit o' Honey.

10   Those are the same primal urges that drive the fashion world. Mario DiFante, who staged New York's first Pet Fashion Week last August, has an elevated view of the place of dogs and cats in the family hierarchy. As he puts it: "Many of us consider pets as the new babies." That means clothing furry little ones in an ever-expanding range of sweaters, raincoats, leather jackets, and dresses. For Lara Alameddine, co-founder of Little Lily, a better word might be "babes." Her four-year-old company clears $1 million a year selling products including doggie slippers, bikinis, and even canine versions of Oscar-night gowns. It's popular with celebrity dog owners such as Paris Hilton, who often dresses up her Chihuahua, Tinkerbell. "We're catering to the owner's sense of style," says Alameddine. "There are no bones on our clothes."

11   Pet products now aim to make people feel they're being extra good to their little ones—much as toymakers have long encouraged parents to spoil kids. Along with doggie spas, there are mobile pet-grooming vans, pedicure services, professional dog walkers, and massage therapy for animals. Trainers like Cesar Millan—better known to millions as the Dog Whisperer—find that their expertise is suddenly in greater demand. Along with having the No. 1 series on the National Geographic Channel, Millan boasts best-selling books, DVDs, a line of products, and his famous Dog Psychology Center of Los Angeles that's a favorite with Hollywood clientele.

12   The growing willingness of owners to spare no expense for their animals has also made the outsourcing of the yucky aspects a burgeoning business. More than 350 service agencies with names such as Doody Duty, Scoopy-Poo, and Pooper Trooper have sprung up solely to relieve owners of the need even to pick up a pet's waste in their yard by doing it for them. With annual growth nearing 50%, "the pooper scooper industry is now experiencing a lot of consolidation," says Jacob D'Aniello of DoodyCalls, which has 20 locations nationwide.

13   But few parts of the business have seen as much diversification and expansion as the pet food business. As with humans, there's a growing concern about the nutrition, taste, and even ethical standards of what goes into a pet's stomach. Owners increasingly mirror their own preferences—for vegetarian cuisine, kosher meals, and even locally sourced food—in feeding their pets. And when things go wrong, the reaction is as explosive as if the victims were children. Consumers were outraged by a massive recall of melamine-contaminated pet food that killed or sickened thousands of U.S. cats and dogs. Because pets are now such valued members of the family, says Duane Ekedahl, president of the Pet Food Institute, "it had a higher impact than maybe it would have had 10 years ago."

14   As food becomes a more emotionally charged issue for people, owners are more inclined to get emotional about what's on their pets' menu. Witness the growth of what one industry executive calls the "Godiva-ization" of food, with a demand for meats fit for human consumption, visible vegetables, and nutritional supplements. It has become common to reach for a canine or cat equivalent of ketchup, such as Iams Co.'s popular "savory sauce" for dogs that comes in Country Chicken, Savory Bacon, and Roasted Beef flavor—descriptions that are, needless to say, lost on the actual consumer.

THOROUGHLY VETTED

15   Fancy food products are easy targets for critics of indulgent pet owners. But a far more controversial issue is animal medicine, especially at a time of urgent national debate about human health care. Americans now spend $9.8 billion a year on vet services. That doesn't include the over-the-counter drugs and other supplies, which add $9.9 billion in costs.

16   The annual compound growth rate for core veterinary services alone has been about 10% over the past decade, and the menu of services is becoming more elaborate by the month. Much of the inflation in pet care is due to medical advances that have people digging deep for everything from root canals for aging cats to cancer surgery for rabbits. "There has been an evolution of the entire profession," says Tom Carpenter, president of the American Animal Hospital Assn. "Pocket pets and animals who wouldn't even have been taken to vets now go for regular visits."

17   Suzanne Kramer of Chicago spent close to $380 on vet visits and drugs to treat a tumor in her hamster, Biffy, before he died last year. "Some might say: Well, he's just a hamster,' but I loved him," says Kramer. Barbara Miers of Rochester, N.Y., also took her son's hamster, Henry, to a vet and bought antibiotics for a tumor, even though the animal was nearing the end of his life span and died shortly after the final treatment. For Miers, the issue had parallels to human health. As she puts it: "Do you not give old people health care because they're old?"

18   No wonder "it's a good time to be in our profession," as Carpenter says. A vet's job has become more wide-ranging and thus more lucrative. There are even animal grief counselors to help families cope with the demise of beloved pets. Not only is state-of-the-art technology such as magnetic resonance imaging, with costs that range around $1,500 a scan, now available in small-town labs, but consumers' expectations of medical care have been transformed. They want the same best-in-class care for their pets that they want for themselves.

19   That's creating a market for new products like Pfizer Inc.'s dog-obesity drug Slentrol, which will cost $1 to $2 a day. Reconcile, a new drug from Eli Lilly & Co, for "canine separation anxiety," is based on the active ingredients in Prozac. Lilly has not suggested a retail price for Reconcile, and vets have a lot of latitude in deciding how much to charge for it. Overall, sales of pet health products have grown at a compound annual growth rate of 8.8% in recent years, more than double the rate in the late 1990s.

20   There's little doubt that human-quality care has helped to extend radically the life span of pets. Dogs routinely live 12 to 14 years now, a big jump from the average a few decades ago. John Payne, acting CEO of Banfield, the Pet Hospital, likes to boast that his cat, Gizmo, stayed perky until he died last November at the advanced age of 23 1/2. More than 60% of new customers of his chain, which has more than 600 locations nationwide, enroll their pets in wellness plans. One reason is that standard pet insurance often doesn't cover preventive care. While pet insurance is still in its infancy, with 1% of owners having coverage, the number of clients is growing by double digits each year. Jamie Ward invested in a $25.77-a-month plan with Veterinary Pet Insurance (VPI) for her American Staffordshire terrier,

Loki, only to discover that it didn't cover any of the $2,000 in expenses for a kneecap injury. (VPI says it abided by the terms of the contract.)

21   The ever-expanding roster of drugs and treatment can run into tens of thousands of dollars in expenses, creating a dilemma for owners. Steve Zane of Hoboken, N.J., choked slightly when a veterinarian presented him and his wife, Lily, an estimate of $3,700 to help cure liver failure in their cat, Koogle, over Christmas. "We looked at each other and said: 'Well, he's family,'" recalls Zane, a graphic designer who's still paying off the final bill for the recovered cat. "If it had been $15,000, I think we would almost have had to say no."

22   The anthropomorphization of pets has also created the perception that they have human problems such as separation anxiety and depression. While a number of vets say such issues are real, especially just after the death of a dog's four-footed chum or the removal of puppies, others say it simply creates yet more opportunities for new products. Americans are expected to spend 52% more on medicines to treat their pets this year than they spent five years ago. Drugmakers love the category because, compared with human drugs, there's less risk of liability, less competition, and less pressure to switch to generics because so few consumers carry pet insurance. Even so, Dawn M. Boothe, a professor of clinical physiology and pharmacology in the Auburn University College of Veterinary Medicine, argues that "the recovery of costs" for drug companies may take a long time as people may scoff at pricey treatments for pets.

23   Much of the attention is going to the growing problem of pet obesity. As many as 40% of dogs are estimated to be overweight or obese, with similarly high rates among cats, thanks to the indulgent habits of their owners. Being plied with carob bonbons all day while getting rolled around in an all-terrain stroller (retail price: about $210) is not an ideal lifestyle for any animal. People who overeat or don't get enough exercise tend to draw their pets into the same behavior, vets say, and the growing inclination to regale pets with treats has come at a cost to their waistline. Along with creating interest in new anti-obesity drugs, it's prompting interest in diet pet food. It has also created a market for procedures including pet liposuction, which is becoming more common in cities like Los Angeles where owners are used to getting nips and tucks for themselves.

24   And for some pet lovers, no medical procedure is too extreme. Plastic surgeons offer rhinoplasty, eye lifts, and other cosmetic procedures to help tone down certain doggy features, from droopy eyes to puggish noses. Root canals, braces, and even crowns for chipped teeth are also becoming more popular.

25   Some might question whether all this primping and pampering of pets has the makings of a bubble that could have owners telling Fido to get his own damn bone once the economy takes a turn. After all, Paola Freccero admits that when she grew up in Massachusetts, "Pets were pets. You didn't dress them, you didn't feed them special food, you didn't take them to play dates." But thanks to the advice of her vet and what she read on the Internet, she wouldn't serve up anything but the best for her puggle (pug/beagle mix), Lucy, including treats at $2 apiece. And from the moment Eric Olander paid $500 for a plane ticket to get a stray chow chow mix from Atlanta to his home in Los Angeles, the dog has been a focal point of his life. "I call him my 401(k) with paws," he says, "because that's where all my money goes."

Case 20

The Battle to Be Top Dog—PetSmart vs. Petco: *PetSmart and Petco Have Adopted Different Strategies as Each Seeks the Dominant Position in the Animal Care Industry*

1   The news hit the Phoenix offices of PetSmart on a Friday afternoon: The U.S. Food & Drug Administration was recalling tainted pet food manufactured in China. PetSmart's Chief Executive Philip Francis told his team to pounce. The company ripped recalled products from shelves, put up informational signs at stores, staffed up at its customer-service call centers, and gave refunds to folks returning tainted products. In some cases, PetSmart paid vet bills for sick animals.

2   Francis didn't stop there. He had the company mine its customer database and send warning notices to folks who'd recently bought recalled products. The move prompted grateful letters and e-mails from customers. "For the first time in my life, a company has sent me something of value," one wrote. Says Francis: "I'd prefer the recall hadn't happened, but from a customer loyalty standpoint, you just can't spend enough on advertising to accomplish what it did for us."

3   Francis has to move quickly these days because he has someone nipping at his heels: His San Diego-based archrival, Petco Animal Supplies. PetSmart and Petco are the two top dogs in the $41 billion animal care industry. Petco is the older of the two, founded in 1965. It was the first retail chain to take the pet food businesses out of dark, smelly mom-and-pop stores and into a modern category-killer format. Today, both companies operate in about as many locations: 908 for PetSmart, 850 for Petco. But they often have different approaches.

4   Petco's stores tend to be smaller and more ubiquitous, almost replacing the neighborhood pet store. They're located in strip malls. PetSmart stores are bigger and tend to be in the larger "power centers," alongside other discount chains. According to a recent analysis from JPMorgan retail analyst Nancy Hoch, PetSmart's prices were on average 8% higher than those of Wal-Mart Stores but 11% below Petco's.

SHIFTING STOCK AND SERVICES

5   A former supermarket executive, Francis joined PetSmart when the company was suffering a crisis in 1998. In much the way Toys 'R' Us and Tower Records struggled in their niches, PetSmart's stock-'em-high warehouse format was no longer working as discounters such as Wal-Mart and Target loaded up on pet supplies, particularly the higher-end products such as Iams dog food that only vets and pet stores had sold previously. Francis shrunk the stores, cutting the typical store size from 28,000 sq. ft. to 20,000 sq. ft. He kept the same assortment of product but stocked less on shelves, sending trucks from central warehouses more frequently to restock and thus avoiding the warehouse look.

6   Most important, he added services: adoption, training, veterinary, grooming, day care, and pet hotels. Last year the company groomed 7.5 million dogs, a 16% increase over the year before. It provided 378,000 training classes, another 16% increase. Overall, services are expected to generate $450 million in sales this year, about 10% of the company's $4.5 billion total, but representing 26% annual growth since the strategy was hatched in 2000.

ROOM AND BOARD

7 Today, the inside of the store looks a lot homier, with a little blue shingled area inside with brick and siding that houses the hotel and day care area. Inside the hotel section, visitors are greeted to slate tiles and wooden reception desk. In the dog area, owners can choose between regular boarding, where dogs congregate in a big room and then sleep alone in kennels, or private suites with raised platform beds and televisions airing the Animal Planet cable network and other pet programming. Since the stores are in strip malls, the company developed a porous pebble floor where the dogs could urinate. There's also a "bone phone" that allows owners to call in and talk to their pets. Cats have quarters with separate air filtration systems so their smell doesn't drive the dogs crazy. The cats also get to watch a live fish tank.

8 Francis says he can add a pet hotel to an existing location for less than half the cost of building a similar standalone location. Plus, the hotel shares the cost of the heating and air conditioning system, parking lot, employee break area, armor car pickups, and other overhead. Overnight stays start at $21 a night, $31 for a suite. Day care starts at $14 a day. After five years the hotels can help boost a store's sales by 29% and double its profitability, both because the hotels are a high-margin business and because customers come more frequently and buy other things when they do. A typical PetSmart store with a hotel earns $879,000 on sales of $7.1 million.

9 Even with numbers such as those, Francis says he's rolling out the hotel concepts slowly. They're in just 62 of the stores today, although Francis says they could ultimately be in 435 stores, or 40% of the chain, by 2010. He's taking it slow because "people get angrier about bad service than a bad product. It's more personal. We have to make sure we get it right."

GROSS-OUT PETS

10 Petco has a different approach. The $2.2 billion company still does two-thirds of its business in dog and cat products, but Petco features a broader selection of goods for other animals, everything from hamsters to tarantulas. The company recently featured a "Reptile Rendezvous" at 200 stores. The events included "in the terrarium" photo contests and demonstrations for products such as a new clay that reptile owners can mold into small hills and caves. Snakes, iguanas, and turtles remain very popular with teenage boys, says Petco's CEO James Myers: "Anything that grosses your parents out."

11 Petco has not embraced the services strategy quite as aggressively as PetSmart. Its stores do prominently feature grooming services, and the company provides doggie day care at some locations. But Petco stores, at about 14,000 sq. ft., aren't as large as PetSmarts and for now Myers is holding back on overnight pet-sitting. "I'm not sure that plays everywhere in America," he says.

12 There is another difference: Petco is privately held. It was bought last year by private equity firms Texas Pacific Group and Leonard Green & Partners. Ironically, it was the second time Los Angeles-based Leonard Green had taken the company private. PetSmart's Francis says he gets calls from time to time from people interested in a buyout. So far he's been against the idea. "I've got all the money I need," he says. "Our goal is to keep our stock price up so nobody can afford to take us private."

Case 21

BusinessWeek

Six Sigma Kick-Starts Starwood: *The Hotel Chain Says Six Sigma Doesn't Have to Stifle Creativity, and Points to Its Success in Developing Profitable New Programs for Guests*

1   In January, 2006, the Westin Chicago River North hotel was picked to pilot a project, dubbed Unwind, for the upscale hotel chain. The purpose: to imagine a set of nightly activities that would draw guests out of their rooms and into the lobby where they could meet, mingle, and develop a greater loyalty to the hotel group. Westin spied an opportunity with Unwind after a study it produced found 34% of frequent travelers feel lonely away from home.

2   Instead of hiring consultants or ethnographers, a common first step for a new initiative, the hotel chain relied on a seemingly stodgy process: Six Sigma. Originally developed by Motorola in the 1980s as a quality-control mechanism, the program has become part of the fabric of Corporate America. With its focus on reducing defects and cutting business costs, the technique has spread from manufacturing to the services sector.

OVERCOMING SKEPTICISM

3   Even 3M has embraced it—with mixed results. The program hurt the inventive Minnesota company's creativity, which is precisely the rap it has among companies trying to innovate. So when Starwood Hotels & Resorts Worldwide, Westin's parent company, introduced Six Sigma in 2001, "there was tremendous skepticism," admits Geoff Ballotti, president of Starwood's North America Div.

4   Under Ballotti, however, Starwood has found Six Sigma's strengths can promote innovation, not stifle it. Combining creativity and efficiency, instead of pitting one against the other, is a delicate managerial maneuver that few service companies have been able to pull off. Starwood is one. Bank of America is another.

5   Starwood has been successful, in part, because it began with a culture of creativity before introducing the management tool. Founder Barry Sternlicht relied heavily on design to distinguish the hospitality company's Sheraton and Westin hotel brands from the competition. He brought in noted architect David Rockwell to help create Starwood's hip W Hotels brand.

QUICK EXECUTION OF CONCEPTS

6   Today, by harnessing Six Sigma processes to the creativity that bubbles up from its hotel units, Starwood is able to quickly turn concepts into reality. Hundreds of projects have been done this way, including a "menu engineering" program that rejiggers the contents of an in-room refrigerator based on their popularity to drive higher profits, and the development several years ago of a pool concierge who helps guests in Latin American resorts book spa appointments and restaurant reservations. "Everybody admires them for how they do this," says Jeneanne Rae, president of Peer Insight, an innovation consulting firm based in Alexandria, Va.

7   Last year, according to Starwood management, programs developed under the famed management technique delivered more than $100 million in profit to its bottom line. As a result, the White Plains (N.Y.) company is one of the world's most profitable hotel

operators: Its net margin is nearly 15%, higher than those of rivals Hilton Hotels and Marriott International (MAR), as well as the industry average of 9%. "We have been driving our margin growth faster than our competitors," says Ballotti. "When people ask why, I point to Six Sigma."

8   The company's Six Sigma group is run by Brian Mayer, who claims the quirky title of vice-president of Six Sigma, Operation Innovation & Room Support. "I grew up in the hospitality industry," says Mayer, whose grandfather and father ran catering businesses. "The joke is that I was born in a chafing dish."

PARTNERING WITH STAFF

9   Since the program launched in 2001, Mayer's crew has trained 150 employees as "black belts" and more than 2,700 as "green belts" in the arts of Six Sigma. Based mostly at the hotels, the specialists are change agents who help dream up and oversee the development of projects. The key to their success is that instead of acting like muckety-mucks imposing their will from "corporate," the Six Sigma specialists operate more like partners who help the hotels to meet their own objectives, Mayer says. Indeed, almost 100% of the creative concepts come from in-house hotel staff. The Unwind program, for instance, was generated by the Westin group. And every project must be overseen by a hotel employee. "By focusing on their goals and budgets it enables us to become a partner in the operation," says Mayer.

10   The process begins when hotel teams pitch Mayer's group on a new idea. "It's competitive," says Mayer. "They fight for our resources." A Six Sigma council composed of Ballotti and his 13 direct reports, including his senior vice-president for operations and sales and marketing, then evaluates an idea's merit based on the division's priorities and the project's expected payoff. If the council approves a project, black belts and green belts are deployed like swat teams to the hotels to execute the project.

11   In the case of Unwind, one Chicago-based black belt and four in-house green belts gathered a group of leaders in January, 2005, from the Westin Chicago River North, including the directors of rooms, food and beverages, and sales, to brainstorm. Then the hotel's fitness director "came up and said, 'Why don't we do massage,'" says Peter Simoncelli, the hotel's general manager.

12   The team liked the idea and started to design the experience. First up was figuring out the logistics: getting the massage chairs, choosing the uniform of the masseuse, determining the best location of the massage table. In October, 2005, the hotel staged a dry run. The team quickly learned they had a problem: The guests wanted the complimentary massage to last longer than the hotel anticipated. "We had to come up with a diplomatic way of saying there is a limited amount of time in the massage chair," says Simoncelli. After completing the pilot in a few weeks, the Six Sigma team turned the project over to its hotel sponsor, in this case the director of rooms. Last year the hotel introduced the activity and found a nice surprise: Revenues from massages in the hotel spa jumped 30%.

REVIEWING RESULTS

13   After rolling out a prototype, green belts shift into analytical mode. At that point they spend a lot of time with the E-Tool, a proprietary Web-based system that allows Starwood to monitor a slew of performance metrics to gauge the success or failure of a new project. In the case of Unwind, the hotel kept close tabs on the massage revenue produced by each room. What's more, E-Tool enables hotel managers to rapidly spread and drive consistent execution of each project.

14   That's no easy task at Starwood, which owns, manages, or franchises 800 hotels, and rolls out new projects to its hotels every two weeks. Green belts enter every single project into the E-Tool, which currently contains 3,000 to 4,000 unique items. The entries are detailed and include photographs and descriptions of the projects as well as how-to instructions. The Unwind program alone produced 120 new features—one for each Westin hotel, including traditional fire dancing in Fiji and Chinese watercolor painting in Beijing. "I probably will make 50% fewer mistakes than if I had rolled out a project myself," says Simoncelli.

SAVINGS IN SAFETY AND ENERGY

15   One project made mandatory for all North American hotels was a workplace safety effort. Starwood launched the initiative in early 2004 after executives noticed that workers' compensation claims were skyrocketing. A Six Sigma team discovered that the biggest cause of accidents were slips and falls, and housekeepers often suffered from back strains and other overexertions. The team developed a series of work processes, including a stretching routine required for all housekeepers and new cleaning tools with longer handles. Then it began tracking the amount of claims and the frequency of claim types. Thanks to the new regimen, Starwood slashed its accident rate from 12 to 2 for every 200,000 work hours.

16   The latest effort is an initiative to drive down the company's energy costs. Starwood is currently hashing out an internal mandate to require compact fluorescent lightbulbs in 75% of its rooms. There was a lot of resistance from hotel staff who felt the new bulbs would not provide the same type of light. But a Six Sigma group gathered and set up a dozen rooms with different bulbs. "We had top leaders figuring out which one was best," says Ballotti. "The collective power of getting these folks together is just amazing."

Source: Reprinted with special permission from "Six Sigma Kick-Starts Starwood." *BusinessWeek,* August 30, 2007. Copyright © 2007 The McGraw-Hill Companies.

Case 22

BusinessWeek

Google's New Role: Venture Capitalist: *The Tech Giant's Startup Investments Are Narrowing Opportunities for VCs. Other Corporations Are Upping Their Venture Investing, Too*   Aaron Ricadela

1   Just as it has done to companies in the software, publishing, and advertising industries, Google is becoming a thorn in the side of venture capitalists. The owner of the world's largest Web search engine is scooping up young tech outfits for a relative pittance, giving itself first dibs on hot-growth technologies and in some cases boxing VC funds out of potential big-bang acquisitions and initial public offerings.

2   Google has begun making VC-style investments to the tune of about $500,000 or less in promising startups, often buying those companies afterward, according to partners at Silicon Valley VC firms who spoke on condition of anonymity. In an effort to keep spotting promising deals, Google has been hiring a stable of finance pros. And it has invested more than $1 million in a Mumbai-based investment firm called Seedfund to gain access to technology such as automatic translation software that could help spur growth in India.

3   "Google has easy money," says Pravin Gandhi, a managing partner at Seedfund, which also has raised some of its $15 million from Motorola and VC firm Mayfield Fund. So far, Seedfund has taken $500,000 to $750,000 stakes in four companies, including an online news site. On the horizon could be investments that help Google add specialized channels, such as information about autos, to its Web site or cultivate technology that can translate Web content from English into Indian languages, Gandhi says. "It's a somewhat less risky way to participate in the Indian growth story," he says.

BEATING VCs TO THE PUNCH

4   By staking startups, Google hopes to avoid paying the higher prices companies can fetch once they take funding from traditional VCs. It's possible that some of its investments are conditioned on Google having first-acquisition rights should a target opt to sell, some VCs speculate. Google didn't respond to calls requesting comment. Making investments in startups also can help Google use more of its $4.5 billion in cash to cultivate tools that complement existing products. Google recently started a program called Gadget Ventures to fund entrepreneurs who build online tools using Google's technology.

5   The zeal for dealmaking at Googleplex mirrors an increase in corporate venture investing to its highest level in years. "They're back, like the swallows returning to Capistrano," says Paul Maeder, a managing general partner at Highland Capital Partners. "We're in a wave now where corporate venturing is increasing again."

6   Companies that aren't full-time investors pumped $1.3 billion into 390 venture capital deals in the first half of 2007, up 30% from the $1 billion invested in about 350 deals a year earlier, according to an Aug. 30 report by PricewaterhouseCoopers and the National Venture Capital Assn. (NVCA), based on data from Thompson Financial. That's the most invested since 2001, just before the bottom fell out of the tech industry. The big spenders include Intel, which invested $112 million in U.S. startups in the first half of 2007, vs. $79 million a year earlier, and Motorola, which invested nearly $30 million in the first half of the year and says its overall 2007 investments should top the record set in 2006.

VCs SEEK ALTERNATIVE SOURCES

7 The incursions don't sit well with many VCs. Combined with the predilection on the part of many entrepreneurs to fund their own ventures, investments by Google and other corporations leave even fewer opportunities for VCs to take big, early stakes. That's especially problematic when venture firms have raised record amounts of cash and need to find places to invest it.

8 "There are a lot of entrepreneurs who aren't making the trip to Sand Hill Road," says Ray Rothrock, managing general partner at Venrock Associates, referring to the Menlo Park (Calif.) thoroughfare that is home to many venture capital firms. "They're going else-where." Venrock, which funds Web startups including women's blogging site BlogHer and search engine ZoomInfo, is considering launching a startup incubator as a way to counter corporations' ability to buy the same companies it wants to fund.

9 A partner at another large VC firm says a tendency by corporate venture arms to buy startups not long after investing in them is "very inconsistent with the venture com-munity's strategy" of providing guidance and making several rounds of investments over the long haul.

WIDESPREAD CORPORATE STAKES

10 Among the reasons for the corporate-investing comeback: an upswing in research-and-development spending after the tech-stock crash; the need to spot promising startups in China, India, and Russia; and increased shareholder willingness to tolerate the quarterly vicissitudes of venture investing in order to create long-term value. Venture investments by pharmaceutical companies to fill their drug-development pipelines also helped boost the first-half numbers, according to the NVCA—Novartis and Johnson & Johnson were among the biggest U.S. investors.

11 In the tech sector, Intel Capital invested $236 million worldwide through the first half, 62% of that overseas. Among its winning investments was a $218.5 million stake in virtu-alization software company VMware, now worth triple that amount after VMware's block-buster Aug. 14 IPO. In 2006, Intel took a $600 million stake in Craig McCaw's Clearwire, which is building a long-range WiMAX network.

12 Intel has restructured its fund to emphasize financial returns and is investing in follow-up rounds in its portfolio companies—something it didn't do before. "There's no strategic value unless each individual investment is successful," says Intel Capital President Arvind Sodhani. "A bankrupt company is not very strategically valuable to Intel—or to anybody for that matter."

NOTHING VENTURED, NOTHING GAINED

13 Cisco Systems too, is parking more venture money in emerging markets. In 2005 the maker of computer-networking gear earmarked $100 million for investment in Indian startups, and since December, 2006, it has opened funds to invest in China and Russia. Closer to home, Cisco took a $150 million stake in VMware. The company averages 15 to 20 investments a year, a spokesman says.

14 In the wireless sector, Motorola Ventures invests about $100 million a year worldwide. Key 2007 deals include Vocel, which makes software for marketing ringtones and mobile applications, and VidSys, which provides video-surveillance technology to the military. And cell-phone chipmaker Qualcomm has been investing in startups that provide TV and payment services for mobile phones.

15   Even Yahoo! is turning its attention to nurturing startups—both inside and outside its walls. The company has set up an in-house incubator called Brickhouse in downtown San Francisco, and in May, Yahoo! hired noted dealmaker Blake Jorgensen as its chief financial officer, signaling an increased willingness to make acquisitions.

RETURNING TO THE FRAY

16   Corporate venturing can be risky. Amid the tech market crash, longtime investors such as Intel booked big investment losses, and some companies, including Dell and Boeing, exited the venture business entirely. "They got burned after the bubble, probably even more than the traditional VCs," says Mark Heesen, president of the NVCA. Other companies, such as Microsoft, IBM, and Hewlett-Packard, scaled way back. Microsoft and HP still make selective startup investments, though not through formal programs. IBM has stopped taking equity stakes entirely, though it works with VCs to strike technology deals with young companies that can help it generate revenue or spot acquisition targets, says Claudia Fan Munce, managing director of IBM's venture capital group.

17   Now the question is whether corporate investors and VCs can shepherd their investments to acquisitions or IPOs after a summer in which stock and credit markets took a beating. "Tech has been down for so long," says the NVCA's Heesen. "Now people are saying: 'Everything else is so bad, maybe tech is a good place to be.'"

18   Google and other corporate venture investors are betting that's true—and they're treading on VCs' turf to make sure they claim some prime acreage.

Source: Reprinted with special permission from "Google's New Role: Venture Capitalist," *BusinessWeek*, September 4, 2007. Copyright © 2007 The McGraw-Hill Companies.

Case 23

BusinessWeek

A Red-Hot Big Blue in India: *From Inking Deals to Hiring the Best Workers, IBM Is Leading Its Tech Services Rivals*

1   Just a few years ago, IBM looked stodgy compared with agile Indian tech players such as Infosys, Wipro, and Tata Consultancy Services. But today, Big Blue has become the leader in the Indian tech services industry, with 10% of the domestic market. Its Indian workforce has more than doubled in two years, to 53,000—about 15% of its worldwide total—and Bangalore and New Delhi are now home to IBM's largest research and development labs outside of the U.S.

2   Since inking a $750 million, 10-year agreement with leading cellular carrier Bharti Airtel Ltd. in 2004, IBM has been racking up deals in India faster than any of its local competitors. In the first half of 2007 alone, it signed some $1.4 billion in long-term contracts. Says Bharti's innovation director, Jay Menon, a former IBMer who now sits on Big Blue's advisory board: "India is the jewel in IBM's global crown."

3   Indeed, the company is so well entrenched in the subcontinent that in 2006, Chief Executive Samuel J. Palmisano was voted "IT leader of the year" by Nasscom, India's software industry association. And local heavyweights view IBM as a formidable competitor, as it has signed up a roster of blue-chip clients such as real estate developer DLF, state-run Canara Bank, and the Indian tax department. "IBM has really understood what India is all about," says Nasscom President Kiran Karnik.

The Stat

53,000

IBM's employees in India, up from 23,000 in 2004 and just 400 in 1995

Source: IBM

4   At the same time, the company has worked hard to integrate India into its worldwide operations. That has allowed IBM to eliminate 20,000 jobs in high-cost markets such as the U.S., Europe, and Japan. The success of this strategy was confirmed this summer when IBM reported second-quarter revenues were up 9%, to $23.8 billion—powered in part by a 10% increase at its IT services group, which suffered mightily at the hands of its Indian rivals in the early part of this decade.

5   IBM hasn't been shy about plowing big bucks into India. Instead of creating a tech services operation from scratch there, which could have taken years, it snapped up call-center operator Daksh for $150 million in 2004; the outfit now handles back-office operations for the likes of Sprint and Dun & Bradstreet. Since then, IBM has spent another $2 billion in India building new facilities and hiring thousands.

6   Research is also a big part of the equation. IBM has set up R&D centers staffed by 3,000 engineers in India, which have become a source of innovation on everything from software to semiconductors to supercomputers. One team, for instance, developed a Web-based program that analyzes a person's accent, grammar, and vocabulary, which is used to evaluate applicants for jobs at IBM's call center operations, and the company says it could be deployed more widely to test language fluency.

7   IBM's rapid expansion in India has turned up the heat in the competition for skilled workers. Big Blue added some 10,000 employees to its India payroll last year—compared with 25,000 for all of the Indian players combined. In Pune, a rapidly developing IT center near

Mumbai, the company has been dispatching vans with signs saying "IBM is hiring" to the gates of rivals at lunch time. "Their hit rate is pretty good," laments a manager at a tech firm that has lost employees to IBM.

8   The company's success is spurring Indian rivals to look for more opportunities in their own backyard after years of focusing on customers overseas. Infosys, for instance, says it will now start bidding for Indian deals, something it hasn't done in the past. "IBM has created a market. Now they will find they will have to share," says Gaurav Gupta, who heads the India business at Everest Group, a tech advisory firm in Bangalore. The folks at IBM are unfazed. "Competition is welcome," says Shanker Annaswamy, IBM's India chief. "No one has the depth we do." And, IBM is doing it in India and in its global, radical collaboration.

Source: Reprinted with special permission from "A Red-Hot Big Blue in India." *BusinessWeek,* September 3, 2007. Copyright © 2007 The McGraw-Hill Companies.

Case 24   BusinessWeek

Radical Collaboration IBM Style

1   By late 2003, IBM's decision three years earlier to pump $5 billion into its chip business wasn't looking so smart. The division had lost more than $1 billion in 2002 and was on its way to losing $252 million more in 2003. Investors urged Big Blue to quit, but that wasn't going to happen. IBM saw leading-edge chip technology as vital to keeping its lead in the highly profitable business of making powerful server computers. Still, clearly, something had to be done.

2   That's why John Kelly, who then ran the semiconductor division, summoned 10 executives to IBM's chip factory in East Fishkill, N.Y. Kelly argued it was time for a new strategy. IBM needed to share its most advanced semiconductor research with a few key allies. The tech giant already had a handful of alliances aimed at improving manufacturing and chip design. Several partners had come forward asking for deeper relationships, including collaboration with scientists working for IBM Research. Kelly expected pushback from his people, and he got it. "It was a real struggle. We had never thrown our doors open before," recalls Bernard Meyerson, who then ran research and development for the chip division and now manages alliances. "We could all envision nightmare scenarios of a decade of research value being lost."

3   After two hours of heated debate, Kelly prevailed. Since then, IBM has built what it calls an "open ecosystem" of chip R&D with nine partners, including Advanced Micro Devices, Sony, Toshiba, Freescale Semiconductor, and Albany Nanontech, a university research center. All told, in five separate alliances, IBM partners have contributed more than $1 billion to help expand the company's facilities and buy the latest chipmaking equipment. But just as important, they're providing brainpower, including more than 250 scientists and engineers who now work in East Fishkill. As a result, IBM's chip operation boomed, and, even now, during a cyclical downturn in the chip industry, it's still making a profit.

4   IBM is reinventing the way it innovates. At one time the tech giant was a true believer in go-it-alone R&D. The feeling was that if a technology wasn't invented by IBMers, it wasn't as good. Now the computer pioneer realizes that no matter how big an organization is, more smart people are going to work outside its walls than inside. So it courts R&D partners aggressively. "We are the most innovative when we collaborate," declares Chief Executive Samuel J. Palmisano.

IN AN ERA OF FIERCE COMPETITION, IT PAYS TO INNOVATE COMMUNALLY

5   IBM's decision to invite in outsiders and open up the innovation process reflects one of the most intriguing concepts in corporate strategy today. Many major companies have concluded that succeeding in the 21st century requires teaming up with other companies—or even individual researchers—to create so-called innovation networks. "These networks allow companies to seamlessly weave internal and external innovation capabilities to optimize profits and speed products to market," says Navi Radjou, an analyst with Forrester Research.

6   Companies no longer compete simply against one another. Now alliances devoted to innovation go head-to-head. bt Group, basf, Boeing, Eli Lilly, Procter & Gamble, and IBM are the pioneers. They all have revamped their strategies to expand collaboration with

outsiders. Forrester estimates that while most major companies are aware of innovation networking, only about 20% to 30% are experimenting with it, and a mere 5% have mastered the practice.

FORGET THE COOKIE CUTTER. GET OUT THE CHAINSAW

7   There's no one-size-fits-all approach to collaborative innovation. What works best overall, strategy consultants say, is to think radically.

8   Some companies turn suppliers of goods and services into something much more valuable—sources of ideas about how to design a product and its components. Boeing, for instance, tapped a global network of suppliers to produce much of the detailed design work for its new 787 Dreamliner jet.

9   Other companies are busy prospecting for valuable new ideas from individuals and start-ups. Britain's bt placed scouts in India, China, and Silicon Valley to spot useful inventions and funnel them into its businesses.

10   Yet another approach: Bring together a handful of companies to sharpen their competitive edge together. Businesses have been doing that sort of thing for more than two decades, but the alliances are different now. Increasingly, they are global, not national. In 1987, hard-pressed U.S. chip companies set up a research consortium, sematech, to counter Japan's growing power in the chip industry. Today, sematech has two Japanese members. Another change: Scientists from different companies work more closely than ever, sharing ideas and intellectual property in ways their research forefathers would never have considered.

11   Some early results are in. Boeing cut 12 months off the time it took to bring the 787 Dreamliner to market. P&G improved its R&D productivity by 60% through its Connect + Develop program, where it links up with individual inventors from around the world. And at bt, teaming up with outsiders on innovation projects has spawned $1 billion in incremental sales for the telecom giant since 2002.

RUST BELT REBIRTH: IBM'S FACTORY OF THE FUTURE

12   Seven years ago, IBM's chip fabrication plant in New York's Hudson Valley was in mothballs. Today it's humming with activity. That's thanks in no small measure to the company's alliance strategy.

13   The 200,000-square-foot factory cost $4.4 billion to rehabilitate and expand. IBM shared the huge cost with its partners. "By ourselves, we'd have to bear expenses that are just enormous—and well beyond our appetite," says William Zeitler, general manager of the company's Systems & Technologies Group.

14   The shared investments buy a load of cutting-edge technology. In the vast plant, you feel like you have crossed into a world where robots are in charge. There are hundreds of giant chipmaking machines as large as locomotives. An automated overhead transport system carries stacks of silicon disks in picnic-cooler-size pods. The pods, lowered on cables, feed the disks into machines that will move them through each step of the assembly process. Within the machines, robotic hands pass the disks from one workstation to the next, where the surfaces are etched, coated with chemicals, or baked. Each disk typically holds 500 to 1,000 chips.

15   And the humans? They're crawling all over the place, dressed in cloth "bunny suits" that keep dust off the disks. Although the chipmaking is highly automated, it's hard to get it right: Engineers and R&D scientists constantly monitor every step in the process and make adjustments or experiment to increase the number of usable chips on each disk.

16   In most chip plants, those who aren't employees typically wear different-colored bunny suits to distinguish them. Not so in East Fishkill. All the scientists and engineers—2,000 IBMers and hundreds more who work for partners—wear the same white outfits. They work together without regard to who issues their paycheck. Sometimes an IBM worker leads a team; other times it's somebody from AMD or Freescale. "We don't work in silos," says John Pellerin, the top AMD manager at the plant. "We're a fully cross-mixed team."

SHRINKING CHIPS. SOARING COSTS. AN INDUSTRY LEARNS TO SHARE AND SAVE

17   In a business where new fabrication plants and advanced research are frightfully expensive, collaboration is nearly a necessity. Only Intel and a handful of other giants can afford to go it largely alone.

18   How expensive is chipmaking? A new factory costs $4 billion or more over two years. Then there's the research into designs, materials, and chipmaking processes needed for a company to remain competitive. R&D costs have been rising at an average of 12% per year while revenues for the industry are growing at just 6%. "The cost of research is kicking them," says Dan Hutcheson, CEO of vlsi Research. Collaboration saves billions. All told, Hutcheson estimates the members of IBM's chip alliances have saved $2 billion to $4 billion on research costs by throwing in together. Market research outfit In-Stat estimates the group will save an additional $7 billion over the next three years.

INNOVATION NETWORKS CAN BE TOUGH TO MANAGE

19   If the benefits of collaborative innovation are easy to spot, so are the pitfalls. Think how hard it is to get people in a single corporation on the same page. Now multiply that by a factor of three or five. Who's in charge? Who owns the innovations? "The complications are always going to be about control and the danger of goals diverging," says Laura Tyson, professor of economics and business at the Haas School of Business at the University of California at Berkeley. "The other big issue is the intellectual property that you create in common. Later, if you break up, you have to be prepared to work through the divorce."

20   Experts say the secret to successful alliances is agreeing on common goals and setting rules of engagement from the start. Then the partners should set up procedures for day-to-day interactions, including spelling out what can be discussed by people from different companies and what's strictly off limits.

21   Just because a company weaves partners into its operations doesn't mean it won't have to change the way it operates. Once P&G CEO A. G. Lafley set a goal of going outside to find half of all innovations, the people he put in charge realized they would have to set up an external department to cherry-pick innovations and bring them into P&G. An in-house team of more than 200 now sizes up more than 2,500 innovations a year. "You have to set up an internal structure so you can digest all this stuff," says Larry Huston of strategy consultancy 4inno, who formerly managed P&G's external innovation programs.

22   In some cases, to avoid conflicts companies target fundamental research they're willing to share, even with rivals. This approach is starting to catch on in the pharmaceutical industry. Lilly and other drugmakers have teamed up to identify "biomarkers," substances that indicate the presence of a disease. With that research in hand, each can separately develop drugs to combat the diseases.

23   Innovation networks do sometimes fail, most often because companies' interests diverge. That's what happened earlier this year when the three partners in the Crolles2 chip research

alliance went their own ways. Netherlands-based nxp Semiconductors was the first to quit, followed by Freescale and STMicroelectronics. The three companies' priorities became out of sync. Being partners "is like being roommates. If one comes in at 3 a.m. and another gets up at 7 a.m., it just doesn't work," says Andrea Cuomo, chief strategy officer for STMicro.

HOW IBM LEARNED TO MIX CULTURES AND MAKE OPEN INNOVATION PAY OFF

24   It's telling that when Crolles2 fell apart, STMicro and Freescale quickly turned around and joined IBM's alliances. Freescale, in fact, joined three of the five. The reason: The Austin (Tex.) company has seen IBM gradually hone its skills at managing such arrangements. "This is not IBM's first rodeo," says Freescale Vice-President Gregg Bartlett. "They have a lot of experience, and there won't be any surprises."

25   IBM's success is hard-won. Some of its earlier collaborations didn't go smoothly. In the 1990s, the Armonk (N.Y.) behemoth formed a venture to develop memory-chip technologies with Germany's Infineon Technologies and Japan's Toshiba, but their national and corporate cultures clashed. At one point, Toshiba engineers accused IBMers of withholding information from them. The problems got so bad that the companies sent 10 people each on a three-day team-building session.

26   Face-to-face with their differences, the engineers mapped out better ways to work together. At IBM, people typically reached decisions by discussing problems in open meetings. Toshiba's engineers preferred to see presentations, read reports, and make decisions later. IBM's dearth of reports made the Japanese engineers suspect they were being kept in the dark. The solution: assigning people to take notes on the meetings and issue reports later.

27   These days IBM managers are particularly sensitive to cultural issues. Mukesh Khare, a project manager, says that typically in group discussions, Toshiba engineers will say "yes" to signal they understand a proposal—not necessarily that they agree. Later, he'll circle back to them and find out what they really think.

28   Mutual respect is also key to making these link-ups succeed. When IBM, AMD, Sony, and Toshiba worked together on a semiconductor breakthrough called low-k, metal gate, which makes it possible to place circuits closer together on a chip, each company brought a particular expertise. AMD, for example, was adept at devising experiments to test the group's theories. "I used to have trepidation about these relationships, but not now," says IBM Fellow Dan Edelstein. "Their work was unassailable."

MOTTO FOR THE 21ST CENTURY: NETWORK OR DIE

29   Alain Kaloyeros isn't your typical college professor. The deeply tanned, 51-year-old physics professor at the University at Albany drives a Ferrari F430 F1 Spider with a 500 horsepower engine and a vanity plate that reads: Dr Nano. Readying for a *BusinessWeek* interview, he tore the tops off of 15 packets of Splenda and poured them into a 16-ounce cup of coffee. "I need sweetness in my life," Kaloyeros explained.

30   This high-octane prof is one of IBM's key partners in its chip research network. And he embodies two of the most important requirements of successful alliances: nerve and commitment.

31   In the late 1990s, Kaloyeros and IBM's John Kelly dreamed up a plan to make the Albany campus of the State University of New York a hotbed of semiconductor research. The pair relentlessly pursued their vision until they got the state and corporate funding

they wanted. Now, 10 years and $4.2 billion later, Albany Nanotech boasts a staff of 1,800 university and corporate scientists and is the most advanced university chip research complex in the world.

32   There, Big Blue and its partners gain access to the latest chipmaking equipment and design the processes that they'll use when those machines are installed in their own manufacturing plants. That gives them a head start on other companies that can't afford such early access. And it gives members of the alliance a chance to make up ground on Intel, which, thanks to its vast resources, is typically a year ahead in advancing to each successive generation of technology.

33   The hookup between IBM and New York State has been something of a high-wire act. Both sides ran into funding hurdles. Now the major investments have been made and the rewards are rolling in. For those who fought the funding wars, the formula for success is simple: Share the risk and stick to the vision. "John Kelly went back to IBM numerous times and said, 'This is going to happen.' He really stuck his neck out," says former New York Governor George Pataki, who backed the project. "Fortunately, the state came through."

34   IBM's alliances with the likes of Albany Nanotech, AMD, and Freescale have paid off just the way its leaders hoped. Now, the company is expanding its innovation ecosystem to include suppliers of chip materials, chemical companies, and chip-design software companies. "This is a model that will not only survive but will prosper," predicts Kelly, who is now director of IBM Research.

35   For pioneers such as Kelly and Kaloyeros, there's no turning back. For other R&D leaders, an open-innovation strategy is still new and risky. But as more companies embrace it, the pressure will be on the holdouts to reach across organizational borders in search of ideas and greater productivity. They can delay, but they could be left far behind if they don't play.

Case 25

BusinessWeek

Jack Daniel's International Strategy: *By Sticking to Its Homespun, Down-Home Story, the Tennessee Sour Mash Whiskey Has Increased Sales at Home and Abroad*

1   For Pok Rui Bin, 29, drinking Jack Daniel's Old No. 7 after 12-hour workdays in Beijing means mixing it with green tea. The advertising copywriter's cocktail of choice is just one of many regional recipes that Global Managing Director Mike Keyes is getting used to now that his brand is available in 135 countries. What appeals to Pok about the Tennessee whiskey, he says, is the smooth smoky flavor, "and how it's hand-crafted and all comes from this one special place . . . I love that American West stuff."

2   Allowances can be made for Pok's poor sense of direction, and for the green tea mixer, since he's never been to the U.S. But he has been to the Jack Daniel's Web site, which is translated into 14 languages. The lifting of trade barriers in several countries, a weakening U.S. dollar, and the spread of cocktail culture to cities such as Beijing, Sofia, Moscow, and New Delhi have been pushing the whiskey brand's export sales by double digits. And though several brands closely identified with America—like Marlboro, Starbucks, McDonald's, and American Express—have been lightning rods for anti-U.S. sentiment overseas, American whiskey has remained so immune that parent company Brown-Forman expects to sell more than 4.8 million cases abroad next year, marking the first time since its founding in 1866 that more Old No. 7 will be poured abroad than in the U.S.

OVERSEAS WHISKEY LOVERS

3   After losing favor and showing almost no growth in the 1980s and into the 90s, whiskey sales, especially of premium and superpremium whiskeys, have been steadily climbing in the U.S.—at the expense of cheaper brands and beer. The drinking tastes of Generations X and Y are proving to be different from those of baby boomers. And that trend is found abroad, too. In Moscow, for example, bar managers say that the younger nightclub set increasingly prefers American whiskey to vodka or the more familiar Scotch whisky.

4   Pavel Kamakin, bar manager of the Moscow nightclub 16 Tonn, hosted a Jack Daniel's birthday concert and party earlier this month as part of a promotion by the local distributor. Kamakin says Jack is a close second in popularity to Jameson Irish Whiskey. And, he adds, customers who plan to drink a lot like those brands for their smoothness over the "hotter" Scotch whisky and ubiquitous vodka. Jack Daniel's sales are up 41% from five years ago, to 45,000 cases.

5   In general, overseas markets have been good to all American whiskey. Fortune Brands' Jim Beam Kentucky Bourbon, Jack Daniel's nearest rival, saw global sales reach nearly 6 million cases, with 45% of that consumed abroad. Fortune's Maker's Mark premium bourbon has shown double-digit growth for 13 straight years, with a growing following outside the U.S. But Jack Daniel's is the first major brand to become a majority exporter.

A STRONG BRAND STORY

6   While a weak dollar has helped, overseas pricing still makes Jack Daniel's a premium pour, especially compared with local brands. A key growth feeder is "the consistency of the brand's story," as reflected in Jack Daniel's marketing of its small-town roots, says Allyson

Stewart-Allen, a director of International Marketing Partners, who studies international brand performance. That, says, Stewart-Allen, is also one of the reasons Jack Daniel's has ducked overseas backlash against brands that are overtly American: "Jack Daniel's is less likely to experience boycotting from overseas markets because of the way it has played on the values of craftsmanship and intimacy via its use of small-town America visuals, in other words, the heartland of the U.S."

7   Marketing Jack Daniel's abroad doesn't differ too much from within the U.S.—with one major consideration: just how much to focus on the 19th century Lynchburg (Tenn.) home and roots. In Britain, Jack Daniel's' second-largest market outside the U.S., the story of the small town—"population 361"—and images of 19th century hillbilly distillers in straw hats and overalls are familiar to all who ride the London underground, where the folksy storytelling ads have long occupied eyeballs waiting for trains. In China, though, where sales are up 125,000 cases per year, 45% higher than five years ago, ads feature the iconic black-and-white bottle, leaving the Lynchburg story to be discovered only in the marketing background—on displays at concerts or on the Web site. "Brits relish the handcrafted, small-town story, but a lot of the young and successful in China and India have moved in from the poorer countryside and don't see the rural imagery as aspirational," says Keyes.

8   It's all a matter of emphasis, but Lynchburg's homey roots play some role in every market. To make sure, Brown-Forman, unlike a lot of spirits marketers, contractually has the last word on ads in all world markets and generates all ads from its U.S. agency, Arnold Worldwide, in Boston. To drive home the brand strategy, Master Distiller Jimmy Bedford travels abroad around 100 days a year, educating new hires at distributors and in the bar trade about Jack Daniel's and American whiskey, going as far as to conduct tastings of Jack Daniel's with and without its signature charcoal filtering.

9   The brand's marketing strategy has been the same since 1957, a consistency that is practically unheard of in advertising circles. Even the TV ads use the simple black-and-white photos rather than moving pictures. And that global consistency has been helped in no small part by Ted Simmons, who has been working on Jack Daniel's ads since 1967. First at his own St. Louis ad agency, and now as a consultant to Arnold Worldwide, Simmons says he learned long ago to avoid putting customers or celebrities in Jack ads. "You don't want to hold a mirror up to people," says Simmons. That, he says, leaves the brand accessible to leather-clad bikers, as well as churchgoing schoolteachers, whether they are in St. Petersburg, Russia, or St. Petersburg, Fla. Both, he says, make up the brand's faithful in large numbers.

SHIFTING THE FOCUS

10   That's not to say there aren't experiments. One rare divergence from Simmons' advice came last year when parent company Brown-Forman tried for more hipness, running a TV ad in the U.S. showing young concertgoers getting backstage access by flashing a bottle of Jack Daniel's to the security guard. If successful, the ad idea could have been translated and exported to urban export markets where clubbing is popular and where Jack Daniel's frequently sponsors concerts. But the spot was short-lived. Keyes maintains that it was a successful campaign, but he nonetheless quickly reverted to the familiar positioning, featuring photographs of Lynchburg residents and distillery employees with a narrative that describes how small-town values can be tasted in Jack Daniel's—the "smooth sippin' Tennessee whiskey."

11   Still, images of 19th century hillbillies and limestone caves don't always resonate right away with today's twentysomething drinkers in the U.S. or abroad. But Simmons says they don't have to, because the campaign establishes uniqueness, compared with fashion-focused ads for other spirits brands or humor-laden beer campaigns. He recalls that Taiwanese

distributors in the early 1990s fought the rural Lynchburg positioning. But focus groups with young Taiwanese men showed that images depicting the purity of water from Tennessee's limestone geological shelf and charcoal filtering stayed in their heads, in part because of bad water quality in places where they had grown up. Today the limestone caves are still a fixture in Taiwanese ads. And though Taiwan is not a huge market, sales are up 21% from five years ago, to about 10,000 cases per year.

THE REAL McCOY

12   The value of being the genuine original is tough to overstate, says independent marketing and design consultant Dennis Keene of Los Angeles. "In a world of constantly changing marketing, consumers find comfort in brands that are consistent and honest, and associate those brands with anticipated experiences." What Jack Daniel's has, more than most brands, says Keene, "is a great sense of its own story . . . a story that people keep coming to, and coming back to." And the bottle's black-and-white label, unchanged since anyone can remember, says Keene, "evokes an almost small-batch craftsmanship that belies its enormous sales."

13   What's clear is that Jack Daniel's seeps into the culture more than most rival liquor brands and has the ability to translate the same message across international lines. Twenty-six percent of the 3.5 million visits to its Web site this year have come from outside the U.S., up from 20% in 2004. On MySpace, nearly 100,000 pages have references and testaments to Jack Daniel's, twice that for Absolut, 20 times that for Johnnie Walker, and five times that of Jim Beam. One reference is a video clip of John Belushi's "Bluto" character in the 1978 film *Animal House*, chugging a fifth of Jack Daniel's like it was iced tea. It's a familiar clip, even to Pok Rui Bin in China. Says Keyes, "Sometimes you just have to accept that the brand belongs to the consumer, and not us—and that's the case all over the world."

Case 26

BusinessWeek

Will Universal Music Take on iTunes? *Universal Chief Doug Morris Is Enlisting Other Big Music Players for a Service to Challenge the Jobs/ iTunes Juggernaut*

1 Relationships in the entertainment world can be famously fraught. And few are more so these days than the one between Steve Jobs and Universal Music chief Doug Morris. You may recall that Morris recently refused to re-up a multi-year contract to put his company's music on Apple's iTunes Music Store. That's because Jobs wouldn't ease his stringent terms, which limit how record companies can market their music.

2 Now, Morris is going on the offensive. The world's most powerful music executive aims to join forces with other record companies to launch an industry-owned subscription service. *BusinessWeek* has learned that Morris has already enlisted Sony BMG Music Entertainment as a potential partner and is talking to Warner Music Group. Together the three would control about 75% of the music sold in the U.S. Besides competing head-on with Apple Inc.'s music store, Morris and his allies hope to move digital music beyond the iPod-iTunes universe by nurturing the likes of Microsoft's Zune media player and Sony's PlayStation and by working with the wireless carriers. The service, which is one of several initiatives the music majors are considering to help reverse sliding sales, will be called Total Music. (Morris was unavailable for comment.)

3 This isn't only about Jobs; Morris badly needs to boost his business, and Apple is the one to beat. The iTunes store has grabbed about 70% of downloads in the U.S. And the iPod—well, what's left to say about that juggernaut? Plus, music companies have been here before. A few years ago they launched services with the aim of defeating Napster-style file-sharing—and failed miserably. And let's not forget that existing subscription services have signed up only a few million people, vs. hundreds of millions of iTunes software downloads.

4 While the details are in flux, insiders say Morris & Co. have an intriguing business model: get hardware makers or cell carriers to absorb the cost of a roughly $5-per-month subscription fee so consumers get a device with all-you-can-eat music that's essentially free. Music companies would collect the subscription fee, while hardware makers theoretically would move many more players. "Doug is doing the right thing taking on Steve Jobs," says ex-MCA Records Chairman Irving Azoff, whose Azoff Music Management Group represents the Eagles, Journey, Christina Aguilera, and others. "The artists are behind him."

5 Morris and Jobs were once the best of allies. When Jobs began pushing his idea for a simple-to-use download store in 2003, Morris backed him. Industry insiders say Jobs felt that Morris, unlike many other music executives, understood that they had to adapt or die. And in the years that followed, Apple and Universal moved in near lockstep.

6 But before long, Morris realized he and his fellow music executives had ceded too much control to Jobs. "We got rolled like a bunch of puppies," he said during a recent meeting, according to people who were there.

Hard Rocker
Morris is a music-industry pugilist. His greatest hits:

February 2005
Yanks music videos off AOL and Yahoo!, which then agree to pay royalties.

September 2006
Declares war on YouTube and MySpace for allegedly not blocking pirates. Later signs deal with YouTube; sues MySpace.

November 2006
Wins $1 for every Zune music player Microsoft sells (plus royalties).

July 2007
Upset with Apple's marketing restrictions, refuses to re-sign multi-year deal with iTunes.

August 2007
Begins selling unprotected music to Amazon.com, Best Buy, and others, but won't loosen copyright protection for iTunes.

And though Morris hasn't publicly blasted Jobs, his boss at Universal parent Vivendi is not nearly so hesitant. The split with record labels—Apple takes 29 cents of the 99 cents—"is indecent," Vivendi CEO Jean-Bernard Levy told reporters in September. "Our contracts give too good a share to Apple."

7   After unilaterally breaking off talks with Apple in July, Morris continued offering Universal's roster—Eminem, 50 Cent, U2, and other artists—to Apple, but on a month-to-month basis. That freed Universal to cut special deals with other vendors, such as cell carriers eager to generate revenues. AT&T is packaging ringtones and music videos of Universal artists and is expected to start selling downloaded tracks with videos soon.

8   That's not all: In August, Morris announced a five-month test with Wal-Mart, Google, and Best Buy. The three companies will sell music downloads that can be played on any device—a freedom not available to buyers of iTunes songs, most of which play only on Apple devices and software. Morris wants to see if the downloads, which won't have copy protection, will help cut into piracy and hike sales. And of course he won't be upset if iPod owners bypass iTunes.

9   With the Total Music service, Morris and his allies are trying to hit reset on how digital music is consumed. In essence, Morris & Co. are telling consumers that music is a utility to which they are entitled, like water or gas. Buy one of the Total Music devices, and you've got it all. Ironically, the plan takes Jobs' basic strategy—getting people to pay a few hundred bucks for a music player but a measly 99 cents for the music that gives it value—and pushes it to its extreme. After all, the Total Music subscriber pays only for the device—and never shells out a penny for the music. "You know that it's there, and it costs something," says one tech company executive who has seen Morris' presentation. "But you never write a check for it."

10   The big question is whether the makers of music players and phones can charge enough to cover the cost of baking in the subscription. Under one scenario industry insiders figure the cost per player would amount to about $90. They arrived at that number by assuming people hang on to a music player or phone for 18 months before upgrading. Eighteen times a $5 subscription fee equals $90. There is precedent here. When Microsoft was looking to launch a subscription service for Zune, Morris played hardball. He got the tech giant to fork over $1 for every player sold, plus royalties. Total Music would take that concept even further. "If the object is to wrest control of the market from Steve Jobs," says Gartner analyst Mike McGuire, "this is a credible way to try it."

11   Of course, Morris still needs Jobs. It's noteworthy that Universal has not pulled its music from iTunes—Morris simply can't afford to do that. Universal's earnings fell 25% in the first half. Jobs, of course, knows that and can afford to be magnanimous. "Doug's a very special guy," the Apple chief told *BusinessWeek*. "He's the last of the great music executives who came up through A&R. He's old school. I like him a lot."

Case 27

BusinessWeek

The Arab World Wants Its MTV: *U.S. Media Giant Viacom Aims to Deliver It, as Well as Nickelodeon, Comedy Central, and More*

1 Matthew Noujaim lives and breathes hip-hop. But the 19-year-old Beirut university student, who raps about "anything and everything, including the Arab cause" in English and Arabic, has struggled to get his music noticed. Although rap is hugely popular among Middle Eastern youth, it's still underground and largely ignored by the region's record labels, radio stations, and music television channels. "There's lots of good hip-hop made here that never gets played," Noujaim says. "No one's willing to promote local talent."

Sumner of Arabia Viacom chief Redstone has big plans for the Middle East

2 That's about to change. MTV Arabia, a new 24-hour free satellite channel, will begin broadcasting in Arabic across the Middle East on Nov. 16. The Viacom-owned network's flagship show, Hip HopNa ("my hip-hop"), will be co-hosted by Saudi rapper Qusai Khidr and Palestinian-American producer Farid Nassar, aka Fredwreck, who has worked with Snoop Dogg, 50 Cent, and other marquee names. The show will visit 10 cities across the Middle East in search of talent, giving would-be Arab rap stars an international platform. Noujaim won the show's first competition, and Fredwreck has produced one of his tracks. "This is a music genre that is bubbling underneath the surface here, and we want to claim it as our own," says Bhavneet Singh, head of emerging markets for MTV Networks International.

Television Launching MTV Arabia in November, with Nickelodeon to follow in 2008. Arabic Comedy Central under discussion.	**Digital** Planning to put MTV on the Net and on phones. Similar deals for Nickelodeon and other brands being considered.
Licensing Selling rights to use SpongeBob SquarePants, Dora the Explorer, and other Nick characters for toys and clothing.	**Hotels** Considering Nickelodeon-branded hotel in Dubai as part of a global relationship with Marriott.
Film Exploring Dubai-based production of Paramount titles and co-production deals for Arabic-language films.	**Theme parks** Planning Nickelodeon-branded section in Dubailand, the world's largest amusement park, set to open in 2011.

GLOBALIZATION A GO-GO

3 How will the likes of Justin Timberlake and Rihanna go down in a region that's not exactly brimming with goodwill toward Americans? Better than you might think. Middle Eastern youth may not agree with U.S. politics, but they can't get enough of Western music and fashion. "The myth about the Arab world is that people go to bed at night hating the U.S. and wake up hating Israel," says James Zogby, president of the Arab American Institute, a think tank in Washington. "But go to any mall in Saudi Arabia, and you'll see kids in jeans and baseball caps hanging out at Starbucks and McDonald's. Globalization is real."

4 For Viacom, MTV Arabia is just the beginning. The region is attractive because it's awash in petrodollars and two-thirds of the population is under 25. Viacom has signed a 10-year licensing deal between MTV Networks and Tecom Investments, controlled by Dubai's ruler. On Oct. 12, Viacom planned to announce another decade-long licensing deal with Tecom for children's channel Nickelodeon Arabia. That's set for the second half of 2008, and the

company reckons an Arabic version of Comedy Central won't be far behind. Also under discussion: Paramount Pictures productions in the region and licensing of Nick's characters for clothing, toys, and games. "The Middle East may be the world's most underappreciated growth story," says Viacom Chairman Sumner M. Redstone.

5   No wonder U.S. media giants are pouring in. NBC Universal in May struck a licensing deal for a $2.2 billion amusement park in Dubai. Days later, Viacom announced plans to create a Nickelodeon section in Dubailand, a $2.5 billion development in the emirate that aims to be the world's largest theme park when it opens in 2011. And in September, Warner Bros. Entertainment announced a multibillion-dollar deal in Abu Dhabi that includes film production, a Warner Bros. theme park and hotel, and a chain of cinemas.

6   The Westerners will face plenty of homegrown competition. More than 50 music TV channels broadcast in the region. The dominant player, Rotana, owned by Saudi Prince Al Waleed bin Talal, is also the Middle East's largest record label and has exclusive contracts with most top-selling pop and folk artists. But MTV is betting it will win viewers by offering an alternative. "No one in this market is going out and asking the viewers what they want," says Abdullatif Al Sayegh, CEO of Arab Media Group, the Tecom unit that runs the channel. "We're spending our time in malls and cafés talking to young people; we're not getting our ideas from watching TV."

7   MTV Arabia is the biggest test to date of the network's two-decade-old localization strategy. MTV's flagship music channel has seen its American TV ratings slip and has struggled online. Management believes the biggest growth will come overseas, and the network now pumps out a blend of international and local tunes from Russia to Indonesia to Pakistan. That has helped MTV and sister operations, such as VH1 and Nickelodeon, reach 508 million households in 161 countries. "This isn't going to be MTV U.S.," Bill Roedy, vice-chairman of MTV Networks, says of the latest offering. "It is Arabic MTV made by Arabs for Arabs."

8   That means it'll be pretty tame by American standards. At noon every Friday, Islam's holiest day, the channel will air an animated call to prayer. During peak family viewing hours from 8 to 11 p.m., shows will introduce audiences to acts from the West and from other emerging markets such as India and Pakistan. And there will be Arabic versions of popular MTV shows such as *Made*, which gives young people coaching in fields like cooking and film.

"EDGY AND FUN"

9   Later in the evening things will loosen up a bit. *Al Hara* ("the neighborhood") is an Arabic version of *Barrio 19*, a program that shows what young people do for fun. In the Middle East, that apparently includes dune-bashing (driving all-terrain vehicles over, and into, steep sand dunes) and water soccer, played in what looks like a vast inflatable kiddie pool. Says Rasha Al Emam, the 30-year-old Saudi woman who heads MTV Arabia's programming production: "The idea is to encourage kids to go out and do something edgy and fun instead of sitting around smoking a *shisha*," or waterpipe.

10   While plenty of U.S. and European videos will never make it into the line-up, others will be sanitized for the Arab audience. At MTV Arabia's offices, a vast warehouse in Dubai, editors from across the region pore over clips frame by frame to remove offensive content. Bad language? Bleep it out. Shots of kissing, revealing outfits à la Britney Spears, or people on a bed? Blur them, or insert some less racy bit of the video.

11   That'll be fine with Maram Alhabib. The 23-year-old Saudi studying special education at Jeddah's Dar Al Hekma University loves metal group Seether and American alternative band Three Doors Down, but she finds many music videos to be too provocative. "The Arab channels are boring, they all play the same music and a lot of the videos . . . are all

about seduction," she says. "If MTV focuses on music and issues Arabs care about, people will watch."

MTV's Bhavneet Singh talks about the challenges of launching MTV Arabia, and the iconic music channel's global strategy

The launch of MTV Arabia is the biggest test to date of a strategy pioneered by the network's international operations more than two decades ago. The iconic music channel may be struggling to keep audience share in the U.S., but international youth can't get enough of their MTV. The network's international operations are its fastest growing, thanks in large part to its local licensing strategy. In the past two years alone, the international division of the network has launched 22 new television channels through a dozen licensing deals. Local partners put up the bulk of the cash while the network gets sizable licensing fees and a share of all revenues. Bhavneet Singh, MTV's managing director for emerging markets, had this to say:

Why has MTV Networks International chosen to expand its global reach through licensing?

The licensing model works well in markets that are difficult to navigate due to either distinctive local cultures and/or regulatory issues. Financially, it's also an effective operating model, with lower risk and attractive returns through strong local partnerships. For us, it's really about tapping into a very capable local player to create a partnership where we're mutually vested in the success of the business. Our take on this model is unique. We invest a lot of resources and support from our global network to work alongside our local partners to ensure they realize all the benefits of our 20 years' experience in this business. By capitalizing on their local consumer and market understanding, as well as their existing infrastructures and talent, we're able to more quickly access markets with an operation that is much more in sync with local audiences and advertisers.

Your MTV partner in the Middle East, Arab Media Group (AMG), is a big media player in the region but has no experience in television. Why did you choose them?

We surprised a lot of people by picking AMG over a number of established, major TV players. What impressed us immediately was they didn't try to gloss over the gaps in their experience, and it didn't concern us too much because we had the TV expertise and they had a ton of other strengths. Most important to us was they demonstrated a deep understanding of the diverse consumers across the Middle East markets. A fundamental tenet of MTVNI's success has been: When you focus on your audiences, the business follows. We saw this was also key to AMG's DNA. The other critical factor: They had the capability and ambition to build a long-term partnership with us across many brands and lines of business, well beyond MTV Arabia. We're already working on the next ventures together.

What are other opportunities for MTV Networks brands in the Middle East region?

The growth trends in the region across all of our industries are some of the most attractive in the world. In fact, when I was closing the MTV deal with Tecom/AMG, our partner said, "This is only a fifth of what I want to do together," and I responded, "It's only a tenth of what I have in mind!" We've just announced plans to launch Nick Arabia in 2008, and earlier this year, we announced that Nick would be an anchor of a new theme park in Dubai. Talks are under way with various partners in digital media, consumer products, hotels, film, and other TV brands.

What is your digital strategy for MTV Arabia?

It's impossible to separate our digital strategies from our TV strategies. They're totally integrated, and we want to make our content accessible across any and all the platforms that matter to Arab youth. We're creating programming blocks where viewers determine via online and mobile what music videos and MTV shows they want to watch. Our Web site design is unlike any other MTV in the world, with an iPod-like interface that will make it easy for young people to blog, chat, and give us feedback. We're building a club where our members will get special access to events, concert promotions, and other one-of-a-kind MTV experiences like tickets to our big events around the world. Ultimately, we'll also have mobile TV channels and downloadable content for mobile and Internet. We're participating in a pilot program for DVB-H (digital video broadcast—handset), which will see mobile users watching broadcast-quality video content in 2008.

You're entering a market with more than 50 music channels. That's a crowded market. How will MTV be different?

We aren't positioning MTV as a music channel. We're a youth lifestyle platform, offering young people a place for self-expression in all aspects of their lives. We've done a lot of research, and we think this is the big gap in the market. Everything we do will reflect what young people are thinking, feeling and experiencing, and we want to empower and inspire them. Purely on the music front, we'll feature underground Arabic music genres like hip-hop, which is incredibly popular, but hasn't been embraced by mass media. And, we're going to play more international music because our audiences have told us they're missing that connection to the global music scene that only MTV can offer.

How difficult has it been to persuade Arab leaders to welcome MTV?

They've welcomed our plans and the most important reason is, the brand has been created by Arabs to reflect and respect Arabic cultural values. MTVN pioneered the local approach to building our brands worldwide, and that credibility mattered. Some had seen our Indian MTV, for example, and they appreciated how MTV was totally reinvented to reflect Indian sensibilities and music tastes. We also found that our vision to create an empowering and uplifting platform for Arab youth is totally in sync with the views of Arab leaders. The officials offered ideas and support for our pro-social platform, which will tap into our audiences' concerns about education and careers through empowering messages and initiatives.

Your businesses span many markets, including Central and Eastern Europe and Russia. What is different about doing business in the Middle East compared to the other regions?

Every region is different in its approach to business, and so is the Middle East. Personal relationships—and most important, one's word—mean more in the Middle East than in any other market. Building trust and understanding is a prerequisite to any deal, and that dynamic has helped my confidence in our choice of partners because we really know each other by the time a deal is done. As a result, the mobile phone rules! Nearly all of my business negotiations were conducted via text and phone conversations, rather than e-mail. It made life difficult for the lawyers, but as we do everywhere, we have to adapt to the way local markets operate.

Sources: Adapted by John Robinson and reprinted with special permission from "The Arab World Wants Its MTV," *BusinessWeek*, October 11, 2007 and "MTV Presses Play in the Middle East," *BusinessWeek*, October 22, 2007. Copyright © 2007 The McGraw-Hill Companies.

Case 28

Big Oil and Ethanol?

1   For some industries, the prospect of $3.5 billion in federal subsidies now, and double that in three years, might be a powerful incentive. But not, apparently, for the oil industry, which is seeing crude oil prices soar to record highs. Despite collecting billions for blending small amounts of ethanol with gas, oil companies seem determined to fight the spread of E85, a fuel that is 85% ethanol and 15% gas. Congress has set a target of displacing 15% of projected annual gasoline use with alternative fuels by 2017. Right now, wider availability of E85 is the likeliest way to get there.

2   At the same time the industry is collecting a 51 cents-per-gallon federal subsidy for each gallon of ethanol it mixes with gas and sells as E10 (10% ethanol and 90% gas), it's working against the E85 blend with tactics both overt and stealthy. Efforts range from funding studies that bash the spread of ethanol for driving up the price of corn, and therefore some food, to not supporting E85 pumps at gas stations. The tactics infuriate a growing chorus of critics, from the usual suspects—pro-ethanol consumer groups—to the unexpected: the oil industry's oft-time ally, the auto industry.

The Stat

$3.5
BILLION

Federal subsidies that go to oil refiners for mixing ethanol into gas—a number that should double by 2010

Data: *BusinessWeek*

3   The industry collects the subsidies, but didn't lobby for them— Congress created them to encourage a larger ethanol market. While oil reps say they aren't anti-ethanol, they are candid about disliking E85. Says Al Mannato of the American Petroleum Institute (API), the chief trade group for oil and natural-gas companies: "We think [ethanol] makes an effective additive to gasoline but that it doesn't work well as an alternative fuel. And we don't think the marketplace wants E85."

4   Those who criticize the industry's stance see it as reminiscent of its attempts to discredit the theory that human use of fossil fuels has caused global warming. Mark N. Cooper, research director at the Consumer Federation of America, authored a recent paper characterizing the situation as "Big Oil's war on ethanol." The industry, he writes, "reacted aggressively against the expansion of ethanol production, suggesting that it perceives the growth of biofuels as an independent, competitive threat to its market power in refining and gasoline marketing."

5   One prong in the oil industry's strategy is an anti-ethanol information campaign. In June the API released a study it commissioned from research firm Global Insight Inc. The report concludes that consumers will be "losers" in the runup to Congress' target of 35 billion gallons of biofuel by 2017 because, it forecasts, they'll pay $12 billion-plus a year more for food as corn prices rise to meet ethanol demand. The conclusions are far from universally accepted, but they have been picked up and promoted by anti-ethanol groups like the Coalition for Balanced Food & Fuel Policy, made up of the major beef, dairy, and poultry lobbies. Global Insight spokesman Jim Dorsey says the funding didn't influence the findings: "We don't have a dog in this hunt."

6   Academia plays a role as well. There is perhaps no one more hostile to ethanol than Tad W. Patzek, a geo-engineering professor at the University of California at Berkeley. A former Shell petroleum engineer, Patzek co-founded the UC Oil Consortium, which studies engineering methods for getting oil out of the ground. It counts BP, Chevron USA, Mobil USA, and Shell among its funders. A widely cited 2005 paper by Patzek and Cornell University professor David Pimentel concluded that ethanol takes 29% more energy to produce than it supplies—the most severe indictment of the biofuel. Michael Wang, vehicle and fuel-systems analyst at the Energy Dept.'s Argonne National Laboratory, says among several flaws in the study is the use of old data and the overestimation of corn farm energy use by 34%. Pimentel defends the study. In a recent update, he and Patzek hiked the estimate of ethanol's energy deficit to 43%.

7   A more moderate conclusion comes from a recent study by the University of California at Davis, which last year received a $25 million grant from Chevron to study biofuels. It said the energy used to produce ethanol is about even with what it generates and that cleaner emissions would be offset by the loss of pasture and rainforest to corn-growing. Only a small part of the research backed by the grant will involve ethanol, says Billy Sanders, UC Davis' research director. The primary focus will be developing alternative processes and feedstocks for biofuel that is not ethanol.

8   Infrastructure problems are behind much of the oil companies' resistance to E85. It adds "too much complexity and cost," says Shell spokesperson Anne Bryan Peebles, since it requires separate pumps, trucks, and storage tanks. Any mix with more than 10% ethanol may cause corrosion and other problems in existing pipelines.

9   That inconvenient truth is one reason oil companies aren't rushing to install E85 pumps. Of the 179,000 pumps at U.S. gas stations, only about 1,000 pump E85. Almost none are at oil-company-owned stations. And if an independent station that operates under, say, the Exxon or Shell brand wants one, it can cost around $200,000 to install a separate pump when all the gas suppliers' restrictions are met. Exxon Mobil Corp. bars branded independents from buying fuel from anyone but Exxon, though it let a handful install E85 pumps for test marketing—as separate machines on separate islands nowhere near Exxon or Mobil signs. ConocoPhillips has a similar policy. But switching existing tanks and pumps to E85 is the cheapest way to offer it, with more than 50% of costs often offset by various subsidies. Mannato says companies want to prevent consumers who don't have flex-fuel vehicles, which run on either gas or E85, from gassing up with E85. Also, they "don't want their brand associated with someone else's product."

A FACE-OFF WITH DETROIT

10   The industry's stance angers carmakers, which have more than 5 million flex-fuel vehicles on the road. General Motors, Ford, and Chrysler all pledge that half of new-vehicle sales should be flex fuel by 2012 but are waiting for bigger commitments to E85 pumps. "Big Oil is at the top of the list for blocking the spread of ethanol acceptance by consumers and the marketplace," says Loren Beard, senior manager for energy planning and policy at Chrysler, referring to the struggle to get E85 pumps installed.

11   The API says its pilot programs show that many consumers fill up once, and not again, after they experience the 25% loss in fuel economy that comes with E85. Some states near ethanol plants, like Indiana, sell E85 as much as 33% cheaper than gas; in others, like New York, E85 costs more than gas.

12   As tension grows between Big Oil and its critics, ethanol production will keep rising. That may pressure oil companies to accept E85. The industry can absorb almost all the 15 billion gallons projected for production by 2012 in the form of E10. After that, without more E85 pumps, there'll be a lot more ethanol on the market than drivers can find to put in their tanks.

Source: Adapted by John Robinson and reprinted with special permission from "Big Oil's Stall on Ethanol," *BusinessWeek*, October 10, 2007. Copyright © 2007 The McGraw-Hill Companies.

Case 29

BusinessWeek

Exxon vs. ConocoPhillips on Going Green: *Rex Tillerson Has Been Portrayed as a Kinder, Gentler CEO. But He Shares His Predecessor's Doubts on the Viability of Alternative Energy*

1   Former President Bush said the nation is addicted to oil. Detroit is rolling out hybrid vehicles. Across the Midwest, farmers are tilling soil to build ethanol plants. But the head of the world's largest energy company isn't jumping on the green bandwagon. "I'm not an expert on biofuels," says Rex Tillerson, the chairman and chief executive of Exxon Mobil. "I'm not an expert in biofuels. I'm not an expert in farming. I don't have much technology to add to moonshine."

2   Tillerson's comments came as part of the opening address at CERAWeek, the annual energy conference sponsored by Cambridge Energy Research Associates, a division of consulting firm IHS. Since the demise of a conference sponsored by the now-defunct accounting firm Arthur Andersen seven years ago, CERAWeek has become the leading confab for energy industry movers and shakers. A record 2,000 attendees packed conference rooms at Houston's Westin Galleria Hotel, turning the city into a kind of Davos on the bayou. The event also featured speeches by Energy Secretary Samuel Bodman and Toyota Motor North America chief Jim Press.

A SKEPTICAL CEO

3   It's Tillerson's remarks that are likely to fuel the most attention. Tillerson, a tall Texan with a baritone voice just this side of John Wayne's, is a long time Exxon exec who took over from the legendary Lee Raymond a little more than a year ago. While Raymond's prickly demeanor and critical comments about global warming studies made Exxon unpopular with many activists, Tillerson has been portrayed as a kinder, gentler CEO. Yet Tillerson made it clear that he shares his predecessor's skepticism about the contribution of fossil fuels to global warming and the opportunity that lies in alternative energy technologies. "We need to remain realistic about the role they can play," he said. "We're not just going to grow crops and solve our energy problems."

4   At a press conference after his address, Tillerson was asked about the report released two weeks ago in Paris by the United Nations Intergovernmental Panel on Climate Change, a consortium of scientists that concluded burning fossil fuels was causing global warming. He said he hadn't read the report, but as he understood it, there is still plenty of uncertainty about what the best course of action is. "There's clearly a change in the climate," Tillerson said. "It's getting warmer. How that all interrelates with industrial activity is not 100% clear."

5   Tillerson indicated that he thinks it's best to avoid piecemeal policies such as caps on carbon emissions or windfall profits taxes that could harm the economy or impede oil production down the road. "It may make people feel better, feel like they're doing something," he said.

SUPPLY CONCERNS

6   In his address at the conference, he said, "Many policymakers think in increments of two, four, or six years, based on election cycles. In contrast, those of us in the energy industry think in increments of two, four, or six decades, based on timelines to gain access to new

acreage, explore for, discover, and bring to production the next sources of supply. This is an important point, because acting impulsively in setting energy policy with the expectation of immediate results will likely have negative consequences that will be felt for decades to come. We must therefore inform the public and policymakers about the long time-frames that define our industry."

7   To prove his point, Tillerson gave the example of Sakhalin-1, a massive oil and natural gas development in Russia that he helped develop as he climbed the corporate ladder. The fields, he noted, were first discovered in the 1970s. It took three decades for the confluence of technology, prices, and political negotiations to bring the project, which started up in October, to the point where it is now producing 250,000 barrels of oil per day. "The problem is the public doesn't see our product as being a result of technological innovation like they do a cell phone or satellite TV."

FOCUSING ON TECHNOLOGY

8   Tillerson said he is trying to make Exxon greener. He said changes at company facilities around the world have helped cut Exxon's carbon dioxide emissions by 11 million tons, the equivalent of taking 2 million cars off the road. Tillerson said he's avoiding investing in ethanol plants, because barriers to entry are low, and the industry seems to have no trouble attracting money from venture capital firms and other investors. Instead, Exxon is working with climate-change researchers at Stanford University to come up with new, more complex forms of biofuels, including ethanol made from plants other than corn. There, Exxon can add value through technology breakthroughs, he said.

9   Asked at the press conference following his speech if he thought energy trading and the money pouring into commodity funds in recent years were having an impact on the price of oil, Tillerson said they were. "I'm always shocked when I hear pension funds are moving into commodities," he said. Tillerson said he figured the "risk premium" associated with trading added between $10 and $15 dollars to the price of a barrel, which should be more like $40 today.

10   Tillerson said Exxon has spent $210 billion since 1991 on exploring and developing oil fields around the world. That was more than the company earned during the period. In spite of today's high prices, he said the company was maintaining its discipline and making sure projects pencil out even at prices much lower than the present. "In times like these we make a lot of money," he said. "But these times don't last forever and in order to make it through the cycle we have to make sure the investments make sense."

CEO Mulva Says the Oil Company is Taking Its Role in Global Warming Seriously and Plans to be More Proactive

CONOCOPHILLIPS' OWN INCONVENIENT TRUTH

11   James Mulva says he's recognizing an inconvenient truth. The chairman and chief executive of ConocoPhillips, the nation's third-largest oil company, acknowledged this month that fossil fuels—his company's core product—are permanently warming the Earth. "The science has become quite compelling," Mulva said in an interview with *BusinessWeek.com.* "We've been studying this for quite a number of years. That is happening."

12   Energy executives, of course, have taken mixed positions on the climate change debate. Exxon Mobil has long been one of the most outspoken skeptics on global warming. Although the position has softened somewhat recently, Chairman and CEO Rex Tillerson

told an industry gathering that he still doubted burning fossil fuels were causing polar ice caps to melt and temperatures to rise.

LEARNING EXPERIENCE

13   BP Group Chief Executive John Browne may be at the other extreme. The company recently unveiled a "green" gas station in Los Angeles with solar panels and low-flush toilets, and Browne has long said that oil companies need to look "beyond petroleum" for solutions to environmental concerns. "It would be unwise and potentially dangerous to ignore the mounting concern," he said back in 1997.

14   Mulva's global warming announcement came amid a flurry of environmental initiatives at the Houston-based company. On Apr. 10, ConocoPhillips pledged $22 million to help Iowa State University develop fuels out of corn and switchgrass. Six days later the company unveiled a joint venture with Tyson Foods to produce diesel fuel out of animal fat. Mulva says that venture will operate on a break-even basis and only then as a result of a $1-a-gallon federal subsidy.

15   The 175 million gallons per year of production is a drop in the bucket compared to the 375 million gallons of gasoline Americans consume every day. Still, Mulva says he hopes the project will be a learning experience leading to other alternative fuel initiatives down the road.

SELF-SERVING PRAGMATISM?

16   To die-hard environmentalists there is something self-serving in oil companies jumping on the green wagon. Are they truly trying to save the planet or merely attempting to ward off environmental legislation that could cost them money and reduce gasoline consumption? "We appreciate their corporate citizenship, but is there something we're not seeing here?" asks Tyson Slocum, director of the energy program at the consumer group Public Citizen. "They want to maximize the benefits for their industries and shareholders. With that you don't get very effective environmental policy."

17   Mulva acknowledges there is an element of pragmatism in his approach. While applauding states such as California that have passed their own requirements to reduce greenhouse gas emissions, Mulva says he'd prefer a national approach that balances environmental concerns with economic ones. Mulva was short on specific policy recommendations, but he did indicate he might embrace a carbon trading system that would give companies the flexibility to meet emissions caps by purchasing credits from greener producers.

ADAPTATION

18   Mulva did have a specific recommendation on the subject of ethanol, the fuel typically made from corn that burns cleaner than gasoline and is used as a smog-reducing additive in many parts of the country. Environmental activists have talked up the prospects of producing much more corn-based ethanol and adopting as a primary fuel something called E85, a blend of 85% ethanol and 15% gasoline. But Mulva said that rather than try to install an entirely new system of pumps and trucks for distributing E85, the industry would do better with a more gradual approach. While now there's usually not more than 5% ethanol used at gas stations across the country, there could be a shift toward a fuel blend that was 10% ethanol across the board. "That's about 15 to 16 billion gallons, which is about the maximum that can be made from corn production," he said. "All of our current vehicles could use it."

19   Mulva, 60, worked his way through the ranks of Phillips Petroleum, which merged with Conoco in 2002. He says he can remember the dark days of 1986, when to fight off corporate raids from T. Boone Pickens and Carl Icahn, Phillips had to buy back half its stock. It took on $9 billion in debt, a huge burden for a company with a stock market value of just $3 billion. Then oil prices collapsed, from $27 a barrel to $10, after a big production increase from Saudi Arabia. "We learned how to adapt," Mulva says.

Sources: Adapted by John Robinson and reprinted with special permission from "Big Oil's Stall on Ethanol," *BusinessWeek,* October 10, 2007, "Exxon's Boss is Cool on Green Policies," *BusinessWeek,* February 14, 2007, and "ConocoPhillips' Own Inconvenient Truth," April 19, 2007. Copyright © 2007 The McGraw-Hill Companies.

Case 30

German Companies Hop on Green Bandwagon: *In the Name of Higher Profits, Powerful Investors Such as Global Banks Are Driving the Adoption of Eco-friendly Business Practices*

1   In the name of increasing profits, of all things, more and more German companies are discovering climate protection. With increasingly stringent emissions laws and energy prices higher than they've been in years, sustainability has suddenly become a factor in economic growth. But can the new trend last?

2   Environmentalists usually devote most of their attention to such garden-variety endangered species as the brooding corncrake. But Winfried Häser, an environmental strategist with Germany's postal service, Deutsche Post, focuses his attention on another, equally sensitive species: the pin-striped financial analyst.

3   Häser regularly meets with the professional financial investors of international banks like Credit Agricole and HSBC to tell them about all the things his Bonn-based, internationally active logistics organization is doing for the environment. Once they've heard Häser's presentation, the investors usually fire back with questions about Deutsche Post's progress on reducing its CO_2 emissions and how many of the company's 130,000 vehicles are already running on biofuels. The financial world suddenly has a burning interest in the answers to these and other questions about preserving the environment.

4   This is quite a sea change. In the past, no more than a handful of concerned shareholders would demand answers to their questions about the environment at annual company meetings. Critics of poor corporate environmental records were usually minor shareholders—the kinds of troublemakers financial executives and CEOs rarely took seriously.

5   But nowadays the people asking the environmentally tough questions often control investments that run into the billions. They work for banks and mutual funds, and they look for attractive investment opportunities for the capital they manage.

CRISIS-PROOF PROFITS

6   Far from being driven by some noble-minded aim of saving the world, these masters of our money are mainly looking for one thing: profit, and as crisis-proof as possible.

7   This new environmental interest among powerful investors is probably the most salient indication of the important role climate change and its consequences now play in the economy. The issue has made it into the corner offices of top executives, and not just in companies already known for their support of environmental issues, such as German mail-order giant Otto and baby food manufacturer Hipp.

8   Companies in all sectors of the economy are suddenly examining their businesses to determine how sustainable and environmentally conscious they are in fact doing business. They are not doing this out of pure altruism. Instead, companies find themselves forced to adjust to new realities, including stricter environmental laws and the ever-rising cost of coal, natural gas, oil and electricity. In the process, some are even discovering ways to develop entirely new businesses.

9   Climate protection is becoming an important competitive factor. For this reason, companies are looking for strategies on how to address the issue in the future.

10   Major German corporations like Allianz, Deutsche Telekom, Bayer and BASF are establishing concrete goals, expressed in tons, for reducing their CO_2 emissions. They are

establishing sustainability departments and issuing mandatory environmental guidelines. They are forming new industry associations like the 2 Degree Initiative, which has set itself the goal of limiting global warming to a temperature increase of no more than 2 degrees Celsius (3.6 degrees Fahrenheit) compared to the pre-industrial age.

11   Meanwhile, they are making sure that the public is well aware of their efforts. Some companies have already launched ad campaigns to hype their efforts to preserve the environment, almost as if they were no longer in the business of producing cars or building power plants, but were suddenly intent on generating cleaner air. Or could it be that it's all nothing but hot air?

12   DaimlerChrysler touts its tiny Smart car as a "CO_2 Champion," all the while raking in most of its revenues with larger vehicles, many of which emit three times as much carbon dioxide as the Smart. German energy utility company RWE seems to think that "Less CO_2 through Innovations" is "An RWE Idea"— and one that the company has only recently come up with. And yet no other German company is a bigger emitter of carbon dioxide.

GOOD DEEDS OR BLUFFING?

13   One could almost be forgiven for suspecting that these and other companies are more interested in green labels than good deeds. Are they serious about their new environmental consciousness or is it all a bluff?

14   One thing is clear, and that is that the issue is more than just a trend. "Sustainability is developing into a central element of corporate strategy," says Martin Koehler, a senior partner at the Boston Consulting Group (BCG). "There is so much demand that we have brought together our experts worldwide to form a separate division."

15   BCG's clients want to be prepared to deal with the fundamental changes in the conditions under which they do business.

16   For utilities that will be required to purchase emissions credits in the future, the CO_2 emissions of their power plants will be the most decisive factor in determining their costs in the future. The automobile and aviation industry will have to adjust to increasingly stringent environmental regulations, and the chemical industry will face much higher electricity costs in the future. Even food manufacturers will see rising costs in raw materials like corn and wheat, which will also be used to generate energy. The Organization for Economic Cooperation and Development (OECD) predicts a 20 to 50 percent rise in the prices of agricultural products within the next 10 years.

17   According to a study by investment bank Lehman Brothers, global warming is a "tectonic force that, like globalization and the aging of society, will gradually but powerfully change the economic landscape."

STUDYING ENVIRONMENTAL IMPACTS TO SAVE COSTS

18   The green wave has long been underway in the United States. Companies like General Electric (GE), DuPont, and Wal-Mart are analyzing the environmental compatibility of their procedures and process chains, with far-reaching consequences. "If Wal-Mart 'asks' its 60,000 suppliers to reduce packaging, this affects product and packaging design worldwide," explains US consultant Andrew Winston.

19   More and more German companies are looking into ways to improve the sustainability of their business operations. Hamburg-based coffee and consumer goods retailer Tschibo, for example, has set up a team to analyze the company's global flows of goods. The group reconstructs the path taken by items like shower curtains, towels and hair brushes, from production site to retail outlet, and analyzes the emissions generated in the process.

The company is preparing this environmental impact study to determine how it can best save on shipping costs.

20   "It's incredibly grueling work," says Kay Middendorf, head of logistics at Tschibo. But the effort is also worthwhile, says Middendorf, who expects a 50 percent increase in shipping costs in the next decade. One of Middendorf's ideas is to reduce the speed at which container ships carrying his company's good travel, which would cut emissions in half. But shippers have been reluctant to cooperate so far.

21   Of course, for some industries adjusting to climate change doesn't always translate into cutting back in one way or another.

22   Steel producer ThyssenKrupp, for example, suffers from high energy prices but is benefiting from the boom in wind energy. Its Dortmund-based subsidiary Rothe Erde (Red Earth) is the world market leader in the production of slewing ring bearings.

23   Electronics giant Bosch is another case in point. The Stuttgart-based company already spends 40 percent of its R&D budget on products designed to help users preserve the environment and save resources—products in the geo and solar power markets, for example. Bosch CEO Franz Fehrenbach is currently developing a new division in which he plans to consolidate the company's efficiency-oriented business. Fehrenbach says he wants to "provide technological answers to ecological questions," adding that "the days are gone when there were only niche markets for regenerative sources of energy."

24   Siemens, another leader in the electronics business, has much to offer in the field of renewable energy. Indeed, energy and efficiency have been part of the company's core business since it was founded. Munich-based Siemens is a leader in such diverse fields as power plant construction, rail vehicles and lighting technology, and yet the public is hardly aware of its role in these sectors.

25   While U.S. rival GE has been conducting its "Ecomagination" campaign for years and CEO Jeffrey Immelt never misses an opportunity to tout his company as a green giant, Siemens is just beginning to see itself as a problem solver when it comes to climate change. Klaus Kleinfeld, who resigned as the company's CEO, had already launched Siemens's strategic reorientation, and his successor Peter Löscher, a former GE executive, apparently plans to continue the effort. Climate change, Löscher recently said, is one of the company's most important challenges.

Part 2: Eco-Friendly Companies Promise Handsome Profits

26   The players in the capital markets couldn't be more pleased. In the past, those who chose to invest in companies with environmentally sustainable business practices could feel good about themselves, but were unlikely to earn impressive returns. "Sustainability and performance were often contradictions," says Holger Boschke of Dresdner Bank. But, says Boschke, this too has changed. Nowadays these companies promise handsome profits.

27   Pension funds, in particular, which generally look for profitable long-term investments, are now restructuring their investment strategies. Knut Kjaer, who heads the Norwegian pension fund, which now manages €220 billion ($303.8 billion) in profits from his country's oil revenues, making it the world's second-largest pension fund, has removed ethically and environmentally suspect companies from his portfolio. In fact, this is the fund's stated policy. Henri de Castries, head of the Axa Group, one of the world's largest financial investment firms, knows that for many industries the risks of climate change are "just as important as interest rates and exchange rate risks."

28   The question is, how does one measure whether a company does in fact conduct its business in a sustainable manner? Merely analyzing the changes in its CO_2 emissions would be too simple. When a company spins off an energy-intensive division—the way German

consumer goods group Henkel once did when it sold its chemical subsidiary Cognis or GE did when it recently spun off its plastics division—it automatically improves its overall environmental impact, but the end effect on the environment amounts to zero.

CALLS FOR CARBON DISCLOSURE

29 The Carbon Disclosure Project (CDP), a group of 280 major investors who manage combined assets of more than $40 trillion, is attempting to provide more accurate answers to these questions. CDP has called upon the world's largest corporations to disclose their climate-related risks and explain their strategies to offset the problem. The organization uses the resulting figures to develop a Climate Leadership Index of 50 companies on the vanguard of climate protection. The index is intended to serve as a guideline for investors.

30 There are a number of surprises on the CDP's list. It includes Bayer and BASF, despite the fact that many still view the chemical industry as suspect when it comes to climate protection. Only recently, for example, BASF CEO Jürgen Hambrecht criticized Berlin's climate protection policies as "fear mongering." Nevertheless, Germany's chemical industry giants have already reduced their emissions by more than 30 percent since 1990 and plan to continue the trend in the coming years.

31 Sustainability ratings like the London-based CDP and the Zürich-based SAM (Sustainable Asset Management) have already become standard tools for evaluating companies. As a result, businesses are taking steps to project a positive image.

32 This has proven to be all too easy for some companies, which buy certificates from organizations like Climatepartner or Atmosfair, which use the money to invest in solar, hydroelectricity and wind energy projects. By purchasing the certificates, the companies hope to save precisely the amounts of greenhouse gases they were previously emitting, making them "climate neutral." The deals have since become the modern equivalent of the selling of indulgences.

"INCREDIBLE NONSENSE"

33 "Carbon neutral" has since become a label that is liberally applied to rock concerts, television sets, computers, air travel and even banks like Credit Suisse and Barclays. Indeed, "carbon neutral" was named The New Oxford American Dictionary's Word of the Year for 2006.

34 Critics say that this method is a temporary solution at best. Although she welcomes such initiatives, Regine Günther of the World Wildlife Fund (WWF) is highly skeptical of the reforestation programs offered by some agencies. "There's an incredible amount of nonsense out there," she says. It also remains to be seen whether these contributions will be sufficient to offset environmental damage being done elsewhere. For example, someone who purchases gold jewelry online from Christ Jewelers through Climatefriends pays a "climate contribution" equal to 4.5 percent of the sale. This is a modest toll, though, considering that, according to the Wuppertal Institute, more than half a ton of earth has to be moved to mine a single gram of gold—not to mention the tremendous volume of water consumed in the process.

35 The efforts of the oil and gas industry also seem highly disingenuous. "We take concerns about the climate very seriously," insists Kurt Döhmel, the head of the German division of Shell. It is true that oil companies like Shell and BP have been investing in renewable energy for years. But these investments are paltry compared to the billions they pump into their polluting core business: the production and sale of oil and gas, which is burned and causes air pollution.

36   But that happens to be the way oil and gas companies make their money, and this is unlikely to change anytime soon. According to Döhmel, fossil fuels will still cover 80 percent of the world's energy needs in 2050.

37   Environmental standards will be even more problematic for the utility industry. According to the WWF, six of Europe's 10 most polluting coal power plants are in Germany, and RWE operates four of them. Nevertheless, power companies still plan to build close to 30 new coal-fired plants.

38   Part of their planning is based on the expectation that a technological solution will soon be developed to capture and sequester CO_2. But it will take years for these technologies to come online, and it remains to be seen whether it will even be possible to retrofit all of the coal-fired plants currently on the drawing boards.

39   Failing to reduce emissions could prove extremely costly for RWE and other German utilities. In the next phase on the emissions trading process, which begins in 2008, governments will reduce quotas for emissions rights even further, likely increasing the cost of polluting from the current price of upwards of 20 euros per ton of CO_2.

40   Energy experts like Georg Erdmann, a professor at Berlin's Technical University, predict that prices could eventually top €100 a ton, a level that would spell economic disaster for utilities like RWE.

THE PAINFUL LESSONS OF THE AUTO INDUSTRY

41   These scenarios offer a taste of the massive impact climate change will have on many businesses. Those who fail to react early on stand to be punished by the consumer, a painful lesson the German auto industry is already learning today.

42   For Toyota, the initial costs of developing its energy-saving hybrid drive ran into the billions. But now the Japanese carmaker, which once suffered from a reliable but somewhat boring image, is suddenly the world leader on both the environmental and technological front. Indeed, Toyota is far more deserving of a slogan coined by German competitor Audi: Vorsprung durch Technik (Progress through Technology).

43   Ultimately, the question is whether sustainability will in fact bring about lasting change within the economy. The advertising industry, at any rate, is skeptical about whether the green economy is a lasting phenomenon. "We've seen this sort of thing before," says Peter Haller, the head of Serviceplan, Germany's largest independent advertising agency.

44   A few years after Haller founded the company in 1970, skyrocketing oil prices led to public debates over the limits of growth. But, as Haller recalls, the issue was soon displaced by concerns over terrorism and unemployment.

45   But the situation in the energy markets quickly normalized after the 1970s oil crisis. Today a similar stabilization seems unlikely, with oil prices remaining above $40 a barrel for the third year in a row. Instead, continually rising energy costs are more likely to force companies to improve their energy efficiency, thereby enhancing climate protection efforts. The European Union, for its part, will continue to increase its pressure on industry by enacting tougher environmental laws.

46   This is why many executives believe that we are unlikely to see a repeat of the early 1970s. In fact, Bosch CEO Fehrenbach is convinced that "we will be dealing with this for decades to come."

Case 31

Aegis Analytical Corporation's Strategic Alliances

Paul Olk and Joan Winn

1   As Gretchen Jahn, cofounder and executive vice president of Corporate Development of Aegis Analytical Corporation, looked over the financial statements for the first half of 2003, she tried to muster the enthusiasm she had had the previous spring when Aegis entered into alliances with two leading pharmaceutical manufacturing distributors. Jahn had expected that the increased visibility in the market would buoy Aegis's lagging sales. Meanwhile, Justin Neway, cofounder of the company, carefully prepared a presentation to potential investors, as they both knew that this round of funding was needed to support Aegis's growth plan and achieve positive cash flow in late 2004.

2   Gretchen L. Jahn and Justin O. Neway formed Aegis Analytical Corporation in 1995 to provide process manufacturing software and consulting services to pharmaceutical and biotech manufacturers. The product, called "Discoverant," helped managers see what was happening during the manufacturing process. It allowed users to connect to multiple databases simultaneously—including electronic data formats and manual inputs taken from paper records—and assemble the data. The user could then develop models to evaluate the performance of specific manufacturing processes. The product greatly reduced the time and effort needed to identify problems in a company's manufacturing processes.

3   In March 2002, Aegis formed an alliance with Honeywell POMS that made POMS a reseller of the Aegis Discoverant product. As an add-on product to the POMS software that monitored manufacturing plant activities, Honeywell agreed to sell the product under the name "POMS Explorer, powered by Aegis." Jahn and Neway believed that combining the products would enhance the sales of each, and that Honeywell's name recognition in the pharmaceutical market would help Aegis gain credibility and visibility.

4   Later that spring, Aegis entered into an agreement with Rockwell Automation to market Aegis's Discoverant with Rockwell's ProPack Data manufacturing software, designed to help companies monitor production operations. Again, because a customer could use the ProPack Data system with Discoverant, both companies hoped the collaboration would increase the sales of each product.

5   Neither relationship had yet produced a single sale, and Aegis began questioning the wisdom of this strategy. Strategic alliances were integral to the company's sales efforts, and after Jahn reflected upon the disappointments of the past year, she and Neway

The authors wish to thank Gretchen Jahn, Justin Neway, and the employees of the Aegis Analytical Corporation for their cooperation in the preparation of this case. The authors also thank Chooch Jewel and Brian Swenson for research assistance and insights. This case is intended to stimulate class discussion rather than to illustrate the effective or ineffective handling of a managerial situation. All events and individuals in this case are real.

debated what actions the much smaller Aegis should take to improve these alliances with the larger companies.

HISTORY OF AEGIS ANALYTICAL

6   In 1995, Gretchen Jahn and Justin Neway cofounded Aegis Analytical Corporation in Lafayette, Colorado. Jahn had 20 years of experience in information technology and integrated resources management prior to starting Aegis. She had recently sold her software consulting company and was working as an independent information technology and management consultant. Neway, a biochemist, had 20 years of experience in pharmaceutical and biotechnology manufacturing. He had moved to Colorado from California in 1990, and taken a job as director of manufacturing for Somatogen, a biotech research company. (Exhibit 1 shows management team profiles.) Both had worked closely with the regulatory, quality-control, and operational issues that plagued pharmaceutical manufacturing processes.

FINDING DEVELOPMENT PARTNERS

7   Jahn, a self-described "serial entrepreneur," had started two companies before Aegis. She had experience with software development and implementation, and understood the importance of manufacturing efficiencies and process improvements in getting drugs through the regulatory process. Neway's experiences in biotech and pharmaceutical manufacturing gave him an in-depth understanding of the difficulties in accessing data from a variety of sources and across many different products and then putting them into a unified format. Originally, Jahn and Neway had hoped to use Somatogen's name as a launching pad for their product. However, when Somatogen began negotiations for its eventual sale to the pharmaceutical company Baxter, they recognized they would need to find an alternative. Neway focused his efforts on courting potential development partners. Jahn recalled,

> We spent several years working out of our respective basements, using our own funds to make invited technical presentations. We made 23 presentations in the United States and Europe to major pharmaceutical companies to demonstrate our product and to get feedback to improve the product and also to see if we could find someone who would be an initial development partner. Eventually Aventis gave us a contract worth $1.3 million to jointly develop our software product with them. This was in 1999. In May and July of 1999, we received our first funding—seed investments of $400,000 and $500,000—from angel investors and Sandlot Capital. We were three people at that time.
>
> So we built this first version and we got office space and then graduated to other office space once we were all sitting on top of each other. And we hired people and subcontracted all kinds of nifty stuff and then we went out for the next round of funding. We closed on that in 2000—right around 4½ million—from GlaxoSmithKline's investment arm, SR One, and Aventis's investment arm, Future Capital, which is in Frankfurt, Germany, as well as Viscardi Ventures, a financial investment firm in Munich, Germany.

GROWING THE ORGANIZATION

8   Aegis had been successful in getting enough financing to develop and test its manufacturing software product, set up a team of applications and technical specialists, a management team, and an advisory board of industry and regulatory experts. It had organized research

EXHIBIT 1
Aegis Management Team, 2003

Gretchen L. Jahn, Cofounder, Executive Vice President, Corporate Development, has over 20 years' experience in IT. Ms. Jahn most recently led the turnaround of the software development of a CEO-less venture-backed start-up company. Previously, Ms. Jahn was a principal and vice president at Mile-High Information Services, a consulting, software development, and product sales company. She has prior experience as a data processing manager and a software specialist for Digital Equipment Corporation. Ms. Jahn received her BA in 1973 from Lawrence University and her MA in 1975 from the University of Colorado.

Justin O. Neway, Ph.D., Cofounder, Executive Vice President, and Chief Science Officer, has over 19 years of experience in pharmaceutical and biotechnology manufacturing, and in software marketing and applications. Prior to joining Aegis, Dr. Neway was director of fermentation R&D at Somatogen, a biotechnology manufacturer. He was the project leader for several technical teams, one of which developed a demonstration system for data analysis and visualization of batch process information. Dr. Neway received his B.Sc. (microbiology, 1975) and M.Sc. (biochemistry, 1977) from the University of Calgary, and his Ph.D. in biochemistry from the University of Illinois in 1982.

John M. Darcy, President and CEO, has over 25 years in proven management and leadership in *Fortune* 50 companies, turnarounds, and start-ups. Mr. Darcy has been an advisor to Aegis, and is providing significant marketing assistance for the Discoverant product launch as director of marketing. Most recently he built three separate start-up companies in the food, agricultural chemicals, and Web imaging businesses. Prior to this, Mr. Darcy was president and chief operating officer at Avis Enterprises, a $2B private investment company with majority equity positions in several industries including automobile rentals and dealerships, and has held management positions at Carnation/Nestle and Pillsbury. Mr. Darcy received his BA in 1967 and his MA in 1969 from the University of California, Los Angeles.

Geri L. Studebaker, Vice President, Marketing, has over 12 years of experience in software marketing and applications. Prior to Aegis, Ms. Studebaker was senior director of worldwide marketing for Webb Interactive, an e-business software provider for small to medium-size business. There she successfully managed overall product redesign and company positioning efforts. Prior to Webb, Ms. Studebaker held several positions with JD Edwards, the most recent being senior marketing manager.

Cheryl M. Boeckman, Vice President, Sales, has over 17 years of experience in executive-level sales. Ms. Boeckman was vice president of sales with SoftBrands Manufacturing/Fourth Shift, where she managed a team selling enterprise resource planning and supply chain management software to tier-one through tier-three manufacturing companies focusing on multiple industries including medical device and pharmaceuticals.

Steve C. Sills, Director, Business Development, has over 10 years of experience in software marketing and business development. Mr. Sills joins Aegis with a broad range of experience in the software industry. Prior to joining Aegis, he was a business development manager with Vitria Technology, a leading enterprise application integration (EAI) vendor.

seminars and conferences with leaders in biotech research and application, and successfully sold and implemented its first product in July 2000. Jahn continued,

> Our next funding in 2001 just about destroyed me. We brought in $14.5 million in October 2001, after the bubble had burst. What's funny is that Aegis is not a dot-com. So during the boom we were discounted because we weren't a dot-com. After the boom, we were discounted because every software company was. The Friday before September 11 (2001), I turned down $4 million because our valuation was so low. Then September 11th happened. We were supposed to have a board meeting on the 14th over in Munich, which we ended up having over the phone, and I said, "Look guys, we don't know what is going to happen . . . we just better get through this." We were one of the few people whose funding got bigger.

Everybody else that I talked to that was raising money at that time had their investors dry up and go away.

9   By 2002, the company had grown to 35 employees. Aegis had entered into sales agreements with eight corporate customers and had 25 sales in the pipeline by the end of that year. Exhibit 2 reports Aegis's financial performance over the last several years. Also in 2002, Jahn hired John M. Darcy, former Avis CEO, as president and CEO to reposition the company with a sales and marketing focus rather than a development focus. Jahn moved into a corporate development role to pursue new markets for the product, and develop alliances and market awareness. Because of its small size, Aegis was able to share information within the organization quickly and did not need to spend a lot of time making decisions. Aegis also prided itself on having an organization that emphasized precision in their work as well as honesty and integrity when dealing with others. Management believed that understanding and concern for customers would be a key to Aegis's success.

THE DISCOVERANT PRODUCT

10   Aegis positioned Discoverant as a manufacturing performance management software system that fulfilled three critical requirements: practical data access, useful data analysis, and ability to communicate results to nonexperts.

11   Aegis's Discoverant enabled manufacturing employees and managers to analyze specific manufacturing processes that crossed database boundaries. Exhibit 3 shows the relationship of Discoverant to disparate data sources and to analysis and results reporting. The software did not require that every piece of corporate data be stored and controlled in a single location. In developing Discoverant, Aegis's developers had incorporated existing software engines, both as a cost savings and implementation aid, building only those parts of the product that were needed to fill the gap and integrate the various systems. Jahn and Neway explained that companies without Aegis's product would have to go through a lot of time and effort to get the same information. Without Discoverant, it was common for a company's IT department to spend 2 to 4 weeks to get appropriate data from multiple systems. After company employees collected the data, it would take them another week to interpret and analyze the data. Discoverant took minutes to perform the same steps. The cost savings became significant when a company that manufactured a defective product or ran invalid experiments searched for the errors in the manufacturing process.

12   The company emphasized Discoverant's ability to "easily access millions of data values from diverse sources, drill down on any operation, make informed proactive decisions by identifying critical process parameters, and enable manufacturing enterprise compliance strategies." A simple point-and-click feature allowed the user to select the relevant data and produce desired statistical analyses, charts, or graphs. A major advantage was the fact that the person running the analyses and reports did not have to have a programming background. Aegis would help the company install the system and develop the data models. Aegis's implementation process required staff from the client company to be active participants. Aegis provided a 2-day user-training session for its customers so that they understood the product's basic functions and tools, and how to use it to evaluate the various manufacturing systems. This included a basic course on statistics so nonstatisticians could use the software. Postimplementation customer support was provided via phone, fax, e-mail, and Internet. Aegis wanted to make sure that everyone in the company who used the software had a complete understanding of Discoverant.

13   Aegis also offered additional consulting services, including follow-up, validation, and advanced technical and user training. These services were offered to companies who needed more assistance or wanted additional advice for improving their manufacturing systems.

EXHIBIT 2 5-Year Financial Performance, 1998–2003[a]

Income Statement Summaries							
Calendar Year Ending:	1998	1999	2000	2001	2002	2003 Jan–June	Cumulative 1998–2003
Revenues	$ 8,053	$ 814,001	$ 670,754	$ 562,741	$2,513,267	$ 352,847	$4,921,663
Operating Expenses	152,189	1,239,510	3,417,575	5,128,508	7,779,047	3,446,349	21,163,178
Net Operating Income	(144,136)	(425,509)	(2,746,821)	(4,565,767)	(5,265,780)	(3,093,502)	(16,241,515)

Consolidated Balance Sheet Summaries (at December 31)					
	1998	1999	2000	2001	2002
ASSETS					
Current Assets					
Cash Equivalent	$ 2,732	$ 193,481	$ 1,393,732	$12,268,918	$ 6,210,001
Accounts Receivable	3,774	248,267	397,581	158,381	364,613
Other Current Assets		25,151	122,732	146,494	406,589
Total Current Assets	6,506	466,899	1,914,045	12,573,793	6,981,203
Long-Term Assets					
Furniture and Equipment (net)[b]	15,103	102,960	340,679	523,743	378,162
Capitalized Lease and Improvements	182,468	38,261	40,061	40,061	
Other Assets (Net)[c]	1,632	227,524	533,581	661,249	297,832
Total Long-Term Assets	16,735	512,952	912,521	1,225,053	716,055
Total Assets	23,241	979,851	2,826,566	13,798,846	7,697,258
LIABILITIES AND EQUITY					
Liabilities					
Accounts Payable	89,941	360,716	255,024	491,971	572,740
Deferred Revenue			291,700	1,580,040	799,000
Capitalized Lease Obligation	4,808	173,760	225,318	252,837	111,753
Total Liabilities	94,749	534,476	772,042	2,324,848	1,483,493
Equity					
Stock and Paid-In Capital	104,313	1,053,474	5,495,757	20,498,977	28,095,497
Retained Earnings	(38,840)	(183,017)	(694,412)	(4,459,213)	(16,615,952)
Net Income	(136,981)	(425,509)	(2,746,821)	(4,565,767)	(5,265,780)
Total Equity	(71,508)	444,948	2,054,524	11,473,997	6,213,765
Total Liabilities and Equity	$ 23,241	$ 979,424	$2,826,566	$13,798,845	$ 7,697,258

Notes: [a]Some figures may be disguised.
[b]Furniture and Equipment is net of depreciation.
[c]Other Assets includes trademarks and patent costs, capitalized software development costs, and Web site development.

Source: Aegis Analytical Corporation documents, 2003.

SALES EFFORTS

14   The keys to selling such a sophisticated product were having a simple way to communicate the benefits of the product, a knowledgeable sales force, and skilled consultants to implement the software for the client. Neway understood that his audience—research scientists who used mathematics and statistics but were not programmers themselves—needed an image of the numeric processes. He worked to put together a visual representation that showed the manufacturing data in a 3-dimensional image. This eventually became Aegis's "visual process signature" used for both sales presentations and actual data tracking.

EXHIBIT 3 **The Discoverant Connectivity Link between Disparate Data Sources and Reports**

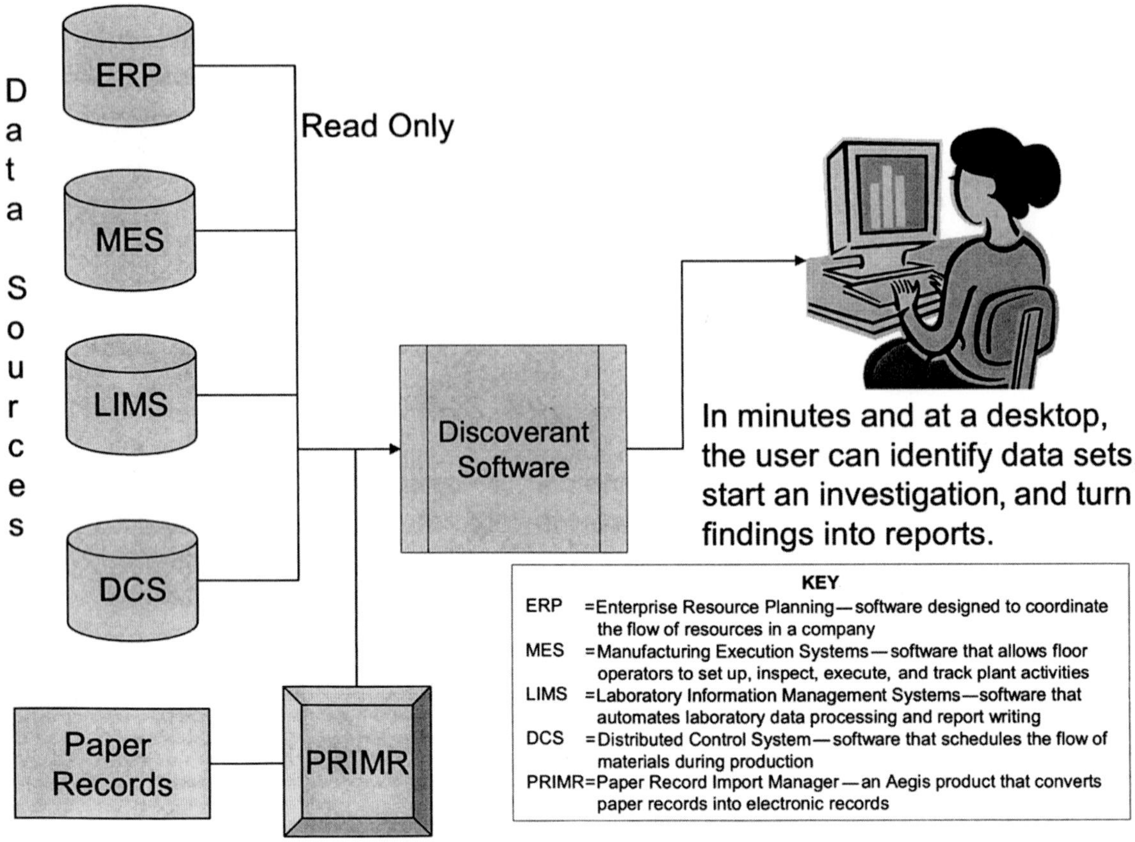
Data Sources
ERP
MES
LIMS
DCS
Read Only
Discoverant Software
Paper Records
PRIMR
In minutes and at a desktop, the user can identify data sets, start an investigation, and turn findings into reports.
KEY
ERP =Enterprise Resource Planning—software designed to coordinate the flow of resources in a company
MES =Manufacturing Execution Systems—software that allows floor operators to set up, inspect, execute, and track plant activities
LIMS =Laboratory Information Management Systems—software that automates laboratory data processing and report writing
DCS =Distributed Control System—software that schedules the flow of materials during production
PRIMR=Paper Record Import Manager—an Aegis product that converts paper records into electronic records

Source: Adapted from Aegis material.

15 To help convey the Discoverant product, Aegis developed a short video clip based on a case study. Aegis management made the video available to potential customers via a CD-ROM and posted it on the company's Web site. The scenario depicted a manager preparing for a meeting the next day where she would need to explain to her superiors why there were batch failures in a drug's tablet dissolution rate. Even though she had all the data she had requested on the manufacturing processes, she did not have weeks to analyze the data and expected that she would have to spend more time collecting additional data. What she needed was immediate access to all of the company's manufacturing data and a program that would help with the analysis. A colleague introduces her to Discoverant. With this program, she has direct access to the raw data stored in the various databases (e.g., LIMS, ERP) and can begin analyzing the manufacturing conditions associated with the batch failures. Discoverant revealed that the failures appeared to be related to the drying process—particularly, to lower dryer air temperature. Through Discoverant's statistical tools, she is able to analyze the relationship and reveal that it is highly significant. Discoverant's reporting tools—including the visual process signature—then enable her to illustrate the relationship between temperature variations and batch variations. Within minutes she has her answer and feels very prepared for the next day's meeting.

16 Beyond these promotional efforts, Aegis set up sales teams to provide long-term consultative relationships that would help customize the product for each customer. A sales account manager led a specialized team of applications and technical specialists organized for each

sales and market effort and was responsible for the relationship with each customer. Full installation and implementation of the product were expected to take between 6 and 9 months. The standard purchase cycle for enterprise software within the pharmaceutical industry started with an evaluation in one facility or production line followed by expansion to other facilities on a global scale. A contract often was negotiated for the full expansion up front in the purchase process. Specific sites were identified and a timeline established. This enabled Aegis to understand the total potential value of a customer at the time of initial phase.

17   The sales cycle itself varied from 7 months to more than 2 years. The delay was due to the multiple sales cycles involved in selling the product. In its initial efforts, Aegis sales teams quickly found that there were really three selling cycles, each requiring multiple visits. Aegis thought it would only have to make the first sale, to the individuals in the company who would actually use the product. The sales team typically started with the head of manufacturing but also spoke with the head of quality and process scientists. Although this effort often took from 3 to 9 months, the product was generally well received, particularly by the IT departments, because it eliminated their having to write numerous queries. After getting commitment by these users, however, Aegis discovered two more cycles. First, Aegis had to help convince upper management to purchase the software. Aegis found that upper management would spend as much time conducting due diligence on the decision to spend an estimated $0.5 to $1.5 million on Discoverant as they would on a $15 million software installation. This cycle typically took between 3 months to a year. After getting approval from upper management, Aegis would then have to work with the company's purchasing and legal department to complete the sale, which could take another 1 to 6 months. This lengthy 3-tier sales cycle process increased the amount of time and effort required by Aegis's sales team.

18   Aegis planned to set up direct sales teams in key geographic areas where there were high concentrations of potential customers. Aegis had already set up a team in Frankfurt, Germany, to provide sales and marketing support for the European market. In geographic areas of lower customer concentration, Aegis planned to use sales agents and alliances to leverage the direct sales force and to provide local coverage and first-line support. Strategic partners would help expand sales and implementation capabilities.

DEMAND FOR MANUFACTURING PROCESS SOFTWARE IN THE PHARMACEUTICAL INDUSTRY

19   To succeed in a global context, pharmaceutical companies continually needed to reduce costs while increasing efficiency, responsiveness, and customer satisfaction. Improving profitability in the manufacturing process depended on reducing the cost of raw materials, energy, and capital, and on increasing the yield from their assets. Profitability also depended upon demonstrating that they could meet quality standards in producing the drug. To meet such regulations, manufacturers made significant investments in software systems to collect information that revealed where, if any, manufacturing problems existed and, after correcting the problems, demonstrated compliance to the regulators. Initially, production processes were automated through distributed control systems (DCS) that used hardware, software, and industrial instruments to measure, record, and automatically control process variables. More recently, process manufacturers had begun to automate key business processes by implementing enterprise resource planning (ERP) and manufacturing execution system (MES) software solutions to enhance the flow of business information across the enterprise, as well as other software programs such as LIMS (Exhibit 3).

20   The implementation of each of these systems led to an accumulation of large amounts of raw data that recorded in detail the performance of each manufacturing process at full

EXHIBIT 4
Market Projections
for 2003

Source: Aegis Analytical
Corporation documents, 2003.

(Dollar Values Are in Thousands.)							
Annual Revenues	**Number of Companies**	**Mfg. Sites**	**Total Cells**	**Licenses $250K**	**Services at 50%**	**Maint. @ 15%**	**Total Value**
$1 Billion +	52	225	1,125	281,250	140,625	42,188	$464,063
$500M—$1B	41	62	186	46,500	23,250	6,975	76,725
$250M—$500M	71	77	154	38,500	19,250	5,775	63,525
Opportunity	164	364	1,465	$366,250	$183,125	$54,938	$604,313

Note: The standard purchase cycle for enterprise software within the pharmaceutical industry starts with an evaluation in one facility or production line followed by expansion to other facilities on a global scale. A contract often is negotiated for the full expansion up front in the purchase process. Specific sites are identified and a timeline established. Therefore, Aegis understands the total potential value of a customer at the time of initial phase. Even under current (sluggish) market conditions, Aegis believes that sales to new pharma accounts can be expected to result in large total sales in the same accounts in the next 18 to 24 months as the initial projects show good results and decisions are made to proceed with wider deployments.

commercial scale over extended periods of time. The proliferation of software products resulted in companies having mountains of data scattered across numerous disparate data sources. Collectively, these held a great deal of information about how to improve manufacturing performance. Prior to 2000, there was no simple way to access all the data and extract the big picture about the manufacturing process. Aegis wanted to become the recognized leader in process manufacturing technology by providing software that could be used to integrate all major functions and provide system-wide information.

21   The demand for Aegis's product was not driven solely by pharmaceutical companies' interest in reducing costs. Increasing pressure from consumer groups and the federal government's Food and Drug Administration (FDA) led Aegis to believe that this market would be highly receptive to any product that shortened and improved the product-to-market cycle time. In 2002 alone, the FDA had issued 755 warning letters about product quality—an increase of more than 40 percent from 1998. The FDA had also increased the number and severity of penalties levied against pharmaceutical manufacturers, including criminal convictions and fines as high as $500 million.

22   Discoverant had no direct competitors. Other companies had products that performed parts of what Discoverant did, but no one besides Aegis had a product that did it all. In 2003, there were several commercial vendors of general statistical and visualization tools such as Mathsoft, Statistica, MatLab, IMSL, SAS, Visual Numerics, and AVS. These tools permitted the analysis of already collected data but did not help in accessing the various databases. Other software companies, such as Aspen Technology, OSI, and Lighthammer, provided process manufacturing software that captured shop floor data for process control and data management, but typically the data had to be inside a single database. These products could not combine data from dissimilar databases. Finally, Spotfire and Aspen Technology had recently announced an alliance to develop data analysis capabilities for manufacturing systems, but the product was not yet available. Although some large pharmaceutical and food production companies had custom in-house systems developed by internal IT departments or third-party consultants, most companies' systems were limited in use and required a team of experts to interpret the disparate data that the systems generated. Someone who was not a programmer could use Discoverant.

23   Aegis had identified a number of pharmaceutical manufacturing companies that would benefit by an integrated manufacturing information system. Though many pharmaceutical manufacturing companies in 2002 were quite small, with annual revenues under $250 million, targeting only those pharmaceutical companies with annual revenues over $250 million would give Aegis access to a potential market of $604 million in license, service, and maintenance fees. Pharmaceutical manufacturers with annual revenues in

excess of $1 billion had the largest IT budget and were therefore most likely to implement manufacturing enterprise software solutions like Discoverant. Importantly, companies of this size accounted for approximately 77 percent, or $464 million, of the total potential market for Aegis's products (Exhibit 4).

AEGIS'S ALLIANCE STRATEGY

24 Jahn and Neway understood the power of brand recognition and company reputation in reaching their target market. They developed research partnerships with top-tier pharmaceutical manufacturing companies such as Merck, Genentech, and Aventis and invited representatives from Abbott, Amgen, Aventis, Merck, Novartis, GlaxoSmithKline, Eli Lilly, Roche, and Wyeth to join discussions at Aegis-hosted conferences in Colorado. Contacts at the University of Newcastle and University College London, two of the top universities in the world known for software technology applicable to manufacturing processes, joined Aegis's Scientific Advisory Board. These relationships fostered an exchange of technical information and ideas, and gave Aegis professional connections and sales leads.

25 In their initial efforts to sell Discoverant, Neway and a small team of sales and technical people made direct calls to large pharmaceutical and biotech manufacturers. Believing that alliances with well-known service providers would give them credibility and visibility in the marketplace, and also permit them to reach more companies than they could alone, Aegis's growth strategy focused on finding partners. Aegis's first partners were client-investors, pharmaceutical companies like Merck and GlaxoSmithKline in California and Hoechst Marion Roussel in Kansas City. Having big company names as successful users of Aegis's Discoverant product provided important testimonials for Discoverant's features. This networking helped form the research and technical partnerships that Aegis used to get its first contracts and secure venture funding.

26 The focus in 2002 was on creating alliances that would enhance sales. Although Aegis had made some sales of Discoverant, as top managers began to understand that the 3-part sales process was the norm, they realized they did not have enough internal resources. Their sales staff could continue to pursue direct sales, but sales might benefit from partners who could help convince top management to purchase Discoverant. These alliances were considered an integral part of the sales force. In choosing sales partners, then, Aegis sought out companies that had complementary products and would agree to promote the Discoverant brand using the Aegis name to distinguish it from perceived competition. While it had started screening potential candidates, in 2002, Aegis was approached by two companies that seemed to be the best candidates with which to partner. In that year, Aegis formed a relationship with Honeywell POMS and another with Rockwell Automation.

HONEYWELL POMS ALLIANCE

27 In 1999, Honeywell acquired the POMS Corporation, a leader in providing manufacturing execution systems (MES) for the pharmaceutical as well as for other industries. POMS had sold over 70 systems to nine of the top 10 pharmaceutical companies in the world. POMS employed 150 people and was headquartered in Herndon, Virginia. Prior to the acquisition, POMS was strictly a reseller of software and, according to an Aegis manager, had a spotty record of implementing and supporting its software offerings.

28 On March 13, 2002, Aegis formed an alliance with Honeywell POMS that made it a reseller of the Aegis Discoverant product in combination with POMS's manufacturing system. Honeywell approached Aegis after a potential customer asked if POMS was compatible with Discoverant. This interest helped Aegis during negotiations. Although Honeywell initially requested an exclusive relationship, Aegis thought that it was not in the company's best interests. Eventually the two sides did come to an agreement that Aegis's product would be packaged and resold under the name "POMS Explorer, powered by Aegis." According to Chris Lyden, vice president and general manager of Honeywell's Industry Solutions Business for Chemicals, Life Sciences, and Consumer Goods,

> By combining Aegis's Discoverant with our the flagship POMS MES product, we will be able to provide added benefits to our customers and further enhance the way they manage their manufacturing systems. Honeywell's new POMS Explorer module, powered by Aegis, can save significant cost for our customers by reducing batch failures, stabilizing the manufacturing operations, and getting products to market faster.

29   Both companies recognized the mutual benefits from the alliance. Aegis believed this alliance was a significant step toward gaining both credibility and visibility within the Life Sciences market. With Honeywell, Aegis aligned itself with an organization that had $24 billion in sales, over 120,000 employees, and operations in 95 countries throughout the world.

30   Aegis was banking on POMS's name recognition and reputation to build market awareness for Aegis and Discoverant. Honeywell POMS, located in the Automation and Control Solutions division, one of four major strategic business units in Honeywell (besides Aerospace, Specialty Materials and Transportation, and Power Systems), viewed Discoverant as an additional software offering that would expand the capability of its MES product. The Aegis software provided POMS customers with the software needed to visually see and analyze the manufacturing data. To help reach these expectations, the two companies put together a relatively standard contract that included the following:

> Honeywell POMS had a nonexclusive, nontransferable, non-sublicensable license to resell Aegis's product.
>
> The agreement would initially run for 2 years with an additional 1-year automatic renewal, unless either party wished to terminate the agreement at least 90 days before the end of the 2-year period.
>
> Aegis and Honeywell POMS agreed to appoint one sales professional to act as the primary representative to the other. The agreement specified that the representatives shall meet in person at least once per calendar quarter to discuss the status of the sales effort and other questions about selling the software. These meetings will alternate between Aegis's and Honeywell POMS's facilities, unless both parties agree to talk telephonically or at another location.
>
> Aegis would provide training sessions for Honeywell POMS sales personnel within 90 days of the start date of the contract.
>
> Honeywell POMS was responsible for the point-of-contact sales support for users. If Honeywell POMS was not able to solve the problem, they would contact Aegis for support. Provisions were provided for the time by which Aegis had to respond.
>
> The parties agreed to prepare mutually agreed press releases to promote the relationship. They also agreed to collaborate on marketing events, on distributing promotional materials, and on promotion of the other's product on its Web sites.
>
> Honeywell POMS would receive a discount on the licensing fees Aegis charged. This was a reduced price on what Aegis would charge Honeywell POMS to resell Discoverant. The more sales Honeywell POMS recorded, the greater the discount.
>
> Termination clauses permitted each party to end the relationship if the other went out of business or if there was a breach of any provisions within the agreement.

31   In considering the agreement, Jahn acknowledged that it had provisions for Honeywell to "make sure that their sales reps would get enough of a commission so that they would be motivated to sell it and also that our sales reps would not be disadvantaged by selling through our partner instead of selling direct....There are lots of ways of arranging [sales incentives plans] and we had lots of conversation with Honeywell to determine what would work best in this particular environment." Aegis's VP of sales also was involved in making sure both sides were aware of the selling message and pricing structures and were present at the training sessions. He had numerous face-to-face meetings with his Honeywell counterparts to discuss the product. They focused on building a relationship first and did that successfully. Further, the Honeywell relationships benefited from Jahn having personal contact with Honeywell's director of business development.

32   However, from her experience in larger companies, Jahn was concerned about Honeywell's commitment to promoting the Discoverant product, and the VP of sales spent much of his time convincing his counterparts of the value of this add-on product. "For Honeywell, we're a line item in their sales catalogue," Jahn later observed. "When the market fell out, their sales reps were concentrating on how to get people to buy their own products, much less other things in the catalogue."

ROCKWELL AUTOMATION AGREEMENT

33   Rockwell Automation purchased ProPack Data in April 2002. ProPack Data, a German company established in 1984, was a market leader of manufacturing execution systems (MES) and electronic batch record systems (EBRS) for the pharmaceutical and other regulated industries. The company employed 230 people and became a part of Rockwell's Process Solutions business. Rockwell Automation had revenues of $4.3 billion, employed 23,000 individuals, and had operations in 80 different countries.

34   Aegis had been approached by ProPack—and had already begun negotiations with them—before the Rockwell acquisition. The ProPack Data manufacturing execution system PMX was designed to help customers reduce operating costs, shorten cycle times, and improve product quality in production operations. The software solution provided by Aegis provided connectivity and visibility to the manufacturing processes that PMX was managing.

35   As with the Honeywell alliance, the relationship with ProPack was designed to make Aegis visible to much larger organizations. The addition of Rockwell into the ProPack equation was a double-edged sword for Aegis's management team. On one hand they were excited by the large size of Rockwell and the possibility to leverage that size to their advantage. However, Jahn was concerned that that those advantages might be offset by increased bureaucracy and added delays.

36   Aegis and ProPack Data set up a sales and marketing agreement for lead generation that was simpler than the Honeywell POMS agreement. If a company's referral led to a sale for the partner, the company would receive a finder's fee. The agreement's primary function was to increase access to new sales territory. Aegis hoped to increase the number of sales leads, thus generating a higher number of sales opportunities. According to Bernhard Thurnbauer, senior vice president of strategic marketing of ProPack Data,

> We are excited about this agreement with Aegis. We feel that this [arrangement] will give ProPack Data a significant edge in providing a true value added solution. Aegis's Discoverant Manufacturing Informatics system meets the need of leading pharmaceutical manufacturers to analyze and visualize all their data in a multitude of disparate sources. Using Discoverant, manufacturers can find and control the key process drivers across their entire manufacturing processes, all the way from raw materials to final product.

37   Each company intended to use the partner's strengths to build interest in its own products and services and committed its sales representatives to prospect for the partner. Once opportunities were identified, various strategies would be employed to close the sale. The sales opportunity itself would dictate how the two companies would work together and who would take the dominant role in the sales process. Each sale would be governed by a separate agreement, which would include a finder's fee for the partner that developed the sale. Additional highlights of the agreement included:

> The agreement committed both Aegis and Propack Data to explore mutually beneficial ways in which they could complement one another's sales and marketing activities.
>
> Both Aegis and Propack Data agreed this was an important relationship and would seek to communicate ideas for improving the relationship.
>
> Each party would assign a person to act as the primary liaison to the other party.
>
> Each party would independently market its respective products and services, but the two companies would prepare mutually agreed press releases to promote the relationship, provide marketing and sales support to each other, and spread the word about the relationship within their respective organization.
>
> The liaisons were to attend quarterly meetings to discuss comarketing of their products and customer leads. The location of the meetings would alternate between Aegis and Propack Data facilities.
>
> Unless there was a sale, there would be no commissions or other type of remuneration owed by one party to the other.
>
> Upon request, each party agreed to provide on-site product training to the other party's employees up to once a year.
>
> A separate agreement would be written up when both parties decided to pursue jointly a product installation and implementation.
>
> The agreement could be terminated at any time without cause with 90 days' written notification.

EFFECTIVENESS OF THE PARTNERSHIPS

38   When, by 2003, neither the Honeywell nor Rockwell relationship had produced a single sale, Jahn began to question the value of these alliances. With sales as the major focus in the alliances, and the primary criterion for evaluating the success of the alliance, Jahn tried to understand possible reasons for the lack of sales. It was easy to blame lagging sales on the struggling economy. With the drug manufacturing industry not experiencing consistent growth, companies were not able to spend money on improving their processes, upgrading software, or revamping production. Budgets cuts and purchasing managers following orders to reduce expenses led to a shrinking market. Unfortunately, the products that Aegis and its alliance partners were selling fell into the category of items that were not essential to current operations. In fact, Honeywell's POMS division, while having some success with other software products, overall had low sales and had recently laid off 25 percent of its sales force, including individuals with whom Aegis had worked. Aegis had also lost some its original sales team. During lean times, the companies that normally would be interested in purchasing Aegis software solutions were looking internally to make incremental improvements.

39   Another reason for the absence of sales might have been the characteristics of the relationships and the partner communication systems and performance metrics that were set up. Effective communication between alliance partners was essential. Was Aegis effectively communicating with either alliance partner? Although there were contractual specifications

about how often they had to meet, communication appeared to be confined to situations when either side had a question or needed clarification on an issue. Communications between Honeywell POMS and ProPack Data had been cordial, but there was no evidence that the partners had a free flow of communication beyond the "need to know" when problems arose.

40   For Honeywell POMS, the Aegis director of business development handled all direct communications. The current agreement allowed the companies to set agendas and develop sales opportunities at a level that met the alliance's needs. Group phone calls, sales calls, and bi-yearly face-to-face meetings were designed to keep the companies in contact with each other. Though initially there was contact between engineers to make sure the technologies were compatible, most communication occurred between the companies' sales teams and corporate management. Communication between sales teams occurred when they were working the same sales together, which they had done on several occasions; then, there was frequent communication. The loss of key personnel in both companies required the new managers to begin to rebuild the communication level and the overall interest in the relationship. At the corporate level, they communicated weekly. Though more frequent communication would perhaps be better, Jahn believed the current level allowed the companies to set agendas and develop sales opportunities at a level that met the alliance's needs. As the alliance developed, Aegis realized it had a good cultural fit with Honeywell POMS and noted very few communication problems. Aegis believed it could share information with Honeywell.

41   The Aegis and ProPack Data agreement was hindered when Aegis's primary contact left ProPack Data, handing off responsibility to someone who did not take an active role, thereby frustrating the Aegis team. On both sides, communication had not extended beyond the contact persons, and the relationship suffered. The two companies had been trying to move beyond these events and had taken steps to improve the channels of communication between the firms.

A DIFFICULT DECISION

42   As Jahn reflected upon the development of the company and these relationships, she wondered about Aegis's alliance strategy and what actions to take. Perhaps it was too early to make changes—these were difficult economic times and Aegis might not have given the relationships enough time to produce sales. Jahn and Neway knew that communication and trust were important to keeping a relationship going through troubled times. Their comfort level and trust increased with each partner as time went on. On the other hand, one could argue that these relationships had already had sufficient time to prove themselves and it did not appear that either would be successful. If Aegis terminated one or both of these relationships, it would need to focus its time and energy on more productive sales options. But what would these be?

43   Relationships with other partners large enough to get the attention of major pharmaceutical companies would likely have some of the same problems as these two relationships and would take time to develop. Rather than terminate these alliances, a more reasonable solution might be to restructure the relationships. This could include changes in the contract with either Rockwell or Honeywell, or in their interactions with one another. Believing they had put together contracts with appropriate incentives to encourage sales, their thoughts turned to improving the relationships with each company. But how would a company of fewer than 40 employees influence either of these large corporations? Further, as a small company between rounds of financing, Aegis did not have a lot of extra financial or staffing resources. Any solution would have to be a low cost one. Each path was filled with risk and difficulties in implementation, but Jahn and Neway knew that for Aegis to attract investments and to succeed would require a quick but thoughtful decision.

Case 32

Citigroup Retail Banking Operations in the U.S. and Abroad:
The Banking Industry   Allyson Papazahariou, Marc E. Gartenfeld,
                                         Dorothy Dologite, and Robert J. Mockler

INTRODUCTION

1   On January 20, 2006, Citigroup announced fourth-quarter earnings of $6.9 billion, or $1.37 per share, which was two cents below the consensus estimate. The failure of Citigroup, one of the world's largest financial services firms, to meet expectations was quite alarming to the company and its investors. Of primary concern to stakeholders was the poor performance of the company's global consumer business, which accounted for about 55% of the company's profits. Earnings for the global consumer business group had fallen 23% to $2.43 billion. The disappointing fourth quarter results for Citigroup, and its global consumer unit in particular, was yet another blow to the company, which had had its share of problems in the last few years, including costly legal mishaps resulting from its connections to the WorldCom and Enron scandals; embarrassing occasions of non-compliance to regulatory statutes abroad (notably in Japan and in the U.K.); major technical glitches involving the privacy of its customers; and, as a result of so much bad publicity, the tarnishing of its corporate image.

2   It seemed the company was plagued by problems since the appointment of new CEO Charles ("Chuck") O. Prince III in 2003. Chuck Prince needed to develop an effective differentiating enterprise-wide strategy if Citigroup was to survive and prosper against aggressive competition over the intermediate and long-term future.

3   Citigroup was the largest bank in the U.S. and the first to reach assets of $1 trillion. Based in the U.S., Citigroup extended its financial services to the far reaches of the earth. Citigroup had more than 3,000 bank branches and consumer finance offices in the US and Canada, plus an additional 1,500 locations in about 100 other countries, supported by 300,000 employees around the world [Citigroup, 2005]. Citigroup was organized into three major business groups: Global Consumer, Corporate and Investment Banking, and Global Wealth Management, as shown Figure 1. In addition, Citigroup held two stand-alone businesses: Citigroup Asset Management and Citigroup Alternative Investments.

4   Although Citigroup was the largest bank in the U.S. by the end of 2005 it was clear that its international growth was outpacing its U.S. growth, a trend that was expected to continue [Citigroup, 2005; National Information Center, 2006]. A good portion of that growth came from Asia. In 2004, Citigroup had acquired KorAm Bank in Korea, Citigroup's largest investment ever in Asia. Also in 2004, Citigroup became one of the first foreign banks to issue credit cards in China. Citigroup's global strategy was a key priority given the vast overseas opportunity presenting itself and the intensive competitive threat from other large financial services companies also planning to take advantage of the global opportunity. In addition to the investments already made in Asia, Citigroup was planning on opening up to 200 bank branches and 500 consumer finance offices outside the US to help foster further international growth.

5   Citigroup was still striving to broaden its reach within the U.S. as well. In 2004, it acquired Principal Residential Mortgage, one of the largest mortgage companies in the U.S. In addition,

This case was prepared by Allyson Papazahariou, Marc E. Gartenfeld, Dorothy Dologite, and Professor Robert J. Mockler of St. John's University. © Robert J. Mockler.

FIGURE 1   **Citigroup**

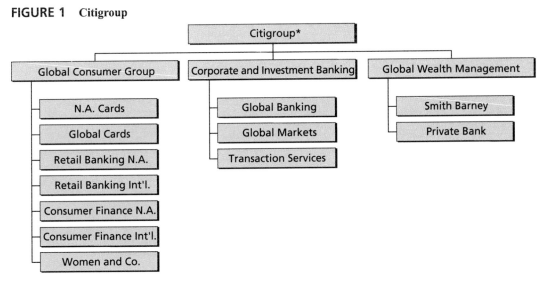

*Citigroup also held two stand-alone businesses: Citigroup Asset Management and Citigroup Alternative Investments

Citigroup had agreed to purchase First American Bank in Texas. However, this acquisition would have to wait: In March 2005, the Federal Reserve banned Citigroup from making any further acquisitions until it cleaned up the regulatory mess it had gotten itself into.

6   In the 1980s and 1990s, industry consensus was that the key to success was based on a combination of the development of financial products and their distribution. By 2006, it appeared that distribution was the primary key to success, with potentially higher returns than new product development. With two-thirds of the global economy outside the U.S., large banks were looking to expand to markets overseas and still maintain a strong presence in the U.S. This was no easy task, considering government and political barriers, cultural differences, technological obstacles and the highly fragmented nature of the non-U.S. financial services industry, where even the lead firm might have had only a very small (low single-digit) market share.

7   Citigroup had been externally focused on acquiring banks and financial services firms from 1997–2005; yet, internally it was experiencing a host of problems that resulted in the firm failing to meet earnings expectations in the fourth quarter of 2005. A key opportunity for improvement was its global consumer business, which is the focus of this paper.

8   In order to bolster earnings for the global consumer group, Citigroup needed to reconsider its domestic and international distribution plan. With Smith Barney under its umbrella, Citigroup also needed to determine if and how it should integrate Smith Barney with Citibank branches. Another decision that needed to be made involved Citigroup's product line. With distribution crossing many borders and cultures, Citigroup needed to investigate whether or not it needed to customize its product line by geography. Customers were yet another area Citigroup needed to further explore, specifically, which consumer segments would be most profitable? Finally, the retail banking business relied heavily on traffic into their branches. Citigroup had to evaluate the branch experience they were offering customers whether it was achieving the desired level of trial and repeat customer visits. The main question to be resolved was how to differentiate Citigroup from its competition and so achieve a winning edge over competitors within intensely competitive, rapidly changing immediate, intermediate, and long-term time frames.

INDUSTRY AND COMPETITIVE MARKET ANALYSIS: FINANCIAL SERVICES

9   The financial services industry comprised companies that provided products and services that facilitated the flow of money, such as accounting firms, regulatory agencies, investment services, credit services, insurance providers, and banks, as shown in Figure 2.

10   Under the Glass-Steagall Act of 1933, banks, insurance companies, and securities firms were not allowed to merge with each other or offer products and services provided by the other types of firms. This changed in 1999 when Congress passed the Gramm-Leach-Bliley (GLB) Act, which eliminated the restrictions of the Glass-Steagall Act and consequently opened new opportunities for banks [Liam, 2004]. Free to engage in insurance and securities activities, many large banks began acquiring insurance and securities firms in order to expand their product lines. A wave of merger and acquisition activity among banks and financial services companies immediately followed the GLB Act. Megamergers—mergers between banks with assets of over $1 billion—became common [Liam, 2004].

Accounting

11   Accounting firms provided accounting and related services to corporations and individuals. There were three main branches of accounting: auditing, financial advisory services, and tax-related services. Auditing was the process by which accountants evaluated the financial statements of an organization and offered an opinion as to whether the financial statements were presented fairly in all material respects and in accordance with Generally Accepted Auditing Standards (GAAS). Financial advisory services consisted of banking services, valuation services, and forensic accounting and litigation services. Tax-related services were concerned with advising clients about the advantages and disadvantages of certain business decisions as they related to federal, state, and local tax implications.

Regulatory Agencies

12   Regulatory agencies, in the form of public and private organizations, regulated securities trading, international trade, and banking and financial services firms. For example, the Federal Reserve, FDIC, and Controller of Currency were regulatory agencies that supervised

FIGURE 2   **Financial Services Industry**

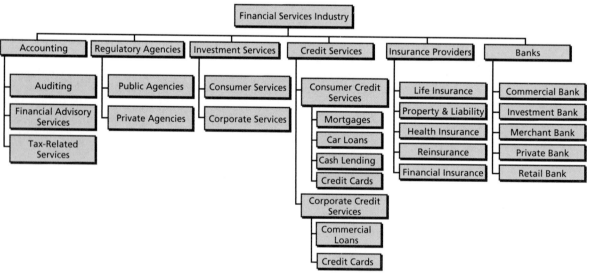

commercial banks. The Securities and Exchange Commission (SEC) and state supervisory agencies were regulatory agencies that supervised financial companies.

Investment Services

13 Investment services provided funding and financing to private individuals (such as mutual funds and retirement funds) and to corporations (such as venture capital for start-up companies or financing for business growth opportunities). Investment services aimed at private individuals was one of the fastest growing segments of the financial services industry. The need for investment services among private individuals was driven by several factors: (1) employers substituting defined contribution plans for traditional pension plans; (2) concerns about the future of Social Security; (3) the rising costs of their children's college education; and (4) increased access to investment services through banks, broker-dealers, and insurance companies and online services.

Credit Services

14 Credit services included companies that provided loans and other credit and financing products to individuals and/or corporations. Consumer credit services included mortgages, car loans, cash lending, and credit cards. Corporate credit services included commercial loans and credit cards.

Insurance Providers

15 Insurance is an "economic device whereby an individual or a business transfers the risk of uncertain financial loss by payment of a premium" [Liam, 2004]. There are five basic types of insurance: life insurance, property and liability insurance, health insurance, re-insurance (which assumes underwriting risks from other insurance companies for a premium), and financial insurance (which provides guarantees for financial obligations such as municipal bonds). The latter two types of insurance are generally not covered by retail banks.

Banks

16 Traditionally, banks had three major roles: intermediary, payor, and guarantor [Liam, 2004]. As intermediaries, banks transformed client savings into credit for private individuals as well as for businesses. As payors, banks made payments on behalf of their customers. As guarantors, banks provided guarantees that their customers would pay their debts. In these roles, banks provided customers with checking and savings accounts; loans, leases, mortgages, and credit cards.

17 By 2004, the banking industry had evolved from offering basic banking services to also providing financial services. This was the result of deregulation (notably the Gramm-Leach-Bliley Act of 1999 described earlier), globalization, advances in technology and consolidation. The lines between banks, financial service providers, and insurance companies had been blurred and they were now all competing with one another. Restrictions posed during the Great Depression that prevented banks from entering other financial services had been lifted, and banks were now free to engage in such activities as asset management, investment banking, and insurance.

18 Despite the fact that banks could engage in many different types of financial activities, there were still distinctions among types of banks (even if they fell under the same holding company). The main types of banks were commercial banks, investment banks, merchant banks, private banks, and retail banks. Commercial banks focused mainly on businesses (offering such services as business loans). Investment banks were concerned with underwriting, acting as intermediaries between issuers of securities and the investing public, facilitating mergers and other corporate reorganizations, and also acting as brokers for institutional clients. Merchant banks were involved mostly in international finance,

FIGURE 3   Retail Banking

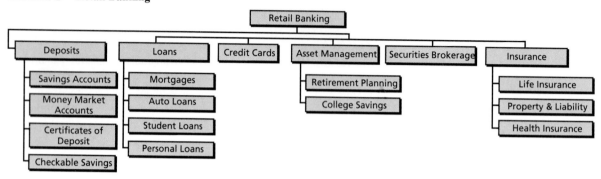

long-term loans for companies, and underwriting. Private banks focused on high net worth clients and offered services such as protecting and growing assets, planning retirement and passing wealth on to future generations. Retail banks served individual consumers in the mass market through local branches, offering such services as deposits, loans, credit cards, asset management, security brokerage, and insurance, as shown in Figure 3.

INDUSTRY AND COMPETITIVE MARKET SEGMENT: RETAIL BANKING

19   Retail banking was conducted by large national banks that had retail branches across many geographic regions of the U.S. (and often abroad) and by state banks that had branches in only one or a few states. National banks offered a full range of products and services to their customers, although some specialized in particular products such as home mortgages. State banks usually offered a more limited array of services and focused on basic banking services such as savings and loans.

How the Retail Banking Segment Works: Business Process Model

20   Retail banks, whether national or regional, raised funds by collecting deposits from consumers and making loans. Retail banks' primary liabilities were deposits and primary assets were loans. Revenue was earned through disproportionate interest rates between the deposits and loans. Banks made money because the interest they charged on loans was higher than the interest rate they paid on deposits. The interest rate a bank charged on loans depended on the number of customers who wanted to borrow money and the amount of money the bank had available to lend [Tripp, 2005]. The amount available to lend also depended on the reserve requirement the Federal Reserve Board set. Interest rates for specific loans also depended on the risk associated with the loan (i.e., the likelihood of the loan being paid back). Besides interest revenue, banks also generated revenue from the fees they charged their customers (such as ATM fees) and from investments and securities.

21   In its most basic form, retail banks operated by acquiring new customers, maintaining customer accounts, increasing share-of-wallet among existing customers and disposing unprofitable customers (such as loan defaulters), as shown in Figure 4.

22   In order to attract new customers, banks relied heavily on branch distribution and marketing. The rationale for extensive distribution was the more accessible the bank, the more customers it would attract. Marketing was also a key element for driving consumer trial. Marketing was used to raise awareness of the bank and its services and to position the bank as a trustworthy institution in which to safeguard and invest assets. Once new customers opened an account at a particular bank, the bank would maintain the account and provide

FIGURE 4 **How Retail Banking Works**

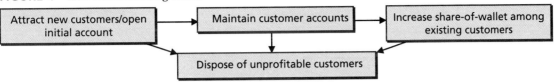

the customer daily transaction services (for payments and withdrawals) and ease of access to information about the account (such as through telephone and online banking and regular account statements).

23 Maintaining accounts was not enough to drive growth and profits. Banks sought to increase the share-of-wallet from each of their customers. For example, if a customer had a savings account at a bank, the bank would try to persuade that customer to also arrange his mortgage, college savings plan, and/or retirement plan at that bank as well. Again, this was accomplished largely through marketing, especially direct selling to customers by financial representatives on-premise in the branches. Not all customers were profitable. Banks tried to unload customers who were not increasing profits, or worse taking away profits, such as a customer who was not making his mortgage payments.

24 Retail banks offered similar basic deposit and loan services (the latter increasingly referred to as consumer financing), and competed with one another by offering different interest rates. However, banks had limited latitude in the interest rates they could offer/charge and still be profitable, so they tried to differentiate themselves through unique products, exceptional customer service, and a superior branch experience. Most banks operated under similar organizational structures, with the national banks having larger product portfolios, greater geographical reach, more advanced technology and more complicated operations to support the products, geography, and technology. Figure 5 displays the typical banking business process model.

Distribution

25 Banks grew via distribution—that is, by increasing their number of branches. For national banks such as Citigroup, J.P. Morgan Chase, and Bank of America, this meant establishing themselves in new markets within the U.S. and abroad.

U.S.

26 Banks increased their distribution in the U.S. through their expertise in de novo branch building (building branches from scratch) and through strategic mergers and acquisitions. For distribution to be successful in the U.S., the branches had to have prime locations (for example, on main streets or within high-traffic strip malls) and good geographic dispersion.

Non-U.S.

27 For success in foreign markets, distribution depended on having in-depth knowledge of the country and culture, adhering to local laws and regulations, building relationships with the local governments and businesses, and recognizing technological limitations within those countries. With the world at their fingertips, banks had to choose wisely which foreign markets they should invest in. In 2006, the "hot" foreign markets were China, India, and Russia.

28 ***China.*** The primary reason banks were looking to China was strong demographics—that is, the sheer number of potential customers. However, bank regulations in China were tight and foreigners could not own banks in China. In order to be successful foreign banks had to set up representative offices that offered services such as letters of credit and financing

FIGURE 5   Retail Banking Business Process Model

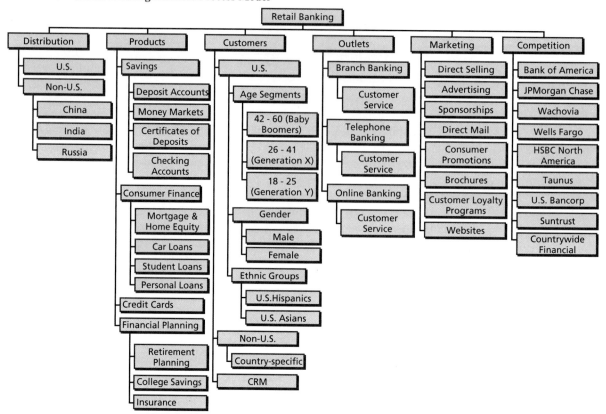

of imports and exports. By establishing a presence in China, banks would have a foothold in case regulations were relaxed in the future.

29   *India.*   Banks looked to India because of the large population base and the increasing number of citizens moving from lower-class to middle-class status. To be successful in India, banks had to aggressively market credit cards since card ownership had become a growing trend. Specifically, the card population had grown from two million to ten million in the last two to three years [Businessline, 2005].

30   *Russia.*   By 2006, Russia had caught the eye of many U.S. banks looking to expand internationally. Unlike China and India, Russia allowed foreigners to own banks. Moreover, there was a lot of potential in the consumer lending business, where most citizens had no housing debt and where bank loans to individuals had quadrupled from 2004 to 2005 [Chazan, 2005]. To be successful in Russia, banks had to market credit cards and consumer lending.

Products

31   There were four types of products banks offered: savings, consumer finance, credit cards, and financial planning.

Savings

32   Savings products took several forms: deposit accounts, money market accounts, certificates of deposits, and checking accounts. Deposit accounts required consumers to have a low minimum balance or no minimum balance and offer a very low amount of interest each

month. Customers could withdraw their money at any time. Certificates of deposit let consumers deposit a specific amount of money that could not be withdrawn for a specified period of time (for example, six months or one year). In exchange for the time commitment, consumers received a higher rate of interest (and the bank could use the money for other purposes). Money market accounts fell in between savings accounts and certificates of deposit. With money market accounts, consumers had limited transaction privileges and received more interest than a savings account and less interest than a certificate of deposit. Checking accounts were a form of savings accounts, and banks could charge a fee on checks. Most checking accounts did not pay interest, with the exception of the negotiable order of withdrawal (or NOW) accounts.

Consumer Finance

33 Consumer finance (loans) came in a wide variety of products, including mortgage and home equity, car loans, student loans, and personal loans. Interest rates on the loans depended on the type of loan, time to maturity, the customer's credit history and other factors.

Credit Cards

34 Credit cards gave consumers a line of credit so they could purchase items and pay for them at a later date. Banks charged high interest rates for this time privilege.

Financial Planning

35 Lastly, banks offered financial planning tools, such as individual retirement accounts (which required consumers to keep their money in the bank until they reached a certain age and for which they will be charged a severe penalty if they withdraw before that age), college savings plans and insurance (usually life insurance).

36   There were two primary keys to success in selling these rather bland products: consumer trust (consumers needed to be confident their money and personal information was secure) and competitive interest rates, as customers wanted to earn as much interest as possible on their assets and pay the least interest possible on their loans. Additional keys to success were:

- A wide variety of products so the customer had the convenience of one-stop shopping (for example, customers could open a savings account, buy life insurance and start a retirement savings plan at the same bank)—and the bank was able to increase share-of-wallet among customers.
- Options within each type of product to allow for greater flexibility in meeting customers' needs (for example, in addition to regular checking accounts, Bank of America offers student checking accounts to meet their unique needs such as a one-time refund on an unexpected service fee).
- Added services such as no fee checking, free direct deposit, overdraft protection and customer rewards programs.
- Easy access to account information (e.g., by phone or the Internet) and easy-to-read account statements.
- The ability to link all the accounts a customer might have with the bank, and provide information about all of the accounts in one account statement.
- Continually updating product portfolios with innovative products to meet customers' evolving needs and reach new consumer segments (for example, Citibank introduced the Construction Loan, whereby customers only need to make interest payments while they are building or renovating, and then begin making principal payments where construction is complete).

Customers

37   Most consumers used banks at least for savings deposit purposes, making it possible for banks to appeal to a mass market. Still, banks typically targeted certain segments of the population with specific products and service. In foreign countries, banks had to tailor their products to the primary needs of the local populations.

U.S. Customers

38   Targets that were of special interest to banks in the U.S. were specific age segments groups, women, and ethnic groups (most notably U.S. Hispanics and Asians).

39   *Age Segments.*   Banks segmented consumers in the U.S. by age. A common segmentation scheme was ages 42–60 (Baby Boomers), 26–41 (Generation X) and 18–25 (Generation Y). Each age group was at a different lifestage and therefore had different banking needs.

40   *Baby Boomers.*   Baby Boomers were people in the U.S. born between 1946 (the end of W.W. II) and 1964. During this time period, 78 million baby boomers (a.k.a. "Boomers") were born [Reynolds, 2004B]. Boomers made up a large majority of the work force and wealth component. Boomers were a prime target for banks because they not only represented the largest age group in the U.S., but it was also the age group with the highest net worth and therefore had the largest amount of assets to invest. Older Boomers were nearing retirement and were concerned with financial planning, health, travel, and their families (spouses, children, and grandchildren).

41   In order to bring Boomers into their franchise and increase their share-of-wallet, retail banks had to offer products that not only helped Boomers save for retirement, but also helped them manage their finances once they retired and had limited cash flowing in. With the exception of reverse mortgages, no banking products existed in 2006 that addressed financial issues related to living as a retired person. Boomers were also interested in life insurance and, increasingly, elder care plans. Elder care plans were special insurance plans that would cover one's expenses for assisted living or a nursing home. Many Boomers were experiencing problems associated with paying for elder care for their parents and did not want their own children to experience the same financial problems caring for them. Thus, the interest in buying elder care insurance was strong among Boomers.

42   Since Boomers craved information about managing their finances during retirement, there was an opportunity for retail banks to draw in customers by holding complimentary financial planning seminars in their branches as well as online in the form of Webcasts.

43   *Generation X.*   Generation X comprised of individuals in their mid-twenties through early forties, made up a much smaller portion of the U.S in terms of population size compared to Baby Boomers—49 million individuals versus 76 million individuals, respectively [Reynolds, 2004A]. Generation X was the best-educated generation in U.S. history and, unlike their Baby Boomer parents, Generation Xers started their careers with technological tools that never existed before. Also unlike their parents, Generation Xers faced unique challenges that resulted in them having to work even harder. These new challenges included raising children with both parents working and unprecedented expenses for their children, specifically child daycare costs in the short-term and astronomical college costs in the long term.

44   Despite their small population size, Generation Xers were a prime target for banks because they were earning good incomes, were in the market for items that required consumer financing (such as houses and cars) and, at the same time, were planning for their futures.

45   In order to attract and maintain Generation X customers, retail banks had to offer products that met their needs, specifically mortgages, college savings plans, and retirement planning services. Moreover, retail banks had to offer these products "under one roof." One-stop shopping would not only meet the product needs of Generation Xers, but also offer them the convenience they needed given their busy lifestyles.

46   In addition, retail banks had to advance their current account linkage systems so that customers would receive a single, comprehensive monthly statement that included information about all their accounts at a given bank (for example mortgage, retirement savings, and college savings information in one statement), plus gave customers the ability to easily transfer funds between these accounts. More advanced account linkage systems would be a great benefit to the hectic Generation Xer. No bank was able to provide such comprehensive account linkages—but the one that was first to market with complete account linkages would gain a strong foothold in the Generation X market.

47   In addition, with the advent of online securities, Generation Xers were likely to be involved in owning securities as investments. No bank had linked its personal securities business to its retail banking services but, again, there would be high rewards to the bank that was first to market with this combined offering.

48   As previously stated, Generation Xers were swamped with work and family responsibilities. To be successful in bringing them into their franchise, a retail bank had to offer services that made life easier for the Generation Xers. In addition, opportunities existed for banks to assign "personal financial assistants" to their customers who would proactively help them manage their accounts and take advantage of new product offers. Another opportunity might be building supervised play areas in branches where Generation X parents could leave their children while they spoke with financial advisors. The supervised play area idea had already been successfully instituted in the resort, casino, and fitness center industries.

49   Lastly, banks were interested in *Generation Y* customers. While they did not have a high level of assets now, they would in the future. It was important to meet Generation Y needs now (specifically student-oriented savings accounts and credit cards) to start building customer loyalty for the future.

50 ***Gender.***   Generation X women were better educated than Generation X men by almost 3% [Packaged Facts, 2004]. This level of education among women has resulted in a stronger presence of women in the workforce and contributions to household income by women that were much greater than preceding generations. Realizing the earning power of women, some banks were creating special products and services geared to their unique needs (such as special credit cards). Unique needs of women included:

- Women living longer and needing to find ways to pay for longer retirements.
- The possibility of having to leave the work force to care for their children or for elderly parents, resulting in loss of current income and lapses in retirement savings.

51   Banks could successfully cater to women's needs by offering them tailored education programs, personal attention to help them with their unique challenges (such as survivor financial counseling), and special savings on products and services to meet their needs (e.g., discounts on selected daycares).

52 ***Ethnic Groups.***   Banks could not ignore the growing U.S. Hispanic population, which jumped 22.4 million people in 1990 to over 40 million in 2003—and was still on the rise [U.S. Census Bureau, 2004]. The financial position of Hispanics was improving as well. According to the "U.S. Hispanic Economy in Transition" report [Hispanic Business, 2005]:

- The net worth of U.S. Hispanics surpassed $534 billion in 2000, up more than 30% in two years.
- Hispanic employment has grown more than 16% since 2000, while overall U.S. employment has barely grown 2%.
- Higher paying managerial and professional jobs were the fastest-growing occupational categories for Hispanics.

53   In order to capture the Hispanic market, banks had to provide Spanish-language brochures and Spanish-speaking financial advisors in branches that were located in high-concentration Hispanic areas. Spanish-speaking telephone representatives had to be made available to Hispanic customers. Since Hispanics were very family-oriented, marketing messages had to focus on the benefit to the family, not the individual. Similarly, customer loyalty programs had to offer rewards to the family, not just the individual [Camacho, 2005].

54   Banks were also very interested in the Asian-American segment. Asian-Americans had the highest median income in the United States and were the best-educated group in the U.S. and had a younger and more rapidly growing population than the Whites [Angell, 2006]. Asian-Americans had more assets to invest at banks than the general population and were likely to take advantage of investment products such as college savings and securities trading.

55   To attract Asian customers, banks had to offer multilingual bankers (e.g., those fluent in Mandarin, Cantonese, Korean, or Vietnamese) at branches located in areas with high populations of Asians (such as San Francisco and New York).

Non-U.S. Customers

56   The non-U.S. market was a very attractive growth area as population growth and migration to the middle class in these areas meant more customer opportunities (these demographic trends were especially strong in China, India, and Russia). To attract customers in foreign countries, banks had to invest in research to thoroughly understand their cultures, behaviors, and financial needs and then develop products to meet their unique needs. Research was also critical for developing culturally appropriate marketing strategies.

CRM (Customer Relationship Management)

57   In trying to meet consumers' needs, banks were turning more and more to customer relationship management (CRM) systems. CRMs were being leveraged for multi-touch marketing, which meant bringing "all sorts of customer data together for sales and service through whatever distribution channels customers use, whether branches, ATMs, telephones or the Internet" [Groenfeldt, 2006]. In 2005, banks spent a little over $4 billion on CRM in North America. Banks that embraced CRM believed that it could use it as a means to offering personalized services to millions of customers. Banks could profile individual customers on the products they used and the transactions they made. Of course, to be of any value, CRMs had to have dedicated analytics personnel and the ability to act on their findings, specifically to use the information to sell more products to each customer thereby increasing share-of-wallet.

Outlets

58   There were three primary outlets for banking: branch banking (traditional retail outlets), telephone, banking, and online banking.

Branch Banking

59   Bank outlets took the form of branch banks, telephone banking, and online banking. In order to attract and maintain customers, outlets had to have a modern design and the atmosphere had to be clean, friendly, and professional. The bank had to provide a positive and distinctive branch experience. Some financial institutions, like Umpqua Bank, Washington Mutual, and U.S. Bancorp, made branches with casual atmospheres, and offered such benefits as free coffee and chocolates, newspapers, and Internet access, and kids' play rooms. Maintaining quality and consistency across the branches was also imperative. In addition, a branch bank had to be easily accessible by consumers—therefore, it had to be in a convenient location and have extended hours of operation.

60   *Customer Service.*   Within each branch there were customer service representatives, namely bank tellers (for serviced basic banking needs) and financial advisors (who usually had their own offices to conduct private discussion with customers about their financial situations). Customer service representatives in the branches had to dress professionally, and be polite, friendly, and knowledgeable about banking products and services so that they could cross-sell the banks products and services.

Telephone Banking

61   For telephone banking to be successful, customers had to have a positive experience on the phone. Automated telephone systems had to be easy to use (the less buttons to press the better).

62   *Customer Service.*   Telephone customer service representatives had to be friendly, polite, and knowledgeable about all banking products and services.

Online Banking

63   Online banking—whereby individuals made account balance inquiries, transfer funds, paid bills, and managed assets such as stocks online—was launched in 1999. Banks welcomed the idea of online banking because it helped cut expenses. However, adoption by customers had been slow: By 2004, only 40% of Americans claimed to have used online banking, a technology that had been in existence for five years [Ipsos, 2004]. A major barrier to entry among consumers was fear of outside companies or hackers gaining access to their personal information. To be successful in online banking, banks had to leverage technology to ensure personal security. In addition, websites had to be visually appealing and user-friendly so that customers could complete their transactions quickly and easily.

64   *Customer Service.*   Since there was no human interface for customers who conducted their banking online, it was critical that customer service representatives be easily accessible. This was typically accomplished by providing 24-hour toll-free telephone assistance. Of course, telephone representatives had to be polite and knowledgeable.

Marketing

65   Marketing was a critical function in the retail banking industry. Retail banking used marketing to attract new customers and increase share-of-wallet among existing customers. Marketing could be accomplished through various vehicles, including direct selling, advertising, sponsorships, direct mail, consumer promotions, brochures, customer loyalty programs, and Websites. Most national banks leveraged most of these vehicles in their marketing mix.

Direct Selling

66   All banks engaged in direct selling in which financial advisors who worked in the branches offered visiting customers new products and services. In order to be successful, financial advisors had to be well-versed in all of the banks' products and be able to communicate the product benefits to the consumer. Part of the selling process involved educating customers on how various financial instruments worked. Staff training on all products was essential.

Advertising

67   Retail banks used advertising to accomplish one or more of the following objectives:

1. Communicate a trustworthy corporate image.
2. Communicate the bank's financial planning expertise.
3. Communicate the launch of new and innovative products.

68   Advertising took the form of TV and print advertising, radio, sponsorships, billboards, and online banners, pop-ups, and key word searches. TV advertising was by far the largest investment due to the high cost of production and television air time. National banks usually hired large, well-known advertising agencies to create and produce their advertising campaigns. In order to be successful, ads had to be memorable, relevant, believable, and persuasive.

69   Retail bank advertising was challenging. Most banking and other financial services were dry and unexciting and getting a consumer to pay attention to the ad was not easy. To be effective, advertising for a retail bank had to be unique and engaging, and yet retain a serious tone as the ads were asking consumers to trust their money with that bank.

Sponsorships

70   Some retail banks used sponsorships to generate awareness of the bank and position the bank in a certain light. For example, Bank of America sponsored various sporting events and teams, including the U.S. Olympic Team, the PGA Tour, and professional and local teams. The keys to success in using sponsorships as part of the marketing strategy were to choose events that fit with the corporate image and ensuring that the events reached a wide audience (for example, making sure that the sponsored event was being televised for national television broadcast on a major TV network).

Direct Mail

71   Direct mail was used largely to promote credit cards. Direct mail pieces might entice a consumer with low credit card interest rates. In order to be successful, direct mail pieces had to have a clear and easy call to action, such as a toll-free number to call to activate the card immediately.

Consumer Promotions

72   Retail banks often used consumer promotions as a tool for increasing trial of their basic banking services. An example of a consumer promotion might be a free iPod for opening an account with the bank. Consumer promotions had to be employed carefully so as not to diminish from the prestige of the bank.

Brochures

73   Retail banks produced brochures about their products (such as college savings and retirement plans) that they made available to consumers in the bank branches. To be effective, brochures had to effectively communicate how the products worked and their benefits to customers. Equally important was that onsite bank representatives distributed the brochures to consumers and not let them sit on a shelf.

Customer Loyalty Programs

74   Banks were increasingly using customer loyalty programs not only to retain customers but also to increase the number of services they used with a particular bank. For example, Bank of America attempted to retain customers with its "Rewards for Airline, Hotel, and Automotive Partners" program, in which customers earned miles for airline travel or points for hotel stays by using Bank of America's partner credit cards (e.g., US Airways Visa, Hawaiian Airlines Visa, and Asiana Visa). Customers were less likely to switch away from these credit cards because they would lose the miles and points they had accumulated. Citibank's "Thank You" program attempted to increase customers' share-of-wallet by offering monthly points based on the number of Citibank products and services the customer used. A customer who used 3 Citibank products or services earned up to 325 points per month, while a customer who used 7 or more Citibank products or services could earn up to 2,400 points per month. The points could be redeemed for credit card account statement credits and lower interest rates.

75 Keys to success for customer loyalty programs were ease of use and relevant rewards.

Websites

76 Websites were an increasingly important element of the marketing mix. Websites could be leveraged to create and bolster the corporate image, provide information about products and services, and educate consumers about financial instruments. However, to be successful, Websites had to be easy-to-navigate.

Competition

77 The largest U.S. bank, in terms of assets, was Citigroup, followed closely by Bank of America Corporation, and J.P. Morgan Chase & Co, as shown in Figure 6. In 2004, J.P. Morgan Chase acquired Bank One and Bank of America acquired FleetBoston, which put both institutions in the range of $1 trillion in assets (but still behind number one bank Citigroup). Future acquisition deals for these super financial institutions would likely focus on smaller, more strategic acquisition to fill gaps in the international market, which most large banks were trying to gain a foothold in.

78 This case study will evaluate Citigroup's two major competitors, Bank of America and J.P. Morgan Chase, in detail. Citigroup's smaller competitors will be evaluated in less detail.

Bank of America

79 Bank of America was the U.S.'s first coast-to-coast bank. It became even stronger in 2004 when it acquired FleetBoston. Bank of America was the second-largest bank in the US in terms of assets (behind Citigroup). Through its expertise in de novo branch banking and smart acquisitions, Bank of America had the country's most extensive branch network, with more than 5,800 locations covering 30 states. Bank of America branches were located in prime locations that were easily accessible to customers, and the company had good geographic dispersion throughout the U.S. In early 2006, Bank of America purchased MBNA credit card company, which doubled its credit card customer base to 40 million active accounts. Global Consumer and Small Business Banking, which included credit cards, was Bank of America's largest segment, and also provided deposits, insurance, loans, treasury services, and financing of car, boat, and RV dealerships. The bank claimed market share leadership in California, Florida, Massachusetts, New Jersey, and Washington State [Bank of America, 2005, 2006].

80 Bank of America also operated in Europe, Asia, Canada, and South America, with adequate knowledge of local cultures, laws, technology, and decent relationships with local governments. Bank of America had a representation in China and sold credit cards in India but did not have a presence in Russia.

FIGURE 6
Top 50 Bank Holding Companies as of 12/31/2005

Source: National Information Center, (2006), "Financial Data and Institutional Characteristics Collected by The Federal Reserve System." [Online]. *http://www.ffiec. gov/ nicpubweb/ nicweb/ Top50Form.aspx.* February 22, 2006.

Rank	Institution Name	Location	Total Assets
1	Citigroup Inc.	New York, NY	$1,494,037,000
2	Bank Of America Corporation	Charlotte, NC	$1,294,312,241
3	J.P. Morgan Chase & Co.	New York, NY	$1,198,942,000
4	Wachovia Corporation	Charlotte, NC	$ 520,755,000
5	Wells Fargo & Company	San Francisco, CA	$ 481,741,000
6	HSBC North America Holdings Inc.	Prospect Heights, IL	$ 395,534,168
7	Taunus Corporation	New York, NY	$ 364,693,000
8	U.S. Bancorp	Minneapolis, MN	$ 209,465,000
9	Suntrust Banks, Inc.	Atlanta, GA	$ 179,712,841
10	Countrywide Financial Corporation	Calabasas, CA	$ 175,085,370

81   Bank of America had not been involved in major scandals or security breaches and was a bank that consumers trusted. Bank of America offered a wide variety of products including savings accounts, checking accounts, credit cards, and home loans—all with competitive interest rates. Moreover, it offered flexible options within each type of product. For example, within checking, it offered regular checking, preferred checking (that offered reward points), MyAccess Checking® (which did not require a minimum balance) and CampusEdge® Checking (to meet students' checking needs). Bank of America offered added services such as a Free Visa® Check Card, free direct deposit, overdraft protections, and free scheduled transfers. Bank of America accounts could be accessed at anytime using their online and telephone banking systems.

82   Bank of America struggled to link accounts beyond checking and savings and to create new and unique products.

83   Bank of America was very strong in attracting Generation X and Generation Y customers, but struggled with the Baby Boomer segment. While Bank of America did offer retirement savings plans and life insurance, it did not offer products or information to help retired persons manage their finances, nor did it offer elder care insurance. Bank of America was strong in offering Generation X the products and services it needed, namely mortgages and one-stop shopping, and offered decent college and retirement savings plans. Similar to its competitors, it lacked comprehensive account statements and advanced account linkage systems. Bank of America had not yet developed innovative services such as personal financial assistants or supervised play areas for children. Bank of America was superior in attracting Generation Y customers as it offered unique Student-oriented savings plans and credit cards.

84   On the other hand, Bank of America did not offer any unique products or services to women, such as tailored education programs, personal attention, or special savings on products or services to meet their needs.

85   Bank of America was also lagging in providing Hispanic customers with products and services they needed, such as in-language branch bankers and marketing messages aimed at the family or customer reward programs that offered family benefits. Bank of America did provide Spanish-speaking telephone representatives. Bank of America was ahead of the curve in marketing to Asian Americans by offering multilingual bankers at branches located in areas with high populations of Asians (e.g., in California).

86   Regarding customers in foreign markets, Bank of America did an average job in investing in research about foreign markets and using research to develop culturally appropriate marketing strategies.

87   Bank of America performed adequately in terms of customer relationship management.

88   Bank of America maintained modern, clean branches, uniquely designed with a "hostess" at the front door and a lounge area with couches and magazines. The Bank of America branch atmosphere provided the customer with an exceptional branch experience that was consistent across branches. Bank of America was on par with competition in terms of convenient locations.

89   Bank of America's telephone banking ease of use and customer service was also on par with competition. Bank of America's online banking was also on par with competition in terms of personal security, visual appeal/ease of navigation, and customer service.

90   Bank of America had a well-oiled machine in terms of marketing. While its direct selling was just on par with competition, the company was known for its innovative ad campaigns, including one that was run in 2002 for their ATM machines which featured a man walking around and running into a Bank of America ATM at every turn as "Jaws-like" music played in the background. Finally, he says, "They're everywhere," meaning the ATM machines.

91   Bank of America's sponsorships (mainly in sports venues targeted to Generation X and Y) fit with its corporate image and reached a wide audience. Bank of America's direct mail and consumer promotions were on par with the competition. Bank of America's brochures made it easy for customers to understand their products and benefits, although distribution to customers was only average, and its Website was easy-to-navigate, with product information clearly displayed in the homepage. Bank of America launched their "Keep the Change" program in 2005. Every time a customer bought something with a Bank of America debit card, Bank of America rounded up the purchase to the nearest dollar and transferred the difference from their checking to their savings account. Plus, for the first 3 months, Bank of America matched the "Keep the Change: Savings at 100%." While this program attempted to provide customers with much valued-cash back, it was somewhat hard to understand.

92   Bank of America's Website was superior in terms of ease of navigation and product information, average in reinforcing the corporate image and poor in educating consumers about financial instruments.

J.P. Morgan Chase

93   In 2001, Chase Manhattan, a retail banking giant, merged with prestigious investment bank J.P. Morgan to form J.P. Morgan Chase & Company. In 2004, J.P. Morgan Chase & Co., then the third-largest financial services firm in the US, acquired Bank One, the sixth-largest bank in the country. Through strategic acquisitions and some de novo branch banking, J.P. Morgan's branch network extended to the Midwest and South and strengthened its retail operations, where the company was already a leader in the U.S. in mortgages and credit cards. Like its competitors, J.P. Morgan Chase branches were located in prime locations [J.P. Morgan Chase, 2005, 2006].

94   J.P. Morgan Chase had operations in 50 countries and had adequate country knowledge and decent relationships with local governments. However, the company had limited retail bank operations in China, India, or Russia.

95   J.P. Morgan Chase was an exceptionally trusted name and offered a wide range of products at competitive interest rates, with flexible options within each type of product. J.P. Morgan Chase was on par with the competition in terms of added services, easy access to account information, account linkages, and product innovation.

96   In terms of its customer base, J.P. Morgan Chase did not have a special positioning with any consumer group. While it offered exceptional retirement savings that appealed to Baby Boomers and Generation Xers, it did not offer any special products or services in the areas of retirement finance management, life insurance, elder care or retirement education. The bank was on par or sub-par with its competition in attracting Generation X customers as its mortgages, college savings plans and one-stop shopping did not offer any unique benefits. Similar to its competition, J.P. Morgan Chase struggled with advanced account statements and linking Chase accounts to J.P. Morgan securities accounts. J.P. Morgan did not offer any innovative services to Generation X, to Generation Y, or to women. By and large, J.P. Morgan was on par with its competition in marketing to Hispanics and to Asian Americans.

97   J.P. Morgan Chase retail banking was not strong abroad and therefore the company had not invested in multinational research. J.P. Morgan was not as adept at using CRMs to connect with consumers as some of its competitors. The company's retail banking branches were in fair condition and consistent, albeit non-descript in appearance. The branches were located in convenient locations. Customer service lagged behind some competitors. Telephone banking and online banking were generally on par with competition. In terms of marketing, J.P. Morgan Chase's financial advisors were average. While the company's sponsorships, direct mail, and consumer promotions were on par with competition, its advertising was lackluster. The company's brochures and distribution of brochures also fell short.

98   J.P. Morgan Chase had yet to develop a marketing plan that showed one face. J.P. Morgan, Chase, and Bank One had separate marketing plans, and separate Websites (although the Chase and Bank One Websites were easy-to-navigate, reinforced their individual company images, and prominently featured their products). J.P. Morgan needed to develop a strategy that demonstrated to the customers the benefits they would reap as a result of the J.P. Morgan/Chase/Bank One merger.

Wachovia

99   Wachovia, the fourth largest bank in the U.S., was formed in 2001 when East Coast banking bought Wachovia (taking the smaller firm's name). Wachovia had more than 3,200 locations that offered retail and corporate banking services in 16 eastern and southern states. Wachovia was known for its expertise in wealth management, mutual funds, insurance, and corporate finance. The company had entered metropolitan markets in Texas by building new branches and opened about 100 new banking locations in 2005, including about a dozen in Manhattan.

Wells Fargo and Company

100   Wells Fargo was the fifth-largest bank in the U.S. It had about 3,000 bank branches covering about 25 states in the western and Midwestern U.S. It also had about 1,000 home mortgage stores across the country. Wells Fargo specialized in consumer and business banking, investment management, venture capital, and international trade. Wells Fargo was the industry leader in insurance brokerage, online banking, and online brokerage services.

HSBC North America Holdings Inc.

101   HSBC North America Holdings, with about 60 million customers, offered personal and commercial banking services, mortgage services, consumer finance, private banking, insurance, and corporate investment banking under the HSBC, HFC, and Beneficial brands. HSBC North America's Retail Services division issues private label credit cards through agreements with about 60 retailers and manufacturers, including Best Buy, Saks Fifth Avenue, and Neiman Marcus.

Taunus Corporation

102   Taunus Corporation was a subsidiary of Deutsche Bank, one of the largest banks in the world. Deutsche Bank offered retail banking services in Germany, and investment banking and asset management business throughout Europe, the Pacific Rim, and the Americas. The company's strategy was to become the "Wal-Mart of asset management." In 2004, Deutsche Bank acquired Berkshire Mortgage, one of the top residential lenders in the U.S.

U.S. Bancorp

103   U.S. Bancorp, which owned U.S. Bank and other subsidiaries, operated nearly 2,500 locations in the U.S. and about two-dozen midwestern and western states, along with more than 4,600 branded ATMs. U.S. Bancorp owned U.S. Bank and other subsidiaries that provided consumer and commercial banking, as well as mortgage banking, international banking, consumer finance, equipment lease financing, and title and business insurance. U.S. Bank planned to open more than 160 branches inside Safeway stores in California, Nevada, and Arizona by 2006.

Suntrust Banks, Inc.

104   SunTrust Bank operated about 1,700 bank branches in southeastern states, including Alabama, the Carolinas, Florida, Georgia, Maryland, Tennessee, Virginia, and Washington, D.C. SunTrust Bank offered retail and commercial banking, trust services, credit cards, mortgage banking, mutual funds, insurance, equipment leasing, asset management, and securities underwriting, and dealing. SunTrust bought National Commerce Financial in 2004, which helped the bank expand in existing territories and gain entry into the growing North Carolina market. SunTrust was focusing on building other fee-based businesses, such as retail brokerage, asset management, and investment banking.

Countrywide Financial Corporation

105 Countrywide Financial Corporation was one of the largest independent residential mortgage-lending firms in the U.S. It also offered home equity loans, property/casualty, health, and credit insurance. Countrywide Financial operated approximately 600 branch offices in all 50 states (except Vermont) and Washington, D.C. The company operated primarily in the US, but processed mortgages through a joint venture Barclays. Countrywide generated 80% of its earnings from mortgage banking.

THE COMPANY

106 Citigroup was the world's largest financial institution. The company organized itself into three major business groups: Global Consumer, Corporate and Investment Banking, and Global Wealth Management. The company also operated two stand-alone businesses: Citigroup Asset Management and Citigroup Alternative Investments. In 2006, the Global Consumer unit was Citigroup's most significant business, accounting for over half of its profits.

History

107 Citigroup's mission was to become the world leader in banking by having the most extensive distribution network in the world.

108 Citigroup's history dates back to 1864 when Predecessor Travelers Group (the first US accident insurer) was founded in Hartford, Connecticut. Travelers expanded into life insurance, annuities, liability insurance, and auto insurance. In the late 1970s and early 1980s, Travelers branched out into financial services. The company experienced problems in the late 1980s when the real estate market declined and as a result their mortgage business suffered. Eventually Travelers sold its home mortgage business and, in its weakened condition, attracted Sanford "Sandy" Weill. Weill had built brokerage firm Shearson Loeb Rhoades and sold it to American Express in 1981. When Weill was forced out of American Express in 1985, he bought Control Data's Commercial Credit unit. In 1988, Weill's Commercial Credit bought Primerica, a financial services company and parent to Smith Barney, Harris Upham & Co. In 1993, Primerica bought Shearson from American Express, as well as Travelers, taking its name and logo.

109 Realizing the company was losing its focus, Weill sold its life subsidiaries and bought Aetna's property/casualty business in 1995. In 1996, he consolidated all property/casualty operations to form Travelers Property Casualty and took it public. In 1997, Travelers bought investment bank Salomon Brothers and formed Salomon Smith Barney Holdings (now Citigroup Global Markets).

110 In 1998, Weill initiated the merger between Travelers and Citicorp. Following the merger, both sides experienced significant losses driven by a slow U.S. economy and overseas turmoil. Citigroup was forced to lay off more than 10,000 employees.

111 In 1999, Citigroup pioneered online banking by launching Internet banking services on AOL. In 2000, the company launched online brokerage under the name Cititrade. The year 2000 was also an important one for Citigroup as it bought subprime lender Associates First Capital (now part of CitiFinancial) in order to expand its consumer product lines and its international presence. Citigroup continued its aggressive domestic and global expansion in 2001 and 2002. In 2001, the company bought European American Bank and Grupo

Financiero Banamex, one of Mexico's biggest banks. In 2002, it bought California-based Golden State Bancorp.

112 The year 2002 marked the start of extensive legal and regulatory problems for Citigroup. Citigroup paid about $215 million that year to settle federal allegations that Associates First Capital made customers unwittingly purchase credit insurance by automatically billing for the service. Citigroup then became entangled in the Enron scandal when it was accused of floating short-term loans to Enron and being used by Enron in transactions with offshore entities to mask debt and inflate cash flow Figures. While Citigroup neither confirmed nor denied the allegations, it earmarked more than $100 million to pay victims who lost money because of Enron's malfeasance.

113 In 2003, the SEC implied that Citigroup issued favorable stock ratings to companies in exchange for investment banking contracts. Again, Citigroup neither confirmed nor denied the allegations but paid over $400 million in fines. During this time, Citigroup decided to separate its stock-picking and corporate advisory businesses and created a retail brokerage and equity research unit called Smith Barney.

114 In 2004, Citigroup was forced to pay $2.65 billion to WorldCom investors because Citigroup was one of the lead underwriters for WorldCom stocks and bonds. Again, Citigroup admitted no wrongdoing. (Between WorldCom and Enron, Citigroup had to set aside an additional $5 billion to cover legal fees.) Also in 2004, Citigroup was forced to shut down its private banking operations in Japan after regulators determined that the company had misled customers regarding the sale of certain structured bonds. Prince forced the resignation of three top executives as a result of the Japanese scandal.

115 Despite its legal troubles, Citigroup produced net profits of nearly $18 billion (on revenues in excess of $94 billion) in 2003, one of the largest annual profits in U.S. corporate history. At the peak of Citigroup's financial success, CEO Sandy Weill stepped down as CEO of Citigroup and named Citigroup corporate and investment bank head Chuck Prince as his successor. In the years that followed, Prince would be challenged by more regulatory scandals, plus corporate image problems and technological mishaps.

Current Situation

116 CEO Chuck Prince seemed to be focused on a strategy of expanded distribution, but with a leaner machine. In 2005, Citigroup sold The Travelers Life and Annuity Company, along with most of its international insurance business to Metlife for nearly $12 billion. Also that year Citigroup sold its commercial truck and trailer leasing and lending business to GE Commercial Finance for $4.6 billion. While J.P. Morgan Chase and Bank of America continued to acquire large domestic competitors (Bank One and FleetBoston, respectively), Citigroup, under Prince's guidance, focused on smaller, more strategic acquisitions to fill gaps in its product line as well as in the global market. Citigroup bought the credit card receivables portfolio of Sears, Roebuck and Co. for $32 billion as well as the credit card business of Federated Department Stores and May Department Stores. Other purchases made under Prince's watch included Principal Financial Group's mortgage business, Hibernia's mortgage services, South Korea's KorAm Bank, and First American Bank in the U.S.

117 Figure 7 provides an overview of Citigroup.

Distribution

118 Citigroup's distribution extended throughout the U.S. and abroad.

U.S.

119 Through an aggressive acquisition strategy and an expertise in de novo branch banking, Citibank had built strong distribution with more than 3,000 bank branches and consumer

FIGURE 7 **Citigroup Overview**

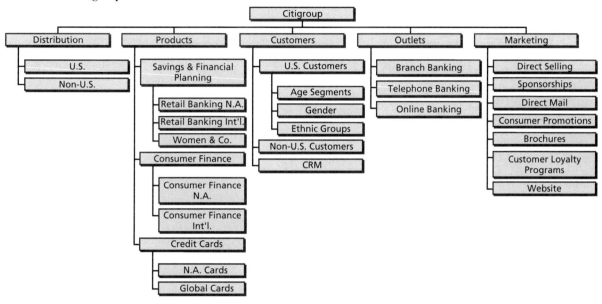

finance offices in the US and Canada. Similar to competitors, Citibank branches were located in prime locations and had good geographic dispersion.

Non–U.S.

120 Citigroup had consumer businesses in 53 countries outside the U.S. Citigroup had made great strides in infiltrating foreign markets: In 2004, the company acquired KorAm Bank in Korea (Citigroup's largest investment ever in Asia), partnered with Shanghai Pudong Development Bank in China, and opened its first branch bank in St. Petersburg, Russia (which offered credit cards and consumer lending) [Citigroup Annual Report 2004, 2005]. Citigroup also had a presence in India where it sold credit cards and promoted credit education. Establishing a presence in each of these countries had required in-depth knowledge of the country and positive relationships with their governments. In fact, CEO Chuck Prince had met personally with President Vladimir Putin "to pitch him on a credit card and discuss the bank's ambitious expansion plans in Russia, one of its priority markets" [Chazan, 2005].

Products

121 The Citigroup Global Consumer businesses comprised a diverse and innovative set of consumer product offerings, including savings and deposits, consumer financing, credit cards, and financial planning in the U.S. and abroad. Products fell into one of several divisions within the Citigroup Global Consumer business unit.

Savings and Financial Planning

122 Within the Citigroup Global Consumer business unit, savings and financial products were organized into three sub-divisions: Retail Banking North America, Retail Banking International, and Women and Co.

123 ***Retail Banking North America.*** Retail Banking North America included branch banking, commercial banking, commercial real estate, commercial financing and leasing, mortgages, student loans, and the Primerica Financial Services distribution channel. Retail Banking North America was operated under the following brand names: Citibanking North America, Commercial Markets/Commercial Real Estate, CitiCapital, CitiMortgage and

My Home Equity, The Student Loan Corporation, Primerica Financial Services, Women in Primerica, Primerica Financial Needs Analysis, The Primerica Opportunity, Primerica Financial Solutions, Primerica African American Leadership Council, and Banamex.

124 *Retail Banking International.* Through its Retail Banking International unit, Citibank offered financial products and services tailored to meet the needs of local customers in over 50 countries.

125 *Women and Co.* Women and Company specialized in the unique financial needs of women.

Consumer Finance

126 Within the Citigroup Global Consumer business unit, consumer finance (lending) products were organized into two sub-divisions: Consumer Finance North America and Consumer Finance International.

127 *Consumer Finance North America.* The Consumer Finance North America unit offered consumer finance and community-based lending services across North America. The unit had a customer base of 4.3 million consumers in the United States, Canada, Mexico, and Puerto Rico, operating under the brand names CitiFinancial and Credito Familiar.

128 *Consumer Finance International.* The Consumer Finance International unit offered consumer finance and community-based lending services in 20 countries outside North America, operating under a number of brands around the world.

Credit Cards

129 Within the Citigroup Global Consumer business unit, credit cards products were organized into two sub-divisions: North America Cards and Global Cards.

130 *North America Cards.* The North America Cards unit offered credit and charge cards such as Mastercard MasterCard®, VISA®, and private labels. North America Cards boasted over 120 million accounts. Citigroup Global Consumer offered four types of cards in North America:

- Reward Cards—Cards for earning Thank You Points®, cash back, travel miles, and other rewards.
- Value Credit Cards—Basic cards.
- Small Business Credit Cards—Cards that included expert financial advice.
- College Student Credit Cards—Cards marketed to help students build credit history (did not require a co-signor).

131 *Global Cards.* The Global Cards unit offered an array of cards to countries outside North America. Global Cards had 20.9 million accounts in 42 countries outside of North America.

132 Citigroup's Global Consumer business offered competitive interest rates, a wide variety of products and flexible options within each product. Citibank's products covered the four categories of deposits, consumer financing, credit cards, and financial planning. Moreover, customers could choose from a variety of options within each of these product types. For example, it offered several varieties of credit cards, including rewards cards, value credit cards, and college student credit cards. Moreover, Citigroup offered added services such as 24/7 access to accounts, overdraft protection and online bill payments and email banking alerts.

133 Citigroup has faced some challenges in the other keys to success, namely trust, account linkage, and product innovation.

134 Citigroup lost some footing in the area of trust when it became embroiled in both the WorldCom and Enron scandals, which gained international attention. In Japan, Citigroup faced more embarrassment when it was forced in 2004 to shut down its private banking operations there after regulators determined that the company had misled customers regarding the sale of certain structured bonds. And, in the U.S., Citigroup lost a box of computer tapes with account information for 3.9 million of its customers, exposing these customers to the possibility of identity theft [Krim, 2005]. In response, Citigroup sent out letters to all of its U.S. customers warning them to watch their financial accounts for suspicious transactions and offering a 90-day service to alert them if someone tried to establish credit in their name. Still, the company was now associated with security breaches by current as well as potential customers.

135   Account linkage was also a challenge faced by Citigroup, as well as other top banks. While basic savings and checking accounts were linked, customers who had accounts at Citibank and Smith Barney could not transfer across accounts and did not enjoy consolidated account statements.

136   Finally, Citibank struggled with new product innovation. In fact, it had shifted its strategy away from product development and more towards distribution, as evidenced by CEO Chuck Weill publicly stating that Citigroup was a "distribution company now." While Citibank had a full service offering, it still needed to make new product development a priority if it were to keep up with competition.

Customers

137   Citigroup's Global Consumer business unit focused on two major customer segments: U.S. customers and non-U.S. Customers. Customer relationship management (CRM) was an important tool used for gaining customer insight.

U.S. Customers

138   U.S. customers were classified by age segments, gender, and ethnicity.

139   *Age Segments.*   Citibank had a history of being all things to all people. It offered products that met the needs of people in all stages of life, from college students to those nearing and in retirement.

140   For its *Baby Boomer* customers, Citibank lagged behind some of its competitors in its retirement savings offer and was on par in its life insurance offer. It had not yet met the emerging needs of Baby Boomers, specifically retirement finance management, elder care insurance, or special education programs about living in retirement.

141   For the *Generation X* customer base, Citibank was weak in its mortgage and retirement savings products, and was competitive in offering college savings plans and one-stop shopping. Citibank had not yet developed a unified, linked account statement or a link between bank accounts and securities accounts (i.e., a link between the Citibank division and the Smith Barney division). There were also opportunities in the industry that Citibank had not taken advantage of, such as personal assistants and supervised play areas in the branches.

142   Citibank was weak in attracting *Generation Y* customers, as it did not offer special services to them, such as student-oriented savings accounts or credit cards.

143   *Gender.*   Citibank recognized the potential of focusing on women, and created a special business unit dedicate to their needs called "Women & Company." This unit provided women with tailored education programs, personal attention to help them with their unique challenges (such as survivor financial counseling), and special savings on products and services to meet their needs (e.g., discounts on selected daycares). No other retail bank provided such specialized services to women.

144   *Ethnic Groups.*   The company provided Spanish-language brochures and Spanish-speaking financial advisors in branches located in high-concentration Hispanic areas and created marketing messages that focused on benefits to the family, not just the individual. Citibank provided Spanish-speaking telephone representatives but did not have specialized Hispanic customer loyalty programs.

145   Citibank still needed to create a strategy for bringing Asian Americans into their customer base.

Non–U.S. Customers

146   Citigroup was at the forefront of integrating themselves in foreign markets. The company invested heavily in research to understand cultures, behaviors, and financial needs and then developed products to meet unique needs. In addition, it used its research to develop culturally appropriate marketing strategies abroad.

Customer Relationship Management

147   Citigroup was on the cutting-edge of customer relationship marketing. The company collected information from credit card transactions, so it could tell what customers bought, where they went on vacation and more [Groenfeldt, 2006]. It used this information to cross-sell its products and create more relevant customer rewards programs.

Outlets

148   Citigroup's consumer banking outlets included branch banking, telephone banking, and online banking.

Branch Banking

149   Citigroup branches were somewhat outdated, with some branches having a better appearance than others. Compared to some of its competitors (like Bank of America) Citibank branches did not offer a positive, distinctive experience.

150   *Customer Service.* Customer service representatives were generally knowledgeable, having been trained on Citibank's Citipro® financial check-up, a tool used to measure consumers' financial needs.

Telephone Banking

151   Citibank's telephone banking was on par with competition in terms of ease of use.

152   *Customer Service.* Telephone customer service representatives met industry standards in terms of knowledge and professionalism.

Online Banking

153   Online banking—whereby individuals made account balance inquiries, transferred funds, paid bills, and managed assets such as stocks online—was launched by Citigroup in 1999. Banks welcomed the idea of online banking because it helped cut expenses. However, adoption by customers had been slow: By 2004, only 40% of Americans claimed to have used online banking [Ipsos, 2004], a technology that had been in existence for five years at that time. A major barrier to entry among consumers was fear of outside companies or hackers gaining access to their personal information. To be successful in online banking, banks had to leverage technology to ensure personal security. Unfortunately, Citibank had lost customer confidence in guaranteeing personal security when it lost customers' records in 2005. There was room for improvement in the visual appeal and ease of navigation of its online banking.

154   *Customer Service.* Online customer service was adequate in terms of knowledge and being easy to reach.

Marketing

155   Citigroup leveraged a variety of marketing tools to inform customers about their products and services and persuaded them to try them. These tools included direct selling, advertising, sponsorships, direct mail, consumer promotions, brochures, customer loyalty programs, and their Website.

Direct Selling

156   Citigroup supported its direct selling by arming each of its financial advisors with the Citipro® financial check-up tool, which allowed them to better understand their customers' needs.

Advertising

157   Citigroup's Global Consumer Group's marketing focused largely on its "Live richly" advertising campaign. Launched in 2001, the campaign won numerous awards. The campaign's objective was to communicate that Citi is "an advocate for a Healthy Approach to Money." The campaign positions Citi as an "active partner in achieving perspective, balance, and peace of mind in finances and in life for its customers." The "Live richly campaign used lively, color imagery and engaged the consumer because it focused on the consumer benefits, but still was not up to par with the creativeness of competitors' advertising.

158   The "Live richly" campaign appeared in television commercials, print ads, phone kiosks, billboards, bus shelters, subway stations, and construction bridges. The outdoor component of the campaign was shown in six cities in the U.S.: New York City, Chicago, San Francisco, Los Angeles, Miami, and Washington D.C.

Sponsorships

159   With sponsorships of variety of well-known charitable organizations, such as the American Red Cross and Habitat for Humanity, Citibank is on par with its competition.

Direct Mail

160   Citigroup made extensive use of direct mail, which educated customers about its various products and made it easy for them to sign-up for cards simply by dialing a toll-free number. Direct mail pieces fit Citibank's brand image.

Consumer Promotions

161   Citigroup's consumer promotions were on level with the competition.

Brochures

162   Citigroup brochures carried out the "Live richly" campaign by using the same imagery and focusing on how Citibank products could help customers live more fulfilling lives by acquiring and renovating their homes, taking vacations and the like. The quality of their brochures and their distribution were average.

Customer Loyalty Programs

163   Citigroup offered an easy-to-understand rewards program called the "Thank You Network®" which enabled customers to earn points for using many of Citibanks's banking services. The program was easier to understand than most competitive programs, although the rewards offered were mediocre.

Website

164   Citibank's Website was weak. The Website mixed corporate information with consumer information, and the links were scattered making it difficult to navigate and, therefore, difficult to find product information and other critical information. Moreover, the website did not feature the imagery or messaging of the "Live richly" campaign used in the company's advertising and brochures. The Website could not be used by customers to educate themselves about financial instruments.

Management Strategy

165   Chuck Prince had been named CEO of Citigroup in October 2003. Filling former CEO Sandy Weill's shoes was not an easy job. Over the last two decades, Weill had built

Citigroup from the ground up into the largest bank in the U.S. and a global financial services powerhouse. Before being named CEO, Prince had served as general counsel under Weill overseeing regulatory matters and not involving much with the strategy or operation of the company. Now, Prince had to develop a vision for Citigroup and implement a strategy that would bolster its global consumer business performance and ensure Citigroup's dominant position into the future.

166   Citigroup's main competitive advantages were its name and scale, and Prince was counting on these strengths to successfully implement his three-prong strategy for Citigroup [Der Hovanesian, 2006].

167   First, Prince was planning to expand Citigroup's consumer business from 53 countries to all 100 countries where Citigroup operated. However, Prince faced obstacles in his plan for global distribution. The Citigroup name was not as well recognized abroad as in the U.S and there was already mistrust in certain markets where regulations were not followed (and thus scandal ensued). Moreover, Citigroup's economies of scale might not have fit neatly into certain foreign markets where customization of Citigroup's products might be needed.

168   Second, Prince was planning on upgrading CitiFinancial, the consumer finance unit and targeting the newly affluent consumer group (i.e., those consumers with $100,000+ in assets). The Citigroup name might not have been as leverageable in attaining this goal either. Citigroup had traditionally followed a strategy of all things to all people, and now it was seeking to specialize in servicing a higher-end customer. It was likely that consumers did not associate Citigroup with higher-end financial services.

169   Third, Prince sought to combine Smith Barney brokers and Citibank retail branches. Smith Barney was the global private wealth management unit of Citigroup. It was a leading provider of comprehensive financial planning and advisory services to high net worth investors, institutions, corporations, and private businesses, governments, and foundations. With approximately 12,100 financial consultants in some 500 offices, Smith Barney offered a full suite of investment services, including asset allocation, private investments and lending services, hedge funds, cash and portfolio management, as well as retirement, education, and estate planning. Smith Barney had more than 7.7 million client accounts, representing $1,015 billion in client assets. While integrating Smith Barney into Citibank retail branches would expand the Citibank product offering and increase Smith Barney distribution, the combination of the Citibank brand name and the Smith Barney brand might send mixed messages to consumers.

170   In order to make his plan a success, Prince would need to make hard decisions about his global distribution plan, his product lines, who his customer base was, and how he would reach them.

LOOKING TOWARDS THE FUTURE

171   CEO Chuck Prince had to form a strategy that would improve Citigroup's Global Consumer unit, which the company depended heavily on for revenue generation. One alternative was to aggressively expand Citibank and CitiFinance branch locations in the U.S. Increasing the number and geographic dispersion of bank branches in the U.S. would attract new customers to the Citibank and CitiFinance franchises, and thus increase revenue for the Citigroup Consumer Business unit.

172   This plan was *feasible* because the Citigroup Consumer unit had a proven expertise for increasing distribution via de novo branch building and through mergers and acquisitions. In addition, Citibank ran national advertising campaigns in the form of TV and print advertising and paid for sponsorships, so the Citibank name was most likely already recognizable in markets where the bank did not yet exist.

173   The *benefit* of this alternative was that Citibank could gain a foothold in markets where it did not exist, and steal market share from its competitors in those areas.

174   This strategy would enable Citibank to *win against the competition,* namely J.P. Morgan Chase, and Bank of America, because Citibank could achieve a greater number of retail branches in the U.S. than its competitors as well as better geographic dispersion. Citibank generally had the same product lines as its competitors, but Citibank also had the Citipro® financial check up and Women & Co. services, which its competitors did not. These unique offerings would give customers in new regions a reason to switch from their current banks to Citibank. Building new outlets would also give Citibank the opportunity to begin developing branch designs that were more modern than the competition, which could then be transitioned to existing Citibank branches. Finally, increasing distribution in the U.S. would give Citibank the opportunity to expand in high-concentration Hispanic areas (such as Texas, California, and Florida) faster than its competition and leverage its Hispanic expertise more than its competition.

175   The *drawback* of this plan is that it focused solely on the U.S. market and ignored the growing opportunities abroad.

176   The *way around this problem* was to focus on cross-selling to U.S. customers to increase share-of-wallet per customer, therefore increasing the profitability per customer rather than just the sheer number of customers.

177   Another alternative was to expand existing Citibank and CitiFinance locations in the U.S., and begin distributing Smith Barney products through Citibank branches.

178   This strategy was *feasible* for Citibank because the Citigroup Consumer unit had a proven expertise in the U.S. for increasing distribution via de novo branch building and through mergers and acquisitions. As for the Citibank/Smith Barney integration, Citigroup was parent to both Citibank and Smith Barney and therefore had complete knowledge of the companies' methods of operations, trade secrets, finances and the like, which would make integration between the companies easier than for a competitor who might try to quickly acquire and integrate a securities brokerage firm into their retail bank branches. Also, as the parent company, Citigroup could encourage collaboration between Citibank and Smith Barney by offering rewards in the compensation packages of Citibank employees who helped sell Smith Barney services and vice versa. From the perspective of the Citibank customer, Smith Barney was already a well-known name and respected brand name, so its appearance in a Citibank branch would bolster the image of Citibank.

179   The *benefit* of this alternative was that Citibank could expand the size of its banking market, and not just depend on stealing market share in current markets. Plus, it was increasing accessibility of Smith Barney products to its customers by conveniently offering Smith Barney products in their Citibank and CitiFinance branches.

180   This strategy would enable Citibank to *win against the competition* by achieving a greater number of retail branches in the U.S. than its competitors as well as better geographic dispersion. By co-branding the Citibank and Smith Barney brand names, Citigroup was positioning itself as a superior financial services firm than Bank of America and J.P. Morgan Chase. Offering Smith Barney products in Citibank branches would also draw in Generation X customers who were more likely to invest in securities than older, more risk-averse customers. Within Generation X, the newly affluent ($100,000 or more in assets) were of special interest as a target market for Smith Barney investment services. Finally, if Citigroup could link Citibank accounts with Smith Barney accounts, thereby providing a very high level of convenience to its customers, it would have a definite competitive edge over J.P. Morgan Chase, Bank of America, and other competitors.

181   The main *drawback* of this plan was that by co-branding Citibank and Smith Barney, Citigroup was attempting to change its image from a basic bank offering traditional products (such as savings and checking accounts) to that of a financial specialty firm (offering securities brokerage and other investment services through Smith Barney). It was likely that consumers did not associate Citibank with the higher-end financial services offered by Smith Barney and might be confused by the Citibank/Smith Barney co-branding strategy.

182 A *way around this drawback* was to re-design its branches and Website. The new design should work to project a higher-end financial services firm, especially if Smith Barney was integrated in the branches. Citibank should also develop a customer loyalty program that rewarded Citibank customers for opening a Smith Barney account, and vice versa. Another way around this drawback was to invest in a targeted marketing plan that would communicate an overall message that Citibank had products and services specifically designed for each customer's unique needs (i.e., customized solutions). The marketing plan would then have sub-messages aimed at each of Citibank's target segments. For example, Citibank would advertise its overall message about customized solutions and a sub-message about its Women & Company services during women's TV shows and in women's magazines. Citibank would advertise its overall message about customized solutions and an investment services sub-message to high-income Generation Xers on finance-related TV shows and in financial publications.

183 These were two alternatives that new Citigroup CEO Chuck Prince would have to consider in order to grow Citigroup and maintain its leading position versus Bank of America and J.P. Morgan Chase & Company. Both alternatives would grow Citigroup, with the second alternative being the riskier—yet potentially more rewarding—of the two. Prince would have to consider these two alternatives, and consider other opportunities that Citigroup might pursue.

LIST OF WORKS CITED

Angell, B (2006). "Ethnic Population too Big to Ignore." [Online]. *http://www.us-banker.com/article.html?id=20040426VHZJ6UKV.* Accessed February 22, 2006.

Bank of America. (2005). "Annual Report 2004." [Online]. *http://investor.bankofamerica.com/ phoenix.zhtml?c=71595&p=irol-reportsannual.* Accessed February 17, 2006.

Bank of America (2006). "Homepage." [Online]. *http://www.bankofamerica.com.* Accessed February 20, 2006Businessline. (2005). "Citibank Launches Credit Education Initiatives." April 6, 2005: p. 1.

Camacho, A. (2005). "Tying Hispanic Cultural Values to Marketing Research: An Ipsos Insight White Paper." [Online]. *http://www.ipsosinsight.com/ KnowledgeCenter/ ConsumerProducts.aspx.* Accessed February 22, 2006.

Chazan, G. (2005). "Russian Banks Prove Tempting; Sale of Tiny KMB Underscores Interest in Country's Growth Story." *Wall Street Journal.* April 5, 2005: p. C.14.

Citigroup (2005). "Annual Report 2004." [Online]. *http://www.citigroup.com/ citigroup/fin/ar.htm.* Accessed February 17, 2006.

Der Hovanesian, M. (2006). "Rewiring Chuck Prince." *Fortune.* February 20: p.75.

Groenfeldt, T. (2006). "Customer Data, Right Here, Right Now." [Online]. *http://www.us-banker.com/article.html?id=20040423DB80IJZW.* Accessed February 22, 2006.

Hispanic Business (2005). "U.S. Hispanic Economy in Transition," March 2005. [Online]. *http://www.hispanicbusiness.com/ news/newsbyid.asp?id=22777.* Accessed February 22, 2006.

Ipsos. (2004). "Retail Banking: 2004 Customer Report." [Online]. *http://www.ipsos-ideas.com/library/IpsosInsight_CR_04Banking.cfm.* Accessed March 2, 2006.

J.P. Morgan Chase (2005). "Annual Report 2004." [Online]. *http://investor. shareholder.com/jpmorganchase/annual.cfm.* Accessed February 17, 2006.

J.P Morgan Chase (2006). "Homepage," [Online]. *http://www.jpmorgan.com.* Accessed February 20, 2006.

Krim, J. (2005). "Customer Data Lost, Citigroup Unit Says; 3.9 Million Affected As Firms' Security Lapses Add Up." *The Washington Post.* June 7, 2005: p. A.01.

Liam, Thomas K. (2004). *Capital Markets.* Mason, OH: Thomson, South-Western.

National Information Center (2006). "Financial Data and Institutional Characteristics Collected by The Federal Reserve System." [Online]. *http://www.ffiec.gov/ nicpubweb/ nicweb/ Top50Form.aspx.* Accessed February 22, 2006.

Packaged Facts. (2004). "The Young Adult Market: Generation X Grows Up." [Online]. *http://www.packagedfacts.com/product/print/?productid=376471.* Accessed March 1, 2006.

Reynolds, C. (2004A). "Overlooked & Under X-Ploited." American Demographics. May 1, 2004. [Online]. *http://www.findarticles.com/p/articles/mi_m4021/is_4_26/ ai_n6047692.* Accessed March 1, 2006.

Reynolds, C. (2004B). "Retirement Goes Boom." American Demographics. April 1, 2004. [Online]. *http://www.findarticles.com/p/articles/mi_m4021/is_3_26/ai_ 114558701.* Accessed March 1, 2006.

Tripp, Robert. (2005). "How Do Banks Make Their Money?" [Online]. *http://www.howbankswork.com/9-2.html.* Accessed February 12, 2006.

U.S. Census Bureau (2004). "Projections, July 2004." [Online]. *http://www.census.gov/ popest/estimates.php.* Accessed February 22, 2006.

ADDITIONAL SOURCES

Citigroup.(2006). "Citigroup Reports Fourth Quarter Earnings." [Online]. *http://www. citigroup.com/citigroup/press/2006/060120a.htm.* Accessed February 17, 2006.

Citigroup.com. (2006). [Online]. *www.citigroup.com.* Accessed February 20, 2006.

Engen, J. (2006). "Fabulous on the Fundamentals." [Online]. *http://www.us-banker. com/article.html?id=20060103R382M4MI.* Accessed February 22, 2006.

Hebeka, M. (2005). "Standard & Poor's Industry Surveys: Banking." August 19, 2004.

Hoovers (2006). "Citigroup and various competitors." [Online]. *http://www.hoovers. com.* Accessed February 5, 2006.

Thefreedictionary.com. [Online]. *http://financial-dictionary.thefreedictionary.com/ Retail+Banking.* Accessed February 20, 2006.

Case 33

The Desert Palms Hotel & Casino

David L. Corsun, Brian Shedd, and Michael Dalbor

1   Robert Hoffman surveyed the empty parking lot and boarded-up exterior of the closed Regency Casino. It was October of 2001, and in his mind he could see a beautiful water park, complete with a lazy river, interlacing tubular waterslides, and throngs of people screaming and enjoying themselves in the hot desert sun. The location of the defunct casino, and his future water park, was ideally placed between the 3000 room Flamingo Laughlin and his own 1420 room Desert Palms Hotel & Casino in Laughlin, Nevada. He had a handshake deal with the owner of the Regency for $1.5 million, a steal for the 1 acre parcel of land that stretched from Casino Drive to the banks of the Colorado River and the River Walk that connected all 9 Laughlin casinos.

2   As General Manager of the Desert Palms, Hoffman knew he had his work cut out for him in selling the corporate office on such an expense. The two National Gaming, Inc. properties (Desert Palms and Desert Wins) were struggling along with the other casinos to deliver a fraction of the revenue seen 5 or 6 years earlier from this market. Maybe a water park was just what the Desert Palms needed to boost occupancy and average daily rate (ADR) in an economy on the brink of recession. He could envision profitable room and park packages that would give his property a distinct competitive advantage. The water park would also draw guests from all the other resorts, giving him an opportunity to capture their gaming play in his casino.

3   The afternoon sun was disappearing behind the Flamingo towers as he turned and walked back inside the Desert Palms. He knew there were several interested parties looking at the Regency property, and he must act quickly to close the deal successfully. He had a meeting with the CEO and Sr. Vice President of Operations for National Gaming in four days to make his pitch. To sell them on it, he had to be absolutely sure of the proposal himself. He arrived in his office and drifted off in thought, thinking of all the changes he had made to the property in his short 6 month tenure there, and what impact they might have on this meeting.

A NEW DAY

4   Just six months earlier, Robert Hoffman had been a happily retired 55-year-old man in the habit of watching Oprah every morning and taking a long afternoon nap. After 30 years in the gaming business, 20 spent as the General Manager of the Gold Strike Inn & Casino in Boulder City, Nevada, he had welcomed retirement with open arms.

5   When the call came from Michael Sharp, CEO of National Gaming, Inc., to consider taking over the helm of the Laughlin property, Hoffman was intrigued by the challenge but reluctant to step out of his comfortable retirement routine. Mr. Sharp was confident in Hoffman's ability to turn the property around in a couple of years, and told him he would be back in retirement before he knew it. The sales pitch worked, and a few weeks later, he arrived on the scene to assume the top spot at the Desert Palms.

6   His initial assessment of the property was that much change was needed. The property was being run in 2001 in much the same manner as it had been in 1995. However, in 1995 the year-end net income for the casino hotel was around $15 million, whereas in 2001 it would be lucky to clear $1 million. Hoffman moved quickly to make some obvious changes that would make a substantial difference on the property's financial statements. He reduced the property staffing by 20%, mostly by repositioning people from overstaffed departments into job openings elsewhere. Some people opted not to move, and the subsequent attrition helped achieve the objective as well.

7   Next, he turned his attention to the operational aspects of the property. He sought to increase efficiency, speed, and service at the property while reducing staffing by several hundred employees. Hoffman met these goals by instituting operational processes already used by the competition. For example, placing cabinets that contained bags of coins underneath all the slot machines on the casino floor eliminated the lengthy wait for customers to have their slot machines filled when they ran out of money. Prior to instituting this procedure, customers waited for a slot technician to get a bag of change from the casino cashier to fill their machines. With the cabinets installed, the technician simply unlocked the cabinet beneath the machine and filled it right then. With the reduced staff levels on the casino floor, this change was essential to maintaining customer service levels.

8   Hoffman then turned his attention to the organizational hierarchy at the property and identified two levels of management he thought didn't need to exist. He saw no need for assistant shift supervisors and assistant shift managers. These positions had been created many years earlier for the few occasions when there were gaps in the managers' schedules. These assistant positions were filled by line-level employees who received an hourly pay differential year-round for occasionally assuming the role of a supervisor during such a scheduling mishap. In the 1980s and early '90s, such positions were common at many casinos. Hoffman eliminated these positions and demanded that the property's managers schedule themselves responsibly, thereby eliminating the gaps.

9   Hoffman's evaluation of the property's processes was thorough and ongoing, touching every department. He examined food costs and what was being served in every restaurant. He scoured purveyors' invoices to identify any waste or over-pricing.

10   Hoffman also significantly reduced the marketing and advertising expenses at the property. "We'll let the other 8 joints pay to get people to Laughlin" he thought, "then we'll get them to come to the Desert Palms." His cutbacks began to show up on the income statement, and only 3 months into his reorganization effort, the property expenses were down 40%. If they were even going to be possible, further substantial cost savings were not obvious to Hoffman. What he needed now were increased revenues.

THE NEW PLAN

11   The Desert Palms was short on amenities. In a market of newer, nicer properties that had spas, bowling alleys, car museums, and tennis courts, the Desert Palms had only a hair salon. Competitor properties were booking Vegas caliber entertainment into their show rooms. Harrah's, for example, brought Earl Turner down from the Rio Suites Hotel in Las Vegas to headline in Laughlin. Hoffman's first move in expanding the property's offerings entailed convincing Krispy Kreme Doughnut Corporation to put a satellite operation in a corner of the property. Not only was Hoffman a big doughnut eater, these tasty morsels had a fanatical following among doughnut enthusiasts and were considered a "big city" brand. Throngs of customers began leaving the surrounding properties to swamp the small outlet, creating long lines and early sold-out inventory.

12   Next, Hoffman introduced the only 25-cent craps game in town, with 100 times odds. Almost immediately, the Desert Palms' low-limit craps table was surrounded by a crowd of vocal players around the clock. Shortly thereafter, he lowered the blackjack table limits to $2, the lowest table limits in Laughlin. The amount of money being handled by the casino was going up; however, the amount of money being kept by the casino as "win" remained the same, or declined slightly as a result of the low table limits.

13   Hoffman needed a real people-draw. He went back to the past—way back. He brought out a 99-cent shrimp cocktail, a common draw on the Las Vegas Strip 20 years earlier. The deli lines grew long with shrimp cocktail fans waiting to take advantage of the bargain price. Then he had an epiphany. What did people consider synonymous with Vegas and gambling? Elvis Presley. He hired a crew of Elvis impersonators and began a daily slot tournament during which a Desert Palms Elvis sang tunes and guests pushed the slot machine buttons in search of cash prizes.

14   The property was taking on a sort of carnival feel, people were talking, and Hoffman was encouraged by what he heard. He changed the property slogan from "The Winning Edge" to "A Fun Place" to help hammer home the message to guests and visitors. In November, the property's fortunes turned in his favor for the first time. The Desert Palms outperformed the prior year's numbers for the first time in 5 years.

15   Unfortunately, the property's occupancy figure was not such a bright spot (see Table 1). Call volume in the reservations office had decreased dramatically since the advertising budget had been slashed, and future room bookings were subsequently down versus the prior year. Steve Sodergraf, the Senior Vice President of Operations for National Gaming, Inc. applauded Hoffman's skills in making financial gains on the Desert Palms' income statement, but grew concerned about the reductions in advertising that had all but eliminated the property presence in the regional newspapers. He advised Hoffman not to forego long-term profitability in favor of short-term gains. Hoffman reevaluated the budget cuts in marketing and agreed to allocate some more funds toward the advertising budget. The regional advertising schedule was increased, but remained less than half of prior years' frequency.

16   To compensate for the reduced advertising budget, the Desert Palms' marketing department implemented an aggressive prospect marketing campaign, utilizing lists purchased from information brokers and offering introductory free stays at the property. Response to the direct mail campaign was dramatic, and successfully spurred call volume up to and

TABLE 1 Desert Palms Hotel & Casino: Occupancy and Average Daily Rate (ADR)

Month	Desert Palms Occupancy % 2000	2001	Laughlin Market Occupancy % 2000	2001	Desert Palms Midweek ADR ($) 2000	2001	Desert Palms Weekend ADR ($) 2000	2001
January	78	84	82.8	85.3	18.02	16.69	45.62	37.20
February	93	91	94.9	92.1	18.54	18.36	39.54	40.14
March	94	94	94.7	95	18.83	19.06	42.60	44.74
April	95	91	93.3	91.9	23.45	25.12	58.78	65.86
May	82	71	89.2	85.7	18.78	21.84	48.39	54.25
June	87	76	93.7	88.1	18.65	20.92	46.76	47.53
July	90	80	92.9	89.0	21.54	22.41	44.10	48.41
August	88	83	93.1	91.6	18.74	21.79	45.93	50.85
September	83	68	86.7	80.5	19.58	22.44	44.60	47.84
October	86	78	89.6	89.6	17.89	19.90	41.59	44.61
November	73	77	78.9	80.2	17.84	19.78	39.58	43.30
December	68	63	71.1	70.6	20.71	24.41	43.14	41.97

beyond prior year levels. The prospect marketing program built membership in the Desert Palms' players' club and introduced hundreds of people to the Laughlin market. The top 5 markets from which the Desert Palms drew are delineated in Table 2 and customer data are included in Table 3.

THE NEXT STEP

17 Since his arrival at the Desert Palms, Hoffman had often looked out his window at the tiny Regency Casino located right next door. With a huge parking lot and only 115 slot machines, this casino seemed trapped in time, a glimpse of when life was simpler. "Such a waste," Hoffman thought, "for that little joint to occupy such prime real estate."

18 The temperature in Laughlin regularly exceeded 100 degrees in the summer, and the area had over 300 days of sunshine a year. Around 6,000 people lived in the Laughlin community, with an additional 60,000 inhabitants within the tri-state area (Bullhead City and Kingman in Arizona, and Needles in California). Laughlin visitor trends are outlined in Table 4. Besides the Colorado River (with a water temperature of about 52 degrees year-round), and Emerald River golf course, there were no other outdoor activities in Laughlin for tourists or locals to enjoy. The Regency Casino lot was ideally suited for just such an attraction, and Hoffman was well aware of how popular and successful water parks like Wet & Wild in Las Vegas were.

19 Things were going well at the Desert Palms, revenues were going up, expenses were coming down, and his employees' biggest complaint was that they were too busy. Reading the local paper one morning, Hoffman saw that the Regency was going out of business. Wasting no time, he arranged a meeting with Larry Long, owner of the Regency, to inquire what the selling price of the casino would be. Long said he would take $2 million, which Hoffman countered with $1.5 million. Long agreed to sell for that amount. The handshake deal would only last as long as other, higher offers were not received.

20 Hoffman was confident a water park was just what Laughlin needed as an additional attraction to golf and the river. He could see a lazy river encircling the park, with water

TABLE 2
Desert Palms Hotel & Casino: Top 5 Markets

Market	Hotel	Casino
California	57.29%	51.36%
Arizona	24.34	22.49
Nevada	3.34	3.19
New Mexico	3.0	3.27
Texas	1.42	2.24
Other	10.61	17.45

TABLE 3
Desert Palms Hotel & Casino: Customer Data

Demographic Characteristic	Fall/Winter	Spring/Summer
Age	50–75	35–54
Marital status	Married	Married
Work status	Retired	Employed
Household income	$20–60,000	$50,000+
Other	Value conscious	Value conscious
		Travels with children
	Average Trip Gaming Worth	**2001 Market mix**
Frequent individual travelers	$151	53.14%
Groups	76	25.72
Casino	234	21.14

TABLE 4
Laughlin Visitor
Trends (2000–2001)

Measure	Year over Year Change
Visitor volume	+2.0%
Room inventory	−1.4
Convention attendance	−5.5
Occupancy %	+2.3
Gaming revenue	+6.0
Air passengers	+23.1
Average daily traffic (Highway 163)	−2.9

slides, food and drink concessions, and maybe even a wave pool. This could be big! He could charge $20 per person for admission for non-hotel guests, and build a discounted admission to the park into his own room packages, realizing a higher average daily rate (ADR) (see Table 1) in the process. He was hoping to increase his ADR by $5 and offer $10 admission for hotel guests. He anticipated that 50% of the 30,000 water park customers he expected to attract each year would be hotel guests. Hoffman believed that the water park would generate some latent demand for the hotel and that about 25% of those water park customers staying at the hotel would represent new business. He figured these new guests would stay an average of approximately 2 nights. The incremental costs associated with these additional room nights would come in at about 30%. Further, anticipating that some parents would leave their kids to enjoy the water park while they gambled, Hoffman thought it was reasonable to expect average additional casino play of $50 for every non-hotel guest visiting the water park and $100 for every hotel guest taking advantage of this new amenity. Revenues were expected to increase by four percent a year over the project's 20-year depreciable life. Hoffman thought these numbers were conservative, particularly because he didn't include any additional food and beverage revenue.

21   Historically, the property's revenue breakdown was approximately 50% gaming, 40% from rooms, and 10% from food and beverage sales. The highest margins were realized via gaming revenue. The house win percentage (percent of gaming play resulting in revenue) in this slot-intensive market was about 20. Other costs associated with generating the gaming revenue ate up about 50% of the revenue generated.

22   Only a concrete block wall separated the pool area of the Desert Palms from the Regency Casino parking lot, custom made for easy access. To make things even easier, National Gaming, Inc. had its own development company, which had constructed its four Las Vegas mega-resorts. The development people had also produced the famous wave pool at Montego Bay, in which professional surfing competitions were held, and a lazy river at the Monte Cristo. Hoffman phoned the National Gaming development offices and asked for a quote on building a water park within the Regency square footage. The quote came back at around $10 million. He could build his park for $11,500,000. Hoffman estimated the annual operating expenses of the water park would run about $175,000, nearly all of which were fixed costs.

23   The only thing left to do was sell his idea to Michael Sharp and Steve Sodergraf. He knew it wasn't going to be easy. National Gaming, along with its competitors, had moved away from the old gaming business model in which food and beverage, entertainment, and other areas were seen as services rather than revenue centers. This water park would have to make money in order to get built. Plus, $11,500,000 would buy a whole lot of capital improvements on the Desert Palms property, as well as the neighboring Desert Wins. He knew further that such an investment in Laughlin was a long-term gamble on a market under constant pressure from Native American casinos opening in California and Arizona. The existing Native American casinos had eroded some of Laughlin's day trip business and there were others coming online, including some casino resorts like the Barona tribe's resort outside San Diego (most of the existing Native American competition consisted of only casinos).

24   There was also Wall Street to consider, and how stockholders would view such an investment. It was a risk, one that could have major financial consequences if the market failed to materialize to support it. Further, National Gaming's top executives had more than the Laughlin market to consider. The company operated 14 casino hotels in three states, and employed over 25,000 people.

25   Hoffman decided to poll existing Desert Palms customers to gain their perspective. Nearly everyone over 40 years old opposed the idea, concerned that such a park would bring more kids and families to a traditionally adult destination and property. The younger demographic thought the idea was great, and would be willing to pay at least $5 per night more for such an amenity. The Desert Palms' customer median age was 57 for most of the year (see Table 3), making the vocal majority a serious concern in the matter. After collecting and analyzing 1,500 questionnaires, Hoffman felt he had enough information to determine the customer perspective. His meeting date was approaching, and he needed to make up his mind.

Case 34

Fortune Magazine: The Magazine Publishing Industry

Catherine Keenan, Marc E. Gartenfeld, Dorothy Dologite, and Robert J. Mockler

INTRODUCTION

1 *Fortune Magazine*, a division of Time Warner, was one of the most popular and successful business magazines. *Fortune Magazine* had been published for the past 75 years. Through these years the business and economic climate, which *Fortune* operated in and reported on, had dramatically changed. In December 2005, the President of *Fortune* was faced with the daunting task of maintaining the magazine's reputation and market leadership.

2 *Fortune Magazine* was facing the same issues as the magazine industry as a whole. After its peak in 2000, advertising pages had experienced a steady decline. The events of September 11, 2001 and the subsequent economic downturn had negatively affected the publishing industry. The business and finance sector, which *Fortune* operated in, had been severely affected. The soft advertising environment was expected to continue into 2006.

3 Shifts in consumers' demands were also affecting the magazine industry. Consumers were no longer solely demanding information in printed form. Digital media and the Internet were gaining increasing popularity. It was clear that on-line media was here to stay. It was announced in November 2005, that the web search engine Google was expected to sell $6.1 billion ads in 2006, which is more advertising sold by any newspaper chain, magazine publisher, or television network [Hansel, 2005].

4 Another issue the magazine industry faced was rising costs of magazine production. If Management kept producing the magazine as it had been produced in the past, the bottom line would take a hit because of these rising expenses. Lower forecasted advertising revenues would not add up to this hit. Mr. Poleway needed to think of ways of producing a high quality product more efficiently, at the lowest cost possible.

5 While the competitive environment was already fierce in the business sector of the magazine industry, Conde Naste, a rival publisher, had just announced its intention to launch a business and industry magazine in 2007. This launch would make the competition even fiercer.

6 Given these issues, the President was still expected to deliver year over year profit increases to Time Warner corporate. It was clear that by maintaining the status quo, Mr. Poleway would not be able to deliver the desired results. *Fortune Magazine* was, therefore, faced with a number of critical long-term decisions. Was the format and style of the editorial content appropriate for meeting the consumers' wants and needs? Was *Fortune* targeting the right consumer demographic? Could production specifications be altered so as to cut costs, while still producing a superior product? Was *Fortune* charging the correct open rate for its advertising pages? Was the right amount of copies of the magazine being entered into the circulation stream? The main question facing the President of *Fortune* was how to differentiate *Fortune* from the competition in order to achieve a winning edge over competitors within a competitive and rapidly changing environment.

INDUSTRY AND COMPETITIVE MARKET ANALYSIS: MEDIA INDUSTRY

7 Media is defined as a means of mass communication. The media industry was comprised of companies that owned, operated, sold, or distributed through forms of communication.

This case was prepared by Catherine Keenan, Marc E. Gartenfeld, Dorothy Dologite, and Professor Robert J. Mockler of St. John's University. © Robert J. Mockler.

As shown in Figure 1, these products included television, film, music and radio, information collection & delivery services, Internet search engines, Internet content providers, and publishing companies [Hoovers, 2005].

8   Total consumer spending on media, in the United States in 2004, was approximately $190 billion. In all segments of the media industry, there was a shift toward spending in digital media. The sectors which had been most impacted by this shift thus far were the television, film, and music industries [Plunkett Research, 2005A].

9   The media industry had substantially evolved over the past decade. Loss of control was the major issue that had faced the media industry. Digital media allowed the consumer to have increased control. The days when viewers would plan their schedules around their favorite TV show and sit through all the ads during that show were long gone. Consumers were now demanding more control over what they watched, read, and listened to. Downloading of songs and recording of shows using Digital Video Recorders (DVRs) and Video on Demand services had put the consumer in control of what they watched and when they watched it. The consumer could choose to skip over all commercials and advertising if desired. Downloading of music allowed the consumer to only purchase the songs they wanted, rather than purchase an entire CD of songs that they might not enjoy.

10   The shift in control had made the traditional business model of the media industry obsolete and had greatly altered the way in which media companies had traditionally operated. Advertising revenue, which traditionally had been the largest revenue component of a media company, was being replaced with soaring revenues from subscription-based vehicles, such as Digital Video Recorders (DVRs and TIVO's), which are devices that allow viewers to record television shows. Programming schedules were losing relevance, while electronic programming guides were becoming more vital [Plunkett Research, 2005A]. Also, an increasing amount of advertising dollars was being displaced from traditional media vehicles and being allocated to the Internet. For instance, in 2005, Internet search engine, Google, had announced that it expected to sell $6.1 billion in ads, which was more than the ad revenue of any newspaper, magazine publisher, or television network [Hansel, 2005].

11   Media companies were being forced to radically change to deal with new demands from consumers. The immediate issues facing this industry included: the rise of multi-purpose cell phones, which were being used for far more and more entertainment purposes, including video and TV programming; the increasing use of DVD's and DVR's; commercial free, legal, and illegal sharing of music; and electronic gaming and gambling.

FIGURE 1   **The Media Industry**

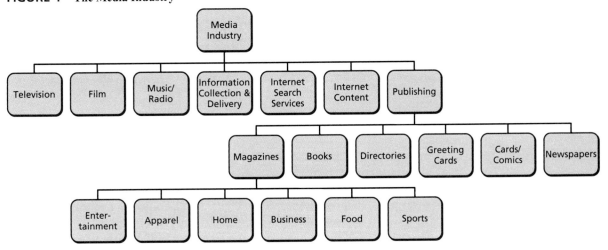

Television

12   For instance, in the television sector, out of the 73 million cable TV subscribers in the United States, 27 million of them were digital cable subscribers. In 2004, the number of homes in the U.S. with DVD recorders was approximately 7 million. This number was expected to grow to 33.5 million by 2008. Also in 2004, there were 19 million video-on-demand subscribers, 2.3 million TIVO subscribers and 7.2 million digital televisions sold. These numbers were all expected to sharply increase over the next few years [Plunkett Research, 2005A].

Film

13   In the film sector in 2004, US box office revenues totaled $9.4 billion; however, DVD rentals and sales in the U.S. in 2004 totaled $21.2 billion. This more than double increase in DVD rentals and sales over box office revenues showed that the consumer would rather watch movies at home, on their own terms [Plunkett Research, 2005A].

Music/Radio

14   In the music sector, in 2004, global music sales were approximately $32 billion; however, only $12 billion came from traditional CD purchases. In 2004, there were approximately 230 legitimate music download sites and 200 million tracks sold off these sites in the U.S. and Europe. There were 4.4 million iPods sold and these numbers were expected to increase in the coming years [Hoovers, 2005]. In the Radio sector, which is the distribution channel for music, in 2004, there were 150 radio stations broadcasting digitally. This number was expected to sharply rise over the coming years [Plunkett Research, 2005A].

Information Collection & Delivery

15   These were companies that collected, retrieved, and delivered various types of information via online services and the Internet.

Internet Search Services

16   These were companies that owned and operated search engines and other websites.

Internet Content Providers

17   These were companies that created or acquired content for distribution via the Internet.

Publishing

18   The publishing segment is the focus of this study and is discussed in detail in the following sections.

INDUSTRY AND COMPETITIVE MARKET: PUBLISHING

19   As shown in Figure 1, the Publishing industry was comprised of companies that published books, directories, greeting cards, baseball cards/comics, newspapers, and magazines [Hoovers, 2005].

20   The publishing industry had also been affected by the digitization of media and had been forced to make changes in its business models. Publishing was no longer only concerned with producing printed pages, but was now about managing content and adapting it to a variety of formats, ranging from printed pages to Web-enabled phones [Pfeiffer Report, 2005].

21   Many publishing operations were questioning their current setup. The publishing industry was currently based on technology that was over a decade old. This may not seem long; however, this was an eternity with respect to digital advances, which had occurred, in the past decade. It would be essential to find a new publishing platform, which would take into account the challenges of the online world. Also, because of the hardware and operating system changes, which were constantly going on, software used for publishing would also have to be rethought.

22   Experts were predicting that the publishing industry was headed for the second wave of Desktop Publishing. The first wave occurred with the arrival of Macintosh and desktop page layout tools, which encouraged most publishing companies to convert their print production to computer-based tools. What was needed were new platforms that supported a web-centric publishing model [Pfeiffer Report, 2005].

23   The area of the publishing industry under study in this case was the Magazine industry.

INDUSTRY AND COMPETITIVE MARKET: MAGAZINE SUB-SEGMENT

24   In 2004, U.S. magazine revenues were approximately $21.4 billion. Even in changing times, magazines remained indispensable to both readers and marketers. Consumers had an emotional bond with their favorite magazines and this helped to give credibility to the advertising in the pages of the magazine, causing consumers to take action. Magazines were constantly developing and growing with the readers [Magazine Publishers Association, 2005].

25   Economic conditions were highly correlated with the profitability of magazines. Magazines earned revenues by either selling ad pages or by consumers purchasing the magazines. In bad economic times, advertising budgets are cut and therefore, ad revenues decline. Also, in bad economic times, consumers have less disposal income to spend on non-essential items. Since magazines were considered to be a non-essential item, the number of copies sold decreases, lowering circulation revenue.

26   According to a survey of adults 18 and over, the popularity of reading was at an all time high. In 1995, people spent 28% of their time reading, 25% watching TV, 8% going to the movies, 2% on the computer and 5% listening to music. In 2004, people spent 35% of their time reading, 21% watching TV, 10% going to the movies, 7% on the computer and 6% listening to music. Of the people surveyed, 84% read magazines. An average reader spent 45 minutes reading each issue [Magazine Publishers Association, 2005].

HOW THE SEGMENT WORKS: ESSENCE OF THE BUSINESS MODEL

27   Figure 2 shows the essence of the magazine business model. The main product of the magazine sub-segment of the media industry was the printed magazine. The first distinguishing factor among the magazines in the industry was frequency. A magazine could be weekly, bi-weekly, monthly, and the like. Magazines were divided by topic of interest. Topics included sports, news, health, beauty, business and finance, and many other topics. The demographic group, or the consumer, that a magazine targeted was in large measure based

FIGURE 2   **Magazine Business Model**

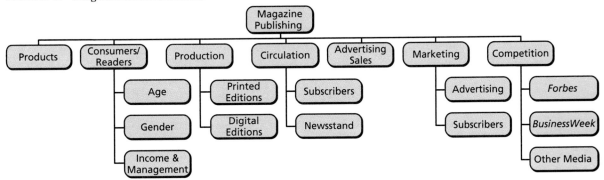

on the topic covered. For instance, home-decorating magazines would generally target people who lived in the suburbs, rather than in urban areas.

28   Magazines were made up of ad and editorial pages. The number of ad pages that a magazine could obtain generally drove the size of the magazine. The production department of the magazine had the role of putting the issue together, based on specific instructions. These instructions included ad and edit placement and separation. For instance, many advertisers did not want their ad positioned near depressing editorial topics, such as 9/11.

29   Once the magazine was put together, files were sent electronically to the printing plants to begin printing and binding the magazines. From the plant, the magazine was sent via trucks to postal facilities or wholesalers for home and newsstand delivery.

30   Marketing tactics for the magazine were aimed at the two sources of revenue for the Company: circulation and advertising. The goal of the magazine was to maximize these revenues, while keeping production costs low, and producing a magazine with strong editorial content, that was different and better than other magazines in the industry. Marketing tactics such as direct mail promotions to obtain new subscribers, cover wraps to retain existing subscribers, and presentations to media planners to garner advertising pages were all used to boost the two revenue streams.

31   The competition in the magazine industry was fierce. Magazines competed against other magazines within the topic of interest covered, as well as other forms of media. For instance, business magazines competed against other business magazines as well as business websites, and all-day business news channels such as CNBC.

Products

32   The main product of the magazine sub-segment was the printed editions, containing a mix of advertising and editorial pages, and digital editions. Another product was the digital editions.

Printed Editions

33   Magazines were defined by topics. Topics ranged from sports to automotive, food, business, beauty, health etc. In 2004, the top three magazine categories, in regards to editorial pages, were entertainment/celebrity (23,767 pages), apparel (19,626 pages), & home furnishings (11,622 pages). Business and Industry ranked number 7 with 10,365 pages [Magazine Publishers Association, 2005].

34   Magazines were also defined by editorial format and style. Magazines could be either formal or informal in nature. They could report the latest news, or they could tell a story. The editorial style of weekly magazines tended to be more newsworthy, usually reporting the events of the past week. Monthly or Bi-monthly magazines tended to blend news stories with more edit that told a story, which was longer and involved more research, rather than hard, factual news. For instance, business magazines tended to be more formal. *BusinessWeek* was a weekly magazine that reported on the economic events that had occurred in the last week. Among other business topics, it focused on the current week's stock market activity and interest rate fluctuations. *Fortune* was a bi-weekly magazine. While *Fortune* would report on significant news stories, the cover story was more editorial in nature, usually spotlighting a particular company or business leader. In-depth research went into these stories to make the reader feel as if he or she was walking down the halls of the company under review.

35   In 2004, on average, a magazine was comprised of 48.1% advertising pages and 51.9% edit pages. In 1994, there were 15,069 magazines for consumers to choose from. This number had grown to 18,821 in 2004. In 2004, there were 480 new magazines introduced into the market [Magazine Publishers Association, 2005].

36   The keys to success when dealing with products were to deliver magazines that consumers wanted and demanded to read in the marketplace. Magazines were tailored to consumer's

interests; therefore they needed to provide relevant information to the consumer. Magazine readers were loyal; therefore an editor needed to be cautious when changing the editorial style of the magazine. Magazines needed to engage the reader. High quality editorial content, through articles and photographs, were key to capturing an audience. Magazines needed to be physically attractive in order to draw readers. The paper type and size needed to be appealing to readers. Also, magazines needed to be trustworthy in order to gain brand recognition and a positive reputation. Finally, advertising should be pertinent to the topic of the magazine, in order to be most effective.

Digital Editions

37 As technology changed, many magazines were introducing digital forms of their magazines to subscribers. A digital magazine was a copy of the printed magazine in digital format. Digital magazines brought in subscription revenues for the magazine. Due to increasing popularity of the Internet, digital magazines were expected to gain popularity in the future. Also, magazines were utilizing individual web sites in order to draw on-line customers to the printed magazine.

38 The keys to success when dealing with digital editions were to deliver a technically superior product. There could be no glitches in the edition and the performance, in terms of picture quality, speed, and readability needed to be up to the viewer's standards. Also, an adept support staff needed to be available to readers if he/she should encounter any problems when reading the digital magazine.

Consumers/Readers

39 The audience was the consumer of the magazine. Audience is defined as the number of people claiming to have read the magazine. It is made up of primary readers, those who have purchased the magazine through either newsstand sales or subscription, and secondary or pass-along readers. Digital readers were a new type of magazine consumer. Consumers could be divided by demographic characteristics. The main demographic categories of the magazine industry were age, gender, and income & level of management.

Age

40 The coveted demographic in the media industry was believed to be the 18–34 year old demographic. It was believed that advertising has the greatest influence on this demographic, due to the fact that people this age tended to spend more money on luxury items and were concerned with being on the cutting edge. The key to success when targeting demographics was to know the audience and deliver appropriate editorial content. Also, the topic had to be relevant for the targeted audience. For example, a children's magazine would have an entirely different editorial style and topic than a business publication, catered to adults. The language also had to be of the correct complexity for the targeted age group. It was believed that the younger the advertising target, the better.

Gender

41 Magazine topic was what determined the gender composition of the audience. For instance, traditionally, men more often than not would be drawn to a magazine like *Sports Illustrated*, while women would be drawn to *InStyle*. In today's society, gender stereotypes were increasingly being broken down. Therefore, a magazine needed to be cognizant of the fact that breadth of readers attracted to a topic was increasing. The topic of the magazine was what drew a specific audience to the product. A change in topic could greatly alter the audience composition. The nature and category of the magazine would determine the target demographic, in terms of gender. The keys to success when dealing with the gender demographic were a consistent and relevant editorial topic. Also, advertising needed to be catered to the gender demographic targeted.

Income & Management Level

42 Generally, magazines wanted to target high-income consumers, since advertisers would be more likely to advertise in magazines read by people who had the money to spend on their products. In the business sector, a coveted demographic characteristic was targeting upper management. Upper Management were the people deemed to be in control of the decision-making aspects of the corporation. Advertisers were inclined to want to focus on this group. For instance, Xerox would want someone in upper management to respond to its ad by having Xerox's copiers installed in the offices, rather than a competitor's brand.

43 The keys to success in regards to income and management level were to target the highest income level possible. In regards to management level, upper management was the targeted demographic. In order to capture the interest of this demographic, the quality of the product needed to be superior. The quality of the product was measured in terms of paper quality, trim size, and editorial quality. Advertising also needed to be appropriate to capture the interest of this demographic. A magazine catering to a high income demographic would feature editorial content about Mercedes, rather than Hyundai.

44 Regardless of demographic targeted, the magazine's format and style were important to reach the correct consumer. For instance, in the business sector, if a consumer was pressed for time and needed to get hard economic facts quickly, a news-focused magazine such as *BusinessWeek* would be more appropriate. However, if a consumer wanted to take the time to thoroughly research a particular company, a magazine like *Fortune*, which contained more in-depth company information, would be more suitable.

45 Since consumers were loyal, switching editorial styles could be detrimental for readership. A magazine wanted to add new readers, while sustaining current readers. Also, the magazine needed to be distributed properly in order to reach the appropriate audience. For instance, women's lifestyle magazine would be appropriately sold in supermarkets. Advertising and promotions needed to be effective, in increasing sales. For instance, selling a health magazine in a health food store may boost sales. Also, research needed to be accurate in order to obtain the correct demographic characteristic information within the target population. For instance, a male magazine wanted to make sure it is reaching male readers. Finally, consumers needed to be attracted to the magazine; it had to have the right look and feel for its price range.

Production

46 Magazine production involved the steps and costs necessary to physically put the book together. The production process was similar across all magazines in the industry. Ads for the magazine were received in advance. Edit then got positioned next to appropriate ads in order to complete the book make-up process. Once the book was put together and approved, the files were sent to the printing plant via computer systems. Before this technology was invented, actual films would need to be delivered to the printing plant. From there, the plant followed instructions and printed and bound the magazine. Magazines were then shipped to wholesalers, trucking agents and postal facilities for either home or newsstand delivery.

47 The three main expenses during the production process were paper costs, printing costs, and distribution costs. These physical costs could represent 35–40% of the total cost base of the magazine. Paper was looked at in terms of cost per ton. The paper industry was a very capital-intensive industry; a paper machine could cost $600m and cost 2 years to build. Paper was priced as a commodity. The paper industry was an oligopoly; there were relatively few suppliers, which gave them strength in the market. No single company had a dominant share and there was increasing industry consolidation. In the current environment, paper prices were on the rise.

48   In the printing industry, 5 suppliers controlled 85% of the market. Because of the low returns in this industry, there had been little capital investment. Three-five year term contracts protected against price variances and justify targeted capital investment.

49   Distribution costs included postal costs and trucking costs. In 2006, postal costs were expected to rise anywhere from 5–15%. This could translate into millions of dollars. Increasing fuel costs would also drive up trucking costs, which could significantly hurt a magazine's bottom line.

50   The key to success of any magazine was to produce a high quality product. Magazine publishers needed to have good relationships with printing plants, which were ultimately responsible for the quality of the magazine. Generally, the more business a magazine publisher gave a printer, the better the relationship. The better the paper prices secured, the cheaper the publisher could produce the magazine. Good relationships with distributors also helped to guarantee that magazines were delivered to newsstand and subscribers in a timely manner, without damage. Low prices in printing contracts would also help to save money. Generally, the more business a printing plant was given, the lower the contractual prices granted.

51   Production specifications could greatly impact the physical costs of the magazine. The magazine also had to have the right look and feel for its price range. Paper quality and trim size were important for creating the look of the magazine. For instance, since a newspaper was cheap, it was okay for it to be on thin paper. However, if a consumer was paying $5 for a magazine, the quality of the paper and printing should reflect the higher price paid. The main specifications that had the greatest impact on costs were number of pages, number of copies produced, type and weight of paper used, size of the magazine, and type of binding (spine or stapled).

Circulation

52   The circulation goal was to deliver the ratebase required of the magazine while maximizing circulation profits. Ratebase is defined as the guaranteed circulation by the publication, which advertising space rates were based upon. The readers per copy was the number of people actually reading the magazine. Readers per copy assumed that the person buying the magazine will pass along their copy to other readers. If a magazine failed to make ratebase, it needed to compensate the advertisers that ran in that magazine. For an average magazine, 46% of magazine revenue stemmed from circulation. The Audit Bureau of Circulation (ABC) was an independent body that reported the circulation information for the magazine industry. Reports, called pink sheets, were then released to examine whether magazines were truthfully making their ratebases as promised to advertisers. Failing a pink sheet could severely hurt the reputation of a magazine in the advertising community [Magazine Publishers Association, 2005].

53   Circulation was divided into two categories: subscriptions and newsstand sales. These were the two main ways that magazines participated in the marketplace. In 2004, 86% of magazines purchased came from subscription sales, while 14% were from newsstand sales. Due to the increasing popularity of digital media, digital subscriptions were expected to obtain an increasingly larger portion of the circulation mix. By 2010, it was expected that digital subscriptions would make up approximately 10% of all subscription sold. In 2004, 70% of circulation revenue was from subscriptions, while 30% was from newsstand sales [Magazine Publishers Association, 2005].

54   The keys to success in regards to circulation were pricing the magazine correctly, and determining the correct ratebase. Too high a ratebase could lead to lower circulation profits because there would be an excess of copies in the marketplace over demand. Also, subscription renewal rates were important for judging the success of the magazine. Another key to success was maintaining a high quality and accurate list of potential subscribers.

A magazine needed to be assured that a subscriber would actually pay for the magazines provided.

Subscriptions

55   Subscriptions were broken down into two categories: renewals and new business. The goal with renewals was to sustain these existing customers. New business could be acquired through agents such as schools, libraries, airlines, and other public places and also through direct ways such as direct mail, TV, gifts, and partnerships. In the 1990's the largest source of subscriptions was sweepstakes companies, such as Publishers Clearing House. However, due to legal reasons, this outlet was no longer available. In 2004, the average basic 1-year subscription rate was $25.93.

56   The keys to success when dealing with subscriptions were high renewal rates. While the consumer would renew their subscriptions if the product was desirable and they felt that they needed it, programs such as continuous service plans helped magazines to keep renewal rates high, since the renewing was automatic. The customer's credit card would get automatically billed. Another key to success was securing the highest price possible for the subscription, meaning the highest average subscription price. Maintaining a high quality and accurate list of subscribers was also important. This tied into the type of demographic which a magazine was targeting. A high quality subscriber was one that has money and would be able to pay for his/her subscription as well as be a likely purchaser of the products advertised in the magazine. Circulation files and mailing lists that located these types of subscribers were the most valuable. Collecting payment from subscribers in a timely manner was also a key to success. Obtaining new subscribers was also a key to success.

Newsstand Sales

57   Newsstand sales, or single copy sales, could arise from various locations. In 2004, 38% of all single copy sales came from supermarkets, 17% from mass merchandisers, 11% from bookstores, 10% from drug stores, 6% from terminals, 7% from convenience stores, and 10% from actual newsstands [Magazine Publishers Association, 2005]. The major key to success affecting single copy sales was price. In 2004, the average cover price on the newsstand was $4.40. This was up from $2.81 in 1994. Another major key to success was to be able to sell the highest number of copies on the newsstand. Other factors affecting single copy sales were the efficiency of the copies on the newsstand, i.e. putting the correct amount of copies in the market. The unsold copies in the newsstand were thrown out. Therefore, costs were incurred to produce these magazines; however, no revenue was received from these copies. Therefore, it was important to not have an excess of copies in the newsstand to avoid this waste. The quality of the displays was also important, so that the magazines looked attractive to potential buyers on the newsstand.

Advertising Sales

58   For an average magazine, advertising revenue represented 54% of a magazine's total revenue. Advertising revenue was acquired by selling ad pages in the magazine. The Publishers Information Bureau (PIB) was an independent agency that tracked advertising pages and set the rules for the consistent auditing of magazines' ratebases.

59   In 2004, there were 234,428 advertising pages sold in magazines. This was equivalent to $21.3 billion in advertising revenues. Since 2000, magazines had held a solid 17% of share of all advertising dollars spent in the media industry [Magazine Publishers Association, 2005].

60   Numerous research studies had been conducted to show that advertising in magazines had benefits over advertising in other forms of media. Multiple studies showed that consumers were more likely to find magazine advertising acceptable and enjoyable compared

to advertising in other media. Also, they found it less interruptive and more trustworthy. It had also been proven that advertising related experience increased magazine usage. Advertising helped to build the nature of the magazine. Studies also showed that readers were more likely to take action from magazine ads than television ads and that allocating more money to magazine advertising improved marketing and advertising ROI (Return on Investment) across a broad range of product categories [Magazine Handbook, 2005].

61   The type of advertisers that advertised in a magazine was also driven by the topic of the magazine. For instance, in *InStyle* the majority of advertisements were for beauty and fashion products. In a business publication, high-end advertisers such as Mercedes and Rolex tended to advertise.

62   A magazine's rate card was a listing of the open-rates, before any discounting occurred, that they charged to advertise in their magazine. In order to entice potential clients, a discount was normally offered off the open rate. A discount was the reduction in the amount that an advertiser actually paid for the unit within the magazine. Examples of discounts included contractual discounts, frequency discounts, waived premiums, corporate discounts, and bonus space. The actual cost that an advertiser paid was called Out of Pocket. This cost included any discount and production premiums paid. The CPM is the cost per thousand. It is a figure used in comparing the cost efficiency of media vehicles. It is calculated by dividing the out-of-pockets costs by the rate base per thousand.

63   The key to success when dealing with advertising sales was to secure as many advertising pages as possible. Correctly calculate the open rates of the magazine, given the competition, economic environment, reader profile, and quality of the reader was also a key to success. For instance, a magazine that targeted high-income readers could legitimately charge a higher base rate since these higher income readers were valued more in the advertising marketplace. Also, the discount level and type of discount offered to an advertiser needed to be at such a level that the advertiser agreed to the business, but the magazine was still making a profit and not giving away pages for free. Another key to success was to closely listen to the demands of the advertiser in term of placement of the ad. The advertiser might be sensitive to certain edit or might not want to be positioned too close to a competing advertiser. If the advertisers stated this and the magazine did not follow instructions, more often than not, the magazine had a responsibility to the advertiser to re-run that ad or a new ad at no additional cost to the advertiser. These make-goods could become very expensive for the magazine. Another key to success was keeping advertising costs low. Travel and Entertainment were often used to secure ad pages. These costs needed to be controlled and watched carefully. Finally, the physical quality of the magazine needed to meet advertisers' expectations. Heavier paper stock and high print quality were extremely important to an advertiser in terms of how attractive the ad would look to the reader. Trim size of the magazine was moderately important in helping to make an advertisement look more attractive.

Marketing

64   A magazine needed to have effective campaigns in order to effectively promote the magazine. The main part of marketing was to build sales for the magazine. Sales were generated from either advertising or circulation.

Advertising

65   The goal of marketing for advertisers was to obtain advertising pages. The sales call was the main way that advertisers were told of the benefits of advertising in a particular magazine. Return on Investment, meaning the return that an advertiser would get from running their ad in terms of increased units sold, was the most important metric to an advertiser.

66   The main way that an advertiser was incentivized to run pages in a magazine was through the discount offered. The advertiser needed to feel that he was being given a good deal.

The discount could be in monetary terms, such as a percentage off the open rate, or in terms of free ad space or special programs.

67   Entertainment was also used to incentivize advertisers to run pages. After hours events were used to convince advertisers to run pages. These events included dinners, shows, sporting events, spa treatments, and the like.

68   The key to success in marketing to advertisers was to create a positive image of the magazine. The advertiser needed to be confident that his ad was associated with a premium, trustworthy product. The way to convince an advertiser of this was through effective presentations, which stressed the statistics that an advertiser wanted to hear, such as household income of readers, level of education readers, and return on investment. Another key to success was to go on as many sales calls as possible. It was important to be in the field in order to create buzz for the magazine.

69   Finding the appropriate discount was also a key to success. The sales representative had to know their clients preferences in terms of offering discounts in terms of percentages, free space, or special programs.

70   A final key to success was utilizing the correct mix of entertainment to lure advertisers to your magazine. The correct people needed to be contacted and their interests needed to be known ahead of time. For instance, someone in the upper 50's would probably not enjoy a rock concert as much as someone in their 20's.

Subscribers

71   The goal of marketing subscribers was to build sales. The goal was to keep existing subscribers, while building new ones.

72   The key to success when marketing to subscribers was to keep renewal rates high. One way to do this was through utilization of continuous service plans. When a customer originally subscribed to a magazine, they could opt to have uninterrupted service; when the year was up, their credit card would still be charged and they would continue to receive the magazine. The renewal rates for continuous service were higher than those under the "bill me" option.

73   Another key to success when marketing to new subscribers was to have effective direct mail offers, which was a combined offer with other magazines. Also, targeting the correct subscribers was important for new business. This could be achieved through renting of mailing lists, which was a cost effective way of obtaining new names.

74   Insert cards in newsstand copies were also keys to obtaining new subscribers. Finally, promotion of the individual magazine web-site could also draw in new subscribers.

Competition

75   *Fortune* magazine directly competed against publications in the business segment of the magazine industry. The two main competitors in the business and industry magazine segment were *Forbes* and *BusinessWeek*. *Fortune* also competed against other forms of media such as the Internet and television, which delivered up to the minute news information.

Forbes

76   Since *Forbes'* inception in 1917, its mission had been to provide information and insights to ensure its readers success, giving the business leaders the tools they needed to compete in the capitalist game. *Forbes* prided itself on being preemptive, predictive, counter-conventional, uncompromising, independent, and concise. *Forbes* claimed to get the news first, report what's next, run against popular opinion, never settle, and get quickly to the point for time-starved executives. *Forbes* was an independent company; therefore it did not have to report its results to Wall Street [*Forbes*, 2005].

77   *Forbes* delivered 26 issues a year and had a North American as well as an Asia editorial edition. Like *Fortune*, *Forbes* had annual editorial lists that defined those corresponding

issues. These lists included The World's Billionaires, The 100 richest celebrities, and the 400 richest People in America. *Forbes'* style, while business based, was more focused on individuals and the secrets of their financial successes. Other items produced by *Forbes* are *Forbes.com*, its up to the minute business web site as well as FYI, *Forbes'* dedicated lifestyle edition. *Forbes* also sponsored conferences and seminars, such as *Forbes Live* and Peer-to Peer networking events.

78   *Forbes* targeted 4.9 million adult readers each issue. Its readers per copy were 5.44 per issue. Eighty-eight percent were male and 12% were female. Ninety-three percent were college educated. *Forbes* targeted a very elite demographic; the median household income was $167,000 and average net worth was $2.1million. Eighty-four percent of *Forbes* readers were employed in business and industry and 67% were in top management. *Forbes* readers also spent their money on luxury goods; 80,000 readers owned a premium luxury car and 20,000 owned a boat, 257,000 have a wine cellar and 113,000 spent over $5k on watches and jewelry in the past year. *Forbes'* readers were also frequent travelers. *Forbes'* readers spent $6.4 billion of all vacation travel in 2004 [*Forbes*, 2005].

79   *Forbes'* magazine measured 8 × 10½" and was printed on 32# paper stock and 80# cover stock. *Forbes* employed computer interfaces when transmitting the pages to the printing plant [*Forbes*, 2005].

80   *Forbes'* circulation was 96% subscription sales and 4% newsstand sales. *Forbes'* ratebase was 900,000 and they generally delivered a 2.7% bonus above ratebase. The publisher's selected 1-year price was $59.95 and the newsstand cover price was $4.99. The average subscription price per copy was $1.52. Nearly 83% of subscriptions came from consumer requests, such as insert cards, or renewal business.

81   In 2005, *Forbes* open rate for a full national page was $91,570. *Forbes* frequency discounts, which were one of the many types of discounts used by Forbes, were as follows: if an advertiser ran 4 insertions, the rate dropped to $80,580. For 8 insertions, the rate dropped to $77,850. Besides frequency discounts, Forbes utilized other forms of discounts such as free pages and special kickers to increase business. *Forbes'* average of total discounts offered to advertisers was aground 60%. *Forbes'* black and white open rate was $62,260. A full color half-page cost $54,940 and a black and white half page cost $37,370. In 2004, *Forbes'* total revenue from advertising was $324 million and it sold 3,460 ad pages [*Forbes*, 2005].

82   Since *Forbes* was a private company, financial results did not need to be reported. This was a benefit since *Forbes* did not need to be held financially accountable to Wall Street for the business decisions that it made.

83   *Forbes* was strong in creating a product that was in high demand in the marketplace and was relevant in topic. *Forbes* received average marks for delivering a high quality editorial product in terms of stories and pictures. *Forbes* ranked average in delivering a physically attractive book; it was on heavy paper stock (32#) and was larger than some competitors (8 × 10½"). *Forbes* was strong in containing appropriate advertising. *Forbes'* highest categories of advertisers were technology and automotive, which fit the business and industry topic. *Forbes* ranked average in delivering a product, which was highly trusted in the industry. *Forbes* was strong in terms of consistency of editorial style. *Forbes* continued to discuss business and economy in terms of individual wealth success stories.

84   *Forbes* was average in targeting the age demographic; the magazine tended to skew older; *Forbes* targeted in the late 40's / early 50's. It did offer appropriate editorial content, a relevant topic and the correct level of language complexity for the age targeted. In regards to gender, *Forbes* was strong in regards to relevance of topic and appropriateness of advertising. It was also strong in consistency of editorial product.

85   In regards to income and level of management, *Forbes* was very strong in targeting a high household income and percentage of upper management targeted.

86   *Forbes* was strong at reaching its correct demographic; it targeted high quality subscribers, had strong newsstand presence and appeared to be priced correctly.

87   *Forbes* was average in producing a high quality product. Because *Forbes* was not a large, multi-title magazine publisher, *Forbes* was probably weak at the following: securing the lowest paper prices in the industry, relationships with printers, contractual printing rates, and relationships with distributors. *Forbes* was also strong in terms of quality of paper used and average in trim size.

88   In regards to subscriptions, *Forbes* was average in terms of ratebase and strong in subscription price. *Forbes*, however, was weak in subscription renewals, average in list maintenance, and strong in collection of payments, since it catered to such a high income demographic. *Forbes* ranked average in terms of obtaining new subscription business.

89   *Forbes* was strong in terms of newsstand price, average in the correct number of copies in the marketplace, and average in sell-through, meaning there was not an excessive amount of copies wasted on the newsstand.

90   *Forbes* ranked strong in terms of number of ad pages secured, as compared to its competition. *Forbes* was average in terms of its open rates. *Forbes* was weak in terms of level of discounts and type of discount offered, its average of 60% was high compared to competitors. *Forbes* was average in terms of advertiser positioning and keeping the number of make-goods low.

91   *Forbes* was probably weak in terms of keeping advertising sales costs low. Since *Forbes* was privately owned, it did not have the corporate mandates to meet Wall Street expectations and keep expenses low. Though *Forbes* had the highest number of advertising pages, it might have been paying a lot for these pages in terms of high client entertainment costs.

92   *Forbes'* sales staff was strong in giving presentations. The sales staff was effective in conveying *Forbes'* positive brand image. *Forbes* went on an average volume of sales calls. The *Forbes'* sales staff was given flexibility to offer discounts, which they felt, would secure business. *Forbes* spent a lot on entertainment expenditures; therefore, this was positive in the eyes of potential advertisers.

93   *Forbes* was weak in keeping subscribers, they had lower renewal rates than competitors. They offered continuous service plans, and tried to build business by offering incentives to opt for the continuous service option. *Forbes* was weak at utilizing direct mail combo offers. Forbes was also strong at utilizing mailing list rentals, insert cards and average at web-site promotions.

BusinessWeek

94   *BusinessWeek* was the business publication of the McGraw Hill Company. *BusinessWeek's* mission for the past 75 years had been to give professionals worldwide the insight, information, and inspiration they needed to make smarter decisions about business, finance, and careers. *BusinessWeek's* edit focused on business issues and events, financial trends and projections, and technology [*BusinessWeek*, 2005].

95   *BusinessWeek* produced 50 issues a year. *BusinessWeek* had a North American edition as well as editions in Europe and Asia. Besides the printed magazine, *BusinessWeek* offered a variety of other products to readers. These products included *BusinessWeek Online*—an up to the minute business website which included a subscription component for the MBA user. *BusinessWeek* also had a weekend television program called *BusinessWeek Weekend*, which was a consumer business and personal finance television program. This show aired in over 79% of the U.S. television market. *BusinessWeek* also sponsored conferences and corporate events [*BusinessWeek,* 2005].

96   *BusinessWeek* targeted 5.8 million readers worldwide every issue. The readers per copy were approximately 5.98 per issue. *BusinessWeek's* audience was made up of 67% male and 33% female. The median age of a reader was 44 years. Fifty-five percent of readers

graduated from college, the median household income was $88,381, and 43% of readers were in professional/managerial positions [BusinessWeek, 2005].

97   *BusinessWeek* magazine measured $8 \times 10\frac{1}{2}$" and was printed on 30# paper stock and 60# cover stock. *BusinessWeek* employed computer interfaces when transmitting the pages to the printing plant.

98   *BusinessWeek's* ratebase was 970,000 per issue and its circulation was comprised of 97% subscribers and 3% newsstand sales. The cover price of *BusinessWeek* on the newsstand was $4.95 and the yearly subscription price was $59.97 [*BusinessWeek,* 2005].

99   In 2005, *BusinessWeek's* open rate for a full national page was $106,500. *BusinessWeek* offered a variety of discounts to attract advertisers. One type of discount was the frequency discount. *BusinessWeek's* frequency discounts were as follows: if an advertiser ran 3 insertions, the rate was $95,850. For 13 insertions a year, the rate was $90,525. For over 26 insertions, rate was $79,875. Other forms of discounts used were free pages and special kickers. *BusinessWeek's* average of the total discounts offered to advertisers was approximately 70%. *BusinessWeek's* black and white open rate was $72,000. A full color half-page cost $66,500 and a black and white half page cost $45,000. *BusinessWeek's* total revenue, in 2004, from advertising was $365 million and it sold 3,164 ad pages [*BusinessWeek,* 2005].

100   *BusinessWeek* was a subsidiary of the McGraw Hill Company. The entire company reported total revenues in 2004 of $5 billion and net income of $756 million [Hoovers, 2005].

101   *BusinessWeek* was strong in creating a product that was in high demand in the marketplace and was relevant in topic. *BusinessWeek* received weak marks for delivering a high quality editorial product in terms of stories and pictures. *BusinessWeek* was strong in containing appropriate advertising. *BusinessWeek's* highest categories of advertisers were technology and automotive, which fit the business and industry topic. *BusinessWeek* ranked low in delivering a product, which was highly trusted in the industry. *BusinessWeek* was strong in terms of consistency of editorial style. It continued to discuss the current week's business and economy news.

102   *BusinessWeek* was strong in targeting the age demographic; the magazine tended to skew younger. It did offer appropriate editorial content, a relevant topic and the correct level of language complexity for the age targeted. In regards to gender, *BusinessWeek* was strong in regards to relevance of topic and appropriateness of advertising. It was also strong in consistency of editorial product.

103   In regards to income and level of management, *BusinessWeek* was weak in targeting a high household income and percentage of upper management targeted.

104   *BusinessWeek* was strong at reaching its correct demographic; it targeted successfully to subscribers, had strong newsstand presence and appeared to be priced correctly.

105   *BusinessWeek* was weak in producing a high quality product. Through *BusinessWeek's* relationship with McGraw Hill, which was not as large of a magazine publisher as Time Inc., it was probably average at the following: securing the lowest paper prices in the industry, relationships with printers, contractual printing rates, and relationships with distributors. *BusinessWeek* was weak in terms of quality of paper used and weak at trim size.

106   In regards to subscriptions, *BusinessWeek* was strong in terms of ratebase and strong in subscription price. *BusinessWeek* was also strong in subscription renewals, average in list maintenance, and average in collection of payments. *BusinessWeek* ranked average in terms of obtaining news subscription business.

107   *BusinessWeek* was average in terms of newsstand price, average in the correct number of copies in the marketplace, average in sell-through.

108   *BusinessWeek* was weak in terms of number of ad pages secured, as compared to its competitive set. *BusinessWeek* was strong in terms of it open rates. *BusinessWeek* was weak in terms of level of discounts and type of discount offered, they had high discount

percents. *BusinessWeek* was average in terms of advertiser positioning and keeping the number of makegoods low. *BusinessWeek* was probably average in terms of keeping advertising sales low.

109   *BusinessWeek*'s sales staff was average at giving presentations. The sales staff was average in conveying *BusinessWeek*'s positive brand image. *BusinessWeek* went on an average volume of sales calls. The *BusinessWeek* sales staff was given flexibility to offer discounts, which they felt, would secure business. *BusinessWeek* was average at entertainment expenditures.

110   *BusinessWeek* was average in keeping subscribers. They offered out the continuous service plans, and tried to build business by offering incentives to opt for the continuous service option. *BusinessWeek* was weak at utilizing direct mail combo offers. *BusinessWeek* was also weak at utilizing mailing list rentals and insert cards, and average at web-site promotions.

Other Media

111   *Fortune* also competed against other forms of media in terms of delivering business news and information. Business websites were the latest form of competition. Business websites, such as Yahoo! Finance and CNN.com had the advantage of having the ability to deliver up to the minute information. On these websites, one could find the latest stock prices as well as detailed analysis. Also, these websites had extensive archives which aided the consumer while researching. These websites were available 24 hours a day and most were free to the user. Subscription fees might apply for more advanced services that these website offered. These vehicles were also becoming major players in the advertising market. As stated earlier, websites such as Google, were becoming the largest areas for advertising expenditures in the industry.

112   Television was another form of media, which business magazines competed against. Financial news networks, such as CNBC and CNNfn also had the ability to deliver up to the minute information. Most of the financial networks had scrolling stock tickers that delivered the latest stock market information. This source of information was essentially free to the consumer.

THE COMPANY

Time Warner

113   Time Warner was considered to be the world's #41 media firm. The company combined new media, such as AOL and New Line Cinemas, with old media spanning film, TV, cable, and publishing. Figure 3 shows the different business units of Time Warner. In 2004, Time Warner's sales totaled $42 billion and its net income was $3.3 billion. Time Warner's top competitors were Viacom and Disney [Time Warner, 2005].

FIGURE 3   Time Warner

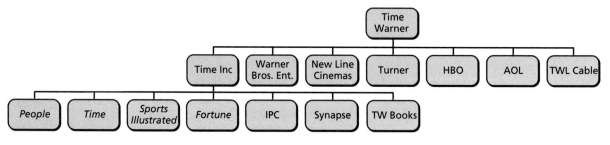

Time inc.

114   Time Inc., a subsidiary of Time Warner, was the leading US consumer magazine publisher with more than 140 magazines. Time Inc.'s magazines included news, sports, celebrity, fashion, women's lifestyle, business, personal finance, entertainment, and the like. The advertising revenues of Time Inc. accounted for nearly a quarter of the advertising revenues of all U.S. consumer magazines. In 2004, 13% of Time Warner's revenue came from Time Inc. [Time Warner, 2005].

115   Time Inc. would continue to maintain its current strategy in the coming years. That strategy was to maintain excellence and reinvention of its core magazines, while overseeing a seamless management of acquisitions, an ongoing cost management program and continuing launches of new magazines. Time Inc.'s main competitors in the magazine industry were Hearst Magazines, Conde Naste and Advance Publications [Time Warner, 2005].

Fortune Magazine

116   *Fortune Magazine* was Time Inc.'s sole purely business magazine. *Fortune*'s mission was to be a global magazine and world-class brand. *Fortune* reached the most sought after leaders in business-offering advertisers incomparable access and prime positioning. *Fortune* served up in-depth, cutting edge editorial coverage and exclusive insider access to the sharpest minds in the world [*Fortune,* 2005].

117   *Fortune*'s first issue was released into the market in 1930, over 75 years ago, for $1 per copy. The magazine was released during the Great Depression, which was a strange time to start a magazine about business. The mission of *Fortune* was to explain how the world really worked [Okrent, 2005].

118   Figure 4 shows the different business departments of *Fortune Magazine*.

Product

119   The main product of *Fortune* was the magazine that was produced 26 times a year domestically, and 23 times a year in Europe and Asia. Today's product was very different in terms of style and editorial content than the product developed by Henry Luce 75 years ago. The

FIGURE 4   *Fortune Magazine*

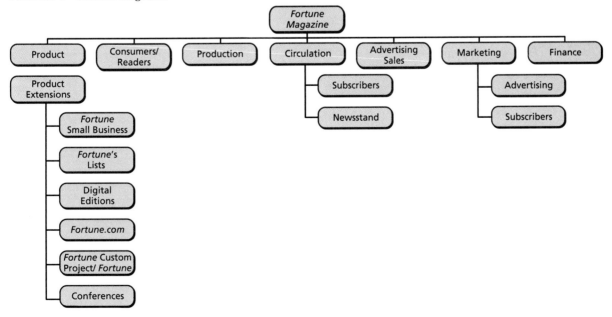

very first issue was extremely large for a magazine of depression times, 11 inches by 14 inches. Also, the paper stock used was much heavier than other publications.

120   Even 75 years ago, *Fortune*'s editorial content set it apart from the competition. At its inception, *Fortune* staffed unknown writers, who were future Pulitzer Prize winners. *Fortune*'s stories took many forms; however, the main story form, which *Fortune* employed, was the company story. The company story was defined by *Fortune* as a long, vivid portrait of one of the major businesses of the day. *Fortune*'s goal was telling its readers how to make money by using real life company stories as examples.

121   Over time, *Fortune* evolved. During harder economic times, the lavishness was toned down. The magazine became smaller and the paper stock, lighter. After the World War II, Luce changed the mission of *Fortune* to be a magazine that "assists in the successful development of American business enterprise at home and abroad" [Okrent, 2005].

122   The editorial content and format of *Fortune* has evolved as well. While *Fortune* still was about storytelling, the focus of the stories has changed. More recent stories had focused on the intersection of business and government, democratization of the capital markets, and the influence of technology. *Fortune* had evolved into more of a business news magazine, rather than simply a Company Storytelling magazine.

123   *Fortune Magazine* was strong in creating a product that was in high demand in the marketplace. *Fortune* received high marks for delivering a high quality editorial product in terms of stories and pictures. *Fortune* also delivered a physically attractive magazine; it was on heavy paper stock (32#) and was larger than competitors (8 × 10⅞"). *Fortune* was strong in containing appropriate advertising. *Fortune*'s highest categories of advertisers were technology and automotive, which fit the business and industry topic. *Fortune* also delivered a product, which was highly trusted in the industry.

124   *Fortune Magazine* was weak in terms of consistency of editorial style. In 2005, with a change in managing editors, *Fortune* changed its format from, that of a "story-telling" magazine to more news-based magazine. Switching editorial style could hurt loyal readers, who were used to the original product.

Product Extensions

125   *Fortune*'s superb reputation in the business community has afforded it the opportunity to expand its brand beyond the actual magazine issue. Following are some of the product extensions of *Fortune Magazine*.

126   ***Fortune Small Business.*** *Fortune Small Business (FSB)* was a separate magazine that was spun-off from *Fortune*. The goal of *Fortune Small Business* was to celebrate the drive, passion, and intensity of small business. *FSB* strived to keep the leading edge of today's entrepreneurs connected. *FSB* shared the advertising sales and production staff of *Fortune* magazine. The name *Fortune* in the title had given *FSB* credibility in the market and while it was still in the investment stages; this magazine was expected to become profitable in its own right in 2006.

127   ***Fortune's Lists.*** *Fortune*'s signature lists, which were published in the magazine periodically, were recognized around the world as a measure of business success. The most famous list was the *Fortune 500 issue*, which ranked the top 500 companies. Other lists included *America's Most Admired Companies*, *50 Most Powerful Women*, and the *100 Fastest Growing Companies* issues. These annual lists increased newsstand sales, created media buzz, and were the most eagerly awaited scorecards in the industry.

128   ***Digital Edition.*** The Digital edition of *Fortune* magazine was an on-line version of the magazine. The digital version of the current issue was, in 2005, being sent to a test group of subscribers on a trial basis. The digital version mirrored the layout of the print version; however, there were some enhanced HTML features in the document, such as video images

of advertising. This service was just launched in September 2005 and was expected to gain presence in the market over the next few months.

129 ***Fortune.com.*** *Fortune.com* was a website that gave more of *Fortune* the magazine. It gave more company news, investor analysis, technology advice—every day. As of 2005, each business unit of Time Inc. had its own separate website. Planned for January 2006, was an integrated website called CNNMoney.com, which would be powered by the business publications of Time Inc.; *Fortune, Money, CNN, Business 2.0,* and *FSB. Fortune.com* would reside within this site. The company believed that this would be the most insightful and comprehensive business and finance destination. Its mission was to produce the premier and most trusted site for business leaders and savvy investors by informing, inspiring, and advising. It was going to contain breaking news and up-to-the minute markets coverage, as well as company and CEO profiles. Personal finance advice would also be available on this website. There will be 35 journalists and editors producing news daily and access to CNN's resources. Ten Thousand magazine articles would be delivered through the website each year [Shah, 2005].

130 ***Fortune Custom Projects/Fortune Marketplace.*** *Fortune Custom Projects* created targeted special advertising sections to provide advertisers an effective and unique way to deliver their message to the business community. The benefit of custom projects was that they drew readers to a specific topic. Clients benefited from this targeted advertising. Examples of *Fortune Custom Projects* were issue or section reprints for a particular advertiser. Also, *Fortune Marketplace* gave direct response advertisers a showcase for their products.

131 ***Conferences.*** *Fortune* was the leading producer of conferences for senior executives. Conferences provided for a unique opportunity for top-level executives to gather with peers and exchange ideas. Programs were strategically oriented; case studies were conducted in order to examine future trends that would shape the business environment. Examples of the conferences offered in 2005 were *The Fortune Boardroom Forum, Fortune Global Forum, The Most Powerful Women,* and *Fortune Innovation Forum*.

Consumers/Readers

132 The reader was the consumer of *Fortune* magazine. The median age of the *Fortune* reader was 49.4 years old. Eighty-three percent of readers had graduated from college and 53% had received a postgraduate degree. The median household income of a *Fortune* reader was $165,200 and the average household income was $347,500. The median personal income was $119,400 and the average personal income was $288,400. The median net worth was $871,900 and the average net worth was $2,223,600. The median value of a reader's investment portfolio was $663,400 and the average value was $1,902,800 [*Fortune*, 2005].

133 Eight-five percent of readers were employed in a business profession. Sixty-four percent were in top management and 35% were either in middle management or were professionals. Almost 90% of all readers owned stocks, used a computer at work and home, had access to the Internet, have traveled by airline in the past year, and owned or leased 2 or more vehicles [*Fortune*, 2005].

134 From the statistics presented above, *Fortune Magazine* targeted a very elite readership based on income and net worth. Most were business professionals and the advertising in the magazine accurately reflected this demographic. An untapped market was MBA students, who were the business leaders of the future. *Fortune* recognized this and planned to increase promotions to build a solid base within this group.

135 *Fortune* was strong at targeting the age demographic. *Fortune* targeted in the upper 40's. It did offer appropriate editorial content, a relevant topic, and the correct level of language complexity for the age targeted. In regards to gender, *Fortune* was strong in regards to relevance of topic and appropriateness of advertising. It was weak, however, in consistency of editorial product.

136   In regards to income and level of management, *Fortune* was strong in targeting a high household income and average in percentage of upper management targeted. *Fortune* was strong in its physical attributes; paper quality and trim size. *Fortune* was strong in regards to editorial quality and appropriateness of advertising.

137   *Fortune* was also strong at reaching its correct demographic; it targeted successfully to subscribers, had strong newsstand presence and appeared to be priced correctly.

Production

138   The domestic edition of *Fortune* magazine was printed 26 times a year in Clarksville, Tennessee. Europe and Asia editions were printed in their respective countries. *Fortune*'s association with Time Inc. allowed it the luxury of obtaining some of the best paper prices and printing rates in the industry. Paper was bought by Time Inc. as a whole company and managed by a Central Production Group. This group then expensed paper costs to the individual magazine titles, based upon the pounds of paper used on an issue. Time Inc., as a large bargaining unit, could obtain more competitive prices in the paper industry than *Fortune* magazine could do on its own.

139   Contracted printing rates worked similar to paper. Time Inc. negotiated printing contracts for the company as a whole, while each individual title had its own price list. Time Inc.'s bargaining power allowed it to gain some of the most competitive printing rates in the industry. *Fortune* magazine benefited from these lower rates.

140   Once the magazine was printed at Clarksville, magazines were sent via trucks either directly to wholesalers or to postal hubs. The costs incurred during this process included trucking freight costs and postage. For the remainder of 2005 and 2006, *Fortune* was expecting to be hit with increased trucking costs, on the 200,000 newsstand copies it put out each issue, due to surging fuel prices. After not raising periodical postage for the past few years, the United States Postal Service was expected to raise periodical postage rates from anywhere between 5% to 15%. This could translate into hundreds of thousands of dollars against *Fortune*'s bottom line.

141   Advertiser production premiums were also included in the magazine. These were special units that an advertiser bought that were intended to make an impact. They were normally produced on heavier paper, which translated into higher paper and postage charges. These could be complex units, such as pop-ups, which translated into higher printing costs as well. Typically, an advertiser would pay for the incremental production costs incurred to produce these units.

142   One way to mitigate the effects of production input increases was to change the production specs of the magazine. Currently, *Fortune* magazine measured $8 \times 10\frac{7}{8}$"and was produced on 32# body stock paper and 80# cover stock paper. *Fortune* was currently larger than its main competitors. The magazine was perfect bound, meaning it had a spine rather than being stapled, and had a UV coating on the cover to give it that glossy look. Currently, the physical costs to produce one average issue of *Fortune* magazine were approximately $1 million. An average issue had approximately 190 pages and an average page cost approximately $4500 to produce. Changes to production specs such as smaller trim size and lighter paper stock could translate into hundreds of thousands of dollars of savings in paper and distribution costs, due to cheaper paper being used and a lighter magazine being mailed out. All changes to the production specs of the magazine needed editorial approval, since the look of the magazine could be greatly altered by these changes. Also, an evaluation needs to be conducted to ensure that the advertising community and the reader accepted the new book.

143   *Fortune* was strong in producing a high quality product. Because of its affiliation with Time Inc, *Fortune* was strong at the following: securing the lowest paper prices in the industry, relationships with printers, contractual printing rates, and relationships with distributors. *Fortune* was also strong in terms of quality of paper used and trim size.

Circulation

144   *Fortune Magazine* guaranteed a ratebase of 830,000. This meant that *Fortune* as guaranteeing that 830,000 readers will see the ads, per issue. On average, *Fortune* delivered a rate base bonus to advertisers of 10%. The total paid circulation for an average issue of *Fortune* was 918,739 copies [*Fortune, 2005*].

Subscribers

145   Close to 96% of copies sold were to subscribers, who paid on average $1.43/issue or $40.16 per year.

146   In regards to subscriptions, *Fortune* was weak in terms of ratebase and subscription price, they were both lower than the industry average. *Fortune*, however, was strong in subscription renewals, list maintenance, and collection of payments. *Fortune* ranked average in terms of obtaining new subscription business.

Newsstand Sales

147   Four percent were newsstand copies, with a cover price of $4.99. A newsstand copy of *Fortune* cost approximately $2 in production and editorial costs. Out of the $4.99, *Fortune* was able to keep over 50%, with the rest going to the newsstand owners.

148   *Fortune* was strong in terms of newsstand price, correct number of copies in the marketplace (200,000), and sell-through, or amount of units sold.

Advertising Sales

149   In 2004, *Fortune* sold 3,405 ad pages. In 2005, a full color page in *Fortune* magazine cost an advertiser $88,500 based on open rates. A black and white full page cost $61,950. A half page color ad cost $53,100 while a half page black and white ad costs $37,200. Advertising on the back cover was the most expensive position in the book. It would cost an advertiser $115,050 to advertise on the back cover [*Fortune*, 2005].

150   The rates listed above were the open, rate card, rates of *Fortune* magazine. Almost never would an advertiser pay the open rates. Pages were discounted in order to entice advertisers to increase business. Discount rates needed to be examined closely to make sure that *Fortune* was not losing money in the deals. A common form of discount was the frequency discount. This discount was based on the total number of National Equivalent Pages run in an advertiser's current year. The more ads that ran, the greater the discount. For *Fortune* magazine, the total of the average discounts were around 50%.

151   In 2004, *Fortune*'s top three advertisers in terms of ad pages were IBM, Hewlett Packard, and the American Stock Exchange. The advertisers in *Fortune* magazine were suitable for the editorial content of the magazine.

152   *Fortune* ranked average in terms of number of ad pages secured, as compared to its competitive set. *Fortune* was weak in terms of it open rates; it was the lowest. *Fortune* was strong in terms of level of discounts and type of discount offered; it had the lowest discount percents. *Fortune* was strong in terms of advertiser positioning and keeping the number of make-goods low.

153   *Fortune*'s strength in Advertising Sales was that the magazine secured advertising pages without having to spend enormous amounts on Travel and Entertainment, in the form of wining and dining clients. Because of budget cuts, sales representatives' T&E expenses were closely monitored. Clients were buying pages in *Fortune* because they were aware that it was a premium product with a high Return on Investment, not because they were being bribed with perks.

154   *Fortune* was strong in terms of paper quality, print quality and trim size, making the magazine attractive to advertisers.

Marketing

155   *Fortune*'s best source of marketing was its reputation. In all campaigns, the *Fortune* brand name was used to draw business. References to the *Fortune* lists and *Fortune Conferences* gave campaigns credibility. Cross promotions with sister publications in Time Inc., especially *Money Magazine*, Time Inc.'s personal finance publication, helped to bring business to *Fortune*.

Advertisers

156   *Fortune Magazine*'s sales staff was strong at giving presentations. The sales staff was effective in conveying *Fortune*'s positive brand image. *Fortune* also went on a high volume of sales calls. The *Fortune* sales staff was given flexibility to offer discounts, which they felt, would secure business. *Fortune* was weak at entertainment expenditures, due to corporate mandates.

Subscribers

157   *Fortune* was strong in keeping subscribers. They offered the continuous service plans, and tried to build business by offering incentives to opt for the continuous service option. *Fortune* was also strong at utilizing direct mail combo offers; it had the benefit of the sister publications of Time Inc. *Fortune* was also strong at utilizing mailing list rentals, insert cards and web-site promotions.

Finance

158   Time Warner corporate always looked to *Fortune* magazine to bring in substantial year over year gains to its divisional income. In 2004, total circulation revenue was approximately $24 million. Total circulation expenses were approximately $16 million. Total advertising revenues were approximately $134 million. Advertising expenses were approximately $28 million. Total physical costs were approximately $30 million. Total divisional income for *Fortune* magazine in 2004 was approximately $35 million.

Management & Strategy

159   The President of *Fortune Magazine* was ultimately responsible for the income delivered to Time Warner corporate. He relied on the heads of *Fortune*'s divisional units to make the best decisions for *Fortune* in order to allow them to be different and better and thus win against the competition.

160   The Publisher of *Fortune* was responsible for the ad sales and advertising and marketing expenses of the magazine. He and his staff aggressively went out into the market and tried to sell as many ad pages as possible.

161   The head of circulation and his staff determined the correct ratebase of the magazine. Issues such as cover prices, subscription price, issue frequency and consumer demographics resided in the circulation division.

162   The managing editor of *Fortune* and his staff were responsible for the editorial content and covers of the magazine.

163   The Production Director of *Fortune* was responsible for printing and distributing the magazine as efficiently and cheaply as possible.

164   The Business Manager heads the business office, which was in charge of setting the open advertising rates and discount level of pages. The business office was responsible for monitoring advertising, marketing, production, and editorial expenses.

165   Given the tough economic environment, one issue facing *Fortune*'s management team was keeping office costs down. It was the responsibility of each department head to currently monitor their department expenses.

LOOKING TOWARDS THE FUTURE

166   The President of *Fortune Magazine* was faced with many crucial decisions affecting the future of the magazine. One very important decision involved production changes for the magazine. The current state of the advertising environment and technological changes, causing changes to consumer preferences, such as digital magazine, has cast a shadow of doubt over the magazine industry. The one thing that was certain was that in order for a magazine to be viable, expenses needed to be kept to a minimum and all processes needed to be running as efficiently as possible. Production specifications were the one area where he could make decisions that could greatly affect the physical costs spent on the magazine.

167   The production decision revolved around two alternatives. The first was to leave the magazine at its current specifications in regards to type of paper used on the magazine and dimensions of the magazine, which was known as trim size. The second alternative would be to lower the weight of paper stock used and to make the book smaller, thus saving money in paper and postage.

168   Alternative 1 (**definition**) proposed that *Fortune* not make any changes to its production specifications. *Fortune* was produced on 32# body paper and 80# cover paper. The trim size of *Fortune* was $8 \times 10\frac{7}{8}$". Since, its inception 75 years ago, *Fortune* had strived to be a premier product with a lavish look. The size of the magazine and type of paper used were associated with the physical quality of the magazine. Business magazines were generally larger and on heavier paper stock than other magazines. For instance, *People Magazine* and *Sports Illustrated* are both on 30# body stock, 60# cover stock and measure $8 \times 10\frac{1}{2}$".

169   By maintaining its current production specifications, *Fortune* would maintain its superior quality among the business publications. *Fortune* was printed on the same body paper as *Forbes*; however its trim size was larger. *Fortune* was on both heavier paper and was larger than *BusinessWeek*. The Managing Editor of *Fortune* wanted strongly for *Fortune* to maintain its current specifications. While his main role in the magazine was the editorial content, he was also concerned about the look and feel of the magazine. In the magazine industry, packaging was almost, if not more, important than content. The **benefit** of keeping production specs the same would be that *Fortune* would maintain its lavishness and rich look, making it more attractive to the reader and advertiser.

170   Keeping production specifications the same is **feasible,** considering *Fortune* would simply have to continue its existing processes. For instance, *Fortune* already has an inventory of 32# paper that is managed by a Central Production group. Also, *Fortune* already has set contracts with its printers; therefore all the necessary equipment to print *Fortune* at its trim size was already in place.

171   By keeping production specifications the same, *Fortune* would **win** against the competition because it was producing a superior product. As stated above, *Fortune* was larger and on better paper than the competition. Assuming consumers were aware of these different production specifications, which market research suggested they were, consumers would choose *Fortune* over the competition. Advertisers would also be attracted to *Fortune* because of its lavishness. The positive physical image of *Fortune* would make the advertisements look better.

172   By maintaining its current production specifications, *Fortune* was expected to be hit hard in 2006. Paper prices were expected to rise 5% and postage costs were expected to rise up to 8%. The combined effects of these 2 increases on *Fortune* magazine were approximately

$1 million. By not making any changes, *Fortune* could expect a $1 million hit directly to its bottom line. Because of the tough economic times that *Fortune* was facing, this hit would be detrimental and would cause *Fortune* to miss profit projections.

173   The **way around the drawback** was to evaluate other parts of the business and make expenditure cuts that were feasible and appropriate. Also, effort would need to be made to build up the revenue streams of the business.

174   Alternative 2 proposes that *Fortune* made some drastic changes to its production specifications. After meeting with people in the Central Production area, the President learned of a new quality of 30# paper which was just entering the market. While the paper did weigh less, it was coated and therefore of better quality than the type of paper used on most weekly publications including *People* and *Sports Illustrated*. Also, *Fortune*'s cover stock could move from 80# to 70# paper. Also, after evaluating the size of the competition's magazines, the President felt that taking down *Fortune*'s trim size to 8 × 10½" would be acceptable.

175   The **benefits** of this strategy would be cost savings. By changing body stock to 30, *Fortune* was expected to save $80k in paper costs (mostly from using less paper) and $175k in postage costs, since the magazines that would be mailed out would be lighter. Changing from 80 to 70 cover stock would save approximately $100k. Lowering the trim size of the magazine would save approximately $500k in paper and postage costs. The combined savings of all these changes was approximately $900k, which was almost the hit that *Fortune* would take if it made no changes.

176   These changes were **feasible** for *Fortune*. Paper was bought by Central Production for the company as a whole. Central Production would have no problem purchasing the new type of paper for *Fortune*. Any inventory of *Fortune*'s old paper stock would either be passed along to other titles or sold outside the company. Since Time Inc. secured some of the lowest paper prices in the industry, this paper could likely be sold outside the company at a slight profit. Changing trim size would be more difficult, though not impossible. Through Time Inc, *Fortune* has set long-term printing contracts with its plants to produce its product. The current contract was based on the current specifications of the magazine. Contracts would need to be altered if this change was to take effect. *Fortune* would need to be printed on a different type of machine if it were to change trim size. Management needed to make sure the current printing plant had the necessary machinery available. If not, *Fortune* might have to switch printing plants, which could be a costly endeavor and cause legal problems, since a contract might need to be broken. However, the printing plant would probably do all possible to help secure *Fortune*'s business for the long term.

177   *Fortune* could **win against the competition** since it would be saving money which could be used in other areas to build its business. This money could be used to build up revenue streams, such as more direct mail to potential subscribers and enhanced sales presentation on sales calls. The saved money could be invested back into the magazine and be used to strengthen the magazine. Money could be used to enhance the editorial content by securing award winning writers and photographers. Money could also be spent on research for stories. Also, this savings could be used to improve circulation research programs to reach new subscribers, and increase marketing programs for the magazine, which would build exposure to *Fortune* and boost advertising and circulation sales.

178   The **drawback** of the alternative was the *Fortune*'s look would be altered. The managing editor would not be happy because the magazine would be smaller and possibly not as rich looking. The smaller size of the magazines would necessitate the changing of edit's templates, which would create additional work. There might also be some backlash on the advertising side. Because the paper would be not as thick, show through might occur. Show through is when an image on one side of the paper bleeds through the other side. The Publisher of *Fortune*, felt that advertisers would be angry if an ad from one side bleeds onto their ad. Advertisers would insist on make-goods, which could be costly for the magazine.

Also, advertisers would be dissatisfied with the smaller size of their ads, due to the smaller trim size of the magazine. They might feel the impact on the reader might not be as great. The consumer would also be getting an inferior product compared to before. *Fortune* would not stand out as much against the current competition. Also, new competition, such as Conde Naste's proposed business launch in 2007, could enter the market with more attractive specifications, taking consumers away from *Fortune*.

179 The **way around the drawback** was to test the new paper and have a prototype of the magazine in its new size before all was committed to the new specifications. Since trim size was only moderately important to advertisers, it would not be as big an issue as the quality of the paper.

180 Since both of these alternatives seemed reasonable, the President had the tough task of deciding what route *Fortune* would take regarding production specifications.

REFERENCES

BusinessWeek (2005). [Online]. *http://www.businessweek.com* Accessed October 21.

CNNMoney.com—Press Release October 2005.

CMI (2005). [Online]. *http://www.cmi.com.* Accessed October 21.

Fortune (2005). [Online]. *http://www.Fortune.com.* Accessed October 18.

Okrent, D. (2005). "How the World Really Works." *Fortune* September 19, 2005.

Shah, V. (2005). "CNNMoney.com Presentation." September.

Forbes (2005). [Online]. *http://www.forbesnedia.com.* Accessed October 21.

Hansel, S. (2005). "Google Wants to Dominate Madison Avenue, Too." [Online]. *http://www.nytimes.com* Accessed November 3.

Hoovers (2005). "Time Inc." [Online] *http://www.hoovers.com/media.* Accessed October 13.

Magazine Publishers Association (2005). "The Magazine Handbook" [Online] *http://www.magazine.org* Accessed October 10.

Pfeiffer Consulting (2005). "Publishing Industry: Towards the Void" [Online] *http://www.pfeifferreport.com/trends.html* Accessed October 13.

Plunkett Research (2005A). "Entertainment Trends" [Online]. *http://www.plunkettresearch.com/entertainment/entertainment_trends.htm.* Accessed October 13.

Plunkett Research (2005B). [Online]. *http://www.plunkettresearch.com/entertainment/entertainment_statistics.htm.* Accessed October 13.

Time Inc. (2005). [Online] *http://www.timeinc.com.* Accessed October 10.

TimeWarner (2005). *Annual Report 2004.*

Case 35

FOX Relocation Management Corp.   Cynthia A. Ingols and Lisa Brem

1   Gretchen Fox smiled as she drove back to her office one afternoon in June 1999. She had just attended an awards banquet for the New England Women Business Owners Association, where she was named Business Woman of the Year.

2   As she drove, Fox reflected on all that had transpired in her career since she earned her MBA in 1987. She had started her business, FOX Relocation Management Corp, a year after graduation. Over the next 11 years, the business, which specialized in moving offices, branches, or entire companies to new locations, had grown from a one-person consultancy to a successful private company employing 40 people. Fox wholly owned the sub-chapter S corporation, and had thus far avoided taking out loans to grow the company, other than the use of an occasional line of credit.

3   Fox had reason to feel that she had "made it." But she also felt that she could not simply sit back and savor her success. Her business continued to have opportunities for growth. For Fox, change was not only inevitable, it was preferable. As she explained:

> The real joy for me comes from founding and growing a business. We are a growing company, and we need sparks of excitement that come from change, from going to the next level. Opening new offices, going national or international, expanding the services we offer, going public—all these things would give us as a company more reasons to be proud. People here are invested in the future. We can't get to the future by standing still.

4   This growth showed the business was prospering, but it also posed urgent problems. For the first time, Fox felt she needed to add another layer of management to her organization. Fox wasn't sure that the compensation and incentive plans currently in place were appropriate for this new layer. She also worried that more hierarchy would ruin the carefully constructed culture of independent thinkers at her company.

5   Fox had built her business by maintaining close contact with both employees and clients. Her vivacious personality, intelligence, and "can do" attitude set the tone for her company. Fox's personal touch was one of the major motivators for her staff and one of the selling points for the company's services. The central question in Fox's mind was how to grow the business without losing the hands-on style that had made the company successful. As Fox explained:

> So much of what we do and who we are is attributable to our small size. We are more like a family than a company. We've always been fairly informal with our employees. Conventional wisdom would say that now we are getting too big to do business that way any more. We have put some formal procedures in place, but will they be enough as we move forward?

AN EASY WAY TO START A CONSULTING COMPANY

6   For Gretchen Fox running a relocation company was a perfect fit. She had moved several times throughout the United States and internationally with her late husband, who was an officer in the U.S. Air Force. In 1983, she settled in the Boston area. She earned her MBA part time while holding down a job and raising two children. Throughout the 1980's she held

administrative management positions at a variety of Boston law and consulting firms. As it happened, a common denominator of all her jobs was moving the office. As Fox recalled:

> All the firms I worked for made major moves, and I ended up managing them. I became something of an expert at it. I preferred the project management aspect of moving rather than the day-to-day maintenance tasks.

7   In August 1987, at the end of her third year of her part-time MBA program, Fox was ready for a change. She felt restless at her job and wanted to try her hand at an entrepreneurial venture.

8   Fox had become increasingly impatient with the rigid hierarchies she saw in the legal firms where she worked. She felt it took too long to make decisions and that steep hierarchies promoted a lack of accountability. Fox explained:

> One reason I really don't like hierarchies is their lack of immediate decision-making. One example that had serious repercussions was when I worked at a law firm and we had a bad snow storm. I wanted to send people home early, but my boss had to go to his boss and on up the chain. By the time I got out of there, I ended up with a seven hour drive home.
>
> The other part of it for me, is that I don't automatically respect someone with a title or position; I'm more interested in a meritocracy. That's personal bias I suppose. The law firms couldn't give underlings decision-making authority because they weren't lawyers. Conversely, I remember a time I was lugging huge water bottles to the cooler and the big, strapping, male lawyers walked right by me, not one stopped to help. Being a partner took precedence over being a person. Those kinds of separations don't make for a cohesive team. I wanted to create a place where I didn't have to live by those rules anymore.

9   She felt she could be successful if she put all her experience with corporate relocation to work in a consulting business. Fox, however, was not sure how to get started—would companies actually pay her to be a "move expert"?

10   In 1988, she had the answer to her question. An office manager from a large Boston law firm called Fox to see if she'd be interested in organizing their upcoming move. The call came as a result of a networking group that Fox had started while she was working for a law firm in Washington D.C. Fox explained the connections that led to her first consulting job:

> I was working for the D.C. satellite office of a large Boston law firm. There was one other Boston firm that also had a satellite office, so I started a lunch group that brought together managers from both companies. I felt as though we probably dealt with similar issues and could benefit from sharing experiences. I got to know the office manager of the other firm pretty well. A couple of years later, after I'd moved back to Boston, the office manager from the Boston firm happened to be talking to the DC office manager. The Boston office manager was looking for someone to manage the firm's move, and my DC friend immediately recommended me.
>
> I interviewed for the job along with about eight other people. The hiring manager told me later that even though he'd interviewed people with a lot more experience—one was a very senior architect—he said my interpersonal skills were so strong that they decided to offer the job to me.

11   The company offered Fox a full-time one-year contract to move its 950-member workforce, giving her the choice of being on payroll or acting as an independent contractor. As Fox recalled:

> There I was—wondering how to start consulting and this job dropped in my lap.
> I decided to go in as an independent contractor. I remember thinking—what easier way to start a consulting company? Of course, I didn't think then of what being a consultant meant. Later, I realized that, in addition to delivering services, I would have to send out invoices, set up a bookkeeping system, and find more clients.

12   Fox set up shop in her Lexington home and worked independently on small projects until 1992, when she accepted a large job at Harvard Business School that eventually developed into a two-year commitment. She hired several temporary employees to help coordinate the move, but realized in August 1992 that she would need permanent help. Fox hired Lori Coletti, a facility management specialist from a large telecommunications company. Coletti had a degree in interior design and experience with business furnishings that complemented Fox's business degree and relocation skills. Although Fox was happy to gain an employee with Coletti's background, hiring a full-time employee was unsettling. As Fox explained:

> Hiring Lori, my first permanent employee, was the first big milestone for the business. It was the hardest thing I have ever had to do. I was suddenly responsible for someone else—for her family—for her livelihood. It was a combination of worrying about not having enough work for her and having to pay her even if the work wasn't coming in. We sort of got around that. We negotiated an hourly wage, figuring that if I didn't need 40 hours per week consistently, I wouldn't have to pay for it. But in reality, Lori ended up working 50 hours a week from the start and that has never really changed. She is still here—and is vice president of the company.

A LOOSE COLLECTION OF CONSULTANTS

13   In the fall of 1992, when a large regional bank hired Fox to move its Massachusetts head-quarters, Fox hired two more employees. From September 1992 through May 1993, FOX Relocation moved 1,500 people for the bank. From that time on, Fox continued to augment the bank's project management staff, managing various aspects of employee relocation on a permanent basis.

14   By 1994, the company had seven hourly employees. The base of operations was still Fox's home, although most of the work was done on-site at client facilities. One long-time employee, Jane Menton, described the start-up phase:

> I started working for Gretchen in 1992. At the time, Fox Relocation wasn't so much a company as a loose collection of consultants. She had one employee—Lori. Mostly, though, Gretchen would hire consultants to get the jobs done. Eventually, she hired me as the second employee.
>
>   It was interesting working out of someone's house. I feel fortunate to have started that way because I was able to work directly with Gretchen. I got to really understand what she expected and how she worked with clients. At the time she was a project manager running projects instead of the more administrative role she plays now as president of the company. I enjoyed those early days. I felt we were all learning at the same time.

15   The energy of starting something new and operating on a shoestring was exciting, but Fox felt the need to become established in a Boston location closer to her client base. "People were trying to do business out of phone booths," she recalled. "It was time we moved downtown."

16   In October 1994 the company's five employees were working with two large clients and managing four smaller projects. Fox decided to sublease space from a Boston real estate management firm. For $500 a month, Fox and her employees shared a small office and had use of the real estate firm's equipment and conference room. Fox felt that this arrangement was a good way to test the waters without incurring significant financial risk. It wasn't long, however, before the company outgrew the space. "We were getting in the way. We were using the conference room more than the company we were subleasing from," Fox explained.

17   By December 1995, FOX Relocation had doubled in size, with enough work to keep ten full time employees busy. The company moved to 2,200 square feet of space on the 11th floor of a downtown Boston office building. Six months later, it increased its office size by another 2,200 square feet. Fox explained the financial risk the company took that year:

> Instead of paying $6,000 a year on rent, we were now paying more than 10 times that amount. It was daunting. But the up side was that our business was expanding as well. By the end of 1996, we had over 20 employees. We had doubled in size in two years.

RELOCATION CONSULTANTS—A NICHE WITHIN THE FACILITY MANAGEMENT INDUSTRY

18   Before 1980, the term "move consultants" was not in Corporate America's vocabulary. Most—if not all—moves were performed by employees. Office managers in small to medium-sized firms, and facility management teams in large firms typically had the dubious honor of managing and executing a move. In the 1980's, however, as the tidal wave of downsizing swept away administrative personnel and departments, corporate executives found that there was no one left with the expertise and the time to plan a large move. The facility management outsourcing industry gave birth to a small subset of firms that chose to specialize in the high-stress world of corporate relocations.

19   Another trend in facilities management, called "workforce churn", also fueled the growth of relocation consultants. Churn was the term used to describe the continual movement of employees as a result of expansion, downsizing, redeployment, or a project-oriented workforce. *The Boston Globe* reported in 1998 that the average churn rate (the percentage of employees who took part in some type of organizational move) was 44 percent nationwide, with the Boston area's rate much higher, at 60 to 70 percent.[1] As one facility management industry magazine wrote:

> American businesses are changing at an ever-increasing rate. Churn rates of 55 to 60 percent are now common compared to 25 to 30 percent just a few years ago. And churn rates of 100 percent are no longer shocking. A Texas computer manufacturer reports moving more than 12,000 people in one city over a one-year period to accommodate a one-third growth in employment and a 100 percent churn rate. An energy company moves more than 800 people, 40 percent of its employees, over a four-month period.[2]

20   The reasons for the high level of churn rates were increases in industry consolidations and corporate mergers, and the rapid expansion of high-tech firms that used fluid teams to perform projects. As the article described:

> It's not unusual for companies to form teams involving up to 300 people, and then as the project nears completion, ramp-down to 20 people. This trend is particularly prevalent among software and computer manufacturers. [. . .] About 15 percent of this activity involves moves into new facilities, consuming more than $10 billion each year in goods and services to do so.[3]

21   In addition to offering an experienced, cost-efficient team to manage moves, relocation consultants also took the heat of a stressful move off an employee or department. Since two-thirds of employees in charge of a move are either fired or quit soon after the move, hiring a move consultant saved companies the cost of hiring and training new personnel.[4]

---

[1] Valigra, Lori, "Helping Firms on the Move," *The Boston Globe*, November 25, 1998.
[2] Fischer, Glenn, "Four Elements of a Successful Move," *Buildings*, March 1998, p. 1.
[3] Ibid.
[4] Valigra.

THE FOX WAY

22   Throughout the early 1990s, Fox experienced growth in number and scope of assignments. She continued to hire project managers in response to the increasing demands of both new and existing clients. In 1995, Fox promoted Lori, her first employee and right arm, to the position of Vice President. This marked a departure from Fox's "loose collection of consultants" and the installation of a rudimentary hierarchy. The bulk of the staff, the project managers, remained on the same level.

23   The company prided itself on its lack of formal titles and status symbols. As Fox explained:

> We are not departmentalized. I didn't set up the company to operate that way. I didn't personally do all that well in hierarchical organizations that typically operated under the more traditional business model. I didn't like it, and I chose not to subject other people to it.
>
> That's not to say we don't have *any* hierarchy or that we have a totally flat organization. Of course we do have some hierarchy—we have hierarchy of experience. We have some people who have been in this business for 25 years and some who have been in it for one. The one with 25 years of experience is much more likely to be managing a project than the person with little experience. But we don't use titles, except for Lori and myself. Its not something that's needed internally.
>
> Despite the lack of titles, it was always clear to the client who to contact if there was a problem or issue. In the beginning they always talked to me, then after I made Lori Vice President, she talked to her clients and I kept mine. There was perhaps more internal than external confusion.

24   Although most of the staff at FOX Relocation were female, Fox asserted that she didn't set out to build an all-female company. The fact was the overwhelming majority of applicants happened to be female. Fox believed the reason for this was that the work lent itself to a traditionally "female" approach to tasks and problem solving. As she explained:

> The way we work is very hands-on. Of course, not all relocation companies work this way. One of our competitors is almost entirely male, and they don't offer the same level of hands-on attention to detail that we do. It's really a different business model.
>
> We are widely known for our incredible ability to coordinate and manage all the details of a move. One of our employees said to me at lunch the other day that a lot of what we do is handholding and giving pats on the back. And that really is important. People are traumatized by moves. Even if they are moving to a different floor in the same building, there is something very unsettling about it. We help communicate with people and listen to their concerns. At the same time we handle a zillion details, from selecting voice/data networks to making sure there are coat hangers in every closet.

25   Employees at FOX Relocation expressed a strong sense of shared values and prided themselves on their customer-service orientation. As Project Manager Robin Dorogusker explained:

> At FOX, we have a style of working that is tightly focused on customer service. We want the customer to be happy and we want to do a good job. Everyone here is willing to get down and dirty and do whatever it takes to get the job done—whether it's designing office space or crawling around on the floor looking for phone jacks.

26   The culture at FOX Relocation was expressed in its code of ethics and mission statement, written in the spring of 1997:

Code of Ethics

- We are a community and our clients are part of that community
- We treat our employees and clients with utmost respect

- We seek continuous improvement
- We have as much fun as our work allows

Mission Statement

Our mission is to provide a full range of corporate real estate program and project management services in a way that supports our clients' culture and fulfills their unique needs so as to ensure that the clients' business operations and revenue stream are not disrupted.

27   The culture at Fox was communicated to new employees in a variety of ways. One employee told of how, the first day on the job, they were added to the company-wide email distribution list. One of the first emails is below:

As you all know, our good friend Bob will be retiring this Spring. The good news is that he has already sold his house. The bad news is that he has to be out of it by the week of January 12—yikes!

We are looking for volunteers to help pack his (4,400sf!) house on the following dates:
Saturday 1/3/03
Saturday 1/10/03
Sunday 1/11/03

Any and all help will be appreciated. Bob will offer snacks, beverages, and even a little pool playing during the breaks! Also—who knows what he will decide not to take? There may be a few cool items to raffle off to helpers! In any case, we will make it fun.

Please understand that this is not a FOX project (not billable) . . . it is merely helping out a fellow FOX (builds good karma)! Please let me know if you are able to help on any of these dates. I will be happy to provide directions as well as coordinating any carpooling if necessary.

Thanks!
Ginny

WORKFLOW AT FOX RELOCATION

28   Client projects at FOX Relocation generally fell into two categories: one-time moves and ongoing facility management. FOX Relocation employees were primarily coordinators. They did not actually pick up and move boxes; rather, they set schedules and coordinated the moving company's activities with the activities of other sub-contractors such as security, electricians, and environmental systems. One-time moves involved anything from a small group relocating to another floor, to 2,500 employees moving to a new building over the course of a single weekend. Teams were formed for each job and were disbanded when a job was completed. Exhibit 1 is a representation of responsibility areas involved in a typical one-time move. It was created as a guideline for a move, a reminder of what should be completed, but the actual implementation was up to the individual assigned the move. It also served as an agenda for the kick off meeting with the client. It made it clear what responsibility areas Fox was willing to take on.

29   The on-going facility work usually entailed at least two people working full-time, or nearly full-time, on-site at a client's facility. On-going work included: space planning; inventorying, refurbishment, or procurement of furniture and art; coordinating new construction and building maintenance; and moving and installing technology. Employees at FOX either worked for several clients and projects at once or were stationed full-time on-site as part of the client's facility management team. Clients included Harvard University Law School, Fleet Bank, BankBoston, and Bell Atlantic.

EXHIBIT 1   **One-Time Move: Areas of Responsibility**

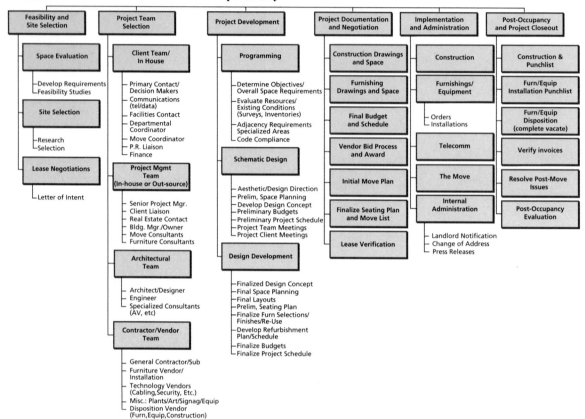

Source: Company Records

30   Fox and Coletti conducted most of the company's marketing, which took the form of networking, nurturing client relationships, following leads, and the occasional write-up in the local press media. Approximately 30% of new jobs came from repeat customers, and most new clients came to FOX Relocation through word-of-mouth. Once a new client or job was identified, Fox or Coletti wrote proposals and conducted negotiations.

31   Coletti maintained a two-month workflow projection based on current jobs and what she and Fox judged to be "in the pipeline." Jobs were assigned to project managers based on their availability and expertise. Employee preferences were taken into account whenever possible. Generally, jobs were given to teams of two or three people. Although one person usually functioned as the primary client contact and maintained a budget and schedule for the project, that person did not have authority over others in the team and did not act as team leader. When the job was completed, members of the team moved on to form new teams around a new project. In large or complex moves, the teams were bigger and Fox or Coletti appointed a team leader to manage the overall move. Fox explained the fluid nature of the project manager roles:

> People are given projects based mainly on availability. They could be managing a large project this month and put on another project that someone else is running next month. So a person is not always in charge, nor is he or she always in the position of underling. This structure really makes a difference to how people see their roles.

32   As Robin Dorogusker explained:

> We don't have politics at FOX. People don't have to vie for position. There's no real hierarchy. People aren't trying to get to the next level, because there is no next level. So there isn't a sense of competition—just a feeling that we want to do a good job on our projects. We enjoy each other's successes and help out from job to job. There is a lot of camaraderie.

33   Since most clients wanted to minimize the downtime associated with relocation, the actual moving was done over a short and convenient period of time—usually at night or over a weekend. The team in charge of the move often needed more people to get the job completed on schedule. In particularly large or complex moves, the entire company could be mobilized. As Project Manager Jane Menton explained:

> We think of ourselves as a team—one that needs to work together. Everyone is very good about that. Because even if you're on a two-person team, you may have a large move and you'll need extra help. I've never seen an instance when someone's needed help and no one has come forward. Sure, there are lots of times when you don't know what people are working on, but there are also the times when everyone—even Gretchen—will pitch in and help with a move. One great example of that was the Suffolk County Courthouse. We had to conduct a huge records inventory for that move. Everyone in the company had to contribute to get it done and they were all willing to help.

HUMAN RESOURCES

34   New employees came to FOX Relocation almost exclusively through word-of-mouth. Even in the low unemployment job market of the late 1990's, the company had never needed to place a help-wanted advertisement. The company received several unsolicited resumes almost every week. Fox and Coletti conducted interviews on an on-going basis. Most of the resumes came from people with art, architecture, interior design, space planning, or facility management backgrounds. Many had experience as project managers for larger companies. Some FOX Relocation employees had previously been downsized as their corporations out-sourced their facility management divisions. Fox felt that despite the word of mouth method of hiring, she was as or more diverse in her hiring practices than most companies in her industry.

35   Project manager Steven Smith recalled why he was attracted to FOX Relocation:

> I wanted to work for a small company. I like to keep a balance between my work life and personal life and be able, for the most part, to maintain a 40-hour work week. I talked to some people who work for big companies and they had war stories about how many hours they put in. One of the benefits of working at FOX Relocation is that Gretchen and Lori recognize that people have a life outside the office, and empower us to manage our own workload and hours.

36   In the early years of the company, all employees interviewed and approved each new hire. Since the company was so small, Fox wanted to ensure that personalities meshed and that every employee understood and fit into the culture. Project Manager Larry Ellsworth, who was stationed full-time at a client site, described a typical FOX Relocation employee:

> We are generally people who can fit in with other people. I like fitting in—I like understanding my client's needs, understanding their organization, and becoming part of it. I keep a reasonable distance while actively taking part in the job and acting in my client's interest. I think most of us here at FOX have that ability. We're chameleons. We can pick up the color of our surrounding environment. It helps to get the job done when you are able to think the way your client thinks.

37   As the company grew, it was no longer feasible for all employees to be involved in hiring decisions. Instead, new hires met with an ad hoc committee of veteran employees. Jane
Menton described the hiring process and what she looked for in an applicant:

> Nervous people don't do well here. This is a high stress job. We are usually the last
> people brought in—after the architect, the builders, and so on. We are also the last people
> standing there after the move is completed, and we end up taking responsibility for decisions
> we didn't make. It's also our job to stay on a bit after the move to make sure everyone is
> settled. Sometime this takes a lot of diplomacy. Lots of people hate their job or hate their
> company, and the way they express that is to say "I hate my chair." People will try to gain
> control over whatever they can. So we change the chair, the employees are happy, and the
> project is a success.
>
> Employees here also need to be comfortable with the lack of formal structure. People
> come from all kinds of backgrounds. Some, who've come from large organizations with a lot
> more structure, have a hard time adjusting to the flexibility we have at FOX. We have to work
> odd hours. We don't have defined roles. And we don't get a lot of formal feedback.

38   Other than annual reviews conducted by either Fox or Coletti, employees were given
feedback and direction on a situational basis. Project managers had considerable autonomy
over their projects. Menton explained the review process:

> There is a form Gretchen uses for employee reviews, but she just uses it as a guide. I haven't
> seen her actually fill it out. We are not managed very closely at all. Basically, Gretchen
> and Lori look at whether we bring our projects in on budget and on time. At the beginning
> of a job, they give us a not-to-exceed price based on a scope of work, and then it is up to us
> to manage the job. We occasionally get feedback from clients through letters or telephone
> calls. Most times we will ask the client if we can use them as a reference. We get a lot of
> our jobs through word-of-mouth, so it's important to have a good on-going relationship
> with our clients.

39   As Steven Smith described his feelings about the way employees were managed:

> One thing I like more than anything else about this job is that, as far as the client is
> concerned, I *am* FOX Relocation. Lori, my boss—who I immediately report to—does
> not check in with us on a regular basis. We manage ourselves and we represent our own
> company. I think it's great that I'm a reflection of our company. I've never fully had that
> feeling before in any other job. It's very satisfying. I have a feeling of ownership without all
> the liability that true ownership would bring.

40   However, Smith, also saw drawbacks to the lack of formal structure:

> I have three people on my team. We are stationed full-time at one of our large corporate
> clients. I am considered the senior person of that team, there is also another project manager
> and what I'd call a junior person on the team. To the client I am considered the team leader,
> but at FOX we're all considered to be on the same level. That's where I think there is
> something lacking in the organization. There is some lack of clarity on our part; our internal
> roles don't always correspond with our external roles. Most people here seem comfortable
> with this ambiguity, so I have not made an issue of it.

41   As one would expect in a service business, payroll and related expenses comprised the
largest percentage of expenses (see Exhibit 2—% Income Statements[5]). All the project managers at FOX Relocation had the choice of being paid on an hourly or salaried basis. Hourly
wages and salaries were negotiated individually, with the applicant naming a preferred rate,
which Fox compared to other employees in the company with similar experience. Occasionally, Fox researched architectural and design firm employee pay rates. However, Fox was

---

[5] Since Fox Relocation is a privately held company, no financial statements were available for publication.

EXHIBIT 2
Profit and Loss Comparisons 1997, 1998, 1999

Source: Company records

	Jan–Dec 1997	Jan–Dec 1998	Jan–Dec 1999
Revenues	100.0%	100.0%	100.0%
Total Revenues	100.0%	100.0%	100.0%
Expenses			
401K Employer Contrib.	2.4%	2.4%	2.4%
Automobile Expense	0.2%	0.4%	0.4%
Dues and Subscriptions	0.1%	0.1%	0.1%
Equipment Rental	0.2%	0.3%	0.3%
Freelancer Expense	7.0%	4.0%	3.8%
Insurance	1.0%	1.0%	1.0%
Interest Expense		0.1%	0.3%
Marketing & Advertising	2.0%	1.1%	1.9%
Medical Insurance	1.0%	1.5%	1.5%
Moving and Storage	0.0%	0.5%	0.2%
Office Supplies	1.2%	1.1%	1.2%
Payroll Expenses			
Salaries and Wages	51.2%	55.0%	54.1%
Payroll Taxes	5.0%	4.5%	4.5%
Postage and Delivery	0.2%	0.2%	0.3%
Printing and Reproduction	0.2%	0.9%	0.3%
Professional Development	0.5%	0.2%	0.2%
Professional Fees	0.5%	0.5%	0.5%
Recruiting	0.2%		0.2%
Rent	3.1%	2.7%	2.2%
Repairs	0.3%	0.9%	0.3%
Taxes	0.2%	0.1%	0.3%
Telephone	1.1%	1.5%	1.3%
Travel & Ent	1.8%	2.5%	2.0%
Utilities	0.2%	0.2%	0.2%
Total Expenses	79.6%	81.7%	79.5%
Net Income	**20.4%**	**18.3%**	**20.5%**

more concerned with maintaining internal wage parity than comparing with other firms. Most employees chose to be paid hourly. As Coletti explained:

> In the early days of the company, people were paid hourly because we weren't sure we could guarantee full time employment. It was fine with the other employees and me—we didn't need the guarantee of a 40-hour salary. Now, paying hourly wages serves as a motivator for people. It's similar to being on a sales force. The employees have some control over how much they make because, in most situations, they can set their schedules. We certainly don't want people working significantly more than 40 hours per week on a regular basis. People know, however, that if they do need to put in that kind of time, they will be paid for it. In certain cases, individuals who are paid hourly make out better on an annual basis than those same individuals would have on salary, so I encourage some people to opt for hourly pay. A few of the people who started out as salaried have eventually asked to go hourly, I have never seen anyone go the other way.

GROWING PAINS

42   As the company grew, one way that Fox kept abreast of employee attitudes and morale was to conduct a workplace satisfaction survey. Fox explained the differences in responses over the last several years:

> Every year, I've sent out a survey to people asking: "What three things do you value in your workplace that you do have here?" and "What three things do you value that you don't have

EXHIBIT 3
Benefit Compensation
Package
As of July 1999

Source: Company records

FOX provides the following employment benefits:	
Tufts Associated Health Plan HMO	Employer pays 100% individual premium
Delta Dental Plan	Employer pays 50% individual premium
UNUM Life Insurance equal to annual Salary	Employer pays 100% premium
UNUM long-term disability policy	Employees voted to pay 100% premium to preserve right to tax-free benefit
Maternity and Family Leave	In accordance with Maternity and Family Leave Act
401 (k) Profit Sharing Plan	25% employer matching contribution (Note: Since plan inception, FOX has matched 100% of contributions)
Year-end Profit-Sharing	For past 5 years, FOX has paid every employee an equal amount from profits
Paid Vacation	1 week in year 1 3 weeks in years 2–5 4 weeks in years 6–10
Paid Holidays	8 plus 1 floating at employee discretion

here?" At first the answer to the second question was health and dental benefits. So we added that. Then the answers were more in the vein of profit sharing and 401 K plans, so we added that. Now we have what I consider a generous and complete benefits package (see Exhibit 3, Benefit Compensation Package). In every year we have had the 401K plan, we have added the maximum amount. Most employees were matched 100%. The profit sharing plan was simple. All employees, excepting me, took an equal share in profits of the company, after an amount was set aside for future growth. I found that satisfaction in incentive plans fell along gender lines. The males seemed to want more to strive for, that they needed a goal. I disagree with that. When one big accounting firm was falling apart, the chairman went to the board to ask for more money, arguing that he needed more pay to get quality work. I have to ask: what are you paying them for now? I don't really believe in incentive pay. I don't think getting more money at the end of the year makes one person work harder than another.

In 1998, 100% of the respondents said they valued most about FOX was the flexibility and number two was the teamwork aspect. One thing they would like to see added now is the ability to have a greater role in firm management.

43   One Fox employee, Steven Smith, described how he saw incentives at Fox:

You have to find ways to continually challenge yourself. After being at one client site for several years, I was able to move around a lot. I managed nine different clients the following year. That was a big change. It's a great incentive for me to be given autonomy to meet and exceed client expectations, to personally represent your entire company, and to be held responsible to stay within a set budget of billable hours. Hourly pay can be an incentive to work longer hours, but I don't abuse it. It does compensate me, though, when I'm working a lot. Salary is just not discussed here. It is a closely guarded secret. No one knows what another person makes.

44   In 1997 and 1998 many of FOX Relocation's bank clients experienced mergers, leading the company to double in size from 20 to 40 employees to meet their clients' relocation needs. Up until this point, the company had enjoyed steady, manageable expansion. Robin Dorogusker explained the impact of this growth spurt:

There was a rough period when we were growing rapidly. It was very difficult. We had some growing pains. We just weren't prepared for the pace at which we grew. We went to

40 employees before we had the infrastructure or the technology to support them. So many people were getting hired so quickly. People felt they were thrown into the lion's den without any training. We didn't have time to train, and we weren't able to communicate with each other. It's hard working in an organization with 38 people when you don't know who some of the new people are.

45 By 1998, Fox realized that the company needed to change the way it trained new employees:

> It became clear that we could no longer train people just by osmosis. We had to institute a more formal training program, which is basically a mentoring system. New people, regardless of how much work experience they have, are partnered with someone more senior on projects until such time as they can go out on their own. There is no rule as to how long the mentoring will last—it depends on the person.

46 Dorogusker agreed that the worst of the transition times seemed past:

> As things slowed down a little, we started making time for meetings, and Gretchen and Lori have made an effort to get people to know each other. They tried to shift around the teams to allow people to work with others they hadn't gotten to know yet. Gretchen started picking names out of a hat and having those people go to lunch with each other. Through all of this rapid growth, Gretchen and Lori have tried to keep up the family atmosphere. For example, they are very tolerant of people's personal lives. Some bring their children to the office now and then. Gretchen and Lori try to understand what is going on with everyone and how their personal lives may or may not interfere with their work.

47 In late 1997, Fox felt the time had come to replace their outdated equipment and second-hand office furniture. She established an employee committee to redesign the office layout, purchase new furniture, and research computer networks. The committee came up with a "partial hoteling" solution, where employees, such as Coletti, Fox and the administrative personnel had permanent desks and offices. The rest of the space was assigned and reassigned based on how much time each employee spent at the office. Employees that were based in the office, but were often at client sites, had a desk and file cabinet. The employees that were stationed full-time on client sites had temporary use of desks; drafting tables, and phones when they visited the office. The new office furniture the committee chose was designed to be lightweight and flexible to allow for easy movement as employee needs changed.

48 In 1998, the company completed the installation of a computer network and in 1999 was in the process of designing a web site. The network made it much easier for Fox to communicate to employees and for employees to communicate with each other. Employees were also given cell phones and beepers, and the company maintained an updated list of all phone, beeper numbers, and employee email addresses to make it easier for employees to keep in touch with the company.

49 Another way Fox communicated with her growing workforce was a two-hour bi-weekly staff luncheon. All employees attended the meetings—even those stationed off-site. At the meetings, people had a chance to apprise others of particular issues or staffing needs they may have on a project. The company also invited vendors or other experts to give presentations as a way to keep staff up to date on industry issues and new products. The company always paid for lunch, and each meeting concluded with a cake and celebration of staff birthdays and distribution of paychecks.

50 Growth at FOX Relocation was not only measured in the increased number of client projects and employees. The company was also expanding its capabilities. New employees brought with them a range of skills that FOX Relocation added to its capacities. In 1994, the company acquired a small interior design firm that had expertise in computer-aided design and computer-aided facilities management. FOX Relocation also developed expertise in art collection management. In addition, the company was handling bigger and more complex moving projects that required larger teams of people and a more formal hierarchy to execute. Dorogusker described the team put in place to conduct the Federal Courthouse move:

> The project was different in that it was much more massive than anything I had experienced before. It was the first time we designated an actual team leader, feeling that one point person would be most efficient. I was the project leader, and I had all the direct client contact. I directed three project managers who worked with the individual courts. I had to keep the project managers focused, maintain the schedules and budgets, and keep a view of the big picture. It was difficult at first. We had never worked in that kind of a structured team. It caused some tension because previously we'd been equals. But we talked it out and came to an understanding that our roles had to be different for this project. In the end we learned that sometimes we need that kind of structure to get the job done.

51   For Fox, growth also meant she was forced to step away from project management and the day-to-day oversight of her company. She refocused her role on marketing and public relations. As the company grew, Coletti shouldered more and more of the daily responsibility of running the company and supervising employees. As Dorogusker described:

> Gretchen and Lori play different roles. Gretchen has become a personality—winning the award and being written about in the paper and that kind of thing. She is now more externally focused and involved in the marketing of the company. Lori is more hands-on. She keeps tabs on staffing and the status of projects. Lori also works with us and is connected to us on a more regular basis. Right now, I report to Lori. I used to work with Gretchen, and I'm fortunate in that respect. Most people here have not worked with Gretchen directly on a project.

52   As Coletti and Fox's roles evolved, some employees expressed a sense of ambiguity concerning reporting relationships and authority. As Larry Ellsworth described:

> It's a little hard to say exactly what the reporting structure is here. Clearly Gretchen is the president of the company. I think about her as the overall strategic "big picture" person. Lori I think of more as the general manager/operations director. But I don't feel I have to go to only one of them about a specific problem. They are more like twin managers.

53   Coletti described the way she saw the reporting process:

> Some employees will come to me, while others go to Gretchen. There is some ambiguity about who makes certain decisions. Sometimes an employee will email both of us with a question. It gets a little sticky when we come back with different answers, but we work it out.

THE FUTURE

54   As Fox sat at her desk, looking out over Boston's teeming business district, she felt satisfied that she had built a reputable company, had a great team of people who were happy to work for her, and had a client base that would continue to expand. She knew that some key questions had to be answered in order to meet the future proactively. In what direction should she take the company? What will be the impact of growing from 50 to 100 people? How much longer could she pay people on an hourly basis? She was sure that soon, she would have to move to a conventional salary model. How would that impact her incentive structure? Fox also felt that she needed to create another layer of management. But should she? What impact would such changes have on teams and leadership of teams?

55   As Fox became more focused externally, how should she change her role and what should that new role be? Are isolated tensions and ambiguities indicative of systemic problems that could be exacerbated as the company grows? Could FOX Relocation maintain its culture, structure, and ability to respond quickly and effectively to client needs throughout this period of rapid growth?

Case 36

Jim Thompson Thai Silk Company
Robert A. Pitts

1   As he looked back on his 20 years as managing director of Jim Thompson Thai Silk Company (JT), Bill Booth felt considerable pride. The company had grown to become, by 1994, Thailand's leading retailer of native silk, commanding an enviable two-thirds share of the premium tourist market. It had also expanded far beyond its original base of merely retailing products produced by others, to become the country's only fully-integrated producer of native silks.

2   Recent developments were threatening to undermine this hard-earned success, however. Bangkok's increasing auto congestion, escalating air pollution, and soaring AIDS infection rate were causing foreign tourists—JT's primary customers—to avoid the city as a travel destination. Since JT's shops were all located in Bangkok, its revenue and profitability were falling. Eager to find a way to reverse this decline, Booth had established strategic planning as a major priority for the coming year.

EARLY HISTORY

3   JT was founded in 1951 by James Thompson, an American who arrived in Thailand at the end of the Second World War as a member of the U.S. Office of Strategic Services, predecessor to the Central Intelligence Agency. A member of a prominent Delaware family and a graduate of Princeton University, Mr. Thompson determined to make a career in Thailand following cessation of hostilities. Becoming interested in the commercial potential of native silk, he opened a retail shop in Bangkok to sell retail fabric produced by local weavers. The store's reputation for superb quality and innovative design made it particularly popular among tourists and foreigners stationed in Bangkok—two groups able to afford its prices, which were well above those of most local competitors.

4   With expansion of tourism and the U.S. troop buildup in South East Asia in connection with the Vietnam War, JT grew rapidly. Then, a strange event occurred. During a 1967 Easter holiday in a Malaysian jungle resort, Mr. Thompson mysteriously disappeared and, despite a lengthy search lasting many months, was never seen again.[1] JT's board appointed as acting managing director an American who had been assistant manager under Mr. Thompson. Seven years later, in 1974, the acting manager died, and Bill Booth was appointed managing director.

5   Booth had arrived in South East Asia in the early 1960s as a member of the U.S. military in Vietnam. Struck by the beauty and vitality of nearby Thailand, he settled there at the completion of his military assignment. Booth devoted his early months in the country to intensive study of the Thai language, and eventually became very fluent. Following an unsuccessful attempt to enter the local silk business on his own, he joined JT in 1964, where he held a variety of positions before becoming managing director.

This case won the 1995 Curtis E. Tate Outstanding Case Research Award for its selection as the best case presented at the 1994 National Case Research Association Annual Meeting. The author thanks company management for their helpful cooperation in developing this material.

EXPANSION

6 Under Booth's direction, JT expanded into each successive stage of the silk production process. The first step in this process began in 1974, when it established a sewing venture in partnership with a prominent Thai business-woman. Four years later it acquired a printing plant in partnership with a West German textile printer. In 1979, it entered the weaving business, choosing to establish this activity on a wholly-owned basis rather than through joint venture, and to locate it not in Bangkok, where its sewing and printing plants were situated, but in Northeastern Thailand, where many of its contract weavers lived. Finally, in 1988 JT entered into sericulture (the breeding of silkworms for production of raw silk fiber) and spinning (twisting together of fibers to produce yarn), establishing these operations on a wholly-owned basis and locating them near its weaving mill in Northeastern Thailand. (Exhibit 1 is a map of Thailand; Exhibit 2 provides basic facts about the country.)

7 The company's expansion into production had been motivated in part by a desire to improve product uniformity. Booth noted, for example, that this objective had influenced JT's entry into weaving.

8 During the early years, we left weaving entirely in the hands of contract weavers. This arrangement worked fine so long as final sales went primarily to tourists buying through our retail outlet. It became a stumbling block to expansion of our home furnishing business, however. Owners of hotels, office buildings, apartments, and condominiums from time to time need to replace wall covering and upholstery fabric, and when they do, they

EXHIBIT 1
Map of Thailand

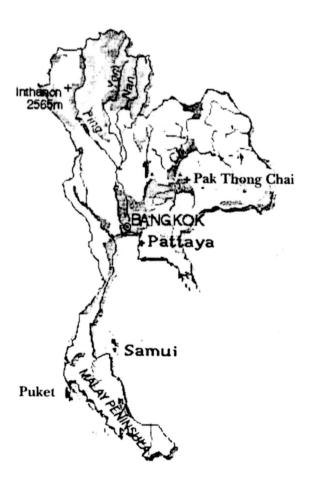

EXHIBIT 2
Facts about Thailand

Sources: *Encyclopedia of the Third World*, Volume III, Facts On File (New York, 1992); *The Statesman's Year-Book, 1994–1995*, St. Martin's Press (New York, 1994); *The World Fact Book 1994–95*, Central Intelligence Agency, Brassey's (Washington, 1994); *The Europa World Yearbook 1994*, Volume III, Europa Publications Limited (Rochester, Kent, England, 1994).

Overview

Size: 198,000 square miles (slightly more than twice the size of Wyoming); 1993 population 59 million; 1993 population growth rate 1.4%; ethnic divisions: Thai 75%, Chinese 14%; religions: Buddhism 95%, Muslim 3.8%; literacy rate 93%; capital city: Bangkok (1993 population 5.9 million); 1992 gross domestic product $103 billion; 1992 per capita gross domestic product $1,800; 1992 annual inflation rate in consumer prices 4.5%.

Government

Until 1932 the country was ruled as an absolute monarchy. Since that date it has experienced a series of relatively bloodless military coups and new constitutions. Though officially a constitutional monarchy, it operates in fact as a benign military dictatorship. It is unique among South Asian nations in never having experienced European rule.

Economy

The economy is relatively free of controls on private enterprise that are common in other developing countries. The dominant sector is private, only 10% of manufacturing output being produced by government-owned entities. The Industries Promotion Act of 1962 provides companies operating in designated industries guarantees against nationalization, and exemptions from import duties, export duties, and many taxes.

Currency

The Thai "baht" is freely convertible into foreign exchange. Its value against the dollar has remained very stable over a long period of time. US$1 = 25.28 baht (April 1993), 25.400 baht (1992), 25.517 baht (1991), 25.585 baht (1990), 25.702 baht (1989), 25.294 baht (1988).

need replacement material that precisely matches the color of original fabric. Our contract weavers were unable to meet this requirement, so we entered weaving ourselves. We can now replicate orders much more precisely.

9   Another objective motivating the company's move into weaving had been a desire to improve delivery capability. Booth provided the following details.

> Contract weavers are sometimes unreliable about meeting delivery schedules. This posed little difficulty as long as our business was primarily retail, since our well-stocked store always contained plenty of merchandise for tourists to make their selection. It became a problem as we tried to expand our home furnishing business, however. Delay in receipt of wall covering or upholstery material can postpone occupancy of a new building, and late occupancy imposes a serious cost on a building's owner. By bringing weaving under our direct control we have significantly improved our ability to deliver on time.

10   A third objective motivating JT's expansion into production had been a desire to establish secure sources of supply. During the 1980s, JT experienced increasing difficulty obtaining raw silk in quantities needed to feed its weaving operation. Shortages were caused in part by a decline in the acreage that Thai farmers devoted to mulberry cultivation. Total acreage devoted to this end fell from about 60,000 hectares in the mid-1970s to less than 40,000 hectares in the early 1990s. (One hectare 10,000 square meters, or 2.417 acres.) This decline was caused by migration of villagers from the depressed silk-producing regions in the Northeast to Bangkok in search of higher-paying jobs, and by conversion on the part of many remaining farmers to other crops—particularly to cassava, the European demand for which was increasing. Since mulberry leaves constitute a silkworm's chief diet, declining mulberry cultivation led to reduction in output of raw Thai silk. Developments in China, where JT historically had obtained a large share of its silk supply, also contributed to the problem. China produced more than half of the world's raw silk output, and supplied almost

90 percent of world exports. The Chinese government had long encouraged silk production, but in the 1980s began to allow silk producers to cultivate other crops. Thus freed from government constraint, many farmers switched out of mulberry into more lucrative crops such as fruits and vegetables. As silk output fell, prices on the world market climbed, leading remaining producers to skirt official channels and sell their output at elevated prices through Hong Kong's black market.

11   A fourth factor motivating JT's expansion into production had been a desire to improve technology. The Thai silk industry was dominated by very small producers employing traditional handicraft methods. As a consequence, the technology employed was generally quite rudimentary. Raw silk, for example, was produced mainly by farm women and children in the poor Northeast portion of the country, while most weaving was carried out by individuals working in very small family operations. These players lacked resources to underwrite significant improvement in technology. JT had undertaken production in part to bring its substantial resources to bear on this problem.

TECHNOLOGY TRANSFER

12   Each successive step into silk production had obliged JT to acquire new technology. Generally, needed expertise was not available in Thailand. Consequently, JT had been obliged to seek it abroad. JT had used several approaches over the years to secure foreign technology. One was to form joint ventures with foreign firms. JT had used this method, for example, to secure initial technology for its printing plant. Its joint venture partner in this activity was a small West German textile printer with a reputation for very high quality. This firm had helped select initial equipment for the printing venture, arrange factory layout, and oversee early startup. In addition the firm had assigned one of its senior engineers—Mr. Czerny—to assist the venture on a continuing basis. Making visits to Thailand four times each year, Czerny had counseled JT not only on printing matters, but on a host of other textile-related issues as well, in the process becoming an integral member of JT's management team.

13   A second method JT had used to obtain foreign technology was to send company personnel abroad for technical training. It had used this device, for example, to obtain technology for its sericulture operation. During early development of this operation, JT employees had made extended visits to China to receive training at the Chinese Sericulture Research Institute. Employees hired to operate the company's spinning machines had also traveled to China for technical training.

14   Yet another device JT had used to obtain technology from abroad was to bring foreign experts to Thailand to train company employees. Experts from China's Sericulture Research Institute, for example, had made numerous trips to Thailand to train JT employees in mulberry cultivation, silk-worm rearing, and cocoon production techniques, and several of its technicians were in Thailand as late as 1994 providing such training. The network of relationships which Booth maintained with knowledgeable foreigners had also helped the company obtain foreign expertise. One key individual in this network was Henry Thompson, nephew of Jim Thompson and heir to his interest in the company. A resident of the United States with extensive business experience and a keen interest in JT's welfare, Henry had provided thoughtful counsel on many occasions during the course of the company's development.

PRODUCTION ACTIVITIES

15   As a result of this expansion, JT by 1994 was no longer simply a retailer of silk fabric made by others, but was involved in each stage of the complex process through which the delicate filament produced by a silkworm is transformed into such products as fabric, articles

EXHIBIT 3
Vertical Production Flow*

Activity	Output	Supply†	Employees	Location
Sericulture	Cocoons	66%	150‡	PTC§
Spinning	Yarn	22%	250	PTC
Weaving	Fabric	100%	1,500	PTC
Printing	Printed fabric	100%	100	Bangkok
Sewing	Accessories	100%	350	Bangkok

*This exhibit describes JT's silk production activities only. The company also produced small quantities of cotton fabric. However, most of the cotton fabric it sold to retail and home furnishing customers was purchased from outside suppliers.
†Percent of JT's requirements supplied internally.
‡JT also utilized approximately 1,500 contract farming families in a broad area surrounding its sericulture facility to raise silkworm eggs to the cocoon stage.
§Pak Thong Chai. Sericulture, degumming, and spinning were carried out in upper Pak Thong Chai Province; weaving was performed in the provincial capital and in a nearby village.

of clothing such as blouses and pillowcases. Key activities JT performed in bringing about this transformation were sericulture, spinning, weaving, printing, and sewing (see Exhibit 3 for summary).

Sericulture

16   Silk thread is made from a fine, lustrous fiber produced by a silkworm when it forms a cocoon near the end of its life cycle. A silkworm's sole diet is mulberry leaves. Silk production therefore commences with the growing of mulberry trees. JT cultivated mulberry trees on a 900-acre plantation at the upper end of a farming valley in Pak Thong Chai Province, about 150 miles Northeast of Bangkok. The 150 workers employed in this operation picked leaves from mulberry trees, conveyed them to a large rearing house, and fed them to silkworms placed there on trays stacked on long racks. Eggs produced by these silkworms were sold to approximately 1500 contract farming families located in a wide area surrounding the facility. Farmers raised the silkworms hatched from these eggs to the cocoon stage, then sold cocoons back to JT.

17   This arrangement was theoretically capable of producing 30,000 boxes of eggs annually which, under proper conditions, would yield 800 tons of fresh cocoons, or 120 tons of raw silk fiber. Adverse developments had caused actual results to fall short of these targets, however. An infestation of flying insects and fungi severely reduced egg output in 1991, and drought the following year devastated the mulberry crop, causing contract farmers to demand fewer eggs. This decline in demand forced JT to place a large inventory of unsold eggs in cold storage. A subsequent surge in world supply of raw silk, accompanied by a corresponding drop in price, further eroded contract farmers' demand for JT's eggs. These adverse developments had caused the amount of cocoons JT repurchased from contract farmers to decrease from a peak of 290 tons in 1990 to only 173 tons in 1993.

18   Despite these setbacks in the production area, JT had made progress on the technical front. Its sericulture operation had succeeded in producing several highly resistant crossbreeds of Chinese white and Thai yellow silkworm species. In addition, its extension activities had helped contract farmers improve production yields, and the average amount of fresh cocoons produced per box of silkworm eggs increased from 23 kilograms in 1992 to 27 kilograms in 1993.

Spinning

19   Each cocoon produced by a silkworm consists of a continuous strand of silk fiber varying in length from 800 to 1200 yards, wound up and bound together by a natural glue. JT released the fiber contained in cocoons by eliminating this glue in a process called "degumming." It then spun the resulting fiber into yarn in a facility adjacent to its sericulture operation.

This activity utilized fourteen automated spinning machines and employed 250 operators. Its output in 1993 was 38.5 tons of yarn, down from a peak of 48.5 tons the previous year.

Weaving

20 Yarn produced by its spinning operation and that procured from outside sources was conveyed to JT's weaving mill located in the town of Pat Thong Chai about 15 miles from the company's sericulture operation. This facility was the largest hand weaving operation in the country. Yarn entering the mill was first dyed to give it a particular color, then woven into fabric on one of the 537 hand looms installed in the facility. In addition to this mill. JT also operated a satellite weaving mill, containing 277 hand looms, in a nearby village. Looms at both locations had been designed and built by company technicians. Most of the company's 1500 weavers were women. Hand weaving was a slow, tedious process. During a typical 8-hour shift, a weaver added only 2 or 3 meters to the length of the fabric being produced on her loom. Fabric width was generally about 1 meter.

JT also operated several power looms at its Pak Thong Chai facility, mainly to weave cotton fabric. Total output from these machines amounted to just 38,000 meters of fabric in 1993, compared to 593,000 meters of fabric produced on the company's hand looms.

Printing

21 A portion of the fabric produced by JT's weaving mills was shipped to its printing joint venture near Bangkok. The latter was equipped with both tables for hand printing and with state-of-the-art machines for high-speed machine printing. In 1993, this facility processed 355,000 meters of hand-printed silk fabric, 191,000 meters of hand-printed cotton fabric, and 984,000 meters of machine-printed cotton and synthetic fabric. Most of this output went for JT's internal use. JT was negotiating to purchase its joint venture partner's 26 percent interest in this operation in exchange for JT stock, with the understanding that the joint venture partner would continue to provide technical help following transfer of ownership. The latter showed interest in this arrangement, but was seeking an increase in the fee it received for technical assistance from the current level of 2 percent of printing revenues to 5 percent. Anticipating favorable conclusion of this negotiation, JT was planning the orderly transfer of printing equipment to a new printing facility it was building adjacent to the company's weaving mill in Pak Thong Chai. The planned move to this facility would enable the company to avoid problems arising from increasingly stringent water pollution regulation in the Bangkok area.

Sewing

22 A portion of the fabric leaving JT's weaving and printing mills went to its sewing joint venture in Bangkok. In 1993 the joint venture operation employed 350 skilled seamstresses to produce more than 500,000 different pieces of merchandise. High-volume items were neckties, purses, and pillowcases. JT was negotiating to buy out its partner in this venture.

OTHER ACTIVITIES

23 In addition to the production operations noted above, JT supported activities in finance, purchasing, design, and sales, among others. (Exhibit 4, which is a list of management personnel by function, shows all areas of operation.)

Finance

24 JT's original capital had been supplied by Jim Thompson and two other Americans (49 percent), and 29 Thai weaving families and silk traders (51 percent). Very few of the shares issued to the latter had subsequently changed hands except by inheritance. The widow

EXHIBIT 4
Management of Jim Thompson Thai Silk Company

Source: 1993 Annual Report.

Managing Director: W. M. Booth

Deputy Managing Director: Pichet Buranastidporn

Division Managers

Production: Surindr Supasavasdebhandu
Purchasing: Supphong Mangkonkarn
Design Advisor: Gerald W. Pierce
Accounting: Mrs Warunee Tanatammatorn

Department Managers

Executive Secretary: Miss Supaporn Tongperm
Miss Nithima Smitharak
Advisor: Chob Pundee
Design: Tinnart Nisalak
Design Liaison: Mrs Sirilak Sirisant
Merchandise/Warehouse: Mrs Panya Yothasiri
Marketing: Mrs Veronique De Champvallier
Retail: Mrs Jeannie Cho Menge
Mrs Lorna M Jarungklin
Mrs Aporn Yordmuang
Computer Processing: Sakda Siriphongwatana
Internal Audit: Kosol Jirabunjongkij
Home Furnishing: Mrs Chidchanok Supavaradom
Dispatching: Mrs Kanchana Pundee
Personnel: Prachuab Chirakarnphong
Somchai Apisithwanich

of one of the original American shareholders had recently sold her 25 percent stake to a large Japanese department store chain for a price reputed to be $25 million. This firm, which operated two stores in Thailand—both located in Bangkok—was now JT's largest shareholder.

25   JT's growth over the years had been financed largely by retained earnings. As a result, the company had issued very few new shares since its inception, and had resorted to no borrowing on a long-term basis. Despite its recent profit decline and its continued dividend payout, which had averaged 30 percent of earnings in recent years, JT was accumulating funds in excess of the amount needed to operate its business. In early 1994, this excess was invested mainly in short-term certificates of deposit. (See Exhibit 5 for a financial summary.)

Purchasing

26   JT purchased large quantities of silk cocoons from suppliers located in Thailand, and significant amounts of silk fiber and silk yarn from both domestic and foreign sources. It also purchased large quantities of cotton fabric from outside sources. To deal with increasing shortages of domestic raw silk, it had established remote buying stations in various parts of Thailand beginning in the early 1980s. In 1993 these stations purchased a total of 90.5 tons of fresh cocoons and 134 tons of silk yarn.

Design

27   Creative design was frequently mentioned by JT managers as one of JT's primary strengths, serving to differentiate the firm from competitors and enabling it to command premium prices. In 1994 the design department employed more than 30 people devoted to developing new fibers, new color formulations, new weave patterns, new print designs, and new garments. A weave designer from Ireland and a print specialist from Taiwan had recently

EXHIBIT 5   Jim Thompson Thai Silk Company

Selected Financial Data (Baht in millions, except as otherwise noted)										
	1993	**1992**	**1991**	**1990**	**1989**	**1988**	**1987**	**1986**	**1985**	**1984**
Revenues	847	810	914	991	931	774	667	481	382	354
Expenses										
Cost of Sales	428	401	462	514	488	400	377	268	213	219
Sell & Adm.	160	147	151	156	139	119	88	75	5	51
Interest	2	0	0	0	0	0	0	1	1	1
Income Tax	77	78	106	111	106	89	70	48	44	33
Total Expenses	667	626	719	782	734	608	535	392	316	304
Net Profit	181	184	195	209	197	167	132	90	66	50
Current Assets										
Cash & S.T. Invest.	288	221	232	158	71	82	172	158	131	88
Receivables	53	32	38	55	35	33	26	24	24	20
Inventories	564	531	473	433	476	414	227	152	135	130
Other	21	20	35	53	7	2	8	6	2	2
Total Current Assets	927	804	778	698	589	531	433	341	292	240
Fixed Assets										
Inv. In Subs.	28	39	77	77	49	34	33	31	21	26
Property, Plant, Eq.	406	395	279	226	201	127	77	62	47	40
Other	8	4	3	1	1	0	2	3	3	0
Total Fixed Assets	442	438	359	304	251	161	112	96	71	66
Total Assets	1,369	1,242	1,137	1,002	840	693	545	438	362	306
Current Liabilities										
Bank Debt	2	2	4	5	4	13	8	12	12	14
Accounts Payable	26	15	12	19	10	11	12	19	17	15
Accrued Expenses	15	19	31	4	6	5	3	4	3	2
Income Tax Payable	40	33	58	57	55	47	39	28	23	17
Other Current Liabilities	8	20	5	22	23	19	9	5	4	3
Total Current Liabilities	91	89	110	107	98	95	71	68	59	51
Shareholders' Equity	1,279	1,153	1,027	895	742	598	474	370	303	256
Total liab. & SH. EQ.	1,369	1,242	1,137	1,002	840	693	545	438	362	306

Source: Annual Reports (errors due to rounding) $1 U.S. = 25.28 Baht (April 1993)

joined the group. Having outgrown its former quarters in the company's headquarters building located in downtown Bangkok, the department had recently moved to a new location on the outskirts of the city.

Sales

28   JT's sales revenue derived from three major markets—retail (80 percent of the 1993 total), home furnishing (9 percent), and export (11 percent).

Retail Sales

29   JT operated five retail outlets, all located in Bangkok. Its flagship store, located next to its headquarters building in the heart of Bangkok's commercial district, was designed to

resembled a Siamese palace of an earlier era, with several tiers of sloping die roofs. The building's sumptuous interior was lined from floor to ceiling with teak shelves containing the largest selection of Thai silk fabric in the world, and its many nooks and crannies contained a vast assortment of colorful purses, neckties, and pillowcases. A mezzanine displayed garments representing the latest ready-to-wear women's fashions. Home furnishing fabrics were displayed on the store's second floor; home decorative merchandise—including sisal carpeting, antique furniture, porcelain vases, hand-painted wall panels, and Oriental room screens—on the third. In addition to its main store, JT operated four "satellite" outlets in other parts of the city. Three of the latter were located in the lobbies of luxury hotels, while the fourth was located on the ground floor of Bangkok's recently opened World Trade Center. All four satellite outlets had been established during the past two years.

30   JT's retail merchandise was typically priced 15 percent to 20 percent above levels charged by rivals. Popular items were printed neckties (priced at $35.70 in early 1994), head scarfs ($31.00), printed cushion covers ($18.90), and printed silk napkins ($11.00). Retail prices were scrupulously maintained, the only exception to this policy being huge clearance sales which JT held twice a year in the ballroom of a large Bangkok hotel. Prices at these biennial events were typically set 50 percent or more below retail list. These sales lasted three Sundays in a row, and were so popular that JT limited attendance to approximately 5000 "invitation only" customers.

31   In early 1994 there were dozens of competitors selling high-priced silk and cotton merchandise to foreign tourists in Bangkok. However, the number of such rivals had decreased over the years, and several powerful competitors of an earlier era had all but collapsed. In the meantime, JT had grown to become the undisputed leader of the industry, commanding an estimated two-thirds of the entire premium market.

Home Furnishing Sales

32   JT sold drapery, wall covering, and upholstery fabric direct to local hotels, office buildings, condominiums, and housing projects. Its sales effort was focused mainly on interior designers who were chief decision makers in this market. It had recently opened a home furnishing showroom dedicated to such designers on the second floor of its headquarters building. Key purchase considerations in this market were design, price, and delivery. Numerous suppliers, many larger and more highly automated than JT, served the market. Despite this handicap, JT's sales of home furnishing fabric had nevertheless grown in recent years. A sizable portion of these sales consisted of cotton fabric, the bulk of which JT purchased from contract suppliers and sold under its own brand.

Export Sales

33   JT's export sales were handled by commissioned agents located in more than two dozen countries throughout the globe. Most export sales consisted of home furnishing fabric. Major export markets were the United States, Japan, United Kingdom, Germany, France, Hong Kong, and Singapore. Sales to Europe had declined somewhat in 1993, but were expected to increase in 1994 as a result of the recent appointment of a new distributor in Germany. Initiatives planned for 1994 included an international advertising program, larger than any ever mounted before; a new showroom scheduled to open in London; and increased effort in several growing Asian markets including Korea, Taiwan, and the Philippines.

REASONS FOR SUCCESS

34   When asked for reasons for the company's success, JT executives cited the following key factors: expertise, innovation, willingness to invest, and leadership.

Outside Experts

35 Frequent use of outside experts was widely cited as a key contributor to the company's success. Surindr Supasavasdebhandu, Production Manager, provided two examples:

> Mr. Czerny has helped us enormously over the years—in identifying the most appropriate machinery for our needs—often relatively inexpensive second hand equipment; in installing new equipment; and in adapting machinery to our particular needs. He is very patient and knows how to work with our employees.

36 At the time we first set up our sericulture operation, two experts from the National Sericulture Institute in China came here to work with us. They provided us a great deal of help getting started. Now, their experts come here for shorter assignments to help us with particular problems as they crop up.

Continual Innovation

37 Surindr explained that JT had not merely duplicated technology brought in from the outside, but had often significantly adapted it to the company's special needs. He offered the following examples. When we first began dyeing we brought in experts from several big organizations in Thailand to advise us on boiler design. We didn't stop there, however. I took a course in thermodynamics so that I could understand what happens inside a boiler. We installed a microprocessor to control the process. As we accumulated knowledge over time, we made continual modifications. I could relate similar stories in our reeling and weaving operations. We are forcing ourselves to continually improve, to compete with ourselves for greater efficiency and higher reliability.

WILLINGNESS TO INVEST

38 The company's willingness to invest, even in projects which did not appear to show adequate return on investment, was felt to be another important contributor to the company's success. Pichet Buranastidporn, deputy managing director, offered the following example:

> It was hard to justify our silk plantation on straight ROI criteria. However, this facility has provided us important intangible benefits. It gives us protection in the event raw silk prices suddenly rise. It also enhances our reputation by making us a fully integrated producer.

Leadership

39 Executive leadership was another factor cited as critical to the company's success. Booth pointed to the exceptional capability of his senior managers, all of whom were Thai.

40 The textile industry is considered low-tech by most Thai managers—not a very exciting area to be in. Because of this stigma, it's hard to attract really good managers to a company like ours. Another problem is the reluctance of many Thai managers to question higher-ups. Because of this trait, even individuals who are very qualified technically often don't have the independence of mind to become really effective managers. We have been very lucky to avoid these difficulties. Pichet and Surindr, for example, approach their jobs with a great deal of independent judgment. This quality has helped them develop into very capable, imaginative managers. Perhaps their strong roots in Chinese culture, which encourages more independence of mind, fosters this quality. It might also come from the fact that the three of us joined the company at about the same time and have grown up here together, so just naturally consider ourselves as equals.

41 Pichet and Surindr, in turn, spoke highly of Booth's contribution. Surindr offered the following details:

> Bill arrives early, and leaves late—seven days a week—setting a good model for the rest of us to follow. He spends much of his time visiting our different operations, raising questions

and providing information everywhere he goes. He doesn't try to make decisions for us, but instead helps us think more clearly about the situations we're facing.

42   Pichet felt that the decision process which had evolved under Booth's leadership had contributed to the company's success.

43   We spend a lot of time discussing an issue before a decision is made. Deliberations usually take place in the evening, often over drinks, and are very informal. This kind of setting helps generate a lot of good ideas. It also provides plenty of opportunity for potential obstacles to surface. When obstacles emerge, we go back to the drawing board to study details more carefully. When a decision finally emerges, we have generally thought it through very thoroughly.

POSSIBLE MARKETING WEAKNESS

44   While extolling JT's many strengths, several executives felt that the company suffered weakness in the area of marketing. One described the problem as follows:

> In the past, demand at our retail store was so strong we didn't have to worry much about marketing. Our big challenge was to produce enough to meet demand. The situation is very different today. With retail sales declining, we must now find new customers, decide which ones we can serve most effectively, devise strategies for reaching new segments, etc. These are essentially marketing tasks. Since we have never had to look too hard for customers, our marketing skills are not yet very well developed.
>
> The condominium market here in Bangkok illustrates the problem. Bangkok has experienced a phenomenal boom in condominium construction over the past decade. These units need to be furnished, their owners have plenty of money to pay for the very best, and Jim Thompson has an outstanding reputation for design and quality. Yet we have garnered very little of this market.
>
> Another illustration of the problem is our experience at the World Trade Center. When we began opening satellite retail outlets a few years ago, our policy was to confine them to luxury hotels. Consequently, we made no effort to secure space in the World Trade Center which was scheduled to open in 1992. Only after an intense sales campaign by the Center's management were we finally persuaded to open an outlet there. To our great surprise, results at the Center have been spectacular.

Booth's Role

45   Close observation of Booth's interactions with staff and others showed him performing a variety of different roles in managing the company. Booth frequently brought together key people whose interaction could benefit the company. He performed this role, for example, during a day-long visit to the company's production operations in Pak Thong Chai. Accompanying him on this visit were a young Thai male named Tamrong who managed the company's printing joint venture, Czerny, and Surindr. A major purpose of the visit was to provide these three an opportunity to plan a proposed move of printing equipment from its current location in Bangkok to the new facility being prepared at Pak Thong Chai. During much of the day the three discussed the logistics of this move.

46   Since Czerny spoke no Thai and Surindr and Tamrong spoke no German, discussions among the three took place in English. For the most part this procedure worked fairly well. However, there were occasions when one of the three became confused. At such moments, Booth would interject a brief clarifying comment—in English to Czerny; in Thai to the other two.

47   Also accompanying Booth on this trip was the representative of a major Brazilian raw silk producer. He had been invited to visit Pak Thong Chai in part to comment on the company's procedures for buying raw silk. He spent the better part of an hour examining raw silk fiber piled on tables in JT's receiving area. During his inspection, he asked numerous questions about location of suppliers, storage procedures, treatment of incoming material, etc. Since he spoke no Thai and JT's purchasing personnel spoke no English, Booth played the role of interpreter.

48   Booth's input to conversations most frequently took the form of questions posed to clarify specific points. For example, during a discussion of spinning defects which took place on the floor of the spinning room in Pak Thong Chai, Booth asked whether the source of the problem might be insufficient maintenance frequency. This question in turn led to extensive discussion of the plant's equipment maintenance procedures.

49   Yet another role which Booth performed on a regular basis was that of gracious host. He took obvious pleasure in treating his Pak Thong Chai visitors to lunch at an outdoor restaurant, and later in the afternoon, during a meeting in the weaving factory's conference room, to cold beverages and appetizers. He also graciously received the steady stream of visitors who arrived at his well-appointed office on the top floor of the company's head-quarters building in Bangkok. Visitors included department managers, lower-level employees, suppliers, customers, and directors. Each was cordially received, offered coffee or tea (in the evening, beer), and engaged in pleasant conversation. Not infrequently, several visitors were seated around the table in his office, engaged in lively discussion of topics ranging from developments in European weaving technology to hazards of restoring antique Thai houses.

RETAIL MARKETING PROBLEMS

50   Dollar sales at JT's flagship retail outlet had declined 11 percent since the peak level reached in 1990, and unit sales had fallen even further. While these declines had been offset somewhat by increases at the company's new satellite outlets, the company's overall retail sales had dropped in recent years.

51   JT managers attributed this decline to a variety of adverse environmental developments occurring in Bangkok. Rapid industrialization was destroying many of the charms which once attracted tourists to the city—its easygoing pace, distinctive Asian architecture, and vast network of canals. Auto congestion was becoming so severe that several hours were sometimes needed to travel just a short distance within the city. This development was of special concern to JT because most customers traveled by taxi to reach its flagship store. Air pollution had reached an alarming level. The city's AIDS infection rate, particularly among the bar girls who constituted an attraction for some male visitors to the city, had received unfavorable publicity in the international press. Recessions in Japan and Europe, which historically supplied a large proportion of JT's customers, also played a role.

52   These developments, together with the Iraq war and a brief military coup occurring in Bangkok in 1991, caused the number of tourists visiting Thailand to decline that year for the first time in many years (see Exhibit 6). While tourist activity had recovered somewhat since then, visitors were beginning to skirt Bangkok and travel directly to resorts elsewhere in the country. An article appearing in a recent issue of the *Bangkok Post* provided the following details about this trend.

53   One of the major areas of concern is visitor arrivals from Japan which have tapered off. Although Japan's economic woes are said to be partly responsible, the TAT [Tourist Authority of Thailand] is also blaming a spate of adverse publicity over sex, AIDS, and environmental problems in Thailand. The main turnoff appears to be more Bangkok than Thailand. Visitor arrivals in January–September 1993 (by nationality) showed a total of 433,485 Japanese visitors to Thailand (down 1.28 percent on the same period in 1992) but 374,138 arrivals at Bangkok airport (down 14.21 percent by Jan–Sept 1992).

EXHIBIT 6
Jim Thompson
Thai Silk Company

Source: Tourism Authority
of Thailand.

I. International Tourist Arrivals in Thailand (in thousands)								
	1986	**1987**	**1988**	**1989**	**1990**	**1991**	**1992**	**1993**
Malaysia	653	765	868	736	752	808	729	830
Japan	259	342	449	556	652	560	570	582
Taiwan	111	195	189	400	503	454	407	525
Singapore	194	240	249	290	336	320	324	364
Germany	119	148	190	222	243	257	276	320
U.S.A.	196	236	258	267	285	248	274	278
Korea	31	37	65	112	148	180	204	271
Hong Kong	84	132	154	396	383	341	291	265
China	—	—	—	—	61	75	129	262
U.K.	147	184	280	200	238	198	236	250
Australia	95	111	138	219	252	203	208	205
France	100	132	157	187	194	173	194	202
Others	829	961	1,234	1,225	1,252	1,270	1,294	1,407
Total	2,818	3,483	4,231	4,810	5,299	5,087	5,136	5,761

II. Tourist Expenditures in Thailand (% of total)			
	1986	**1990**	**1993**
Shopping	27.4	39.0	42.8
Accommodations	26.6	23.1	23.0
Food & Beverages	16.9	15.1	15.1
Local Transit	15.6	13.3	10.7
Entertainment	10.0	7.6	5.1
Other	3.5	1.9	3.3
Total	100.0	100.0	100.0

54   This indicates that more Japanese are bypassing Bangkok and taking advantage of the increasing number of direct flights to Puket [a popular resort on Thailand's southwest coast]. Japanese tour operators note that the environment-and-safety conscious Japanese are showing strong signs of general disgust with the capital city's traffic problems. Strong marketing by new Puket developments like the Pacific Islands Club and the new Sheraton Grande [Puket is an island off the south coast, in the Indian Ocean] are also diverting the Japanese from Bangkok.[2]

OPTIONS FOR IMPROVEMENT

55   In light of these developments, JT managers were seeking ways to reduce the company's dependence on Bangkok's tourist market. During the early weeks of 1994, four options for achieving this objective were under consideration.

1. Develop a mail order catalogue displaying accessories such as neckties, purses, blouses, etc., and target the catalogue to foreigners who had already purchased JT products during visits to Bangkok.

2. Open a retail store in a major foreign city such as New York, Paris, or Tokyo.

3. Open a retail shop at a Thai beach resort such as Puket, Samui (an island in the Gulf of Siam), or Pattaya (a resort on the Gulf of Siam's east coast). All three locations were growing very rapidly. Puket and Samui were still relatively unspoiled. Pattaya, however,

was beginning to experience its own brand of environmental degradation. An article appearing in a 1991 issue of *The Economist* provided the following details.

> Twenty-five years ago Pattaya was a sleepy fishing village. Then it was discovered by American soldiers on R&R from Vietnam, and the Thai brand of sun, sea, and sex was invented, beginning a boom in tourism. Today Pattaya is a mess. Uncontrolled building has ruined its shoreline. The sea is coated with a film of raw sewage. Last year so many tourists died in mysterious circumstances that even the shady mafia that controls the town was embarrassed. An alarming proportion of the bar girls, many of whom are in fact transvestites, are HIV positive. Lucky is the hotel with 10 percent of its rooms occupied.[3]

4. Expand sales to the domestic home furnishing market.

56   JT managers were particularly enthusiastic about the last of these options, for several reasons. The domestic home furnishing market experienced little adverse affect from the city's traffic congestion. Indeed, the market may have actually benefited from such congestion, since an increasing number of people were moving from the outskirts of Bangkok to down-town condominiums near their work locations to avoid traffic jams during commuting hours. A heady construction boom was taking place in the city, and new units being built needed furnishing. And JT's reputation for creative design and good quality were highly prized by interior decorators, who acted as prime decision makers in the market.

57   The home furnishing market presented JT a major challenge, however. Most home furnishing sales consisted of relatively low-priced cotton fabric produced by suppliers utilizing high-speed mechanical looms. JT's weaving expertise, by contrast, lay in hand weaving. To compete more effectively in the home furnishing market, JT would need to significantly improve its high-speed mechanical weaving capabilities.

58   In an effort to improve its ability in this area, JT had purchased six secondhand high-speed mechanical looms over the past several years from a German company, Rohleder GMBH. JT's personnel had experienced difficulty operating the equipment, however, and trained operators were not available in Thailand. To overcome this obstacle, JT had sent several of its operators to Germany to receive training from Rohleder. Rohleder was the world's eighth largest, and Germany's second largest, manufacturer of upholstery fabric used for couches, chairs, etc. When difficulties persisted following the trainees' return to Bangkok, JT had approached Rohleder for further assistance. Ensuing conversations revealed that Rohleder was interested in establishing its own weaving facility in Asia in order to gain access to low-cost Asian labor and to better serve its growing base of Asian customers. Lacking operating experience in the region, it hoped to secure an Asian partner, and inquired whether JT would consider joining it in constructing a jointly-owned weaving mill in Thailand.

59   Investigation revealed that Rohleder's existing weaving mill, located near Frankfurt, was one of the most technically advanced in the world. Its entire output of fabric was sold to wholesalers who in turn sold, often under their own brands, to interior decorators and furniture manufacturers. Wholesalers generally gave Rohleder very high marks for quality and technical sophistication. Though more than 70 years old, Rohleder was still controlled by its founding family.

60   While Rohleder's skill in mechanical weaving—the very capability JT needed to improve its position in the home furnishing market—made the proposed venture with Rohleder attractive, Booth felt that the other options under consideration also offered promise. He hoped that the planning effort scheduled for the coming weeks would help clarify the pros and cons of all the options open to the company, so that he and his managers could make an optimal decision regarding the company's future direction.

ENDNOTES

1. For an excellent account of this search, see William Warren, *Jim Thompson: The Legendary American of Thailand,* Jim Thompson Thai Silk Company, 1993.
2. *Bangkok Post,* December 30, 1993, p. 45.
3. *The Economist,* July 6, 1991, p. 78.

Case 37

Killer Coke: *The Campaign against Coca-Cola*[1]   Henry W. Lane

> . . . the world of Coca-Cola, a world filled with lies, deception, immorality and widespread labor, human rights and environmental violations.
> —*Ray Rogers,* Director, Campaign to Stop Killer Coke[2]

> The people who are part of the [Killer Coke] campaign are trying to use the [Coca-Cola] brand to advance a political agenda that has nothing to do with the company.
> —*Pablo Largacha,* Communications Manager for Colombia, The Coca-Cola Company[3]

1   When Douglas Daft, CEO of Coca-Cola, arrived at the Hotel du Pont in Delaware to address the company's annual shareholders meeting, he was greeted by a crowd of protesters gathered near the hotel entrance. Most were there to denounce Coca-Cola's alleged complicity in the murders of union leaders in Colombia. The issue had garnered considerable media attention, and Daft knew that shareholders were wondering how the company planned to deal with the issue. He now hoped to put their concerns to rest. "Some in organized labor have been working overtime in college campuses to keep allegations about Colombia alive through misinformation and a twisting of the facts," he began.

> The charges linking our company to atrocities in Colombia are false and they are outrageous. Now what is happening in Colombia today is a tragedy. And during the past 40 years, 60,000 people have died as victims of terrorism and civil war there. We all know employees, colleagues, and friends, who have been victims of that violence, which we absolutely abhor. But the Coca-Cola Company has nothing to do with it.
>
> Our bottling partners have been good employers in Colombia for more than 70 years and have good relationships with a number of unions there. We contribute to an improved standard of living for Colombians, and that is why we continue to operate in that country.

2   Later, when Daft opened the floor to discussion, the first to the podium was Ray Rogers, a 60-year-old activist and director of the Campaign to Stop Killer Coke. "You lied about the situation in Colombia," he declared.

> You said that at no time was any union leader ever harmed by paramilitary security forces at any of your plants. Yet Isidro Gil was assassinated—murdered—in one of your bottling plants

David Wesley wrote this case under the supervision of Professor Henry W. Lane solely to provide material for class discussion. The authors do not intend to illustrate either effective or ineffective handling of a managerial situation. The authors may have disguised certain names and other identifying information to protect confidentiality.

[1] This case has been written on the basis of published sources only. Consequently, the interpretation and perspectives presented in this case are not necessarily those of the Coca-Cola Company or any of its employees.

[2] NYU students move to ban Coke products from college campuses, *Northeastern News,* December 7, 2005.

[3] Diez universidades de Estados Unidos y Europa vetaron el consumo de Coca-Cola por presuntos nexos con 'paras', *El Tiempo (Colombia),* January 4, 2006.

in Colombia. The next day, those same paramilitary security forces went into the plant and rounded up the workers. Coca-Cola managers in the plant had prepared resignation forms. Those workers were told that if they did not resign by 4 p.m. that day, they too would be murdered like their union officer, Isidro Gil. They all resigned en masse and the wages in that plant went from $380 a month down to $130 a month.

3   As Rogers continued to cite cases of alleged abuses, Daft interrupted. "Mr. Rogers, could you please finish?"

4   "I'm not done. I will finish very shortly," replied Rogers. When his microphone was cut off, Rogers raised his voice.

> Right now, there are five colleges and universities that have terminated Coca-Cola contracts over the Colombia issue. They have banned Coca-Cola products from all student-owned and operated facilities. Do stockholders know that? That was University College Dublin. Trinity College soon followed. In the United States, Carleton College, Lake Forest College and Bard College . . .

5   Suddenly Rogers was struck on the back by a security guard, followed by a number of others who forced him to the floor.

6   Appalled by what had happened, Daft pleaded with the security guards to "be gentle." He then turned to one of his executives and whispered, "We shouldn't have done that."

7   With Rogers ejected, the meeting was allowed to proceed. Civil rights activist Reverend Jesse Jackson rose to the podium and upbraided Daft for having Rogers silenced.

> Mr. Daft and members of the board let me say at the outset that while many disagreed with the first person making a comment, the violent removal was beneath the dignity of this company, it was by the security forces an overreaction and if he had been hurt and if he is hurt, that would be another lawsuit. It was an excessive use of power.

8   One by one, activist shareholders rose to rebuke Daft, many focusing on the human rights situation in Colombia. When one challenged Daft to "have an objective investigation," Daft rose to the company's defense.

> There have been objective evaluations and investigations. In every case, the company was cleared and any allegation was dismissed. The independent investigation has taken place.

THE REPUBLIC OF COLOMBIA: A BRIEF HISTORY

9   Colombia was established as a colony of Spain in 1525, and remained under Spanish colonial rule until the early 19th century. The peace was broken in 1810 when several regions in the colony declared independence. The resulting civil war lasted 13 years, and ended with independence for most of South America. It also firmly established a culture of internal conflict.

10   While Spain no longer governed Colombia, the Catholic church continued to exert great influence in political matters. A civil war between liberals, who opposed the influence of the church, and conservatives, who supported it, began in 1840 and lasted until 1903. When the liberal government confiscated all church-owned lands in 1861, a wide-spread guerrilla war erupted.

11   Between 1863 and 1885, Colombia saw more than 50 armed insurrections and 42 separate constitutions. "The army and the police force were kept small and weak to exclude them from politics, and as a consequence, law enforcement, especially in rural areas of the country, was left in private hands."[4] The war reached its climax between 1899 and 1903, following a

---

[4] H. F. Kline, *Colombia: Democracy Under Assault,* Harper Collins, 1995.

collapse in the economy and increasing disparity of wealth under the liberal administration. By 1903, more than 100,000 lives had been lost and Colombia was in ruins.

12   Growing worldwide demand for coffee, oil and bananas helped Colombia to recover from the war and post strong growth during the next two and a half decades. In the early 1930s, a liberal government confiscated dormant land from mainly conservative land owners. When the conservatives were returned to power in 1946, they quickly seized the opportunity to reclaim their land. Many desired to return to the "glories" of Spanish colonial rule and looked to Spanish president Francisco Franco "as the sole defender of Christian civilization."[5]

La Violencia

13   In rural areas of the country, liberal-backed guerrilla groups, which were the precursors for modern-day Marxist guerrillas, formed in order to violently defend land that conservative land owners were trying to reclaim. In 1948, they went on a rampage, burning churches in the colonial city of Santa Fe de Bogotá. This deeply offended the religious sentiments of many Colombians and created deep and long-lasting wounds. It also became the basis for the most violent period in Colombia's history, one that saw the loss of some 200,000 lives and became known as *La Violencia* (The Violence). "Toward the end of *La Violencia* a new generation of young Colombians who had been socialized to think that violence was a normal way of life . . . increasingly took to banditry."[6] In a successful effort to reestablish order, the military seized control of the country in 1953.

14   The military government offered amnesty to guerrillas who surrendered their weapons. And most did. However, liberal guerrilla groups included a large number of communists who refused to surrender their arms, but instead retreated to isolated areas of the country where they continued to operate with impunity.

The Revolutionary Armed Forces of Colombia

15   Civilian rule was restored in 1958 after moderate conservatives and liberals, with the support of the military, agreed to unite under a coalition known as the National Front. Meanwhile, communists successfully established their own government in a remote region of the country, known as the "republic" of *Marquetalia*. The government ignored the growing influence of communists until 1964 when, under pressure by conservatives, the Colombian army razed the communist controlled "republic."

16   Following the attack, the guerrillas reorganized under the banner *Fuerzas Armadas Revolucionarias de Colombia* (FARC). While the group officially came into existence in 1964, it continued to be led by former liberal guerrillas, and therefore "was the continuation of the revolutionary movement that had begun in 1948."[7] As FARC continued to grow, it established itself throughout the country in semi-autonomous fronts.

17   FARC financed itself through kidnapping ransoms, extortion and protection of the drug trade. Fronts also overran small communities in order to distribute propaganda and, more importantly, to pillage local banks. Businesses operating in rural areas, including agricultural, oil and mining interests, were required to pay vaccines (monthly payments) which "protected" them from attacks and kidnappings. An additional, albeit less lucrative, source of revenue was highway blockades where guerrillas stopped motorists and buses in order to confiscate jewelry and money.

18   Over time, fewer recruits joined the organization for ideological reasons, but rather as a means to escape poverty. "FARC's narcotics-related income for 1995 reportedly totaled

[5] Ibid.

[6] Ibid.

[7] J. P. Osterling, *Democracy in Colombia: Clientelist Politics and Guerrilla Warfare.* Transaction Publishers, 1989.

$647 million."[8] And per capita income for Colombian guerrilla fighters was at least 40 times the national average.[9]

19   By 1998, FARC's ranks had swelled to approximately 15,000 guerrilla fighters, up from 7,500 in 1992, and effectively controlled about half the country. They were also "better armed, equipped, and trained than the Colombian armed forces."[10] Over a period of 10 years, the war had cost the lives of an estimated 35,000 civilians and reduced the country's GDP by four percent.[11]

United Self-Defense Forces of Colombia

20   The United Self-Defense Forces of Colombia (AUC)[12] was formed in April 1997 in an effort to consolidate local and regional paramilitary groups in Colombia. Its mission was to protect local economic, social and political interests from leftist rebels. While FARC and other guerrilla groups were obvious targets, the AUC also targeted trade unions, human rights workers and others suspected of having leftist sympathies. The AUC's paramilitary fighters were funded primarily through the production and sale of illegal narcotics and from businesses that paid the AUC for "protection."

21   Trade unionists were frequently victims of paramilitary death squads. According to a U.S. State Department report on human rights in Colombia, 1,875 labor activists were killed between 1991 and 2002, and "labor leaders nationwide continued to be attacked by paramilitaries, guerrillas, and narcotics traffickers." Although the Colombian government "operated a protection program for threatened human rights workers, union leaders, journalists, mayors, and several other groups," AUC members acted with relative impunity. Accordingly, only five of the more than 300 labor-related murder cases investigated since 1986 resulted in a conviction.[13]

22   FARC was also implicated in the murder of unionists, albeit to a lesser extent. In 2002, leftist guerillas were linked to 19 murders of trade unionists, 17 attempted murders, 189 death threats, 26 kidnappings, and 8 disappearances.[14]

23   The human rights situation noticeably improved following the election of Álvaro Uribe Vélez in 2002. Under his administration, the government began to take a harder line against all armed groups in Colombia, including the AUC. With more than $3 billion in support from the United States under "Plan Colombia," Uribe significantly augmented military capacity. By 2004, homicides, kidnappings and terrorist attacks in Colombia decreased to their lowest levels in almost 20 years, resulting in unprecedented public support for the Colombian president.[15]

COCA-COLA COLOMBIA

24   Coca-Cola Colombia was a wholly-owned subsidiary of Coca-Cola U.S.A. with corporate offices in Bogotá (for a timeline of major Coca-Cola events, see Exhibit 1). It was responsible for manufacturing and distributing Coke products to its Colombian bottlers. Major

---

[8] Drug Control: U.S. Counternarcotics Efforts in Colombia Face Continuing Challenges. United States General Accounting Office, February 1998.

[9] Colombia: Guerrilla Economics, *The Economist*. January 13, 1996.

[10] The Suicide of Colombia, Foreign Policy Research Institute, September 7, 1998.

[11] Las FARC lamentan expectativas exageradas, *El Nuevo Herald,* April 22, 1999.

[12] Autodefensas Unidas de Colombia.

[13] Colombia: Country Reports on Human Rights Practices, U.S. Department of State, Bureau of Democracy, Human Rights, and Labor, March 31, 2003.

[14] Ibid.

[15] Background Note: Colombia, U.S. Department of State, Bureau of Western Hemisphere Affairs, February 2005.

EXHIBIT 1
Coca-Cola Timeline

Date	Event
1894	Coca-Cola is first produced in a candy store in Vicksburg, Mississippi.
1899	Exclusive bottling rights sold to three Chattanooga, Tennessee lawyers for one dollar.
1904	Coca-Cola becomes the most recognized brand in America.
1905	Cocaine is removed from the Coca-Cola formula.
1920–1939	First international plants were opened in France, Guatemala, Honduras, Mexico, Belgium, Italy and South Africa. By 1939, Coca-Cola had bottling operations in 44 countries.
1940	Coca-Cola Colombia is founded in Medellín. In its first year, Coca-Cola Colombia sells 67,761 cases of soda.
1945	"Coke" becomes a registered trademark of Coca-Cola.
June 1993	Coca-Cola acquires 30% of FEMSA Refrescos S.A de C.V., a Mexican producer of carbonated beverages.
1994–1996	Paramilitary death squads murder five Sinaltrainal union leaders at a Coca-Cola bottling plant in Carepa, Colombia.
February 1996	Coca-Cola FEMSA acquires 100% of Coca-Cola's bottling operations in Argentina.
July 20, 2001	The United Steelworkers and the International Labor Rights Fund bring suit against Coca-Cola and its Colombian bottlers on behalf of Sinaltrainal, a Colombian union.
March 31, 2003	Coca-Cola is dismissed as a defendant in Sinaltrainal v. Coca-Cola Co., United States District Court For The Southern District Of Florida
May 2003	Coca-Cola FEMSA acquires 100% of Panamerican Beverages, Inc. creating the second-largest Coca-Cola bottler in the world, accounting for almost 10% of Coca-Cola's global sales.
December 31, 2003	Coca-Cola ends the year with record net earnings of $4.3 billion on revenues of $21.0 billion.
April 13, 2003	Labor activist Ray Rogers begins "Killer Coke" campaign
2004	Coca-Cola launches cokefacts.org to promote its side of the Colombia controversy. The site receives only 800 visitors a month compared with killercoke.org's 25,000 visitors a month.
July 21, 2005	Interbrand, the world's leading international brand consultancy, ranks Coca-Cola first among the world's leading brands for the fifth consecutive year. It estimates the company's brand value at $67.5 billion.
December 8, 2005	New York University bans Coca-Cola products from its campus.
December 29, 2005	University of Michigan bans Coca-Cola products from its campus.
December 31, 2005	Coca-Cola ends the year with record net earnings of $4.9 billion on revenues of $23.1 billion.

decisions concerning production, distribution and marketing came from the company's U.S. headquarters, while Coca-Cola Colombia was responsible for ensuring that these directives were carried out by the company's bottlers and other contractors.

25   Bebidas y Alimentos de Urabá (Bebidas) was a small corporation owned by two Florida residents, Richard Kirby and his son, Richard Kielland. Kirby was responsible for overall company strategy, while Kielland, as manager of plant operations, implemented company policy at the Colombian plants. The company operated one plant in Colombia, in Carepa, Urabá, a town of 42,075 inhabitants, located approximately 200 miles north of Medellín.

26   Coca-Cola beverages were also produced in 17 plants owned by Panamerican Beverages, a publicly traded corporation headquartered in Miami. In addition to its Colombian plants,

Panamerican Beverages was the "anchor bottler" for Coca-Cola in Brazil, Costa Rica, Guatemala, Mexico, Nicaragua and Venezuela. In 2003, Panamerican Beverages was purchased by Coca-Cola FEMSA, a subsidiary of Coca-Cola U.S.A.[16]

THE CASE AGAINST COCA-COLA AND ITS COLOMBIAN BOTTLERS

Background

27   Although union members at several Coca-Cola bottling plants were targeted by paramilitaries, Coca-Cola's troubles centered on the events at one particular plant, the Bebidas plant in Carepa, Urabá. According to an Amnesty International report, Urabá was one of the most violent regions in the country, a place where reprisal killings of civilians by communist guerillas and paramilitaries was commonplace.

28   In the mid-1990s, paramilitaries:

> launched major offensives from the northern municipalities of the Urabá region of Antioquia and pushed southwards rooting out and killing those they considered guerrilla collaborators or sympathizers. FARC guerrilla forces, operating in alliance with dissident groups, responded by carrying out a number of massacres of [civilians] they considered to be supporting army or paramilitary forces.
>   Armed opposition groups have been responsible for forced displacement of communities who have fled their homes as a result of death threats or the deliberate and arbitrary killings of those accused of collaboration with the security or paramilitary forces. Many families have also fled their homes in order to escape forcible recruitment of their children by armed opposition groups.[17]

Torture Victims Protection Act Claim

29   In 2001, Sinaltrainal and representatives of several slain union leaders brought suit against Coca-Cola and Bebidas under the Alien Tort Claims Act (ATCA) and the Torture Victims Protection Act (TVPA) (see Exhibit 2).[18] The petition, filed by lawyers from the International Labor Rights Fund and the United Steel Workers of America, argued that Coca-Cola and Bebidas "contracted with or otherwise directed paramilitary security forces that utilized extreme violence and murdered, tortured, unlawfully detained or otherwise silenced trade union leaders."[19] The suit also named Panamerican Beverages as a defendant for its alleged complicity in the kidnappings and murders of several union members and their relatives at three Panamerican plants in northern Colombia.

30   The use of ATCA in such cases was not without precedent. According to Michael Ratner, vice-president of the Center for Constitutional Rights, "courts in the United States pioneered the use of civil remedies to sue human rights violators."

> Litigation under the Alien Tort Claims Act and the Torture Victim Protection Act have resulted in billions of dollars in judgments, and have had an important impact on plaintiffs and human rights both in the United States and internationally. Such cases do not require official approval; they can be brought by individuals who have control over the lawsuits and thus are less subject to political vagaries.

[16] Coca-Cola FEMSA was a joint venture between Mexican brewer Fomento Económico Mexicano, S.A. de C.V. (FEMSA) (46 per cent) and the Coca-Cola Company (40 per cent). The remaining shares were publicly held.

[17] Return to Hope, Forcibly displaced communities of Urabá and Medio Atrato region, Amnesty International Report 23/023/2000, June 1, 2000.

[18] The Torture Victims Protection Act was enacted in 1992 and added as a provision under the Alien Tort Claims Act.

[19] Coca-Cola Accused, *The New York Times,* July 29, 2001.

EXHIBIT 2   **The Alien Tort Claims Act (28 USCS § 1350)**

§ 1350. Alien's action for tort

The district courts shall have original jurisdiction of any civil action by an alien for a tort only, committed in violation of the law of nations or a treaty of the United States.

HISTORY:
(June 25, 1948, ch 646, § 1, 62 Stat. 934.)
HISTORY; ANCILLARY LAWS AND DIRECTIVES

Prior law and revision:
Based on title 28, U.S.C., 1940 ed., § 41(17) (Mar. 3, 1911, ch. 231, § 24, P 17, 36 Stat. 1093).
Words "civil action" were substituted for "suits," in view of Rule 2 of the Federal Rules of Civil Procedure. Changes in phraseology were made.

Other provisions:
Torture Victim Protection Act of 1991. Act March 12, 1992, P.L. 102–256, 106 Stat. 73, provides:
"Section 1. Short title

"This Act may be cited as the 'Torture Victim Protection Act of 1991'.

"Sec. 2. Establishment of civil action

"(a) Liability. An individual who, under actual or apparent authority, or color of law, of any foreign nation—

"(1) subjects an individual to torture shall, in a civil action, be liable for damages to that individual; or

"(2) subjects an individual to extrajudicial killing shall, in a civil action, be liable for damages to the individual's legal representative, or to any person who may be a claimant in an action for wrongful death.

"(b) Exhaustion of remedies. A court shall decline to hear a claim under this section if the claimant has not exhausted adequate and available remedies in the place in which the conduct giving rise to the claim occurred.

"(c) Statute of limitations. No action shall be maintained under this section unless it is commenced within 10 years after the cause of action arose.

"Sec. 3. Definitions

"(a) Extrajudicial killing. For the purposes of this Act, the term 'extrajudicial killing' means a deliberated killing not authorized by a previous judgment pronounced by a regularly constituted court affording all the judicial guarantees which are recognized as indispensable by civilized peoples. Such term, however, does not include any such killing that, under international law, is lawfully carried out under the authority of a foreign nation.

"(b) Torture. For the purposes of this Act—

"(1) the term 'torture' means any act, directed against an individual in the offender's custody or physical control, by which severe pain or suffering (other than pain or suffering arising only from or inherent in, or incidental to, lawful sanctions), whether physical or mental, is intentionally inflicted on that individual for such purposes as obtaining from that individual or a third person information or a confession, punishing that individual for an act that individual or a third person has committed or is suspected of having committed, intimidating or coercing that individual or a third person, or for any reason based on discrimination of any kind; and

"(2) mental pain or suffering refers to prolonged mental harm caused by or resulting from—

"(A) the intentional infliction or threatened infliction of severe physical pain or suffering;

"(B) the administration or application, or threatened administration or application, of mind altering substances or other procedures calculated to disrupt profoundly the senses or the personality;

"(C) the threat of imminent death; or

"(D) the threat that another individual will imminently be subjected to death, severe physical pain or suffering, or the administration or application of mind altering substances or other procedures calculated to disrupt profoundly the senses or personality."

Civil remedies include damage awards for injuries and punitive damages meant to deter future abusive conduct as well as send a message to others that such conduct is unacceptable. In addition to any money that can be collected, these cases are important to the victims and their families. Plaintiffs are allowed to tell their stories to a court, can often confront their abusers, and create an official record of their persecutions. This in turn could lead to a criminal prosecution.[20]

The Murder of Isidro Segundo Gil

31 The plaintiffs sought compensation specifically for the murder of 27-year-old Isidro Segundo Gil, an employee of the Carepa plant, as well as other murdered union members at the Carepa plant and at three plants owned by Panamerican Beverages.[21]

32 In 1996, Bebidas hired Ariosto Milan Mosquera to manage the Carepa bottling plant. Mosquera allegedly began threatening to destroy the union. He allowed paramilitaries access to the plant and made a specific agreement with local paramilitary leaders to drive the union out of the Bebidas plant by using threats and violence, if necessary.

33 On September 27, 1996 Sinaltrainal submitted a letter to both Bebidas and Coca-Cola Colombia accusing Mosquera of working with the paramilitary to destroy the union, and urging Bebidas to protect trade unionists from the paramilitaries who were threatening employees.

34 On the morning of December 5, 1996, two paramilitaries approached Gil as he arrived at work. They said they needed to enter the Bebidas plant. When Gil opened the door, the paramilitaries shot and killed him. Witnesses claimed the murderers were the same para-militaries who had met with Mosquera at the plant. Two days later, paramilitaries arrived at the Bebidas plant, where they assembled the employees and told them that unless they resigned from the union, they would face the same fate as Gil. The employees then entered Mosquera's office and signed resignation forms that he had prepared. Many union members permanently fled Carepa after the forced resignations and continued to live in hiding.[22] For a more detailed summary of the Carepa events, see Exhibit 3.

35 Coca-Cola's initial response was to deny any wrongdoing. "We adhere to the highest standards of ethical conduct and business practices and we require all of our companies, operating units and suppliers to abide by the laws and regulations in the countries that they do business," a company spokesperson explained.[23]

36 For nearly two years, both sides presented evidence to back up their cases. In 2003, the court agreed that Mosquera colluded with paramilitaries in an effort to break the union. It further argued,

Bebidas have not produced any evidence to refute the allegation that Bebidas had ties to Mosquera's decision to hire the paramilitary to impede Sinaltrainal's union activity at Bebidas.[24]

37 However, while the Bottler's Agreement between Coca-Cola and Bebidas granted Coca-Cola U.S.A. the right to supervise and control the quality, distribution and marketing

[20] Michael Ratner, "Civil Remedies for Gross Human Rights Violations," *PBS.org*. February 2, 1999 (www.pbs.org/wnet/justice/law_background_torture.html).

[21] Five of the eight murder cases cited by Coca-Cola opponents took place between 1994 and 1996 at the Carepa plant owned and operated by Bebidas & Alimentos de Urabá.

[22] The account of Gil's murder is summarized from: Sinaltrainal v. Coca-Cola Co., United States District Court for the Southern District of Florida, 256 F. Supp. 2d 1345; 2003 U.S. Dist. LEXIS 7145; 16 Fla. L. Weekly Fed. D 382, March 28, 2003, Decided, March 31, 2003.

[23] "Union Says Coca-Cola in Colombia Uses Thugs," *The New York Times,* July 26, 2001.

[24] Sinaltrainal v. Coca-Cola Co., United States District Court for the Southern District of Florida, 256 F. Supp. 2d 1345; 2003 U.S. Dist. LEXIS 7145; 16 Fla. L. Weekly Fed. D 382, March 28, 2003, Decided, March 31, 2003.

EXHIBIT 3   **Court Filing (July 20, 2001) The Events at Bebidas y Alimentos in Carepa (Abridged)**

In April of 1994, paramilitary forces murdered Jose Eleazar Manco David and Luis Enrique Gomez Granado, both of whom were workers at Bebidas y Alimentos and members of Sinaltrainal. The paramilitary forces in Carepa then began to intimidate other Sinaltrainal members as well as the local leadership of Sinaltrainal, telling them, upon threat of physical harm, to resign from the union or to flee Carepa altogether. The management of Bebidas y Alimentos permitted these paramilitary forces to appear within the plant to deliver this message to Union members and leaders. A number of Union members began leaving town as a result. And, in April of 1995, following more death threats, every member of the executive board of the Sinaltrainal local representing the Bebidas y Alimentos workers fled Carepa in fear for their lives.

In June of 1995, the Sinaltrainal local union elected a new executive board to replace the one that had fled. Isidro Gil was elected as a member of this new board as was an individual named Dorlahome Tuborquia. Shortly thereafter, in July of 1995, Bebidas y Alimentos began to hire members of the paramilitaries who had threatened the first Union executive board into fleeing. These members of the paramilitaries were hired both into the sales and production departments.

In September of 1995, Ariosto Milan Mosquera took over as the manager of the Bebidas y Alimentos plant in Carepa. Mosquera proceeded to discharge Dorlahome Tuborquia. Sinaltrainal challenged this discharge through the legal process, and a judge, finding the discharge to be unlawful, ordered Bebidas y Alimentos to rehire Tuborquia. He returned to work at Bebidas y Alimentos in December of 1995. Shortly after the return of Tuborquia, Mosquera announced that he had given an order to the paramilitaries to carry out the task of destroying the union. In keeping with these threats of Mosquera, the paramilitaries began to renew threats against Sinaltrainal members, including Dorlahome Tuborquia. Specifically, the paramilitaries threatened to kill Tuborquia. In response to these threats, Tuborquia fled Carepa and went into hiding. The paramilitaries then seized Tuboquia's home to use for their operations.

Throughout 1996, Sinaltrainal members witnessed Mosquera socializing with members of the paramilitary forces and providing the paramilitaries with Coke products for their parties. Meanwhile, Bebidas y Alimentos and Sinaltrainal began negotiating a new labor agreement. These negotiations included Sinaltrainal's proposals for increased security for threatened trade unionists and a cessation of Mosquera's threats against the union as well as his collusion with the paramilitaries. Defendant Richard Kirby Keilland personally participated in these negotiations on behalf of Bebidas y Alimentos and he flatly refused the union's requests.

In response, Sinaltrainal began a national campaign in August of 1996 to call upon Bebidas y Alimentos, as well as Panamco Colombia and Coca-Cola Colombia, to protect the Sinaltrainal leadership and members in Carepa from what it feared was the imminent threat of attack by the paramilitaries. By letter dated September 27, 1996, national leaders of Sinaltrainal accused Mosquera of working with the paramilitaries to destroy the union, and they urged that Bebidas y Alimentos ensure the security of the workers in the Carepa plant in the face of the paramilitary threats. Copies of this letter were contemporaneously sent to Coca-Cola Colombia as well as Panamco Colombia. In response to this letter, Mosquera told the union to retract its accusations.

On December 5, 1996, at 9:00 in the morning, two paramilitaries approached Isidro Gil, who was then involved in negotiations on behalf of the union with Bebidas y Alimentos, as he stood in the entrance of the Bebidas y Alimentos plant. The paramilitaries stated that they needed to go into the plant to talk to someone inside. Isidro Gil proceeded to open the door and the two paramilitaries then shot him to death inside the plant. That same night, these same paramilitaries went to the local union hall of Sinaltrainal and started a fire.

On December 6, 1996, paramilitaries approached several more members of the local Sinaltrainal executive board. These paramilitaries told the union board members that they killed Isidro Gil and burned the union office and that they would kill the remaining board members if they did not leave town. The paramilitaries also explained that they would have a meeting with the workers at the Bebidas y Alimentos plant the next day to tell them that they would have to resign from the union or face being killed.

On December 7, 1996 at 8:00 a.m., the paramilitaries appeared at the Bebidas y Alimentos plant as threatened. They assembled the workers and told them that Bebidas y Alimentos did not want the union at the plant. The paramilitaries explained that the workers had the option of either resigning from the union or leaving Carepa altogether lest they be killed. The paramilitaries then proceeded to direct the workers into the manager's office to sign resignation forms which were prepared by Defendant Bebidas y Alimentos itself. As a result of the threats of the paramilitaries, workers resigned en masse from Sinaltrainal.

(continued)

EXHIBIT 3   **Court Filing (July 20, 2001) The Events at Bebidas y Alimentos in Carepa (Abridged)   cont.**

In fear for their life, fourteen Sinaltrainal members, including the remainder of the local Sinaltrainal executive board, fled Carepa after this meeting on December 7, 1996. As a result of the flight of these individuals and the resignation of the other workers from the union, the local Sinaltrainal union in Carepa was destroyed. This union has never returned to Carepa. The Sinaltrainal members who fled Carepa on December 7, 1996 continue to fear for their lives and remain in hiding, moving frequently from house to house. Plaintiff Sinaltrainal, as it does for all such displaced members, helps provide support to these individuals.

After the murder of Isidro Gil, the paramilitaries presented themselves at the Bebidas y Alimentos plant with the medical cards of workers which they had taken from the local union office before they burned it. Bebidas y Alimentos paid the paramilitaries remuneration in the amount owed under these cards. The paramilitaries repaired the union office which they had burned and took it over for the purpose of storing their weapons. On December 26, 1996, the paramilitaries killed another Bebidas y Alimentos worker, José Herrerra. The same paramilitaries later killed the wife of Isidro Gil in 2000, leaving their two children without parents.

In 1997, Peggy Ann Keilland, a close relative of Defendants Richard I. Kirby and Richard Kirby Keilland, took over as the Manager of the Bebidas y Alimentos plant in Carepa. Very shortly after taking over, Ms. Keilland worked with the Chief of the Colombian military in the zone to ensure that the paramilitaries were kept out of the plant. Also in 1997, Defendants Richard I. Kirby and Richard Kirby Keilland asked Defendant Coke if they could sell the Bebidas y Alimentos business along with the Carepa plant. Defendant Coke denied them this request and these Defendants still maintain ownership of the Carepa operations, under the direction and control of Defendants Coke and Coke Colombia.

of its products, including the right to terminate or suspend a bottler's operations for non-compliance with its terms and conditions, it did not give Coca-Cola direct control over plant operations. As such, the court determined that Coca-Cola U.S.A. and Coca-Cola Colombia were not agents that conspired or acted jointly with the paramilitary through Bebidas. As such, the court dismissed Coca-Cola as a defendant because it lacked jurisdiction over Coca-Cola under ATCA.[25]

38   Bebidas and Panamerican Beverages, on the other hand, could be held liable as "an individual who, under color of law of any foreign nation, subjects another person to torture or extrajudicial killing," thereby overruling the company's defense that a private corporation is not an "individual" in the legal sense, and should not be held liable for acts of torture and killing in foreign countries.

THE ANTI-GLOBALIZATION MOVEMENT

39   The incidents at Coca-Cola's bottling plants in Colombia coincided with the rise of the anti-globalization movement, which targeted large multinational corporations as symbols of "the damaging effects of globalization." The movement's goals included labor rights, environmental protection, preservation of indigenous peoples and cultures, food safety and social welfare. It found wide support on college campuses in North America and Europe, as well as from environmental organizations such as Greenpeace. Much of the criticism of globalization focused on alleged exploitation of workers in less-developed countries, such as the use of sweatshops by Nike, the Gap and others.

The Case of Nike: A Model for Change

40   Anti-globalization protesters viewed Nike, in particular, as a model for social change brought about through public pressure. In the 1990s, Nike came under scrutiny for alleged

---

[25] After Coca-Cola acquired a stake in Panamerican Beverages in 2003, the plaintiffs moved to have Coca-Cola reinstated as a defendant. The court agreed to consider the motion, but as of 2005 had not made a ruling.

human rights violations by its outsourcing contractors in Asia. The company denied any wrongdoing and, to prove its case, hired Goodworks International, an Atlanta-based non-profit organization, to audit its Asian contractors. In early 1997, Goodworks director and former civil rights leader, Andrew Young, led the investigation. After a two-week tour of China, Vietnam and Indonesia, Young returned to the United States to report that Nike was "doing a good job."

> We found Nike to be in the forefront of a global economy. Factories we visited that produce Nike goods were clean, organized, adequately ventilated and well lit.[26]

41   Young further cited Ernst & Young audits of particular plants.

> I did not find in the audit reports or in my own conversations with workers at these factories or in our other research a pattern of these factories violating national laws, local laws or the [Nike] Code of Conduct as relates to age or working conditions.[27]

42   Following Young's report, a widely criticized *New York Times* article reported "no evidence of widespread or systematic mistreatment of workers."[28] Medea Benjamin of San Francisco-based CorpWatch, who had expected Young to "maintain his credibility as a defender of the poor," was sorely disappointed.

43   A few months later, a disgruntled Nike employee handed CorpWatch a copy of one of the Ernst & Young audits. In contrast to Young's report, it cited gross human rights violations at company plants in Vietnam. Feeling that it had been misled, *The New York Times* lambasted Nike. A front page headline read, "Nike Shoe Plant in Vietnam is Called Unsafe for Workers." It continued,

> In an inspection report that was prepared in January for the company's internal use only, Ernst & Young wrote that workers at the factory near Ho Chi Minh City were exposed to carcinogens that exceeded local legal standards by 177 times in parts of the plant and that 77 percent of the employees suffered from respiratory problems. The report also said that employees at the site, which is owned and operated by a Korean subcontractor, were forced to work 65 hours a week, far more than Vietnamese law allows, for $10 a week.[29]

44   Within months a proliferation of newspaper articles reported similar abuses at factories throughout Asia and Latin America. Almost overnight, anti-globalization organizers mobilized a worldwide movement against Nike that eventually forced the company to rethink its business practices.

45   Nike created a department to monitor suppliers in less-developed countries. Todd McKean, the company's new Director of Corporate Responsibility Compliance recognized that some Nike factories violated worker rights and that the company had to improve the way it monitored working conditions. "How much do we really know about issues in all of these factories?" he asked.

> Not enough. Every time we look closer, we find another thing wrong. Too much overtime. Wage errors. Too much heat. Involuntary pregnancy testing. An abusive supervisor. Every time we peel another layer off the onion we find another complex set of issues that our compliance and production people work with factory management to try to resolve.[30]

---

[26] Andrew Young, and H. Jordan, *The Nike Code of Conduct Report,* Good Works International, June 27, 1997.

[27] Ibid.

[28] "Nike's Asian Factories Pass Young's Muster," *The New York Times,* June 25, 1997.

[29] "Nike Shoe Plant in Vietnam is Called Unsafe for Workers," *The New York Times,* November 8, 1997.

[30] Factory Monitoring Practices, Labor Practices, Nike, 2001.

46 The company also hired independent agencies, such as the Fair Labor Association, to regularly monitor its 700 contract factories. When audits uncovered abusive practices, Nike required its contractors to implement changes or risk losing their contracts.

47 For CorpWatch, it was a major victory.

> Student organizers demanding that universities doing business with Nike hold the company to higher standards kept Nike's labor practices in the spotlight. Meanwhile, faced with the increasing clout of activist groups, falling stock prices and weak sales, Nike announced major concessions to its critics in May, 1998.[31]

48 While some continued to criticize Nike's labor practices, most anti-globalization activists focused their efforts elsewhere.

KILLER COKE CAMPAIGN

49 Shortly after the U.S. court dismissed Coca-Cola as a defendant in 2003, Ray Rogers mounted the Killer Coke campaign. The organization's website, killercoke.org (see Exhibit 4), dubbed Coca-Cola "the New Nike," and urged students to pressure colleges to cancel their Coca-Cola contracts. "Like Nike, Coke will only remedy its practices with significant pressure and the fear of a tarnished image," exclaimed a web article.[32]

50 Rogers, a long-time activist for labor rights, began his career as a labor organizer for the Amalgamated Clothing Workers of America. In 1978, *The New York Times* recognized Rogers as the moving force behind a successful campaign against J. P. Stevens, a large textile company, which forced the resignation of the chairman of Stevens and the chairman of the New York Life Insurance Co. from each other's board of directors. "The important thing isn't just organizing people into unions," explained Rogers. "It's disorganizing the power structure."[33]

51 Rogers' early success allowed him to create Corporate Campaign, Inc., a public relations and labor strategy firm. In the 1980s, Corporate Campaign confronted Consolidated Edison Utilities, Hormel Foods, American Airlines, Bank of Boston, Campbell Soup, and International Paper, often winning important victories for labor unions. Tactics included walkouts, consumer boycotts, demonstrations and letter-writing campaigns. "I'd much rather see rich businessmen fight it out in the boardroom," Rogers asserted. "You can't embarrass them. You have to make them deal with real economic or political pressure."[34]

52 Rogers' strategy often pitted one company against another. For example, he encouraged trade unions to put pressure on financial institutions that managed union funds to withdraw support from companies opposed to union organizing activities. Other times he would target the largest company in an industry hoping that competitors would use it to their advantage.

> You have to create a situation where you're beating on one institution. They're taking heavy losses, and all the other institutions are standing behind them saying, "Whatever you do, don't set a precedent, don't give in." But finally the institution you're putting pressure on is going to say, "Hey, wait a minute. We're losing a lot of business. And where is that business going? It's going to you, our competitors, and to your banks. You're benefiting at our expense. So if you don't want to set a precedent, then don't you set it, but we're getting out of this thing."[35]

[31] CorpWatch Takes on Nike, Sweatshops (www.corpwatch.org), February 17, 2006.

[32] Tremendous Victories on Campus, *Campaign to Stop Killer Coke Update,* May 20, 2005 (www.killercoke.org/nl0520.htm) February 17, 2006.

[33] Rogers' Tough, Unorthodox Tactics Prevail In Stevens Organizing Fight. *The Wall Street Journal,* October 21, 2006.

[34] Labor's Boardroom, *Time.* June 20 1988.

[35] An Interview with Ray Rogers, *Working Papers Magazine.* January/February 1982.

EXHIBIT 4 Killercoke.org Home Page

53   Killer Coke was a continuation of Rogers' tradition of activism, and it followed many of the same grass-roots tactics. Campaign flyers distributed to university students as part of the "Coke Organizing Manual" demanded that Coca-Cola,

- Denounce the violence that is occurring in the name of Coca-Cola in Colombia.
- Respect the fundamental rights to free association and to organize trade unions, as reflected in Colombian law, Article 22 of the International Covenant on Civil & Political Rights, as well as Conventions 87 & 88 of the International Labor Organization.

- Announce publicly in Colombia its intention to participate in an investigation of the violence at its bottling plants.
- Reinforce Coca-Cola's public stance against violence by directing all bottling plants in Colombia to stop dealing with any armed groups that are participating in violence against trade unionists.
- Establish a complaint and reporting process which will allow union members to report violations occurring in Coca-Cola bottling plants to an official of the company who will then investigate and take swift remedial action against these violations.
- Provide compensation to the known victims of violence at Coca-Cola bottling plants.[36]

54   Serving as a conduit of information, the website sought to foment support on college campuses. Pamphlets, banner templates, web icons, news links, and other resources were provided to help students put pressure on university administrators to suspend contracts with the Coca-Cola Company.

COKE FACTS

55   When the Killer Coke campaign brought Coca-Cola increased notoriety among young consumers, some business analysts began to criticize the company's decision not to investigate the murders in Colombia.[37] Coca-Cola responded by sending high level executives to college campuses to explain its side of the story, and by creating a company-owned website (cokefacts.org) to counter the Killer Coke website (see Exhibit 5).[38] Finally, it hired Cal-Safety Compliance Corporation to audit its Colombian bottling plants.[39]

56   In an article on cokefacts.org, Ed Potter, director of Global Labor Relations for Coca-Cola, criticized the anti-Coke campaign. "I would stand our Company's labor relations practices alongside any other company on the planet," he wrote.

> These unjustified attacks do a disservice to the men and women of Coca-Cola; they mislead the public and impede progress for workers' rights worldwide. The Coca-Cola system is one of the most highly unionized multinational corporations in Colombia and throughout the world. Last year, the Company signed a joint statement with the IUF, the international organization for food and beverage unions, confirming that Coca-Cola workers are "allowed to exercise rights to union membership and collective bargaining without pressure or interference."
>
> Two different judicial inquiries in Colombia have found no evidence to support allegations that bottler management there conspired to intimidate or threaten trade unionists. An additional independent assessment conducted by Cal-Safety Compliance Corporation [see Exhibit 6], an international social compliance auditor certified by the Fair Labor Association and Social Accountability 8000, confirmed that workers in Coca-Cola plants in Colombia enjoy freedom of association, collective bargaining rights and an atmosphere free of anti-union intimidation.[40]

---

[36] Coke Organizing Manual, July 8, 2002.

[37] The Real Story: How did Coca-Cola's management go from first-rate to farcical in six short years? *Fortune,* May 31, 2004.

[38] Other company URLs, such as killercoke.com and stopkillercoke.org, redirected visitors to the cockefacts.org site.

[39] Cal Safety Compliance Corporation, a subsidiary of Specialized Technology Resources, Inc., was part of a worldwide organization "dedicated to ensuring the integrity of its clients' products and technologies." Services included compliance, inspection, and quality assurance testing. Specialized Technology Resources Inc. History & Highlights (www.struk.co.uk/comphistory.htm) February 23, 2006.

[40] The Coca-Cola Company Addresses "False and Inflammatory" Allegations Made by Teamsters, Cokefacts.org, February 7, 2006.

EXHIBIT 5
Cokefacts.org Home Page

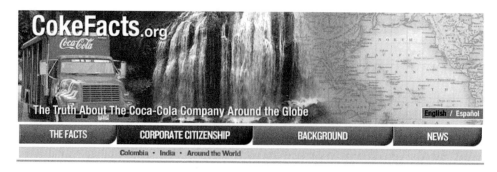

Colombia: Community Building

Working with Colombians to Create a Stronger Nation

The Coca-Cola Company has been operating in Colombia for more than 70 years. Our bottling partners distribute products to about a half million retailers, including everyone from supermarkets like the internationally owned Carrefour and the Colombian-owned Alkosto supermarkets, as well as the small, family-run bodegas that still control about 40 percent of the retail market in Colombia. As a community partner, our bottlers contribute significant resources – through donations and volunteer hours – to address such issues as hunger relief, education and the environment.

Over the past seven decades, Colombia has experienced internal conflict, which affects trade union activists and other civilians from all walks of life. Despite the volatile environment, The Coca-Cola Company and our bottling partners have maintained operations and worked to provide safe, stable economic opportunities for the people of Colombia.

Read More >>

Colombia: Rebuilding Shattered Lives – One Child at a Time

Reaching Across Continents to Help the Youngest Victims of War

No society can be made whole after decades of strife if the needs of its children are not addressed first. That's why The Coca-Cola Company is proud to be a founding sponsor of Colombianitos, the brainchild of a group of Colombian professionals living in Atlanta, Georgia, striving to rescue a generation of children whose lives have been shattered by Colombia's ongoing conflict. The plight of children in Colombia is acute. More than 6.5 million live in abject poverty, and children represent nearly a third of the victims of Colombia's countless land mines.

But Colombianitos is making a difference. Its land mine program provides prosthetic devices and the physical – and psychological – support required to master them. Additionally, scores of children are touched by other Colombianitos programs, which are helping turn back the tide on the drugs, violence and poverty that are robbing young Colombians of their childhoods. It is of course not possible to erase the past. But by matching resources with a passion for change, it is possible to rewrite the future – one child at a time.

57   According to Pablo Largacha, Communications Manager for Colombia, the problem was one of perception. Foreigners simply didn't understand the political reality that is Colombia. "In general," he explained, "Colombians have a better sense of what is happening."

> We have a better understanding of the political situation and the history of armed conflict. The vast majority believe that these are unfounded accusations. Last year, in 2005, Coca-Cola was ranked in Portafolio magazine as the company with the third best reputation in Colombia, with the best marketing, and as one of the best places to work. Therefore, given

EXHIBIT 6
Cal-Safety Workplace
Assessment Colombia
(Overview)[1]

Perhaps most significant about the CSCC auditors' Colombia findings was what they did not find based on private interviews with employees.

Workers were not afraid to speak to outside auditors.

Employees did not ask to be excluded from interviews or for union representation during the interview process.

Auditors found no cases of improper disciplinary action against workers by plant supervisors and managers.

There were no threats by management discovered nor attempts to attack or intimidate a worker for being affiliated with a union, or for being a union organizer or for being a union official. Nonunion workers did not indicate that they were pressured to remain non-union and they were not pressured to join a union.

Security guards were not being used to harass, intimidate or threaten workers.

Auditors *did* find union officials of the plants able to operate in these facilities "free from obstruction and discrimination."

> **It should be noted that in the assessment of our Colombian bottling partners' plants, not one worker was afraid to speak to the CSCC auditors; none asked for a union leader to be present during the interview; and no one showed any sign of concern about responding to very direct questions related to management labour relations during the interview process.**

CSCC was told of demonstrations by some of our bottler's workers, all peaceful, all without reprisals.

Several of these demonstrations even involved employees showing their support for workers laid off at other plants within the Coca-Cola system. Both union and non-union workers felt free to exercise their rights of dissent and unionized workers referenced a number of examples when they freely used the broad range of tools available to them under freedom of association and collective bargaining.

The auditors recorded several complaints about management not adhering to the terms of their collective bargaining agreements. The auditors examined each complaint, and in each instance they found documents indicating that plant managers followed proper procedures in dealing with disagreements with the union over contract terms, without intimidation or harassment on either side; thereby indicating compliance with the terms of collective bargaining agreements and adherence to proper procedures.

In addition, CSCC looked at the entirety of the workplace experience for workers at six facilities, five of which are owned by Panamco Colombia, S.A., a subsidiary of Coca-Cola FEMSA, S.A. de CV., and the sixth by the family-owned company Bebidas & Alimentos de Uraba. Unfortunately, at a few of the plants, shortcomings were found that cannot be ignored. Areas that need attention and improvement have been highlighted in this report and a blueprint for improving plant conditions is provided. Our bottling partners have committed to addressing these findings immediately.

We will work diligently with our bottling partners as they take action to ensure compliance with all laws and regulations that apply to workplace practices and conditions.

---

[1] Workplace Assessments in Colombia, Conducted by Cal Safety Compliance Corporation for The Coca-Cola Company 2005.

the better understanding of the situation, that Coca-Cola is an economic engine driving the advancement of this country, people here have a radically different opinion.[41]

AN INTERNATIONAL CAUSE CÉLÈBRE

58   While the company attempted to defend its position, the Killer Coke campaign continued to gain momentum. On December 31, 2005, the University of Michigan joined Rutgers, NYU, and several other U.S. colleges in banning all Coke products from its campus.[42]

59   The university's board of directors had earlier rejected Coca-Cola's audit of its Colombian bottlers through Cal-Safety Compliance Corporation, calling it "problematic."[43] As a for-profit corporation hired by Coca-Cola to undertake the audit, Cal-Safety did not meet the university's definition of independent. The university essentially agreed with the United Students against Sweatshops, a U.S.-based network of college students working to end sweatshops. It noted Cal-Safety's documented history of giving favorable reports to factories that were later discovered to have been involved in gross human rights violations.[44] The fact that factory audits typically took three hours and involved interviewing employees in offices provided by plant managers was also deemed unacceptable.

60   Taking its cue from the United Students against Sweatshops, the University of Michigan demanded,

- Unannounced factory visits to deny management the opportunity to hide abuses.
- More extensive interviews of employees in off-site locations. "U.S. Department of Labor investigations take roughly 20 hours to complete," it noted. "Worker Rights Consortium investigations often take hundreds of person hours over a period of months."
- Audits conducted by non-profit organizations with "experience or expertise investigating violations of associational rights overseas."[45]

61   In its coverage of the Michigan decision, the *Financial Times* noted that "Coke's public relations offensive [had] so far failed to slow the [Killer Coke] campaign's momentum." Furthermore,

> The value of the Coke brand has been edging down in recent years, following a series of blows to its reputation. Over recent years, the deaths [in Colombia] have become an international cause célèbre for labour rights groups and student activists, who accuse Coke of turning a blind eye to the murders. Anti-Coke campaigns have spread across more than 100 university campuses throughout the U.S., Canada and Europe, including the U.K., where activists are pushing for a nationwide student boycott.[46]

---

[41] Translated from an interview by El Tiempo. Diez universidades de Estados Unidos y Europa vetaron el consumo de Coca-Cola por presuntos nexos con 'paras', *El Tiempo (Colombia)*, January 4, 2006.

[42] In the fiscal year 2005, the University of Michigan had 13 contracts for selling Coca-Cola products, totaling $1.4 million. Products sold by Coca-Cola included Sprite, Dasani water, Minute Maid juice and PowerAde. U. of Michigan Becomes 10th College to Join Boycott of Coke, *The New York Times*, December 31, 2005.

[43] University of Michigan seeks probe of Coke's Colombia operations, *Atlanta Journal-Constitution*, June 17, 2005.

[44] United Students Against Sweatshops Statement, April 15, 2005 (www.killercoke.org/usascal.htm).

[45] Ibid.

[46] Coke struggles to defend positive reputation, *The Financial Times*, January 6, 2006.

Case 38

Managing Sexual Harassment at Coors (A)

Deanna L. Wittmer and Dennis P. Wittmer

1   In May 1996, morning dawned over Golden, Colorado. A cloudless sky bore its uniquely deep Colorado-blue shade. Above the sprawling buildings of the Adolph Coors Brewing Company, North Table Mountain and South Table Mountain stood like angry, red guardians of the small western town and its enormous brewery. Tracy Brown, director of the conditioning department at Coors, reflected on the events of a 2-month investigation. She was dismayed, disgusted, and exhausted. The past few months had been a tangle of deceit and shock. And today, she knew, would be no less difficult.

2   A decision-making committee, composed of Coors managers and investigators, had to choose which of its long-standing employees to believe about alleged sexual harassment. The team had to sort through a significant amount of conflicting information to establish what would be best for Coors and everyone involved. There were issues of credibility of the alleged victim and perpetrator. There were even issues of defamation related to the claims made about the perpetrator, because even criminal charges had been brought against him. The lurid details revealed in the investigation made this quite a mess. Brown's recommendations would weigh heavily on the team in its final decision. Brown knew she would play an important role in determining the future of her department and of Coors.

THE PROBLEM

3   The committee had to bring closure to a complex investigation and decide what disciplinary action, if any, to take concerning charges of sexual harassment. An investigation began concerning issues of theft, time card fraud, and unauthorized drinking in the conditioning department. Brown was relieved that she had gotten rid of some reprehensible employees regarding these violations, but the process had been complex and frustrating. Those involved had gotten more than they bargained for, including a death threat.

4   But the specific issue today involved alleged sexual harassment on the part of Ernie Adams against Lynn Thomas, coworkers in the conditioning unit of Coors Brewery. In the course of the larger investigation involving theft and time card fraud, allegations of sexual harassment

Material for this case preparation came from public sources. Principal sources include *James v. Coors Brewing Co. and Yvonne Mannon, 73 F Supp 2d 1250 (D. Colo. 1999); Citizen Coors* by Dan Baum, 2000; and stories from the *Denver Post, Rocky Mountain News,* and *The Wall Street Journal.* Names have been changed in light of the sensitive nature of the material included. This case was prepared for class discussion and learning, rather than to illustrate effective or ineffective handling of a management situation. Special thanks and appreciation are extended to Tara Scherlschligt for her information, insights, and for reviewing drafts. Thanks to Tara for assisting in the preparation of the case so that other managers might be better able to anticipate and deal with situations presented in this case. Thanks also to John Flanders, corporate counsel for Coors Brewing, and Dan Satriana, Jr., of Hall & Evans and counsel to Coors, for their assistance and for reviewing drafts of the case. Readers should be aware that some language is quite explicit and potentially offensive. The authors have retained the language in order to provide a realistic portrayal of the situation. Finally, the authors wish to thank the anonymous reviewers and the *CRJ* editors who reviewed manuscripts and recommended important changes to make the case more clear and useful. Such reviewers often receive little more than the professional satisfaction of contributing to their profession.

had surfaced, and an investigation into these charges was complete. Lynn Thomas alleged that Adams had sexually harassed her numerous times over a several-year period. The allegations were serious, including the alleged assault that resulted in criminal charges being filed against Adams. Now a committee had to decide what, if any, disciplinary action was warranted against Ernie Adams. In fact, what Brown didn't yet know about this day and this coming meeting was that the decision that would be made concerning Ernie Adams' fate would drive her and Coors into a complicated battle for their professional reputations.

5   By the spring of 1996, Tracy Brown had been at Coors for 22 years. She had extensive technical training and had worked in several departments. She started at the Coors porcelain company in 1974, and she advanced to positions as tour guide, warehouse clerk, and beer flow coordinator. Later, she held several supervisory and managerial positions before she was promoted to director of conditioning in 1994. When Brown took the helm in conditioning, it didn't take long for rumors to start that she wanted to "clean up" the department. Soon after assuming her duties as director of conditioning, she began efforts to understand and correct the workings of the department.

6   The conditioning department had a reputation as a tough place to work. After Coors beer was brewed, it went to conditioning, where it was aged, blended, filtered, and checked for purity and alcohol content. The department was spread throughout several buildings, spanning miles of area. It included basement sections and dark tank storage. It was cold, damp, and remote. Although in 1996 it had 300 to 400 employees, very few women worked in the conditioning department. On March 5, 1996, one of those women, Barbara Winters, came to Brown in distress. Winters reported that Lynn Thomas, whose job it was to scrub the glass-lined, 1,400-barrel beer tanks, had left work at the end of the day in tears. "I'm never coming back," Thomas had said. She had been harassed and her life had been threatened, she told Winters. Winters told Brown that the problem might be rooted in ongoing illicit activities within the department.

7   Two days later, Brown met Thomas to discuss the situation. They met in downtown Golden at a small drugstore restaurant away from Coors; Thomas was too frightened to set foot on the company's premises. As the story began to unfold over the next several weeks, Brown was shocked. It was like peeling an onion: The complexities of the situation were deeply layered, and it made you want to cry.

8   Thomas told of schemes within the department to change time cards and earn overtime. Employees were stealing Coors property and drinking on the job. They were also sneaking away from the Coors grounds for 2- and 3-hour breakfasts and lunches; their pagers worked for a 10-mile radius, and they could be back at work in minutes if required. Two men were at the center of these activities. Two of the conditioning unit employees and reputably ring leaders of the schemes, Bob Jacobsen and John Leaver, devised a way to keep fellow workers from snitching: They drew people into their circle by giving them overtime hours that were never worked. "Hey, we gave you a few extra hours this week," they'd say. Suddenly, their fellow employees were in on it and risked punishment if the plan was uncovered.

9   Soon a rumor leaked that one of the women in the department might tell director Brown. Jacobsen and Leaver took action to protect themselves. On March 5, at the end of the workday, they allegedly trapped Thomas in "the cage," a small room in the basement used for breaks and storage. According to Thomas, Leaver poked her in the chest and said, "You dumb c***, you better learn to keep your mouth shut. How would you like a shotgun blast to the back of your f****** head? How would you like me to snatch your pretty little daughter out of her bed?" They yelled at her for 45 minutes before she escaped crying and fled home. Two days later, at the meeting in downtown Golden, she divulged all she knew to Brown and a massive investigation was launched.

10   On April 4, an anonymous letter was received in Coors's in-house mail. It threatened the lives of Tracy Brown, her children, and two Coors investigators. A police psychologist and his staff assessed the threat to be very real. That weekend, Coors housed those who were

threatened, as well as Barbara Winters, at a hotel under tight security. As an extra step of caution, Coors put the spouses and children of those threatened into the hotel as well. Prior to the death threat, Thomas' dog had been poisoned and her furnace had been tampered with. After the threat was received, Coors installed security systems in the houses of all of these families and increased security at Thomas' home to 24 hours a day. In addition, all of those involved went through self-defense training and counseling.

11   The Jefferson County Sheriff's Department became involved in the case when the threats were made. Sheriff's deputies interviewed Thomas about Jacobsen and Leaver, and restraining orders were issued against them. On April 23, deputy sheriffs interviewed Thomas again. When they asked her if there was anyone else she was having trouble with at Coors, she brought up the name of Ernie Adams, an African-American senior specialist making about $59,000 a year in the conditioning department. She alleged that Adams had sexually harassed her 300 to 400 times over the 8 years she worked in conditioning.

12   That was the first any investigators had heard of Adams in 2 months of questioning. Thomas had not mentioned his name until then, she said, because there had been more pertinent and dangerous issues. Once she had restraining orders against Jacobsen and Leaver and 24-hour security at her house, she could think about other harassment she had encountered. "Ernie Adams was not on my mind," she said. "My life had been threatened, my daughter's life had been threatened. That's [Ernie Adams] not what was on my mind." Adams was then included in the ever-growing probe into the conditioning department.

13   In addition to its internal investigators, Coors hired two independent investigators. Ralph and Chuck Richardson, who were brothers, were hired from an outside firm. In the following year, Coors' internal investigators, human resources manager Kurt Barnes, conditioning supervisor Paul Walker, Brown, and the Richardsons conducted over 150 interviews on more than 75 people. Thomas was interviewed more than 20 times.

14   By the end of April 1996, three employees from the conditioning department were terminated: Leaver, Jacobsen, and Tom Ross (another employee in the conditioning unit). Leaver was fired for gross misconduct (which includes falsifying company records and all forms of harassment) and dishonesty, Jacobsen for gross misconduct, and Ross for dishonesty. Each of them brought their cases to the Coors appeals board, a process where the appellant challenges his or her termination in front of a panel of five randomly chosen Coors employees. Three peers and two managers comprised the board, along with one nonvoting chairman from human resources. Ross retained his job with written warnings and a suspension. The terminations of Leaver and Jacobsen were upheld. In addition, front-line supervisor Charlie Martin resigned. Ernie Adams, along with several others, remained to be dealt with.

15   The investigation was enormous. In the course of a year, Coors interviewed 76 employees and spent nearly $600,000. In a place where gossip spread faster than the plague, the whole brewery talked about it. Of considerable concern were the employees of the conditioning department, who were expected to continue work as though there was nothing troubling the department. Although Brown met repeatedly with her department and revealed any information she could, many details were kept back. In-house and outside investigations remained underway, including criminal inquiries by Jefferson County. The press demanded information. Employees in the department felt a pressure unfamiliar to them.

16   Brown and her colleagues worried about morale at Coors. The company needed to stand behind its employees and protect its reputation.

THE LEGACY OF COORS

17   Adolph Coors Brewing Company boasted a history unique to today's fast-moving, colorful business world. The beer brewed in Golden was made with spring water born more

than 10,000 feet above sea level. It was flushed through 25 miles of rocky canyon walls, and in the place where Clear Creek ends its descent from the high country, Adolph Coors envisioned a brewery with deep integrity. Good, clean water, he believed, was the root of brewing the finest beer. He compromised little in his drive to make high-quality beer like he learned to do in his home of Prussia. In 1873, after stealing away to the United States, Coors and a partner began making beer in what is now Golden, a western suburb of Denver with its own unique heritage. Today, even, a sign hangs over Washington Street, the main drag in town, proudly declaring, "Welcome to Golden: Where the West Lives." Upon entering town, the distinct aroma of hops hangs heavy in the air. There is no mistaking the largest business in town: Coors Brewing Company.

18   Coors is a family business, run for most of its tenure like a "Mom and Pop" place. Adolph Coors, Adolph Coors, Jr., Bill Coors, and Peter Coors, four generations of chief executive officers and presidents between 1873 and 1993, walked the brewery halls, calling their employees by name and inquiring about their families. During Prohibition, Adolph Coors turned the brewery into a malted milk factory and kept almost all employees on payroll, even when there was no work. Employees were proud of their product, believing they brewed the finest beer in the country. Several times during the twentieth century Coors held over 70 percent of the market in many Western states.

19   The Coors family was in business to make high-quality beer, not just money. They refused to cut corners. Instead of cheap dry, milled corn, they used expensive rice. Bill Coors believed that the heat of pasteurization ruined freshly brewed beer, so he invented cold filtering. He insisted his distributors invest in refrigerated trucks and warehouses if they wanted to carry Coors beer, knowing of course that no distributor west of the Rocky Mountains could afford not to carry Coors. In opposition to the litter created by steel cans and pull tabs, Coors pioneered recycling programs and later invented aluminum cans and press tabs (the predecessor to what is now used to open aluminum cans). When other breweries began to fail or declared bankruptcy, the Coors men insisted that their employees not prey on the fallen operations to steal their business. Coors gave millions in philanthropy to schools, libraries, hospitals, and charities, but kept it hushed. "We give because it's right," said Adolph Coors, Jr. "This country has been very good to the Coors family and we owe a debt in return."

20   Coors' powerful history of vertical integration gave the family control over almost every aspect of their company. Within 2 years of opening his brewery, Adolph Coors built a malthouse, steam mill, bottling plant, and icehouse. Over the next 100 years, a can factory, bottle factory, porcelain/pottery company, energy company, construction company, and advertising agency were added. This mass authority, however, meant that the Coors family ran its business the way it wanted—no compromises.

21   Although the Coors family felt it was operating with integrity, Coors struggled with labor issues. While Adolph, Sr., had accepted unions, they were not known as particularly strong. Serious struggles with unions emerged in the late 1950s, and Coors became determined to rid the business of unions. A common strategy was to force a strike and then replace the strikers. In the 1960s, 15 building-trade locals were eliminated. Local 366 of the AFL-CIO called a strike in 1976, and although they spearheaded a nationwide boycott, the union was destroyed. Coors has been nonunion since then. Coors was not alone in not supporting unionization. As a percentage of the nonagricultural labor force, unions grew from the 1930s until the high point in the 1940s and 1950s. About a third of the workforce was unionized in the early 1960s, and that fell to a quarter during the 1970s, falling to a mere 12 percent in 1990.[1]

22   Over the last 40 years, Coors had confrontations with many organized groups. Like many businesses, Coors has had to deal with discrimination issues and claims. After Colorado ratified the Equal Rights Amendment in 1970, Coors hired its first women as production

workers. In the 1970s, the Equal Employment Opportunity Commission (EEOC) filed discrimination charges on behalf of Hispanics and African-Americans for its hiring policies. Gays were upset with the sexual-preference questions of lie detector tests used at Coors. In 1984, after several rather inefficient individual boycotts, groups representing women, Hispanics, blacks, homosexuals, and organized labor banded together to wage a 7-year boycott against Coors.

23   Human resources and employee relations offices at Coors replaced some of the functions performed by unions in terms of employee issues and problems. Coors had a values statement and strong policies related to discrimination, sexual harassment, and other workplace issues. For example, their employee handbook contained clear prohibitions against any form of discrimination or sexual harassment, including procedures for complaints and sanctions for violations of policies. In addition, Coors developed a conflict-resolution process that applied to all employees and management. This process allowed employees to file discrimination and sexual harassment claims directly to the Office of Employee Relations. Coors also developed an elaborate appeals process to deal with disputes about disciplinary actions. It was notable that three of five voting members were the peers of employees.

24   Despite challenges and troubles at Coors, most employees were happy. The money and perks flowed freely, as did the beer. However, the familial atmosphere of the company stunted its efficiency. By the early 1990s, there were employees who had been there more than 40 years, a few without defined jobs. Some of the employees had been there longer than the lifetime of Peter Coors, president at the time. Profits were shrinking and Coors' ranking in the beer market was declining. Thus, when Leo Kiely was drafted in 1993 as the first non-Coors president in the history of the company, it was to clean up the place. None of the Coors men had the heart, it seemed. Kiely cut the Coors payroll by almost 70 percent and told reporters, "I am here for the stockholder." A new chapter in Coors history began.

POLICIES AND CULTURE AT COORS

25   Despite its increasing efficiency and financial success, Coors faced employee conflict during the mid-1990s. In 1994, Coors rolled out a revised sexual harassment and discrimination policy, and all employees went through new training. The policy stated, "Coors Brewing Company is dedicated to an environment of trust, support and caring about our employees. . . . Any employee who engages in discrimination or harassment or retaliates against an employee because the employee made a complaint . . . is subject to immediate discipline, up to and including discharge." On February 23, 1996, Kiely issued a memo reiterating Coors' "zero tolerance" policy on harassment. "I want employees to know the importance of keeping our work environment positive for everyone," he wrote to all managers, supervisors, and team leaders. "It is your responsibility . . . to take such matters seriously and notify Human Resources of any complaint received. When harassment occurs it is a lose/ lose situation for both employees and the company." The zero tolerance policy stated, "Discrimination or harassment, in any form . . . is inappropriate, offensive and illegal. It is strictly prohibited in the workplace. . . . No employee who complains about improper conduct will be retaliated against for raising the concern."

26   Women at Coors, a support group dealing with women's issues at the company, worked with executives to design the 1994 policy. At the time, tank scrubber Lynn Thomas, a Coors employee since 1973, was on the board of Women at Coors. Although she was not on the subcommittee for sexual harassment, she helped women deal with work-related gender issues on a regular basis. In fact, she said she discussed several problems she herself was having with her work environment. Although she didn't use names, she described how her department was generally unfriendly to women. She was called a "brain-dead d**** b**

w****" on a regular basis. "B****," "c***," and "g***" were a typical part of workplace dialogue, even if they weren't always directed at her. Some men would leer at her, lick their lips, or try to grab her. Most mornings, she claims, as soon as she got to work she was asked about her sexual activities the previous night. She was uncomfortable with much of this behavior, but at the same time she wanted to fit into the unit. In fact, it was a "guy environment," said one of her coworkers and "a lot of people thought she was one of the guys."

27   Amy Chester, who was on the board of Women at Coors with Thomas, said that Thomas would discuss her workplace problems on a regular basis. Thomas reported to the group that she was physically harassed and called vulgar names. Men would relieve themselves in floor drains, Thomas told them. "Women were so intimidated there that they ate their lunches in the locker room because they couldn't stand to be in the lunchrooms," Chester said. Chester said Thomas reported an incident where a coworker "grabbed her in a remote area of production and she thought that she was going to be physically assaulted." Chester also remembered Thomas telling the group that she "complained to her supervisors on a regular basis, and in many cases the supervisors were in on this, so it was difficult to be heard in a situation like that."

28   Eventually, as Thomas became witness to many rule-breaking activities within her department, the harassment increased. When Bob Jacobsen and John Leaver cornered her in "the cage" at work and threatened her life, she had had enough. She refused to return to work.

CLAIMS AND COUNTERCLAIMS

29   After Thomas told Jefferson County sheriff's deputies that she had been sexually harassed, Coors began interviewing Adams about his relationship with Thomas. Pending investigation, he was suspended from work with pay on April 26 after a meeting with Barnes (human resources manager), Walker (Adams' supervisor), and two investigators. In this meeting, after a discussion about sexual harassment, Adams said, "There is no reason why a woman would say I've done anything inappropriate." In fact, Adams reported, Thomas "wasn't like an ordinary girl." He said he had seen her grab her male supervisor, Charlie Martin, in the crotch area. Thomas and Adams would joke around, Adams said, and hug each other. She would consistently use bad language, make off-color comments, and touch her coworkers. "She was like one of the guys," Adams described. "I didn't think she carried herself in a lady's way." When they did touch each other, they'd play and tease, put their arms around each other. "She never told me to stop," he said. Adams declared, however, that he had never touched her breasts or her buttocks.

30   Thomas told a different story. She claimed that on at least one occasion Adams had attacked her and tried to remove her clothing. He had also "felt her up" by putting his hand on her crotch and her breasts, she said. Other times, he had bumped her in the butt, grabbed her, tried to kiss her, and pressed his body against her. She would squirm and try to get away. Thomas' work partner Roy Pena said that when Thomas would tell Adams to leave her alone, Adams would just laugh. Thomas also claimed that she would ask Pena to protect her from Adams' advances.

31   Thomas admitted horsing around, telling dirty jokes, and using bad language. When men called her names, she said, she would call them "c***s*****" in return. She felt it was her only choice. During her first 3 years in the conditioning department, Thomas reported, no one even talked to her outside of necessary workplace conversations. Participating in the vulgar environment was the only way to make peace and make friends in the department, she said. Trying to behave differently would only earn you trouble. "In order for you to survive in this department, you did what these people said," Thomas said. Pena agreed. "I would have to say three-fourths of the conditioning department broke rules," he said.

"If you didn't go along with the whole group, you weren't part of the group." Don Williams, senior Coors investigator, said his first impression when talking to Thomas was "she was very much traumatized and in fear for her life and the life of her family."

32   Thomas said she had complained to several supervisors about the department's hostile atmosphere, but according to Coors records there was very little proof she had ever spoken of harassment to anyone. Besides the witnesses from Women at Coors, only one complaint could be found. Adams' supervisor at the time the investigation started, Paul Walker, had written a memo to Brown dated March 25, 1996, that said Thomas had "divulged that she was also being told things by some of the guys that made her feel bad. Specifically that the area smelled like tuna." No other documented complaints of sexual harassment could be found. "Supervisors didn't document things, they didn't take women's issues seriously. They were good friends. They were all in this good' ol boy situation," Thomas said. "Tracy was the first person out of 8 years that tried to do something." Investigator Chuck Richardson said he believed Thomas had tried to report the harassment but that it "fell on deaf ears."

33   Thomas' direct supervisor, Charlie Martin, later admitted to knowing that Thomas was being harassed and in fact said he had done nothing to prevent it. Martin, who was the supervisor to whom Thomas would first report her complaints, also covered for Leaver and Jacobsen in some of their illicit activities. When he was interviewed during the investigation, Martin was angered. "You're asking me to testify and burn people for things that have been going on for years," he said. Although he was aware of his employees' wrongdoing, no one in his department was ever written up, he said. In fact, Martin was the first person Thomas called after the incident in the "cage" with Jacobsen and Leaver. "Lynn, I know what's going on," Thomas reported Martin said to her. "I can't control these men. I'm going to lose my job. I have been here for 35 years. I can't control them." Martin also admitted that he thought his supervisor, Tracy Brown, had gotten her job because she was a woman. Overall, it seemed he contributed significantly to the subculture where many troublesome issues festered. "I rely on the team leaders to know what's going on in their area and to react to things appropriately," Brown said. "I don't believe that Charlie [Martin] was doing that, because we had a lot of bad stuff going on." As the investigation revealed this, Brown told Martin that he was incompetent. She gave him the option of resigning before she fired him. He took his severance package and left Coors.

34   According to investigator Chuck Richardson, Thomas "was intimidated and lived in fear." Richardson was also skeptical of Adams' sincerity, he said, because in interviews Adams repeatedly returned to the subject of Thomas, even when her name was not raised by any of the interviewers. "Adams became irate, and it just wasn't—it wasn't appropriate to become irate at that point," Richardson said. During investigative interviews, a few women admitted that they regularly steered clear of Adams. Lily Sellers, who at the time of the investigation had worked for 17 years in the can plant and the brewery, said Adams had a reputation as a harasser at Coors: "Somebody you wanted to stay away from. Just not somebody you want to be caught alone with." Hanna Jones, a 12-year veteran of the conditioning department, said Adams had a reputation as a womanizer. She also said Thomas had told her of several occasions she had been harassed by Adams.

TIME FOR A DECISION

35   On May 7, 1996, Brown and three investigators met again with Adams. "She has one of the nastiest mouths in the whole brewery," Adams reported about Thomas. He said, "What have I done to anybody to make them bring me into something like this? I was an outsider." Adams insisted repeatedly that he was telling the truth. He asked that investigators speak with Charlie Martin, Rick Alvarez, and Roy Pena to confirm his stories about Thomas' crude behavior. When investigators tried to confirm Thomas' claims that she had reported

Adams to her supervisors, there was no paper trail. There was documentation, however, of two formal complaints she had made before 1994, demonstrating her ability to successfully use the "system" to lodge protest.

36   On May 14, 1996, Adams met with Barnes of human resources, Adams' direct supervisor Paul Walker, and Coors investigator Larry Smith. Before the meeting, their third meeting with Adams, Tracy Brown and the decision-making team had to decide his fate. This decision was difficult, and it had repercussions either way. Thomas was obviously distressed and scared, but there had been many issues for her to deal with. Some of her coworkers, especially from Women at Coors, said she had talked about her struggles with Adams, yet others could not corroborate her stories. She said she had gone to several managers, but there was very little proof of this. According to Adams, he and Thomas had an amicable relationship, one that included sexual jokes and crude banter. But Thomas said it had gone much further; she said Adams had touched her inappropriately and at least once had pinned her down and tried to tear off her clothes. Thomas said she repeatedly asked her work partner Pena to protect her from Adams' physical advances, yet she continued to use restrooms and telephones near Adams' office.

37   The prior months had also uncovered negligence on the part of Thomas' supervisor, and there was no doubt she had been subject to harassment from John Leaver and Bob Jacobsen. But the charges against Adams were purely for sexual harassment, not theft, fraud, or drinking. It seemed obvious that the predominately male workplace was difficult for women and that there were many barriers for them. Coors had revamped its sexual harassment policy in 1994 and had announced its "zero tolerance" for harassment. Thomas and Adams had each worked over 20 years at Coors. They had not been problem employees. The team's decision would affect the entire conditioning department and perhaps set an important tone for every employee at Coors.

38   Brown knew that swift, firm action had to be taken. It was time for the group to make a decision about Adams. What should she recommend the group decide about Adams and the sexual harassment charges against him?

ENDNOTE

1. For further information about American labor unions, trends, and discussions of worker rights in the context of government and union roles, see Richard Edwards, *Rights at Work: Employment Relations in the Post-Union Era* (1993) and Thomas Kochan, Harry Katz, and Robert McKersie, *The Transformation of American Industrial Relations* (1994).

EXHIBIT 1
Organizational Chart of Key Players in the Conditioning Unit

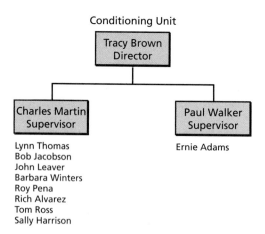

Conditioning Unit

Tracy Brown
Director

Charles Martin
Supervisor

Paul Walker
Supervisor

Lynn Thomas
Bob Jacobson
John Leaver
Barbara Winters
Roy Pena
Rich Alvarez
Tom Ross
Sally Harrison

Ernie Adams

EXHIBIT 2   Coors Discrimination and Harassment Policy

Coors Brewing Company
Golden, Colorado

PERSONNEL POLICY
CI—18:1-D

VICE PRESIDENT, HUMAN RESOURCES	TITLE D-1: DISCRIMINATION & HARASSMENT	EFFECTIVE DATE July 27, 1994		
Rwzlnt (signature)	ORIGINAL ISSUE DATE 4/20/92	REVISION 2	PAGE 1	OF 2

Coors Brewing Company (CBC) is dedicated to an environment of trust, support and caring about our employees as defined by "Our Values". We strive to create an atmosphere of mutual respect for all employees and job applicants. Discrimination, harassment of any sort and intimidation in the workplace are, therefore, prohibited, whether committed by supervisory or non-supervisory personnel. Any employee who engages in discrimination or harassment or retaliates against an employee because the employee made a complaint of discrimination or harassment or participated in an investigation of a claim of discrimination or harassment, is subject to immediate discipline, up to and including discharge. It is the responsibility of management, supervisors and all CBC employees to comply with this policy.

DISCRIMINATION
Discrimination is against the law and is against Company policy and will not be tolerated. CBC handles all matters pertaining to employees and job applicants without discrimination based on race, religion, color, national origin, age, gender, sexual orientation, disability or veteran status.

SEXUAL HARASSMENT
Sexual harassment is against the law and is against Company policy and will not be tolerated. Sexual harassment is defined as unwelcome sexual advances, requests for sexual favors and other verbal or physical conduct of a sexual nature when:

- Submission to such conduct is an explicit or implicit condition of employment,

- Submission to or rejection of such conduct is used as a basis for employment or promotion decisions, or

- Such conduct unreasonably interferes with an employee's work performance or creates an intimidating, hostile or offensive working environment.

Whether a particular behavior is sexual harassment may depend on the circumstances and it is not possible to provide a complete list of behavior constituting sexual harassment. Clear examples include unwanted physical contact or sexually-oriented propositions. Foul language, obscene gestures and sexually explicit jokes, remarks or pictures may also create an intimidating, hostile or offensive work environment. Employees who are offended by such behavior are encouraged to advise the offending party and ask him or her to stop.

EXHIBIT 2   (continued)

Page 2 of 2

HARASSMENT AND INTIMIDATION

Any other forms of harassment or intimidation based on
personal characteristics are offensive and are inappropriate
in the workplace. Harassment or similar unacceptable
behaviors that create a hostile, intimidating, or offensive
environment, or that are used as a condition of employment or
a basis for a personnel decision, are specifically prohibited
by CBC.

COMPLAINTS AND VIOLATIONS

Any employee who is found to engage in discrimination,
harassment or intimidation in the workplace will be subject to
disciplinary action, up to and including dismissal for the
first offense (see policy W-3: Work Rules & Corrective
Discipline). An employee may be held individually liable for
discrimination, harassment, or intimidation and subject to the
same financial penalties that may be imposed upon employers
under state or federal law.

Employees with complaints about discrimination or other forms
of harassment should report the matter to any one or more of
the following:

- their supervisor or team leader, or their supervisor's or
  team leader's management,

- an Employee Relations Representative (on weekends and
  evenings, through pager 234-4254; deaf employees add a *1
  after entering their phone number),

- any attorney in the CBC Law Department.

All complaints will be kept confidential among those parties
involved (including the accused) to the extent possible.
Employee Relations must be notified of any complaints
received. All complaints will be investigated to the extent
appropriate. In some cases, investigation or resolution of
the problem may require additional disclosure; e.g. to legal
counsel. Retaliation or intimidation resulting from a
complaint of discrimination or harassment is prohibited.
Filing a false complaint, however, is subject to policy W-3:
Work Rules & Corrective Discipline; specifically, dishonesty.

EXHIBIT 3
Coors' Zero
Tolerance Policy for
Harassment

Zero Tolerance for Harassment

As set forth in its policy on Discrimination and Harassment, Coors Brewing Company will not tolerate discrimination or harassment, in any form, whether on the basis of race, religion, color, national origin, age, gender, sexual orientation, disability, veteran status or other personal characteristics.

Such behavior is inappropriate, offensive and illegal. It is strictly prohibited in the workplace.

Harassment is verbal or physical conduct that belittles or shows hostility or aversion toward individuals or groups because of these characteristics.

Harassing behavior includes, for example:

1. Epithets, slurs, jokes, negative remarks or stereotyping;
2. Threatening, intimidating or hostile acts;
3. Or, written or graphic material that demeans, belittles or shows hostility or aversion toward individuals or groups and that is sent to another employee, or posted or circulated in the workplace.

Employees who engage in such harassment are subject to disciplinary action up to and including discharge for the first offense.

Any employee with a complaint of harassment should report the matter as set forth in the Discrimination and Sexual Harassment policy, which is attached to this statement.

No employee who complains about improper conduct will be retaliated against.

EXHIBIT 4   Coors Values Statement

Our Values

Our corporate philosophy can be summed up by the statement, "Quality in all we are and all we do." This statement reflects our total commitment to quality relationships with customers, suppliers, community, stockholders and each other. Quality relationships are honorable, just, truthful, genuine, unselfish and reputable.

We are committed first to our customers for whom we must provide products and services of recognizably superior quality. Our customers are essential to our existence. Every effort must be made to provide them with the highest quality products and services at fair and competitive prices.

We are committed to build quality relationships with suppliers because we require the highest quality goods and services. Contracts and prices should be mutually beneficial for the Company and the supplier and be honorably adhered to by both.

We are committed to improve the quality of life within our community. Our policy is to comply strictly with all local, state and federal laws, with our Corporate Code of Conduct and to promote the responsible use of our products. We strive to conserve our natural resources and minimize our impact on the environment. We pay our fair tax share and contribute resources to enhance community life. We boldly and visibly support the free enterprise system and individual freedom within a framework which also promotes personal responsibility and caring for others.

We are committed to the long-term financial success of our stockholders through consistent dividends and appreciation in the value of the capital they have put at risk. Reinvestment in facilities, research and development, marketing and new business opportunities which provide long-term earnings growth take precedence over short-term financial optimization.

These values can only be fulfilled by quality people dedicated to quality relationships within our Company. We are committed to provide fair compensation and a quality work environment that is safe and friendly. We value personal dignity. We recognize individual accomplishment and the success of the team. Quality relationships are built upon mutual respect, compassion and open communication among all employees. We foster personal and professional growth and development without bias or prejudice and encourage wellness in body, mind and spirit for all employees.

1/16/86   Adolph Coors Company

Case 38

Managing Sexual Harassment at Coors (B)

Deanna L. Wittmer and Dennis P. Wittmer

1   Paul Walker, Ernie Adams' supervisor, began the May 14, 1996, meeting with Adams by informing him that he was terminated for sexual harassment and dishonesty. Adams became irate. He cried and yelled. He asked if Coors investigators and managers had contacted the witnesses he had mentioned. There were people who could corroborate his stories, he said. In previous meetings, he had requested that these coworkers be interviewed. According to investigators, some had been contacted, but they didn't provide nearly enough information to free Adams from accusations. "Lynn Thomas is the worst f****** bitch in the whole company," Adams said before he left the room. "Everyone on the floor will tell you she's a slut."

INTERNAL APPEAL

2   At the May 14 meeting, Adams was informed that he could appeal his termination if he wished, and he immediately filled out the necessary paperwork to commence the process. Coors had an in-house appeal process available to anyone who wished to challenge Coors during a termination or other disciplinary action. This process allowed the terminated employee to present his or her case to five voting Coors employees. The appeal board was comprised of three peers and two members of management. The peers were from the same pay group as the appellant (examples might be production classification or construction classification). A nonvoting board chairperson from human resources (HR) was included to coordinate and oversee the appeals process.

3   Before the appeal hearing, a representative from HR was assigned to assist the terminated employee in the appeal process in order to assure that he received all of the information and guidance he needed. To construct the appeal board, the HR representative presented the appellant with randomly generated lists of Coors employees. Each list had three names. According to Coors policy, the appellant started with five lists total: three of peers and two of management members. The appellant was allowed to strike one name from each list, for a total of five names. The appellant was not required to strike any names. The final five

Material for this case preparation came from public sources. Principal sources include *James v. Coors Brewing Co. and Yvonne Mannon, 73 F Supp 2d 1250 (D. Colo. 1999); Citizen Coors* by Dan Baum, 2000; and stories from the *Denver Post, Rocky Mountain News,* and *The Wall Street Journal.* Names have been changed in light of the sensitive nature of the material included. This case was prepared for class discussion and learning, rather than to illustrate effective or ineffective handling of a management situation. Special thanks and appreciation are extended to Tara Scherlschligt for her information, insights, and for reviewing drafts. Thanks to Tara for assisting in the preparation of the case so that other managers might be better able to anticipate and deal with situations presented in this case. Thanks also to John Flanders, corporate counsel for Coors Brewing, and Dan Satriana, Jr., of Hall & Evans and counsel to Coors, for their assistance and for reviewing drafts of the case. Readers should be aware that some language is quite explicit and potentially offensive. The authors have retained the language in order to provide a realistic portrayal of the situation. Finally, the authors wish to thank the anonymous reviewers and the *CRJ* editors who reviewed manuscripts and recommended important changes to make the case more clear and useful. Such reviewers often receive little more than the professional satisfaction of contributing to their profession.

Coors employees that will make up the appeal board were then randomly chosen from the remaining names on the lists. In Adams' case, Kurt Barnes presented Adams with seven lists of peers and five lists of managers. According to Barnes, he told Adams he could strike one name from each list. Adams struck five names total.

4   Typically, the immediate supervisor of the appellant presented Coors' side of the case. In Adams' appeal, director of conditioning Tracy Brown presented an overview of the investigation into the conditioning department. This provided appeal board members with information about the events leading up to Adams' termination. Brown mentioned that some conditioning department employees had been fired for fraud, theft, harassment, dishonesty, and drinking on the job. Next, Paul Walker, Adams' direct supervisor, presented Coors' case, explaining the action that was taken against Adams and why it was taken. Finally, Adams presented his case. Both Walker and Adams handed out packets of supporting information to the board.

5   Following the presentations, the appeal board requested to hear testimony from investigator Don Williams, who told the board that he felt at least one other woman had been subjected to harassment from Adams. Walker and Adams both left the room while the board called Williams to testify. It is up to the chairperson of the board to determine if any witnesses will be called. Williams was the only witness to testify.

6   The appeal board voted unanimously to uphold Adams' termination. "There are many different issues going on in the conditioning department," the board report said. "You can't tolerate people being subjected to harassment." Although the board thought that some of the presented information was rumor, a substantial amount was fact. "The board felt sorry for both Ernie and Lynn and felt the whole situation was tragic," the report said.

7   In the following 5 months, four more male Coors employees were fired in relation to the larger investigation. Three were fired for gross misconduct, and one was fired for sexual harassment and gross misconduct. Two of these men, including the one fired for sexual harassment, won their appeals and were given unpaid suspensions and written warnings. The other two terminations were upheld. By the time the investigation drew to a close, eight men had been fired. Three got their jobs back through the appeal process. Among the eight, Adams was the only African-American.

LAWSUITS ABOUND

8   Even after the last Coors employee was fired in the enormous investigation, security measures continued. Some people chose to discontinue the security because they no longer felt endangered or because they felt imprisoned, but others opted to continue for many more months. There had not been any further death threats. However, the first one was taken extremely seriously, especially by Thomas. The *Denver Rocky Mountain News* reported that even months after the death threat, "at home, with workplace rumors identifying her as a snitch, [Thomas] said she feared she was being stalked by some of her former coworkers." Thomas also reported seeing Adams drive by her house. "I didn't think I would live a year [after the threats]," Thomas told KUSA-TV in November 1997. In all, Coors used hotels, security systems, bodyguards, cell phones, self-defense classes, and the Jefferson County Sheriff's Department to protect current and former employees. Coors spent over $600,000 on the investigation, security, and preventative action. Of that amount, $325,000 paid for personal security services for Thomas, Coors wrote in a letter to the U.S. Equal Employment Opportunity Commission. Coors had supported Thomas all along and continued to stand behind her, even providing long-term disability until May 1998. Nonetheless, in November 1997, after Coors had so carefully watched and protected her, Lynn Thomas sued the company. She claimed she had been subjected to a hostile work environment, in violation

of Title VII of the Civil Rights Act of 1964. She also claimed Coors had provided negligent supervision in allowing this hostile environment.

9   Meanwhile, Ernie Adams had already filed his own suit against Coors Brewing Company, Lynn Thomas, and director of conditioning Tracy Brown. His suit alleged that Coors subjected him to disparate treatment on the basis of gender, disparate impact on the basis of race, breach of contract and/or promissory estoppel, negligence, intentional infliction of emotional distress, abuse of process, and defamation. Against Thomas personally, he asserted intentional interference with a contractual relationship, defamation, and abuse of process. Although Thomas would not talk with reporters, court documents included accusations that Adams tried to "squeeze her, kiss or touch her every time they met. Thomas alleged a 'near-rape' incident in March 1995. She said that Adams grabbed her from behind, took off her top and pulled her pants down."[1]

10   News stories abounded. Articles appeared in *The Wall Street Journal, Rocky Mountain News, Denver Post,* and *Denver Westward.* KUSA-TV, Denver's NBC affiliate, covered the story as well. In a November 13, 1997, *Denver Post* article, Coors spokeswoman Amee St. Clair said, "We're being caught in the middle. We're being sued by both sides, by the person whose complaint we took action on and who now doesn't feel it's enough, and by the person we acted against, who says we didn't do the right thing. . . . We're damned if we do and damned if we don't. But at the end of the day we at Coors knew we did the right thing, listened to folks, acted ethically and took corrective action."

11   Thomas settled out of court with Coors for an undisclosed but purported amount of about $200,000. Ernie Adams' case, however, went to trial. The U.S. District Court in Denver began hearing the case of Ernie Adams versus Coors Brewing Company, Lynn Thomas, and Tracy Brown in July 1999. The court threw out the claims of intentional infliction of emotional distress against all parties, and the claims of negligence and interference with a contract against Brown were eliminated.

12   Adams' remaining allegations were numerous. His suit claimed that Coors should have easily ascertained the falsities of Thomas' stories. Thomas was lying to cover up her own misconduct on the job, Adams claimed, and she behaved so crudely he could have sued her for harassment. The company was afraid of a sexual harassment lawsuit, Adams alleged, so Coors automatically took Thomas' side and dismissed the possibility that Adams could have been the victim.

13   Adams also accused Coors of breaking promises to contact the coworkers he said would support his stories. In the May 7 meeting with investigators and managers, Adams had specifically asked that Charlie Martin, Rick Alvarez, and Sally Harrison be interviewed. Coors had not done so, he claimed. In response, Coors representatives said there had been several roadblocks to using these sources. Charlie Martin, Thomas' direct supervisor who had admitted to knowing about most of the misconduct in the conditioning department, had already resigned. Although investigators claimed they had tried unsuccessfully to reach Martin by telephone, he was deemed largely dishonest and untrustworthy as a witness, and negligent as a supervisor, and therefore investigators could not rely on his opinion.

14   Sally Harrison, a Coors employee who grew up with Adams' wife, offered little information. Although Thomas claimed that Harrison had walked in on the "near rape" incident where Adams tried to take off her clothes, Harrison said she had seen nothing. Harrison did say, however, that she had repeatedly warned Adams to stay away from Thomas, or she (Harrison) would tell Adams' wife.

15   Rick Alvarez, another Coors employee who considered himself a friend to seven of the eight terminated men, was not interviewed by Coors until September 3, 1996. He told Chuck Richardson that Thomas talked about sex on a regular basis and that he had seen her grab a coworker in the crotch area. This information was vital to the investigation, Adams claimed, but it was not gathered until long after he was terminated.

16 Adams also alleged that the appeal process was unfair on several counts and that Coors failed to follow set procedures. Adams was presented with 11 pages of names of potential board members, while policy says it will only be five pages. "We don't just do two pages of management and three pages of peers simply because we would never fill an appeal board. People are too busy, just too tight," Barnes explained. HR had gone to the practice of using about twice as many lists as required so that a larger pool from which to draw appeals board members would be available. Although Adams struck only five names from the 11 lists, his supervisor Walker struck seven. Barnes said Adams didn't want to strike any others; Adams said he wasn't given the chance. Also, Adams claimed he struck the name of Sue Johnson, yet she sat on his appeal board. When Adams arrived at his appeal and saw her there, he did not raise any objection. During the trial, Coors pressed Adams for a reason he had not objected. Adams could not produce one.

17 Coors policy said that one representative from human resources would be present at the appeal: the nonvoting board chairperson. In Adams' appeal, Kurt Barnes was also present as a secretary. Barnes was there to take notes and then write the board's final decision, Barnes said. He did not participate in the appeal, nor did he have a vote.

18 Adams' suit asserted that he was denied information he requested prior to his appeal, such as interview transcripts. His notice of the appeal date also said it would be on Friday, June 7, which was actually a Wednesday. In addition, Coors policy says that one Coors supervisor, the direct supervisor of the appellant, will present the case for Coors. In Adams' appeal, there were two Coors supervisors. Brown presented an overview of the investigation, and Walker presented the evidence against Adams.

19 Adams said that the table of contents given to him prior to the hearing was different from the one given to him at the appeal. In the first, "Security—background report on the investigation" is listed; on the second, it says, "Background report on the investigation—Tracy Brown." He was unaware Brown would speak until the day of his appeal. All of these factors kept Adams from preparing a proper defense, he claimed. After Brown gave her overview, Adams said she refused to clarify that he was not involved in the harassment, theft, drinking, and fraud, even after he requested she do so. This was the basis of Adams' defamation charge against Brown, the only complaint that went to trial against her. In response, Brown said it is against policy for anyone to ask questions at that point of the appeal and does not remember Adams doing so. According to Barnes, at no time during the appeal or during the board's deliberation did anyone raise the issue of whether Adams was involved in theft, time card fraud, or threatening witnesses.

20 The chairperson of the appeal board determined any deviations from appeal policy, and Brown was in fact given permission by the chairperson to speak before Walker. The chairperson also determined whether witnesses would be called to testify. Although the board members could ask to hear from a witness, neither the appellant nor his supervisor could ask for witness testimony. In Adams' case, the board heard only from Coors investigator Don Williams, even though Adams had witnesses on Coors premises, ready to testify. In the appeal of the other man who was fired for sexual harassment, Gary Weishaupl, a witness for the appellant was allowed to testify. Weishaupl won his appeal. Adams lost his.

21 In her overview to the appeal board, Brown said Thomas was fearful that her life was in danger. In fact, Thomas had been threatened, her dogs had been poisoned, and her furnace had been tampered with. Although Adams had been spotted driving by Thomas' house, he was not included as a suspect. Because of Brown's statement, the board was misled to think that Thomas was directly afraid of Adams, he claimed. The judge disagreed with that point. He also disagreed with the allegation that Brown's overview made the board believe Adams had been involved in theft, fraud, and drinking. Halfway through the trial, he dismissed the single charge of defamation against Brown. Although Brown was no longer legally involved, she continued to attend the trial until its end. She had also been present at almost all of the depositions taken for the trial.

22 Adams further alleged that Thomas had given interviews to a TV station and newspapers, in which she defamed him by discussing his termination for sexual harassment. He had been labeled in the public as a sexual molester, Adams said, thus harming his professional and personal reputations. According to the defense, Thomas had talked with one newspaper, but her attorney had done an interview with the TV station, and Thomas had turned down countless other interviews.

23 Finally, Coors pressed the Jefferson County Sheriff's Department into pursuing a criminal investigation without foundation, Adams claimed. The county charged him with six counts of misdemeanor sexual assault. Thirteen months later, with Thomas' permission, the charges were dropped due to lack of evidence.

24 The trial lasted just over 3 weeks. The jury took 8 hours to deliberate. When Adams was awarded $1.4 million dollars, he banged on the table, pumped his fist in the air, and whooped with delight. The judge had to ask for decorum in the courtroom. The jury found in favor of Adams on every count except gender discrimination.

25 Those at the Coors table sat in disbelief. Coors managers and employees had exposed an ugly mess in one of their departments. They did what they thought was appropriate, and Coors representatives stood strongly behind their decisions in support of the people that they thought were the victims. It had not worked out to their advantage.

26 In a Denver *Rocky Mountain News* article on August 10, 1999, Coors spokeswoman Aimee St. Clair said the company had been caught in the middle in trying to enforce its "zero tolerance" sexual harassment policy. "We were sued by both sides, but at the end of the day, we believe we did the right thing, the best any corporation could do in that kind of situation." In another story in the *Rocky Mountain News,* "Workplace experts say the Coors case, though an extreme example, illustrates the minefield employers sometimes face in their stepped-up efforts against sexual harassment. Some suggest it could become a classic example in harassment seminars for corporate managers of everything that can go wrong no matter how careful an employer treats a worker's complaint."[2]

27 After Coors filed an appeal in the Tenth Circuit Court, the parties settled out of court. The settlement was not disclosed.

28 Senior management at Coors had much about which to reflect. What lessons could be learned from this difficult ordeal they had endured? What should Coors do to protect the company from future liability involving sexual harassment? As in any business, management must constantly be assessing, learning, and improving.

ENDNOTES

1. *Rocky Mountain News,* March 28, 1999. Adams sued Tracy Brown personally for negligent supervision, intentional interference with contract, and defamation. As reported in an Associated Press story, "He [Adams] said the brewery was out of line when it called in local law enforcement authorities and pressed them to file criminal charges against him, charges which were eventually dropped for lack of evidence." Of course, the allegations of sexual harassment surfaced in the investigation related to the death threats, and the charges were filed by the government, not Coors.

2. *Rocky Mountain News,* March 28, 1999.

Case 39

Morgan Stanley: A Leading Global Financial Services Firm

Suril Patel, Marc E. Gartenfeld, Dorothy Dologite, and Robert J. Mockler

INTRODUCTION

1   In June of 2005, in an extraordinary capitulation to a group of dissident former executives known as the "Gang of Eight," Morgan Stanley CEO Philip Purcell announced his resignation. Although Purcell tried to portray his departure as a dignified response to personal attacks against him, a continuing exodus of Morgan Stanley's senior executives, seemed to have finally turned the board of directors against the embattled chief.

2   In a letter to Morgan Stanley's 50,000 employees, Purcell said he would step down at the firm's next shareholder meeting in March 2006, unless the board finds a replacement before then. On June 30, 2005 a replacement was duly announced, John Mack a Morgan Stanley veteran of twenty five years would take over with immediate effect.

3   Purcell's departure was the latest chapter in a long-running battle between two cultures that have been at war since the investment bankers of Morgan Stanley agreed to merge with the retail stock salesmen of Dean Witter in 1997.

4   Morgan Stanley was originally founded in New York on September 5, 1935 as an investment bank by Henry S. Morgan, and Harold Stanley of J. P. Morgan & Co. along with others from Drexel & Co. In 1964, Morgan Stanley created the first computer model for financial analysis. By 1971 the Mergers & Acquisitions business was established along with Sales & Trading. In 1986, Morgan Stanley Group, Inc. became publicly listed.

5   On February 5, 1997, the company was acquired by Dean Witter, Discover & Co. (a.k.a. Dean Witter Reynolds) the spun-off financial services business of Sears Roebuck. The merged company was briefly known as "Morgan Stanley Dean Witter Discover & Co." until 1998 when it was known as "Morgan Stanley Dean Witter & Co." until late 2001. To foster brand recognition and marketing the Dean Witter name was dropped and the firm became "Morgan Stanley." The merger was controversial, and the firm lost some of its blue chip status with its corporate client base. The two firms could not have been more different. Morgan Stanley, a Wall Street investment bank founded in 1935, specialized in lucrative financing deals around the globe. Dean Witter, a chain of retail stockbrokers acquired by Sears in 1981, catered to small-time investors of limited means.

6   While Purcell's strategy for consolidating power at the firm succeeded, Purcell's vision of "one-stop shopping" in the financial marketplace faltered. Purcell, as Dean Witter's CEO, convinced Morgan Stanley that the financial supermarket concept could work by combining investment banking services with a strong sales force pushing stocks to Main Street investors at the retail level. Morgan Stanley Dean Witter, as the combined firm was originally called, could do everything from the financing of initial public offerings to the sale of that new stock to investors across the country. Citigroup and Merrill Lynch have succeeded in fusing high finance with retail commerce, but Morgan Stanley stumbled in its attempts.

7   The bursting of the dot-com bubble in 2000 hurt all the investment banks, but Morgan Stanley had the most difficult time recovering. In the preceding years, rivals such as Goldman Sachs, Lehman Bros. and Bear Stearns had outperformed it significantly.

This case was prepared by Suril Patel, Marc E. Gartenfeld, Dorothy Dologite, and Professor Robert J. Mockler of St. John's University. © Robert J. Mockler.

8   The situation got so bad that a coalition of eight former Morgan Stanley bankers sent a confidential letter to the company's board on March 3, 2005, suggesting some steps the directors might take to improve the company's performance. Instead, on March 28, Purcell demoted Stephan Newhouse, the firm's Morgan-Stanley-bred president, and replaced him with Zoe Cruz and Stephen Crawford, two loyalists from the Dean Witter side of the house. The next day several members of Morgan Stanley's management committee resigned from the firm. The Gang of Eight went public with their criticism of Purcell's management style, taking out newspaper ads to explain their views [Group of Eight, 2005].

9   In response to the criticism, Purcell agreed to spin off the firm's Discover card unit but maintained an iron grip on the levers of power at Morgan Stanley. But the high-level defections from the once-vaunted investment bank continued in April 2005, when 18 more executives departed for rival firms.

10   "The drip, drip, drip of top leadership at Morgan Stanley convinced institutional investors that the dissident group was right," says Richard Ferlauto, director of pension and investment policy at AFSCME.

11   In his resignation letter, Purcell focused on the Gang of Eight's unrelenting criticism of him and insisted that Morgan Stanley's one-stop shopping concept would eventually succeed.

12   "It has become clear that in light of the continuing personal attacks on me and the unprecedented level of negative attention our firm and each of you has had to endure, that this is the best thing I can do for you, our clients and our shareholders," Purcell wrote.

13   "I feel strongly that the attacks are unjustified, but unfortunately, they show no signs of abating. A simple reality check tells us that people are spending more time reading about the acrimony and not enough time reading about the outstanding work that is being accomplished by our firm."

14   John Mack in his acceptance speech as CEO of the firm said, "I am proud to return home to the world's premier financial services company and to the most talented team on Wall Street. Morgan Stanley remains the gold standard for client service, product excellence, teamwork and integrity in our industry. I look forward to working shoulder-to-shoulder with my colleagues old and new, across all of the Firm's businesses. I am eager to hear and execute their ideas on how we can bring out the best in Morgan Stanley and continue delivering innovation for our clients, growth for our shareholders, and opportunity for our employees."

15   Mr. Mack added, "I see four key priorities for our Firm. First, we need to ensure that we have the right people in place and that everyone is working together as a united team toward common goals. Second, we must ensure that we have the right strategy to enhance profitability in the face of intense global competition. Third, we need to focus relentlessly on our clients, delivering them the outstanding service and innovative solutions they expect from Morgan Stanley. And finally, we must assure productive working relationships with regulatory and public officials and other key constituencies of the Firm."

16   The main problem to be resolved was how to improve Morgan Stanley's company wide position against its competition and to achieve a winning edge over competitors within an intensely competitive industry. One key decision to be made was whether the company should offer a one stop shop service as advocated by previous management or focus on their core activities.

OVERALL INDUSTRY DESCRIPTION: FINANCIAL SERVICES INDUSTRY

17   Financial Services industry, as shown in Figure 1, was a term used to refer to the services provided by the finance industry. Financial services described organizations that dealt with

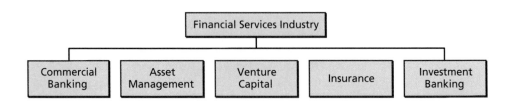

FIGURE 1
The Financial
Services Industry

the management of money. Commercial banks, investment banks, insurance companies, asset management firms, stock brokerages and venture capitalists are examples of the types of firms that comprised the industry, which provided a variety of money and investment and related services. The Financial services industry was the largest industry category in the world, in terms of earnings; as of 2004, the industry represented 20% of the market capitalization of the S&P 500 [Yahoo, 2006A].

Commercial Banking

18   This sector consisted of financial intermediaries that raised funds by collecting deposits from businesses and consumers via checkable deposits, savings deposits, and time deposits. It made loans to businesses and consumers. It also bought corporate bonds and government bonds. Its primary liabilities were deposits and its primary assets were loans and bonds. The term "commercial" was used to distinguish it from an investment bank.

Asset Management

19   This sector was comprised of mutual fund firms or divisions of financial services company. Often times this segment includes revenues from separate accounts, which can be thought of as "a mutual fund for one person" where the investment manager controls almost all the decisions. In banks, this segment has traditionally included the revenues and profits from money market funds sold to large corporations, or even a specialized money market fund set up for an individual corporation (this is called liquidity management). Typically, large corporations only keep in their bank accounts as much cash as required by the bank to offset the fees charged by that bank. Excess cash is then usually invested in a money market mutual fund or a short-term series of bonds. The fees earned by a bank for this management is often described under the "asset management" category [Morgan Stanley, 2006A].

Venture Capital

20   Venture capital is capital provided by outside investors for financing of new, growing or struggling businesses. Venture capital investments generally are high risk investments but offer the potential for above average returns. A venture capitalist is a person who makes such investments. A venture capital fund is a pooled investment vehicle (often a partnership) that primarily invests the financial capital of third-party investors in enterprises that are too risky for the standard capital markets or bank loans.

Insurance

21   The insurance industry consists mainly of insurance carriers, insurance agencies and brokerages. In general, insurance carriers are large companies that provide insurance and assume the risks covered by the policy. Insurance agencies and brokerages sell insurance policies for the carriers. While some of these establishments are directly affiliated with a particular insurer and sell only that carrier's policies, many are independent and are thus free to market the policies of a variety of insurance carriers. In addition to supporting these two primary components, the insurance industry includes establishments that provide

other insurance-related services, such as claims adjustment or third-party administration of insurance and pension funds.

Investment Banking

22 This sector consisted of banks that assisted public and private corporations in raising funds in the capital markets (both equity and debt), as well as in providing strategic advisory services for mergers, acquisitions and other types of financial transactions. They also acted as intermediaries in trading for clients. Investment banks differed from commercial banks, which take deposits and make commercial and retail loans.

INDUSTRY & COMPETITIVE MARKET SEGMENT: INVESTMENT BANKING

Overview

23 The original purpose of an investment bank was to raise capital and advice on mergers and acquisitions and other corporate financial strategies. As banking firms diversified investment banks came to fill a variety of roles. Figure 2 highlights how investment banks evolved and how the lines between commercial banks and investment banks began to become blurred as firms from both sectors attempted to deliver a one stop shop financial service to individual and institutional clients.

Institutional Securities

24 The Institutional securities business offered a full range of investment banking, sales & trading and research services. Investment Banking was the traditional aspect of investment banks which involved helping customers raise funds in the Capital Markets as well as in providing strategic advisory services for mergers, acquisitions and other types of financial transactions. Investment bankers prepared idea pitches that they brought to meetings with

FIGURE 2   **Investment Banking**

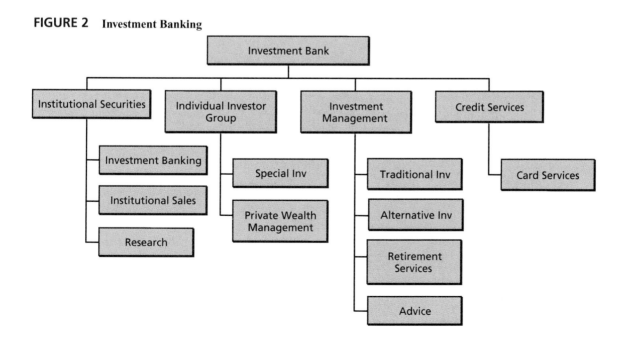

their clients, with the expectation that their efforts would be rewarded with a mandate when the client was ready to undertake a transaction. Once mandated, an investment bank would be responsible for preparing all materials necessary for the transaction as well as the execution of the deal, which may have involved subscribing investors to a security issuance, coordinating with bidders, or negotiating with a merger target.

25   Institutional sales and trading was often the most profitable area of an investment bank. In the process of market making, traders would buy and sell financial products with the goal of making an incremental amount of money on each trade. *Sales* was the term for the investment banks sales force, whose primary job was to call on institutional and high-net-worth investors to suggest trading ideas and take orders. Sales desks then communicate their clients' orders to the appropriate trading desks, who could price and execute trades, or structure new products that would fit a specific need [Morgan Stanley, 2006B].

26   The Research division of an Investment bank would review companies and write reports about their prospects, often with "buy" or "sell" ratings. While the research division generated no revenue, its resources were used to assist traders in trading, the sales force in suggesting ideas to customers, and investment bankers by covering their clients.

Individual Investor Group

27   The Private Wealth Management division of an investment bank provided wealth management solutions for high net worth individuals and their families. The wealth management business was typically built by securing, developing and managing relationships with wealthy individuals and family groups. The division aimed to build and protect client assets through effective asset allocation, risk analysis, strategy implementation, investment manager selection and implementation, client portfolio reviews and world class client service.

28   The Special Investments division was responsible for the structuring and marketing of alternative investment strategies developed and sponsored by the investment bank concerned. Typical alternative investment strategies employed by investment banks, included private equity, real estate and hedge funds.

Investment Management

29   The premise in the Investment Management division was to help clients meet their financial goals whether it be via the use of traditional investments or alternative investments. The division worked with a wide-ranging product line that featured advanced portfolio management techniques.

30   Responsibilities of the investment management division included developing and managing customized investment portfolios and discretionary funds for institutions, corporations, governments and foundations, designing and managing families of mutual funds, managing relationships with investors, and providing a full range of reporting and accounting services.

31   The Traditional investments division comprised of investing client assets into the traditional investment bond and equity markets, mutual funds, unit investment trusts and variable annuities. The Alternative investment division included Hedge Fund Strategies, managed futures, real estate and private equity.

32   The Retirement services division was concerned with assisting institutions and individuals with planning appropriate retirement procedures and policies so as to be in line with client goals and objectives. The Advice division comprised of financial planning, asset allocation services, trust services and estate planning. This division often assisted other divisions to help select appropriate strategies.

Credit Services

33   Many investment banks moved into the lucrative Credit service markets targeting both individual and institutional clients. Many capitalized on their well recognized global brand

names and introduced Credit cards to the general public. The companies cards grew rapidly and many became industry leaders globally challenging the more established credit card companies.

HOW THE INDUSTRY SEGMENT WORKS: THE BUSINESS PROCESS MODEL

34 The Investment banking industry was comprised of various segments as shown in Figure 3. The industry had evolved from its earlier foundations. The industry had forayed into industries that previously had been dominated by specialist financial services companies, e.g. credit services or had been dominated by Commercial banks.

35 Much of the change in the structure of the Investment and Commercial banks in the U.S. related to the Glass-Steagall Act being repealed by the Gramm-Leach-Bliley Act in 1998. The Glass-Steagall Act was initially created in the wake of the Stock Market Crash of 1929, which prohibited banks from both accepting deposits and underwriting securities. When the act was repealed many Commercial and Investment banks started to offer products and services that traditionally had been offered only by the other.

Products & Services

36 The Investment Banking industry as mentioned previously constantly evolved. One of the main courses of evolution was with investment banking products. Investment banks constantly invented new products, which were usually accompanied by very high profit margins since buyers were not sure how to value them. However, since these products could not be patented or copyrighted, they were very often copied quickly by other Investment Banks, and margins were forced downward as the pricing approached commodity pricing.

37 Throughout Investment Banking history, many theorized that all investment banking products and services would be commoditized, and the concentration of power in the bulge bracket would be eliminated. This however failed to happen, because while many products became commoditized, new ones were constantly being invented. For example, whilst trading stocks for customers became a commodity style business, creating stock derivative contracts were a very high margin business since the contracts were difficult to evaluate. In addition, while many products became commoditized, an increasing amount of investment bank profit came from proprietary trading, where size creates a positive network benefit (since the more trades an investment bank does, the more it knows about the market, allowing it to theoretically make better trades).

FIGURE 3 **Investment Banking: The Business Model**

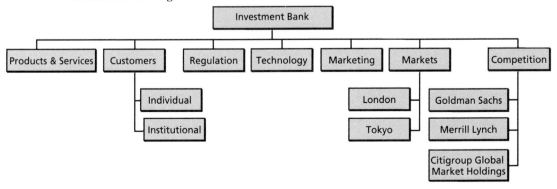

Public Offerings of Debt & Equity Securities

38   The public offering of debt and equity Securities was the foundation of investment banking. Typically there were four types of public offerings that investment banks conduct: IPO's of securities issued by companies that have never been issued any public securities. IPO's of new securities that companies that are already public have not previously issued. Further public offerings by issuing companies of securities that are already publicly traded. Finally public offerings by company shareholders of securities that are already publicly traded [Kuhn, 1990].

Public Trading of Debt and Securities

39   Most large investment banks maintained strong trading capabilities, especially the bulge bracket firms (the most prestigious firms such as Morgan Stanley, Goldman Sachs and Merrill Lynch). The trading focus of firms differed from firm to firm. The largest Wall Street securities firms maintained full-line services for retail customers; all bulge bracket investment banks performed block trading for institutional investors.

40   Securities underwriting was the process of floating securities of all kinds in the primary public markets. Groupings under this category would have been investment grade corporate bonds, high yield bonds, convertible debentures and preferred and common stock.

Mergers & Acquisitions

41   The original purpose of an investment bank was to raise capital and advise on mergers and acquisitions and underwrite securities. M&A was often the most visible and one of the most dynamic departments of an investment bank. In fact M&A took on such a significance providing a healthy percentage of corporate profits that the department grew towards independence from corporate finance at some investment banks. Subgroups within M&A specialized in specific industries.

Investment Research & Security Analysis

42   Research was a foundational pillar of the investment banking industry, supporting both the securities trading and investment banking operations. It was very important for large investment banks to field a top team of analyst stars. It symbolized a firms relative strength and expertise and as such were used to attract corporate clients and institutional investors.

43   As banking firms have diversified, investment banks came to fill a variety of roles such as offering brokerage services to public & institutional investors, providing financial advice to corporate clients, especially on security issues, providing financial security research to investors and corporate customers, market-making, in particular securities. Investment banks also moved into foreign exchange markets, private banking, asset management and bridge financing.

44   The keys to success when dealing with products and services were to offer a range of both to meet the many demands of various different types of clients both individual and institutional and utilise market opportunities to create further wealth for the companies shareholders. Additionally it is vital if the company were to succeed in meeting all the needs of clients that its staff be experts in their respective fields and have access to industry expertise. Also it was paramount that the full range of services were offered to all clients regardless of their geographic base. It was essential that both products and services were priced competitively in order for companies to retain and expand their respective client bases. Additionally it was essential that firms had established relations with the largest money managers to ensure a steady revenue stream. Client focus was arguably the most important aspect of the product and services categories, with appropriate focus it was likely that individual client objectives would be met and that client retention would be high.

Customers

45   Traditionally one of the fundamental differences between Investment and Commercial banks was the clientele that each carried out services for.

Individual Customers

46   As previously mentioned individual customers are those individuals that were primarily targeted by the commercial banks. These individuals made up the mass market.

47   These groups did however become targeted by the investment banking firms that had significant brokerage divisions offering clients full financial services solutions. Additionally the Investment banks also served those individuals known to the industry as high net worth individuals and families who typically were able and willing to invest half a million dollars minimum in specialized products and services.

48   The keys to success in the customer segment were that the quality of service was professional so as to meet all customer needs and wants, for example through the offering of innovative financial solutions through possibly the offering of customized products and services to improve returns on investments. Additionally the support services and the personal attention paid to clients and customers must be in place to address customers and client's questions, concerns and demands, this factor could be achieved largely through the deployment of a personal banker for the clients assisted by access to specialist teams of individuals to offer industry best advice and resources. Additionally a strong brand reputation is essential if a company is to secure and retain clients' and customers' business.

Institutional Clients

49   Whilst Commercial banks aimed their financial products and services at the mass market the Investments banks tailored the products and services to meet the needs of institutional investors like Pension funds, Mutual insurance groups, Governments, Financial Institutions and mid-large scale organizations.

50   Institutional investors carried great clout in the investment banking world. They often represented tens of thousands of employees, accounting for an extremely large pool of savings and contributions looking for appropriate investment paths. Institutional investors were very lucrative sources of business and as such competition to secure their business was very intense. However the bottom line for these clients as to who would win their business was that performance of the soliciting firm, along with reputation and industry experience and of course competitive fees.

51   Institutional investors were a largely risk averse group of investors as they represented the savings of many retirees and like minded conservative individuals. The institutional investors looked to invest in a variety of investment products to diversify their portfolio of investments and alternatively lessen their risk exposure to any one type of activity.

52   The keys to success in ensuring institutional investors were successfully served were varied. It was of primary importance that the quality of service offered to clients was above and beyond client expectations so as to retain their business.

53   The quality of the service was ranked highly if companies offered innovative financial solutions and engineering to client investment problems, for transferring derivative holdings to bespoke hedge fund investments. Also it was also important to institutional clients that companies had quality research departments with high quality staff and industry best knowledge as to what lucrative market opportunities the clients to invest in to meet financial objectives.

54   It was very important that personal attention was granted to corporate clients so as to ensure all clients' needs were noted and addressed appropriately and business was retained. It was especially important to provide specialist teams to offer clients customized solutions and advice to their particular problems and concerns. Finally it was also of importance that a firm had a leading reputation and brand name in the industry often attained through years of stable and above market performance and limiting regulatory problems. This was of extreme importance as a choice of well known and respected bank would be preferred by the members in the institutional pool.

Regulation

55 The Investment banking industry as mentioned previously went through substantial change due to improvements in technology, deregulation of financial services, regulatory changes, the globalization of the marketplace, and demographics. The Internet, along with high-speed computer systems, dramatically altered the way in which securities and commodities were bought and sold, almost completely automating the transaction process. At the same time, the number of financial services being offered is rising as firms look for new ways to attract the business of an increasingly wealthy and investment-savvy public.

56 The Securities and Exchange Commission (SEC) was the main regulatory body in the USA that oversaw the key participants in the securities world, including securities exchanges, securities brokers and dealers, investment advisors, and mutual funds, all functions of the investment banking industry. The SEC was primarily concerned with promoting the disclosure of important market-related information, maintaining fair dealing, and protecting against fraud. However crucial to the SEC's effectiveness in each of these areas was its enforcement authority. Each year the SEC brought hundreds of civil enforcement actions against individuals and companies for violation of the securities laws. Typical infractions include insider trading, accounting fraud, and providing false or misleading information about securities and the companies that issue them.

57 Though it was the primary overseer and regulator of the U.S. securities markets, the SEC worked closely with many other institutions, including Congress, other federal departments and agencies, the self-regulatory organizations (e.g. the stock exchanges), state securities regulators, and various private sector organizations.

58 In particular, the Chairman of the SEC, together with the Chairman of the Federal Reserve, the Secretary of the Treasury, and the Chairman of the Commodities Futures Trading Commission, served as a member of the President's Working Group on Financial Markets.

59 The keys to success when dealing with regulation was to ensure that the company met all SEC requirements and did not partake in any activities that would result in large penalties and damage the reputation of firms significantly enough to lead to an exodus of clients. It was key that the company conducted all its operations with integrity and in a professional manner meeting the highest ethical standards. Additionally the company should be seen to be proactive in the field of regulation and ethics by contributing to investor protection and the general integrity of the securities industry by participating in industry wide schemes.

Management

60 Many of the investment banks regarded their most important assets as their management and employees. Almost all employees were considered managerial level once they had graduated from their starting analysts roles. The senior management of the companies played major roles in guiding the firms to meet short and medium term targets as well as ensuring the firms where strategically enabled to continue to expand and grow according to future objectives in the long term. From the year 2000 onwards there was an increase scrutiny and interest in the management of firms and senior ranking officials after many high profile corporate scandals, all time high regulatory penalties and jail terms. It was of the utmost importance that management were respected, reputable and experienced in the industry in which they where working in.

61 The keys to success in the management category were that first management had the relevant experience and expertise in the respective fields and divisions to ensure industry best guidance and decision making. Additionally the reputation of management was extremely important often judged by management credentials, skills and regulatory compliance with guidelines. This was an especially important factor in the success of management due to high profile corporate scandals during the period in question. Related to the previous regulatory point it was essential that management were seen to have a strong corporate governance ethic instilled in the firm, a good way of ensuring this was to actively pursue a top down ethic instillation process to make sure selected principles were adhered to. Additionally it was essential that training and pay were of an industry best standard to allow the firm to retain and develop a management team that would guide the firm in a positive direction. Finally the firm should also be seen to promote diversity in the workforce by promoting women, the disabled and ethnic minorities to positions of management, this would help to enhance the firms reputation and brand as well as encourage all like minded and top potential management regardless of background to view the firm as an appealing firm to work in.

Operations & Technology

62　Every major investment bank relied upon considerable amounts of in-house software, created by their respective Technology teams, who were also responsible for Computer and Telecommunications-based support. Technology played a great part in shaping the business practices of the Investment Banking industry. In order to maintain competitive advantage, many firms embraced the technical challenge by making use of cutting edge technologies, pushing such technologies to the limit in order to drive business forward. The scope of the IT department in an investment bank ranged from the development of technical solutions to the provision of essential services, including network infrastructure, database servers and physical computational hardware.

63　The keys to success in regards to technology were that firstly a company be innovative in its IT operations. This would allow it to offer unmatched services to potential clients in regards to passing on efficiency savings specifically addressing cost and time expenses. Another key to success was to have systems and processes that were secure to protect confidential client information.

64　Innovation and security would be deliverable dependent on the caliber and competence of staff, therefore a high quality IT personnel were needed. Online tools and information were also a key to success as part of a firm's marketing, sales and information commitments to all stakeholders of the firms. Without a significant web presence firms would be unable to operate and compete on a global scale. Finally due to the timely nature of arbitrage opportunities and the general sensitive nature of the financial markets as a whole it is extremely important that the systems and operations in place allow the company to deliver time sensitive documents quickly and efficiently.

Marketing

65　Marketing was viewed as an important activity in the field of Investment banking. Many firms differentiated themselves by the marketing and sales efforts and brand name in the industry was an essential key to success. The user friendliness of the company's online resources was especially important due to the fact that this was the global access point to the firm's results, strategies and what differentiated the firm from others. In addition the firm's sales and distribution channels and cross selling of products and services was essential to the ongoing revenue generating activities of the firm.

Geographic Scope

66　The Geographic scope of a firm was an important factor in determining to what degree a firm would penetrate lucrative foreign markets. It was essential that firms had divisions and representatives so as to develop a reputable name in foreign markets from which to secure highly sought government, institutional and high net worth investor clients. Most of the larger firms had an established traditional markets based in North America, Europe and Japan.

67 These markets had delivered tremendous gains over the past few decades and growth and expansion still remained, however the most potential lucrative opportunities were to be seen in the newly formed emerging markets.

68 The emerging markets comprised of India, China, Brazil, Russia and other high growth largely Asian and South American countries. These countries offered many opportunities for growth for the investment banks and with the cooling down of traditional markets the firms to remain competitive were extremely interested in pursuing and establishing operations in these markets.

Competition

69 The business of investment banking was intensely competitive and the general trend towards one stop shopping and globalization had made it even more so. The blurring lines of competition between the heavily backed commercial banks and the specialist investment banks had also added to increase in competitive intensity within the industry. The main emerging competitors of Morgan Stanley in their Investment banking activities were Goldman Sachs, Merrill Lynch and Citigroup Global Market Holdings.

Goldman Sachs

70 Goldman Sachs traditionally possessed the Midas touch in the investment banking world. A global leader in mergers and acquisitions advice and securities underwriting, Goldman offered an array of investment banking and asset management services to corporate and government clients, as well as institutional and individual investors. It owned Spear, Leeds & Kellogg Specialists, one of the largest market makers on the NYSE, and was also a leading market maker for fixed income products, currencies, and commodities. The firm was a focused, specialist firm with a highly centralized management structure.

71 Goldman's business fell into three segments: Investment Banking; Trading and Principal Investments; and Asset Management and Securities Services. As Goldman's perennial rank among the top companies in its industry attests, the world's most venerable and profitable companies entrusted Goldman with their corporate financial and advisory needs.

72 Goldman had some government and high-net-worth individual clients, but unlike some of its rivals that rushed to diversify operations and income sources, Goldman focused almost exclusively on institutional clients, a large part of Goldman's revenues came from the lucrative trading and M&A markets.

73 Goldman Sachs aggressively pursued international expansion. The firm acquired a 7% stake in Sumitomo Mitsui Financial Group, Japan's second-largest banking group, that boosted both its presence and its ability to win potentially lucrative M&A business in Japan. The firm also formed a joint venture with Gao-Hua Securities to offer investment banking services in mainland China.

74 Additionally, Goldman also established a foothold in Australia by acquiring a 45% stake in JB Were, one of Australia's largest brokerages [Hoovers, 2006A].

75 Goldman Sachs was strong in offering a wide range of products and services, Goldman concentrated primarily on institutional clients focusing upon its Mergers and Acquisitions division in particular. In addition its staff were regarded as the highest caliber in the industry and its industry expertise was second to none. In regards to pricing the company operated at a premium pricing level but this did not harm its profitability as clients were willing to compromise price for the quality of service advice and products the firm offered. In addition Goldman also had established relations with the largest money managers in the industry allowing them to secure large institutional clients and block others from tapping this large revenue stream.

76 The firm was rated as moderate in regards to its global presence. Although the firm operated in the major markets its significantly lower personnel number highlighted in Figure 4 did not allow for the same global expansion as its competitors.

77   In regards to the customer category once again Goldman Sachs performed well. The company offered a quality of service that was amongst the best in the industry to both its institutional and individual clients and customers.

78   The company was able to offer a superior service largely due to its expert specialist teams and highly trained personnel. Clients both institutional and individual were attracted to the firm largely due to its excellent reputation and brand name.

79   One area where Goldman did lag behind others was in regards to the attention it paid to its customers. Due to personnel constraints it was unable to focus as much time as competitors, however this was largely confined to less lucrative individual customers. Institutional clients received an industry leading service. Institutional clients also had access to quality market performance reports, strategies and recommendations that the firm's research department developed for each client individually.

80   Goldman Sachs performed admirably in the regulation category. The highly publicized financial scandals seemed to have not affected Goldman as significantly as they have many of the financial services firms. The firms integrity, professionalism and high ethical standards are regarded as excellent to both individual and institutional investors. Additionally the company regularly sponsors and participates in industry organizational ethical and corporate governance events and thus ranks highly in this category. Also, the high ranking in the previous two categories leads to the firm key strength of reputation being so high. However the company has not escaped unscathed from this category and recent scandals such as that involving the company having to pay $2 million to settle charges of improperly trying to promote initial public stock offerings before they received regulatory approval does dent the company's strict compliance with rules and regulations category.

81   According to the SEC, traders on Goldman Sachs' New York Asian Shares Sales Desk sent e-mails to institutional investors promoting four IPOs in 1999 and 2000 during the SEC-mandated waiting period between the IPO's registration filing and the SEC's approval. The e-mails contained abbreviated sales pitches, whereas only a full prospectus may be used to promote sales during the waiting period. However once again it must be stated that the company's ethical and corporate governance is a key strength of the company and it is certainly an industry leader in regards to this aspect.

82   Goldman's management was a key strength of the firm. Their expertise, and their training and pay were viewed with high regard. However corporate governance was viewed as being moderate in strength due to the scandals mentioned before. Diversity of management was also seen as moderate as the ranks were dominated by white, middle class, males.

83   Operations and technology at the investment bank often referred to as the back office played an essential component of the bank. Goldman strength lay in the firm's security and confidentiality of documents and online resources. Additionally the company also was strong in leveraging technologies to allow it to deliver time sensitive documents quickly. In regards to innovation of technologies, online tools and information resources and quality of IT personnel the firm performed moderately well. This was due to the fact that it lacked the capital investment capabilities of many of its larger rival firms.

84   Marketing was regarded as of great importance in the financial services industry and as such was regarded as of the highest importance by Goldman. The firm was strong in the user friendliness of its online system as well as its cross selling of products and services. The firm ranked fairly moderately in wide sales and distribution channels due to the smaller number of offices the firm has compared to its significantly larger rivals in regards to personnel size.

85   Goldman was seen to be moderate in terms of geographical presence. The firm concentrated largely on the established European, American and Asian markets with most of its resources and personnel being largely deployed in the U.S. The firm did not aggressively pursue the emerging markets limited largely by its lack of personnel and its more focus established markets strategy.

Merrill Lynch

86   Merrill Lynch, once the undisputed leader of the herd, found itself in a bullfight for dominance with fellow retail/wholesale financial supermarkets. The firm, known as "The Bull," offered financial services for private, institutional, and government clients, including mutual fund, insurance, annuity, trusts, and clearing services, in addition to traditional investment banking and brokerage. The company had operations in more than 35 countries around the world. The firm was a diversified products and services firm with a centralized management structure.

87   Merrill Lynch merged its Merrill Lynch Investment Managers unit with asset manager Black-Rock and the resulting company, had approximately $1 trillion in assets under management. Merrill Lynch unlike Goldman Sachs but similarly to Morgan Stanley tried to position itself as a one-stop financial services provider by offering banking services, mortgages, and credit cards to its clients. The company's Global Private Client Group provided individual investors with brokerage services, mutual funds, and life insurance and annuities. The Global Markets and Investment Banking Group offers investment banking and capital market services to corporations, institutions, and governments worldwide. Merrill Lynch was seen by many to have not adequately controlled its growth at a steady rate and as such was viewed to be un-cohesive as well as being highly bureaucratic and slower than its competition at responding to market changes and seizing opportunities in the constantly changing business environment.

88   The decline from undisputed dominance made the firm look like a possible takeover candidate as it faced off with traditional competitors such as Morgan Stanley and Citigroup from above and Charles Schwab from below. Nevertheless, Merrill Lynch remained one of the more consistent profit-generators among American companies.

89   The strengths of Merrill Lynch were that firstly the firm offered a great range of products and services catering for a vast range of institutional and individual clients. The company also had significant industry expertise and global reach. Having been established before many of its competition it truly was a global firm.

90   The company was also strong in its relations with the largest money managers having developed these relations through many years of trading.

91   Additionally the company was viewed as being strong in regards to being client focused. The large personnel at its disposal allowed the firm to give personal attention to institutional and individual clients.

92   In regards to customers Merrill Lynch was viewed as moderate across most of the categories. Its quality of service for both institutional and customer clients and customers, lack of specialist teams and therefore poorer reputation as a result meant that the firm had much room for improvement in this category. It was also likely that the firm's poorer showing in this category was part of the reason why it had lost market share to others over the past decade in the investment banking sector. In regards to personal attention to clients and customers the firm was strong, its large number of staff allowed the firm to cater for a close relationship. The firm's quality of market performance and economic research department to help institutional clients produce above market returns also lagged behind the other bulge bracket firms largely due to the firm's unfocused strategy stretching personnel and resources across commercial and banking activities.

93   The firm was strong across the category in the field of regulations. The firm had managed to keep out of the corporate scandal spotlight that had been focused on many of its rivals. As such the firm Integrity, professionalism and reputation were seen as of the highest quality. In addition the firm continued to contribute to the securities industries efforts to improve ethical behavior.

94   The expertise of Merrill Lynch management was strong however its reputation was viewed as moderate due to the fact the firm had lost market share over the past decade its

smaller more flexible rivals. The firm's corporate governance was also viewed as being strong however diversity was moderate. Once again white, middle class males dominated the management ranks. However the firm's African-American CEO Stanley O'Neal did signal that he intended to address this issue. Training of management was seen as a strength. The firm had over the years produced many in house CEO's and CFO's and continued to fill its management ranks with in house trained employees. In regards to pay the firm lagged behind some its rivals.

95   In regards to operations and technology the firm was largely moderate in regards to innovation, online tools and the quality of its people. It was strong in regards to security and the delivery of time sensitive documents quickly.

96   The firm was strong in marketing. It had a wide range of sales and distribution channels. In addition the firm was an expert in the cross selling of products, especially to the individual investor whom they targeted with individual financial representatives.

97   In regards to geographic presence the firm ranked moderately. Like its major rivals it concentrated largely on the established US, European and Asian markets. It had curtailed its global operations in recent years in a bid to concentrate on the core American market and improve efficiencies and cross departmental synergies.

98   However the firm did pursue the emerging markets seeing them as in line with their present firm wide strategy of straddling both the commercial and investment banking sectors.

Citigroup Global Market Holdings

99   Citigroup Global Markets was comprised of three business segments, Investment Services, Private Client Services, and Asset Management—and was part of Citigroup's broader Global Corporate and Investment Banking Group (GCIB). GCIB's business also is divided into three parts: Global Banking, Global Capital Markets (equity and fixed income underwriting, sales, and trading), and Global Transaction Services (custody, clearing, and fund services). The investment banking behemoth provides a range of investment banking, brokerage, asset management, research, and advisory services to corporations, governments, and consumers. It had a presence in approximately 100 countries. The firm had a centralized management structure.

100   Like several of its competitors, Citigroup Global Markets was battered by the sluggish economy and slump in M&A activity. The firm also continues to deal with the fallout from a far-reaching settlement with government regulators over alleged conflicts-of-interest between the research and investment banking operations of several of Wall Street's top players. Citigroup was fined $300 million the largest amount assessed in the matter—and was required to pay an additional $100 million toward providing independent research and education to investors.

101   The settlement also banned IPO "spinning" (giving special IPO allocations to key clients in exchange for investment banking business), and required that the company and its competitors strengthen the firewall between their research and investment banking operations.

102   In anticipation of the settlement, Citigroup created a separate equity research and private client division, Smith Barney, and placed Sallie Krawcheck at the helm amid much fanfare. (The former Sanford Bernstein CEO has been dubbed "Mrs. Clean" of Wall Street.) Today, the Smith Barney unit provides financial services to individual and institutional investors through more than 500 offices. Krawcheck, however, switched roles with Citigroup CFO Todd Thomson in late 2004.Other units of Citigroup Global Markets deal in trading of commodities such as petroleum products, natural gas, and metals (Connecticut-based Phibro) and make markets for some 2,000 Nasdaq-listed securities [Hoovers, 2006B].

103   Citigroup ranked strong in its range of product and service offerings. Additionally the group had a wealth of industry experience and personnel expertise and this allowed it too

FIGURE 4
Investment Banking:
Competitor
Comparison

Source: Hoovers, 2006C

	Morgan Stanley	Citigroup	Goldman Sachs	Merrill Lynch
Market Cap ($Mill):	64,084	0	62,854.3	70,326
Employees:	53,284	40,000	21,928	50,600
Annual Revs ($Mill):	52,081	23,065	43,391	32,465
Revenue growth:	30.9%	11.3%	45.4%	17.0%
P/E Ratio:	13.46	N/A	16.52	15.56
P/S Ratio:	1.24	N/A	1.45	1.61

remain competitive against many of the more established investment banks. However one area where the firm was moderate was in its global strategy and reach, Citigroup had until very recently concentrated it operations largely in the Americas however the company had made moves to establish a foothold in the large European markets. Due to the group's large commercial presence, reputation and resources the firm was able to establish relations with the largest money managers.

104   Citigroup offered a moderate quality of service and personal attention to clients. It also managed to rate only moderately in regards to offering of specialist teams and individuals and alternatively the reputation of the firm was viewed by customers as being moderate.

105   The firm's market performance and economic research department is ranked considerably lower than other competitors. The firm's brand name and reputation were ranked moderate by both institutional and individual clients and customers largely due to its smaller investment division and relative recent entry into the industry.

106   In terms of integrity, high ethical standards the firm ranks only moderately. It also suffers in the strict compliance to regulations. This was due to scandals such as being accused of helping Enron and other companies hide their losses by loaning money to those companies in a special way that would reduce liabilities visible on the balance sheet. The company paid $2.65 billion to settle a class action lawsuit brought on behalf of purchasers of WorldCom securities. Additionally the firm was also embroiled in euro bond scandals and mutual fund scandals that had adverse effect on the aforementioned regulatory classes and the company's overall reputation which was ranked as being moderate.

107   In terms of management the firm's infancy compared to other investment banks was shown in the moderate ranking of management expertise, reputation, training, pay and diversity. The majority of Citigroup's management team had been trained at other banks a brought knowledge of various processes, procedures from a variety of banking houses. As such the firm did not differentiate itself from the other companies in terms of culture and was seen by its rivals as a bit part player in the industry that relied upon legacy systems and processes that were already obsolete.

108   Citigroup was only moderate in its innovation of technologies and online tools and information resources. However like many of it competitors the firm delivered a strong level of security and confidentiality and time sensitive delivery of documents. In addition the quality of the group's back office was seen as moderate.

109   In terms of marketing Citigroup was viewed as being relatively strong. It was seen as moderate to strong in the sales and distribution channels and user friendliness of its online system. However the firm was seen as being strong in the cross selling of products and services.

110   Citigroup ranks moderately to poor in regards to its geographical presence. Outside of the US the firm has a very limited presence and is not recognized as a globally operated firm. However in recent years the firm has attempted to address this issue and has established a major European headquarters in London, England employing over 3000 employees. Due to the firm's recent expansion into the European markets the emerging markets had largely been ignored and it lagged behind major competitors in accessing these markets.

111   Figure 4 shows a financial comparison among the major competitors within the Investment Banking industry.

Markets

112   Due to the tightly wired world of international finance and globalization of corporations Investment banks were presented many opportunities for growth by rapidly expanding foreign markets being spurred on the Asian tiger economies along with the many newly industrialized countries all over the globe.

Traditional Markets

113   Many Investment banks expanded dramatically into London as a stepping stone into the lucrative European Union forming; additionally Tokyo was also targeted for expansion due to the value of the rising Yen and similarly as a stepping stone into the lucrative Asian markets.

Emerging Markets

114   However the greatest opportunities for continued expansion by the Investment banks were in the emerging markets. The term emerging markets was commonly used to describe business and market activity in industrializing or emerging regions of the world. These markets signified a business phenomenon that was not fully described by or constrained to geography or economic strength; such countries were considered to be in a transitional phase between developing and developed status. Examples of emerging markets include China, India, Brazil, Malaysia, countries in Eastern Europe, and parts of Africa.

115   A key to success in regards to markets was to ensure that a company had a significant presence in all the major financial markets as well as the fastest growing markets of the world. This would allow it to compete on a global and target suitable clientele and service there in order meet clientele expectation.

THE COMPANY

116   Morgan Stanley was a leading global financial services firm, offering a wide variety of products and services. A partial list of these products and services included:

- Investment banking services such as advising, securities underwriting
- Institutional sales and trading, including both equity and fixed income investment
- Research services
- Individual investor services such as credit lending (Discover Card), private wealth management, and financial and estate planning
- Traditional investments such as mutual funds and separately managed accounts
- Alternative investments such as hedge funds, managed futures, and real estate

117   Despite offering such a diverse array of services, Morgan Stanley continued to be an industry leader in many areas, particularly equity and debt underwriting and investment banking. The company considered its brand name and reputation as a longtime leading financial firm among its most valuable assets.

118   Morgan Stanley was founded in New York on September 5, 1935, by Henry S. Morgan, and Harold Stanley of J. P. Morgan & Co. along with others from Drexel & Co. This split of the commercial and investment banks came as a result of the Glass-Steagall Act. Within its first year it achieved 24% of market share among public offerings. In 1964 Morgan Stanley created the first computer model for financial analysis. By 1971 the Mergers & Acquisitions business was established along with Sales & Trading. In 1986 Morgan Stanley Group, Inc. became publicly listed.

119 In 1996, Morgan Stanley acquired Van Kampen American Capital (website), a respected mutual fund company.

120 On February 5, 1997, the company was acquired by Dean Witter, Discover & Co. (a.k.a. Dean Witter Reynolds) the spun-off financial services business of Sears Roebuck. The merged company was briefly known as "Morgan Stanley Dean Witter Discover & Co." until 1998 when it was known as "Morgan Stanley Dean Witter & Co." until late 2001. To foster brand recognition and marketing the Dean Witter name was dropped and the firm became "Morgan Stanley." The merger was controversial, and the firm lost some of its blue chip status with its corporate client base.

121 The following section will provide a detailed analysis of Morgan Stanley's business model as depicted in Figure 5.

Products & Services

122 The firm offered a wide selection of products and services through its various departments that catered for a range of individual investor preferences. The firm aimed to eventually offer a one stop shop for financial products and services. Morgan Stanley offered both commercial and investment banking products and services such as Mergers and Acquisition services, Securities underwriting and credit lending services. The following section will describe three specific product sections that many investment banks were divided into. Each section catered for separate clientele objectives. With each of these services in place along with the core values of commitment, teamwork, integrity, professional excellence and entrepreneurial spirit Morgan achieved its objectives of helping their clients meet their overall financial objectives.

Global Capital Markets

123 Morgan Stanley's Global Capital Markets (GCM) group responds with market judgments and ingenuity to clients' needs for capital. Whether executing an IPO, a debt offering or a leveraged buyout, GCM integrates our expertise in Sales and Trading and in Investment Banking to offer clients seamless advice and sophisticated solutions. The firm originated, structured and executed public and private placement of a variety of securities: equities, investment-grade and non-investment-grade debt and related products. With fresh ideas and distribution capabilities in every major market, GCM worked to help clients get the most value from each stage of a transaction. GCM also continually developed capital market solutions to enable clients to mitigate strategic, operational, credit and market risks.

FIGURE 5 **Company Analysis: Morgan Stanley Business Model**

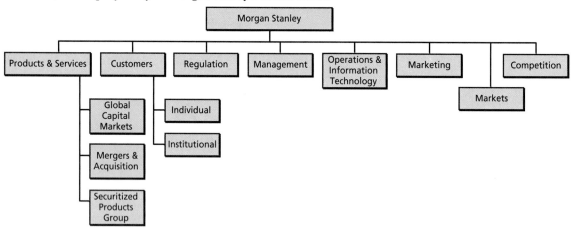

Mergers & Acquisitions

124 Morgan Stanley's Mergers and Acquisitions (M&A) department devised and executed innovative, customized solutions to meet their clients' most challenging issues. The M&A team excelled in domestic and international transactions including acquisitions, divestitures, mergers, joint ventures, corporate restructurings, recapitalizations, spin-offs, exchange offers, leveraged buyouts and takeover defenses as well as shareholder relations. Morgan Stanley applied its extensive experience with global industries, regions and banking products to meet our clients' short- and long-term strategic objectives.

Securitized Products Group

125 The Securitized Products Group (SPG) engaged in a wide array of activities that included structuring, underwriting, and trading collateralized securities across the globe. SPG made active markets and took proprietary positions in the full range of asset-backed, residential mortgage-backed, commercial-backed and collateralized debt obligation securities in both the cash and synthetic markets. In addition, SPG originated commercial mortgage and single-family loans through conduit and loan purchase activities, and advised clients on securitization opportunities. Bringing together Morgan Stanley's Fixed Income and Investment Banking divisions, SPG drew on their expertise in finance, capital markets, trading and research to give clients the best of securitization finance [Liaw, 1999].

126 Morgan Stanley was strong in its product offerings; the company offered a wide range of products and services to both institutional clients and individual customers, its aim was to eventually offer a one stop shop financial service. In addition the company was also strong in its wealth of personnel expertise as the company employed the brightest and best talent in the financial services industry; the firm was also seen as being strong in its industry expertise with many years of market activities. The firm was also rated strong in its relations with the leading money managers. The firm did however charge a premium price for its industry renowned products and services and hence was rated as moderate in the competitive pricing section. In regards to Global strategy and reach Morgan Stanley was strong. The firm was the first ever into the expected to be lucrative Chinese and Indian markets. The firm provided products and services that were client focused and offered specialist terms and adjusted product and service packages to its clients.

Customers

127 Morgan Stanley through its various financial service departments offered both individual and institutional customers tailored products and services to meet their varying requirements. The mass customization approach was a way in which to offer services and products to all financial clients and customers from the low to high net worth individuals and all differing sizes of corporations from sole proprietor company to large scale corporation.

Individual Investors

128 Morgan Stanley through its Asset Management division offered open and closed-end funds and separately managed accounts to individual investors through affiliated and unaffiliated broker-dealers, banks, insurance companies and financial planners. A small number of unaffiliated broker dealers accounted for a substantial portion of the Van Kampen fund sales. Morgan Stanley also sells Van Kampen funds through numerous retirement plan platforms. Internationally, Morgan Stanley distributes investment products to individuals outside the U.S through non-proprietary distributors.

129 Additionally the firm also catered for its individual investors with an emphasis on the affluent and high net worth investors through its Retail brokerage division. Morgan Stanley's products and services were delivered through several channels. Morgan Stanley's wholly owned subsidiary Morgan Stanley DW Inc. (MSDWI), Retail brokerage's network of financial advisors and wealth advisors provided solutions designed to accommodate individual investment objectives, risk tolerance and liquidity needs for high net worth and affluent investors, and call centers are available to meet the needs of emerging affluent clients.

130   Morgan Stanley ranked strong in the customer quality of service category, and personal attention to customers. In addition the firm also ranked strong in regards to its brand name and reputation. The one area were the company was ranked slightly poorer in the moderate to strong category was that of the specialist teams and individuals the firm provided to clients. This inability to focus on individual clients was largely due to personnel being stretched due to expansive growth objectives under the firms previous CEO who strived for a one stop shop financial services firm and thus stretched personnel capacity to its maximum.

Institutional Investors

131   Morgan Stanley provided an array of products and services to institutional investors worldwide, including pension plans, governments, mid-large scale organizations, financial institutions, private funds, endowments and a number of securities services. Products and services were available to institutional investors primarily through separate accounts, U.S. mutual funds and other pooled vehicles.

132   Morgan Stanley investment management division also sub-advised funds for various unaffiliated financial institutions and intermediaries. The firm's global sales force and a team that was dedicated to covering the investment consultancy industry served institutional investors. Morgan Stanley additionally offered clients alternative investment products primarily through alternative investment partners which utilized a fund of funds strategy to invest in hedge funds and private equity funds.

133   In regards to institutional investors Morgan Stanley ranked highly for all related categories. The firm had been servicing this client base for many years and had developed extremely successful operations to meet client objectives and overall satisfaction with the firm.

134   The firm was seen as strong in the quality of service it offered to clients through its innovative financial products that differentiated the firm's strategies from other less sophisticated methods. The firm's research department was also ranked strong having developed into a knowledgeable and well utilized resource for the professionals in the firm to ensure correct investment strategies were pursued. The firm was also ranked strong in its personal attention paid institutional clients through its specialist teams and individuals. Due to the positive ranking of aforementioned categories the firm's brand name and reputation were ranked highly by all investors.

Regulation

135   Most aspects of Morgan Stanley's business were subject to stringent regulation by U.S. federal and state regulatory agencies and securities exchanges and by non-U.S. government agencies or regulatory bodies and securities agencies. Aspects of Morgan Stanley's public disclosure, corporate governance principles, internal control environment and the roles of auditors and counsel were subject to the Sarbanes-Oxley Act of 2002 and related regulations and rules of the SEC and the NYSE.

136   New laws or regulations or changes to existing laws and regulations either in the U.S. or elsewhere could have materially adversely affected the financial condition or results of operations of Morgan Stanley. As a global financial institution, to the extent that different regulatory regimes impose inconsistent or iterative requirements on the conduct of its business, Morgan Stanley faced complexity and additional costs in its compliance efforts [Morgan Stanley annual report, 2004].

137   In regards to integrity, professionalism and ethical standards the firm ranks moderate. In addition Morgan Stanley ranks moderate in strict compliance with rules and regulations largely due to the firm being embroiled in January, 2005, with the New York Stock Exchange imposing a $19 million fine on Morgan Stanley for alleged regulatory and supervisory lapses. Morgan Stanley's reputation on regulatory issues is seen as being moderate to strong having weakened recently due to high profile corporate scandals and the high profile fight with the group of eight directors. The firm was seen as strong in its efforts in contributing to investor protection and the overall integrity of the securities industry by its sponsoring of events and publications for industry wide education.

Management

138   As mentioned previously Morgan Stanley was in a period of change in regards to its management during the timeline of this report. The Purcell, Dean Witter "One stop shop" era had just ended and the Mack, Morgan Stanley "Investment banking specialist" era had just begun.

139   The firm adopted a centralized management structure to ensure its employees followed a top down management focused and controlled strategy. Management of the firm were paid based according to performances of the divisions in which they managed.

140   Morgan Stanley's management expertise and training leading to in house retention were strong. In fact the new CEO was a Morgan Stanley veteran who had been with the company over twenty years and had started as a management trainee. However due to the high profile group of eight conflict with the previous management and the general exodus of top quality management that had left the company under the previous CEO Morgan's management reputation had suffered greatly and was ranked as only moderate. Due to the scandals mentioned previously and additional SEC penalties the firm was ranked moderate in its management's corporate governance principles. In regards to diversity the firm was also only moderate and had recently been reprimanded by the SEC for discrimination against women at the managerial level. However the firm was in line to improve its management stature as it gave amongst the most generous compensation packages to management in the industry.

Operations & Information Technology

141   Morgan Stanley's Operations and Technology departments provided the process and technology platform that supported Institutional sales and trading activities, including post-execution trade processing and related internal controls over activities from trade entry through to settlement and custody, including asset servicing. This was done for proprietary and customer transactions in listed and OTC transactions in commodities, equity and fixed income securities, including both primary and secondary trading, as well as listed, OTC and structured derivatives in markets around the world. This activity was undertaken through Morgan Stanley's own facilities as well as through membership in various clearing and settlement organizations globally. The departments also provided the platforms to support the firm's Retail and Brokerage activities from trade capture through to custody. The departments also supported the asset management business by supporting activities such as mutual fund accounting, transaction processing and certain fiduciary services on behalf of institutional, retail and intermediary clients. Another division that relied heavily on the departments was Morgan Stanley's Discover card credit services division; it relied upon the departments to be able to perform the functions required to service and operate card accounts. The functions included new account solicitation, application processing along with a number of other critical activities.

142   Morgan Stanley was considered the industry leader in information technology, with an IT budget rivaling the operating budget of many medium and large software companies. Its

IT department also received accolades from the open source community for its continual work in commercial proliferation and improvement of OSS, including such projects as the A+ programming language and a computing architecture which led to the Stateless Linux project for Fedora Core.

143   Morgan Stanley as mentioned previously was an industry leader in information technology. The firm was ranked as strong in its innovation of technologies, security and confidentiality, Quality of IT and Operations employees and delivery of time sensitive documents quickly. The only area where the firm was ranked in the moderate class was that of its online tools and resources which some viewed as a possible area for improvement.

Marketing

144   Morgan Stanley often cited its brand name and reputation as its most valuable assets. The firm made a number of efforts to differentiate itself from the competition and had managed to carve out a name for itself through largely producing high quality gains and growth over a number of successive periods.

145   The firm used its brokerage offices and the internet to spread through word of mouth and controlled media coverage the advantages of its benefits and services throughout all global markets. The firm avoided the using of the mass media to retain the specialist and premium brand image it had created. However due to increased public scrutiny over many financial corporate scandals that had taken place from 2000 and onwards the firm had an increasingly harder time in the control of its imaging.

146   The firm was ranked as being strong in the scope of its sales and distribution channels. The firm was also ranked strong in its cross selling product and service strategies. One area however where the firm did not excel at and was ranked as being moderate to strong was in the user ease of use of its online internet system, due the fact that this was the premium way for the firm to market its services and differentiate itself from the competition. The firm did not provide as well equipped website and one would have hoped for.

Geographic Scope

147   Morgan Stanley operated globally, in all the major markets of the world. However the majority of its revenues came from its vast operations in the North American market.

148   Morgan Stanley's business continued to expand around the world, as global markets became ever more tightly linked by technology, by the breaking down of regulatory

FIGURE 6
Morgan Stanley's Global Presence

Source: Morgan Stanley Online, 2006

FIGURE 7
Morgan Stanley's
Summarized
Comparative Income
Statement

Source: Yahoo! Online, 2006

Income Statement Data					
	2005	**2004**	**2003**	**2002**	**2001**
Total revenues:	52,081	39,341	34,776	32,926	43,550
Less—expenses:	44,720	15,633	13,959	13,852	21,542
Net revenues	7,361	23,708	20,817	19,074	22,008
Less—other expenses	2,422	19,222	17,030	16,086	18,519
Net income	4,939	4,486	3,787	2,988	3,489

FIGURE 8
Morgan Stanley's
Summarized
Comparative
Balance Sheet

Source: Yahoo! Online, 2006

Balance Sheet and Other Operating Data					
	2005	**2004**	**2003**	**2002**	**2001**
Total assets:	898,523	747,334	602,843	529,499	482,628
Consumer loans, net	22,916	20,226	19,382	23,014	19,677
Total capital	125,891	110,793	82,769	65,936	61,633
Long-term borrowing	96,709	82,587	57,902	44,051	40,917
Shareholders equity	29,182	28,206	24,867	21,885	20,716
Return on average common shareholders equity	17.3%	16.8%	16.5%	14.1%	18.0%

barriers, and by the increasingly global needs of their clients. Half of the firm's institutional business came from outside the United States. The firm's 53,718 people represented over 120 nationalities worked in 600 offices in 28 countries.

149   Figure 6 highlights the geographical presence that Morgan Stanley's global operations had and the markets it focused its businesses on. Some of the most notable markets that the company had a significant presence in were, Greater China, India, Japan and Europe. Morgan Stanley was ranked moderate in its geographical presence.

Competition

150   All aspects of Morgan Stanley's businesses were highly competitive and Morgan Stanley expected them to remain so. The company competed in the U.S. and globally for clients, market share and human talent in all aspects of its business segments. Morgan Stanley's competitive position depended on its reputation, the quality of its products, services and advice. Morgan Stanley's ability to sustain or improve its competitive position also depended substantially on the firms ability to continue to attract and retain qualified employees while managing its compensation costs.

151   Morgan Stanley's competitive position depended greatly on innovation, execution capability and relative pricing. Morgan Stanley competed in the U.S. and globally with other securities and financial services firms, brokers and dealers, and with others on a regional or product basis. The firm competed with commercial banks, insurance companies, the sponsors of mutual funds, hedge funds, energy companies and other such companies that offered financial services in the U.S. globally and through the internet. Morgan Stanley's ability to access capital at competitive rates (dependent on the company's credit ratings) and to commit capital efficiently also affected its competitive position.

152   Over time certain sectors of the financial services industry became considerably more concentrated as financial institutions in a broad range of financial service industries were acquired or merged with other firms. These convergences often resulted in Morgan Stanley's competitors gaining greater capital and other resources, such as a broader range of products and services and geographic diversity.

153   Additionally the complementary trends in the financial services industry of consolidation and globalization present amongst other things, technological, risk management,

regulatory and other infrastructure challenges that required effective resource allocation in order for Morgan Stanley to remain competitive (Morgan Stanley annual report, 2004).

154   Additionally Morgan Stanley also experienced intense price competition to some of its businesses. In particular the ability to execute trades electronically through the internet and other alternative trading systems increased the pressure on trading commissions.

Financial Analysis

155   Morgan Stanley maintained leading market positions in each of its business segments — institutional securities, Retail brokerage, Asset management and Discover. The company recorded net income of $4939 million and diluted earnings per share of $4.57 in fiscal 2005, an increase of 10% and 13%, respectively, from the prior year. Net revenues rose 13% to $26.8 billion in fiscal 2005, and return on average common equity was 17.3% compared to 16.8% in the prior year.

156   Net interest expenses of 19.4% increased 15% from the prior year, primarily due to higher compensation expense and professional services expense associated with increased business activity and legal and consulting costs, compensation and benefit expenses associated with increased business activity and legal and consulting costs. Other notable costs to the firm were those associated with certain legal matters, including those associated with the Coleman litigation and Parmalat settlement.

157   A breakdown of Morgan Stanley's divisions reveals the following; Institutional securities for 2005 recorded income of $4.8 billion, an 11% from the prior year. Investment banking advisory revenues for the same period rose 28% to $1.5 billion whilst underwriting revenues rose 8% from last year to $2.0 billion. Fixed income sales and trading revenues were a record $6.8 billion, up 22% from the prior year. The Retail brokerage division recorded pre-tax income of $585 million, up 58% from the prior year. Asset management recorded pre-tax income of $1.0 billion a 22% increase from the prior year due to higher investment gains and an increase in asset management fees. Finally Discover's pre-tax income was 25% lower then the previous year reported at being $921 million. Overall most of the divisions were seen to be posting gains and Morgan Stanley's financial positioning seemed to be comfortable [Hoovers, 2006].

158   Figures 7 and 8 provide a comparative snapshot of the firm's financial performance over the past five years.

Management Strategy

159   During 2005 Morgan Stanley made substantial changes to its senior management and this in turn lead to certain organizational and strategic changes that the firm's management believed would improve its performance in future periods.

160   The reason for these changes came from concerns about prior year concerns over lackluster performance. Eight former senior Morgan Stanley executives, including S. Parker Gilbert, who had been chairman of Morgan Stanley several years before the merger, and Robert Scott, who had been President under Phillip Purcell the CEO of the company who resigned in March 2005 before being pushed out, sent a letter to the Board on March 3, 2005, requesting immediate replacement of Purcell. On March 29, Purcell announced that he would be replacing then President Stephan Newhouse, a 26 year Morgan Stanley veteran and former Navy officer, with Zoe Cruz and Steve Crawford, two of Purcell's most recognized supporters. Three days later, on March 31, the so called "Group of Eight" published a full-page advertisement in the *Wall Street Journal* revealing their position.

161   The dispute, which the eight former executives claim represented a groundswell within the company, amid concerns of Phil Purcell's alleged neglect for Morgan Stanley's traditional and most profitable institutionally ingrained business, investment banking. Key to

the firm's future was Joe Perella, the head of investment banking and former head of M&A at CSFB (Credit Suisse First Boston). (Perella joined Bruce Wasserstein to form the former Wasserstein Perella & Co. (aka "Wasserella") specialist firm dealing mainly in mergers and later sold to Dresdner Bank.) Perella left Wasserella to join Morgan Stanley and managed the Investment Banking Division at Morgan Stanley for a time (Group of Eight, 2005).

162 It was announced on April 13, 2005 that Perella was also leaving Morgan Stanley. At that time, Purcell retained support of the Morgan Stanley board, which some say he "packed." On May 12, 2005, dissidents announced a plan to split up Morgan Stanley into two firms: one retail (as former Dean Witter) and one institutional firm (as former Morgan Stanley), saying Purcell's plans to merge these two entities has not worked over the past eight years.

163 Purcell had announced plans to spin off the Discover Card division, a heavy earner for Morgan Stanley, as steadily hiking fees have increased profits while the number of card holders has remained the same. However, his successor (see below) announced that the division would be kept with the firm.

164 Former CEO Purcell announced on June 13, 2005 that he will retire as CEO when a successor is found, but no later than March of 2006. As of June 30, 2005 he was officially succeeded by John Mack in both capacities. Debate continues over Purcell's strategy of keeping the firm as a "financial supermarket" to all investors (both retail and institutional). The focus of Morgan Stanley had historically been on institutional clients.

165 Former President John Mack was chosen to succeed Purcell and his appointment was made official by the board of directors on June 30, 2005. Mack announced he does not want the $25 million per year guaranteed him in his rehiring, preferring instead to be paid based on performance. How his performance will be measured is unclear.

166 John Mack's performance priorities upon succeeding were to pursue the following strategic initiatives in order to improve the company's net revenues, profit margins and return on common shareholders equity [Morgan Stanley 10-K, 2005].

- Leverage global scale, franchise and integration across businesses.
- Increase principal activity in order to strike a better balance between principal and customer activity.
- Invest to optimize growth opportunities and achieve "best in class" status in all businesses.
- Aggressively pursue new opportunities, including a "bolt on" acquisitions.
- Improve operating margins by creating productivity and efficiency gains.
- Create a cohesive "one firm" culture.

LOOKING TOWARDS THE FUTURE

167 In 2006, CEO John Mack and his newly established management team decided that Morgan Stanley needed to deploy a strategic direction to the firm that would allow it to remain competitive as the industry started to become even more competitive with large, powerfully backed commercial banks and established competitors seeking rapid global expansion. This situation placed Morgan Stanley in direct competition with a number of companies but those most aligned to the company's current practices and thus direct competition were Goldman Sachs, Merrill Lynch and Citigroup Global Holdings Inc. Morgan Stanley therefore was faced with the task of differentiating itself from these aforementioned companies to retain it shrinking market share and improve its medium to long-term growth prospects.

168 One alternative proposed by John Mack and his team was that Morgan Stanley should scale back its operations and focus on what the company does best its core Investment banking activities. Mack stressed the need for the company to focus on its distinctive competence

and not be distracted by other non core business divisions, such as the Retail brokerage side or Credit lending services.

169   The **benefit** of this particular alternative was the company would be able to organize its workforce more cohesively and management would not remain as disbanded as it had previously been done so. This approach would enable the company to repair its reputation in the markets after recent scandals and not blur its well respected investment banking name with those of the less favored commercial banks amongst potential institutional clients and high net worth individuals.

170   This alternative was **feasible** because it followed a similarly successful path that had greatly aided the company's growth and success in the past.

171   This alternative would **win against the competition** because it would lead to the firm becoming a leaner, fitter increasingly flexible and adapt organization allowing the firm to offer a superior quality of service to its customers. It would lead the firm to better utilizing resources more effectively amongst its prime operations and rid itself of operations that were not bringing synergy to the firm in the way in which it desired.

172   A **drawback** to this alternative was the risk of not having a wide range of services to help diversify its revenue generating operations in case the core operations were to be affected in an adverse manner through economic issues or large regulatory penalties, a common occurrence in the financial services sector.

173   A **way to get around this drawback** would be to introduce other revenue generating services and products from various divisions or possibly keeping select divisions that could hedge against an investment banking downfall.

174   Another alternative being considered by John Mack and his newly appointed management team was that in order to differentiate itself from the competition, Morgan should choose to focus on niche businesses within its current portfolio of businesses and services. It should focus on the Investment banking division but also diversify its revenue stream by investing in those areas of the business that seemed to be flourishing and have good growth prospects for the future, whilst also not diluting the company's cohesiveness and making it too separate and bureaucratic.

175   The **benefit** of this alternative would be that as opposed to the first alternative where the company's revenue streams would be diversified and therefore it would not be so duly affected if its core investment banking division were to suffer a downturn. Additionally this approach would allow Morgan to harness those divisions that had proven to be successful and redirect cost savings from those investments that had not lived up to expectations. The extra capacity of personnel and cash resources would also enable the firm to better focus on high revenue client needs. The firm could invest more resources on the development of specialist teams in the investment banking sector that would no doubt satisfy any client's desire for a focused and attentive service.

176   This alternative was **feasible** because the company was already a market leader in the industry offering a wider array of services, including some not so suitable ones. This alternative would merely prove to be more of restructuring and refocus of the group to a more than feasible option.

177   This approach could **win against the competition** simply because it would allow the company to become a market leader and industry dominator in its selected niche industries as well as staying true to its successful investment banking function and reputation. The company could refocus its attention and financial resources to beefing up those segments of its business that would really prove fruitful and not just drain the company's coffers.

178   A **drawback** of this alternative would have been the unforeseen risks associated with the possible dilution of the company's current revenue streams. A number of competitor banks would offer a one stop shop service for a number of financial services that Morgan would not be catering for if it followed this particular alternative, therefore certain high net worth and institutional clients may be tempted to switch for the sake of deriving cross service and product benefits.

179 **A way around this drawback** would be through marketing and sales targeted at these individuals to convince them of the highly specialist services and products the company offers through its expert staff that can no way be bettered at larger, less focused competitors

180 John Mack agreed that these were both valid alternatives and therefore management needed further deliberation to decide upon which course of action would prove best for the company if it where to meet management and shareholder expectations.

REFERENCES

Group of Eight (2005). [Online]. *http://futureofms.com.* Accessed February 23, 2006.

Hoovers (2006A), [Online]. *http://www.hoovers.com/morgan-stanley.* Accessed February 29th.

Hoovers (2006B), [Online]. *http://www.hoovers.com/citigroup.* Accessed February 29th.

Hoovers (2006C), [Online]. *http://www.hoovers.com/morgan-stanley.* Accessed March 22nd.

Kuhn, R. *Investment Banking*, New York, NY: Harper Row, 1990.

Liaw, K. *The Business of Investment Banking,* New York, NY: John Wiley & Sons, 1999.

Morgan Stanley (2006A).[Online]. *http://www.morganstanley.com/about/inside/ orgchart.* Accessed March 1st.

Morgan Stanley (2006B).[Online]. *http://www.morganstanley.com/about/inside/ orgchart.* Accessed March 1st.

Morgan Stanley 10-K (2005). [Online]. *http://www.morganstanley.com.* Accessed March 3rd.

Morgan Stanley annual (2004).[Online] *http://www.morganstanley.com/about/ir/ annual04.* Accessed March 15th.

Rupert, R. *The New Era of Investment Banking*, Chicago, Illinois, Probus Publishing, 1993.

Yahoo! (2006A). [Online] *http://biz.yahoo.com/ic.* Accessed March 17th.

Yahoo! (2006B). [Online] *http://finance.yahoo.com/q/ks?s=MS.* Accessed March 9th.

Case 40

Procter & Gamble: *The Beauty/Feminine Care Segment of the Consumer Goods Industry*

Ivie Agenmonmen, Marc E. Gartenfeld, and Robert J. Mockler

INTRODUCTION

1   In 2005, A.G. Lafley, chairman, president, and chief executive of Procter & Gamble (P&G), told the shareholders that since 2000 sales had grown more than 40% to $57 billion and profit had more than doubled [P&G Annual Report, 2005]. P&G was a global manufacturing, distribution, and marketing company focusing on providing branded products with superior quality and value. Two billion times a day, P&G brand products touched the lives of people around the world. The company provided over 300 brands reaching consumers in about 140 countries.

2   P&G was formed in 1837 by William Procter and James Gamble. It all started by making and selling soaps and candles. On August 22, 1837, they formalized their business relationship by pledging $3,596.47 apiece; in early 2006, the company made approximately $68 billion annually in sales. In 1862, during the civil war, the company was awarded several contracts to supply soap and candles to the Union armies. These orders kept the factory busy day and night, building the Company's reputation as soldiers returned home with their P&G products. Since then P&G had continued to grow in sales and in the introduction of new products [P&G Company Information, 2006].

3   Over the years P&G has acquired new product brands and companies such as Iams, Clairol, and Wella. The most recent one was on October 1, 2005, when P&G added Gillette to expand the Company's product mix to 22 brands. The Gillette Company was a manufacturer and distributor of various types of consumer goods in the following five areas/brands: Blades and Razors, Duracell (batteries), Oral Care, Braun (small appliances), and Personal Care. The merger with Gillette made P&G a more balanced company in terms of brands, employees, and sales against its competitors over the intermediate and long-term future.

4   The consumer goods industry was changing drastically in the last few years leading up to 2006. Retail power was increasing and today's consumers were more confidently deciding when, where, and how to shop, and at what price to buy. There were various reasons for these changes, such as more variety of products in the marketplace. In addition, according to the Bureau of Economic Analysis (BEA), personal income increased to $41.1 billion and disposable personal income (DPI) increased to $35.5 billion, in December 2005 [BEA, 2006].

5   P&G, as illustrated in Figure 1, was structured into four organizational units: Market Development Organization (MDO), Global Business Services (GBS), Corporate Functions (CF), and Global Business Unit (GBU).

- **Market Development Organizations (MDO)** studied consumers to build local understanding which was used as a foundation for marketing campaigns. Interacting with consumers helped ensure that the company's marketing plans and campaigns were structured to change the game to favor P&G at the point of purchase.

- **Global Business Services (GBS)** provided business technology and services that drove business success and won customers and consumers. This unit provided services and

This case was prepared by Ivie Agenmonmen, Marc E. Gartenfeld, and Professor Robert J. Mockler of St. John's University. © Robert J. Mockler.

FIGURE 1 Procter & Gamble's Structure Division

solutions that enabled the company to operate efficiently around the world, collaborate effectively with business partners, and helped employees to become more productive.

- **Corporate Functions (CF)** worked to maintain P&G's place as the leader of the consumer goods industries. This unit ensured that the functional capability integrated into the rest of the company remained on the cutting edge of the industry.
- **Global Business Unit (GBU)** created strong brand equities, robust strategies, and ongoing innovation in products and marketing to build major global brands [P&G Corporate Information, 2006]. The main philosophy of the GBU was to think globally instead of locally. This case study will concentrate on this unit to get a better understanding of the global operations of P&G. In early 2006, P&G had 5 divisions in its GBU: Baby/Family care, Fabric/Home care, Snacks and Beverage, Health care, and Beauty/Feminine care.

6 With the acquisition of Gillette, P&G's product mix of billion-dollar brands was well-balanced. In early 2006, the company had 12 billion-dollar brands in Baby/Family care and Fabric/Home care, and 10 billion-dollar brands in Beauty/Feminine care and Health care [P&G Annual Report, 2005]. The effects on the Beauty/Feminine care segment due to the acquisition of Gillette and the natural fast growth nature of this segment will be further discussed in detailed later in this case. It is also important to note that even though this division is named Beauty/Feminine care, most people would assume it focuses just on products for females, but in reality quite a few products in this division are geared towards men.

7 P&G was always creating and acquiring new products. To make the public aware of these products, the company had high advertising and marketing expenses. It also had a very good distribution channel that acted as a revenue source for the company, when it partnered with other companies to help distribute its products. Some of the threats facing P&G were the increase in commodity costs and competition in the consumer goods industry. There were a couple of strategic business decisions that P&G could focus on: it could produce more products with natural ingredients and more men's products because these were the growing trends in the industry; or it could focus on one of its product segments such as skin products for a while and then later introduce its other products. All these were possible alternatives, but the main question to be resolved was how to differentiate P&G from its competition, and so achieve a winning edge over competitors within intensely competitive, rapidly changing immediate, intermediate, and long-term time frames.

THE OVERALL INDUSTRY AND COMPETITIVE MARKET ANALYSIS: THE CONSUMER GOODS INDUSTRY

8 Consumer goods companies were those that provided services primarily to consumers. The industry, as shown in Figure 2, was divided into durable goods and nondurable goods.

Durable Goods

9 Durable goods were items with a normal life expectancy of three years or more, such as furniture, household appliances, jewelry, and mobile homes. Due to the nature of these

FIGURE 2
The Consumer Goods Industry

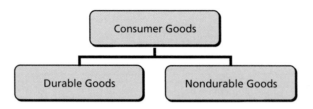

goods, the durable good industry was sensitive to business cycles. Business cycles were predictable long-term patterns of alternating periods of economic growth (recovery) and decline (recession), characterized by changing employment, industrial productivity, and interest rates [Webster Dictionary, 2006].

Nondurable Goods

10   On the other hand, nondurable goods were items that generally lasted for only a short time (three years or less), such as petroleum, beverages, apparel, tobacco, pharmaceutical, and beauty/feminine care products. Nondurable goods were not responsive to any economic conditions such as interest rate, inflation, business cycle, and the likes. They were not responsive, because some of these products met the needs of people. Consumers had to buy these products such as food, medicine, and apparel to survive. They also bought these goods when they needed them because of their short life span; they did not want to buy a lot in bulk and then would not be able to use them. In the United States, the Bureau of Economic Analysis (BEA) released reports stating that nondurable goods manufacturing turned up in 2004—increasing 2.7% after decreasing 1.2% in 2003 [BEA, 2006].

INDUSTRY AND MARKET SEGMENT: THE NONDURABLE GOODS INDUSTRY

11   As mentioned above, examples of nondurable goods were petroleum, beverages, apparel, tobacco, pharmaceutical, and beauty/feminine care products, as shown in Figure 3.

Petroleum

12   Petroleum products were divided into three major categories: fuels, finished nonfuel products, and feedstocks

- **Fuels**—These are products such as motor gasoline and distillate fuel oil (diesel fuel).
- **Finished Nonfuel Products**—These are products such as solvents and lubricating oils.
- **Feedstocks**—These products were for the petrochemical industry such as naphtha and various refinery gases.

13   Petroleum products were used by everyone: from gasoline used to fuel cars to heating oil used to warm homes. The demands for these products varied dramatically, but the greatest demand was for products in the fuels category, especially motor gasoline [EIS, 2005]. In the United States (US), petroleum products contributed about 40.2% of the energy used, more than that of natural gas, coal, nuclear, and hydroelectric. It was estimated that by 2025, the US would increase its consumption of these products to 27.9 million barrels per day [EIS, 2005].

Beverages

14   This industry group included alcoholic beverage and non-alcoholic beverage products.

- **Alcoholic Beverage**—These were drinks that contained ethanol. There were two types, those that included low-alcohol-content which were produced by the fermenting of sugar

FIGURE 3 The Nondurable Goods Industry

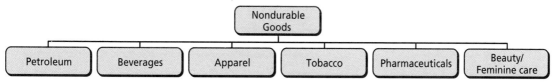

of starch containing products and high-alcohol-content beverages produced by distillation of the low alcohol content beverage [Wikipedia, 2006]. Examples of these products were beer, wine, ale, and cider.

- **Non-alcoholic Beverage**—These were drinks that did not contain ethanol, such as coffee, juice, tea, and soda water.

Apparel

15   This industry group included products for men, women, children, and infants. The products consisted of both inner and outerwear clothes.

Tobacco

16   This industry group included products that were made from tobacco, which was a plant that grew in a wide range of soil and climate conditions. Its non edible leaf was dried and used to manufacture products such as cigarettes, pipe tobacco, cigars, chewing tobacco, and snuff. Companies who produced these products constantly had problems because of the health risk associated with using their products. According to the World Health Organization (WHO), tobacco killed more than two and a half million people prematurely every year.

Pharmaceuticals

17   This industry group included companies that researched, developed, produced, and sold chemical or biological substances for medical or veterinary use. These substances included prescription, generic, and OTC drugs; vitamins and nutritional supplements; drug delivery systems; and diagnostic substances [Hoovers, 2006].

18   The Beauty/Feminine care industry, the focus of this study, is discussed in details in the following section.

INDUSTRY AND COMPETITIVE MARKET: BEAUTY/FEMININE CARE GOODS

19   The desire to be beautiful is as old as civilization. This desire created an industry which generates $160 billion a year. Americans spent more each year on beauty than they did on education [*Economist,* 2006]. The industry, as shown in Figure 4, encompassed some of the following products: hair, products, skin products, feminine products, fine fragrances, cosmetics, and personal cleansing.

20   Companies that produced beauty/feminine care products were influenced by fashion, seasons, and culture. The latest trends to affect this market were the movement by consumers towards natural products and the increased interest by men to look clean and well groomed, creating a large emerging men's market. From 2003 to 2008, as shown in Figure 5, the sale of most beauty/feminine care products, such as hair products, cosmetics, and skin products increased. Each of these beauty/feminine care products is further described in the following section.

FIGURE 4
Beauty/Feminine Care Goods Segment

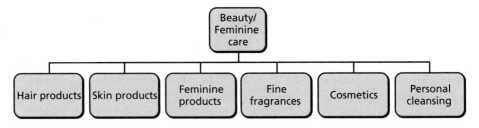

FIGURE 5
Projected U.S. Retail Dollar Sales of Ethnic Specific Cosmetics, 2003–2008 (in millions)

Source: Package Facts (2005). "The U.S. Market for Ethnic HBC Products". [Online]. *http://cpprod.stjohns.edu/cp/ tag.b9b8fA3031868bbe.render. userLayoutRootNode.uP?uP_ root=root&uP_sparam= activeTab&activeTab= U1l1lS39&uP_ tparam=frm&frm=fram.* Accessed January 25, 2006.

	Hair Care		Cosmetics		Skin Care		Total
Year	$	% Change	$	% Change	$	% Change	$
2003	$1,030	-4.0%	$367	5.6%	$118	3.3%	$1,515
2004	1,009	-2.0	387	5.5	121	2.5	1,517
2005	1,019	1.0	410	6.0	124	2.5	1,553
2006	1,035	1.5	437	6.5	129	4.0	1,601
2007	1,055	2.0	463	6.0	132	2.3	1,650
2008	1,030	2.5	493	6.5	137	3.6	1,712

How Industry Segment Works: The Business Process Model

21 The beauty/feminine care industry was comprised of various segments as shown in Figure 6. This industry included companies that manufactured goods that were used to fulfill the needs of consumers.

22 The products these companies produced included hair products, skin products, feminine products, fine fragrances, cosmetics, and personal cleansing products.

23 Consumers used each product for their own personal reasons, but the main purposes were to make people look beautiful and feel clean. The consumers for these products included both females and males from all age groups. Even though it was called beauty/feminine care, males were actually a large part of the consumer base because they used a lot of beauty products. Consumers also included people from different ethnic group, marital status, and also low income consumers.

24 Consumers seemed to be more confident about what they wanted and this played a major role in determining what products were manufactured. In early 2006, a national survey of consumer goods executives showed that a majority of respondents believed that their organizations were well on the way to becoming demand-driven. Demand-driven enterprises were defined as those that not only identified real-time changes in demand, but were also organizationally prepared to profitably respond to these opportunities. The benefits of becoming more demand-driven were that the companies had 15% less inventory, a 17% better perfect-order performance, and a 35% shorter cash-to-cash cycle time [Findarticles, 2006]. So as consumers changed, the companies also changed in order to remain in the competition with their competitors.

25 These products were produced in factories all over the world with raw materials ranging from materials as simple as water to chemicals such as stearic acid and sodium hydroxide. These materials were mixed in unique ways to make each product. Regardless of the raw materials or procedures used to make them, each product had to meet regulatory standards. In the United States of America, an example of such a regulatory body was the U. S. Food and Drug Administration (FDA). These standards varied by country, and they helped to ensure that these products were safe enough to be used by the consumers.

26 After production, these products were packaged and distributed to consumers through various distribution channels such as distribution companies, individual stores, and chain store outlets. Packaging was another important factor in selling products, for example male

products had to be packaged in a different way to attract them. Most times, the packets for men's products were normally dark colored to make the products look more masculine. Distribution companies were companies that bought and sold large amount of products to various retailers, who then sold to the consumers. Individual stores were stores that were owned by companies and these companies sold their products directly to the consumers from these stores. While the chain store outlets included some multinational companies such as Costco and Wal-Mart, which carried a variety of products, these stores were located in different parts of the world, such as Africa, Asia, Australia, Europe, Latin America, and North America, providing products to consumers there.

27   Manufacturing companies had to decide if they wanted to make or buy their manufacturing materials. If they decided to buy any item they usually looked for the cheapest and most efficient source to buy from. This process was called Sourcing and it was a process that had to be continuously reviewed in order to maintain the best deals that suited the company.

28   Advertisement was the promotion of goods, services, companies and ideas, usually by an identified sponsor. Companies used advertisement as part of an overall promotional strategy for their products. They advertised through different media such as television, Internet, print, and radio. Advertising helped to bring some awareness about the products to the consumers, so they could go out and purchase them.

29   Due to the variety in customers and consumers, technology played a major role in this industry, making it a capital intensive industry. They required highly mechanized assembly lines which were designed for long production runs and flexibility, so that it could be easily changed to produce the same products with minor alterations.

30   Some of the companies that produced beauty/feminine care products were Unilever, Colgate-Palmolive, Playtex products, Avon, and Estee Lauder. Since they produced products that appealed to people all over the world, they had to take into consideration various factors such as differences in skin types, body types, hair types, values and beliefs, to efficiently meet their needs. These differences were seriously considered during production in each part of the world to produce products that could be used by consumers and sold for a profit.

31   Figure 6 illustrates the beauty/feminine care goods segment business model. It serves as the framework in discussing this segment.

Products

32   The life span of these products were three years or more. This industry had a wide variety of products and they could be used on different parts of the body, by either males or females. Each product had its own brand with different value, quality, and quantity. Companies in the beauty/feminine care segment produced various products, as illustrated in Figure 6.

Hair Products

33   Hair products included products such as hair shampoo, hair color, hair conditioner, hair spray, hair perms, hair accessories, and the likes. The hair care market was a billion dollar market, with an estimated $7.6 billion in 2004 from retail market, excluding sales of products through professional channels such as salons [Packaged Facts, 2005]. As shown in Figure 7, hair products was estimated to top $3.5 billion at retail in mass and prestige channels combined, as of 2010. Also from 2004-2010, the category would gain 22.9%, or $657 million. The resultant compound annual growth rate (CAGR) for the six years would be 3.5% [Packaged Facts, 2005].

34   Over the past few years, there has been a growing trend toward natural hair remedies and treatments. Consumers were more aware of, and growing wary of chemicals, that could be some mass-market hair treatment products. The other trend mentioned above about men's

FIGURE 6 Beauty/Feminine Care Goods Industry

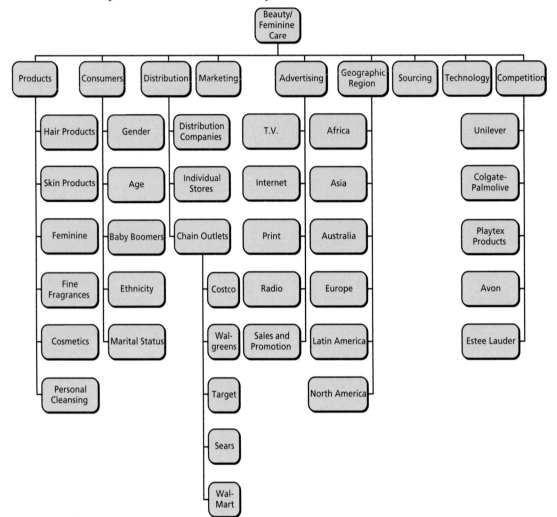

interest, was also obvious in the hair care industry, because there was an increased effort by men to keep their hair well groomed.

35 The keys to success included several factors. The hair products had to be competitively priced and affordable. There had to be a wide selection of these products available to the consumers. The quality of these products had to be considered during production to maintain the company's brand quality reputation. Brand recognition was also an important factor because consumers had to feel as if they could relate with the brand and its attributes. Location and distribution were also important to ensure that these products had a mass market presence. They also had to frequently introduce new products. The packaging for the products had to be designed to attract the right consumer.

Skin Products

36 Skin products were further divided into two product classes: mass-market products, which were generally lower priced and sold in such mass outlets as drugstores, discount store, and food stores. And prestige products, which were higher priced, which usually were packed

FIGURE 7 Projected U.S. Retail Dollar Sales of Beauty Products, by Category, 2004–2010 (in millions)

Year	Skincare	% Change	Hair care	% Change	Make-up	% Change	Total	% Change
2010	$8,849	5.0%	$3,524	4.0%	$3,981	4.5%	$16,454	4.7%
2009	8,523	5.0	3,389	4.0	3,809	4.0	15,721	4.5
2008	8,117	5.0	3,258	3.5	3,663	4.0	15,038	4.4
2007	7,730	5.5	3,148	3.5	3,522	4.0	14,400	4.7
2006	7,327	6.5	3,042	3.0	3,386	4.0	13,755	5.1
2005	6,880	7.0	2,953	3.0	3,256	3.5	13,089	5.2
2004	6,430	7.3	2,867	2.8	3,146	3.9	12,443	5.4

Source: Package Facts (2005). "The U.S. Sale of beauty products". [Online]. *http://cpprod.stjohns.edu/cp/tag.b9b8fA3031868bbe.render. userLayoutRootNode.uP?uP_root=root&uP_sparam=activeTab&activeTab=U1l1lS39&uP_tparam=frm&frm=fram.* Accessed January 25, 2006.

stylishly and contained special ingredients, they were often sold in departmental and specialty stores. Skin products included moisturizers, cleansers, gels, conditioners, toners, and the likes. Factors that affected this segment of this industry were the aging U.S. consumers, technological development; mass market went upscale and new products which were introduced into the market. As illustrated in Figure 7, it was estimated that the sale of skin care products would reach $8.9 billion in combined mass and prestige channels in 2010. This segment would grow a total of 39.2%, or $2.5 billion, during 2004–2010. That translated into a highly desirable 5.7% CAGR over the six years [Packaged Facts, 2005].

37   The way people looked after their skin was often dictated by the degree of affluence. In rural parts of Africa, men and women still made crude bars of soap using crude potassium hydroxide produced from burnt tree bark. Many used coconut oil as a moisturizer. In addition many people tried to lighten their skin by using skin creams containing certain drugs. Steroid creams were freely available for sale in some places, as were creams containing skin-lightening ingredients called hydroquinone. In the developed world, these ingredients could legally be incorporated in low concentrations in well-formulated cosmetic preparations [P&G Skin care, 2003].

38   The keys to success included several factors. The skin products had to be competitively priced and affordable. There had to be a wide selection of these products available to the consumers. The quality of these products had to be considered during production to maintain the company's brand quality reputation. Brand recognition was also an important factor because consumers had to feel like they could relate with the brand and its attributes. Location and distribution were also important to ensure that these products had a mass market presence. They also had to develop these products according to fashion trends. The packaging for the products had to be designed to attract the right consumer.

Feminine Products

39   Feminine products were the only products under the beauty/feminine care segment that were used only by females. They included products such as sanitary pads, tampons, heat patches, and disposable cups. In early 2006, the trends were that consumers wanted products that were more comfortable and easy to use. Some of these products affected the health of the consumers, so companies who produced them had to warn consumers about the possible side effects from using these products. An example of a product that came with such warnings was tampons. A possible side effect from using these products was Toxic Shock Syndrome, which was caused by a particularly virulent and penicillin resistant strain bacterium.

40   The keys to success included several factors. There had to be a wide variety of these products available to the consumers. These products had to be competitively priced and affordable. The quality of these products had to be considered during production to maintain the company's brand quality reputation. Brand recognition was also an important factor.

Location and distribution were also important to ensure these products had a mass market presence. The packaging for the products had to be designed to attract the right consumer.

Fine Fragrances

41 The fragrance industry was a growing industry with companies like Estee Lauder, Calvin Klein, Tommy Hilfiger, and the likes. It was a billion dollar industry and it was constantly changing due to the trends in fashion. In early 2006, many people enjoyed using these fragrances so they could smell clean and attractive.

42 The keys to success included several factors. Quality of these products had to be maintained to retain the company's brand quality reputation. These products had to be competitively priced. Brand recognition was also important. Location and distribution were also important to ensure these products had a mass market presence. They also had to develop these products according to fashion trends. The packaging for the products had to be designed to attract the right consumer.

Cosmetics

43 The cosmetic industry was constantly changing according to its customer's need, but early 2006, the growth in the industry was tremendous. Cosmetics have a temporary benefit and effect, so it has to be reapplied on a regular basis depending on the particular customer. This temporariness of the product made the market a continuous and strong one, because customers had to constantly go out and purchase new products. There were various products in this industry, which included concealers, powders, blushers, and the likes, which were for the skin, and those for the lips which included lip gloss, lip sticks, lip liner, and the likes. It was estimated, as shown in Figure 7 that cosmetics (for face, lips, and eyes) should be worth just under $4 billion in 2010, in mass and prestige channels combined. From 2004–2010, this segment would expand by 26.5%, or $835 million. Cosmetic's CAGR for the same span was therefore calculated at 4% [Packaged Facts, 2005].

44 The cosmetic industry was also divided based on the customer's skin type. An example was the ethnic color specific cosmetics which were the best in this category and were predicted, as shown in Figure 5, to push to $493 million at retail by 2008.

45 The keys to success included several factors. The cosmetics products had to be competitively priced. Brand recognition was also an important factor because consumers needed to feel like they could relate with the brand and its attributes. Availability of variety of these products was required to suit all consumers' needs. Location was also important, so that the companies manufacturing these products could maintain their brand quality reputation. New products had to be frequently developed according to fashion trends. Location and distribution were also important to ensure these products had a mass market presence. The packaging for the products had to be designed to attract the right consumer.

Personal Cleansing

46 The personal cleansing products included products such as soap bars, body wash, body scrubbers, and the like. This segment of the industry had witnessed tough times as its sales declined by 11.9% from 2000 to 2004. This decline was largely due to consumers substituting bath products with higher multi-benefit skin care products at comparatively lower prices. The sales of personal cleansing product were projected to continue to decline by $210.3 million, from an estimated $2.4 billion in 2005, to $2.2 billion in 2010 [Packaged Facts, 2005].

47 The keys to success included several factors. The personal cleansing products had to be competitively priced. Availability of variety of these products was required to suit all consumers' needs. Brand recognition was also an important factor. Location and distribution were also important to ensure these products had a mass market presence. The manufacturing companies had to maintain their brand quality reputation. They had to also frequently introduce new products. The packaging for the products had to be designed to attract the right consumer.

Consumers

48   Consumers were those that ultimately used the products. Consumers made better purchasing decisions when they were aware of the products in the market. When they knew about the products, such as their price and quality, they had the choice to make a better purchase. The common mistakes that some consumers made were instinctive purchases and ignorantly following trends that did not necessarily affect them. There was a wide variety of products in the market place so most consumers could easily get the products they wanted. Consumers for this industry's products could be segmented into gender, age, ethnicity, marital status, and low income consumers.

Gender

49   While most people thought that beauty/feminine care products were just for females, this was not the case because most of the products in this division were also used my males. Both groups needed these products to meet their basic needs such as cleansing products to keep their bodies clean. For many years, women represented a larger part of the customer and consumer base because of several factors such as, women were usually the ones that bought products for their homes and families and some segments of this industry, like the feminine care, only manufactured products that could be used by women. But in early 2005, there was a trend for men to beautify themselves. This trend made manufacturing companies to increase their production of men's products.

50   The keys to success included several factors. The beauty/feminine care products had to be competitively priced and affordable. There had to be a wide selection of these products available to the consumers, distributed through various channels. The quality and value had to be high for each of the products. Brand loyalty was also an important factor because some consumers had always used these products and wanted to continue using them. Location and distribution of these products were also important because these products had to have mass market presence. The packaging for the products had to be designed to attract the right consumer. Consumers had to have promotions targeted at them. An example of a promotion that attracted male consumers was to get a popular male celebrity to promote products.

Age

51   Age was another major factor that companies considered when analyzing the market. What was the age for their consumers? The answer was everyone, from infants to senior citizens. Everyone used beauty/feminine products. The manufacturing companies addressed each age group differently, for example, the baby boomers age group, which included consumers that were born during the period of an increased birth rate when economic prosperity arose in many countries following World War II. This term was commonly used to refer to the generation which demographic popularizers had identified as people who were born between 1946 and 1964 [Wikipedia, 2006].

52   In the United States the baby boomers made up the lion's share of the cultural, political, academic leadership and industrial class. They therefore were a group of people that had significant influence on the beauty/feminine care products. An example of their effect on a particular product can be seen using the hair care products. The number of men in their 55–64 years age group, which represented half of the baby boomers, was expected to grow from 11.39 million in 1999 to 17.39 million in 2010, thus increasing as percentage of the total male population from 8.3% to 11.5% [Packaged Facts, 2005]. As men grew older they were faced with issues like loss and dryness of hair. This forced them to spend more on hair care products. Companies were aware of this trend and were willing to produce these products because of the increase in that particular target age group.

53   The keys to success included several factors. The beauty/feminine care products had to be competitively priced and affordable. There also had to be a wide selection of these

products available to the consumers. Brand recognition was also an important factor because consumers needed to feel like they could relate with the brand and its attributes. Location and distribution of these products were also important because these products had to have mass market presence. These products had to have a strong brand image. Brand loyalty was also an important factor because some consumers had always used their products.

Ethnicity

54   An ethnic group was a human population whose members identified with each other, usually on the basis of a common genealogy or ancestry. Ethnic groups were also usually united by common cultural, linguistic, religious, and behavioural practices [Wikipedia, 2006].

55   Each ethnic group had distinct taste, look, and needs. It was important that the companies manufactured productss that were suitable for them to use. To meet these different ethnic needs, the manufacturers had to perform in-depth research into each group. For example, in the United States, the populations of the African Americans and Hispanics, which were big buyers of the hair care products, were very high. The Hispanics were estimated to increase from 12.6% in 2000 to 15.5% in 2010, while the African Americans would increase from 12.7% in 1999 to 13.1% in 2010. On the other hand, non-Hispanic whites were estimated to decline from 69.4% to 50.1% of the total population during 2000–2050 [U.S. Census Bureau, 2004].

56   Although ethnicity was an issue for manufacturers in the United States, it was not necessarily and issue for manufacturers in countries with one main ethnic group like Ghana. Consumers in countries like Ghana, generally had the same hair type, skin types, beliefs and the likes. These differences in countries were issues that manufacturing companies had to take into consideration before manufacturing and promoting any products.

57   The keys to success included several factors. The beauty/feminine care products had to be competitively priced and affordable. There also had to be a wide selection of these products, tailored to meet the needs of each ethnic group. The products had to be of high quality and value. Brand loyalty was also an important factor because some consumers had always used their products. Brand recognition was also an important factor because consumers needed to feel like they could relate with the brand and its attributes. There also always had to be the development of products according to fashion trends.

Marital Status

58   In 1998, 110.6 million adults (56% of the adult population) were married and living with their spouses [USCB, 1998]. This meant that there was a bigger part of the adult population which were buying things in bulk because they had to buy for the family. If 56 percent of the adult population was married, it meant that the remaining 44 percent were single. Single consumers had more disposable income, because they had more to spend on themselves. These consumers also spent a lot on beauty care products, because they wanted to keep themselves looking good and probably attract people to them.

59   The keys to success included several factors. The beauty/feminine care products had to be competitively priced and affordable. There also had to be a wide selection of these products available to the consumers that were tailored to meet their needs. The products had to be of high quality and value. Brand recognition was also an important factor because consumers needed to feel like they could relate with the brand and its attributes. The products had to be distributed properly to ensure that there was mass market presence. Brand loyalty was also an important factor because some consumers had always used their products.

Low Income Consumers

60   The indebtedness of American households grew substantially in the last decade. The outstanding balance of all consumer credit, excluding mortgage debt, was $800 billion at the end of 1990 [Wikipedia, 2006]. This group of consumers was a very large part of the beauty/feminine care industry. Companies in this industry had to manufacture products that would be affordable for them. Some of the methods used to reduce the costs of the products were reducing the size of the package and reducing the quality of the packaging.

61 The **keys to success** included several factors. The beauty/feminine care products had to have a wide selection of these products available to the consumers that were tailored to meet their needs. Brand recognition was also an important factor because consumers needed to feel like they could relate with the brand and its attributes. Brand loyalty was also an important factor because some consumers had always used their products. There also had to be mass market presence. The packaging for the products had to be designed to attract the right consumer.

Distribution

62 Distribution was the act of dispersing products from the point of production to the final consumer. Most distribution channels had a designated sales force which was in charge of selling and promoting their products. The sales force included individuals who were recruited to move from place to place encouraging customers to purchase their products. These individuals were encouraged to do a better job by offering them incentives such as days off and monetary incentives. Companies had various channels of distributions, such as distribution companies, individual stores, and chain store outlets.

Distribution Companies

63 These were the middle men that purchased directly from the manufacturers and resold them to the retailers for a profit. They were experts at moving things into the market. To do this most of them generally had a good transportation system. These companies normally bought in bulk to control their inventory and increase their profits.

64 The keys to success included several factors. Distribution companies had to offer competitive pricing. Prices they set were not only competitive with that of their competitors but also that of the manufacturing companies which sold directly to the outlet store chains. Distributors had to also establish goods relationships with the store managers to get good product display and shelf space. Some companies also incorporated supply chain technology with their retailers to ensure proper distribution of their products. Distribution companies had to recruit good employees and offer incentives for them to work hard.

Individual Stores

65 Individual stores were stores that were owned by companies, where consumers could walk into and purchase the product they wanted. An advantage of this kind of service provided by companies was that they were able to remove the extra price allocated by the middlemen. It also gave them a chance to relate with their consumers and learn what they liked and disliked about their products, especially the male consumers who were generally not thought to purchase beauty/feminine care products. They also learned trends amongst their consumers and were able to educate them on their products. Also the presence of these stores in different communities helped to build a household name amongst the consumers.

66 The keys to success included several factors. Individual stores had to competitively price their products. Employees in these stores had to be willing to interact with customers to get their opinion about the products. The companies had to offer incentives to their employees to do a good job. These stores had to have a variety of products. Brand recognition was also an important factor. These stores had to be located in prime locations to attract more consumers.

Chain Store Outlets

67 All over the world, the numbers of chain outlets were growing. In Taiwan the total number of chain store outlets grew 11% to 62,637 in 2004, according to a survey released in late April by the Taiwan Chain Store and Franchise Association. These were stores that sold a variety of products. In the United States, a large percentage of the population purchased beauty/feminine products in these types of stores. There were different types of chain stores outlets, some were specialized chain stores, where they sold a wide variety of products and offered very good customer service. Another kind of store was the discount store, that offered a limited variety of products and did not spend too much of their resources on customer services. These stores had to pay special attention to its customers especially the male customers by offering sales and promotions on products that they thought these customers might be interested in. Some of these chain store outlets were Costco, Walgreen, Target, Sears, and Wal-Mart.

68 *Costco.* Costco was the largest membership warehouse club chain in the world. It was a discount chain store with about 456 locations worldwide. In 2004, the company's store sales rose 13% to $47.1 billion and its main competitor was Wal-Mart's owned Sam's Club [Wikipedia, 2006]. Since it was a discount chain store, it sold very high volume products for low prices, by keeping overhead low and using idiosyncratic inventory practices. They also bulk-packaged their products and sold primarily to large families and small businesses [Costco Services, 2006].

69 *Walgreen.* Walgreen was the nations leading drugstore chain. It was a specialized chain store with about 4,000 locations. In January of 2005, their sales increased by 11.8% [Walgreen's Corporate News, 2006]. They provided a wide array of products and were totally geared to providing their customers with complete satisfaction.

70 *Target.* Target was an upscale discounter that provided high-quality, on-trend merchandise at attractive prices in clean, spacious and guest-friendly stores. In addition, Target operated an online business, Target.com [Target Corporate News, 2006]. They had 1397 locations and had revenue of $15.2 billion for the last quarter of 2005.

71 *Sears.* Sears was a specialty outlet stores that provided a wide variety of services to its customers. It had revenues in 2004 of $36.1 billion. It had more than 2,400 Sears-branded and affiliated stores in the U.S. and Canada, which included approximately 870 full-line and 1,100 specialty stores in the U.S. Sears also offered their services through sears.com, landsend.com, and specialty catalogs [Aboutsears, 2006]. It was also the only retailer where consumers could find each of the Kenmore, Craftsman, DieHard, and Lands' End brands together.

72 *Wal-Mart.* Wal-Mart was a discount store outlet that sold to more than 138 million customers worldwide each week, with more than 1,500 locations. The company was growing constantly and had over $56 billion in international sales in 2005. They operated like Costco which is described above [Wikipedia, 2006].

73 The keys to success included several factors. Chain store outlets had to be competitively priced. The store had a variety of products for each consumer. They offered sales and promotion that attracted more consumers. They also provided free samples and trials for their consumers. The company also provided a website that made it more convenient for consumers to shop from home. These stores were located in prime locations to attract more consumers. These stores had to recruit and maintain quality employees. Also they had to offer incentives to their employees. Manufacturers had to build strong relationships with these retailers to get shelf space, store promotion and product display area.

Advertising

74 Advertising was used in the beauty/feminine care product industry to make consumers aware of the products that were available. It was done through various forms, but companies had to be careful in choosing the form that would be suitable to convey their message to their target consumers. Advertising could be done through television, Internet, print, radio, and sales and promotions.

Television

75   Television was a very good form for advertising products because it had a large audience. Companies advertised through different methods. Some would produce commercials that focused on their products, while some would introduce their products in shows that they thought their target audience regularly watched. An example of a show that companies spent a lot of money on advertising was the Super Bowl in 2006. Some companies paid $3.5 million for 30 seconds to advertise their products. They believed that advertising their product during the show would help create awareness of their product.

76   The keys to success included several factors. Television stations had to be competitively priced. Manufacturers had to choose the appropriate channels and shows to advertise on. To do this successfully, they had to choose the audience they wanted to target for each product. The rating of the shows was an important factor that most companies considered before advertising on them. Sales promotion, coupon, and free products were a good way to attract the consumers.

Internet

77   Globally, the Internet was quickly becoming the most popular form of advertising because it was accessible to potential customers all over the world. The Internet affected many aspects of consumers' lives—the way they worked, played, and communicated, etc. The keys to success included several factors. Websites had to be competitively priced. Manufacturers had to choose the appropriate sites to advertise on. To do this successfully, they had to choose the audience they wanted to target for each product. Sales promotion, coupon, and free products were a good way to attract the consumers.

Print

78   This advertisement included those in the newspapers, magazines, and the likes. In early 2006, companies were gradually reducing the use of newspaper for advertising. They were moving to other forms of advertising, because in the United States, studies showed that people were reading less. These made some companies change from this form of advertising to others that they were sure their products information would reach their target audience. The keys to success included several factors. Printing media had to be competitively priced. Manufacturers had to choose the appropriate books, magazine, and newspaper to advertise on. To do this successfully, they had to choose the audience they wanted to target for each product. Sales promotion, coupon, and free products were a good way to attract the consumers.

Radio

79   Radio was another effective form of advertising. There were no visuals in radio advertising, just vocal information of the products. It had a large audience especially people listening at work or in their cars. In 2005, the XM satellite radio was launched and it offered a variety of channels including commercial free music channels. These features would encourage more people to listen to radio, creating a better channel for advertisement. The keys to success included several factors. Radio stations had to be competitively priced. Manufacturers had to choose the appropriate channels and shows to advertise on. To do this successfully, they had to choose the audience they wanted to target for each product. The rating of the shows was an important factor that most companies considered before advertising on them. Sales promotion, coupon, and free products were a good way to attract the consumers.

80   Advertisement was important to this industry. It helped educate the consumers on their products. It made them aware of the products, informed them of the uses, and encouraged them to go out and purchase them.

Sales and Promotions

81   Various sales and promotions such as free samples, coupons, and discounts were used by companies to attract more consumers. These methods were especially effective for new products. Sales and promotions for these products normally encouraged the consumers to take the risk and try the new product. Chain store outlets also used these methods to attract more customers. The keys to success included several factors. Customers and consumers had to be aware of the sales and promotions. They also had to be easy to use and be available to the consumers and customers.

Geographic Region

82　A geographic region was a term used to refer to a separated place on earth, such as Africa, Asia, Australia, Europe, Latin America, and North America.

- **Africa**—Africa was a continent with countries like Botswana which had a population of 1,640,115 people and Nigeria which had a population of 128,771,988 as of January, 2006 [CIA, 2006]. Most people in this continent had dark colored skin, and thick curly hair.
- **Asia**—Asia was a continent with countries like China which had a population of 1,306,313,812 people and Taiwan with a population of 22,894,384 people [CIA, 2006]. Most people in this continent had light colored skin with straight black hair.
- **Australia**—Australia was the sixth largest country in the whole world with about 20,090,437 people [CIA, 2006]. It was known for its uniqueness.
- **Europe**—Europe was a continent with countries like the United Kingdom which had a population of about 60,441,457 people and Spain with about 40,341,462 people [CIA, 2006].
- **South America**—South America included countries like Brazil with about 186,112,794 people and Colombia with about 42,954,279 people [CIA, 2006].
- **North America**—This was a continent with countries like the United States of America, which had a population of about 295,734,134 people and Canada with about 32,805,041 people [CIA, 2006].

83　These geographical regions had people who consumed beauty/feminine care products. So they were important for the existence of this industry. The keys to success included several factors. They had to be tailored to meet the needs of the consumers. For example in Asia manufacturers had to produce hair products that were suitable for straight hair and not kinky, curly hair. Brand recognition was also an important factor because consumers needed to feel like they could relate with the brand and its attributes. Products had to be competitively priced, and companies had to have a mass market presence in these regions.

Sourcing

84　Sourcing was a systematic procurement process that continuously improved and re-evaluated the purchasing activities of a company. It was a form of supply chain management. It involved various processes, such as formally selecting a vendor to supply a particular product or service that was routinely purchased by the company. This process included the definition of product and service requirements, identification of qualified suppliers, negotiation of pricing, service, delivery and payment terms, and supplier selection. Most times, the end result of the sourcing process was a negotiated contract with a preferred supplier [ICG Commerce, 2006].

85　Some manufacturing companies chose to outsource some or all of their processes to other companies in the same country they operated in or in another country. There were various reasons why companies outsourced. Some did it because it was cheaper, while others did it because they lacked the expertise required to make their products better.

86　The keys to success included several factors. Sources who wanted to sell to these manufacturing companies had to make their products competitively priced. They also had to be conveniently located to the manufacturing companies. Lastly they had to have a good transportation system to move these materials to and from the manufacturing company.

Technology

87   The beauty/feminine care industry was a capital intensive industry. The companies that manufactured these products required highly mechanized assembly lines which were designed for long production runs and flexibility. These companies constantly manufactured the same products over and over again, so they had to have machines that could run for long periods of time. Also due to the differences in their consumers, products sometimes had to be manufactured with some differences. An example was in the production of moisturizers; some consumers had oily skin while some had dry skin. During production, the companies had to make slight changes in the ingredients for their products to suit these differences in their consumers. In order to achieve this, the machines used had to be designed in a way that it allowed such changes and flexibility.

88   The Internet made business easier for some companies because it provided a fast and efficient way for them to communicate amongst themselves, with their customers, suppliers, and distributors. It also gave them the opportunity to research and get more information that helped to make their products better. With the introduction of the Internet, companies created and designed websites that helped their consumers and customers learn more about them, it gave them an opportunity to purchase things from the companies without leaving their homes.

89   The keys to success included several factors. The companies had to use high quality machines and technology systems, so they continuously had problems with them. These equipments also had to be flexible in their functions so they could be used to manufacture different products. They also had to be competitively priced so that it was affordable by these companies. The websites had to be designed properly so that they were easy to use.

Competition

90   Competition in beauty/feminine products was based on price, brand quality reputation, mass market presence, variety of products, brand recognition, and introduction of new products. Some of the companies in the beauty/feminine care industry were Unilever, Colgate-Palmolive, Playtex products, Avon, and Estee Lauder.

Unilever

91   Unilever was founded in 1930 in England, it was an international manufacturer of leading brands in foods, home care and personal care, such as Axe, Dove, Lux, Pond's, Rexona, Sunsilk, and Vaseline. Every day 150 million people in over 150 countries used one of their products. Unilever believed that most of their brands gave the benefits of feeling and looking good. The trends the company addressed in early 2006 were ageing populations, urbanization, changing diets, and lifestyles [Unilever Annual Report, 2005].

92   In regard to hair products, Unilever was strong brand quality reputation, price competition, mass market presence, variety of products, and brand recognition. It was moderately competitive in frequently introducing new products. In regard to skin product, Unilever was also strong in all keys to success except for development of products according to fashion trends, in which the company was only moderately competitive. Lastly in regards to the company's cleansing product, it was strong in all keys to success except for frequent new product introduction, in which the company was only moderately competitive. In early 2006, Unilever, did not manufacture feminine products, fine fragrances, and cosmetics.

93   In regard to Gender and age, it was strong in all keys to success. In regard to Ethnicity, Unilever was strong in all keys to success except for manufacturing products that were tailored to meet their needs and developing products according to trends, in which the

company was a weak competitor. In regards to marital status, it was strong in all keys to success except for manufacturing products that were tailored to meet their needs, high quality and value, and mass market presence, in which the company was only moderately competitive. In regards to low income consumers, Unilever was strong in all keys to success except for manufacturing products that were tailored to meet their needs, in which it was only moderately competitive.

94   In regard to distribution companies, it was moderately competitive in all keys to success except for competitive price in which the company was strongly competitive. In regards to chain store outlets, Unilever was strong in all keys to success except for recruiting quality employees, offering them incentives, and developing strong relationship with the store managers, in which it was only moderately competitive.

95   In regards to television advertising, the company was strong in all keys to success. The company was strong in all keys to success relating to Internet advertising. In regards to print advertising, the company was strong in all keys to success. The company was strong in all keys to success relating to radio advertising. In regards to geographic regions, it was strong in all keys to success except for mass market presence, in which it was moderately competitive. And in regards to sourcing, operations, and technology, Unilever was strong in all keys to success.

Colgate-Palmolive

96   Colgate-Palmolive was a $10.6 billion global consumer goods company, operating in more than 200 countries, with approximately 70% of its sales coming from international operations. The Company focused on strong global brands in its core businesses—Oral Care, Personal Care, Home Care, and Pet Nutrition. Its worldwide sales were up 5.5% on unit volume growth of 4.5%, on top of 9.0% volume growth in 2005 [Colgate Corporate News, 2006]. Worldwide they sold more than 40 different products and encouraged customers to try products by offering an array of sales promotions, such as coupons, free products, and discounts. Their beauty/feminine care products were Irish springs, Palmolive, Softsoaps, Colgate, Protex, Speed Sticks, and Lady Sticks.

97   In regards to skin products, Colgate-Palmolive was strong in brand recognition, variety of products, brand quality reputation, price competition, and mass market presence. The company was moderately competitive in the development of products according to fashion trends. Also in regards to the company's cleansing products, Colgate-Palmolive was strong in all keys to success except for frequent new product introduction, in which the company was only moderately competitive. In early 2006, Colgate-Palmolive, did not manufacture hair products, feminine products, fine fragrances, and cosmetics.

98   In regards to gender, age, and marital status, it was strong in all keys to success. In regards to ethnicity, the company was strong in all keys to success except for manufacturing products that were tailored to meet their needs and development of products according to fashion trends, in which it was a weak competitor. And in regards to low income consumers, it was moderately competitive in all keys to success.

99   In regard to distribution companies, it was strong in all keys to success. In regards to chain store outlets, Colgate-Palmolive was strong in all keys to success except for developing strong relationship with the store managers, in which it was only moderately competitive.

100   In regards to television advertising, the company was strong in all keys to success. The company was strong in all keys to success relating to Internet advertising. In regards to print advertising, the company was strong in all keys to success. The company was strong in all keys to success relating to radio advertising. In regards to geographic regions, it was strong in all keys to success except for mass market presence, in which it was moderately competitive. And in regards to sourcing, operations and technology, the company was strong in all keys to success.

Playtex Products

101 Playtex Products was a leading manufacturer and distributor of personal care products. It was founded in 1932 as the "International Latex Corporation" in Rochester, New York, selling latex products under the "Playtex" name. In January 1994, the Company went public as Playtex Products, Inc. Since then, Playtex has acquired many leading consumer brands, including Banana Boat, Wet Ones, Mr. Bubble, Ogilvie, Binaca, Diaper Genie and Baby Magic. Approximately 98% of the Company's net sales were from products that were number one or two in their respective markets. Net sales for the company from October 1, 2004 to October 1, 2005 were $651 million, continuing the Company's upward trend in sales of non-divested brands [Playtex Products Corporate news, 2006].

102 The company's Feminine Care products were leading the plastic applicator and deodorant tampon categories with brands like Gentle Glide, Beyond, and Portables. Also its skin care segment included Banana Boat sun care, Wet Ones hand and face wipes and Playtex Gloves. The Banana Boat brand offered a full spectrum of sun block, tanning, sunless tanning, and after-sun products. Banana Boat was the number two brand overall and the number one brand in after-sun care. Wet Ones and Playtex Gloves were both leaders in their markets [Playtex Products Corporate News, 2006].

103 In regards to skin products, Playtex Products was strong in brand quality reputation and price competition. It was moderately competitive in its variety of products and mass market presence and it was competitively weak in terms of brand recognition and development of products according to fashion trends. In regards to feminine products, the company was strong in all keys to success except for brand recognition and variety of products in which the company was only moderately competitive. In early 2006, Playtex Products did not manufacture hair products, fine fragrances, cosmetics, and personal cleansing products.

104 In regards to genders, it was strong in all keys to success except for various distribution channels and mass market presence in which the company was only moderately competitive. In regards to age, Playtex Products was moderately competitive in all keys to success except in competitive pricing, in which it was strongly competitive. In regards to marital status, it was moderately competitive in all keys to success. And in regards to low income consumers, it was moderately competitive in all keys to success except for brand recognition in which it was a weak competitor.

105 In regard to distribution companies and chain stores outlets it was moderately competitive in all keys to success. In regards to television advertising, the company was strong in all keys to success. The company was strong in all keys to success relating to Internet advertising. In regards to print advertising, the company was strong in all keys to success. The company was strong in all keys to success relating to radio advertising. In regards to geographic regions, it was moderately competitive in all keys to success, except for competitive pricing, in which it was strongly competitive. And in regards to sourcing, operations and technology, Playtex Products was strong in all keys to success.

Avon

106 Avon was the world's largest direct seller with almost 5 million representatives. Its products were available to consumers in 100 countries, with its representative earning about $3 billion annually. It all started in 1886 in the United States. In 2005, it became the world leader in anti-aging skin care products [Avon Annual Report, 2005].

107 The company's skin care brands included, Anew—a ground-breaking line of anti-aging skincare products. This brand contained popular products like Anew Retroactive+ and Anew Ultimate. Other products were the new blockbuster, Anew Clinical brands, a brand of targeted skin treatments that offered at-home alternatives to professional cosmetic treatments, and also Avon solutions—which was a full line of products that simplified the process of buying skincare without compromising results. Their hair care brands included, Advance

Techniques—which offered high performance hair products for every hair type, age group, and ethnic background to accommodate a diverse worldwide consumer base, and all of the products were formulated with conditioning ingredients that prevented long-term damage to hair. Avon was also the world's largest sellers of perfumes, with brands like Treselle, Perceive, Today, Tomorrow, and Always Trilogy. In early 2006, Avon did not manufacture hair products, and feminine products.

108   In regards to skin products, Avon was strong in brand quality reputation, price competition, and mass market presence. The company was moderately competitive in terms of brand recognition, variety of products, and development of products according to fashion trends. In regards to fine fragrances, the company was strong in brand quality reputation, price competition, and mass market presence. It was moderately competitive in brand recognition and development of products according to fashion trends. In the cosmetics segment of Avon, the company was strong in brand quality reputation, price competition, and mass market presence. It was moderately competitive in the variety of products, brand recognition, development of new products according to fashion trends. The cleansing products manufactured by Avon were strong in all keys to success except for brand recognition and frequent introduction of new products, in which it was moderately competitive.

109   In regards to genders, it was strong in all keys to success except for various distribution channels and mass market presence in which the company was only moderately competitive. In regards to age, Avon was moderately competitive in all keys to success except in competitive pricing, in which it was strongly competitive. In regards to ethnicity, the company was strongly competitive in price competition and high quality and value, it was moderately competitive in tailoring products to meet their needs, brand recognition, and brand loyalty, and a weak competition when it came to the development of products according to fashion trends. In regards to marital status, it was moderately competitive in all keys to success except for competitive pricing and high quality and value, in which it was strongly competitive. And in regards to low income consumers, it was moderately competitive in all keys to success.

110   In regard to distribution companies and chain stores outlets it was moderately competitive in all keys to success, except for competitive pricing, in which it was strongly competitive. In regards to television advertising, the company was strong in all keys to success. The company was strong in all keys to success relating to Internet advertising. In regards to print advertising, the company was strong in all keys to success. The company was strong in all keys to success relating to radio advertising. In regards to geographic regions, it was moderately competitive in all keys to success, except for competitive pricing, in which it was strongly competitive. And in regards to sourcing, operations and technology, Avon was strong in all keys to success.

Estee Lauder

111   Estee Lauder was founded in 1946; this technologically advanced, innovative company has gained a worldwide reputation for elegant, luxurious products in over 100 countries. The Company distributed their various products through department and specialty stores. The company was very involved in the breast cancer awareness program, being the largest corporate sponsor of The Breast Cancer Research Foundation, founded by Evelyn H. Lauder in 1993 [Estee Lauder Annual Report, 2005].

112   Their skin care segment included brands such as Re-Nutriv—which was an anti-aging cream for the eyes, Self-Tan—an air-brush self-tan spray for body, and Perfectionist—an anti-aging product for skin and lips. The cosmetics segments also included brands such as Pure Color Crystals, Graphic Color Eye Shadow Quad, Double wear, and Prime FX. Lastly their fragrance segment included brands like Beautiful, Pleasure, Intuitions, and Paradise. In early 2006, Estee Lauder did not manufacture hair products, feminine products, and personal cleansing products.

113   In regards to skin products, Estee Lauder was strong in brand quality reputation and price competition. It was moderately competitive in its variety of products and mass market presence and it was competitively weak in terms of brand recognition and development of products according to fashion trends. In regards to fine fragrances, the company was strong in brand quality reputation, price competition, and mass market presence. It was moderately competitive in brand recognition and development of products according to fashion trend. In the cosmetics segment of Estee Lauder, the company was strong in brand quality reputation, and price competition. It was moderately competitive in the variety of products, and brand recognition. In terms of mass market presence, and the frequent development of new products according to fashion trends, the company was competitively weak.

114   In regards to genders, it was moderately competitive in all keys to success except for high quality and value and promotion targeted to them, in which Estee Lauder was strongly competitive. In regards to age and marital status, it was moderately competitive in all keys to success. And in regards to low income consumers, it was a weak competitor in all keys to success, except for brand recognition in which it was moderately competitive.

115   In regard to distribution companies and chain stores outlets it was moderately competitive in all keys to success. In regards to television advertising, the company was strong in all keys to success. The company was strong in all keys to success relating to Internet advertising. In regards to print advertising, the company was strong in all keys to success. The company was strong in all keys to success relating to radio advertising. In regards to geographic regions, it was moderately competitive in all keys to success. And in regards to sourcing, operations, and technology, Estee Lauder was strong in all keys to success.

THE COMPANY

116   P&G was a company that manufactured, distributed and marketed consumer goods products. It was established in 1837 in the United States. It later started expanding to other countries and in early 2006 it was one of the global leaders in the consumer goods industry. It acquired its first overseas subsidiary with the purchase of Thomas Hedley & Sons Company, UK, in 1930. Also in 1915, P&G built a manufacturing facility in Canada, its first outside the US [Datamonitor, 2006].

117   In early 2006, the company had its headquarters in Cincinnati, Ohio. In the United States, the company owned and operated 35 manufacturing facilities which were located in 21 different states. Worldwide, the company owned and operated 83 manufacturing facilities in 42 countries. P&G provided branded products and services of superior quality and value that improved the lives of consumers all over the world. And as a result, it believed that the consumers rewarded it with leadership sales, profit, and value creation. These results allowed its people, shareholders, and the communities in which they lived and worked to prosper [P&G Company Information, 2006].

118   P&G's top 10 customers were Ahold, Albertson's, Carrefours, Costco, Kmart, Kroger, Metro, Target, Tesco, and Wal-Mart The company always acquired new brands and products, either my creating them or by merging with other companies. An example of these mergers was in 1985, P&G expanded its over-the-counter and personal health care business with the acquisition of Richardson-Vicks, owners of Vicks respiratory care and Oil of Olay product lines. Also in 1988, the company announced a joint venture to manufacture products in China. This marked the company's foray into the largest consumer market in the world [Datamonitor, 2006].

119   One of the threats that P&G faced was intense competition. It operated in an industry with rivals such as Unilever, Colgate-Palmolive, Playtex Products, Avon, and Estee Lauder. These companies operated and sold their products worldwide. Their presence in the same industry put

pressure on P&G to competitively price its products and continually strive to develop innovative products. Another threat was the increase in prices of raw materials. These prices were subject to price volatility caused by weather, supply conditions, and other unpredictable factors.

120   Lastly, the risk associated with merger integration was another threat for this company. In September 2003, P&G acquired Wella, owning 79.2 percent of the company's total shares. This acquisition contributed about $3.3 billion in sales to P&G's overall beauty business—around $1.6 billion in the professional hair care segment; $1 billion in the retail hair care segment and $800 million in fragrances. However, Wella's results (as of October 2003) were falling below P&G's stated long-term targets, giving an early indication of disruptions post its takeover [Datamonitor, 2006]. Other brands acquired by P&G were Clairol from Bristol-Myers Squibb in 2001 and Gillette in 2005.

121   In 2004, P&G did not manufacture products that were specifically for different ethnic groups, such as Hispanics and African Americans, and products that were made with natural ingredients. There was a high demand for these types of products because some consumers wanted to use products that were made from natural ingredients and some consumers wanted products that were made for their ethnic group.

122   In the United States it was virtually impossible to calculate the absolute number of companies that produced and marketed beauty/feminine care products. The field of competition was highly fragmented, for example, between those companies active in mass channels (supermarkets, chain drugstores, and mass merchandisers) and prestige channels, not to mention those active in the natural food and beauty care channel. The company size was another factor, between globally-oriented mega-corporations like P&G and kitchen table-based entrepreneurs limited to regional or even local distribution.

123   Although it was impossible to calculate the number of companies that produced and marketed beauty/feminine care products. It was obvious that P&G was one of the leaders in this industry because, as illustrated in Figure 8, P&G was well ahead of the industry.

124   P&G faced various challenges in 2006, such as consumers' interest in natural products. This trend was as a result of consumers questioning the ingredients used in making products and their effects. Some activists claimed that these products contained toxic chemicals known to cause cancer, fertility problems, and birth defects. Another challenge was the stagnant sales of some products due to low product development and innovation. Duane Reade Inc.'s Divisional Merchandise Manager, Mike Cirilli, said that "The market's poor sales will only turn around with the launch of dramatically different products. We need the leaders in these categories, such as P&G and L'Oreal to come out with some revolutionary products, spend $100 million on them in advertising and get all the consumers excited again. We need excitement. Excitement and advertising spending will bring sales dollars to these categories" [Packaged Facts, 2005].

FIGURE 8
Financial Information of P&G and the Industry

Source: Yahoo! Finance (2006). "Procter & Gamble 2006." [Online]. *http://finance.yahoo.com/q/co?s=PG.* Accessed March 17, 2006.

	P&G	Industry
Market capital	202.67B	275.79M
Employees	110,000	2.81K
Quarterly revenue growth	26.90%	10.40%
Revenue	61.68B	1.74B
Gross margin	51.05%	36.68%
EBITDA	14.42B	262.13M
Operating margins	19.95%	7.40%
Net income	7.77B	13.16M
EPS	2.733	1.23
P/E	22.55	22.50
PEG (5 yr expected)	2.02	2.02
P/S	3.28	2.05

125   The emerging men's market was another trend that was affecting the industry. The number of men spending time in front of the mirror, grooming themselves had increased. The acquisition of Gillette helped P&G to start to address this trend with products like Gillette's complete skin care for men and Gillette's Fusion. This was some of the steps that P&G decided to take to remain at the top in the beauty/feminine care segment. Following were detailed analyses of P&G's business model, as illustrated below in Figure 9. It serves as the framework in discussing the company's strategy on business development.

Products

126   When the company started in 1837, it was producing only two products, candles, and soap. In early 2006, P&G was manufacturing, marketing, and distributing close to a hundred different brands. These brands and products were sold to consumers worldwide.

127   In 2005, the beauty/feminine care segment of P&G delivered its third consecutive year of double digit growth in volume, sales, and profit. Volume increased 12%, sales increased 14%, and net earnings increased 22%. The industry leading performance was driven mainly by broad-based organic growth across geographies and brands. Each of its top 10 countries delivered higher sales than 2004, with solid gains in both developed and developing markets. Global market shares continued to grow, with most of its leading brands at record highs [P&G Annual Report, 2005].

128   P&G produced products that were used by males and females. With the growing trend for men to use beauty products, the company started manufacturing more products for them. They designed the products so that it would attract male consumers, by using dark color for the packaging so that it looked more masculine. Some of P&G's products were hair products, skin products, feminine products, fine fragrances, cosmetics, and personal cleansing products.

Hair Products

129   P&G offered a variety of hair products. These products passed through different processes before they reached the consumers. A major process was the testing phase. These products were developed for different types of hair—normal, dry, greasy, permed, bleached, and so

FIGURE 9   **P & G**

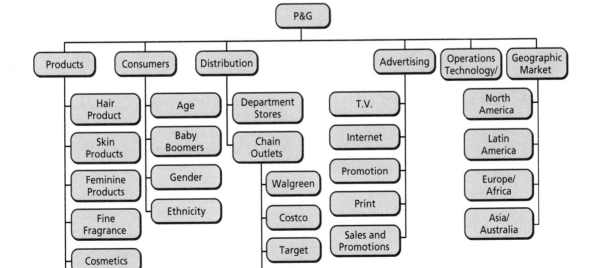

on. So each product had to be tested, not only as a formulation that was to be stored for months in a bottle or tube and then sold, but also as a product that was to be used on human hair and scalp.

130   The process started in the laboratory; the experimental formulation was thoroughly tested on cut lengths of human hair . . . before production was considered.

131   The products under test were applied to the hair and rinsed off, and an experienced technician judged the amount of tangling, stretching, perming, and coloring that resulted. After that, a complex computer-assisted technology assessed many aspects of the product's performance. If all went well, the products were evaluated in real life conditions, on the hair of clients in salons. This was an essential part of testing, because it was the only way to judge whether the new product was acceptable to consumers. Only when these tests were completed safely and satisfactorily did the products go on the open market for the consumers to try. This whole process might have involved thousands of tests and took up to a couple of months or even years to complete [P&G Hair Care, 2003].

132   Some of the hair products brands which were produced by P&G were: Herbal Essence—this brand offered a variety of shampoo, conditioners and styling aids, Infususium 23—this brand included shampoos, conditioners, specialty care products, leave-ins, Physique—these products included cutting-edge technology formulas, Pantene—these products included amino pro-v complex, Aussie—these products were produced using Australian ingredients, and Head & Shoulders—products used to eliminate dryness, irritation, and itchiness of the scalp.

133   In regards to hair products, P&G was strong in brand quality reputation, price competition, mass market presence, variety of products, and brand recognition. It was moderately competitive in frequently introducing new products.

Skin Products

134   P&G tried to address the three main types of skin. Which were oily, normal, and dry. Some of the skin care products brands it produced were: Noxzema—this included facial cleansers in the form of creams, pads, and astringents, Gillette—this included shave multigel, facial moisturizers, razors, shaving sticks, and skin soothing after shave, and Olay—this brand offered products that provided multiple benefits that were designed for women of all ages.

135   Each product was made for a different function. The skin cleanser was used to remove surface dirt, make-up, top layer of dead skin cells and potentially harmful micro-organisms (bacteria). Skin toner was used after cleansing to ensure complete removal from the skin of all cleansing preparations, and also after a face mask to remove all traces of the mask. These products were based on plant extracts and sometimes contained alcohol. Skin moisturizers hydrated the skin, and/or protected the skin from dehydration. That is, it was designed to improve water retention in the skin. They could be in the form of creams, lotions or serums [P&G Skin Care, 2003].

136   In regards to skin products, P&G was strong in brand recognition, variety of products, brand quality reputation, price competition, and mass market presence. It was moderately competitive in the development of products according to fashion trends.

Feminine Products

137   Some of the feminine products brands produced by P&G were: Tampax—this brand included different size of tampons. Another brand was Always, which included different styles and sizes of sanitary pads. Always was the world's leading feminine care brand, it grew in volume by 11% and reached record-high global market share of 22% [P&G Annual Report, 2005]. Feminine products were specifically for females to use during their menstrual cycles. The target consumers for these products were generally females from the ages of 12 to 40 years old.

138   In regards to feminine products, P&G was strong in brand quality reputation, price competition, mass market presence, variety of products, and brand recognition.

Fine Fragrances

139   P&G was a major distributor of fine fragrances brands such as: Giorgio Beverly Hills—this included products such as Giorgio, G and Red. Another brand was Hugo Boss—which included Hugo Deep Red, Hugo Woman and Hugo Energise, which were used by either men or women. Hugo Boss, along with Lacoste—which was now 10 times bigger than when P&G acquired the license in 2001—further strengthened its global leadership position in men's fine fragrances [P&G Annual Report, 2005].

140   In regards to fine fragrances, P&G was strong in brand quality reputation, price competition, brand recognition, and mass market presence. It was moderately competitive in the development of products according to fashion trends.

Cosmetics

141   P&G's target consumer for cosmetics were women of all ages. The cosmetics included those for lips, face, nails, eyes, etc. P&G had two major brands for cosmetics. First was Covergirl, which was for women who wanted to have a clean, fresh, and natural look. It included foundation, loose powder, eye shadow, mascara, etc. The other brand was Max Factor, which gave women a more edgy look, making them look more like celebrities. This brand also included various products, such as lip gloss, mascara, eye shadow, etc.

142   In regards to cosmetics, P&G was strong in variety of products, brand quality reputation, brand recognition, price competition, and mass market presence. It was moderately competitive in the development of products according to fashion trends and in frequently introducing new products.

Personal Cleansing

143   P&G had a couple of brands that included personal cleansing products. These products included bar soaps, body wash and cleansing bars, that were used for cleaning the body. The target consumers for these products were everybody. People needed to stay clean to reduce infections, illness, and smell that were related to dirt. One of the brands that P&G provided was Zest. It believed that this product was refreshingly different from ordinary soap. It rejuvenated the consumer with a combination of great, refreshing scent and clean-rinsing lather that would not dry skin like soap [P&G Product Information, 2006]. Other products were Camay, which was a moisturizing bar soap enriched with perfumes of French inspiration that P&G believed would leave skin feeling fresh, soft and sensual. And Noxzema, which included creams, astringent, and pad, used for deep cleaning.

144   In regards to personal cleansing products, P&G was strong in brand recognition, price competition, variety of products, brand quality reputation, and mass market presence. It was moderately competitive in frequently introducing new products.

Consumers

145   Consumer goods were used by everyone. Consumers for P&G's products could be segmented into age, gender, ethnicity, and low-income consumers.

Age

146   P&G addressed each age group differently and produced products that were suitable for them to use. An example was the group of people that were showing signs of aging. P&G understood that as people aged, their skin's vitality and radiance were reduced. So in the skin care segment, the company produced products that would address these issues. One of the products it produced was the Olay's total effect. Which it believed would fight seven signs of aging. These products diminished the appearance of fine lines and wrinkles, smoothed skin texture, evened skin tone, improved surface dullness, gave skin a radiant, healthy glow, minimized the appearance of pores, visibly reduced the appearance of blotches and age spots, and soothed dry skin [P&G Product Information, 2006].

147   When it came to the company's hair products, an example of the group of people it considered was the baby boomers and senior citizens. These people had similar issues such as loss and dryness of hair. P&G produced products like Head & Shoulders, which eliminated dryness, itchiness, and irritations. Another product which P&G produced that could be used by these age groups was the Pantene Sheer Volume, because it increased hair volume and made it look healthier.

148   In regards to age, P&G was strong in brand image, brand recognition, price competition, variety of products, brand loyalty, mass market presence.

Gender

149   P&G manufactured products that could be used by both men and women. Some products could be used by both groups, while others were specifically for either one of them.

150   In 2005, the men beauty market was emerging and growing at a very fast rate. Men were more interested in grooming themselves and looking good. Some people called this group of men, metrosexuals, because they liked to groom and take care of themselves. P&G acknowledged this trend and in late 2005, the company acquired Gillette. This acquisition put P&G at the top of this market. It produced products like Gillette fusion, Gillette complete skin care, and Gillette MacH3, which were used by men to keep themselves looking good.

151   Women on the other hand, have always been interested in looking beautiful. P&G had various products that satisfied their needs, from Olay's base moisturizers, that smoothened and softened skin to Covergirl cosmetics that was used to put on the most beautiful face possible [P&G Product Information, 2006]. P&G Beauty segment was focused on delivering consumer understanding that reached beyond functional needs to connect at a deeper emotional level. It was a leader in innovation that went beyond science to include sophisticated design that created a total beauty experience and delight for consumers [P&G Annual Report, 2005]. These processes made the consumers to connect with the company and its attributes, building consumer loyalty and brand recognition.

152   In regards to gender, P&G was strong in price competition, high quality and value, brand loyalty, promotion targeted to them, various distribution channels, and mass market presence.

Ethnicity

153   P&G understood that their consumers belonged to different ethnic groups. It produced products that would suit their different needs. To be very effective in reaching these groups, P&G set up strategies to market these groups. In 2005, P&G was one of the leaders in multicultural marketing and was awarded for their jobs by agencies. An example of an agency that awarded the company was the Association of Hispanics Advertising Agencies.

154   Another ethnic group that P&G was actively involved with was the African-Americans. In 2005, Anne Sempowski Ward, the Associate Marketing Director for the African-American Marketing team of P&G released the following statement:

> P&G's commitment to African-Americans is stronger today than ever before. It has spanned more than a century and is still growing—collective accomplishment rooted in the vision and actions of our leadership, the involvement of our local plants, and the interest of individual employees. African-American ideas, experiences, customs and lifestyles are represented throughout our advertising and packaging and have inspired several product innovations. We look forward to the next 100 years, and thank you for your support as P&G continues to make journeys of hope, freedom and success possible. [P&G Ethnic Echoes, 2005].

155   An example of how P&G incorporated ethnicity into its products was in the hair care segment, for ethnic groups such as Caucasians which included people who had different color of hair. The company produced Clairol's highlighting and blonding, which helped to color and maintain the color of hair.

156   In regards to ethnicity, P&G was strong in products tailored to meet their needs, brand recognition, developing products according to fashion trends, price competition, high quality and value, and brand loyalty.

Low-income Consumers

157   P&G was constantly innovating ways to reach more consumers. The low income consumers were a group that the company really wanted to target. It understood that these people had low disposable income and decided to manufacture products that they could afford. Some ways it reduced the prices of its products were to reduce the sizes of these products. It also changed some of its packages, so that the product was cheaper and easier to store. An example was changing the package from boxes to bags.

158   In regards to low-income consumers, P&G was strong in products tailored to meet their needs, brand recognition, mass market presence, and brand loyalty.

Distribution

159   P&G had a very effective distribution system. It was used to distribute their products to their consumers. This function was also a form of capital for the company, when it helped other companies distribute their products. P&G had various distribution centers all over the world. In June 2005, P&G built a new Canadian Distribution Center in Brantford, Ontario. This center was built to serve the company's $2 billion national business. The site employed more than 150 people and the total investment was estimated to be $70 million [P&G Annual Report, 2005].

160   In the United States, a major distribution center was the Brown Summit, which was located in Greensboro, North Carolina. The center held over 1,000 different products. Most of these products were from U.S. plants shipped when orders where made by the customers. The distribution channels of P&G included departmental store, such as Macy's and JCPenny and discount stores such as Wal-Mart and Costco. P&G's biggest customer is Wal-Mart. In 1980s, the two giants built a software system that linked P&G up to Wal-Mart's distribution centers. This system was called the Supply Chain System (SCS). It was used to facilitate the coordination with outside business entities. In the case of P&G and Wal-Mart, whenever the inventory level of P&G's products at Wal-Mart's distribution centers reached re-order point, the system automatically alerted P&G to ship more products. This process helped to manage inventory and increase profit. P&G distributed its products through distribution companies and chain store outlets.

161   In regards to distribution, P&G was strong in all keys to success, such as price competition, variety of products, recruiting good employees, offering incentives to employees, strong relationship with store manager, and store sales and promotion.

Advertising

162   With over 300 brands to market, P&G was specialized in advertising its products. For the past 5 years, the company has constantly increased its advertising cost, as shown in Figure 10, to accommodate its growing brands. The company used various media to reach its consumers, such as the television, Internet, radio and print. It offered sale promotions, such as free trials, discounts and coupons. These advertisements served different purposes for the company. First they made consumers aware of the products. These advertisements were sometimes made to be interactive, so that they held the consumer's attention. They also served to make the consumers aware of sale promotions that were going on at a particular

FIGURE 10

Advertising Expenses

Source: P&G Annual Report
(2005). [Online]. *http://www.
pg.com/annualreports/2005/
pdf/pG2005annualreport.pdf.*
Accessed March 17, 2006.

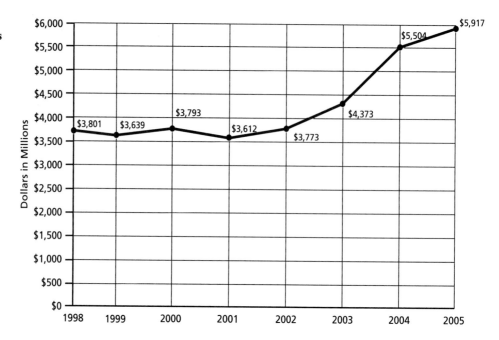

time. And lastly it helped to convince consumers that they needed the product, so they actually went out and purchased them.

163   In each segment of the company, P&G hired employees who were responsible for marketing their products. These representatives would move from store to store, selling its products to the store managers. These interactions helped to build a better relationship with the store managers, because these managers helped increase and maximize shelf space and also provided better displays for P&G's product. P&G advertised on television, Internet, print, and radio.

Television

164   P&G created commercials and it was careful to choose the right channels and shows that it hoped its target consumers viewed. Most of its commercials showed people using its products and their experiences after using them.

Internet

165   P&G used the Internet to advertise because it could reach its consumers worldwide. It did this advertisement through various methods, such as posters on websites, emailing codes for samples and discounts, and the likes.

Print

166   In 2000, advertising on prints such as newspapers, magazines, and the likes was declining. In early 2006, P&G still used this form of advertising to reach those consumers that read these prints. It advertised its products by showing picture of people using their products or just by showing its products and explaining their uses.

Radio

167   P&G also advertised on radio because it was effective in reaching some consumers. Since radio was audio, P&G did not have to spend money on creating and directing visual commercials.

Sales and Promotions

168 P&G also used various sales and promotions such as free samples, coupons, and discounts. These methods were used by the company to attract more consumers. These methods were especially effective for new products. Sale and promotion for these products normally encouraged the consumers to take the risk and try the new product. P&G's consumers had to be made aware of the sales and promotions so they could go out and use them to purchase the products.

169 In regards to advertising, P&G was strong in all keys to success, such as ratings, audience, price of advertisement, offering coupons and samples, availability, easy to use, and awareness.

Operations/Technology

170 P&G was a manufacturing company that prided itself on the quality of its products. To achieve such high quality, the company had to ensure it had the right machines and facilities required to manufacture its products. When the company could not effectively manufacture parts of its product, it outsourced that function to another company to help it do it better.

171 With the introduction of the Internet, P&G moved to greater heights. It created numerous ways for the company to do business in a faster and more efficient way. It was easier for it to communicate with their customers, suppliers, and distributors. It also gave P&G the opportunity to research and get more information that helped to make its products better. With the introduction of the Internet, P&G created and designed its website that helped its consumers and customers learn more about the company; it gave them an opportunity to purchase things from the company without leaving their homes.

172 In regards to operations/technology, P&G was strong in all keys to success, such as high quality machines and technology, flexibility, competitive price, affordability, and properly designed websites.

Geographical Regions

173 In early 2006, the geographical regions that P&G operated in were Africa, Asia, Australia, Europe, South America, and North America. The company did not operate in all countries in these continents. Some of the countries it did not operate in had a high demand for consumer goods such as Togo in Africa.

174 It was strong in all keys to success such as products tailored to needs, brand recognition, price competitive, and mass market presence.

Financial Analysis

175 For the past 5 years, P&G's net sales have grown, as shown in Figure 11. The company was a global leader with sales growth of more than 40%, increasing to $57 billion. P&G's profit also more than doubled in 2005 and they generated more than $30 billion in free cash flow. Shareholders received $11 billion in cash through dividends and this increased their value with another $60 billion by nearly doubling the price of P&G stock. The company has increased sales per employee nearly 40% over the past five years and even though Research and Development (R&D) investment has increased over the past years, R&D as a percentage of sales has declined from 4.8% in 2000 to 3.4% in 2005. More than 80% of initiatives succeeded in creating shareholder value, an improvement of 25% over the past three years. The productivity of P&G's product supply organization has increased at a high single-digit rate since 2000 and there had been a decrease in P&G's Global Business Services (GBS) costs by more than 15% on base business services since 2000.

176 Companies tried to increase profit by various methods. One of these methods was to reduce cost. P&G reduced capital spending as a percentage of sales since 2000 from nearly 8% to less than 4%, without foregoing any strategic investment in growth. They also added

FIGURE 11
**P&G'S Financial
Data—Net Sales**

Source: P&G Annual Report
(2005). [Online]. *http://www.
pg.com/annualreports/2005/
pdf/pG2005annualreport.pdf.*
Accessed March 17, 2006.

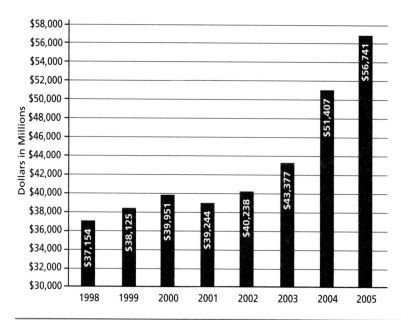

Amounts in millions except per share amounts	Years Ended June 30					
	2005	**2004**	**2003**	**2002**	**2001**	**2000**
Net sales	$56,741	$51,407	$43,377	$40,238	$39,244	$39,951
Operating income	10,927	9,827	7,853	6,678	4,736	5,954
Net earnings	7,257	6,481	5,186	4,352	2,922	3,542
Net earnings margin	12.8%	12.6%	12.0%	10.8%	7.4%	8.9%
Basic net earnings per common share	$2.83	$2.46	$1.95	$1.63	$1.08	$1.30
Diluted net earnings per common share	2.66	2.32	1.85	1.54	1.03	1.23
Dividends per common share	1.03	0.93	.082	0.76	0.70	0.64

an incremental growth point to the company's top line over the past two years with marketing Return on Investment (ROI) initiatives [P&G Annual Report, 2005].

Management Strategy

177   One of P&G's strategies was to build existing core businesses into stronger global leaders. In 2005, the company grew market share, profit, and sales in all its core categories, such as its beauty and health segments. These increases were achieved by the decision to reach more consumers, especially low income consumers and the acquisition of Gillette. This acquisition increased the brands, products, and consumers of the company. Another strategy was to develop faster-growing, higher-margin, more asset efficient businesses with global leadership potential. In 2005, this was evident in the beauty segment, where sales nearly doubled to $19.5 billion and profit more than doubled to $2.9 billion. This growth was also noticed in the Health Care segment, where sales doubled to $7.8 billion and profit more than tripled to $1 billion. These two segments made up 47% of P&G's sales and 50% of the company's profit [P&G Annual Report, 2005].

178   Internationally, P&G tried to regain growth momentum and leadership in Western Europe, by introducing new products and increasing advertisements. In 2005, the Western Europe volume went up mid-single digit and on average it went up twice the rate of

Western Europe Gross Domestic Profit (GDP) growth. At the end of the year, the company's brands growing share in categories accounted for more than half of Western Europe sales. Another major strategy for P&G was to increase growth among lower-income consumers in developing markets, such as Nigeria and Ghana. To attract these consumers, P&G changed the package, making them small and reducing the quality of the packaging, so it was more affordable for these consumers. This strategy has delivered mid-teens volume growth, on average, in these countries.

LOOKING TOWARDS THE FUTURE

179   Since 2000, A.G. Lafley and his colleagues have been successful in trying to maximize the strengths of the company, while also reducing its weaknesses. They have worked to increase P&G's brands, net sales, and profit. In 2005, male consumers became more interested in beauty products, and to satisfy this need and other issues the company were facing, P&G acquired Gillette. It also entered a major multimedia marketing partnership with Viacom Plus in 2001, to create more ways to reach its consumers.

180   On various occasions, the executives and employees of P&G discussed strategies that would make P&G a better company and put it ahead of its competitors, such as Unilever, Colgate-Palmolive, Playtex Products, Avon, and Estee Lauder. Some of the strategies they discussed are as follows:

181   The first alternative was for P&G to expand and build existing core businesses, such as the health and beauty segments. It decided to do this by reaching more consumers, especially the low income consumers. These segments would be expanded to include new brands and products which would attract such consumers. The already existing products would be altered by reducing their sizes and changing their packages to reduce their prices. Doing this would make it easier for consumers to buy them.

182   The **benefit** of this strategic alternative was that P&G would only have to expand on products and services it already had. It would not have to spend a lot of money on research and development, reducing the cost for the company. At the same time it would reach more customers just by altering some of its products.

183   This alternative was **feasible** because P&G had already built strong brand recognition and loyalty with its consumers. Consumers would need little conviction to buy another product from the same company. P&G had also already built a strong relationship with most of the large chain store outlets, such as Wal-Mart. So the distribution process would remain effective for the new products that would be introduced into the market. The company already had the expertise within each of its segments required to support the introduction of new brands. From 2000 to 2005, P&G's net income increased, so the company had the financial resources to create or acquire new brands. It would also be able to afford the costs that would be attributed to these brands, and at the same time maintain its position as the global leader in the Consumer goods industry.

184   This alternative would **win against the competition** such as multinational firms like Unilever, Colgate-Palmolive, Playtex Products, Avon, and Estee Lauder, because P&G would increase its brands and products to reach more consumers. The company would do this by merging with other companies to create more products and specifically targeting the low income consumers. These consumers represented a large part of the consumer base and changing its products by reducing the packaging size and quality would reduce the price of the products making it more attractive and affordable for these consumers. These changes would increase its sales and make its products more price competitive.

185   The **drawback** of this alternative was the reduction in its expertise in one particular product. P&G had so many products, that it was difficult to appropriately manage each and every one of them. Another drawback was the lack of enough prestigious products, such as very expensive fragrances. There was not enough attention given to high earning consumers who were able to afford such products. This alternative also did not address consumers who were interested in products that contained natural ingredients. The current trend was to use products with natural ingredients because of the uncertainty that came with using products manufactured with chemicals. People feared that using such products resulted in health problems, such as cancer and infertility. **A way around this drawback** was to get more qualified employees so P&G could continue to appropriately manage each product. The company also needed to manufacture products that incorporated the trends as mentioned above.

186   The second alternative was for P&G to focus and expand just on its skin care segment of the beauty/feminine care segment. The company would focus and specialize just on these products. It would produce different types of products for each ethnic group, products that had natural ingredients (such as herbs), and more skin products for men. It would have to sell all its other products, such as its hair products, cosmetics, feminine products and fine fragrances. The money from the sale of these products would be used to acquire more brands and products in the skin care segment.

187   The **benefit** of this alternative was that it would enable the company to focus just on one segment of the beauty/feminine care division and do it well. P&G would be able to apply all its resources and skills to this segment. Its employees would all be working in the same field, making it easier to share information between each other. The marketing team would only need to collect information from its consumers about skin products, making it easier to market and advertise these products.

188   This alternative was **feasible** because P&G already had a skin care segment. It just had to expand its products to incorporate every trend. P&G was financially capable of doing this, especially after selling of its other segments. The company already had a strong relationship with most of the large chain stores outlet, such as Costco and Wal-Mart. So the distribution process would remain effective for the new products that would be introduced into the market. P&G's employees already had the expertise within this segments required to support the introduction of new brands.

189   This alternative would **win against the competition** because P&G would increase its products and expertise in the skin care segment. The company would offer a wider variety of skin care products that would satisfy more consumers' needs. Satisfying more consumers would increase the company's sale and number of consumers, allowing P&G to win against its competitors such as Unilever, Colgate-Palmolive, Playtex Products, Avon, and Estee Lauder. Concentrating on this segment would also create a better environment for P&G to create more innovative products according to trends and this would keep it ahead of its competitors.

190   The **drawback** of this alternative was the loss of its other segments. The company would lose those consumers that wanted other products, such as hair products, cosmetics, fine fragrances, and feminine products. P&G's employees would also lose the flexibility of moving from one segment to the other. This flexibility would have allowed them to learn about different segments in the consumer goods industry. **A way around this drawback** was to allow another company such as Unilever who sold products in these other segments to use P&G's name to sell its products. This would satisfy the needs of those consumers who would prefer to use products associated with P&G. And also those employees who wanted to get more experience and flexibility could also go to this other company and work for a while.

191   Lafley and his colleagues had a tough choice to make. These and other alternatives needed to be considered very carefully before reaching a decision which will impact the Company's future substantially.

LIST OF WORKS CITED

Aboutsears (2006). [Online]. *http://www.aboutsears.com/*. Accessed February 15, 2006.

Avon Annual Report (2005). [Online]. *http://www.avoncompany.com/investor/annual-report/index.html*. Accessed February 15, 2006.

BEA (2006). "News release". [Online]. *http://www.bea.gov/bea/newsrel/pinewsrelease. htm*. Accessed January 25, 2006.

CIA (2006). "The world fact book". [Online]. *http://www.cia.gov/cia/publications/ factbook/fields/2119.html*. Accessed March 21, 2006.

Colgate Corporate News (2006). [Online]. *http://www.colgate.com/app/Colgate/US/ Corp/ChairmansMessage.cvsp*. Accessed February 15, 2006.

Costco Services (2006). [Online]. *http://www.costco.com/*. Accessed February 15, 2006.

Datamonitor (2006). "Procter and Gamble". [Online]. *http://cpprod.stjohns.edu/cp/tag. b9b8fA3031868bbe.render.userLayoutRootNode.uP?uP_root=root&uP_sparam=activ eTab&activeTab=U1l1lS39&uP_tparam=frm&frm=frame*. Accessed March 17, 2006.

Economist (2006). "Pots of promise". [Online]. *http://www.economist.com/printedi-tion/displayStory.cfm?Story_ID=1795852*. Accessed January 25, 2006.

EIS (2005). [Online]. *http://www.eia.doe.gov/neic/infosheets/petroleumproducts.htm*. Accessed February 12, 2006.

Estee Lauder Annual Report (2005). [Online]. *http://www.esteelauder.com/home.tmpl*. Accessed February 15, 2006.

Hoovers (2006). "Companies information". [Online]. *http://www.hoovers.com/ company-information/--HICID__1486--/free-ind-factsheet.xhtml*. Accessed February 12, 2006.

ICG Commerce (2006). "Strategic Sourcing". [Online]. *http://www.icgcommerce.com/ corporate/doc/html/resource/procurement_terms.htm*. Accessed March 17, 2006.

Packaged Facts (2005). - A division of marketresearch.com. "The U. S. Market for hair products". [Online]. *http://cpprod.stjohns.edu/misc/timedouT2.html*. Accessed January 25, 2006.

Playtex Products Corporate News (2006) [Online]. *http://www.playtexproductsinc. com/index.htm*. Accessed February 15, 2006.

Procter & Gamble 2005 Annual Report (2006). [Online]. *http://www.pg.com/ annualreports/2005/pdf/pG2005annualreport.pdf*. Accessed January 22, 2006.

Procter & Gamble Corporate News (2006). [Online]. *http://pg.com/news/index.jhtml. http://ccbn.mobular.net/ccbn/7/1142/1201/*. Accessed January 22, 2006.

Procter & Gamble Company Information (2006). [Online]. *http://www.pg.com/ company/index.jhtml*. Accessed February 22, 2006.

Procter & Gamble Hair Care (2003). [Online]. *http://www.pg.com/science/haircare/ hair_twh_116.htm*. Accessed February 27, 2006.

Procter & Gamble Skin Care (2003). [Online]. *http://www.pg.com/science/skincare/ Skin_tws_toc.htm*. Accessed February 27, 2006.

Procter & Gamble Product Information (2006). [Online]. *http://www.pg.com/product_ card/brand_overview.jhtml*. Accessed February 27, 2006.

Procter & Gamble Ethnic Echoes (2005). [Online]. *http://www.pg.com/images/company/ who_we_are/diversity/multi/echo_feb_april05.pdf*. Accessed March 5, 2006.

Target Corporate News (2006) [Online]. *http://sites.target.com/site/en/corporate/page. jsp?contentId=PRD03-000482*. Accessed February 15, 2006.

Unilever Annual Report (2005). [Online]. *http://www.unilever.com/ourcompany/ investorcentre/.* Accessed February 22, 2006.

U.S. Census Bureau (2004). "U. S. Interim projections by Age, Sex, Rave and Hispanic origin". [Online]. *http://www.census.gov/prod/99pubs/P20-514u.pdf.* Accessed February 12, 2006.

Wal-Mart Corporate news (2006). [Online]. *http://www.walmartstores.com/ GlobalWMStoresWeb/navigate.do?catg=316.* Accessed February 15, 2006.

Webster Dictionary (2006). [Online] *http://www.webster.com/.* Accessed February 10, 2006.

Wikipedia (2006). [Online]. *http://en.wikipedia.org/wiki/Main_Page. http://en.wikipedia.org/wiki/Baby_boomer* Accessed January 30, 2006.

Walgreen Corporate News (2006). [Online]. *http://investor.walgreens.com/home.cfm.* Accessed February 15, 2006.

Case 41

Provide Commerce Inc: *The Organic Perishable Goods Industry*

Anthony Onwugbenu, Marc E. Gartenfeld, Dorothy Dologite, and Robert J. Mockler

INTRODUCTION

1 Bill Strauss, CEO of Provide Commerce, stated, "We are pleased with out Valentine's Day shipments which delivered more than six million stems of roses and more than two million stems of tulips during the holiday period. Our value pricing, targeted marketing and extensive floral product selection continued to drive growth." Strauss continued, "We believe that our direct business model which delivers fresh, high quality flowers every day, will continue to drive growth and customer satisfaction. We look forward to building on this momentum throughout the remainder of fiscal 2005."

2 Provide Commerce Inc operated an e-commerce marketplace of websites for perishable organic goods that consistently delivered fresh, high-quality products direct from the supplier to the customer at competitive prices. The company's platform combined an online storefront, proprietary supply chain management technology and established supplier relationships to create a market platform that bypassed traditional supply chains of distributors and retailers.

3 The increasing pervasiveness of the Internet was driving growth in online shopping and changing the manner in which companies merchandised and distributed products. Consumer Internet purchases were being driven by heightened awareness and a first hand experience regarding its convenience, security, and usability. In addition, consumers were also using the Internet to access products and shopping experiences not previously available through traditional retail channels.

4 The company launched proflower.com, a floricultural division, in 1998 to retail organic floricultural products, through a website, fresher than its competitors by utilizing a business model that sourced organic products directly from the producers and brought them straight to the consumers. With the success of the initial website, the company had leveraged its business model onto two organic categories: cherry moons.com, a division which retailed organic agricultural produce and, uptownprime.com, a division which retailed organic meat products. With the continued success of its three divisions, the company was faced with a new challenge of continuing the momentum and identifying new organic categories to expand into. In light of the challenge, management was faced with answering key decisions such as should Provide Commerce Inc explore the undeveloped children's market? Should the company enter the organic wellness market which strives to satisfy a wide consumer base? How should the company improve on its brand recognition in an industry where organic goods were uniform? The main strategic question to be resolved was what organic categories the company could expand into while utilizing its business model to offer higher quality organic goods than its competitors.

INDUSTRY AND COMPETITIVE MARKET: THE NONDURABLE GOODS INDUSTRY

5 Nondurable goods were tangible products that could be stored or inventoried and had an average life of less than three years. As shown in Figure 1, this industry consisted of paper,

This case was prepared by Anthony Onwugbenu, Marc E. Gartenfeld, Dorothy Dologite, and Professor Robert J. Mockler of St. John's University. © Robert J. Mockler.

FIGURE 1 The Nondurable Goods Industry

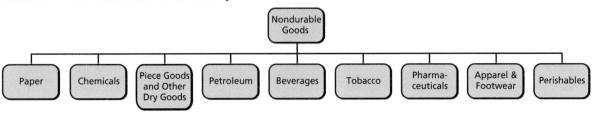

chemicals, piece goods and other dry goods, petroleum, beverages, tobacco, pharmaceuticals, apparel and footwear, and perishables. According to the Bureau of Economic Analysis, the nondurable goods contributed a positive 0.73 annual percent change in real domestic product (GDP) for fiscal year 2004, a .18 percent increase from 2003 [BEA, 2005].

Paper

6   This industry group was comprised of paper products that were segmented into three subdivisions: industrial and personal service, printing and writing, and stationery and office supplies.

Industrial and Personal Service

7   This subdivision focused on craft wrapping and other coarse paper, paperboard, and converted paper.

Printing and Writing

8   This subdivision focused on bulk printing and/or writing paper generally on rolls for further processing. This type of paper was used in newspapers and school notebooks.

Stationery and Office Supplies

9   This subdivision focused on stationery, office supplies and/or gift wrap. Examples were bonded paper and letter writing paper.

Chemicals

10   This industry group focused on industrial and consumer goods chemicals.

Industrial

11   This subdivision focused on dyes used on fabrics, ammonia used in fertilizers, additives used in cement, adhesives, sealants, pesticides, and acids.

Consumer Goods

12   This subdivision focused on detergents, cleaning compounds, and bleaches.

Piece Goods and Other Dry Goods

13   This industry group included piece goods which in turn included belts, buckles and zippers, fabrics, knitting and industrial yarns, thread, and hair accessories.

Petroleum

14   This industry group was comprised of crude oil, jet fuel, gasoline, liquefied petroleum gas (LPG), and lubricating oils and greases. The instability in the Middle East region, which accounted for one-third of the world's oil reserves and the continued phenomenal growth of the Chinese economy raised the price per barrel above $50 in 2004. Recent Syria and Lebanese tensions, continued insurgence in the Iraq, and the imminent global threat of terrorism would influence the volatility of oil prices. With China's dependence on oil imports

forecasted to rise 45% by 2010 due to its phenomenal economic growth and rapidly expanding middle class, oil prices would continue to be high [Brookings, 1999].

Beverages

15 This industry group comprised of alcoholic products that included beer, ale, porter, wine, neutral spirits and ethyl alcohol used in blended wines and distilled liquors, and other fermented malted beverages; and non-alcoholic products that include juices, soda drinks, and tropical nectar.

Tobacco

16 This industry group was comprised of tobacco products, such as cigarettes, snuff, cigars, and pipe tobacco.

Pharmaceuticals

17 This industry group included biological and medical products; botanical drugs and herbs; and pharmaceutical products intended for internal and external consumption in such forms as ampoules, tablets, capsules, vials, ointments, powders, solutions, and suspensions. In September 2003, the pharmaceutical industry was shaken by industry giant Merck & Co.'s voluntarily withdrawal of its blockbuster arthritis pain medication Vioxx following an extended clinical trial that linked the drug to heart attacks and stroke. Fears of drug safety and a dearth of new products continued to challenge the industry.

Apparel and Footwear

18 This industry group consisted of men's, women's, children's, infants', unisex clothing, athletic sneakers, and footwear made of leather, rubber, and other materials.

19 The perishable goods industry, the focus of this study, is discussed in the following section.

INDUSTRY AND MARKET SEGMENT: THE PERISHABLE GOODS INDUSTRY

20 The perishable goods industry group has two general segments: industrial agriculture and organic production, as shown in Figure 2.

Industrial Agriculture

21 Industrial agriculture viewed the farm as a factory with "inputs" (such as pesticides, feed, fertilizer, and fuel) and "outputs" (such as corn and chicken). The goal was to increase yield per acre and decrease costs of production, usually by exploiting economies of scale. The key feature of industrial agriculture was the cultivation of a single crop, a practice called monoculture. Monoculture was the farming practice that devoted acres of farmlands towards the cultivation of single crop such as corn, soybeans, and wheat. It was also a farming practice with two problems. Firstly, monoculture restricted crop rotation which was the process of alternating between two or more crops for each planting season. For instance, corn planted

FIGURE 2
The Perishable Goods Segments

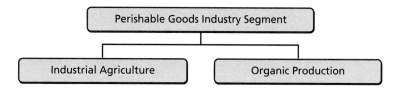

this year was rotated with soybeans for next year's planting season. Crop rotation allowed for the replenishment of the soil's nutrients, a vital factor which influenced the yield produced per acre. Secondly, monoculture increased the susceptibility of disease because it fostered the cultivation of a genetically uniform crop base. Growing thousands of acres of crop plants that were genetically similar made the food supply venerable to disease. In 1970, the Southern Corn Leaf Blight destroyed 60 percent of the US corn crop in one summer, clearly demonstrating that a genetically uniform crop base was a disaster waiting to happen.

22   Industrial agriculture relied heavily on pesticides and fungicides. Pesticides were chemicals sprayed on crops to kill pest such as insects. Fungicides were chemicals sprayed on crops to prevent the growth of fungus. Industrial agriculture also consumed enormous amounts of fertilizer. The United States had seen remarkable increases in agricultural productivity throughout the twentieth century. Between 1920 and 1980, for example, US corn yields soared 333 percent from 21 to 91 bushels an acre and were still improving; success in the increases could be attributed to improved planet varieties, fertilizers, pesticides, and mechanization [Union of Concerned Scientists, 2004].

Organic Production

23   "Organic" was a labeling term that denoted products produced under the authority of the Organic Foods Production Act. The products in this segment were categorized into food and non-food. Organic foods were edible products such as meats and produce. On the other hand, non food organic goods were products manufactured for human use such as soaps and candles. The principal guidelines for organic production were to use materials and practices that enhanced the ecological balance of natural systems and that integrated the parts of the farming system into an ecological whole. Organic food handlers, processors, and retailers adhered to standards that maintained the integrity of organic agricultural products. Organic agriculture was an ecological production management system that promoted and enhanced biodiversity, biological cycles, and soil biological activity. It was based on minimal use of off-farm inputs and on management practices that restored maintained and enhanced ecological harmony. The primary goal of organic agriculture was to optimize the health and productivity of interdependent communities of soil life, plants, animals, and people.

24   The organic food industry is the focus of this report and will be discussed in depth in the following sections.

INDUSTRY AND COMPETITVE MARKET: ORGANIC PERISHABLE GOODS

25   More than one-half of Americans (54 percent) had tried organic food, with nearly one-third (29 percent) claiming to consume more organic foods and beverages than one year ago [Whole Foods Market, 2004]. The overwhelming majority (69 percent) of "frequent organic eaters" (eat organic several times a week) claimed they were eating more organic foods than one year ago; meanwhile, 43 percent of "occasional organic eaters" (eat organic several times a month) and 16 percent of "infrequent organic eaters" (have tried, but did not consume regularly) reported eating more organic foods than one year ago. Price remained the biggest barrier for consumers who did not eat organic foods to try them. Nearly, seven out of ten (69 percent) who did not eat organic foods claimed price was a major factor in their decision. However, due to the industry growth and consumer demand, the price of organic foods was becoming more competitive.

26   According to Figure 3, produce continued to be the primary gateway into organics accounting for 72 percent of consumer purchases. However, consumers were purchasing more organic foods in expanding categories. The next categories accounting for significant

FIGURE 3
Categories of
Organic Goods
Purchased by
Consumers

Source: Whole Food Market
(2004). "Categories of Organic
Goods". [Online]. *http://www.*
wholefoodsmarket.com/issues/
org_reasons.html. Accessed
May 2005

Categories	Percent
Produce	72 %
Bread / Baked Goods	30 %
Non-Dairy Beverages (e.g., soymilk or juice)	29 %
Packaged Goods (e.g., soup or pasta)	24 %
Dairy	23 %
Meat	19 %
Frozen Foods	17 %
Prepared Foods / ready-to-go-Meals	12 %
Baby Food	7 %

consumer purchases are: baked goods, non dairy beverages, packaged goods, and soymilk
at 30 percent, 29 percent, 24 percent, and 23 percent respectively.

How Industry Segment Works: The Business Process Model

27   The organic goods industry was comprised of various segments as shown in Figure 4.

28   The industry under study cultivated agriculture, livestock, and floriculture products
organically. Agriculture and floriculture were grown by farmers who used a traditional
farming method. In the traditional farming method, seeds from crop harvest and plant
flowers were used to start the new planting season. Farmers used natural fertilizers in the
form of either compost or manure to accelerate the development of crops and flowers. Soil
preservation was an essential part of the process. Land was tilled using simple farming tools
and the drip irrigation method, the slow delivery of water through an extensive network of
pipes brings water to the crops and plants. Harmful plant organisms were controlled through
the use of birds and imported insects.

29   Livestock which included beef, pork, and poultry was raised by ranchers who used the
free ranch method. Under the free ranch method, livestock were allowed to graze freely
over acres of farm. As organically designated livestock, the farmlands which the animals
graze over were free from chemical pesticides and were grown with natural fertilizers.
Furthermore, animal feed given to the livestock were natural in content and were without
growth hormones or any artificial additives. The livestock matured naturally and were then
slaughtered and processed into consumable products such as filet mignon.

30   The products within this industry were distributed either through distribution companies
or directly from point of origin such as farms and ranches. Distribution companies, in
principal, were intermediaries whose function was to buy in bulk direct from farms and
ranches and resell to various retail outlets such as supermarkets. The advantage of distribution companies was they served as a one-stop supply source for retailers. They were able
to offer a diverse selection of products at competitive prices because they individually
negotiated with the big farms and ranches and wielded considerable leverage due to their
ability to bulk purchase. Retailers could also buy directly from farms and ranches. Without
the mediation of distribution companies, retailers purchasing directly had to find sourcing
for a wide variety of products to offer consumers and negotiate pricing and delivery terms
from the point of origin to their respective point of sale locations.

31   Supermarkets, specialty stores, catalogs, and the Internet were four retail outlets organic
goods were sold through. Supermarkets offered a diversity of goods at a physical location.
Qualified assistance was also available. Specialty stores specialized in and carried a particular type of product. For instance, butcher shops processed and offered a variety of meat
products. Catalogs offered convenience shopping because of the relative ease of purchase.
Customers browsed through goods displayed on a printed medium and could place an order
over the phone. Internet was another form of convenience shopping but unlike catalogs

FIGURE 4 The Organic Perishable Goods Industry

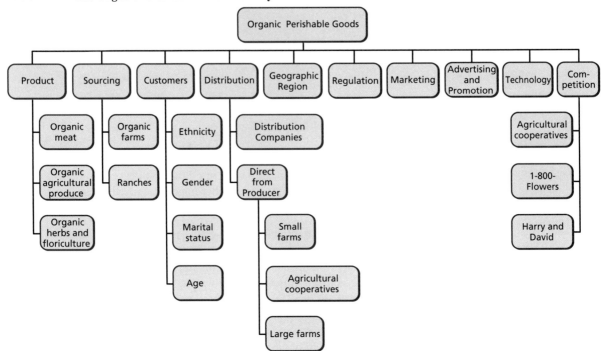

products were displayed on a website. Similar to catalogs, customers browsed for goods and placed orders directly through the website or via telephone.

32   Consumers of this industry covered diverse demographics. These consumers were motivated by their concern about toxic pesticides, growth hormones and antibiotics on their health.

33   Organic products were sold domestically and internationally.

34   The United States Department of Agriculture (USDA) was the regulatory body that presided over food, agriculture, and natural resources. The National Organic Program (NOP) was a program mandated by the USDA to oversee all issues related to organic agriculture. Under the NOP program, the term organic was defined and applied to the qualifying products. It also advised on the proper production, handling, labeling, and certification of organic products.

35   Advertising was performed through various multimedia outlets such as the Internet, radio, television, and print. Promotion tended to be on special events such as Valentine's Day, Mother's Day, and Christmas.

36   Competition was stiff with supermarkets, specialty retailer, catalog companies, and e-commerce retailers vying for market share. Valued add services offered the most effective way for differentiating each competitor from the other.

Products

37   The products sold in the industry were meats, agriculture produce, and herbs, and floriculture. They were organically produced base on ecologically-based practices such as biological pest management and composting.

Organic Meats

38   Organic meats came from animals raised under organic management. The animals were breed without growth-producing hormones or antibiotics. The animals received preventive medical care, such as vaccines, and dietary supplements of vitamins and minerals. They

also consumed 100 percent organically produced feed, free of animal byproducts. Livestock intended for meat products such as cows, pigs, and chicken were provided with living conditions that accommodated their natural behavior. These animals had access to the outdoors, adequate shade, exercise areas, fresh air, and direct sunlight suitable to their species.

39   Diet was a reason for enthusiasm towards organic meat. In the US alone, an estimated 59 million adults were currently on the popular low-carbohydrate, high-fat Atkins diet, according to figures from the Valen Group. According to Jim Long, meat analyst and CEO of the genetics company Genesus, "The Atkins diet had had a huge effect on meat demand in North America. Meat was a good source of protein, and this had been identified as a good thing. And in North America, meat protein was also relatively cheap compared to the rest of the world." The organic poultry segment continued to be of importance in the North American market for organic meat products. Organic chicken had been widely available in retail outlets for a number of years due to the short production cycle, integrated production method, and low price premium of the product. In contrast, organic beef and pork were still rarely found in retailers because of the low production volume and the high prices, which could be up to three times higher than conventional beef and pork.

40   The keys to success include several factors. The meat products must be competitively priced. There must be a wide selection of organic meat products such as beef and pork. Organic integrity of the meat product must be ensured by adhering to the National Organic Program standards such as providing ample farm land that accommodates the natural behavior of the livestock and ensures livestock feed was free from growth-hormones and natural in content. The quality of the meat products must be maintained by ensuring the quick delivery to the destination point and using storage and transportation systems that provide proper temperature and other conditions necessary for freshness.

Organic Agricultural Produce

41   Organic agricultural produce were fruits and vegetables that were produced using ecologically based practices, such as biological pest management. Crops grown were free from chemicals and modified fertilizers; crop nutrients were derived from manure, crop wastes materials, and composting. Soil fertility was managed through tillage and cultivation practices such as crop rotation and cover crops. Crop pest, weeds, and diseases were controlled through physical, mechanical, and biological control management methods such as insect-eating birds.

42   Fruit and vegetables were the normal gateway into organic foods. Consumer health concerns continued to spur the demands for organic produce. According to O'Mama Report, organic produce as a category was growing by approximately 8 percent per year in the United States [O'Mama Report, 2001].

43   Certified organic agricultural land increased by 74 percent between 1997 and 2001, according to the latest figures from the U.S. Department of Agriculture (USDA). This remarkable growth in organic acreage gives organics the distinction of being the fastest growing segment of U.S. agriculture. If this trend continues, the portion of overall agricultural land certified as organic would double in the next four years.

44   The keys to success include several factors. Organic agricultural produce must be competitive priced. There must be a wide selection of organic produce such as oranges and apples. Organic integrity of the produce must be ensured by adhering to the National Organic Program standards such as using manure as crop nutrients. The quality of the produce must be maintained by ensuring the quick delivery to the destination point and using storage and transportation systems that provide proper temperature and other conditions necessary for freshness.

Organic Herbs and Floriculture

45   Organic herbs and floriculture was the cultivation and management of cut flowers, potted flowering plants, foliage plants, cut cultivated greens, and herbs based on ecological

practices such as biological pest control and composting. Herbs and floricultural products were free from chemicals and modified fertilizers; crop nutrients were derived from manure, crop wastes materials, and composting. Soil fertility was managed through tillage and cultivation practices such as crop rotation and cover crops. Pests, weeds, and diseases were controlled through physical, mechanical, and biological control management methods such as insect-eating birds. They were predominantly grown under protective cover such as plastic or glass greenhouses.

46   Organic herbs were used for culinary purposes, dietary supplements such as St. John's Wort, and for personal care such as body lotion and soaps. In 1997, producers grew certified organic herbs for culinary and medicinal uses in 32 states. California was the largest producer of cultivated organic herbs, with 1,062 acres, followed by Washington (846 acres), and Illinois (797 acres). In addition, Idaho had 52,000 acres of St. John's Wort, a popular medicinal herb. Florida had 25,000 acres of certified organic palmetto berries which had medicinal uses, and maypop which had both medicinal and culinary uses. Finally, Oregon had 6,000 acres of lake algae which had medicinal uses.

47   US consumption of floriculture crops totaled $5.5 billion in 2001, up 3 percent from 2000. Although domestic production had risen by 89 percent between 1989 and 2001, foreign supply of cut flowers, majority from South America, comprised about 50 percent of total floriculture and nursery crops [University of Florida, 2003]. Foreign growers remain competitive due to lower labors, smaller climate-control investments, and favorable exchange rates.

48   The keys to success rest on several factors. Organic herbs and floricultural products must be competitively priced. Organic integrity of the produce must be ensured by adhering to the National Organic Program standards such as using manure as crop nutrients. The quality of the floriculture and herbs must be maintained by ensuring quick delivery to the destination point and using storage and transportation systems that provide proper temperature and other conditions necessary for freshness. Producers must maintain product diversity by growing a variety of herbs and floricultural products such as organic roses and daisies.

Sourcing

49   Sourcing referred to the products' initial point of origins. Products under this industry were sourced from farms and ranches that implemented an organic systems plan and required factors of production.

Organic Farms

50   Organic farms were land devoted to agricultural purposes that utilized an Organic Systems Plan (OSP). The Organic Systems Plan was a plan that described how a farm would ensure compliance with organic standards. The first measure of compliance was to have distinct, defined boundaries and buffer zones that prevented the unintended application of a prohibited substance onto land under organic management. Prohibited substances included the use of synthetic fertilizers and pesticides in the cultivation of crops. The second measure was using organic seeds during the planting season. The third measure was to submit audits and receive evaluations by the National Organic Program. Finally, the farm had to implement sustainable farming methods such as crop rotation. Crop rotation was the process of alternating between two or more crops for each planting season. It allowed for the replenishment of the soil's nutrients, a vital factor which influenced the yield produced per acre.

51   Organic farming required three factors of production which were land, inputs, and labor. Money was spent to secure these factors of production. Land was purchased directly by the farm or leased from a landlord. After the land was secured, the farm purchased the inputs necessary for planting. Inputs included the purchase of machines used to till the land, the purchase of organics seed and manure, and purchase of harvesting equipment. Organic farming was labor intensive and required the use of workers called farm hands. Farm hands were used for the dispersion of seeds, application of manure, and inspection of crops for pests.

52   Capital expenditures varied according to the scale of production. Larger farms had more capital expenditures because they needed to purchase more factors of production to support large scale production of organic products. On the other hand, although smaller farms had smaller expenditures relative to the larger farms, they still purchased factor productions necessary to support their scale of production. Financing was available according to the scale of production. For large scale farming operations, the Department of Agriculture provided low interest agricultural loans which were used to maintain operations such as the purchase of land and the paying of expense. For small scale farms, the Small Business Administration (SBA), a government agency that supported small enterprises, provided micro loans to support operations. Small farms could also obtain financing from community development financial institutions (CDFIs). Community development financial institutions were small banks and credit unions that provided micro-loans to small enterprises.

53   After the crops had grown to maturity, they were harvested and stored in large silos on the farming premises. In those silos, temperature, humidity levels, and other conditions were monitored in order to maintain freshness. As organically designated crops, the silos were also free from any preservatives and additives. They continued to remain in the silos until they were ready for distribution.

54   The keys to success included several factors. Organic farms had to obtain sufficient financing to support their scale of production. Organic farms had to adhere to the National Organic Program standards. Organic farms had to exercise financial discipline on the expenditure for the factors of production. Motivated labor needed to be employed to execute the necessary organic farming processes such as the planting of seeds and the monitoring of crop pests. The farms had to provide adequate storage facilities that conform to the organic standards and maintain the freshness of products until they were ready for distribution.

Ranches

55   Organic ranches were land devoted to raising livestock using an Organic Systems Plan (OSP). The Organic Systems Plan was a plan that described how a ranch would ensure compliance with organic standards. The first measure of compliance was to provide living conditions that accommodated the natural behavior of the animals. For instance, in the free ranch method, ruminants (including cows, sheep, and goats) were given access to pasture. The second measure was to ensure the animals were fed organic feed. The third measure was to submit audits and receive evaluations by the National Organic Program. Finally, the ranch had to implement sustainable animal management techniques. Although, organic livestock and poultry could be vaccinated for diseases, ranchers might not use antibiotics, hormones or medications. Instead, livestock diseases and parasites were controlled largely through preventive measures such as balanced diet, sanitary housing, and stress reduction.

56   Organic ranches required three factors of production which were land, inputs, and labor. Money was spent to secure these factors of production. Land was purchased directly by the farm or leased from a landlord. After the land was secured, the ranch purchased the inputs necessary for ranching. Inputs included the purchase of housing facilities for the livestock land, the purchase of organics feed, and the purchase of slaughtering machinery. Organic farming was also labor intensive and required the use of workers called farm hands. Farm hands vaccinated, fed, and monitored the development of livestock. Farm hands also cleaned the housing facilities of the livestock and ensured that they were taken out for their exercise. Financing was available according to the scale of production. For large scale farming operations, the Department of Agriculture provided low interest agricultural loans which were used to maintain operations such as the purchase of land and the paying of expense. For small scale farms, the Small Business Administration (SBA), a government agency that supported small enterprises, provided micro loans to support operations. Small farms could also obtain financing from community development financial institutions (CDFIs). Community development financial institutions were small banks and credit unions that provided micro-loans to small enterprises.

57 After the livestock had grown to maturity, they were slaughtered, processed into consumable products, and stored in refrigerated storage facilities on the ranches. In the storage facilities, temperatures were monitored to ensure the product remained fresh. As organically designated meat products, the storage facilities were also free from any preservatives and additives. They continued to remain in the storage facilities until they were ready for distribution.

58 The keys to success include several factors. Ranches had to obtain sufficient financing to support their scale of production. Ranches had to adhere to the National Organic Programs standard. Ranches had to exercise financial discipline on the expenditure for the factors of production and employ motivated labor to execute the necessary organic ranching processes such as cleaning the housing facilities and feeding the livestock organic feed. The ranches had to provide adequate storage facilities that conformed to the organic standards and maintain the freshness of products until they were ready for distribution.

Consumers

59 Consumers of organic goods were motivated by their concerns about chemicals used in food production and their desire to maintain a healthy lifestyle.

Ethnicity

60 According to the Institute for Public Policy and Business Research, Caucasians were more willing to pay higher prices for organic produce. They were also found to be less price elastic in their produce purchase. This means that as produce prices increased, the quantity of produce purchased declined more slowly. Caucasians were more likely to purchase their organic product from a variety of outlets which included supermarkets, specialty retailers, directly from farms, catalogs, and over the Internet. On the other hand, African-Americans, Hispanics, and Asians were more motivated by family reasons to purchase organic goods because of their perceived health benefits. Due to their strong culture of preparing cooked meals, these three ethnic groups were extremely concerned on the quality of the goods and were apt to shop from outlets were they could physically examine the goods prior to purchase. For this reason, these three ethnic groups were more likely to purchase their organic goods from supermarkets, specialty retailers, and directly from farms.

61 The keys to success rest on several factors. Organic products had to be competitively priced. Organic integrity of the produce had to be ensured by adhering to the National Organic Program standards such as using manure as crop nutrients. The quality of produce had to be maintained by ensuring quick delivery to the destination point and using storage and transportation systems that provided proper temperature and other conditions necessary for freshness. Store display cases had to be aesthetically pleasing and customer friendly allowing for easy access. Producers had to maintain product diversity which accommodated different ethnic tastes by growing a variety of organics goods such as plantains. Proper organic labeling, appropriate certification, and nutritional content had to be on organic products available for sale.

Gender

62 Purchasers of organic goods tended to be women. According to the Institute for Public Policy and Business Research, women tended to be the primary food shoppers of a household and were more aware of food issues. In addition, they were more educated on food production topics such as pest management and were willing to pay more for organic produce than men.

63   The keys to success rest on several factors. Organic products had to be competitively priced. Organic integrity of the produce had to be ensured by adhering to the National Organic Program standards such as using manure as crop nutrients. The quality of produce had to be maintained by ensuring quick delivery to the destination point and using storage and transportation systems that provided proper temperature and other conditions necessary for freshness. Proper organic labeling, appropriate certification, and nutritional content had to be on organic products available for sale.

Marital Status

64   According to the Institute for Public Policy and Business Research, both single men and single women had a higher willingness to pay for organic goods than married men and women. Surprisingly, a small percentage of married couples with children actually bought organic even though an overwhelming majority believed they were better for their children. Packaged Facts, a division of *MarketResearch.com,* claimed cost and a limited selection of organic products for kids might be factors contributing to the unwillingness of married couples to spend extra money to actually purchase them. On the other hand, young married couples without families exhibited a strong propensity to purchase organic goods due to having more disposable income.

65   The keys to success rest on several factors. Organic products had to be competitively priced. Organic integrity of the produce had to be ensured by adhering to the National Organic Program standards such as using manure as crop nutrients. The quality of produce had to be maintained by ensuring quick delivery to the destination point and using storage and transportation systems that provided proper temperature and other conditions necessary for freshness. Proper organic labeling, appropriate certification, and nutritional content had to be on organic products available for sale.

Age

66   The biggest consumers of organic foods were among the Gen Y and Baby Boomer generations (in the Walnut Acres/RoperASW survey, Gen Ys were defined as between ages 18 and 24 and Boomers as between 35 and 49). Fully 80 percent of Gen Y, and 75 percent of Boomers, had bought organic food at some point [The Big O, 2000]. Baby boomers were more likely to buy organic because of health reasons. Some preferred the healthier medicinal benefits that organic herbs offered relative to the more conventional form of medicine.

67   The keys to success rest on several factors. Organic products had to be competitively priced. Organic integrity of the produce had to be ensured by adhering to the National Organic Program standards such as using manure as crop nutrients. The quality of produce had to be maintained by ensuring quick delivery to the destination point and using storage and transportation systems that provided proper temperature and other conditions necessary for freshness. A diversity of organic products should be offered with a selection boosting medicinal benefits. Proper organic labeling, appropriate certification, and nutritional content had to be on organic products available for sale.

Distribution

68 Distribution was the process through which goods were sourced from the point of origin and brought to customers at a point of sale. Distribution companies and direct from producers were two methods organic products were brought before consumers.

Distribution Companies

69 Distribution companies were intermediary entities that purchased directly from farmers and ranchers and resold to retail outlets. In essence, they typically served as a one-stop supply source. They wielded considerable purchasing power because of their ability to purchase in bulk. This financial strength also allowed them to carry a wide selection of products. As an intermediary, distribution companies sold products to retail outlet such as a supermarket.

70   An interested retailer would enter an exclusivity agreement with a prospective distribution company. The terms of the agreement restricted retailers from sourcing organic products elsewhere. Organic products not under the current holding of the distribution company had to initially be brought to the attention of the company. The distribution company was allowed to perform a best effort sourcing of the products on behalf of the retailer. However, in the event the distribution company was unsuccessful in procuring the sought after organic product, retailers were given the discretion to negotiate their own supply of the product. This was the only time retailers were allowed to break from the exclusivity provisions of their agreement with the distribution companies. In addition to offering a wide variety of organic products, distribution companies were responsible for the logistics of bringing products from their large distribution centers to the retailers' point of sale. At times, supply chain management technology was employed between the distribution company and the retailers. Electronic signals were sent to the nearest distribution centers of a specific parent company of impending shortages of choice products and immediate replenishment delivery was scheduled. For the retailers without such supply-chain technology, inventory was taken every week, shortages were tabulated, and purchase orders were sent to the distribution company for processing and delivery. Due to the bulking purchase ability of distribution companies, they maintained several fleets of delivery vans and trucks to deliver organic products. They also maintained a sizable amount of delivery men who were responsible for ensuring the delivery of the organic products. The delivery trucks and vans complied with the organic standards. Under the organic standards, the storage units on the trucks and vans had to be free of fungicides and other prohibited chemicals such as pesticides. In addition to comply with the organic standards, the storage units were equipped to maintain all the necessary conditions of freshness such as the monitoring of temperature levels. Furthermore, under the terms of agreement, the distribution companies were also responsible for displaying products on the shelves. Delivery men were assigned to restock products on the shelves and dispose of expired items.

71   The keys to success include several factors. Distribution companies had to offer competitive pricing. Distribution companies had to offer various product categories to maintain exclusivity agreements with purchasers. Distribution companies had to integrate supply chain technology with retailers to ensure the timely replenishment of organic products. The delivery systems had to comply with the organic standards and offer conditions necessary to maintain the freshness of products such as proper refrigeration. Distribution companies had to offer superior customer service to the retailers such as having delivery men that restocked shelves and disposed of expired items in a timely manner.

Direct from the Producer

72   Direct from producer was a method of distribution that brought organic product from the producer directly to the consumer.

73   *Small Farms*   Small farms also employed a direct from producer sales model through two methods. On-farm sale was the direct sale of organic products to the customer on the farm premises. Customers traveled to the farm to purchase and take their goods. Farmers were in regular contact with consumers because they were on site to purchase their goods. As relationship between the farmers and consumers developed, consumers became more comfortable with the services offered by the farms and tended to remain loyal. Another method was community-supported agriculture (CSA) which was an innovative direct arrangement between organic farmers and consumers. Consumers subscribed to the harvest of a CSA farmer for the entire upcoming season, and paid for their organic produce in advance. Given the small scale of production, after the harvest, the farmers were responsible for delivering the organic products directly to the consumers. The delivery trucks and vans complied with the organic standards. Under the organic standards, the storage units on the trucks and vans were free of fungicides and other prohibited chemicals such as pesticides. In addition to comply with the organic standards, the storage units of the delivery vehicles were equipped to maintain all the necessary conditions of freshness such as the monitoring of temperature levels. Under a CSA arrangement, consumers shared the production risks and variable harvests of the farmer.

74   The keys to success included several factors. The quality of the organic products had to be maintained by ensuring quick delivery to the customer after harvest and using storage and transportation systems that provided proper temperature and other conditions necessary for freshness. Organic integrity of the products had to be ensured by adhering to the National Organic Program standards such as using manure as crop nutrients. A wide selection of organic products had to be offered. The farmers had to offer superior customer service such as having enthusiastic and knowledgeable farmers to offer assistance.

75   *Agricultural Cooperatives*   An organic agricultural cooperative was an incorporated business that was owned and ran by a group of farmers or producers growing organic products adhering to the National Organic Program. Each farmer or producer became a member of the cooperative through his/ her equity contribution which was a direct contribution in the form of either paid membership fees or purchase of stock. Should the cooperative fail, each member's liability was limited to the amount he/she invested. The cooperative was controlled by a board of directors who were elected by the members. Each member had only one vote in the selection of directors regardless of the amount of equity invested. The directors were also users of cooperatives and their responsibilities, among others, were to hire a manager, define his/her duties, and authority, and formally review his/her performance annually; adopt general policies to guide the manager such as expenditures that needed board approval; finally, develop business strategies for the cooperative. Members of the cooperative were compensated according to a patronage refund system. After the fiscal year was over, a cooperative computed its earnings on business conducted on a cooperative basis. Those earnings were returned to the members as cash or equity allocations on the basis of how much business each member had done with the cooperative during the year. These distributions were called patronage refunds. For example, if a cooperative had earnings from business conducted on a cooperative basis of $100,000 for the year, Mr. Mockler, a member, who did two percent of the business with the cooperative would receive a patronage refund of $2,000. Members could also choose not to do business with the cooperative. After the cooperative computed its earning after the fiscal year, the members who had not done business with the cooperative would not receive patronage refunds.

76   Organic agricultural cooperatives were beneficial to members for two major reasons. First and foremost, cooperatives had access to supplies and services at reasonable cost. By banding together and purchasing business supplies and services as a group, individual farmers were able to offset the market power advantage of firms providing those supplies. Members were able to gain access to volume discounts and could negotiate for favorable pricing, delivery terms, credit terms, and other arrangements. The larger the group purchasing supplies and services through the cooperative, the greater the potential savings for members that conducted business through the cooperative. Finally, cooperatives had increased clout in the market place. Each member was able to distribute his her organic products under a collective effort and receive favorable pricing on products sold to buyers. Organic agricultural cooperatives differed in size and could serve a variety of geographic regions. Local organic cooperatives operated in a relatively small geographic area, typically a single county or an area within a radius of 10 to 30 miles. They usually had only one or two locations, from which to serve members. Super local cooperatives operated in two or more counties, often with several branch locations. Regional cooperatives served an area

comprised of numerous counties, an entire state or a number of states. National cooperatives served a major portion or most of the United States. International cooperatives operated in more than one country, with headquarters in the United States or another country.

77   Agricultural cooperative sold their products directly to the consumers, retail outlets, and distribution companies. Consumers were able to drive to the facilities of local cooperatives or super local cooperatives and purchase their products directly. Farmers were in regular contact with consumers because they were on site to purchase their goods. As relationship between the farmers and consumers developed, consumers become more comfortable with the services offered by the local cooperatives and tended to remain loyal. For the larger cooperative serving larger geographic regions, the products were marketed and sold directly to the consumer over the Internet. Cooperatives also sold their products to larger purchasers such as supermarkets, specialty retailers, catalogs, and distribution companies. Similar to large farms, regional and national cooperatives were able to maintain an integrated supply management technology with the large purchasers who may have had regional or national presence. The supply management technology linked cooperative and retailers together under a uniform platform and allowed for communication between the two so shortages were kept to a minimum. Given their size, cooperatives could maintain either a couple of delivery trucks or a fleet of delivery vans and trucks to deliver organic products. The delivery trucks could be driven by members or by employed delivered men. The delivery trucks and vans complied with the organic standards. Under the organic standards, the storage units on the trucks and vans were free of fungicides and other prohibited chemicals such as pesticides. In addition to comply with the organic standards, the storage units were equipped to maintain all the necessary conditions of freshness such as the monitoring of temperature levels.

78   The keys to success hinged on several factors. A diversity of products had to be offered by maintaining a group of members producing a variety of products. The democratization ethos of the cooperative had to be maintained, despite the size, to ensure active participation and willingness to pool resources. That meant members had to receive patronage refunds that were equal to the amount of business conducted with the cooperative. Organic integrity of the produce had to be ensured by adhering to the National Organic Program standards such as using manure as crop nutrients. The quality of the organic products had to be maintained by ensuring quick delivery to the customer after harvest and using storage and transportation systems that provided proper temperature and other conditions necessary for freshness. The organic agricultural cooperatives had to maintain an integrated supply management system to service the larger purchaser such as supermarkets. The organic agricultural cooperatives had to offer superior customer service such as having enthusiastic and knowledgeable farmers to offer assistance.

79   *Large Farms*   Organic large farms by definition had numerous acres of farmland that were used to grow agricultural products adhering to the standards of the National Organic Program. Some large farms had an all inclusive operation where they were responsible for the growing, processing, packaging, proper labeling, and logistical support of the products. Large farms sold to bulk purchasers such as distribution companies and regional and national supermarkets. Terms were negotiated in advance prior to the harvest on issues such on product selection, pricing, and delivery scheduling to mitigate the risk to the farms. Depending on the arrangement, the distribution companies and supermarkets coordinated technology systems with the farms to monitor inventory levels at their retail outlets or distribution centers. The farm became responsible for ensuring the delivery of organic goods to the purchaser's point of sale when inventory levels of products were low. The farm employed delivery men and maintained delivery vehicles that were used to transport the organic goods. Other farms also outsourced the logistical support to a third party. The delivery trucks and vans used complied with the organic standards. Under the organic standards, the storage units on the trucks and vans were free of fungicides and other prohibited chemicals such as pesticides. In addition to comply with the organic standards, the storage units were equipped to maintain all the necessary conditions of freshness such as the monitoring of temperature levels. The large farms had storage facilities that kept the organic products. In these storage facilities, temperature, humidity levels, and other conditions were monitored in order to maintain freshness. Due to the organic nature of the products, the storage facilities were also free from fungicide and prohibited chemicals such as pesticides.

80   The keys to success involve several factors. Large farms had to negotiate with large purchasers and receive commitments prior to the harvesting season. Organic integrity of designated produce had to be ensured by adhering to the National Organic Program standards such as using manure as crop nutrients. The quality of produce had to be maintained by ensuring reliable, quick delivery to the destination point and using storage and transportation systems that provide proper temperature and other conditions necessary for freshness. The large farms had to maintain an integrated supply management system to service their bulk purchasers.

Retail Outlets

81   Retail outlets were the final medium through which goods were brought to consumers. Each retail outlet was marked by distinctive characteristics that made it appealing to consumers.

Supermarkets

82   Supermarkets were self serve retail outlets which carried a variety of consumer products. Supermarkets purchased from distribution companies. This retail outlet was especially appealing to consumers because of the wide variety of organic products that were offered. They were also able to satisfy the need of diverse demographics. For instance, professionals were able to purchase organic snacks that catered to their working schedules while the aging population was able to purchase produce to satisfy their healthy lifestyle. Qualified representatives were also available in supermarkets to offer customers assistance on organic related questions. Supermarkets were also appealing as point of purchase because they permitted consumers to inspect goods for purchase and compare brands. Consumers who were more likely to cook for their families such as Hispanics, African-Americans, and Asians tended to shop from supermarkets because they valued the ability to physically inspect the organic products prior to purchase. According to a report from the Natural Marketing Institute, Hispanic consumers, the largest minority group in the United States with a population of 38.8 million, were significantly more interested in natural and organic products than was the general population, more likely to shop the natural products channel, and more likely to want their stores to carry natural and organic products.

83   The keys to success involve several factors. Products had to be competitively priced. The organic integrity and quality of produce had to be maintained by ensuring quick delivery to the supermarkets through the use of storage and transportation systems that provided conditions necessary for freshness and making certain the storage units on the delivery trucks complied with organic standards. Supermarkets had to offer variety of organic goods to satisfy a diverse consumer base. Supermarkets had to offer superior customer service such as having qualified representatives to answer organic related questions.

Specialty Retail

84   Specialty retail involved the retailing of a specific type of organic product. Organic goods retailed through specialty outlets tend to be localized with an emphasis on serving the demands of the community. A butcher was an example of specialty retailer. Butchers purchased organic meat products directly from the producers, ranches and agricultural cooperatives. The butcher either had the organic products delivered by the ranches and

agricultural cooperatives or picked up the products by themselves. If the delivery responsibility fell on the butcher, he/she maintained vehicles and drivers to pick up the organic goods from the producers. The delivery trucks and vans used complied with the organic standards. Under the organic standards, the storage units on the trucks and vans were free of fungicides and other prohibited chemicals such as pesticides. In addition to comply with the organic standards, the storage units were equipped to maintain all the necessary conditions of freshness such as the monitoring of temperature levels. The value the butcher added was the ability to offer a wider selection of special cuts of the organic meats to the consumers. For example, the consumer was able to purchase an organic shank, a special cut of beef, from the butcher. Butchers were also in regular contact with consumers because consumers had to come to the butcher shop to purchase their organic goods. As relationship between the butcher and consumers developed, consumers became more comfortable with the services offered by the butcher and tended to remain loyal.

85   The keys to success involved several factors. Products had to be competitively priced. The organic integrity and quality of produce had to be maintained by ensuring quick delivery to the supermarkets through the use of storage and transportation systems that provided conditions necessary for freshness and making certain the storage units on the delivery trucks complied with organic standards. The special retailer had to offer valued added services such as selective meat cuts to the consumer. The specialty retail had to offer superior customer service such as having qualified butchers to answer organic related questions.

Catalog

86   Catalogs were printed matter prepared for soliciting business that was mailed directly to consumers. Catalog companies retailing organic goods offered a wide range of organic goods with intent of satisfying a wide range of consumer demand. Similar to distribution companies, catalog companies retailing organic goods purchased in bulk directly from large producers such as large farms. Depending on the delivery agreement, the catalog company negotiated to have the goods delivered to its distribution center by the producer to its large storage facilities, which served as a distribution center, strategically located throughout their business region. Due to the organic nature of the products, the storage facilities complied with organic standards and thus were free from fungicide and prohibited chemicals such as pesticides. The organic goods were retailed directly to the consumers. A consumer placed an order over the telephone requesting an item from the catalog to the catalog company's call center. The catalog company maintained customer representatives in those call centers to take orders, process payment, send the order to the distribution center, and offer customers additional assistance if so needed. After the order was taken and payment had been processed, the order was sent to the distribution center closest to the consumer. The organic good was packaged under organic standard and remained ready for delivery. Catalog companies outsourced the delivery of goods to third party carriers. Third party carriers, such as FedEx, were responsible for picking up the organic goods and having them delivered directly to the customer.

87   The keys to success rest on several factors. Products had to be competitively priced by negotiating with reputable large producers. Organic, product, and quality integrity had to be maintained by ensuring safe delivery from the producer, to the distribution centers, and eventually to the consumer by using storage and transportation systems that provided proper handling, maintain conditions necessary for freshness, and comply with the organic standards. The catalog company had to give superior customer services such as employing trustworthy and knowledgeable representatives. The catalog company's technology system had to be fully integrated to ensure proper dissemination of information from the call center, to the distribution center, and to the third party carriers. The catalog company had to ensure timely delivery of goods to the customer by outsourcing logistical support to nationally recognized and reputable third party carriers such as FedEx. The catalog had to be well presented. This means the catalog had to be logically organized, easy to navigate, and aesthetically pleasing.

E-commerce

88 E-commerce was the use of an interface, websites, to facilitate the commerce between sellers and consumers over the Internet. Organic goods retailed in e-commerce were sold through a website on the Internet. Organic e-commerce retailing was pursued directly by the producer such as agricultural cooperatives or indirectly by an independent company.

89 Agricultural cooperatives produced the organic products collectively by their members and, depending on the size of the cooperative, had them stored in storage facilities located either on site or strategically located around their business region. The cooperative maintained a website where the organic goods were marketed. The website was advertised directly as banners on web portal such as Yahoo! or indirectly as links after key word search as "organic." The website was informative and served as a place for consumers to purchase organic goods. Information on the cooperative's organic products selection was available for the customer to browse through. Information on the cooperative's history, mission statement, and organic production processes and accreditation was presented on the website. Additional educational resource tools such as industry news and organizations were available to consumers. The website also served as a place to purchase organic goods. On the website, the consumer browsed through the cooperative's selection of organic goods. The consumer could either purchase the organic goods directly on the website or he/she placed an order over the telephone through a telephone number made available on the website.

90 If the organic goods were purchased online, the order was taken, payment was processed, and the confirmed order was sent directly to the storage facilities. If the organic goods were purchased over the telephone, the order was directed to a call center. In the call center, the cooperative maintained representatives that received orders, processed payment, and sent the confirmed orders to the storage facilities. Once the order was received, the organic good was packaged under organic standards and remained ready for delivery. The cooperative delivered the organics goods to the customers if their business region was local. Under this scenario, the cooperative maintained delivery men and vehicles. The delivery trucks and vans used complied with the organic standards. Under the organic standards, the storage units on the trucks and vans were free of fungicides and other prohibited chemicals such as pesticides. In addition to comply with the organic standards, the storage units were equipped to maintain all the necessary conditions of freshness such as the monitoring of temperature levels. From the storage facilities, packaged organic goods were delivered directly to the consumer. The cooperative may outsource delivery to the customers to third party carrier. The delivery trucks and vans used complied with the organic standards. Under the organic standards, the storage units on the trucks and vans were free of fungicides and other prohibited chemicals such as pesticides. In addition to comply with the organic standards, the storage units were equipped to maintain all the necessary conditions of freshness such as the monitoring of temperature levels. From the storage facilities, the third-party carrier picked up the organic goods and delivered them to the consumer.

91 An independent company could pursue e-commerce retailing of organic goods. The independent company negotiated with various producers to offer organic goods under its brand. The producers were strategically located around the company's area of business. The producers were responsible for growing the organic products and storing them in storage facilities on site. The company maintained a proprietary website where its organic goods were marketed. The website was advertised directly as banners on web portal such as Yahoo! or indirectly as links after key word search as "organic." The website was informative and served as a place for consumers to purchase its organic goods. Information on the company's organic products selection was available for the customer to browse through.

Information on the company's history, mission statement, and accreditation was presented on the website. Additional educational resource tools such as company news and organizations were available to consumers.

92   The website also served as a place to purchase organic goods. On the website, the consumer browsed through the company's selection of organic goods. The consumer could either purchase the organic goods directly on the website or he/she could place an order over the telephone through a telephone number made available on the website. If the organic goods were purchased online, the order was taken, payment was processed, and the confirmed order was sent directly to the storage facilities. If the organic goods were purchased over the telephone, the order was directed to a call center. In the call center, the company maintained representatives that received orders, processed payment, and sent the confirmed orders to the storage facilities. Once the order was received, the organic good was packaged under organic standards and remained ready for delivery. The company outsourced delivery to the customers to third party carriers. The third party carrier, such as FedEx, went to the producers' storage facilities, picked up the packaged organic goods, and delivered them to the customer. The delivery trucks and vans used complied with the organic standards. Under the organic standards, the storage units on the trucks and vans were free of fungicides and other prohibited chemicals such as pesticides. In addition to comply with the organic standards, the storage units were equipped to maintain all the necessary conditions of freshness such as the monitoring of temperature levels.

93   The keys to success involved several factors. Products had to be competitively priced. Organic e-commerce retailers had to maintain good websites. By definition, this meant the website had to be informative such as offering additional resources on the organic industry and serve as a place for consumers to purchase organic goods. On the website, the products had to be logically presented and aesthetically pleasing. The website had to be easy to navigate. Organic e-commerce retailers had to maintain reliable technology system to ensure the timely and accurate dissemination of information from the point of purchase, to the storage facilities, and to the delivery system. Organic e-commerce retailers had to maintain customer service such as telephone representatives to take orders and technicians to offer assistance on technical issues. E-commerce retailers had to effectively advertise such as placing banners on web portals. Organic and product quality integrity had to be maintained by ensuring quick delivery from the storage facilities by using storage and transportation systems that provided proper handling, maintain conditions necessary for freshness, and comply with the organic standards.

Geographic Region

94   Geographic region was defined as the territory in which goods were sold. Organic goods were sold both in the continental United States and internationally. For the purpose of this report, the domestic market would be discussed. Organic goods were sold in the United States through various retail outlets. The supermarket was the popular destination when purchasing organic goods especially for the ethnic consumers. Organic goods were also retailed through specialty markets and catalogs or over an e-commerce platform involving the use of the Internet. Retailing over an e-commerce platform gave vendors of organic goods a broader medium to reach consumers.

95   The keys to success rest on several factors. Products had to be competitively priced. Organic and product quality integrity had to be maintained by ensuring quick delivery from the storage facilities by using storage and transportation systems that provided proper handling, maintained conditions necessary for freshness, and complied with the organic standards. There had to be sufficient market intelligence to ascertain local trends and demands. An aggressive advertising campaign had to be pursued across various media outlets to promote brand recognition.

Regulation

96   The United States Department of Agriculture (USDA) was the regulatory body that presided over food, agriculture, and natural resources. The organizational structure of the department was as follows: the Secretary of the Department of Agriculture, the director of the entire department, was responsible for the development and execution of strategies according to the directives of Congress and the President; the Deputy Secretary directly reported to the Secretary of the Department and was responsible for the deployment of directives of Secretary of the Department. Reporting to the Deputy Secretary were various subordinate positions which included: the Chief Information Officer; Chief Financial Officer; Inspector General; Executive Operations; Director of Communications; General Counsel; Under Secretary for Natural Resources and Environment; Under Secretary for Farm and Foreign Agricultural Services; Under Secretary for Rural Development; Under Secretary for Food, Nutrition, and Consumer Services; Under Secretary for Food Safety; Under Secretary for Research, Education, and Economic; Under Secretary for Marketing and Regulatory Programs; Assistant Secretary for Congressional Relations; Assistant Secretary for Administration; and finally, Assistant Secretary for Civil Rights.

97   Under the direction of the Agricultural Marketing Service (AMS), an arm of the United States Department of Agriculture (USDA), National Organic Program (NOP or program) was established by the authorization of Organic Foods Production Act of 1990. The National Organic Program facilitated domestic and international marketing of fresh and processed food that was organically produced and assured consumers that such products meet consistent, uniform standards. The program established national standards for the production and handling of organically produced products, including a National List of substances approved for and prohibited from use in organic production and handling. In addition, the program established a national-level accreditation program administered by AMS for State officials and private persons who wanted to be accredited as certifying agents. Under the program, certifying agents certified that production and handling operations were in compliance with the requirements of regulation and initiated compliance actions to enforce program requirements. Finally, the program set requirements for domestic labeling products as organic and containing organic ingredients and ensured the importation of organic agricultural products from foreign programs had equivalent organic program requirements consistent with the United States national organic standards for the production, processing, and certification of organic foods.

98   The key to success was to ensure organic designated products conform to all the organic standards established by the National Organic Program.

Marketing

99   Organic certification was critical to the commercial success of any organically produced goods. This meant the goods had to be certified organic by accredited organizations under the National Organic Program (NOP) and labeled with the "USDA Organic" seal of approval. Besides obtaining certification, some companies pursued a consumer awareness initiative designed to educate the consumers on the principles of organic goods. For example, simple issues such as the lack of agricultural pesticides in the production process were discussed on the short blurbs on the products' packaging whereas complex issues such as the sustainability of organic production may be discussed on company websites. Developing a brand could be difficult because organic goods were produced under uniform organic standards. Companies tried to differentiate their organic products by marketing characteristics that helped to distinguish their brand and shape consumer perception. For instance, an organic retailer offering goods of higher quality would explain the process of how the organic goods were brought to customer (i.e. sourcing, storage,

and delivery) with a little blurb on the product's packaging and more extensively on the company's website.

100   The keys to success involved several factors. Organic products had to have proper certification visible on the product's packaging. Consumers had to be educated on the organic concept and its related issues. This could be achieved by addressing organic health benefits on product packaging and a more comprehensive presentation of issues on websites. A brand name should be developed by creating a consumer perception. For instance, an organic retailer offering goods of higher quality should explain the process of how the organic goods were brought to customer (i.e. sourcing, storage, and delivery) with a little blurb on the product's packaging and more extensively on the company's website.

Advertising and Promotion

101   Advertising was the use of print, radio, television, and the Internet to raise consumer awareness on a product. Supermarkets circulated weekly booklets that displayed offerings available to consumers. These booklets could be found in the entrances of supermarkets; they were also inserted within the pages of local newspapers or they were delivered directly to consumers by handlers. Catalogs companies advertised product offerings in printed catalogs which were mailed directly to consumers. Within the catalogs, the products were vividly displayed and accompanied by short descriptions highlighting the contents and use of the product. Local farmers, cooperatives, and specialty retailers were more likely to advertise in local newspapers that served their area of business. Agricultural cooperatives, supermarkets, e-commerce retailers, catalog companies were more likely to advertise over the radio because they had the financial capabilities to support such strategy. With a consumer base that stretched beyond the local area, the radio became better suited in reaching a wider audience.

102   Television advertisement presented a budgetary challenge to most of the retail outlets and was not the most preferred medium to advertise. If television advertisement was considered as a strategy, its utilization rate was highly infrequent and more likely to be pursued by larger organic retailers because of their financial strength. Internet advertisement was more likely to be pursued by producers such as farmers' cooperatives and organic e-commerce retailers selling directly to the consumers. Internet advertisement was predicated on word searches. These producers placed banners or links with searches associated with trigger words or phrases. For example, a producer might place a link to searches involving the word "organic." Promotion involved the offering of incentives to motivate the purchase of a product. Organic goods were typically promoted with price incentives. Given the relative price differentials between organic and inorganic goods, producers and retailers tried to motivate purchases by offering limited discount periods. For instance, during key holiday such as Valentine's Day and Mother's Day, organic floricultural retailers would offer discounts on flowers and plants to stimulate purchases. Discounts were also utilized when introducing a new product. Given the initial apprehension of customers to try a new product, producers and retailer might run a limited promotional discount to motivate interest.

103   The keys to success rested on several factors. The financial strength of the organic retailer had to be strong enough to support the intended advertising medium. Organic retailers had to utilize the best advertising medium more likely to reach intended consumer markets. Organic retailers had to offer discounts and additional promotional incentives to motivate consumer purchases.

Technology

104   Websites and supply-chain management systems were used in the organic goods industry.

Websites

105 E-commerce retailers of organic goods used websites to sell organic goods. Websites offered the retailer to reach a broader consumer base. On the websites, the consumer viewed the categorized organic goods that were offering by selecting the products tab. The consumer selected the organic goods that he/she desired. A brief description of the product was displayed alongside the picture of the organic product. Information such as its origin, weight, nutritional content, and any additional characteristics such as its effect on health were displayed on the website. The desired organic product was selected for purchase. On the purchase screen, the consumer input billing and personal information such as home address and credit information. The information was secured and a confirmation was either given immediately or later sent to the consumer's email address. Some websites offered the consumer the option of tracking the transit of the confirmed purchase with the confirmation number. On the websites, customer assistance contact information was available. The retailer's term of transactions and legal disclosures were both available on the websites. Additional useful links to information pertaining to the organic industry might also be available on the website.

Supply Chain Management

106 Large farms selling to distributors used supply chain management technology to manage inventory levels of organic products at the distribution centers. Inventory levels of organic goods were electronically tabulated as they left the distribution center towards the destination points. If the inventory level of particular goods fell below a threshold, an electronic message was sent to the farm to prepare the needed amount for delivery to the distribution center. If the system was not fully integrated between the large farm and the distribution center, an electronic message would be sent to the main terminal at the distribution center alerting the low inventory level of particular organic goods. A purchase order would be later sent to the distribution center. This process was also true for distribution companies selling to the retail outlets. Direct from producers, such as agricultural cooperatives, offered organic products that were sold directly to consumers who also employed supply-chain management technology. These direct from producer integrated their technology with e-commerce retailers and catalog companies to ensure a proper and timely dissemination of product availability. If the organic product was in shortage of supply, the information was relayed to the retailers' system and the product offering was temporarily suspended until adequate supply became available at the producers' facilities. However, if the organic product was available, the purchased and confirmed order was sent directly to the producer's system. The producer's responsibility was to fulfill the order.

107 The keys to success involved several factors. The website had to be logically organized, easy to navigate, and informative. The website had to have customer service. The website had to be secure to handle sensitive consumer information and it had to have a good technology infrastructure to monitor the inventory level properly and communicate shortages appropriately.

Competition

108 Competition in the organic goods industry was intense. The agricultural cooperatives were a group of farmers that were able to retail organic goods directly to the customers but were financially restricted. 1-800-Flowers was a gift retailing company whose strong brand recognition extended to organic perishable goods. Harry and David was a family-owned gift retailing company that sold goods through the Internet, catalogs, and at various companies operated stores scattered across the United States.

Agriculture Cooperatives

109   An organic agricultural cooperative was an incorporated business that was owned and run by a group of farmers or producers growing organic products adhering to the National Organic Program. As a group, members purchased business supplies and services at volume discounts and negotiated for favorable pricing, delivery terms, credit terms, and other arrangements for their organic products. The organic agricultural cooperatives major strength was that they were the original source for organic products. They mainly consisted of farmers and growers who actually produced the organic products. The resource pooling ability of agricultural cooperatives gave them strength in having sufficient financing to support any scale of production. As organic producer, they were strong in their ability to adhere to National Organic Programs standards. Given the egalitarian structure of organic agricultural cooperatives, members conferred on issues affecting the group as a whole. This structure also gave organic agricultural cooperatives strength in exercising financial discipline on the expenditures of factors of production. Organic agricultural cooperatives were also strong in the quality of organic goods because they used storage and transportation systems that provided the necessary conditions to bring the organic goods to the consumer in good quality. They were also strong in properly labeling the organic goods and ensuring the appropriate certification and nutritional content on the packaging of the organic goods.

110   However, organic agricultural cooperatives also had several weaknesses. Organic agricultural cooperatives did not have strong brand recognition. Advertising strategies could not be pursued extensively because they did not have the sufficient financial strength to do so. Organic agricultural cooperatives tended to focus on producing edible organic products and thus were weak in their ability to offer additional product categories such as wellness products and organic flowers. The egalitarian structure of the cooperative restricted the possibility of any expenditure without uniform members' consent. For this reason, organic agricultural cooperatives pursuing e-commerce retailing were weak in product presentation on the websites through which they sold.

1-800-Flowers

111   1-800-FLOWERS.COM®, was a publicly traded (NASDAQ: FLWS), gift retailing company, founded by CEO, Jim McCann in 1976.

112   1-800-Flowers.com major strength resided in its strong brand recognition. The success of its floricultural division had helped to shape consumer perception of convenience, reliability, and quality. The company's brand recognition was attributed to that fact it had the financial strength to successfully utilize any advertising medium to reach its intended audience. Since a majority of its sales were derived from the Internet, the company strategically placed a link on the Yahoo! home page. For instance, consumers seeking to purchase flowers were presented with no other options but to purchase from the company as a result of its strategy. The company also occasionally advertised on television which further strengthened its brand recognition. Given its e-commerce strategy, the company had strength in maintaining a well presented and secured website. Products were logically organized under the appropriate category which made finding a desired product easy. Consumers were also able to safely purchase goods online because the company was strong in maintaining a secure website. However, 1-800-Flowers.com also had several weaknesses. The company was weak in offering a wide selection of different organic goods and various organic product categories to the consumer. It offers a few organic produce selections to the consumer. The company was not strong in offering quality products because the organic goods were not sent directly to the consumers. The company purchases from large distribution centers and from large farmers where the organic goods might have been in storage for a couple of days. The company was also weak in its consumer education initiatives. Information on

the organic industry or related resources was not readily available to the consumer on the company's websites.

Harry and David

113 Harry and David was a privately-owned gift retailing company, formed by two brothers Harry and David in 1914. The company retailed goods over several company-operated stores, via catalogs, and over the Internet throughout the domestic United States.

114 Harry and David's major strength resided in wide selection of organic products retailed through a catalog and website, www.harryanddavid.com. The company offered a wide selection of organic produce and fruits such as organic tomatoes and organic apples. The company also scored highly in ensuring the organic products offered to the consumers adhered to the National Organic Program standards. The organics products were properly labeled and had the appropriate certification on the products' packaging. Harry and David purchased organic goods from large distribution companies and maintained reliable supply chain and technology systems with them. Since the company also retailed organic goods from its stores, it had the necessary technology to maintain appropriate inventory levels of organic goods at each of its stores. The company also retails organic goods over the Internet. It was strong in the product presentation and maintenance of a good and secure website. Organic goods were aesthetically pleasing and were logically organized in the appropriate product category. The website was also easy to navigate. Customers could conveniently purchase goods online through a secure platform. The company also scored highly on customer service. Customer representative were available, knowledgeable, and willing to help at the company-owned stores and at its call centers.

115 However, Harry and David also had several weaknesses. The company was weak on consumer education initiatives. Useful resources on the organic industry were not readily available on the company's website. The company had relative weak brand recognition. Though the company had the financial strength to pursue advertising strategy, it did not aggressively pursue advertising on any medium with the intention of reaching consumers. The company relied on word-of-mouth advertisement from existing customers to attract new customers. Although the company offered a wide selection of organic produce, it was weak in offering different organic product categories such as organic wellness products. Since the company purchased from distribution companies, it scored low in the quality of organic goods. Distribution companies, by definition, were intermediaries that purchased goods in bulk and had them stored in storage facilities. The organic goods were not as fresh as if purchased directly from the producer.

THE COMPANY

116 Provide Commerce Inc, was an e-commerce marketplace of websites for perishable goods. The company employed a business platform that delivered products direct from the supplier to the consumer. Its business was segmented into three divisions which included: Proflower.com, a floriculture division that offered fresh cut flower and plants; Uptown Prime, a gourmet food division which offered natural premium meats and seafood; finally, Cherry Moon, a produce division which offered fresh organic premium fruits. The company had exclusivity agreements with its producers that allowed the company to get more favorable terms of trade. Following were detailed analyses of Provide Commerce Inc's business model as shown below in Figure 5. Each section focuses on opportunities and strength and weakness in key to success areas.

Products

117 The company retailed organic meats, agricultural produce, and flowers.

FIGURE 5 Company Analysis: Provide Commerce Inc Business Model

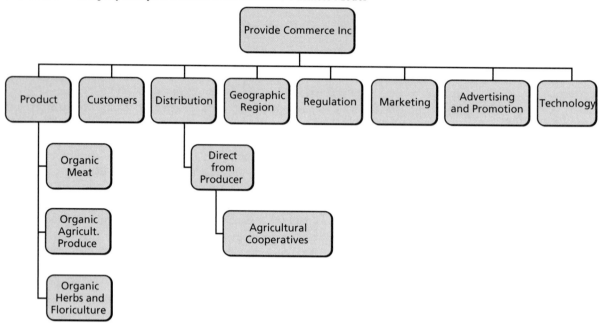

Meats

118 The Uptown Prime division offered organic meat products through a website, www.uptownprime.com. The company was able to offer a variety of organic meat products such as beef, pork, and lamb. It offered a variety of cuts of its organic beef. The filet mignon, "king of steaks," was cut from the heart of the tenderloin and was the tenderest of all steak cuts. The side muscle was removed and was triple trimmed to remove all exterior fat. The NY Strip was cut from the top loin and was leaner than other cuts. The top sirloin was cut from the center of the sirloin and typically perfect for grilling. Organic burgers and roast round up the remaining organic beef offering. The "Kobe" pork known for its texture was the organic pork selection offered by the company. The company's pricing on organic meats was competitive because of the exclusivity agreements it had with its producers. Provide Commerce Inc business offered these organic meat products fresher than its competitors because it used a direct-from-producer business model rather than sourcing through an intermediary such as a distribution company. The process began when the customer purchased a selection of organic meat from the company's website. Once the order was confirmed, it was sent directly to producer to be fulfilled. The order was processed, packaged, and readied for delivery. The company maintained an agreement with FedEx to provide logistical support from the producer to the customer. The next day FedEx picked up the packaged good and had it delivered to the consumer. FedEx was a reputable third-party carrier that maintained storage systems that provided temperature and other conditions necessary for freshness. This helped to preserve the quality of the organic meats while in transit to the customer. Given the organic nature of the products, producers adhered to the standards of the National Organic Program standards. This meant the livestock was fed organic feed and was provided housing conditions that supported the animals' natural behavior. In addition, FedEx also ensured its storage units used in the transportation of the organic meats conformed to the organic standards.

119   Although the company had a strong offering of organic goods, it needed to extend its product categories. Organic meats could be offered as snacks and prepared as children's meals. Organic product offered for children continues to be undeveloped despite the inherent demand by parents who wanted to offer their children a healthier alternative. Organic snacks such as meat jerky could be a strong addition to the company's current offering. The appeal of the organic snacks was that it could be enjoyed by all consumer base given their relative demands.

Agricultural Produce

120   The Cherry Moon division offered organic fruits and vegetable through a website, www. cherrymoon.com. On the website, all the organic produce was categorized under a link named "Organic." The company current organic offerings included organic pineapples, pears, oranges, mangoes, apples, bananas, and kiwis. It also offered organic fruit baskets. The company's pricing on agricultural produce was competitive because of the exclusivity agreements with its producers. Provide Commerce Inc business offered these organic agricultural produce fresher than its competitors because it used a direct-from-producer business model rather than sourcing through an intermediary such as a distribution company. The process began when the customer purchased a selection of organic produce from the company's website. Once the order was confirmed, it was sent directly to producer to be fulfilled. The order was processed, packaged, and readied for delivery. The company maintained an agreement with FedEx to provide logistical support from the producer to the customer. The next day FedEx picked up the packaged good and had it delivered to the consumer. FedEx was a reputable third-party carrier that maintained storage systems that provided temperature and other conditions necessary for freshness. This helped to preserve the quality of the organic agricultural produce while in transit to the customer. Given the organic nature of the products, producers adhered to the standards of the National Organic Program standards. This meant there was sufficient separation between the organically cultivated produce and the traditionally cultivated produce. In addition, FedEx also ensured its storage units used in the transportation of the organic meats conform to the organic standards.

121   Although the company had a strong offering of organic agricultural produce, it needed to extend its product categories. Organic fruits could also be offered as snacks such as apple chips. Organic product offered for children continues to be undeveloped despite the inherent demand by parents who wanted to offer their children a healthier alternative. Organic snacks such as apple chips could be a strong addition to the company's current offering. The appeal of the organic snacks was that it could be enjoyed by all consumer base given their relative demands.

Organic Herbs and Floriculture

122   The Proflowers division offered natural flowers and plants through a website, www. proflowers.com. The company current floricultural offerings included roses, daisies, and lilies. The company's pricing on floricultural products was competitive because of the exclusivity agreements with its producers. Provide Commerce Inc offered these floricultural produce fresher than its competitors because it used a direct-from-producer business model rather than sourcing through an intermediary such as a distribution company. The process began when the customer purchased a selection of organic produce from the company's website. Once the order was confirmed, it was sent directly to producer to be fulfilled. The order was processed, packaged, and readied for delivery. The company maintained an agreement with FedEx to provide logistical support from the producer to the customer. The next day FedEx picked up the packaged good and had it delivered to the consumer. FedEx was a reputable third-party carrier that maintained storage systems that provided temperature and other conditions necessary for freshness. This helped to preserve the quality of the floricultural products while in transit to the customer. Given the organic nature of the products,

producers adhered to the standards of the National Organic Program standards. This meant there was sufficient separation between the organically cultivated floricultural products and herbs from the traditionally cultivated floricultural products and herbs.

123   Although the company had a strong offering of flowers, it needed to expand its offering within the floricultural division to include organic herbs. Organic herbs presented a unique opportunity to offer a healthy medicinal alternative to the aging population who already purchased organic goods based on health benefits. Organic herbs such as St. John's Wort that had medicinal properties could be offered in a new wellness division.

Consumers

124   The company retailed organic products to a wide consumer base. Pricing on products offered to its consumers were competitive because of the exclusivity agreements the company maintained with its organic producers. Consumers purchasing organic goods wanted assurance that the goods were in fact what they claimed to be and were labeled with all the necessary certification. The producers that supplied organic goods to Provide Commerce Inc were checked by certifying agents under the jurisdiction of the National Organic Program. Before any producers could apply the organic label to any goods, the production process had to conform to the established standards. The company's strength was that all its producers offering organic goods were certified and label their products accordingly with the USDA "Organic" seal of approval. Customers of organic goods demanded a high quality of products that they purchased. The company offered higher quality organic goods to the consumer because it sourced directly from the producers.

125   The process began when the customer purchased a selection of organic produce from the company's website. Once the order was confirmed, it was sent directly to producer to be fulfilled. The order was processed, packaged, and readied for delivery. The company maintained an agreement with FedEx to provide logistical support from the producer to the customer. The next day FedEx picked up the packaged good and had it delivered to the consumer. FedEx was a reputable third-party carrier that maintained storage systems that provided temperature and other conditions necessary for freshness. This helped to preserve the quality of the organic agricultural produce while in transit to the customer. Good customer service was highly appreciated by consumers. At times, consumers might have industry-specific questions on the organic production process and certification process or they might simply want friendly advice on goods they wanted to purchase. The company supported a strong customer service. Representatives were all always available to answer basic issues such as web-related problems. For the more complex issues such as industry-specific questions, a supervisor was also available to provide assistance.

126   The company remained weak in the various organic product categories it offered to the consumer. The diversity of the organic consumers presented opportunities in unexplored areas. Organic goods for children continue to remain an undeveloped product category even though there continues to be an expressed demand by parents. A children's division would be developed to satisfy the demand for this specific category. Products for the children would include complete packaged school lunches either with meat entrees or exclusively vegetarian. Schools lunches provided a healthy alternative to working families with children who were pressed for time in the morning to prepare school lunches and were concerned over the unhealthy state of lunches offering at the school cafeterias. Organic snacks were another product category which could be further developed. The appeal of organic snacks was that it was not relegated to a specific consumer group and thus could satisfy all consumers. Organic snacks such as dried peaches could serve as a tasty and convenience snack for the single, busy professional or it could be offered to children as tea-time snacks before dinner was prepared. Finally, a wellness division offering organic herbs should be introduced. The appeal of organic wellness products was that they were able to satisfy a wide consumer

base. For instance, the herbal compound, or mixture of various herbs, of Reishi Mushroom, Maitake Mushroom, Shiitake Mushroom, Codonopsis, Siberian Ginseng and Astragalus was used therapeutically for deep immune support. Likewise, the herbal compound of fresh Helonias, fresh Black Cohosh, Chasteberry, Dang gui, fresh Partridge Berry, fresh Angelica, fresh Ginger and Licorice was a female tonic formula that nourished the full genito-urinary system, balanced the hormonal functions and supported blood circulation, digestion, and liver function.

Distribution

127 The company applied a direct from distributor model which involved purchasing from the producer and retailing directly to the consumers. The company negotiated exclusivity agreements with its producers to maintain the control over the product quality and branding. This exclusivity agreement also afforded the company the flexibility to introduce new products without the fear of losing proprietary information to competitors. Because of the exclusivity agreement, producers were more willing to entertain the competitive pricing requests on products by the company. The distribution process began with the product selection. Both the company and producers agreed on the organic products which should be grown to and exhibited on the company's e-commerce websites. Because the company's business geographic scope spanned the domestic United States, the company maintained agreements with organic agricultural cooperatives. The participatory nature of agricultural cooperatives gave these producers an infinite size and production capacity. It also increased the variety of organic goods produced which increased the selection offered to the company. For this reason, the company was strong in the selection of organic goods which it retailed over its e-commerce website. The producers supplying organic goods through the cooperatives were checked by certifying agents under the jurisdiction of the National Organic Program. Before any producers could apply the organic label to any goods, the production process had to have conformed to the established standards. The company's strength was that all its producers offering organic goods were certified and label their products accordingly with the USDA "Organic" seal of approval.

128 Once the company and the agricultural cooperatives had reached an agreement, the cooperatives were responsible for ensuring confirmed orders were processed and readied for delivery. The process began when the customer purchased a selection of organic produce from the company's website. The company was strong in having a reliable supply chain and technology with its producers. The company's technological systems supporting the websites were linked with those of the producers. This integration allowed for timely transfer of information and for an effective supply management of organics goods retailed over the company's websites. For instance, confirmed orders were transmitted simultaneously to the producer's system for processing. Likewise, shortages of choice products were displayed as "Sold Out" on the company's websites so as not to cause consumer disappointments. If customers required personal assistance, representatives could be reached via telephone on a number listed on the website.

129 Consumers demanded a high quality of organic goods and the company satisfied this demand better than its competitors. The strength of the company lay in its strategic relationship with FedEx which required FedEx to provide logistical support from the producer to the customer. Traditional forms of distribution required that organic goods to be purchased by large distribution companies, stored at the facilities, and eventually delivered to consumers through various retail outlets. This method reduced the life of the organic products before they reached the consumer. However, by contracting the logistical support to the third-party carrier and requiring a next-day pick-up at the producers' premises, the company ensured the freshness of the products to the consumer. Furthermore, by bypassing the traditional distribution method, the company did not need storage facilities during the interim period before it was retailed to the consumer nor did it need to support proprietary transportation systems supported by employees.

Geography

130   The company's primary market was the United States. Through its e-commerce platform, the company's products were available in all 50 states.

Technology

131   The company's retailed organic products from its three online storefronts: proflowers.com focused on floricultural products; cherrymoon.com focused on organic agricultural produce; uptownprime.com focused on organic meats. Its technology infrastructure was consistently strong in each of the key to success areas.

132   The company had a strong website presentation and secure infrastructure to protect consumer information. The process began with the initial purchase of an organic product through the company's website. Products were logically displayed and properly categorized. For instance, all organic tulips were organized under a link called "Tulips." The products were also lush with vibrant colors, though a bit more accentuated than the real thing made them both aesthetically pleasing and delectable. Products that were currently available were displayed on the website but products were not available were marked with a "Sold Out" banner. By clicking on the "Buy" link, the customer was redirected to a detailed product page. On this product page, pricing information was available, a comprehensive product description and sourcing information was displayed, and an "Order" link was provided. By selecting the "Order" link, the customer was redirected to customer information page where the customer's contact, billing, and delivery date and information were inputted. The company accepted all major credit cards such as MasterCard, Visa, and Discover for online purchases. Prior to the submission of the customer's information for processing, a pop-up screen appeared giving the customer the opportunity to make any changes. By selecting the "Confirm" link, the order was submitted for processing and if successful a confirmation number was displayed and also sent electronically to the customer's email address. If the order could not be processed, the customer was redirected to the information page and was asked to make the necessary changes. A privacy policy was available on the website and pledged the customer information inputted on the website would not be made available to third party vendors such as marketing companies.

133   Good customer service was highly appreciated by consumers. At times, consumers had industry-specific questions on the organic production process and certification process or they simply wanted friendly advice on goods they wanted to purchase. The company supported a strong customer service. Representatives were all always available to answer basic issues such as web-related problems. For the more complex issues such as industry-specific questions, a supervisor was also available to provide assistance.

Marketing

134   As an organic retailer of organic products, the Provide Commerce Inc was strong in ensuring the packaging of products was labeled with proper certification. Organic products were appropriately labeled with the USDA "Organic" seal of approval. In order to be awarded the right to label a product organic, the producers had to conform to the National Organic Program standards. The producers that supplied the company's organic products were checked and verified by certifying agents under the jurisdiction of their production processes.

135   Organic goods such as oranges were uniform across all retail outlets. As organic goods, they all conformed to the same standards of production and thus made product differentiation a bit difficult. However, brand recognition was important within this industry. Due

to the uniformity of goods, creating a consumer perception on a company's brand could positively affect the revenues of the company. The company lacked a weak brand image because it did not aggressively strive to tout qualities that differentiated itself from its other competitors. The company stood to improve its brand recognition but touting the process organic products was brought to the customers fresher than its competitors. Unlike its other major two competitors, 1-800-Flowers and Harry and David, Provide Commerce Inc delivered organic goods directly from the producers. By eliminating the transitory phases that its competitors utilized such as storage facilities or purchasing from distribution companies which typically decreased the products' freshness, the company was able to bring organic goods fresher to the customer. To market the better quality of its organic goods, the company needed to aggressively present comparisons between the traditional retailing of organic goods and its direct from producer model. This should be aggressively marketed on the product's packaging, on the company's websites, and in aggressive advertisement campaigns. This strategy would create a brand image associated with quality. To appeal to the underdeveloped children's market, the company should introduce "Veggie" characters such as "C-Carrot," "Mr. Z (zucchini), "Monster Mango," and "Lucy Lemon." The "Veggie" characters would be a marketing strategy to educate children on the organic process and the benefits of organic products. Each character would have distinctive personality in an attempt to appeal to all diversity. The marketing efforts would feature Veggie placements in TV advertisements on children programs and station such as Sesame Street and Cartoon Network, on the children's website division, and on the product packaging.

136 Consumer education initiatives were important in developing further knowledge on the concept of organics. An explanation of the organic production process plus the benefits on health should be made available. This information only seeks to further strength the resolves of consumers to purchase organically cultivated products. The company lacked strong consumer education initiatives. Links to organic resources were not readily available on the company's website. The company stood to improve its education initiatives by providing customers with additional resources to increase their understanding and possibly strengthen their purchasing commitments towards organically produced goods.

Advertising and Promotion

137 Provide Commerce Inc advertised on the Internet and over the radio. The company had an online marketing agreement to secure web advertising. The agreement was a non-cancelable advertising contract. Under this agreement, the company received certain search keywords such as "organic fruits," "premium meat" and "flowers" and featured site placement designed to deliver consumers to the company's website from search results on web portal such as Yahoo!. When a consumer entered either of those keywords searches on a web portal such as Yahoo!, a link to the respective division was generated along with other search results. The company was strong in running promotional seasonal campaigns to motivate consumer purchases. Discounts were typically offered during key holidays such as Valentine's Day and Mother's Day. During these periods, price was reduced on organic products and complimentary next day shipping was included. The company did not aggressively utilize its financial strength to engage in a broader advertising strategy. Television advertisements on certain nationally syndicated shows such as Oprah should be included into the advertising mix. By advertising on television programs catered to women, the company would be able to reach the decision makers on household shopping. Furthermore, advertisement on children's programs and channels would allow the company to introduce organic products to children.

Financial Analysis

138 The company was financially strong. The company improved considerably in fiscal 2004. According to Hoover's Online [Hoovers 2005], net sales amounted to $128 million, an

FIGURE 6
**Provide Commerce
Inc Financial Data**

Source: Hoover's Online (2005).
[Online] *http://jerome.stjohns.
edu:839/subscribe/co/fin/
comparison.xhtml?ID=59885.*
Accessed May 2005

Financial	Company	Industry
Current Ratio	3.65	1.40
Quick Ratio	3.3	1.3
Leverage Ratio	1.33	2.25
Total Debt/Equity	0.00	0.50

increase of 45.2% from $88.7 million in fiscal 2003. Net income amounted to $18 million for fiscal year 2004 as compared to $4.3 million for fiscal 2003. This stellar performance was attributed to the growth in consumer patronage. The company's database of consumers grew to approximately 3.1 million from 69,000 as of 1999. Further analysis that highlighted Provide Commerce financial resources in 2004 showed that the company was financially stronger than the industry average, as shown in Figure 6. The company had a current ratio of 3.65, as shown in Figure 6, relative to an industry average of 1.40. This ratio indicated the company had short assets which could meet current liabilities 4 times. Furthermore, the company had a quick ratio of 3.3 relative to an industry average of 1.33. This ratio indicates the company's ability to meet short term liabilities with cash and cash equivalent assets was 3 times great than its peers. As shown in Figure 6, the company's debt to equity was 0.00 as compared to the industry average of 0.50. This number translated into percent indicates how much of the company's assets were financed by borrowed capital. The company exhibited less business risk with a negligible debt to equity percent.

Management Strategy

139   Provide Commerce Inc's strategy would be focused on expanding its offering of organic perishable goods. Since the initial launch of proflowers.com, a floricultural division, the company had successfully launched two additional websites to retail organic products: uptown prime, a division retailing various selections and cuts of organic; and cherrymoons, a division retailing organic agricultural produce. The company would continue to leverage its direct from producer model consistently across other organic product categories to bring organic products that were fresher than those of its competitors. A newly created children's division offering organic products such as organic meals was an opportunity which could be explored. The undeveloped children's market continued to be insufficient within the organic industry though there was strong evidence of demand by purchasing parents. In addition, the snacks division offered an opportunity for the development of convenient organic products which could satisfy a large consumer base. Finally, the wellness division presented an opportunity to offer a healthier alternative to ailments of everyday living in place of the traditional forms of medication.

140   The success of these strategies hinged on the developing a strong brand recognition. In an industry where either goods were uniform such as organic apples or remain undeveloped such as children's organic product, consumers had to have faith in the brand offered to them. They had to be assured that the products were of the highest quality, inexpensive, and would be conveniently accessible. By marketing and explaining the direct from producer model, the company poised to create a brand recognition associated with quality. Eventually, the long-term strategy would be to continuously evaluate organic perishable goods which could be applied to direct from producer model and added to the company's e-commerce portfolio.

LOOKING TOWARDS THE FUTURE

141   After the successful launch of three organic divisions, proflowers.com, cherrymoons.com, and uptownprime.com, Provide Commerce Inc was seeking to expand into other organic

categories within the organic industry. Consumers motivated by their desire to maintain a healthy lifestyle were demanding more organically produced goods. The company sought to leverage its unique direct from producer model onto new product categories and continue its momentum within the organic industry.

142   The first alternative was for Provide Commerce Inc to expand into two new organic categories: wellness and organic snacks. The wellness division would focus on retailing organic health supplements and medicinal herbs. Furthermore, the organic snacks would focus on retailing various organic snacks as apple crisps and beef jerky. Both divisions would offer various new organic products with the intent of satisfying a wide consumer base.

143   The benefit of this strategic alternative was that Provide Commerce Inc would be entering into two undeveloped organic product categories which had not been adequately pursued by its competitors. By offering new organic products, the company would be in essence differentiating its offering from the more uniform goods retailed by its competitors. This strategy would pay dividends because the consumers continue to exhibit strong demand for organic goods in general.

144   This alternative was feasible because the company maintained exclusivity agreements with agricultural cooperatives who were the primary producers of all organic products. The introduction of new organic products would require careful planning. The participatory nature of agricultural cooperatives would allow the producers to obtain the necessary capital needed to support the introduction of the new organic product categories. New members who may already have had expertise within these new organic product categories but may not have had the market power of an agricultural cooperative would be motivated to join. Furthermore, the prospect of diversifying goods sold through the cooperatives may force existing members to produce products within the new organic categories. The agricultural cooperative also had the necessary expertise, factors of production, storage facilities and financial planning required for the production of the new organic product categories.

145   This alternative would win against the competition because Provide Commerce Inc would offer the new organic products fresher than its competitors. The company sourced directly from producers eliminating the intermediary use of distribution companies otherwise used by its competitors, 1-800-Flowers and Harry and David. The quality of the organic goods would also be maintained because of the company's use of the third party carrier FedEx. FedEx's reputation as third party carrier would ensure the organic products were brought from the producers' premise directly to the consumers in a timely manner while using the appropriate storage systems that would preserve the product quality.

146   The drawback to this alternative was the company's lack of brand recognition may make consumers apprehensive to purchase the new organic product categories. Brand recognition was important given the uniformity of the organic goods within the industry. Consumers want to associate a brand with a perception whether it be reliability, quality, or convenience. One way around this drawback was for the company to aggressively market its ability to source directly from producer. The company would have to explain its business model by inserting blurbs on its product packaging and pursuing a consumer education initiative on its websites. The company would also have to advertising aggressively. Given the financial strength of the company, it could afford to include television into its advertising mix. Television was an underutilized advertising medium within the organic industry. By advertising on a medium not pursued by its competitors, the company would have the unbridled ability to spread its message to consumers.

147   The second alternative considered by Provide Commerce Inc would be to expand organic offering within its three existing divisions to include more exotic organic products. Proflowers.com, the floricultural division, would introduce new organic flowers such as hibiscus. Cherrymoons.com, the agricultural produce division, would introduce new organic produce such as guava. Finally, the Uptownprime.com, organic meat division, would introduce organic meat such as bison.

148   The benefit of this alternative was that Provide Commerce Inc would be differentiating the company's organic offering from product categories already established within the industry. The uniformity in production and types of organic goods would give the company a competitive edge if the company expands the selection of its organic goods.

149   This alternative was feasible because the company maintained exclusivity agreements with agricultural cooperatives who were the primary producers of all organic products. The expansion into new exotic organic products would require careful planning. The participatory nature of agricultural cooperatives would allow the producers who currently had necessary expertise, factors of production, storage facilities and financial planning required for the production of the exotic organic products to join.

150   This alternative would win against the competition because Provide Commerce Inc had considerable strength within the selection of organic meats and agricultural produce than 1-800-Flowers and Harry and David respectively. The quality of the organic goods would also be maintained because of the company's use of the third party carrier FedEx. FedEx's reputation as third party carrier would ensure the organic products were brought from the producers' premise directly to the consumers in a timely manner while using the appropriate storage systems that would preserve the product quality.

151   The drawback to this alternative was a possible consumer reluctance to try organic products unfamiliar to them. One way around this drawback would be for Provide Commerce Inc to offer discount and promotional incentives to motivate purchases. The company would seek to offer an introductory price possibly lower than the current organic offering for a trial period. After the trial period, the prices would be elevated to sufficient levels adequate to its exotic nature.

LIST OF WORKS CITED

BEA (2005). "Gross Domestic Product: First Quarter 2005 (Advance)" [Online]. *http://www.bea.doc.gov/bea/newsrel/gdpnewsrelease.htm*. Accessed April 17, 2005.

Brookings (1999). "China's Changing Oil Strategy and its Foreign Policy Implications" [Online]. *http://www.brookings.edu/fp/cnaps/papers/1999_troush.htm*. Accessed April 17, 2005.

Hoover's Online (2005). [Online] *http://jerome.stjohns.edu:839/subscribe/co/fin/comparison.xhtml? ID=59885*. Accessed May 2005.

O'Mama Report (2001). "Organic Offering: More Than Just Produce" [Online]. *http://www.theorganicreport.com/pages/17_organic_offerings.cfm*. Accessed May 2, 2005.

Union of Concerned Scientists (2004). "The Costs and Benefits of Industrial Agriculture" [Online]. *http://www.ucsusa.org/food_and_environment/sustainable_agriculture/page.cfm?pageID=350*. Accessed April 18, 2005.

University of Florida (2003). "Production, Marketing, and Distribution of Cut Flowers in the United States and Brazil" [Online]. *http://hortbusiness.ifas.ufl.edu/Cut%20Flowers%20Brazil-US.pdf* Accessed March 23, 2005.

Whole Food Market (2004). "Categories of Organic Goods" [Online]. *http://www.wholefoodsmarket.com/issues/org_reasons.html*. Accessed May 2005.

Case 42

Regal Entertainment Group: *The Movie Theater Segment of the Entertainment Industry*

Ho-Sung Lee, Marc E. Gartenfeld, and Robert J. Mockler

INTRODUCTION

1   Regal Entertainment Group (REG), the US's largest movie theater chain had more than 6,273 screens at about 580 theaters in 40 states through its Regal Cinemas, Edwards' Theatres, United Artists Theatre Company, and Hoyts Cinema brands. During the summer of 2005, Hollywood sank into one of its largest slumps since the 1980s. By the middle of the busy summer season, box office revenues were significantly down from the year before for a staggering 19 straight weeks. In December 2005, Michael L. Campbell, the chairman and CEO of Regal Entertainment Group, faced the task of developing an effective differentiating enterprise-wide strategy if REG was to survive and prosper against aggressive competition over the intermediate and long-term future.

2   The industry under study was the Entertainment industry which consisted of live entertainment, T.V. & radio broadcasting, theme park, electronic home entertainment and movie theaters. As individual incomes had been rising, the entertainment industry had been growing very rapidly. The segments of the entertainment industry were also expanding rapidly which in turn was attracting new competitors.

3   Another issue in the entertainment industry was the change from analog to digital formats of film technology. The customers who spent their time in entertainment industry wanted more and more convenient and high technological services.

4   REG was faced with a number of critical long-term decisions. Some of these strategic decisions included: How could the company reduce cost? What kind of services should the company offer to their customers? Should they dramatically implement digital delivery technology? The main question to be resolved was how to differentiate REG from its competition to achieve a winning edge over competitors within intensely competitive, rapidly changing immediate, intermediate, and long-term time frames.

OVERALL INDUSTRY DESCRIPTION: THE ENTERTAINMENT INDUSTRY

5   Entertainment was an amusement or diversion intended to hold the attention of an audience or its participants. The entertainment industry was comprised of live entertainment, T.V. broadcasting, theme parks, electronic home entertainment, and movie theater chain companies that provided, operated, or engaged in performing arts theaters, sports, video games, home theaters, second-run (discount) theaters, art theaters, adult theaters, IMAX, and first run theaters as shown in Figure 1 [Encyclopedia, 2005].

6   In late 2005, consumers, especially younger ones, demanded more and more control over what they watched, read, and listened to. Issues relating to control included pricing of media usage (including free, illegal downloads versus authorized, paid downloads or pay-per-view) and portability (including the ability for a consumer to download once, whether legally or illegally, and then used a file on multiple platforms and devices).

FIGURE 1 The Entertainment Industry

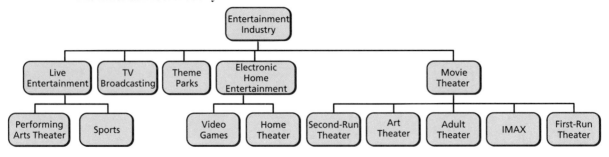

7 Electronic offerings such as DVDs, personal video recorders, video-on-demand, and MP3 players had vastly altered the way consumers enjoyed entertainment. People watched and listened according to their own desires and whims. If someone missed the season finale of his/her favorite television show, the DVD could be bought or rented. If someone was interested in only one track from a recording artist's new CD, that single track could be bought and downloaded from the Internet. If someone loved prime-time drama on a major network but disliked the commercial breaks, the usage of a personal digital video recorder (such as TiVo) would do the trick.

8 The source of information for news, weather, and sports was also changing the landscape of the entertainment industry. News, weather, and sports used to be accessed only through public network television, radio broadcasting, and newspapers. Today consumers had more choices for the same type of information via the Internet, paid programming television, and satellite radio.

Live Entertainment

9 Live entertainment consisted of live performances in the performing arts and sports.

Performing Arts

10 Performing arts were defined as art where the actions of an individual or a group at a particular place and in a particular time, constitute the work. One main type of performing arts was musical theaters.

11 Musical theater was a form of theatre combining music, songs, dance, and spoken dialogue. In late 2005, the musicals were being pulled in a number of different directions. The days when a sole producer made musicals had gone. Corporate sponsors dominated Broadway, and often alliances were formed to stage musicals which required an investment of $10 million or more [Encyclopedia, 2005].

Sports

12 Sports had been organized and regulated from the time of the Ancient Olympics up to the present. The Industrial Revolution and mass production brought increased leisure which allowed increases in spectator sports, less elitism in sports, and greater accessibility. Professionalism became prevalent, it had helped increase the popularity of sports, as had the need to have fun and take a break from a hectic workday or to relieve unwanted stress [Encyclopedia, 2005].

TV Broadcasting

13 Television was a telecommunication system for broadcasting and receiving moving pictures and sound over a distance. The term had come to refer to all the aspects of television programming and transmission as well. Recently, the market for LCD(Liquid Crystal Display) televisions was booming. In October 2004, 40" to 45" televisions were widely available and

Sharp Corporation had announced the successful manufacture of a 65" panel. Also in 2004, Samsung and Sony joined forces to build a factory in South Korea intended to produce 60,000 panels a month, and in March 2005, Samsung announced an 82" HDTV TFT Panel [Encyclopedia, 2005].

Theme Parks

14 Amusement parks was a more generic term for a collection of amusement rides and other entertainment attractions assembled for the purpose of entertaining a fairly large group of people. From the large corporate parks, like those in the Disney and Six Flags families, to small family-owned and operated parks, the nation's landscape was dotted with acres of thrilling rides, attractions, and much more [Wikipedia, 2005].

Electronic Home Entertainment

15 Electronic home entertainments consisted of video games and home theaters.

Video Games

16 Over the past two decades, the video game industry had rapidly advanced and become a valuable contributor to the entertainment business. The estimated break-down of gamers in US households was 61% male and 39% female, with 47% of gamers between 13 and 24 years old, 30% between 25 and 39 years old, and 23% over 40 years old. Video games consisted of PC-based and console-based games. Console based games required proprietary hardware and game titles from companies such as Sony, Nintendo, and Microsoft. PC games required a PC and game software [VNU, Inc, 2005].

Home Theaters

17 In 1980, only a small percentage of households in the United States had cable television, and VCRs were a brand-new luxury item. Sound systems, for the most part, were limited to the small speaker built into the television, and not many people had a screen larger than 27 inches. There was certainly no mistaking the typical TV room for a home theater—home theaters were expensive setups with actual film projectors and wide screens.

18 In late 2005, a home theater system was a combination of electronic components designed to recreate the experience of watching a movie in a theater. When watching a movie on a home theater system, the viewer was more immersed in the experience than when watching it on an ordinary television.

Movie Theater

19 Movie theaters, the focus of this study, are discussed in detail in the following sections.

INDUSTRY AND COMPETITIVE MARKET: THE MOVIE THEATER INDUSTRY

20 About 16 new major features were introduced to the theatrical marketplace each month, playing 800 to 2,500 screens, or an average of about 1,650 screens. The average studio feature ("A-Picture") was in first-run release for approximately 8 weeks garnering between 1,000 and 2,700 screens and grossing $10 to $40 million over this period. The same picture was in second-run theaters for the balance of its theatrical life, this being approximately 6 months. Independent pictures grossed much more modest sums, but their production and marketing budgets were considerably less as well.

21 Since first-run was usually 8 weeks, it meant that between 12,800 and virtually all of the existing 26,500 screens (during the peak times of Summer and Christmas holidays), were booked with major studio productions, leaving, at best, between 6,850 and 13,700 screens

available for independent productions for limited periods of time or during off-season periods. Each independent production played on about 5 to 75 screens (or an average of approximately 40 screens) making it possible for about 260 pictures to be absorbed by the market in each 6-month period.

22   Box office receipts soared to a new record in 2004, although the actual number of movie-goers declined for a second year in a row. Movies took in $9.4 billion in 2004 at the domestic box office, according to tracking firm Exhibitor Relations. But the record gross was due more to rising prices than attendance. Factoring in a nationwide average ticket price of $6.21 in 2004, attendance fell about 1.7 percent to 1.53 billion during that time. Attendance in 2003 was 1.57 billion, down 4.3 percent from 2002. The average ticket price in 2002 year was $6.03 [Matrixx Entertainment Corporation, 2003].

Types of Movie Theaters

23   As shown Figure 1, the movie theater industry consisted of companies that operated second-run theaters, art theaters, adult theaters, IMAX, and first-run theaters [Encyclopedia, 2005].

Second-Run (Discount) Theaters

24   Second-run or discount theaters were theaters that ran films that had been pulled from the first-run theaters and were presented at a lower ticket price.

Art Theaters

25   An Art Theater was a theater that presented alternative and art films as well as second-run and classic films. Art films, foreign films, and documentaries were usually art house films but from time to time they caught the appeal of the mainstream viewing audiences. Some recent examples of such break-out films included Life is Beautiful (Italy, 1998) and the documentary Fahrenheit 9/11 (United States, 2004).

Adult Theaters

26   An adult theater specialized in showing pornographic movies; often called "adult" movies. With the advent of the Internet and DVDs, the production and distribution of pornographic movies had become even easier and it is a huge business involving hundreds of filmmakers and thousands of performers all over the world. With 20,000 feature length films a year in the US alone, the adult movie industry was the largest branch of film industry in the world.

IMAX

27   IMAX (for Image Maximum) was a film projection system that had the capacity to display images of far greater size and resolution than conventional film display systems. A standard IMAX screen was 22 m wide and 16 m high (72.6 × 52.8 ft), but could be larger. IMAX was the most successful large-format special-venue film presentation system.

28   IMAX theaters could show conventional movies, but the major benefits of the IMAX system were only available when showing movies filmed using it. While a few mainstream feature films had been produced in IMAX, IMAX movies were often documentaries featuring spectacular natural scenery, and might be limited to the 45-minute length of a single reel of IMAX film. IMAX films, at times were also filmed in 3-D format. Viewers needed to wear special glasses, which decodes the format into a 3-dimensional image.

First-Run Theaters

29   First-run theaters, the focus of this study, is discussed in the following section.

FIGURE 2
Total US Admissions

Source: National Association of Theater Owners (2005). [Online]. *http://www. natoonline.org/* Accessed November 15.

Year	2004	2003	2002	2001	2000
Admissions ($billions)	1.53	1.57	1.63	1.49	1.42

INDUSTRY AND COMPETITIVE MARKET: FIRST-RUN THEATERS

30   A first-run theater was a theater that ran primarily mainstream film fare from the major film companies and distributors, during the initial release period of each film. Hollywood movies were usually considered mainstream [Encyclopedia, 2005].

31   The first-run theater industry emphasized megaplexes (16 or more screens), multiple story stadium seating, and digital sound and picture. While megaplexes worked well in large metropolitan areas, smaller cities might not have had the population or density to support such large developments. Not every market supported a megaplex, and there was a demand for everything from single screens and multiplexes (8 to 16 screens) on up.

Major Trends

32   Believing bigger and better screens would bring greater demand for movies; exhibitors began a costly building frenzy of state-of-the-art multiplex theaters in the late 1990s. To some extent the demand did grow, but the new multiplexes tended to cannibalize sales from the exhibitors' older theaters, which did not close down as quickly as expected, leaving a glut of screens open. Nearly 14,000 new screens were built in the 1990s. Consequently, between 2000 and 2001 a dozen major theater circuits filed for Chapter 11 bankruptcy reorganization.

33   During the summer of 2005, Hollywood sank into one of its largest slumps since the 1980s. By the middle of the busy summer season, box office revenues were significantly down from the year before for a staggering 19 straight weeks. As shown in Figure 2, the number of movie theater admissions in U.S had been decreasing for the last 2 years. There were several factors that contributed to the decline, including rising ticket prices, customer dissatisfaction with the theater experience, consumers' shift to watching movies sent directly to their mailbox by Netflix or Blockbuster, or to buy movies from cable TV's pay per-view channels, as well as the building of their own movie libraries by purchasing cheap DVDs from mass retailers like Best Buy. Hollywood's obsession with big opening weekend grosses also did not help, since the exhibitor's percentage of a movie's gross increased the longer the film played in the theaters. When a big film was burned out by the second or third week of its release, there was not much business left to fill the theater seats [Hoover, 2005].

Essence of the Business Model

34   Figure 3 shows the essence of first run movie theater business model. The first run movie theater model catered to the mass market movie goers who were interested in watching new blockbuster releases advertised by the movie studios.

35   There were 5 main types of movies: *action, comedy, science fiction, horror,* and *drama.*

36   Customers ranged across all ages depending on the movies that were just released. Customers can be categorized by demographics, including age, gender, and ethnic group, and rating systems.

37   All first run movie theaters were located within a large geographic area, usually in a metropolitan city. The product and services provided by the first run movie theaters included:

FIGURE 3 **First-Run Movie Theater Business Model**

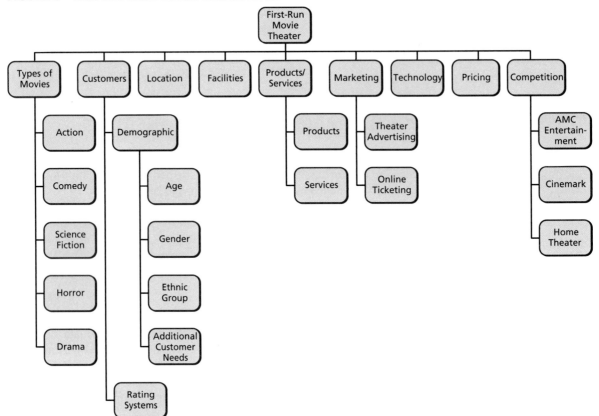

viewing of motion pictures, concessions which included food and beverages, and video game arcades for waiting patrons.

38   Another service provided by many first run movie theaters was screen advertising for promotions. Companies were attempting to find innovative ways to bring in revenue. Additional revenue sources for the movie theaters were promotional and advertising content from advertisers shown before the movie. Advertising on the screens was becoming the standard, even though movie patrons repeatedly express annoyance at the increase of ads at the movies. Movie theater firms were also experimenting with showing concerts or sporting events on their screens and some were even offering new types of foods and adding alcoholic beverages.

39   Marketing was defined as the process of planning and executing the pricing, promotion, and distribution of goods, ideas, and services to create exchanges that satisfied individual and organizational goals. There were two main types of marketing strategies. One of them was advertisement of movie theaters and the other one was online marketing. The first run movie theaters marketed their locations and movies through local newspaper movie listings and online movie portals. Theater advertising was done through local newspaper's movie listings, where new releases were advertised with locations of the movie theaters screening the movie with the time. Another commonly used advertising method was through movie phone services which allowed customers to call a number to find a movie, show-times, and locations of the movie they wished to watch. Online ticketing allowed customers to purchase movie tickets online and access show times, movie reviews, and trailers.

40   With new investments in technology, first run movie theaters were confident that the moviegoers would be willing to pay for the improvements in movie quality that could not

be easily duplicated at home. The technology used to deliver the movies to the big screen was still mostly analog. With the evolution of new technologies the first run movie theaters were starting to adopt digital technology within their theaters to improve the delivery, sound, and viewing quality. The industry's newest trend, digital cinema, was already making a huge impact on the exhibition market. Cheaper for producers in virtually every way, digital technology was the future of 21st century moviemaking (George Lucas shot both *Star Wars—Episode II: Attack of the Clones* and *Star Wars—Episode III: Revenge of the Sith* digitally). Yet, there were still few theaters with the necessary digital projectors because many of the major exhibitors had little or no capital for new investments [Hoover, 2005].

41   Pricing was the manual or automatic process of applying prices to purchase and sales orders, based on factors such as: a fixed amount, quantity break, promotion or sales campaign, specific vendor quote, combination of multiple orders or lines, and many others. Most theaters employed some form of price discrimination, such as discounts for seniors and students. But with the major exception of matinee rates, each moviegoer paid the same price for all movies at any time. The price of movie tickets had increased steadily over the years even though moviegoers had declined. The price ranged from $6.50 to $10.50 depending on factors such as location and time of showings.

Types of Movies

42   There were 5 main types of movies; *action movies* were defined as usually involving a fairly straightforward story of good guys versus bad guys, where most disputes were resolved by using physical force. Action films were largely derived from crime films and thrillers, by way of westerns and to some extent war films. A *comedy* movie was a film laced with humor or that sought to provoke laughter from the audience. *Science fiction* had been a film genre since the earliest days of cinema. Science fiction films had explored a great range of subjects and themes, including many that could not be readily presented in other genre. Science fiction films had been used to explore sensitive social and political issues, while often providing an entertaining story for the more casual viewer. Today, science fiction films were in the forefront of new special effects technology, and the audience had become accustomed to displays of realistic alien life forms, spectacular space battles, energy weapons, faster than light travel, and distant worlds. The *horror genre* was characterized by the attempt to make the viewer experience dread, fear, terror, disgust, or horror. Its plots often involved the intrusion of an evil force, event, or personage, sometimes of supernatural origin, into the mundane world. *A drama* was a film that depended mostly on in-depth character development, interaction, and highly emotional themes. In a good drama film, the audiences were able to experience what other characters were feeling and identify with someone. This genre could be especially useful by challenging the ignorance from stereotypes or any other overly simplistic generalizations by bringing it down to a more personal and complex level. As well, such movies could also be therapeutic by showing how characters coped with their problems, challenges, or issues, and to the extent the viewer could identify with the characters with his or her own world [Encyclopedia, 2005].

Customers

43   Customers could be categorized into demographics and rating systems. The Motion Picture Association of America publishes an annual Movie Attendance Study entitled, "US Movie Attendance Study." Some key findings from the 2004 report are discussed in the following paragraphs.

Demographics

44   Demographics of movie viewers included age, gender, and ethnic group. At the end of this discussion the study also provides additional customer needs that could not be put into any of the demographic categories listed here.

45   *Age*   The 12–29 age group represented almost half of annual theater admissions. Frequent moviegoers (those attending at least once per month in a year) made up 81 percent of total admissions. The most frequent moviegoers were those aged 18–20 years old (53 percent). Of the total population aged 12 and over in 2003, 72 percent were moviegoers. While families, teenagers, college students and young couples were essential to movie ticket sales, it was important not to overlook any demographic. A community with a sizable retirement population might want to program special daytime screenings. The presence of a local film society could also encourage sizable ticket and concession sales at the movie theater. A large number of stay-at-home parents with younger children might support daytime programming of family films. A large teenage population might sustain midnight screenings on weekend nights. Collaborations with local groups and organizations along with targeted marketing and promotions might provide the needed boost in admissions.

46   Certain types of movie were usually targeted at specific age groups. The first group was the age from 1–12 years old. The types of movies for targeting this group were cartoon and adventure movie. However, this group was not the main movie theater customers. The second group was from 13 to 17 years old. This group mostly watched the action movie and educational movie such as humanism movies. However, this group was restricted by some movie genres. Theme, language, violence, nudity, sex, and drug use were among those content areas considered in the decision-making process. Third group was from 17 years to 40 years old. This group was the main customers for movie theaters and they covered most of film genres depending on their preference. The last group was from 41 years old to senior group and this group mostly liked to watch romantic and drama genre of movies.

47   *Gender*   There were "women's films" and there were "men's films," conventional wisdom holds. Women's films were not simply "romance" films. They concerned films where the story was told from the woman's point of view such as "The Piano" and "Muriel's Wedding," the woman was the clear protagonist or heroine, or the story centers around women and women's issues. "Men's films" tended to focus more on action, adult (rather than romance) and competition. If conventional wisdom was accurate, it would be expected that favorite films should express a gender bias such that males would be partial to "men's films," and females would be partial to "women's films." These expectations were consistent with Social Identity Theory which held that people seek out particular messages which supported their social identity (Abrams & Hogg, 1990). Harwood (1997) extended the theory to selective choices in media viewing as a form of social identity gratification. Film preference which was consistent or congruent with gender identity was what Fischoff's 1994 study revealed [Media Psychology Research Institute, 1998].

48   The gender-genre differences were most dramatically expressed in the age group below 26 yrs., i.e., the Young. For example, Young males accounted for only 13% of all male-cited Drama films but accounted for 31% of male-cited Action films. Thus, they cited 1/3 more than their proportionate share of male-cited Action films and 1/3 less than their proportionate share of male-cited Drama films. Young females, on the other hand, were less polarized on the issue of Action versus Drama. They cited 45% of all Drama films for women. On the other hand, they cited 61% of all female-cited Action films. Age, therefore, did nothing to enhance or dull female's appreciation of Drama films; but it strongly affected their appreciation of Action films [Media Psychology Research Institute, 1998].

49   *Ethnic Groups*   Another type of customer was an ethnic group. For example, there were 38.8 million Hispanics in the USA, according to Census Bureau estimates released 2002. This showed a 9.8% increase since the Census was taken in April 2000. The U.S. population grew 2.5% to 288.4 million in the same period. Hispanics accounted for half of the national increase. Non-Hispanic blacks, including people who said they were black and another race, grew at a much slower rate than Hispanics, up 3.1%, to 36.6 million. Hispanics made up 13% of the nation's population. Hispanics represented 15% of movie-ticket sales, higher than their share of the population. The number of Asians also surged. They were up 9% to 13.1 million [USA Today, 2005].

50 ***Additional Customer Needs***   The key to success factor in attracting customers was being able to provide convenience. When a new movie was released waiting on long lines to purchase tickets could be a nuisance for the moviegoer. Alternative ticketing via online websites was crucial for movie theater owners because with this type of alternative ticketing the customers had a choice of purchasing their tickets ahead of time to secure a seat. Another benefit of online ticketing was that customers could see which showed time tickets were available before coming to the theater. Another key to success was being able to provide activities for the customers while waiting for their movies. For example customers could play video games in the arcade. A company's brand recognition was important for customers to choose movie theaters because, if a movie theater had a good reputation regarding its services such as concessions, customers would remember and go back to that particular movie theater. Competitive pricing and package plans were also important factors that affected customers' choice of particular movie theater such as matinees, incentive for group ticketing, age group discount, and discount for watching 2 movies in same day.

Rating Systems

51   In the United States today, many of the products were from Hollywood, and each product was defined by Motion picture rating systems. Motion picture rating systems were issued to give moviegoers an idea of the suitability of a movie for children and/or in terms of issues such as sex, violence and profanity. Therefore, customers could also be divided into such a rating system, including G, PG, PG-13, R, and NC-17 categories.

- G: General Audiences—All ages were admitted. This rating signified that the film contained nothing most parents would consider offensive for even their youngest children to see or hear. Nudity, sex scenes, and scenes of drug use were absent, violence was minimal, snippets of dialogue might go beyond polite conversation but did not go beyond common everyday expressions.

- PG: Parental Guidance Suggested—Some material might not be suitable for children. This signified that the film might contain some material parents might not like to expose their young children to—material that clearly needed to be examined or inquired about before children were allowed to attend the film. Explicit sex scenes and scenes of drug use were absent; nudity, if present, was seen only briefly, horror and violence did not exceed moderate levels.

- PG-13: Parents Strongly Cautioned—Some material might be inappropriate for children under the age of 13. It signified that the film might be inappropriate for pre-teens. Parents should be especially careful about letting their younger children attend. Rough or persistent violence was absent; sexually-oriented nudity was generally absent; some scenes of drug use might be seen; some use of one of the harsher sexually derived words might be heard.

- R: Restricted—Under the age 17 required accompanying parent or adult guardian (age varied in some jurisdictions). This rating signified that the film might contain some adult material. Parents were urged to learn more about the film before taking their children to see it. An R might be assigned due to, among other things, a film's use of language, theme, violence, sex, or its portrayal of drug use.

- NC-17: No One 17 and Under Admitted—Signifies that the rating board believed that most American parents would feel that the film was patently adult and that children age 17 and under should not be admitted to it. The film might contain explicit sex scenes, an accumulation of sexually-oriented language, and/or scenes of excessive violence. The NC-17 designation did not, however, signify that the rated film was obscene or pornographic in terms of sex, language, or violence.

52   In some jurisdictions, they might impose legal obligations of refusing the entrance of children or minors to certain movies; in others, while there was no legal obligation to do so strictly speaking, movie theaters enforced the restrictions. The system was not designed to serve the function of "critic." The ratings did not determine or reflect whether a film was "good" or "bad." The system was not intended to approve, disapprove or censor any film; it merely assigned a rating for guidance—leaving the decision-making responsibilities to the parents. The rating system was strictly voluntary and carried no force of law. Could a rating be changed? The answer was "Yes." The rules permitted movie producers to re-edit their films and re-submit them in hopes of receiving another rating. Producers might also appeal a rating decision to the Rating Appeals Board, which was composed of men and women from the industry organizations that sponsored the rating system. A two-thirds secret ballot vote of those present on the Appeals Board might overturn a rating board decision. While the decision to enforce the rating system was purely voluntary, the overwhelming majority of theaters followed the Classification and Rating Administration's guidelines and diligently enforced its provisions. The key to success was that movie theaters made specific rating system properly in order to satisfy customers.

Location

53   Since the 1980s, most theater chains had developed a policy of co-locating their theaters in shopping centers (as opposed to the old practice of building stand-alone theaters) and metropolitan areas. The key to success factor for location was being close to the customers. The location was crucial because it had to be located in a heavily populated area of a city.

54   When a new movie theater was planning on entering a competitive market (where competitors were located close by), the question arose if it be able to get access to its preference of first run prints. Often when movie theaters were geographically close together they might be unable to run the same movie. This was a concern if only one movie theater in a community could book a popular film and made a good profit on concessions for weeks on end. In markets with large chain movie theaters, it was harder for smaller or independent movie theaters to gain the advantage [Center for Community Economic Development, 2005].

55   Population growth was always a factor in locating a business in a community. Considering which population segments were growing quickly and to what extent they would continue to grow over 10 to 20 years was important. Also, comparing the population growth to that of other communities in and around the trade area was crucial for success [Center for Community Economic Development, 2005].

56   International markets were also important. Most big movie theater chains in U.S acquired movie theaters overseas. For example, AMC movie theaters could be found in Canada, France, Hong Kong, Japan, Portugal, Spain, and the UK. Cinemark could be found in several other countries, mostly in Latin America.

Facilities

57   Recent trends in the movie exhibition industry emphasized megaplexes (16 or more screens), multiple story stadium seating, and digital sound and picture. While Megaplexes might work well in large metropolitan areas, smaller cities might not have the population or density to support such large developments. The large blueprints required for these developments might not fit in with downtown plans focusing on creating pedestrian friendly districts emphasizing a sense of history and place. Not every market would support a megaplex, and there was a demand for everything from single screens, miniplexes (2 to 7 screens) and multiplexes (8 to 16 screens) on up.

58   The question of the number of screens was an important one. Single or twin screen movie theaters were often not first run, due to the contractual limitations of running first run movies (holding the movie for a certain number of weeks and sometimes guaranteeing a certain attendance or gross). The current trend was to build movie theaters with a minimum of 6 or 8 screens featuring a few larger auditoriums, with the remaining auditoriums of increasingly smaller sizes. As a movie "ages" it drew a smaller audience, it could be moved to the smaller auditoriums while the newly opening films could be screened in a larger one. In this way, the risk of choosing a poor performing movie was spread out over enough theaters so that ticket sales should not suffer too greatly.

59   Renovation of an existing facility, whether an historic movie theater or other building being converted, brings its own set of issues. The main factors to consider when considering renovation or reuse of an existing facility included but were not limited to the following: What was the capacity of the movie theaters?, What were conditions of seats, lobby, screen, restrooms, etc?, and Were there concession areas/equipment available? [Center for Community Economic Development, 2005].

60   Depending on the location, the movie theater could have parking facilities or could be easily reached through public transportation, and be able to provide security for their customers.

Products/Services

61   Products and services made up this section.

Products

62   The main product of the first run movie theater was the delivery of motion picture movies to moviegoers. Film was a term that encompassed motion pictures as individual projects, as well as the field in general. The origin of the name came from the fact that photographic film (also called filmstock) had historically been the primary medium for recording and displaying motion pictures. Many other terms existed—motion pictures (or just pictures), the silver screen, photoplays, the cinema, picture shows, flicks—and most commonly movies [Encyclopedia, 2005].

63   A recent extension of product was a video network through which it distributed digital content to theaters. This was the move of movie theater product from the analog to the digital method. With this new type of formatting the cost of delivery from the distributors to the audience was lower without decreasing the quality of the product. Another added benefit with this new type of delivery service was that the product could be downloaded instead of the storage required for traditional film reels.

64   As stated above in the customer section, the minorities had been increasing sharply in USA. Offering independent movies and foreign movies were also attractive for particular groups. In metropolitan areas, there existed a large mix and large numbers of minorities, such as Hispanic, African Americans, and Asian. Importing foreign movies with English subtitles for majorities groups and English speakers would give a movie theater an additional revenue source.

65   Some movie theaters provided real motion products. For example, movie theaters sometimes offered big events such as music concert, movie sneak preview, comedies shows, Broadway plays, opera, and ballet using its movie theaters. These events were good for its reputation and attractive to customers.

Services

66   Recent multiplex movie theater had 10 to 15 screens in a building. The key to success here was that a theater should show the most popular movies on more screens and extended show times. Another key to success was getting the rights to show movies before mass release dates. For example, movies like Star Wars were a guaranteed blockbuster and some theaters were able to show the movie earlier.

67   Another service movie theater offers was concession. Movie theaters usually sold various snack foods and drinks at concession stands which often represented another major source of income; movie studios in the US traditionally drove hard bargains entitling them to more than 70, 80, or 90% of the gross ticket revenue during the first week (and then the balance changed in 10% increments per week from there). Some movie theaters forbid eating and drinking inside the viewing room (restricting such activities to the lobby), while others encouraged it, e.g. by selling large portions of popcorn. Concession was currently a huge area of expansion with many companies in the US offering a wider range of snacks, including hot dogs and nachos. The noise of people eating, including the opening of wrappers, was frowned upon by many moviegoers.

68   In addition, it is quite common for the lobby to include an arcade game area so that customers could spend their spare time before the movie played. The key to success was offering more choices of various foods and drinks that could be consumed while watching a movie. In some movie theater chains they had mini food courts that offered well known food franchises such as Taco Bell and Nathan's.

69   Advertising services of movie theaters provided a new advertising channel for any merchants to advertise to movie goers while they were waiting for the movie. Movie theaters generated advertising revenue from providing this service to a captive audience. Pre-Feature Advertising: "On-Screen" product was the farthest reaching cinema advertising product in existence. A company combined that reach with the impact of the big screen with digital image and sound and a company had the most powerful advertising alternative in existence.

70   Lobby Promotional Elements surrounded a company's customer with multiple touch points throughout the movie going experience with lobby elements. Elements included Popcorn Bag Advertising, Soft Drink Cups, Danglers and Banners, Window Clings, Posters and One Sheets, Restroom Advertising, and In-lobby promotions and exhibits.

71   Movie theaters also helped the merchants which wanted to advertise their products with various ways such as video editing and post production, animation and full Motion Graphics and ad design.

72   Many types of businesses chose movie theatres for meetings, special events, and customer seminars. Movie theaters lent their space and received service charge. This service could be one of revenue source for movie theaters.

Marketing

73   There were two main types of marketing strategies: advertisement of movies theaters and online ticketing.

Theater Advertising

74   Movie theaters advertised their own theaters through couple of channels. Theater advertising was done through local newspaper's movie listings, where new releases were advertised with locations of the movie theaters screening the movie with the time. Another commonly used advertising method is through movie phone services which allowed customers to call a number to find a movie, show-times, and locations of the movie they wished to watch. The key to success was that a movie theater had up to date new movie information and a movie theater was using newspapers and online channels so that customers could reach this information easily. Besides up to date new movie information, movie theaters were able to effectively advertise through these newspaper and phone services by offering promotions such as discount price for group ticketing.

Online Ticketing

75   Online ticketing allowed customers to purchase movie tickets online and access show times, movie reviews, and trailers. The company allowed moviegoers to print out their own tickets and to avoid waiting in lines at the box office or ticket kiosks to verify that a ticket

FIGURE 4
**Average U.S.
Ticket Prices**

Source: National Association
of Theater Owners (2005).
[Online]. *http://www.
natoonline.org/* Accessed
November 15.

Year	Price ($)
2004	6.21
2003	6.03
2002	5.80
2001	5.65
2000	5.39

was purchased online. The key to success was that a movie theater had their own website in which customers could buy tickets and also the theater had to have various joint ventures, such as movietickets.com, which offered a theater's location, show times and ticketing.

Technology

76   Mostly films in recent decades had been recorded using analog video technology similar to that used in television production. Modern digital video cameras and digital projectors were gaining ground. These approaches were extremely beneficial to moviemakers and movie theaters, especially because footage could be evaluated and edited without waiting for the film stock to be processed, not only did it improve the delivery, it also improved the sound and viewing quality. Yet the migration was gradual, and as of 2005 most major motion pictures were still recorded on film [Encyclopedia, 2005].

77   The key to success here was for the movie theater operator to seamlessly change from the existing analog technology to digital with as little disruption to movie showing. Another critical success factor was the implementation, updating, and maintaining the new technology with skilled staff.

Pricing

78   The price of movie tickets had increased steadily over the years even though moviegoers had declined. The price ranged from $6.50 to $10.50 depending on factors such as location and time of showings. Figure 4 shows the average price of a movie tickets in U.S for last 5 years.

79   Movie theater operators offered different prices for admissions, prices which varied by the movie and the times of showing. For example, movie theaters offered special pricing for matinees movies shown during off-peak hours, usually during the day. Another incentive was for Senior citizens who were offered discounts on tickets as well as concession items. Children under a certain age, usually under the ages of 3, were often allowed free admissions. Some theaters also offered student discounts.

80   Some movie theaters offered package plans. For example, a movie theater gave a discount to customers when they were watching 2 or 3 movies in a same day.

81   The key to success in pricing for the products and services was by offering discounts and incentives by segments and cross promotional coupons. For example movie theater operators offered coupons with a purchase of admission for future purchases of concession items. Some offered online-only promotions to promote more online ticketing.

82   Besides discount plan, most movie theaters suggested customers had a membership card. This membership card offered couple of benefit for customers. Whenever customers used this card, they earned points. After they received particular points, they earned rewards such as 100 points for a free soda and 200 for a free movie.

83   Another competitive promotion pricing was a discount price for group ticketing. This meant that movie theaters gave any group or customers discount price for minimum number of ticket purchasing.

Competition

84   Regal Entertainment Group (REG) was the US's largest chain theater. The next two largest movie theaters in the USA were AMC Entertainment Inc. and Cinemark, Inc, which were the main competitors of REG. REG also competed against home theaters.

AMC Entertainment Inc.

85   AMC Entertainment shined when the lights went down. One of the biggest movie theater chains in the US owned about 230 theaters that housed almost 3,550 screens, about 75% of which were in multiplexes and megaplexes (units with more than 14 screens and stadium seating). Stadium seating was defined as a technique used in movie theaters to allow more guests to see the movie screen with less blockage than traditional seating. Like seating in a football or baseball stadium, stadium seating in theaters was usually a 30 degree slope stepped upwards from the bottom of the theater, as opposed to the approximately 15 degree gentle slope in traditional theaters. AMS's theaters could be found in 27 states and the District of Columbia, as well as in Canada, France, Hong Kong, Japan, Portugal, Spain, and the UK.

86   AMC Entertainment generated more than two-thirds of its revenue from ticket sales, while more than 25% came from the concession stand. The company also sold digitally projected on-screen advertising and pre-show entertainment videos through its National CineMedia joint venture with Regal Entertainment Group and Cinemark. National CineMedia was formed in early 2005 when AMC merged its National Cinema Network with Regal's CineMedia subsidiary. The new company could now deliver ads and programming to more than 13,000 screens in North America. (Cinemark later bought a 21% stake in National Cinemedia. The deal reduced AMC's initial interest in the venture to 29%.)

87   The unbridled expansion of megaplexes (and the failure to close smaller, older locations) had left the theater industry with a glut of screens. However, as one of the few theater chains to avoid Chapter 11 in the last few years, AMC Entertainment had expanded with the purchases of rival exhibitors Gulf States Theatres and GC Companies. Merger talks with Loews Cineplex were once abandoned in 2004, but AMC finally agreed to purchase Loews the following year. The combined company would retain the AMC Entertainment name, with AMC CEO Peter Brown continuing in his position [Hoover, 2005].

88   In 1995, AMC introduced a new idea that transformed the moviegoing experience. AMC's first megaplex premiered in Dallas, Texas with the opening of The Grand 24. With what was then the largest screen-count theatre in the U.S., this 24-auditorium complex was an instant hit. Since then, AMC had built more than 2,000 megaplex screens and offered megaplexes (some with more than 30 screens) throughout the U.S. and the world—far more than any other exhibition company.

89   In a megaplex environment, moviegoers received the ultimate in selection and convenience. At an AMC megaplex, moviegoers enjoyed a wider selection of features and showtimes, as well as longer running dates. There was always something for everybody—and it was all under one roof.

90   Many types of businesses chose AMC movie theatres for meetings, special events, and customer seminars. AMC Theaters offered from one to 24 "meeting rooms" (auditoriums), depending on the location. AMC auditoriums varied in size and configuration. Multiple auditoriums could be rented at the same time and location to meet the needs of larger groups and/or separate, concurrent events. Satellite broadcast allowed participants from coast to coast to "attend" the same meeting from great distances. All auditorium rentals included access to spacious lobbies.

91   AMC offered the local and other companies opportunities that companies could reach consumers age 18–49 with high disposable income and active lifestyles with National Cinema Network's Cinema Media Solutions—fully integrated ad campaigns that showcased companies' brand on the big screen, in surround-sound, throughout the lobby, and even online—everywhere moviegoers went.

92   The more tickets customers bought, the bigger their bonus. Customers received one Free Promotional Pass for each purchase of 100 AMC Gold Experience or AMC Silver Experience tickets.

93   A customer could give someone special the ultimate getaway with the AMC Entertainment Card. It was a great gift they could use toward both movie tickets and concessions. Plus, the AMC Entertainment Card was available in dollar increments from $10 to $100, so it appealed to any budget. Whether they used it to catch the latest blockbuster movie, or to enjoy their favorite concession items, the AMC Entertainment Card made a great gift that everyone was sure to enjoy.

Cinemark, Inc.

94   Cinemark had left its mark on the cinema landscape. Another large movie exhibitor in the US had more than 3,200 screens in more than 300 theaters in the US and several other countries, mostly in Latin America. Cinemark operated multiplex theaters (the ratio of screens to theaters was about 12 to 1) in smaller cities and suburban areas of major metropolitan markets. Some larger theaters operated under the Tinseltown name; others were "discount" theaters showing no first-run films. Chairman and CEO Lee Roy Mitchell shared ownership of the company with private investment firm Madison Dearborn Partners which paid about $1.5 billion for a stake in Cinemark.

95   All of Cinemark's theaters were multiplexes. About 15% of its theaters were "discount" cinemas. The company preferred to build new theaters in midsized markets or in suburbs of major cities where the Cinemark theater was the only game in town. Cinemark's theaters could be found in 33 US states and 14 other countries. Cinemark had also teamed up with IMAX Corporation to build 5 Cinemark IMAX Theatres in Colorado, Illinois, New York, Oklahoma, and Texas.

96   The company spent the late nineties upgrading into one of the most modern and technologically advanced movie chains. About two-thirds of the current screens had been built since 1996; about 65% of its North American first run screens and 75% of its international screens feature stadium seating—a trend that began in the 1990s. In 2005, it joined Regal Entertainment and AMC Entertainment in National CineMedia, a joint venture that delivered ads and pre-movie entertainment to more than 13,000 screens in the US and Canada via a private digital network. Regal owned 50%, AMC 29%, and Cinemark 21%.

97   Cinemark, along with the rest of the movie theater industry, struggled through the late 1990s as numerous bankruptcies abounded thanks to overbuilding. Things seemed to be on the upswing in early 2002, and Cinemark responded by filing an IPO. However, the overall decline of the stock market forced the firm to postpone its IPO offering later that year. Cinemark had since abandoned plans to take the company public in favor of bringing in major investors. Investment firms Madison Dearborn and Quadrangle Group both bought seats in the Cinemark show [Hoover, 2005].

98   Cinemark offered particular customers promotional reward plan for simply submitting surveys. Cinemark Field Trip Giveaway (the "Sweepstakes") was open to legal residents of the fifty United States and the District of Columbia who were at least eighteen (18) years old at the time of entry and who were professionals in education, such as teachers, librarians, principals, education paraprofessionals, district professionals and after school leaders. The customers had a chance to win a free field trip.

99   Most of Cinemarks sold Gift Cards which were used to purchase tickets and concessions both at the theatre and online. Cinemark Supersaver Discount Movie Tickets provided up to a 40% discount off the regular adult admission price at Cinemark Theatres. Supersavers were great for Recognition, Employee Rewards or Gifts, Client or Customer Appreciation,

Promotion and Marketing Programs, Gifts for Family and Friends. For example, Cinemark Platinum Supersavers provided up to 30% off regular adult ticket prices at Cinemark Theatres. Supersavers were accepted at any Cinemark Theatre and expired one year from the date of purchase. A minimum of 50 supersavers had to be purchased. Additional supersavers might be purchased in increments of 10 (60, 70, etc.)

100   Cinemark offered special promotion discount prices for special season such as holiday and group ticketing. For example, Cinemark had a discount day for every Monday beginning June 27th. Cinemark Theatres would be hosting Family Time—a special discount day—at Cinemark Valley Fair 9 in West Valley City every Monday starting Monday, June 27, 2005. Family Time was a discounted family event that would take place every Monday with reduced ticket prices and special concession offers. For groups of 3 or more, admission would be 50 cents per person of any age. Concession offers included a $2.50 kiddie combo (a kid size drink and popcorn) or a popcorn tub for $5.75. Each week there were balloons, games, and prizes for children. Family Time was the perfect opportunity for families to see a movie at a discount, enjoy special concession offers and have a good time together at the theatre.

Home Theater

101   The basic home theater system was designed to imitate the movie going experience. The basic elements of a home theater system were: television, sound, video programming, and lighting. Customers might be tempted to simply make do with their current *televisions*, and this might well be a viable alternative, depending on the television. The most optimal visual impact would be obtained from a high-definition television (HDTV) or a flat screened monitor. *Surround sound* was a term that defined the ability to receive sound from various areas such as the rear, the front and the side. Customers should first attempt to control the amount of outside *lighting* by hanging heavy drapes over the windows. Customers could apply dimmer switches to their overhead lights and to lamps in order to dim the lights to the desired degree. The final element for home theater system was the *video programming* equipment which customers most likely already owned. A good quality DVD and VHS player would allow them to play and record various types of programming [Minerva WebWorks LLC, 2005].

102   The home theater offered the convenience of home viewing. With new home theater technology viewers could reproduce the visual and sound similar to movie theaters without leaving home and paying admissions.

103   Disadvantages for the home theater were the smaller screen sizes currently available for home viewing and the quality of surround sound and acoustics.

THE COMPANY

104   Regal Entertainment Group (NYSE: RGC) was the largest motion picture exhibitor in the world. The Company's theatre circuit, comprising Regal Cinemas, United Artists Theatres, and Edwards Theatres operated 6,273 screens in 558 locations in 40 states. Regal operated approximately 18% of all indoor screens in the United States including theatres in 43 of the top 50 U.S. markets and growing suburban markets.

105   The company developed, acquired, and operated multi-screen theatres primarily in mid-sized metropolitan markets and suburban growth areas of larger metropolitan markets throughout the U.S. The company sought to locate each theatre where it would be the sole or leading exhibitor within a particular geographic film-licensing zone. Management believed that as of December 30, 2004, approximately 87% of its screens were located in film licensing zones in which the company was the sole exhibitor [Regal Entertainment Group, 2005].

FIGURE 5 **Shows the Different Business Segments of Regal Entertainment Group.**

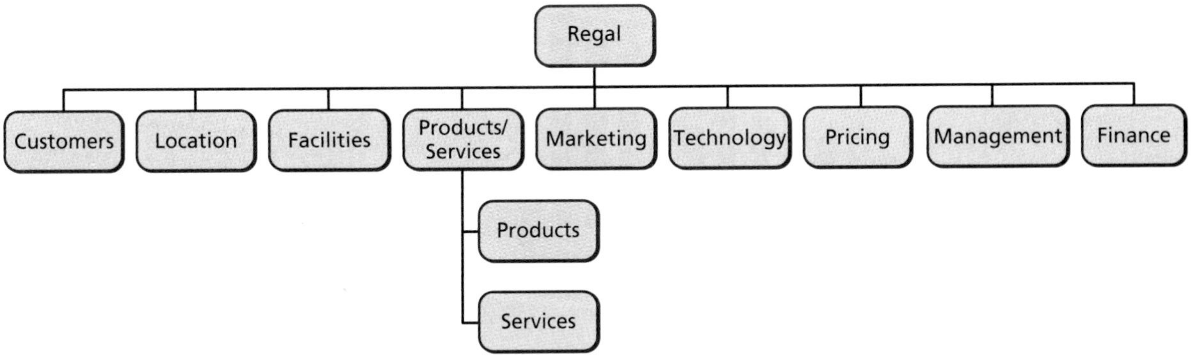

Customers

106 As shown in Figure 6, although the movie theater industry decreased in their revenue and attendance, REG had increased revenues and attendance.

107 REG had approximately 400 million movie goers per year. About 55% of these customers were between 18 and 29 years of age and 59% had an annual income of over $50,000 per year [Regal Entertainment Group, 2005]. Fifty-one percent were male and 49% were female. REG covered all ratings. The Company was weak, however, in targeting minority groups. It had a satisfactory amount of ticket booths available to keep the waiting times of purchasing tickets fairly short. REG offered an up-to-date website on which customers could purchase tickets online using credit cards. The Company was strong in reaching various customer groups by offering differing pricing and package plans. It also had strong brand recognition. In providing non-movie activities, such as arcade games, especially for the younger customer groups, REG was weak.

Location

108 The Company's theater circuit operated 6,273 screens in 558 locations in 40 states. Regal operated approximately 18% of all indoor screens in the United States including theatres in 43 of the top 50 U.S. markets and growing suburban markets. REG developed, acquired, and operated multi-screen theatres primarily in mid-sized metropolitan markets and suburban growth areas of larger metropolitan markets throughout the U.S. As of December 30, 2004, approximately 87% of its screens were located in film licensing zones in which the company was the sole exhibitor. Being the sole exhibitor in a film licensing zone provided the company with access to all films distributed by major distributors and eliminated its need to compete with other exhibitors for films in that zone. As the sole exhibitor in a particular zone, the company could exhibit all commercially successful films on its screens, subjected to a successful negotiation with the distributor, and had the ability to compete for attendance generated from commercially popular films [Regal Entertainment Group, 2005].

Facilities

109 REG's theaters housed an average of 11 screens, and more than 60% of its screens were in theaters with stadium seating which defined as a technique used in movie theaters to allow more guests to see the movie screen with less blockage than traditional seating. Like seating in a football or baseball stadium, stadium seating in theaters was usually a 30 degree slope stepped upwards from the bottom of the theater, as opposed to the approximately 15 degree gentle slope in traditional theaters. REG had demonstrated it ability to enhance revenues and realize operating efficiencies through the successful acquisition and integration of 15 theater circuits since 1995. REG had generally achieved immediate cost savings at acquired

FIGURE 6
Steady Box Office of Regal Growth

Source: Regal Entertainment Group (2004). [online]. *http://www.regalcinemas.com/ corporate/about.html* Accessed November 24.

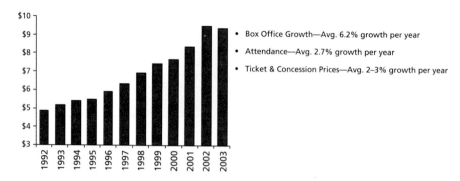

- Box Office Growth—Avg. 6.2% growth per year
- Attendance—Avg. 2.7% growth per year
- Ticket & Concession Prices—Avg. 2–3% growth per year

theater and improved their profitability through the application of its consolidated operating functions and key supplier contracts.

Products/Services (Revenue Model)

110 As shown in Figure 7, 67% of REG's revenue came from ticket sales and 26% from concessions. Advertising was the main "other" revenue source. In the near future, more advertising was expected to be noticed at REG cinemas through National CineMedia's deal with content providers such as NBC, Universal Studios, and Turner Broadcasting. Pre-movie low-budget slide shows for local merchants were replaced with what the company called "The 2wenty": twenty minutes worth of promotional clips and ads beamed via satellite to digital projectors in REG theaters through the company's Digital Content Network [Hoover, 2005].

Products

111 The Regal Entertainment Group was proud to offer Cinema Art: Critically-acclaimed films, alternative productions, restored classics, and first-run foreign movies. Since 1999, REG had provided this diversity of film choices under the Regal Cinema Art brand. More than 50 theatres across the country showcased these alternative and independent movies through a national network of Regal Cinema Art theatres. REG offered customers Big Screen Concerts about once a month. As soon as customers signed in on REG's website, they received the latest scoop on which bands were playing and how to get tickets for these concerts. The kinds of event included music events, movie sneak preview, one night romantic comedies, Broadway plays, opera, and ballet.

Services

112 REG's "On-Screen" product was the farthest reaching cinema advertising product in existence. With over 400 million movie goers in 43 of the top 50 markets, any merchant's customers were watching. REG combined that reach with the impact of the big screen and with digital image and sound to offer the most powerful advertising alternative in existence. Lobby Promotional Elements surrounded the Company's customer with multiple touch points throughout the movie going experience. Such elements included Popcorn Bag Advertising, Soft Drink Cups, Danglers and Banners, Window Clings, Posters and One Sheets, Restroom Advertising, and In lobby promotions and exhibits. REG offered help in the production of a merchant's ad or content with the following services: Video Editing and Post Production, Animation and Full Motion Graphics, Corporate Ad Design, Sound Design and Editing, and Print and Interactive. REG operated its assets very efficiently during non-peak periods from the rental of auditoriums on a single site and networked basis for seminars, business conferencing, distance learning, and other business meetings and from the distribution of alternative digital programming in the music, education, entertainment and sports categories.

FIGURE 7
Regal Entertainment Group's 2004 Sales

Source: Regal Entertainment Group (2005). [Online] *http://www.regalcinemas.com/ corporate/about.html* Accessed November 24.

	$ mil.	% of total
Admissions	1,658	67
Concessions	636	26
Other	174	7
Total	2,468	100

Marketing

113 REG utilized local newspapers' movie listings, where new releases were advertised with locations of the movie theaters screening the movie at the time. Another commonly used advertising method was utilizing movie phone services which allowed customers to find a movie, show-times, and locations of the movie they wished to watch by calling an automated telephone service. In addition, REG customers could purchase movie tickets online on the Company's own website as well as on third party websites, which were in a joint-venture agreement with REG.

Technology

114 While REG admitted that digital projection technologies required to screen movies in theaters were not yet commercially viable, the Company was focusing on this lower-cost digital video and communications tool to digitally distribute in-theatre advertising, as well as complement its business of renting out theaters for corporate meetings, seminars, and distance learning programs. Regal had outfitted nearly 80% of its locations with digital projectors and other ancillary digital equipment for marketing and advertising purposes. Regal would not yet digitally project feature-length films, but its system could be fully upgraded once the industry adopted a set of digital standards [Hoover, 2005].

Pricing

115 The price of movie ticket admissions at REG theaters differed from location to location. For example, in certain cities in California matinee's were priced at $7.50 before 6 P.M. and $9.50 for general adult admissions after 6 P.M. REG also offered senior discount pricing of $7.00. In New York City the Company charged $10.75 for general adult admissions without any discounts for matinees. For senior citizens they offered $7.00 admissions. For children they charged $7.00 in both California and New York City. Joining the Regal Crown Club customers could earn rewards for going to the movies. When customers joined the Regal Crown Club, they received free movies, popcorn, and soft drinks. Regal Crown Club members would receive 1 credit per dollar spent on ticket purchases at the box office, with a maximum of 12 credits per card, per day. All members earned extra credits on concession purchases. Two extra credits were earned for a concession transaction, or 4 extra credits were earned for a specified promotional transaction, such as a Candy Combo. Members received rewards each time 40 credits were earned. REG offered the following pricing discount packages/deals:

- PREMIERE SUPER SAVER TICKET: These tickets were accepted for any movie at any time (even opening night of blockbuster films), this unrestricted movie ticket was customers best value at $7.00 each. Plus, customers could add free custom messaging on the back of the ticket for a personal touch. A 50 ticket minimum purchase was required.

- VIP SUPER SAVER TICKET DATE was not accepted during the first twelve days of selected new releases, this restricted movie ticket offered the best savings at $6.00 each. 50 Minimum purchase required.

- ULTIMATE PREMIERE MOVIE PACK: A pack included two unrestricted Premiere movie tickets and a $10 gift certificate good towards any concession or box office purchase. 25 Minimum purchase required.

Management

116   REG was the largest domestic motion picture exhibitor with nearly twice as many screens as the nearest competitor. The quality and size of REG theatre circuit was a significant competitive advantage for negotiating attractive national contracts and generating economies of scale. REG had significant experience identifying, completing, and integrating acquisitions of theatre circuits. REG had demonstrated the ability to enhance revenues and realize operating efficiencies through the successful acquisition and integration of 15 theatre circuits since 1995. REG had generally achieved immediate cost savings at acquired theatres and improved their profitability through the application of its consolidated operating functions and key supplier contracts. The company had developed a proven operating philosophy focused on efficient operations and strict cost controls at both the corporate and theater levels. At the corporate level, REG was able to capitalize on its size and operational expertise to achieve economies of scale in purchasing food & beverages and marketing functions. REG had developed an efficient purchasing and distribution supply chain that generated favorable concession margins. At the theater level, management devoted significant attention to cost controls through the use of detailed management reported and performance-based compensation programs to encourage theater managers to control costs effectively and increase concession sales.

Finance

117   REG had invested over $2.1 billion in capital expenditures since 1997 to expand and upgrade its theater circuit. As a result, REG did not expect to require major capital reinvestments in the near term to maintain its operations. The combination of its operating margins and its limited need to make maintenance capital expenditures would allow the company to generate significant cash flow from operations. For the thirty-nine weeks ended 29 September 2005, Regal Entertainment Group's revenues increased 1% to $1.85B. Net income decreased 2% to $56.7M. Revenues reflected vendor marketing programs and the purchase of theaters. Net income was offset by higher film rental & advertising costs, an increase in interest expense and the presence of equity in earnings joint venture including former employee compensation expenses [Regal Entertainment Group, 2005].

LOOKING TOWARDS THE FUTURE

118   Michael L. Campbell, the chairman and CEO of Regal Entertainment Group, was faced with many crucial decisions affecting the future of his theater. One very important decision involved the future locations of the Company's theaters. The location decision revolved around two alternatives: to expand to foreign regions, such as Asia, or to existing domestic high population and high-income areas.

119   Alternative 1 proposed that REG expand his movie theaters into metropolitan areas of international markets, such as capital cities of various Asian countries. **Define**

120   REG was the industry leader and based on Porter's Competitiveness Model, the Company could expand into international markets without great risk. Based on its expertise, the company would reap the benefits of reaching new customers and therefore increase market share. **Benefit**

121   Expansion was feasible for REG because they were financially stable. To be able to expand the current business model into international markets would require substantial investments, for which the capital was available, in building new movie theaters as well as acquiring and renovating newly acquired theaters.

122   The main competitors against REG were AMC and Cinemark. AMC launched theaters in international markets in Europe and Asia, and Cinemark had its own movie theaters in South American countries. Because the competitors were either not present (Cinemark) or weak (AMC) in Asian markets, REG would beat the competitors head-to-head and could become the market leader there. In the Asian markets, REG could improve its reputation and expand its brand recognition by building new theaters. The markets were very large, with China, for example, having over 3 billion citizens as of early 2005. By acquiring existing movie theaters in Asian markets, REG could save money. These savings could be invested into replacing old facilities with new ones, developing new technologies, and providing variety of concessions. By doing so, REG would win against the competition. By providing Hollywood movies as well as Asian movies, REG could expand its revenue source and would keep leading the global movie theater industry. **Winning**

123   The drawback of this alternative was the lack of real estate available to build huge multiplex screen movie theaters in Asian metropolitan area. Another drawback was the costly investment required to build new movie theaters especially with the rise of real estate prices in heavily populated areas in Asian countries.

124   One way around the drawback was to purchase the land required to build new movie theaters. Up-front cost would be expensive but the land would appreciate and they would not have to pay rent. Another way around the drawback was acquisition of existing movie theaters. If REG would pay only for building and facilities which already existed, REG saved costs to build new movie theaters and buy new facilities.

125   Alternative 2 proposed that REG expand movie theaters in large population areas in the US, even though there were already theaters in the same territory. In order to cover the high population the company could increase their theaters in domestic metropolitan areas. Currently, REG has 105 theaters in California, 52 theaters in New York, 45 theaters in Florida, and additional ones in other areas, and was in the process of opening new theaters in high income areas for the purpose of targeting special, niche markets. **Define**

126   REG could open new movie theaters and acquire existing theaters in new heavily populated areas the company currently did not have a presence in. The benefit was to bring the movie theaters closer to more moviegoers while developing a presence within the new areas. The benefit of expanding in high income areas was not limited only to large population areas. So, even though the population and the number of customers were not very large in certain areas, if their income was considered high enough and higher than another territory, the company would invest in new facilities in that region.

127   Expansion was feasible for REG because they were financially stable. To be able to expand using the current business model would require substantial investments in building new movie theaters as well as acquiring and renovating newly acquired theaters. This alternative was also feasible because the capital investment would be significantly lower than building in highly populated areas and there was little difficulty in finding new locations.

128   REG could beat their competitors because of their financial strength and good reputation. Currently, REG was the industry leader with the most theater locations in the World. Being the only publicly traded company within the industry, REG was in a winning position to expand. REG could win against the competition since it would save money which would be used to build small facilities and with those save money. By specializing products and services, REG would have various customers, which would give REG opportunities to keep leading the movie theater industry because customers were one of the most important factors in the movie theater business model. By providing specialized products and services, REG would gain much better reputation. Brand recognition would be very attractive to customers. By expanding movie theaters into special niche areas, REG would need special services as well. The most effective services for customers would be concessions. Various concessions and services such as waiter service would be one of the most dramatic differentiations from its competitors. **Winning**

129   The drawback of this alternative was the lack of real estate available to build multiplex movie theaters. Another drawback was the costly investment required to build new movie theaters especially with increasing real estate prices in heavily populated areas. The drawback of expanding into high income areas was that there could be existing big movie theaters in new areas and REG needed money for research specialists to find higher income areas.

130   The way around the drawback was to purchase the land required to build new movie theaters. Up-front cost would be expensive but the land would appreciate and they would not have to pay rent. Another way around the drawback was acquisition of existing movie theaters. The way around the drawback of high income areas was to specialize the new movie theater. REG offered the highest quality service, the newest technology, and the best facilities in order to be attractive to higher income customers.

131   Both alternatives seemed reasonable. Deciding among the two alternatives under consideration and other strategic decision areas was now the problem REG was facing.

REFERENCES

AMC Company (2005). [Online]. *http://www.amctheatres.com/*. Accessed November 22, 2005

Cinemark Company (2005). [Online]. *http://www.cinemark.com/*. Accessed November 22, 2005

Center for Community Economic Development (2005). [Online]. *http://www.uwex.edu/ces/cced/dma/12.html*. Accessed December 02, 2005

Convex Company (2005). "How Stuff Works". [Online]. *http://electronics.howstuffworks.com/home-theater1.htm*. Accessed November 14, 2005

D&B Company (2005). [Online]. *http://www.hoovers.com*. Accessed November 14, 2005

Encyclopedia Company. [Online]. *http://en.wikipedia.org/wiki/Entertainment_industry*. Accessed November 14, 2005

Knot Magazine (2005). [Online]. *http://www.knotmag.com/*. Accessed December 03, 2005

LML Company (2005). [Online]. *http://themeparksonline.com*. Accessed November 14, 2005

M/Cyclopedia of New Media (2005). [Online]. *http://wiki.media-culture.org.au/index.php/Main_Page*. Accessed December 03, 2005

Matrixx Entertainment Corporation (2005). [Online]. *http://www.mecfilms.com/moviepubs/memos/moviein.htm*. Accessed November 21, 2005

Media Psychology Research Institute (2005). [Online]. *http://www.calstatela.edu/faculty/sfischo/media3.html*. Accessed December 09, 2005

Minerva WebWorks LLC (2005). [Online]. *http://www.bellaonline.com/subjects/5808.asp*. Accessed December 05, 2005

National Association of Theater Owners (2005). [Online]. *http://www.natoonline.org/*. Accessed November 15, 2005

Regal Entertainment Group (2005). [Online]. *http://www.regalcinemas.com/corporate/about.html*. Accessed November 24, 2005

USA Today (2005). [Online]. *http://www.usatoday.com/news/nation/census/2003-06-18-Census_x.htm*. Accessed December 01, 2005

VNU, Inc. (2005) [Online]. *http://store.vnuemedia.com/nielsenentertainment/store/product_view.jsp*. Accessed November 15, 2005

Case 43

Ruth's Chris: *The High Stakes of International Expansion*

Allen H. Kupetz and Ilan Alon

"Well, I was so lucky that I fell into something that I really, really love. And I think that
if you ever go into business, you better find something you really love, because
you spend so many hours with it . . . it almost becomes your life."

Ruth Fertel, 1927–2002
Founder of Ruth's Chris Steak House

1   In 2006, Ruth's Chris Steak House (Ruth's Chris) was fresh off a sizzling initial public
offering (IPO). Dan Hannah, vice-president for business development since June 2004, was
responsible for the development of a new business strategy focused on continued growth
of franchise and company-operated restaurants. He also oversaw franchisee relations. Now
a public company, Ruth's Chris had to meet Wall Street's expectations for revenue growth.
Current stores were seeing consistent incremental revenue growth, but new restaurants
were critical and Hannah knew that the international opportunities offered a tremendous
upside.

2   With restaurants in just five countries including the United States, the challenge for
Hannah was to decide where to go to next. Ruth's Chris regularly received inquiries from
would-be franchisees all over the world, but strict criteria—liquid net worth of at least
US$1 million, verifiable experience within the hospitality industry, and an ability and
desire to develop multiple locations—eliminated many of the prospects. And the cost of a
franchise—a US$100,000 per restaurant franchise fee, a five per cent of gross sales roy-
alty fee, and a two per cent of gross sales fee as a contribution to the national advertising
campaign—eliminated some qualified prospects. All this was coupled with a debate within
Ruth's Chris senior management team about the need and desire to grow its international
business. So where was Hannah to look for new international franchisees and what countries would be best suited for the fine dining that made Ruth's Chris famous?

THE HOUSE THAT RUTH BUILT

3   Ruth Fertel, the founder of Ruth's Chris, was born in New Orleans in 1927. She skipped several grades in grammar school, and later entered Louisiana State University in Baton Rouge
at the age of 15 to pursue degrees in chemistry and physics. After graduation, Fertel landed a
job teaching at McNeese State University. The majority of her students were football players

Richard Ivey School of Business
The University of Western Ontario

who not only towered over her, but were actually older than she was. Fertel taught for two semesters. In 1948, the former Ruth Ann Adstad married Rodney Fertel who lived in Baton Rouge and shared her love of horses. They had two sons, Jerry and Randy. They opened a racing stable in Baton Rouge. Ruth Fertel earned a thoroughbred trainer's license, making her the first female horse trainer in Louisiana. Ruth and Rodney Fertel divorced in 1958.

4   In 1965, Ruth Fertel spotted an ad in the *New Orleans Times-Picayune* selling a steak house. She mortgaged her home for US$22,000 to purchase Chris Steak House, a 60-seat restaurant on the corner of Broad and Ursuline in New Orleans, near the fairgrounds racetrack. In September of 1965, the city of New Orleans was ravaged by Hurricane Betsy just a few months after Fertel purchased Chris Steak House. The restaurant was left without power, so she cooked everything she had and brought it to her brother in devastated Plaquemines Parish to aid in the relief effort.

5   In 1976, the thriving restaurant was destroyed in a kitchen fire. Fertel bought a new property a few blocks away on Broad Street and soon opened under a new name, "Ruth's Chris Steak House," since her original contract with former owner, Chris Matulich, precluded her from using the name Chris Steak House in a different location. After years of failed attempts, Tom Moran, a regular customer and business owner from Baton Rouge, convinced a hesitant Fertel to let him open the first Ruth's Chris franchise in 1976. It opened on Airline Highway in Baton Rouge. Fertel reluctantly began awarding more and more franchises. In the 1980s, the little corner steak house grew into a global phenomenon with restaurants opening every year in cities around the nation and the world. Fertel became something of an icon herself and was dubbed by her peers *The First Lady of American Restaurants.*

6   Ruth's Chris grew to become the largest fine dining steak house in the United States (see Exhibit 1) with its focus on an unwavering commitment to customer satisfaction and its broad selection of USDA Prime grade steaks (USDA Prime is a meat grade label that refers to evenly distributed marbling that enhances the flavor of the steak). The menu also included premium quality lamb chops, veal chops, fish, chicken and lobster. Steak and seafood combinations and a vegetable platter were also available at selected restaurants. Dinner entrees were generally priced between US$18 to US$38. Three company-owned restaurants were open for lunch and offered entrees generally ranging in price from US$11 to US$24. The Ruth's Chris core menu was similar at all of its restaurants. The company occasionally introduced new items as specials that allowed the restaurant to offer its guests additional choices, such as items inspired by Ruth's Chris New Orleans heritage.[1]

7   In 2005, Ruth's Chris enjoyed a significant milestone, completing a successful IPO that raised more than US$154 million in new equity capital. In their 2005 Annual Report, the company said it had plans "to embark on an accelerated development plan and expand our footprint through both company-owned and franchised locations." 2005 restaurant

EXHIBIT 1
Fine Dining Steak Houses by Brand in the United States (2005)

Source: Ruth's Chris Steak House files.

Company Name	Number of Restaurants
Ruth's Chris	92
Morton's	66
Fleming's	32
Palm	28
Capital Grille	22
Shula's	16
Sullivan's	15
Smith & Wollensky	11
Del Frisco	6

[1] Ruth's Chris Steak House 2005 Annual Report, pg. 7.

FIGURE 1
Ruth's Chris
Restaurant Growth
by Decade

Source: Ruth's Chris Steak
House files.

Decade	New Restaurants (total)	New Restaurants (company-owned)	New Restaurants (franchises)
1965–1969	1	1	0
1970–1979	4	2	2
1980–1989	19	8	11
1990–1999	44	19	25
2000–2005	25	12	13
	93*	42	51

*Due to damage caused by Hurricane Katrina, Ruth's Chris was forced to temporarily close its restaurant in New Orleans, Louisiana.

FIGURE 2
Restaurant Growth
Paths*

*This diagram is based on
Ansoff's Product/Market
Matrix, first Published in
"Strategies for Diversification,"
Harvard Business Review,
1957.

	Restaurant Brands	
	Existing	New
Existing	**Penetration** (more restaurants) *Same market, same product*	**Product development** (new brands) *Same market, new product*
Market New	**Market development** (new markets) *New market, same product*	**Diversification** (new brands for new market) *New product, new market*

sales grew to a record US$415.8 million from 82 locations in the United States and 10 international locations including Canada (1995, 2003), Hong Kong (1997, 2001), Mexico (1993, 1996, 2001) and Taiwan (1993, 1996, 2001). As of December 2005, 41 of the 92 Ruth's Chris restaurants were company-owned and 51 were franchisee-owned, including all 10 of the international restaurants (see Exhibit 2).

8   Ruth's Chris's 51 franchisee-owned restaurants were owned by just 17 franchisees, with five new franchisees having the rights to develop a new restaurant, and the three largest franchisees owning eight, six and five restaurants respectively. Prior to 2004, each franchisee entered into a 10-year franchise agreement with three 10-year renewal options for each restaurant. Each agreement granted the franchisee territorial protection, with the option to develop a certain number of restaurants in their territory. Ruth's Chris's franchisee agreements generally included termination clauses in the event of nonperformance by the franchisee.[2]

A WORLD OF OPPORTUNITIES

9   As part of the international market selection process, Hannah considered four standard models (see Figure 2):

1. Product development—new kinds of restaurants in existing markets
2. Diversification—new kinds of restaurants in new markets
3. Penetration—more of the same restaurants in the same market
4. Market development—more of the same restaurants in new markets

10   The product development model (new kinds of restaurants in existing markets) was never seriously considered by Ruth's Chris. It had built a brand based on fine dining steak houses

[2] Ruth's Chris Steak House 2005 Annual Report, pg. 10.

EXHIBIT 2 Ruth's Chris Locations in the United States (2005)

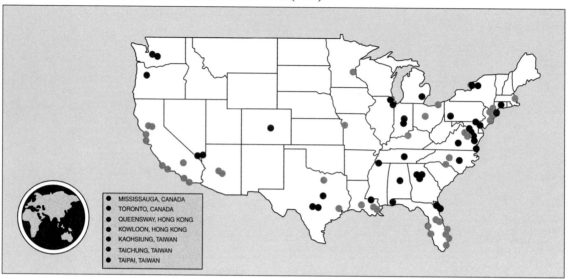

MISSISSAUGA, CANADA
TORONTO, CANADA
QUEENSWAY, HONG KONG
KOWLOON, HONG KONG
KAOHSIUNG, TAIWAN
TAICHUNG, TAIWAN
TAIPAI, TAIWAN

● Company-owned

● Franchisee-owned

Source: Ruth's Chris Steak House files.

and, with only 92 stores, the company saw little need and no value in diversifying with new kinds of restaurants.

11   The diversification model (new kinds of restaurants in new markets) was also never considered by Ruth's Chris. In only four international markets, Hannah knew that the current fine dining steak house model would work in new markets without the risk of brand dilution or brand confusion.

12   The penetration model (more of the same restaurants in the same market) was already underway in a small way with new restaurants opening up in Canada. The limiting factor was simply that fine dining establishments would never be as ubiquitous as quick service restaurants (i.e. fast food) like McDonald's. Even the largest cities in the world would be unlikely to host more than five to six Ruth's Chris steak houses.

13   The market development model (more of the same restaurants in new markets) appeared the most obvious path to increased revenue. Franchisees in the four international markets—Canada, Hong Kong, Mexico and Taiwan—were profitable and could offer testimony to would-be franchisees of the value of a Ruth's Chris franchise.

14   With the management team agreed on a model, the challenge shifted to market selection criteria. The key success factors were well-defined:

• Beef-eaters: Ruth's Chris was a steak house (though there were several fish items on the menu) and, thus, its primary customers were people who enjoy beef. According to the World Resources Institute, in 2002 there were 17 countries above the mean per capita of annual beef consumption for high-income countries (93.5 kilograms—see Exhibit 3).[3]

• Legal to import U.S. beef: The current Ruth's Chris model used only USDA Prime beef, thus it had to be exportable to the target country. In some cases, Australian beef was able to meet the same high U.S. standard.

[3] Ruth's Chris Steak House 2005 Annual Report, pg. 10.

EXHIBIT 3   Meat Consumption per Capita* (in kilograms)

Region/Classification	2002	2001	2000	1999	1998	Growth Rate 1998–2002
World	39.7	38.8	38.6	38.0	37.7	5.31%
Asia (excluding Middle East)	27.8	26.9	26.6	25.7	25.4	9.45%
Central America/Caribbean	46.9	45.7	44.8	42.9	41.3	13.56%
Europe	74.3	72.5	70.5	70.6	73.1	1.64%
Middle East/North Africa	25.7	25.7	26.0	25.1	24.7	4.05%
North America	123.2	119.1	120.5	122.2	118.3	4.14%
South America	69.7	68.4	69.1	67.6	64.2	8.57%
Sub-Saharan Africa	13.0	12.9	13.1	12.8	12.6	3.17%
Developed countries	80.0	78.0	77.2	77.3	77.6	3.09%
Developing countries	28.9	28.1	28.0	27.1	26.6	8.65%
High-income countries	93.5	91.9	92.0	92.2	90.9	2.86%
Low-income countries	8.8	8.6	8.4	8.3	8.2	7.32%
Middle-income countries	46.1	44.6	43.9	42.7	42.3	8.98%

*World Resources Institute, "Meat Consumption: Per Capita (1984–2002)," retrieved on June 7, 2006 from http://earthtrends.wri.org/text/agriculture-food/variable-193.html.

- Population/high urbanization rates: With the target customer being a well-to-do beef-eater, restaurants needed to be in densely populated areas to have a large enough pool. Most large centers probably met this requirement.
- High disposable income: Ruth's Chris is a fine dining experience and the average cost of a meal for a customer ordering an entrée was over US$70 at a Ruth's Chris in the United States. While this might seem to eliminate many countries quickly, there are countries (e.g. China) that have such large populations that even a very small percentage of high disposable income people could create an appropriate pool of potential customers.
- Do people go out to eat? This was a critical factor. If well-to-do beef-eaters did not go out to eat, these countries had to be removed from the target list.
- Affinity for U.S. brands: The name "Ruth's Chris" was uniquely American as was the Ruth Fertel story. Countries that were overtly anti-United States would be eliminated from—or at least pushed down—the target list. One measure of affinity could be the presence of existing U.S. restaurants and successful franchises.

WHAT SHOULD RUTH'S CHRIS DO NEXT?

15   Hannah had many years of experience in the restaurant franchising business, and thus had both personal preferences and good instincts about where Ruth's Chris should be looking for new markets. "Which markets should we enter first?" he thought to himself. Market entry was critical, but there were other issues too. Should franchising continue to be Ruth's Chris exclusive international mode of entry? Were there opportunities for joint ventures or company-owned stores in certain markets? How could he identify and evaluate new potential franchisees? Was there an opportunity to find a global partner/brand with which to partner?

16   Hannah gathered information from several reliable U.S. government and related websites and created the table in Exhibit 4. He noted that many of his top prospects currently did not allow the importation of U.S. beef, but he felt that this was a political (rather than a cultural) variable and thus could change quickly under the right circumstances and with what he felt

EXHIBIT 4
Data Table

Country	Per Capita Beef Consumption (kg)	Population (1,000s)	Urbanization Rate (%)	Per Capita GDP (PPP in US$)
Argentina	97.6	39,921	90%	$13,100
Bahamas	123.6	303	89%	$20,200
Belgium	86.1	10,379	97%	$31,400
Brazil	82.4	188,078	83%	$8,400
Chile	66.4	16,134	87%	$11,300
China	52.4	1,313,973	39%	$6,800
Costa Rica	40.4	4,075	61%	$11,100
Czech Rep	77.3	10,235	74%	$19,500
France	101.1	60,876	76%	$29,900
Germany	82.1	82,422	88%	$30,400
Greece	78.7	10,688	61%	$22,200
Hungary	100.7	9,981	65%	$16,300
Ireland	106.3	4,062	60%	$41,000
Israel	97.1	6,352	92%	$24,600
Italy	90.4	58,133	67%	$29,200
Japan	43.9	127,463	65%	$31,500
Kuwait	60.2	2,418	96%	$19,200
Malaysia	50.9	24,385	64%	$12,100
Netherlands	89.3	16,491	66%	$30,500
Panama	54.5	3,191	57%	$7,200
Poland	78.1	38,536	62%	$13,300
Portugal	91.1	10,605	55%	$19,300
Russia	51	142,893	73%	$11,100
Singapore	71.1	4,492	100%	$28,100
South Africa	39	44,187	57%	$12,000
South Korea	48	48,846	80%	$20,400
Spain	118.6	40,397	77%	$25,500
Switzerland	72.9	7,523	68%	$32,300
Turkey	19.3	70,413	66%	$8,200
UAE/Dubai	74.4	2,602	85%	$43,400
U.K.	79.6	60,609	89%	$30,300
United States	124.8	298,444	80%	$41,800
Vietnam	28.6	84,402	26%	$2,800

Source: World Resources Institute, "Meat Consumption: Per Capita (1984–2002)," retrieved on June 7, 2006 from http://earthtrends.wri.org/text/agriculture-food/variable-193.html and World Bank Key Development Data & Statistics, http://web.worldbank.org/WBSITE/EXTERNAL/DATASTATISTICS/0,,contentMDK:20535285~menuPK:232599~pagePK:64133150~piPK:64133175~theSitePK:239419,00.html, retrieved on June 7, 2006.

was the trend toward ever more free trade. He could not find any data on how often people went out to eat or a measure of their affinity toward U.S. brands. Maybe the success of U.S. casual dining restaurants in a country might be a good indicator of how its citizens felt toward U.S. restaurants. With his spreadsheet open, he went to work on the numbers and began contemplating the future global expansion of the company.

"If you've ever had a filet this good, welcome back."

Ruth Fertel, 1927–2002
Founder of Ruth's Chris Steak House

Case 44

Schwartz & Co. LLP: *The Accounting Services Industry*
Brian Pagano, Marc E. Gartenfeld, and Robert J. Mockler

INTRODUCTION

1   In September of 2001, a major scandal involving the Enron Corporation brought about drastic changes within the accounting profession. In 2006, one could still feel the results of this scandal, and the rapidly changing accounting environment had brought about many challenges for all accounting firms. Schwartz & Co, LLP, a small accounting firm based in Long Island, had been forced to make adjustments to the way it did business in the same way that the Big Four had.

2   Schwartz & Co's main office was located in Bellmore, NY, and it also had satellite offices in Manhattan and Boca Raton, Florida. The key decision makers of the company were the two partners: Michael J. Schwartz, CPA, and Joseph Boyce, CPA. They employed 14 other people full time as well as 3 interns. The company provided both audit and tax services to over 1,000 clients, which included individuals, partnerships, corporations, and trusts, with a specialization in investment partnerships. The task here was to develop an effective differentiating enterprise-wide strategy if Schwartz & Co. was to survive and prosper against aggressive competition in the face of a rapidly changing environment over the intermediate and long-term future.

3   All firms had been forced to re-evaluate the way they did business as a result of the Enron scandal. Besides simply planning for expansion, every firm had to devote substantial resources to familiarizing their employees with the legislation passed as a result of Enron. If Schwartz & Co, or any accounting firm for that matter, could not find out how to most effectively use the resources they had for this purpose, then they would encounter major problems affecting their survival.

4   In light of all this, Michael Schwartz and Joseph Boyce had to make certain decisions in key areas. They had to decide what geographical areas they would like to operate in, what types of clients to focus on, what types of services to provide to those clients, what kind of employee growth they were looking for (for example, whether they should sacrifice quality in order to get more employees), and whether they should hire new employees straight out of school or workers with more experience. The main question to be resolved was how to differentiate Schwartz & Company from its competition and so achieve a winning edge over competitors within intensely competitive, rapidly changing immediate, intermediate, and long-term time frames.

OVERALL INDUSTRY AND COMPETITIVE MARKET: THE PROFESSIONAL SERVICES INDUSTRY

5   The accounting industry was only one of several branches of the overall professional services industry, as shown in Figure 1. The other two industry branches included law firms and financial services. What set each of these industries apart from many others were the type of service and the level of personalized service that they provided for their clients.

Law Firms

6   Lawyers were some of the most well known providers of personal professional services. Law firms assisted their clients both by directing them in legal proceedings against others

This case was prepared by Brian Pagano, Marc E. Gartenfeld, and Professor Robert J. Mockler of St. John's University. © Robert J. Mockler.

FIGURE 1   Relevant Branches of the Professional Services Industry

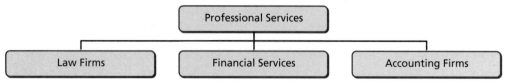

when they had been wronged and by defending them when others brought charges against them. Law firms could specialize in different areas such as business law or criminal law, or they could overlap into other professional service fields, for example tax law.

Financial Services

7   Financial services could include banks or actuarial services. Banks served both as a place to safely deposit cash and as a place to allow your cash to grow. Many commercial banks dealt with individuals, but there were also larger banks that dealt exclusively with larger corporations. Banks could also specialize in providing various specialty loans, for example mortgages or auto loans. All banks were insured by the Federal Deposit Insurance Corporation, meaning the first $100,000 were insured by the government in case the bank ever failed. Banks paid interest on deposits made with them and generated the money for this by investing with the cash they had. Due to the immense importance of banking in America, however, banks were not permitted to invest in stocks. They were only allowed to invest in bonds ranked as having the lowest risk of default on payments.

8   Actuarial services generally worked with insurance, calculating risks involved in various areas. Perhaps the best known actuarial services dealt with insurance. These firms calculated what amount the insurance company could expect to pay out in a given time frame, which was then used to determine what sort of premium they should charge. The different financial services also overlapped with other sectors, as they had their own unique laws and accounting practices.

Accounting Firms

9   Accounting firms provided many different types of services to their clients. Accountants could perform audits, give advice on tax planning, or compile financial records for their clients, to name a few of their activities. Many companies had their own accounting departments within them, but there were also firms that practiced accounting exclusively. These firms ranged in size from small sole practitioners, which might have only a single employee to the Big Four, which employed thousands of people worldwide.

Industry Segment: Accounting

10   Accounting firms could divide their operations, as shown in Figure 2, into three major areas: Tax, Audit, and Consulting. Each area could then be further divided into smaller areas.

Services Provided in General

11   Although not every firm had operations in every area shown in Figure 2, accounting firms would traditionally perform services in any of those shown. The major factor that would determine whether a firm provided more or less services would be the size. Naturally, a larger firm would be able to provide more services than a smaller one.

Tax

12   Many accounting firms would prepare taxes for their clients. While a great deal of money was made by actually preparing the actual tax returns for clients, this was not the

FIGURE 2   **The Accounting Sector: Services Provided**

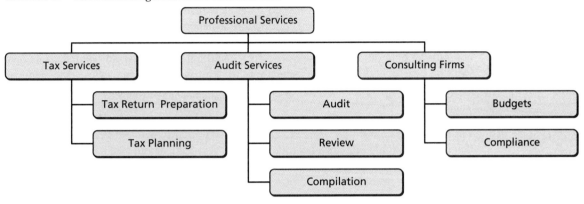

only source of income for firms in the tax area. Firms could meet with their clients for discussions regarding tax planning. For example, a firm might recommend a client to invest in certain types of bonds that might offer a tax break. Or, accountants might explain the different consequences that could result depending on whether a firm wanted to buy a piece of residential or non-residential property. The tax code was very large and very diverse, and providing clients with people who were familiar with it and could use it to help save them money was an important source of income for many accounting practices.

Audit

13   Audit services provided by firms could be further broken down, just as tax services could. An audit, by definition, consisted of an accounting firm testing the financial statements of a company to ensure that the five basic assumptions of management (namely existence and occurrence, completeness, rights and obligations, valuation, and financial statement presentation and disclosure) were all fairly presented in the financial statements. After performing various tests of transactions and balances, the auditors would then sign an opinion statement. This opinion might be unqualified if the financial statements were presented fairly in accordance with Generally Accepted Accounting Principals (GAAP), qualified if they were presented with certain departures from GAAP that did not result in information being presented that was misleading or altogether incorrect, or adverse if the financial statements were not presented fairly. In certain instances auditors might also sign a disclaimer, stating that they were not making an opinion on the financial statements of a company. Audit services were very important for firms because in order to trade on the New York Stock Exchange, it was required that they issued annual reports with audited financial statements. Even if a firm did not trade publicly, finding investors willing to put money into a company that had not been audited would be very difficult.

14   Cheaper and less in-depth than an audit was a review. The idea behind this service provided was the same, however. An accounting firm would go over the financial statements of the client searching for misstatements. However, in a review no official opinion would be issued. And where in an audit the accounting firm would say that in their opinion the financial statements were presented fairly (called positive assurance), in a review the assurance given would be negative. This meant that the accountants only said that, based on what they had seen, there did not appear to be any material misstatements in the financial statements of the company. Review services were not permitted in place of an audit, but for smaller companies that were not publicly traded this might be acceptable for investors to place their trust in them. The lower assurance level also resulted in a lower cost, which made it desirable for those who might not have been able to afford an in-depth audit.

15   Financial statement compilation was slightly different from audit and review services in that here the accounting firm issued no statements at all as to the reliability of the client's financial statements. Rather, they collected information from the client and actually organized it into financial statements themselves. The firm preparing these compilations could not issue an opinion on them because a firm could not legally give an opinion on its own work because of independence issues. Another firm might still audit these statements as usual, however.

Consulting

16   The strength of accounting firms had always rested primarily with their employees. Besides being able to simply prepare a tax return or audit financial statements, they could also take advantage of their knowledge to assist in the management of certain clients. Legal issues forbade a firm from auditing and providing consultation for the same client, but provided the accountants did not participate in the audit, they would then be permitted to assist in the management of other companies.

17   One important aspect of management was budgeting. Various regulations in GAAP could make it difficult to determine exactly what effect a certain project might have on net income. Different valuation standards or accounting estimates were just two difficulties that might arise. Accountants could assist in setting up budgets for any task that required one, including production, labor, and inventory purchases. Accountants could show managers how to most effectively and efficiently meet financial goals over time.

18   Compliance was another aspect of consulting that tied in closely with many other areas. It could take on a legal viewpoint. For example, an item might need to be allocated over several years or it might need to be expensed immediately. Compliance could also take on a tax viewpoint. For example, a client might have unknowingly claimed a larger deduction than they were allowed to, which the accountants would point out, potentially saving the client thousands of dollars in interest and penalties if they were audited by the government. Accountants could also provide compliance testing on behalf of investors. For example, many investors required firms in which they had an investment to keep their debt financing below a certain percentage. It would be up to the accountants to monitor this percentage and make sure the company's debt was where the investors required it to be.

How the Industry Segment Works: The Essence of the Business Process

19   As shown in Figure 3, the accounting segment of the professional services industry had several different facets: services provided, types of clients serviced, staff characteristics, industry regulation, geographical regions, and competition. Each area could be further broken down as shown in the model.

Services

20   Accounting firms provided services to their clients in audit, tax, and consulting, as described earlier. The environment in each of these areas was changing very rapidly for various reasons. If a firm was to succeed over its competition, it had to be able to adapt to these changes more quickly and efficiently than anyone else.

Tax

21   Tax rules in the United States would change every year. Some rules, such as the amount of a standard deduction, were adjusted every year for factors such as inflation, while other rules might come in sporadically, including one new regulation stating that taxpayers could now file for an automatic six-month extension where in the past only the first three months were automatically given with the next three needing a valid reason [IRS, 2006].

FIGURE 3 **Accounting Segment Business Model**

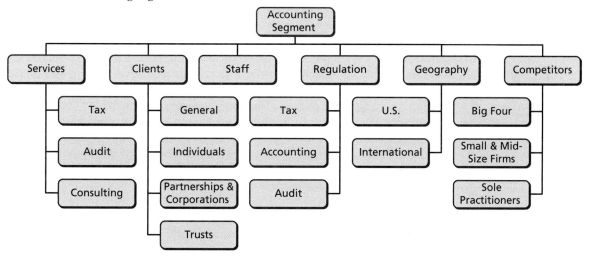

22   In order to succeed in the tax field, an accounting firm would need a staff that was knowledgeable about the changes in the tax law, dealing both with what the law was and what the law was expected to change to. Failure to be current on as many aspects of the tax law as possible could result in returns having to be amended and in taking a much longer time to prepare each return. The firm had to also have efficient tax programs. Preparing tax returns by hand was still acceptable for the IRS as of 2006, and it might be easier when dealing with the simplest returns, but the clients that paid more for tax return preparation were those that had more complicated returns. It was therefore practically necessary that the firm used a computer program for tax preparation and that the staff was properly trained in its use. Another key to success in the tax field was the surest way to satisfy your client: the minimization of the tax the client had to pay. The complexity of the tax code could also be very vague at times, and the preparer could use this fact to put certain items where they would yield the greatest benefit to the taxpayer. Obviously, if Firm A told a client that he owed $1,000 and Firm B told that same client he was entitled to a $500 refund, then that client would obviously go back to Firm B in the future.

23   Another key to success in the tax area relating to clients was the level of personalization the firm could provide with the service. The process of preparing a tax return could be very intrusive on an individual's personal life, requiring information such as the client's social security number, marital status, and job status. Sometimes people could be very reluctant to discuss these issues, so it was important for the firm to handle each client in a friendly, personal way that made the client feel comfortable.

24   Finally, within the firm it was important that tax documents were properly organized. While the client might not directly know whether or not papers were kept properly, it was particularly important for the staff within the firm. This was because when a firm prepared many tax returns, it could not always finish the entire return at once. Questions might arise that required the firm to get answers from the client, and these answers could not always be obtained right away. So that the process of preparing a tax return from beginning to end could go as smoothly as possible, important papers should be kept in a consistent, logical order.

Audit

25   Audit had been most substantially affected by the passing of the Sarbanes Oxley Act in 2001. This act had several effects, both intended and unintended, on accounting firms and

their clients. Just some of the effects listed by Jo Lynne Koehn and Stephen C. Del Vecchio were "contraction of the audit market," "decreased competitiveness of the audit market," "increase in accounting costs," and "consulting was booming" [Koehn, 2004]. Contraction of the audit market referred to the regulation that audit firms be registered with the Public Company Accounting Oversight Board. Many smaller accounting firms in the US could not afford to comply with this, which resulted in a drop in the number of firms from over 850 before the act was passed to less than 600 in 2003. The "decreased competitiveness of the audit market" primarily referred to the Big Four. A recent study by the General Accounting Office revealed that the Big Four audited over 78% of all public companies in the US, and 99% of all public company sales [Bloom, 2005]. The increase in accounting costs was expected due to all of the additional requirements imposed by the act, but the fact remained that accounting costs were in fact rising, and some accounting firms were better equipped than others to handle these rising costs.

26   Staff dealing with an audit generally should be experienced rather than simply knowledgeable. Of course, knowing exactly what the audit procedure was helped, but with experience came knowledge as well as efficiency, which was especially important in light of the rising costs of performing an audit. Being able to perform a proper audit in the shortest amount of time was a major advantage for any firm because it would lower its costs per audit.

27   As mentioned above, the audit process was one that was often required by banks or investors to ensure that financial statements were presented fairly. Because nobody liked being told they might be wrong, the audit service was generally not one the client necessarily wanted to have done. It was therefore important that an accounting firm kept the client comfortable and performed the procedures with as little inconvenience to the client as possible. The audit process that the client didn't even know was happening was the one that would be enjoyed the most.

28   Internally, review procedures should be standardized within the firm. The audit process itself was very similar for different clients, especially for clients in the same industry. Therefore, to promote efficiency, necessary papers and templates should be put together in such a way that staff could easily move from one audit to the next without having to get familiarized with a new client. The more efficiently this could be done, the less time it would take per audit, and the lower the cost of the audit as a result.

Consulting

29   The boom in consulting mentioned by Koehn and Del Vecchio was a direct result of Sarbanes Oxley as well. All of the extra rules combined with harsher penalties for noncompliance resulted in the upper management of public companies be willing to pay the extra money required to ensure that they did not find themselves in the same situation as Enron for any reason. Accounting firms could, therefore, find more clients to whom they could provide all sorts of consulting services, whether it was legal or ethical issues.

30   Similar to tax, staff involved in consulting should be knowledgeable in whatever area it was they were giving advice about. Clients expected to call with a question and have it answered immediately. However, even if the staff of a firm didn't know everything there was to know, it was still possible to succeed in this area by having ready access to the information clients were seeking. Whether this came from good record-keeping or subscriptions to Internet tax updates or some other means was all the same, as long as the information was there for the firm to access.

31   Clients would seek consulting services from an accounting firm because they wanted to know how they could run their business better. Clients also wanted to see that the firm knew this. The best way a firm could demonstrate they knew how its clients could improve their business was to be proactive with them. Rather than wait for a question to arise about why a certain process was not working or how it could be improved, the firm should take

the initiative and point it out even before the client knew anything was wrong. This would prove to the client not only that the firm knew how to improve the business, but that it was genuinely interested in improving the business.

Clients

32   Firms could provide their services for different types of clients. These types were individuals, partnerships, corporations, and trusts. Each one had different characteristics, but all required the same of the firm if the firm wanted to succeed. The most important differentiator for a firm was the connection it had with its clients. A friendly attitude in all forms of communication with the client was therefore essential. This could be as simple as saying "How could I help you?" over the phone or asking someone how they preferred to be addressed. It showed that the client's needs always came first.

33   Regarding work done for any client, it was important the work be completed in a timely manner and at a reasonable cost. Depending on the complexity of the service provided, some work would take longer or be more expensive than other work. This was to be expected, and need only be explained to the client in advance when something was going to take longer than usual. Being able to keep promises to clients regarding time and cost for a service would show the firm could be trusted to keep its word.

34   Sometimes clients would have questions for the firm as well. In this case, it was important that someone always be available to address any client questions whenever they might arise. Staff could have access to emails outside of the office, or several people might be familiar with a project in the event that one person was not available to take a phone call. Clients should never have to wait for an answer.

35   The primary reason clients came to a firm was that they wanted the firm to add value to them. The clients felt that, for whatever reason, the firm could do a given service better than they could, and that it outweighed the additional costs involved. If a firm could not deliver on that assumption, the client would not return in the future. A firm could ensure that it could deliver by familiarizing its staff with the appropriate areas for any and all clients they would be working with.

36   The bottom line when dealing with clients that would bring them back year after year was respect. A firm needed to demonstrate any time that they dealt with a client that they respected that client. Staff should never talk down to or belittle a client, as it was perhaps the most harmful thing to a working relationship necessary with any professional service firm. The firm and client had to be on the same level for the best relation possible.

Individuals

37   In addition to the general keys to success for all clients, individuals looked for certain traits within an accounting firm that other types of clients might not. When a firm was preparing a personal tax return for a client, building just the right relationship became key. This could be best achieved by matching up clients with the staff that best suited them. For example, pair a young professional just out of college with a client just out of college. People would naturally work best with people that were similar to them. Additionally, because here it was the person that was being served, any types of meetings should be scheduled according to what was most convenient for the individual client. If the clients would prefer to meet at their house on a Saturday morning, then that was where the meeting should be. The clients would realize that the firm was catering to their needs and would appreciate it.

Partnerships and Corporations

38   Partnerships and corporations operated in largely the same fields, differing mainly in ownership structure rather than in the types of services they provided. As such, the keys to success for these types of clients did not differ substantially. In addition to the general keys to success mentioned above, it was important to notice that partnerships and corporations operated in various industries and in various states. As a result, the firm had to be familiar with the various standards within the industry and with the applicable laws in any states the client operated in. Reference materials such as legal books or databases could be used to familiarize the staff in any relevant areas.

Trusts

39   Trusts were simply entities set up by a client to expand and cheaply transfer wealth to somebody else at a given point in time. Though they might vary greatly in size, they were all set up for the same purpose. Although the way trusts operated might be complicated, their purpose was very simple, and as a result no additional keys to success besides the general ones mentioned earlier applied.

Staff

40   The staff of an accounting firm could be divided between accounting and tax departments, or all of the staff could do whatever work there was to do. The biggest factor involved here was the size of the firm. The bigger the firm and the more diverse the work it did, the more likely it was to divide its staff between different service areas. In addition to this division, firms also employed both full-time employees and interns, who might only be temporary or might stay with the firm and ultimately go full-time.

41   The firm that succeeded with its staff was one that could successfully hire and retain the best employees. One way to achieve this was a successful college recruiting program. A firm could build working relationships with local universities to build a presence on campus and make its name known to achieve this.

42   A firm had to also show that it was the best place for its employees to work. If a firm could not keep employees, it had to incur recurring costs to continually train new employees. High employee retention was a good way for a firm to keep costs down. Some ways to achieve a high retention rate included building trust within team members, encouraging interpersonal relations among staff as more than just coworkers, allow opportunities for personal and career growth to employees, and cater to the needs and wants of staff whenever possible. A pleasant working environment was one of the surest ways to keep employees happy in their work. In addition to these items keeping employees in the firm, they would also encourage teamwork and promote efficiency.

43   Staff had to also be treated like people and not just cogs in a machine to keep them satisfied. Employees might work well as a team, but if they were not respected by higher management, it would likely cause problems in the future. Management should therefore encourage comments from employees about how they could improve and take every comment seriously. Management had to also pay attention to the amount of work the staff could handle compared to what they were doing. If staff was overworked for long periods of time with no reaction from management, it would lower morale and lead to problems within the firm.

44   Staff should also have diverse experience so that the firm did not become overly specialized. If a firm generated 90% of its income from providing tax services for farmers in Kansas, they ran the risk that one bad harvest year could cause their revenues to drop substantially until the farmers recovered enough to be able to pay. A firm with diverse staff could handle diverse clients and would not subject itself to risks such as that.

Regulations

45   Just as in any professional services industry, the accounting sector had its own sets of rules and regulations. There were rules such as the Internal Revenue Code governing tax, and various codes regarding auditing and accounting in general. Accounting firms had to be familiar with these regulations and fully comply with them or face potentially serious penalties.

Tax Regulations

46 The Internal Revenue Code (IRC) was the broad set of rules that regulated taxes in the United States. The IRC included definitions such as who qualified as a dependent or what was a municipal bond, and it also included financial guidelines including how to calculate alternative minimum tax or what the maximum itemized deduction was that a person could take. The IRC had to be followed when preparing taxes, and if was not the consequences would generally be that the taxpayer had to amend their return to report the correct amount of taxes owed and pay interest and penalties in addition.

47 Tax laws changed every year in the United States. Sometimes the changes were simple, such as the amount of a personal exemption increasing to reflect inflation. Sometimes the rules were slightly more complicated, such as altering the definition of who qualified as a dependent. In order to succeed, a firm dealing with tax had to have knowledge of what laws would change even before they actually took effect. Failure to do so could be very time-consuming for the firm. For example, a firm might prepare a return for a client with three dependents and arrived at a certain amount of tax due or overpaid. However, after the return was complete, the firm discovered that, based on a new tax law, the client only had two dependents. This could have a major effect on the deductions available to the taxpayer, and the entire return had to then be reevaluated.

48 It was equally important that the firm had knowledge of current laws, not only changes to be enacted in the future. To continue with the previous example, assumed now that the client's return was prepared assuming two dependents although under current definitions the client actually had three. While the IRS would not complain if people claim fewer dependents than they were allowed, the end result was that the client was paying more than necessary, and the firm would need to explain why. Tax services were deadline-driven, so it was the responsibility of the accounting firm to make sure all necessary services were finished at the proper time. Whether they were working with corporate tax returns that had to be filed by March 15 or individual returns to be filed by April 15, the firm had to be aware of all the clients they were working on, when the deadline was for that client, and if the time remaining was enough to finish all of the work required.

Accounting Regulations

49 Accounting regulations related to all aspects of reporting and documentation of a company's financial performance. There were various types of accounting regulations, both local and international. Three sets of accounting regulations were GAAP, the Financial Accounting Standards Board, and the International Accounting Standards Board.

50 Generally Accepted Accounting Principals (GAAP) related to accounting practices of all firms. Public companies were required to follow GAAP when preparing financial statements so that their financial position was fairly represented and was comparable to that of their competitors, which would of course show their own financial statements in the same format. If a company deviated from GAAP in their financial statements, then their auditors were required to give them an adverse opinion, which could result in investors pulling their money out of the company, or even in lawsuits against the company if the investors faced losses as a result of misrepresentation. Accounting firms had to be familiar with GAAP so that they could let their clients know if they needed to make changes to their financial statements in order to be in compliance.

51 The Financial Accounting Standards Board (FASB) was the group responsible for releasing accounting standards that might ultimately become GAAP in the US. They released concept statements that described what the purposes of various accounting concepts were or should be or what the problems were with existing practices and suggestions to remedy them. Accounting firms had to stay current on what the newest releases were from FASB because they could easily become GAAP soon after, so they had to know how it would affect their clients' financial statements.

52   The International Accounting Standards Board (IASB) was very similar to FASB except they issued statements that would become international rather than local standards. Currently, IASB standards were not GAAP in the US, but there had been a major push recently towards international convergence due to the rapid globalization of business. Many companies did business in more than one country, and differences in accounting standards could result in statements showing different financial positions for the same set of circumstances based on what country they were reported in. While not as important as FASB right now in the US, IASB was still something accounting firms should be aware of, particularly any differences between FASB and IASB, as that was something the FASB would probably re-evaluate sooner rather than later.

53   The conceptual framework of accounting standards was fairly straightforward. Namely, financial statements were supposed to fairly represent the performance of a company. All firms were therefore required to be familiar with these standards in general. What a firm needed in order to succeed over its competition then was more than mere knowledge. One helpful tool was reference material. The exact format required for presentation could vary based on circumstances, so reference material showing examples help to ensure that the firm prepared statements correctly the first time around. The reference materials could be anything from college textbooks to court cases, depending on the complexity of the situation. Employees dealing with accounting had to also be able to tell which standards were applicable in any situation. A simple example of this would be that a company that only had operations in China would not need to follow GAAP. By taking unnecessary regulations out of the picture, a firm could increase its efficiency by being able to better focus its attention on only those standards that were applicable.

54   Accounting standards, both local and international, were built around concepts. The most important part of a standard was not the one saying what had to be done, but why it should be done. A firm had to be aware of the conceptual background of each standard so that it could explain to its clients why it was doing what it was doing.

Audit Regulations

55   Audit regulations have undergone the most substantial changes of all of the different regulations. The most important audit regulations, the Public Company Accounting Oversight Board and the Sarbanes-Oxley Act of 2002, were both the direct result of scandals that were able to occur because of faulty audit procedures. These new audit regulations were designed to make this type of fraud much more unlikely to go undiscovered again, but in order to achieve this increased reliability on audits the regulations had to be relatively harsh.

56   The Public Company Accounting Oversight Board (PCAOB) was created in 2002 as part of the Sarbanes-Oxley Act. In a sense, it audits auditors. The PCAOB reviewed accounting firms that were registered with it on a regular basis to insure that they were following sound practices relating to audits. Penalties for a poor review from the PCAOB could include losing certification to audit public companies, which would be a very harsh blow to any firm because public companies generally had a great deal of money.

57   After the Enron scandal of 2001, there have been major changes regarding laws and regulations about accounting. Enron had been using faulty accounting practices to conceal major losses on their financial statements, and instead showed that the company had been doing well over the past several years. This all came to light when the company filed for bankruptcy in 2001 and it was discovered that they in fact had almost no money. Enron's auditors, Arthur Andersen, were implicated in the scandal and shut down as a result. Accounting had always been a highly trusted profession in America in the past, but the sheer number of people and amount of money involved in the Enron scandal became a problem for the entire accounting profession.

58   The US government's response to all this was the Sarbanes Oxley Act of 2002. This act took accounting, which had always been a self-regulating industry prior to 2001, and placed very strict regulations on it. First, it made accountants legally responsible in the event that fraud was involved in a company's financial statements that were not discovered in an audit. Whether the auditors knew of the fraud being committed or not did not change anything. It also increased the scope of an audit to include not only testing the numbers on the financial statements themselves, but also the internal controls of a company to see that the process of arriving at these numbers was an acceptable one and that it was carried out. The Sarbanes Oxley Act also put greater responsibility in the hands of the highest level executives of the companies being audited.

59   In the Enron case, the defense of the executives was always that they were unaware of what was happening within the firm. What Sarbanes Oxley did to counter this in the future was to require the CEO and CFO to sign off on all financial statements issued by the company. This increased legal liability for the executives naturally resulted in a demand for much more detailed audits that could find anything that might put these executives in a position that they could get fired, fined, or even put in jail. The increased pressure from companies being audited, combined with the additional requirements from the government created a sharp increase in the demand for accountants since the law was passed. As a result, many companies found themselves with a severe shortage of employees. The new hires they had been making in the past were suddenly not enough to cover the drastic increase in the amount of work to be done. Besides the additional accountants needed to perform all this additional work, new hires were also necessary for the legal departments of accounting firms to be able to analyze the new law to figure out what could and could not be done now that might not have been an issue in the past.

60   As with accounting standards, all accounting firms were required to follow these audit standards, so the key to overcoming the competition had to be in more than simply following them. The key to successful compliance with audit standards lied primarily in records kept by the firm. One important item for the firm was detailed documentation of activities from prior periods. Combined with this, the firm should also have templates for documents that would need to be used repeatedly, or for documents that needed few modifications for different clients. This promotes efficiency by saving time on preparing long or repetitive documents such as opinion letters and giving the firm more time for field work or other audit tasks.

61   The harsh penalties for noncompliance with new audit standards made it more important than ever that a firm be aware of independence issues with its clients. A firm dealing with large numbers of clients had to be aware of what services it provided for each one so that it could then be aware of what services it could not legally provide for each client. If a firm provided an audit that it could not legally do because of independence issues, the accounting firm would possibly face sanctions from the government, and the client would have to pay for another audit from a different firm.

Geography

62 Individuals, partnerships, corporations, and trusts were not localized to a single area, and so accounting firms shouldn't be either. Smaller accounting firms might be very local and only cater to a certain area, while the largest firms might have hundreds of offices in dozens of countries all over the world.

United States

63 Within the US, a firm could either be local, regional, or national. Some firms might have a single office in a suburban area, some firms might only operate in major cities, or some might operate right out of the owner's house in a small town. Just a few factors to consider when dealing with location were the number of employees the firm had to spread out, the likelihood of attracting new clients by moving to a different area, and the cost of the different areas.

64 What then determined if a firm could win over its competition in a given area were such factors as whether or not the firm had an office where the client was located, the firm's ability to get its staff to wherever the client was, and whether the firm was recognized in that geographical area. These three areas could interrelate, particularly with the larger firms.

International

65 An accounting firm might have ten offices across the United States, but still be considered local. As stated earlier, business was becoming increasingly global. Besides foreign companies having operations in the US, US companies also often had offices in other countries around the world. Accounting firms with clients that fell into either of these categories might need to open an office in a foreign country in order to provide their services to clients operating in that country or risk losing them to another firm.

66 Once a firm leaves the United States, there were other factors that came into play besides just whether or not staff could get to a certain area. First, the firm had to have knowledge of what standards the foreign company used (whether international, local, or US standards) and then make sure it was familiar with those standards. Second, the firm had to be able to communicate with clients in the foreign country, so knowledge of the language and familiarity with local customs was very important as well. Finally, as in the United States, the firm had to be established in an area as a recognized provider of high quality services to succeed over the competition.

67 Because international expansion was very expensive, and because at the time Schwartz & Company's size indicated that international expansion at this time would be impractical, this area is not considered in great detail.

Competition

68 Competition within the accounting sector could be best divided into three distinct classes: The Big Four, small and mid-sized firms, and sole practitioners. Each of these three areas had its own set of strengths and weaknesses in each of the key to success areas.

Big Four

69 The Big Four accounting firms were Price Waterhouse Coopers, Ernst & Young, Deloitte & Touche, and KPMG. Their main offices were in New York, but they had offices all over the world. They provided all kinds of services for their clients, and as mentioned earlier, they performed the audits for over 75% of the publicly traded companies in the US. They worked with all types of clients and employed full-time staff as well as a great deal of interns right out of college.

70 The smallest of the Big Four firms had over 20,000 employees in the US alone. No matter where their clients were located, they either already had an office close by or were able to easily get employees to that client. They also had offices in and employees from over 90 countries worldwide [Accounting Jobs, 2006]. This allowed any of the Big Four firms as a whole to be familiar with languages and customs of nearly every major area in the world. This also gave each of the Big Four recognition internationally as well as locally. Naturally, their size alone allowed them to offer very high salaries to students coming out of college, so their college recruiting programs were very successful. However, the long hours created a stressful work environment, and many private companies hired accountants out of Big Four firms for an even higher salary, so employee turnover was high. This high turnover made it difficult for interpersonal relations to flourish within the firm.

71 The Big Four accounting firms all offered services in tax, audit, and consulting, and due to the number of people they employed, it was a safe assumption to make that for any of these areas they had several employees both knowledgeable and experienced. They also serviced all types of clients: individuals, partnerships, corporations, and trusts. The Big Four firms were also able to take advantage of economies of scale due to their size, and were therefore able to service the biggest clients at the best prices.

Small and Mid-Sized Firms

72   Smaller accounting firms might share many traits of the Big Four such as international offices and providing all types of services, but they fell short in terms of size. Mid-sized and smaller accounting firms were still present, however, in each segment of the industry.

73   The biggest weakness of these smaller firms was that they had much less exposure than Big Four firms. While college students learned about the Big Four in class, it was the responsibility of the smaller firms to get their names recognized however they could. This weakness also extended to acquiring new clients. Entities looking for an accounting firm already knew about the Big Four and what their merits were, but few knew of the qualities of smaller firms. The impression given by the words "small firm" had never been a good one, as it seemed to imply a lower level of service.

74   Depending on the size of the firm, it could offer all types of services to all types of clients, but it could also have been limited if it didn't have enough employees to diversify its client base. The increased costs associated with both making its name known to potential employees and clients, and with expanding into new areas if necessary, could flow down into higher costs for clients or a more stressful work environment for employees.

75   Smaller accounting firms that were able to overcome this major weakness were then able to turn it into a major strength. That strength was that smaller firms' employees were generally much more loyal to the firm than employees of Big Four firms. Although smaller firms might not be able to pay as well as Big Four, and they might not have been as conveniently located in general, the fact remained that the environment tended to be one that promoted trust and teamwork by being free of internal office politics and that promoted growth among its employees.

Sole Practitioners

76   Sole practitioners were generally the smallest practices in the field, but their small size helped them to excel in their relationships with clients. The small number of clients made it easier for these practices to build personal relations with each one. They normally would have relatively few clients, and they would often specialize in one type of client, such as individuals or sole proprietorships. This could result in a greater level of knowledge in the fields of each of their clients. Because sole practitioners worked directly with their clients, the issue of friendly attitudes and respect was much easier to achieve than in larger firms.

77   A weakness of sole practitioners was their limited recognition outside of their geographical area of operation. Because they had few employees, diversification was very difficult to achieve, and there would be virtually no team to develop trust within.

THE COMPANY

78   Schwartz & Company, LLP was a small firm in terms of the number of professionals it employed, but was closer to a mid-sized firm in terms of revenues generated. Figure 4 shows areas that the firm was concerned with [Interview, 2006A].

Services

79   Although Schwartz & Company was a relatively small firm, it did not limit the services it provided because of its size. Just like mid-sized and larger firms, Schwartz & Company provided tax, audit, and consulting services.

FIGURE 4   Schwartz & Company, LLP Areas of Operation

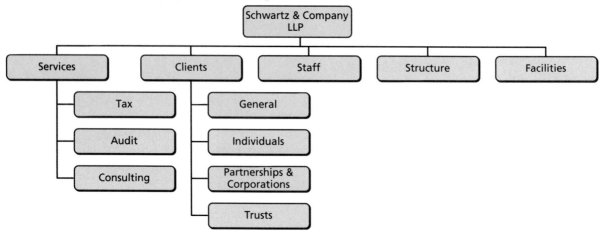

Tax

80   Schwartz & Company's greatest strength in the tax field was the personalization of the services it provided. The staff worked closely with clients and stayed on top of tax issues from year to year. Tax projections were also provided at the end of the year, allowing major tax questions to be discussed months before tax deadlines in April.

81   Schwartz & Company was very helpful in that it kept its employees aware of current tax regulations. Meetings were held regularly regarding important tax issues to be aware of and how to work with them on the tax preparation software the firm used. Emails were sent out within the office, and contact between staff members was encouraged when any questions arose. The firm was also efficient in its organization of tax documents. Management made it clear what they were looking for, and those expectations remained consistent from year to year.

Audit

82   The greatest strength Schwartz & Company had in the audit department was its experienced staff. Before the formal process would start, management would sit down with staff and discuss with each of them what was expected and how to go about performing the audit. A large percentage of the firm worked with audits over time and was especially familiar with the way they were done at Schwartz & Company.

Consulting

83   The higher level staff at Schwartz & Company gave specialized consulting services to clients in the areas of tax planning, financial planning, and wealth management, among others. The firm's greatest strength here was the staff's commitment to excellence. Staff at Schwartz & Company would always be proactive with clients, solving problems the client never even knew existed. This commitment to improving the client's position first helped Schwartz & Company grow completely through client referrals.

84   A weakness of the firm in this field was its lack of access to information. While the staff was very knowledgeable in most areas, they had no large reference materials or Internet databases to go to in the event that staff did not already know something. Information was still available over the Internet, but was more difficult to navigate than a company database might be.

Clients

85 Schwartz & Company provided services for all types of entities. Just to name a few, the firm would prepare tax returns for individuals, perform audits and reviews of partnerships and corporations, and offer wealth management consulting services to trusts. However, as Michael J. Schwartz, general partner at Schwartz & Company put it, "We have no clients; we have lots of relationships" [Interview, 2006B]. The greatest strength of Schwartz & Company was always its relation to its clients. In the business world, there was any number of accounting firms a person could go to for the services they needed. What made them choose Schwartz & Company was the relations they built above and beyond the standard business relationship they could find anywhere else.

86   Regarding the acquisition of new clients, the firm would ask certain questions regarding potential new clients before it accepted them. Namely, research would be done regarding the integrity of the client, whether the firm could provide a value-adding service for the client, whether the client would recognize the value that Schwartz & Co, LLP added, and whether the potential client wanted a relationship or not. These standards were the same, regardless of whether the potential client was an individual, partnership, firm, or trust.

General

87 One way Schwartz & Company was able to build such strong relations with its clients was its size. Where with a large firm clients could run the risk of being moved around between staff, clients with Schwartz & Company would deal with the same people every time. This continued contact helped create a friendly atmosphere for each client, no matter what they came looking for.

88   Staff at Schwartz & Company also did their best to ensure that work for the client was done on time. Deadlines were set, and while office hours were set, the general mood of the firm was that the office closed when the work was finished. Therefore, whatever the actual amount of time needed to complete a project might be, the firm would ensure its clients that a certain date was reasonable and that the work would be finished by then.

89   Although Schwartz & Company was a small firm, they were not generally difficult to contact as might be expected at a small firm. There would almost always be someone in the office between 8:30 a.m. and 7 p.m., and many staff were issued Blackberries so that clients could contact them outside of normal office hours in case of emergencies.

90   Schwartz & Company was also careful with its selection of clients. The firm did not set up any restrictions on whether or not a client would be accepted based on industry or size; however, all potential clients would be interviewed before they were accepted, and an important point Schwartz & Company would look for in this interview was whether it could add value to this client. Only after this was determined would the client be accepted, and in this way the firm would be able to be sure that their clients would walk away satisfied.

Individuals

91 Because Schwartz & Company placed such an important emphasis on the importance of connecting with the individual, it was able to develop strong relations with clients there for individual services. The priority of the firm was always the client. Therefore, clients would be assigned to employees that could best relate to them, and the firm operated around what the client needed first.

Partnerships and Corporations

92 What made partnerships and corporations different from individuals was that the services partnerships and corporations required were more extensive. It more often required knowledge of regulations in various states, which Schwartz & Company was able to handle.

However, there were also various practices depending on the industry the client was in. A weakness of Schwartz & Company was that although it specialized in investment partnerships, its experience in other fields was more limited, and it had no clients at all in the construction and apparel industries.

Trusts

93 As mentioned earlier, the purpose of a trust was very straightforward, and did not differ between different trusts. Trusts therefore did not have any keys to success in addition to the ones basic to all clients. Schwartz & Company's strengths in the general field made it inherently strong with trusts as well.

Staff

94 Schwartz & Company's small size gave it certain advantages over its larger competitors, while at the same time its large size gave it certain advantages over its smaller competitors.

95 The firm had less than 20 employees, all working in one office. The constant contact among team members helped an atmosphere of trust and friendship to grow within the firm. Because the firm was fairly large in comparison to sole proprietorships and other small firms, it was able to cater to the wants and needs of its employees. For example, if an employee working primarily on audits preferred to go into tax, then the firm was able to accommodate that employee. A smaller firm with fewer employees might not have been able to move the employee out of the audit field if nobody could fill the vacancy.

96 Schwartz & Co's policy regarding employees was to settle for nothing less than the best. The way it went about achieving this was through its internship program. Besides allowing the intern to get a feel for a smaller accounting firm as opposed to a Big Four firm, it would also gives the firm an opportunity to evaluate performance to decide whether it would be a good idea to keep the intern on as full time. This had been a very successful method of keeping only employees with a strong work ethic and that work very well together as a team.

97 The small size of the firm, on the other hand, allowed for personal growth opportunities that would likely not be found in larger firms. Interns and new staff at Schwartz & Company were needed on projects right away, where in a Big Four environment newer staff would generally be used for the tasks not directly related to accounting, such as photocopying and mailing. Therefore, where personal growth would be delayed in larger firms, at Schwartz & Company challenges and growth were a daily occurrence. Management at the firm realized this, and was eager to have staff share what they learned and if they had any ideas as to how the firm could operate better.

98 The firm offered incentives to its employees to achieve certain goals, whether they would result in the growth of the firm itself or the growth of the individual within the firm. For example, an employee might choose a self-improvement book to read, or might be asked to bring in a certain number of resumes in a given year. Each employee would be given a unique set of goals each year with progress evaluated quarterly. The employee's progress towards achieving these goals would then be figured into that employee's bonus.

99 Many members of the staff at Schwartz & Company were recently graduated from college. A familiarity with local campuses helped its college recruiting program greatly.

100 Training for new staff members was mostly an informal process. There were no off-site meetings or formal processes that all new employees had to undergo. Rather, new employees would work closely with more experienced staff at first and would learn how the firm worked by actually doing the work. Additionally, each employee was assigned a mentor from higher level management to act as someone that he or she could go to with any questions, comments, complaints, or observations about any aspect of the firm.

101 The one major weakness Schwartz & Company had with staff was a relatively small number of employees compared to clients. The high standards the firm set when hiring new employees led to a small rate in hiring new employees compared to the number of new clients acquired.

Structure

102 Schwartz & Company, LLP's organizational structure consisted of two partners at the top, followed by managers, staff, and interns moving down the chain. However, while the chain of command was very clear within the firm, responsibilities were not broken down into such clear areas. For example, a first year staff could still be in charge of performing an audit. Tasks were given to employees based on expectations built from previous work rather than simply based on number of years of experience.

103 Because Schwartz & Company was a fairly small firm, and because all the staff would have experience in several areas, the firm was not broken down into distinct departments for different services or client types.

Facilities

104 Schwartz & Company, LLP had offices located in Bellmore, Manhattan, and Boca Raton, Florida. The Bellmore office served as the main office, while the other two offices had no permanent employees but were used when staff needed to be in the area.

LOOKING TOWARDS THE FUTURE

105 At a recent informal meeting at Schwartz & Company, various suggestions were made regarding how the firm could increase revenues among the services provided for individual clients. One staff member, Mark Lundin, suggested that the firm move into a new market, namely preparing returns for college students. Another staff member, Peter Costalas, suggested that the firm would be better off staying on its current course of catering to high net-worth individuals.

106 The first alternative to expand into the college student market, would result mostly in an increase in the number of tax returns prepared by the firm, as college students generally did not own large businesses or have investments of millions of dollars in different ventures.

107 The benefit of the first alternative was that it would allow the firm to make its name known to college students without any additional costs besides that of implementing the change within the firm. Students would know about the firm because of the services it would provide for them, and the internship program could be promoted and explained to each individual student one-on-one.

108 This alternative was feasible because the firm had very good relationships with several colleges on Long Island. Schwartz & Company could use these existing relationships and making these schools the first ones the new program was brought to. Once the program proved successful, Schwartz & Company could use these first schools as an example and expand into other schools in the area.

109 This alternative would win against the competition because it would greatly strengthen its college recruiting program. On-campus publicity was very important for a firm to get its name out to students, because if nobody knew the firm existed then nobody would apply to work there. Smaller firms and sole practitioners that didn't have enough employees to spare to send to a college campus two or three days a week would not be able to get this publicity. Additionally, employees of Schwartz & Company could speak directly with students in a very informal manner promoting the firm and giving the students a direct look at the kind of environment the firm promoted. Big Four firms that came in and spoke to large audiences had to give a general speech, but a one-on-one conversation would allow Schwartz & Company to speak to the needs of each student individually.

110   The firm would also be able to win by providing a much more personalized service than its competitors. Schwartz & Company could send its younger staff to the campuses, as students would have a much easier time relating with professionals close to their own age. College-age staff at Big Four accounting firms generally were not given the type of experience that first-year staff at Schwartz & Company got, so the Big Four firms should have a difficult time finding employees capable of providing the service and the personalized relationships at the same time. Because smaller firms would probably not be able to implement this plan in the first place, they would be able to provide neither the service nor the personalization.

111   A drawback to the first alternative was the existence of the Volunteer Income Tax Assistance (VITA) program. This program was provided by college students that currently attended classes at the university where the services were provided, and they provide these services free of charge. Therefore, although the university was not actually a competitor of Schwartz & Company, this program could discourage students from paying even a discounted rate to Schwartz & Company when they could have their tax returns prepared for free by people they already know from class.

112   A way around this drawback was the limitations of the VITA program. The VITA program did have certain rules for those providing the service. For one, state returns could not be prepared; only federal. Also, there were limitations regarding how much income someone could have and what deductions they could take before students in the VITA program could not prepare a return for that person. The services offered by Schwartz & Company would have no such limitations.

113   A second alternative would be to keep the firm focused on high net-worth individuals. Under this alternative, the only new individuals Schwartz & Company would take on as clients would be those with a net-worth of $1 million and over.

114   The benefit of this alternative was that Schwartz & Company would be continuing to work with what it knew best. The firm had grown since 1991 serving individuals classified as high net-worth, so it would be able to continue working around its strength.

115   This second alternative was feasible because the firm would not need to make any changes to its structure or existing practices. It would only need to continue what it had been doing since its foundation.

116   This second alternative would win against the competition because it would be able to use its experience with a certain type of client over time in order to work more efficiently and thus keep costs down for the client. Smaller firms and sole practitioners might be able to reduce costs through efficiency gained by experience as well, but their size would not allow them to do this for as many clients as Schwartz & Company could. While the Big Four firms could take even more advantage of economies of scale than Schwartz & Company, their major clients were large corporations and individuals of even higher net-worth than those targeted by Schwartz & Company under this alternative. Thus, Schwartz & Company should have the lowest costs in that particular niche.

117   Another way that this alternative would win against the competition would be the firm's ability to add value for its clients. Just as the saying goes, it takes money to make money. This could be applied to clients, in that those that already had more value were the ones whose value could be increased more. While not much value could be added to college students by simply preparing their tax returns, value could be added to those with a high net-worth. For example, those operating businesses could be informed of practices that could reduce their tax liability. Smaller firms and sole practitioners could do this equally well with the clients they have experience with; however, they could not take full advantage of it because the end result should ultimately be client recommendations, and the smaller the firm was the less capable it was of handling large increases in number of clients. Big Four firms, on the other hand, service clients that were so large that practices to save a client

$1 million might not be material to that client. Schwartz & Company should be able to add more value relative to the client's size than Big Four firms could.

118 A drawback to this alternative would be that, unlike college students, high net-worth individuals were not as uniform in the services they need provided for them. While one employee could likely provide a high level of service for dozens of college students, clients with higher net-worth require more time per service provided, and Schwartz & Company could have a hard time being able to maintain a high level of service with an increasing number of clients due to the comparatively small number of staff.

119 A way around this drawback would be that Schwartz & Company already had a specialization in dealing with high net-worth individuals. This existing experience would lead to a fairly small learning curve, and fewer new employees should have to be hired to cover the increased client base as compared to how a different firm might have to change its hiring practices.

120 Both alternatives had many positive features to them as well as drawbacks. Michael Schwartz and Joseph Boyce would have to carefully consider each alternative and consider any additional possibilities thoroughly before committing to any single decision.

LIST OF WORKS CITED

Anonymous (2006). "Accounting Jobs and Careers: Vault Employment Channels." [Online]. *http://vault.com/hubs/501/channelhome_501.jsp?ch_id=253.* Accessed on March 20, 2006.

Bloom, Robert and David C. Schirm (2005). "Consolidation and Competition in Public Accounting." *CPA Journal.* [Online]. *http://www.nysscpa.org/cpajournal/2005/605/infocus/p22.htm.* Accessed on February 28, 2006.

Interview (2006A). Personal interview with Maria Sanjurjo. April 5, 2006.

Interview (2006B). Personal interview with Michael J. Schwartz. April 7, 2006.

IRS (2006). "Highlights of 2005 Tax Law Changes." [Online]. *http://www.irs.gov/newsroom/article/0,,id=152307,00.html.* Accessed on February 28, 2006.

Koehn, Jo Lynne and Stephen C. Del Vecchio (2004). "Ripple Effects of the Sarbanes-Oxley Act." *CPA Journal.* [Online]. *http://www.nysscpa.org/cpajournal/2004/204/essentials/p36.htm.* Accessed on February 28, 2006.

Case 45

The Apollo Group, Inc. [University of Phoenix]   Richard B. Robinson

1   John G. Sperling was a late bloomer as an entrepreneur. A Cambridge University PhD who had spent most of his career teaching at San Jose State University after brief stints at Maryland, Ohio State and Northern Illinois, he didn't launch Apollo Group Inc.—parent of the University of Phoenix—until 1976, when he was 55. But what Sperling lacked in precociousness he more than made up for in ambition: His goal was nothing less than to turn conventional higher education on its head.

2   Rather than catering to 18- to 22-year-olds looking to find themselves, Sperling focused on the then-neglected market of working adults. And he recruited working professionals as teachers, rather than tenured professors. Although UOP and its online campus, University of Phoenix Online, have more than 18,000 faculties, only about 450 are full-time. Most radical of all, while nearly all other universities are nonprofits, Sperling ran his university to make money. Those ideas sparked overwhelming resistance from the education establishment, which branded UOP a "diploma mill." The result? "We faced failure every day for the first 10 years," said Founder Sperling, who turned 88 in 2009.

3   From an IPO adjusted price of $0.76 to a mid-2005 high of $98, Apollo's stock reflected a company *BusinessWeek* considered among the top 50 performing companies on Wall Street. The Phoenix-based company, whose day-to-day operations were still generating average annual revenue growth exceeding 30% over that time, saw its revenues reach $2.5 billion in 2006 with net income exceeding $414 million. With a price-earnings ratio of 76, Apollo has one of the richest price-earnings multiples on Wall Street at the time.

4   Tuition at Apollo averages only $10,000 a year, 55% of what a typical private college charges. A key factor, says Sperling, is that universities for the young require student unions, sports teams, student societies, and so on. The average age of a UOP student is 35, so UOP doesn't have those expenses. It also saves by holding classes in leased office spaces around the country. By 2005, over 135,000 of its 275,000 students studied at University of Phoenix Online.

5   By 2006, Phoenix Online had become the dominant player in the online education market that still has lots of potential for growth. The bricks-and-mortar University of Phoenix was one of the first institutions to identify and serve the burgeoning market for educating working adults. In the late 1980s, long before the Web debuted, the school began to experiment with offering its classes online. It got off to a slow start, "and we lost money for a number of years," recalled Brian Mueller, Apollo's President.

6   As a result of this head start, however, Phoenix Online was ready to capitalize on an online-education market that began exploding in the mid-1990s. Today, about 15% of the 600,000 or so U.S. students earning a degree via the Net are enrolled at Phoenix Online. Phoenix Online also garners an outsize share of the industry's revenues—about one-third of the total. That's because as the market leader, it can charge higher tuition than most rivals. Undergraduates pay a little more than $10,000 a year at Phoenix Online, while students seeking a master's degree pay nearly $12,500. "They're by far the giant in this industry," says Eduventure market analyst Sean Gallagher. Appendix A at the end of this case lists some of the other key players or "competitors."

7   Is the best yet to come? Both Phoenix Online and the broader industry are still in their infancy. "There are 70 million working adults in this country who don't have a college degree," says Gallagher. Increasingly, they realize that they need a degree to get ahead. But because they often have a family as well as a job, studying online is the most convenient solution. Howard Block, an analyst at Banc of America Securities, predicts "dramatic enrollment growth" for Phoenix Online. He expects that half of the students in post-secondary education will one day make at least some use of the Internet to earn their degrees.

GLOBAL OUTREACH

8   Phoenix Online began to tap the international market in 2005, initially "bringing in about 500 students a month," said Mueller. "But that's just the tip of the iceberg." Though Phoenix Online started offering classes only in English, it has begun to offer courses in Spanish and plans to introduce Mandarin soon as well. Ironically, one of the hottest tech stocks of recent years has done all this with plain-vanilla technology. While other companies charged into online education with dazzling digital content, Phoenix Online offers a text-heavy format that can easily be accessed with dial-up modems.

9   This might sound like a recipe for failure. But Phoenix Online realized that interaction with humans—the professor and other students in the class—was far more important to success than interaction with the digital content. Thus, Phoenix Online keeps its classes small, averaging just 12 students. And to combat the Achilles heel of distance education—a high dropout rate—it offers its students plenty of hand-holding, including round-the-clock tech support. The result: 65% of its students go on to graduate.

10   Some see plain technology as a potential negative for the virtual college. "At some point, Phoenix Online will need to upgrade the sophistication of its platform," warns Trace Urdan, an analyst with ThinkEquity Partners, a boutique investment bank. That will require more spending on research and development and information technology, he warns, which could crimp margins. Still, any extra spending could be easily offset if Phoenix Online bumped up its class size to 15 students, argues Block. Even with today's small classes, operating profit margins now top 30%.

THE ONLINE TREND

11   The dot-com bubble may have burst in the world of commerce, but the promise of harnessing the Internet for paradigm-changing growth—and even profits—still thrives in the halls of academia. At the University of Maryland University College, enrollment in classes offered over the Net soared to 63,000 in the past academic year, up 50% from the year before. UMUC students can now earn some 70 degrees and certificates entirely online. The University of Phoenix Online saw revenues jump some 76% in the fiscal year ended Aug. 31, to $181 million, while profits grew 82%, to $32 million.

12   Since the U.S. Army began rolling out an e-learning program in 2001, annually more than 10,400 soldiers are taking classes and earning degrees online from 24 participating colleges. Students at eArmyU, as it's known, receive a free laptop and printer and 100% of their tuition. The Army enrollment hit 80,000 after it took the program Army-wide in 2006.

13   Nearly seven years after the dot-com fizzle began, e-learning has emerged from the wreckage as one of the Internet's most useful applications. Nearly 75% of the 4,000 major colleges and universities in the U.S. now offer classes over the Internet or use the Web to enhance campus classes, according to market researcher International Data Corp. About

FIGURE 1
Corporations Are Charging into E-Learning

Data: International Data Corp.

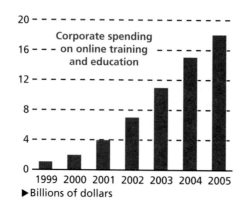

Corporate spending on online training and education

▶ Billions of dollars

FIGURE 2
The E-Learning Explosion

Data International Data Corp., Eduventures.com. IDC. U.S. Distance Learning Assn.

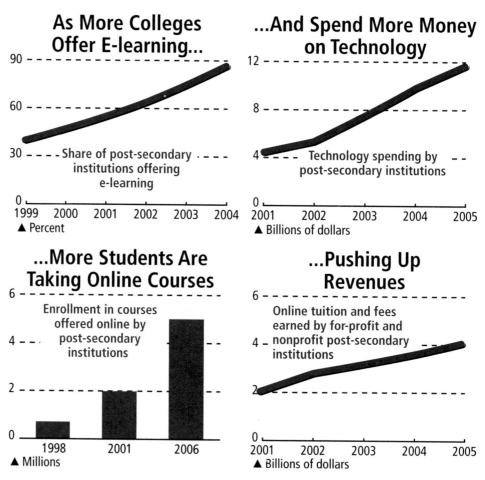

As More Colleges Offer E-learning...

Share of post-secondary institutions offering e-learning

▲ Percent

...And Spend More Money on Technology

Technology spending by post-secondary institutions

▲ Billions of dollars

...More Students Are Taking Online Courses

Enrollment in courses offered online by post-secondary institutions

▲ Millions

...Pushing Up Revenues

Online tuition and fees earned by for-profit and nonprofit post-secondary institutions

▲ Billions of dollars

6 million students take online classes from U.S. higher-ed institutions in 2007 according to John G. Flores, head of the U.S. Distance Learning Assn., a nonprofit trade group outside Boston. And it's not just a U.S. phenomenon: students from developing countries are jumping online, too.

14   These classes are opening new horizons for the fastest-growing segment of higher education: working adults, who often find it difficult to juggle conventional classes with jobs and families. Adults over 25 now represent nearly half of higher-ed students; most are employed and want more education to advance their careers.

15   E-learning is an influence in the traditional college class as well. Online classes won't replace the college experience for most 18- to 24-year-olds. But from the Massachusetts Institute of Technology to Wake Forest University in North Carolina, colleges are using the Web in on-campus classes to augment textbooks and boost communication.

16   There are still plenty of hurdles to clear before the e-learning world can take off. For one thing, most of the success is with established universities, like UMUC, which can leverage their brand names to reach out to working adults. The for-profit start-ups, by contrast, have struggled with accreditation and poor name recognition. Many have fallen by the wayside, including BigWords.com, an Amazon-like purveyor of textbooks, while only a handful make money, like UOP Online.

MASS MARKET?

17   Quality is a problem, which is a key reason why many online students drop out. That will force a further shakeout, eliminating mediocre players. Many colleges grapple with such issues as how much time their faculty should devote to e-teaching. And long-established rules make it difficult for online students to get financial aid. Even as these problems are resolved, "online learning will never be as good as face-to-face instruction," argues Andy DiPaolo, director of the Stanford Center for Professional Development, which offers online graduate classes to engineers.

18   Ultimately, the greatest e-learning market may lie in the developing world, where the population of college-age students is exploding. Just as cell phones leapfrogged land-based telephones in many developing countries, so may e-learning help to educate the masses in countries that lack the colleges to meet demand—and can't afford to build them.

ROAD WORK

19   Looking way out, as far as mid-century, e-learning could "become the environment in which the majority of human beings are educated beyond the secondary level," asserts University of Melbourne President Alan Gilbert. His school, along with Canada's McGill University and more than a dozen other universities, is part of U21 Global, a virtual university being created through a joint venture with textbook giant Thomson Learning. It aims to enroll 100,000 students by the decade's end, mostly in Asia.

20   Meanwhile, e-learning demand in the U.S. is rising, driven by higher education's changing demographics. Take Dr. Michael Kaner, a 43-year-old dentist in suburban Philadelphia who's halfway through adding a law degree to his credentials. Attending a night program at an area law school wasn't practical, he says, since it would have required 12 hours of commuting a week. So in 1999, Kaner signed up for Kaplan's Concord law program. Although the classes require 25 to 30 hours a week, there's no commute and he studies when it suits him. "This is the only way I could pursue a law degree," says Kaner, who hopes to build a part-time legal practice in dental issues.

21   Judy Rowe, who dropped out of college in the 1960s after running out of money, earned a bachelor's degree in psychology from UMUC last year while working as a flight attendant for American Airlines Inc. "I took my laptop with me and did my assignments on the road," says Rowe, who's now thinking about a second career in psychology.

COST-EFFECTIVE

22   E-learning is a good fit with the military, where frequent transfers complicate pursuing a degree. The U.S. Army awarded PWC Consulting a $453 million, five-year contract to

create an electronic university that allows soldiers to be anywhere and study at Kansas State University or any of the 24 colleges involved in the program.

23   eArmyU already has changed the perspective of soldiers like Sergeant Jeremy Dellinger, 22, who had been planning to leave the Army to go back to school when his basic enlistment ends. Then he enrolled in eArmyU to earn his bachelor's degree from Troy State University in Alabama. "Now I can get my degree and still do the work I love" as a supply sergeant, says the Fort Benning (Ga.)-based soldier. Like Dellinger, about 15% of those who have signed up so far have reenlisted or extended their commitment. By cutting turnover, "eArmyU could almost pay for itself," says program director Lee Harvey, since it costs nearly $70,000 to train green recruits.

24   Corporations, too, see e-learning as a cost-effective way to get better-educated employees. Indeed, corporate spending on e-learning is expected to more than quadruple by 2005, to $18 billion, estimates IDC. At IBM, some 200,000 employees received education or training online last year, and 75% of the company's Basic Blue class for new managers is online. The move cut IBM's training bill by $350 million last year, because online classes don't require travel.

25   Even as online higher-ed catches on, however, few private-sector providers are turning a profit. During the boom years, venture capitalists pumped some $5 billion into e-learning companies, says Adam Newman, a senior analyst at Eduventures.com. Roughly $1 billion went to companies that have already flamed out, he says. Beyond Phoenix, probably only half a dozen companies are making money now. Lack of name recognition is the biggest problem for companies like Capella, Jones International, and Cardean, UNext's virtual campus. And winning accreditation—crucial for attracting students—is tough going, too. It took Capella five years to make the grade; Jones waited four years. Concord's grads can sit for the California Bar Exam, but the American Bar Assn. still hasn't granted it accreditation.

CAUTIOUS ELITES

26   Phoenix Online aside, the big e-learning winners so far are the traditional nonprofit universities. They have captured nearly 95% of online enrollments, figures A. Frank Mayadas, head of e-learning grants at the Alfred P. Sloan Foundation. Most active are state and community colleges that started with strong brand names, a faculty, and accreditation, says Mayadas, as well as a tradition of extension programs.

27   By contrast, many elite universities have been far more cautious about diluting the value of their name. Harvard Business School believes it would be impossible to replicate its classroom education online. "We will never offer a Harvard MBA online," vows professor W. Earl Sasser, chairman of HBS Interactive, which instead develops e-learning programs for companies. MIT faculty nixed teaching classes online, fearing "it would detract from the residential experience," says former faculty chair Steven Lerman.

28   That didn't stop MIT from embracing the Internet in a different way. Over the next five years, MIT plans to post lecture notes and reading assignments for most of its 2,000 classes on the Web for free, calling the effort "OpenClassWare." Lerman says "it's a service to the world," but he says it's no substitute for actual teaching, so faculty aren't worried about a threat to classroom learning.

29   A few other top schools see profit-making opportunities. Since 1996, Duke University's Fuqua School of Business has been offering MBAs for working executives. In these blended programs, some 65% of the work is done online and Just 35% in classes held during required residencies that consume 9 to 11 weeks over two years. Duke charges up to $90,000 for these programs—vs. $60,000 for its traditional residential MBA. Yet they have been so popular that by next year, "we'll have more students in nontraditional programs than the

daytime program," says Fuqua Dean Douglas T. Breeden. The extra revenues are helping Fuqua to double its faculty.

The Adult Education Market

30   The adult education market is a significant and growing component of the post-secondary education market, which is estimated by the U.S. Department of Education to be a more than $275 billion industry. According to the U.S. Department of Education, over 6 million, or 40% of all students enrolled in higher education programs are over the age of 24. This number is projected to reach 6.7 million in 2011. The market for adult education in the U.S. is expected to increase as working adults seek additional education and training to update and improve their skills, to enhance their earnings potential, and to keep pace with the rapidly expanding knowledge-based economy.

31   Many working adults are seeking accredited degree programs that provide flexibility to accommodate the fixed schedules and time commitments associated with their professional and personal obligations. UOP's format since its inception has focused on working adult students by providing an accredited collegiate education that enables them to attend classes and complete classwork in a schedule and manner more convenient to the constraints their work life imposes on their ability to obtain a college or advanced degree. UOP has long felt that most colleges and universities as well as newer emerging technology-based education and training companies do not effectively address the unique requirements of working adult students. They often cite the following attributes of the traditional, not-for-profit education industry:

- Traditional universities and colleges were designed to fulfill the educational needs of conventional, full-time students aged 18 to 24, who remain the primary focus of these universities and colleges.
- This focus has resulted in a capital-intensive teaching/learning model in typical state and private colleges and universities that may be characterized by:
  - a high percentage of full-time tenured faculty with doctoral degrees;
  - fully-configured library facilities and related full-time staff;
  - dormitories, student unions, and other significant plant assets to support the needs of younger students;
  - often major investment in and commitment to comprehensive sports programs;
  - major administrative overhead for all the various university functions,
  - politically-based funding;
  - major resistance to change in any academic programs, even in the face of rapid global change across disciplines and professions;
  - an emphasis on research and the related staff and facilities; and
  - faculty with PhDs & a research focus but limited practical experience, even in key programs like business and other working-related professions.
- The majority of accredited colleges and universities continue to provide the bulk of their educational programming from September to mid-December and from mid-January to May. As a result, most full-time faculty members only teach during that limited period of time.
- While this structure serves the needs of the full-time 18- to 24-year-old student, it limits the educational opportunity for working adults who must delay their education for up to five months during these spring, summer, and winter breaks.
- Traditional universities and colleges are also limited in their ability to market to or provide the necessary customer service for working adult students because it requires the development of additional administrative and enrollment infrastructure.

THE APOLLO GROUP, INC.

32 The Apollo Group, Inc. [AGI] has provided higher education to working adults for over 30 years through its four subsidiaries listed below. They enrolled and served slightly over 275,000 students enrolled in 2005.

- **The University of Phoenix [UOP]**—the largest private university in the U.S. and source of the majority of the Apollo Group's revenue.
- **Institute for Professional Development**—provides adult-education program development and management consulting services to 23 regionally accredited private colleges and universities.
- **The College for Financial Planning Institutes**—one of the nation's leading providers of financial services education for individuals and corporations in the financial services industry.
- **Western International University**—adapts the Apollo model with younger professionals that seek individualized instruction through campuses in Arizona, and more recently China, India and the Netherlands.

33 Revenue during the last five fiscal years for the UOP versus the other three parts of The Apollo Group have almost tripled with combined revenues up 140% companywide. They were as follows the last five years [in $millions]:

	FY2006	FY2005	FY2004	FY2003	FY2002
Univ. of Phx	$2,075	$2,014	$1,697	$1,251	$ 931
Other 3 Schs	$ 402	$ 235	$ 97	$ 87	$ 78
Corporate	$ 1	$ 1	$ 4	$ 1	$ 0.2
	$2,478	$2,251	$1,798	$1,339	$ 1,009.2

34 The Apollo Group network spanned 101 campuses and 165 learning centers in 39 states and five other countries in 2007. UOP locations identified on its website were as follows in mid-2007:

The University of Phoenix Strategy

35 The University of Phoenix [UOP] strategy includes six key elements.

1. **Establish New University of Phoenix campuses and Learning Centers.** The University of Phoenix [UOP] plans to continue the addition of campuses and learning centers

throughout the United States and Canada. New locations are selected based on an analysis of various factors, including the population of working adults in the area, the number of local employers and their educational reimbursement policies, and the availability of similar programs offered by other institutions. Chairman Todd Nelson offered this comment relative to establishing new locations:

> Even after 30 years we are still in only 35 states. So we still have 15 states to go, including New York and Connecticut. And in many states there are multiple markets. So we probably easily have another 35 to 40 new markets to expand into in the U.S. Over the next ten years our plan is to have a physical campus not only in every state but also in every major U.S. metropolitan area.

2. **International Expansion.** The UOP believes that the international market for UOP's services is a major growth opportunity. The U.S. is the most common destination for international students studying abroad. They believe that more working adult students would opt for a U.S. education that does not involve living in the U.S. because they could do so without leaving their employment and incurring the high travel and living costs and stringent visa requirements associated with studying abroad. UOP's belief is supported by the fact that University of Phoenix Online has students located in approximately 75 countries despite having used only limited advertising. In addition, many U.S. residents live and work in foreign countries and would benefit from the opportunity to continue their education while abroad. UOP plans to offer the University of Phoenix educational model at physical campuses in international markets. The UOP now has a location in Juarez, Mexico, and expects a Mexico City campus soon. Its Western University operation has a location in China, India Dubai and the Netherlands from which AGI expects to expand into a UOP presence.

3. **Enhance Existing Educational Programs.** UOP's current enrollment by college is spread across eight core programs:

College of Undergraduate Business	41%
College of Graduate Business	18
College of Info Systems & Technology	11
College of Social & Behavioral Sciences	8
College of General & Professional Studies	8
College of Education	7
College of Health Sciences and Nursing	6
School of Advanced Studies	1
	100%

President Mueller notes several strengths he believes are underpinnings of these programs that the UOP works continuously to improve:

3a. **Accredited Degree Programs.** UOP currently offers 15 degree programs across these eight core program areas that are accredited by The Higher Learning Commission or the regional accrediting associations.

3b. **Experienced Faculty Resources.** While substantially all of UOP's faculty are working professionals, UOP requires each member of AGI's faculty to possess either a Masters or Doctoral degree and to have five years of recent professional experience in a field related to the subject they teach. UOP's classes are designed to be small, with an average of one instructor for every fifteen students. Faculty members are also required to be accessible to students by maintaining office hours. The UOP now claims to have over 17,500 instructors available on a regular basis with advanced degrees and currently working in relevant professional positions as well as having completed rigorous instructor training and evaluation programs to ensure the quality of their instruction content and approach.

3c. **Current and Relevant Standardized Programs.** UOP uses content experts selected from AGI's approximately 17,600 faculty to design UOP's curriculum. This enables UOP to offer current and relevant standardized programs to UOP's students.

3d. **Emphasize Input from Employers of UOP Students.** The employers of UOP's students often provide input to faculty members in designing curriculum, and class projects are typically based on issues relevant to the companies that employ AGI's students. AGI's classes are taught by a practitioner faculty that emphasizes the skills desired by employers. In addition, the time flexibility provided by AGI's classes further benefits employers since it avoids conflict with their employees' work schedules. A recent survey by University of Phoenix showed that approximately 60% of its students receive some level of tuition assistance from their employers. Two pedagogical innovations described below were developed at the UOP based on input from several major global companies and employers of UOP students seeking improvements on the realism in business course materials and greater options for incorporating both online and in-person learning. Pres. Mueller offered this comment:

> We consider the employers that provide tuition assistance to their employees through tuition reimbursement plans or direct bill arrangements UOP's secondary customers.

3e. **Pedagogical Innovations.** FlexNet® is one example of UOP adapting its means of delivering course material to accommodate different learner needs. Described earlier in this case, FlexNet® combines online and face-to-face instruction allowing any UOP student to choose among three approaches to receive course instruction and interaction. Virtual Organizations represent another innovation—six composite businesses, schools, health care and government organizations that have been developed as learning tools by subject matter experts and professionals in those fields. These virtual organizations allow UOP students and their instructors to immerse them inside virtual real-world settings to include Internet and intranet sites to provide a more realistic form of experiential learning than case studies and simulations while also fostering critical thinking and resourcefulness as the students engage the virtual organization learning experience.

3f. **Small class-size with quality instructor contact.** The UOP has long sought to overcome the "diploma mill" perception long associated with non-tradition collegiate education by structuring quality instruction into its daily approach. One way this has steadily paid off and separated UOP from that perception has been through having every class remain small. The UOP has recently allowed its average online course to increase in size from 10 to 12 students. The average on-ground class has gone from 14 students to 15 students. President Mueller offered these recent observations on this cornerstone aspect of the UOP strategy:

> Yes, we've take the average class size from 10 to 12 online, and 14 to 15 on-ground. That has actually reduced instructional costs because of our overall size. We will never have large classes compared to other universities. A classroom environment with 20 students or less, like we offer, is better than a strategy class with 50 students or a lecture class with 200 students like most public universities offer. At the UOP we know that a good education means students need access to their faculty, easily.

And he went on to suggest that the acid test for quality of UOP instruction versus other non-traditional universities or even traditional universities can be measured by students' employers willingness to reimburse for taking UOP classes:

> This is a free-market economy. If we don't provide value, the companies that are reimbursing students [to take UOP courses] are not going to pay. We are not seeing any deterioration in this area. Rather, we are seeing just the opposite.

3g. **Offer a Low Cost Advantage.** UOP's tuition is running about $10,000 annually, for a full load. It is increasing at an average 4%–5% annually. The average traditional university tuition is running about $15–$20,000 annually, and increasing approximately 10% annually. The variance is even more pronounced for graduate programs, where an MBA, for example, costs slightly over $12,500 at UOP versus an average $28,000 nationwide.

4. **Expand Educational Programs.** UOP regularly evaluates and responds to the changing educational needs of working adults and their employers by introducing new undergraduate and graduate degree programs as well as training programs. To its degree offerings, University of Phoenix recently added the Master of Business Administration in Health Care Management and specializations in Marketing and Human Resources Management to its Master of Business Administration; specializations in Elementary and Secondary Education and Adult Education and Distance Learning to its Master of Arts in Education; and a specialization in Educational Counseling to its Master of Counseling. To its certificate programs, University of Phoenix has recently added graduate certificates in e-Business, Technology Management, and Global Management, as well as a certificate in Operations and Supply Chain Management. UOP believes that expanding its program offerings will help it improve UOP's market position as a provider of higher education and training for working adults.

President Mueller made this observation regarding new courses and degrees UOP may add soon:

We always have new programs being developed. Criminal justice is a big area of growth. Engineering is a possibility. And some new nursing programs—for registered nurses and licensed practical nurses—are a possibility in 2007.

5. **Serve a Broader Student Age Group.** The UOP has built tremendous success focusing on the working adult student population in the U.S. Based on recent surveys of incoming students, the average age of University of Phoenix's students is in the midthirties, approximately 54% are women and 46% are men. Approximately 67% of University of Phoenix's students have been employed on a full-time basis for nine years or more. The approximate age percentage distribution of incoming UOP students is:

Age	Percentage of Students
25 and under	16.5%
26 to 33	38.0%
34 to 45	34.7%
46 and over	10.8%
	100.0%

Recently, the UOP has adapted this focus and initiated a conscious effort to direct more attention to younger students, to include targeting high school students as they make decisions to consider college. President Mueller offered these comments about this new emphasis at UOP on the traditional collegiate market of 18- to 22-year-old students:

If you look at the higher education market, at least half your students are in this [18- to 22-year-old] age group, and over the next decade, this will be the fastest area of growth. Also, we've had literally tens of thousands of 18- to 22-year-olds who have shown interest. We're not going to add dormitories. We're not after the traditional younger student [who goes off to live at college]. We're going after the younger student who is working. And they have similar needs to [our working adult students], including the flexibility of classes that can start any time of the day, evening or weekend.

6. **Market Aggressively.** The Apollo Group spent $545 million in the last fiscal year marketing its academic programs, mostly the UOP. This is a staggering amount when you consider that few traditional universities spend even close $10 million in direct marketing expenditures. Yet Apollo's earnings almost doubled since 2003 and revenue grew by over 90% during the same period.

Barmak Nasirian, associate director of the American Association of Collegiate Registrars and Admissions Officers, warns: "This rate of growth may not be sustainable." His group represent traditional colleges, many of which are critical of Apollo and the UOP. President Mueller at the Apollo Group offered this observation:

> We had enrollment growth, so you would have expected marketing costs to rise comparably. Two things are behind the increase. First, the cost of leads are more expensive. And second, because we were having a good year financially, we felt it was wise to spend aggressively in the marketing area.

The Apollo Group Looks to the Future

36   The Apollo Group's reputation was sullied in late 2005 with the release of a U.S. Education Dept. report depicting a high-pressure sales culture at the UOP that resembled a telemarketing boiler room more than a university admissions office. "Phoenix recruiters soon find out that UOP bases their salaries solely on the number of students they recruit," the report charged. That's prohibited by federal law. One recruiter who started at $28,000, for instance, was bumped to $85,000 after recruiting 151 students in six months. But another who started at $28,000 got just a $4,000 raise after signing up 79 students. Websites like www.uopsucks. com have emerged as blog-like forums for former students and employees unhappy with or distrustful of the UOP's offerings.

37   Ultimately, such violations could have led the government to bar Phoenix from the federal student loan program, crippling the university. Former CEO Nelson called the report "very misleading and full of inaccuracies." But he says he decided to settle rather than wage a protracted legal fight. The Apollo Group agreed to change its compensation system and pay a $9.8 million fine without admitting guilt. Still, Apollo's defenders note that the point of the law is to prevent for-profits from luring unqualified students. If the UOP is doing that, it hasn't showed up in student-loan default rates, which remain a low 6%—below the average for traditional colleges and universities.

38   With the regulators off its back, and with tuition growth surging 30% during the quarter following the release of the report, the UOP once again focused on growth. The online program, with approximately 150,000 students, was seen as far from saturated. And for the first time the UOP started targeting high school graduates, who are expected to hit a record later this decade as a "baby boomer echo" factor. Similarly, the UOP has barely begun to scratch the international market, where experts see huge demand for U.S.-style education. Phoenix opened its first Mexican campus in 2005, and has big hopes for China, where Apollo's Western International University now has just 50 students, and India.

39   But the UOP will have to fill acres of classroom seats to keep up its pace—and it is paying an ever-increasing cost to do so. The company already has over 270,000 students. Some 90% of those are enrolled at the University of Phoenix, making it by far the nation's largest private university. Given that size, it had to add nearly 57,000 students—the equivalent of another University of Texas at Austin—in 12 months just to make its growth target. And that has proven very difficult to accomplish at Apollo since it experienced successively lower enrollment growth for nine straight quarters through Q1, 2007. Adding to these problems has been an SEC investigation of stock option grant irregularities in late 2006 that have resulted in a restatement of financial statements to be completed in 2007.

40   "Since early 2007 we have focused on making significant changes in two major areas of our business: marketing and retention," said President Mueller. "Much of the work required to launch our marketing and branding efforts is complete and we are already seeing evidence of its effectiveness." Mueller added that retention and academic strategies take longer to implement, but that he's confident that investments in such improvements will benefit students and stockholders in the long run.

Acquisition Activity

41   Mueller and the Apollo Group may see other ways to grow student counts. In early 2007 Apollo announced the acquisition of Insight Schools, a company that runs online charter schools in Washington state, for $15 million. Competitor Kaplan followed several months later with the acquisition of Sagemont Virtual, a company that runs the University of Miami Online High School. Apollo's entry into high schools began in 2005 when it formed a partnership with Orange Lutheran High School in California. It converted many of the school's courses so they could be delivered in an online format, a move that was embraced by the school's students and faculty, according to Mueller. "We became convinced we could provide that service to high school students, and it would have the same kind of value educationally—if not greater—at the high school level than even at the higher educational level," said Mueller. That sounds quite familiar to the start founder John Sperling engineered over thirty years ago.

42   About 700,000 public pre-collegiate students were enrolled in at least one online or blended course in 2007. Online high school courses are becoming popular with states with large rural areas and those seeking to expand both high level offerings as well as special course offerings. Some analysts think an educational setting with 50 million high school students might well be attractive as a growth vector when compared to a mature higher education market, domestically, with about 15 million students.

43   And, when you consider the number of high school aged students worldwide, and the special delivery needs in needy areas that online options may assist, you have to wonder if this may be a major new trend. Then, too, if a high schooler gets comfortable with an online approach, that may well feed directly into an online higher educational choice. Meanwhile, Barbara Stein, manager of 21st century education at the National Education Assn., is concerned that students who attend virtual high schools may be loosing out on the benefits of a traditional high school experience. "We think those are not a great idea. Most students do not do that well when they have no face-to-face interactions," says Stein. "There may be extreme situations where that is the appropriate recourse, but for most students it is not."

APPENDIX A   Guide to Online Universities
As e-learning has exploded, here is a brief look at the range of providers:

1. University of Maryland University College

The largest state university provider of online classes, it moved online in the mid-90s, building on its long heritage of offering extension classes. Last year, enrollments in its online classes hit 63,000, up 50% in one year. Students can now earn 70 different degrees and certificates online. In addition to classes, UMUC provides a comprehensive array of online student services, from applications to academic advising and financial aid consulting.

COST: Same as for UMUC's traditional classroom classes. That means Maryland residents are charged just $197 per semester hour for undergrad classes, and $301 per semester for graduate classes. But out-of-state residents must pay over 50% more.

2. University of Phoenix Online

The nation's largest for-profit virtual university, offering the same kind of business, education and technical classes for working adults that have made its bricks-and-mortar counterpart, the University of Phoenix, such a success. In business, students may earn everything from undergraduate degrees in accounting, management and marketing to an MBA and even a Doctor of Management in Organizational Leadership. Phoenix Online provides lots of attention to its students. Classes are kept small, and instructors insist on participation.

COST: $400 to $500 per credit; an MBA degree costs about $23,000.

3. eArmyU (The U.S. Army's Virtual University)

Since January, eArmyU has allowed enlisted soldiers to take classes and earn degrees from 24 different institutions, ranging from Central Texas College to Utah State. So far, 10,400 soldiers have signed up on the three Army bases where it's offered. The plan is to offer it Army-wide by 2003.

COST: Free to soldiers, who receive a laptop, printer, Internet connection and 100% of tuition. Civilians are not eligible for eArmy.

4. Western Governors University

Virtual university founded by 19 western states in 1997. A pioneer in "competency-based degrees," which require students to demonstrate mastery of a subject, rather than complete a certain number of credit hours. In practice, this means students are assessed when they enter a program. An individual class of study is then developed for each student to fill the gaps in their knowledge. The result is that the length of time needed to complete a degree varies widely, and is dependent on what the student knows. While it may sound radical, WGU is backed by some two-dozen corporate sponsors, including IBM, AOL and Microsoft.

COST: WGU charges about $4500 for the assessment and mentoring needed for a two-year degree. Students must pay separately for classes, which are offered by some 40 different institutions.

5. Concord Law School

Launched by Kaplan Inc., a unit of the Washington Post Co, Concord has grown to become the nation's largest virtual law school, with 800 students at present. Kaplan argues that the law is ideally suited to online learning, because it facilitates communication (via e-mail) among students and professors. While the program is not yet accredited by the American Bar Association, students may sit for the California Bar Exam.

COST: $6,000 per year, or $24,000 for four-year law degree.

6. Duke's Fuqua School of Business

"Blended" MBA programs for working executives, in which 65% of the work is done over the Net, and 35% in classes that meet for 9 or 11 weeks during 20-month programs. There are two blended programs. The "Global Executive" program is designed for executives who manage a large international business unit or a global staff. The average global student has 14 years of professional experience. In contrast, the "Cross Continent" program is aimed at more junior managers—with an average of six years of experience—who have already demonstrated success at the department level.

COST: Up to $90,000 for "Global Executive" program, versus $60,000 for normal daytime MBA. The extra costs cover the residential program, which in the case of Global Executive is held in various spots around the world, including Europe, Asia and the Duke campus.

APPENDIX A   Guide to Online Universities—continued
As e-learning has exploded, here is a brief look at the range of providers:

7. Cardean University

The virtual university founded by UNext.com, one of the highest profile e-learning start-ups. UNext partnered with some of the world's best known universities—including Stanford, the University of Chicago and Columbia—to develop its cutting edge Business curriculum. It is now offering classes to employees of General Motors and a number of other companies, and will shortly begin marketing its Business classes to consumers.

COST: About $25,000 for MBA.

8. Jones International University

The virtual university founded in 1993 by cable pioneer Glenn R. Jones, who earlier offered distance classes via cable TV through his Mind Extension University. Jones offers more than 40 executive and professional education programs. Students may earn a bachelor's degree in business, an MBA, as well as various masters' degrees in education.

COST: 3-credit class runs $925; MBA costs about $12,000.

9. Capella University

A for-profit virtual university that offers some 500 online classes every quarter. Students may choose from 15 different degree programs, and some 80 different specializations. Most of the 4,000 students study business, education or information technology.

COST: Classes (which offer 3 to 5 credits) tend to cost from $1150 to $1600. A master's degree runs about $20,000, and a Ph.D. about $34,000.

10. Walden University

Originally founded in 1970 to offer graduate degrees, Walden moved online in the mid-1990s. Walden is 41% owned by Sylvan Learning Systems, which has other online education programs as well. Walden specializes in graduate programs in business, education, psychology, public health and human services.

COST: An MBA runs about $20,000, while a PhD can cost $47,000.

11. The Electronic campus of the Southern Regional Education Board

A sweeping smorgasbord of online classes organized by the Southern Regional Education Board, an organization formed to promote education reform in 16 southern states. The electronic campus offers over 5,000 online classes from 325 different schools, ranging from Auburn University to West Virginia University.

COST: Tuition varies widely, since it is set by the college that actually offers a given class. As one example, a class on American History since 1865 offered by Oklahoma State costs $365.

12. Harvard Extension School

Your best chance to take an online class from Harvard, these classes are offered by Harvard's extension school. While the Harvard Extension School currently offers over 500 classes in the traditional classroom setting, only about three dozen are currently available online. However, the plan is to expand the number of online offerings. Most of the classes available this year are computer science classes, on topics like website development and algorithms.

COST: Same as for attending a class at the extension school. The cost ranges from $275 for a class on American Constitutional History taken without credit, to $1,750 for the class on website development.

13. UT TelecampUS

An excellent example of the expanding e-learning programs offered by state university systems, the UT TelecampUS was launched in 1998 by the University of Texas system. Students may earn an MBA, Masters in Computer Science, and various other online degrees from a school within the UT system. Students who wish to earn a degree must first apply and be admitted to one of the universities in the UT system. That campus will then serve as the student's "home" campus, and ultimately award the degree.

COST: Texas residents pay about $300 for a 3-credit undergraduate class, and $500 for a 3-credit graduate class. Non-residents are charged roughly twice as much.

APPENDIX A   Guide to Online Universities—continued
As e-learning has exploded, here is a brief look at the range of providers:

14. Stanford Center for Professional Development

One of the most challenging and prestigious online programs. The Stanford Center offers both online degrees and non-degree classes from Stanford's School of Engineering and affiliated departments. The center now provides over 250 online credit classes in electrical engineering, mechanical engineering, computer science, etc. These are not watered down classes. They are taught by the Stanford faculty, and students must be admitted, just like on-campus students. The online classes are designed strictly for employed engineers and scientists. The attraction is that they may keep working, while furthering their education.

COST: About $3,000 for a credit class, 40% more than it would cost to take a similar class on campus. Typically, the companies employing the students pick up the tab.

APPENDIX B   Apollo Group Financial Information

	August 31,				
	2006	**2005**	**2004**	**2003**	**2002**
			Restated(1)		
Revenues:					
Tuition and other, net	$2,477,533	$2,251,114	$1,800,047	$1,338,982	$1,007,936
Costs and expenses:					
Instructional costs and services	1,112,660	956,631	781,437	630,566	531,332
Selling and promotional	544,706	485,451	383,800	272,348	198,889
General and administrative	149,928	94,485	84,326	61,314	54,388
Goodwill impairment	20,205	—	—	—	—
Share based compensation(2)	—	16,895	100,283	—	—
Total costs and expenses	1,827,499	1,553,462	1,349,846	964,228	784,609
Income from operations	650,034	697,652	450,201	374,754	223,327
Interest income and other, net	18,054	16,787	16,305	14,238	11,181
Income before income taxes	668,088	714,439	466,506	388,992	234,508
Provision for income taxes	253,255	286,506	186,421	153,109	99,107
Net income	$ 414,833	$ 427,933	$ 280,085	$ 235,883	$ 135,401

(1) See Note 3, "Restatement of Consolidated Financial Statements" included in Item 8 of this Form 10-K.
(2) Share based compensation in 2005 and 2004 is related to the 2004 conversion of the UPX Online stock options into Apollo Group Class A stock options. Share based compensation expense resulting from the revised measurement dates is included in instructional costs and services, selling and promotional, and general and administrative expenses.

	August 31,				
	2006	**2005**	**2004**	**2003**	**2002**
			Restated(1)		
Total cash, cash equivalents, restricted cash and securities, and marketable securities	$ 646,995	$ 685,748	$ 993,875	$1,045,802	$ 688,656
Total assets	$1,283,005	$1,281,548	$1,487,750	$1,417,388	$1,018,659
Current liabilities	$ 595,756	$ 566,745	$ 525,239	$ 384,520	$ 297,632
Long-term liabilities	82,876	80,583	67,546	48,072	44,562
Total shareholders' equity	604,373	634,220	894,965	984,796	676,465
Total liabilities and shareholders' equity	$1,283,005	$1,281,548	$1,487,750	$1,417,388	$1,018,659
Operating Statistics:					
Degreed enrollments at end of year(2)	282,300	271,400	238,400	189,800	144,400
Number of locations at end of year:					
Campuses	99	90	82	71	65
Learning centers	163	154	137	121	111
Total number of locations	262	244	219	192	176

(1) See Note 3, "Restatement of Consolidated Financial Statements" included in Item 8 of this Form 10-K.
(2) Restated Degreed Enrollments includes only UPX and Axia College and represent individual students enrolled in our degree programs that attended a course during the quarter and did not graduate as of the end of the quarter (including Axia students enrolled in UPX and WIU). Previously, the Company used a different definition of enrollment. Previously reported enrollment numbers are restated above.

The following table presents the most significant components as percentages of total tuition and other, net revenue for the years ended August 31, 2006, 2005 and 2004:

	Year Ended August 31,					
	2006		**2005**		**2004**	
			Restated(1)		**Restated(1)**	
($ in millions)						
Tuition revenue	$2,304.3	93.0%	$2,114.1	93.9%	$1,679.0	93.3%
IPD services revenue	74.4	3.0%	69.5	3.1%	62.6	3.5%
Application and related fees	33.8	1.4%	36.4	1.6%	28.7	1.6%
Online course material revenue	138.7	5.6%	104.5	4.6%	69.1	3.8%
Other revenue	31.7	1.3%	33.8	1.5%	23.0	1.3%
Tuition and other revenue, gross	2,582.9	104.3%	2,358.3	104.7%	1,862.4	103.5%
Less: Discounts	(105.4)	(4.3)%	(107.2)	(4.7)%	(62.4)	(3.5)%
Tuition and other revenue, net	$2,477.5	100.0%	$2,251.1	100.0%	$1,800.0	100.0%

Information about our tuition and other net revenues by reportable segment on a percentage basis is as follows:

	Year Ended August 31,		
	2006	**2005**	**2004**
UPX	83.7%	89.5%	94.4%
Other Schools	16.2%	10.4%	5.4%
Corporate	0.1%	0.1%	0.2%
Tuition and other, net	100.0%	100.0%	100.0%

Instructional costs and services increased by 16.3% in 2006 versus 2005, and 22.4% in 2005 versus 2004. The following table sets forth the increases in significant components of instructional costs and services:

	Year Ended August 31,			% of Revenues Year Ended August 31,			% Change 2006 vs.	% Change 2005 vs.
	2006	2005	2004	2006	2005	2004	2005	2004
			Restated (1)			Restated (1)		Restated (1)
($ in millions)								
Employee compensation and related expenses	$ 382.3	$343.9	$282.5	15.4%	15.3%	15.7%	11.2%	21.7%
Faculty compensation	212.3	195.1	154.2	8.6%	8.7%	8.6%	8.8%	26.5%
Classroom lease expenses and depreciation	193.4	171.3	145.1	7.8%	7.6%	8.1%	12.9%	18.1%
Other instructional costs and services	158.2	142.0	122.3	6.4%	6.3%	6.8%	11.4%	16.1%
Bad debt expense	101.6	57.2	31.1	4.1%	2.5%	1.7%	77.6%	83.9%
Financial aid processing costs	52.5	43.3	32.4	2.1%	1.9%	1.8%	21.2%	33.6%
Share based compensation	12.4	3.8	4.0	0.5%	0.2%	0.2%	226.3%	(5.0)%
U.S. Department of Education settlement	—	—	9.8	N/A	N/A	0.5%	N/A	N/A
Instructional costs and services	$1,112.7	$956.6	$781.4	44.9%	42.5%	43.4%	16.3%	22.4%

(1) See Note 3, "Retatement of Consolidated Financial Statements," included in Item 8 of this Form 10-K.

Selling and promotional expenses increased by 12.2% in 2006 versus 2005, and 26.5% in 2005 versus 2004. The following table sets forth the increases in significant components of selling and promotional expenses:

	Year Ended August 31,			% of Revenues Year Ended August 31,			% Change 2006 vs.	% Change 2005 vs.
	2006	2005	2004	2006	2005	2004	2005	2004
			Restated (1)			Restated (1)		Restated (1)
($ in millions)								
Enrollment advisors' compensation and related expenses	$254.3	$204.6	$155.6	10.3%	9.1%	8.6%	24.3%	31.5%
Advertising	231.6	224.0	174.6	9.3%	10.0%	9.7%	3.4%	28.3%
Other selling and promotional expenses	56.5	56.2	52.9	2.3%	2.5%	2.9%	0.5%	6.2%
Share based compensation	2.3	0.6	0.7	0.1%	0.0%	0.1%	283.3%	(14.3)%
Selling and promotional expenses	$544.7	$485.4	$383.8	22.0%	21.6%	21.3%	12.2%	26.5%

(1) See Note 3, "Retatement of Consolidated Financial Statements," included in Item 8 of this Form 10-K.

Summary financial information by reportable segment is as follows:

	Year Ended August 31,		
	2006	2005	2004
		Restated	Restated
($ in thousands)			
Tuition and other revenue, net			
UPX	$2,074,443	$2,014,124	$1,699,005
Other Schools	402,051	235,183	96,982
Corporate	1,039	1,807	4,060
Total tuition and other revenue, net	2,477,533	$2,251,114	$1,800,047
Income from operations:			
UPX	605,708	$ 636,463	$ 478,639
Other Schools	65,790	70,417	15,665
Corporate/Eliminations	(21,464)	(9,228)	(44,103)
	650,034	697,652	450,201
Reconciling items:			
Interest income and other, net	18,054	16,787	16,305
Income before income taxes	$ 668,088	$ 714,439	$ 466,506

Case 46

Tiffany & Co.: *A Specialty Fine Jewelry Retailer*
Anne Orji, Marc E. Gartenfeld, Dorothy Dologite, and Robert J. Mockler

INTRODUCTION

1   On January 31, 2003, Tiffany & Co. (commonly known as Tiffany) announced that William R. Chaney would retire as Chairman of the Board, but would continue to serve on Tiffany's Board of Directors. Michael J. Kowalski would assume the role of Chairman of the Board and continue as Chief Executive Officer (CEO). As CEO, Michael J. Kowalski faced the continuing pressures as CEO to implement strategies that would better position Tiffany and continue to create long-term shareholder value in an increasingly competitive environment. In such leadership roles, he faced the pressures of developing an effective differentiating enterprise-wide strategy for Tiffany if the company was to survive and prosper against growing global competition over the intermediate and long term future as the world's premier luxury brand of fine jewelry [Tiffany & Co., 2001].

2   Fine jewelry is known for its quality, craftsmanship, value, price, and brand. Its quality is nearly perfect with minimal flaws. The craftsmanship is characterized by excellence since time and patience are required to create each fine jewelry piece. The value is determined by the fine jewelry's quality and craftsmanship. If these criteria are strong and superior, then the value is strong. The prices of fine jewelry are usually high because of its quality, craftsmanship, and value attributes. Fine jewelry brands are well known since they offer the highest standard.

3   Tiffany is a retailer, designer, manufacturer and distributor of luxury fine jewelry. As of January 31, 2002, Tiffany had 44 company-operated stores in the United States and 82 company-operated international stores. Jewelry represented approximately 79% of their net sales in 2001 followed by 6% for tableware and 4% for timepieces with all other categories aggregating 11%. Tiffany had jewelry designs sold under the Tiffany brand and exclusively at company-operated stores, online or via catalog. In 2003, Tiffany has the following fine jewelry collections:

> 1837, Atlas, Elsa Peretti, Etoile, Garland, Paloma Picasso, Return to Tiffany, Schlumberger, The Tiffany Mark, Tiffany Biscayne, Tiffany Bubbles, Tiffany Lace, Tiffany Pearls and Tiffany Roundel [Tiffany & Co. Website, 2003].

4   In addition to the United States, Tiffany had stores in Canada, Mexico, Brazil, England, France, Germany, Italy, Switzerland, Australia, China, Guam, Hong Kong, Japan, Korea, Malaysia, Singapore, and Taiwan. The United States represented approximately 59% of Tiffany's net sales. Its international presence brought in net sales of 28% from Japan, 6% from other Asia-Pacific countries, 4% from Europe with the remainder from Canada, Latin America and the Middle East in 2001. However, its international presence produced less than 42% of net sales even though the number of company-operated stores outside the United States was nearly double the number of United States stores [Tiffany & Co. Website, 2003].

5   With international stores nearly doubling the number of domestic stores, but producing less net sales, Tiffany had to incorporate into its enterprise-wide strategy ways to increase its international net sales. One way was to explore developing potential overseas markets.

This case was prepared by Anne Orji, Marc E. Gartenfeld, Dorothy Dologite, and Professor Robert J. Mockler of St. John's University. © Robert J. Mockler.

As China became a member of the World Trade Organization (WTO) in 2002, for example, every major organization in the fine jewelry industry positioned itself in the emerging fine jewelry trade in China. China's membership to the WTO has opened an opportunity for the fine jewelers both because of its growing consumer market and because it has low cost production for custom work and fine craftsmanship [Gomelsky, 2003]. Tiffany tried to capitalize on the market share by establishing one company-operated store, in December 2001, at The Palace Hotel in Beijing, China. It was also to accommodate for the growing tend in high-end luxury brands desired by the Chinese economies with sales growing during 2000 and 2001. However, Tiffany quickly realized that it takes more than just one company-operated store to be successful in the promising fine jewelry market of China, as well as in other potentially strong markets such as Brazil and Canada.

6   Besides China, Brazil was also a potential market because the fine jewelry industry was growing due to lower design and operation costs. This caused fine jewelers to migrate to Brazil and position themselves in the growing market to utilize the low costs. Tiffany opened a company-operated store in San Paolo, Brazil where it was able to tap the market's potential to help increase net sales. However, similar to the case in China, Tiffany needed to do more than just open one company-operated store there.

7   Canada is another growing market in the fine jewelry industry because of the growing popularity of diamonds. Most of the thriving diamond industry and diamond mines are in this area. Fine jewelers were looking to be the first to monopolize market share in Canada by investing in Canadian diamond mines. Being a pioneer in the fine jewelry industry by investing in diamond mines, was expected to help hold a specialty fine jeweler's diamond holdings and help streamline its sourcing process. As a result of larger holdings of diamonds, this generally also meant a larger portion of the market share could be obtained [Gomelsky, 2003].

8   As Tiffany started to make its way into potential overseas markets, its competitors' proactive efforts in expansion and innovation became increasingly aggressive in those potential markets, as well as in the existing markets. Tiffany's competitors' aggressiveness in the industry was taking a toll on Tiffany's stock price. Tiffany had to increase its stock price and maximize shareholder profits because as shown in Figure 1, Tiffany's stock price had dramatically declined to a price of $23.06 per share as of March 2003 from a high of $41.38 per share back in January 2003. This decline was attributed to factors such as increased competition, economic recession post September 11th, and most recently, severe acute

FIGURE 1
Tiffany & Co.
5-Year Stock Price

Source: Hoover's Online (2003B). "Tiffany & Co. 5 Year Quote". [Online]. *http://quotes. hoovers.com/thomson/chart. html?p=&t=TIF&n=Tiffany+% 26+Co.&e=NYSE&c=11481& templ=4&frame=5+Year& index=&ticker=TIF&threed= 2&x=5&y=7.* Accessed February 25.

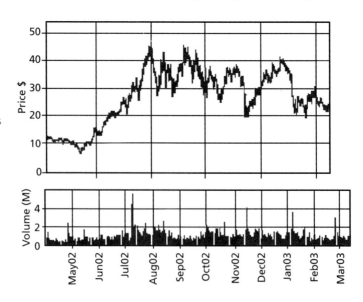

respiratory syndrome (SARS). The SARS epidemic affected retail sales from tourists since many people were hesitant to travel.

9   In light of these internal problems and increasing competition, the strategic question that Tiffany needed to resolve is how to expand on its product designs, customer base, manufacturing operations, retail stores, and international presence while enhancing, not hurting, its brand image. In doing this, Tiffany's most important focus of strategic concern was how to differentiate itself from its competitors in the global arena, and ultimately achieve a winning edge over its competitors in the immediate, intermediate, and long-term time periods.

INDUSTRY & COMPETITIVE MARKET: RETAIL INDUSTRY

10   Retailing involves the selling of products and services to consumers for their personal, family, or household use [Harris, 2002]. It encompasses both durable (expected to last at least three years) and non-durable consumer goods. As shown in Figure 2, this can be further divided into two categories: general retailers that include department stores, discount stores, warehouse clubs and variety stores, and specialty stores that include apparel stores, office supply stores, consumer electronic stores, beauty supply stores, food stores, toy stores, home furnishing stores, sports equipment stores, building material stores, auto stores, and jewelry stores [WetFeet, 2003].

11   For many retailers, 2001 was a difficult year. Due to the economic challenges after the tragic events of September 11th, many retailers did not meet their forecasted numbers. The economic recession caused by September 11th was not only affecting retail sales in the United States, but affecting international sales as well. Sales from tourists declined since many people did not want to travel.

12   In 2003, many retailers, such as Wal-Mart and many department stores, reported lower than expected sales in February due to the inclement weather conditions [Standard & Poor's Online, 2003]. As retailers faced challenges from the economy, competitors, technology, the weather, and the like, they constantly explored strategic ways to remain ahead of the competition and to overcome business market difficulties.

FIGURE 2   **Retail Industry**

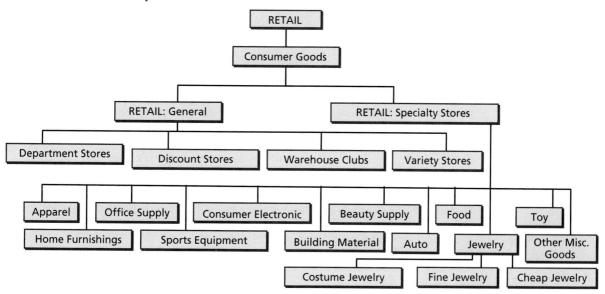

Consumer Goods

13   Consumer goods are goods purchased by an individual for personal, family, or household purposes. It can be either a durable good or a non-durable good purchased at general retail stores or specialty retail stores.

Retail: General

14   General retailers include department stores, discount stores, warehouse clubs and variety stores. These stores sell a variety of consumer goods and general merchandise lines with limited inventory. Cheap jewelry and costume jewelry are sold at these general retail stores, as well as through specialty retail stores. Wal-Mart Stores with over $2 billion in jewelry sales in 2000 was the nation's largest jewelry retailer [Vargas, 2001].

15   The quality, craftsmanship, value, price, and brand of cheap jewelry are lower in general retail stores and cheap jewelry stores than at fine jewelry stores. The quality of cheap jewelry is poor because it has imperfections, flaws, and is slightly irregular. The craftsmanship of cheap jewelry is also poor since the designs are not intricate and plated gold may be used. The quality and craftsmanship, together, determine the value and the price of the item. If the quality and craftsmanship are poor, the value will be poor and the price will be low. An example of a cheap jewelry store is Treasure Palace in New York. A detailed definition of costume jewelry, fine jewelry, and cheap jewelry is given in the following pages.

16   *Department Stores*   Major department stores include Macy's (Federated Department Stores), JC Penney and Sears. Department stores consisted of units mainly engaged in a significant proportion of retail sales in commodities. Examples of commodities include furniture, soft goods, clothing, footwear, leather goods, glassware, porcelain, housewares, watches, perfumes, cosmetics, electronics, and household appliances.

17   The market share of many department stores has eroded over the past decade because of competition from discount stores, like Wal-Mart and Target, and specialty stores. Department stores, such as Abraham & Strauss and Alexander's have, in the past, filed Chapter 11 due to the intense competition [Ernst & Young, 2002].

18   *Discount Stores*   Discount stores, such as Wal-Mart, K-Mart and Target, offer low prices. They convey the image of high-volume, fast turnover outlet selling a variety of merchandise at very competitive prices [U.S. Census Bureau, 1992]. Discount stores have taken business away from many department stores and specialty retailers. The reason for this is because the slow economy pushes consumers toward spending less, even though department stores and specialty retailers offer a better selection compared to discount stores. Wal-Mart, a discount store, is the nation's largest jewelry retailer for cheap jewelry, and is known for its exceptional customer service and low prices.

19   *Warehouse Clubs*   Warehouse clubs are also known as membership warehouse clubs. They include BJ's, Costco, and Sam's Club. Warehouse clubs engage in the retail sale of general lines of merchandise such as groceries, automotive tires, batteries, parts and accessories, audio and video equipment, household appliances, office equipment and supplies, jewelry, apparel, and books through warehouse-based operations. Today's warehouse clubs are a $70 billion industry in the US. With an annual growth rate of about 10%, warehouse clubs are expanding at twice the rate of retail sales in general [Hoovers Online, 2003A].

20   *Variety Stores*   Variety stores are primarily engaged in the retail sale of a variety of merchandise in the low and popular price ranges. An example of a variety store is Woolworth's. Sales usually are made on a cash-and-carry basis. The stores do not carry a complete line of merchandise, are not departmentalized, and do not deliver.

Retail: Specialty

21   Specialty retailers are businesses selling a distinct product category. Specialty retailers include apparel stores, office supply stores, consumer electronic stores, beauty supply

stores, food stores, toy stores, home furnishing stores, sports equipment stores, building material stores, auto stores, and jewelry stores.

22   Specialty stores focus on customer needs and cater to that specific category of need. With their large variety and selection in that category, they are able to offer more to a customer in that category than if a customer went to a general retail store where the selection is limited in each category. The knowledge of the sales staff and various designs that specialty stores offer is another reason why customers enjoy shopping at specialty stores.

23   Sales in specialty stores were flat during the 2002 holiday sales. This means that sales were about the same in specialty stores as in 2001 comparing November and December figures for both years. The biggest sales increase came from home furnishings and furniture with an increase of 7.4%, while music, video and home entertainment showed the greatest decline in sales of 8.1%. This was attributed to a soft employment market and nagging geopolitical concerns according to Michael Baker, the Director of Research for the International Council of Shopping Centers [The Business Journal-Tampa Bay, 2003].

24   *Apparel Stores*   These retail stores sell clothing and accessories for men, women and children. For example, H&M and the Gap are specialty apparel stores that sell clothing and accessories for men, women and children with a large selection of products in each product category.

25   *Home Furnishing/Furniture Stores*   These retail stores sell goods used for furnishing the home. These goods include furniture, beds, springs, mattresses, floor covering, draperies, glass and chinaware, domestic stoves, refrigerators, and other household electric and gas appliances. Seaman's is an example of a major home furnishing/furniture store.

26   *Office Supply Stores*   These stores are engaged in selling office supplies and equipment to businesses and individuals. The main competitors in this category are Staples, Office Max, and Office Depot.

27   *Sports Equipment Stores*   Sporting equipment stores sell a general line of sporting goods and equipment for hunting, camping, fishing, skiing, riding, tennis, golf, basketball, baseball, gymnasium, and playground equipment. The main competitors in this category are Modell's, Sports Authority, and Princeton Ski Shops.

28   *Consumer Electronic Stores*   Consumer electronic stores are engaged in the sale of radios, television sets, compact disc players, record players, cameras, computers, computer peripheral equipment, hi-fi sound reproducing equipment, compact discs, digital video discs, and videos. The main competitors in this category are Circuit City, Best Buy, and The Wiz.

29   *Building Material Stores*   These stores sell lumber and a general line of building materials to the general public. These establishments may also sell to contractors in addition to the general public. Lumber includes rough and dressed lumber, flooring, molding, doors, sashes, frames and other millwork. Building materials include roofing, siding, shingles, wallboard, paint, brick, tile, cement, sand, gravel, and other building materials and supplies. Hardware is also included in the line of retail building materials and lumber that is sold in home centers. Most home centers, such as Home Depot and Lowes Home Improvement Centers, sell lumber, building materials, and hardware. In addition, these home centers sell at least 5 of the following merchandise lines: housewares, tools (power and hand), floor coverings, electrical supplies, kitchen cabinets, plumbing and bath supplies, lawn and garden products, paints and/or sundries, windows and/or doors, roofing, wallcoverings, ceiling products and materials, lawn and garden supplies, and appliances.

30   *Beauty Supply Stores*   Beauty supply stores sell hair products, hair accessories, nail enamel, brushes, beauty kits, make-up, and other beauty essentials for businesses and individuals. Ricky's and Essentials are beauty supply stores.

31   *Auto Stores*   Auto stores sell auto supplies such as automotive batteries, parts, fluids, accessories, and sundry supplies such as polishes, paint, and decorative items. Pep Boys and R&S are auto stores where customers can purchase auto supplies.

32   *Food Stores*   Food stores sell food for home preparation and consumption. Food includes canned or frozen foods such as vegetables, fruits and soups, dairy products. It also includes packaged or bulk dry groceries such as tea, coffee, cocoa, dried fruits, spices, sugar, flour and crackers, meats, fish and poultry, and other process foods and nonedible grocery items. Supermarkets, food stores, grocery stores, and food warehouses fall in this category. The main competitors in this category are Waldbaums, Key Food, and StopNShop. Customers normally make large, volume purchases from these stores.

33   *Toy Stores*   Toy stores sell toys, games, hobby and craft kits, and supplies. Toys R Us is a major competitor in this category.

34   *Other Miscellaneous Goods Stores*   These stores include bookstores, pet stores, bakeries, shoe stores, drug stores, flower shops, religious stores, stationery stores, optical goods, tobacco/smoker's stores, and other miscellaneous stores not mentioned above.

35   *Jewelry Stores*   There are three types of jewelry stores: costume jewelry stores, fine jewelry stores, and cheap jewelry stores. It is also important to understand the differences among three types of jewelry: costume jewelry, cheap jewelry, and fine jewelry in order to understand the position of fine jewelry specialty retail stores, the focus of this study.

36   *Costume jewelry stores* such as 1928 Jewelry Co., a chain of fashion jewelry stores that sell Vatican inspired fashion jewelry, special occasion adornments, evening accessories, and wedding fashion jewelry, sell costume jewelry, also known as fashion jewelry. It does not contain precious gems and probably is not composed of precious materials, such as 14 karat gold or above. Molded glass stones, and sometimes, plated metal are used to make costume jewelry. It usually is fun to wear and some of the pieces are collectibles. Costume jewelry may be collectible since the pieces are made, and inspired, by an era in history. For instance, there are Victorian and Edwardian era costume jewelry pieces, post-war inspired costume jewelry pieces, art-deco pieces, and many more [About.com, 2003]. 31% of households are buying costume jewelry [Danziger, 2002B].

37   *Cheap jewelry stores*, such as Treasure Palace in New York and Shhh, a unit of Paradise Shop, which sells jewelry for less than $9.95 in airports, sell low quality, mass production designs, and very inexpensive jewelry. Cheap jewelry is sold in general retail stores like department stores, warehouse clubs, discount stores, variety stores, and in cheap jewelry stores. The nation's largest cheap jewelry retailer is Wal-Mart stores with over $2 billion in cheap jewelry sales in 2000 [Unity Marketing, 2002]. Cheap jewelry has imperfections, flaws, and is slightly irregular. Based on the low quality found in cheap jewelry, it is lower in price. Cheap jewelry is made up of plated gold or karat gold less than 14, such as 8 karat, 10 karat, or 12 karat. Sometimes, it may contain synthetic stones or semi-precious gemstones of poor quality.

38   In Figure 3, the projected 1998 jewelry sales in millions include cheap jewelry, costume jewelry (other jewelry), and fine jewelry. The total jewelry sales dollars and percentages are combined sales amongst department stores, discount stores, warehouse clubs, variety stores, costume jewelry stores, fine jewelry stores, and cheap jewelry stores. As shown in Figure 3, sales in percentage and dollars by product include diamonds, pearls, other gemstone jewelry, loose gems, karat jewelry and watches. Diamonds account for the largest percentage of total store sales followed by karat gold jewelry. Other jewelry consists of platinum and sterling silver, and all other merchandise such as giftware, bridal collections, tableware, and the like. Establishments that sell costume jewelry, cheap jewelry, and fine jewelry also repair jewelry.

39   *Fine jewelry stores* engage in the wholesale distribution and/or retail sale of fine jewelry such as diamonds, precious stones, semi-precious stones, rings, bracelets, cufflinks, pendants, necklaces, brooches, earrings, and related specialty items such as timepieces, stationery, gifts and accessories, chinaware, and sterling silverware. Fine jewelry is made up of

FIGURE 3
1998 Projected Sales in Department Stores, Discount Stores, Warehouse Clubs, Variety Stores, Costume Jewelry Stores, Fine Jewelry Stores, and Cheap Jewelry Stores

Source: Professional Jeweler (2003). "Jewelry Store Sales by Products Stats". [Online], *http://www.professionaljeweler. com/archives/features/stats/ stats_prod.html*, Accessed February 25.

Sales in Stores	% of Total Store Sales	Sales by Product (millions)
Diamonds	35.7%	$ 7,959,315
Pearls	3.4%	$ 758,030
Other Gemstone Jewelry	12.1%	$ 2,697,695
Loose Gems	3.6%	$ 802,620
Karat Gold Jewelry	20.0%	$ 4,459,000
Watches	10.6%	$ 2,363,270
Estate/Antique	2.1%	$ 468,195
Other Jewelry	4.2%	$ 936,390
All Other Merchandise	5.2%	$ 1,159,340
Repair	3.1%	$ 691,145
Total store sales	100.0%	$22,295,000

Note: Figures are calculated based on using Commerce Department 1992 percentages for jewelry store sales by product times the current year jewelry store sales total. The 1992 percentages are the most current figures available for use in determining individual jewelry product sales in stores only. These figures are not total US sales for each product.

jewelry made from precious or semiprecious stones (such as diamonds, rubies, sapphires, emeralds, and other stones), metals that are 14 karat gold and above, sterling silver, or platinum. It is more intricate in detail and has minimal flaws, compared to cheap jewelry. Fine jewelry is based on quality, craftsmanship, value, price, and brand name that are reflected in its high price range. It is sold almost exclusively in specialty fine jewelry retail stores. The main competitors include Tiffany & Co., Zales Corp., Harry Winston and David Yurman in this retail sector. Besides the competition amongst one another, there is fierce competition coming from department stores, discount stores, warehouse clubs, and variety stores. Even though these establishments may not sell fine jewelry, customers sometimes decide to purchase costume jewelry or cheap jewelry, instead of fine jewelry, because of its lower prices, as a result, taking away business from fine jewelers.

40   Fine jewelry stores, the focus of this paper, are discussed in detail in the following section.

INDUSTRY & COMPETITIVE MARKET: SPECIALTY FINE JEWELRY RETAIL

41   In the first half of 2002, consumers' desire to buy fine jewelry was growing. Even though the economy was in a recession and jewelry store sales, in general, dropped in the third quarter after September 11th, the luxury, fine jewelry store sales continued to grow that year and were up .7% over 2001. Fine jewelry store sales performance in the second quarter of 2002 were even better with sales 4.3% ahead of 2001 [Unity Marketing, 2002].

42   Half of all U.S. households bought jewelry in 2002, with some 39% of households buying fine jewelry. Fine jewelry in particular is a passion for the high-income households that spend over two times the national average on fine jewelry [Danziger, 2002B]. High-income households have higher disposable income and enjoy spending on luxury items. However, fine jewelry stores are facing competition from general retail stores, which include department stores, warehouse clubs, discount stores, and variety stores that sell cheap jewelry. Since the prices for these items are considerably cheaper at these establishments, some customers, including high-income individuals, shop here for jewelry even though it may not be fine jewelry. Even though high-income individuals enjoy luxuries, they also enjoy a good bargain for their money. Currently, cheap jewelry stores, costume jewelry stores, and general retail stores represent the single largest retail store sales of jewelry [Unity Marketing, 2002].

43   Since many women and men have become more fashion conscious and choose luxury items, such as fine jewelry, as purchases, there are more sales and distribution channels for them to conveniently shop at. The retail market for fine jewelry is broadening where customers can conveniently shop through catalog, company websites, and retail stores.

How the Industry Segment Works: The Essence of the Business Process

44   The industry under study sells fine jewelry and gifts and accessories to high-income individuals, all genders, and mainly Baby Boomers, Generation X and Generation Y. Figure 4 outlines the specialty fine jewelry retail segment business model. As defined earlier, fine jewelry is made up of jewelry made from precious or semiprecious stones, 14K gold and above, sterling silver or platinum. Fine jewelry has several sub-categories such as: bracelets, brooches, cuff links, necklaces, rings, earrings, pendants, timepieces, wedding bands, and engagement rings. Gifts and accessories include writing instruments, flatware, hollowware, vases, stemware, crystal, frames, fragrance, key rings, and wedding gifts fabricated from precious metals, precious metal alloys, and their imitations as defined by the Federal Trade Commission [Federal Trade Commission, 2003].

45   As convenience has become a growing trend in influencing customer purchases, many fine jewelry retailers are offering their products online, via direct catalog mail, or through traditional retail stores.

46   When customers visit the company website, the navigation around the site must be easy and convenient for customers to shop. Therefore, searching for their product of choice should be easy to find on the website. Some company websites offer a search feature, list its products by category or collection, have pictures available, or list products based on price range. These accessible features allow customers to find what they are looking for easily and quickly. Otherwise, the customers will go to competitors or another sales channel to look for their product.

47   Direct catalog mail is another convenient sales channel offered to customers. The collection of customer data such as their preferences based on purchase history via catalog, the Internet, or through the retail store allows a company to offer products that are appealing to the customer. The data is convenient for advertising and promoting products for all these channels.

48   The convenience trend is also true for retail store selling. Customers want to be able to find the store easily, so location is very important. Once the customers are in the store, they should feel comfortable shopping and finding the product of their desire. The store design, décor and layout should, therefore, be comfortable and easy for customers to navigate. Also, it is the product knowledge, product selection and customer service that has given specialty

FIGURE 4   Specialty Fine Jewelry Retail Segment Business Model

Specialty Fine Jewelry Retail Segment								
PRODUCTS	CUSTOMERS	SALES AND DISTRIBUTION	OPERATIONS	MANUFACTURING AND DESIGNING	TECHNOLOGY	ADVERTISING	GEOGRAPHIC REGION	COMPETITION
Fine Jewelry Zales Corporation	Gender	Catalog	Inventory Control	In-House	MFG/PRO eB2	Print	Domestic	Zales Corporation
Gifts and Accessories Harry Winston	-Males	internet	JIT	Outsource	QAD eQ	Television	International	Harry Winston
	-Females	Retailing			Real-Time Data	Outdoor		David Yurmin
David Yurman								
	Age -Seniors -Baby Boomers -Generation X -Generation Y							

fine jewelry retail stores increased sales and awareness. Well-trained sales forces, implemented by training programs, are therefore ways to help provide customers with strong product knowledge and excellent customer service.

49   Specialty fine jewelry retailers have a choice: manufacture their products in-house or outsource to an outside vendor. Manufacturing products in-house allows specialty fine jewelry retailers to have control over the manufacturing process. However, this process is very costly causing most specialty fine jewelry retailers to outsource to an outside vendor. The control is turned over to the outsourcer who controls the manufacturing process. Contracts are drawn up to clearly define the terms of the agreement between company and vendor. In the case of outsourcing, relationships with suppliers and vendors are important to improve communication and meet customer demands. Building supplier relationships through communication and through enhanced technology is helpful in meeting customer needs and discovering consumer trends.

50   Specialty fine jewelers also have a choice of opening their own stores or having boutiques in leased space in high-end department stores. Use of such boutiques is expected to decline. Specialization has flourished in certain categories causing the number of department stores to decline in the last 30 years. For example, Angela Cummings, a fine jewelry designer is closing her leased boutiques in Bergdorf Goodman and Neiman Marcus, both of which are high-end department stores. With the economy in a recession causing difficulties in the retail environment, the jewelry designers say that department stores are trying to squeeze more money from them. According to Ms. Cummings, "It's very difficult for a small business, without big funding in back of us. It's hard to keep coming up with new things when we pay for everything; so much was on consignment" [Rozhon, 2003]. Many fine jewelers have decided to start off on their own as opposed to leasing a boutique in a department store. The costs and monies associated with department stores are high. It makes it harder for the fine jewelers to create new products because they're constantly paying the department store back with little funding to spend on creating new products.

51   Specialty retailers strive to give customers exactly what they need without wasting the customer's time since the stores are specialized in a particular product category [Hoover, 1996]. Specialization is a focus on a particular category and extending it to offer the most out of it. More women are entering the work force with less time set aside for shopping. The specialization of retail stores is visible to the customer and will value her time. Therefore, she would prefer to go to a specialty retailer. The fine jewelry industry is taking advantage of this flourishing phenomenon [Hoover, 1996]. The industry remains highly fragmented with opportunities for market share capitalization. The capitalization of market share is gaining and increasing market share through discovering opportunities and creating keys to success factors based on these opportunities, which will be discussed in the following sections.

Products

52   Specialty fine jewelry retailers sell a variety of fine jewelry such as diamonds, precious stones, semi-precious stones, rings, bracelets, cufflinks, pendants, necklaces, brooches, earrings, and gifts and accessories that include timepieces, stationery, crystal, chinaware, and sterling silverware. Product differentiation is a major success factor, as in most luxury item categories. This is done through developing innovative products or collections that are not currently offered by competitors that help build brand image. Creating trendy and fashionable pieces that can be worn with various outfits and complement various personalities are also ways to differentiate a brand. Utilizing different metals and stones to create high quality, durable pieces are other ways to differentiate product brands. High quality pieces are made up of quality grade diamonds, precious stones, semi-precious stones, and high craftsmanship with minimal flaws in the detailed designs.

53 It is important to have a strong brand image in addition to other driving success factors that keep the consumers happy. Brand image is a positive idea positioned in the consumer's mind about the company and its products. In addition to the brand building steps described above, specialty fine jewelers would have advertising campaigns to position an idea that would easily equate the idea to the brand. The idea of status or an everlasting fine jewelry piece would be examples an advertisement would promote brand image. Another way to build brand image is to have celebrities wear the fine jewelry piece so there's high visibility and attention towards the product. Oftentimes, customers pay attention to what celebrities wear. When the customers see the product worn by celebrities, many customers want to purchase the product. Finally, offering the customer a positive personal shopping experience with the company and its products also helps build brand image. A positive shopping experience that would not be forgotten by the customer would be to offer superior customer service, product differentiation, quality products, and beautiful packaging and gift-wrapping, as well as understanding and catering to their needs paying close attention to enhancing the customers' overall shopping experience. Brand image helps promote and sell products. Oftentimes, fine jewelers stamp their brand on the fine jewelry piece itself to help promote the brand's name. This seal indicates that the company stands behind its products and can be worn with pride. When the customer wears the piece of fine jewelry, he or she will feel proud to own the fine jewelry branded piece. All these elements help promote brand image.

54 Inventory management and replenishment of products are important in keeping the store stocked with goods for customers and order of shipment for timely arrival. By maintaining merchandise inventory, offering diversified brand and product portfolio, training a knowledgeable sales force and selling quality, value and craftsmanship fine jewelry, customers are more likely to be satisfied in this competitive industry both domestically and internationally.

55 Building brand image and customer loyalty will lead to continued and repeated future purchases. However, there is a problem: there are fine jewelry design imitations that cost a fraction of the price at cheap jewelry stores and general retail stores. This competition makes it hard for customers to be loyal to fine jewelry stores because the customers can purchase a similar design at a fraction of the price. At the same time, it is hard for fine jewelers because the competition from imitators is hurting their sales and brand image of what fine jewelry characteristics represent—quality, craftsmanship, value, and price.

Fine Jewelry

56 Fine jewelry is made from precious or semiprecious stones (such as diamonds, rubies, sapphires, emeralds, and other stones), metals that are 14 karat gold and above, sterling silver, or platinum. Fine jewelry has several sub-categories such as: bracelets, brooches, cuff links, necklaces, rings, earrings, pendants, watches, wedding bands and engagement rings.

57 As commissioned by *Advertising Age* and conducted by Ziccardi Partners Frierson Mee, the luxury study shown in Figure 5 found that high-income consumers now say that quality, value, design/style, and price are drivers of luxury good purchases.

58 The first driver, quality, is a characteristic that determines a product's value or worth in the market and how well it will perform the functions for which it is designed. The better the quality, the more durable and expensive the product will be. Quality and value are based on standards set by the customer's own experience and knowledge of the product. Utilizing different metals and stones in a fine jewelry piece can help differentiate and boost the quality of the product. For instance, instead of using traditional 14k gold, platinum metal may be used. This is equated to quality since it maintains its luster through the years. Also, "D" color quality diamonds may be used instead of lesser quality such as "H" color. A "D" color diamond is the best color diamond there is, followed by "E", "F", "G", "H", and so on alphabetically.

FIGURE 5 Jewelry/Timepiece Purchase Drivers

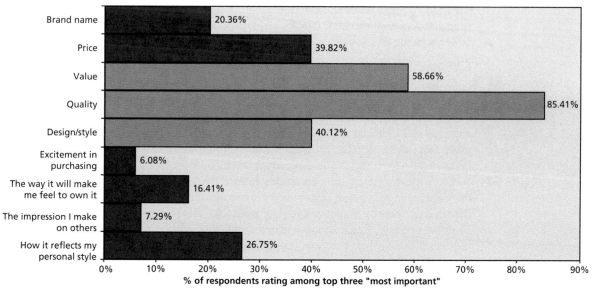

Source: Advertising Age (2002). [online]. *http://www.adage.com/news.cms?newsId=34174.* Accessed February 26, 2003.

59   The second driver, value, is a product's monetary or material worth. By using quality metals and stones, the fair market value will be maintained through the years. When purchasing fine jewelry, it is like making an investment. Products should maintain their value even after a certain amount of years.

60   The design or style of a product defines its functional purpose and can be varied for differentiation. Its designs and styles should be functional to accommodate different personalities and to enable wearing products with various outfits.

61   The last driver, price, is a monetary unit assigned to products based on the preceding drivers. When customers purchase a fine jewelry piece, the quality, value and design should be equivalent to the price tag as well as the brand name. By offering various price ranges, fine jewelers are able to compete at various levels including market, category, and price. The creation of price competitiveness is based on the products that competitors are offering in the same price range. In order to compete in price, an added value of the product should be offered if prices are higher or value should be altered if prices are lower. Added value may include better quality, innovative design, and the like. Similarly, prices can be lowered to compete with competition by changing certain attributes of the product, such as the materials used. For instance, incorporating a sterling silver collection, which is less costly than gold may help a fine jeweler compete in the lower price range. At the same time, the fine jeweler would be able to be price competitive since it has various price ranges to offer the customer. These drivers are keys to success in the specialty fine jewelry retail store industry.

62   Some specialty fine jewelry retail stores, such as Tiffany, are losing millions of dollars each year to imitations and counterfeiters. The imitation designs are sold at a fraction of Tiffany's costs since the quality, craftsmanship, and value are much lower. However, there have been recent events that have highlighted fine jewelry stores', such as Tiffany, efforts to find and prosecute counterfeiters. For example, on April 23, 2003, the owners of Enddi Silver and Starglam.com were arrested in conjunction with selling Tiffany knockoff jewelry and signature blue packaging [Molofsky, 2003]. Another event was on January 17, 2003, when Tiffany obtained a preliminary injunction to prevent a Philadelphia jewelry company,

Katz Imports Inc., from selling counterfeit Tiffany jewelry on eBay and through its web site at www.pennsylvaniadiamondexchange.com [Green, 2003]. In light of these events, counterfeiters and imitation may be reduced to a minimum, but will always be internal problem facing fine jewelry retailers.

Gifts and Accessories

63   Gifts and accessories include timepieces, stationery, chinaware, crystal, sterling silverware, fragrance, frames, and key rings. Timepieces include clocks and watches. Stationery includes planners and writing instruments such as pens and pencils made from precious metals, precious metal alloys and their imitations. Picture frames and key rings are also made from these metals. Chinaware, usually given as wedding gifts, includes flatware, hollowware, vases, and stemware made from china, crystal, and sterling silver.

64   A key trend for gifts and accessories category is a new bridal market boom. Babies of the baby boom generation born after 1976 are reaching 26 in 2002, which corresponds to their average year of first marriage [Danziger, 2002A]. This generation accounts for about 71 million people, which is larger than their parents' generation, the baby boomers. Since they are planning their first wedding, the bridal registry should be available to them. The fine jewelry stores, the online website, and the catalogs should offer an array of products for this growing segment.

65   In addition, the men are more involved with shopping for his apartment and being actively involved in the bridal registry and baby registry. This trend is largely due to their working mothers who sent them out to do the grocery shopping, or run errands. This trend is a great opportunity to cater to the needs and lifestyle of the bridal market boom.

66   The last key trend in the gifts and accessories category is the growing number of business relationships. As a result of this, many companies are buying writing instruments, key rings, or picture frames as a reward to employees, gifts to business partners, and important customers.

Customers

67   Specialty fine jewelry retailers cater to all genders, specific age groups, and high-income individuals. They cater to individuals who are able to afford these luxury goods. Overtime, the products offered to this target market must meet its needs in an ever-changing environment. At the same time, an appropriate business strategy had to be developed around anticipating change, evolving with the changing environment, and catering to a changing market composition.

68   Strong customer relations will help define and cater the needs of the customers regardless of the changes. By building a strong relationship with the customer, a specialty fine jewelry retailer can better understand and meet the needs of its clients, and react quickly to growing trends in the industry. Building a relationship with a customer develops over time. Remembering details, such as the customer's first name, date of birth, color preference, likes, dislikes, size, and the like, help build a strong tie between the customer and the company. This makes the customer feel that the company he/she is purchasing from cares about his/her wants and needs.

69   Consumers are three times more likely to respond that "feeling good about myself" is more important rather than "making an impression." They are also 10 times more likely to prefer "well-being" to "status." This desire for well-being shows in all aspects of their lives, from the demand for more service at retail stores to not giving up luxurious accommodations while traveling, to indulging oneself and loved ones with fine jewelry [Advertising Age, 2002]. Other top purchase motivators for luxury goods are buying things that last, enjoying favorite brands, indulging oneself, feeling successful, and other motivators discussed in Figure 10. It is an opportunity to seize these segments and fulfill their desire for well-being by offering goods and services that make them feel good.

Gender

70 Specialty fine jewelry retailers cater to both males and females. Jewelry has become an affordable luxury for fashion-forward women and men as well as a favorite gift item in all price ranges [Unity Marketing 2003].

71 *Males* Males have a lower purchase incidence of fine jewelry compared to females: 36% for men in 2001, and 48% females. Non-adult males and females accounted for 16% of the remaining purchases. However, males spend significantly more money on fine jewelry purchases than females. Most of the jewelry purchases by males are gifts. When purchasing fine jewelry, men fall in two segments: either the personal Indulger who loves to buy fine jewelry for himself and takes the time to find the right piece for him; or the Gifter who feels that jewelry is a great gift to others [Unity Marketing, 2002].

72 Males often look for durability of products, that is, quality products that last for a long time. Various metals and stones are used to create the high quality products. As a result, the pieces maintain their luster through the years. Another trend in young males (18-34 years of age) is that they were the first to grow up in households with working mothers who had little time to do any shopping for them. They were sent to the mall to purchase their own clothing, do the grocery shopping, and run errands. These men are marrying later. They actively participate in the selections that go with the bridal registry and baby registry [WSL Strategic Retail, 2003]. Men have been more involved in the shopping experience. However, there are limited stores that actually cater to their needs and to growing male shopping trends.

73 *Females* Females have a higher incidence of jewelry purchases with 48% in 2001. When purchasing jewelry, women fall into three segments: the Fashionista, the Expert, and the Thriftier. The Fashionista wears jewelry as part of her everyday life, as every new outfit and new occasion is an opportunity to purchase fine jewelry accessories [Danziger, 2002B]. When purchasing fine jewelry, females look for beautiful, fashionable styles and convenience to accommodate their lifestyle. The Expert is knowledgeable about fine jewelry and knows that high quality jewelry comes with price. The last segment is the Thriftier who makes jewelry purchase decisions based on price, not the quality, craftsmanship, or latest trend [Unity Marketing, 2002].

74 Women represent a significant growth potential, since many females are entering the workforce. With little time to shop, offering ease and convenience of shopping are keys to success with this segment. Convenience may entail location of retail stores near the workplace, extended hours of operation for working females, and easy return and exchange policies. The convenience factor will increase shopping, traffic, and sales. If hours of operation were extended, females would be able to conveniently shop after work. This accommodates for their busy schedule. Also, the easy return and exchange policy would allow working females to return or exchange items in the most convenient way for them. They can either return via mail or through retail store if the item was purchased online or via catalog. This offers choice to the customer. With these added accommodations for working females, it shows that the specialty fine jewelry retailer values her time.

Age

75 For the purpose of this case study, customers can be divided into the following age groups: Seniors, Baby Boomers, Generation X, and Generation Y.

76 *Seniors* This generation is 65 and older. By 2015, they were expected to comprise nearly 15 percent of the U.S. population. Companies had to cater to the needs of this group with features such as brighter lighting, larger signs, and convenient parking. Classic and antique jewelry designs were very popular with this age group.

77 *Baby Boomers* This generation is 38 to 56 years old. The majority of these individuals who fall in the baby boom group have families, are focusing on saving for retirement, and paying for tuition for their kids. The baby boom generation is focused on luxury, travel, and leisure. Since this group represents 40 million credit card users, owning almost 50% of the credit cards in the United States, they have over 50% of discretionary spending power that is 2.5 times the average per capita [E-Com Profits, 2003]. By offering store credit cards or the acceptance of major credit cards as a means of payment is a key to attract this segment. Another key in attracting this age group is to offer a wide product assortment and exclusive fine jewelry items to fulfill their focus of luxury.

78   *Generation X* This generation is born between 1965 and 1976. They are between 26 and 37 years of age. Children of the baby boomers, Generation Xers experienced high divorce rates and separation among their parents. Due to this, they look for a sense of community in other things such as the Internet, their small group of friends, and the like. Generation Xers are born in the era of the Information Age. Specialty retailers should give the Generation Xers experiences that fit their lifestyle and aspirations and information that keeps them informed. Purchases via the Internet are high in this age group. So the acceptance of credit cards and secure shopping online should be offered to target this market.

79   *Generation Y* Born between 1977 and 1994, Generation Y consumers are between the ages of 8 and 25 years of age. At 60 million strong, more than three times the size of Generation X, Generation Y is the biggest generation to hit the American scene since the 72 million baby boomers. They make their own choices and purchases, yet are influenced by their parents' spending habits.

80   For specialty fine jewelry retailers to be successful with Generation X and Generation Y, they have to offer fashionable and trendy fine jewelry pieces to fit their fast and ever-changing lifestyles. The fine jewelry pieces had to be versatile to fit their personality and style. At the same time, shopping convenience and security, excellent customer relations, high quality products, strong craftsmanship, high value, competitive prices, strong brand, acceptance of credit cards, and sense of well-being were keys to success.

Income

81   Specialty fine jewelry retailers target high-income individuals who are affluent and enjoy luxury items. Generally, high-income individuals have higher disposable income. Therefore, they would spend more on luxury items rather than products of need. Related to making a high salary is the ability to spend what you make. High-income individuals have a high-disposable income with the ability to purchase large-ticketed items. They spend on luxury items to match their high salary and lifestyle. They often live in the suburbs and earn more than $85,000 a year. 34% are in homes headed by directors or managers, 21% are from the professional classes, a further 21% are self-employed, and 24% are retired. In the next few years, the number of families with household incomes of over $100,000 in the United States and Europe is forecasted to grow about 20% [Retail Industry, 2001]. These individuals use credit cards as payments and look for easy payment transactions as opposed to carrying large amounts of cash.

82   In order to be successful with this retail segment, a specialty fine jeweler had to offer competitive prices along with quality products. Competitive prices were based on the quality, craftsmanship, value, price, and brand of the product. These drivers determined, not only, sales but also price. The higher price, the better the quality, craftsmanship, and value of the product. The opposite was true for lower priced items.

83   Since this segment is concerned with luxury, brand recognition is also important. High prices are associated with high quality and status. However, there seems to be a shift in spending behavior. Consumers, who made purchases at specialty fine jewelry retailers, were also making purchases at cheap jewelry stores and general retail stores, which include department stores, warehouse clubs, discount stores, and variety stores. So, status

did not seem like a driving factor, but rather the importance of quality for the money and well-being—how the individual felt when wearing the product.

Sales/Distribution

84 Specialty fine jewelry retailers sell their products through a traditional sales distribution channel, such as a retail store. Some fine jewelry retailers engage in retail and wholesale sales distribution of products to other businesses in the industry. Non-traditional distribution channels include non-store retailing such as mail order catalogs, television, and company Internet websites [Danziger, 2002B]. Certain product lines can be offered in certain distribution channels to cater to certain markets or even used to test new product lines. The greater presence the specialty fine jewelry retailer has in various sales and distribution channels, the more convenient it is for their consumers to purchase their products and for fine jewelers to distribute their products.

Catalog

85 This is an alternate sales medium for specialty fine jewelry retailers. As shown in Figure 6, catalog sales are expected to increase to $160.2 billion from both consumer and business sales by 2006 with a compound annual growth rate of 5.95.

86 Catalogs that have an attractive cover design help gain customer attention. When customers receive catalogs through the mail, if the cover does not have an appealing design or picture, they may not open it. Another way to gain customer attention is to use quality paper stock. The quality paper stock reflects what the fine jeweler is offering in the catalog.

87 Since aesthetics is a large part of the fine jewelry industry, the pictures of the fine jewelry should be displayed and laid out in the most attractive manner. Catalog sales, unlike retail sales, do not have a sales person to give product knowledge or description of the item. So, a clear description and an attractive picture should be available for each item—offered for sale.

88 An assortment of products should be available in the catalog to cater to the competitive pricing of competitors. So for instance, silver jewelry could be included in the catalog to fulfill the lower price range. Other fine jewelry that may include diamonds could also be included to fulfill the higher price range. Competitive pricing is offered to customers through an assortment of products at various price ranges.

89 Competitive pricing for shipping rates is also important for catalog sales. Since the sale is made through the mail, customers look for the best shipping rates. The best shipping rates can be offered by type of delivery. For instance, Priority Mail or Next Day Air would cost more compared to Ground Mail or Two-Day Air. Another way to offer competitive shipping rates is to offer one standard flat fee for shipping regardless of the weight, price, or number

FIGURE 6
United States Catalog Sales ($ in Billions) and Compound Annual Growth Rate

Source: Retail Industry (2001). "Catalog Sales Growth Continues to Outpace Overall Retail Growth". [Online], *http://retailindustry.about.com/library/bl/q2/bl_dma060401a.htm,* Accessed February 25, 2003.

	Sales				
	1996	**2000**	**2001**	**2002**	**2006**
Total	69.5	110.2	120.0	128.2	160.2
Consumer	42.8	67.4	73.3	78.1	96.6
Business	26.7	42.8	46.7	50.1	63.6
Compound Annual Growth Rate					
	1996–2001			**2001–2006**	
Total	11.53			5.95	
Consumer	11.34			5.68	
Business	11.83			6.38	

*Numbers may not add up due to rounding.

of items purchased, or to offer free shipping for a minimum price purchase order (over $200, for example).

90   Gathering customer information is important in developing a personality profile based on customer purchases. Through catalog purchases, fine jewelers were able to gather information about the customers and analyze spending habits based on their purchases. This information is helpful in assisting the specialty fine jewelry retailer understand who their consumers are and help fulfill their needs.

91   In addition, customer information is helpful in developing new products as well as target new areas. This information would assist in developing and introducing new products, categories, and designs in this medium. Assortment of product should be readily available when purchasing through this channel. Customers want to be able to find the same products via catalog as if they were to go to the retail store. However, most fine jewelers who offered products via catalog had a limited selection.

Internet

92   The DMA study, Economic Impact: U.S. Direct and Internet Marketing Today, notes that although Internet sales are slowing from their triple-digit growth rate in recent years, the Internet remains the fastest-growing direct marketing medium compared to catalog sales. As shown in Figure 7, web-generated sales are expected to reach $37.1 billion in 2001, an increase of 32 percent over 2000 sales of $28 billion. After the events of September 11th, and also the SARS epidemic, Asians may have been reluctant to travel, but there were no signs that they would stop buying at home via the Internet [Retail Industry, 2002].

93   Another reason for the continuing increase in Internet sales is the convenience and secure online shopping. Easy to navigate sites and secure shopping online are what determine convenience for customers. When customers visit the company website, the navigation around the site must be easy and convenient for customers to shop. Therefore, searching for their product of choice should be easy to find on the website. Some company websites offer a search feature, list its products by category or collection, have pictures available, or list products based on price range. These accessible features allow customers to find what they are looking for easily and quickly. Also, secure shopping online stresses privacy and security of personal information being distributed online. Company websites have encryption so credit card numbers, personal information, and identity can be guaranteed usually if a company is registered with the Verisign logo on its website. This is a symbol that indicates secure shopping online.

94   Convenience and price are what determine where people shop. By offering convenience and competitive prices, fine jewelers are able to compete in the industry. The creation of price competitiveness is based on the products that competitors are offering in the same price

FIGURE 7
United States Internet Sales ($ in Billions) and Compound Annual Growth Rate

Source: Retail Industry (2001). "Catalog Sales Growth Continues to Outpace Overall Retail Growth". [Online], *http://retailindustry.about.com/library/bl/q2/bl_dma060401a.htm,* Accessed February 25, 2003.

	Sales				
	1996	**2000**	**2001**	**2002**	**2006**
Total	.75	28.0	37.1	61.3	181.4
Consumer	.24	10.0	13.5	22.6	68.7
Business	.51	18.0	23.6	38.7	112.7
Compound Annual Growth Rate					
	1996–2001			**2001–2006**	
Total	118.3			37.3	
Consumer	124.2			38.5	
Business	115.3			36.7	

range. In order to compete in price, an added value of the product should be offered if prices are higher or value should be altered if prices are lower. Added value may include better quality, innovative design, and the like. It is up to the consumer to decide what products to choose based on the value added. For instance, incorporating a sterling silver collection, which is less costly than gold may help a fine jeweler compete in the lower price range. At the same time, the fine jeweler would be able to be price competitive since it has various price ranges to offer the customer.

95 Many customers are taking advantage of the shopping experience offered online. However, it is important that brand recognition and positive brand image is established. Brand recognition and positive brand image can be established through advertisement in various mediums including celebrity sponsors, through continued customer relationships, through offering a positive shopping experience, and through brand stamped pieces. All these ways help build brand image. At the same time, these ways help position an idea or brand in the consumer's mind. Customers have to feel comfortable purchasing from a company they know of and trust especially via the Internet medium. This sales channel may be the easiest way to reach the target market, but it is also the hardest to convince customers to trust and to shop with confidence unless brand image is established and security is in place especially when selling fine jewelry. Many times, fine jewelry retailers try to capture their market and build the customers' confidence by offering an unforgettable shopping experience on the Internet as they would at the retail store. This includes offering exceptional customer service through 24-hour live customer representative chat boxes, offering high quality and competitively priced items by offering a large selection of products at various price ranges, and preparing beautiful packaging and gift-wrapping.

96 The Internet may be a major fine jewelry outlet, next to retail stores. However, limited products are offered through this sales channel. The reason for this is because fine jewelry can range from one hundred dollars to a few hundred thousand dollars. To offer the more expensive products online may not be feasible since a more personalized shopping experience is needed. In addition, the fine jewelry piece may be lost during delivery or payments are not received. These are some security issues that still have to be ironed out.

97 Since all orders are shipped, an important successful factor for specialty fine jewelers is to offer competitive shipping rates. The products that are being shipped are very expensive fine jewelry items, so packaging and availability of insurance for the product are also very important.

98 While both catalog and Internet-generated sales are expected to grow at a slower pace from 2001 through 2006, this trend is consistent with a projected slowing of overall retail sales.

Retailing

99 The sale of fine jewelry is mainly through company-operated retail stores, but some sell through leased spaces (boutiques) at department stores.

100 Retail stores are the main distribution channels for specialty jewelry retailers. As shown in Figure 8, with about 3.5 trillion dollars in sales, customers are still visiting retail stores despite their access to the Internet because the experience the retail store provides is still a part of the excitement of shopping. For example, the elegant décor, bright lighting, attractive merchandising, superior customer service, and beautiful gift-wrapping all add to the shopping experience. By offering a greater experience per square foot of retail floor selling space, customers will remember the experience as well as the company brand name which will help to keep them coming back.

101 To offer a greater shopping experience per square foot, fine jewelers can offer more products, greater customer service, and better shopping features at the retail store. More products can be offered through development of new product designs and categories. Greater customer service can be offered through sales training programs on how to cater to

FIGURE 8
United States Retail Sales ($ in Trillions) and Compound Annual Growth Rate

Source: Retail Industry (2001). "Catalog Sales Growth Continues to Outpace Overall Retail Growth". [Online], *http://retailindustry.about.com/library/bl/q2/bl_dma060401a.htm*, Accessed February 25, 2003.

Sales	1996	2000	2001	2002	2006
Total	2.5	3.2	3.3	3.5	4.1

Compound Annual Growth Rate	
	1996–2001	2001–2006
Total	5.91	4.08

the customers' needs and to satisfy their shopping experience. Finally, visibility of security guards, displaying attractive merchandising, offering customers food, drinks, and entertainment while shopping, and having models showcase the fine jewelry pieces are features of an improved shopping experience. If a retail store is 10,000 square feet and a customer purchases an item for $10,000, this means that $1 worth of items are sold for every square foot of retail selling space in that store. Expanding the shopping experience for its customers, as noted above, can contribute to increased sales per square foot.

102   Prime retail location and space are what makes these stores visible to the market and a success factor in the specialty retail fine jewelry industry. Oftentimes, luxury items are considered luxury because of the brand or based on the price tag. Since many specialty fine jewelry stores offer luxury items that have attractive brand and price, the retail location should be in an exclusive area as well. Finding the right location is based on extensive research and monitoring of an area. Where does one begin to do the research? Find an area where the demographics fit the specialty fine jewelry industry. Look at potential markets and markets where competitors have already begun operations. For instance, location should be in high-end areas such as Madison Avenue in New York City or Manhasset Americana in Long Island, New York where only exclusive retailers occupy the retail space. Luxury retailers located in these areas project an image of luxury, style, and class. One must monitor volume of traffic, demographics, infrastructure, visibility of the store for a period of time to determine if these elements fit the market being catered to. Forecasted financials based on traffic observations and spending habits of individuals in that area produce the needed revenue to open a new location.

103   Fine jewelers consider having a large number of company-operated retail stores rather than larger square foot of selling space as determining success in a particular area. Sales per square feet of selling space, another key to success factor, involves a greater shopping experience per square feet to result in greater purchases by the customer.

104   A greater retail shopping experience is offered in a number of ways. The retail shopping experience may be the help and knowledge the sales staff offers, strong customer relations, beautiful packaging, wide payment acceptance, wide portfolio of products, readily available inventory, cleanliness, modern décor and layout, elegant atmosphere, calm music, bright lighting, and tight security that add to the experience. The retail experience also includes offering various acceptances of payment for the convenience of the customer. Since many customers prefer not to carry cash, the convenience of personal checks and credit cards should be offered. Offering a wide portfolio of products and readily stocked inventory signifies that the company is ready to do business and cater to all the customer's needs. Finally, the aesthetics of the retail store such as modern décor and layout, elegant atmosphere, bright lighting and clean retail store offers a comfortable shopping environment. The modern décor such as the Industrial look of matte metal signifies tastes and innovative trends. The higher the purchase per visit by a customer, the higher the value per square feet of selling space. Therefore, this generates increased sales revenue for that store.

105 Customers should be able to easily find the store as well as capture the retail experience. Every little detail counts because it indicates that the fine jeweler take pride and has confidence in its company and its products. All of the above mentioned add to the retail shopping experience. It gives the customer a sense of what the company stands for and what it has to offer.

106 Some fine jewelers sell through leased space (boutiques) at department stores. However, in recent years, the number of department stores has declined and so has the number of fine jewelers in them. The reason for this is the high costs associated with department stores. Department stores are asking for more money, pushing fine jewelers to sell on consignment. The high costs cause them to find other sales channels, such as catalog, or Internet website to operate their business. The overhead is less and costs are lower than the leased spaces in department stores. At the same time, fine jewelers are able to make choices freely and develop their business without having to pay third party high costs in order to operate.

Operations

107 Strategic decisions in operations involve products and services produced in anticipation of demand. When to produce, how much to produce and what to produce are questions that need to be answered when strategic decisions are made in operations. Also, questions regarding facilities for domestic and international operations, human resources, quality, sourcing and operating systems that support customer and worker demands for rapid access, storage and retrieval of information should also be considered [Russell & Taylor, 2003]. Specialty fine jewelry retailers stand behind their values, products and employees. Proper sales force training programs to build product knowledge, linking communications between stores, controlling inventory levels, shortening product lead times, and minimizing operating costs help determine the success of the specialty fine jewelry retailer. The use of technology and upgradeable systems help with inventory and operations management. The close monitoring of operations helps reduce operation cost by producing appropriate quantities with minimal excess. If there is excess inventory, extra costs are paid for its storage or valuable space is wasted for other inventory. Knowing when to produce, how much to produce and what to produce eliminates wastes and overstock items. Also, this controls the ordering schedule for timely delivery and shipments.

108 Real-time data is very important in maintaining effective and efficient company operations. This is particularly important if there are domestic as well as international operations. Today, it is done through advanced software and technology adopted by the company. However, many companies are not ready to do this because its information systems are not upgradeable. So, large investments are needed to support these new types of technology. If the systems are upgradeable, the transition is easier and would not be as costly. Timing and delivery of information and products are ways to determine the success of the specialty fine jewelry sector.

Manufacturing and Designing

109 Many specialty jewelry retailers either manufactured in-house or outsourced depending on their available technology or diamond mine resources.

In-House

110 Manufacturing products in-house is expensive because they have no experience in the manufacturing process. However, specialty fine jewelry retailers have control over what to produce, what materials to use, and how much to produce to meet demands. Many specialty fine jewelers purchase a portion of their supply chain and vertically integrate. This allows specialty fine jewelers to commit to quality since they are involved with the manufacturing and designing process. At the same time, this allows for flexibility in operations and control.

111   In-house manufacturing and designing still remain very costly. So, some specialty fine jewelry retailers are trying to streamline their process by purchasing their suppliers and vertically integrate operations. Vertically integrating is an important key factor in the fine jewelry retail industry. Usually by vertically integrating, the fine jeweler purchases its suppliers, giving it more control over manufacturing and designing processes. As a result, the more control a company has over its suppliers and operations, the more control it will have in the industry's market share. By streamlining and gaining control of the manufacturing and designing processes, a fine jeweler is able to react quicker to changing customer needs and trends by altering the process.

112   One way fine jewelers have started to vertically integrate is by buying diamond mines. In doing so, the fine jeweler is able to hold diamonds for its future needs. In addition, the ownership of diamond mines allows the fine jeweler to decide on the diamonds' use, as well as how much of it will be used for current designs and future designs. By vertically integrating, the fine jeweler is given choices and is not limited by anyone.

113   The availability of certain technology allows specialty fine jewelry retailers such as David Yurman to select the QAD software to help with its worldwide manufacturing operations. The QAD software is an enterprise platform used for more effective manufacturing and distribution operations. It uses accurate real-time information to achieve operational efficiencies, improve collaboration with suppliers and major retail customers, and support the company's future expansion [QAD Inc., 2002]. The use of QAD gives the fine jewelry retailer a competitive edge when delivery of products and timing are key factors.

Outsource

114   Outsourcing to an outside vendor is a less costly process compared to in-house manufacturing. Contracts have to be drawn up to clearly define the terms of the agreement between company and vendor. Product specification, delivery schedule, number of products to be produced, quality of products, and types of materials used are considered when drawing a contract. In the case of outsourcing, relationships with suppliers and vendors are important to improve communication and meet customer demands. Building supplier relationships through communication and through enhanced technology is helpful in meeting customer needs and discovering consumer trends.

115   Outsourcing still remains to be a decision strategy for most fine jewelry retailers since in-house manufacturing is a costly process. Outsourcing allows outside vendors to take over an agreed manufacturing or designing process to help speed up production. At the same time, outsourcing offers expertise in a particular area. This allows for higher productivity, which otherwise, would have taken the fine jeweler a longer period of time to produce if it had not outsourced.

116   Total quality management is used to monitor production and quality of production. Therefore, a good supplier relation is very important so that products are of quality production and designs satisfy criteria set forth in the contract. Constant communication with suppliers and close monitoring help a fine jewelry retailer maintain its brand image and continue to offer high quality products.

Technology

117   The use of technology offers fine jewelry retailers the ability to produce products efficiently and effectively while minimizing costs. One way is the adoption of advances in technology such as the use of MFG/PRO eB2 and QAD eQ. These allow for accurate real-time information, improve collaboration with suppliers, help collect customer information, and improve operational efficiencies, and in these ways support a company's future expansion. Using such technology gives a competitive edge over other fine jewelry retailers in the industry because collection of customer data and improved collaboration with suppliers through

this technology is helpful in developing products fit for the customer's needs and using real-time accurate information to communicate amongst suppliers and sales forces. The use of technology such as MFG/PRO eB2 and QAD eQ helps support fine jewelry retailers' operations, as well as position them at the forefront of the industry.

118   Since convenience is a growing trend, the Internet allows for easy access to shopping. Many fine jewelry retailers have seized this opportunity to cater to existing and new customers via the Internet by offering their products online. The availability of shopping online for fine jewelry has opened gateways to existing target markets as well as potential markets. The Internet medium and its technology capabilities, to connect business to business, business to customer, and customer to customer, allow for easy access to communicate. With Internet technology capabilities, fine jewelry retailers offer secure, safe, convenient, and reliable shopping.

Advertising

119   Through growing forms of advertising channels such as television, magazine, newspaper, outdoor, Internet, radio, and the like, fine jewelry retailers are able to reach their audience and position their message in the consumer's mind. Currently, print advertising is the largest medium, but many retailers are including the Internet as part of their advertising medium since it is the fastest growing. Fine jewelry retailers spend millions of dollars on advertising brand image and product each year.

120   Advertising expenses are a fine jeweler's largest expense. Not only do they spend money on advertising mediums to promote brand image and product, money is also spent on researching mediums that are most effective in reaching the target market. Researching the lifestyles and interests of a target demographic is costly. Nielsen Media Research provides various reports for advertisers. There are reports that indicate certain target demographic television viewing. There are also reports, through Nielsen's Ad*Views software, that gives a breakdown of advertising expenditures by medium for a certain industry, company, product category, and others. These reports may be costly, but are helpful in determining what medium to advertise in and to what your competitors are doing as far as advertising is concerned [Nielsen Media Research Website, 2003].

Print

121   Print advertising includes magazines and newspapers. Print advertising helps a company project a message or position an idea in the consumers' mind. So the message must be effective, as well as clear to the consumer.

122   Fine jewelers spend their advertising dollars on mediums with the highest target market reach and frequency. For instance, when advertising in magazines, fine jewelry retailers advertise in a fashion, high quality, or monthly magazine such as InStyle, Allure, MarieClaire, Cigar Aficianado, and the like because it reaches a large audience, and the appropriate target audience. When advertising in newspapers, fine jewelry retailers consider the size of the ad space, its cost, and focus on capturing the target audience's attention. Of course, the larger the advertising space, the more expensive the ad will be. For instance, many fine jewelers advertise in The New York Times and The Wall Street Journal because these will reach their target market. Also, the frequency for these newspapers is high. As a result, advertising expenses in print media, with a high daily or monthly circulation, are expensive. However, it is an expense that is important and necessary in building and promoting brand image [Nielsen Media Research Website, 2003].

Television

123   Television reaches a large audience as well. To insure advertising dollars are spent on networks and shows that reach the target audience, specialty fine jewelry retailers have to

research what type of network and shows their audience watches. This is based on the target market's lifestyle and interests. The best way to Figure out what type of shows their audience watches is through Nielsen ratings data. It offers demographic information for all television shows and network view, indicates the type of shows the target demographic watches, indicates what commercials are watched by the specific demographic group, and specifies the ratings data for that demographic group during certain time slots. In choosing the networks to advertise on, specialty fine jewelry retailers look at the ratings data of that network, time slots its target audience watches television, and shows the audience watches in determining when it is a good time to advertise [Nielsen Media Research Website, 2003].

124   Fine jewelry retailers use the media to advertise their products and to gain visibility. Often times, celebrities wear a fine jeweler's product at an awards ceremony. Fine jewelry retailers look for celebrity sponsors months in advance of an award show or charity event to help promote brand image and products. Generally, fine jewelers look for high-profile individuals or celebrities to wear their fine jewelry pieces. The reason for this is because the celebrity gains public attention when walking down the red carpet and the public wants to know what the celebrity is wearing. The media focuses in on what celebrities are wearing, everything from fine jewelry, clothes, shoes, sunglasses, makeup, and hair. Using celebrities can be an effective form of advertising and promoting.

Outdoor

125   Bus depots or billboards on major highways and routes are the most visible form of outdoor advertising. They are used to attract the lower to higher income individuals since these individuals take mass transit to work or drive to certain destinations. Fine jewelry retailers look for areas with high traffic to advertise their brand image or product. Outdoor advertising is very effective since it reaches a large target market. It also provides for greater visibility and reinforcement of brand image and recognition of a product.

Geographic Region

126   Specialty fine jewelry retailers have both domestic stores and international stores. There are many markets that have been tapped into domestically and internationally. Yet, many markets are still new and expanding. Presence of stores in major cities, potential markets, and in prime retail locations where target demographic profile individuals are populated in are important keys to success for fine jewelers.

Domestic

127   Many specialty fine jewelers have a large presence in the United States before going abroad. In doing so, fine jewelers establish a name for themselves domestically before going internationally. Fine jewelers saturate areas that are more densely populated because this is where targeted demographics are located—major United States cities. For example, fine jewelers do business in major United States cities such as New York City, San Francisco, Miami, Austin, Chicago, Beverly Hills, and other large populated United States cities.

128   As fine jewelers saturate the United States market, competition amongst each other, as well as local competitors force movement towards international markets and potential markets. However, the costs associated with international expansion are high and are not possible without a solid financial situation. So fine jewelers look into markets that could help reduce costs, whether operational costs, production costs, labor costs, or material costs and the like.

International

129   The visibility and increase in number of stores are important in major cities and markets. Japan is one of the leading countries purchasing luxury fine jewelry resulting in greater

sales revenue in this area alone. Most fine jewelers cater to the Japanese by establishing retail stores in the densely populated areas of Japan. While other fine jewelry retailers are expanding into markets that have potential growth such as China, Brazil, and Canada.

130   The expansion of free trade has reduced the global cost of production, when China became a member of the World Trade Organization in 2002. At the same time, rising global trades increased economies of scale and companies looking for low-cost source of production. China's membership to the World Trade Organization opened an opportunity for fine jewelers [Gomelsky, 2003].

131   With China having direct business ties with diamond manufacturers, fine jewelers could pursue building supplier relationships with the Chinese to help secure future diamond needs. While China was only in eighth place in the purchase of polished diamonds, within two to three years it was expected to be among the top three markets [Gomelsky, 2003]. However, fine jewelers needed to look into additional potential markets or develop other strategies that would help it gain increased market share and increase net sales in existing operating geographic areas, as well as in potential new areas.

132   The growing desire for fine jewelry in Brazil has created it to be a potential market. In addition, its low design and operation costs cause fine jewelers to expand in this market. Due to Brazil's low costs, many fine jewelers are licensing with Brazilian designers. This is a mutual benefit because the Brazilian designers want to work for a luxury brand fine jeweler and the fine jewelers wanted to utilize the low cost design and operations in Brazil. At the same time, many fine jewelers began licensing with Brazilian designers. This was a mutual benefit because the Brazilian designers longed to work for a luxury brand fine jeweler and the fine jewelers wanted to utilize the low cost design and operations in Brazil. In addition, with the Brazilian market growing, Brazil's jewelry confederation began to channel its energy into providing technical support, market research, and promotional incentives for Brazilian jewelry designers as part of a large effort to increase jewelry exports to $500 million by 2003 [Gomelsky, 2003]. This posed a threat to fine jewelers in other countries because not only was it receiving competition from other fine jewelers in the area, but the Brazilian designers were trying to filter into the competition too.

133   Canada is another potential market in the fine jewelry industry because of its thriving diamond industry and mines in the area. The purchase of mines can help control the diamonds needs and prices. For instance, the more mines and control of diamonds a company has, the company can control the pricing based on its availability. Fine jewelers were looking to be the first to monopolize market share in Canada by investing in Canadian mines. Being a pioneer in the fine jewelry industry by investing in diamond mines, was expected to help hold a specialty fine jeweler's diamond holdings and help streamline its sourcing process. As a result of larger holdings of diamonds, this generally also meant a larger portion of the market share could be obtained [Gomelsky, 2003].

134   Competitors such as Zales have presence in Canada and are expanding its operations. When expanding beyond the domestic borders, companies consider their financial situation. Having financial resources to back store expansion and renovation, to purchase a new location, and to research the potential market, can help better situate a company in that market. The use of technology allows for communication across the globe. It helps with operation efficiency and increases competition. Some things to consider when expanding internationally are demographics, location, culture, economy, technology, tradition, and infrastructure. Another thing to consider is local competition. Louis Vuitton Moet Hennessy Group (LVMH) and DeBeers are competitors in the fine jewelry industry, as well as other local stores located, for example, in the Diamond District of New York. LVMH and the De Beers diamond group decided to form a jewelry company under independent management that is relying on the strong potential of the De Beers name and the LVMH group's expertise in the global management of luxury brands. With headquarters in London, De Beers LV

intends to build a high-end global jewelry chain with the first store scheduled to open in late 2002, or 2003 [LVMH Website, 2003].

Competition

135   Competition is intense in the fine jewelry sector. There is competition from retail stores, catalogs, and the Internet. Fine jewelers compete through differentiation. Some offer differentiation through quality, craftsmanship, value, price, and brand. Others offer specialized pieces that are not available from any other retailer. For example, a specialized piece may be a signature piece that helps identify the company when worn, display the power of the brand, and anchor a strong category.

136   The major competitors in fine jewelry retail sector are: Zales Corporation, Harry Winston, and David Yurman.

Zales Corporation

137   Zales is one of North America's largest specialty fine jewelry retailers. It sells diamonds, colored stones, and gold jewelry (diamond fashion rings, semi-precious stones, earrings, gold chains), watches, and gift items. With about 2,300 stores, primarily in malls, throughout the United States, Canada, and Puerto Rico, Zales operates four large chains aimed at different jewelry markets: Bailey Banks & Biddle Fine Jewelers, Gordon's Jewelers, Zales Jewelers, and Piercing Pagoda. Also, with more than 90 jewelry outlet stores and about 170 stores in Canada under the Peoples Jewelers and Mappins Jewelers names, Zales has extensive retail store distribution, as well as online distribution [Hoover's Online, 2003A].

138   Zales has a strong product category offering a diversified product portfolio of signature products, bridal products, and men's products at competitive prices. For instance, Zales has the Zales Diamond Three Stone Band and the Zales Diamond Anniversary Band that are signature products to help it compete in the industry. A band is usually a wider engagement or wedding ring. Zales is strong in the extensive men's product line because other competitors lack a men's product line. In addition, Zales is able to identify trends in the industry and is successful in producing innovative line extensions such as the Zales Diamond Anniversary Band and the Zales Diamond Three Stone Band to anchor a strong and growing bridal category.

139   Zales has a large presence in major domestic cities. However, it has limited presence in international countries. This is largely due to its technology, which can be upgraded in the near future to improve communications and operation efficiency. Instead, Zales expanded its international operations by utilizing other large fine jewelry stores to sell its Zales brand and products in other countries. By outsourcing and using other fine jewelers' resources, Zales is able to compete. It uses the other large fine jewelry stores' operations as a combined effort to compete in the international market and simultaneously minimize costs.

140   Through Zales' well-trained sales force which develops through effective training programs, Zales' customer service is strong. Its customer service is able to provide product information, help customers find what they are looking for, and assist customers in their shopping experience. The acceptance of credit card payments at Zales allows customers to conveniently shop and the easy return and exchange policies allow customers to shop with confidence. However, its uninspired retail store décor and dim lighting weaken the customers' shopping experience.

141   Its competitive prices offer customers a selection of fine jewelry pieces at various price ranges. It is hard for Zales to gain customer loyalty because lower price equates with lower quality. However, its signature pieces have given Zales brand recognition and image. Although Zales' advertising campaigns can be improved to promote quality and brand, Zales uses its signature pieces as a way of advertising. When customers wear the signature piece, it promotes brand image and recognition. For example, its signature Zales Diamond

Three Stone Band is the trendiest engagement ring today, as noted by Albert Gad, President of Diamonds International [Diamonds International Website, 2003].

142 With focus on high volume products always kept in inventory, Zales can position itself in the market. With differentiated and diverse brands, innovative marketing and merchandising, and an experienced team of supporting store personnel, Zales has used these success factors to leverage itself in the specialty fine jewelry retail market, and gain a position there.

Harry Winston

143 Harry Winston, who was the son of a New York jeweler, established the House of Harry Winston in 1932. The company buys, designs, and sells diamonds and gems. With retail stores in New York and Paris, the company's clientele includes sultans, starlets, and other affluent types who can afford the average $100,000 price tag for a Winston bauble. To broaden its clientele, Harry Winston is seeking to shed some of its exclusive aura and adopt a more approachable image. Private-equity firm Fenway Partners acquired a significant stake in the company in 2000 [Hoover's Online, 2003A].

144 Harry Winston offers quality fine jewelry pieces. Its utilization of different metals, quality grade precious stones, detailed designs, high craftsmanship, and innovative signature brands has attracted an elite, exclusive client base. Its client base of individuals, such as the most powerful industrialists, wealthiest potentates, prominent royal families and celebrated stars, have bought their most treasured jewels from Harry Winston and continue to do so today. Its quality products result in a high price tag that can be afforded by its elite, exclusive client base. In many cases where large-ticketed items are sold, the fine jeweler does not compete in price to differentiate itself, but rather, compete on quality. These individuals enjoy secure shopping since they pay large ticketed prices.

145 Celebrities advertising Harry Winston's latest trends, especially during Golden Globes, Academy Awards, and other galas, helps gain brand recognition. Many customers often desire Harry Winston pieces because the fine jewelry piece is seen worn by a celebrity. The notion that customers seek to imitate celebrities is an innovative way to advertise. The fine jewelry industry knows this that is why it seeks to have celebrities wear its products for greater visibility and advertisement of the brand image and product. It has built a strong brand image that has appealed to its target market for decades.

146 Its specialized operation of cutting the rough diamond, polishing, designing, and creating the finished jewel, is conducted in Winston's New York building on Fifth Avenue. This specialization gives them an advantage over its competitors who outsource this operation. Also, innovative product designs that Harry Winston first introduced when he began to employ light, flexible, platinum settings allowed for three-dimensional arrangements of precious stones. This produced new levels of brilliance that emphasized the jewels' own shapes that brought a whole new level to the fine jewelry industry [Harry Winston Website, 2003].

147 Harry Winston has prime retail location stores to accommodate shoppers, but its saturation in markets is weak. Harry Winston may have operations in exclusive retail stores in New York, Geneva, Paris, Beverly Hills and in Tokyo, but it generally has limited store locations in China, Brazil, Canada, and other potential markets. Also, since convenience is a growing shopping trend, Harry Winston's unwillingness to offer online shopping has affected its potential growth.

David Yurman

148 David Yurman's strength are its nature blend of sculptural design and fine craftsmanship in precious and semi-precious materials. David Yurman quickly achieved its status as a leading luxury jewelry brand since its establishment in 1979. Its pieces can be found at authorized dealers, like luxury department store retailers such as Saks Fifth Avenue, Neiman Marcus, and Carlyle and Co. as well as its company operated stores in New York and in California

[QAD Inc., 2002]. However, its retail store presence is very weak internationally. It depends on the trust and integrity that it has built over many years with its customers to compete in the industry.

149   This internationally acclaimed designer has masterfully combined the aesthetics and craftsmanship of fine jewelry with fashion. David Yurman paved the way for a new era in fine jewelry with wearable, classic designs that carry a distinctive signature cable look. Utilizing its unique cable motif, David Yurman creates a blend of classic and contemporary styles incorporated into its sterling silver, 18 karat gold Cable Collection, and David Yurman Timepieces for men and women. One of David Yurman's strengths is its innovative signature cable motif product that helps promote brand recognition. However, with the growing trend of brides-to-be and men making fine jewelry purchase, David Yurman is weak in providing and extensive line of products for these growing markets.

150   David Yurman has selected MFG/PRO eB2 to serve as its enterprise platform for effective manufacturing and distribution operations and QAD eQ for streamlined, intelligent order management. Its strength in technology has positioned it to operate, manufacture and distribute more efficiently. With MFG/PRO eB2 and QAD eQ, David Yurman uses real-time, accurate information to achieve operational efficiencies, improve collaboration with suppliers and major retail customers, and support the company's future expansion. The new platform, incorporated into its operation in December 2002, helped automate and streamline sales order management and analysis, procurement, production planning and execution, quality management, and distribution logistics. The QAD solutions also offer David Yurman supplier and customer collaboration capabilities. QAD solutions is crucial for its business. Since styles are introduced or discontinued throughout the year, accurate order commitments are crucial to its seasonal business and business operations that require production to-stock, production to-order, for consignment, as well as support for foreign currencies. The use of technology and real-time information has been beneficial in David Yurman's expansion in the fine jewelry retail segment [QAD Inc., 2002]. Its improved technology may help David Yurman's presence internationally since it is currently limited.

Other Competition

151   Besides Zales Corporation, Harry Winston, and David Yurman, fine jewelers also face competition from imitators and counterfeiters. Oftentimes, imitation jewelry is made from small companies that mainly sell through websites. Selling through websites allows them to reach a large audience. Their strength is low prices for luxury fine jewelry look-alikes. Customers know that the jewelry piece is not quality, but because of its significantly low prices, at a fraction of luxury fine jewelry costs, customers purchase it.

152   When budget is a consideration, many fine jewelry aficionados turn to imitation, or simulated, gemstones, many of which offer much of the stunning beauty of the original gems. Legally, only actual gems can be called by their true names. Imitations are typically given similar names to identify them as imitation. For example, imitation names such as balas ruby (spinel), herkimer diamond (quartz), and even emerald (essentially any greenish stone). New names for imitations are created as needed [Retail Jewelers Organization Website, 2002].

153   Imitators advertise through the Internet, since a large portion of their business is through this channel. However, the imitators may face prosecution if a fine jeweler decides to press charges for selling imitation jewelry and trademark infringement. For example, on April 23, 2003, the owners of Enddi Silver and Starglam.com were arrested in conjunction with selling Tiffany knockoff jewelry and signature blue packaging [Molofsky, 2003]. Emitations.com and Overstockjeweler.com also sell imitation designs made by Tiffany & Co., Harry Winston, and David Yurman, which are damaging to these companies' revenues and reputation.

THE COMPANY

History

154 Tiffany & Co. is a retailer, designer, manufacturer, and distributor of fine jewelry. Its product category has expanded since it established in 1837 as a stationery store in downtown Manhattan, New York. Established by Charles Lewis Tiffany and his schoolmate John Young, Tiffany's first day of sales in 1837 totaled $4.98. Today, fine jewelry makes up about 79% of its sales. Other products include timepieces, stationery, chinaware, crystal, sterling silverware, fragrances, and gifts and accessories. It has stores in the United States as well as in international markets around the world. With Charles' vision of establishing the grandest preeminent house of design and the world's premier jewelry house, his vision has held true even over a century later [Tiffany & Co. Website, 2003].

155 Tiffany operates three channels of sales and distribution: domestic and international company-operated retail stores, catalog, and the Internet. It shows a strong retail store presence both domestically and internationally. However, its international retail sales are less than domestic retail sales, even though the number of international retail stores are nearly double that of the United States. Tiffany has hit the "2001 Top 40 Plus," National Jeweler's Annual Report that ranks the largest United States and Canadian retail jewelry chain sales. With four new stores in the United States, Tiffany's rank increased five notches to rank 17. Its focus on expanding company-operated stores both domestically and internationally is a strength in increasing its revenue, brand image, and respectable reputation. However, there are markets outside the United States where the fine jewelry retail sector is rapidly expanding. Other competitors have started to expand in the Canadian, Brazilian, and Chinese markets with very little presence. Tiffany has one store in each of these growing markets and is slowly expanding. It is more concerned with expanding the number of company-operated retail stores and neglecting what matters the most—customers. Tiffany has to improve its offerings per store to satisfy the needs of the customers. This can be done through enhancing the retail shopping experience: offering more products and offering superior service per square feet of retail selling space. The international market share is at risk. It is a future external problem if Tiffany has not rethought its management strategy and cash in on the growing fine jewelry retail expansion and trend in these international areas.

156 Tiffany's Internet sales are strong because it provides a secure shopping site that is easy to navigate. Its products are easy to search for on the website which makes it convenient for its customers to shop. Products can be found by category or collection. Its secure shopping site with the Verisign approved logo and encryption codes for security allow customers to shop with confidence.

157 Tiffany's inventory is readily available when customers shop in the retail store, catalog, or the Internet. This is largely due to its technology that helps it collect customer information to predict sales and trends. However, improvements in its technology and upgrade to QAD solutions can help streamline processes.

158 With its strong advertising programs that promote quality, craftsmanship, value, price, and brand of its products, Tiffany has established a strong reputation. All this can be incorporated into the enhanced retail shopping experience per square feet of retail sales. The shade of blue known as the trademark "Tiffany Blue" symbolizes elegance and exclusivity only available at Tiffany stores, which is one of its keys to success in the industry [Tiffany & Co. Website, 2003]. However, other advertising campaigns can help strengthen its position, for example, its weak use of celebrities to sponsor its products. The use of celebrities to wear Tiffany's fine jewelry could help gain awareness of its products as well as its brand.

159 Another weakness of Tiffany is its products are geared towards women. Its product lines have a few selection of pieces geared towards men. While the company may sell luxury and exclusive items mainly marketed towards women and high-income customers, there are other demographics groups such as males and middle-income individuals that Tiffany can target. These demographic groups are areas of opportunity for Tiffany since males spend the most money on a piece of adornment and shop the most for luxury jewelry gifts. Middle-income individuals are also willing to pay high-prices to own quality fine jewelry.

160   An internal problem that Tiffany currently faces now and in the near future is the imitations and counterfeits of its products. As a result of this, Tiffany loses millions in revenue each year to the counterfeiters. At the same time, it is both costly and damaging to its reputation of quality, craftsmanship, value, price, and luxury brand.

161   With advances in communication and technology, there are low trade barriers in the fine jewelry industry. Low-cost sourcing is available to almost everyone in the pipeline allowing for globalization and eliminating possible middlemen. This allows for the newest trends and developments in the industry to be communicated faster. For example, the customer tells the sales staff what he/she is interested in. If a number of customers request a similar piece of fine jewelry, this message is then relayed to the manufacturer. As a result, the trends and needs of the customers are communicated quickly with a faster turnaround time for fine jewelers to react to the changing needs.

Products

162   Fine jewelry makes up about 79% of Tiffany's sales in 2001. Other products include time-pieces, stationery, chinaware, crystal, sterling silverware, fragrances, and gifts and accessories [Tiffany & Co., 2001]. Known for its quality, craftsmanship, and value, Tiffany has established a brand name for itself in the specialty fine jewelry retail sector of luxury goods. Through its strong advertising campaigns, diversified portfolio of products, and license arrangements with third-party designers such as Elsa Peretti and Paloma Picasso, Tiffany is able to produce innovative designs that are signature Tiffany style brands. These signature products contribute to Tiffany's established brand name and success in the industry.

FIGURE 9   **Tiffany & Co.**

Tiffany & Co.								
PRODUCTS	CUSTOMERS	SALES AND DISTRIBUTION	OPERATIONS	MANUFACTURING AND DESIGNING	TECHNOLOGY	ADVERTISING	GEOGRPAHIC REGION	COMPETITION

Fine Jewelry
- Rings
- Necklaces
- Earrings
- Pendants
- Bracelets
- Cuff Links
- Diamonds
- Precious Stones
- Semi Precious Stones
- Brooches
 	
Timepieces
- Watches
- Clocks
Stationery
- Writing Instruments
 	
Chinaware
 	
Crystal
Sterling Silverware
Fragrance
 	
Gifts & Accessories
- Frames
- Keyrings
	Gender
	  Males
	  Females
	Age
	- Seniors
	- Baby Boomers
	- Generation X
	- Generation Y
	High Income
		Retailing
		Catalog
		Internet
			Linked Communications
			JIT
			Training Programs
			Inventory Control
			Quality Control
				Domestic Facilities
				In-House Designers
				Global Facilities
				Outsource
					QAD
					Real Time
						Media
						Print
						Outdoor
							North America
							- United States
							Northeast
							Southeast
							Midwest
							Southwest
							West
							Hawaii
							Canada
							Mexico
							
							Australia
							-Melbourne
							-Sydney
							Asia-Pacific
							
							South America
							- Brazil
							China
							Europe
							- England
							- France
							- Germany
							- Italy
							- Switzerland
								Zales
								Harry Winston
								David Yurman

163   Its strong quality and durable pieces help project a positive brand name. With its utilization of different metals and stones, and detailed designs and styles with minimal flaws, Tiffany is able to offer quality and durable pieces. Simultaneously, it provides strong brand name and long-term value synonymous with the Tiffany name. Its strong differentiated products through signature products such as "Return To Tiffany" collection, that are trendy and fashionable pieces, offer an everlasting piece for every occasion to its customers.

164   Tiffany also offers various price ranges to compete in the industry. It offers a sterling silver collection that is priced less than its other fine jewelry pieces. This attracts a market that makes purchase decisions based on price.

165   When Tiffany's fine jewelry pieces are worn, it maintains its luster through the years and fulfill the desire for well-being. The desire for well-being and how it makes a customer feel is one of the top purchase motivators for luxury goods. Figure 10 shows the "Top Purchase Motivators for Luxury Goods" surveyed by *Advertising Age* and conducted by Ziccardi Partners Frierson Mee.

Customers

166   Tiffany caters to Seniors, Baby Boomers, Generation X, and Generation Y. By capturing these age groups that can readily spend and generations that are highly influenced, Tiffany can strategically position itself to be a brand representing preeminence for years to come for men, women, and all generations. Tiffany's reacts to new market trends that strategically help position itself in the market by developing products desired by its target market.

Gender

167   Specialty fine jewelers catered to both males and females.

168   *Males*   Males purchased jewelry pieces for themselves as well as expensive fine jewelry as gifts for others. Also, men are more involved in shopping since they grew up in households where their mothers were career women. So, their mothers would send them to purchase their own clothes, buy groceries for the house and run errands. Men also became more involved with shopping for apartment furniture and selecting items for the bridal registry. This was an opportunity for Tiffany to cater to this market.

169   *Females*   Females were entering the workforce and relied more on convenience when shopping. They enjoy purchasing fine jewelry to lavish themselves and decorate their style. More women were entering the workforce with little time to shop. This opportunity encouraged Tiffany to use Internet technology to cater to this group.

FIGURE 10
Top Purchase Motivators for Luxury Goods

Source: Advertising Age (2002). [Online]. *http://www.adage.com/news.cms?newsId=34174.* Accessed February 26, 2003.

Top Purchase Motivators for Luxury Goods/Services	Respondents Rating among Their Top 5
To buy things I know will last	76.65%
For my well-being	61.10%
To enjoy my favorite brands	51.74%
To feel good about myself	50.47%
To indulge myself	49.53%
To express myself	46.37%
To be able to rationalize my purchase	36.28%
To feel successful	30.60%
To be optimistic	29.97%
To be lighthearted	23.34%
To make an impression	17.03%
To be impulsive	12.62%
To be fabulous	7.89%
As a status symbol	6.00%

Age

170   **Seniors**   This generation, 65 years and older, were expected to comprise nearly 15 percent of the United States population by 2015. Tiffany caters to this group with features such as bright lighting, large signs, convenient parking, and mass transportation near retail stores. Since classic and antique jewelry designs were very popular with this age group, Tiffany offers antique looking designs such as its Tiffany Bubbles collection.

171   **Baby Boomers**   This generation, ages 38 to 56 years, focuses on luxury, travel and leisure. With their kids not living at home, this generation is also known as the "Empty Nesters." They also represent 40 million credit card users, which is about 50% of credit card owners in the U.S. [E-Com Profits, 2003]. Tiffany caters to their discretionary income and focus on luxury with the different Tiffany collections, diamonds, and gemstones by offering luxury and diversified products. Tiffany also offers store credit cards to further reiterate brand and reach the Baby Boomer generation since they prefer to make purchases with credit cards.

172   *Generation X*   This generation was born between 1965 and 1976. Generation Xers were 26 to 37 years of age in 2002 and were born in the era of the Information Age. Specialty retailers give the Generation Xers experiences that fit their lifestyle and aspirations and information that keeps them informed. Purchases via the Internet are high in this age group. Tiffany offers sales via the Internet for this age group and others for the convenience and ease of shopping. Also, its sterling silver collection (i.e. Return to Tiffany and Elsa Peretti) is priced accordingly to cater to this age group. This makes its collections more price competitive with other specialty fine jewelry retailers in this market.

173   *Generation Y*   Generation Y comprises 8 to 25 year olds. They make their own purchase choice, but are influenced by their parents' spending habits. This age segment that is starting to work is price conscious and makes many purchase decisions based on price. Tiffany targets this group with its lower priced collections, such as Return to Tiffany & Co. sterling silver jewelry and gifts, while still offering the Tiffany brand that represents quality, craftsmanship, value, and brand in each fine jewelry piece.

High Income

174   High-income individuals are affluent and enjoy luxury items. With their taste for luxury, Tiffany offers diamonds, gemstones, and higher karat metals to these individuals. The Tiffany brand provides status that high-income individuals seek. Also, the pricing of products denotes quality, craftsmanship, and value synonymous to its price range that high-income level individuals look for.

Sales and Distribution

175   Tiffany operates three channels of sales and distribution. The first is United States and international retail through company-operated retail stores. Secondly, is Internet sales and wholesale sales to independent retailers and distributors in certain markets. Finally, direct marketing via catalog sales and Internet sales in the United States [Tiffany & Co., 2001]. By offering product quality, craftsmanship, value and innovative designs as well as expanding its channels of sales and distribution, Tiffany has strategically positioned itself in both the domestic and international markets. However, there is always room for expansion in new channels of sales and distribution.

Retail Stores

176   Tiffany stores are located in prime retail space areas that have high visibility and high-traffic. This contributes to the convenience factor for working women and for target markets. The locations of the stores are in high-end areas to support the high-income level individuals it targets. The stores are company-operated with a knowledgeable sales

staff of its products. With the bright lighting, attractive "Tiffany Blue" displays, beautiful packaging, well-trained sales staff, acceptance of all forms of payment, and well-stocked inventory, customers are attracted to the shopping experience Tiffany offers when entering the retail store.

177 To differentiate itself, Tiffany offers a memorable shopping experience. Tiffany offers a memorable shopping experience by offering a greater retail store experience per square foot of selling space. This means expanded selections of products, presented in an elegant, warm environment that celebrates the Tiffany name. This experience is offered to increase revenue per square foot of retail selling space and to increase repeated customer purchases. Tiffany is changing its strategies on expansion of the number of company-operated stores, to expand selling per square foot by offering customers a shopping experience they would never forget.

178 Besides selling its products in company-operated retail stores, Tiffany also sells to independent retailers and distributors in certain markets. For instance, its fragrances and timepieces may be found in department stores. However, Tiffany's core operations of selling fine jewelry remain in its company-operated retail stores.

Catalog

179 Tiffany offers a Tiffany Business catalog, a Tiffany Diamond and the Measure of Brilliance catalog, and a Tiffany Selections catalog. Each catalog contains product lines that fall into the category that fit the individual customer or customer's choice of purchase. The Tiffany Business catalog offers business related products such as writing instruments, business cardholders, and the like. These are gifts designed for clients or for colleagues in mind. The catalogs have limited inventory compared to shopping in the retail store. However, there are items offered in the catalog that are exclusive giving customers an incentive to shop via the catalogs.

180 The convenient policy of returning catalog purchases at retail stores is a key to its catalogs' success. Customers seek hassle-free returns and exchanges when making purchases and Tiffany offers this through either returning the item via mail where postage is paid by Tiffany or by bringing the item to a Tiffany retail store.

Internet

181 Tiffany offers its products via the company website, www.tiffany.com. The security and easy navigation that the site offers are keys to its success. The site is divided into collections as well as product categories so search for a particular product is made easy. The online shop also provides the Verisign secure logo which indicates that shopping on the Tiffany website is secure. This is a main concern of customers especially when their credit card numbers are given out. Each fine jewelry piece purchased is individually wrapped and delivered in the famous "Tiffany Blue" packaging. The shopping experience online from the quality product being purchased down to the last little detail of beautiful individually wrapped items in the "Tiffany Blue" box and bag are things that keep the customer satisfied and coming back for repeated purchases.

182 When a customer visits the website, the technology allows for automatic collection of information about the customer. For instance, the web server automatically recognizes only the visitor's domain name (not the email address) and records the visitor's browser and platform type (such as Netscape browser or Microsoft platform). Cookies are used to record the visitor's session such as the visitor's shopping selections when ordering. User-specific information is also recorded such as the pages the visitor selects for viewing. Also, visitor-keyed information such as registrations and transaction information is kept to build its customer database, to later reach the customers through other means such as via catalog or send them notifications of promotions. All this data is helpful to Tiffany and are keys in

helping it improve its Internet website, promote brand image, promote brand recognition, and understand customer needs.

183   Tiffany acquired an approximate 5.4% equity interest in Della.com Inc. in February 2000. Della.com is a provider of online wedding gift registry services. After the acquisition, the company entered into a gift registry service agreement and the company offered its products through Della's site. Della developed an online wedding gift registry for Tiffany. Later in 2000, Della.com merged with the WeddingChannel.com. Tiffany saw the growing bridal trend and was proactive in developing a gift registry for this segment. Noticing the growing trend in the bridal market, Tiffany has tried to incorporate products that are relevant to this category. For instance, Tiffany's signature solitaire engagement ring has made the Tiffany brand more popular. The "Tiffany Solitaire" name is a universal name used for six prongs, solitaire diamond ring setting in the fine jewelry industry. By establishing a popular, signature product, Tiffany is able to help promote its brand image through this product in an industry that equates brand to quality, craftsmanship, and value.

Operations

184   Tiffany's linked communication between suppliers and personnel has allowed a strong relationship to be built. It helps in its operation of sales by replenishing inventory and meeting customer demands through real-time data. The supplier relation Tiffany has helps with quality management, inventory control, and just-in-time operations. Feedback and constant communication helps build the relationship stronger, and as a result, create quality products effectively, and in the most cost effective manner.

185   The supplier and company relationship is like a marriage. There has to be communication of expectations in order to develop a trusting relationship. Once the products are produced, the timely delivery of the products (for just-in-time) is important as well. Tiffany's inventory management and schedule are timely and effective so that inventory will always be on hand.

186   When products are received by the retail store, there is a knowledgeable sales force that sells the fine jewelry. Besides purchasing a fine jewelry piece, customers receive information about what they are purchasing through the trained sales force.

Manufacturing/Designing

187   Tiffany has manufacturing plants both domestically and internationally. It recently set up a factory in the tundra town of Yellowknife, Canada to cut part of the mine's production, which it sources through an agreement with junior partner Aber Resources. The $70 million cost of the strategic investment in Aber was a strategic move since Aber holds a 40% interest in the Diavik Diamonds Project in Canada's Northwest Territories, an operation being developed to mine gem-quality diamonds. In addition, Tiffany has entered into a diamond purchase agreement with Aber. This relationship will help Tiffany secure a good portion of its future diamond needs. This suggests that Tiffany is becoming more streamlined especially by purchasing a diamond mine.

188   Also, Tiffany has licensed agreements with designers such as Elsa Peretti and Paloma Picasso who specifically design for Tiffany. Their innovative designs, sold exclusively at Tiffany, provide added leverage in the competitive environment.

Advertising

189   With its marketing and advertising programs that promote the quality, craftsmanship, value, and design of its products, Tiffany enhances customer awareness through various forms of advertising mediums and markets that it serves. The shade of blue known as the trademark "Tiffany Blue" symbolizes elegance and exclusivity only available at the Tiffany stores, which is a key to success for establishing its brand image and awareness. Tiffany's main advertising mediums are print, television, and outdoor. These mediums are used for visibility of brand awareness and help sustain long-term sales growth.

Print

190 Tiffany advertises in high-end, luxury and fashion magazines with a large circulation. Print ads appeared in InStyle, New Yorker, Cigar Aficionado, and the like. By doing so, Tiffany reaches a larger number of people who read these particular magazines. Print also includes advertising in newspapers. Large ads are taken out in newspapers for greater visibility, such as a quarter of the page in The New York Times. The affluent market, the market that Tiffany caters to, reads the New York Times and high-end, luxury, fashion magazines. These print channels allow for greater reach and frequency catering Tiffany's market.

Television

191 Since this is the largest and usually the most expensive medium, financial resources have to be available for this type of advertising. Tiffany spent about $68.1 million on media (includes television), $65.4 million on production, and $57.3 million on catalogs in 2002. Media is the most expensive because it causes the most impact on the target market. Production costs are the costs associated with producing television ads and print advertising such as drawing the ad, using quality paper stock, and using quality photography.

192 Since costs associated to advertising are expensive, choosing the right medium that has the largest reach and frequency is important to not waste financial resources. Research is implemented in choosing the right medium. This is based on the target market's lifestyle and interests. Tiffany uses Nielsen Television ratings data to maximize its advertising dollars by researching its target market's television programming choice and network based on its lifestyle and interests. It offers demographic information for all television shows and network view, indicates the type of shows the target demographic watches, indicates what commercials are watched by the specific demographic, and specifies the ratings data for that demographic during certain time slots.

Outdoor

193 Tiffany advertises on billboards where there is high traffic and high visibility. Advertisements along the side of major highways or routes are where a Tiffany billboard can be found.

194 Bus depots are another place where Tiffany advertises in the United States, as well as abroad. This helps with promoting the brand image and Tiffany's products by conditioning the consumer's mind with these messages or pictures advertised. The outdoor medium reaches its high-income market who may drive, the women who take mass transit to work, as well as other potential target markets.

Geographic Region

195 Tiffany has 44 United States company-operated retail stores and 82 international company-operated retail stores. Its United States' sales are greater even though its number of international company-operated stores is nearly double. Before Tiffany decides to expand and open another company-operated store, its biggest concern is to focus on how to increase sales revenue in its international stores.

Domestic

196 Tiffany's strength is its presence in major United States cities such as New York, San Francisco, St. Louis, and other major cities. Tiffany's focus on expanding company-operated stores both domestically and internationally is a strength in helping it increase its revenue, brand image, and respectable reputation.

197 Another strength of Tiffany is its location in these major United States cities. Its domestic retail stores are located in prime retail space that is accessible by mass transit or driving based on nearby infrastructure. Tiffany's large presence in targeted demographic areas allow for its target market to easily shop. However, since most of the high-income individual lived in suburbs, Tiffany had limited presence in these areas. Its stores were mainly located in urban areas, similar to its competitors.

International

198 Tiffany has 82 company-operated retail stores internationally. Its strong presence in international markets has helped it build brand image as well as generate revenues to help with future expansion. Its largest international market is in Japan, generating the highest international sales. However, its overall international sales were lower, even though its number of international retail stores were nearly double that of the United States. By using its Japan retail store as an example for other international stores to follow, Tiffany may be able to increase its international sales revenue. Japan offered a greater shopping experience per square feet of selling space through its product offering, sales staff, store layout and décor, and even through its "Tiffany Blue" packaging. All these factors contributed to the higher purchase per visit by a customer per square feet of selling space.

199 Tiffany opened one company-operated store in each potential market, such as China, Brazil, and Canada. Since China's membership in the World Trade Organization in 2002, expansion of free trade reduced the global cost of production and caused rising global trades. Since rising global trades increased economies of scale, Tiffany looked for low-cost source of production in China and in Brazil. China was excellent for custom designing and cheap labor, while Brazil was great for its low design and operation costs. This new collaboration with the Brazilians and Chinese helped Tiffany with low-cost source of production and producing innovative products. Tiffany's strength is not only producing innovative and fashionable pieces to cater to its market, but also its streamlined process. Since Canada's growing trend in diamonds, Tiffany purchased a diamond mine in Canada to help it gain a holding of the diamonds in the industry and to cater to the growing trend.

Financials

200 Tiffany was in a good financial position in 2002 as shown in Figure 11. Its liquidity needs are expected to remain the same because of its seasonal working capital and capital expenditures, which have increased due to its expansion. Working capital (current assets less current liabilities) and the corresponding current ratio (current assets divided by current liabilities) were $612,978,000 and 2.8:1 at January 31, 2002 compared to $667,647,000 and 3.0:1 at January 31, 2001.

201 Capital expenditures and payment of a capital lease purchase obligation were $210,291,000 in 2001 and $108, 382,000 in 2000. A portion of the capital expenditures was related to the renovation and expansion of stores, investment in new systems, office facilities, and internal jewelry manufacturing.

202 Tiffany suffered a loss in 2001 due to economic conditions, especially post September 11th results. Many retailers suffered due to people being out of jobs with very little discretionary income, especially for luxury goods. Tiffany's stock price has decreased. However, Michael J. Kowalski will continue to improve Tiffany's financial position, increase its stock price, and build brand image. His ongoing strategy will help Tiffany maintain competitiveness as well as produce greater presence in the fine jewelry retail industry. Tiffany's continued expansion will increase total sales area by 25%.

203 As a specialty fine jewelry retailer, the company's business is seasonal in nature. This means that typically the fourth quarter represents a greater percentage of annual sales, and earnings from operations and cash flow.

FIGURE 11
Tiffany & Co.
Financial Highlights
2001 & 2002

Source: Tiffany & Co. Annual
Report 2002

In Thousands, Except per Share Amounts and Percentages	2002	2001	Increase (Decrease)
Net Sales	$1,706,602	$1,606,535	6%
Worldwide Comparable Store Sales (on a Constant Exchange Rate Basis)	$1,382,808	$1,393,836	(1)%
Earnings from Operations	$319,197	$309,897	3%
Earnings from Operations as a Percentage of Net Sales	18.7%	19.3%	
Net Earnings	$189,894	$173,587	9%
Net Earnings as a Percentage of Net Sales	11.1%	10.8%	
Net Earnings per Diluted Share	$1.28	$1.15	11%
Weighted Average Number of Diluted Common Shares	148,591	150,517	
Return on Average Assets	10.7%	10.9%	
Return on Average Stockholders' Equity	16.9%	17.7%	
Net-Debt as a Percentage of Total Capital	13.8%	8.6%	
Cash Dividends per Share	$0.16	$0.16	

The Company's fiscal year ends on January 31 of the following calendar year. All references to years relate to fiscal years rather than calendar years.

Management and Strategy

204   Tiffany's management strategy has grown and continues to evolve in the luxury goods and specialty fine jewelry retailer sector. With new stores opened in 2002, Tiffany is making a presence domestically as well as abroad. With its recent acquisition of Little Switzerland, Tiffany will have a wholly owned subsidiary. Little Switzerland is headquartered in St. Thomas, U.S. Virgin Islands and is a specialty retailer of luxury items. It has operating stores in the Caribbean and Alaska, which help cater to the tourists in that area [Tiffany & Co. Website, 2003].

205   Tiffany has expanded its operations in the last few years. Tiffany recently renovated its New York flagship store, opened 4 more company-operated stores, and expanded into potential markets such as Brazil, China and Canada. Additionally, the investment of Aber Resources would help Tiffany secure a portion of its future diamond needs giving it control over some of the resources. Tiffany's proactive nature has helped it change its strategy and ways to conform to the ever-changing lifestyle and trends of the environment.

206   When China entered the World Trade Organization in 2001, China became the newest potential market for specialty fine jewelry retailers. This market has the greatest potential for expansion as well as the fastest growing fine jewelry market in Asia due to its low-cost production. Considerations of expanding in potential markets like China, as well as Brazil and Canada, are part of the management strategy. Expanding on the number of company-operated retail stores in untapped markets and expanding per square foot of retail space in already existing stores are considerations in the growth of Tiffany and its management.

207   While tapping into potential markets may be a big step, building brand image, and brand recognition are very important when dealing with international markets. The international market should be able to recognize the Tiffany name in order to be successful in that market. New products and designs catering the markets' culture will help the customers realize that Tiffany is sensitive to the markets' culture and its needs. What may work in the United States may not work overseas. This is highlighted in its lower international sales revenue compared to domestic sales revenue. Research in the new potential markets is important in succeeding and generating increased sales revenues. With Michael J. Kowalski as Chairman of the Board and CEO, Tiffany's future is in his hands based on his strategy decisions. It is also his decisions that will mark a new era in the Tiffany timeline.

LOOKING TOWARDS THE FUTURE

208   Although Tiffany has increased its brand awareness that stands for luxury brand quality, craftsmanship, and value jewelry, it still faces the increasing competition and environmental pressures. As Tiffany continues to expand the number of company-operated retail stores in domestic and international markets, it continues to face decisions that need to be made to improve its strategy in order to remain competitive. Decisions regarding product, customers, sales and distribution, operations, manufacturing and design, technology, advertising, and geographic scope are in the hands of Michael J. Kowalski. His decisions will determine the fate of Tiffany as a specialty fine jewelry retailer.

209   The *first alternative* considered was to expand in potential markets like Brazil, Canada, and China.

210   The benefit of this alternative was that these new markets are unsaturated because its competition such as Zales only had a company-operated retail store in Canada with unsaturated markets by Tiffany's other competitors in China and Brazil. Brazil is a growing market for precious and semi-precious jewelry with innovative designs. Canada has diamond mines that can be beneficial to operations and China's membership into the World Trade Organization made it a potential market for low-cost sourcing. Tiffany also had one company-operated store in each of these potential markets giving it leverage in obtaining a larger market share since other competitors have not shown much presence in the areas.

211   The alternative was feasible because Tiffany had brand recognition in these areas, which is needed to be successful when expanding in potential markets. The branded fine jewelry pieces with the Tiffany name symbolized its pride behind each product's work. Tiffany wanted its customers to be proud to wear the fine jewelry purchases branded with the Tiffany name. This not only helped promote brand image and recognition for Tiffany, but it gave the customers a sense of "status" and "well-being" when the fine jewelry piece was worn. The "Tiffany Blue" symbolizes exclusive luxury fine jewelry which is a brand already recognized by all markets both potential and in which it operates.

212   Another reason why this alternative is feasible is because Brazil and China offered manufacturing and production facilities that were less costly. Besides cost effectiveness in these markets, the fine jewelry trend was vastly growing in these areas as well as Canada. Tiffany had the ability to outsource some of its processes if needed in these areas since it was cost effective in these areas. So catering to the potential markets was easy because of outsourcers and manufacturing facilities in these areas.

213   This alternative could win against competition because competition, like David Yurman, has little international presence. Its major presence is in New York and California. Zales Corporation has dominantly a large presence in North America, while Harry Winston has stores in major cities such as New York, Paris, Beverly Hills, Geneva, and Tokyo. Since Tiffany retail stores are company-operated stores, its close relationships with the customers help better understand what the customers needs are in those markets and cater to them. Unlike its competition that sells a larger portion of its fine jewelry through major department stores or other independent retailers, Tiffany is a company-operated retail store. Therefore, the high prices that department stores are forcing some of Tiffany's competitors to pay are holding Tiffany's competitors from producing innovative fine jewelry pieces that are important in staying ahead in the industry. Tiffany already has one company-operated store in each of the potential markets of Brazil, Canada, and China. Tiffany's head start in these potential markets gives it a strong leverage to win over the competition. Many of its competitors do not have any presence in these markets or even strong international presence for that matter.

214   The drawback with this alternative was that Tiffany had to be prepared to face competitive pressure if they decided to expand in the Brazilian, Canadian, and China markets.

Tiffany needed more than one company-operated store in these regions. Even though Tiffany was one of the earlier fine jewelers to grab the market share in the potential markets, this would not prevent competitors like Harry Winston and David Yurman from reacting to Tiffany's expansion. In addition, Tiffany would face competition from local competitors in the potential markets. The local competitors have been established for many years and the residents of that area recognize the local competitors' brand.

215   A way around this drawback was to expand per square foot in each of the stores it already had established as opposed to expand on number of stores. With a flagship store already established with the brand name, customers will recognize and feel the experience that Tiffany has to offer. The product lines, customer relations, value, quality, craftsmanship, and experience will be offered to the customers all under one roof. The local competitors would find it hard to compete with Tiffany because of its enormous size and offerings per square foot of selling space.

216   The *second alternative* was to expand in the suburbs of the United States.

217   The benefit of this alternative was to saturate the area where the target market lived. Most competitors were located in major cities where the target market worked. While most individuals travel to work, they may not be willing to travel on the weekends to the city where most fine jewelers were located. By expanding in the suburbs where the target market lives, this would offer greater accessibility for them to shop.

218   This alternative was feasible because Tiffany already had a presence surrounding the suburbs—in the major city. Its brand name has already been established in the few mile radius from the city. In addition, it would be one of the first amongst its competitors to open a freestanding retail store in the suburbs.

219   Tiffany would be able to win against competition because it would be able to offer a greater shopping experience to its target market in the suburbs. Overall in retail store size, Tiffany has greater retail space compared to Zales, David Yurman and Harry Winston. Zales stores do not give the customer a sense of luxury feel when walking into the store. However, Tiffany does just by its heavy metal doors giving the feel of walking into a palace. David Yurman fine jewelry can be found in luxury department stores, but its selection and space are limited. By offering product knowledge, quality of products, excellent customer relations, fresh and clean space, beautiful packaging, and a well-stocked inventory, the shopping experience would be an unforgettable experience in the suburbs that would otherwise only be found in the city.

220   The drawback of this alternative was that it takes a large amount of financial resources to expand in the suburbs.

221   The way around this drawback was for Tiffany to renovate certain stores and expand per square foot. By slowly renovating certain stores, expanding per square foot and generating more revenue, then expansion of stores in the suburbs could be possible.

222   The two alternatives have advantages and disadvantages. To implement ways to increase revenue, continue to build brand image, and to target existing and potential areas seem to be the underlying strategic factors. Michael J. Kowalski will have to be proactive in this strategic department and make the right decisions to maintain the brand image status that Tiffany has—quality, craftsmanship, and value. At the same time, carry out Charles Lewis Tiffany's vision established over a century ago—establishing the grandest preeminent house of design and the world's premier jewelry house.

REFERENCES

About.com (2003). [Online]. *http://jewelry.about.com/cs/costumejewelry/index.htm.* Accessed March 24.

Advertising Age (2002). [Online]. *http://www.adage.com/news.cms?newsId=34174.* Accessed February 26, 2003.

The Business Journal—Tampa Bay (2003). "Holiday Sales Fall Flat for Specialty Stores." [Online]. *http://tampabay.bizjournals.com/tampabay/stories/2003/01/06/daily7.html.* Accessed January 6.

Danziger, Pam (2002A). "The Tabletop Report, 2002: The Market, The Competitors, The Trends." [Online]. *http://retailindustry.about.com/library/bl/02q4/bl_um101002.htm.* Accessed February 25, 2003.

Danziger, Pam (2002B). "Today's Jewelry Market." [Online]. *http://www.refresher.com/!umi.html.* Accessed April 28, 2003.

Diamonds International Website (2003). "Couples Confirm 'Love Is In The Air'". [Online]. *http://www.diamondsintl.com/about.cfm?page=press.* Accessed May 6.

E-Com Profits (2003). "Baby Boomer Facts". [Online]. *http://e-comprofits.com/babboomfac.html.* Accessed February 26.

Ernst & Young (2002). "Retail Newsletter". [Online]. *http://www.ey.com.* Accessed February 26, 2003.

Forbes.com (2003). "Tiffany & Co. Stock". [Online]. *http://www.forbes.com/finance/mktgguideapps/compinfo/Company Tearsheet.jhtml?tkr=TIF.* Accessed February 19.

Federal Trade Commission (2003). [Online]. *http://www.ftc.gov/.* Accessed February 19.

Green, Barbara (2003). "Tiffany Granted Preliminary Injunction Against Counterfeit Jewelry Sales". *National Jeweler Online.* [Online]. *http://www.nationaljeweler.com/nationaljeweler/search/search_display.jsp?vnu_content_id=1798850.* Accessed May 5.

Gomelsky, Victoria (2003). "China: The Once and Future Kingdom". *National Jeweler Online.* [Online]. *http://www.national-jeweler.com/.* Accessed February 12.

Harris, Judy (2002). "What is Retailing?" [Online]. *http://www.fiu.edu/~retail/whatis.html.* Accessed February 18, 2003.

Harry Winston Website (2003). [Online]. *http://www.harrywinston.com.* Accessed February 20.

Hoover, Gary E (1996). "What Happens After All the Categories Are Killed?" *Arthur Anderson—Retailing Issues Letter.* Volume 8, Issue 4, p.1–4, 1996.

Hoover's Online (2003A). "Company Capsule". [Online]. *http://www.hoovers.com/co/capsule/1/0,2163,11481,00.html.* Accessed March 12.

Hoover's Online (2003B). "Tiffany & Co. 5 Year Quote". [Online]. *http://quotes.hoovers.com/thomson/chart.html?p=&t=TIF&n=Tiffany+%26+Co.&e=NYSE&c=11481&templ=4&frame=5+Year&index=&ticker=TIF&threed=2&x=5&y=7.* Accessed February 25.

LVMH Website (2003). [Online]. *http://www.lvmh.com.* Accessed May 5.

Molofsky, Randi (2003). "FBI Raids Manhattan for Fake Tiffany Jewels". [Online]. *http://www.nationaljeweler.com/nationaljeweler/search/search_display.jsp?vnu_content_id=1871560.* Accessed, May 5.

Nielsen Media Research Website (2003). [Online]. *http://www.nielsenmedia.com.* Accessed April 29.

Popcorn, Faith (2002). "Trends for 2003: Popcorn Report". [Online]. *http://retailindustry.about.com/library/bl/02q4/bl_trends2003.htm.* Accessed February 19, 2003.

Professional Jeweler (2003)."Jewelry Store Sales by Products Stats". [Online]. *http://www.professionaljeweler.com/archives/features/stats/stats_prod.html.* Accessed February 25.

QAD Inc. (2002). "David Yurman Selects QAD To Make Its Worldwide Manufacturing Operations Sparkle". [Online]. *http://biz.yahoo.com/bw/021202/20232_1.html.* Accessed March 2, 2003.

Retail Industry (2001). "Catalog Sales Growth Continues to Outpace Overall Retail Growth". [Online]. *http://retailindustry.about.com/library/bl/q2/bl_dma060401a.htm.* Accessed February 25, 2003.

Retail Industry (2002). "The Global Luxury Retailing Sector". [Online]. *http://retailindustry.about.com/library/bl/02q1/bl_ri020602.htm.* Accessed February 25, 2003.

Retail Jewelers Organization Website (2002). "Buying Fine Jewelry". [Online]. *http://www.rjo.polygon.net/docs/buyingfine.html.* Accessed May 6, 2003.

Rozhon, Tracie (2003). "Squeezed, A Jewelry Designer Closes Shop". *The New York Times,* [Online]. *http://www.nytimes.com/2003/04/04/business/04GEMS.html.* Accessed April 4.

Russell, Roberta S. and Taylor III, Bernard W.(2003). *Operations Management Fourth Edition.* Pages 33–53, Prentice Hall Inc.

Standard & Poor's Online (2003). "Stocks Remain in the Red". [Online]. *http://www.standardandpoors.com.* Accessed February 24.

Tiffany & Co. (2001). *Annual Report.*

Tiffany & Co. (2002). *Annual Report.*

Tiffany & Co. Website (2003). [Online]. *http://www.tiffany.com.* Accessed February 15, 2003.

Unity Marketing (2002). "Consumers' Appetite for Jewelry Is Vigorous in the First Half of 2002". [Online]. *http://www.unitymarketingonline.com/reports/jewelry/pr1.html.* Accessed August 16, 2003.

U.S. Census Bureau (1992). "1992 Census of Retail Trade, Definitions of Industries". [Online], *http://www.census.gov/epcd/www/rc92sics.html.* Accessed February 24, 2003.

Vargas, Melody (2001). "Jewelry Sales Reach $39.8 Billion". [Online]. *http://retailindustry.about.com/library/bl/q2/bl_um041701.htm.* Accessed February 25, 2003.

Vargas, Melody (2002). "Consumer Spending: Tabletop Market's Growth Slows". [Online]. *http://retailindustry.about.com.* Accessed February 25, 2003.

WetFeet (2003). "Retail Industry Profile". [Online]. *http://www.wetfeet.com/asp/industryprofiles_overview.asp?industrypk=28.* Accessed February 19.

WSL Strategic Retail (2003). "Convenience is Key". [Online]. *http://retailindustry.about.com/library/uc/02/uc_wls1.htm.* Accessed February 26.

CASE 47

TIME For Kids Magazine

Evan Giamanco, Marc E. Gartenfeld, and Robert J. Mockler

INTRODUCTION

1   TIME For Kids Magazine (*TFK*) was established in 1995 and is the sister publication to TIME Magazine. In 2004, *TFK* appointed Jodi Kahn as its President. Mrs. Kahn was faced with many issues that needed to be addressed. While its subscribing teachers held *TFK* in high regard, general awareness of the product was lacking. Furthermore, potential advertisers had a difficult time understanding *TFK*'s business model because it differed from purchasing an ad page. Since *TFK* was a publication delivered to schools it was not permitted to run advertisements as a traditional magazine would. Because of this *TFK* created sponsored programs for advertisers, which could be purchased and shipped along with the weekly issues to the classroom. These sponsored programs had to have an educational element.

2   *TFK* was a news magazine which was published weekly during the elementary and middle school year (26 weeks) in late 2005. *TFK*, in the fall of 2005, published three age-appropriate editions for grades K−7 that were delivered to classes via paid teacher subscriptions. These issues were accompanied by a teacher's guide that connected to the classes' curricula.

3   Given the current state of *TFK*, decisions needed to be made in many important areas. How could *TFK* increase the awareness around its product as well as its circulation? It was also tackling the challenge of gaining more advertisers to sponsor programs and renew these programs in the following years. *TFK*'s managers were faced with answering these and other questions if they were to differentiate *TFK* from the competition and so achieve a winning edge over competitors within an intensely competitive and rapidly changing industry.

OVERALL INDUSTRY DESCRIPTION: THE MEDIA INDUSTRY

4   The industry under study is the media industry, which consisted of companies that owned, operated, engaged in, or sold media properties, services, and products, including: film and video production, distribution, replication, and products; television production, broadcasting, distribution, programming, and products; music production, distribution, publishing, and products; radio broadcasting; newspaper, book, magazine, electronic, and specialty publishing; and Internet content and delivery services [Hoover's, 2005].

5   Over the last 20 years, the general focus of the industry had shifted towards the Internet as a more preferred form of media, and its popularity continued to grow rapidly. In an age where people were working more hours and the amount of free time available was at a minimum, one was looking to get the information he/she wanted, and only that information, quickly. By using the Internet one had the ability to find specifically what he/she was looking for within seconds, while minimizing the amount of unwanted information consumed. Although thousands of new magazines were launched each year, the early years of the 21st century had been extremely difficult for the publishing industry, especially magazines as the majority had seen a decrease in revenue. Many consumers felt that the content being provided was not specific or current enough in comparison to the Internet. This had ultimately led to a decrease in overall customer magazine subscriptions, which had forced

This case was prepared by Evan Giamanco, Marc E. Gartenfeld, and Professor Robert J. Mockler of St. John's University. © Robert J. Mockler.

many companies to focus their advertising dollars elsewhere, resulting in a decrease in ad sales across the industry.

6   This paper will focus on the current state and future of the magazine industry; however first it is important to establish a general understanding of the media industry and its components, as is done in the following section.

7   The media industry could be segmented into Digital and Electronic Media, Television, Film and Video, and the Publishing Industry, as shown in Figure 1.

Digital and Electronic Media

8   All types of media that were related to the Internet and any electronic form of media fell into this area. This segment included: Information Collection and Delivery Companies, Internet Search and Navigation Providers, and Internet Content Providers.

Information Collection and Delivery

9   Information Collection and Delivery Companies were companies such as *Ask Jeeves Inc.* that collected, retrieved, and delivered various types of information, including real-time news and financial data via online services, electronic transmission, the Internet, or other means.

Internet Content Providers

10   Internet Content Providers were companies such as *America Online Inc.* that created or acquired content, including editorial and multimedia content, for distribution via the Internet. This also included distribution of paid-placement content. Paid-placement was when a marketer paid to have a highly visible listing for a specific keyword or term in a search engine, typically presented as a sponsored or paid link.

Internet Search and Navigation Providers

11   Internet Search and Navigation Providers were companies such as *Google Inc.* that own and operate search engines and other categorized Web sites used to find information on the Internet.

Television

12   Television companies were those companies that engage in television production, broadcasting, distribution, and programming. This includes cable and satellite television as well.

Film & Video

13   Film companies were those that owned, operated, engaged in, sold, or provided: film and video production, distribution, and replication; products, equipment, and services that support film and video production, pre-production, post-production, distribution, and replication, such as audio, film, and video imaging and editing equipment and services; and CD, DVD, and video duplication services.

FIGURE 1   **Industry Chart—Media Industry**

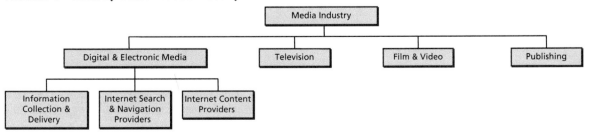

FIGURE 2 **Industry Chart—Publishing Industry**

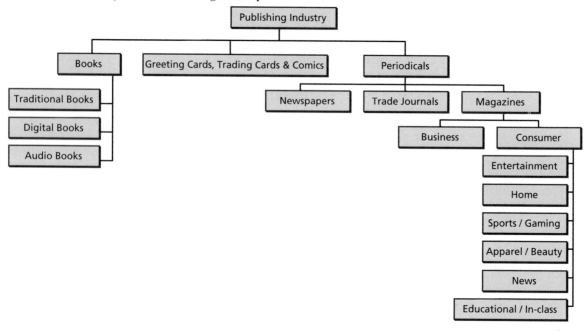

Publishing

14 The Publishing Industry, as shown in Figure 2, consisted of companies that published books, trading cards, greeting cards, comics, and periodicals.

Books

15 This category was broken down into three categories: traditional books, digital books, and audio books.

16 *Traditional Books*   These were a set of written, printed, or blank pages fastened along one side and encased between protective covers.

17 *Digital Books*   These were books composed or converted into digital format to be displayed on a computer. They may be sold or purchased through the Internet, in a retail store (burned onto CDs, floppy discs, etc.), and through mail and/or phone order [Mockler, 2005].

18 *Audio Books*   Books composed and/or converted into audio form. The books could be listened to as a digital file on tape, Internet or CD. They may be sold or purchased through the Internet, in a retail store, or through mail and/or phone order.

Greeting Cards, Trading Cards & Comics

19 This category was broken down into companies that publish and market comic books, baseball and trading cards, greeting cards, and similar products. These products were sold and purchased through the Internet, in a retail store, and through mail and/or phone.

Periodicals

20 This publishing category was broken down into newspapers, trade journals, and magazines.

Newspapers

21 This type of periodical was generally published daily but could be published weekly, monthly, bi-monthly, and quarterly. It covers current events, and caters to the general public and to professional organizations and others.

Trade Journals

22   This medium, which is similar to a magazine in some respects, was a periodical featuring articles written with a more specialized focus. Such publications typically carried little or no advertising. Journals were generally published monthly, bi-monthly, quarterly, and bi-annually. This medium generally catered to academia, professional, and trade consumers. Examples of trade journals were Architectural Review and Building Stone Magazine.

Magazines

23   These were periodic publications containing pictures and stories and articles of interest to those who purchased it or subscribed to it [WordNet, 2005]. Magazines were typically published weekly, biweekly, monthly, bimonthly or quarterly, with a date on the cover that is in advance of the date it is actually published. They were often printed in color on coated paper, and were bound with a soft cover.

24   According to the National Directory of Magazines, 18,821 magazine titles were available in the United States in 2004, up from 13,541 in 1988 [MarketResearch, 2005A].

25   The largest growth in the United States and Canada, from 1994 to 2004, came in the area of college and alumni publications, according to the National Directory of Magazines. There were 1,013 college and alumni publications in 2004, up from 707 in 1994 [Market-Research, 2005B].

26   Other high-growth magazine segments were agricultural supplies, medicine, travel, interior design and decoration, automotive, collectibles, golf, football and dogs.

27   It has been the opinion of many analysts that the growing rise of popularity surrounding the Internet is going to destroy the magazine industry. Recent trends have proven otherwise [Husni, 2005A].

28   Both the U.S. and worldwide magazine industries bounced back in 2004 after three years of little or no growth. U.S. magazine advertising revenue for September increased for the fifth consecutive month and topped the previous September by more than 17%. Ad revenue for the first nine months of 2004 was 10% higher than for the first nine months of 2003.

29   Internet advertising, which included online magazines, was expected to reach $10 billion in 2004, which would mark a 34% increase over 2003 and would top the record 2000 amount [MSN Advertising, 2005].

30   An annual guide to new magazine launches—published by Samir Husni, a professor at the University of Mississippi—reported that the 949 new titles in 2003 represented the most new introductions since 1998. Nearly 800 new launches through the first 10 months of 2004 indicated that 2004 start-ups might equal that figure [Husni, 2005B].

31   2004 however, also saw a troubling trend with the outsourcing of magazine design and content development to foreign firms. Folio magazine reported in June that firms in India and the Philippines had contracted with a number of small-circulation American magazines to do various aspects of their production work. Copy editors and graphic designers were among the employees cited as most at risk of losing their jobs to overseas competitors [FolioMag, 2005].

32   Magazines fell into two broad categories: business magazines and consumer magazines. In practice, magazines were a subset of periodicals, distinct from those periodicals produced by scientific, artistic, academic or special interest publishers, which were subscription-only, more expensive, narrowly limited in circulation, and often had little or no advertising.

33   ***Business Magazines***   Business magazines carried news and other information relevant to a particular profession or industry. These magazines were sold through retail outlets, and by subscription. Some of the most general ones such as *Forbes* and *BusinessWeek* were in many respects similar to the current-affairs-oriented consumer magazines.

34   Many business magazines were available only, or predominantly, by subscription. In some cases these subscriptions were available to any person prepared to pay; in others, free

subscriptions were available to readers who met a set of criteria established by the publisher. This practice, known as *controlled circulation*, was intended to guarantee to advertisers that the readership was relevant to their needs. Very often the two models, of paid-for subscriptions and controlled circulation, were mixed. Advertising was an important source of revenue for business magazines.

35 **Consumer Magazines**   The other broad category of magazines, consumer magazines, was aimed at the public and was usually available through retail outlets and by subscriptions. They ranged from general-interest titles such as TIME, People and Sports Illustrated, which appealed to a broad spectrum of readers, to highly specialized titles covering particular hobbies, leisure pursuits or other interests. Among the hundreds or thousands of topics covered by specialized magazines were, for example, computer games, fishing, particular models of automobile, particular kinds of music, and particular political interests.

36 While most of these magazines were available in the whole of the country in which they were published, some were specific to a local area, and a relatively small number were available internationally—often through localized editions so that, for example, the copy of *Maxim* bought in the USA did not contain the exact same articles as the edition on sale in the UK. Some, such as *TV Guide* were even tailored for local markets within a country. Most made the bulk of their money from advertising, and earned a smaller amount from the purchase price paid by readers; a few were free.

37 Under the consumer magazine umbrella, magazines were even further divided into the following categories: Entertainment, Home, Sports/Gaming, Apparel/Beauty, News, and Educational/In-class.

INDUSTRY AND COMPETITIVE MARKET ANALYSIS: IN-CLASS MAGAZINES

38 In-class magazines were news/general interest magazines that were distributed into classrooms in elementary, middle school and/or high schools. Various editions were produced to ensure that the content found in the issues was educationally relevant to the grade that had subscribed. These issues provided students with current event and non-fiction articles that tied into the teacher's curriculum. These magazines were typically published weekly during the academic school year and did not run during weeks where most schools were closed (Christmas and Easter break). Subscriptions to in-class magazines were purchased by the teacher of that particular class and they were not available on the newsstand. The average cost of a class subscription (25 children per class) was roughly $109.00.

39 Today most in-class magazine publishers were trying to increase circulation by allowing single subscriptions to be purchased online through the issue's branded website. The target market of in-class magazines has changed over the last 10 years and has developed into a very computer savvy group. The rapidly growing popularity of the Internet as a source for news, homework help and research amongst students has made publishers rethink the in-class business model. Creating valuable online content for students and teachers that ultimately ties back to the printed product had become more of a focus for in-class publishers.

The Essence of the Business Segment Model: In-Class Magazines

40 The major participants in the In-class magazine industry consisted of subscribers (teachers) and advertisers who were responsible for purchasing the two types of issues offered: weekly issues (teachers) and sponsored issues (advertisers). In-class magazines generated revenue by selling subscriptions to teachers and by selling sponsored programs to advertisers.

On the average, 54% of an in-class magazine's revenue came from the sale of sponsored programs, the other 46% came from subscription sales [TFK Research, 2005A].

41   In-class magazines published multiple editions of the weekly issues, whose editorial content was geared towards the grade(s) the edition serviced. For example, *TIME For Kids* magazine published 3 editions that were all written differently. One edition was written for Kindergarten and 1st graders, another edition was written for 2nd and 3rd graders, and the last was written for 4th through 7th graders.

42   Sponsored programs were any other issue, guide or property that was produced outside of the weekly issues. Sponsored programs typically consisted of a student magazine and a teacher's guide with a poster on the back that could be hung in the classroom. Other possible components of a sponsored program were a teacher's guide (no poster on back), trading cards, bookmarks, contests and or sweepstakes. The concept for a sponsored program was created by the marketing team based on the request of a potential advertiser. These advertisers were solicited by the sales force of the in-class publication. The sales team would present the concept for a sponsored program to an advertiser who would then decide whether or not to purchase it. If the advertiser decided to purchase a sponsored program, the sales team would notify the marketing team, who would then create it.

43   When advertisers purchased a sponsored program they frequently bought a program that would be distributed across multiple grade editions. Unlike the weekly issues, the editorially content of the sponsored programs typically did not differ if the issue went across editions. Once a teacher subscribed to a specific edition, the teacher received all of the weekly issues published that year as well as any sponsored programs that ran. The only way to receive the sponsored programs was to be a subscriber of the weekly issues. One was not able to subscribe just to the sponsored programs. The sponsored programs were considered a bonus to the subscribers of the weekly issues.

44   In order to get teachers to subscribe to the weekly issues, in-class magazines purchased a list of teachers' names and school addresses from outside vendors and then took these names and mailed them information and order forms for the in-class magazine. The in-class magazines also contacted school principals as well as school district heads and tried to sell their product to them as well. This approach allowed an in-class magazine to gain a larger number of subscribers more quickly, as opposed to trying to sell to each individual teacher. Regardless of who actually decided to subscribe (teacher, principal, district head), the teacher was never responsible for the actual payment of the issues. Either the school or the district paid for in-class magazine subscriptions. If the school was paying for the subscription it was common for the money to come from the school's PTA (Parent Teachers Association). The PTA was a group of parents who had students in the school, and teachers who would meet regularly to discuss issues regarding their particular school. The PTA made decisions regarding activities, and donated/collected money to support possible programs or helped teachers with supplies for the class. Although the teachers didn't physically pay for the subscriptions, more times than not the in-class magazines billed the actual teacher, who would then have to see that his/her school paid for the subscription.

45   Weekly issues were distributed directly to the classrooms in shrink-wrapped bundles. This is discussed in detail in the **PRODUCTS** section. Each bundle contained a student magazine for each child and a teacher's guide.

46   Sponsored programs were handled very differently. Once a class subscribed to an in-class magazine, any sponsored program an advertiser purchased that year to go to a grade specific edition(s) would also be distributed to the class along with their weekly issue. Advertisers were given the opportunity to run a sponsored program for any week that the weekly issues were published. When a sponsored program was purchased it would ship in the bundle along with the grade edition the advertiser had paid for it to be distributed to. It was the job of the sales and marketing department to find advertisers and get them to purchase a sponsored program. Sales representatives met with potential advertisers and explained what their in-class magazine was capable of, typically highlighting the fact they had the ability to reach a large number of children, which was something that advertisers had a difficult time accomplishing. Once an advertiser showed interest, the marketing department created a proposal that would suggest possible ideas for sponsored programs that the advertiser could purchase. Advertisers were also given a list of pricing options, which came from the in-class magazine business office, depending on how much they wanted to spend for a sponsored program. Advertisers were also given the option of selecting which students their program would be distributed to. Advertisers were able to select which grade edition they would like their sponsored program to ship with. Once an advertiser purchased a sponsored program the marketing department began to develop it.

47   In-class magazines relied heavily on their marketing teams and the editorial staff. The marketing team was responsible for creating the concepts of the sponsored programs and overseeing the design of the issues. The editorial staff was responsible for writing the articles found in the weekly issues. Occasionally the editors wrote the content in the sponsored programs, but typically freelancers were hired to complete issues that were part of a sponsored program. The editorial staff had to make sure the articles found in the weekly issue were appropriate for the grade the issue serviced. Certain publishers made it a requirement of the editorial staff to tie the content of each weekly issue into that grade's curriculum. This was possible since there was a national standard of education that detailed the curriculum schools in the United States were required to follow. This was put in place by the National Board for Professional Teaching Standards. This set of standards detailed what lessons needed to be taught for each academic subject and when they should be covered during the school year. The lessons taught on a daily basis needed to address the points and cover the material that the standards required. Because of this, both the weekly issues and the sponsored programs needed to make sure that the content was aligned with the national standards. Figure 3 presented the business model of the in-class magazine publishing segment.

Products

48   For the in-class magazine industry, there were two main types of magazine products that were created, sold and distributed. They were Weekly Issues and Sponsored Programs. Both the weekly issues and the sponsored programs were distributed into the classroom to the students, and each type of issue had a teacher's guide which outlined possible lesson plans, activities and ways a teacher could use the in-class magazine as a valuable part of the curriculum. The content found in these magazines contained news, current event and general interest related articles. The magazine's content (weekly and sponsored issues) was always educational and typically included a game or puzzle for the students.

FIGURE 3   In-Class Magazine Publishing—The Business Model

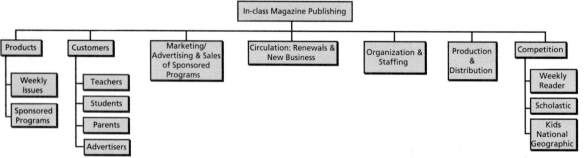

Weekly Issues

49   Weekly issues referred to the news issues that the magazines published on a weekly basis. The weekly issues were distributed to the subscribing classrooms in a bundle. The bundles contained a student magazine for every child and one teacher's guide for the teacher. The bundle was shrink-wrapped and delivered to the classroom. When a teacher subscribed he/she indicated how many children were in their class and ordered the appropriate number of subscriptions. The bundles ranged in size but contained a minimum of 10 student subscriptions. For this particular segment of the industry, these pieces contained 100% original editorial content. These issues came in two forms, a student magazine and a teacher's guide. The teacher's guide had instructions for the teacher on how to work the magazine into their daily curriculum. There were 26 weekly issues printed each year, and the magazine only published when school is in session. Since these issues serviced several grades, it was necessary to print multiple editions so the content could be tailored to be age appropriate.

50   A key to success with the weekly issues was to have them contain current event articles that were appropriately written to the grade(s) they were servicing. Another key was to have the teacher's guides contain lessons that directly corresponded with what the grade's curriculum was covering that particular week the issue is delivered. It was also important for the magazines' editors to be mindful that some news, although current and important, was not appropriate to discuss with certain aged students.

Sponsored Programs

51   Since schools did not permit companies to advertise in the weekly issues distributed to the classrooms as one would be able to do with a traditional magazine, sponsored programs were sold to generate revenue.

52   Once a class subscribed to an in-class magazine, any sponsored program an advertiser purchased that year to go to a specific grade edition(s) would also be distributed to the class along with their weekly issue. Advertisers were given the opportunity to run a sponsored program for any week that the weekly issues were published. When a sponsored program was purchased it would ship in the bundle along with the edition the advertiser had paid for it to be distributed to. It was the job of the sales and marketing department to find advertisers and get them to purchase a sponsored program. Sales representatives would meet with potential advertisers and attempt to sell them a program. Advertisers were given the option of selecting which students their program would be distributed to. Advertisers were able to select which edition they would like their sponsored program to ship with. Once an advertiser purchased a sponsored program the marketing department would develop it.

53   Sponsored programs worked on the same principal as an advertorial would with one major difference. An advertorial was an item written and paid for by an advertiser that looked like a news article or editorial. The only difference in this case between an advertorial and a sponsored program was that a minimum of 25% of the editorial content must have been written by the magazine's edit staff and not the advertiser. These sponsored programs typically included a student magazine and teacher guide (with or without a poster); however, they also included other forms of media such as bookmarks, or trading cards. Most commonly the sponsored programs took the form of a student magazine and a teacher's guide that had a classroom poster on the backside. Similar to the weekly issues, the teacher's guide had instructions for the teacher on how to work the magazine into their daily curriculum, as well as reproducible pages that teacher's photocopied and distributed to the students.

54   Typically companies that had an educational or corporate awareness initiative purchased sponsored programs although it was not uncommon for television networks and film companies to purchase a program to promote a show or movie launch. Regardless of the companies' goals, an educational message must have been present in the piece.

55   The number of sponsored programs being purchased by advertisers for in-class distribution had grown over recent years as corporations tried to strengthen their image in the public eye. Scandals such as the one involving Enron Corporation in 2002 had tainted the views of the general public, leaving large corporations responsible for regaining the peoples' trust. Corporations have been much more active with funding their social awareness and educational initiatives and saw the sponsored programs offered by in-class magazines as an excellent means to do so. For example in 2004 Toyota took a literacy initiative for children in elementary school. In order to get Toyota's message out to students, parents, teachers, and the general public Toyota partnered with *TIME For Kids* magazine to create a sponsored program for 5th, 6th and 7th grade students. The program consisted of a student magazine, a teacher's guide that had a poster printed on the back of it, a sweepstakes and a set of student bookmarks. The program gave students a reading list and encouraged them to complete the list by a certain date. All students who completed the list would get their teacher's signature on an entry form and mailed it in for the chance to win a Toyota vehicle.

56   A key to success with the sponsored programs was to have them contain editorial content that was relevant and appropriately written for the grade(s) the program was servicing.

57   Another key was to have the teacher's guides contain lessons that directly corresponded with what the school curriculum was covering that particular week the issue was delivered.

58   Another key to success was to be able to create a sponsored program that captured the advertiser's message while maintaining the integrity of the magazine's brand. In-class magazines did not want to create a program that would come across as purely promotional with a weak educational message.

Customers

59   In the In-class industry segment under study there were four main customers targeted: students, teachers, parents and advertisers. Paying attention and fulfilling the needs of all four of these customer profiles was extremely important to be successful in this market.

Teachers

60   Teachers of both elementary and middle schools were considered to be the main customer of this type of magazine because they were the only ones who could currently purchase subscriptions. As for sponsored programs, teachers did not have the option of not receiving them because they came with their weekly bundle. However the teacher made the final decision on whether or not they were used in the classroom. The age range of teachers was quite large and can be anywhere from early 20's to late 70's. Both genders were represented; however, there were a higher percentage of women teachers in the elementary/middle school segment.

61   As stated earlier, in order to get teachers to subscribe to the weekly issues, in-class magazines would purchase a list of teachers' names and schools addresses from outside vendors and then take these names and mail them information and order forms for the in-class magazine. The in-class magazines would also contact school principals as well as school district heads and try to sell their product to them as well. This approach allowed an in-class magazine to gain a larger number of subscribers more quickly, as opposed to trying to sell to each individual teacher. Regardless of who actually decided to subscribe (teacher, principal, district head), the teacher was never responsible for the actual payment of the issues. Either the school or the district would pay for in-class magazine subscriptions. If the school was paying for the subscription it was common for the money to come from the school's PTA (Parent Teachers Association). The PTA was a group of parents who had students in the school, and teachers who would meet regularly to discuss issues regarding their particular school. The PTA would make decisions regarding activities, and donate/collect money to support possible programs or help teachers with supplies for the class. Although the teachers didn't actually pay for the subscriptions more times than not the in-class magazines was billed to the actual teacher, who would then have to see that his/her school, paid for the subscription.

62   Teachers had a very strict curriculum that had been put in place by the National Board for Professional Teaching Standards. This set of standards detailed what lessons need to be taught for each academic subject and when they should be covered during the school year. The lessons taught on a daily basis needed to address the points and cover the material that the standards required.

63   A key to success with teachers was having the weekly issues contain relevant curriculum so that the magazines could facilitate learning in the classroom, leaving teachers more inclined to use them. Having the lessons meet the National Teaching Standards could be one way to accomplish this.

64   A key to success with teachers was having the sponsored programs contain relevant curriculum so that they could facilitate learning in the classroom, leaving teachers more inclined to use them. Having the lessons meet the National Teaching Standards could be one way to accomplish this.

65   Another key to success in regard to the class teachers was to have the teachers include the in-class magazine as part of their students' homework. By including concepts and activities that coincide with the curriculum, teachers would then feel comfortable using the issues as part of their homework assignment. Since most teachers assign their students a current event reading regularly, the weekly in-class issues could also mention in the teacher's guide to have the in-class magazine serve as their student's current events reading.

Students

66   Students in both elementary school and middle school were the main customers actually reading the magazines. The students targeted were both male and female and were between the ages of 5–12.

67   A key to success here was to keep the content within the weekly issues both fun and educational in order to keep the students engaged and excited about learning. A key to keeping the issue fun would be to include games, such as a word search activity, or crossword puzzle.

68   A key to success here was to keep the content within the sponsored programs both fun and educational in order to keep the students engaged and excited about learning. A key to keeping the issue fun would be to include games, such as a word search activity, or crossword puzzle.

69   Another key to success for the students was to make the sponsored programs interactive by including more contests and sweepstakes. Children loved to compete and were eager to participate in an activity if they had a chance to win a prize. Having these contests/sweepstakes offer great prizes would also increase their popularity. This would increase the level of enjoyment that the students received from the sponsored programs.

Parents

70   Parents of the above mentioned students were also key customers. Since theses magazines were typically brought home and used in the student's homework, it was important that the parents felt the content in both the weekly issues and the sponsored programs were appropriate for their children.

71   A key to success with the parents was to prove the weekly magazines were a safe, trusted source for their children to learn about real-world events. This could be done if the editors wrote the articles in an age appropriate manner and the parents were able to see that sensitive subjects were written about in a way that was sensitive to the student reading it.

72   Another key to success here was to have the weekly issues' content foster a parent-child dialogue. This could be done if the weekly issues were part of their child's homework

assignment. Most parents helped their children complete their homework each night, and more times than not their children had questions. If their questions were a result of what was read in the weekly in-class magazine, a conversation would be struck between the child and their parent around the issue. This would strengthen communication between parents and their kids at a young age, which was something that all parents value.

Advertisers

73   Companies seeking to advertise were also a main customer type of an in-class magazine. The other three customer types mentioned were all tied to the weekly issues of an in-class magazine, but advertisers purchased the sponsored programs. Typically companies that had an educational or corporate awareness initiative purchased sponsored programs although it was not uncommon for television networks and film companies to purchase a program to promote a show or movie launch. Regardless of the companies' goals, an educational message needed to be part of the program.

74   A key to being successful with advertisers was to create a program that either drove the customer to purchase a product (Toyota would hope a customer bought a car), service (Citibank would hope to gain more customers) or donate money (UNICEF would hope to have people support their global health programs) to the advertiser. This could be done by having a sponsored student magazine include the advertiser's logo, giving the advertiser's website or by including photographs relevant to the advertiser's product or service in the sponsored magazine. Another way would be to create a contest or sweepstakes where the prize would be advertiser's product or service. Toyota could give one lucky winner a free car, or Citibank could give a free checking account as a grand prize.

75   To be viewed as a valuable means of advertising for those advertisers looking to spread the message of a corporate initiative and increase their brand image, it was key for an in-class magazine to include statistics that could help the advertiser quantify the program's success. Since there would not be a direct drive to purchase something, it was important that the advertiser has the ability to quantify the program's reach. This could be accomplished by tracking the number of impressions the program generated and by providing the advertiser with post program research which gave the advertiser an in depth look at how their program was received. Pre-program research could also be helpful to an in-class magazine because it would allow the advertiser to have a better sense of what the class would think of their program before it was created which would allow the advertiser and the in-class magazine to make adjustments, making the program more valuable to the class.

76   Another key to success with advertisers was to provide a sponsored program that was unique from any other type of advertising they might have done in the past. Since it was probable that the advertiser has had little or no exposure in schools, creating a fun and educational student magazine or poster could be unique enough. The addition of contests and sweepstakes that get students, teachers and parents involved could also be unique to an advertiser because the program would require the involvement of three different types of customers, which was not typical of most sweepstakes/contests.

Marketing/Advertising and Sales of Sponsored Programs

77   Advertising involves proclaiming the qualities or advantages of a product or business so as to increase sales.

78   The type of "Sales" being referred to in this section deals only with the selling of sponsored programs. Subscription sales of weekly issues are covered in the **CIRCULATION** section below.

79   Sales across the publishing industry have taken a hit in the early 2000's, mainly after September 11th 2001. Traditional magazines saw ad pages fall as much as 40% as the nation began to recover. While magazine advertising had generally increased since 2003, in-class magazines were having difficulty selling sponsored programs. Advertisers have had a difficult time gauging the success of sponsored programs and because of that, have been skeptic to purchase.

80   The marketing and sales teams were responsible for developing, selling and creating the sponsored programs that were sold by in-class publications. The weekly issues were written and created by the editorial staff and operated completely separate of the sponsored programs.

81   It was the job of the sales and marketing department to find advertisers and get them to purchase a sponsored program. Sales representatives would meet with potential advertisers and explain what their in-class magazine was capable of, typically highlighting the fact they had the ability to reach a large number of children, which is something that advertisers had a difficult time accomplishing. Once an advertiser showed interest, the marketing department would create a proposal that would suggest possible ideas for sponsored programs that the advertiser could purchase. Advertisers would also be given a list of pricing options, which came from the in-class magazine business office, depending on how much they wanted to spend for a sponsored program. Advertisers were also given the option of selecting which students their program would be distributed to. It was typical for there to be several sponsored program proposals requested in a given week from possible advertisers to the in-class magazine, which led to heavy work load for the marketing department. Advertisers were able to select which grade edition they would like their sponsored program to ship with. For example if an advertiser wanted to sponsor a *TIME For Kids* program and was interested in reaching 2nd and 3rd graders, the advertiser could purchase a program that would only be distributed to these grades. In the case of TFK there was 1 edition that was distributed to 2nd and 3rd graders. Once an advertiser purchased a sponsored program the marketing department would begin to develop it.

82   The role of the marketing team at an in-class publication was essential to the magazine's success. The marketing team for an in-class publication played a very significant role because they were responsible for creating the concepts behind each sponsored program as well as executing them. The sales team was essentially responsible for presenting the program to the client and negotiating the price. While the marketing team was responsible for creating the concepts behind the sponsored programs, generally freelance writers and designers were hired to actually create the pieces. The marketing and sales department granted final approval on any aspect of a sponsored program that was created by a freelancer.

83   For the in-class magazine industry traditional ads were not permitted to run in the classroom. This decision had been made by the education system. Since magazines usually depend on ad sales to generate approximately 54% of their revenue, in-class magazines had to depend on the sale of sponsored programs to make up this percentage of revenue. These sponsored programs could be expensive with prices ranging from $50,000 to over $1,000,000 depending on the number of components that were included (e.g. student magazine, teacher's guide, etc.).

84   In the past it had been difficult for advertisers to gauge the effectiveness of an in-class magazine's sponsored programs. Companies wishing to advertise in magazines were very concerned with the number of impressions they would receive for each ad that they run. Impressions were the amount of different people that actually saw the ad.

85   Traditional magazines had the metrics to provide potentials advertisers with statistics on impressions because the Publishers Information Bureau (PIB) audited the majority of traditional magazines. PIB was an independent agency that tracked advertising pages and set the rules for the consistent auditing of magazine advertising. In-class magazines, however, were not audited so advertisers seeking to sponsor an in-class program did not have the same type of statistical information needed to evaluate the in-class product. Advertisers typically had to rely on research, which was generally conducted by a research department hired by the

in-class publication directly. As a result, advertisers could be a bit skeptical in regard to the results found in these research reports and could also have a difficult time understanding them. This had left the magazine's sales team with a difficult task of trying to not only pitch their brand and its value over the competition to advertisers, but also be able to quantify the in-class magazine's reach.

86   When advertising, companies were also interested in the CPM a magazine can guarantee them. The CPM was the Cost Per Thousand and was used in comparing the cost efficiency of media vehicles. This was calculated by dividing the out-of-pockets costs by the rate base per thousand. In-class magazines had the ability to provide advertisers with a CPM although it was calculated differently than a traditional magazine would. Since advertisers could not purchase an individual page like they would in a traditional magazine, the CPM for an in-class magazine was as follows: cost of program / number of pages of all components combined/number of subscribers. For instance, if an advertiser purchased a sponsored program for $300,000 that consisted of an 8-page student magazine and a 4-page teacher's guide going to 2 million subscribers the CPM would be:

$$300{,}000/8 = 25{,}000; 2{,}000{,}000/25{,}000 = \$80 \text{ CPM}$$

87   The components of an in-class sponsored program had become formulaic over recent years, almost always consisting of a student magazine and a classroom poster with a teacher's guide printed on the reverse side. Advertisers were always looking for a fresh new approach so it was the job of these in-class magazines to find new and interesting ways of changing the components offered. In-class publishers had looked to insert CD-ROMs into the student and teacher's guides that contain streaming video, educational games and/or class lessons for the students to view and complete. In-class magazine sponsored programs also began to include sweepstakes and contests in their student magazines and teacher's guides to get students and teachers to engage more with their product. The prizes awarded for winning had been the advertiser's products or something that related to their program's message. For example, one in-class magazine had created a sponsored program for Swatch Watch Inc. that taught young children how to tell time. A sweepstakes offered in the student magazine awarded a child with a Swatch watch and a trip to the Warner Brothers Studio for him/her and their family.

88   A key to success was to have sales representatives who had experience selling sponsored programs. By looking to hire employees that had worked in sales at other in-class magazines, would be one way to obtain this.

89   Another key to success here was being able to explain to potential advertisers how to quantify the success of a sponsored program. Focusing on the impressions the sponsored program generates could help advertisers understand the value of an in-class sponsored program. You needed to be able to give them some means of quantifying value for the money spent on the program, which would ultimately lead to them sponsoring a program in this type of magazine. Focusing on the CPM since it was quantifiable and typically high for in-class magazines was a key to getting advertisers to buy.

90   Incorporating more sweepstakes and contests into the in-class magazine's sponsored programs was another key to success. By creating contests and sweepstakes in-class magazines would increase a buzz generated by the sponsored programs for their advertisers, while also promoting their products, services, and/or messages. Advertisers would also be informed of how many entries were received for their contest/sweepstakes, which would give them a means to quantify the success of the program.

91   Another key to success was to focus on the fact that in-class magazine's sponsored programs were giving advertisers the ability to reach a very specific audience in a trusted environment, the classroom. It is very difficult to reach a large amount of children at the same time and the in-class magazine allowed one to do so. This advantage should be leveraged when negotiating with advertisers to sell a program.

92   For the marketing department a key to success was the ability to fulfill proposal requests relatively quickly, while making sure that they have captured the message the advertiser was looking to deliver to its audience.

93   It was key to sell as many sponsored programs as possible to generate the greatest amount of revenue possible for the in-class magazine. By having the sales force aggressively seek potential advertisers this would be possible. A key to finding these advertisers was to have the sales force research companies that they felt had important messages that could be made into an educational program. The sales force could register for online sales databases, which give company information and tell the user what the advertiser is trying to market and who their audience is. This would help the in-class magazines' target advertisers with the greatest potential of choosing the in-class product.

Circulation: Renewals & New Business

94   Circulation was the focus of the Subscription Sales department of a magazine. This department sought to increase subscriptions sales. For an average in-class magazine, 46% of magazine revenue stemmed from circulation with the remaining 54% coming from the sale of sponsored programs [TFK Research, 2005B]. Their objectives were to deliver the circulation required of the magazine while maximizing circulation net profits.

95   For in-class magazines, subscriptions were purchased through direct mail, renewal campaigns and the Internet. Since the only way to receive the sponsored programs was to purchase the weekly issues (they're not offered separately) all aspects of maintaining and increasing circulation were specific to the weekly issue product.

96   Subscriptions could be segmented into Renewals and New Business. Renewals referred to retaining present subscribers, while New Business was exactly that—gaining new subscribers. In 2004, the average basic 1-year subscription rate was $82.00 [General Presentation, 2005].

97   Typically an in-class magazine had a renewal effort at least once a month. Renewal efforts were done by mailing letters, sending postcards, and attaching a cover wrap onto the subscriber's issue of the in-class publication. A cover wrap was a 4-page unit that was wrapped over the front and back cover of a magazine.

98   To attract new business, in-class magazine publishers purchased names and addresses of teachers, principals and district supervisors through list rentals. Once the magazine had the list of names they then solicited subscriptions through direct mail efforts.

99   In all direct mail efforts a form was mailed to either the potential subscriber or the renewing subscriber (depending on what campaign is running) that explained the in-class magazines and the possible ordering options that were available. Typically there was too much information put on these forms, which could confuse the potential/renewing customer.

100   Customer Service centers were designated to take subscription orders over the phone and helped customers with any questions or concerns they may have had. These customer service centers also had a few employees solicit subscriptions over the phone in order to aid the direct mail efforts.

101   The keys to success in regards to increasing circulation for in-class magazines were to carefully construct renewal campaigns as well as direct mail campaigns that clearly explained what the product options were to the subscriber. Since there were several grade editions to choose from and different ordering options that all need to be explained in one form, important information could be missed by the potential subscriber. It was important to make the forms as clear and concise as possible.

102   Another key was to decide what was the best number of campaigns to run as well as when to run them throughout the year. By choosing the best time to run these campaigns, in-class magazines could increase their circulation. This could be at the end of the summer when teachers are getting ready to begin the school year or at end of the school year, in preparation for the following class.

103   Another key to success was to hire a strong customer service staff that was very personable and enjoyed dealing with customers over the phone. By hiring such employees to work the phones, new and/or renewing subscribers would enjoy their experience more and be more inclined to do business with the in-class magazine.

Organization & Staffing

104   Magazine staffs were typically divided into 2 segments—Publishing and Editorial. The editorial department was responsible for writing and designing all of the content found in the magazine's standard issues, not necessarily the sponsored programs. The publishing department typically consisted of a Marketing/Promotions department, Sales department, Production department, Finance department and a Subscription Sales department. The departments found on the publishing side's main responsibility was to market and sell the weekly issues and sponsored programs while making sure both were produced to its specifications in an efficient manner, ultimately making the magazine profitable.

105   The keys to success on the editorial side were to have excellent writers who truly enjoyed what they are writing about. This would lead to rich content, which would increase the value to the reader. On the publishing side the keys to success were creating sponsored programs that were valuable to both teachers and students.

106   A key to success relevant to the finance department was the ability to keep excellent records of past programs. Since magazine staffs on the publishing side generally changed every 3–5 years it was important that a completely new staff be able to understand what had been done in the past.

107   Another key to success was to implement strict, consistent pricing methods, which helped in-class magazines start to establish sound records. This could be done by creating some type of pricing chart that would include price points for all possible components of a sponsored program.

108   It was also key to price the sponsored programs so that the margin the magazine made was maximized but didn't discourage a potential advertiser. By taking a look at past programs purchased and having a general idea of how much advertisers were willing to pay for a program could lead to success in this area. Having the sales force be able to get the advertiser to give their budget range for a sponsored program would also increase the in-class magazine's ability to create the most efficient program they could at the highest margin possible.

Production & Distribution

109   The magazine production process for in-class magazines was fairly different from that found in traditional magazines in the industry. These magazines were produced at a printing plant on a web press. A web press was a printing press that printed at extremely high speeds while giving you the ability to print on both sides of the paper at the same time. The finished product was then dried and folded as it left the press. Paper was delivered into the press off of large roles. There were three ways in which any magazine could bind: perfect bound, saddle-stitched or collated. Perfect-bound magazines were bound with glue and had a perfect flat binding panel like a book, on which may be displayed title and issue information. *GQ* and *Cigar Aficionado* were currently perfect-bound. Saddle-stitched magazines were bound with one or more staples and had the advantage of being able to lay open by themselves without breaking the binding. *Newsweek* and *People* are saddle-stitched [City Newsstand, 2005]. In-class publications were collated, meaning the pages were held together with glue. These magazines were also nested, meaning there was 1 issue placed inside every issue. The nested magazines were stacked one on top of another in shrink-wrapped bundles and distributed in bundles. The bundles could include a minimum of 10 issues but could hold anywhere over 500 if needed. Magazines were then shipped to trucking agents and postal facilities for delivery.

110   There were three main expenses during the production process of the weekly issues and sponsored issues (if the sponsored programs includes an issue component which is usually the case): paper costs, printing costs and distribution costs. These physical costs could represent 35–40% of the total cost base of the magazine. Paper was looked at in terms of cost per ton. There were very few suppliers in the paper industry, which gave them strength in the market. No single company had a dominant share and there was increasing industry consolidation. Paper prices typically increased 6% every year.

111   In the printing industry, 5 suppliers control 85% of the market. Because of the low returns in this industry, there had been little capital investment. Three to five year term contracts protected against price variances.

112   Distribution costs include postal costs and trucking costs. In 2006, postal costs were expected to rise 11% for in-class publications. Since the magazines were educationally based and distributed in schools, they qualified for the 3rd class postal rate, which was significantly cheaper. Traditional magazines mail 1st class, which was very costly.

113   A key to success in regards to production was to evaluate the magazine to see if there was anything one could do differently to minimize your cost. Possible options would be reducing the paper weight of the issue which would reduce your postage cost. Another option could be to reduce the size of the magazine, by something as small as 1/8th.

Competition

114   The direct competitors to *TFK* were Scholastic News and Weekly Reader.

Scholastic News

115   *Scholastic*, a global children's publishing and media company, had a corporate mission supported through all of its divisions of instilling the love of reading and learning for lifelong pleasure in all children. Recognizing that literacy was the cornerstone of a child's intellectual, personal and cultural growth, *Scholastic*, for more than 80 years, had created quality products and services that educated, entertained and motivated children and were designed to help enlarge their understanding of the world around them [Scholastic, 2005].

116   *Scholastic* lived by the credo—"We strive to present the clearest explanation of current affairs and contemporary thought, and to encourage literacy appreciation and expression consistent with the understanding and interests of young people at all levels of learning."

117   *Scholastic News* produced weekly student magazines that were accompanied by a teacher's guide. Their teacher's guides as well as their student guides aligned to the National Teaching Standards, which increased the use of the magazine in the classroom. *Scholastic News* also produced sponsored programs that were also used within the classroom.

118   *Scholastic News* published 5 editions that were entitled *Grade 1*, *Grade 2*, *Grade 3*, *Grade 4* and *Grade 5–6*. *Grade 1* serviced kindergarten and 1st grade, *Grade 2* serviced 2nd grade, *Grade 3* serviced 3rd grade, *Grade 4* serviced 4th grade, and *Grade 5–6* serviced 5th and 6th grade. Having 5 editions allowed *Scholastic* to really tailor the content in the issues even more so to meet the curriculum standards of the serviced grade. Both the weekly issues and the sponsored programs showed the edition name on the cover. The average price per subscription was $4.50, $112.50 for a class of 25 students. *Scholastic News* currently had 4.9 million subscribers across the United States. *Scholastic News* saw their student penetration increase between the years of 1997–2004 from 14% to 20% for grades K–6 in the United States [TFK Research, 2005C].

119   *Scholastic News* had sold many sponsored programs over the years, 13 programs specifically in 2004–05. While advertisers seem to choose to sponsor *Scholastic News* programs frequently, students felt that the issues were boring at times. Teachers were very pleased with all *Scholastic* issues (weekly and sponsored) because they were aligned with the national teaching standards and therefore could be easily worked into their daily lessons.

120   *Scholastic News* was very strong in the product category and made sure that the editorial content found in both the weekly issues and the sponsored programs was written in an appropriate manor for the grade(s) the edition serviced. *Scholastic News* also did an excellent job of making it clear which edition serviced which grade(s). *Scholastic News* included the grade each issue services on the cover (either front or back) of that edition.

121   *Scholastic News* also did well at creating effective renewal/new business and direct mail campaigns. *Scholastic News* saw their student penetration increase between the years of 1997–2004 from 14% to 20% for grades K–6 in the United States [TFK Research, 2005D].

Weekly Reader

122   The Weekly Reader Corporation was a unit of WRC Media, Inc. Weekly Reader was an exciting company and a leader in the field of education. They were publishers of materials for elementary and secondary schools, with over 90% of the school districts in the United States using their materials. The 90% presence included all products published by Weekly Reader, not just the in-class magazines [Weekly Reader, 2005].

123   Weekly Reader Corporation, which began with the publication of the first Current Events on May 20, 1902, had been publishing for over 100 years. In that span of time, Weekly Reader publications have covered all the major events of the 20th century, from the Boer War to the election of George W. Bush.

124   *Weekly Reader* was the best-known publication of Weekly Reader Corp. Weekly Reader classified itself as a "newspaper for children in the elementary grades" although it was a magazine. *Weekly Reader* was founded in 1928 by Eleanor Johnson, then director of elementary schools in York, Pennsylvania.

125   *Weekly Reader* came in 7 grade-specific editions, and served more than 4.9 million school-children in 50,000 schools. This number was less than Scholastic's circulation by 700,000 subscribers but higher than TFK's circulation by 800,000 subscribers. An individual subscription of Weekly Reader had cost an average of $4.64, $116.13 for a class of 25 students.

126   *Weekly Reader* saw their student penetration decrease between the years of 1997–2004 from 22% to 17% for grades K–6 in the United States [TFK Research, 2005E]. This was partially due to both *TIME For Kids* and *Scholastic News* gaining more of the market share.

127   *Weekly Reader* produced Student magazines that were accompanied by a Teacher's Guide. Their teacher's guides as well as their student guides aligned to the National Teaching Standards, which increased the use of the magazine in the classroom. *Weekly Reader* also produced sponsored programs, which were also used within the classroom.

128   *Weekly Reader* was very strong in the product category and made sure that the editorial content found in both the weekly issues and the sponsored programs was written in an appropriate manor for the grade(s) the edition serviced. *Weekly Reader* also did an excellent job of making it clear which edition serviced which grade(s). *Weekly Reader* included the grade each issue services on the cover (either front or back) of that edition.

129   *Weekly Reader* had sold many sponsored programs over the years, 11 programs specifically in 2004–05. Teachers were very pleased with all *Weekly Reader* issues (weekly and sponsored) because they were aligned with the national teaching standards and therefore could be easily worked into their daily lessons.

130   The *Weekly Reader* issues were currently very short, which limited the amount of time a teacher could utilize the product in the classroom.

THE COMPANY

Time Warner

131   Time Warner was considered to be the world's #1 media firm. The company combined new media, such as AOL and New Line Cinema, with old media spanning film and TV, cable,

FIGURE 4   Time Warner: Entities Structure

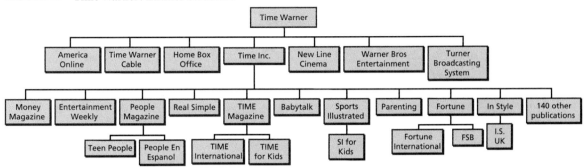

and publishing. Figure 4 shows the different business units of Time Warner. In 2004, Time Warner's sales totaled $42 billion and its Net Income was $3.3 billion.

Time Inc.

132   With 155 magazines worldwide, Time Inc. was well positioned across the most popular consumer magazine sectors—news, sports, celebrity, fashion, women's lifestyle, business, personal finance, entertainment, shelter, epicurean and regional. In 2004, one in two U.S. adults read a Time Inc. magazine every month. Over that same year, 60% of adults in the U.K. read a magazine published by Time Inc.'s IPC Media, the U.K.'s largest consumer magazine company [Time Warner, 2005A].

133   The advertising revenues of Time Inc accounted for nearly a quarter of the advertising revenues of all U.S. consumer magazines. In 2004, 13% of Time Warner's revenue came from Time Inc. [Time Warner, 2005B].

134   Time Inc.'s main competitors in the magazine industry were Hearst Magazines, Conde Naste and Advance Publications.

135   Time Inc continued to maintain excellence and reinvention of its core magazines, while overseeing a seamless management of acquisitions, an ongoing cost management program and continuing launches of new magazines.

TIME For Kids Magazine

136   Using the most current news and real-life, non-fiction articles, *TFK* connected 4.1 million kids to the world every week. Delivered directly to classrooms, *TFK* was a fun, interactive way to motivate kids to read, develop their critical thinking skills and ultimately inspire a confident, life-long curiosity in the events of the world around them. *TFK*'s mission statement was as follows:

> *TIME For Kids* brings real news and enlightening information to young people so that they develop a lifelong interest in, and a connection to, world events. *TFK* enables its readers to become literate, critical thinkers and informed, responsible citizens.

Products

137   *TFK* was a weekly publication that was delivered to schools via teacher paid subscriptions. *TFK* printed 26 weeks per year (Big Picture is an exception) that coincided with the elementary and middle school year. *TFK* published three age appropriate editions of its weekly issues entitled Big Picture, News Scoop, and World Report.

Weekly Issues

138   The Big Picture edition was for Kindergarten and 1st grade students. This edition printed only once a month since the audience was fairly young. The current circulation of Big

FIGURE 5   TIME For Kids Business Model

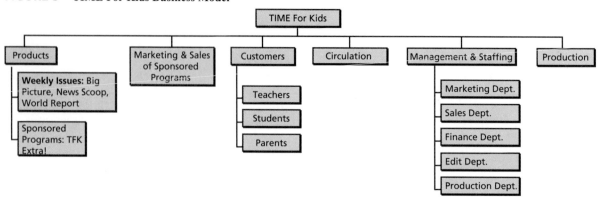

Picture was 650,000 students and 30,000 teachers across the United States. The issue printed on 60# paper stock and was 4 pages. It was accompanied by a 12-page teacher's guide.

139   The News Scoop edition was for 2nd and 3rd grade students. This edition printed weekly and the current circulation is 1,240,000 students and 55,000 teachers across the United States. The issue printed on 38# paper stock and was 4 pages. It was accompanied by a 6 page teacher's guide.

140   The World Report edition was for 4th through 7th grade students. This edition printed weekly and the current circulation is 2,200,000 students and 85,000 teachers across the United States. The issue printed on 38# paper stock and was 8 pages. A 6-page teacher's guide accompanied the issue as well.

141   The issue names were printed on the magazine covers; however the grade they targeted was not specified.

142   The material in the teacher's guide coincided with the school curriculum for that grade.

143   The weekly issues shipped to the classroom in bundles and typically arrived on either a Wednesday or a Thursday. This was 4 to 5 days before the actual cover date of the issue.

144   *TFK* did an excellent job of making sure the editorial content found in the weekly issues was written in an appropriate manor for the grade(s) the edition serviced and censored materials it felt were inappropriate for certain grades. *TFK* only published 3 editions. Some employees felt this was not enough. *TFK* also did not make it clear which edition was responsible for servicing which grade. *TFK*'s three editions, Big Picture, News Scoop and World Report, did not tell readers which grades each edition serviced. The issues had the edition name on the cover. In some cases, this had confused both students and parents who were unclear how the editions differed. Teachers would be aware of which editions serviced which grade because they had placed the subscription and this information is clear on the order form.

Sponsored Programs

145   The other type of issues *TFK* published were their sponsored programs, which were branded "*TFK Extra!*" All subscribers of the weekly issues received any sponsored programs that ran as well. Sold sponsored programs were responsible for 54% of *TFK*'s revenue. These programs were unique for every advertiser that purchased them. These programs took the place of traditional ads in a magazine and could cost anywhere between $50,000 to over $1,000,000 depending on what was created. The editorial staff that was responsible for writing the weekly issues did NOT write or have input on the *TFK Extra!* Issues. These issues were both written and designed by freelancers who were once part of *TFK*'s editorial staff.

146   The main components of the sponsored programs were typically a *TFK Extra!* (student magazine), and/or a 16-panel poster (8 pages front and back) that had a teacher's guide on the back of it. Other components although not typically produced, could be trading cards, bookmarks, CDs and stickers. These items were not typically sold due to the high costs associated with producing them.

147   The sponsored programs must have contained a minimum of 25% original *TFK* editorial content. This was due to the fact that *TFK* received a 3rd class postage rate for being an educational periodical and could be in jeopardy of paying a 1st class rate if it did not meet this requirement. Traditional magazines paid a 1st class rate which was much more costly.

148   Typically advertisers would purchase a *TFK Extra!* and request that the program go to more than one grade edition. When this was done, the editorial content was not adjusted to meet academic level of both editions. This meant that the material found in a student magazine that a 2nd grader was using may have been written for a 5th grader. TFK made an effort to have the *TFK Extras!* written in a way that tried to capture both audiences although they were not always successful. If one were to purchase a program going to both News Scoop (grades 2–3) and World Report (grades 4–7) subscribers, they would be targeting grades 2–7. There was not much of a difference between 3rd and 4th graders. However, there was an academically large difference between a 2nd and 7th grader.

149   *TFK* did not frequently incorporate lessons into the teacher guides of the sponsored programs (if there was a teacher guide) that directly corresponded with the appropriate grades curriculum. This limited the use of the sponsored programs in the classroom and resulted in them being sent home to read.

150   When a sponsored program ran it would be delivered along in the regular weekly bundles. Copies of the sponsored program would be placed on the bottom of the bundle that was shipped to the classroom.

151   Most companies who purchased *TFK Extras!* were those who had an educational objective or who sought to fulfill a corporate awareness initiative, such as Toyota and their literacy program for children, or the Florida Department of Citrus and their health initiative that promoted a balanced diet amongst kids.

Marketing and Sales of Sponsored Programs

152 *TFK*'s sales staff had minimal experience at selling sponsored programs in an in-class atmosphere. With that being said, *TFK* only did a fair job of explaining how the in-class magazine business model worked and quantifying the value of a sponsored program to advertisers. *TFK* did a fair job as well at explaining the value of being able to reach a large number of students in the classroom to potential advertisers. This was a difficult task in general for an in-class publication since the majority of advertisers were accustomed to purchasing ad pages in traditional magazines. Over the last 2 years both Weekly Reader and Scholastic News had won business that *TFK* competed for.

153 *TFK* also did only a fair job of getting sponsors to renew their programs over consecutive years. Three of the six programs sold by *TFK* in the 2005–06 school year were renewed programs. The competition was strong at getting advertisers to renew programs and had averaged a 63% renewal rate on sponsored programs between the years of 2002–2005 [Hilliard, 2005].

154   Since *TFK* was not what the industry considers a traditional print buy, meaning you're not buying an ad page as you would in most magazines, *TFK* was not typically considered when a company was planning its advertising for a specific year. Because of this companies generally ran programs with *TFK* if they had available dollars in any of their budgets, not necessarily the print budget. The dollars spent though were usually those that were leftover after planning is complete. One of the challenges facing *TFK* was to find a way to get advertisers to commit to purchase a sponsored program at the start of the advertising planning process. Because of this challenge, it was important for *TFK* to be able to fulfill advertisers' proposal requests quickly. *TFK* had done a fair job of this.

Customers

155   *TFK*'s current customers were directly teachers of grades K–7. However, students, their parents and advertisers were also considered "customers," as well even though they were not purchasing subscriptions. These teachers, students, parents and advertisers were located in the United States.

156   The curriculum found in the weekly issues of *TFK*, while relevant did not meet national standards of the grade that was receiving it. This was also true for the content found in the sponsored programs. Because of this teachers did not use *TFK* as part of their homework assignment as frequently as *TFK* would have liked.

157   Students found *TFK* fun to read and felt like they really learned a lot from both the weekly issues and sponsored programs. In a recent focus group conducted by *TFK*, students did state that they wish *TFK* ran more contests and sweepstakes. Students also felt that the prizes offered for winning these contests/sweepstakes were not the most exciting. When *TFK* ran a program with the Florida Department of Citrus, the sweepstakes winner received a visit from an orange grower to the child's class. Children felt this was a boring prize.

158   *TFK* was very strong at proving to parents and teachers that *TFK* was a trusted source for information and that the magazine operated with the highest of ethics. *TFK* made sure that the content found in the weekly issues was covered responsibly in cases where an article may deal with a very sensitive topic/issue. *TFK* had received numerous letters from teachers and parents, thanking the magazine for teaching their students/children about events that were going on in the world without having them lose hope. Other letters received by *TFK* from the parents thanked them for bringing these parents closer to their children and increasing the amount of time they spent having a conversation with their children about the magazine.

159   *TFK*'s customers for sponsored programs were advertisers of midsize companies such as Triaminic, large corporations such as Toyota and government agencies such as the Department of Health and Human Services. These advertisers were looking to find a large audience of children to either market their product to or to increase awareness of an educational initiative the advertiser may have.

160   *TFK* exemplified educational responsibility when running the sponsored programs. *TFK* had turned down advertisers who wished to purchase a sponsored program in the past if they felt the advertiser's message was too promotional, or not appropriate for the classroom. For example, Trident had approached *TFK* several times to create a program, but the magazine would not partner with Trident because their product was gum and gum isn't allowed to be chewed in school. By being selective about whom *TFK* allows to sponsor a program, the magazine has been able to increase teachers' and parents' trust alike.

161   *TFK* did a good job at creating programs that drove the advertiser's customers to purchase the advertiser's product, service or donate money. An example of this would be the increase in sales for Toyota of their Sienna vehicle that was being showcased as part of a sponsored program in 2004. Toyota experienced an 8% increase in sales of the Sienna during a six-month span (3 months where there was a *TFK* contest and the following 3 months) in the markets *TFK* provided the Toyota *TFK Extra!* to.

162   *TFK* also provided all of their advertisers with research after a sponsored program had run. The research was conducted every 4 months and would include information on all sponsored programs that were issues during that span. Most advertisers found the research quite helpful. No pre-research was conducted.

163   Advertisers seemed to feel that the sponsored programs created by *TFK* were unique, although past advertisers had mentioned that they wish a contest and/or sweepstakes had been recommended or included in *TFK*'s program.

CIRCULATION

164   *TFK* currently had 4.1 million student subscribers and 170, 000 teacher subscribers who received *TFK* during their 26 week publishing cycle. They published their first 2005 school year issue on September 2nd and will run their last issue for this school year May 5th 2006. *TFK* currently charged $4.30 per subscription, which would be $107.50 for a class subscription for 25 students. *TFK* was delivered directly into the classroom of the subscribing teacher.

165   In 2005 *TFK* changed their publishing schedule to print 1 week earlier than they did for the 2004–05 school year. *TFK* also decided to run their renewal campaigns one week later than they did in 2003. This had a negative impact on the rate of renewals in September although they did rebound with a strong October and November. *TFK*'s direct mail campaigns which were used to solicit new business did a fair job of doing so. *TFK* did see its circulation increase from 2004 to 2005 by 100,000 subscribers.

166   *TFK*'s order forms were fairly easy to understand and fill out, and its customer service was good.

167   It was also believed that natural disasters such as Hurricane Katrina and the hurricanes in Florida that occurred at the beginning of the 2005–06 school year had a negative impact on the renewed subscriptions of those areas.

Management & Staffing

168   The editorial staff, which was responsible for creating the weekly issues, was very strong. The majority of the editorial staff was with *TFK* when the title launched back in 1995. The publishing staff (marketing, sales, and business office) on the other hand was faced with some challenges.

169   In November of 2005 Mrs. Kahn decided that major change was needed if she was to better the magazine's business. Mrs. Kahn decided to hire a completely new team, keeping only her production manager, finance manager and her assistant. Because of this *TFK*'s current management staff was fairly junior in experience. Mrs. Kahn's first hires, which came in November 2005, were 2 sponsored program sales representatives and one sales & development manager. *TFK*'s business manager was hired in March of 2005 and immediately went on maternity leave in April 2005 so she did not really get settled into the job until October of 2005. The marketing director was hired in May of 2005 and a marketing project manager was hired in June 2005.

170   Mrs. Kahn was an extremely caring Publisher, who valued quality of life above and beyond work. As a mother of 2, she felt it was important to create a flexible working environment that would allow parents to work and have enough time to spend with their family. Mrs. Kahn hired 2 sales people in a job sharing arrangement. Each worked only 3 days per week, having only one day per week that both would be in the office at the same time. The sales team was responsible for covering the East, West, and Mid-West regions. They were both stationed in New York City. The marketing director worked 2 days in the office and one from home, totaling 3 days per week. The following employees worked 5 days per week: finance manager, business manager, production manager, marketing project manager and the sales & development manager.

171   Having both members of the sales staff only work 3 days per week was a hindrance for *TFK* as a whole. One sales person worked Monday, Tuesday and Thursday, while the other worked Wednesday, Thursday and Friday. This meant that for only half of the week one person was out trying to sell a *TFK Extra!* The sponsored programs were responsible for 54% of *TFK*'s revenue and having one person out in the field almost every day definitely made it difficult to maximize sales. There was also no presence in the West and Mid-West markets, an area where *TFK* did a fair amount of business. It was difficult for the sales people to find time to cover their home territory (East coast) and try to find business on the West coast as well.

172   Having the marketing director 3 days per week (2 in the office) was actually fairly manageable. The marketing director was very experienced and did a tremendous job when in the office. She also made sure she was accessible on her days off if needed. The marketing director was very creative and in her brief time with *TFK* had overseen the creation of several sponsored programs that were received well by advertisers and classes.

173   *TFK*'s new business manager was a very bright woman who had a difficult job in front of her. The financial practices that were followed before her hiring were poor and inconsistent. There was no system as to how much each component of a sponsored program should be sold for, nor was there any records of the profitability of the sponsored programs that had run. When looking back at programs that ran in 2004, it seemed that *TFK* sold programs with profit margins ranging between 20% and 60%. This was no way for a magazine to handle its finances and it needed to be corrected. The new business manager was responsible for monitoring the profitability of all sponsored programs sold as well as creating consistent methods for pricing programs. One of the first things she implemented as new business manager was a book that contained all possible components that could be sold as part of a sponsored program. In this book was the cost to *TFK* for each component as well as the cost the business office wanted the sales team to sell the component for. This was definitely a step in the right direction since it helped *TFK* maximize the margin made on each program more frequently.

174   While Mrs. Kahn was a very nurturing person, her management style was fairly loose and lacked direction at times. Frequently she would meet with her direct reports and assign them tasks that she would later decide were not valuable. Having her staff work on projects that were never executed was a misuse of time and money. There were also several instances where Mrs. Kahn would assign her team tasks and give very little direction on how she wanted them to be completed. This frustrated the staff and forced them to guess on how to go about completing certain projects. With such a junior management staff in place it seemed as though a more structured approach was needed.

Production

175   The weekly edition of *TFK* magazine printed 26 times a year in Dallas, Texas. The magazine was produced on a web press. *TFK* magazines were also nested, meaning there is 1 issue nested inside every issue. These magazines were also distributed in bundles, which were shrink-wrapped. The bundles included a minimum of 10 issues but could hold anywhere over 500 depending on the subscription order. The average bundle size contained 25 copies.

176   It cost approximately 5 cents to produce 1 copy of *TFK* (weekly issue or sponsored issue). The approximate cost of an average size classroom bundle (25 issues) was $1.30 [Kelliher, 2005].

177   *TFK*'s association with Time Inc allowed it the luxury of obtaining some of the best paper prices and printing rates in the industry. Paper was bought by Time Inc as a whole company and managed by a Central Production group. This group then expensed paper costs to the individual magazine titles, based upon the pounds of paper used on an issue. Time Inc as a large bargaining unit could obtain more competitive prices in the paper industry than *TFK* could do on its own.

178   Contracted printing rates worked similar to paper. Time Inc. negotiated printing contracts for the company as a whole, while each individual title had its own price list. Time Inc.'s bargaining power allowed it to gain some of the most competitive printing rates in the industry. *TFK* benefited from these lower rates.

179   Once the magazine printed at Dallas, magazines were sent via trucks directly to schools or to postal hubs. The costs incurred during this process include trucking freight costs and postage. For the remainder of 2005 and 2006, *TFK* was expecting to be hit with increased trucking costs due to surging fuel prices. After not raising periodical postage for the past

few years, the United States Postal Service has raised periodical postage rates up 11%. The cost of paper will also increase 2006 at a rate of 6%. This could translate into hundreds of thousands of dollars against *TFK*'s bottom line.

180   One way to mitigate the effects of production input increases was to change the production specs of the magazine. Currently, *TFK*'s student magazine measures 8" × 10 ½" and was produced on 38# stock paper. The teacher's guides measured 8" × 10 ½" and was produced on 60# stock paper. The magazines varied in page size depending on the edition. The *Big Picture* edition was 4 pages and its teacher's guide was 12 pages. The *News Scoop* edition was 4 pages and its teacher's guide is 6 pages. The *World Report* edition was 8 pages and its teacher's guide was 6 pages. The magazine was collated, meaning it was glued rather than being stapled or having a spine.

181   Changing the production specs, such as having a smaller trim size and lighter paper stock, could translate into hundreds of thousands of dollars of savings in paper and distribution costs. This was due to cheaper paper being used and a lighter magazine being mailed out. All changes to the production specs of the magazine needed editorial approval, since the look of the magazine can be greatly altered by these changes. Also, an evaluation needed to be conducted to ensure that the new magazine would be received well by the teachers, students and parents.

Management and Strategy

182   Jodi Kahn, the President of *TIME For Kids* Magazine, was ultimately responsible for the income delivered to Time Warner corporate. Mrs. Kahn relied on the heads of *TFK*'s divisional units to make the best decisions for *TFK* in order to allow them to be different and better and thus win against the competition.

183   Eileen Masio was the Marketing Director of *TFK*. She was responsible for creating the sponsored programs and any marketing partnerships. She and her staff aggressively went out into the market and tried to sell as many ad pages as possible.

184   Jill Finnegan and Elise Perlmutter were the Sales Directors of *TFK*. They were responsible for finding potential advertisers and selling them sponsored programs. Both women went out into the market and tried to sell as many sponsored programs as possible.

185   Michelle Mitchell was the head of circulation. She and her staff were responsible for increasing *TFK*'s subscriber base. Issues such as subscription price, issue frequency and consumer demographics resided in the circulation division.

186   Martha Pickerell was the managing editor of *TFK*. She and her staff were responsible for the editorial content and design of the magazine's weekly issues.

187   Gary Kelliher was the Production Manager of *TFK*. He was responsible for printing and distributing the magazine (weekly issues and sponsored programs) as efficiently and cheaply as possible.

188   Michelle Kedem was the Business Manager. She heads the business office, which was in charge of setting the rates of the sponsored program components and had the authority to grant discounts to potential advertisers if she saw fit. The business office was responsible for monitoring advertising, marketing, production and editorial expenses for both weekly issues and sponsored programs.

189   Given the competitive environment, one issue facing *TFK*'s management team was to create editorial content in both the weekly issues and the sponsored programs that was completely appropriate for the grade it was used in. Each department played a role in making this possible.

LOOKING TOWARDS THE FUTURE

190   In 2004 Jodi Kahn decided that *TIME For Kids* needed to develop a strategy to differentiate the company from the other in-class magazines, increase their circulation and increase the

number of advertisers that sponsor programs. In order to push *TIME For Kids* ahead of the competition, Jodi Kahn was faced with various strategic alternatives. Two possible strategies involve modifying the different editions offered to the various grade levels.

191   The first alternative considered by Jodi Kahn was to create an edition for each of the eight grades that *TFK* currently services (kindergarten through seventh). *TFK* would still keep the current edition names that they used (*Big Picture, News Scoop*, and *World Report*) but would now have variations under these names. For example, there would be 2 versions of the *Big Picture*, one going to Kindergarten students and one going to 1st graders. *News Scoop* would have different versions for 2nd, 3rd, and 4th graders. *World Report* would have an issue versioned for 5th, 6th, and 7th graders. Each edition included the grade level on the cover and all would be different in content. This would be for both the periodical issues as well as the sponsored programs.

192   A benefit of this strategic alternative for *TFK* was to create content that would possibly increase its circulation. Each issue would be editorially focused for a specific grade making the material more relevant. Another benefit for *TFK* would be the ability for advertisers to sponsor programs for a narrower target market.

193   This alternative was feasible because the teachers that already subscribed to *TFK* were accustomed to receiving one of three different issues a different issue depending on what grade they were teaching in a given year. Currently only three editions were offered. Furthermore the *TFK* editorial staff already included former teachers of all seven grades that are serviced, so the knowledge was there to create academically relevant, age appropriate editions.

194   By offering teachers a more relevant student magazine for their classes, *TFK* would be brought up to par with what the competition was offering. Pairing this with *TFK*'s superior editorial content would enable *TFK* to win against the competition. Having eight editions would also give advertisers the opportunity to reach a specific grade rather than market to those that they do not wish to target but are forced to because a portion of their audience falls within an edition's grade range. This would minimize the frustration advertisers are currently dealing with when they are forced to campaign outside their target audience, which would increase their chances of running another program at a later date. If advertisers ran additional sponsored programs, *TFK* would generate additional revenue as well as gain business over their competitors. This alternative would also in all likelihood increase the positive responses reported in *TFK*'s semi-annual research. Better research results would help *TFK* strengthen their image with both advertisers and teachers. Implementing this alternative would increase the magazine's circulation as well as increase the number of sponsored programs sold, which would ultimately increase *TFK*'s revenue.

195   A drawback to choosing this alternative would be that *TFK* would now need to create different content for each edition which would be very time consuming, especially since they are a weekly publication and time is of the essence. This would also increase the editors' workload significantly and would most likely require *TFK* to hire more writers.

196   A way around this drawback would be to bring on a combination of freelance writers/designers and full-time employees to help create these editions. By bringing on some freelancers, *TFK* would be able to save money, as they would not be responsible for providing the benefits that a full-time employee would receive. These benefits were typically 40% of the employee's current salary, meaning if your salary was $50,000 the company would see the total cost of employing you as $70,000.

197   Another way around this drawback would be to keep the themes and concepts in each issue consistent but made sure the way the issues were written are grade appropriate. This would allow the editors to focus more on creating the relevant teacher curriculum rather than creating eight completely unique issues with different edit.

198   The second alternative would be to create a fourth edition. As stated earlier *TFK* currently produces 3 editions: *Big Picture, News Scoop* and *World Report*. This alternative

would have the *World Report* edition service only 4th and 5th graders and create a newly titled edition going to 6th and 7th graders. The edition would be named *Senior Review*. All editions would have the grade indicated next to the issue name as well. This would be for both the periodical issues as well as the sponsored programs.

199   A benefit of this strategic alternative for *TFK* was to create content that would possibly increase its circulation. The *World Report* edition would now be more focused since it would have an edition reaching only 2 grades, making the material more relevant.

200   Another benefit for *TFK* would be the ability for advertisers to sponsor programs for a narrower target market.

201   This alternative was feasible because the teachers that already subscribe to *TFK* are accustomed to receiving a different issue depending on what grade they are teaching in a given year. Currently only three editions are offered. Furthermore the *TFK* editorial staff already creates a *World Report* edition so they would only need to make minor changes to the current version to create an academically relevant, age appropriate edition.

202   This alternative would win against the competition because *TFK* would be offering teachers a more relevant student magazine for their classes, which is something that not all of their competitors offered in regard to the periodical editions provided. This would help differentiate *TFK* from the competition. Having four editions would also give advertisers planning on purchasing a sponsored program the opportunity to reach a narrower grade range rather than market to those that they did not wish to target but were forced to because a portion of their audience fell within an edition's grade range. This would minimize the frustration advertisers were currently dealing with when they were forced to campaign outside their target audience, which would increase their chances of running another program at a later date. They would no longer feel like a portion of their money was being spent unwisely. This alternative would also in all likeliness increase the positive responses reported in *TFK*'s semi-annual research. Better research results would help *TFK* strengthen their image with both advertisers and teachers. Implementing this alternative would increase the magazine's circulation as well as increase the number of sponsored programs sold, which would ultimately increase *TFK*'s revenue.

203   A drawback to choosing this alternative would be that *TFK* would now need to create different content for each *World Report* edition which would be time consuming, especially since they are a weekly publication and time is of the essence. This would also increase the editors' workload and would most likely require *TFK* to hire another writer.

204   A way around this drawback would be to promote the Associate Editors of both *World Report* student magazine and teacher's guide to be managing editors of *Senior Review* student magazine and teacher's guide. It was conceivable to think that the associate editors would be able to make the modifications needed to make the issues more age appropriate. They would also have the option of bringing in freelance writers to assist with the issue if need be. The issues would maintain the same art and image direction, so changes would not need to be made to the magazine's layout.

205   Both alternatives would help *TIME For Kids* increase its editorial focus and help advertisers target a more specific age range. Jodi Kahn was left with a difficult decision about these and other alternatives.

REFERENCES

City Newsstand (2005). "Magazines 101" [Online] *http://www.citynewsstand.com.* Accessed November 8.

FolioMag (2005). "Magazine Outsourcing" [Online] *http://www.foliomag.com.* Accessed November 10.

General Presentation (2005). "TFK General Presentation." Accessed September 8th.

Hilliard, Marcell (2005). "Competitive Analysis." Presented August 4.

Hoovers (2005). "Time Warner" [Online] *http://www.hoovers.com.* Accessed October 14.

Husni, Dr. Samir A. (2005A). "The State of Magazines: A Presentation to Time Inc."
  Presented May 20.

Husni, Dr. Samir A. (2005B). "The State of Magazines: A Presentation to Time Inc."
  Presented May 20.

Kelliher, Gary (2005). "TIME For Kids Efficiency Report" Provided November 20.

MarketResearch (2005A). "Magazines" [Online] *http://www.marketresearch.com.*
  Accessed October 19.

MarketResearch (2005B). "Magazines" [Online] *http://www.marketresearch.com.*
  Accessed October 19.

Mockler, Robert J. & Gartenfeld, Marc E. (ed) (2005). Cases In Domestic & Multinational Strategic Management (VII), New York, N.Y. pgs C10-5.

MSN Advertising (2005). "Internet Advertising" [Online] *http://advertising.msn.com.*
  Accessed October 27.

Scholastic (2005). "About Us"[Online] *http://www.scholastic.com.* Accessed October 16.

Time Warner (2005A), "Our Company" [Online] *http://www.timewarner.com.*
  Accessed November 1.

Time Warner (2005B), "Our Company" [Online] *http://www.timewarner.com.*
  Accessed November 1.

TFK Research (2005A), "Penetration Analysis Report" Presented September 14.

TFK Research (2005B), "Penetration Analysis Report" Presented September 14.

TFK Research (2005C), "Penetration Analysis Report" Presented September 14.

TFK Research (2005D), "Penetration Analysis Report" Presented September 14.

TFK Research (2005E), "Penetration Analysis Report" Presented September 14.

Weekly Reader (2005). "About Us"[Online] *http://www.weeklyreader.com.* Accessed
  October 16.

WordNet (2005). "Magazines" [Online] *http://wordnet.princeton.edu.* Accessed
  October 14.

Case 48

TiVo, Inc: *TiVo vs. Cable and Satellite DVR; Can TiVo Survive?*

Alan N. Hoffman, Rendy Halim, Rangki Son, and Suzanne Wong

BACKGROUND

"With TiVo, TV fits into your busy life, NOT the other way around"

1   The evolution history of Television started way back in 1939 with an original purpose of providing people with entertainment and enjoyment in life. It was then followed by an invention of the remote control in 1950 known as the "lazy bones." Perhaps, this has been one of the biggest breakthroughs and most influential forms of entertainment we all have appreciated and enjoyed up until now. However after the Lazy Bones was invented, the next generation of TV watching tools evolved; one of them was TiVo, every couch potato's dream. Thanks to two Silicon Valley veterans with their creative and smart ideas, they took the initiative to recreate innovative and advanced technology developments in a radically different approach. TiVo, was created not only just that entertainment, but "TV Your Way." Fundamentally designed, "With TiVo, TV fits into your busy life, NOT the other way around."

2   Now, many people may have heard the name TiVo . . . mentioned on popular TV shows, movies and many talk shows . . . even Oprah wonders in her September 2005 issue of her "O" magazine that why can't life be like TiVo . . . but not so many know what TiVo really is about.

ONCE UPON A TIVO . . .

3   Pioneered by Mike Ramsay and Jim Barton, TiVo redefined entertainment in many other ways, delivering the promise of technologies that were much hyped. Incorporated in Delaware and originally named their firm "Teleworld," the playback of TiVo started in August 4, 1997. As proposed, the original idea was to create a home network-based multimedia server where content to thin clients would stream out throughout the home. In order to build such product, solid software foundation is much needed and the device created has to operate flawlessly perfect, reliable and handle power failure gracefully for the consumers. At that time, both were still working in Silicon Graphics (SGI) and were very much involved in the entertainment industry. Jim Barton, though was involved with on-demand video system; he was the executive sponsor of an effort to port an open source system called Linux to the SGI Indy workstation, while Mike Ramsay, was responsible for products that create movies' special effects for such companies as ILM and Pixar. With the combination of both worlds, these two SGI veterans thought Linux software would well serve TiVo as the operating system foundation. As for the hardware, it was designed solely by TiVo Inc and manufactured with the help of various OEMs including Philips, Sony, Hughes, Pioneer,

The authors would like to thank Audrey Ballara, Will Hoffman and Ann Hoffman for their research and contributions to this case. Please address all correspondence to: Dr. Alan N. Hoffman, MBA Program Director, LAC295D, Bentley College, 175 Forest Street, Waltham, MA 02452-4705, voice (781)891-2287, ahoffman@bentley.edu, fax (781)459-0335. Printed by permission of Dr. Alan N. Hoffman.

Toshiba, and Humax. Combined they created a product that is very much interactive with real people, delivering a commitment where those people will be able to take charge of their own entertainment whenever they want to and wherever they need to.

From the Server Room to the Living Room

4   Swaying from their original idea to create a home network device, they later developed the idea to record digitized video on a hardware storage drive. Inside the Silicon Valley headquarters of TiVo in Alviso, California, both veterans created a so called "fantasy living room," depicting a room full of executives who hope that will be a prototype for 100 million living rooms across North America. At that time, they both knew it would be so cool to exploit and develop the idea into an actual product with a promising future, a dream of most start-up companies. In the early days, Mike Ramsay said that they used to have thoughts of things like "Wow, you know, you can pause live television—isn't that a cool thing?" Jim Barton then got a computer to store a live TV signal and made it to play it back. Then . . . that was the start of TiVo—providing people with more than the original purpose of TV as just simply a tube to be watched, resulted with an invention to create the world's very first interactive entertainment network, where luxury of entertainment and control is in the viewers' own hands. As of March 31, 1999, TiVo shipped its first unit and because that day was a blue moon, an engineering staff code named TiVo's first version DVR as the "Blue Moon." Both Jim Barton and Mike Ramsay were psyched as the introduction to market a disruptive technology had just begun. Teleworld was then renamed to TiVo in July 1999. Now that the living room is filled only with an oval coffee table and a comfy chair just like any other living room in the households, the only objects that can be distinctively seen and left is what's on the table surface—a telephone and TiVo's distinctive peanut-shaped remote control. The sofa and chairs all face an entertainment center containing a big-screen television that is linked to several TiVo boxes (a few are available; a few are works in progress).

TIVO ACCLAMATION

5   Now where the success of on demand programs and online streaming are flocking TV networks, still many people have found DVR to be an essential part of their digital home entertainment center, catering more to people's viewing habits. Consumers would slip into stores such as big box retailers Best Buy, Circuit City, Target and Wal-Mart and sales people would refer them to TiVo as TiVo has been commonly associated as the "DVR." Reminiscing back to the history of DVR, TiVo was actually never a beginner, but ReplayTV. The two early consumer DVRs, ReplayTV and TiVo, both launched their product in 1999 Consumer Electronics Show in Las Vegas. ReplayTV won the "Best of Show" award in the video category and was later acquired by SoniceBlue and D&M Holdings later in the years. However, it wasn't ReplayTV, the pioneer of DVRs in the DVR industry, the brand that made it to the world producing a cult like product, but TiVo. TiVo's success also includes still currently being the only standalone DVR company in the industry. According to Forrester, from a scale of 1 to 5, TiVo's brand trust among regular users scores 4.2, while its brand potential among aspiring users scores A with 11.1 million potential users.

6   Spending approximately 13 months for full development of the first TiVo box, the wait was worthwhile as the revolutionary nature of TiVo won itself an Emmy award in August 19, 2006. This recognition was given to TiVo for providing innovative and interactive services that enhance television viewing to a whole new level. Other finalists for this particular Emmy award include AOL Music on Demand, CNN Enhanced and DirecTV Interactive Sports. With a cult like product, TiVo has transformed into a verb. TiVo established a top-notch brand that has become the "it" word among its fervidly loyal customers and even

non customers. In general, people would say "TiVo it," meaning to record or zap (make something disappear). A working wife, who has an important business dinner meeting that night and was rushing through the door, could speedily ask her husband "Could you TiVo Desperate Housewives for me tonight dear?" On the other hand, TiVo felt that this verb transformation will jeopordize TiVo and associate its products as a generic brand of DVR when people say, "I want two TiVo's." However, with all the TiVo buzz, TiVo became public on September 30th, 1999 at a price offering of $16 per share with a total of 5.5 million number of shares listed under the NASDAQ. On its way to the IPO, TiVo established one of the most rapid adoption rates in the history of consumer electronics. Quoted recently in an April 2007 article by PC World, TiVo became the third on the list of 50 best technology products of all time—saluted amazing products that changed our lives forever.

7   The acknowledgement has well served the young West Coast Company who is currently available in four countries which includes United States, United Kingdom, Canada and Taiwan. In addition, though it is not sold yet, TiVo's technology has been modified by end users so it could fit in another four countries such as Australia, New Zealand, Netherlands and South Africa. However TiVo has never come close to winning the number of customers (market share) nor generated a profit since it launched in 1997. Considered to be the best DVR system out there by variety of top notch publications such as *BusinessWeek, New York Times* and *Popular Science,* TiVo hit a 3 million subscriber milestone only by February, 18th, 2005. Not long after, TiVo finally made its first profitable quarter. TiVo's subscribers include diverse and loyal subscribers from the infamous Oprah Winfrey, Brad Pitt and entrepreneur Craig Newmark (the owner of Craigs List). Though, the business philosophy of TiVo is relatively simple: TiVo connects consumers to the digital entertainment they want, where, and when they want it.

THE BRAIN INSIDE THE BOX

"It's not TiVo unless it's a TiVo"

The Surf & Turf

8   As people's daily life became busier and demanded more and more to attain the pleasure of watching TV, Digital Video Recorders became the tool to suffice that trend. The trend resulted in audiences wanting to have more direct allegiance with particular programs. TiVo then revolutionized that new way to watch TV, with the introduction of the Digital Video Recording system (DVR). Hard as it seems to be described in a sentence or two, the best way to describe what TiVo really is, is by the things that it does.

9   The DVR platform has created massive opportunity for TiVo to continue developing creative and sophisticated applications, features and services. Unlike a VCR (videocassette recorder), TiVo as a Digital Video Recorder issues only Linux based software and allows users to capture any TV programming and record them into internal hard disk storage for later viewing. Its patented feature, "Trick Play" that allows viewers to stop, pause, rewind and slo-mo live shows are what TiVo is originally best at.

10   The TiVo device also allows users to watch their programs without having to watch the commercials if they don't want to. Users are exposed to promotional messages but are not forced to watch them. While this feature seems very attractive to consumers, understandably, not to television networks and advertising agencies. However, unlike ReplayTV that allows users to automatically and completely skip advertisements and was hit by several lawsuits by ad agencies and TV networks, TiVo managed to take a different approach.

11   With its inventive advertisement feature, TiVo offered to help, turning a difficult situation into a business opportunity, which has become TiVo's hallmark. TiVo surely knows that advertisements are a source of revenue. TiVo then started testing its "pop-up" feature. While recording or watching, there are some advertisements that pop up at the bottom of the TV screen. If a customer is interested in any of these advertisements, he has the ability to click to get more information about the product being advertised. People then have the choice to get advertisers' information or not depending on what they have interest in. "Product Watch" lets users choose the products, services, or even brands that interest them and it will automatically find and deliver the requested/relevant products straight to your list. Surprisingly, during the 2002 Super Bowl, TiVo tracked the viewing patterns of 10,000 of its subscribers and found that TiVo's instant replay feature was used more on certain commercials, notably the Pepsi ad with Britney Spears, than on the game itself. As of today, TiVo has included 70 "showcase" advertising campaigns in its TiVo platforms for companies such as Acura, Best Buy, BMW, Buick, Cadillac, Charles Schwab, Coca-Cola, Dell, General Motors, GMC, New Line Cinema, Nissan, Pioneer, Porsche, and Target.

12   Beyond the key functions above, there are much more for users to surf throughout the integral functionality of a TiVo device. While a "Season Pass Manager" is to avoid conflict resolution such as overlapping recordings, a "Wish List" platform allows viewers to store their search according to their specifics such as actor, keyword, director, etc. So far, no other companies have yet been able to match these two TiVo's recording features. In addition, the catchy remote control with its distinctive "Thumbs Up and Down" feature allows users to rate the shows they have watched purportedly for the use of others and themselves so that TiVo could assist and provide users with the movie similar to what they have rated. The remote itself has won design awards from the Consumer Electronics Association. Jakob Nielsen, a technology consultant of the Nielsen Norman Group, called the oversize yellow pause button in the middle of the remote "the most beautiful pause button I've ever seen." Steve Wozniak, the co-founder of Apple Computer mentioned "TiVo adjusts to my tastes" and that its remote has been the most ergonomic and easy to use one that he has had encountered in many years.

13   In addition, being portable is now the hottest thing in television right now. Nowadays, that people have yet become more tech savvy, "TiVoToGo," its newest feature launched in January 2005, allows users to connect their TiVo to a computer with an internet or a home network, transferring recorded shows from TiVo boxes to users' PCs. Then, through a software program developed with Sonic, customers are able to edit and conserve their TiVo files. Later in August 2005, TiVo released a software that allows customers to transfer MPEG2 video files from their PC to their TiVo boxes to play the video on the DVR.

14   TiVoToGo feature also includes TiVo's "Central Online" which allows users to schedule recordings on its website 24/7, and "MultiRoom Viewing" which allows users to transfer recordings between TiVo units in multiple rooms, download any programs in any format they want into the TiVo box, and transfer them into a device such as an IPOD, laptop or other mobile devices such as cellular phones. This provides the pleasure of viewing them anytime and anywhere the users desire to do so. On top of that, with the partnerships TiVo has established in regards to 3rd party network content, viewers now can access weather, traffic condition, even purchase a last minute movie ticket at Fandango.com and have the pleasure to enjoy "Amazon Unbox," allowing users to buy/rent the latest movies and TV shows to be downloaded into the TiVo box.

"Behind the Box"—The Hardware Anatomy of TiVo 101

15   So, many people would ask, how TiVo actually operates. "Even my mother can use TiVo with no problem!" This is the phrase that TiVo wants their people to say.

16   Technically speaking, installing TiVo units have been pretty much self explanatory because they are designed to be simple enough for everyone to install and operate. Parts that go into the device and its internal architecture have been made to be less complex. Online self installation guide with a step by step pictured instruction has been the tool to suffice complete this request, however, options do come in handy, with a teamed up "door to door" professional installation service with Best Buy or a set up appointment with 1-877-Geek Squad.

17   In basic sense, TiVo is simply a cable box, with hard drive that gives the ability to record, and the fancy user interface. The main idea at the beginning, however, was to free people up from being locked by the network schedule. With TiVo, the watchers can watch anytime they want with extra features such as, pause, rewind, fast forward, slow motion, and many other great features, including the commercial-free watching experience.

18   Initially, the box will receive the signals coming from cable, antenna, or satellite. Then the signals received by the box will be divided into many frequencies and selected with the tuner that is built-in the box. The signals with the right selected frequencies will be sent and encoded through the encoder, stored in the hard drive, and then decoded again for the watchers to view anytime.

19   TiVo's earlier model Series2 was supported with USB ports that have been integrated into the TiVo system to support network adapters which includes wired Ethernet and WiFi. It also provides the possibility to record over-the-air. The new TiVo series 3 has been built with two internal cable-ready tuners and it supports a single external cable or satellite box. As a result, TiVo gives the ability to record two shows at once, unlike other DVRs. Moreover, the latest version of the TiVo box has a 10/1000 Ethernet connection port and a SATA port which can support external storage hardware. It also has a HDMI plug which provides an interface between any compatible digital audio/video source, such as a DVD player, a PC, or a video game system. In other words, with the new TiVo box, customers don't even need their cable box anymore. Some recent models even contain DVD-R/RW drives which transfer recordings from the TiVo box to a DVD disc.

20   TiVo hardware can work as a normal digital recorder by itself. People might sometimes want to keep the hardware and cancel their subscriptions with TiVo, which is very damageable for the company revenue model.

What the Hack!

21   Where there is technology involved, there are incentives for hackers to challenge the system. Some people have hacked the TiVo boxes to improve the service, and to expand the recording capacity or/and storage. Others have aimed at making TiVo available in countries where TiVo is not currently available. In the latest version of TiVo, improved encryption of the hardware and software has made it more difficult for people to hack the systems.

THE TIVOPERATION—BEHIND THE SCENES . . .

". . . and I never miss an episode. TiVo takes care of the details"

Marketing:

Feel the Buzzzzzz—Hail Thy TiVo

22   When it comes to new technology, penetrating consumers markets is usually difficult as customers are slower to embrace new products than forecasters predict and opt to choose using old and easier technology like the VCRs. Mike Ramsay would get upset in the early days, when someone says, "oh, that's just like a VCR." He would then reply to them and say "no, no, no, no, no. It's much more than a VCR, it does this, it does that, let's personalize it

and all that stuff." At that point, it gets so difficult to describe what TiVo actually is, leading into a five to ten minute conversation instead of a 30 second TiVo pitch.

23   However, this problem has not hindered TiVo from being a great product. Early on, TiVo has tried the traditional way of getting the product across with a result of repetitive stumbles in marketing its products. The millions of dollars spent on advertisements did not help consumers understand what TiVo actually does. A customer claims, "I personally remember seeing TiVo ads on 'TV before I even knew what a TiVo was, and it took seven years for me to finally see one, in the flesh.'"

24   What makes TiVo DVRs different from other generic DVRs, can only be felt and experienced and not seen even though the feature differences can be seen in Exhibit 1. According to Gartner analyst Van Baker, "For cable and satellite DVRs, the interface stinks. They do a really bad job of it." TiVo would rally people to change their lives by continuously preaching its brand and products, creating cause and evangelism with a result of many people claiming TiVo changed their lives. According to a survey reported on the TiVo website, 98% of users said that they could not live without their TiVo.

25   The one word that explicitly describes the cult like product is "interactive" in many ways. So when TiVo subscribers feel the buzz, they show and tell, the story goes on and on and on. Between 1999 and 2000, TiVo's subscriptions increased by 86%. In addition to capitalizing on its tens of thousands of customer evangelists to move the product into the mainstream, TiVo's word-of-mouth strategy focuses on celebrity endorsements and television show product placement. The firm began giving its product away to such celebrities as Oprah, Sarah Michelle Gellar, Drew Bledsoe and many more, turning them into high-profile members of the cult, while Jay Leno and Rosie O'Donnell helped much influence TiVo's consumers in a very positive way.

The Market Research Team

26   The need to create such unique emotional connection between people and this product is significant to TiVo. Another way for a firm like TiVo to always be a step ahead and develop ways to improve and measure promotions and viewer behavior is to do continuous intensive market research. TiVo's market research team is considered as one of its functional units that are driving the company which includes Lieberman Research Worldwide and Nielson Media Research. With Lieberman, the first ever DVR based panel was established in August 2002. Internally, TiVo also has built a platform in their system that sends detailed information on its customers watching TV behavior back to TiVo. TiVo also fully embraced the community with its TiVo community and hackers programs so that TiVo research team know what people needs are, when and where they need them.

Financial:

Fast Forward or Rewind TiVo's Stock?

27   TiVo started with a price of $16 during its IPO in 1999. TiVo reached the highest in its stock price history after its IPO at $78.75 with its first eye catching ad "Hey, if you like us, TiVo us" which then became its first milestone. After the rush rapid growth, TiVo's stock price shot down to a price as low as $2.25, the lowest in history around 2002. TiVo's stock price then started to pick up in 2003 when FCC Chairman Michael Powell announced that he uses TiVo, claiming TiVo is a "God's Machine," and when White House Press Secretary Ari Fleischer was found too to be a loyal user of TiVo. Around mid 2003, TiVo hit its first 1 million subscribers, significantly increased its stock price to reach around $14.00/share then inched back down to a low $3.50 per share as a result from the resignation of its CEO, Mike Ramsay. With the new CEO in place, TiVo finally reached a 3 million subscribers milestone by mid 2005, reaching to a current average stock price of $6–$7 range per share. Now, the question is, how to appease investors without killing a feature that helps sell the product?

EXHIBIT 1

	TiVo Series2™ Boxes	Leading Cable Service DVR*	Satellite DVR**	DIRECTV DVR with TiVo©
Record from multiple sources	Yes combine satellite, cable, or antenna, depending on product.	No Digital cable only	No Satellite only	No DIRECTV only
Easy search: Find shows by title, actor, genre, or keyword	Yes	Titles only browsing only	Title, subject, and actor only	Yes
Online scheduling: Schedule recordings from the Internet	Yes	No	No	No
Dual Tuner: Record 2 shows at once[1]	Yes	Yes	Yes	Yes
Movie and TV Downloads: Purchase or rent 1000's of movies and television shows from Amazon Unbox and have them delivered directly to your television.[2]	Yes	No	No	No
Home Movie Sharing: Edit, enhance, and send movies and photo slideshows from your One True Media account to any broadband connected TiVo box.[3]	Yes	No	No	No
Online services: Yahoo! weather, traffic & digital photos, Internet Radio from Live365, Podcasts, & movie tickets from Fandango	Yes	Limited	Limited	No
Built-In Ethernet: Broadband-ready right out of the box—connecting to your home network is a snap[4]	Yes	No	No	No
TiVoToGo transfers to mobile devices: Transfer shows to your favorite portable devices, laptop or burn them to DVD.[3,5]	Yes	No	No	No
Home media features: Digital photos, digital music and more	Yes	No	No	No
Transfer shows between boxes: Record shows on one TV and watch them on another.[3]	Yes	No	No	No

*Leading cable services compared to Time Warner/Cox Communications Explorer® 8000™ DVR and Comcast DVR
**Leading satellite services compared to DISH Network 625 DVR
[1]On the TiVo® Series2™ DT DVR, you can record basic cable channels, or one basic cable and one digital cable channel, at once.
[2]Requires broadband cable modem or DSL connection.
[3]Requires your TiVo box to be connected to a home network wirelessly or via Ethernet
[4]Available on the new TiVo® Series2™ DT DVR and the TiVo® Series3™ DMR
[5]In order to burn TiVoToGo transfers to DVD you will need to purchase software from Roxio/Sonic Solutions.

Source: http://www.tivo.com/1.0.chart.asp

Multiroom Solutions

	Digeo/Moxi	Motorola	Scientific-Atlanta	Echostar	TiVo	Microsoft
Main DVR	Cable DVR*	Cable DVR†	Cable DVR†	Satellite DVR*	TiVo box	Media Center PC
Set-top box on additional TV(s)	IP terminal	Cable box‡	Cable box	None	TiVo box	XBox 360
How boxes share content	IP	IP	Digital broadcast	Analog broadcast	IP§	IP
Physical connection	Coax	Coax	Coax	Coax	Home network	Home network
Features available on additional TVs:						
Play back recorded programs	✓	✓	✓	✓	✓	✓
Record programs	✓	✓		✓	✓	✓
Pause programs	✓	✓		✓	✓	✓
View Internet content	✓	✗			✓	✓
View personal digital content	✗	✗			✓	✓

*New product specifically designed for multiroom use   "×"= Available, but operators have not yet deployed
†Standard cable DVR plus modifications for multiroom use
‡Requires additional IP dongle on standard digital set-top box
§Requires transferring files from one TiVo box to the other

Source: Forrester Research Inc., 2006

TiVo DVRs

SAVE $150 INSTANTLY†

80-hr TiVo® Series2™ DT DVR

SAVE $150 INSTANTLY†

180-hr TiVo® Series2™ DT DVR

300-hr TiVo® Series3™ HD Digital Media Recorder

Comcast.

Motorola Set-Top Box

Scientific Atlanta Set-Top Box

DIRECTV·

Deconstructing TiVo

28 Since it was founded in 1997, TiVo has accumulated more than $400 million in losses. Looking at TiVo's revenues and costs structures in Exhibit 2, TiVo, an enigmatic company, has much divided its revenues and costs in variety of forms which includes service, technology, hardware and shared revenues. Being a company that lives under a great shadow of Wall Street pessimism, the question then becomes what value can TiVo add besides hyping their latest technology developments? Service revenues for example, TiVo needs to know what is the actual value of TiVo-owned subscribers and not TiVo's partnerships subscribers such as to DirecTV and Comcast. Deconstructing the value of just this one particular matter then leads to longer questions which includes, how long does a TiVo subscriber remain a subscriber, how much do each of them pay and are willing to pay, how much advertising revenue do users produce for every tag they click, moreover, how long and how can TiVo maintain its subscribers to be TiVo-owned subscribers?

29 In one way, the chicken and egg problem may have been the bulk of the TiVo's hardware revenues problem where people would say "What, huh, TiVo, personalizing your own TV network? What the hell are you talking about?," but not being able to gain the economies of scale that it desires, it should be TiVo's point of concern. Even though rebates are being offered, still, TiVo has not reached its price point that really attracts people. TiVo offers three types of boxes depending on the hours of programming storage capacity which range from an 80 hour TiVo Series to 300 hour TiVo Series HD. For the basic TiVo Series2 box of 80 hours and 180 hours has a one time fee of $99.99 and $199.99, while the HD TiVo box costs $799.99 with a 300 hours storage capacity.

30 TiVo also has been a heavy user of mail-in rebates which is reflected as one of their forms of revenues shown in Exhibit 2. According to *BusinessWeek,* $5 million in additional revenue was recognized because nearly half of TiVo's 100,000 new subscribers failed to apply for a $100 rebate. This slippage type of strategy is known to marketers as the "shoebox effect" and this usage of promotional practice has caused a large positive impact for TiVo.

Operation:

Research and Development—The "A" Team

31 Again, the word "interactive" is the buzz word. TiVo's R&D team makes sure that they build TiVo from the user's perspective and viewing habits. TiVo forms forums of communication through TiVo community.com and TiVo hackers. In this forum, criticisms are allowed and even encouraged, so long as they are constructive and help TiVo to grow. Users and aspiring users of TiVo are allowed to say what they like and dislike and voice what they expect to see TiVo in the future. Ideas generated through this forum will help TiVo's R&D team and developers to continuously be on hand and future innovaters accordingly to the need of people's ever changing lifestyle. TiVo is also concerned how its platform could actually be used the wrong way by kids these days. With this concern, TiVo has collaborated with parents to build a new feature called TiVo Parental Zone that allows parents to control what their kids are actually watching. Privacy concern has also been an issue nowadays in the advance technology industry. TiVo manages to protect its community regarding privacy concern by storing such information on a computer behind its "firewall" in a secure location, and often restricts the number of employees internally who can access such data.

32 Previously TiVo's R&D team only consists of contract based engineers; now, TiVo makes sure that its R&D team consists of a diverse, utmost creative and detailed staff engineers. Its intensive research principle is that benefits must extend existing people's behaviors. The design team has every little detail of steps to follow to fit the needs of lifestyle. As an example of TiVo's meticulous product design process, TiVo created a remote control that combines personalization and interconnectivity. TiVo's remote

EXHIBIT 2   Tivo Inc. Condensed Consolidated Statements of Operations (In thousands, except per share and share amounts) (unaudited)

	Three Months Ended October 31,		Nine Months Ended October 31,	
	2006	**2005 Adjusted**	**2006**	**2005 Adjusted**
Revenues				
Service and technology revenues	$ 52,616	$ 43,197	$ 160,605	$ 123,891
Hardware revenues	27,978	24,652	53,666	39,827
Rebates, revenue share, and other payments to channel	(14,934)	(18,234)	(32,932)	(27,860)
Net revenues	65,660	49,615	181,339	135,858
Cost of revenues				
Cost of service and technology revenues (1)	13,826	8,508	44,256	24,832
Cost of hardware revenues	31,925	24,667	68,678	48,006
Total cost of revenues	45,751	33,175	112,934	72,838
Gross margin	19,909	16,440	68,405	63,020
Research and development (1)	12,221	9,712	37,973	30,394
Sales and marketing (1)	10,123	10,006	25,856	24,410
General and administrative (1)	9,811	11,702	35,961	26,249
Total operating expenses	32,155	31,420	99,790	81,053
Loss from operations	(12,246)	(14,980)	(31,385)	(18,033)
Interest income	1,291	826	3,341	2,184
Interest expense and other	(133)	(10)	(165)	(13)
Loss before income taxes	(11,088)	(14,164)	(28,209)	(15,862)
Provision for income taxes	(4)	—	(35)	(51)
Net loss	$ (11,092)	$ (14,164)	$ (28,244)	$ (15,913)
Net loss per common share-basic and diluted	$ (0.12)	$ (0.17)	$ (0.32)	$ (0.19)
Weighted average common shares used to calculate basic and diluted net loss per share	91,930,061	84,200,655	87,680,571	83,362,402
(1) Includes stock-based compensation expense (benefit) as follows:				
Cost of service and technology revenues	$ 365	$ —	$ 1,035	$ —
Research and development	1,608	(6)	4,177	(131)
Sales and marketing	474	20	1,264	(20)
General and administrative	1,636	151	4,257	199

The accompanying notes are an integral part of these condensed consolidated statements.

	1998	1999	2000	2001	2002	2003	2004	2005
Consolidated Statement of Operations Data: Revenues								
Service revenues	$ 3,782	$ 989	$ 19,297	$ 39,261	$ 61,560	$ 107,166	$167,194	
Technology revenues	$ -	$ -	$ 100	$ 20,909	$ 15,797	$ 8,310	$ 3,665	
Hardware revenues	$ -	$ -	$ -	$ 45,620	$ 72,882	$ 111,275	$ 72,093	
Rebates, revenue share, and other payment to the channel	$ (5,029)	$ (630)	$ -	$ (9,780)	$ (9,159)	$ (54,696)	$(47,027)	
Net Revenues	$ (1,247)	$ 359	$ 19,397	$ 96,010	$141,080	$ 172,055	$195,925	
Cost and Expenses								
Cost of service revenues	$ 18,734	$ 1,719	$ 19,852	$ 17,119	$ 17,705	$ 29,360	$ 34,179	
Cost of technology revenues	$ -	$ -	$ 62	$ 8,033	$ 13,609	$ 6,575	$ 782	
Cost of hardware revenues	$ -	$ -	$ -	$ 44,647	$ 74,836	$ 120,323	$ 84,216	
Research and development	$ 25,070	$ 2,544	$ 27,205	$ 20,714	$ 22,167	$ 37,634	$ 41,087	
Sales and marketing	$ 151,658	$ 13,946	$ 104,897	$ 48,117	$ 18,947	$ 37,367	$ 35,047	
General and administrative	$ 15,537	$ 1,395	$ 18,875	$ 14,465	$ 16,296	$ 16,593	$ 38,018	
Total Costs	$ 210,999	$ 19,604	$ 170,891	$ 153,095	$163,560	$ 247,852	$233,329	
% Costs over Revenues	-16921%	5461%	881%	159%	116%	144%	119%	
Net Loss from operations	$ (212,246)	$(19,245)	$(151,494)	$ (57,085)	$(22,480)	$ (75,797)	$(37,404)	

has a feature of thumbs up and down to be clicked on for users to rate shows so that TiVo will know what to record. In addition, TiVo allows the Braille ability on its remote for eye impaired users. Other R& D processes includes product testing & development of its softwares and platforms, product integration of software to satellite system and product integration such as the integration of a DVD burner and Tivo recorder. Besides developing its main products, the TiVo R&D team also tried to design platforms and technology that can be used with any other products and enhance the demand of TiVo's main products such as the ability to connect with computers, other home theater technologies and especially, cable and satellites.

33   Since the intensified competition exists in this DVR industry, TiVo found the need to patent its advance software and technology platform. TiVo licensed its TiVoToGo software to chip maker AMD, digital media software companies such as Sonic Solutions and giant companies such as Microsoft in order to enable video playback on pocket PCs and smart phones. As of today, TiVo has 85 patents granted and still 117 applications patents pending, which include domestic and foreign patents that further leave rivals scratching their heads. TiVo licenses its patents through several of its trusted partners such as Sony, Toshiba, Pioneer and DirecTV. TiVo believes that licensing its technology to third parties has been its best business model.

Executive Team & Management

34   TiVo's top management is always on hands with its operations and promotions. Former CEO, Mike Ramsay, would make overseas trips such as to Japan to conduct meetings and seminars with consumer electronic makers. This effort is as an attempt to convince the makers to embed TiVo's software into their products. In order to make sure everything goes well and accordingly, the ex CEO has been focusing on maintaining partnerships. He would rarely be in his office, instead on the road talking to companies that can help TiVo build software and subscribers. However, many mistakes were made throughout his history being a CEO which includes employee layoffs twice in 2001. 80 employees (approx 25% of workforce) were laid off in 5th of Apr 2001 and 40 employees (approx 20% of workforce) were laid off in 31st Oct 2001. TiVo's previous CEO, Mike Ramsay was just an engineer on the block. He knows how to be creative and build great machines, but doesn't really know

TiVo Inc. Condensed Consolidated Balance Sheets (In thousands, except share amounts) (unaudited)

	October 31, 2006	January 31, 2006 Adjusted
ASSETS		
CURRENT ASSETS		
Cash and cash equivalents	$ 78,898	$ 85,298
Short-term investments	28,067	18,915
Accounts receivable, net of allowance for doubtful		
accounts of $121 and $56	27,300	20,111
Finished goods inventories	34,107	10,939
Prepaid expenses and other, current	4,327	8,744
Total current assets	172,699	144,007
LONG-TERM ASSETS		
Property and equipment, net	10,874	9,448
Purchased technology, capitalized software, and		
intangible assets, net	17,580	5,206
Prepaid expenses and other, long-term	597	347
Total long-term assets	29,051	15,001
Total assets	$ 201,750	$ 159,008
LIABILITIES AND STOCKHOLDERS' EQUITY/(DEFICIT)		
LIABILITIES		
CURRENT LIABILITIES		
Accounts Payable	$ 28,278	$ 24,050
Accrued liabilities	32,553	37,449
Deferred revenue, current	56,596	57,902
Total current liabilities	117,427	119,401
LONG-TERM LIABILITIES		
Deferred revenue, long-term	51,550	67,575
Deferred rent and other	2,208	1,404
Total long-term liabilities	53,758	68,979
Total liabilities	171,185	188,380
COMMITMENTS AND CONTINGENCIES (see Note 10)		
STOCKHOLDERS' EQUITY/(DEFICIT)		
Preferred stock, par value$ 0.001:		
Authorized shares are 10,000,000;		
Issued and outstanding shares-none	—	—
Common stock, par value$ 0.001:		
Authorized shares are 150,000,000;		
Issued shares are 96,922,295 and 85,376,191,		
respectively and outstanding shares are 96,841,792		
and 85,376,191, respectively	97	85
Additional paid-in capital	753,373	667,055
Deferred compensation	—	(2,421)
Accumulated deficit	(722,335)	(694,091)
Less: Treasury stock, at cost - 80,503 shares	(570)	—
Total stockholders' equity (deficit)	30,565	(29,372)
Total liabilities and stockholders' equity (deficit)	$ 201,750	$ 159,008

the industry very well, moreover manage the company and steer TiVo from drowning further. As a result, Mike Ramsay resigned in mid 2005; a change of CEO was implemented, where the new CEO hired was the former president of NBC Cable, Tom Rogers, a new strength to TiVo's management.

35   In addition, TiVo's Board of Directors consists of individuals from very diverse backgrounds and companies; however, this actually poses as one of TiVo's concern. TiVo needs more members that are from TiVo's industry related background and can influence future DVR/Cable industry; possibly they would make better decisions.

SLEEPING WITH THE ENEMIES

". . . So Long, TiVo! Hello DVR! . . ."

The Industry

36   The Digital Video Recorder or Personal Video Recorder market is located at the convergence of these 4 established industries: Broadcasting and TV, Software and Programming, Electronic Instrument, and Communications Equipment.

37   For TiVo, introducing a disruptive technology into the industry was full of obstacles. When a Digital Video Recording has the potential to be considered as a "disruptive technology," which means that the technology creates something new which "usurps existing products, services, and business model." According to Mike Ramsay, the DVR phenomenon has established that "people really want to take control of television, and if you give them control, they don't want you to take it back." Though TiVo has innovatively added all the great software, platforms and services that a standalone TiVo DVR has to offer, the viewing will not work/be greater without a connection to a cable network or satellite signals. Therefore, users who want a TiVo DVR, will need to subscribe to TiVo, pay a onetime fee for the TiVo box and subscribe to companies that provides cable or satellite signals such as Comcast and DirecTV. Because this is the case, the TiVo DVR has made itself to be readily equipped with a built in cable-ready tuner for use with any external cable box or satellite receiver. TiVo has made many alliances and at the same time even competed with cable operators and satellite networks. With cable, satellite, and electronics companies pushing to have their own DVRs, the DVR industry is expected to grow rapidly.

38   Market share wise, TiVo claims to cover the entire US market:

Friends or Foe?

39   In 2000, AOL invested $200 million in TiVo and became the largest shareholder of the company and one of its main service partners. The deal allowed TiVo to release a box that provided both TiVo's capabilities and AOL services. Aside AOL, TiVo established other service partnerships. TiVo and Discovery Communication and NBC agreed on a $8.1

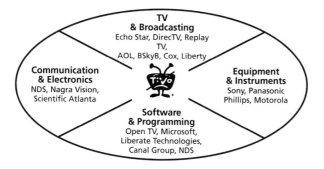

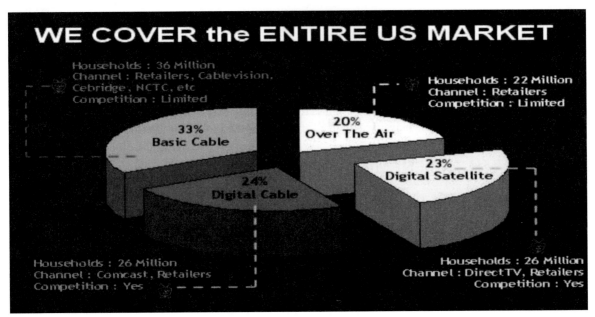

Source: Natexis Bleichroeder, Inc, July 2005.

million deal in the form of advertising and promotional services. Later on, an additional $5 million was paid to NBC for promotions. It also collaborated on Research and Development and allowed TiVo to use a portion of its satellite network. AT&T helped TiVo to market and sell the service in Boston, Denver and Silicon Valley areas. BSkyB was the service partner for TiVo in the United Kingdom. Creative Artists Agency marketed and gave promotional support of the personal video recorder and was given in exchange 67,122 shares of preferred stock.

40   Despite all the partnerships that TiVo was able to enjoy, TiVo has actually been faced by a difficult challenge, that is cable and satellite operators who can be either TiVo's buddy or enemy—now that they offer digital video recorder-equipped set-top boxes of their own. Cable operators like Time Warner Cable and Cox Communications offer built-in DVR capability in set-top boxes and provide the equipment "free" to subscribers, and in late August 2003, Echostar announced a free DVR promotion, which was an unprecedented move in the industry. TiVo's fairly expensive retail priced unit could possibly jeopardize the company's ability to stay. There are relatively few cable and satellite providers, leaving TiVo with little power over them. These companies have the ability to dictate pricing of the TiVo technology because these huge cable companies can always develop or purchase their own generic DVR unit to market to their subscription base. Although TiVo had to give up a cut of profits to partners, still TiVo decided to have strategic relationship with competitors and cable companies for distribution and credit on its sales force.

41   Previously, DirecTV has been the backbone of TiVo, the service partner that has been fruitfully fueling most of TiVo's growth. In addition, TiVo's current 4.4 million subscribers have mostly come from its deal with DirecTV. As of early 2002, subscribers to TiVo service through DirecTV have increased from 230,000 to 2.1 million, representing more than half of all DVR subscriptions through satellite. Earlier on when DirecTV began the talk with TiVo, the satellite provider was already equipped with a DVR service through its partnership with Microsoft's Ultimate TV. For users to be able to watch their shows, subscriptions to DirecTV channels range from $29.99/month providing 40 channels to $65.99/month with over 250 channels.

42 Now that DirecTV is developing their own DVR device with the NDS Group and mentioned in 2005 that it would stop marketing and selling TiVo's digital recorders to its satellite TV subscribers starting in 2007, will TiVo become history? Though, DirecTV's DVR still costs users $299 onetime fee, but it includes unique features such as the ability to jump to a specific scene in the program as well as allowing users to pay for any downloaded pay-per-view movies only when they are being viewed. In 2006, TiVo and DirecTV reached a commercial extension agreement for three years. The agreement will allow existing DirecTV customers using the TiVo digital video recorder to continue to receive maintenance and support from DirecTV. As part of the agreement, TiVo and DirecTV also said they wouldn't sue each other over patent rights. Since the agreement with DirecTV was facing to expiration date, TiVo has been rushing to differentiate its product and struggling to strike other distribution deals.

43 In July 2000, Comcast, a cable operator, agreed to a trial offering TiVo boxes to its subscribers, hoping that the trial would lead to a bigger deal where Comcast would integrate TiVo software into Comcast cable boxes. Upon knowing it, Comcast balked and was unwilling to concede. In April 2001, when another trial was struck up to lead to a larger deal, TiVo laid off approximately 25% of its staff. November 2001, a full bloom of hope became hopeless when ATT Broadband agreed to offer TiVo DVRs to its customers with the fact that within a few weeks after, Comcast ended up killing the deal by acquiring the cable provider and its 14 million customers. In addition, in 2002, cable operators such as Comcast ended up developing their own DVR boxes with makers such as Motorola and Scientific-Atlanta. However, similar to DirecTV, Comcast, the nation's cable company, announced in March 2005, that it would offer its customers a video recorder service from TiVo and even will allow TiVo to develop its software for Comcast's DVR platform. Comcast and TiVo agreed working to make TiVo's DVR service and interactive advertising capability (ad management system) available over Comcast's cable network and its set-top DVR boxes. This agreement also included that under TiVo brand name, the first of their co-developed products would be available in mid- to late-2006.

44 Subscriptions to Comcast's basic or standard cable cost users $8.63 or $52.55. To want to have a DVR feature, users need to add $13.94 with Comcast in addition to the subscriptions to TiVo which ranges from $12.95 to $16.95/month depending on the lifetime plan chosen that varies from one to three years. Due to the agreement with Comcast, TiVo's shares closed up nearly 75%, or $2.87 per share, to $6.70. Investors were positive about the news, some upgrading TiVo's investment rating from a sell to hold; even though, sparking investors had concern over TiVo's future, since DirecTV started using a second company, NDS, to provide DVR service, a deal with Comcast puts to rest some of those concerns by opening up a large new potential audience for TiVo's service. According to a filing with the SEC, TiVo receives an upfront payment from Comcast for creating a new DVR that works with Comcast's current service. TiVo also receives a recurring monthly fee for each Comcast subscriber who uses TiVo through Comcast.

45 Both TiVo's deal with a cable operator such as Comcast and a satellite broadcaster such as DirecTV were made merely because of the technological differences that can be tweaked around. Rolling out new technologies such as DVR, will be easier for satellite broadcasters because changes can be made in a central location. While as for cable operators, technology will have to be deployed gradually as they have different equipment in different areas. With all these deals, could TiVo's opportunities be beyond TV and that it helps TiVo to become what it has always wanted to be: a software provider?

46 In addition, with the hype of being portable, lately, TiVo and BellSouth FastAccess DSL agreed on a variety of co-marketing. With strong southeastern presence and renowned customer satisfaction of BellSouth, TiVo can turn a DSL Internet connection into a pipeline for video content delivered directly to the television. To expand program recording to a cellular phone, its latest TiVo Mobile feature, TiVo struck up a deal with Verizon to bring the digital video recording pioneer's capabilities beyond its set-top-boxes and the television, and directly to cellphones for the first time. In terms of contents, TiVo also has engaged in new partnerships with CBS Corp, Reuters Group PLC, and Forbes magazine, not to mention New York Times Co., National Basketball Association and some other firms. This will make "news and entertainment programs available for downloading onto TiVo's." International Creative Management is to recommend films, television shows and Internet videos that TiVo users can download onto their boxes. Finally TiVo has decided to open up to amateur videos through a deal with One True Media Inc., "an Internet start up that operates a Web Service designed to help users easily edit their raw footage into slick home movies.

THE TALKATIVO

"... Bring 'em on! We are talking the HD language now ... Yeah!."

HD Trend

47   High Definition sets in the entertainment industry are now the most important new consumer electronic items. HD products focus more toward quality of what is being seen and heard rather than the compactness like we saw a decade ago. High Definition sets include HDTV, HD broadcasting, HD DVD, HD Radio, HD Photo and even HD Audio.

48   Of which TiVo is linked particularly to, High Definition TV (HDTV) was first introduced in the United States during the 1990s and it is basically a digital television broadcasting system using a significantly higher resolution than the traditional formats such as NTSC, PAL and SECAM. The technology at that time was very expensive. Nowadays, as the prices have decreased, HDTV is going mainstream. A significant number of people have already bought HDTV; most people are planning to buy an HDTV soon. As of 2007, HDTVs are available in 24 million US households. By 2009, HDTV will have replaced all the old Standard Definition TVs. With the price of the hard-drive becoming lower and lower, and the increasing technology of HDTV, the demands for the HD products are also increasing multiple times. With HDTV, users are potentially being offered a much better picture quality than standard television, with greater picture on screen clarity and smoother motion, richer and more natural colors and surround sound.

HD TiVo

49   Lately, TiVo issued the TiVo Series3 which will allow customers to record HD television and digital cable. As people experience HDTV, TiVo service will be increasingly appealing. Once again, TiVo has set up the technological standards in the environment. The TiVo Series 3, HD version allows the consumers to do many additional great things and deliver both the audio and visual in HD.

50   TiVo realizes that great quality videos need to be supported by great quality audio, thus, they put a lot of efforts in the audio development, and received the certification of being the first digital media recorder to meet their performance standard in HDTV. THX is very well known to have developed highest standard of audio, mainly the surround systems in the entertainment, as well as the media industry.

TiVo SERIES 3

51   The new Hi-Def TiVo Series3 which is being sold for $799, has the ability to record two HD programs simultaneously while playing back a third previously recorded one. It also has two signal inputs and it accepts cable TV and over-the-air signals. It replaces the existing as well as the 30-second commercial skip. In addition, the new HD Tivo is different because there is no lifetime membership anymore for the HD TiVo compared to the older DVR products. Is this the shift of TiVo revenue model to aim at the subscription based revenue stream?

52   Despite that the capability of TiVo being able to record and playback at Hi-Def level, there are still many considerations for people before buying the TiVo. The downside of the HD TiVo, however, the price is overly expensive for most people especially when there are some DVRs being offered for free by the cable companies.

HD TiVENemies

53   Now that the HD trend is flocking the entertainment industry, TiVo competitors are also offering HD DVRs on their own and not just a DVR.

54   As for a cable operator such as Comcast, Comcast allows its subscribers to rent their DVR boxes for $13.94/month as they do not offer to sell their DVR boxes to their customers. With their HD DVR boxes manufactured by Motorola and Scientific Atlanta, users are able to navigate their own preferences just like using a TiVo, except that TiVo may have better and more features built into the TiVo boxes. Then with the Comcast DVR boxes, users will be able to watch the variety of cable channels offered by Comcast with an additional monthly subscription fee to cable channels.

55   Once a best friend, now may soon be a foe, DirecTV, a satellite operator, allows subscribers to add an additional DVR subscription service for $4.99 monthly on top of the chosen monthly subscription service package to DirecTV cable channels which ranges from $29.99 to $65.99. Same as Comcast not allowing users to keep their DVR boxes, if a user is in need of an HD DVR box, the user will need to pay an upfront cost of $299 with $100 rebate. As for the basic DVR, DirecTV charges $99.99 upfront cost.

REFERENCES

http://www.tivo.com/

http://en.wikipedia.org/wiki/TiVo

http://en.wikipedia.org/wiki/High-definition_television

http://egotron.com/ptv/ptvintro.htm

http://news.com.com/TiVo,+Comcast+reach+DVR+deal/2100-1041_3-5616961.html

http://news.com.com/TiVo+and+DirecTV+extend+contract/2100-1038_3-6060475.html

http://www.technologyreview.com

http://www.fastcompany.com/magazine/61/tivo.html

http://iinnovate.blogspot.com/2006/09/mike-ramsay-co-founder-of-tivo.html

http://www.acmqueue.org/modules.php?name=Content&pa=showpage&pid=53&page=7

http://www.internetnews.com/stats/article.php/3655331

http://thomashawk.com/2006/04/tivo-history-101-how-tivo-built-pvr_24.html

http://www.tvpredictions.com/tivohd030807.htm

http://www.tivocommunity.com/tivo-vb/showthread.php?threadid=151443

Case 49

Warner Music Group Inc.: *Recorded Music Segment—Entertainment and Media Industry*

Algirdas Dembinskas, Marc E. Gartenfeld, and Robert J. Mockler

INTRODUCTION

1   In 2006, Edgar Bronfman Jr., the Chief Executive Officer of the Warner Music Group, had to develop a strategy to survive against the competition and declining sales in the recorded music industry. Companies in the recorded music industry had experienced decline in sales since the year 1999. There was a common misconception that the decline in sales was caused by one single reason—piracy. However, there was another reason that caused the decline in record companies' sales—the change in the distribution of the musical content. Edgar Bronfman's task was to develop an effective differentiating enterprise-wide strategy if Warner Music Group was to survive and prosper against aggressive competition over the intermediate and long-term future.

2   Warner Music Group was home to a collection of well-known record labels in the music industry including Asylum, Atlantic, Bad Boy, Cordless, East West, Elektra, Lava, Maverick, Nonesuch, Reprise, Rhino, Sire, Warner Bros., and Word. Warner Music International, a leading company in national and international repertoire operated through numerous international affiliates and licensees in more than 50 countries. Warner Music Group also included Warner/Chappell Music, one of the world's biggest music publishers, with a catalog of more than one million copyrights worldwide. Warner/Chappell Music was a global music publisher and held the rights to more than one million copyrights from more than 65,000 songwriters and composers. Publishing had become a very profitable business for Warner Music Group, because it accounted for about 20 percent of sales. Warner Music Group also had an alternative distribution alliance, which helped the company to focus on the independent music market. The WEA Corporation was a part of Warner Music Group, and it served the distribution purpose. Figure 1 shows the structure of the Warner Music Group Company.

3   From 1990 to 1999, the U.S. recorded music industry grew at a compound annual growth rate of 7.6 percent, twice the rate of total entertainment spending. This growth was driven by demand for music, the replacement of LPs and cassettes with CDs, price increases and strong economic growth. The industry began experiencing negative growth rates in 1999, on a global basis, primarily driven by an increase in digital piracy. Other drivers of this decline were the overall recessionary economic environment, bankruptcies of record retailers and wholesalers, growing competition for consumer discretionary spending and retail shelf space, and the maturation of the CD format, which has slowed the historical growth pattern of recorded music sales. Since that time, annual dollar sales of physical music products in the U.S. were estimated to have declined at a compound annual growth rate of 4 percent, although there was a 2.5 percent year-over-year increase recorded in 2004 (through November 20, 2005 U.S. recorded music sales (excluding sales of digital tracks) were down approximately 7.6 percent year-over-year, however). Similar declines had occurred in international markets, with the extent of declines driven primarily by differing penetration levels of piracy-enabling technologies, such as broadband Internet access and CD-R technology, and economic conditions [Warner Music Group, 2006].

This case was prepared by Algirdas Dembinskas, Marc E. Gartenfeld, and Professor Robert J. Mockler of St. John's University. © Robert J. Mockler.

FIGURE 1
Warner Music Group, Divisions

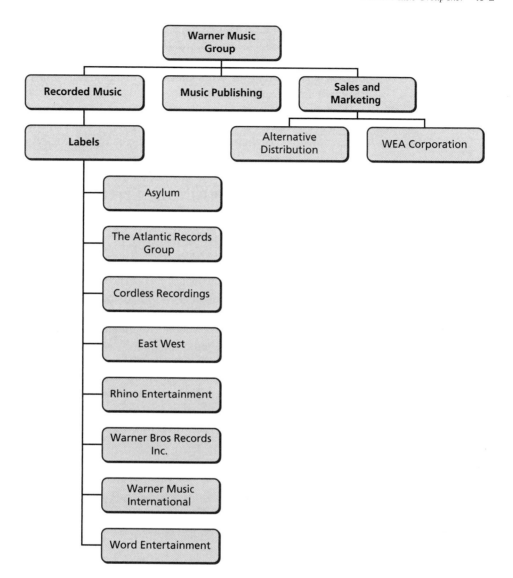

4   The decision makers at the Warner Music Group had to implement a strategic corporate decision. The proposed decision for the Warner Music Group was to enter into the distribution with telecommunications companies. The distribution through telecommunication devices would lead to very effective distribution of musical content to consumers. Consumers would be able to get musical and video content informing them about new releases from the Warner Music Group's artists. Furthermore, brand and direct marketing techniques had to be implemented in order to win against the competition. Brand and direct marketing would help Warner Music Group to collect market intelligence, connect with consumers, and establish two way communications between Warner Music Group and its consumers. The decision maker's task was to develop an effective differentiating enterprise-wide strategy if Warner Music Group was to survive and prosper against aggressive competition over the intermediate and long-term future.

5   The decision makers at the Warner Music Group also had other critical decisions to make. One of the critical decisions was to focus on online and wireless distribution of

musical content. Warner Music Group had already entered into the agreements with Sprint, Verizon, and France Telecom, and it sold their musical content in the form of ring tones, ring back tones, and master tones. The proposed strategy suggested selling and marketing new releases with the use of telecommunication companies. Another suggestion was to apply brand and direct marketing techniques to market products more effectively.

6   The main question that was to be resolved was how to differentiate Warner Music Group from its competition and so achieve a winning edge over competitors within intensely competitive, rapidly changing immediate, intermediate, and long-term time frames, the major focus of the course.

INDUSTRY AND COMPETITIVE ANALYSIS: ENTERTAINMENT AND MEDIA INDUSTRY

Overall Industry Description

7   The entertainment and media industry consisted of companies that operated and sold media properties, services, and products, as well as provided entertainment in the form of recreation. The industry included film and video production and distribution; television production, broadcasting, distribution, programming, and products; music production, distribution, publishing, and products; radio broadcasting; newspaper, book, magazine, electronic, and specialty publishing; theme and amusement parks, and Internet content and delivery services. The players in the industry were highly interrelated. Music was interrelated with videos, movies, publishing, radio, and Internet especially. Music companies delivered their content through radio, television, and films. Music companies advertised in newspapers, magazines, Internet, and radio. The media industry was probably the most interrelated of all industries, as shown in Figure 2.

FIGURE 2   **Entertainment and Media Industry Segments**

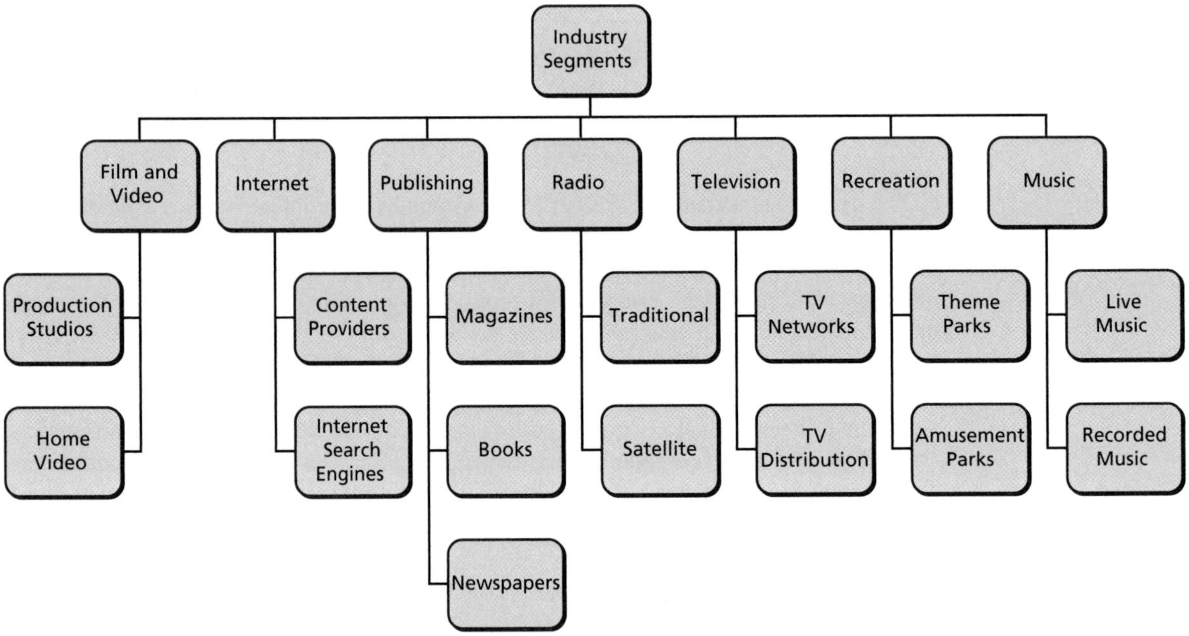

Film and Video

8   Film and Video companies have always been a major player in the media industry. Those companies operated and sold film and video production and engaged in distribution of the production. The major players in the film and video industry segment were: The Walt Disney Company, Time Warner Inc., Sony Corporation, Miramax Film Corporation, MTV Networks Company, and Warner Bros. Entertainment. Two types of companies that belonged to this sector were production studios and home video companies.

Production Studios

9   Production studios were responsible for pre-production and post-production of audio, films, video imaging; as well as duplication services such as CD, DVD, and video Entertainment.

Home Video

10   Companies in the Home Video segment produced audio and films, and distributed them in the form of VHS and DVD.

Internet

11   Internet was becoming a more and more important channel for distribution of musical content, as well as advertising, and direct marketing. Internet segment consisted of content providers and Internet search engines.

Content Providers

12   These were the companies that created or acquired content, editorial and multimedia, for distribution via the Internet. Companies in this segment also were responsible for the distribution of paid-placement content. Major Companies were: Yahoo Corporation, The Walt Disney Company, Time Warner Inc., CBS Corporation, and The New York Times Company. A very important player in this segment was Yahoo Corporation, because as one of the most visited websites, yahoo.com had a lot of multimedia content, and served an important role in the marketing and distribution of the musical content.

Internet Search Engines

13   Internet Search Engines were companies that owned and operated search engines and other categorized Web sites used to find information on the Internet. The major players were Google Corporation, America Online Inc., Yahoo Inc, and Microsoft Corporation. Microsoft was an important player because musical content was distributed through Microsoft applications such as windows media player. Microsoft, the biggest software provider, also planned to launch a portable audio player, which could have had a significant impact on the distribution of the musical content.

Publishing

14   The publishing segment of the media industry consisted of companies that published magazines, books and newspapers. The publishing segment of the media industry had significant effect on the music industry, because many players in the recorded music industry advertised heavily in the publications, such as magazines that covered trends in the music. Major recorded music companies in the publishing segment were: The Walt Disney Company, Time Warner Company, Verizon Communications Inc., and The New York Times Company.

Magazines

15   Magazines were very important and popular marketing channels for recorded music companies. The major magazines that cover the recorded music industry were: The Rolling Stone, Vibe, Source, and many others.

Books

16 Book publishing consisted of companies that published book in print as well as in electronic format. Apple Corporation's iTunes software was an important channel for the distribution of electronic books.

Newspapers

17 Newspapers mainly served as a vehicle for the distribution of news. It was relevant to recorded music industry, because of the potential of publicity campaigns and advertising. The most popular newspapers were USA Today, New York Times, and Washington Post.

Radio

18 The radio segment of the media industry was experiencing a change. Introduced satellite radio stations were changing the radio landscape. Traditional radio stations were still popular among consumers, however satellite radio stations offered more exclusive shows and programs.

Traditional Radio

19 The traditional radio industry was an important component of the media landscape. In 2005, there were about 11,000 commercial stations competing for audiences in local markets across the country, and like their television brethren, these stations got their revenue primarily through advertising sales [Hoovers, 2006].

Satellite Radio

20 Sirius Satellite Radio Company and XM Satellite Radio Holdings Company were becoming more and more popular. It was expected that the popularity of the satellite radio and the number of subscribers would increase in the near the future. The change in the radio segment had important implications for the music industry. Satellite radio served as a good channel for niche marketing, because subscribers to the satellite radio service had an opportunity to listen to many channels that were targeted at consumers with different tastes of music. Satellite radio stations were the opposite of regular radio stations, which took a more commercial approach.

Television

21 The television segment was made up of companies that provided cable, over the air, subscription and pay-per-view services. Television has always been an important and effective channel for advertising and promotions. The television segment consisted of TV networks and TV distribution companies. Both played important roles for the recorded music companies.

TV Networks

22 TV Networks consisted of companies, such as MTV Networks. The recorded music companies were highly interrelated with MTV Networks Company, because MTV was one of the most important marketing channels for musical content and videos. Furthermore, the acquisition of Pixar animation studios by the Walt Disney Company, showed how interrelated companies in the media industry could become (Steve Jobs, the chief executive officer of the Pixar Company and Apple Corporation, has become a board member of the Walt Disney Company). "MTV reached more than 87 million subscriber households (Sister network, MTV2, which featured more music-oriented programming, reached 53 million households)" [Hoovers, 2006].

TV Distribution

23 TV Distribution consisted of companies that distributed the television programming to direct users. Companies included, The Walt Disney Company, Time Warner Company, and Apple Computer, among others.

Recreation

24 Recreation segment consisted of outdoor entertainment, such as theme parks and amusement parks. Theme parks and amusement parks provided outdoor entertainment for paid and non-paid admission.

Music

25 Music segment consisted of live music performers and recorded music. Music in general was always an important part of entertainment industry, because it was interrelated with all other segments of entertainment industry.

Live Music

26 Live music performers performed on television shows, concerts, charity events, sports events, award ceremonies, and in many other places. Live music artists performed for a salary and had contracts with record music companies, music clubs, and bars.

Recorded Music

27 Recorded music segment, the chosen topic for the research project, was the most satisfying segment for consumers. According to the research conducted by the Recording Industry Association of America in 1997, consumers felt that, compared to TV, movies, and books and magazines, recorded music did a better job of satisfying the wants and needs that prompted them to buy the product in the first place [Consumer Purchasing Trends, 2006]. Recorded music was one of the primary mediums of entertainment for consumers worldwide and in 2004, generated $33.6 billion in retail sales.

28 Recorded music companies played an integral role in virtually all aspects of the music value chain, from discovering and developing talent to producing albums and promoting artists and their product. Revenues were generated through the marketing, sale and licensing of recordings in various physical and digital formats. The major recorded music companies have built significant recorded music catalogs, which were long-lived assets that were exploited year after year. The sale of catalog material was typically more profitable than that of new releases, given lower development costs and more limited marketing costs. In first three quarters of calendar 2005, 38 percent of all U.S. physical unit sales were from recordings more than 18-months old, and 25 percent were from recordings more than three years old. According to the study by the Recording Industry Association of America, the most popular genres in 2004 were shown in Figure 3.

FIGURE 3
Most Popular Genres of Music

Source: Recording Industry Association of America (2006B). Purchasing Trends. *http://www.riaa.com/news/ marketingdata/purchasing.as0.* Accessed February 15, 2006.

Genre	Percent of Sales
Rock	23.9%
Rap/Hip Hop	12.1%
R&B/Urban	11.3%
Country	13.0%
Pop	10.0%
Religious	6.0%
Classical	2.0%
Jazz	2.7%
Soundtracks	1.1%
Oldies	1.4%
New Age	1.0%
Children's	2.8%
Other	8.9%

INDUSTRY AND MARKET SEGMENT: THE RECORDED MUSIC INDUSTRY

29 Recorded music was one of the primary mediums of entertainment for consumers world-wide and in calendar 2004, generated $33.6 billion in retail sales [Warner Music Group Annual Report, 2006]. The recorded music industry consisted of companies that engaged in the recording, production, publishing, distribution, manufacturing and marketing of recorded music and music videos. Companies attracted the best talent, recorded, distributed, manufactured and marketed the musical content. Major record companies that dominated the market were: Universal Music Group, Sony BMG Music Entertainment, EMI, and Warner Music Group.

How the Recorded Music Industry Works: The Business Process Model

30 The recorded music industry consisted of products (recorded music, talent, and copyrights), consumers, sales and marketing, distribution, manufacturing and competition, as shown in Figure 4.

31 Companies in the recorded music industry collected revenues from sales of musical content and copyrights. Companies sold and distributed musical content through records in the form of CD, DVD, cassette, and digital formats. Digital distribution of music content consisted primarily of music originally accessed over the Internet or wirelessly through digital download or subscription models, which could be transferred to a portable music player. Companies in the recorded music industry entered into agreements with numerous partners, such as iTunes, MusicNet, musicmatch, Rhapsody, Yahoo! and MSN to provide musical content for sale through their music service offerings. Companies entered into agreements with mobile carriers, such as T Mobile and Verizon, to distribute the music content.

FIGURE 4 Recorded Music Industry

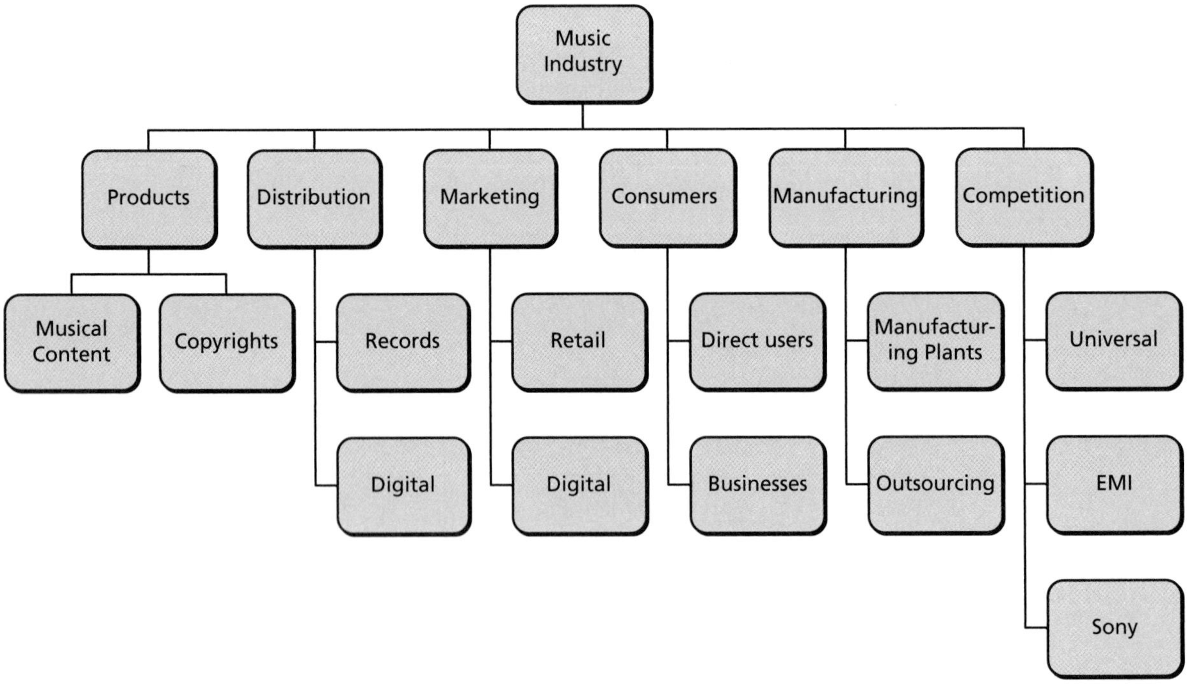

32   Companies in the recorded music industry identified potentially successful recording artists, signed them to recording agreements, collaborated with them to develop recordings of their work, marketed and sold finished recordings to retail stores and legitimate online channels. Companies had a specific job position called A&R (Artists and Repertoire). People who occupied this position listened to demo recordings sent to them by potential new artists. If the artist appeared to have a potential to be successful in the recorded music industry, companies signed the artist to one of their labels. Being successful in the recorded music industry meant that an artist had to be appealing to the audience and sell at least one hundred thousand of singles and/or albums.

33   Artists recorded musical content in the form of singles and albums. Singles consisted of one or few songs and were released in the form of CD and/or Vinyl. Digital versions were also available. Albums consisted of ten to twenty songs compiled together. Albums were released in the form of CD, vinyl, cassette, and digital format. The key to success in the recording music industry was to release at least one album in a three-year span (1E).

34   Musical content was marketed through various media channels. Channels included: radio, television, and mobile. Companies in the recorded music industry contracted radio and television stations, which marketed their products by playing them on air. It worked in the following way: recorded music companies sent the newly recorded material to radio or television station; the station aired the recorded material. In most cases it was the first time the newly recorded song was presented to consumers.

35   Another key to success was to administer copyrights to film studios, advertising agencies, and other businesses. This part of the business was called publishing. It worked in the following way: the publisher worked on behalf of the song's composer and songwriter. The composer and songwriter owned the actual copyrights for the song, and the publisher represented them in all business transactions. Publisher promoted, placed and marketed the creative work of the songwriter for a share of revenues that were generated. Revenues from publishing included revenues from the following sources: mechanical, performance, synchronization, and other.

36   Revenues from mechanical sources were royalties received by the licensor with respect to compositions embodied in recordings sold in any format or configuration, including singles, albums, CDs, digital downloads and mobile phone ringtones [Warner Music Group Annual Report, 2006]. Revenues from performance source were royalties received by the licensor when the composition was performed publicly. Revenues from the synchronization source were defined as royalties or fees received for the right to use the composition in combination with visual images (e.g., in films, television commercials and programs and videogames). Revenues from other sources included revenues received from stage performances.

Products

37 In the recorded music industry, companies offered two types of products: musical content and copyrights.

Musical Content

38 The musical content was offered in the physical forms of CD, DVD, vinyl, and cassette; as well as digital formats, such as mp3, etc. The key to success in the musical content area was to record an award winning material. Contracting professional producers who overlooked the final versions of recorded musical content was one way of doing it. Artists created the musical content; therefore it was important to attract the best artists at low cost. Other keys to success were huge market penetration in all genres of music, musical content appealing to the American audience, and strong Artists and Repertoire department that discovered new talent. It was also very important for artists to release at least one album in a three-year span, because consumers had to be reminded about artists' existence in the market.

39   The opportunities in this area included collaboration with award winning producers and songwriters. The key to success was to have a rich catalog of music, because it made companies strong in the publishing business. Having a rich catalog enabled companies to sell more copyrights to businesses. The biggest threat was the loss of the best talent to the competitors.

Copyrights

40   Copyrights were the intellectual property of recorded music companies. Recorded music companies either owned or controlled rights to musical compositions. The key to success in this product category included being able to administer copyrights to businesses.

Distribution

41   Companies in the music industry competed on the basis of distribution. Distribution has changed over the years, as more and more consumers started buying music content on the Internet. There were two types of distribution: records and digital.

Records

42   Companies in the recorded music industry distributed their musical content through records, which were sold in retail and independent stores. Records were sold at retailers such as Virgin Megastore, Tower Records, Best Buy, Circuit City, and Target. Records were also sold on the Internet, by online retailers, such as Amazon.

Digital Distribution

43   Digital distribution of music content consisted of music originally accessed over the Internet or wirelessly through digital download or subscription models, which could be transferred to a portable music player. Companies also distributed the musical content through the mobile channels, such as sold musical content in the form of ring tones, and full track downloads using the cellular phone.

44   As the popularity of Internet grew, companies started to distribute their products on the Internet. Major distribution companies were Apple Inc., and its iTunes software, as well as Napster, and many other Internet websites and file sharing software. The biggest threat in this area was growing piracy. Piracy was unauthorized reproduction and distribution of musical and video content. In other words, it was copyright infringement. With digital technology, most modern piracy involved an exact and perfect copy of the original made from a hard copy or downloaded over the Internet. Illegal copying of copyrighted material occurred through organized black market reproduction and distribution channels. Piracy consisted of digital and counterfeiting. Musical content downloaded illegally over the Internet was considered digital piracy. Musical content could be shared on peer-to-peer software that worked on most personal computers. The mass production of illegal CDs and cassettes was considered as counterfeiting.

45   The keys to success in the distribution area were having strong understanding about the digital distribution, being well positioned in the digital distribution, and good working relations with Internet companies. Other keys to success were big market penetration and partnerships with telecommunication companies.

Marketing

46   Marketing in the music industry was a very important part of a business. The goal of marketing was to maximize the likelihood of success for new releases as well as stimulate the sales of previous releases. The companies' goal was to maximize the value of each artist and release, and to help artists develop an image that maximized appeal to consumer. The marketing activities included helping the artist develop creatively in each release. It was done by strategically scheduling album releases and selecting singles for release, creating concepts for videos that were complementary to the artists' work, and coordinating promotion of albums to radio and television outlets [Warner Music Annual Report, 2006]. Marketing activities consisted of retail marketing and digital marketing activities.

Retail

47 Retail Marketing included marketing activities that were performed in physical locations. Music companies promoted their products to retailers, consumers, and businesses that bought copyrights. Products were advertised on billboards, magazines, internet, television, brochures, and many other places. Promotions included concerts, charity events, and appearances on television by artists. Other Aspects of promotion included in-store appearances, displays and placement in album listening stations. These activities were overseen by marketing staff to ensure that maximum visibility was achieved for the artist and the release. Public relations included articles about artists' personal affairs. Sales promotions included bonus materials that came along with the purchase of the musical content. Bonuses included: unreleased songs, videos, interviews, ringtones, posters, tickets to shows, as well as many other materials. Newly released records were sold at lower prices.

Digital

48 Digital Marketing included marketing activities performed on the Internet or using telecommunications. Record companies marketed the musical content through the mobile channel. The mobile channel consisted of cellular phones and telecommunication providers, which marketed musical content in the form of cellular phone ring tones. Consumers were able to download a digitally re-mastered ring tone of the newly released song. It was very important for companies to be in marketing partnerships with digital telecommunication companies and digital distributors such as iTunes.

49 The marketing process started when the new artist was signed to the label. The first step was to make the public aware of the artist. Key to success was playing artist's music on the radio and airing videos on music television stations, such as MTV. Another key to success was to create awareness by publicity. Companies in the recorded music industry hired public relations companies to write press releases about new artists. Such press releases appeared in the magazines that covered music business, such as Rolling Stones and Vibe. Artists also appeared on the television shows and performed in concerts and television shows. After the artist's awareness was created, companies marketed the musical content of the artist by advertising the new products through aforementioned channels. Companies' websites also served as venues for marketing. Marketing on websites enabled companies to have a well-targeted audience, because consumers subscribed to newsletters.

50 Other keys to success in this category were effective promotional bonuses, such as pre-released songs and never seen before footage of artists' life. The timing was also very important. The most profitable times of the year for new releases were months of June, September and December. June was important because of the end of school year, September was important because of the start of school year, and December was important because it was holiday season and consumers were eager to spend more in those months. It was also very important for artists to collaborate with other artists in order to keep their name known. Among other keys to success, coordinated promotion of albums to radio and television outlets was important; as well as effective media planning and buying.

Consumers

51 There were two groups of customers that companies in the music industry dealt with. One group was direct users, who bought musical content for their own use. The other group was businesses that bought musical content, talent, and copyrights.

Direct Users

52   Direct users of the Warner Music Group included people of all ages and most ethnic groups. The target market was consumers aged 10–45. The consumers could be classified in groups by their age, ethnicity and lifestyle [Recording Industry Association of America (2006A)]. According to the study, the biggest segment of music buyers were people aged 15–19. Figure 5 shows music buyers with regard to their age.

53   As shown in Figure 5, there was small difference between buyers with regard to their age, therefore major record companies focused on consumers of all ages. Lifestyle and ethnicity were two important and interrelated factors.

54   The segment of people 10–19 years of age listened to pop music, which was heavily played on radio and television. The segment of 20–24 consisted mostly of college students who were also heavily affected by the music marketed on radio and television. The music that was heavily played on radio and television was hip-hop/r&b and pop music. The segment of people 25–29 years of age preferred various types of music, especially rock music. The segment of consumers age 30–44 preferred rock music as well as classical, country, jazz, and religious music. The segment of consumers age 45+ preferred classical, religious, and oldies genres of music.

55   Income was another basis for segmentation. Consumers who earned forty thousand or more dollars per year were the heaviest buyers of music. In this segment the most important factors was consumers' accessibility to digital distribution channels. If a consumer earned more than forty thousand dollars a year, it meant that it was highly expected that a consumer had a portable music player and was buying music online.

56   As shown in Figure 4, Rock was the most popular genre followed by country, hip-hop, rhythm and blues, and pop genres. Country music was popular among the American audience, defined as people who were at least third generation Americans, most of them living in the west of the United States. Hip-hop and rhythm and blues were most popular in cities with a large percentage of minorities. One of the most significant ethnic groups was Hispanics. According to U.S. census bureau, as of July 1, 2004, the Hispanic population in the United States of America has reached 41.3 million [Recording Industry Association of America (2006D)]. The Hispanic recorded music market has been expanding and it was important for recorded music companies to focus on this market. According to the Recording Industry Association of America, there were over 16 million Hispanics under the age of 24 in the year 2005. The heaviest segment of Hispanic music purchasers was people between 14 and 29 years of age. The mean average of CD purchases per year was 43, and 46 percent purchased more than 50 CDs per year. A half of Hispanic consumers considered that listening to music was very important to them. Most Hispanic consumers' buying decisions were highly influenced by radio. Hispanics preferred to purchase music records at independent stores, malls, and flea markets and nightclubs [Recording Industry Association of America (2006C)].

FIGURE 5
Buyers with Regard to Age

Source: Recording Industry Association of America (2006B). Purchasing Trends. *http://www.riaa.com/news/marketingdata/purchasing.asp.* Accessed February 15, 2006.

Age Groups	Percentage of Buyers
10–14 years	9.4%
15–19 years	11.9%
20–24 years	9.2%
25–29 years	10.0%
30–34 years	10.4%
35–39 years	10.7%
40–44 years	10.9%
45+	26.4%

57 The key to success in the consumer segments were:

10–19 Years of Age

58 Companies in the recorded music industry had to market their musical content on radio and television, because this segment was highly susceptible to radio and television.

20–24 Years of Age

59 Companies in the recorded music industry had to market their musical content on college campuses and on radio and television. Companies also had to supply this segment with hip-hop/r&b music.

25–29 Years of Age

60 Companies in the recorded music industry had to supply this segment with rock music, as well as to have big penetration in other genres of music, because this segment liked various musical genres.

30–44 Years of Age

61 Companies in the recorded music industry had to record popular rock, classical, country, jazz and religious musical content to satisfy this segment of consumers.

45+ Years of Age

62 Companies in the recorded music industry had to have a rich catalog of music, such as oldies, in order to be successful in this segment.

63 Other keys to success were having strong market intelligence and effective market segmentation.

Businesses

64 The second group of customers in the recorded music industry consisted of businesses, such as advertising agencies, movie production companies, radio stations, television stations, restaurants, venues, as well as many other service providers. Those groups of consumers bought copyrights to songs and used them for their businesses.

65 It was essential for the company to have a rich catalog of music, because it enabled them to serve other businesses more effectively. Companies with rich catalogs of music were able to offer bigger song selection; therefore they served their clients more effectively. The opportunities in this area included new movies and new television shows, which needed musical content to accompany the visual composition. The threats in this area included the loss of partnerships with movie production companies, television stations, radio stations, and other businesses.

66 The key to success in this area was being able to sell copyrights to television, radio, cable, and satellite stations. Another key to success was to administer copyrights to advertising agencies, video game producers, nightclubs and movie theaters.

Manufacturing

67 Companies in the recorded music industry either owned manufacturing plants or outsourced the manufacturing function.

Manufacturing Plants

68 Some companies in the recorder music industry owned the manufacturing plants in which they manufactured CDs and DVDs. Other companies outsourced the manufacturing of the CDs and DVDs.

Outsourcing

69 Companies in the recorded music industry also outsourced the manufacturing function by making agreements with other companies. Warner Music Group, which owned the manufacturing company before the year 2004, has decided to sell it and outsource the manufacturing to the same company.

70 Keys to success in this category were efficient management of the manufacturing plants (3A), and profitable partnerships with manufacturing companies (outsourcing).

Competition

71 In 2004, the four largest players in music industry were: Universal, Sony BMG, EMI, and Warner Music Group, which accounted for approximately 72 percent of worldwide recorded music sales in 2004. There were many mid-sized and smaller players in the industry as well. Recorded music was one of the primary mediums of entertainment for consumers worldwide and in the year 2004, generated $33.6 billion in retail sales. Universal was the market leader with a 26 percent global market share in 2004, followed by Sony BMG with a 22 percent share. EMI and WMG held a 13 percent and 11 percent share of global music sales in 2004, respectively [Warner Music Group Annual Report, 2006].

72 Revenues in the music industry were generated through the marketing, sale and licensing of recordings in various physical and digital formats. Looking at the global picture of the music industry, the top five territories (U.S., Japan, U.K., Germany and France) accounted for 73 percent of the recorded music market in 2004. The U.S. was the largest end-market, constituting 36 percent of total 2004 recorded music sales [Warner Music Group Annual Report, 2006].

Universal Music Group

73 Universal Music Group was the largest recording company in the world. It consisted of the many record labels including Def Jam and Geffen, in addition to the following departments: Universal Music Publishing Group, Universal Music Group Nashville, Universal Music Enterprises, The Verve Music Group, Universal eLabs, and Universal Music and Video Distribution. Universal Music Group had a roster of such artists as Eminem, Sheryl Crow, Sting, and U2, among many others.

74 Universal Music Publishing Group controlled the rights to more than a million songs, including rights to songs of legends such as the Beach Boys, Isaac Hayes, and Otis Redding. The company collected royalties for mechanical reproduction and licensed its songs for use in movies and television.

75 Universal Music Group Nashville made both kinds of music: country and western. It operated some of the top country music labels in the US, including MCA Nashville and Mercury Nashville. UMG Nashville also operated Lost Highway Records, which specialized in alternative country artists such as Ryan Adams [Hoovers, 2006].

76 Universal Music Enterprises generated revenue from old recordings through several repackaging and marketing operations. Its Universal Chronicles unit marketed compilations and reissued albums through traditional retail channels, while its UTV Records developed repackaged CDs to sell though television campaigns. Universal Music Enterprises also created custom recorded products for customers through its Special Markets unit. The division was launched by UMG in 1999 [Hoovers, 2006].

77 The Verve Music Group was one of the leading jazz record companies in the US. It also reissued recordings from its back catalog including classic tracks by John Coltrane, Count Basie, Ella Fitzgerald, Charlie Parker, and Sarah Vaughan.

78 Universal eLabs was responsible for the development of electronic commerce initiatives. eLabs worked closely with and supported all Universal Music Group's record labels and other businesses to enhance opportunities for music driven by new technologies, while protecting the value of recorded music [Hoovers, 2006].

79 In the U.S., Universal Music and Video Distribution handled distribution and sales for Universal Music Group's artists [Warner Music Group Annual Report, 2006].

80 Universal Music Group was the number one recorded music company in the world. It had many strengths, such as big presence in all genres of music, it offered effective promotional bonuses, and it was successful in the administration of copyrights. The Universal Music Group had award-winning artists on their roster, such as Eminem and U2. Universal Music Group was able to attract the best talent, as shown by their artists' roster. Artists, such as Eminem released at least one album in three-year period and that helped Eminem to remain in consumers' minds.

81 Among other strengths was effective communication with radio and television stations, effective in store displays of new albums, effective publicity, effective placement of artists in concerts and other events, effective timing of album releases, and creative videos that represented artists work. Universal Music Group owned its own production plant and was managing it effectively. The Company had partnerships with many physical and digital retailers that distributed its products, such as Best Buy, Target, and iTunes. Universal Music Group had strong market intelligence and applied effective market segmentation. Additionally Universal Music Group was strong in selling administering copyrights to television, radio, cable, and satellite stations. Also, Universal Music Group was strong in administering copyrights to other businesses, such as film producers and film studios, advertising agencies, video game producers, nightclubs and movie theaters. An example of this was the successful soundtrack to the movie Bad Boys 2, which became one the best selling soundtracks in the recorded music industry.

82 Universal Music Group's only weakness was its lack of partnerships with telecommunication companies, which helped to market and distribute musical content.

EMI Music Group

83 EMI Music Group consisted of records labels such as Capitol and Virgin, EMI Publishing Group, Caroline Distribution Company, Capital Records Nashville, EMI Music Publishing Latin America, and Blue Note Jazz label. EMI Music Group included artists: Kylie Minogue, Moby, and Robbie Williams, among others.

84 EMI Publishing administered the rights to more than a million songs. EMI Music Publishing licensed its music for use in movies, television shows, and advertising. EMI Music Publishing accounted for more than 20 percent of its parent's total business in the year 2004.

85 Caroline was one of the leading distribution companies for independent music. It serviced hundreds of independent record labels by getting their CDs, tapes, and vinyl records into retail outlets throughout the country.

86 Capitol Records Nashville operated one of the top labels in country music. In addition to music, the label produced and distributed comedy albums by the likes of Roy D. Mercer and Tim Wilson [Hoovers, 2006].

87 EMI Music Publishing Latin America was a part of EMI Music Publishing. It collected royalties from CD manufacturing as well as fees for live performances. It licensed its songs for use in movies, television programs, and advertising.

88 Blue Note Records was a jazz label, with a catalog that included such greats as Art Blakey, John Coltrane, Miles Davis, and Thelonious Monk. The label continued to release re-issues from such masters as Cannonball Adderley, Stan Kenton, and Jimmy Smith while promoting new artists including Terence Blanchard, Norah Jones, and Amos Lee [Hoovers, 2006].

89 EMI music group's strengths included effective copyright administration and huge penetration in various genres of music. Among other strengths was effective communication with radio and television stations, effective in store displays of new albums, effective publicity, effective placement of artists in concerts and other events, effective timing of album releases, and creative videos that complemented artists' work. EMI music group offered promotional bonuses with the purchases of albums, such as exclusive DVDs. The Company was effective in dealing with radio and television stations, because the musical content recorded by EMI artists was constantly played on radio and television.

90   EMI music group outsourced its manufacturing to other companies, because they believed it was more important to focus on digital distribution of musical content. EMI had partnerships with many physical and digital retailers that distributed its products, such as Best Buy, Target, and iTunes. EMI had strong market penetration, as evidenced by recording artist Norah Jones' album, which was sold at many Starbucks stores.

91   EMI music group had strong market intelligence and applied effective market segmentation, because they had artists such as Jermaine Dupri who appealed to younger consumers and Depeche Mode who appealed to older consumers. Additionally EMI was strong in selling administering copyrights to television, radio, cable, and satellite stations. EMI was strong in administering copyrights to other businesses as well, such as film producers and film studios, advertising agencies, video game producers, nightclubs and movie theaters.

92   EMI music group was based in England and it had a roster of artists that were more appealing to European market. Such artists included, Robbie Williams and Kylie Minogue. The lack of appeal among the American audience was one of the weaknesses of EMI music group. Another weakness was its weak positioning in the digital market. Weak partnerships with telecommunication companies were another weakness of EMI music group.

Sony BMG

93   Sony BMG was created as a joint venture between Sony Corporation of America and media company Bertelsmann. Sony BMG Music Entertainment was the second largest record company in the world (behind Universal Music Group). Sony BMG consisted of record labels such as Columbia, Jive, La Face. Sony BMG had the following divisions: Sony Music Nashville, RED Distribution, RCA Music Group, Epic Records, and Columbia Records.

94   Sony Music Nashville was one of the top producers of country music. In included artists such as Jace Everett, Shelly Fairchild, and Miranda Lambert.

95   RED Distribution was an independent record distributor that handled releases for some 40 record labels. The leading independent distributor in the US, RED distributed for labels including Fat Wreck Chords, Trustkill Records, and Victory Records, its top-selling label [Hoovers, 2006].

96   RCA Music Group operated RCA Records. RCA had many award winning artists that were appealing to the American audience and appealing to different market segments. Artists included Christina Aguilera, Dave Matthews Band, The Foo Fighters, Kelly Clarkson, and Avril Lavigne.

97   Epic Records Group was one of the leading recording labels in the US, with artists that included Audioslave, Good Charlotte, Jennifer Lopez, Oasis, and Shakira. It has also released the soundtracks to such films as Chicago, Garden State, and Forest Gump. Additionally Epic Records Group was strong in selling administering copyrights to television, radio, cable, and satellite stations. Epic Records Group was strong in administering copyrights to other businesses as well, such as film producers and film studios, advertising agencies, video game producers, nightclubs and movie theaters. In addition to recorded CDs, the label marketed DVDs and videos and it offered streaming audio and downloadable songs on the Internet.

98   Columbia Records Group was one of the leading recording labels in the US. It included artists such as Aerosmith, Dixie Chicks, Beyonce Knowles, Will Smith, and Bruce Springsteen.

99   One of the strengths of Sony music group was its artists' roster that was highly appealing to the American audience. Other strengths included effective communications with radio and television stations, effective promotional bonuses and exclusive offerings, effective publicity, effective marketing through artists' websites, efficient production plant management, award winning musical content, collaboration between artists, artists' appearances in stores, effective in store displays, effective timing of albums releases, and huge market penetration in most genres of music. Sony music group's weaknesses were weak positioning in the digital market, and weak partnerships with telecommunication companies. Sony owned its manufacturing plant and was running its operations effectively.

THE COMPANY

History

100   Warner Music Group was founded in 1929, when Jack Warner, president of Warner Bros. Pictures, Inc., founded Music Publishers Holding Company ("MPHC") to acquire music copyrights as a means of providing inexpensive music for films. In 2002, Warner Music Group acquired Word Entertainment to expand its presence in the Christian music genre. Warner Music Group was acquired by the Investor Group from Time Warner Inc. ("Time Warner") in March 2004. Warner Music Group became the only stand-alone music company with publicly traded common stock in the United States in May 2005 [Warner Music Annual Report, 2006]. Figure 6 shows the structure of the Warner Music Group.

Products

101   Warner music group offered two types of products: musical content and copyrights.

Musical Content

102   Warner Music Group had artists in all major music genres, including pop, rock, jazz, country, R&B, hip-hop, rap, reggae, Latin, alternative, folk, blues, gospel and other Christian music. The strength of Warner Music Group was its wide talent base and strong Artist and Repertoire. In the U.S., Warner Music Group has designed an incubator system, which helped independent distribution network to identify major acts of the future at a lower

FIGURE 6   Warner Music Group

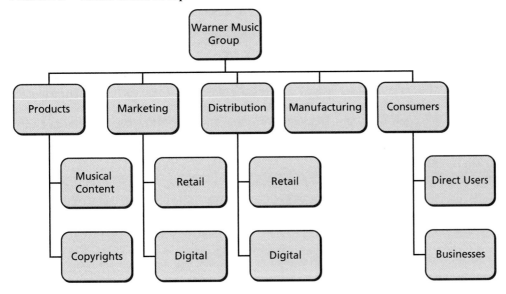

cost. In addition, Warner Music Group had Cordless Recordings, which was an "e-label" that gave its artists the ability to come to market with one or several songs in the digital world without the need to create an entire album. These strategies helped Warner Music Group to take advantage of the changing marketplace and to find and develop new recording artists and songwriters. Among other strengths, Warner music group had artists that appealed to the American audience. Artists included, Kid Rock, T.I., Lil' Kim, and Bruce Springfield. Warner Music Group's artists were able to record at least one album in a three-year span. Examples included T.I., Kid Rock and Lil' Kim. Warner music group also had artists who recorded award-winning musical content, such as a song from the motion picture "Hustle and Flow" that won an Oscar award for the best song at the 78th Academy Awards [Warner Music Group, (2006A)]. Other winners included Red Hot Chili Peppers (Grammy award for best rock music group), and others. The weakness in the product area was the lack of hip-hop artists. Warner Music Group had only 9 artists in the year 2006 [Warner Music Group Annual Report, 2006].

Copyrights

103   Copyrights were the intellectual property of recorded music companies. They consisted of recorded musical works by artists. The key to success in this product category included being able to administer copyrights to film studios, television stations, advertising agencies, venues, and restaurants. Warner Music Group was among market leaders in the music publishing and held 16 percent of shares of the market in 2004. The only company that held more shares in the publishing market was EMI publishing, which held 16.3 percent [Warner Music Group Annual Report, 2006].

Marketing

104   WEA Corporation marketed most of Warner Music Group's releases. Warner Music Group marketed musical content and copyrights to direct users and businesses. The Company engaged in retail marketing and digital marketing.

Retail Marketing

105   Retail Marketing included marketing activities that were performed in physical locations; they included in store promotions and appearances, advertising on billboards, internet, and magazines such as The Rolling Stone, The Source, Vibe, and many others. Warner Music Group's artists, such as T.I., P.Diddy, Red Hot Chili Peppers, and Madonna appeared on television shows and award ceremonies such as Grammy and MTV music awards. Warner Music Group also engaged in effective sales promotions by offering never before released musical content that came as a bonus with the new albums. Artists that were a part of Warner Music Group released at least one album in a three-year period. An example of such an artist was a hip-hop artist T.I. who released albums in the following years: 2003, 2004, and 2006. Warner Music Group also engaged in effective publicity. An effective element of publicity was artist's appearances in the retail store. Another important strategy that Warner Music Group applied effectively was the timing of album releases. Most Warner Music Group albums were released in the months of June, August, or December.

Digital Marketing

106   Digital Marketing included marketing activities performed on the Internet or using telecommunications. Warner Music Group's labels had well-developed websites that served as venues for marketing. For example, Atlantic Records had a website that contained musical samples and cover art of albums of its artists T.I. and Missy Elliot among others. Warner Music Group was the first recorded music company to offer music videos to Cingular Wireless customers [Warner Music Group, (2006B)]. Warner Music Group had an agreement with MTV Networks for the use of the Warner Music Group's music videos in mobile content.

107 The weakness in the marketing area was the lack of collaboration between artists. This weakness was attributed to the weakness in the product category, specifically in the hip-hop genre where Warner Music Group had only 9 hip-hop artists. In comparison, Universal Music Group had over 25 hip-hop artists, which made it easier for hip-hop artists to feature on each other's material. It was very important to have many hip-hop artists because hip-hop was one of the best selling genres of music and consumers who listened to hip-hop were among heaviest users of music.

Distribution

108 The Warner Music Group's WEA Corporation was the first major music distribution company in the U.S. WEA Corporation distributed audio and video releases from Warner Bros., Elektra, Atlantic Rhino Entertainment, Asylum Records, Word Entertainment, Time-Life Music, Warner Music Latina and Curb Records, as well as several other labels. WEA Corporation's E-Commerce department worked with online and traditional retailers for all commercial, digital and wireless transactions. The department developed and created marketing programs to promote Warner Music Group's artists to online retailers and telecommunication partners, such as Sprint Mobile. In addition to the WEA Corporation, The Alternative Distribution Alliance was created in 1993 to focus on the independent music market. The Alternative Distribution Alliance was distributor of independent record labels, including labels such as SubPop, Matador, Tommy Boy, and many others. WEA Corporation and Alternative Distribution Alliance marketed and sold products to record stores, mass merchants and other retailers throughout the country [Warner Music Group Annual Report, 2006].

Retail Distribution

109 Warner Music Group distributed musical content in the form of records, such as CDs and DVDs. CDs and DVDs were distributed through retailers, such as Virgin Megastore, FYE, Best Buy, Circuit City and others.

Digital Distribution

110 The strength of Warner Music Group was its good positioning in digital distribution and emerging technologies. Warner Music Group had partnerships with a broad range of online digital and mobile providers, such as iTunes, MusicNet, Musicmatch, Rhapsody, Sprint, Verizon and Cingular. Those partnerships gave Warner Music Group an advantage over competition in the key to success areas. For example, a week before the release of T.I.'s fourth album titled "The King" (March of 2006), the clients of Sprint telecommunications were able to download the exclusive tracks and ring tones through Sprint mobile.

111 In January 2006, Warner Music Group became the first recoded music company that entered into the distribution and marketing agreement with Skype Company, which provided Internet communications. Skype had 74 million registered users who used Skype to make voice calls to other users all over the world. Warner Music Group provided Skype users with the opportunity to download ring tones from artists, such as Madonna, T.I., Green Day and others [Warner Music Group, (2006C)]. The agreement gave Warner Music Group a good positioning in the digital distribution, big penetration in the communications area, and it proved that managers of Warner Music Group had a good understanding of technology and digital distribution.

Manufacturing

112 Warner Music Group has sold its manufacturing and packaging operations to Cinram Corporation, but was able to enter into the profitable agreement with Cinram Corporation that continued to manufacture Warner Music Group's CDs and DVDs. However, the absence of the manufacturing plant was Warner Music Group's weakness, because Warner Music Group had less control over manufacturing of CDs and DVDs.

Consumers

113   Warner Music Group has two types of consumers: direct users who used musical content for their own entertainment, and businesses who bought copyrighted songs and used them in their businesses.

Direct Users

114   Warner Music Group had good market intelligence and was effective in segmenting the consumer into segments. It was evidenced by their artist roster. Artists such as Sean Paul and T.I. appealed to younger audience including segments of 10–19 and 20–24 years of age. Artists such as Red Hot Chili Peppers and Green Day appealed to the segments of 25–29 and 30–44 years of age. Warner Music Group also had artists to satisfy the segment of consumers of age 45+ with artists such as, Fleetwood Mac, Phil Collins, and Tracy Chapman. Warner Music Group's strength included having big artist roster that included artists representing all genres of music. However, the weakness was the small number of hip-hop artists.

Businesses

115   Warner Music Group was effective in marketing the copyrights to businesses. Warner Music Group administered copyrights to television, radio, cable, and satellite studios (5C). It also administered copyrights to film producers and film studios. For example, in 2006 the movie called ATL had soundtrack of musical content recorded by Warner Music Group recording artists T.I. Other businesses that Warner Music Group administered copyrights to included advertising agencies, video game producers, nightclubs and movie theaters.

Financials

116   Recorded Music revenues increased by $65 million to $2.924 billion for the twelve months ended September 30, 2005, compared to $2.859 billion for the twelve months ended September 30, 2004 [Duhigg, C. (2006)]. Recorded Music revenues represented approximately 83 percent of consolidated revenues for the twelve months ended September 30, 2005 and 2004. The increase in Recorded Music revenue was primarily due to the increase in digital sales of $105 million to $137 million in the twelve months ended September 30, 2005. The increase in revenues from the sale of music in digital formats related to the development and increased consumer usage of legal, online distribution channels for the music industry. For the twelve months ended September 30, 2005, digital sales increased to 5 percent of Recorded Music revenues. Digital sales in the U.S. increased by $79 million to $105 million or 7 percent of U.S. Recorded Music revenues and more than offset the decline in fiscal 2005 U.S physical unit sales. International sales of music in digital formats rose by $26 million to $32 million or 2 percent of international Recorded Music revenues. Excluding the increase in digital sales and an approximate $86 million favorable impact of foreign currency exchange rates, physical sales of Recorded Music formats declined by approximately $124 million in the twelve months ended September 30, 2005 as compared with the twelve months ended September 30, 2004. The decline reflected the continued impact of industry-wide piracy, particularly in the international Recorded Music Business where $111 million of this decline occurred [Warner Music Group Annual Report, 2006].

117   Recorded Music OIBDA increased by $114 million to $380 million for the twelve months ended September 30, 2005, compared to $266 million for the twelve months ended September 30, 2004. Expressed as a percent of Recorded Music revenues, Recorded Music OIBDA was 13 percent and 9 percent for the twelve-month periods ended September 30, 2005 and 2004 respectively [Warner Music Group Annual Report, 2006].

Management Strategy

118 ***Management Team*** Edgar Bronfman, Jr. was the Chairman of the Board and CEO of the Warner Music Group since March 1, 2004. Lyor Cohen was the Chairman and CEO of U.S. Recorded Music operations since March 1, 2004. Paul-René Albertini has served as President of Warner Music International since 2002 and led Warner Music International as Chairman and CEO.

119 The decision makers at the Warner Music Group were pursuing aggressive strategy to expand into the digital distribution. Managers believed in the development of online and mobile distribution. Distribution agreements with Skype Company and Sprint Mobile showed that managers at Warner Music Group had good understanding of the new technologies. Management Team thought that the legitimate online distribution channels offered advantages to illegal peer-to-peer sites, including greater ease of use, higher quality and more consistent music product, faster downloading, better search capabilities, and better integration with portable digital music players. For example, legitimate online operations such as Apple's iTunes, MusicNet, musicmatch and Rhapsody have been launched since the beginning of 2003 and offered a variety of models, including per-track pricing, per-album pricing and monthly subscriptions [Warner Music Group Annual Report, 2006].

120 To emphasize the importance of digital distribution the Company has been restructured and has sold its manufacturing, packaging and physical distribution operations to Cinram Company. It was expected that the Company would continue moving towards new digital distribution solutions.

LOOKING TOWARDS THE FUTURE

121 The Chairman and CEO Edgar Bronfman Jr. had to implement strategic decisions in order to win against the competition of Universal Music Group, EMI and Sony Music. All major competitors were expanding into the digital distribution; however, physical distribution remained a very important means of distribution. Bronfman had to focus on digital distribution, but at the same time stay competitive in the physical distribution area.

122 The first alternative to be considered was to expand its focus on physical distribution channels, such as record stores, independent stores, and retail outlets. It suggested that the Warner Music Group explored new physical channels, such as Starbucks coffee stores and retail stores around college campuses to reach the customers. The benefit of this alternative was that it would increase the market penetration, and Warner Music Group would be able to segment the market effectively.

123 This alternative was feasible because Warner Music Group has been in business for many years and it had developed good relationships with retailers and had good understanding of physical distribution. It was also feasible because Warner Music Group had artists in their roster that fitted the college students segment of the market. Furthermore, distribution to Starbucks coffee stores guaranteed access to other market segments, which were potentially profitable.

124 This alternative would win against the competition of companies like Sony Music, Universal Music Group, and EMI, because Warner Music Group would have the biggest market penetration and would be able to reach well-targeted audience. It would also help Warner Music Group artists to be more visible if consumers saw their products in most record stores, Starbucks coffee shops, and stores around campuses. Such visibility combined with marketing activities, such as marketing on radio and television, would provide the synergy and increase sales.

125   The drawback of this alternative is that by focusing on physical distribution channels, Warner Music Group could lose its strong presence in the digital distribution area. Another drawback was associated with the fact that other companies, such as EMI, were already supplying their musical content to Starbucks coffee stores. There were other drawbacks associated with distribution to college students, for example the lack of potential retailers around college campuses that would be interested to sell records.

126   The way around this drawback was to hire more people who would be responsible for digital distribution strategies and would help the Company to stay competitive in the digital distribution. Additionally, the Warner Music Group could invest more money into physical distribution by paying bonuses to Starbucks for distributing their products. The way around the drawback associated with distribution to college students was to hire street marketing teams who would promote and sell records around campuses.

127   The second alternative was to further expand its presence in the digital and mobile distribution. The alternative suggested that Warner Music Group focus more on digital distribution, while maintaining the focus on physical distribution as well. The alternative also suggested that Warner Music Group develop its own digital distribution channel, such as file sharing program with monthly subscription. The benefit of this alternative was that costs associated with physical distribution, such as manufacturing, distribution and inventory costs, did not apply. Another benefit was that focusing on digital distribution guaranteed more effective reach of consumers. Consumers would not have to visit physical locations to buy musical content.

128   Another benefit associated with this alternative was that Warner Music Group would be able to reach more favorable terms of distribution with physical retailers. It would happen, because retailers are highly dependent on record music companies that distribute the music content through them. If distribution of musical content shifted to digital distribution many physical retailers would go out of business.

129   Another benefit associated with this alternative was that focusing on digital distribution would enable the Warner Music Group to respond to latest trends in the marketplace and would strengthen its position in the digital distribution.

130   This alternative was feasible because Warner Music Group already had partnerships with file sharing companies, such as iTunes, Napster and others. Warner Music Group also had Partnerships with telecommunication providers such as Verizon and Cingular and Internet telecommunications company Skype. It was also feasible because Warner Music Group had good understanding of digital distribution, and was well positioned in it.

131   The alternative would win against the competition of firms like Sony Music, because Warner Music Group would increase its competitiveness in the digital market. It would win also because no other company had developed its own file-sharing program. Therefore, Warner Music Group would attract more consumers, because of its presence in the digital market.

132   The drawback of this alternative was piracy. The digital piracy was the biggest threat, because file-sharing programs were easy to obtain. Furthermore, the anti-piracy laws have not been strongly established. Another drawback associated with this alternative was the fact that major competitors were in the digital distribution as well.

133   The way around this drawback was to enter into distribution agreements with illegal fire sharing networks, such as Limewire. Many users who used illegal fire sharing networks would be forced to pay for the musical content. No other competitor has ever entered into agreement with illegal file sharing network, and it would put Warner Music Group ahead of competition.

134   Another way around this drawback was to contribute to the industry-wide battle against the piracy and to invest in market intelligence, which enabled it to follow consumer trends, such as to detect the most popular illegal file sharing networks.

REFERENCES

Duhigg, C49(2006) "Warner Music's Earnings Nearly Double;" [Online]. The Los Angeles Times Online. *http://www.latimes.com/entertainment/news/music/la-fi-warner15feb15,1,5064962.story?coll=la-entnews-music.* Accessed February 15, 2006.

Recording Industry Association of America (2006A). Consumer Segmentation Study *http://www.riaa.com/news/marketingdata/segementation.asp.* Accessed February 15, 2006.

Recording Industry Association of America (2006B). Purchasing Trends. *http://www.riaa.com/news/marketingdata/purchasing.asp.* Accessed February 15, 2006.

Recording Industry Association of America (2006C). Hispanic Consumer Trends. *http://www.riaa.com/news/marketingdata/hispanic.asp.* Accessed February 15, 2006.

Recording Industry Association of America (2006D). Hispanic Population. *http://www.census.gov/Press=Release/www/releases/archives/population/005164.htm.* Accessed February 15, 2006.

Hoovers. *http://www.hoovers.com.* Accessed February 9, 2006.

Warner Music Group Annual Report (2006) [Online]. *http ://library.corporate-ir.net/library/18/182/182480/items/181572/2005_AR.pdf.* Accessed February 9, 2006.

Warner Music Group (2006A). "Hustle & Flow Earns Oscar for Original Song for its Hard Out There for a Pimp". [Online]. *http://www.wmg.com/news/story.jsp?article=29720018.* Accesses February 9, 2006.

Warner Music Group (2006B). "Music Choice Extends The Reach of its Video-on-Demand Network to Cingular Wireless Customers". [Online]. *http://www.wmg.com/news/story.jsp?article=29720020.* Accessed February 9, 2006.

Warner Music Group (2006C). "Warner Music Group Announces Landmark Ringtone Agreement with Skype, Global Internet Calling Company". [Online]. *http://www.wmg.com/news/story.jsp?article=29320018.* Accessed February 9, 2006.

Case 50

Whole Foods Market 2007: *Will There Be Enough Organic Food to Satisfy the Growing Demand?*

Patricia Harasta and Alan N. Hoffman

1   Reflecting back over his three decades of experience in the grocery business, John Mackey smiled to himself over his previous successes. His entrepreneurial history began with a single store which he has now grown to the nations leading natural food chain. While proud of the past, John had concerns about the future direction the Whole Foods Market chain should head. Whole Foods Market was an early entrant into the organic food market and they have used their early mover advantage to solidify their position and continue their steady growth.

2   In 2005 Whole Foods Market acquired the Wild Oats Food chain. Wild Oats operates 100 full service stores in 24 states and Canada. With the changing economy and a more competitive industry landscape, John Mackey is uncertain about how to meet the company's aggressive growth targets. Whole Foods Market's objective is to reach $12 billion in revenue with 300+ stores by 2010 without sacrificing quality and their current reputation. This is not an easy task and John is unsure of the best way to proceed.

COMPANY BACKGROUND

3   Whole Foods carries both natural and organic food offering customers a wide variety of products. "Natural" refers to food that is free of growth hormones or antibiotics, where "certificated organic" food conforms to the standards, as defined by the U.S. Department of Agriculture in October 2002. Whole Foods Market® is the world's leading retailer of natural and organic foods, with 193 stores in 31 states and Canada and the United Kingdom. John Mackey, current president and cofounder of Whole Foods, opened "Safer Way" natural grocery store in 1978. The store had limited success as it was a small location allowing only for a limited selection, focusing entirely on vegetarian foods. John joined forces with Craig Weller and Mark Skiles, founders of "Clarsville Natural Grocery" (founded in 1979), to create Whole Foods Market. This joint venture took place in Austin, Texas in 1980 resulting in a new company, a single natural food market with a staff of nineteen.

4   In addition to the supermarkets, Whole Foods owns and operates several subsidiaries. Allegro Coffee Company was formed in 1977 and purchased by Whole Foods Market in 1997 now acting as their coffee roasting and distribution center. Pigeon Cove is Whole Foods' seafood processing facility, which was founded in 1985 and known as M & S Seafood until 1990. Whole Foods purchased Pigeon Cove in 1996, located in Gloucester, MA. The Company is now the only supermarket to own and operate a waterfront seafood facility. The last two subsidiaries are Produce Field Inspection Office and Select Fish, which is Whole Foods' West Coast seafood processing facility acquired in 2003. In addition to the above, the Company has eight distribution centers, seven regional bake houses and four commissaries.

The authors would like to thank Ann Hoffman, Christopher Ferrari, Robert Marshall, Julie Giles, Jennifer Powers and Gretchen Alper for their research and contributions to this case.

Please address all correspondence to: Dr. Alan N. Hoffman, AGC 320, Department of Management, Bentley College, 175 Forest Street, Waltham, MA 02452-4705, voice (781) 891-2287, ahoffman@bentley.edu, fax (781) 459-0335. Printed by permission of Dr. Alan N. Hoffman, Bentley College.

5   "Whole Foods Market remains uniquely mission driven: The Company is highly selective about what they sell, dedicated to stringent quality standards, and committed to sustainable agriculture. They believe in a virtuous circle entwining the food chain, human beings and Mother Earth: each is reliant upon the others through a beautiful and delicate symbiosis." The message of preservation and sustainability are followed while providing high quality goods to customers and high profits to investors.

6   Whole Foods has grown over the years through mergers, acquisitions and several new store openings. Today, Whole Foods Market is the largest natural food supermarket in the United States. The Company consists of 32,000 employees operating 193 stores in the United States, Canada and United Kingdom with an average store size of 32,000 square feet. While the majority of Whole Foods locations are in US, the Company has made acquisitions expanding its presence in the UK. European expansion provides enormous potential growth due to the large population and it holds "a more sophisticated organic-foods market than US in terms of suppliers and acceptance by the public." Whole Foods targets their locations specifically by an area's demographics. The Company targets locations where 40% or more of the residents have a college degree as they are more likely to be aware of nutritional issues.

WHOLE FOODS MARKET'S PHILOSOPHY

7   Their corporate website defines the company philosophy as follows, "Whole Foods Market's vision of a sustainable future means our children and grandchildren will be living in a world that values human creativity, diversity, and individual choice. Businesses will harness human and material resources without devaluing the integrity of the individual or the planet's ecosystems. Companies, governments, and institutions will be held accountable for their actions. People will better understand that all actions have repercussions and that planning and foresight coupled with hard work and flexibility can overcome almost any problem encountered. It will be a world that values education and a free exchange of ideas by an informed citizenry; where people are encouraged to discover, nurture, and share their life's passions."

8   While Whole Foods recognizes it is only a supermarket, they are working toward fulfilling their vision within the context of their industry. In addition to leading by example, they strive to conduct business in a manner consistent with their mission and vision. By offering minimally processed, high quality food, engaging in ethical business practices and providing a motivational, respectful work environment, the Company believes they are on the path to a sustainable future.

9   Whole Foods incorporates the best practices of each location back into the chain. This can be seen in the Company's store product expansion from dry goods to perishable produce, including meats, fish and prepared foods. The lessons learned at one location are absorbed by all, enabling the chain to maximize effectiveness and efficiency while offering a product line customers love. Whole Foods carries only natural and organic products. The best tasting and most nutritious food available is found in its purest state—unadulterated by artificial additives, sweeteners, colorings, and preservatives.

10   Whole Foods continually improves customer offerings, catering to its specific locations. Unlike business models for traditional grocery stores, Whole Foods' products differ by geographic regions and local farm specialties.

EMPLOYEE & CUSTOMER RELATIONS

11   Whole Foods encourages a team based environment allowing each store to make independent decisions regarding its operations. Teams consist of up to eleven employees and a team

leader. The team leaders typically head up one department or another. Each store employs anywhere from 72 to 391 team members. The manager is referred to as the "store team leader." The "store team leader" is compensated by an Economic Value Added (EVA) bonus and is also eligible to receive stock options.

12   Whole Foods tries to instill a sense of purpose among its employees and has been named one of the "100 Best Companies to work for in America" by Fortune Magazine for the past six years. In employee surveys, 90% of its team members stated that they always or frequently enjoy their job.

13   The company strives to take care of their customers, realizing they are the "lifeblood of our business," and the two are "interdependent on each other." Whole Foods' primary objective goes beyond 100% customer satisfaction with the goal to "delight" customers in every interaction.

COMPETITIVE ENVIRONMENT

Natural Products Sales Top $45 Billion in 2004

American shoppers spent nearly $45.8 billion on natural and organic products in 2004, according to research published in the *24th Annual Market Overview* in the June issue of *The Natural Foods Merchandiser.* In 2004, natural products sales increased 6.9% across all sales channels, including supermarkets, mass marketers, direct marketers, and the Internet. Sales of organic products rose 14.6% in natural products stores. As interest in low-carb diets waned, sales of organic baked goods rose 35%. Other fast-growing organic categories included meat, poultry and seafood, up 120%; coffee and cocoa, up 64%; and cookies, up 63%.

14   At the time of Whole Foods' inception, there was almost no competition with less than six other natural food stores in the United States. Today, the organic foods industry is growing and Whole Foods finds itself competing hard to maintain its elite presence. As the population has become increasingly concerned about their eating habits, natural foods stores, such as Whole Foods, are flourishing. Other successful natural food grocery chains today include Trader Joe's Co., and Wild Oats Market.

15   Trader Joe's, originally known as Pronto Markets was founded in 1958 in Los Angeles by Joe Coulombe. By expanding its presence and product offerings while maintaining high quality at low prices, the Company has found its competitive niche. The Company has 215 stores, primarily on the west and east coasts of the United States. The Company "offers upscale grocery fare such as health foods, prepared meals, organic produce and nutritional supplements." A low cost structure allows Trader Joe's to offer competitive prices while still maintaining its margins. Trader Joe's stores have no service department and average just 10,000 square feet in store size. A privately held Company, Trader Joe's enjoyed sales of $2.5 million in 2003, a 13.6% increase from 2002.

16   Additional competition has arisen from grocery stores, such as Stop 'N Shop and Shaw's, which now incorporate natural foods sections in their conventional stores, placing them in direct competition with Whole Foods. Because larger grocery chains have more flexibility in their product offerings, they are more likely to promote products through sales, a strategy Whole Foods rarely practices.

17   Despite being in a highly competitive industry, Whole Foods maintains its reputation as "the world's # 1 natural foods chain." As the demand for natural and organic food continues to grow, pressures on suppliers will rise. Only 3% of US farmland is organic so there is limited output. The increased demand for these products may further elevate prices or result in goods being out of stock, with possible price wars looming.

THE CHANGING GROCERY INDUSTRY

18 Before the emergence of the supermarket, the public was largely dependent upon specialty shops or street vendors for dairy products, meats, produce, and other household items. In the 1920s, chain stores began to threaten independent retailers by offering convenience and lower prices by procuring larger quantities of products. Appel explains that the emergence of the supermarkets in the 1930s was a result of three major changes in society:

1. The shift in population from rural to urban areas
2. An increase in disposable income
3. Increased mobility through ownership of automobiles.

19 Perhaps the earliest example of the supermarket as we know it today is King Kullen, "America's first supermarket," which was founded by Michael Cullen in 1930. "The essential key to his plan was volume, and he attained this through heavy advertising of low prices on nationally advertised merchandise." As the success of Cullen's strategy became evident, others such as Safeway, A&P, and Kroger adopted it as well. By the time the United States entered World War II, 9,000 supermarkets accounted for 25% of industry sales.

20 Low prices and convenience continue to be the dominant factors driving consumers to supermarkets today. The industry is characterized by low margins and continuous downward pressure on prices made evident by coupons, weekly specials, and rewards cards. Over the years firms have introduced subtle changes to the business model by providing additional conveniences, such as the inclusion of bakeries, banks, pharmacies, and even coffee houses co-located within the supermarket. Throughout their existence, supermarkets have also tried to cater to the changing tastes and preferences of society such as healthier diets, the Atkins diet, and low carbohydrate foods. The moderate changes to strategy within supermarkets have been imitated by competitors, which are returning the industry to a state of price competition. Supermarkets themselves now face additional competition from wholesalers such as Costco, BJ's and Sam's Club.

A DIFFERENT SHOPPING EXPERIENCE

21 The setup of the organic grocery store is a key component to Whole Foods' success. The store's setup and its products are carefully researched to ensure that they are meeting the demands of the local community. Locations are primarily in cities and are chosen for their large space and heavy foot traffic. According to Whole Foods' 10K, "approximately 88% of our existing stores are located in the top 50 statistical metropolitan areas." The Company uses a specific formula to choose their store sites that is based upon several metrics, which include but are not limited to income levels, education, and population density.

22 Upon entering a Whole Foods supermarket, it becomes clear that the Company attempts to sell the consumer on the entire experience. Team members (employees) are well trained and the stores themselves are immaculate. There are in-store chefs to help with recipes, wine tasting and food sampling. There are "Take Action food centers" where customers can access information on the issues that affect their food such as legislation and environmental factors. Some stores offer extra services such as home delivery, cooking classes, massages and valet parking. Whole Foods goes out of their way to appeal to the above-average income earner.

23 Whole Foods uses price as a marketing tool in a few select areas, as demonstrated by the 365 Whole Foods brand name products, priced less than similar organic products that are carried within the store. However, the Company does not use price to differentiate itself from competitors. Rather, Whole Foods focuses on quality and service as a means of standing out from the competition.

24   Whole Foods only spent 0.5% of their total sales from the fiscal year 2004 on advertising; they rely on other means to promote their stores. The Company relies heavily on word-of-mouth advertising from their customers to help market themselves in the local community. They are also promoted in several health conscious magazines, and each store budgets for in-store advertising each fiscal year.

25   Whole Foods also gains recognition via their charitable contributions and the awareness that they bring to the treatment of animals. The Company donates 5% of their after tax profits to not-for-profit charities. The Company is also very active in establishing systems to make sure that the animals used in their products are treated humanly.

THE AGING BABY BOOMERS

26   The aging of the Baby Boomer generation will expand the senior demographic over the next decade as their children grow up and leave the nest. Urban singles are another group who has extra disposable income due to their lack of dependents. These two groups present an opportunity for growth for Whole Foods. Americans spent 7.2% of their total expenditures on food in 2001, making it the seventh highest category on which consumers spend their money. Additionally, US households with income of more than $100,000 per annum represent 22% of aggregate income today compared with 18% a decade ago.

27   This shift in demographics has created an expansion in the luxury store group, while slowing growth in the discount retail market. To that end, there is a gap in supermarket retailing between consumers who can only afford to shop at low cost providers, like Wal-Mart, and the population of consumers who prefer gourmet food and are willing to pay a premium for perceived higher quality. "The Baby Boomers are driving demand for organic food in general because they're health-conscious and can afford to pay higher prices" says Professor Steven G. Sapp, a sociologist at Iowa State University who studies consumer food behavior.

28   The perception that imported, delicatessen, exotic and organic foods are of higher quality, therefore commanding higher prices, continues to bode well for Whole Foods Market. As John Mackey, explains "we're changing the [grocery-shopping] experience so that people enjoy it. It's a richer, [more fun], more enjoyable experience. People don't shop our stores because we have low prices." The consumer focus on a healthy diet is not limited to food. More new diet plans emerged in America in the last half of the 20th century than in any other country. This trend has also increased the demand for nutritional supplements and vitamins.

29   In recent years, consumers have made a gradual move toward the use of fresher, healthier foods in their everyday diets. Consumption of fresh fruits and vegetables, pasta and other grain-based products has increased. This is evidenced by the aggressive expansion by consumer products companies into healthy food and natural and organic products. "Natural and organic products have crossed the chasm to mainstream America." The growing market can be attributed to the acceptance and widespread expansion of organic product offerings, beyond milk and dairy. Mainstream acceptance of the Whole Foods offering can be attributed to this shift in consumer food preferences as consumers continue to cite taste as the number one motivator for purchasing organic foods.

30   With a growing percentage of women working out of the home, the traditional role of home cooked meals, prepared from scratch, has waned. As fewer women have the time to devote to cooking, consumers are giving way to the trend of convenience through prepared foods. Sales of ready-to-eat meals have grown significantly. "The result is that grocers are starting to specialize in quasi-restaurant food." Just as women entering the work force has propelled the sale of prepared foods; it has also increased consumer awareness of the need for the one-stop shopping experience. Hypermarkets such as Wal-Mart, that offer non-food

items and more mainstream product lines, allow consumers to conduct more shopping in one place rather than moving from store to store.

31   The growth in sales of natural foods is expected to continue at the rate of 8−10% annually, according to the National Nutritional Foods Association. The sale of organic food has largely outpaced traditional grocery products due to consumer perception that organic food is healthier. The purchase of organic food is perceived to be beneficial to consumer health by 61% of consumers, according to a Food Marketing Institute (FMI)/Prevention magazine study. Americans believe organic food can help improve fitness and increase the longevity of life. Much of this perception has grown out of fear of how non-organic foods are treated with pesticides for growth and then preserved for sale. Therefore, an opportunity exists for Whole Foods to contribute to consumer awareness by funding non-profit organizations that focus on educating the public on the benefits of organic lifestyles.

OPERATIONS

32   Whole Foods purchases most of their products from regional and national suppliers. This allows the company to leverage its size in order to receive deep discounts and favorable terms with their vendors. The company still permits stores to purchase from local producers to keep the stores aligned with local food trends and is seen as supporting the community. The company owns two procurement centers and handles the majority of procurement and distribution themselves. Whole Foods also owns several regional bake houses, which distribute products to their stores. The largest independent vendor is United Natural Foods which accounted for 20% of Whole Foods' total purchases for fiscal year 2004. Product categories at Whole Foods include, but are not limited to:

- Produce
- Seafood
- Grocery
- Meat and Poultry
- Bakery
- Prepared Foods and Catering
- Specialty (Beer, Wine and Cheese)
- Whole body (nutritional supplements, vitamins, body care and educational products such as books)
- Floral
- Pet Products
- Household Products

33   While Whole Foods carries all the items that one would expect to find in a grocery store (and plenty that one would not), their ". . . heavy emphasis on perishable foods is designed to appeal to both natural foods and gourmet shoppers." Perishable foods accounted for 67% of their retail sales in 2004 and are the core of Whole Foods' success. This is demonstrated by their own statement that, "We believe it is our strength of execution in perishables that has attracted many of our most loyal shoppers."

34   Whole Foods also provides fully cooked frozen meal option through their private label Whole Kitchen, to satisfy the demands of working families. For example, the Whole Foods Market located in Woodland Hills, CA has redesigned its prepared foods section more than three times in response to a 40% growth in prepared foods sales.

35   Whole Foods doesn't take just any product and put it on their shelves. In order to make it into the Whole Foods grocery store, products have to undergo a strict test to determine if they are "Whole Foods material." The quality standards that all potential Whole foods products must meet include:

- Foods that are free of preservatives and other additives
- Foods that are fresh, wholesome and safe to eat
- Promote organically grown foods
- Foods and products that promote a healthy life

36   Meat and poultry products must adhere to a higher standard:

- No antibiotics or added growth hormones
- An affidavit from each producer that outlines the whole process of production and how the animals are treated
- An annual inspection of all producers by Whole Foods Market
- Successful completion of a third party audit to attest to these findings

37   Also, due to the lack of available nutritional brands with a national identity, Whole Foods decided to enter into the private label product business. They currently have three private label products with a fourth program called Authentic Food Artisan, which promotes distinctive products that are certified organic. The three private label products: (1) 365 Everyday Value: A well recognized and trusted brand that meets the standards of Whole Foods and is less expensive than the regular product lines; (2)Whole Kids Organic: Healthy items that are directed at children; and (3) 365 Organic Everyday Value: All the benefits of organic food at reduced prices.

38   When opening a new store, Whole Foods stocks it with almost $700,000 worth of initial inventory, which their vendors partially finance. Like most conventional grocery stores, the majority of Whole Foods inventory is turned over fairly quickly; this is especially true of produce. Fresh organic produce is central to Whole Foods existence and turns over on a faster basis than other products.

FINANCIAL OPERATIONS

39   Whole Foods Market focuses on earning a profit while providing job security to its workforce to lay the foundation for future growth. The company is determined not to let profits deter the Company from providing excellent service to its customers and quality work environment for its staff. Their mission statement defines their recipe for financial success.

> Whole Foods, Whole People, Whole Planet—emphasizes that our vision reaches far beyond just being a food retailer. Our success in fulfilling our vision is measured by customer satisfaction, Team Member excellence and happiness, return on capital investment, improvement in the state of the environment, and local and larger community support.

40   Whole Foods also caps the salary of its executives at no more than fourteen times that of the average annual salary of a Whole Foods' worker; this includes wages and incentive bonuses as well. The company also donates 5% of their after tax profits to non-profit organizations.

41   Over a five-year period from 2000 through 2004, the Company experienced an 87% growth in sales, with sales reaching $3.86 billion in 2004. Annual sales increases during that period were equally dramatic: 24% in 2001, 18% in 2002, 17% in 2003 and 22% in 2004. They achieved $5.6 billion in sales in 2006 which was up from $4.7 billion in 2005, resulting in a yearly increase of 19.2%. On average the company's sales have grown 19.4% over the past five years. In fiscal 2006, Whole Foods achieved 11% comparable-store sales growth (CSSG), which is well above the industry average This growth is perhaps more impressive, given the relatively negative economic environment and recession in the United States.

42   Whole Foods strategy of expansion and acquisition has fueled growth in net income since the company's inception. This is particularly evident when looking at the net income growth in 2002 (24.47%), 2003 (22.72%) and 2004 (27.94%). In 2006 the company earned $204 million, a 50% increase from the $136 million it earned in 2005.

43   The Ticker for Whole Foods, Inc. is WFMI. In reviewing the performance history of Whole Foods stock since its IPO reveals a mostly upward trend. The 10- year price trend shows the Company increasing from under $10 per share to a high of over $100 per share, reflecting an increase of over 1,000%. In 2007, the stock has been on a downward trend due to slowing same store sales. The current price of $47 with 140 million shares outstanding gives the Company a market valuation of $6.7 billion (Apr, 2007). As of 2006, Whole Foods had only $8.6 million in long term debt, while having $256.2 million in cash and cash equivalent balances.

THE CODE OF CONDUCT

44   From its inception, the Company has sought to be different from conventional grocery stores, with a heavy focus on ethics. Besides and emphasis on organic foods, the Company has also established a contract of animal rights, which states the Company will only do business with companies that treat their animals humanely. While they realize that animal products are vital to their business, they oppose animal cruelty.

45   The Company has a unique fourteen-page Code of Conduct document that addresses the expected and desired behavior for its employees. The code is broken down into the following four sections:

- Potential Conflicts of Interest
- Transactions or situations that should never occur
- Situations where you may need the authorization of the Ethics committee before proceeding and finally
- Times when certain actions must be taken by executives of the company or team leaders of individual stores.

46   This Code of Conduct covers, in detail, the most likely scenarios a manager of a store might encounter. It includes several checklists, that are to be filled out on a regular, or at least an annual basis by team leaders and store managers. After completion, the checklists must be signed and submitted to corporate headquarters and copies retained on file in the store. They ensure that the ethics of Whole Foods are being followed by everyone. The ethical efforts of Whole Foods don't go unrecognized; they were ranked number 70 out of the "100 Best Corporate Citizens."

POSSIBLE SCARCE RESOURCES: PRIME LOCATIONS AND THE SUPPLY OF ORGANIC FOODS

47   Prime store locations and the supply of organic foods are potential scarce resources and could be problematic for Whole Foods Market in the future.

48   Whole Foods likes to establish a presence in highly affluent cities, where their target market resides. The majority of Whole Foods' customers are well-educated; thereby yielding high salaries enabling them to afford the Company's higher prices. Whole Foods is particular when deciding on new locations, as location is extremely important for top and bottom line growth. However, there are a limited number of communities where 40% of the residents have college degrees.

49   Organic food is another possible scarce resource. Organic crops yield a lower quantity of output and are rarer, accounting for only 3% of US farmland usage. Strict government requirements must be satisfied; these are incredibly time consuming, more effort intensive, and more costly to adhere to. With increased demands from mainstream super markets also carrying organics, the demand for such products could outreach the limited supply. The market for organic foods grew from $2.9 billion in 2001 to $5.3 billion in 2004, an 80.5% increase in the three-year period. Currently, there are about 10,000 American farmers on about 2.3 million acres of land. Many companies have already started to look for resources outside of the U.S. to meet its growing customer demands. As organics become more main stream, people are worried that standards will be lowered and farmers and businesses might resort to questionable farming practices. The Organic Trade Association estimates that the organic foods industry makes up about 2.5 percent of total U.S. food sales. This figure is up from 0.8 percent in 1997, and represents annual sales increases of between 15 and 21 percent, compared to total U.S. food sales of approximately 2 to 4 percent.

50   In 2005, consumer sales of organic foods totaled $13.8 billion. Whole Foods is the largest natural foods chain and with its acquisition of Wild Oats it now represents $3.2 billion of total organic food dollars. Together these two companies represent 47% of the U.S. organic foods market. Roughly 46% of total organic food dollar volume was sold through the mass-market channel, which includes supermarkets/grocery stores, mass merchandisers, and club stores. The remaining 7% was made up of farmer's markets food service, and other non-retail sales. Whole Foods recognizes that the increased demand for organic foods may adversely affect their earnings and informs their investors as such. "Changes in the Availability of Quality Natural and Organic Products Could Impact Our Business. There is no assurance that quality natural and organic products will be available to meet our future needs. If conventional supermarkets increase their natural and organic product offerings or if new laws require the reformulation of certain products to meet tougher standards, the supply of these products may be constrained. Any significant disruption in the supply of quality natural and organic products could have a material impact on our overall sales and cost of goods."

EXHIBIT 1
Sales

	Sales (In Millions)						
Company	**2000**	**2001**	**Growth%**	**2002**	**Growth%**	**2003**	**Growth%**
Whole Foods Market[i]	$1,838.60	$2,272.20	23.60%	$2,690.50	18.40%	$3,148.60	17.00%
Trader Joe's Company[ii]	$1,670.00	$1,900.00	13.80%	$2,200.00	15.80%	$2,500.00	13.60%
Wild Oats Market[iii]	$838.10	$893.20	6.60%	$919.10	2.90%	$969.20	5.50%

[i] Hoovers Online: http://www.hoovers.com/whole-foods/−ID_10952−/free-co-factsheet.xhtml: December 1, 2004.
[ii] Hoovers Online: http://www.hoovers.com/trader-joe's-co/−ID-47619−/free-co-factsheet.xhtm: December 1, 2004.
[iii] Hoovers Online: http://www.hoovers.com/wild-oats-markets/−ID_41717−/fee-co-factsheet.xhtml: December 1, 2004.

WHOLE FOODS MARKET, INC. Unaudited Five-Year Historical Data[6]

	Avg Wkly Sales	Sales (000)	YOY Increase[1]	Comparable Store Sales Growth	2-Year Comps[2]	Identical Store Sales Growth	2-Year Idents[2]	Ending S.F.	YOY Increase	Wtd. Avg YOY Increase[3]	# of New Stores	Acquired Stores	Relocated/ Closed Stores	Ending Store Count	Gross Margin	Store Contribution[4]
1Q02	$376,335	$ 780,799	21.3%	9.4%	16.7%	7.5%	14.0%	3,841,559	16.4%	18%	2	3	3	128	33.9%	8.6%
2Q02	$395,062	$ 622,789	20.5%	10.1%	19.7%	9.1%	17.3%	3,974,266	16.8%	16%	3	0	0	131	35.0%	10.3%
3Q02	$406,019	$ 648,763	21.1%	10.5%	20.7%	9.5%	18.2%	4,040,492	16.5%	17%	4	0	2	133	34.9%	10.0%
4Q02	$395,831	$ 638,124	19.9%	10.5%	20.7%	9.6%	18.4%	4,098,492	13.9%	16%	2	0	0	135	35.1%	9.6%
FY02	$392,837	$2,690,475	20.7%	10.0%	19.2%	8.7%	16.8%	4,098,492	13.9%	17%	11	3	5	135	34.6%	9.5%
1Q03	$414,571	$ 923,760	18.3%	10.5%	19.9%	10.1%	17.6%	4,287,368	11.6%	11%	5	0	0	140	34.0%	8.6%
2Q03	$422,554	$ 725,139	16.4%	7.0%	17.1%	6.4%	15.5%	4,423,052	11.3%	12%	3	0	0	143	34.4%	9.4%
3Q03	$432,906	$ 749,042	15.5%	7.6%	18.1%	7.0%	16.5%	4,463,883	10.5%	11%	1	0	0	144	34.5%	9.4%
4Q03	$429,020	$ 750,651	17.6%	8.8%	19.3%	8.3%	17.9%	4,545,433	10.9%	10%	3	0	2	145	34.2%	8.7%
FY03	$424,095	$3,148,593	17.0%	8.6%	18.6%	8.1%	16.8%	4,545,433	10.9%	11%	12	0	2	145	34.2%	9.0%
1Q04[5]	$478,666	$1,118,148	21.0%	14.7%	25.2%	14.3%	24.4%	4,578,933	6.8%	8%	1	0	0	146	34.4%	9.1%
2Q04[5]	$488,908	$ 902,140	24.4%	17.1%	24.1%	17.0%	23.4%	4,759,050	7.6%	7%	3	7	0	156	35.4%	9.9%
3Q04	$483,560	$ 917,355	22.5%	14.1%	21.7%	13.7%	20.7%	5,004,963	12.1%	9%	5	0	1	160	34.5%	9.1%
4Q04	$478,165	$ 927,306	23.5%	14.0%	22.8%	13.3%	21.6%	5,145,261	12.1%	13%	3	0	0	163	34.6%	8.6%
FY04	$482,061	$3,864,950	22.8%	14.9%	23.5%	14.5%	22.6%	5,145,261	12.1%	9%	12	7	1	163	34.7%	9.2%
1Q05	$516,277	$1,368,328	22.4%	11.4%	26.1%	10.7%	25.0%	5,258,601	14.8%	15%	3	0	0	166	34.6%	9.1%
2Q05	$539,003	$1,085,158	20.3%	11.6%	28.7%	10.2%	27.2%	5,399,604	13.5%	13%	4	0	2	168	35.7%	10.2%
3Q05	$556,912	$1,132,736	23.5%	15.2%	29.3%	13.2%	26.9%	5,536,424	10.6%	13%	3	0	1	170	35.2%	10.0%
4Q05	$541,987	$1,115,067	20.2%	13.4%	27.4%	11.9%	25.2%	5,819,413	13.1%	12%	5	0	0	175	35.3%	7.2%
FY05	$536,986	$4,701,289	21.6%	12.8%	27.8%	11.5%	26.0%	5,819,413	13.1%	13%	15	0	3	175	35.1%	9.1%
1Q06	$584,554	$1,666,953	21.8%	13.0%	24.4%	12.0%	22.7%	6,056,121	15.2%	15%	5	0	0	180	34.5%	9.0%
2Q06	$601,908	$1,311,520	20.9%	11.9%	23.6%	10.9%	21.1%	6,172,105	14.3%	14%	3	1	1	183	35.3%	10.1%
3Q06	$605,365	$1,337,885	18.1%	9.9%	25.1%	9.6%	22.8%	6,225,756	12.5%	14%	1	0	1	183	35.3%	10.2%
4Q06	$584,498	$1,291,017	15.8%	8.6%	22.0%	8.4%	20.3%	6,379,817	9.6%	11%	4	0	1	186	34.8%	9.2%
FY06	$593,439	$5,607,376	19.3%	11.0%	23.8%	10.3%	21.8%	6,376,817	9.6%	13%	13	1	3	186	35.0%	9.6%
1Q07	$619,966	$1,870,731	12.2%	7.0%	20.0%	6.2%	18.2%	6,581,347	8.7%	8%	4	0	1	189	34.3%	8.4%

[1] Excludes extra week in FY01

[2] Sum of two years of comparable and identical store sales increases

[3] Defined as increase in current year weighted average square footage over prior year weighted average square footage

[4] Defined as gross profit minus direct store expenses

[5] Results positively impacted by strikes at conventional grocery stores in Southern California for majority of Q1 and half of Q2

[6] FY03-FY05 gross margins and store contribution are restated

Sales of a store are deemed to be "comparable" commencing in the fifty-third full week after the store was opened or acquired. Identical store sales exclude sales from remodels with expansions of square for greater than 20% and relocations. Store closed for seven or more days due to unusual events such as fires, snowstorms or hurricanes are excluded from the comparable and identical store base in the first week of closure until re-opened for a full fiscal week.

Whole Foods Market, Inc. Consolidated Quarterly Statements of Operations (In thousands, except per share amounts)

Fiscal Year 2006	1st Qtr January 15, 2006		2nd Qtr April 09, 2006		3rd Qtr July 02, 2006		4th Qtr September 24, 2006		YTD September 24, 2006	
Sales	$	1,666,953	$	1,311,520	$	1,337,886	$	1,291,017	$	5,607,376
Cost of goods sold and occupancy costs		1,092,018		848,020		866,260		841,436		3,647,734
Gross profit		574,935		463,500		471,626		449,581		1,959,642
Direct store expenses		424,438		330,470		335,555		331,505		1,421,968
Store contribution		150,497		133,030		136,071		118,076		537,674
General and administrative expenses		50,889		43,421		43,955		42,979		181,244
Operating income before pre-opening		99,608		89,609		92,116		75,097		356,430
Pre-opening expenses		7,823		5,696		6,604		11,935		32,058
Relocation costs		668		1,628		1,256		1,811		5,363
Operating income		91,117		82,285		84,256		61,351		319,009
Other income (expense):										
Interest expense		(3)		—		(8)		(21)		(32)
Investment and other income		6,082		4,068		5,581		5,005		20,736
Income before income taxes		97,196		86,353		89,829		66,335		339,713
Provision for income taxes		38,878		34,542		35,931		26,534		135,885
Net income	$	58,318	$	51,811	$	53,898	$	39,801	$	203,828
Basic earnings per share	$	0.42	$	0.37	$	0.38	$	0.28	$	1.46
Weighted average shares outstanding		137,532		139,450		140,712		140,215		139,328
Diluted earnings per share	$	0.40	$	0.36	$	0.37	$	0.28	$	1.41
Weighted average shares outstanding, diluted basis		145,317		145,546		145,925		143,462		145,082
Dividends per share	$	2.15	$	0.15	$	0.15		—	$	2.45

The notes in the company's Form 10K for fiscal year 2005 are an integral part of these condensed consolidated financial statements.

Whole Foods Market, Inc. Consolidated Balance Sheets (In thousands) September 24, 2006 and September 25, 2005

Assets		2006		2005
Current assets:				
Cash and cash equivalents	$	2,252	$	308,524
Short-term investments—available-for-sale securities		193,847		—
Restricted cash		60,065		36,922
Trade accounts receivable		82,137		66,682
Merchandise inventories		203,727		174,848
Prepaid expenses and other current assets		33,804		45,965
Deferred income taxes		48,149		39,588
Total current assets		623,981		672,529
Property and equipment, net of accumulated depreciation and amortization		1,236,133		1,054,605
Goodwill		113,494		112,476
Intangible assets, net of accumulated amortization		34,767		21,990
Deferred income taxes		29,412		22,452
Other assets		5,209		5,244
Total assets	$	2,042,996	$	1,889,296

Liabilities and Shareholders' Equity		2006		2005
Current Liabilities				
Current installments of long-term debt and capital lease obligations	$	49	$	5,932
Trade accounts payable		121,857		103,348
Accrued payroll, bonus and other benefits due team members		153,014		126,981
Dividends payable		—		17,208
Other current liabilities		234,850		164,914
Total current liabilities		509,770		418,383
Long-term debt and capital lease obligations, less current installments		8,606		12,932
Deferred rent liability		120,421		91,775
Other long-term liabilities		56		530
Total liabilities		638,853		523,620
Shareholders' equity:				
Common stock, no par vale, 300,000 shares authorized; 142,198 and 136,017 shares issued 139,607 and 135,908 shares outstanding in 2006 and 2005, respectively		1,147,872		874,972
Common stock in treasury at cost		(99,964)		—
Accumulated other comprehensive income		6,975		4,405
Retained earnings		349,260		486,299
Total shareholders' equity		1,404,143		1,365,676
Commitments and contingencies				
Total liabilities and shareholders' equity	$	2,042,996	$	1,889,296

The accompanying notes are an integral part of these consolidated financial statements.

Glossary

A

adaptive mode   The strategic formality associated with medium-sized firms that emphasize the incremental modification of existing competitive approaches.

adverse selection   An agency problem caused by the limited ability of stockholders to precisely determine the competencies and priorities of executives at the time they are hired.

agency costs   The cost of agency problems and the cost of actions taken to minimize them.

agency theory   A set of ideas on organizational control based on the belief that the separation of the ownership from management creates the potential for the wishes of owners to be ignored.

agile organization   A firm that identifies a set of business capabilities central to high-profitability operations and then builds a virtual organization around those capabilities, allowing the agile firm to build its business around the core, high-profitability information, services, and products. Creating an agile, virtual organization structure involves outsourcing, strategic alliances, a boundaryless learning approach, and web-based organization.

ambidextrous organization   Organization structure most notable for its lack of structure wherein knowledge and getting it to the right place quickly is the key reason for organization. Managers become knowledge "nodes" through which intricate networks of personal relationships—inside and outside the formal organization—are constantly, and often informally, coordinated to bring together relevant know-how and successful action.

B

balanced scorecard   A management control system that enables companies to clarify their strategies, translate them into action, and provide quantitative feedback as to whether the strategy is creating value, leveraging core competencies, satisfying the company's customers, and generating a financial reward to its shareholders. A set of four measures directly linked to a company's strategy: financial performance, customer knowledge, internal business processes, and learning and growth.

bankruptcy   When a company is unable to pay its debts as they become due, or has more debts than assets.

barriers to entry   The conditions that a firm must satisfy to enter an industry.

benchmarking   Evaluating the sustainability of advantages against key competitors. Comparing the way a company performs a specific activity with a competitor or other company doing the same thing.

board of directors   The group of stockholder representatives and strategic managers responsible for overseeing the creation and accomplishment of the company mission.

boundaryless organization   Organizational structure that allows people to interface with others throughout the organization without need to wait for a hierarchy to regulate that interface across functional, business, and geographic boundaries.

breakthrough innovation   An innovation in a product, process, technology, or the cost associated with it that represents a quantum leap forward in one or more of these ways.

business model   A clear understanding of how the firms will generate profits and the strategic actions it must take to succeed over the long term.

business process outsourcing   Having an outside company manage numerous routine business management activities usually done by employees of the company such as HR, supply procurement, finance and accounting, customer care, supply-chain logistics, engineering, R&D, sales and marketing, facilities management, and management/development.

business process reengineering   A popular method by which organizations worldwide undergo restructuring efforts to remain competitive. It involves fundamental rethinking and radical redesigning of a business process so that a company can best create value for the customer by eliminating barriers that create distance between employees and customers.

C

cash cows   Businesses with a high market share in low-growth markets or industries.

CCC21   A world-famous, cost-oriented continuous improvement program at Toyota (Construction of Cost Competitiveness for the 21st Century).

chaebol   A Korean consortia financed through government banking groups to gain a strategic advantage.

company creed   A company's statement of its philosophy.

company mission   The unique purpose that sets a company apart from others of its type and identifies the scope of its operations. The unique purpose that sets a company apart from others of its type and identifies the scope of its operations in product, market, and technology terms.

concentrated growth   A grand strategy in which a firm directs its resources to the profitable growth of a single product, in a single market, with a single dominant technology.

concentration   The extent to which industry sales are dominated by a few firms.

concentric diversification   A grand strategy that involves the operation of a second business that benefits from access to the first firm's core competencies. A strategy that involves the acquisition of businesses that are related to the acquiring firm in terms of technology, markets, or products.

conglomerate diversification   A grand strategy that involves the acquisition of a business because it presents the most promising investment opportunity available. A strategy that involves acquiring or entering businesses unrelated to a firm's current technologies, markets, or products.

consortia Large interlocking relationships between businesses of an industry.

continuous improvement A form of strategic control in which managers are encouraged to be proactive in improving all operations of the firm. The process of relentlessly trying to find ways to improve and enhance a company's products and processes from design through assembly, sales, and service. It is called *kaizen* in Japanese. It is usually associated with incremental innovation.

core competence A capability or skill that a firm emphasizes and excels in doing while in pursuit of its overall mission.

corporate social responsibility The idea that business has a duty to serve society in general as well as the financial interest of stockholders.

D

dashboard a user interface that organizes and presents information from multiple digital sources simultaneously in a user-designed format on the computer screen.

debt financing Money "loaned" to an entrepreneur or business venture that must be repaid at some point in time.

declining industry An industry in which the trend of total sales as an indicator of total demand for an industry's products or services among all the participants in the industry has started to drop from the last several years with the likelihood being that such a trend will continue indefinitely.

differentiation A business strategy that seeks to build competitive advantage with its product or service by having it be "different" from other available competitive products based on features, performance, or other factors not directly related to cost and price. The difference would be one that would be hard to create and/or difficult to copy or imitate.

discretionary responsibilities Responsibilities voluntarily assumed by a business, such as public relations, good citizenship, and full corporate responsibility.

disruptive innovation A term to characterize breakthrough innovation popularized by Harvard Professor Clayton Christensen; usually shakes up or revolutionizes industries with which they are associated even though they often come from totally different origins or industry settings than the industry they "disrupt."

divestiture A strategy that involves the sales of a firm or a major component of a firm.

divestiture strategy A grand strategy that involves the sales of a firm or a major component of a firm.

divisional organization Structure in which a set of relatively autonomous units, or divisions, is governed by a central corporate office but where each operating division has its own functional specialists who provide products or services different from those of other divisions.

dogs Low market share and low market growth businesses.

downsizing Eliminating the number of employees, particularly middle management, in a company.

dynamic The term that characterizes the constantly changing conditions that affect interrelated and interdependent strategic activities.

E

eco-efficiency Company actions that produce more useful goods and services while continuously reducing resource consumption and pollution.

ecology The relationships among human beings and other living things and the air, soil, and water that supports them.

economic responsibilities The duty of managers, as agents of the company owners, to maximize stockholder wealth.

economies of scale The savings that companies achieve because of increased volume.

emerging industry An industry that has growing sales across all the companies in the industry based on growing demand for the relatively new products, technologies, and/or services made available by the firms participating in this industry.

empowerment The act of allowing an individual or team the right and flexibility to make decisions and initiate action.

entrepreneurial mode The informal, intuitive, and limited approach to strategic management associated with owner-managers of smaller firms.

entrepreneurship The process of bringing together the creative and innovative ideas and actions with the management and organizational skills necessary to mobilize the appropriate people, money, and operating resources to meet an identifiable need and create wealth in the process.

equity financing Money provided to a business venture that entitles the provider to rights or ownership in the venture and which is not expected to be repaid.

ethical responsibilities The strategic managers' notion of right and proper business behavior.

ethical standards A person's basis for differentiating right from wrong.

ethics The moral principles that reflect society's beliefs about the actions of an individual or group that are right and wrong.

ethnocentric orientation When the values and priorities of the parent organization guide the strategic decision making of all its international operations.

expert influence The ability to direct and influence others because they defer to you based on your expertise or specialized knowledge that is related to the task, undertaking, or assignment in which they are involved.

external environment The factors beyond the control of the firm that influence its choice of direction and action, organizational structure, and internal processes.

external interface boundaries Formal and informal rules, locations, and protocol that separate and/or dictate the interaction between members of an organization and those outside the organization—customers, suppliers, partners, regulators, associations, and even competitors.

F

feedback The analysis of postimplementation results that can be used to enhance future decision making.

formality The degree to which participation, responsibility, authority, and discretion in decision making are specified in strategic management.

fragmented businesses Businesses with many sources of advantage, but they are all small. They typically involve differentiated products with low brand loyalty, easily replicated technology, and minimal scale economies.

fragmented industry An industry in which there are numerous competitors (providers of the same or similar products or services the industry involves) such that no single firm or small group of firms controls any significant share of the overall industry sales.

functional organization   Structure in which the tasks, people, and technologies necessary to do the work of the business are divided into separate "functional" groups (e.g., marketing, operations, finance) with increasingly formal procedures for coordinating and integrating their activities to provide the business's products and services.

functional tactics   Detailed statements of the "means" or activities that will be used by a company to achieve short-term objectives and establish competitive advantage. Short-term, narrow scoped plans that detail the "means" or activities that a company will use to achieve short-term objectives.

G

generic strategy   A core idea about how a firm can best compete in the marketplace. Fundamental philosophical option for the design of strategies.

geocentric orientation   When an international firm adopts a systems approach to strategic decision making that emphasizes global integration.

geographic boundaries   Limitations on interaction and contact between people in a company based on being at different physical locations domestically and globally.

global industry   An industry in which competition crosses national borders on a worldwide basis. Industry in which competition crosses national borders.

globalization   The strategy of approaching worldwide markets with standardized products.

golden handcuffs   A form of executive compensation where compensation is deferred (either a restricted stock plan or bonus income deferred in a series of annual installments).

golden parachute   A form of bonus compensation designed to retain talented executives that calls for a substantial cash payment if the executive quits, is fired, or simply retires.

grand strategy   A master long-term plan that provides basic direction for major actions directed toward achieving long-term business objectives. The means by which objectives are achieved.

grand strategy cluster   Sets of grand strategies that may be more advantageous for firms to choose under one of four sets of conditions defined by market growth rate and the strength of the firm's competitive position.

grand strategy selection matrix   A four-cell matrix that helps managers choose among different & grand strategies based upon 1) whether the business is operating from a position of strength or weakness and 2) whether it must rely solely on its own internal resources versus having the option to acquire resources externally via merger or acquisition.

growth industry strategies   Business strategies that may be more advantageous for firms participating in rapidly growing industries and markets.

H

holding company   Structure in which the corporate entity is a broad collection of often unrelated businesses and divisions such that it (the corporate entity) acts as financial overseer "holding" the ownership interest in the various parts of the company, but has little direct managerial involvement.

horizontal boundaries   Rules of communication, access, and protocol for dealing with different departments or functions or processes within an organization.

horizontal integration   A grand strategy based on growth through the acquisition of similar firms operating at the same stage of the production-marketing chain. A strategy based on growth through the acquisition of one or more similar firms operating at the same stage of the production-marketing chain.

I

ideagora   A Web-enabled, virtual marketplace which connects people with unique ideas, talents, resources, or capabilities with companies seeking to address problems or potential innovations in a quick, competent manner.

implementation control   Management efforts designed to assess whether the overall strategy should be changed in light of results associated with the incremental actions that implement the overall strategy. These are usually associated with specific strategic thrusts or projects and with predetermined milestone reviews.

incremental innovation   Simple changes or adjustments in existing products, services, or processes.

industry   A group of companies that provide similar products and services.

industry environment   The general conditions for competition that influence all businesses that provide similar products and services.

information power   The ability to influence others based on your access to information and your control of dissemination of information that is important to subordinates and others yet not otherwise easily obtained.

innovation   A grand strategy that seeks to reap the premium margins associated with creation and customer acceptance of a new product or service. A strategy that seeks to reap the initially high profits associated with customer acceptance of a new or greatly improved product. The initial commercialization of invention by producing and selling a new product, service, or process.

intangible assets   A firm's assets that you cannot touch or see but that are very often critical in creating competitive advantage: brand names, company reputation, organizational morale, technical knowledge, patents an a unique "bundle of resources"—tangible and intangible assets and organizational capabilities to make use of those assets.

intrapreneurship   A term associated with entrepreneurship in large established companies; the process of attempting to identify, encourage, enable, and assist entrepreneurship within a large, established company so as to create new products, processes, services, or improvements that become major new revenue streams and/or sources of cost savings for the company.

intrapreneurship freedom factors   Ten characteristics identified by Dr. Gordon Pinchot and elaborated upon by others that need to be present in large companies seeking to encourage and increase the level of intrapreneurship within their company.

invention   The creation of new products or processes through the development of new knowledge or from new combinations of knowledge.

isolating mechanisms   Characteristics that make resources difficult to imitate. In the RBV context these are physically unique resources, path-dependent resources, causal ambiguity, and economic deterrence.

J

joint venture   A grand strategy in which companies create a co-owned business that operates for their mutual benefit. Commercial companies created and operated for the benefit of the co-owners; usually two or more separate companies that come together to form the venture.

K

keiretsus   A Japanese consortia of businesses that is coordinated by a large trading company to gain a strategic advantage.

L

leadership development   The effort to familiarize future leaders with the skills important to the company and to develop exceptional leaders among the managers employed.

leader's vision   An articulation of a simple criterion or characterization of what a leader sees their company must become in order to establish and sustain global leadership. IBM's former CEO, Lou Gerstner, described IBM as needing to become the leader in "network-centric computing" is an example of such a characterization.

learning organization   Organization structured around the idea that it should be set up to enable learning, to share knowledge, to seek knowledge, and to create opportunities to create new knowledge. It would move into new markets to learn about those markets rather than simply to bring a brand to it, or find resources to exploit in it.

legal responsibilities   The firm's obligations to comply with the laws that regulate business activities.

liquidation   A strategy that involves closing down the operations of a business and selling its assets and operations to pay its debts and distribute any gains to stockholders.

long-term objectives   The results that an organization seeks to achieve over a multiyear period.

low-cost strategies   Business strategies that seek to establish long-term competitive advantages by emphasizing and perfecting value chain activities that can be achieved at costs substantially below what competitors are able to match on a sustained basis. This allows the firm, in turn, to compete primarily by charging a price lower than competitors can match and still stay in business.

M

market development   A grand strategy of marketing present products, often with only cosmetic modification, to customers in related marketing areas. A strategy of marketing present products, often with only cosmetic modification, to customers in related marketing areas by adding channels of distribution or by changing the content of advertising or promotion.

market focus   This is a generic strategy that applies a differentiation strategy approach, or a low-cost strategy approach, or a combination—and does so solely in a narrow (or "focused") market niche rather than trying to do so across the broader market. The narrow focus may be geographically defined, or defined by product type features, or target customer type, or some combination of these.

market growth rate   The projected rate of sales growth for the market being served by a particular business.

matrix organization   The matrix organization is a structure in which functional and staff personnel are assigned to both a basic functional area and to a project or product manager. It provides dual channels of authority, performance responsibility, evaluation, and control.

mature industry strategies   Strategies used by firms competing in markets where the growth rate of that market from year to year has reached or is close to zero.

milestone reviews   Points in time, or at the completion of major parts of a bigger strategy, where managers have predetermined they will undertake a go–no go type of review regarding the underlying strategy associated with the bigger strategy.

modular organization   An organization structured via outsourcing where different parts of the tasks needed to provide the organization's product or service are done by a wide array of other organizations brought together to create a final product or service based on the combination of their separate, independent, self-contained skills and business capabilities.

moral hazard problem   An agency problem that occurs because owners have limited access to company information, making executives free to pursue their own interests.

moral rights approach   Judging the appropriateness of a particular action based on a goal to maintain the fundamental rights and privileges of individuals and groups.

multidomestic industry   An industry in which competition is segmented from country to country.

O

operating environment   Factors in the immediate competitive situation that affect a firm's success in acquiring needed resources.

opportunity   A major favorable situation in a firm's environment.

organizational capabilities   Skills (the ability and ways of combining assets, people, and processes) that a company uses to transform inputs into outputs.

organizational culture   The set of important assumptions and beliefs (often unstated) that members of an organization share in common.

organizational leadership   The process and practice by key executives of guiding and shepherding people in an organization toward a vision over time and developing that organization's future leadership and organization culture.

organizational structure   Refers to the formalized arrangements of interaction between and responsibility for the tasks, people, and resources in an organization.

outsourcing   Obtaining work previously done by employees inside the companies from sources outside the company.

P

parenting framework   The perspective that the role of corporate headquarters (the "parent") in multibusiness (the "children") companies is that of a parent sharing wisdom, insight, and guidance to help develop its various businesses to excel.

passion (of a leader)   A highly motivated sense of commitment to what you do and want to do.

patching   The process by which corporate executives routinely "remap" their businesses to match rapidly changing market opportunities—adding, splitting, transferring, exiting, or combining chunks of businesses.

peer influence   The ability to influence individual behavior among members of a group based on group norms, a group sense of what is the right thing or right way to do things, and the need to be valued and accepted by the group.

perseverance (of a leader)   The capacity to see a commitment through to completion long after most people would have stopped trying.

planning mode   The strategic formality associated with large firms that operate under a comprehensive, formal planning system.

policies   Broad, precedent-setting decisions that guide or substitute for repetitive or time-sensitive managerial decision making. Predetermined decisions that substitute for managerial discretion in repetitive decision making.

pollution   Threats to life-supporting ecology caused principally by human activities in an industrial society.

polycentric orientation   When the culture of the country in which the strategy is to be implemented is allowed to dominate a company's international decision-making process.

portfolio techniques   An approach pioneered by the Boston Consulting Group that attempted to help managers "balance" the flow of cash resources among their various businesses while also identifying their basic strategic purpose within the overall portfolio.

position power   The ability and right to influence and direct others based on the power associated with your formal position in the organization.

premise control   Management process of systematically and continuously checking to determine whether premises upon which the strategy is based are still valid.

primary activities   The activities in a firm of those involved in the physical creation of the product, marketing and transfer to the buyer, and after-sale support.

principles (of a leader)   A leader's fundamental personal standards that guide her sense of honesty, integrity, and ethical behavior.

private equity   Money from private sources that is invested by a venture capital or private equity company in start-ups and other risky—but potentially very profitable—small and medium-size enterprises.

privatization   A restructuring in which the ownership structure of a publicly traded corporation is converted into a privately held company.

process   The flow of information through interrelated stages of analysis toward the achievement of an aim.

product development   A grand strategy that involves the substantial modification of existing products that can be marketed to current customers. A strategy that involves the substantial modification of existing products or the creation of new but related products that can be marketed to current customers through established channels.

product differentiation   The extent to which customers perceive differences among products and services.

product life cycle   A concept that describes a product's sales, profitability, and competencies that are key drivers of the success of that product as it moves through a sequence of stages from development, introduction to growth, maturity, decline, and eventual removal from a market.

product-team structure   Assigns functional managers and specialists (e.g., engineering, marketing, financial, R&D, operations) to a new product, project, or process team that is empowered to make major decisions about their performance responsibility, evaluation, and control.

punitive power   Ability to direct and influence others based on your ability to coerce and deliver punishment for mistakes or undesired actions by others, particularly subordinates.

Q

question marks   Businesses whose high growth rate gives them considerable appeal but whose low market share makes their profit potential uncertain.

R

referent influence   The ability to influence others derived from their strong desire to be associated with you, usually because they admire you, gain prestige or a sense of purpose by that association, or believe in your motivations.

regiocentric orientation   When a parent company blends its own predisposition with those of its international units to develop region-sensitive strategies.

relative competitive position   The market share of a business divided by the market share of its largest competitor.

remote environment   Economic, social, political, technological, and ecological factors that originate beyond, and usually irrespective of, any single firm's operating situation.

resource-based view   A new perspective on understanding a firm's success based on how well the firm uses its internal resources. The underlying premise is that firms differ in fundamental ways because each firm possesses a unique "bundle of resources"—tangible and intangible assets and organizational capabilities to make use of those assets.

restricted stock   Stock given to an employee who is prohibited or "restricted" from selling the stock for a certain time period and not at all if they leave the company before that time period.

restructuring   Redesigning an organizational structure with the intent of emphasizing and enabling activities most critical to a firm's strategy to function at maximum effectiveness.

retrenchment   A business strategy that involves cutting back on products, markets, operations, or other strategic commitments of the firm because its overall competitive position, or its financial situation, or both are not able to support the level of commitments to various markets or the resources needed to sustain or build its operations in some, usually declining or increasingly competitive, markets. Unlike liquidation, retrenchment would have the firm sell some assets, or ongoing operations, to rechannel proceeds to reduce overall debt and to support the firms efforts to rebuild its future competitive posture.

reward power   The ability to influence and direct others that comes from being able to confer rewards in return for desired actions or outcomes.

S

Sarbanes-Oxley Act of 2002   Law that revised and strengthened auditing and accounting standards.

self-management   Allowing work groups or work teams to supervise and administer their work as a group or team without a direct supervisor exercising the supervisory role. These teams set parameters of their work, make decisions about work-related matters, and perform most of the managerial functions previously done by their direct supervisor.

short-term objective   Measurable outcomes achievable or intended to be achieved in one year or less. Desired results that provide specific guidance for action during a period of one year or less.

simple organization   Structure in which there is an owner and a few employees and where the arrangement of tasks, responsibilities, and communication is highly informal and accomplished through direct supervision.

Six Sigma   A continuous improvement program adopted by many companies in the last two decades that takes a very rigorous and analytical approach to quality and continuous improvement with an objective to improve profits through defect reduction, yield improvement, improved customer satisfaction, and best-in-class performance.

social audit   An attempt to measure a company's actual social performance against its social objectives.

social justice approach   Judging the appropriateness of a particular action based on equity, fairness, and impartiality in the distribution of rewards and costs among individuals and groups.

special alert control   Management actions undertaken to thoroughly, and often very rapidly, reconsider a firm's strategy because of a sudden, unexpected event.

specialization businesses   Businesses with many sources of advantage. Skills in achieving differentiation (product design, branding expertise, innovation, and perhaps scale) characterize winning specialization businesses.

speed-based strategies   Business strategies built around functional capabilities and activities that allow the company to meet customer needs directly or indirectly more rapidly than its main competitors.

stakeholder activism   Demands placed on a global firm by the stakeholders in the environments in which it operates.

stakeholders   Influential people who are vitally interested in the actions of the business.

stalemate businesses   Businesses with few sources of advantage, most of them small. Skills in operational efficiency, low overhead, and cost management are critical to profitability.

stars   Businesses in rapidly growing markets with large market shares.

stock options   The right, or "option," to purchase company stock at a fixed price at some future date.

strategic alliances   Alliances with suppliers, partners, contractors, and other providers that allow partners in the alliance to focus on what they do best, farm out everything else, and quickly provide value to the customer. Contractual partnerships because the companies involved do not take an equity position in one another. Partnerships that are distinguished from joint ventures because the companies involved do not take an equity position in one another.

strategic business unit   An adaptation of the divisional structure in which various divisions or parts of divisions are grouped together based on some common strategic elements, usually linked to distinct product/market differences.

strategic control   Management efforts to track a strategy as it is being implemented, detect problems or changes in its underlying premises, and make necessary adjustments. Tracking a strategy as it is being implemented, detecting problems or changes in its underlying premises, and making necessary adjustments.

strategic intent   A leader's clear sense of where they want to lead their company and what results they expect to achieve.

strategic management   The set of decisions and actions that result in the formulation and implementation of plans designed to achieve a company's objectives.

strategic positioning   The way a business is designed and positioned to serve target markets.

strategic processes   Decision making, operational activities, and sales activities that are critical business processes.

strategic surveillance   Management efforts to monitor a broad range of events inside and more often outside the firm that are likely to affect the course of its strategy over time.

strategic thrusts or projects   Special efforts that are early steps in executing a broader strategy, usually involving significant resource commitments yet where predetermined feedback will help management determine whether continuing to pursue the strategy is appropriate or whether it needs adjustment or major change.

strategy   Large-scale, future-oriented plans for interacting with the competitive environment to achieve company objectives.

strength   A resource advantage relative to competitors and the needs of the markets a firm serves or expects to serve.

structural attributes   The enduring characteristics that give an industry its distinctive character.

support activities   The activities in a firm that assist the firm as a whole by providing infrastructure or inputs that allow the primary activities to take place on an ongoing basis.

SWOT analysis   SWOT is an acronym for the internal Strengths and Weaknesses of a firm, and the environmental Opportunities and Threats facing that firm. SWOT analysis is a technique through which managers create a quick overview of a company's strategic situation.

T

tactics   Specific actions that need to be undertaken to achieve short-term objectives, usually by functional areas.

tangible assets   The most easily identified assets, often found on a firm's balance sheet. They include production facilities, raw materials, financial resources, real estate, and computers.

technological forecasting   The quasi-science of anticipating environmental and competitive changes and estimating their importance to an organization's operations.

threat   A major unfavorable situation in a firm's environment.

turnaround   A grand strategy of cost reduction and asset reduction by a company to survive and recover from declining profits.

U

utilitarian approach   Judging the appropriateness of a particular action based on a goal to provide the greatest good for the greatest number of people.

V

value chain A perspective in which business is seen as a chain of activities that transforms inputs into outputs that customers value. Customer value derives from three basic sources: activities that differentiate the product, activities that lower its cost, and activities that meet the customer's need quickly.

value chain analysis An analysis that attempts to understand how a business creates customer value by examining the contributions of different activities within the business to that value.

vertical boundaries Limitations on interaction, contact and access between operations and management personnel; between different levels of management; and between different organizational parts like corporate vs. divisional units.

vertical integration A grand strategy based on the acquisition of firms that supply the acquiring firm with inputs or new customers for its outputs. A strategy based on the acquisition of firms that supply the acquiring firm with inputs such as raw materials or new customers for its outputs, such as warehouses for finished products.

virtual organization Corporations whose structure has become an elaborate network of external and internal relationships. In effect, a temporary network of independent companies—suppliers, customers, subcontractors, and businesses around the core, high-profitability information, services, and products. Creating an agile, virtual organization structure involves outsourcing, strategic alliances, a boundaryless learning approach, and web-based organization.

vision statement A statement that presents a firm's strategic intent designed to focus the energies and resources of the company on achieving a desirable future.

volume businesses Businesses that have few sources of advantage, but the size is large—typically the result of scale economies.

W

weakness A limitation or deficiency in one or more resources or competencies relative to competitors that impedes a firm's effective performance.

Photo Credits

Chapter 1

© PRNewsFoto/McDonald's Corporation, p. 9

Chapter 2

Courtesy of Questar Corporation, pg. 30

Chapter 3

© AP Photo/Kirsty Wigglesworth/WPA pool, p. 73

Chapter 4

Courtesy of Robert Half International, p. 95

Chapter 5

Courtesy of Cognizant Technology Solutions, p. 138

Chapter 6

© Julie Cordeiro/Boston Red Sox, p. 158

Chapter 7

© AP Photo/Chuck Burton, p. 205

Chapter 8

© AFP/Getty Images, p. 258

Chapter 9

Courtesy of International Business Machines Corporation. Unauthorized use not permitted, p. 287

© Handout/epa/Corbis, p. 292

© Kim Kulish/Corbis, p. 298

Chapter 10

Courtesy of Symantec Corporation, p. 307

Chapter 12

© AP Photo/Reed Saxon, p. 378

Chapter 13

© AP Photo/Michel Euler, p. 420 (top left)

© AP Photo/Bell Atlantic, p. 420 (bottom left)

© AP Photo/General Electric Company, p. 420 (top right)

© AP Photo/Paul Sakuma, p. 420 (bottom right)

Chapter 14

© ISSEI KATO/Reuters/Corbis, p. 430

Name Index

Subject Index

Case Study Index